Pet Friendly
Places to Stay
2011

D0529273

AA Lifestyle Guides

Please contact Advertisement Sales: advertisingsales@theaa.com
Editorial Department: lifestyleguides@theaa.com
AA Hotel & Guest Accommodation enquiries: 01256 844455
AA Campsite enquiries: 01256 491577

Typeset/Repro: Servis Filmsetting Ltd, Stockport
Printed in Italy by Printer Trento SRL, Trento.

Directory compiled by the AA Lifestyle Guides Department and managed in the Librios Information Management System and generated from the AA establishment database system.

Published by AA Publishing, a trading name of AA Media Limited, whose registered office is Fanum House, Basing View, Basingstoke, Hampshire RG21 4EA. Registered number 06112600

A CIP catalogue record for this book is available from the British Library

ISBN: 978-0-7495-6741-5

A04464

Maps prepared by the Mapping Services Department of AA Publishing.

Maps © AA Media Limited 2010.

Contents

Welcome to the Guide

This guide is perfect for pet owners who are reluctant to put their animals into kennels or catteries while they go on holiday. In these pages you can find not only places where dogs and cats are welcome, but also where horses can be stabled on site or very close by.

Hints on booking your stay

As this guide shows, there are a great many hotels, bed and breakfasts and campsites that offer a warm welcome and an extensive range of facilities to both pet lovers and their animal companions. Though all the establishments listed have told us they are happy to admit animals, some go out of their way to make you and your pet feel at home, offering animal welcome packs, comfortable dog baskets, water bowls, special blankets, home-made treats and comprehensive information on local country walks.

Do remember though, that even the pet-friendliest of proprietors appreciate advance warning if you intend to bring your animal with you. See pages 12-15 for helpful hints and tips on planning your trip. While summer is an obvious time to book a holiday, you might like to consider taking an off-peak break when animals – dogs in particular – are more likely to enjoy cooler temperatures and crowd-free destinations.

And just a friendly word of warning. On sending us information for this guide many establishments stated that they very much welcome pets but they must be accompanied by well behaved owners!

How to Use the Guide

1 Locations The guide is divided into countries. Each country is listed in county order and then alphabetically in town/village order within a county.

2 Map reference Each town/village is given a map reference for the atlas section at the back of the guide. For example:

Map 03 SY29

03 refers to the page number of the atlas section at the back of the guide

SY is the National Grid lettered square (represents 100,000sq metres) in which the location will be found

2 is the figure reading across the top or bottom of the map page

9 is the figure reading down each side of the map page

Campsites (and some B&Bs) include a 6-figure National Grid reference as many are located in remote areas.

A county map appears before the atlas section at the back of the guide.

3 Which pets are accepted Five symbols show at a glance what type of animal is welcome – dogs, cats, small caged animals, caged birds and horses. 🐾 indicates places that provide kennels.

4 Establishment name & rating For further information on AA ratings and awards see page 10. If the name of the establishment appears in italic type this indicates that not all the information has been confirmed for 2011.

Within each location hotels are listed first, in descending order of stars and % score, followed by B&Bs in descending orders of stars, then campsites in order of their pennant rating (see page 11).

5 Contact details

6 Directions Short details of how to find the establishment or campsite.

---

1 → **AXMINSTER**   **Map 3 SY29** ← **2**

3 → 🐾 😺

15 → LOGO

4 → ## Fairwater Head Hotel
★★★ **75%** ⊛ HOTEL
Hawkchurch EX13 5TX
5 → ☎ 01297 678349 📠 01297 678459
e-mail: stay@fairwaterheadhotel.co.uk
web: www.fairwaterheadhotel.co.uk
6 → **dir:** *Off B3165 (Crewkerne to Lyme Regis road). Hotel signed to Hawkchurch*

7 → **PETS: Bedrooms** (8 GF) unattended **Sep accom** outside pen area **Public areas** except dining room on leads **Grounds** on leads disp bin **Exercise area** surrounding countryside **Facilities** food (pre-bookable) food bowl water bowl dog chews scoop/disp bags leads pet sitting washing facs cage storage walks info vet info **On Request** fridge access torch towels **Other** charge for damage **Resident Pets:** Mocca (Springer/Cocker
8 → Spaniel), Lollipop (Black Labrador)

14 →

This elegant Edwardian country house provides a perfect location for anyone looking for a peaceful break. Surrounded by extensive gardens and rolling countryside, the setting guarantees relaxation. Bedrooms are located both within the main house and the garden wing; all provide good levels of comfort. Public areas have much appeal and include lounge areas, a bar and an elegant restaurant. Food is a highlight with excellent local produce prepared with care and skill.

13 →

9 → **Rooms** 16 (4 annexe) (8 GF) **S** £77.50-£180; **D** £97.50-£195 (incl. bkfst)* **Facilities** FTV Library Xmas New Year Wi-fi **Parking** 30 **Notes** LB Closed 1-30 Jan

12   **10**   **11**

7 Pet facilities (**PETS:**)

Bedrooms GF Ground floor bedrooms; **unattended** indicates that the establishment allows a pet to be left unattended in the bedroom; **sign** indicates that a sign is provided to hang on the door stating an animal is in the room.

Sep accom (separate accommodation) some places have kennels or outbuildings available. Check when booking that this is suitable for your pet.

Public areas indicates that pets are allowed in public areas. Any exceptions are as stated. Most hotes and B&Bs in this guide request that dogs are kept on leads when passing through public areas to the bedrooms.

Charges £ (€ Republic of Ireland) Some establishments charge a fee for accommodating a pet: the price shown is the charge per animal per night, per week or per stay.

Grounds Establishments that allow pets access to their gardens or grounds, or in the case of campsites there may be specified areas for exercise.

Exercise area The type of area available (ie fields, beach, coastal path etc) and the distance from the establishment (ie 100yds).

Facilities Information and specific facilities that guests who are staying with their pets might find useful. Campsites may sell certain pet related items in their on-site shop.

Other Additional information supplied by the establishment.

Restrictions Certain establishments have rules on the number of pets, or the size or the breed of dog allowed.* We strongly advise readers to check with the hotel, B&B or campsite at the time of booking that their pet will be permitted to accompany them during their stay.

*Some establishments have stated that they do not accept 'dangerous dogs'. The following breeds are covered under the Dangerous Dogs Act 1991 – Pit Bull Terrier, Japanese Tosa, Dogo Argentino and Fila Brazilierio.

For further details see:

www.defra.gov.uk/wildlife-pets/pets/dangerous/index.htm

8 Resident Pets Lists the names and breeds of the proprietors' own pets.

9 Rooms The number of bedrooms, and whether they are en suite, family or ground floor rooms. **Prices** These are per room per night. These are given by the proprietors in good faith, and are indications only, not firm quotations. (☀ indicates 2010 prices). At the time of going to press up-to-date prices for campsites were not available. Please check the AA website **theAA.com** for current information. Smoking is not permitted in the public areas of hotels and guest houses, but some bedrooms may be set aside for smokers. Please check with the establishment when you book your room. Please note that not all bedrooms in B&Bs have TVs.

10 Facilities **Leisure facilities** are as stated in the entries. **Child Facilities** (Ch fac), these vary from place to place so please check at the time of booking that the establishment can meet your requirements.

11 Parking Shows the numbers of spaces available for the use of guests. This may include covered parking. Please note that some establishments make a charge to use their car park.

12 Notes This section can include the following: **No Children** followed by an age indicates that a minimum age is required (ie No children 4yrs) **RS** (Restricted Service) Some establishments have a restricted service during quieter months and some of the listed facilities may not be available. **LB** Some establishments offer leisure breaks. **Dinner (B&Bs only)** indicates that an evening meal is available, although prior notice may be needed. **Licensed (B&Bs only)** indicates that the establishment is licensed to serve alcohol. **Payment** The majority of establishments in this guide accept credit and debit cards. 🚫 This symbol indicates those that don't.

13 Description This is written by the AA Inspector at the time of their visit.

14 Photograph Establishments may choose to include a photograph in their entry.

15 Hotel logo If a symbol appears in the entry it indicates that the hotel belongs to a group or consortium.

Symbols and Abbreviations

Key to symbols

🐾	Dogs
🐱	Cats
🐹	Small caged animals e.g. rabbits, hamsters
🐦	Caged birds
🐕	Kennels available
🐴	Horses (stables or paddock)
★	The best hotels (see page 10)
★	The best B&Bs (see page 10)
★	Hotel and B&B rating (see page 10)
%	Merit score (see page 10)
U	AA Rating not confirmed (see page 11)
❀	AA Rosette Award for quality of food (see page 11)
▶	Campsite rating (see page 11)
🏛	Holiday Centre (see page 11)

🚫	No credit cards
✳	2010 prices
🏊	Heated indoor swimming pool
⚲	Outdoor swimming pool
⚲	Heated outdoor swimming pool
🎾	Tennis court/s
🏑	Croquet lawn
⛳	Golf course
🎵	Entertainment

Bed & Breakfast only

🍽	A very special breakfast, with an emphasis on freshly prepared local ingredients
🍽	A very special dinner, with an emphasis on freshly prepared local ingredients

Key to abbreviations

Air con	Air conditioning		RS/rs	Restricted services
BH/bank hols	Bank Holidays		S	Single bedroom
Ch fac	Special facilities for children		STV	Satellite television in bedrooms
D	Double bedroom		Spa	Establishment has own spa facilities
Etr	Easter		Whit	Whitsun Bank Holiday
Fmly	Family bedroom		Wi-fi	Wireless network access
Fr	From		wk	Week
FTV	Freeview television in bedrooms		wkend	Weekend
GF	Ground floor bedroom		Xmas	Special Christmas programme
hrs	Hours			
incl. bkfst	Including breakfast		**Bed & Breakfast only**	
LB	Special leisure breaks		Cen ht	Full central heating
m	Miles		Last d	Last time dinner can be ordered
mtrs	Metres		pri facs	Bedroom with separate, private facilities
mdnt	Midnight			
New Year	Special New Year programme		rms	Bedrooms in main building
No Children	No children can be accommodated		Tea/coffee	Tea & coffee making facilities
rdbt	Roundabout		TVL	Television lounge

AA Classifications and Awards

Hotel and Guest Accommodation Ratings

In collaboration with VisitBritain, VisitScotland and VisitWales, the AA uses Common Quality Standards for inspecting and rating accommodation. All Hotels and B&Bs in this guide have received an inspection under these standards.

Hotel Ratings

If you stay in a **one-star** hotel you should expect a relatively informal yet competent style of service and an adequate range of facilities. The majority of the bedrooms are en suite, with a bath or shower room always available. A **two-star** hotel is run by smartly and professionally presented management and offers at least one restaurant or dining room for breakfast and dinner, while a **three-star** hotel includes direct-dial telephones, a wide selection of drinks in the bar and last orders for dinner no later than 8pm. A **four-star** hotel is characterised by uniformed, well-trained staff, with additional services, a night porter and a serious approach to cuisine. A **five-star** hotel, offers many extra facilities, attentive staff, top quality rooms and a full concierge service.

   The Merit Score (%) AA inspectors supplement their reports with an additional quality assessment of everything the hotel offers, including hospitality, based on their findings as a 'mystery guest'. This results in a overall Merit Score. Shown as a pecentage score beside the hotel name, you can see at a glance that a hotel with a percentage score of 69% offers a higher standard than one in the same star classification but with a percentage score of 59%. To gain AA recognition initially, a hotel must achieve a minimum quality score of 50%.

★ Red stars The very best hotels within each star category are indicated by red stars.

There are six descriptive designators for establishments in the Hotel Recognition scheme:

HOTEL Formal accommodation with full service. Minimum of six guest bedrooms but more likely to be in excess of 20.

TOWN HOUSE HOTEL A small, individual city or town centre property, which provides a high degree of personal service and privacy.

COUNTRY HOUSE HOTEL A rurally and quietly located establishment with ample grounds.

SMALL HOTEL Has less than 20 bedrooms and is personally run by the proprietor.

METRO HOTEL A hotel in an urban location that does not offer dinner.

BUDGET HOTEL Inexpensive group lodge accommodation, usually purpose built by main roads and motorways and in town or city centres.

Guest Accommodation Ratings

Stars in the AA Guest Accommodation scheme reflect five levels of quality, from one at the simplest level to five offering the highest quality. The criteria for eligibility is guest care plus the quality of the accommodation rather than the choice of extra facilities. Guests should receive a prompt, professional check in and check out, comfortable accommodation equipped to modern standards, regularly changed bedding and towels, a sufficient hot water supply at all times, well-prepared meals and a full continental breakfast.

★ Yellow stars The top 10% of three, four and five star establishments are indicated by yellow stars.

There are six descriptive designators for establishments in this scheme:

B&B A private house run by the owner with accommodation for no more than six paying guests.

GUEST HOUSE Run on a more commercial basis than a B&B, the accommodadtion provides for more than six paying guests and there are more services.

FARMHOUSE The B&B or guest house accommodation is part of a working farm or smallholding.

INN The accommodation is provided in a fully licensed establishment. The bar will be open to non-residents and provide food in the evenings.

RESTAURANT WITH ROOMS This is a destination restaurant offering overnight accommodation, with dining being the main business, and open to non-residents. The restaurant should offer a high

standard of food, and restaurant service at least five nights a week. A liquor licence and maximum of 12 bedrooms.

GUEST ACCOMMODATION Any establishment that meets the minimum entry requirements is eligible for this general category.

⚜ AA Rosettes

The AA awards Rosettes for the quality of food. These range from one Rosette for food prepared with care, understanding and skill, up to five Rosettes for the very finest cooking that stands comparison with the best cuisine in the world.

AA AA Campsite Ratings

AA sites are classified from one to five pennants according to their style and the range of facilities they offer. 1 pennant – these parks offer a fairly simple standard of facilities. 2 pennants – offer an increased level of facilities, services, customer care, security and ground maintenance. 3 pennants – have a wide range of facilities and are of a very good standard. 4 pennants – these parks achieve an excellent standard throughout that will include landscaped grounds, natural screening and immaculately maintained toilets. 5 pennant Premier Parks – the very best parks with superb mature landscaping and all facilities, customer care and security will be of exceptional quality.

Campsites have shortened entries in this guide. For more detailed information visit our website **theAA.com** and follow the 'Places to Stay' link.

Holiday Centres

This category indicates parks which cater for all holiday needs including cooked meals and entertainment.

U A small number of establishments in the guide have this symbol because their star or pennant rating was not confirmed at the time of going to press. This may be because there has been a change of ownership, or because the establishment has only recently joined one of the AA rating schemes.

To find out more about AA ratings and awards please visit our website **theAA.com**

Useful Information

Britain
Fire Regulations
The Fire Precautions Act does not apply to the Channel Islands, Republic of Ireland, or the Isle of Man, which have their own rules. As far as we are aware, all establishments listed in Great Britain have applied for and not been refused a fire certificate.

Licensing laws
These laws differ in England, Wales, Scotland, Northern Ireland, the Republic of Ireland, the Isle of Man, the Isles of Scilly and the Channel Islands.

Public houses are generally open from mid morning to early afternoon, and from about 6 or 7pm until 11pm, although closing times may be earlier or later and some pubs are open all afternoon. Unless otherwise stated, hotels listed in this guide are licensed. (For guest accommodation, please refer to the individual gazetteer entry. Note that licensed premises are not obliged to remain open throughout the permitted hours.) Hotel residents can obtain alcoholic drinks at all times, if the licensee is prepared to serve them. Non-residents eating at the hotel restaurant can have drinks with meals. Children under 14 (or 18 in Scotland) may be excluded from bars where no food is served. Those under 18 may not purchase or consume alcoholic drinks. A club licence means that drinks are served to club members only. 48 hours must elapse between joining and ordering.

Prices
The AA encourages the use of the Hotel Industry Voluntary Code of Booking Practice, which aims to ensure that guests know how much they will have to pay and what services and facilities that includes, before entering a financially binding agreement. If the price has not previously been confirmed in writing, guests should be given a card stipulating the total obligatory charge when they register at reception.

The Tourism (Sleeping Accommodation Price Display) Order of 1977 compels hotels, travel accommodation, guest houses, farmhouses, inns and self-catering accommodation with four or more letting bedrooms, to display in entrance halls the minimum and

maximum prices charged for each category of room. Tariffs shown are the minimum and maximum for one or two persons but they may vary without warning.

Facilities for disabled guests
The final stage (Part III) of the Disability Discrimination Act (access to Goods and Services) came into force in October 2004. This means that service providers may have to consider making permanent physical adjustments to their premises.

For further information, see the government website **www.direct.gov.uk/en/disabledpeople/ RightsandObligations/DisabilityRights/ DG_4001068** We indicate in entries if an establishment has ground floor rooms, and if a hotel tells us that they have disabled facilities this is included in the description. The establishments in this guide should all be aware of their responsibilities under the Act. We recommend that you telephone in advance to ensure that the establishment you have chosen has appropriate facilities.

Useful websites:
www.holidaycare.org.uk
www.dptac.gov.uk/door-to-door

Northern Ireland and Republic of Ireland

Licensing Regulations

Northern Ireland:

Public houses open Mon-Sat 11.30-23.00. Sun 12.30-22.00. Hotels can serve residents without restriction. Non-residents can be served 12.30-22.00 on Christmas Day. Children under 18 are not allowed in the bar area and may neither buy nor consume liquor in hotels.

Republic of Ireland:

General licensing hours are Mon-Thu 10.30-23.30, Fri & Sat 10.30-00.30. Sun 12.30-23.00 (or 00.30 if the following day is a Bank Holiday). There is no licensed service (except for hotel residents) on Christmas Day or Good Friday.

Fire Regulations

The Fire Services (NI) Order 1984. This covers establishments accommodating more than six people, which must have a certificate from the Northern Ireland Fire Authority. Places accommodating fewer than six people need adequate exits. AA inspectors check emergency notices, fire fighting equipment and fire exits here.

The Republic of Ireland safety regulations are a matter for local authority regulations. For your own and others' safety, read the emergency notices and be sure you understand them.

Telephone numbers

Area codes for numbers in the Republic of Ireland apply only within the Republic. If dialling from outside check the telephone directory (from the UK the international dialling code is 00 353). Area codes for numbers in Britain and Northern Ireland cannot be used directly from the Republic.

For the latest information on the Republic of Ireland visit the AA Ireland's website: **AAireland.ie**

Useful websites for pet owners:

www.thekennelclub.org.uk The Kennel Club provides lots of information on microchipping and runs a pet reunification scheme. The website also includes information on lost micro-chipped pets: The European Pet Network has access to several animal databases from various European countries.

If a lost micro-chipped and registered pet is found, the EPN aims to find the owner.

www.petsbureau.co.uk A national missing pets register.

www.defra.gov.uk/wildlife-pets/pets/travel/index. htm for details of the Pet Travel Scheme and for comprehensive information and advice on travelling with your pet.

www.rcvs.org.uk website of the Royal College of Veterinary Surgeons that will help you find a vet near your holiday destination.

Bank and Public Holidays 2011

1st January	New Year's Day
4th January (Scotland)	New Year's Holiday
22nd April	Good Friday
25th April	Easter Monday
2nd May	Early May Bank Holiday
30th May	Spring Bank Holiday
2nd August (Scotland)	August Holiday
29th August	Late Summer Holiday
25th December	Christmas Day
26th December	Boxing Day

Away from Home

At first, the prospect of taking your pet away with you may seem a little daunting. There is their welfare to think of and the responsibility of trying to ensure they fit comfortably into their new surroundings. Many proprietors have cats and dogs of their own and will quickly build up a good rapport with your pet. This can play a vital role in the success of your holiday, and if all goes well, owners who are genuine animal lovers will be welcoming you back year after year. On the whole, proprietors report favourably on their pet guests, often commenting that their behaviour is at least as good as their owners!

We all love our pets and want to give them the care they deserve, but holidays can mean a certain amount of stress for us and also for our pets. Changes in routine can upset an animal as much as its owner. So keep them to their regular mealtimes if possible, take plenty of water for them on your journey, especially in hot weather.

Planning ahead

Always remember to advise the proprietor when booking that you intend bringing your pet with you. This gives you both the opportunity to establish whether the accommodation really is suitable for your pet's needs. Some establishments impose restrictions on the type, size or number of animals permitted; for example, those that accept dogs may not accommodate the larger breeds. Many establishments can provide foods but is it advisable to take the food your pet is familiar with.

Not all rooms will necessarily be available to guests with animals and some rooms may be set aside for people with allergies.

When booking, you should also check the establishment's supervision policy. Some may require your pet to be caged when unattended, or may ask you not to leave your pet alone at all.

The gazetteer entry in this guide indicates whether you should expect to pay an additional charge or deposit for your pet, but we recommend that you confirm the amount when booking.

The countryside

For your family holiday to be a complete success, you'll need to do a little research and planning. As well as finding somewhere suitable to stay, you might like to contact the tourist board for leaflets and brochures on pet-friendly places of interest, or you might find the ideal place listed in the AA Days Out guide. Remember to 'Mind that Pet!' and keep your dog under tight control when visiting local attractions.

Time to adjust

Remember that an animal shut in a strange hotel room for long periods may become distressed. We have stories from our hotels and B&Bs of dogs chewing up furniture or howling mournfully while their owners are out and these are symptoms of boredom and separation anxiety, particularly if your pet is a rescue animal.

On arrival, give your pet time to adjust to the new surroundings and if you think he will be upset and bark or howl, don't leave him alone in your room.

Watching our pets let off steam in a different environment is one of the pleasures of a good holiday, but although they are cherished members of the family who provide many hours of fun and enjoyment, owners have a duty to ensure that their pet is kept under proper control at all times.

In the case of dogs, allowing them to socialise with people and other animals from an early age means that, under your supervision, they will be at ease with other residents and their pets during your stay. It's not uncommon to end up swapping dog stories with guests or even members of staff. Lasting friendships are sometimes formed this way!

House rules

Unless otherwise indicated by the management, please don't allow your pet on the furniture, or in the bed. If he or she likes to sleep on the bed, remember to take a sheet, a blanket or a bedspread of your own, unless the proprietor provides one. Remember also to take an old towel to dry your pet after a walk in the rain and don't use the bath or shower for washing your animal.

Clean up after your pet immediately – inside the room and out – and leave no trace of them on departure. Take a supply of supermarket carrier bags with you and poop scoop anywhere in the hotel or grounds. Management will advise on disposal of the bags – some hotels/B&Bs have an animal toilet area and provide bags. If something has been damaged by your pet, notify the management immediately. It's really a case of simple common sense.

If the hotel/B&B allows you to take animals into public areas, be sure that you keep your pet under control at all times. Keep dogs on leads, especially when around small children. Your dog may be easily distracted by the sights and smells of unfamiliar surroundings, and may not respond to your commands as well as at home.

Bear in mind that dogs need to be exercised regularly – even on holiday – and time should be set aside for this as often as possible, especially if they have been travelling with you in the car for most of the day. Most country hotels and B&Bs will have plenty of good walks on the doorstep, which makes the chore of exercising your dog that much more enjoyable.

A lot of the establishments listed in this guide are surrounded by farmland so please remember to keep your dog under strict control near livestock – even letting your dog walk in the same field as farm animals may be considered as "worrying". (Remember a farmer is entitled to kill your dog if it is worrying livestock.)

Just in case

One final tip is to check your insurance for the level of cover it offers before taking your pet away. Pet insurance may not cover personal liability but your house insurance might. Should your pet chew the furniture or take a nip at a passing ankle, you would be well advised to have covered this eventuality by having the appropriate, up-to-date insurance policy.

The AA offers Pet Insurance.
Please visit **theAA.com** or call **0800 294 2713** for further information.

Quality-assured accommodation at over 6,000 establishments throughout the UK & Ireland

- ✓ Quality-assured accommodation
- 🔒 Secure online booking process
- 🏢 Extensive range and choice of accommodation
- ⓘ Detailed, authoritative descriptions
- ⭐£ Exclusive discounts for AA Members

Microchipping your pet

Reliable identification

Microchipping was introduced more than 20 years ago, and adopted worldwide as a reliable method of pet identification because collars can be lost and tattoos may fade or be altered.

For your much loved dog or cat this is definitely a worthwhile procedure, for as much as every responsible owner endeavours to know the whereabouts of their pet every hour of the day, there could be a moment when they make a dash for freedom. For cats, certainly known to be independently-minded in their daily habits, being microchipped is an obvious choice for the owner. But it has to be remembered that many thousands of dogs also go missing each year, and it is estimated that less than half will be reunited with their owners.

The Control of Dogs Order 1992 states that all dogs (with a few specified exceptions), when in a public place or on a highway, must wear a collar showing the owner's name and address on a plate or disk attached to it; ideally it should also include their telephone number. Any dog seen without a collar in public place may be seized by the local authority and treated as a stray*. The owner may be prosecuted and fined.

How microchipping works

Microchipping can be undertaken at most veterinary practices in the UK, through some local authorities and also by animal welfare organisations. For any pet other than a dog or cat a veterinary surgeon should be consulted as the correct positioning of the chip is vitally important.

In a quick procedure, where an anaesthetic is not normally required, the chip is implanted under the skin, usually between the shoulder blades; the discomfort to the animal is no worse than a vaccination injection. The microchip will last for the pet's lifetime.

The microchip is a small electronic device, only the size of a grain of rice, which has a unique number that can be read by a scanner. The scanner's low frequency radio waves activate the chip so that the unique number can be read.

This number (now comprising 15-digits) is held, together with the owner's details, on a national

database. Scanners are used by vets, local authority dog wardens and animal welfare groups to check stray cats and dogs; if a chip is in place, and providing the contact details are up-to-date, the owner can be easily and quickly contacted.

Microchipping events

June is National Microchipping Month. This is an initiative started by The Kennel Club (and endorsed by the RSPCA) to promote this method of pet ID. Each year a list of microchipping events, held throughout England, Wales and Scotland, can be found on the Kennel Club's petlog ® website.

Travelling abroad

If you are thinking of taking your pet abroad with you, it is a requirement under the PETS Travel Scheme (see page 19) to have your pet microchipped before your journey. Having fulfilled this particular requirement you can feel reassured that, should your pet go astray, there is more likelihood of a reunion.

*Under the Environmental Protection Act 1990 your stray dog can to be seized and sold, re-homed or destroyed if unclaimed after a seven day period.

Useful websites for further information
www.petlog.org.uk
www.rspca.org.uk
www.nationalpetregister.org
www.petsbureau.co.uk
www.europetnet.com
www.worldpetregister.com

The Pet Travel Scheme (PETS)

Pets are on the move. They now travel more often with their owners in the United Kingdom and, because of changes in quarantine regulations, pets can now be taken abroad and then return to the UK, subject to certain conditions.

The Pets Travel Scheme* gives information about the countries involved in the scheme; regulations; documentation required; microchip ID tags; help finding a vet; guidance on looking after pets during transportation; bringing your pet from a long-haul country; authorised routes; approved transport companies; charges; a latest news section and lots more besides.

Pets that are resident anywhere in the UK can travel unrestricted within Britain, and are not subject to quarantine regulations or to the PETS rules unless they are entering this country from overseas. There are no requirements for pets travelling directly between the UK and the Republic of Ireland.

The PETS scheme, which only applies to dogs (including assistance dogs), cats, ferrets, and certain other pets, enables pets resident in the UK to enter, without quarantine restrictions, certain (listed) countries throughout the world and then return to Britain. Thanks to the relaxation of quarantine controls in this country, they can go straight home on arrival. In order to bring your pet into, or back into, the UK from one of the listed countries the scheme requires that your pet must be fitted with a microchip, be vaccinated against rabies, pass a blood test and be issued with a pet passport. Before entering the UK, your animal will also need to receive both tapeworm and tick treatments. Naturally, careful thought should

be given to the welfare of your pet and whether a holiday abroad is appropriate, but if you decide to go ahead, remember it is necessary for your pet to have passed a satisfactory blood test at least 6 calendar months before travel commences. Your pet cannot travel under this scheme unless this time has elapsed.

*The European Parliament and Council have agreed that existing regulations are applicable until at least 31.12.11

From 26.5.10 The European Parliament and Council introduced a limit of five animals (dogs, cats and ferrets only) per person for all importations into and around the European Union, regardless of the exporting country. This is applicable to all listed countries.

For detailed information about the PETS scheme contact:
PETS Helpline: 0870 241 1710
(8am–6pm (UK time) Monday to Friday)
E-mail: quarantine@ animalhealth.gsi.gov.uk
(Please include your postal address and daytime telephone number in your e-mail).
Website: www.defra.gov.uk/wildlife-pets/pets/travel/pets/index.htm

Remember, whether in the UK or abroad animals can die if left in a vehicle in direct sunlight or high temperatures.

England

ENGLAND

BEDFORDSHIRE

ASPLEY GUISE — Map 4 SP93

Best Western Moore Place
★★★ 74% HOTEL
The Square MK17 8DW
☎ 01908 282000 📄 01908 281888
e-mail: manager@mooreplace.com
dir: M1 junct 13, take A507 signed Aspley Guise & Woburn Sands. Hotel on left in village square

PETS: Bedrooms (16 GF) Stables Charges Public areas except restaurant & bar area on leads Grounds on leads disp bin Exercise area 10 mins Facilities cage storage walks info vet info On Request fridge access torch Other charge for damage max 2 dogs per room Restrictions no very large dogs; no St Bernards, Newfoundlands, Alsatians or Mastiffs

This impressive Georgian house, set in delightful gardens in the village centre, is very conveniently located for the M1. Bedrooms do vary in size, but consideration has been given to guest comfort, with many thoughtful extras provided. There is a wide range of meeting rooms and private dining options.

Rooms 62 (27 annexe) (16 GF) S £49-£107; D £65-£119* Facilities Xmas New Year Wi-fi Parking 70 Notes LB RS 27-31 Dec

BERKSHIRE

ASCOT — Map 4 SU96

MACDONALD HOTELS & RESORTS

Macdonald Berystede Hotel & Spa
★★★★ 78% HOTEL
Bagshot Rd, Sunninghill SL5 9JH
☎ 0844 879 9104 📄 01344 872301
e-mail: general.berystede@macdonald-hotels.co.uk
web: www.macdonald-hotels.co.uk/berystede
dir: A30/B3020 (Windmill Pub). Continue 1.25m to hotel on left just before junct with A330

PETS: Bedrooms (33 GF) unattended sign Stables 1m Charges £10 per night £70 per week Public areas except restaurant on leads Grounds on leads disp bin Exercise area 0.5m Facilities dog walking walks info vet info On Request fridge access Other charge for damage Restrictions small & medium size dogs only

This impressive Victorian mansion, close to Ascot Racecourse, offers executive bedrooms that are spacious, comfortable and particularly well equipped. Public rooms include a cosy bar and an elegant restaurant in which creative dishes are served. An impressive self-contained conference centre and spa facility appeal to both conference and leisure guests.

Rooms 126 (61 fmly) (33 GF) Facilities Spa STV ⊛ ᛦ Gym Leisure complex including thermal & beauty treatment suites Outdoor garden spa Xmas New Year Wi-fi Services Lift Parking 200

BRACKNELL — Map 4 SU86

Coppid Beech
★★★★ 75% ⊛ HOTEL
John Nike Way RG12 8TF
☎ 01344 303333 📄 01344 301200
e-mail: sales@coppidbeech.com
web: www.coppidbeech.com
dir: M4 junct 10 take Wokingham/Bracknell onto A329. In 2m take B3408 to Binfield at rdbt. Hotel 200yds on right

PETS: Bedrooms (16 GF) sign Charges £10 per night £70 per week Public areas only for access on leads Grounds on leads disp bin Exercise area 0.5m Facilities cage storage walks info vet info On Request fridge access towels Other charge for damage

This chalet designed hotel offers extensive facilities and includes a ski-slope, ice rink, nightclub, health club and Bier Keller. Bedrooms range from suites to standard rooms - all are impressively equipped. A choice of dining is offered; there's a full bistro menu available in the Keller, and for more formal dining, Rowan's restaurant provides award-winning cuisine.

Rooms 205 (6 fmly) (16 GF) S £135-£205; D £155-£225 (incl. bkfst) Facilities Spa STV ⊛ Gym Ice rink Dry ski slope Snow boarding Freestyle park ♬ New Year Wi-fi Services Lift Air con Parking 350 Notes LB

FINCHAMPSTEAD — Map 4 SU76

California Chalet & Touring Park (SU788651)
▶ ▶ ▶
Nine Mile Ride RG40 4HU
☎ 0118 973 3928 📄 0118 932 8720
e-mail: enquiries@californiapark.co.uk
dir: From A321 (S of Wokingham), right onto B3016 to Finchampstead. Follow Country Park signs on Nine Mile Ride to site

PETS: Charges 2+ dogs £1 per night Public areas on leads disp bin Exercise area adjacent woods Facilities walks info vet info Other prior notice required

Open all year Last arrival 21.00hrs Last departure noon

A peaceful woodland site with secluded pitches among the trees, adjacent to the country park. Several pitches have a prime position beside the lake with their own fishing area. A 5.5 acre site with 30 touring pitches, 30 hardstandings.

Notes No ground fires, no ball games, no washing of caravans

The Bear Hotel

★★★ 80% ◉◉ HOTEL

41 Charnham St RG17 0EL

☎ 01488 682512 🖹 01488 684357

e-mail: info@thebearhotelhungerford.co.uk

web: www.thebearhotelhungerford.co.uk

dir: *M4 junct 14, A338 to Hungerford for 3m, left at T-junct onto A4, hotel on left*

PETS: Bedrooms (24 GF) unattended **Public areas** on leads **Grounds Exercise area** canal & common nearby **Facilities** food (pre-bookable) bedding walks info vet info **On Request** fridge access **Resident Pets:** Bear (cat)

Situated five miles south of the M4 this hotel dates back as far as early 13th century and was once owned by King Henry VIII. It now has a contemporary feel throughout. Bedrooms are split between the main house, the courtyard and Bear Island. The award-winning restaurant is open for lunch and dinner, and lighter snacks are available in the bar and lounge. Guests can enjoy the sun terrace in the summer and log fires in the winter.

Rooms 39 (26 annexe) (2 fmly) (24 GF) **Facilities** FTV Xmas New Year Wi-fi **Parking** 68

 ■■LEGACY
■HOTELS.

Legacy Three Swans Hotel

★★★ 70% HOTEL

117 High St RG17 0LZ

☎ 01488 682721 🖹 01488 681708

e-mail: info@threeswans.net

web: www.threeswans.net

dir: *M4 junct 14 follow signs to Hungerford. Hotel half way along High St on left*

PETS: Bedrooms (5 GF) unattended **Stables** 0.75m **Charges** £10 per night **Public areas** only in public bar **Grounds** on leads **Facilities** water bowl bedding dog chews walks info vet info **On Request** torch **Other** charge for damage prior notice required

Centrally located in the bustling market town of Hungerford this charming former inn, dating back some 700 years, has been renovated in a fresh and airy style. Visitors will still see the original arch under which the horse-drawn carriages once passed. There is a wood panelled bar, a spacious lounge and attractive rear garden to relax in. The informal restaurant is decorated with a range of artwork by local artists. Bedrooms are well appointed and comfortable.

Rooms 25 (10 annexe) (1 fmly) (5 GF) (3 smoking) **Facilities** FTV Access to local private gym Xmas New Year Wi-fi **Parking** 30

The Pheasant Inn

★★★★ ▭ INN

Ermin St, Shefford Woodlands RG17 7AA

☎ 01488 648284 🖹 01488 648971

e-mail: enquiries@thepheasant-inn.co.uk

web: www.thepheasant-inn.co.uk

dir: *M4 junct 14, 200yds N on A338 turn left onto B4000 towards Lambourn*

PETS: Bedrooms Public areas Grounds Facilities food bowl bedding walks info **Other** charge for damage

The Pheasant Inn is a friendly, traditional property conveniently located 400 yards from the M4 and close to the racing centre of Lambourn and Newbury racecourse. Horseracing is popular in the area and the theme runs throughout the traditional pub and restaurant where lunch and dinner are served daily. Bedrooms in contrast are contemporary in style providing guests with comfortable accommodation; all feature flat-screen TVs, free Wi-fi and in-room beverage making facilities.

Rooms 11 en suite (4 GF) **Facilities** FTV TVL tea/coffee Dinner available Cen ht Wi-fi **Parking** 100

Hurley Riverside Park *(SU826839)*

▶▶▶▶▶

Park Office SL6 5NE

☎ 01628 824493 & 823501 🖹 01628 825533

e-mail: info@hurleyriversidepark.co.uk

dir: *Signed off A4130 (Henley to Maidenhead road), just W of Hurley*

PETS: Charges £2 per night **Public areas** on leads disp bin **Exercise area** large riverside picnic grounds adjacent **Facilities** walks info vet info **Other** dogs must be kept on leads; pet supplies available in village shop

Open Mar-Oct Last arrival 20.00hrs Last departure noon

A large Thames-side site with a good touring area close to river. A quality park, there are three beautifully appointed toilet blocks, which include quality, fully-serviced unisex facilities. Level grassy pitches are sited in small, sectioned areas, and this is a generally peaceful setting. Furnished tents for hire. A 15 acre site with 200 touring pitches, 12 hardstandings and 290 statics.

Notes No unsupervised children, dogs must be kept on leads, quiet park policy

Days Inn Membury

BUDGET HOTEL

Membury Service Area RG17 7TZ

☎ 01488 72336   📄 01488 72336

e-mail: membury.hotel@welcomebreak.co.uk

web: www.welcomebreak.co.uk

dir: *M4 between junct 14 & 15*

PETS: Bedrooms (17 GF) **Public areas** only for access to bedrooms **Grounds**

This modern building offers accommodation in smart, spacious and well-equipped bedrooms, suitable for families and business travellers, and all with en suite bathrooms. Continental breakfast is available and other refreshments may be taken at the nearby family restaurant.

Rooms 38 (32 fmly) (17 GF) (5 smoking) **S** £29-£59; **D** £29-£69*

Elephant at Pangbourne

★★★ 78% @ HOTEL

Church Rd RG8 7AR

☎ 0118 984 2244 & 07770 268359   📄 0118 976 7346

e-mail: annica@elephanthotel.co.uk

web: www.elephanthotel.co.uk

dir: *A4 Theale/Newbury, right at 2nd rdbt signed Pangbourne. Hotel on left*

PETS: Bedrooms (4 GF) unattended **Charges** £15 per night £105 per week **Public areas** except restaurant on leads **Grounds Exercise area Facilities** food bowl water bowl bedding cage storage walks info vet info **On Request** torch towels **Other** charge for damage pets allowed in one bedroom only

Centrally located in this bustling village, just a short drive from Reading. Bedrooms are individual in style but identical in the attention to detail, with handcrafted Indian furniture and rich oriental rugs. Guests can enjoy award-winning cuisine in the restaurant or bistro-style dining in the bar area.

Rooms 22 (8 annexe) (2 fmly) (4 GF) **Facilities** FTV ⛳ Xmas New Year Wi-fi **Parking** 10

Millennium Madejski Hotel Reading

★★★★ 80% @ HOTEL

Madejski Stadium RG2 0FL

☎ 0118 925 3500   📄 0118 925 3501

e-mail: sales.reading@millenniumhotels.co.uk

web: www.millenniumhotels.co.uk

dir: *M4 junct 11 onto A33, follow signs for Madejski Stadium Complex*

PETS: Bedrooms Charges Public areas except restaurants & bar on leads **Grounds** on leads disp bin **Exercise area** 100mtrs **Facilities** walks info vet info **Other** charge for damage **Restrictions** small dogs only

A stylish hotel, that features an atrium lobby with specially commissioned water sculpture, is part of the Madejski stadium complex, home to both Reading Football and London Irish Rugby teams. Bedrooms are appointed with spacious workstations and plenty of amenities; there is also a choice of suites and a club floor with its own lounge. The hotel also has a fine dining restaurant.

Rooms 201 (39 fmly) (19 smoking) **D** £60-£200* **Facilities** Spa STV 🐕 supervised Gym Wi-fi **Services** Lift Air con **Parking** 250 **Notes** LB RS Xmas & New Year

The Mill House Hotel

★★ 79% @ HOTEL

Old Basingstoke Rd, Swallowfield RG7 1PY

☎ 0118 988 3124   📄 0118 988 5550

e-mail: info@themillhousehotel.co.uk

web: www.themillhousehotel.co.uk

dir: *M4 junct 11, S on A33, left at 1st rdbt onto B3349. Approx 1m after sign for Three Mile Cross & Spencer's Wood, hotel on right*

PETS: Bedrooms unattended **Grounds** on leads **Exercise area** fields at rear of hotel **Facilities** cage storage walks info vet info **On Request** fridge access torch **Other** charge for damage

This smart Georgian house hotel enjoys a tranquil setting in its own delightful gardens, making it a popular wedding venue. Guests can enjoy fine dining in the conservatory-style restaurant or lighter meals in the cosy bar. Well-equipped bedrooms vary in size and style and include a number of spacious, well-appointed executive rooms.

Rooms 12 (2 fmly) **Facilities** FTV Wi-fi **Parking** 60 **Notes** Closed 25-30 Dec RS Sun evenings

ENGLAND

Ibis Reading Centre

BUDGET HOTEL

25A Friar St RG1 1DP

☎ 0118 953 3500   📠 0118 953 3501

e-mail: H5431@accor.com

web: www.ibishotel.com

dir: *Exit A329 into Friar St. Hotel near central train station*

PETS: Bedrooms Charges £5 per night **Other** charge for damage dogs are required to be muzzled

This hotel is situated in the main shopping area of Reading has handy NCP parking behind it. All bedrooms are well equipped and comfortable, and both dinner and breakfast are available in La Table restaurant.

Rooms 182 (36 fmly) **D** £29-£110*

Holiday Inn Reading M4 Jct 10

Holiday Inn

U

Wharfedale Rd, Winnersh Triangle RG41 5TS

☎ 0118 944 0444   📠 0118 944 0033

e-mail: reservations@hireadinghotel.com

dir: *M4 junct 10/A329 (N) towards Reading (E), 1st exit signed Winnersh/Woodley/A329, left at lights into Wharfesale Rd. Hotel on left*

PETS: Bedrooms Charges £10 per night **Grounds** on leads **Other** charge for damage **Restrictions** max weight of dog - 7.5kg

Currently the rating for this establishment is not confirmed. This may be due to a change of ownership or because it has only recently joined the AA rating scheme. For further details please see the AA website: theAA.com

Rooms 174 (25 fmly) (16 smoking) **S** fr £68; **D** fr £68*
Facilities FTV Gym Treatment room Xmas New Year Wi-fi
Services Lift Air con **Parking** 120 **Notes** LB

Wellington Country Park *(SU728628)*

▶ ▶ ▶

Odiham Rd RG7 1SP

☎ 0118 932 6444   📠 0118 932 6445

e-mail: info@wellington-country-park.co.uk

dir: *M4 junct 11, A33 south towards Basingstoke. M3 junct 5, B3349 north towards Reading*

PETS: Stables 1m **Charges** £2 per night **Public areas** on leads disp bin **Exercise area** on site **Exercise area** nearby **Facilities** food bowl water bowl scoop/disp bags vet info **Other** prior notice required

Open Mar-Nov Last arrival 17.30hrs Last departure 13.00hrs

A peaceful woodland site set within an extensive country park, which comes complete with lakes and nature trails. There's also a herd of Red and Fallow deer that roam the meadow area. Ideal for M4 travellers. A 80 acre site with 72 touring pitches, 10 hardstandings.

Notes No open fires.

The Swan at Streatley

★★★★ 77% HOTEL

High St RG8 9HR

☎ 01491 878800   📠 01491 872554

e-mail: sales@swan-at-streatley.co.uk

web: www.swanatstreatley.co.uk

dir: *From S right at lights in Streatley, hotel on left before bridge*

PETS: Bedrooms (12 GF) unattended **Charges** £15 per night **Public areas** except restaurant on leads **Grounds** disp bin **Facilities** water bowl walks info vet info **Other** charge for damage

A stunning location set beside the Thames, ideal for an English summer's day. The bedrooms are well appointed and many enjoy the lovely views. The hotel offers a range of facilities including meeting rooms, and the Magdalen Barge is moored beside the hotel making an unusual, yet perfect meeting venue. A motor launch is available for hire from April to October. The spa includes an indoor heated mineral pool and offers a range of treatments. Cuisine is accomplished and dining here should not be missed.

Rooms 45 (12 GF) **Facilities** Spa STV supervised Fishing Gym Electric motor launches for hire Apr-Oct Xmas New Year Wi-fi **Parking** 170

Christopher Hotel

★★★ 77% HOTEL

110 High St, Eton SL4 6AN

☎ 01753 852359   📠 01753 830914

e-mail: reservations@thechristopher.co.uk

web: www.thechristopher.co.uk

dir: *M4 junct 5 (Slough E), Colnbrook Datchet Eton (B470). At rdbt 2nd exit for Datchet. Right at mini rdbt (Eton), left into Eton Rd (3rd rdbt). Left, hotel on right*

PETS: Bedrooms (22 GF) **Charges** £10 per night **Public areas** except restaurant on leads **Grounds** on leads **Exercise area** large field adjacent **Facilities** food (pre-bookable) food bowl water bowl feeding mat washing facs cage storage walks info vet info **On Request** fridge access torch towels **Other** charge for damage **Resident Pet:** Magic (cat)

This hotel benefits from an ideal location in Eton, being only a short stroll across the pedestrian bridge from historic Windsor Castle and the many other attractions the town has to offer. The hotel has comfortable and smartly decorated accommodation, and a wide range of dishes is available in the informal bar and grill. A stylish room is available for private dining or for meetings.

Rooms 34 (23 annexe) (10 fmly) (22 GF) **S** £110-£125;
D £155-£173 **Facilities** FTV Xmas New Year Wi-fi **Parking** 19
Notes LB

ENGLAND

WINDSOR *continued*

Clarence Guest House

★★★ GUEST HOUSE

9 Clarence Rd SL4 5AE
☎ 01753 864436 📄 01753 857060
e-mail: clarence.hotel@btconnect.com
web: www.clarence-hotel.co.uk
dir: *M4 junct 6, dual-carriageway to Windsor, left at 1st rdbt onto Clarence Rd*

PETS: Bedrooms Facilities walks info vet info **On Request** towels **Other** charge for damage

This Grade II listed Victorian house is in the heart of Windsor. Space in some rooms is limited, but all are well maintained and offer excellent value for money. Facilities include a lounge with a well-stocked bar, and a steam room. Breakfast is served in the dining room overlooking attractive gardens.

Rooms 20 en suite (6 fmly) (2 GF) (18 smoking) **S** £40-£76; **D** £49-£85 **Facilities** FTV TVL tea/coffee Cen ht Licensed Wi-fi Sauna **Parking** 4

BRISTOL

BRISTOL	Map 3 ST57

Hotel du Vin Bristol

★★★★ 74% ⊛ TOWN HOUSE HOTEL

The Sugar House, Narrow Lewins Mead BS1 2NU
☎ 0117 925 5577 📄 0117 925 1199
e-mail: info.bristol@hotelduvin.com
web: www.hotelduvin.com
dir: *From A4 follow city centre signs. After 400yds pass Rupert St NCP on right. Hotel on opposite carriageway*

PETS: Bedrooms Charges £10 per night **Public areas** except restaurant **Facilities** food bowl water bowl bedding washing facs walks info vet info **On Request** fridge access torch towels **Other** charge for damage

This hotel is part of one of Britain's most innovative and expanding hotel groups that offer high standards of hospitality and accommodation. Housed in a Grade II listed, converted 18th-century sugar refinery, it provides great facilities with a modern, minimalist design. The bedrooms are exceptionally well designed and the bistro offers an excellent menu and wine list.

Rooms 40 (10 fmly) **S** £125-£160; **D** £125-£320* **Facilities** STV FTV Xmas New Year Wi-fi **Services** Lift **Parking** 12

Novotel Bristol Centre

★★★★ 70% HOTEL

Victoria St BS1 6HY
☎ 0117 976 9988 📄 0117 925 5040
e-mail: H5622@accor.com
web: www.novotel.com
dir: *At end of M32 follow signs for Temple Meads station to rdbt. Final exit, hotel immediately on right*

PETS: Bedrooms Charges £8 per night **Public areas** except food areas (ex assist dogs) muzzled and on leads **Exercise area** 5 mins walk **Facilities** walks info vet info **On Request** towels

This city centre hotel provides smart, contemporary style accommodation. Most of the bedrooms demonstrate the Novotel 'Novation' style with unique swivel desk, internet access, air-conditioning and a host of extras. The hotel is convenient for the mainline railway station and also has its own car park.

Rooms 131 (20 fmly) **Facilities** STV Gym Wi-fi **Services** Lift **Parking** 120

The Berkeley Square

★★★ 78% ⊛⊛ HOTEL

15 Berkeley Square, Clifton BS8 1HB
☎ 0117 925 4000 📄 0117 925 2970
e-mail: berkeley@cliftonhotels.com
web: www.cliftonhotels.com/chg.html
dir: *M32 follow Clifton signs. 1st left at lights by Nills Memorial Tower (University) into Berkeley Sq*

PETS: Bedrooms (4 GF) unattended **Charges Public areas** except restaurant on leads **Grounds** on leads **Exercise area** adjacent to park **Facilities** walks info vet info **Other** charge for damage cats must be caged

Set in a pleasant square close to the university, art gallery and Clifton Village, this smart, elegant Georgian hotel has modern, stylishly decorated bedrooms that feature many welcome extras. There is a cosy lounge and stylish restaurant on the ground floor and a smart, contemporary bar in the basement. A small garden is also available at the rear of the hotel.

Rooms 43 (4 GF) **Facilities** Use of local gym & swimming pool **Services** Lift **Parking** 20

Arnos Manor Hotel

★★★ 74% HOTEL

470 Bath Rd, Arno's Vale BS4 3HQ

☎ 0117 971 1461 📠 0117 971 5507

e-mail: arnos.manor@forestdale.com

web: www.arnosmanorhotel.co.uk

dir: *From end of M32 follow signs for Bath. Hotel on right of A4 after 2m. Next to ITV West TV studio*

PETS: **Bedrooms** (7 GF) unattended sign **Charges** £7.50 per night **Public areas** except restaurant/bar on leads disp bin **Exercise area** 50mtrs **Facilities** food (pre-bookable) food bowl water bowl cage storage walks info vet info **On Request** fridge access torch towels **Other** charge for damage **Restrictions** no dangerous breeds (see page 7)

Once the home of a wealthy merchant, this historic 18th-century building is now a comfortable hotel and offers spacious, well-appointed bedrooms with plenty of workspace. The lounge was once the chapel and has many original features, while meals are taken in the atmospheric, conservatory-style restaurant.

Rooms 73 (5 fmly) (7 GF) **S** £74-£105; **D** £87-£145 (incl. bkfst)* **Facilities** FTV Xmas New Year Wi-fi **Services** Lift **Parking** 200 **Notes** LB

Rodney Hotel

★★ 76% ⊛ HOTEL

4 Rodney Place, Clifton BS8 4HY

☎ 0117 973 5422 📠 0117 946 7092

e-mail: rodney@cliftonhotels.com

dir: *Off Clifton Down Rd*

PETS: **Bedrooms** (2 GF) on leads **Grounds Exercise area** park 0.5m **Facilities** vet info **On Request** fridge access **Other** charge for damage **Restrictions** small dogs only

With easy access from the M5, this attractive, listed building in Clifton is conveniently close to the city centre. The individually decorated bedrooms provide a useful range of extra facilities for the business traveller; the public areas include a smart bar and small restaurant offering enjoyable and carefully prepared dishes. A pleasant rear garden provides additional seating in the summer months.

Rooms 31 (1 fmly) (2 GF) **S** £46-£92; **D** £60-£110 (incl. dinner)* **Facilities** FTV Wi-fi **Parking** 10 **Notes** Closed 22 Dec-3 Jan RS Sun

Clifton

★★ 75% HOTEL

St Pauls Rd, Clifton BS8 1LX

☎ 0117 973 6882 📠 0117 974 1082

e-mail: clifton@cliftonhotels.com

web: www.cliftonhotels.com/clifton

dir: *M32 follow Bristol/Clifton signs, along Park St. Left at lights into St Pauls Rd*

PETS: **Bedrooms** (12 GF) unattended **Charges Public areas** except restaurant **Exercise area** 0.5m **Facilities** food (pre-bookable) walks info vet info **On Request** fridge access torch towels **Other** charge for damage

This popular hotel offers very well equipped bedrooms and relaxed, friendly service. There is a welcoming lounge by the reception, and in summer months drinks and meals can be enjoyed on the terrace. Racks Bar and Restaurant offers an interesting selection of modern dishes in informal surroundings. There is some street parking, but for a small charge, secure garage parking is available.

Rooms 59 (2 fmly) (12 GF) (9 smoking) **Facilities** STV Wi-fi **Services** Lift **Parking** 12 **Notes** LB

Washington

★★★ GUEST HOUSE

11-15 St Pauls Rd, Clifton BS8 1LX

☎ 0117 973 3980 📠 0117 973 4740

e-mail: washington@cliftonhotels.com

dir: *A4018 into city, right at lights opp BBC, house 200yds on left*

PETS: **Bedrooms** unattended **Public areas** except breakfast room **Grounds Exercise area** 0.25m **Facilities** food (pre-bookable) vet info **On Request** fridge access torch towels **Other** charge for damage

This large terraced house is within walking distance of the city centre and Clifton Village. The bedrooms, many refurbished, are well equipped for business guests. Public areas include a modern reception lounge and a bright basement breakfast room. The property has secure parking and a rear patio garden.

Rooms 46 rms (40 en suite) (4 fmly) (10 GF) (7 smoking) **S** £36-£71; **D** £44-£87* **Facilities** FTV tea/coffee Direct Dial Cen ht Licensed Wi-fi **Parking** 16 **Notes** Closed 23 Dec-3 Jan

ENGLAND

AYLESBURY — Map 4 SP81

Hartwell House Hotel, Restaurant & Spa

★★★★ ◉◉◉ HOTEL

Oxford Rd HP17 8NR
☎ 01296 747444 📠 01296 747450
e-mail: info@hartwell-house.com
web: www.hartwell-house.com
dir: From S: M40 junct 7, A329 to Thame, then A418 towards Aylesbury. After 6m, through Stone, hotel on left. From N: M40 junct 9 for Bicester. A41 to Aylesbury, A418 to Oxford for 2m. Hotel on right

PETS: Bedrooms (10 GF) unattended Charges Public areas Grounds disp bin Exercise area Facilities food bowl water bowl dog chews scoop/disp bags cage storage walks info vet info On Request fridge access torch towels Other charge for damage pets allowed in Hartwell Court suites only Restrictions 1 large or 2 small dogs only

This beautiful, historic house is set in 90 acres of unspoilt parkland. The grand public rooms are truly magnificent, and feature many fine works of art. The service standards are very high; guests will find that the staff offer attentive and traditional hospitality without stuffiness. There is an elegant, award-winning restaurant where carefully prepared dishes use the best local produce. Bedrooms are spacious, elegant and very comfortable. Most are in the main house, but some, including suites, are in the nearby, renovated coach house, which also houses an excellent spa.

Rooms 46 (16 annexe) (3 fmly) (10 GF) S £170-£200; D £200-£380 (incl. bkfst)* Facilities Spa STV ⊗ supervised 🏊 🎣 Gym Sauna treatment rooms Steam rooms 🎵 Xmas New Year Wi-fi Services Lift Parking 91 Notes LB No children 4yrs RS Xmas/New Year

BUCKINGHAM — Map 4 SP63

Best Western

Best Western Buckingham Hotel

★★★ 75% HOTEL

Buckingham Ring Rd MK18 1RY
☎ 01280 822622 📠 01280 823074
e-mail: info@thebuckinghamhotel.co.uk
dir: Follow A421 for Buckingham, take ring road S towards Brackley & Bicester. Hotel on left

PETS: Bedrooms (31 GF) unattended Charges £10 per night Public areas on leads Grounds on leads disp bin Facilities vet info On Request torch Restrictions small dogs only

A purpose-built hotel, which offers comfortable and spacious rooms with well designed working spaces for business travellers. There are also extensive conference facilities. The open-plan restaurant and bar offer a good range of dishes, and the well-equipped leisure suite is popular with guests.

Rooms 70 (6 fmly) (31 GF) S £40-£99; D £49-£129*
Facilities STV FTV ⊗ supervised Gym Xmas New Year Wi-fi
Parking 200 Notes LB

CHENIES — Map 4 TQ09

The Bedford Arms Hotel

★★★ 79% ◉ HOTEL

WD3 6EQ
☎ 01923 283301 📠 01923 284825
e-mail: contact@bedfordarms.co.uk
web: www.bedfordarms.co.uk
dir: M25 junct 18/A404 towards Amersham, hotel signed after 2m on right

PETS: Bedrooms (8 GF) Charges disp bin Exercise area 20yds Facilities water bowl walks info vet info Other charge for damage Restrictions no very large dogs

This attractive, 19th-century country inn enjoys a peaceful rural setting. Comfortable bedrooms are decorated in traditional style and feature a range of thoughtful extras. Each room is named after a relation of the Duke of Bedford, whose family has an historic association with the property. There are two bars, a lounge and a cosy, wood-panelled restaurant.

Rooms 18 (8 annexe) (2 fmly) (8 GF) S £60-£110; D £95-£140 (incl. bkfst)* Facilities STV Wi-fi Parking 60 Notes Closed 27 Dec-4 Jan

HIGH WYCOMBE — Map 4 SU89

Fox Country Inn

★★★ 64% SMALL HOTEL

Ibstone HP14 3XT
☎ 01491 639333 📠 01491 639444
e-mail: info@foxcountryinn.co.uk
dir: M40 junct 5 follow signs to Ibstone, hotel 1.5m on left

PETS: Bedrooms (10 GF) unattended sign Sep accom prior notice required for kennels Stables 1m Charges from £20 per night from £90 per week Public areas disp bin Exercise area 100yds Facilities food (pre-bookable) food bowl water bowl bedding pet sitting dog walking washing facs dog grooming cage storage walks info vet info On Request fridge access torch towels Other charge for damage bedding & blankets charged

This delightful inn has become a small family-run hotel. The bedrooms are very well appointed with many added extras, and are designed with comfort in mind. Public areas are modern, and external decking provides further seating in summer months. There is a wide ranging choice of dishes including a Thai menu.

Rooms 18 (3 fmly) (10 GF) Facilities FTV Xmas New Year Wi-fi Parking 45 Notes LB

MACDONALD
HOTELS & RESORTS

Macdonald Compleat Angler

★★★★ ◉◉◉ HOTEL

Marlow Bridge SL7 1RG

☎ 0844 879 9128 📠 01628 486388

e-mail: compleatangler@macdonald-hotels.co.uk
web: www.macdonald-hotels.co.uk/compleatangler
dir: *M4 junct 8/9, A404(M) to rdbt, Bisham exit, 1m to Marlow Bridge, hotel on right*

PETS: Bedrooms (6 GF) unattended sign **Stables** 3m **Charges** £10 per night **Grounds** on leads **Exercise area** 400mtrs **Facilities** cage storage walks info vet info **On Request** fridge access **Other** charge for damage

This well-established hotel enjoys an idyllic location overlooking the River Thames and the delightful Marlow weir. The bedrooms, which differ in size and style, are all individually decorated and are equipped with flat-screen TVs, high speed internet and air conditioning. Aubergine has three AA Rosettes and offers modern French cuisine; Bowaters serves British dishes and has gained two AA Rosettes. Staff throughout are keen to please and nothing is too much trouble.

Rooms 64 (6 fmly) (6 GF) **D** £115-£230 **Facilities** STV Fishing Fly and coarse fishing River trips (Apr-Sep) ♫ Xmas New Year Wi-fi **Services** Lift **Parking** 100 **Notes** LB

NOVOTEL

Novotel Milton Keynes

★★★ 73% HOTEL

Saxon St, Layburn Court, Heelands MK13 7RA

☎ 01908 322212 📠 01908 322235

e-mail: H3272@accor-hotels.com
web: www.novotel.com
dir: *M1 junct 14, follow Childsway signs towards city centre. Right into Saxon Way, straight across all rdbts, hotel on left*

PETS: Bedrooms (40 GF) **Charges** £10 per night **Public areas** only for access on leads **Grounds** on leads disp bin **Exercise area** 50mtrs

Contemporary in style, this purpose-built hotel is situated on the outskirts of the town, just a few minutes' drive from the centre and mainline railway station. Bedrooms provide ample workspace and a good range of facilities for the modern traveller, and public rooms include a children's play area and indoor leisure centre.

Rooms 124 (40 fmly) (40 GF) **Facilities** 🏊 Gym Steam bath **Services** Lift **Parking** 130

Campanile

Campanile Milton Keynes

BUDGET HOTEL

40 Penn Road (off Watling St), Fenny Stratford, Bletchley MK2 2AU

☎ 01908 649819 📠 01908 649818

e-mail: miltonkeynes@campanile.com
dir: *M1 junct 14, A4146 to A5. S'bound on A5. 4th exit at 1st rdbt to Fenny Stratford. Hotel 500yds on left*

PETS: Bedrooms (26 GF) **Charges** £5 per night **Public areas** on leads **Exercise area** canal walk nearby **Other** please phone for further details of pet facilities

This modern building offers accommodation in smart, well-equipped bedrooms, all with en suite bathrooms. Refreshments may be taken at the informal bistro.

Rooms 80 (26 GF) **S** £55-£62; **D** £55-£62*

DAYS INN

Days Inn Milton Keynes East M1

BUDGET HOTEL

Newport Pagnell MK16 8DS

☎ 01908 610878 📠 01908 216539

e-mail: newport.hotel@welcomebreak.co.uk
web: www.daysinn.com
dir: *M1 junct 14-15. In service area - follow signs to Barrier Lodge*

PETS: Bedrooms muzzled and on leads **Grounds** on leads **Exercise area Facilities** (pre-bookable) walks info vet info **Other** charge for damage

This modern building offers accommodation in smart, spacious and well-equipped bedrooms, suitable for families and business travellers, and all with en suite bathrooms. Refreshments may be taken at the nearby family restaurant.

Rooms 90 (54 fmly)

ENGLAND

Cliveden Country House Hotel

★★★★★ ◎◎ COUNTRY HOUSE HOTEL

SL6 0JF

☎ 01628 668561   📠 01628 661837

e-mail: info@clivedenhouse.co.uk

web: www.clivedenhouse.co.uk

dir: *M4 junct 7, A4 towards Maidenhead for 1.5m, onto B476 towards Taplow, 2.5m, hotel on left*

PETS: **Bedrooms** (10 GF) **Stables** 2m **Public areas** except restaurants, spa & walled garden on leads **Grounds** on leads disp bin **Exercise area** woodland walk **Facilities** food (pre-bookable) food bowl water bowl bedding pet sitting dog walking washing facs cage storage walks info vet info **On Request** fridge access **Other** charge for damage charge for pet food

This wonderful stately home stands at the top of a gravelled boulevard. Visitors are treated as house-guests and staff recapture the tradition of fine hospitality. Bedrooms have individual quality and style, and reception rooms retain a timeless elegance. Exceptional leisure facilities include cruises along Cliveden Reach and massages in the Pavilion. The Terrace Restaurant with its delightful views has two AA Rosettes. The Rosette award for Waldo's, which offers innovative menus in discreet, luxurious surroundings, is temporarily suspended due to a change of chef; a new award will be in place once our inspectors have completed their assessments of meals cooked by the new kitchen team.

Rooms 39 (10 GF) **S** £210-£1745; **D** £210-£1745 (incl. bkfst)* **Facilities** Spa STV FTV ⊛ ⊰ ⊛ ⊌ Gym Squash Full range of beauty treatments 3 vintage boats 🎵 Xmas New Year Wi-fi **Services** Lift **Parking** 60

Days Inn Cambridge

BUDGET HOTEL

Cambridge Extra Services, Junction A14/M11 CB3 8WU

☎ 01954 267176   📠 01954 267864

e-mail: cambridge.hotel@welcomebreak.co.uk

dir: *A14/M11 Cambridge Extra Services*

PETS: **Bedrooms** (40 GF) unattended **Grounds** on leads disp bin **Exercise area** **Facilities** cage storage walks info vet info **On Request** towels

This modern, purpose built accommodation offers smartly appointed, well-equipped bedrooms, with good power showers. There is a choice of adjacent food outlets where guests may enjoy breakfast, snacks and meals.

Rooms 82 (14 fmly) (40 GF) (19 smoking) **S** £29-£49; **D** £29-£69

Stanford Park (TL578675)

►►►

Weirs Drove CB25 0BP

☎ 01638 741547 & 07802 439997

e-mail: enquiries@stanfordcaravanpark.co.uk

dir: *Signed from B1102*

PETS: **Public areas** disp bin **Exercise area**

Open all year Last arrival 20.00hrs Last departure 11.00hrs

A secluded site on the outskirts of Burwell set in four large fields with several attractive trees. The amenities are modern and well kept, and there are eight hardstandings hedged with privet. A 20 acre site with 100 touring pitches, 20 hardstandings.

Notes No group bookings 🐾

Hotel Felix

★★★★ 82% ◎◎ HOTEL

Whitehouse Ln CB3 0LX

☎ 01223 277977   📠 01223 277973

e-mail: help@hotelfelix.co.uk

web: www.hotelfelix.co.uk

dir: *M11 junct 13. From A1 N, take A14 onto A1307. At 'City of Cambridge' sign left into Whitehouse Ln*

PETS: **Bedrooms** (26 GF) unattended **Grounds** on leads **Exercise area** field behind hotel **Facilities** cage storage walks info vet info **On Request** fridge access **Other** charge for damage please phone for further details of pet facilities

A beautiful Victorian mansion set amidst three acres of landscaped gardens, this property was originally built in 1852 for a surgeon from the famous Addenbrookes Hospital. The contemporary-style bedrooms have carefully chosen furniture and many thoughtful touches, whilst public rooms feature an open-plan bar, the adjacent Graffiti restaurant and a small quiet lounge.

Rooms 52 (5 fmly) (26 GF) **Facilities** STV Xmas New Year Wi-fi **Services** Lift **Parking** 90

Hotel du Vin Cambridge

★★★★ 74% ⊛ TOWN HOUSE HOTEL

15-19 Trumpington St CB2 1QA

☎ 01223 227330 📄 01223 227331

e-mail: info.cambridge@hotelduvin.com

web: www.hotelduvin.com

dir: *M11 junct 11 Cambridge S, pass Trumpington Park & Ride on left. Hotel 2m on right after double rdbt*

PETS: Bedrooms (6 GF) unattended **Charges** £10 per night **Public areas** except restaurant & bar on leads **Facilities** food bowl water bowl bedding feeding mat walks info vet info **On Request** towels **Other** charge for damage

This beautiful building, which dates back in part to medieval times, has been transformed to enhance its many quirky architectural features. The bedrooms and suites, some with private terraces, have the company's trademark monsoon showers and Egyptian linen. The French-style bistro has an open-style kitchen and the bar is set in the unusual labyrinth of vaulted cellar rooms. There is also a library, specialist wine tasting room and private dining room.

Rooms 41 (3 annexe) (6 GF) **Facilities** STV Xmas New Year Wi-fi **Services** Lift Air con **Parking** 24

Best Western The Gonville Hotel

★★★ 78% HOTEL

Gonville Place CB1 1LY

☎ 01223 366611 & 221111 📄 01223 315470

e-mail: all@gonvillehotel.co.uk

web: www.bw-gonvillehotel.co.uk

dir: *M11 junct 11, on A1309 follow city centre signs. At 2nd mini rdbt right into Lensfield Rd, over junct with lights. Hotel 25yds on right*

PETS: Bedrooms (5 GF) **Grounds** on leads **Exercise area** adjacent **Facilities** vet info **Other** charge for damage cats in cages only

A well established hotel situated on the inner ring road, a short walk across the green from the city centre. The air-conditioned public areas are cheerfully furnished, and include a lounge bar and brasserie; bedrooms are well appointed and appealing, offering a good range of facilities for both corporate and leisure guests.

Rooms 73 (1 fmly) (5 GF) **S** £70-£136; **D** £76-£159.50*

Facilities FTV New Year Wi-fi **Services** Lift **Parking** 80 **Notes** LB RS 24-29 Dec

Royal Cambridge

★★★ 75% HOTEL

Trumpington St CB2 1PY

☎ 01223 351631 📄 01223 352972

e-mail: royal.cambridge@forestdale.com

web: www.theroyalcambridgehotel.co.uk

dir: *M11 junct 11, signed city centre. At 1st mini rdbt left into Fen Causeway. Hotel 1st right*

PETS: Bedrooms (3 GF) sign **Charges** £7.50 per night **Public areas** except restaurant on leads **Facilities** food food bowl water bowl cage storage walks info vet info

This elegant Georgian hotel is situated in the heart of Cambridge. The bedrooms are well equipped and provide great comfort. The stylish restaurant and bar are a popular choice with locals and guests alike. The complimentary parking proves a real benefit in this city centre location.

Rooms 57 (5 fmly) (3 GF) **S** £85-£125; **D** £104-£164 (incl. bkfst)*

Facilities FTV Xmas New Year Wi-fi **Services** Lift **Parking** 80 **Notes** LB

DUXFORD   Map 5 TL44

Duxford Lodge

★★★ 75% ⊛ HOTEL

Ickleton Rd CB22 4RT

☎ 01223 836444 📄 01223 832271

e-mail: admin@duxfordlodgehotel.co.uk

web: www.duxfordlodgehotel.co.uk

dir: *M11 junct 10, onto A505 to Duxford. 1st right at rdbt, hotel 0.75m on left*

PETS: Bedrooms (4 GF) **Charges Grounds** on leads **Facilities** walks info vet info **On Request** towels **Other** charge for damage **Restrictions** no large dogs; no Rottweilers or Bull Terriers

A warm welcome is assured at this attractive red-brick hotel in the hart of a delightful village. Public areas include a cosy relaxing bar, separate lounge, and an attractive restaurant, where an excellent and imaginative menu is offered. The bedrooms are well appointed, comfortable and smartly furnished.

Rooms 15 (4 annexe) (2 fmly) (4 GF) **S** £78.50-£93.50; **D** £108-£128.50 (incl. bkfst)* **Facilities** FTV Wi-fi **Parking** 34 **Notes** Closed 25 Dec-2 Jan

ENGLAND

Castle Lodge
★★★ GUEST HOUSE
50 New Barns Rd CB7 4PW
☎ 01353 662276   📠 01353 666606
e-mail: castlelodgehotel@supanet.com
dir: *Off B1382 Prickwillow Rd, NE from town centre*

PETS: **Bedrooms** unattended **Charges** **Public areas** except restaurant on leads **Grounds** on leads **Exercise area** field nearby **Facilities** food (pre-bookable) food bowl water bowl pet sitting dog walking cage storage walks info **On Request** fridge access torch **Other** charge for damage

Located within easy walking distance of the cathedral, this extended Victorian house offers well-equipped bedrooms in a variety of sizes. Public areas include a traditionally furnished dining room and a comfortable air-conditioned bar lounge. Service is friendly and helpful.

Rooms 11 rms (6 en suite) (3 fmly) **Facilities** TVL tea/coffee Dinner available Direct Dial Cen ht Licensed Wi-fi **Parking** 6

The Old Bridge Hotel
★★★ 86% ◉◉ HOTEL
1 High St PE29 3TQ
☎ 01480 424300   📠 01480 411017
e-mail: oldbridge@huntsbridge.co.uk
web: www.huntsbridge.com
dir: *From A14 or A1 follow Huntingdon signs. Hotel visible from inner ring road*

PETS: **Bedrooms** (2 GF) unattended **Stables** 5m **Charges** **Public areas** on leads **Grounds** on leads **Exercise area** adjacent **Facilities** walks info vet info **On Request** towels **Other** charge for damage

An imposing 18th-century building situated close to shops and amenities. This charming hotel offers superb accommodation in stylish and individually decorated bedrooms that include many useful extras. Guests can choose from the same menu whether dining in the open-plan terrace, or the more formal restaurant with its bold colour scheme. There is also an excellent business centre.

Rooms 24 (2 fmly) (2 GF) **S** £99-£140; **D** £135-£199 (incl. bkfst) **Facilities** STV FTV Fishing Private mooring for boats Xmas New Year Wi-fi **Services** Air con **Parking** 50 **Notes** LB

Huntingdon Boathaven & Caravan Park
(TL249706)
►►►
The Avenue, Godmanchester PE29 2AF
☎ 01480 411977   📠 01480 411977
e-mail: boathaven.hunts@virgin.net
dir: *S of town. Exit A14 at Godmanchester junct, through Godmanchester on B1043 to site (on left by River Ouse)*

PETS: **Public areas** except toilet block; dogs must be kept on leads **Exercise area** field adjacent to site **Facilities** vet info **Other** prior notice required

Open all year rs Open in winter when weather permits Last arrival 21.00hrs

A small, well laid out site overlooking a boat marina and the River Ouse, set close to the A14 and within walking distance of Huntingdon town centre. Clean, well kept toilets. A pretty area has been created for tents beside the marina, with wide views across the Ouse Valley. Weekend family activities are organized throughout the season. A 2 acre site with 24 touring pitches, 18 hardstandings.

Notes ◎

The Willows Caravan Park *(TL224708)*
►►►
Bromholme Ln, Brampton PE28 4NE
☎ 01480 437566
e-mail: willows@willows33.freeserve.co.uk
dir: *Exit A14/A1 signed Brampton, follow Huntingdon signs. Site on right close to Brampton Mill pub*

PETS: **Charges** 50p per night **Public areas** dogs must be kept on leads disp bin **Exercise area** along river bank **Facilities** walks info vet info **Other** prior notice required **Resident Pet:** dog

Open all year Last arrival 20.00hrs Last departure noon

A small, friendly site in a pleasant setting beside the River Ouse, on the Ouse Valley Walk. Bay areas have been provided for caravans and motorhomes, and planting for screening is gradually maturing. There are launching facilities and free river fishing. A 4 acre site with 50 touring pitches, 10 hardstandings.

Notes Ball games on field provided, no generators, no groundsheets, 5mph one-way system. ◎

PETERBOROUGH — Map 4 TL19

Best Western Orton Hall

★★★ 81% @ HOTEL

Orton Longueville PE2 7DN
☎ 01733 391111 📠 01733 231912
e-mail: reception@ortonhall.co.uk
dir: Off A605 E, opposite Orton Mere

PETS: Bedrooms (15 GF) Charges £15 per night Public areas
except restaurants on leads Grounds Exercise area park
0.25m Facilities water bowl On Request towels Other charge
for damage

An impressive country-house hotel set in 20 acres of woodland
on the outskirts of town and with easy access to the A1. The
spacious and relaxing public areas include the baronial Great
Room and the Orton Suite for banqueting and for meetings, and
the oak-panelled, award-winning Huntly Restaurant. The on-site
pub, Ramblewood Inn, is an alternative, informal dining option.

Rooms 73 (2 fmly) (15 GF) S £40-£130; D £40-£140*
Facilities STV ✈ Gym Sauna Steam room 2 joggers 2 cross
trainers Xmas New Year Wi-fi Parking 200 Notes LB

Days Inn Peterborough

BUDGET HOTEL

Peterborough Extra Services, A1 Junction 17, Great North Road,
Haddon PE7 3UQ
☎ 01733 371540 📠 01733 391594
e-mail: peterborough.hotel@welcomebreak.co.uk
dir: A1(M) junct 17 Peterborough Extra Services

PETS: Bedrooms (40 GF) Public areas on leads Grounds on
leads disp bin Facilities cage storage walks info vet info
On Request towels Other charge for damage

This modern, purpose-built accommodation block offers smartly
appointed, particularly well-equipped bedrooms with good power
showers. There is a choice of adjacent food outlets where guests
can enjoy breakfast, snacks and meals.

Rooms 82 (13 fmly) (40 GF) (13 smoking) S £29-£79; D £29-£79

ST NEOTS — Map 4 TL16

The George Hotel & Brasserie

★★★ 86% @ HOTEL

High St, Buckden PE19 5XA
☎ 01480 812300 📠 01480 813920
e-mail: mail@thegeorgebuckden.com
web: www.thegeorgebuckden.com
dir: Just off A1 at Buckden, 2m S of A1/A14 interchange

PETS: Bedrooms Charges £8 per night Public areas only in
foyer area on leads Grounds on leads Exercise area 0.5m
Facilities food bowl water bowl cage storage walks info vet
info On Request fridge access

Ideally situated in the heart of this historic town centre and just a
short drive from the A1. Public rooms feature a bustling ground-
floor brasserie, which offers casual dining throughout the day
and evening; there is also an informal lounge bar with an open
fire and comfy seating. Bedrooms are stylish, tastefully appointed
and thoughtfully equipped.

Rooms 12 (1 fmly) S £90-£140; D £110-£140 (incl. bkfst)*
Facilities STV Xmas Wi-fi Services Lift Parking 25 Notes LB

WISBECH — Map 5 TF40

Elme Hall

★★★ 70% HOTEL

Elm High Rd PE14 0DQ
☎ 01945 475566 📠 01945 475666
e-mail: elmehallhotel@btconnect.com
web: www.elmehall.co.uk
dir: Off A47 onto A1101 towards Wisbech. Hotel on right

PETS: Bedrooms Stables 5m Charges £5 per night £25 per
week Public areas on leads Grounds Exercise area Facilities
cage storage walks info vet info On Request towels Other
charge for damage Restrictions single budget bedrooms
unsuitable for medium to large dogs

An imposing, Georgian-style property conveniently situated on
the outskirts of the town centre just off the A47. Individually
decorated bedrooms are tastefully furnished with quality
reproduction pieces and equipped to a high standard. Public
rooms include a choice of attractive lounges, as well as two bars,
meeting rooms and a banqueting suite.

Rooms 8 (3 fmly) S £58; D £78-£245 (incl. bkfst)* Facilities FTV
♬ Wi-fi Parking 200

ENGLAND

WISBECH *continued*

Little Ranch Leisure *(TF456062)*

▶▶▶

Begdale, Elm PE14 0AZ
☎ 01945 860066 📠 01945 860114
dir: *From rdbt on A47 (SW of Wisbech) take Redmoor Lane to Begdale*

PETS: Public areas disp bin **Exercise area** 10-acre orchard **Facilities** vet info

Open all year

A friendly family site set in an apple orchard, with 25 fully-serviced pitches and a beautifully designed, spacious toilet block. The site overlooks a large fishing lake, and the famous horticultural auctions at Wisbech are nearby. A 10 acre site with 25 touring pitches, 25 hardstandings.

Notes 😊

CHESHIRE

AUDLEM
Map 7 SJ64

Little Heath Farm *(SJ663455)*

★★★★ FARMHOUSE

CW3 0HE
☎ 01270 811324   Mrs H M Bennion
e-mail: hilaryandbob@ukonline.co.uk
dir: *Off A525 in village onto A529 towards Nantwich for 0.3m. Farm opposite village green*

PETS: Bedrooms Charges £5 per night **Public areas** except dining room **Grounds** on leads disp bin **Exercise area** on farm **Other** charge for damage prior notice required

The 200-year-old brick farmhouse retains much original character, including low beamed ceilings. The traditionally furnished public areas include a cosy sitting room and a dining room where guests dine family style. The bedrooms are stylish, and the friendly proprietors create a relaxing atmosphere.

Rooms 3 en suite (1 fmly) **Facilities** TVL tea/coffee Cen ht **Parking** 6 **Notes** 😊 50 acres mixed

BURWARDSLEY
Map 7 SJ55

The Pheasant Inn

★★★★★ 🍴 INN

Higher Burwardsley CH3 9PF
☎ 01829 770434 📠 01829 771097
e-mail: info@thepheasantinn.co.uk
dir: *From A41, left to Tattenhall, right at 1st junct & left at 2nd Higher Burwardsley. At post office left, signed*

PETS: Bedrooms unattended **Charges** £10 per stay **Public areas** on leads **Grounds Exercise area** 10mtrs **Facilities** water bowl washing facs cage storage walks info vet info **On Request** fridge access torch towels

This delightful 300-year-old inn sits high on the Peckforton Hills and enjoys spectacular views over the Cheshire Plain. Well-equipped, comfortable bedrooms are housed in an adjacent converted barn. Creative dishes are served either in the stylish restaurant or in the traditional, beamed bar. Real fires are lit in the winter months.

Rooms 2 en suite 10 annexe en suite (2 fmly) (5 GF) **S** £65-£95; **D** £85-£130* **Facilities** FTV tea/coffee Dinner available Direct Dial Cen ht Wi-fi **Parking** 80

CHESTER
Map 7 SJ46

Grosvenor Pulford Hotel & Spa

★★★★ 74% HOTEL

Wrexham Rd, Pulford CH4 9DG
☎ 01244 570560 📠 01244 570809
e-mail: reservations@grosvenorpulfordhotel.co.uk
web: www.grosvenorpulfordhotel.co.uk
dir: *M53/A55 at junct signed A483 Chester/Wrexham & North Wales. Left onto B5445, hotel 2m on right*

PETS: Bedrooms (21 GF) unattended **Charges** £10 per stay **Public areas** except restaurant on leads **Grounds** disp bin **Exercise area** 100mtrs **Facilities** washing facs cage storage walks info vet info **On Request** fridge access torch towels

Set in rural surroundings, this modern, stylish hotel features a magnificent spa with a large Roman-style swimming pool. Among the bedrooms are several executive suites and others containing spiral staircases leading to the bedroom sections. A smart brasserie restaurant and bar provide a wide range of imaginative dishes in a relaxed atmosphere.

Rooms 73 (10 fmly) (21 GF) (6 smoking) **S** £90-£120; **D** £130-£175 (incl. bkfst)* **Facilities** Spa STV FTV 🏊 💆 Gym Steam room Sauna Xmas New Year Wi-fi **Services** Lift **Parking** 200 **Notes** LB

Dene Hotel

★★ 75% HOTEL

95 Hoole Rd CH2 3ND

☎ 01244 321165 🖹 01244 350277

e-mail: info@denehotel.com

web: www.denehotel.com

dir: *M53 junct 12 take A56 for 1m towards Chester. Hotel 1m from M53 adjacent to Alexander Park*

PETS: Bedrooms (20 GF) unattended **Public areas** except restaurant **Grounds** disp bin **Exercise area** 2 mins walk **Facilities** walks info vet info **On Request** towels

This friendly hotel is part of a small privately owned group and is located close to both the city centre and M53. The bedrooms are very well equipped and many are on ground floor level; family rooms and interconnecting rooms are available. In addition to bar meals, an interesting choice of dishes is offered in the welcoming Castra Brasserie which proves very popular with locals.

Rooms 52 (8 annexe) (5 fmly) (20 GF) **S** £35-£60; **D** £50-£80 **Facilities** FTV New Year Wi-fi **Parking** 55 **Notes** LB

DISLEY Map 7 SJ98

Best Western Moorside Grange Hotel & Spa

★★★ 72% HOTEL

Mudhurst Ln, Higher Disley SK12 2AP

☎ 01663 764151 🖹 01663 762794

e-mail: sales@moorsidegrangehotel.com

web: www.moorsidegrangehotel.com

dir: *Exit A6 at Rams Head in Disley, onto Buxton Old Rd for 1m, right onto Mudhurst Ln, hotel on left*

PETS: Bedrooms unattended **Charges Public areas** except restaurants on leads **Grounds** disp bin **Exercise area Facilities** water bowl scoop/disp bags walks info vet info **On Request** fridge access torch towels **Other** charge for damage please contact hotel for details of charges for dogs

Situated on the edge of the Peak District National Park, and with spectacular views of the moors above Higher Disley, this large complex is in an area considered a walkers' paradise. The hotel has excellent conference and function facilities, a well-equipped leisure centre and two tennis courts in the extensive grounds. Suites, and bedrooms with four-poster beds, are available.

Rooms 98 (3 fmly) **Facilities** Spa ⓢ supervised ⛳ Putt green Gym Squash Xmas New Year Wi-fi **Services** Lift **Parking** 250

KNUTSFORD Map 7 SJ77

The Longview Hotel & Stuffed Olive Restaurant

★★ 81% HOTEL

55 Manchester Rd WA16 0LX

☎ 01565 632119 🖹 01565 652402

e-mail: enquiries@longviewhotel.com

web: www.longviewhotel.com

dir: *M6 junct 19 take A556 W towards Chester. Left at lights onto A5033, 1.5m to rdbt then left. Hotel 200yds on right*

PETS: Bedrooms (5 GF) unattended **Charges** £10 per night **Grounds** on leads **Exercise area** across road **Facilities** vet info **Other** charge for damage

This friendly Victorian hotel offers high standards of hospitality and service. Attractive public areas include a cellar bar and foyer lounge area. The restaurant has a traditional feel and offers an imaginative selection of dishes. Bedrooms, some located in a superb renovation of nearby houses, are individually styled and offer a good range of thoughtful amenities, including broadband internet access.

Rooms 32 (19 annexe) (1 fmly) (5 GF) **Facilities** FTV Wi-fi **Parking** 20 **Notes** RS 19 Dec-4 Jan

Rostherne Country House

★★★★ GUEST ACCOMMODATION

Rostherne Ln, Rostherne WA16 6RY

☎ 01565 832628

e-mail: info@rosthernehouse.co.uk

PETS: Bedrooms unattended **Stables Charges** £2.50 per night **Public areas** lounge only **Exercise area** adjacent **Facilities** vet info **Other** charge for damage small paddock available; cats must be caged **Restrictions** no dangerous dogs (see page 7)

Set in its own spacious gardens in the village of Rostherne, this elegant Victorian house retains much original charm with spacious, well-equipped bedrooms and character lounges with open fires. It is a wonderful relaxing base for exploring the delights of Cheshire and dinner is available by arrangement. Other facilities include an honesty bar and a paddock for guests' horses. Courses in various subjects are also available.

Rooms 4 rms (3 en suite) (1 pri facs) (1 fmly) **Facilities** FTV TVL tea/coffee Dinner available Cen ht Wi-fi **Parking** 12

ENGLAND

ENGLAND

The Lymm Hotel
★★★ 73% HOTEL

Whitbarrow Rd WA13 9AQ
☎ 01925 752233 📄 01925 756035
e-mail: general.lymm@macdonald-hotels.co.uk
web: www.macdonaldhotels.co.uk/lymm
dir: *M6 junct 20, B5158 to Lymm. Left at junct, 1st right, left at mini-rdbt, into Brookfield Rd, 3rd left into Whitbarrow Rd*

PETS: Bedrooms (11 GF) **Charges** £20 per night **Grounds** on leads **Exercise area Facilities** walks info vet info **Other** charge for damage

In a peaceful residential area, this hotel benefits from both a quiet setting and convenient access to local motorway networks. It offers comfortable bedrooms equipped for both the business and leisure guest. Public areas include an attractive bar and an elegant restaurant. There is also extensive parking.

Rooms 62 (38 annexe) (5 fmly) (11 GF) **S** £55-£78; **D** £63-£88 (incl. bkfst)* **Facilities** STV Xmas New Year Wi-fi **Parking** 75 **Notes** LB

Best Western Crown Hotel & Restaurant
★★ 73% HOTEL

High St CW5 5AS
☎ 01270 625283 📄 01270 628047
e-mail: info@crownhotelnantwich.com
web: www.crownhotelnantwich.com
dir: *A52 to Nantwich, hotel in town centre*

PETS: Bedrooms unattended **Facilities** walks info vet info **On Request** fridge access torch towels **Other** charge for damage **Resident Pets:** Bertie (Shih Tzu)

Ideally set in the heart of this historic and delightful market town, The Crown has been offering hospitality for centuries. It has an abundance of original features and the well-equipped bedrooms retain an old world charm. There is also a bar with live entertainment throughout the week and diners can enjoy Italian food in the atmospheric brasserie.

Rooms 18 (2 fmly) (1 smoking) **Facilities** FTV 🎵 Wi-fi **Parking** 18 **Notes** LB Closed 25 Dec

Campanile

Campanile Runcorn
BUDGET HOTEL

Lowlands Rd WA7 5TP
☎ 01928 581771 📄 01928 581730
e-mail: runcorn@campanile.com
dir: *M56 junct 12, take A557, then follow signs for Runcorn rail station/Runcorn College*

PETS: Bedrooms (18 GF) **Charges** £5 per night **Grounds** on leads **Exercise area** grassed area **Facilities** walks info vet info **On Request** fridge access towels **Other** please phone for further details of pet facilities

This modern building offers accommodation in smart, well-equipped bedrooms, all with en suite bathrooms. Refreshments may be taken at the informal bistro.

Rooms 53 (18 GF) **D** £43-£70*

Willington Hall
★★★ 78% COUNTRY HOUSE HOTEL

Willington CW6 0NB
☎ 01829 752321 📄 01829 752596
e-mail: enquiries@willingtonhall.co.uk
web: www.willingtonhall.co.uk
dir: *3m NW off unclass road linking A51 & A54, at Clotton exit A51 at Bulls Head. Follow signs*

PETS: Bedrooms unattended **Stables** nearby **Charges** £10 per stay **Public areas** except restaurant **Grounds** disp bin **Exercise area** woods 0.25m **Facilities** cage storage walks info vet info **On Request** fridge access torch towels

Situated in 17 acres of parkland and built in 1829, this attractively furnished country-house hotel offers spacious bedrooms, many with views over open countryside. Service is courteous and friendly, and freshly prepared meals are offered in the dining room or in the adjacent bar and drawing room. A smart function suite confirms the popularity of this hotel as a premier venue for weddings and conferences.

Rooms 10 (4 fmly) **S** £80; **D** £120-£130 (incl. bkfst)* **Facilities** Fishing 🎣 New Year Wi-fi **Parking** 60 **Notes** LB Closed 25 & 26 Dec

The Bear's Paw

★★★★★ INN

School Ln CW11 3QN
☎ 01270 526317
e-mail: info@thebearspaw.co.uk
dir: *M6 junct 17 onto A534/A533 signed Middlewich/Northwich. Continue on A533, left onto Mill Ln, left onto Warmingham Ln. Right onto Plant Ln, left onto Green Ln*

PETS: Bedrooms unattended **Stables** 10m **Charges** £10 per stay **Public areas** except restaurant on leads **Grounds** **Exercise area** 10mtrs **Facilities** food bowl water bowl washing facs walks info vet info **On Request** fridge access **Other** charge for damage

Located beside a small river within a rural Cheshire village, this 19th-century inn, totally refurbished in 2009, provides very comfortable and well equipped boutique bedrooms with a wealth of thoughtful and practical extras. A friendly team deliver imaginative food, utilising quality seasonal produce, in an attractive open-plan dining room, and a choice of sumptuous lounge areas is also available.

Rooms 14 en suite (4 fmly) **S** £75-£90; **D** £90-£130*
Facilities STV FTV tea/coffee Dinner available Direct Dial Cen ht Wi-fi **Parking** 75 **Notes** LB

The Park Royal

★★★★ 77% HOTEL

Stretton Rd, Stretton WA4 4NS
☎ 01925 730706 📠 01925 730740
e-mail: parkroyalreservations@qhotels.co.uk
web: www.qhotels.co.uk
dir: *M56 junct 10, A49 to Warrington, at lights turn right to Appleton Thorn, 1st right into Spark Hall Close, hotel on left*

PETS: Bedrooms (34 GF) **Stables** 2m **Charges** £10 per stay **Grounds** on leads **Facilities** walks info vet info **On Request** torch **Other** charge for damage **Restrictions** small dogs only

This modern hotel enjoys a peaceful setting, yet is conveniently located just minutes from the M56. The bedrooms are modern in style and thoughtfully equipped. Spacious, stylish public areas include extensive conference and function facilities, and a comprehensive leisure centre complete with outdoor tennis courts and an impressive beauty centre.

Rooms 146 (3 fmly) (34 GF) **S** £60-£155; **D** £70-£165 (incl. bkfst)* **Facilities** Spa FTV 🏊 Gym Dance studio Xmas New Year Wi-fi **Services** Lift **Parking** 400

Holiday Inn Warrington

★★★ 72% HOTEL

Woolston Grange Av, Woolston WA1 4PX
☎ 0871 942 9087 📠 01925 838859
e-mail: nicola.crowley@ihg.com
web: www.holidayinn.co.uk
dir: *M6 junct 21, follow signs for Birchwood*

PETS: Bedrooms (9 GF) **Charges** £10 per night **Grounds** on leads **Exercise area Facilities** cage storage walks info vet info **On Request** fridge access towels **Other** charge for damage

Ideally located within the M62 and M56 interchange, this hotel provides the ideal base for all areas of the north-west region for both corporate and leisure guests. Rooms are spacious and well equipped, and a wide choice of meals is available in the comfortable restaurant and cosy bar. Meeting and conference facilities are also available.

Rooms 96 (26 fmly) (9 GF) (7 smoking) **Facilities** STV Xmas New Year Wi-fi **Services** Lift Air con **Parking** 101

Paddington House

★★ 74% HOTEL

514 Old Manchester Rd WA1 3TZ
☎ 01925 816767 📠 01925 816651
e-mail: hotel@paddingtonhouse.co.uk
web: www.paddingtonhouse.co.uk
dir: *1m from M6 junct 21, off A57, 2m from town centre*

PETS: Bedrooms (6 GF) unattended **Charges** £5 per night **Public areas Grounds** on leads disp bin **Exercise area Facilities** water bowl vet info **On Request** fridge access towels **Other** charge for damage **Restrictions** no large dogs

This busy, friendly hotel is conveniently situated just over a mile from the M6. Bedrooms are attractively furnished, and include four-poster and ground-floor rooms. Guests can dine in the wood-panelled Padgate Restaurant or in the cosy bar. Conference and function facilities are available.

Rooms 37 (9 fmly) (6 GF) (6 smoking) **S** £45-£55; **D** £55-£65 (incl. bkfst) **Facilities** FTV New Year Wi-fi **Services** Lift **Parking** 50 **Notes** LB

ENGLAND

ENGLAND

WYBUNBURY
Map 7 SJ64

Lea Farm *(SJ717489)*
★★★ FARMHOUSE
Wrinehill Rd CW5 7NS
☎ 01270 841429   Mrs J E Callwood
e-mail: leafarm@hotmail.co.uk
dir: *1m E of Wybunbury church on unclassified road*

PETS: **Bedrooms Sep accom** outdoor kennel, barns **Stables**
Charges £2 per night **Public areas Grounds** on leads disp
bin **Exercise area** adjacent **Facilities** food bowl water
bowl bedding washing facs cage storage walks info vet
info **On Request** fridge access torch towels **Other** charge for
damage **Resident Pet:** Lucy (Collie)

This working dairy farm is surrounded by delightful gardens and
beautiful Cheshire countryside. The spacious bedrooms have
modern facilities and there is a cosy lounge. Hearty breakfasts
are served in the attractive dining room, which looks out over the
garden with its resident peacocks.

Rooms 3 rms (2 en suite) (1 fmly) **S** £28-£36; **D** £50-£60
Facilities FTV TVL tea/coffee Cen ht Fishing Pool Table
Parking 24 **Notes** 150 acres dairy/beef

CORNWALL & ISLES OF SCILLY

CROOKED INN

Stoketon Cross
Trematon
Saltash
Cornwall PL12 4RZ
Tel: 01752 848177
Fax: 01752 843203

◆

*Overlooking the beautiful Lyhner Valley, our family
run inn offers you real food and an atmosphere you
are not likely to forget.*

*Our numerous family pets would love to meet your
pets, whilst you all stay with us in our luxurious
AA 3 ★★★
en-suite accommodation.*

Email us (if you must): info@crooked-inn.co.uk

ASHTON
Map 2 SW62

Boscrege Caravan & Camping Park
(SW595305)
▶▶▶
TR13 9TG
☎ 01736 762231   📄 01736 762152
e-mail: enquiries@caravanparkcornwall.com
dir: *From Helston on A394 turn right in Ashton by Post Office into
lane. Site in 1.5m, signed*

PETS: **Charges** £2 per night £14 per week **Public areas** on
leads disp bin **Exercise area** 6-acre meadow **Exercise area**
200yds **Facilities** walks info vet info **Other** prior notice required
Resident Pets: Ozzy (German Shepherd), Molly, Topsey, Tilly &
Ginge (cats), 12 chickens

Open Mar-Nov Last arrival 22.00hrs Last departure 11.00hrs

A quiet and bright little touring park divided into small paddocks
with hedges, and offering plenty of open spaces for children to
play in. The family-owned park offers clean, well-painted toilets
facilities and neatly trimmed grass. In an Area of Outstanding
Natural Beauty at the foot of Tregonning Hill. A 14 acre site with
50 touring pitches and 26 statics.

BLACKWATER
Map 2 SW74

Chiverton Park *(SW743468)*
▶▶▶▶
East Hill TR4 8HS
☎ 01872 560667   📄 01872 560667
e-mail: chivertonpark@btopenworld.com
dir: *Exit A30 at Chiverton rdbt (Starbucks) onto unclass road
signed Blackwater (3rd exit). 1st right, site 300mtrs on right*

PETS: **Charges** £2.50 per night £15 per week **Public areas** disp
bin **Facilities** walks info vet info **Other** prior notice required
Resident Pets: Tolley (German Longhaired Pointer), Grogley
(Golden Retriever)

Open 3 Mar-3 Nov rs Mar-May & mid Sep-Nov limited stock kept
in shop Last arrival 21.00hrs Last departure noon

A small, well-maintained site with some mature hedges dividing
pitches, sited midway between Truro and St Agnes. Facilities
include a good toilet block and a steam room, sauna and gym.
A games room with pool table, and children's outside play
equipment prove popular with families. A 4 acre site with 12
touring pitches, 10 hardstandings and 50 statics.

Notes No ball games.

BODMIN
Map 2 SX06

Trehellas House Hotel & Restaurant
★★★ 74% SMALL HOTEL
Washaway PL30 3AD
☎ 01208 72700 📠 01208 73336
e-mail: enquiries@trehellashouse.co.uk
web: www.trehellashouse.co.uk
dir: A389 from Bodmin towards Wadebridge. Hotel on right 0.5m beyond road to Camelford

PETS: Bedrooms (5 GF) unattended Grounds disp bin Exercise area Facilities food bowl water bowl leads washing facs cage storage walks info vet info On Request fridge access torch towels Resident Pets: Bonnie & Clyde (Chocolate Labradors)

This 18th-century former posting inn retains many original features and provides comfortable accommodation. Bedrooms are located in both the main house and adjacent coach house - all provide the same high standards. An interesting choice of cuisine, with an emphasis on locally-sourced ingredients, is offered in the impressive slate-floored restaurant.

Rooms 12 (7 annexe) (2 fmly) (5 GF) S £50-£75; D £55-£160 (incl. bkfst)* Facilities FTV ⚡ Xmas New Year Wi-fi Parking 32 Notes LB

Westberry
★★ 80% HOTEL
Rhind St PL31 2EL
☎ 01208 72772 📠 01208 72212
e-mail: westberry@btconnect.com
web: www.westberryhotel.net
dir: On ring road off A30 & A38. St Petroc's Church on right, at mini rdbt turn right. Hotel on right

PETS: Bedrooms (6 GF) unattended sign Charges Public areas Grounds on leads disp bin Exercise area 300yds Facilities food bowl water bowl litter tray scoop/disp bags cage storage walks info vet info On Request fridge access Other charge for damage

This popular hotel is conveniently located for both Bodmin town centre and the A30. The bedrooms are attractive and well equipped. A spacious bar lounge and a billiard room are also provided. The restaurant serves a variety of dishes, ranging from bar snacks to a more extensive carte menu.

Rooms 20 (8 annexe) (2 fmly) (6 GF) S £48-£78; D £58-£78 (incl. bkfst)* Facilities STV Full sized snooker table Wi-fi Parking 30 Notes LB

Mount Pleasant Farm
★★★ GUEST ACCOMMODATION
Mount PL30 4EX
☎ 01208 821342
e-mail: info@mountpleasantcottages.co.uk
dir: A30 from Bodmin towards Launceston for 4m, right signed Millpool, continue 3m

PETS: Bedrooms Public areas except dining area on leads Grounds on leads disp bin Exercise area moor adjacent Facilities pet sitting dog walking washing facs cage storage walks info vet info On Request fridge access torch towels Other no charge for pets in B&B, £10 per week in cottage Resident Pets: Poppy, Penny & Molley (Springer Spaniels), Toffee (cat), Happy & Misty (horses)

Set in 10 acres, this is a wonderfully peaceful base from which to explore the delights of Cornwall. Originally a farmhouse dating back to the 17th century, there is something here for all the family with extensive facilities including a games barn and heated swimming pool. Cosy bedrooms are well furnished, while public areas include a spacious sun lounge and extensive gardens. Breakfast, served in the well-appointed dining room, features local produce and is a highlight of any stay; home-cooked evening meals are available by prior arrangement.

Rooms 6 en suite (3 fmly) S £32-£37; D £54-£74* Facilities FTV TVL tea/coffee Dinner available Cen ht ⚂ Pool Table Parking 8 Notes LB 🐾

BOLVENTOR
Map 2 SX17

Colliford Tavern Campsite (SX171740)
▶▶▶
Colliford Lake, St Neot PL14 6PZ
☎ 01208 821335 📠 01208 821661
e-mail: info@colliford.com
dir: Exit A30 1.25m W of Bolventor onto unclass road signed Colliford Lake. Site 0.25m on left

PETS: Charges £1 per night Public areas except bar & restaurant on leads disp bin Exercise area dog walking area Facilities washing facs walks info vet info

Open all year Last arrival 22.00hrs Last departure 11.00hrs

An oasis on Bodmin Moor, a small site with spacious grassy pitches, and the advantage of a comfortable lounge bar and restaurant in the tavern. Attractions for children are greatly enhanced by the merger of the site with the neighbouring children's play park. A 3.5 acre site with 40 touring pitches, 8 hardstandings.

| BRYHER (ISLES OF SCILLY) | Map 2 SV81 |

Hell Bay Hotel

★★★ ◉◉◉ HOTEL

TR23 0PR

☎ 01720 422947 📠 01720 423004

e-mail: contactus@hellbay.co.uk

web: www.hellbay.co.uk

dir: *Access by helicopter or boat from Penzance, plane from Bristol, Exeter, Newquay, Southampton, Land's End*

PETS: Bedrooms (15 GF) unattended **Charges** £12 per night **Public areas** except bar & lounge **Grounds** on leads disp bin **Exercise area** public coastal path adjacent **Facilities** food bowl water bowl bedding feeding mat cage storage walks info vet info **On Request** fridge access torch towels **Resident Pets:** Suzie (Springer Spaniel)

Located on the smallest of the inhabited islands of the Scilly Isles on the edge of the Atlantic, this hotel makes a really special destination. The owners have filled the hotel with original works of art by artists who have connections with the islands, and the interior is decorated in cool blues and greens creating an extremely restful environment. The contemporary bedrooms are equally stylish and many have garden access and stunning sea views. Eating here is a delight, and naturally, seafood features strongly on the award-winning, daily-changing menus.

Rooms 25 (25 annexe) (3 fmly) (15 GF) **Facilities** STV ⤢ ⚓7 Gym Wi-fi **Notes** LB Closed Nov-Feb

| BUDE | Map 2 SS20 |

Hotel Penarvor

★★ 74% SMALL HOTEL

Crooklets Beach EX23 8NE

☎ 01288 352036 📠 01288 355027

e-mail: hotel.penarvor@boltblue.com

dir: *From A39 towards Bude for 1.5m. At 2nd rdbt right, pass shops. Top of hill, left signed Crooklets Beach*

PETS: Bedrooms Charges £6 per night **Public areas** except restaurant on leads **Grounds** on leads disp bin **Exercise area Facilities** vet info **On Request** fridge access **Other** charge for damage **Resident Pets:** Bonnie (Old English/Border Collie cross), Charlie (Cocker Spaniel)

Adjacent to the golf course and overlooking Crooklets Beach, this family owned hotel has a relaxed and friendly atmosphere. Bedrooms vary in size but are all equipped to a similar standard. An interesting selection of dishes, using fresh local produce, is available in the restaurant; bar meals are also provided.

Rooms 16 (6 fmly) **Parking** 20

The Cliff at Bude

★★★★ GUEST HOUSE

Maer Down, Crooklets Beach EX23 8NG

☎ 01288 353110 & 356833 📠 01288 353110

e-mail: cliff-hotel@btconnect.com

web: www.cliffhotel.co.uk

dir: *A39 through Bude, left at top of High St, pass Sainsburys, 1st right between golf course, over x-rds, premises at end on right*

PETS: Bedrooms unattended sign **Stables** 2m **Charges** dog £2.50 per night **Public areas** except restaurant & lounge on leads **Grounds** on leads disp bin **Exercise area** adjacent to hotel **Facilities** pet sitting washing facs cage storage walks info vet info **On Request** torch **Other** charge for damage **Resident Pets:** Janus & Crystal (Boxers), 10 rabbits

Overlooking the sea from a clifftop location, this friendly and efficient establishment provides spacious, well-equipped bedrooms. The various public areas include a bar and lounge and an impressive range of leisure facilities. Delicious dinners and tasty breakfasts are available in the attractive dining room.

Rooms 15 en suite (15 fmly) (8 GF) **S** £45.54-£52.50; **D** £75.90-£87* **Facilities** FTV TVL tea/coffee Dinner available Direct Dial Cen ht Licensed 🕮 ⚓ ⚓ Gymnasium Pool Table **Parking** 18 **Notes** LB Closed Nov-Mar

Budemeadows Touring Park *(SS215012)*

►►►►

Widemouth Bay EX23 0NA

☎ 01288 361646 📠 0870 7064825

e-mail: holiday@budemeadows.com

dir: *3m S of Bude on A39. Follow signs after turn to Widemouth Bay. Site accessed via layby*

PETS: Charges £1.50-£2.50 per night **Public areas** except pool & playground disp bin **Exercise area** beach 1m, lane, public footpaths 100mtrs **Facilities** food food bowl water bowl walks info vet info **Other** prior notice required disposal bags available

Open all year rs mid Sep-late May shop, bar & pool closed Last arrival 21.00hrs Last departure 11.00hrs

A very well kept site of distinction, with good quality facilities. Budemeadows is set on a gentle sheltered slope in nine acres of naturally landscaped parkland, surrounded by mature hedges. Just one mile from Widemouth Bay, and three miles from the unspoilt resort of Bude. A 9 acre site with 145 touring pitches, 24 hardstandings.

Willow Valley Holiday Park *(SS236078)*

►►►►

Bush EX23 9LB

☎ 01288 353104

e-mail: willowvalley@talk21.com

dir: *On A39, 0.5m N of junct with A3072 at Stratton*

PETS: Charges £1.50 (Jul-Aug), £1 (Sep-Jun) per night **Public areas** except children's park disp bin **Exercise area** field available **Facilities** vet info **Other** prior notice required **Resident Pets:** Treacle & Smudge (cats)

Open Mar-end Oct Last arrival 21.00hrs Last departure 11.00hrs

A small sheltered park in Strat Valley with a stream running through and level grassy pitches. The friendly family owners have improved all areas of this attractive park, including a smart toilet block, and offering four pine lodges for holiday hire. The park has direct access off the A39, and only two miles from the sandy beaches at Bude. A 4 acre site with 41 touring pitches and 4 statics.

Notes 📧

Juliot's Well Holiday Park *(SX095829)*

►►►►

PL32 9RF

☎ 01840 213302 📠 01840 212700

e-mail: juliotswell@breaksincornwall.com

dir: *Through Camelford, A39 at Valley Truckle turn right onto B3266, then 1st left signed Lanteglos, site 300yds on right*

PETS: Charges £5 per night £35 per week **Public areas** disp bin **Exercise area** fields, walks around lake **Exercise area** nearby **Facilities** food walks info vet info **Other** prior notice required pet shop in town, 1m **Resident Pets:** Rambo (Greyhound), Riley (Labrador)

Open all year Last arrival 20.00hrs Last departure 11.00hrs

Set in the wooded grounds of an old manor house, this quiet site enjoys lovely and extensive views across the countryside. A rustic inn on site offers occasional entertainment, and there is plenty to do, both on the park and in the vicinity. The superb, fully-serviced toilet facilities are very impressive. There are also self-catering pine lodges, static caravans and five cottages. A 33 acre site with 39 touring pitches and 82 statics.

Lakefield Caravan Park *(SX095853)*

►►►

Lower Pendavey Farm PL32 9TX

☎ 01840 213279

e-mail: lakefieldcaravanpark@btconnect.com

dir: *From A39 in Camelford turn right onto B3266, then right at T-junct, site 1.5m on left*

PETS: Stables Charges stabling £20 per night **Public areas** on leads **Exercise area** 5-acre field **Facilities** washing facs vet info **Other** prior notice required full equestrian facilities on site **Resident Pets:** Mo (Border Collie), Bill & Luna (Border Terriers), Spock (Papillon cross), Puss-Puss (cat), 40 horses

Open Etr or Apr-Sep Last arrival 22.00hrs Last departure 11.00hrs

Set in a rural location, this friendly park is part of a specialist equestrian centre, and offers good quality services. Riding lessons and hacks always available, with BHS qualified instructor. A 5 acre site with 40 touring pitches.

CARLYON BAY   Map 2 SX05

East Crinnis Camping & Caravan Park
(SX062528)

►►►

Lantyan, East Crinnis PL24 2SQ
☎ 01726 813023 & 07950 614780 📱 01726 813023
e-mail: eastcrinnis@btconnect.com
dir: *From A390 (Lostwithiel to St Austell) take A3082 signed Fowey at rdbt by Britannia Inn, site on left*

PETS: Charges £1.50 per night £10 per week **Public areas** except children's play area & shower block on leads disp bin **Exercise area** wildlife area with large pond **Facilities** washing facs walks info vet info **Other** prior notice required disposal bags **Resident Pets:** Alfie (Labrador), Bonnie (working Collie), Lola (Retriever)

Open Etr-Oct Last arrival 21.00hrs Last departure 11.00hrs

A small rural park with spacious pitches set in individual bays about one mile from the beaches at Carlyon Bay, and just two miles from the Eden Project. The friendly owners keep the site very clean and also offer three self-catering holiday lodges. A 2 acre site with 25 touring pitches, 6 hardstandings.

CAWSAND   Map 2 SX45

Wringford Down
★★★ GUEST ACCOMMODATION

Hat Ln PL10 1LE
☎ 01752 822287
e-mail: andrew@wringford.co.uk
dir: *A374 onto B3247, pass Millbrook, right towards Cawsand & sharp right, 0.5m on right*

PETS: Bedrooms Sep accom kennel **Stables** 0.5m **Charges** £5 per night £35 per week **Grounds** on leads disp bin **Exercise area** on site **Exercise area** adjacent **Facilities** washing facs cage storage walks info vet info **On Request** fridge access torch towels **Other** charge for damage **Restrictions** no dangerous dogs (see page 7) **Resident Pets:** Daisy (Golden Retriever), Dotty (Springer Spaniel), Baby (cat), Sylvester, Truffle & Toffee (ponies), ducks & peacocks

This family-run establishment has a peaceful location near Rame Head and the South West Coast Path, and is particularly welcoming to families. There is a nursery, swimming pool, games room, and gardens with play areas. A range of rooms, and some suites and self-catering units are available. Breakfast and dinner are served in the dining room.

Rooms 5 en suite 2 annexe en suite (4 fmly) (5 GF) **S** £44-£60; **D** £68-£100* **Facilities** FTV TVL tea/coffee Dinner available Cen ht Licensed Wi-fi 🔊 🏌 Golf 18 Pool Table **Parking** 20 **Notes** LB

CONSTANTINE   Map 2 SW72

Trengilly Wartha Inn
★★★ 🍴 INN

Nancenoy TR11 5RP
☎ 01326 340332 📱 01326 340332
e-mail: reception@trengilly.co.uk
web: www.trengilly.co.uk
dir: *Follow signs to Nancenoy, left towards Gweek until 1st sign for inn, left & left again at next sign, continue to inn*

PETS: Bedrooms unattended **Stables** 1m **Charges** £3 per night **Public areas** except restaurant on leads **Grounds** disp bin **Exercise area Facilities** food (pre-bookable) food bowl water bowl bedding dog chews feeding mat scoop/disp bags leads dog walking washing facs cage storage walks info vet info **On Request** fridge access torch towels **Resident Pets:** Kerris & Tara (mongrels), goats, chickens

Located in a very peaceful wooded valley, just one and a half miles from the village of Constantine, this inn offers cosy, comfortable accommodation with nicely appointed and well equipped bedrooms. An interesting menu is offered in the restaurant together with a well balanced wine list; there is also a wide selection of bar meals available at lunch and dinner.

Rooms 6 en suite 2 annexe en suite (2 fmly) (2 GF) **S** £50; **D** £80-£96* **Facilities** tea/coffee Dinner available Direct Dial Cen ht Wi-fi **Parking** 60 **Notes** LB RS 25 Dec No food

COVERACK   Map 2 SW71

Little Trevothan Caravan & Camping Park
(SW772179)

►►►

Trevothan TR12 6SD
☎ 01326 280260
e-mail: sales@littletrevothan.co.uk
dir: *A3083 onto B3293 signed Coverack, approx 2m after Goonhilly ESS, right at Zoar Garage onto unclass road. Approx 1m, 3rd left. Site 0.5m on left*

PETS: Charges £1.50 per night **Public areas** except children's play areas on leads disp bin **Exercise area** fenced-off area **Facilities** washing facs walks info vet info **Other** prior notice required **Restrictions** no Rottweilers or Pit Bull Terriers **Resident Pets:** 2 Weimaraners, 2 cats

Open Mar-Oct Last arrival 21.00hrs Last departure noon

A secluded site near the unspoilt fishing village of Coverack, with a large recreation area. The nearby sandy beach has lots of rock pools for children to play in, and the many walks both from the park and the village offer stunning scenery. A 10.5 acre site with 70 touring pitches, 10 hardstandings and 40 statics.

Notes

Bears & Boxes Country Guest House

★★★ GUEST HOUSE

Penrose, Dizzard EX23 0NX
☎ 01840 230318
e-mail: rwfrh@btinternet.com
web: www.bearsandboxes.com
dir: *1.5m NE of St Gennys in Dizzard*

PETS: Bedrooms unattended **Public areas Grounds** disp bin
Exercise area 100yds **Facilities** food (pre-bookable) food
bowl water bowl bedding dog chews feeding mat scoop/disp
bags leads pet sitting dog walking washing facs cage storage
walks info vet info **On Request** fridge access torch towels

Dating in part from the mid 17th century, Bears & Boxes is a
small, family-run guest house situated 500yds from the coastal
path. Guests are welcomed with a tray of tea and home-made
cake, and the caring owners are always around to help and
advise about the locality. The cosy bedrooms have numerous
thoughtful extras, and evening meals, using the very best of local
ingredients and cooked with flair, are served by arrangement.

Rooms 3 en suite (1 GF) **S** fr £32; **D** fr £64* **Facilities** FTV TVL
tea/coffee Dinner available Cen ht Wi-fi **Parking** 6

Crantock Plains Camping & Caravan Park

(SW805589)

▶ ▶ ▶

TR8 5PH
☎ 01637 830955 & 07967 956897
e-mail: matthew-milburn@btconnect.com
dir: *Exit Newquay on A3075, 2nd right signed to park & Crantock.
Site on left in 0.75m on narrow road*

PETS: Charges £1.20 per night **Public areas** on leads disp bin
Exercise area Facilities walks info vet info **Other** prior notice
required

Open Last arrival 22.00hrs Last departure noon

A small rural park with pitches on either side of a narrow lane,
surrounded by mature trees for shelter. The family-run park has
modern toilet facilities appointed to a good standard. A 6 acre
site with 60 touring pitches.

Notes No skateboards

THE INDEPENDENTS
HOTEL ASSOCIATION

Green Lawns

★★★ 77% HOTEL

Western Ter TR11 4QJ
☎ 01326 312734 📠 01326 211427
e-mail: info@greenlawnshotel.com
web: www.greenlawnshotel.com
dir: *On A39*

PETS: Bedrooms (11 GF) unattended **Stables** 6m **Charges**
£12.50 per night disp bin **Exercise area** 0.25m **Facilities** cage
storage walks info vet info **On Request** fridge access torch
towels

This attractive property enjoys a convenient location close to the
town centre and within easy reach of the sea. Spacious public
areas include inviting lounges, an elegant restaurant, conference
and meeting facilities and a leisure centre. Bedrooms vary in size
and style but all are well equipped and comfortable. The friendly
service is particularly noteworthy.

Rooms 39 (8 fmly) (11 GF) (2 smoking) **S** £60-£120; **D** £110-£210
(incl. bkfst)* **Facilities** FTV 🏊 Gym Squash Sauna Steam room
Spa bath New Year Wi-fi **Parking** 69 **Notes** LB Closed 24-30 Dec

RICHARDSON

Falmouth

★★★ 75% HOTEL

Castle Beach TR11 4NZ
☎ 01326 312671 & 0800 019 3121 📠 01326 319533
e-mail: reservations@falmouthhotel.com
web: www.falmouthhotel.com
dir: *A30 to Truro then A390 to Falmouth. Follow signs for beaches,
hotel on seafront near Pendennis Castle*

PETS: Bedrooms unattended **Charges** £8 per night **Grounds** on
leads **Exercise area** beach (winter only) & countryside **Facilities**
walks info vet info **On Request** fridge access torch towels
Other charge for damage

This spectacular beach-front Victorian property affords wonderful
sea views from many of its comfortable bedrooms, some of
which have their own balconies. Spacious public areas include
a number of inviting lounges, a choice of dining options and an
impressive range of leisure facilities.

Rooms 71 (16 fmly) **S** £60-£70; **D** £120-£240 (incl. bkfst)*
Facilities Spa FTV 🏊 Putt green Gym Beauty salon & Therapeutic
rooms 🎵 Xmas New Year Wi-fi **Services** Lift **Parking** 120
Notes LB

ENGLAND

ENGLAND

Penmorvah Manor

★★★ 72% HOTEL

Budock Water TR11 5ED

☎ 01326 250277 📄 01326 250509

e-mail: reception@penmorvah.co.uk

web: www.penmorvah.co.uk

dir: *A39 to Hillhead rdbt, take 2nd exit. Right at Falmouth Football Club, through Budock. Hotel opposite Penjerrick Gardens*

PETS: **Bedrooms** (10 GF) **Charges** £7.50 per night **Public areas** except restaurant on leads **Grounds** disp bin **Exercise area** **Facilities** water bowl cage storage vet info **On Request** torch towels **Resident Pets:** Millie (Cocker Spaniel), Toffee & Minky (cats)

Situated within two miles of central Falmouth, this extended Victorian manor house is a peaceful hideaway, set in six acres of private woodland and gardens. Penmorvah is well positioned for visiting the local gardens, and offers many garden-tour breaks. Dinner features locally sourced, quality ingredients such as Cornish cheeses, meat, fish and game.

Rooms 27 (1 fmly) (10 GF) **S** fr £65; **D** £100-£150 (incl. bkfst)* **Facilities** Xmas Wi-fi **Parking** 100 **Notes** LB Closed 31 Dec-Jan

Pennance Mill Farm Touring Park *(SW792307)*

▶▶▶

Maenporth TR11 5HJ

☎ 01326 317431 📄 01326 317431

dir: *From A39 (Truro to Falmouth road) follow brown camping signs towards Maenporth Beach. At Hill Head rdbt take 2nd exit for Maenporth Beach*

PETS: **Charges** £2 (dogs & cats) per night **Public areas** except playground on leads **Exercise area** field & woodland walk **Facilities** walks info vet info **Other** prior notice required **Resident Pets:** 9 farm cats

Open Etr-Xmas Last arrival 22.00hrs Last departure 10.00hrs

Set approximately half a mile from the safe, sandy bay at Maenporth, this is a mainly level, grassy park in a rural location sheltered by mature trees and shrubs and divided into three meadows. It has a modern toilet block. A 6 acre site with 75 touring pitches, 8 hardstandings and 4 statics.

Notes 🐾

von Essen hotels

Fowey Hall

★★★★ 77% ◉◉ HOTEL

Hanson Dr PL23 1ET

☎ 01726 833866 📄 01726 834100

e-mail: info@foweyhallhotel.co.uk

web: www.foweyhallhotel.co.uk

dir: *In Fowey, over mini rdbt into town centre. Pass school on right, 400mtrs right into Hanson Drive*

PETS: **Bedrooms** (6 GF) **Charges** £7 per night **Public areas** except restaurant on leads **Grounds** on leads disp bin **Exercise area** beach **Facilities** food bowl bedding washing facs cage storage walks info vet info **On Request** fridge access towels **Other** prior notice required max 2 dogs in hotel at any time; pets allowed in courtyard bedrooms only disposal bags available

Built in 1899, this listed mansion looks out on to the English Channel. The imaginatively designed bedrooms offer charm, individuality and sumptuous comfort; the Garden Wing rooms adding a further dimension to staying here. The beautifully appointed public rooms include the wood-panelled dining room where accomplished cuisine is served. Enjoying glorious views, the well-kept grounds have a covered pool and sunbathing area.

Rooms 36 (8 annexe) (30 fmly) (6 GF) **Facilities** Spa STV FTV ⊙ 🎾 Table tennis Basketball Trampoline Pool table Xmas New Year Wi-fi **Parking** 30

Trevanion

★★★★ GUEST ACCOMMODATION

70 Lostwithiel St PL23 1BQ

☎ 01726 832602

e-mail: alisteve@trevanionguesthouse.co.uk

web: www.trevanionguesthouse.co.uk

dir: *A3082 into Fowey, down hill, left onto Lostwithiel St, Trevanion on left*

PETS: **Bedrooms** unattended **Public areas** except dining room **Exercise area** directly across road **Facilities** food food bowl water bowl leads pet sitting walks info vet info **On Request** fridge access towels **Other** please phone for further details of pet facilities **Resident Pet:** Poppy (parrot)

This 16th-century merchant's house provides friendly, comfortable accommodation within easy walking distance of the historic town of Fowey and is also convenient for visiting the

Eden Project. A hearty farmhouse-style, cooked breakfast, using local produce, is served in the attractive dining room; other menu options are available.

Rooms 5 rms (4 en suite) (1 pri facs) (2 fmly) (1 GF) **S** £35-£40; **D** £55-£70* **Facilities** FTV tea/coffee Dinner available Cen ht Wi-fi **Parking** 5 **Notes** LB 🐾

Penmarlam Caravan & Camping Park

(SX134526)

► ► ►

Bodinnick PL23 1LZ
☎ 01726 870088 📠 01726 870082
e-mail: info@penmarlampark.co.uk
dir: *From A390 at East Taphouse take B3359 signed Looe & Polperro. Follow signs for Bodinnick & Fowey, via ferry. Site on right at entrance to Bodinnick*

PETS: Public areas only assist dogs in toilet/shower block & shop disp bin **Exercise area** adjacent **Facilities** food dog chews cat treats washing facs walks info vet info **Other** all animals must be kept under strict control disposal bags available **Resident Pets:** Rusty (Border Terrier), Pippa (Collie cross), chickens

Open Apr-Oct Last departure noon

A tranquil park set above the Fowey Estuary in an Area of Outstanding Natural Beauty, with access to the water. Pitches are level, and sheltered by trees and bushes in two paddocks, while the toilets are well maintained. A 4 acre site with 63 touring pitches and 1 static.

GOONHAVERN	Map 2 SW75

Silverbow Park *(SW782531)*

► ► ► ► ►

Perranwell TR4 9NX
☎ 01872 572347
dir: *Adjacent to A3075, 0.5m S of village*

PETS: Charges £1.50 per night **Public areas** on leads disp bin **Exercise area** large field (off lead) **Facilities** washing facs walks info vet info **Other** charge for damage prior notice required free biodegradable disposal bags available **Resident Pets:** 1 German Shepherd, 1 cat, rabbits & ducks

Open May-end Sep Last arrival 22.00hrs Last departure 10.30hrs

This park has a quiet garden atmosphere, and appeals to families with young children. The landscaped grounds and good quality toilet facilities, including four family rooms, are maintained to a very high standard with attention paid to detail. A 14 acre site with 100 touring pitches, 2 hardstandings and 15 statics.

Notes No cycling, no skateboards. 🐾

Penrose Farm Touring Park *(SW795534)*

► ► ► ►

TR4 9QF
☎ 01872 573185 📠 01872 571972
e-mail: info@penroseholidaypark.com
dir: *From Exeter take A30, past Bodmin & Indian Queens. Just after Wind Farm take B3285 towards Perranporth, site on left on entering Goonhavern*

PETS: Charges Jul-Aug £2 (£1 low season) per night **Public areas** except bathrooms on leads disp bin **Exercise area** dog field (off lead) **Facilities** walks info vet info **Other** prior notice required disposal bags available **Resident Pets:** Marley (Springer Spaniel), Kai & Tia (Northern Inuits)

Open Etr or Apr-Oct Last arrival 21.30hrs

A quiet sheltered park set in five paddocks divided by hedges and shrubs, only a short walk from the village. Lovely floral displays enhance the park's appearance, and the grass and hedges are neatly trimmed. Four cubicled family rooms are very popular, and there is a good laundry. A 9 acre site with 110 touring pitches, 48 hardstandings and 24 statics.

Notes Families & couples only.

Roseville Holiday Park *(SW787540)*

► ► ►

TR4 9LA
☎ 01872 572448 📠 01872 572448
dir: *From mini-rdbt in Goonhavern follow B3285 towards Perranporth, site 0.5m on right*

PETS: Stables 1m **Charges** high season £1-£3 per night **Public areas** on leads disp bin **Exercise area** field **Facilities** vet info **Other** prior notice required pet shop in village **Restrictions** no Rottweilers or Pit/Staffordshire Bull Terriers

Open Whit-Oct rs Apr-Jul, Sep-Oct shop closed Last arrival 21.30hrs Last departure 11.00hrs

A family park set in a rural location with sheltered grassy pitches, some gently sloping. The toilet facilities are modern, and there is an attractive outdoor swimming pool complex. Approximately two miles from the long sandy beach at Perranporth. A 8 acre site with 95 touring pitches and 5 statics.

Notes Families only. 🐾

GORRAN	Map 2 SW94

Treveague Farm Caravan & Camping Site
(SX002410)

▶ ▶ ▶

PL26 6NY

☎ 01726 842295 📠 01726 842295

e-mail: treveague@btconnect.com

dir: *From St Austell take B3273 towards Mevagissey, past Pentewan at top of hill, turn right signed Gorran. Past Heligan Gardens towards Gorran Churchtown. Follow brown tourist signs from fork in road*

PETS: **Public areas** on leads disp bin **Exercise area** field **Exercise area** nearby **Facilities** food food bowl water bowl vet info

Open Apr-Oct Last arrival 21.00hrs Last departure noon

Spectacular panoramic coastal views can be enjoyed from this rural park, which is well equipped with modern facilities. A stone-faced toilet block with a Cornish slate roof is an attractive and welcome feature, as is the building that houses the smart reception, shop and café. A footpath leads to the fishing village of Gorran Haven in one direction, and the secluded sandy Vault Beach in the other. A 4 acre site with 40 touring pitches.

Notes 🐾

GORRAN HAVEN	Map 2 SX04

Trelispen Caravan & Camping Park
(SX008421)

▶ ▶

PL26 6NT

☎ 01726 843501 📠 01726 843501

e-mail: trelispen@care4free.net

dir: *B3273 from St Austell towards Mevagissey, on hilltop at x-roads before descent into Mevagissey turn right on unclass road to Gorran. Through village, 2nd right towards Gorran Haven, site signed on left in 250mtrs*

PETS: **Public areas** **Exercise area** 50yds **Facilities** vet info **Other** prior notice required

Open Etr & Apr-Oct Last arrival 22.00hrs Last departure noon

A quiet rural site set in three paddocks, and sheltered by mature trees and hedges. The simple toilets have plenty of hot water, and there is a small laundry. Sandy beaches, pubs and shops are nearby, and Mevagissey is two miles away. A 2 acre site with 40 touring pitches.

Notes 🐾

GWITHIAN	Map 2 SW54

Gwithian Farm Campsite *(SW586412)*

▶ ▶ ▶ ▶

Gwithian Farm TR27 5BX

☎ 01736 753127

e-mail: camping@gwithianfarm.co.uk

dir: *Exit A30 at Hayle rdbt, take 4th exit signed Hayle, 100mtrs. At 1st mini-rdbt turn right onto B3301 signed Portreath. Site 2m on left on entering village*

PETS: **Stables** 0.5m **Charges** £1 per night £7 per week **Public areas** except shop & shower block on leads disp bin **Facilities** walks info vet info **Resident Pets:** Charcoal & Barnaby (Pygmy goats), Tiggy (cat), 5 guinea pigs

Open 31 Mar-1 Oct Last arrival 22.00hrs Last departure 17.00hrs

An unspoilt site located behind the sand dunes of Gwithian's golden beach, which can be reached directly by footpath from the site. The site boasts a superb toilet block with excellent facilities including a bathroom and baby-changing unit. There is a good pub opposite. A 7.5 acre site with 87 touring pitches, 12 hardstandings.

HAYLE	Map 2 SW53

Atlantic Coast Caravan Park *(NW580400)*

▶ ▶ ▶

53 Upton Towans, Gwithian TR27 5BL

☎ 01736 752071 📠 01736 758100

e-mail: enquiries@atlanticcoastpark.co.uk

dir: *From A30 into Hayle, turn right at double rdbt. Site 1.5m on left*

PETS: **Charges** £30 per week **Public areas** disp bin **Exercise area** adjacent **Facilities** food food bowl water bowl dog chews cat treats leads washing facs walks info vet info **Other** prior notice required disposal bags available, pet shop (5 min drive) **Resident Pet:** Bonny (German Shepherd/Flat Coated Retriever cross)

Open Mar-early Jan Last arrival 20.00hrs Last departure 11.00hrs

Fringed by the sand-dunes of St Ives Bay and close to the golden sands of Gwithian Beach, the small, friendly touring area offers fully serviced pitches. There's freshly baked bread, a takeaway and a bar next door. This park is ideally situated for visitors to enjoy the natural coastal beauty and attractions of south-west Cornwall. Static caravans for holiday hire. A 4.5 acre site with 15 touring pitches and 50 statics.

Notes No commercial vehicles, gazebos or day tents.

Higher Trevaskis Caravan & Camping Park
(SW611381)

▶▶▶

Gwinear Rd, Connor Downs TR27 5JQ

☎ 01209 831736

dir: *At Hayle rdbt on A30 take exit signed Connor Downs, in 1m turn right signed Carnhell Green. Site 0.75m just past level crossing*

PETS: Public areas except toilet block, shower block & shop disp bin **Exercise area** lanes & bridleway adjacent **Facilities** walks info vet info **Other** prior notice required max 2 dogs per pitch **Restrictions** no Pit Bull Terriers or Rottweilers; no dangerous breeds (see page 7)

Open mid Apr-Sep Last arrival 20.00hrs Last departure 10.30hrs

An attractive paddocked park in a sheltered rural position with views towards St Ives. This secluded park is personally run by owners who keep it quiet and welcoming. Three unisex showers are a great hit with visitors. Fluent German spoken. A 6.5 acre site with 82 touring pitches, 3 hardstandings.

Notes Max speed 5mph, balls on field only. 🌐

Parbola Holiday Park *(SW612366)*

▶▶▶

Wall, Gwinear TR27 5LE

☎ 01209 831503

e-mail: bookings@parbola.co.uk

dir: *At Hayle rdbt on A30 take Connor Downs exit. In 1m turn right signed Carnhell Green. In village right to Wall. Site in village on left*

PETS: Charges £4 per night £28 per week **Public areas** except swimming pool area, shop, games room, launderette & children's play areas **Exercise area** surrounding area **Facilities** walks info vet info **Other** prior notice required dogs not allowed in Jul & Aug (ex assist dogs) **Restrictions** small to medium size dogs only **Resident Pets:** birds in aviary

Open all year rs Etr-end of Jun & Sep shop closed, unheated pool Last arrival 21.00hrs Last departure 10.00hrs

Pitches are provided in both woodland and open areas in this spacious park in Cornish downland. The park is centrally located for touring the seaside resorts and towns in the area, especially nearby Hayle with its three miles of golden sands. A 16.5 acre site with 110 touring pitches, 4 hardstandings and 28 statics.

The Gwealdues Hotel

★★ 76% HOTEL

Falmouth Rd TR13 8JX

☎ 01326 572808 📠 01326 561388

e-mail: thegwealdueshotel@hotmail.co.uk

web: www.gwealdueshotel.com

dir: *Off rdbt on A394. On town outskirts*

PETS: Bedrooms (1 GF) unattended **Charges** £5 per night **Public areas** except food areas during service on leads **Exercise area** 100yds **Facilities** walks info vet info **Other** dogs only to be left unattended at meal times **Restrictions** no very large dogs; no dangerous dogs (see page 7); dog owners must be aware of small children staying at hotel **Resident Pets:** Mr B (cat), Honey (rabbit)

A family owned and run hotel that is within easy access of the coast and the cathedral city of Truro. The staff are friendly and attentive. The comfortable bedrooms include family rooms. There is a well stocked bar and a traditionally styled restaurant.

Rooms 18 (2 fmly) (1 GF) **Facilities** FTV Wi-fi **Parking** 50 **Notes** LB

Poldown Caravan Park *(SW629298)*

▶▶▶

Poldown, Carleen TR13 9NN

☎ 01326 574560

e-mail: stay@poldown.co.uk

dir: *From Helston follow Penzance signs for 1m, right onto B3302 to Hayle, 2nd left to Carleen, 0.5m to site*

PETS: Charges £1 per night **Public areas Exercise area** adjacent **Facilities** washing facs walks info vet info **Other** prior notice required **Resident Pet:** 1 dog (Retriever)

Open Apr-Sep Last arrival 21.00hrs Last departure noon

A small, quiet site set in attractive countryside with bright toilet facilities. All of the level grass pitches have electricity. This sunny park is sheltered by mature trees and shrubs. A 2 acre site with 13 touring pitches, 2 hardstandings and 7 statics.

Notes 🌐

ENGLAND

ENGLAND

HELSTON *continued*

Skyburriowe Farm *(SW698227)*

►►►

Garras TR12 6LR

☎ 01326 221646

e-mail: bkbenney@hotmail.co.uk

dir: *From Helston A3083 to The Lizard. After Culdrose naval airbase continue straight at rdbt, in 1m left at Skyburriowe Ln sign. In 0.5m right at Skyburriowe B&B/Campsite sign. Pass bungalow to farmhouse. Site on left*

PETS: Stables 4m **Public areas** on leads **Exercise area** 0.5m lane on farm **Facilities** walks info vet info **Other** prior notice required **Resident Pets:** Finlee & Candy (Golden Retrievers)

Open Apr-Oct Last arrival 22.00hrs Last departure 11.00hrs

A leafy no-through road leads to this picturesque farm park in a rural location on the Lizard Peninsula. The toilet block offers excellent quality facilities, and most pitches have electric hook ups. There are some beautiful coves and beaches nearby. A 4 acre site with 30 touring pitches, 2 hardstandings.

Notes Quiet after 23.00hrs 😊

HOLYWELL BAY   **Map 2 SW75**

Trevornick Holiday Park *(SW776586)*

TR8 5PW

☎ 01637 830531   🖺 01637 831000

e-mail: info@trevornick.co.uk

dir: *3m from Newquay off A3075 towards Redruth. Follow Cubert & Holywell Bay signs*

PETS: Charges £4-£4.95 per night £28-£34.65 per week **Public areas** on leads **Exercise area** designated fields for walking dogs **Facilities** walks info vet info **Other** prior notice required free dog scoop on arrival

Open Etr & mid May-mid Sep Last arrival 21.00hrs Last departure 10.00hrs

A large seaside holiday complex with excellent facilities and amenities. There is plenty of entertainment including a children's club and an evening cabaret, adding up to a full holiday experience for all the family. A sandy beach is just a 15-minute footpath walk away. The park has 68 ready-erected tents for hire. A 20 acre site with 593 touring pitches, 6 hardstandings.

Notes Families & couples only.

KENNACK SANDS   **Map 2 SW71**

Gwendreath Farm Holiday Park *(SW738168)*

►►►

TR12 7LZ

☎ 01326 290666

e-mail: tom.gibson@virgin.net

dir: *From A3083 turn left past Culdrose Naval Air Station onto B3293. Right past Goonhilly Earth Station signed Kennack Sands, left in 1m. At end of lane turn right over cattle grid. Right, through Seaview to 2nd reception*

PETS: Charges £25 per week **Public areas** disp bin **Exercise area** adjacent to park **Facilities** walks info vet info **Other** prior notice required

Open May-Sep Last arrival 21.00hrs Last departure 10.00hrs

A grassy park in an elevated position with extensive sea and coastal views, and the beach just a short walk through the woods. Campers can use the bar and takeaway at an adjoining site. Please telephone to book before arrival. A 5 acre site with 10 touring pitches and 17 statics.

Notes 😊

Silver Sands Holiday Park *(SW727166)*

►►►

Gwendreath TR12 7LZ

☎ 01326 290631   🖺 01326 290631

e-mail: enquiries@silversandsholidaypark.co.uk

dir: *From Helston follow signs to Future World Goonhilly. After 300yds turn right at x-roads signed Kennack Sands, 1m, left at Gwendreath sign, site 1m*

PETS: Stables 2m **Charges** £1.80-£2.50 per night (camping area) **Public areas** except in toilet block & reception; dogs must be on leads in main field disp bin **Exercise area** field available **Exercise area** beach (15 mins) **Facilities** food bowl water bowl washing facs walks info vet info **Other** prior notice required disposal bags available **Resident Pets:** George (Rough Collie), Whisky & Crispy (Jack Russells)

Open Etr-Sep Last arrival 20.00hrs Last departure 11.00hrs

A small park in a remote location, with individually screened pitches providing sheltered suntraps. A footpath through the woods from the family-owned park leads to the beach and the local pub. A 9 acre site with 34 touring pitches and 16 statics.

Notes No groups

KILKHAMPTON — Map 2 SS21

Upper Tamar Lake *(SS288118)*

▶ ▶

Upper Tamar Lake EX23 9SB
☎ 01288 321712
e-mail: info@swlakestrust.org.uk
dir: *From A39 at Kilkhampton onto B3254, left in 0.5m onto unclass road, follow signs approx 4m to site*

PETS: Public areas except café on leads disp bin **Exercise area** around lake, spacious grass areas **Facilities** vet info

Open Apr-Oct

A well-trimmed, slightly sloping site overlooking the lake and surrounding countryside, with several signed walks. The site benefits from the excellent facilities provided for the watersports centre and coarse anglers, with a rescue launch on the lake when the flags are flying. A good family site, with Bude's beaches and surfing waves only eight miles away. A 2 acre site with 36 touring pitches.

LANDRAKE — Map 2 SX36

Dolbeare Park Caravan and Camping
(SX363616)

▶ ▶ ▶ ▶

St Ive Rd PL12 5AF
☎ 01752 851332   📠 01752 547871
e-mail: reception@dolbeare.co.uk
dir: *A38 to Landrake, 4m W of Saltash. At footbridge over A38 turn right, follow signs to site (0.75m from A38)*

PETS: Charges £1-£2 per night **Public areas** except shower block, laundry, shop & children's play area on leads **Exercise area** dog friendly beaches **Facilities** food leads walks info vet info **Other** prior notice required disposal bags available **Restrictions** please phone to confirm which breeds are accepted; no dangerous breeds (see page 7)

Open all year Last arrival 18.00hrs Last departure noon

A mainly level grass site with trees and bushes set in meadowland. The keen and friendly owners set high standards, and the park is always neat and clean. The toilet block has an inviting interior and spacious family rooms are particularly impressive. A 9 acre site with 60 touring pitches, 54 hardstandings.

Notes No cycling, no kite flying

LANIVET — Map 2 SX06

Mena Caravan & Camping Park *(SW041626)*

▶ ▶ ▶

PL30 5HW
☎ 01208 831845   📠 01208 831845
e-mail: mena@campsitesincornwall.co.uk
dir: *Exit A30 onto A389 N signed Lanivet & Wadebridge. In 0.5m 1st right & pass under A30. 1st left signed Lostwithiel & Fowey. In 0.25m right at top of hill. 0.5m then 1st right. Entrance 100yds on right*

PETS: Charges £1-£2 per night £7-£14 per week **Public areas** disp bin **Exercise area** adjacent fields & woods (11 acres) **Facilities** food food bowl water bowl dog chews leads washing facs walks info vet info **Other** kennels nearby, dog friendly beach, guides & disposal bags available **Resident Pets:** Molly (Springer Spaniel), Jess (Labrador cross), Daisy (Labrador), Thomas, Maisy & Ruby (cats), Rodney & Del (Kune Kune pigs)

Open all year Last arrival 22.00hrs Last departure noon

Set in a secluded, elevated location with high hedges for shelter, and plenty of peace. This grassy site is about four miles from the Eden Project and midway between the north and south Cornish coasts. There is a small coarse fishing lake on site and two static caravans for holiday hire. A 15 acre site with 25 touring pitches, 1 hardstanding and 2 statics.

LANLIVERY — Map 2 SX05

The Crown Inn

★ ★ ★ INN

PL30 5BT
☎ 01208 872707   📠 01208 871208
e-mail: thecrown@wagtailinns.com
web: www.wagtailinns.com
dir: *Signed off A390, 2m W of Lostwithiel. Inn 0.5m down lane into village, opp church*

PETS: Bedrooms Public areas except restaurant on leads **Grounds** on leads **Exercise area** footpath adjacent **Facilities** water bowl dog chews scoop/disp bags washing facs cage storage walks info vet info **On Request** fridge access torch towels **Other** charge for damage

This character inn has a long history, reflected in its worn flagstone floors, aged beams, open fireplaces and ancient well. Dating in part from the 12th century, The Crown has undergone a faithful restoration. Dining is a feature and menus offer a wide choice of fresh fish, local produce and interesting dishes. The attractive bedrooms are more contemporary and are impressively appointed. The garden is a delight.

Rooms 2 en suite 7 annexe en suite (7 GF) **Facilities** FTV tea/coffee Dinner available Cen ht Wi-fi **Parking** 50

ENGLAND

Redgate Smithy

★★★★ BED AND BREAKFAST

Redgate, St Cleer PL14 6RU

☎ 01579 321578

e-mail: enquiries@redgatesmithy.co.uk

web: www.redgatesmithy.co.uk

dir: *3m NW of Liskeard. Off A30 at Bolventor/Jamaica Inn onto St Cleer Rd for 7m, B&B just past x-rds*

PETS: Bedrooms unattended **Public areas** except at breakfast **Grounds** disp bin **Exercise area** adjacent lane **Facilities** food bowl bedding dog chews scoop/disp bags washing facs cage storage walks info vet info **On Request** fridge access torch towels **Restrictions** small, friendly dogs only; no Rottweilers, Staffordshire Bull Terriers or Rhodesian Ridgebacks **Resident Pet:** Sinbad (Cocker Spaniel)

This 200-year-old converted smithy is on the southern fringe of Bodmin Moor near Golitha Falls. The friendly accommodation offers smartly furnished, cottage style bedrooms with many extra facilities. There are several dining options nearby, and a wide choice of freshly cooked breakfasts are served in the conservatory.

Rooms 3 rms (2 en suite) (1 pri facs) **S** £45; **D** £70 **Facilities** FTV tea/coffee Cen ht Wi-fi **Parking** 3 **Notes** LB No Children 12yrs Closed Xmas & New Year

Trelaske Hotel & Restaurant

★★★ **79%** HOTEL

Polperro Rd PL13 2JS

☎ 01503 262159 📠 01503 265360

e-mail: info@trelaske.co.uk

dir: *B252 signed Looe. Over Looe bridge signed Polperro. 1.9m, hotel signed on right*

PETS: Bedrooms (2 GF) unattended sign **Charges** £6.50 per night **Grounds** on leads disp bin **Exercise area** **Facilities** food bowl water bowl dog chews cat treats feeding mat walks info vet info **On Request** fridge access torch towels **Resident Pet:** Moe (Blue Fronted Amazon Parrot)

This small hotel offers comfortable accommodation and professional yet friendly service and award-winning food. Set in its own very well tended grounds and only minutes away from Looe and its attractions.

Rooms 7 (4 annexe) (2 fmly) (2 GF) **S** £70-£105; **D** £97.50-£105 (incl. bkfst) **Facilities** FTV Wi-fi **Parking** 50 **Notes** LB

THE INDEPENDENTS
HOTEL ASSOCIATION

Hannafore Point

★★★ **64%** HOTEL

Marine Dr, West Looe PL13 2DG

☎ 01503 263273 📠 01503 263272

e-mail: stay@hannaforepointhotel.com

dir: *A38, left onto A385 to Looe. Over bridge turn left. Hotel 0.5m on left*

PETS: Bedrooms unattended sign **Charges** £10 per night **Public areas** except terrace & bar on leads **Exercise area** adjacent **Facilities** water bowl washing facs cage storage walks info **Other** charge for damage

With panoramic coastal views of St George's Island around to Rame Head, this popular hotel provides a warm welcome. The wonderful view is certainly a feature of the spacious restaurant and bar, creating a scenic backdrop for both dinners and breakfasts. Additional facilities include a heated indoor pool and gym.

Rooms 37 (5 fmly) **S** £48-£60; **D** £80-£120 (incl. bkfst)* **Facilities** STV ③ Gym Spa pool Steam room Sauna ♫ Xmas New Year Wi-fi **Services** Lift **Parking** 32

Coombe Farm

★★★★ GUEST ACCOMMODATION

Widegates PL13 1QN

☎ 01503 240223

e-mail: coombe_farm@hotmail.com

web: www.coombefarmhotel.co.uk

dir: *3.5m E of Looe on B3253 just S of Widegates*

PETS: Bedrooms **Charges** £3.50 per night £20 per week **Public areas** **Grounds** on leads disp bin **Exercise area** 2m **Facilities** walks info vet info **On Request** fridge access torch **Other** charge for damage dogs must be on leads immediately outside cottages (be aware there are peacocks in grounds) **Resident Pets:** Daisy (Golden Retriever), Lordy & Barney (Shetland/Welsh pony), Snowy (guinea pig), peacocks, rabbits

Set in ten acres of grounds and gardens, Coombe Farm has a friendly atmosphere. The bedrooms are in a converted stone barn, and are comfortable and spacious. Each has a dining area, with breakfast delivered to your room.

Rooms 3 annexe en suite (1 fmly) (3 GF) **S** £45-£55; **D** £75-£82* **Facilities** STV FTV tea/coffee Direct Dial ⚐ Golf 18 **Parking** 20 **Notes** Closed 15 Dec-5 Jan

Little Harbour
★★★ GUEST HOUSE

Church St PL13 2EX
☎ 01503 262474
e-mail: littleharbour@btinternet.com
web: www.looedirectory.co.uk
dir: *From harbour, West Looe, right into Princess Sq, guest house on left*

PETS: Bedrooms Public areas Facilities water bowl washing facs walks info vet info **On Request** fridge access towels **Other** charge for damage **Restrictions** no dangerous dogs (see page 7) **Resident Pets:** Katamia Gingerbean (Persian cat), Biscuit (guinea pig)

Little Harbour is situated almost on Looe's harbourside in the historic old town; it has a pleasant and convenient location and parking is available. The proprietors are friendly and attentive and bedrooms are well appointed and attractively decorated. Breakfast is served freshly cooked in the dining room.

Rooms 5 en suite (1 fmly) **S** £20-£35; **D** £40-£60 **Facilities** FTV tea/coffee Cen ht Wi-fi **Parking** 3 **Notes** LB No Children 12yrs

Camping Caradon Touring Park *(SX218539)*
▶▶▶▶

Trelawne PL13 2NA
☎ 01503 272388 📠 01503 272858
e-mail: enquiries@campingcaradon.co.uk
dir: *Site signed from B3359 near junct with A387, between Looe & Polperro*

PETS: Charges £1-£2 per night **Public areas** except shop, bar & club room disp bin **Exercise area** 0.25m **Facilities** walks info vet info **Resident Pet:** rabbit

Open all year rs Nov-Mar by booking only Last arrival 22.00hrs Last departure noon

Set in a quiet rural location between the popular coastal resorts of Looe and Polperro, this family-run park is just 1.5 miles from the beach at Talland Bay. The owners have upgraded the bar and restaurant, and are continuing to improve the park. A 3.5 acre site with 85 touring pitches, 23 hardstandings.

Polborder House Caravan & Camping Park
(SX283557)

▶▶▶

Bucklawren Rd, St Martin PL13 1NZ
☎ 01503 240265
e-mail: reception@polborderhouse.co.uk
dir: *Approach Looe from E on A387, follow B3253 for 1m, left at Polborder & Monkey Sanctuary sign. Site 0.5m on right*

PETS: Stables 2m **Charges** £1 per night **Public areas** disp bin **Exercise area** 10yds **Facilities** food food bowl water bowl dog chews cat treats scoop/disp bags leads washing facs walks info vet info **Other** prior notice required disposal bags available **Restrictions** no fighting breeds **Resident Pet:** St Bernard

Open all year Last arrival 22.00hrs Last departure 11.00hrs

A very neat and well-kept small grassy site on high ground above Looe in a peaceful rural setting. Friendly and enthusiastic owners. A 3.3 acre site with 31 touring pitches, 19 hardstandings and 5 statics.

Tencreek Holiday Park *(SX233525)*
▶▶▶

Polperro Rd PL13 2JR
☎ 01503 262447 📠 01503 262760
e-mail: reception@tencreek.co.uk
dir: *Take A387 1.25m from Looe. Site on left*

PETS: Charges variable **Public areas** except public buildings disp bin **Exercise area** designated area **Exercise area** footpath from site **Facilities** food walks info vet info **Other** prior notice required disposal bags available

Open all year Last arrival 23.00hrs Last departure 10.00hrs

Occupying a lovely position with extensive countryside and sea views, this holiday centre is in a rural spot but close to Looe and Polperro. There is a full family entertainment programme, with indoor and outdoor swimming pools, an adventure playground and an exciting children's club. A 24 acre site with 254 touring pitches and 101 statics.

Notes Families & couples only

ENGLAND

Best Western Restormel Lodge

★★★ 73% HOTEL

Castle Hill PL22 0DD

☎ 01208 872223 ᐧ 01208 873568

e-mail: bookings@restormellodgehotel.co.uk

web: www.restormellodgehotel.co.uk

dir: *On A390 in Lostwithiel*

PETS: **Bedrooms** (9 GF) **Charges** £10 per night £60 per week **Grounds** on leads **Exercise area** 500mtrs **Facilities** washing facs vet info **On Request** fridge access torch towels Resident Pet: Monster (cat)

A short drive from the Eden Project, this popular hotel offers a friendly welcome to all visitors and is ideally situated for exploring the area. The older building houses the bar, restaurant and lounges, with original features adding to the character. Bedrooms are comfortably furnished, with a number overlooking the secluded outdoor pool.

Rooms 36 (12 annexe) (2 fmly) (9 GF) **Facilities** FTV ⚡ Xmas New Year Wi-fi **Parking** 40

Lostwithiel Hotel Golf & Country Club

★★★ 67% HOTEL

Lower Polscoe PL22 0HQ

☎ 01208 873550 ᐧ 01208 873479

e-mail: reception@golf-hotel.co.uk

web: www.golf-hotel.co.uk

dir: *Off A38 at Dobwalls onto A390. In Lostwithiel turn right & hotel signed*

PETS: **Bedrooms** (15 GF) unattended sign **Charges** £8 per night **Public areas** except restaurant on leads **Grounds** on leads **Facilities** washing facs walks info vet info **On Request** torch towels **Other** charge for damage

This rural hotel is based around its own golf club and other leisure activities. The main building offers guests a choice of eating options, including all-day snacks in the popular Sports Bar. The bedroom accommodation, designed to incorporate beamed ceilings, has been developed from old Cornish barns that are set around a courtyard.

Rooms 27 (2 fmly) (15 GF) (2 smoking) **Facilities** FTV ⚡ ℒ 18 ⚡ Putt green Fishing Gym Undercover floodlit driving range Indoor golf simulator Xmas New Year Wi-fi **Parking** 120

Penrose B&B

★★★★ GUEST ACCOMMODATION

1 The Terrrace PL22 0DT

☎ 01208 871417 ᐧ 01208 871101

e-mail: enquiries@penrosebb.co.uk

web: www.penrosebb.co.uk

dir: *A390 Edgecombe Rd, Lostwithiel onto Scrations Ln, 1st right for parking*

PETS: **Bedrooms** **Public areas** except dining room at breakfast **Grounds** on leads disp bin **Exercise area** 0.25m **Facilities** pet sitting washing facs cage storage walks info vet info **On Request** fridge access torch towels **Resident Pet:** Chocky (cat)

Just a short walk from the town centre, this grand Victorian house offers comfortable accommodation and a genuine homely atmosphere. Many of the bedrooms have the original fireplaces and all are equipped with thoughtful extras. Breakfast is a generous offering and is served in the elegant dining room, with views over the garden. Wi-fi access is also available.

Rooms 7 rms (6 en suite) (1 pri facs) (3 fmly) (2 GF) **D** £40-£100 **Facilities** FTV tea/coffee Cen ht Wi-fi **Parking** 8 **Notes** LB ⊗

Eden Valley Holiday Park *(SX083593)*

▶▶▶▶

PL30 5BU

☎ 01208 872277 ᐧ 01208 871236

e-mail: enquiries@edenvalleyholidaypark.co.uk

dir: *1.5m SW of Lostwithiel on A390 turn right at brown/white sign in 400mtrs*

PETS: **Stables** 100yds **Charges** £1-£2 per night **Public areas** except children's play area disp bin **Exercise area** field set aside **Facilities** walks info vet info **Other** prior notice required **Restrictions** no Dobermans, Rottweilers, German Shepherds or Staffordshire Bull Terriers **Resident Pet:** Pippin (Cairn Terrier)

Open Etr or Apr-Oct Last arrival 22.00hrs Last departure 11.30hrs

A grassy park set in attractive paddocks with mature trees. A gradual upgrading of facilities continues, and both buildings and grounds are carefully maintained. This park is ideally located for visiting the Eden Project, the nearby golden beaches and sailing at Fowey. Two self-catering lodges. A 12 acre site with 56 touring pitches, 12 hardstandings and 38 statics.

Croft Farm Holiday Park *(SX044568)*

► ► ►

PL30 5EQ

☎ 01726 850228   📠 01726 850498

e-mail: enquiries@croftfarm.co.uk

dir: *Exit A30 at Bodmin onto A391 towards St Austell. In 7m left at double rdbt onto unclass road towards Luxulyan/Eden Project, continue to rdbt at Eden, left signed Luxulyan. Site 1m on left. (NB Do not approach any other way as roads are very narrow)*

PETS: Charges £1.50 per night £10.50 per week **Public areas** except public buildings & playing field; dogs must be exercised on dog-walk area only   disp bin **Exercise area** woodland walk **Facilities** washing facs walks info vet info **Other** prior notice required disposal bags available

Open 21 Mar-21 Jan Last arrival 18.00hrs Last departure 11.00hrs

A peaceful, picturesque setting at the edge of a wooded valley, and only one mile from The Eden Project. A 10.5 acre site with 52 touring pitches, 42 hardstandings and 45 statics.

Notes No skateboarding, ball games only in playing field, quiet between 23.00hrs-07.00hrs

Godolphin Arms

★ ★ ★ ★ INN

TR17 0EN

☎ 01736 710202   📠 01736 710171

e-mail: enquiries@godolphinarms.co.uk

dir: *From A30 follow Marazion signs for 1m to B&B. At end of causeway to St Michael's Mount*

PETS: Bedrooms Stables 1m **Charges Public areas** on leads **Grounds** on leads disp bin **Exercise area** 100yds **Facilities** water bowl dog chews feeding mat walks info vet info **On Request** fridge access torch towels **Other** charge for damage

A traditional inn overlooking St Michael's Mount and beyond, The Godolphin Arms is the heart of the community and caters for all ages. Bedrooms have been refurbished and the staff are friendly. Food is served daily, and there are often special themed evenings. There's good reserved parking for guests.

Rooms 10 en suite (2 fmly) (2 GF) **Facilities** STV tea/coffee Dinner available Direct Dial Cen ht Wi-fi **Parking** 10 **Notes** No coaches

Wheal Rodney Holiday Park *(SW525315)*

► ► ►

Gwallon Ln TR17 0HL

☎ 01736 710605

e-mail: reception@whealrodney.co.uk

dir: *Exit A30 at Crowlas, signed Rospeath. Site 1.5m on right. From Marazion centre turn opposite Fire Engine Inn, site 500mtrs on left*

PETS: Charges £1.50 per night **Public areas** except buildings disp bin **Exercise area** 200yds **Facilities** food food bowl water bowl dog chews cat treats washing facs walks info vet info **Other** prior notice required early prior booking arrangements advised disposal bags available **Resident Pets:** Citroen, Harry, Badger (Sheep Dogs), Naughty Ralph, Pippin & Fudge (cats)

Open Etr-Oct Last arrival 20.00hrs Last departure 11.00hrs

Set in a quiet rural location surrounded by farmland, with level grass pitches and well-kept facilities. Just half a mile away are the beach at Marazion and the causeway or ferry to St Michael's Mount. A cycle route is just 400yds away. A 2.5 acre site with 30 touring pitches.

Notes Quiet after 22.00hrs

Budock Vean-The Hotel on the River

★ ★ ★ ★ 79% ⊚ COUNTRY HOUSE HOTEL

TR11 5LG

☎ 01326 252100   & 0800 833927   📠 01326 250892

e-mail: relax@budockvean.co.uk

web: www.budockvean.co.uk

dir: *From A39 follow tourist signs to Trebah Gardens. 0.5m to hotel*

PETS: Bedrooms sign **Stables** 5m **Charges** £7.75 per night £43.75 per week **Grounds** on leads disp bin **Exercise area** **Facilities** feeding mat scoop/disp bags walks info vet info **On Request** fridge access torch **Other** charge for damage

Set in 65 acres of attractive, well-tended grounds, this peaceful hotel offers an impressive range of facilities. Convenient for visiting the Helford River Estuary and the many local gardens, or simply as a tranquil venue for a leisure break. Bedrooms are spacious and come in a choice of styles; some overlook the grounds and golf course.

Rooms 57 (2 fmly) **S** £68-£130; **D** £136-£260 (incl. bkfst & dinner)* **Facilities** Spa ⊛ ♨ 9 🏌 Putt green 🛥 Private river boat & foreshore 🎵 Xmas New Year Wi-fi **Services** Lift **Parking** 100 **Notes** LB Closed 3 wks Jan

MAWNAN SMITH *continued*

Meudon

★★★ 85% COUNTRY HOUSE HOTEL

TR11 5HT
☎ 01326 250541 📠 01326 250543
e-mail: wecare@meudon.co.uk
web: www.meudon.co.uk
dir: *From Truro A39 towards Falmouth at Hillhead (Anchor & Cannons) rdbt, follow signs to Maenporth Beach. Hotel on left 1m after beach*

PETS: Bedrooms (15 GF) unattended Charges £10 per night
Public areas Grounds disp bin Exercise area 8.5-acre gardens & private beach Facilities walks info On Request fridge access
Resident Pet: Felix (cat)

This charming late Victorian mansion is a relaxing place to stay, with friendly hospitality and attentive service. It sits in impressive nine-acre gardens that lead down to a private beach. The spacious and comfortable bedrooms are situated in a more modern building. The cuisine features the best of local Cornish produce and is served in the conservatory restaurant.

Rooms 29 (2 fmly) (15 GF) S £88-£140; D £176-£280 (incl. bkfst & dinner)* Facilities FTV Fishing Private beach Hair salon Yacht for skippered charter Sub-tropical gardens Xmas Wi-fi Child facilities Services Lift Parking 50 Notes LB Closed 28 Dec-Jan

The Plume of Feathers

★★★★ INN

TR8 5AX
☎ 01872 510387 & 511122 📠 01872 511124
e-mail: enquiries@theplume.info
dir: *Just off A30 & A3076, follow signs*

PETS: Bedrooms Charges Public areas on leads Grounds on leads disp bin Exercise area Facilities food bowl water bowl walks info vet info On Request fridge access towels Other charge for damage

A very popular inn with origins dating back to 16th century, situated close to Newquay and the beaches. The restaurant offers a varied menu which relies heavily on local produce. The stylish bedrooms are decorated in neutral colours and have wrought-iron beds with quality linens. The garden makes an ideal place to enjoy a meal or a Cornish tea. The staff are very friendly.

Rooms 7 annexe en suite (1 fmly) (5 GF) S £58.75-£88.75; D £80-£120* Facilities FTV tea/coffee Dinner available Cen ht Wi-fi Parking 40 Notes LB No coaches

Mullion Cove Hotel

★★★ 77% HOTEL

TR12 7EP
☎ 01326 240328 📠 01326 240998
e-mail: enquiries@mullion-cove.co.uk
dir: *A3083 towards The Lizard. Through Mullion towards Mullion Cove. Hotel in approx 1m*

PETS: Bedrooms (3 GF) unattended Stables 2m Charges free in low season otherwise £7 per night Public areas dogs allowed in specific lounge only on leads Grounds on leads disp bin Exercise area Facilities dog chews scoop/disp bags washing facs dog grooming walks info vet info On Request fridge access torch Other charge for damage

Built at the turn of the last century and set high above the working harbour of Mullion, this hotel has spectacular views of the rugged coastline; seaward facing rooms are always popular. The stylish restaurant offers some carefully prepared dishes using local produce; an alternative option is to eat less formally in the bar. After dinner guests might like to relax in one of the elegant lounges.

Rooms 30 (3 fmly) (3 GF) S £65-£225; D £130-£300 (incl. bkfst & dinner)* Facilities FTV ᕯ Xmas New Year Wi-fi Services Lift Parking 60 Notes LB

Polurrian

★★★ 77% HOTEL

TR12 7EN
☎ 01326 240421 📠 01326 240083
e-mail: relax@polurrianhotel.com
web: www.polurrianhotel.com
dir: *A394 to Helston, then follow The Lizard & Mullion signs, onto A3083. Approx 5m, right onto B3296 to Mullion. Follow one-way system to T-junct, turn left signed Mullion Cove. 0.5m turn right, follow hotel sign. Hotel at end of road*

PETS: Bedrooms (8 GF) unattended sign Stables 2m Charges £8 per night Public areas except lounge & restaurant Grounds on leads disp bin Exercise area adjacent Facilities water bowl bedding feeding mat scoop/disp bags walks info vet info On Request fridge access torch towels Other charge for damage

With spectacular views across St Mount's Bay, this is a well managed and relaxed hotel where guests are assured of a warm welcome from the friendly team of staff. In addition to the formal

eating option, the High Point restaurant offers a more casual approach, open throughout the day and into the evening. The popular leisure club has a good range of equipment. Bedrooms vary in size, and the sea-view rooms are always in demand of course.

Rooms 39 (4 fmly) (8 GF) **S** £57-£199; **D** £114-£220 (incl. bkfst & dinner)* **Facilities** FTV ⌖ ⌇ ⌣ Gym Children's games room & outdoor play area Xmas New Year Wi-fi **Parking** 60 **Notes** Closed Jan-5 Feb

 **Mullion Holiday Park** *(SW699182)*
Ruan Minor TR12 7LJ
☎ 0844 335 3756   📠 01326 241141
e-mail: touringandcamping@parkdeanholidays.com
dir: *A30 onto A39 through Truro towards Falmouth. A394 to Helston, A3083 for The Lizard. Site 7m on left*

PETS: Charges max 2 pets £30 per week disp bin **Exercise area** small meadow **Facilities** food food bowl water bowl scoop/disp bags leads walks info vet info **Restrictions** no dangerous dogs (see page 7)

Open Apr-Oct rs 17 May-20 Sep outdoor pool open Last arrival 22.00hrs Last departure 10.00hrs

A comprehensively-equipped leisure park geared mainly for self-catering holidays, and set close to the sandy beaches, coves and fishing villages on The Lizard peninsula. There is plenty of on-site entertainment for all ages, with indoor and outdoor swimming pools and a bar and grill. A 49 acre site with 69 touring pitches, 9 hardstandings and 305 statics.

Notes Family site

NEWQUAY	Map 2 SW86

Headland
★★★★ 79% ⊚ HOTEL
Fistral Beach TR7 1EW
☎ 01637 872211   📠 01637 872212
e-mail: reservations@headlandhotel.co.uk
web: www.headlandhotel.co.uk
dir: *A30 onto A392 at Indian Queens, approaching Newquay follow signs for Fistral Beach, hotel adjacent*

PETS: Bedrooms unattended **Charges** £13 per night **Public areas** except restaurant on leads **Grounds** on leads disp bin **Exercise area** beach 50yds **Facilities** food water bowl bedding dog chews feeding mat scoop/disp bags pet sitting dog walking walks info vet info **Resident Pets:** Twiglet (Airedale Terrier), Hasna (Lakeland/Jack Russell cross), Tean (Lakeland/Parsons Russell cross) & Gypsy (Jack Russell)

This Victorian hotel enjoys a stunning location overlooking the sea on three sides - views can be enjoyed from most of the windows. Bedrooms are comfortable and spacious. The grand public areas, with impressive floral displays, include various lounges and in addition to the formal dining room, Sands Brasserie offers a relaxed alternative. Self-catering cottages are available, and guests staying in these can use the hotel facilities.

Rooms 97 (40 fmly) **S** £69-£139; **D** £79-£349 (incl. bkfst)* **Facilities** STV FTV ⌖ ⌇ ♣ 9 ⌣ Putt green ⚘ Harry Potter playroom In house surf school New Year Wi-fi Child facilities **Services** Lift **Parking** 400 **Notes** LB Closed 24-27 Dec

Hotel California
★★★ 66% HOTEL
Pentire Crescent TR7 1PU
☎ 01637 879292 & 872798   📠 01637 875611
e-mail: info@hotel-california.co.uk
web: www.hotel-california.co.uk
dir: *A392 to Newquay, follow signs for Pentire Hotels & Guest Houses*

PETS: Bedrooms (13 GF) unattended **Stables** 1m **Charges** £8 per night **Grounds** disp bin **Exercise area Facilities** walks info vet info **On Request** fridge access torch **Other** charge for damage dogs are required to be muzzled

This hotel is tucked away in a delightful location, close to Fistral Beach and adjacent to the River Gannel. Many rooms have views across the river towards the sea, and some have balconies. There is an impressive range of leisure facilities, including indoor and outdoor pools, and ten-pin bowling. Cuisine is enjoyable and menus offer a range of interesting dishes.

Rooms 70 (27 fmly) (13 GF) **S** £35-£50; **D** £70-£100 (incl. bkfst)* **Facilities** FTV ⌖ ⌇ Squash 10 pin bowling alley Billiard room Table tennis ♫ Xmas New Year Wi-fi **Services** Lift **Parking** 66 **Notes** LB Closed 3 wks Jan

Dewolf Guest House
★★★★ GUEST HOUSE
100 Henver Rd TR7 3BL
☎ 01637 874746
e-mail: holidays@dewolfguesthouse.com
dir: *A392 onto A3058 at Quintrell Downs rdbt, guest house on left just past mini-rdbts*

PETS: Bedrooms sign **Public areas** except dining room on leads **Grounds** on leads disp bin **Exercise area** beach, walks less than 5 mins **Facilities** food bowl water bowl dog chews pet sitting walks info vet info **On Request** fridge access towels **Other** charge for damage one bedroom available with private enclosed area plus small fridge; phone for further details of pet facilities **Resident Pet:** Alsatian/Collie cross

Making guests feel welcome and at home is the priority here. The bedrooms in the main house are bright and well equipped, and there are two more in a separate single storey building at the rear. The cosy lounge has pictures and items that reflect the host's interest in wildlife. The guest house is just a short walk from Porth Beach.

Rooms 4 en suite 2 annexe en suite (2 fmly) (3 GF) **S** £30-£45; **D** £60-£90 **Facilities** FTV tea/coffee Cen ht Licensed **Parking** 6 **Notes** LB

ENGLAND

NEWQUAY *continued*

The Three Tees

★ ★ ★ GUEST ACCOMMODATION

21 Carminow Way TR7 3AY
☎ 01637 872055   📠 01637 872055
e-mail: greg@3tees.co.uk
web: www.3tees.co.uk
dir: *A30 onto A392 Newquay. Right at Quintrell Downs rdbt signed Porth, over x-rds & 3rd right*

PETS: Bedrooms Charges £1 per night **Public areas** except dining room **Grounds** disp bin **Exercise area** 2 mins walk **Facilities** water bowl dog chews cage storage walks info vet info **Restrictions** no very large dogs **Resident Pet:** Poppy (Border Collie)

Located in a quiet residential area just a short walk from the town and beach, this friendly family-run accommodation is comfortable and well equipped. There is a lounge, bar and a sun lounge for the use of guests. Breakfast is served in the dining room, where snacks are available throughout the day; the bar serves light snacks in the evenings.

Rooms 8 rms (7 en suite) (1 pri facs) 1 annexe en suite (4 fmly) (2 GF) **D** £60-£70* **Facilities** FTV TVL tea/coffee Cen ht Licensed Wi-fi **Parking** 11 **Notes** LB Closed Nov-Feb

  ## Hendra Holiday Park *(SW833601)*

TR8 4NY
☎ 01637 875778   📠 01637 879017
e-mail: enquiries@hendra-holidays.com
dir: *A30 onto A392 signed Newquay. At Quintrell Downs over rdbt, signed Lane, site 0.5m on left*

PETS: Charges £80 per week **Public areas Exercise area** dog walking areas **Facilities** walks info vet info **Other** prior notice required **Restrictions** no Pit Bulls, Tosas, Argentino Brazilieros, Rottweilers, Dobermans, Akitas, Wolf Hybrids, Rhodesian Ridgebacks, Presa Canaros (see also information on page 7)

Open Apr-Oct rs Apr-Spring BH, Sep-Oct outdoor pool closed Last arrival dusk Last departure 10.00hrs

A large complex with holiday statics and superb facilities including an indoor fun pool and an outdoor pool. There is a children's club for the over 6s, and evening entertainment during high season. The touring pitches are set amongst mature trees and shrubs, and some have fully-serviced facilities. All amenities are open to the public. An 80 acre site with 548 touring pitches, 28 hardstandings and 283 statics.

Notes Families and couples only

Trebellan Park *(SW790571)*

► ► ►

Cubert TR8 5PY
☎ 01637 830522   📠 01637 830277
e-mail: enquiries@trebellan.co.uk
dir: *4m S of Newquay, turn W off A3075 at Cubert sign. Left in 0.75m onto unclass road*

PETS: Charges £2 per night £14 per week **Public areas** except swimming pool area on leads disp bin **Exercise area** footpaths & open fields **Facilities** washing facs walks info vet info **Other** prior notice required **Resident Pets:** Missus, Bob, Beastie & Ginge (cats), peacocks, ducks, aviary

Open May-Oct Last arrival 21.00hrs Last departure 10.00hrs

A terraced grassy rural park within a picturesque valley with views of Cubert Common, and adjacent to the Smuggler's Den, a 16th-century thatched inn. This park has three well-stocked coarse fishing lakes on site. An 8 acre site with 150 touring pitches and 7 statics.

Notes Families and couples only

Treloy Touring Park *(SW858625)*

► ► ►

TR8 4JN
☎ 01637 872063 & 876279   📠 01637 872063
e-mail: treloy.tp@btconnect.com
dir: *Off A3059 (St Columb Major-Newquay road)*

PETS: Stables 0.5m **Charges** £1-£2.50 per night **Public areas** disp bin **Exercise area** dog walking area **Facilities** food vet info **Other** prior notice required **Restrictions** no Pit Bull Terriers or similar breeds

Open May-15 Sep rs Sep pool, takeaway, shop & bar Last arrival 21.00hrs Last departure 10.00hrs

Attractive site with fine countryside views, within easy reach of resorts and beaches. The pitches are set in four paddocks with mainly level but some slightly sloping grassy areas. Maintenance and cleanliness are very high. An 18 acre site with 223 touring pitches, 24 hardstandings.

Trethiggey Touring Park (SW846596)

▶▶▶

Quintrell Downs TR8 4QR
☎ 01637 877672 📠 01637 879706
e-mail: enquiries@trethiggey.co.uk
dir: *A30 onto A392 signed Newquay at Quintrell Downs rdbt, left onto A3058, pass Newquay Pearl centre. Site 0.5m on left*

PETS: Charges Public areas except playground, shop & restaurant on leads disp bin Exercise area field Facilities food bowl water bowl dog chews cat treats scoop/disp bags walks info vet info Other prior notice required please phone for details of pet charges Resident Pets: Bex (Springer Spaniel), Brook (Border Collie)

Open Mar-Dec Last arrival 22.00hrs Last departure 10.30hrs

A family-owned park in a rural setting that is ideal for touring this part of Cornwall. Pleasantly divided into paddocks with maturing trees and shrubs, and offering coarse fishing and tackle hire. A 15 acre site with 145 touring pitches, 35 hardstandings and 12 statics.

PADSTOW	Map 2 SW97

The Metropole

RICHARDSON

★★★★ 70% ⚜ HOTEL

Station Rd PL28 8DB
☎ 01841 532486 📠 01841 532867
e-mail: info@the-metropole.co.uk
web: www.the-metropole.co.uk
dir: *M5/A30 pass Launceston, follow Wadebridge & N Cornwall signs. Take A39, follow Padstow signs*

PETS: Bedrooms (2 GF) unattended sign Charges £10 per night Public areas except restaurant & café bar on leads Grounds on leads disp bin Facilities scoop/disp bags washing facs walks info vet info On Request fridge access torch towels Other charge for damage can provide details of day care for dogs

This long-established hotel first opened its doors to guests back in 1904 and there is still an air of the sophistication and elegance of a bygone age. Bedrooms are soundly appointed and well equipped; dining options include the informal Met Café Bar and the main restaurant, with its enjoyable cuisine and wonderful views over the Camel estuary.

Rooms 58 (3 fmly) (2 GF) Facilities FTV ⚡ Swimming pool open Jul & Aug only Xmas New Year Wi-fi Services Lift Parking 36

St Petroc's Hotel and Bistro

★★ 85% ⚜ SMALL HOTEL

4 New St PL28 8EA
☎ 01841 532700 📠 01841 532942
e-mail: reservations@rickstein.com
dir: *A39 onto A389, follow signs to town centre. Follow one-way system, hotel on right on leaving town*

PETS: Bedrooms (3 GF) unattended Charges 1st night £20; thereafter £5 per night Public areas except restaurant on leads Exercise area beach - 2 mins walk Facilities food bowl water bowl bedding pet sitting dog grooming walks info vet info On Request fridge access torch towels Other charge for damage take home 'Chalky's Pal' blanket (included in price)

One of the oldest buildings in town, this charming establishment is just up the hill from the picturesque harbour. Style, comfort and individuality are all great strengths here, particularly so in the impressively equipped bedrooms. Breakfast, lunch and dinner all reflect a serious approach to cuisine, and the popular restaurant has a relaxed, bistro style. Comfortable lounges, a reading room and lovely gardens complete the picture.

Rooms 14 (4 annexe) (3 fmly) (3 GF) D £135-£270 (incl. bkfst)*
Facilities FTV Cookery school New Year Wi-fi Services Lift
Parking 12 Notes Closed 1 May & 25-26 Dec RS 24 Dec eve

The Old Ship Hotel

★★ 72% HOTEL

Mill Square PL28 8AE
☎ 01841 532357 📠 01841 533211
e-mail: stay@oldshiphotel-padstow.co.uk
web: www.oldshiphotel-padstow.co.uk
dir: *From M5 take A30 to Bodmin then A389 to Padstow, follow brown tourist signs to car park*

PETS: Bedrooms sign Stables 5m Charges £5 per night Public areas except restaurant on leads Grounds on leads disp bin Exercise area 0.1m Facilities water bowl dog chews washing facs walks info vet info On Request fridge access torch towels Other charge for damage Resident Pets: Harley (Boxer), Sox (cat)

This attractive inn is situated in the heart of the old town's quaint and winding streets, just a short walk from the harbour. A warm welcome is assured, accommodation is pleasant and comfortable, and public areas offer plenty of character. Freshly caught fish features on both the bar and restaurant menus. On site parking is a bonus.

Rooms 14 (4 fmly) S £30-£65; D £70-£135 (incl. bkfst)*
Facilities STV ♫ Xmas New Year Wi-fi Parking 20 Notes LB

PADSTOW *continued*

The Seafood Restaurant

★ ★ ★ ★ ★ ◉ ◉ ◉ ≣ RESTAURANT WITH ROOMS

Riverside PL28 8BY

☎ 01841 532700 📄 01841 532942

e-mail: reservations@rickstein.com

dir: *Into town centre down hill, follow round sharp bend, restaurant on left*

PETS: Bedrooms unattended **Charges** 1st night £20, thereafter £5 per night **Public areas** except restaurant on leads **Exercise area** beach nearby **Facilities** food bowl water bowl bedding pet sitting dog grooming walks info vet info **On Request** fridge access torch towels **Other** charge for damage

Food lovers continue to beat a well-trodden path to this legendary establishment. Situated on the edge of the harbour, just a stone's throw from the shops, the Seafood Restaurant offers stylish and comfortable bedrooms that boast numerous thoughtful extras; some have views of the estuary and a couple have stunning private balconies. Service is relaxed and friendly; booking is essential for both accommodation and a table in the restaurant.

Rooms 14 en suite 6 annexe en suite (6 fmly) (3 GF); **D** £135-£300* **Facilities** FTV tea/coffee Dinner available Direct Dial Cen ht Lift Wi-fi **Parking** 12 **Notes** LB Closed 24-26 Dec RS 1 May restaurant closed No coaches

Rick Stein's Café

★ ★ ★ ★ BED AND BREAKFAST

10 Middle St PL28 8AP

☎ 01841 532700 📄 01841 532942

e-mail: reservations@rickstein.com

dir: *A389 into town, one way past church, 3rd right*

PETS: Bedrooms unattended **Charges** 1st night £20, thereafter £5 per night **Public areas** except restaurant on leads **Exercise area** beach - 2 mins walk **Facilities** food bowl water bowl bedding pet sitting dog grooming walks info vet info **On Request** fridge access torch towels **Other** charge for damage

Another Rick Stein success story, this lively café by day, restaurant by night, offers good food, quality accommodation, and is just a short walk from the harbour. Three rooms are available, all quite different but sharing high standards of cosseting comfort. Friendly and personable staff complete the picture.

Rooms 3 en suite (1 fmly) **Facilities** tea/coffee Dinner available Cen ht Licensed **Notes** Closed 1 May BH RS 24-26 Dec

Little Pentyre

★ ★ BED AND BREAKFAST

6 Moyle Rd PL28 8DG

☎ 01841 532246

e-mail: JujuLloyd@aol.com

dir: *From A389, right onto Dennis Rd, bear right onto Moyle Rd*

PETS: Bedrooms unattended **Public areas** pets must be under control at all times **Grounds** on leads disp bin **Exercise area** 50mtrs **Facilities** food bowl water bowl bedding dog chews cat treats feeding mat scoop/disp bags leads washing facs cage storage walks info vet info **On Request** fridge access torch towels **Resident Pets:** 12 chickens

Within easy, level walking distance of the town centre, Little Pentyre is situated in a quiet residential area, adjacent to the Camel Estuary and Trail. The comfortable bedrooms are well equipped and guests enjoy a freshly cooked breakfast, featuring eggs from the hens in the rear garden.

Rooms 2 en suite (2 GF); **D** £55* **Facilities** FTV tea/coffee Cen ht **Parking** 2 **Notes** No Children 10yrs ◉

Padstow Touring Park *(SW913738)*

► ► ► ►

PL28 8LE

☎ 01841 532061

e-mail: mail@padstowtouringpark.co.uk

dir: *1m S of Padstow, on E side of A389 (Padstow to Wadebridge road)*

PETS: Charges £1.50 per night £10.50 per week **Public areas** except shop & amenity blocks disp bin **Exercise area** adjacent public footpaths **Facilities** food food bowl water bowl dog chews cat treats scoop/disp bags walks info vet info **Other** prior notice required **Resident Pets:** Lottie (Border Terrier), Poppy (Yorkshire Terrier)

Open all year Last arrival 21.00hrs Last departure 11.00hrs

A much upgraded park set in open countryside above the quaint fishing town of Padstow which can be approached by footpath directly from the park. It is divided into paddocks by maturing bushes and hedges to create a peaceful and relaxing holiday atmosphere. A 13.5 acre site with 150 touring pitches, 27 hardstandings.

Notes No groups

Dennis Cove Camping *(SW919743)*

▶ ▶ ▶

Dennis Ln PL28 8DR
☎ 01841 532349
e-mail: denniscove@freeuk.com
dir: *Approach Padstow on A389, right at Tesco into Sarah's Ln, 2nd right to Dennis Ln, follow to site at end*

PETS: Stables 2m **Charges** £1.30-£2 per night **Public areas** on leads disp bin **Exercise area** adjacent **Facilities** walks info vet info **Other** prior notice required shop 0.25m **Restrictions** disciplined dogs only **Resident Pet:** Milly (Border Collie)

Open Apr-end Sep Last arrival 21.00hrs Last departure 11.00hrs

Set in meadowland with mature trees, this site overlooks Padstow Bay, with access to the Camel Estuary and the nearby beach. The centre of town is just a 10 minute walk away, and bike hire is available on site, with the famous Camel Trail beginning right outside. A 3 acre site with 42 touring pitches.

Notes Arrivals from 14.00hrs

PENTEWAN | Map 2 SX04

Sun Valley Holiday Park *(SX05486)*

▶ ▶ ▶ ▶

Pentewan Rd PL26 6DJ
☎ 01726 843266 & 844393 📠 01726 843266
e-mail: reception@sunvalley-holidays.co.uk
dir: *From St Austell take B3273 towards Mevagissey. Site 2m on right*

PETS: Charges £25 per week **Public areas** except restaurant during food service disp bin **Exercise area** separate dog walk on site **Exercise area** adjacent **Facilities** food washing facs walks info vet info **Other** prior notice required disposal bags available (free of charge) **Resident Pets:** Sunny (cat), Jenny & Joe (donkeys), Milly & Lilly (goats), rabbits

Open all year rs Winter - pool, restaurant & touring field Last arrival 22.00hrs Last departure 10.30hrs

In a picturesque valley amongst woodland, this neat park is kept to an exceptionally high standard. The extensive amenities include tennis courts, indoor swimming pool, licensed clubhouse and restaurant. The sea is one mile away, and can be accessed via a footpath and cycle path along the river bank. A 20 acre site with 29 touring pitches, 13 hardstandings and 75 statics.

Notes No motorised scooters/skateboards or bikes at night

PENZANCE | Map 2 SW43

Hotel Penzance

★ ★ ★ 83% HOTEL
Britons Hill TR18 3AE
☎ 01736 363117 📠 01736 350970
e-mail: reception@hotelpenzance.com
web: www.hotelpenzance.com
dir: *From A30 pass heliport on right, left at next rdbt for town centre. 3rd right onto Britons Hill. Hotel on right*

PETS: Bedrooms (2 GF) **Stables** 5m **Charges** dogs £10 per night **Public areas** except restaurant on leads **Grounds** **Exercise area** 300mtrs **Facilities** feeding mat walks info vet info **On Request** fridge access torch towels **Other** charge for damage **Resident Pets:** Tom & Jerry (Birman cats)

This Edwardian house has been tastefully redesigned, particularly in the contemporary Bay Restaurant. The focus on style is not only limited to the decor, but is also apparent in the award-winning cuisine that is based on fresh Cornish produce. Bedrooms have been appointed to modern standards and are particularly well equipped; many have views across Mounts Bay.

Rooms 25 (2 GF) **S** £80-£85; **D** £120-£185 (incl. bkfst)*
Facilities FTV Xmas New Year Wi-fi **Parking** 12 **Notes** LB

ENGLAND

PENZANCE *continued*

Queens

★★★ 72% HOTEL

The Promenade TR18 4HG

☎ 01736 362371 📠 01736 350033

e-mail: enquiries@queens-hotel.com

web: www.queens-hotel.com

dir: *A30 to Penzance, follow signs for seafront pass harbour into promenade, hotel 0.5m on right*

PETS: **Bedrooms** sign **Charges** £10 per night (varies) **Public areas** except restaurant on leads **Facilities** cage storage walks info vet info **On Request** fridge access torch towels **Resident Pets:** Bilbo & Cleo (Jack Russells), Logan & Murphy (Labradors)

With views across Mounts Bay towards Newlyn, this impressive Victorian hotel has a long and distinguished history. Comfortable public areas are filled with interesting pictures and artefacts, and in the dining room guests can choose from the daily-changing menu. Bedrooms, many with sea views, vary in style and size.

Rooms 70 (10 fmly) **Facilities** FTV Yoga weekends Xmas New Year Wi-fi **Services** Lift **Parking** 50 **Notes** LB

See advert on page 61

Mount View

★★★ INN

Longrock TR20 8JJ

☎ 01736 710416 📠 01736 710416

dir: *Off A30 at Marazion/Penzance rdbt, 3rd exit signed Longrock. On right after pelican crossing*

PETS: **Bedrooms** unattended **Public areas** bar only **Exercise area** beach & field 50yds **Facilities** walks info vet info **Resident Pet:** Muppet (Beagle)

This Victorian inn, just a short walk from the beach and half a mile from the Isles of Scilly heliport, is a good base for exploring West Cornwall. Bedrooms are well equipped, including a hospitality tray, and the bar is a popular with locals. Breakfast is served in the dining room and a dinner menu is available.

Rooms 5 rms (3 en suite) (2 fmly) (2 smoking) **S** £20-£32.50; **D** £40-£55* **Facilities** FTV tea/coffee Dinner available Pool Table **Parking** 8 **Notes** RS Sun closed 4.30-7pm

Penmorvah

★★★ GUEST ACCOMMODATION

61 Alexandra Rd TR18 4LZ

☎ 01736 363711

dir: *A30 to Penzance, at railway station follow road along harbour front pass Jubilee pool. At mini-rdbt, right onto Alexandra Rd*

PETS: **Bedrooms** **Public areas** except dining room on leads **Exercise area** park 400yds **Facilities** food bowl water bowl feeding mat walks info vet info **On Request** fridge access torch towels **Other** charge for damage **Resident Pet:** Marbles (dog)

A well situated establishment offering comfortable rooms, all of which are en suite. Penmorvah is just a few minutes walk from the seafront with convenient on-street parking nearby.

Rooms 10 en suite (2 fmly) (3 GF) **Facilities** FTV TVL tea/coffee Cen ht **Notes** 🐾

Bone Valley Caravan & Camping Park

(SW472316)

▶▶▶

Heamoor TR20 8UJ
☎ 01736 360313 📠 01736 360313
e-mail: wardmandie@yahoo.co.uk
dir: *Exit A30 at Heamoor/Madron rdbt. 4th on right into Josephs Ln. 800yds left into Bone Valley. Entrance 200yds on left*

PETS: Stables 100yds **Public areas** on leads **Exercise area** field 100yds **Facilities** walks info vet info **Other** prior notice required

Open all year Last arrival 22.00hrs Last departure 10.00hrs

A compact grassy park on the outskirts of Penzance, with well maintained facilities. It is divided into paddocks by mature hedges, and a small stream runs alongside. A 1 acre site with 17 touring pitches, 6 hardstandings and 3 statics.

PERRANPORTH	Map 2 SW75

St Georges Country House

★★★★ GUEST ACCOMMODATION
St Georges Hill TR6 0ED
☎ 01872 572184
e-mail: info@stgeorgescountryhouse.co.uk

PETS: Bedrooms Charges £5 per night **Public areas** except bar/restaurant on leads **Grounds Exercise area Facilities** walks info vet info **Resident Pet:** Mollie (Border Collie)

Situated in an elevated position above Perranporth, St Georges is a very friendly and comfortable establishment. The owners and staff are attentive, and very welcoming. Food is served most evenings and there is also a bar and large sitting room with comfy sofas and lots of books.

Rooms 7 en suite (2 fmly) **S** £40-£50; **D** £70-£110* **Facilities** FTV TVL tea/coffee Dinner available Cen ht Licensed Wi-fi **Parking** 10 **Notes** LB Closed 1wk fr 23 Dec

Tollgate Farm Caravan & Camping Park

(SW768547)

▶▶▶▶

Budnick Hill TR6 0AD
☎ 01872 572130 & 0845 166 2126
e-mail: enquiries@tollgatefarm.co.uk
dir: *Off A30 onto B3285 to Perranporth. Site on right 1.5m after Goonhavern*

PETS: Stables 1m **Public areas** disp bin **Exercise area** excercise field & sand dunes adjacent **Facilities** washing facs walks info vet info **Other** disposal bags available

Open Etr-Sep Last arrival 21.00hrs Last departure 11.00hrs

A quiet site in a rural location with spectacular coastal views. Pitches are divided into four paddocks sheltered and screened by mature hedges. Children will enjoy the play equipment and pets' corner. The three miles of sand at Perran Bay are just a walk away through the sand dunes, or a 0.75m drive. A 10 acre site with 102 touring pitches, 10 hardstandings.

Notes No large groups, no single sex parties

Higher Golla Touring & Caravan Park

(SW756514)

▶▶▶

Penhallow TR4 9LZ
☎ 01872 573963 & 572116 📠 01872 572116
e-mail: cornish.hair@btconnect.com
dir: *A30 onto B3284 towards Perranporth. (Straight on at junct with A3075). Approx 2m. Site signed on right*

PETS: Charges £2 per night **Public areas** on leads disp bin **Exercise area** 20-acre field (subject to stock & crops) **Facilities** walks info vet info **Other** prior notice required maximum 2 dogs per pitch; dogs must be under strict control **Restrictions** no Pit Bull Terriers or Rottweilers, no dangerous breeds (see page 7) **Resident Pet:** Zorro (Labrador/Retriever cross)

Open Etr-mid Oct Last arrival 20.00hrs Last departure 10.30hrs

Extensive country views can be enjoyed from all pitches on this quietly located site. The facilities are very simple (2 WCs and 1 cold washbasin). Every pitch has electricity and a water tap. A 1.5 acre site with 18 touring pitches and 2 statics.

Notes No kite flying, quiet between 21.00hrs-08.00hrs

POLPERRO   Map 2 SX25

Talland Bay Hotel
★★★ 85% ◉◉ COUNTRY HOUSE HOTEL
Porthallow PL13 2JB
☎ 01503 272667 🖹 01503 272940
e-mail: info@tallandbayhotel.co.uk
web: www.tallandbayhotel.co.uk
dir: *From Looe over bridge towards Polperro on A387, 2nd turn to hotel*

PETS: Bedrooms (3 GF) sign Charges £7.50 per night Grounds on leads disp bin Exercise area surrounding countryside Facilities bedding feeding mat leads washing facs cage storage walks info vet info On Request fridge access torch towels Other charge for damage Resident Pets: Flo & Jonty (cats)

This hotel has the benefit of a wonderful location, being situated in its own extensive gardens that run down almost to the cliff edge. A warm and friendly atmosphere prevails and many bedrooms have sea views. Public areas and a number of the bedrooms have undergone a major refurbishment. Accomplished cooking, with an emphasis on carefully prepared local produce, remains a key feature here.

Rooms 20 (2 fmly) (3 GF) S £75.50-£105.50; D £90-£175 (incl. bkfst)* Facilities FTV ⚓ Xmas New Year Wi-fi Parking 22 Notes LB Closed 2 Jan-3 Feb

Penryn House
★★★ GUEST ACCOMMODATION
The Coombes PL13 2RQ
☎ 01503 272157 🖹 01503 273055
e-mail: enquiries@penrynhouse.co.uk
web: www.penrynhouse.co.uk
dir: *A387 to Polperro, at mini-rdbt left down hill into village (ignore restricted access). 200yds on left*

PETS: Bedrooms unattended Stables 5m Public areas except restaurant Grounds on leads disp bin Exercise area 200yds Facilities food bowl water bowl leads pet sitting washing facs cage storage walks info vet info On Request fridge access torch towels Resident Pet: Ella (Great Dane)

Penryn House has a relaxed atmosphere and offers a warm welcome. Every effort is made to ensure a memorable stay. Bedrooms are neatly presented and reflect the character of the building. After a day exploring, enjoy a drink at the bar and relax in the comfortable lounge.

Rooms 12 en suite (3 fmly) S £40-£45; D £70-£100* Facilities FTV tea/coffee Licensed Wi-fi Parking 13 Notes LB

POLZEATH   Map 2 SW97

South Winds Caravan & Camping Park
(SW948790)

▶ ▶ ▶

Polzeath Rd PL27 6QU
☎ 01208 863267 🖹 01208 862080
e-mail: info@southwindscamping.co.uk
dir: *Exit B3314 onto unclass road signed Polzeath, site on right just past turn to New Polzeath*

PETS: Charges £2 per night Public areas on leads Exercise area Facilities washing facs walks info vet info Other shop nearby

Open Mar-Sep Last arrival 21.00hrs Last departure 10.30hrs

A peaceful site with beautiful sea and panoramic rural views, within walking distance of a golf complex, and 0.75m from beach and village. A 16 acre site with 100 touring pitches.

Notes No disposable BBQs, no noise 23.00hrs-07.00hrs, families & couples only

Tristram Caravan & Camping Park *(SW936790)*

▶ ▶ ▶

PL27 6TP

☎ 01208 862215 📠 01208 862080

e-mail: info@tristramcampsite.co.uk

dir: *From B3314 onto unclassified road signed Polzeath. Through village, up hill, site 2nd right*

PETS: Stables Charges £2-£3 per night **Public areas** on leads **Exercise area** field adjacent **Other** prior notice required

Open Mar-Nov Last arrival 21.00hrs Last departure 10.00hrs

An ideal family site, positioned on a gently sloping cliff with grassy pitches and glorious sea views. There is direct, gated access to the beach, where surfing is very popular. The local amenities of the village are only a few hundred yards away. A 10 acre site with 100 touring pitches.

Notes No ball games, no disposable BBQs, no noise between 23.00hrs-07.00hrs

PORTHTOWAN	Map 2 SW64

Porthtowan Tourist Park *(SW693473)*

▶ ▶ ▶ ▶

Mile Hill TR4 8TY

☎ 01209 890256

e-mail: admin@porthtowantouristpark.co.uk

dir: *Exit A30 at junct signed Redruth/Porthtowan. Take 3rd exit at rdbt. 2m, right at T-junct. Site on left at top of hill*

PETS: Charges peak season £1 per night **Public areas** except buildings & children's play area disp bin **Exercise area** short walk & fenced area **Facilities** walks info vet info **Other** prior notice required disposal bags available

Open Apr-Sep Last arrival 21.30hrs Last departure 11.00hrs

A neat, level grassy site on high ground above Porthtowan, with plenty of shelter from mature trees and shrubs. The superb toilet facilities considerably enhance the appeal of this peaceful rural park, which is almost midway between the small seaside resorts of Portreath and Porthtowan, with their beaches and surfing. A 5 acre site with 80 touring pitches, 2 hardstandings.

Notes No bikes/skateboards during Jul-Aug

Wheal Rose Caravan & Camping Park
(SW717449)

▶ ▶ ▶

Wheal Rose TR16 5DD

☎ 01209 891496

e-mail: les@whealrosecaravanpark.co.uk

dir: *Exit A30 at Scorrier sign, follow signs to Wheal Rose. Site 0.5m on left (Wheal Rose to Porthtowan road)*

PETS: Public areas except children's play park on leads disp bin **Exercise area** adjacent tram road **Facilities** food food bowl water bowl dog chews cat treats leads cage storage walks info vet info **On Request** fridge access torch **Other** charge for damage prior notice required **Resident Pets:** Pebbles & Oscar (Labradors)

Open Mar-Dec Last arrival 21.00hrs Last departure 11.00hrs

A quiet, peaceful park in a secluded valley setting, central for beaches and countryside, and two miles from the surfing beaches of Porthtowan. The friendly owners work hard to keep this park immaculate, with a bright toilet block and well-trimmed pitches. A 6 acre site with 50 touring pitches, 6 hardstandings and 3 statics.

Notes 5mph speed limit, minimum noise after 23.00hrs, gates locked 23.00hrs

REDRUTH	Map 2 SW64

THE INDEPENDENTS

Crossroads Lodge

★ ★ **63%** HOTEL

Scorrier TR16 5BP

☎ 01209 820551 📠 01209 820392

e-mail: crossroads@hotelstruro.com

web: www.crossroadstravelinn.co.uk

dir: *A30 onto A3047 towards Scorrier*

PETS: Bedrooms (8 GF) **Charges** £4.50 per night **Public areas** except restaurant on leads **Grounds** on leads **Exercise area** adjacent **Facilities** cage storage walks info vet info **On Request** fridge access towels **Other** charge for damage

Situated on an historic stanary site and conveniently located just off the A30, this hotel has a smart appearance. Bedrooms are soundly furnished and include executive and family rooms. Public areas include an attractive dining room, a quiet lounge and a lively bar. Conference, banqueting and business facilities are also available.

Rooms 36 (2 fmly) (8 GF) **S** fr £52; **D** fr £72 (incl. bkfst)*
Facilities Xmas New Year Wi-fi **Services** Lift **Parking** 140

ENGLAND

REDRUTH *continued*

Lanyon Holiday Park (SW684387)

▶ ▶ ▶

Loscombe Ln, Four Lanes TR16 6LP

☎ 01209 313474

e-mail: info@lanyonholidaypark.co.uk

dir: *Signed 0.5m off B2397 on Helston side of Four Lanes village*

PETS: Bedrooms Stables Charges £5 per night £25 per week (+ £50 damage deposit) **Public areas** except toilets/showers & launderettes on leads disp bin **Exercise area** large dog walking paddock **Facilities** (pre-bookable) walks info vet info **On Request** fridge access **Other** charge for damage prior notice required

Open Mar-Oct Last arrival 21.00hrs Last departure noon

Small, friendly rural park in an elevated position with fine views to distant St Ives Bay. This family owned and run park continues to be upgraded in all areas, including two holiday lodges, and is close to a cycling trail. Stithian's Reservoir for fishing, sailing and windsurfing is two miles away. A 14 acre site with 25 touring pitches and 49 statics.

Notes Family park

REJERRAH   **Map 2 SW75**

 Monkey Tree Holiday Park (SW803545)

Scotland Rd TR8 5QR

☎ 01872 572032   🖷 01872 573577

e-mail: enquiries@monkeytreeholidaypark.co.uk

dir: *Exit A30 onto B3285 to Perranporth, 0.25m right into Scotland Rd, site on left in 1.5m*

PETS: Stables 3m **Charges** £3 per night **Public areas** except bar, restaurant, children's play areas, pool, clubhouse, takeaway & toilet/shower facilities disp bin **Exercise area** dog walking area **Facilities** food walks info vet info **Other** prior notice required disposal bags available **Restrictions** no Pit Bull Terriers, Japanese Tosas, Dogo Argentinos & Fila Brasilieros (see also dangerous dogs information on page 7)

Open all year Last arrival 22.00hrs Last departure 10.00hrs

A busy holiday park with plenty of activities and a jolly holiday atmosphere. Set close to lovely beaches between Newquay and Perranporth, it offers an outdoor swimming pool, children's playground, two bars with entertainment, and a good choice of eating outlets including a restaurant and a takeaway. A 56 acre site with 505 touring pitches, 17 hardstandings and 48 statics.

Notes Family park & couples

Newperran Holiday Park (SW801555)

▶ ▶ ▶ ▶

TR8 5QJ

☎ 01872 572407   🖷 01872 571254

e-mail: holidays@newperran.co.uk

dir: *4m SE of Newquay & 1m S of Rejerrah on A3075. Or A30 Redruth, exit B3275 Perranporth, at 1st T-junct right onto A3075 towards Newquay, site 300mtrs on left*

PETS: Stables 2m **Charges** £2.50 per night **Public areas** except children's play area on leads disp bin **Exercise area** dog walks & field **Facilities** washing facs walks info vet info **Other** prior notice required **Resident Pet:** Hamish (West Highland Terrier)

Open Etr-Oct Last arrival mdnt Last departure 10.00hrs

A family site in a lovely rural position near several beaches and bays. This airy park offers screening to some pitches, which are set in paddocks on level ground. High season entertainment is available in the park's country inn, and the café has an extensive menu. A 25 acre site with 357 touring pitches, 14 hardstandings and 6 statics.

Notes Families & couples only. No skateboards.

ROSUDGEON   **Map 2 SW52**

Kenneggy Cove Holiday Park (SW562287)

▶ ▶ ▶

Higher Kenneggy TR20 9AU

☎ 01736 763453

e-mail: enquiries@kenneggycove.co.uk

dir: *On A394 between Penzance & Helston, turn S into signed lane to site & Higher Kenneggy*

PETS: Charges dogs £3 per night **Public areas** except children's play area, shop, toilets & laundry disp bin **Exercise area** 50mtrs **Facilities** food food bowl water bowl scoop/disp bags washing facs walks info vet info **Other** dogs allowed on Kenneggy Sands all year **Restrictions** no dangerous breeds (see page 7) **Resident Pets:** Hugo & Tickle (Wire Haired Dachshunds), Ginger (cat)

Open 17 May-4 Oct Last arrival 21.00hrs Last departure 11.00hrs

Set in an Area of Outstanding Natural Beauty with spectacular sea views, this family-owned park is quiet and well kept. A short walk along a country footpath leads to the Cornish Coastal Path, and on to the golden sandy beach at Kenneggy Cove. A 4 acre site with 50 touring pitches and 7 statics.

Notes No large groups 😊

Music Water Touring Park *(SW906685)*

►►►

PL27 7SJ

☎ 01841 540257

dir: A39 at Winnards Perch rdbt onto B3274 signed Padstow. Left in 2m onto unclass road signed Rumford & St Eval. Site 500mtrs on right

PETS: Stables Charges £2-£3 per night **Public areas** except bar **Exercise area** short dog walk **Facilities** walks info vet info **Other** prior notice required max 2 dogs per pitch **Restrictions** no Pit Bulls or Rottweilers **Resident Pets:** pets' corner on site (donkeys, dog, chickens, rabbits)

Open Apr-Oct Last arrival 23.00hrs Last departure 11.00hrs

Set in a peaceful location yet only a short drive to the pretty fishing town of Padstow, and many sandy beaches and coves. This family owned and run park has grassy paddocks, and there is a quiet lounge bar and a separate children's games room. A 8 acre site with 55 touring pitches, 2 hardstandings and 2 statics.

Notes One tent per pitch

Rose-in-Vale Country House

★★★ 81% ◉ COUNTRY HOUSE HOTEL

Mithian TR5 0QD

☎ 01872 552202 📠 01872 552700

e-mail: reception@rose-in-vale-hotel.co.uk

web: www.rose-in-vale-hotel.co.uk

dir: A30 S towards Redruth. At Chiverton Cross at rdbt take B3277 signed St Agnes. In 500mtrs follow tourist sign for Rose-in-Vale. Into Mithian, right at Miners Arms, down hill. Hotel on left

PETS: Bedrooms (5 GF) **Stables** 3m **Charges** £6 per night **Public areas** except restaurant on leads **Grounds** on leads disp bin **Exercise area Facilities** walks info vet info **Other** charge for damage **Restrictions** dogs accepted only at manager's discretion **Resident Pets:** Daisey & Rosie (Black Labradors)

Peacefully located in a wooded valley this Georgian manor house has a wonderfully relaxed atmosphere and abundant charm. Guests are assured of a warm welcome. Accommodation varies in size and style; several rooms are situated on the ground floor. An imaginative fixed-price menu featuring local produce is served in the spacious restaurant.

Rose-in-Vale Country House

Rooms 20 (3 annexe) (2 fmly) (5 GF) **Facilities** FTV 🎾 ⚓ Xmas New Year Wi-fi **Parking** 52 **Notes** No children 12yrs

Beacon Country House Hotel

★★ 81% HOTEL

Goonvrea Rd TR5 0NW

☎ 01872 552318

e-mail: info@beaconhotel.co.uk

dir: From A30 take B3277 to St Agnes. At rdbt left onto Goonvrea Rd. Hotel 0.75m on right

PETS: Bedrooms (2 GF) **Charges** discretionary **Grounds** on leads disp bin **Exercise area** 0.12m **Facilities** pet sitting dog walking washing facs cage storage walks info vet info **On Request** fridge access torch towels **Other** charge for damage max 2 dogs per room

Set in a quiet and attractive area away from the busy village, this very friendly, relaxed hotel has splendid views over the countryside and along the coast to St Ives. Guests are assured of a very warm and friendly stay. Bedrooms are comfortable and well equipped and many benefit from glorious views.

Rooms 11 (2 GF) **S** £58-£117; **D** £88-£132 (incl. bkfst)* **Facilities** FTV Xmas New Year Wi-fi **Parking** 12 **Notes** LB No children 8yrs Closed 4-31 Jan

ST AGNES *continued*

Driftwood Spars

★★★★ GUEST ACCOMMODATION

Trevaunance Cove TR5 0RT

☎ 01872 552428   🖷 01872 553701

e-mail: info@driftwoodspars.co.uk

dir: *A30 to Chiverton rdbt, right onto B3277, through village. Driftwood Spars 200yds before beach*

PETS: Bedrooms Stables 3m **Charges** £3 per night £21 per week **Public areas** except restaurant on leads **Grounds Exercise area** 500yds beach **Facilities** vet info **On Request** fridge access **Other** charge for damage **Resident Pet:** Treacle (cat)

Partly built from shipwreck timbers, this 18th-century inn attracts locals and visitors alike. The attractive bedrooms, some in an annexe, are decorated in a bright, seaside style with many interesting features. Local produce, including delicious seafood, is served in the informal pub dining room and in the restaurant, together with a range from hand-pulled beers.

Rooms 9 en suite 6 annexe en suite (4 fmly) (5 GF) **S** £45-£66; **D** £86-£102* **Facilities** tea/coffee Dinner available Direct Dial Cen ht Licensed Wi-fi Pool Table **Parking** 40 **Notes** LB RS 25 Dec no lunch/dinner, no bar in evening

Penkerris

★★ GUEST HOUSE

Penwinnick Rd TR5 0PA

☎ 01872 552262   🖷 01872 552262

e-mail: info@penkerris.co.uk

web: www.penkerris.co.uk

dir: *A30 onto B3277 to village, on right after village sign*

PETS: Bedrooms Stables 1m **Grounds** disp bin **Facilities** walks info vet info **On Request** fridge access **Resident Pet:** Monty (cat)

Set in gardens on the edge of the village, Penkerris is an Edwardian house with a relaxed atmosphere. The best possible use is made of space in the bedrooms, and home-cooked evening meals using local produce are served by arrangement. Ample parking available.

Rooms 7 rms (4 en suite) (3 fmly) **S** £20-£50; **D** £50-£100 **Facilities** FTV TVL tea/coffee Dinner available Licensed Wi-fi **Parking** 9 **Notes** LB

Beacon Cottage Farm Touring Park

(SW705502)

▶ ▶ ▶

Beacon Dr TR5 0NU

☎ 01872 552347 & 553381

e-mail: beaconcottagefarm@lineone.net

dir: *From A30 at Threeburrows rdbt take B3277 to St Agnes, left into Goonvrea Rd, right into Beacon Dr, follow brown sign to site*

PETS: Charges £2 per night **Public areas** disp bin **Exercise area** field available **Facilities** washing facs walks info vet info **Resident Pets:** Rusty (cat), Folly (horse)

Open Apr-Oct rs Etr-Whit shop closed Last arrival 20.00hrs Last departure noon

A neat and compact site on a working farm, utilizing a cottage and outhouses, an old orchard and adjoining walled paddock. The unique location on a headland looking north-east along the coast comes with stunning views towards St Ives, and the keen friendly family owners keep all areas very well maintained. A 5 acre site with 70 touring pitches.

Notes No large groups

Presingoll Farm Caravan & Camping Park
(SW721494)

► ► ►

TR5 0PB
☎ 01872 552333   ▤ 01872 552333
e-mail: pam@presingollfarm.co.uk
dir: *From A30 Chiverton rdbt take B3277 towards St Agnes. Site 3m on right*

PETS: Public areas dogs must be on leads at all times disp bin
Exercise area adjacent meadow with disposal bins **Facilities**
walks info vet info **Resident Pets:** working farm with cattle, pigs
& horses; family dogs (Collies & Dalmatians)

Open Etr/Apr-Oct Last departure 10.00hrs

An attractive rural park adjoining farmland, with extensive
views of the coast beyond. Family owned and run, with level
grass pitches, and modernised toilet block in smart converted
farm buildings. There is also a campers' room with microwave
and free coffee and tea. A 5 acre site with 90 touring pitches, 6
hardstandings.

Notes No large groups 🐾

ST AUSTELL   Map 2 SX05

Cooperage
★ ★ ★ ★ BED AND BREAKFAST
37 Cooperage Rd, Trewoon PL25 5SJ
☎ 01726 70497 & 07854 960385
e-mail: lcooperage@tiscali.co.uk
web: www.cooperagebb.co.uk
dir: *1m W of St Austell. On A3058 in Trewoon*

PETS: Bedrooms Public areas except breakfast room **Grounds**
disp bin **Exercise area** 500yds **Facilities** dog chews feeding
mat leads pet sitting washing facs walks info vet info
On Request fridge access torch towels **Other** pets are only
accepted by prior arrangement **Resident Pet:** Jack (Black
Labrador)

Situated on the edge of the town, this late Victorian, semi-
detached granite house has been renovated in a contemporary
style. The comfortable bedrooms are well equipped and feature
beautifully tiled en suites. Guests are assured of a friendly and
relaxed welcome here and the property is conveniently positioned
for the numerous amenities and attractions locally.

Rooms 4 rms (3 en suite) (1 pri facs) **S** £40-£45; **D** £55-£65*
Facilities FTV tea/coffee Cen ht Wi-fi **Parking** 6 **Notes** LB No
Children 5yrs

Sunnycroft
★ ★ ★ ★ GUEST ACCOMMODATION
28 Penwinnick Rd PL25 5DS
☎ 01726 73351   ▤ 01726 879409
e-mail: enquiries@sunnycroft.net
dir: *600yds SW of town centre on A390*

PETS: Bedrooms Grounds on leads disp bin **Exercise area**
10-15 mins **Facilities** food bowl water bowl dog chews leads
washing facs cage storage walks info vet info **On Request**
fridge access torch towels **Other** dogs only accepted by prior
arrangement **Resident Pet:** Benje (dog)

Just a short walk from the town centre, this 1930s house is
conveniently situated for the Eden Project. The bright bedrooms
offer good levels of comfort, and ground-floor rooms are
available. Tasty and substantial breakfasts are served in the
light and airy conservatory dining room. Ample off-road, secure
parking is available too.

Rooms 5 en suite **S** £50-£70; **D** £55-£120* **Facilities** FTV tea/
coffee Dinner available Cen ht Wi-fi Golf 18 **Parking** 10 **Notes** LB
Closed 24-26 Dec

River Valley Holiday Park *(SX10503)*
► ► ► ► ►
London Apprentice PL26 7AP
☎ 01726 73533
e-mail: mail@cornwall-holidays.co.uk
dir: *Direct access to site signed on B3273 from St Austell at
London Apprentice*

PETS: Charges £25 per week **Public areas** disp bin
Exercise area Facilities food food bowl water bowl walks info
vet info **Other** prior notice required

Open Apr-end of Sep Last arrival 21.00hrs Last departure
11.00hrs

A neat, well-maintained family-run park set in a pleasant river
valley. The quality toilet block and attractively landscaped
grounds make this a delightful base for a holiday. A 2 acre site
with 45 touring pitches, 45 hardstandings and 40 statics.

ST AUSTELL *continued*

Court Farm Holidays *(SW953524)*

► ► ►

St Stephen PL26 7LE

☎ 01726 823684   📠 01726 823684

e-mail: truscott@ctfarm.freeserve.co.uk

dir: *From St Austell take A3058 towards Newquay. Through St Stephen (pass Peugeot garage). Right at St Stephen/Coombe Hay/Langreth/Industrial site sign. 400yds, site on right*

PETS: Charges charge for horses only **Public areas** on leads disp bin **Exercise area** adjacent fields **Facilities** walks info vet info **Other** prior notice required **Resident Pets:** 2 cats, 3 dogs & 4 horses

Open Apr-Sep Last arrival by dark Last departure 11.00hrs

Set in a peaceful rural location, this large camping field offers plenty of space, and is handy for the Eden Project and the Lost Gardens of Heligan. Coarse fishing and star-gazing facilities are among the attractions. A 4 acre site with 20 touring pitches, 5 hardstandings.

Notes No noisy behaviour after dark

ST BLAZEY GATE   Map 2 SX05

Doubletrees Farm *(SX060540)*

► ► ►

Luxulyan Rd PL24 2EH

☎ 01726 812266

e-mail: doubletrees@eids.co.uk

dir: *On A390 at Blazey Gate. Turn by Leek Seed Chapel, almost opposite BP filling station. After approx 300yds turn right by public bench into site*

PETS: Public areas except showers & toilet blocks on leads disp bin **Exercise area** 5 acres **Facilities** walks info vet info **Resident Pets:** Ben (Border Collie), chickens, ducks

Open all year Last arrival 22.30hrs Last departure 11.30hrs

A popular park with terraced pitches offering superb sea and coastal views. Close to beaches, and the nearest park to the Eden Project, it is very well maintained by friendly owners. A 1.57 acre site with 32 touring pitches, 6 hardstandings.

Notes ⊛

ST COLUMB MAJOR   Map 2 SW96

Southleigh Manor Naturist Park (SW918623)

► ► ►

TR9 6HY

☎ 01637 880938   📠 01637 881108

e-mail: enquiries@southleigh-manor.com

dir: *Exit A30 at junct with A39 signed Wadebridge. At Highgate Hill rdbt take A39. At Halloon rdbt take A39. At Trekenning rdbt take 4th exit. Site 500mtrs on right*

PETS: Charges £1.50 per night **Public areas** dogs only allowed adjacent to owner's pitch on leads **Exercise area** dogs must be exercised off site **Facilities** walks info vet info **Other** prior notice required **Restrictions** no dangerous breeds (see page 7) **Resident Pets:** Wenna (Old English Sheepdog)

Open Etr-Oct rs Peak times shop open Last arrival 20.00hrs Last departure 10.30hrs

A very well maintained naturist park in the heart of the Cornish countryside, catering for families and couples only. Seclusion and security are very well planned, and the lovely gardens provide a calm setting. There are two lodges and static caravans for holiday hire. A 4 acre site with 50 touring pitches.

Notes ⊛

ST IVES   Map 2 SW54

Garrack Hotel & Restaurant

★ ★ ★   77% ⊛ HOTEL

Burthallan Ln, Higher Ayr TR26 3AA

☎ 01736 796199   📠 01736 798955

e-mail: aa@garrack.com

dir: *Exit A30 for St Ives. fFrom B3311 follow brown signs for Tate Gallery, then Garrack signs*

PETS: Bedrooms (3 GF) unattended **Charges** max £10 per night **Grounds** disp bin **Exercise area** country lane & cliff walks nearby **Facilities** washing facs walks info vet info **On Request** fridge access towels **Other** charge for damage prior notice required pets allowed in certain bedrooms only

Enjoying a peaceful, elevated position with splendid views across the harbour and Porthmeor Beach, the Garrack sits in its own delightful grounds and gardens. Bedrooms are comfortable and many have sea views. Public areas include a small leisure suite, a choice of lounges and an attractive restaurant, where locally sourced ingredients are used in the enjoyable dishes.

Rooms 18 (2 annexe) (2 fmly) (3 GF) **S** £78-£103; **D** £128-£206 (incl. bkfst)* **Facilities** FTV ⊛ Gym New Year Wi-fi **Parking** 30 **Notes** LB

Old Vicarage

★★★★ 🏠 GUEST HOUSE

Parc-an-Creet TR26 2ES

☎ 01736 796124

e-mail: stay@oldvicarage.com

web: www.oldvicarage.com

dir: *From A3074 in town centre take B3306, 0.5m right into Parc-an-Creet*

PETS: Bedrooms Charges £5 per night £35 per week **Public areas** except dining room **Grounds** disp bin **Exercise area Other** pets must be well behaved **Resident Pet:** Tiger (cat)

This former Victorian rectory stands in secluded gardens in a quiet part of St Ives and is convenient for the seaside, town and St Ives Tate. The bedrooms are enhanced by modern facilities. A good choice of local produce is offered at breakfast, plus home-made yoghurt and preserves.

Rooms 5 en suite (4 fmly) **Facilities** TVL tea/coffee Cen ht Licensed Wi-fi ⅃ **Parking** 12 **Notes** Closed Dec-Jan

Trevalgan Touring Park (SW490402)

▶ ▶ ▶ ▶

Trevalgan TR26 3BJ

☎ 01736 792048

e-mail: recept@trevalgantouringpark.co.uk

dir: *From A30 follow holiday route to St Ives. B3311 through Halsetown to B3306. Left towards Land's End. Site signed 0.5m on right*

PETS: Charges max £2.50 per night **Public areas** except children's play area disp bin **Exercise area** 100mtrs **Facilities** food washing facs walks info vet info

Open Etr-Sep Last arrival 22.00hrs Last departure 10.00hrs

An open park next to a working farm in a rural area on the coastal road from St Ives to Zennor. The park is surrounded by mature hedges, but there are extensive views out over the sea. There are very good toilet facilities including family rooms, and a large TV lounge and recreation room with drinks machine. A 4.9 acre site with 120 touring pitches.

Penderleath Caravan & Camping Park

(SW496375)

▶ ▶ ▶

Towednack TR26 3AF

☎ 01736 798403

e-mail: holidays@penderleath.co.uk

dir: *From A30 take A3074 towards St Ives. Left at 2nd mini-rdbt, approx 3m to T-junct. Left then immediately right. Next left*

PETS: Charges £1.50-£3 per night **Public areas** except toilets, bar area & shop on leads disp bin **Exercise area** except August **Facilities** scoop/disp bags walks info vet info **Other** prior notice required dogs must be well behaved; maximum 2 dogs per pitch disposal bags & pet toys available **Resident Pet:** Buster (Jack Russell)

Open Etr-Oct Last arrival 21.30hrs Last departure 10.30hrs

Set in a rugged rural location, this tranquil park has extensive views towards St Ives Bay and the north coast. Facilities are all housed in modernised granite barns, and include a quiet licensed bar with beer garden, breakfast room and bar meals. The owners are welcoming and helpful. A 10 acre site with 75 touring pitches.

Balnoon Camping Site (SW509382)

▶ ▶

Halsetown TR26 3JA

☎ 01736 795431

e-mail: nat@balnoon.fsnet.co.uk

dir: *From A30 take A3074, at 2nd mini-rdbt 1st left signed Tate/ St Ives. In 3m right after Balnoon Inn*

PETS: Public areas disp bin **Facilities** walks info vet info **Other** prior notice required **Restrictions** no Staffordshire Bull Terriers or similar breeds

Open Etr-Oct Last arrival 20.00hrs Last departure 11.00hrs

Small, quiet and friendly, this sheltered site offers superb views of the adjacent rolling hills. The two paddocks are surrounded by mature hedges, and the toilet facilities are kept spotlessly clean. The beaches of Carbis Bay and St Ives are about two miles away. A 1 acre site with 23 touring pitches.

Notes 🐾

ENGLAND

ST JUST (NEAR LAND'S END)	Map 2 SW33

Trevaylor Caravan & Camping Park
(SW368222)

► ► ►

Botallack TR19 7PU
☎ 01736 787016
e-mail: trevaylor@cornishcamping.co.uk
dir: *On B3306 (St Just-St Ives road), site on right 0.75m from St Just*

PETS: Public areas dogs must be kept on leads at all times disp bin **Exercise area** 50mtrs **Facilities** food food bowl water bowl dog chews cat treats washing facs walks info vet info **Other** prior notice required

Open Fri before Etr-Oct Last departure 11.00hrs

A sheltered grassy site located off the beaten track in a peaceful location at the western tip of Cornwall. The dramatic coastline and the pretty villages nearby are truly unspoilt. Clean, well-maintained facilities and a good shop are offered along with a bar serving bar meals. A 6 acre site with 50 touring pitches and 5 statics.

ST JUST-IN-ROSELAND	Map 2 SW83

Trethem Mill Touring Park *(SW860365)*

► ► ► ►

TR2 5JF
☎ 01872 580504 ▤ 01872 580968
e-mail: reception@trethem.com
dir: *From Tregony on A3078 to St Mawes. 2m after Trewithian, follow signs to site*

PETS: Charges £1 per night **Public areas** except in buildings disp bin **Exercise area** 5-acre dog walk **Facilities** walks info vet info **Other** disposal bags available

Open Apr-mid Oct Last arrival 20.00hrs Last departure 11.00hrs

A quality park in all areas, with upgraded amenities including a reception, shop, laundry, and disabled/family room. This carefully-tended and sheltered park is in a lovely rural setting, with spacious pitches separated by young trees and shrubs. The very keen family who own it are continually looking for ways to enhance its facilities. A 11 acre site with 84 touring pitches, 50 hardstandings.

ST KEVERNE	Map 2 SW72

Gallen-Treath Guest House
★★★ GUEST HOUSE
Porthallow TR12 6PL
☎ 01326 280400 ▤ 01326 280400
e-mail: gallentreath@btclick.com
dir: *1.5m SE of St Keverne in Porthallow*

PETS: Bedrooms unattended **Charges** £2 per night £14 per week **Public areas** except restaurant/dining room **Grounds** disp bin **Exercise area** 2 mins walk to beach, coastal path & fields **Facilities** food (pre-bookable) food bowl water bowl bedding dog chews cat treats scoop/disp bags washing facs walks info vet info fridge access torch towels **Other** charge for damage all pet facilities by prior request only; pets may be left unattended in bedrooms only at meal times **Resident Pet:** J.D.(Bearded Collie/Lurcher cross)

Gallen-Treath has super views over the countryside and sea from its elevated position above Porthallow. Bedrooms are individually decorated and feature many personal touches. Guests can relax in the large, comfortable lounge complete with balcony. Hearty breakfasts and dinners (by arrangement) are served in the bright dining room.

Rooms 5 rms (4 en suite) (1 pri facs) (1 fmly) (1 GF) **S** £25-£32; **D** £50-£64* **Facilities** FTV TVL tea/coffee Dinner available Cen ht Licensed **Parking** 6

ST MERRYN (NEAR PADSTOW)   Map 2 SW87

Trevean Caravan & Camping Park *(SW875724)*

▶▶▶

Trevean Ln PL28 8PR
☎ 01841 520772   🖷 01841 520772
e-mail: trevean.info@virgin.net
dir: *From St Merryn take B3276 to Newquay for 1m. Turn left for Rumford. Site 0.25m on right*

PETS: Stables 1m **Charges** £1 per night £7 per week **Public areas** disp bin **Exercise area Facilities** food washing facs walks info vet info **Other** prior notice required pets accepted on camping & touring pitches only

Open Apr-Oct rs Whit-Sep shop open Last arrival 22.00hrs Last departure 11.00hrs

A small working farm site with level grassy pitches in open countryside. The toilet facilities are clean and well kept, and there is a laundry and good children's playground. A 1.5 acre site with 68 touring pitches and 3 statics.

SALTASH   Map 2 SX45

Crooked Inn

★★★ GUEST ACCOMMODATION
Stoketon Cross, Trematon PL12 4RZ
☎ 01752 848177   🖷 01752 843203
e-mail: info@crooked-inn.co.uk
dir: *1.5m NW of Saltash. A38 W from Saltash, 2nd left to Trematon, sharp right*

PETS: Bedrooms unattended sign **Charges Public areas Grounds** disp bin **Exercise area** fields **Facilities** water bowl pet sitting dog walking washing facs walks info vet info **On Request** fridge access torch towels **Other** charge for damage phone for further details of pet facilities **Resident Pets:** Laddie (pony), Dumbo Fancy Rats, Giant African Land Snails, geese, ducks

The friendly animals that freely roam the courtyard add to the relaxed country style of this delightful property. The spacious bedrooms are well equipped, and freshly cooked dinners are available in the bar and conservatory. Breakfast is served in the cottage-style dining room.

Rooms 18 annexe rms 15 annexe en suite (5 fmly) (7 GF) **Facilities** tea/coffee Dinner available Cen ht Licensed 🕱 **Parking** 45 **Notes** Closed 25 Dec

See advert on page 40

SUMMERCOURT   Map 2 SW85

Carvynick Country Club *(SW878564)*

RV ▶▶▶▶

TR8 5AF
☎ 01872 510716   🖷 01872 510172
e-mail: info@carvynick.co.uk
dir: *Off A3058*

PETS: Public areas on leads **Exercise area** adjacent lane **Facilities** vet info **Other** dogs must be exercised off site

Open all year rs Jan-early Feb restricted leisure facilities

Set within the gardens of an attractive country estate this spacious dedicated American RV Park (also home to the 'Itchy Feet' retail company) provides all full facility pitches on hard standings. The extensive on-site amenities, shared by the high quality time share village, include an excellent restaurant with lounge bar, indoor leisure area with swimming pool, fitness suite and badminton court. 47 touring pitches.

TRURO   Map 2 SW84

Polsue Manor Farm *(SW858462)*

★★★ FARMHOUSE
Tresillian TR2 4BP
☎ 01872 520234   Mrs G Holliday
e-mail: geraldineholliday@hotmail.com
dir: *2m NE of Truro. Farm entrance on A390 at S end of Tresillian*

PETS: Bedrooms Stables Charges horses - fee on application **Grounds Exercise area** woods 0.5m **Facilities** walks info vet info **Other** dogs allowed in non en suite bedrooms only; dogs must be on leads at all times (working farm) **Resident Pets:** Polly & Penny (Yellow Labradors)

The 190-acre sheep farm is in peaceful countryside a short drive from Truro. The farmhouse provides a relaxing break from the city, with hearty breakfasts and warm hospitality. The spacious dining room has pleasant views and three large communal tables. Bedrooms do not offer televisions but there is a homely lounge equipped with a television and video recorder with a selection of videos for viewing.

Rooms 5 rms (2 en suite) (3 fmly) (1 GF) **S** £30-£35; **D** £54-£60* **Facilities** TVL tea/coffee **Parking** 5 **Notes** LB Closed 21 Dec-2 Jan 190 acres mixed/sheep/horses/working

TRURO *continued*

Carnon Downs Caravan & Camping Park
(SW805406)

▶▶▶▶▶

Carnon Downs TR3 6JJ
☎ 01872 862283   📠 01872 870820
e-mail: info@carnon-downs-caravanpark.co.uk
dir: *Take A39 from Truro towards Falmouth. Site just off main Carnon Downs rdbt, on left*

PETS: **Public areas** except toilets, wash-up & showers disp bin
Exercise area good dog walks **Facilities** walks info vet info
Other walks book provided **Resident Pet:** Jaz (Collie)

Open all year Last arrival 22.00hrs Last departure 11.00hrs

A beautifully mature park set in meadowland and woodland close to the village amenities of Carnon Downs. The four toilet blocks provide exceptional facilities in bright modern surroundings. Extensive landscaping allows for more spacious pitch sizes, and there is an exciting children's playground with modern equipment, and a football pitch. A 33 acre site with 150 touring pitches, 80 hardstandings and 1 static.

Notes No children's bikes Jul-Aug

Truro Caravan and Camping Park *(SW772452)*

▶▶▶▶▶

TR4 8QN
☎ 01872 560274   📠 01872 561413
e-mail: info@trurocaravanandcampingpark.co.uk
dir: *Exit A390 at Threemilestone rdbt onto unclass road towards Chacewater. Site signed on right in 0.5m*

PETS: **Stables** 2m **Public areas** disp bin **Exercise area**
Facilities washing facs walks info vet info **Other** prior notice required

Open all year Last arrival 21.00hrs Last departure 10.30hrs

An attractive south facing park divided into paddocks by mature hedging, and with quality modern toilets. It is located on the fringes of an urban area a few miles from the city, and almost equidistant from both the rugged north coast and the calmer south coastal areas. There is a bus from the gate to the city of Truro. A 8.5 acre site with 51 touring pitches, 26 hardstandings and 49 statics.

Notes No bicycles or skateboards

Cosawes Park *(SW768376)*

▶▶▶▶

Perranarworthal TR3 7QS
☎ 01872 863724   📠 01872 870268
e-mail: info@cosawes.com
dir: *Exit A39 midway between Truro & Falmouth. Direct access at site sign after Perranarworthal*

PETS: **Public areas** except residential area; dogs must be on leads at all times; **Exercise area** large riverside field **Facilities** washing facs vet info **Other** local kennels will take 'day borders' with valid vaccination certificate disposal bags available
Resident Pet: Benson (cat)

Open all year Last departure noon

A small touring park in a peaceful wooded valley, midway between Truro and Falmouth, with toilet facilities that include two smart family rooms. Its stunning location is ideal for visiting the many nearby hamlets and villages on the Carrick Roads, a stretch of tidal water which is a centre for sailing and other boats. A 2 acre site with 40 touring pitches, 25 hardstandings.

Summer Valley *(SW800479)*

▶▶▶

Shortlanesend TR4 9DW
☎ 01872 277878
e-mail: res@summervalley.co.uk
dir: *3m NW off B3284*

PETS: **Charges** 50p per night **Public areas** except toilet block disp bin **Exercise area** **Facilities** food food bowl water bowl walks info vet info **Other** disposal bags available
Resident Pet: Parsley (cat)

Open Apr-Oct Last arrival 20.00hrs Last departure noon

A very attractive and secluded site in a rural setting midway between the A30 and the cathedral city of Truro. Keen owners maintain the facilities to a good standard. A 3 acre site with 60 touring pitches.

The Laurels Holiday Park (SW957715)

▶ ▶ ▶

Padstow Rd, Whitecross PL27 7JQ
☎ 01209 313474
e-mail: info@thelaurelsholidaypark.co.uk
dir: *Off A389 (Padstow road) near junct with A39, W of Wadebridge*

PETS: Charges £2 per night **Public areas** except toilets & laundry on leads disp bin **Exercise area** fenced exercise area **Facilities** walks info vet info **Other** prior notice required

Open Apr or Etr-Oct Last arrival 20.00hrs Last departure 11.00hrs

A very smart and well-equipped park with individual pitches screened by hedges and young shrubs. The dog walk is of great benefit to pet owners, and the Camel cycle trail and Padstow are not far away. A 2.2 acre site with 30 touring pitches, 2 hardstandings.

Notes No group bookings, family park

Watergate Bay Touring Park (SW850653)

▶ ▶ ▶ ▶

TR8 4AD
☎ 01637 860387   ▤ 0871 661 7549
e-mail: email@watergatebaytouringpark.co.uk
dir: *4m N of Newquay on B3276 (coast road)*

PETS: Charges Jul-Aug £2 per night **Public areas** except swimming pool area, clubroom, cafeteria & recreational area disp bin **Exercise area** 2-acre exercise field **Facilities** food walks info vet info **Other** prior notice required

Open all year rs Oct-Etr restricted bar, cafe, shop & pool Last arrival 22.00hrs Last departure noon

A well-established park above Watergate Bay, where acres of golden sand, rock pools and surf are seen as a holidaymakers' paradise. Toilet facilities are appointed to a high standard, and there is a wide range of activities including a regular entertainment programme in the clubhouse. A 30 acre site with 171 touring pitches, 14 hardstandings and 2 statics.

The Gurnard's Head

★★★ ◉◉ INN

Treen TR26 3DE
☎ 01736 796928
e-mail: enquiries@gurnardshead.co.uk
dir: *5m from St Ives on B3306, 4.5m from Penzance via New Mill*

PETS: Bedrooms unattended **Public areas** except restaurant **Grounds Exercise area** adjacent fields & footpaths **Facilities** food bowl water bowl **On Request** towels

Ideally located for enjoying the beautiful coastline, this inn offers atmospheric public areas. The style is relaxed and very popular with walkers, keen to rest their weary legs. A log fire in the bar provides a warm welcome on colder days and on warmer days, outside seating is available. Lunch and dinner, featuring local home-cooked food, is available either in the bar or the adjoining restaurant area. The dinner menu is not extensive but there are interesting choices and everything is home made, including the bread. Breakfast is served around a grand farmhouse table.

Rooms 7 en suite **S** £65-£110; **D** £90-£160* **Facilities** tea/coffee Dinner available Wi-fi **Parking** 40 **Notes** Closed 25 Dec & 4 days mid Jan No coaches

Lowbyer Manor Country House

★★★★ GUEST HOUSE

Hexham Rd CA9 3JX
☎ 01434 381230   ▤ 01434 381425
e-mail: stay@lowbyer.com
web: www.lowbyer.com
dir: *250yds N of village centre on A686. Pass South Tynedale Railway on left, turn right*

PETS: Bedrooms Charges £5 per night **Public areas** except restaurant on leads **Grounds** disp bin **Exercise area** 0.5m **Facilities** scoop/disp bags washing facs cage storage walks info vet info **On Request** fridge access torch towels

Located on the edge of the village, this Grade II listed Georgian building retains many original features, which are highlighted by the furnishings and decor. Cosy bedrooms are filled with a wealth of thoughtful extras and day rooms include an elegant dining room, a comfortable lounge and bar equipped with lots of historical artefacts.

Rooms 9 en suite (1 fmly) **S** £35-£50; **D** £70-£84* **Facilities** tea/coffee Cen ht Licensed **Parking** 9 **Notes** LB

AMBLESIDE — Map 7 NY30

Waterhead Hotel

★★★★ 77% ⊛ TOWN HOUSE HOTEL

Lake Rd LA22 0ER
☎ 015394 32566   ▤ 015394 31255
e-mail: waterhead@elhmail.co.uk
web: www.elh.co.uk/hotels/waterhead.htm
dir: A591 to Ambleside. Hotel opposite Waterhead Pier

PETS: Bedrooms (7 GF) Charges £25 per stay Public areas bar
only on leads Grounds on leads Exercise area 50yds Facilities
food bowl water bowl walks info vet info On Request fridge
access torch towels Other charge for damage pets by prior
arrangement only Restrictions no Rottweilers or dangerous dogs
(see page 7)

With an enviable location opposite the bay, this well-established
hotel offers contemporary and comfortable accommodation with
CD/DVD players, plasma screens and internet access. There is
a bar with a garden terrace overlooking the lake and a stylish
restaurant serving classical cuisine with a modern twist. Staff
are very attentive and friendly. Guests can enjoy full use of the
Low Wood Hotel leisure facilities nearby.

Rooms 41 (3 fmly) (7 GF) S £110-£298; D £110-£328 (incl.
bkfst)* Facilities FTV Free use of leisure facilities at sister hotel
(1m) Xmas New Year Wi-fi Parking 43 Notes LB

Skelwith Bridge

★★★ 75% HOTEL

Skelwith Bridge LA22 9NJ
☎ 015394 32115   ▤ 015394 34254
e-mail: info@skelwithbridgehotel.co.uk
web: www.skelwithbridgehotel.co.uk
dir: 2.5m W on A593 at junct with B5343 to Langdale

PETS: Bedrooms (1 GF) Charges £5 per night Public areas
except restaurant Grounds Exercise area 100mtrs Facilities
water bowl pet sitting washing facs cage storage walks info
vet info On Request torch towels Other charge for damage

This 17th-century inn is now a well-appointed tourist hotel
located at the heart of the Lake District National Park and
renowned for its friendly and attentive service. Bedrooms include
two rooms with four-poster beds. Spacious public areas include
a choice of lounges and bars, and an attractive restaurant
overlooking the gardens to the bridge from which the hotel takes
its name.

Rooms 28 (6 annexe) (2 fmly) (1 GF) S £45-£63; D £45-£85 (incl.
bkfst)* Facilities Xmas New Year Parking 60 Notes LB

Skelwith Fold Caravan Park (NY355029)

►►►►

LA22 0HX
☎ 015394 32277   ▤ 015394 34344
e-mail: info@skelwith.com
dir: From Ambleside on A593 towards Coniston, left at
Clappersgate onto B5286 (Hawkshead road). Site 1m on right

PETS: Public areas except shop & children's playground disp bin
Exercise area Facilities food dog chews washing facs vet info
Other disposal bags available

Open Mar-15 Nov Last arrival dusk Last departure noon

In the grounds of a former mansion, this park is in a beautiful
setting close to Lake Windermere. Touring areas are dotted in
paddocks around the extensively wooded grounds, and the all-
weather pitches are set close to the many facility buildings. There
is a 5-acre family recreation area which has spectacular views
of Loughrigg Fell. A 130 acre site with 150 touring pitches, 150
hardstandings and 300 statics.

APPLEBY-IN-WESTMORLAND — Map 12 NY62

Hall Croft

★★★★ ▤ BED AND BREAKFAST

Dufton CA16 6DB
☎ 017683 52902
e-mail: hallcroft@phonecoop.coop
dir: 3m N of Appleby. In Dufton by village green

PETS: Bedrooms Public areas except dining room at breakfast
Grounds disp bin Exercise area woods nearby Facilities
food (pre-bookable) food bowl water bowl washing facs
cage storage walks info vet info On Request fridge access
torch towels Other charge for damage pet sitting on request
Resident Pets: Monty (Collie cross), Shep (Border Collie)

Standing at the end of a lime-tree avenue, Hall Croft, built in
1882, has been restored to its original glory. Bedrooms are
comfortably proportioned, traditionally furnished and well
equipped. Breakfasts, served in the lounge-dining room, are
substantial and include a range of home-made produce. Guests
can enjoy the lovely garden, which has views of the Pennines.

Rooms 3 rms (2 en suite) (1 pri facs) Facilities FTV tea/coffee
Cen ht Parking 3 Notes Closed 24-26 Dec ⊛

Wild Rose Park *(NY698165)*

▶▶▶▶▶

Ormside CA16 6EJ

☎ 017683 51077 🖹 017683 52551

e-mail: reception@wildrose.co.uk

dir: *Signed on unclass road to Great Ormside, off B6260*

PETS: Charges £1.50 per night **Public areas** except shop & restaurant on leads disp bin **Exercise area** fenced exercise area **Facilities** food food bowl water bowl dog chews scoop/disp bags leads washing facs walks info vet info **Other** prior notice required **Restrictions** no Rottweilers, Pit Bulls or Dobermans; no dangerous dogs (see page 7)

Open all year rs Nov-Mar shop & pool closed, restaurant rs Last arrival 22.00hrs Last departure noon

Situated in the Eden Valley, this large family-run park has been carefully landscaped and offers superb facilities maintained to an extremely high standard, including four wooden wigwams for hire. There are several individual pitches, and extensive views from most areas of the park. Traditional stone walls and the planting of lots of indigenous trees help it to blend into the environment, and wildlife is actively encouraged. A 85 acre site with 226 touring pitches, 140 hardstandings and 273 statics.

Notes No unaccompanied teenagers, no group bookings

ARMATHWAITE   **Map 12 NY54**

The Dukes Head Inn

★★★ INN

Front St CA4 9PB

☎ 016974 72226

e-mail: info@dukeshead-hotel.co.uk

web: www.dukeshead-hotel.co.uk

dir: *In village centre opp post office*

PETS: Bedrooms unattended **Stables** 1m **Charges** £5 per stay **Public areas** except lounge bar & restaurant **Grounds** disp bin **Exercise area** surrounding countryside, public footpaths **Facilities** food bowl water bowl cage storage walks info vet info **Other** charge for damage day kennels nearby dog walking & grooming can be arranged with prior notice

Located in the peaceful village of Armathwaite close to the River Eden, the Dukes Head offers comfortable accommodation in a warm friendly atmosphere. There is a relaxing lounge bar with

---

open fires and a wide choice of meals are available either here or in the restaurant.

Rooms 5 rms (3 en suite) (2 pri facs) **S** £42.50; **D** £62.50*

Facilities FTV tea/coffee Dinner available Cen ht Wi-fi **Parking** 20

Notes LB Closed 25 Dec

AYSIDE   **Map 7 SD38**

Oak Head Caravan Park *(SD389839)*

▶▶▶

LA11 6JA

☎ 015395 31475

dir: *M6 junct 36, A590 towards Newby Bridge, 14m. From A590 bypass follow signs for Ayside*

PETS: Public areas disp bin **Exercise area** **Facilities** vet info **Other** disposal bags available **Restrictions** no Rottweilers

Open Mar-Oct Last arrival 22.00hrs Last departure noon

A pleasant terraced site with two separate areas - grass for tents and all gravel pitches for caravans and motorhomes. The site is enclosed within mature woodland and surrounded by hills. A 3 acre site with 60 touring pitches, 30 hardstandings and 71 statics.

Notes No open fires 😊

BASSENTHWAITE   **Map 11 NY23**

Armathwaite Hall Country House & Spa

★★★★ 81% COUNTRY HOUSE HOTEL

CA12 4RE

☎ 017687 76551 🖹 017687 76220

e-mail: reservations@armathwaite-hall.com

web: www.armathwaite-hall.com

dir: *M6 junct 40/A66 to Keswick rdbt then A591 signed Carlisle. 8m to Castle Inn junct, turn left. Hotel 300yds*

PETS: Bedrooms (8 GF) unattended sign **Charges** £15 per night **Grounds** on leads disp bin **Exercise area** 400-acre estate **Facilities** food (pre-bookable) bedding dog chews cat treats scoop/disp bags pet sitting dog walking washing facs walks info vet info **On Request** fridge access torch **Other** charge for damage dog grooming can be arranged **Resident Pets:** Ben & Millie (Belgian Shepherds), Chrissy (Labrador)

Enjoying fine views over Bassenthwaite Lake, this impressive mansion, dating from the 17th century, is peacefully situated amid 400 acres of deer park. Comfortably furnished bedrooms are complemented by a choice of public rooms featuring splendid wood panelling and roaring log fires in the cooler months.

Rooms 42 (4 fmly) (8 GF) **Facilities** Spa STV 🏊 supervised 🎾 Fishing 🚣 Gym Archery Clayshooting Quad & mountain bikes Falconry Xmas New Year Wi-fi **Services** Lift **Parking** 100

ENGLAND

BASSENTHWAITE *continued*

The Pheasant
★★★ 83% ⊛ HOTEL

CA13 9YE
☎ 017687 76234 📄 017687 76002
e-mail: info@the-pheasant.co.uk
web: www.the-pheasant.co.uk
dir: *Midway between Keswick & Cockermouth, signed from A66*

PETS: Bedrooms (2 GF) **Sep accom** sleeping boxes **Charges** £5 per night **Public areas** except lounge at meal times on leads **Grounds** on leads disp bin **Exercise area Facilities** bedding walks info vet info **On Request** torch towels **Other** dogs allowed in certain bedrooms only; please phone for further details of pet facilities

Enjoying a rural setting, within well-tended gardens, on the western side of Bassenthwaite Lake, this friendly 500-year-old inn is steeped in tradition. The attractive oak-panelled bar has seen few changes over the years and features log fires and a great selection of malt whiskies. The individually decorated bedrooms are stylish and thoughtfully equipped.

Rooms 15 (2 annexe) (2 GF) **Facilities** New Year Wi-fi **Parking** 40 **Notes** No children 12yrs Closed 25 Dec

---

| BOOT | Map 7 NY10 |

Eskdale Camping & Caravanning Club Site
(NY178011)

►►►►►

CA19 1TH
☎ 019467 23253 & 0845 130 7633
dir: *Exit A595 at Gosforth or Holmbrook to Eskdale Green & then to Boot. Site on left towards Hardknott Pass after railway*

PETS: Public areas Exercise area surrounding countryside **Other** prior notice required

Open Mar-14 Jan Last arrival 20.00hrs Last departure noon

Stunningly located in Eskdale, a feeling of peace and tranquillity prevails at this top quality Club site, with the sounds of running water and birdsong the only welcome distractions. Although mainly geared to campers, the facilities here are very impressive, with a smart amenities block, equipped with efficient modern facilities including an excellent fully-serviced wet room-style family room with power shower, and the surroundings of mountains, mature trees and shrubs create a wonderful 'back to nature' feeling. There's a nest of camping pods under the trees, with gravel access paths and barbeques, and a new adults-only backpackers' area. Expect great attention to detail and a high level of customer care. The park is only a quarter of a mile from Boot station on the Ravenglass/Eskdale railway ('Ratty'). An 8 acre site with 80 touring pitches.

Notes Site gates closed 23.00hrs-07.00hrs

| BORROWDALE | Map 11 NY21 |

Lodore Falls Hotel
★★★★ 77% HOTEL

CA12 5UX
☎ 017687 77285 & 0800 840 1246 📄 017687 77343
e-mail: info@lodorefallshotel.co.uk
web: www.lodorefallshotel.co.uk
dir: *M6 junct 40 take A66 to Keswick, then B5289 to Borrowdale. Hotel on left*

PETS: Bedrooms unattended **Charges** £10 per night **Public areas** except restaurant & lounge bar on leads **Grounds** on leads disp bin **Exercise area Facilities** food bowl water bowl pet sitting dog walking cage storage walks info vet info **On Request** torch towels **Other** charge for damage

This impressive hotel has an enviable location overlooking Derwentwater. The bedrooms, many with lake or fell views, are comfortably equipped; family rooms and suites are also available. The dining room, bar and lounge areas are appointed to a very high standard. One of the treatments in the hotel's Elemis Spa actually makes use of the Lodore Waterfall!

Rooms 69 (11 fmly) **S** £122.85-£147.85; **D** £216.30-£457.80 (incl. bkfst & dinner) **Facilities** Spa STV FTV 🏊 ⚕ ♨ Fishing Gym Squash Sauna Xmas New Year Wi-fi **Services** Lift **Parking** 93 **Notes** LB

Borrowdale Gates Country House Hotel
★★★ 79% COUNTRY HOUSE HOTEL

CA12 5UQ
☎ 017687 77204 📄 017687 77195
e-mail: hotel@borrowdale-gates.com
dir: *From A66 follow B5289 for approx 4m. Turn right over bridge, hotel 0.25m beyond village*

PETS: Bedrooms (10 GF) unattended **Charges Grounds** on leads **Exercise area** adjacent countryside **Facilities** walks info vet info **Other** charge for damage

This friendly hotel is peacefully located in the Borrowdale Valley, close to the village but in its own three acres of wooded grounds. Public rooms include comfortable lounges and a restaurant with lovely views. Bedrooms vary in size and style.

Rooms 27 (10 GF) **S** £75-£135; **D** £150-£240 (incl. bkfst & dinner)* **Facilities** FTV Xmas New Year Wi-fi **Services** Lift **Parking** 29 **Notes** Closed 3 Jan-4 Feb

Lake District Hotels

Borrowdale Hotel
★★★ 75% HOTEL
CA12 5UY
☎ 017687 77224 ▤ 017687 77338
e-mail: borrowdale@lakedistricthotels.net
dir: 3m from Keswick, on B5289 at S end of Lake Derwentwater

PETS: Bedrooms (2 GF) unattended Sep accom small kennel in car park Charges £5 per night Public areas except restaurant, and bar at lunch Grounds Exercise area 50mtrs Facilities water bowl washing facs walks info vet info On Request fridge access torch Restrictions no Pit Bull Terriers

Situated in the beautiful Borrowdale Valley overlooking Derwentwater, this traditionally styled hotel guarantees a friendly welcome. Extensive public areas include a choice of lounges, traditional dining room, lounge bar and popular conservatory which serves more informal meals. Bedrooms vary in style and size including two that are suitable for less able guests.

Rooms 36 (3 fmly) (2 GF) S £72-£90; D £144-£224 (incl. bkfst)* Facilities STV FTV Leisure facilities available at nearby sister hotel Xmas New Year Wi-fi Parking 30 Notes LB

The Royal Oak
★★★ INN
CA12 5SY
☎ 017687 78533 ▤ 017687 78533
e-mail: info@royaloak-braithwaite.co.uk
web: www.royaloak-braithwaite.co.uk
dir: In village centre

PETS: Bedrooms unattended Charges £3 per night Public areas except in bar/restaurant during food service Grounds disp bin Facilities water bowl leads washing facs walks info vet info On Request fridge access torch towels

The Royal Oak, in the pretty village of Braithwaite, has delightful views of Skiddaw and Barrow, and is a good base for tourists and walkers. Some of the well-equipped bedrooms are furnished with four-poster beds. Hearty meals and traditional Cumbrian breakfasts are served in the restaurant, and there is an atmospheric, well-stocked bar.

Rooms 10 en suite (1 fmly) S £42-£45; D £70-£80* Facilities STV tea/coffee Dinner available Cen ht Wi-fi Parking 20 Notes LB

Farlam Hall
★★★ ⊕ HOTEL
CA8 2NG
☎ 016977 46234 ▤ 016977 46683
e-mail: farlam@relaischateaux.com
web: www.farlamhall.co.uk
dir: On A689 (Brampton to Alston). Hotel 2m on left, (not in Farlam village)

PETS: Bedrooms (2 GF) Public areas except restaurant Grounds disp bin Exercise area 1m Facilities food bowl water bowl washing facs cage storage walks info vet info On Request fridge access torch towels Other charge for damage only 2 dogs permitted in bedroom field available for horses Resident Pets: 2 llamas

This delightful family-run country house dates back to 1428. Steeped in history, the hotel is set in beautifully landscaped Victorian gardens complete with an ornamental lake and stream. Lovingly restored over many years, it provides the highest standards of comfort and hospitality. Gracious public rooms invite relaxation, whilst every thought has gone into the beautiful bedrooms, many of which are simply stunning.

Rooms 12 (1 annexe) (2 GF) S £155-£185; D £290-£350 (incl. bkfst & dinner)* Facilities FTV ⤸ New Year Wi-fi Parking 25 Notes LB No children 5yrs Closed 24-30 Dec & 4-13 Jan

ENGLAND

Crown

★★★ 81% HOTEL

Station Rd, Wetheral CA4 8ES

☎ 01228 561888   📄 01228 561637

e-mail: info@crownhotelwetheral.co.uk

web: www.crownhotelwetheral.co.uk

dir: *M6 junct 42, B6263 to Wetheral, right at village shop, car park at rear of hotel*

PETS: **Bedrooms** (3 GF) unattended **Stables** 10m **Charges** £10 per night **Public areas** except restaurant on leads **Grounds** on leads disp bin **Exercise area** 1-2m **Facilities** water bowl bedding walks info vet info **On Request** fridge access torch towels **Other** charge for damage **Resident Pets:** Bubble & Squeak (cats)

Set in the attractive village of Wetheral and with landscaped gardens to the rear, this hotel is well suited to both business and leisure guests. Rooms vary in size and style and include two apartments in an adjacent house ideal for long stays. A choice of dining options is available, with the popular Waltons Bar an informal alternative to the main restaurant.

Rooms 51 (2 annexe) (10 fmly) (3 GF) **S** £70-£90; **D** £80-£100 (incl. bkfst)* **Facilities** Spa STV ⊗ supervised Gym Squash Children's splash pool Steam room Beauty facilities Sauna Xmas New Year Wi-fi **Parking** 80

Angus House & Almonds Restaurant

★★★ ⇔ GUEST ACCOMMODATION

14-16 Scotland Rd CA3 9DG

☎ 01228 523546   📄 01228 531895

e-mail: hotel@angus-hotel.co.uk

web: www.angus-hotel.co.uk

dir: *0.5m N of city centre on A7*

PETS: **Bedrooms** unattended **Charges** £6 per stay **Public areas** except restaurant **Facilities** walks info vet info **On Request** fridge access **Restrictions** no Rottweilers or Bull Terriers

Situated just north of the city, this family-run establishment is ideal for business and leisure. A warm welcome is assured and the accommodation is well equipped. Almonds Restaurant provides enjoyable food and home baking, and there is also a lounge and a large meeting room.

Rooms 10 en suite (2 fmly) **S** £53; **D** £74 **Facilities** FTV tea/coffee Dinner available Direct Dial Cen ht Licensed Wi-fi **Notes** LB

Green Acres Caravan Park *(NY416614)*

▶ ▶ ▶

High Knells, Houghton CA6 4JW

☎ 01228 675418

e-mail: info@caravanpark-cumbria.com

dir: *Exit M6/A74(M) junct 44, A689 towards Brampton for 1m. Left at Scaleby sign. Site 1m on left*

PETS: **Public areas** disp bin **Exercise area** small woodland area **Facilities** vet info **Resident Pet:** Molly (Labrador/Beagle Cross)

Open Apr-Oct Last arrival 21.00hrs Last departure noon

A small touring park in rural surroundings close to the M6 with distant views of the fells. A convenient stopover, this pretty park is run by keen, friendly owners who maintain high standards throughout. A 3 acre site with 30 touring pitches, 30 hardstandings.

Notes 🎫

Aynsome Manor Hotel

★★ 79% ◉ COUNTRY HOUSE HOTEL

LA11 6HH

☎ 015395 36653   📄 015395 36016

e-mail: aynsomemanor@btconnect.com

dir: *M6 junct 36, A590 signed Barrow-in-Furness towards Cartmel. Left at end of road, hotel before village*

PETS: **Bedrooms Charges** £3 per night **Exercise area** 0.75m **Other** charge for damage guests must bring dogs own bedding; dogs to be on leads at all times

Dating back, in part, to the early 16th century, this manor house overlooks the fells and the nearby priory. Spacious bedrooms, including some courtyard rooms, are comfortably furnished. Dinner in the elegant restaurant features local produce whenever possible, and there is a choice of lounges to relax in.

Rooms 12 (2 annexe) (2 fmly) **S** £80-£135; **D** £90-£135 (incl. bkfst)* **Facilities** FTV New Year **Parking** 20 **Notes** LB Closed 2-31 Jan RS Sun

CLEATOR
Map 11 NY01

Ennerdale Country House

OXFORD
HOTELS & INNS

★★★ 75% HOTEL

CA23 3DT

☎ 01946 813907 📠 01946 815260

e-mail: reservations.ennerdale.ennerdale@ohiml.com

web: www.oxfordhotelsandinns.com

dir: M6 junct 40 to A66, A5086 for 12m, hotel on left

PETS: Bedrooms (10 GF) unattended **Charges** £10 per night £50 per week **Grounds Facilities** food bowl water bowl vet info **Other** charge for damage **Restrictions** no Rottweilers or Pit Bull Terriers

This fine Grade II listed building lies on the edge of the village and has landscaped gardens. Impressive bedrooms, including split-level suites and four-poster rooms, are richly furnished, smartly decorated and offer a range of facilities. Attractive public areas include a stylish restaurant and an American themed bar which offers a good range of bar meals.

Rooms 30 (2 fmly) (10 GF) **Facilities** STV Xmas New Year Wi-fi **Parking** 40

COCKERMOUTH
Map 11 NY13

Shepherds Hotel

★★★ 73% HOTEL

Lakeland Sheep & Wool Centre, Egremont Rd CA13 0QX

☎ 0845 459 9770 📠 01301 703327

e-mail: info@argyllholidays.com

web: www.shepherdshotel.co.uk

dir: At junct of A66 & A5086 S of Cockermouth, entrance off A5086, 200mtrs off rdbt

PETS: Bedrooms (13 GF) unattended **Charges** £5 per night **Grounds** disp bin **Exercise area** adjacent **Facilities** cage storage walks info vet info **Other** pets accepted by prior arrangement only **Resident Pets:** dogs, geese

This hotel is modern in style and offers thoughtfully equipped accommodation. The property also houses the Lakeland Sheep and Wool Centre, with live sheep shows from Easter to mid November. A restaurant serving a wide variety of meals and snacks is open all day.

Rooms 26 (4 fmly) (13 GF) **Facilities** FTV Pool table Play area for small children Wi-fi **Services** Lift **Parking** 100 **Notes** Closed 25-26 Dec & 4-18 Jan

CROOKLANDS
Map 7 SD58

Waters Edge Caravan Park (SD533838)

▶ ▶ ▶

LA7 7NN

☎ 015395 67708

e-mail: dennis@watersedgecaravanpark.co.uk

dir: From M6 follow signs for Kirkby Lonsdale A65, at 2nd rdbt follow signs for Crooklands/Endmoor. Site 1m on right at Crooklands garage, just beyond 40mph limit

PETS: Public areas except bar & toilets on leads **Exercise area** walks & canal banks 300yds **Facilities** food food bowl water bowl dog chews scoop/disp bags vet info **Other** dog grooming available nearby

Open Mar-14 Nov rs Low season bar not always open on wk days Last arrival 22.00hrs Last departure noon

A peaceful, well-run park close to the M6, pleasantly bordered by streams and woodland. A Lakeland-style building houses a shop and bar, and the attractive toilet block is clean and modern. Ideal either as a stopover or for longer stays. A 3 acre site with 26 touring pitches, 18 hardstandings and 20 statics.

CROSTHWAITE
Map 7 SD49

Damson Dene

★★★ 72% HOTEL

LA8 8JE

☎ 015395 68676 📠 015395 68227

e-mail: info@damsondene.co.uk

web: www.bestlakesbreaks.co.uk

dir: M6 junct 36, A590 signed Barrow-in-Furness, 5m right onto A5074. Hotel on right in 5m

PETS: Bedrooms (9 GF) unattended **Public areas** except restaurant & leisure club on leads **Grounds** disp bin **Exercise area Facilities** walks info vet info

A short drive from Lake Windermere, this hotel enjoys a tranquil and scenic setting. Bedrooms include a number with four-poster beds and jacuzzi baths. The spacious restaurant serves a daily-changing menu, with some of the produce coming from the hotel's own kitchen garden. Real fires warm the lounge in the cooler months and leisure facilities are available.

Rooms 40 (3 annexe) (7 fmly) (9 GF) **S** £69-£89; **D** £108-£148 (incl. bkfst) **Facilities** Spa 🏊 Gym Beauty salon Xmas New Year Wi-fi **Parking** 45 **Notes** LB

CROSTHWAITE *continued*

Crosthwaite House

★★★★ GUEST HOUSE

LA8 8BP

☎ 015395 68264 📠 015395 68264

e-mail: bookings@crosthwaitehouse.co.uk

web: www.crosthwaitehouse.co.uk

dir: *A590 onto A5074, 4m right to Crosthwaite, 0.5m turn left*

PETS: Bedrooms unattended Public areas Grounds disp bin Facilities leads pet sitting washing facs cage storage walks info vet info On Request fridge access torch towels Other charge for damage

Enjoying stunning views across the Lyth Valley, this friendly Georgian house is a haven of tranquillity. Bedrooms are spacious and offer a host of thoughtful extras. The reception rooms include a comfortable lounge and a pleasant dining room with polished floorboards and individual tables.

Rooms 6 en suite S £28-£33; D £56-£66* Facilities FTV TVL tea/coffee Cen ht Wi-fi Parking 10 Notes Closed mid Nov-Mar RS early Nov & Feb-Mar

DALSTON   Map 11 NY35

Dalston Hall Holiday Park *(NY378519)*

▶▶▶

Dalston Hall CA5 7JX

☎ 01228 710165

e-mail: info@dalstonhoildaypark.com

dir: *M6 junct 42 signed for Dalston. 2.5m SW of Carlisle, just off B5299*

PETS: Charges £1 per night Public areas Exercise area wooded area (approx 1 acre) Facilities food food bowl water bowl walks info vet info Resident Pet: Billy (German Shepherd)

Open Mar-Jan Last arrival 22.00hrs Last departure noon

A neat, well-maintained site on level grass in the grounds of an estate located between Carlisle and Dalston. All facilities are to a good standard, and ongoing improvements include new hardstanding pitches and extra hook-ups. Amenities include a 9-hole golf course, a bar and clubhouse serving breakfast and bar meals, and salmon and trout fly fishing. A 5 acre site with 70 touring pitches, 50 hardstandings and 32 statics.

Notes No commercial vans, gates closed 22.00hrs-07.00hrs

GLENRIDDING   Map 11 NY31

Lake District Hotels

The Inn on the Lake

★★★ 83% ◉ HOTEL

Lake Ullswater CA11 0PE

☎ 017684 82444 📠 017684 82303

e-mail: info@innonthelakeullswater.co.uk

web: www.lakedistricthotels.com

dir: *M6 junct 40, A66 to Keswick. At rdbt take A592 to Ullswater Lake. Along lake to Glenridding. Hotel on left on entering village*

PETS: Bedrooms (1 GF) unattended Charges £10 per night Public areas bar/conservatory only on leads Grounds disp bin Exercise area countryside On Request fridge access Other pets in certain bedrooms only Resident Pet: Chrissy (Black Labrador)

In a picturesque lakeside setting, this restored Victorian hotel is a popular leisure destination as well as catering for weddings and conferences. Superb views can be enjoyed from the bedrooms and from the garden terrace where afternoon teas are served during warmer months. There is a popular pub in the grounds, and moorings for yachts are available to guests. Sailing tuition can be arranged.

Rooms 47 (6 fmly) (1 GF) Facilities ♨ 9 Putt green Fishing Gym Sailing 9 hole pitch & putt Bowls Lake Bathing Xmas New Year Wi-fi Services Lift Parking 200

Best Western Glenridding Hotel

★★★ 70% HOTEL

CA11 0PB

☎ 017684 82228 & 82289 📠 017684 82555

e-mail: glenridding@bestwestern.co.uk

dir: *N'bound M6 junct 36, A591 Windermere then A592, for 14m. S'bound M6 junct 40, A592 for 13m*

PETS: Bedrooms (8 GF) Charges £10 per night Public areas except dining room, restaurant, lounge & library on leads Grounds on leads disp bin Exercise area Facilities dog chews walks info vet info Other charge for damage Restrictions small dogs only

This friendly hotel benefits from a picturesque location in the village centre, and many rooms have fine views of the lake and fells. Public areas are extensive and include a choice of dining options including Ratchers Restaurant and a café. Leisure facilities are available along with a conference room and a garden function room.

Rooms 36 (7 fmly) (8 GF) Facilities STV Sauna Snooker Table tennis Xmas New Year Wi-fi Services Lift Parking 30

GRANGE-OVER-SANDS	Map 7 SD47

Hampsfell House

★★ 78% HOTEL

Hampsfell Rd LA11 6BG

☎ 015395 32567 📠 015395 35995

e-mail: enquiries@hampsfellhouse.co.uk

web: www.hampsfellhouse.co.uk

dir: A590 at junct with B5277, signed to Grange-over-Sands. Left at rdbt into Main St, right at 2nd rdbt & right at x-rds. Hotel on left

PETS: Bedrooms Charges from £5 per night **Public areas** except restaurant on leads **Grounds** on leads **Exercise area** adjacent **Facilities** pet sitting walks info vet info **On Request** fridge access torch towels **Resident Pets:** Maissie (small Terrier), Pepsi (Whippet), Bertie (Pug)

Dating back to 1800, this owner managed hotel is peacefully set in two acres of private grounds yet is just a comfortable walk from the town centre. Bedrooms are smartly decorated and well maintained. There is a cosy bar where guests can relax and enjoy pre-dinner drinks. Comprehensive and imaginative dinners are taken in an attractive dining room.

Rooms 8 (1 fmly) **S** £40-£55; **D** £50-£90 (incl. bkfst)* **Facilities** New Year Wi-fi **Parking** 20

GRASMERE	Map 11 NY30

Grasmere

★★ 80% ❀ HOTEL

Broadgate LA22 9TA

☎ 015394 35277 📠 015394 35277

e-mail: enquiries@grasmerehotel.co.uk

web: www.grasmerehotel.co.uk

dir: From Ambleside take A591 N, 2nd left into Grasmere. Over humpback bridge, past playing field. Hotel on left

PETS: Bedrooms (2 GF) unattended **Charges** £5 per stay **Grounds** on leads **Exercise area** park 20yds **Facilities** washing facs cage storage walks info vet info **On Request** fridge access torch towels **Other** charge for damage some bedrooms are not suitable for large dogs **Restrictions** no dangerous dogs (see page 7)

Attentive and hospitable service contribute to the atmosphere at this family-run hotel, set in secluded gardens by the River Rothay. There are two inviting lounges (one with residents' bar) and an attractive dining room looking onto the garden. The thoughtfully prepared dinner menu makes good use of fresh ingredients. Pine furniture is featured in most bedrooms, along with welcome personal touches.

Rooms 14 (1 annexe) (2 GF) **Facilities** Full leisure facilities at nearby country club Free fishing permit available Xmas New Year Wi-fi **Parking** 14 **Notes** No children 10yrs Closed 3 Jan-early Feb

HAWKSHEAD	Map 7 SD39

Kings Arms

★★★ INN

LA22 0NZ

☎ 015394 36372 📠 015394 36006

e-mail: info@kingsarmshawkshead.co.uk

web: www.kingsarmshawkshead.co.uk

dir: In main square

PETS: Bedrooms Stables Public areas except restaurant (bar only) on leads **Exercise area** surrounding countryside **Facilities** food bowl water bowl washing facs walks info vet info **On Request** fridge access torch towels

A traditional Lakeland inn in the heart of a conservation area. The cosy, thoughtfully equipped bedrooms retain much character and are traditionally furnished. A good choice of freshly prepared food is available in the lounge bar and the neatly presented dining room.

Rooms 8 en suite (3 fmly) **S** £42-£51; **D** £74-£92 **Facilities** FTV tea/coffee Dinner available Direct Dial Cen ht Wi-fi ⛳ Golf 18 Fishing Riding **Notes** LB Closed 25 Dec

ENGLAND

| HELTON | Map 12 NY52 | IREBY | Map 11 NY23 |

Beckfoot Country House

★★★★ GUEST ACCOMMODATION

CA10 2QB

☎ 01931 713241   📠 01931 713391

e-mail: info@beckfoot.co.uk

dir: *M6 junct 39, A6 through Shap & left to Bampton. Through Bampton Grange & Bampton, house 2m on left*

PETS: Bedrooms Stables Charges dog £2.50 per night, horse £10 per stay **Public areas** except dining room, lounges & conservatory on leads **Grounds** on leads disp bin **Exercise area** paddock **Exercise area** 200yds **Facilities** food bowl water bowl bedding dog chews cat treats feeding mat scoop/disp bags cage storage walks info vet info **On Request** fridge access **Other** charge for damage no more than 2 dogs per bedroom **Restrictions** no Rottweilers, Pit Bulls or Staffordshire Bull Terriers **Resident Pets:** Turbo & Tweaky (cats), Storm & Fleur (Shetland ponies)

This delightful Victorian country house stands in well-tended gardens surrounded by beautiful open countryside, and is only a short drive from Penrith. Bedrooms are spacious and very well equipped. The four-poster room is particularly impressive. Public areas include an elegant drawing room, where guitar workshops are occasionally held, an oak-panelled dining room and a TV lounge.

Rooms 7 en suite 1 annexe en suite (1 fmly) (1 GF) **S** £37-£45; **D** £80-£110* **Facilities** STV TVL tea/coffee Cen ht Licensed Wi-fi **Parking** 12 **Notes** LB Closed Dec-Feb

Overwater Hall

★★★ 82% ◉◉ COUNTRY HOUSE HOTEL

CA7 1HH

☎ 017687 76566   📠 017687 76921

e-mail: welcome@overwaterhall.co.uk

dir: *From A591 take turn to Ireby at Castle Inn. Hotel signed after 2m on right*

PETS: Bedrooms (1 GF) unattended **Public areas** except restaurant & drawing room **Grounds** disp bin **Exercise area** 18-acre gardens **Exercise area** adjacent **Facilities** food bowl water bowl scoop/disp bags pet sitting washing facs cage storage walks info vet info **On Request** fridge access torch towels **Other** charge for damage **Resident Pets:** Oscar & Bafta (Black Labradors), Carina (cat)

This privately owned country house dates back to 1811 and is set in lovely gardens surrounded by woodland. The owners have lovingly restored this Georgian property over the years paying great attention to the authenticity of the original design; guests will receive warm hospitality and attentive service in a relaxed manner. The elegant and well appointed bedrooms include the more spacious Superior Rooms and the Garden Room; all bedrooms have Wi-fi. Creative dishes are served in the traditional-style dining room.

Rooms 11 (2 fmly) (1 GF) **S** £100-£170; **D** £180-£280 (incl. bkfst & dinner)* **Facilities** FTV Xmas New Year Wi-fi **Parking** 20 **Notes** LB

Map 11 NY22

Skiddaw
★★★ 77% HOTEL
Main St CA12 5BN
☎ 017687 72071 ▤ 017687 74850
e-mail: info@skiddawhotel.co.uk
web: www.skiddawhotel.co.uk
dir: A66 to Keswick, follow town centre signs. Hotel in market square

PETS: Bedrooms unattended Public areas except food areas Grounds on leads Exercise area Facilities food bowl water bowl walks info vet info

Occupying a central position overlooking the market square, this hotel provides smartly furnished bedrooms that include several family suites and a room with a four-poster bed. In addition to the restaurant, food is served all day in the bar and in the conservatory bar. There is also a quiet residents' lounge and two conference rooms.

Rooms 43 (7 fmly) (3 smoking) S £71-£105; D £120-£195 (incl. bkfst) Facilities STV Use of sister hotels leisure facilities (3m away) Xmas New Year Wi-fi Services Lift Parking 35 Notes LB

Cragside
★★★★ GUEST ACCOMMODATION
39 Blencathra St CA12 4HX
☎ 017687 73344 ▤ 017687 73344
e-mail: wayne-alison@cragside39blencathra.fsnet.co.uk
dir: A591 Penrith Rd into Keswick, under rail bridge, 2nd left

PETS: Bedrooms Charges £3 per night £18 per week Public areas except dining room on leads Exercise area park 2 mins walk Facilities walks info vet info Other charge for damage Restrictions small-medium size dogs only; no dangerous dogs (see page 7)

Expect warm hospitality at this establishment, located within easy walking distance of the town centre. The attractive bedrooms are well equipped, and many have fine views of the fells. Hearty Cumbrian breakfasts are served in the breakfast room, which overlooks the small front garden. Visually or hearing impaired guests are catered for, with Braille information, TVs with teletext, and a loop system installed in the dining room.

Rooms 4 en suite (1 fmly) S £40-£55; D £50-£65 Facilities FTV tea/coffee Cen ht Wi-fi Notes No Children 4yrs

The Hollies
★★★★ GUEST HOUSE
Threlkeld CA12 4RX
☎ 017687 79216
e-mail: info@theholliesinlakeland.co.uk
dir: M6 junct 40 W on A66 towards Keswick. Turn right into Threlkeld, on main village road opp village hall

PETS: Bedrooms Charges £5 per night Grounds disp bin Exercise area adjacent Facilities walks info vet info Resident Pet: West Highland Terrier

The Hollies is located in the picturesque village of Threlkeld with commanding views up to Blencathra and across to the Helvellyn range. A warm and genuine welcome awaits, along with refreshments and home baking. Bedrooms are well appointed and comfortable with thoughtful extras provided as standard. Quality breakfasts are served on individual tables.

Rooms 4 en suite S £37.50-£53.50; D £60-£77* Facilities FTV tea/coffee Cen ht Wi-fi Parking 6 Notes Closed 25 Dec

Keswick Lodge
★★★★ INN
Main St CA12 5HZ
☎ 017687 74584
e-mail: info@keswicklodge.co.uk

PETS: Bedrooms unattended Charges dog £10 per night Public areas except restaurant Exercise area Facilities food bowl water bowl cage storage walks info vet info On Request fridge access towels Other charge for damage

Located on the corner of the vibrant market square this large, friendly 18th-century coaching inn offers a wide range of meals throughout the day and evening, fully stocked bar and cask ales. Bedrooms vary in size but all are contemporary, smartly presented and feature quality accessories such as LCD TVs. There is also a drying room.

Rooms 18 en suite (1 fmly) S £42.50-£90; D £85-£99* Facilities FTV tea/coffee Dinner available Cen ht Notes LB

KESWICK *continued*

Low Nest Farm B&B

★★★★ GUEST ACCOMMODATION

Castlerigg CA12 4TF

☎ 017687 72378

e-mail: info@lownestfarm.co.uk

dir: *2m S of Keswick, off A591 (Windermere road)*

PETS: Bedrooms unattended **Sep accom** kennel block **Stables** adjacent farm **Charges** £3 per night **Public areas Grounds** disp bin **Exercise area** 5-acre adjacent field **Facilities** food bowl water bowl bedding dog chews scoop/disp bags leads pet sitting dog walking washing facs cage storage walks info vet info **On Request** fridge access torch towels **Other** charge for damage **Resident Pets:** Sophie, Billie, Erik, Max & Lucy (Weimaraners), Pepsi (Poodle), Jasper (parrot), 3 goats, 2 sheep

Low Nest Farm is a small, family-run farm set in some typically breath-taking Cumbrian scenery. Bedrooms are very comfortable with smart en suites and lovely views. There are of course, any number of walks available in the area, and Keswick is just two miles away.

Rooms 6 en suite (4 GF) **Facilities** FTV TVL tea/coffee Cen ht Wi-fi **Parking** 8 **Notes** LB No Children 14yrs Closed mid Dec-mid Feb ❷

KIRKBY LONSDALE   **Map 7 SD67**

The Sun Inn

★★★★★ ◉ INN

6 Market St LA6 2AU

☎ 015242 71965   ≣ 015242 72485

e-mail: email@sun-inn.info

web: www.sun-inn.info

dir: *From A65 follow signs to town centre. Inn on main street*

PETS: Bedrooms unattended **Charges** £10 per stay **Public areas** except restaurant on leads **Exercise area** adjacent **Facilities** water bowl

A 17th-century inn situated in a historic market town, overlooking St Mary's Church. The atmospheric bar features stone walls, wooden beams and log fires with real ales available. Delicious meals are served in the bar and more formal, modern restaurant. Traditional and modern styles are blended together in the beautifully appointed rooms with excellent en suites.

Rooms 11 en suite (2 fmly) **S** £70-£130; **D** £90-£150*
Facilities FTV tea/coffee Dinner available Cen ht Wi-fi ⛳ Golf 18 **Notes** LB No coaches

New House Caravan Park *(SD628774)*

▶▶▶▶

LA6 2HR

☎ 015242 71590

e-mail: colinpreece9@aol.com

dir: *1m SE of Kirkby Lonsdale on A65, turn right into site entrance 300yds past Whoop-Hall Inn*

PETS: Public areas except toilet block **Exercise area** adjacent **Facilities** walks info vet info **Other** prior notice required **Resident Pets:** 1 Lurcher, 4 cats, 1 tortoise, 2 cockatiels

Open Mar-Oct Last arrival 20.00hrs

A very pleasant base in which to relax or tour the surrounding area, developed around a former farm. The excellent toilet facilities are purpose built, and there are good roads and hardstandings, all in a lovely rural setting. A 3 acre site with 50 touring pitches, 50 hardstandings.

Notes No cycling ❷

KIRKBY STEPHEN   **Map 12 NY70**

Brownber Hall Country House

★★★★ GUEST HOUSE

Newbiggin-on-Lune CA17 4NX

☎ 01539 623208

e-mail: enquiries@brownberhall.co.uk

web: www.brownberhall.co.uk

dir: *6m SW of Kirkby Stephen. Off A685 signed Great Asby, 60yds right through gatehouse, 0.25m sharp left onto driveway*

PETS: Bedrooms Public areas must be under supervision **Grounds Exercise area Resident Pets:** Sooty & Polar Bear (cats)

Having an elevated position with superb views of the surrounding countryside, Brownber Hall, built in 1860, has been restored to its original glory. The en suite bedrooms are comfortably proportioned, attractively decorated and well equipped. The ground floor has two lovely reception rooms, which retain many original features, and a charming dining room where traditional breakfasts, and by arrangement delicious dinners, are served.

Rooms 6 en suite (1 GF) **Facilities** tea/coffee Dinner available Cen ht Lift **Parking** 12

Camelot Caravan Park *(NY391666)*

▶ ▶

CA6 5SZ
☎ 01228 791248
dir: *M6 junct 44, A7, site 5m N, & 1m S, of Longtown*

PETS: Public areas on leads disp bin **Exercise area** adjacent field **Facilities** washing facs walks info vet info

Open Mar-Oct Last arrival 22.00hrs Last departure noon

A very pleasant level grassy site in a wooded setting near the M6, with direct access from the A7, and simple, clean toilet facilities. The park is an ideal stopover site. A 1.5 acre site with 20 touring pitches and 2 statics.

Notes ⊛

Grange Country House

★★ 74% SMALL HOTEL

CA13 0SU
☎ 01946 861211 & 861570
e-mail: info@thegrange-loweswater.co.uk
dir: *Exit A5086 for Mockerkin, through village. After 2m left for Loweswater Lake. Hotel at bottom of hill on left*

PETS: Bedrooms (1 GF) unattended **Charges** £5 per night **Public areas** except dining room **Grounds** disp bin **Exercise area** across road **Facilities** food bowl water bowl scoop/disp bags leads washing facs cage storage walks info vet info **On Request** fridge access torch towels **Other** charge for damage **Resident Pet:** Toby (Labrador/Collie cross)

This delightful country hotel is set in extensive grounds in a quiet valley at the north-western end of Loweswater, and continues to prove popular with guests seeking peace and quiet. It has a friendly and relaxed atmosphere, and the cosy public areas include a small bar, a residents' lounge and an attractive dining room. The bedrooms are well equipped and comfortable, and include four-poster rooms.

Rooms 8 (2 fmly) (1 GF) **S** £58-£60; **D** £92-£96 (incl. bkfst)*
Facilities FTV National Trust boats & fishing Xmas **Parking** 22
Notes RS Jan-Feb

Larches Caravan Park *(NY205415)*

▶ ▶ ▶ ▶

CA7 1LQ
☎ 016973 71379 & 71803 ⊫ 016973 71782
dir: *On A595 (Carlisle to Cockermouth road)*

PETS: Public areas except toilet block & swimming pool on leads **Exercise area Facilities** food litter tray scoop/disp bags dog grooming walks info vet info **Resident Pets:** Nemo (German Shepherd), Tigger, Tibby, Blacky & Sam (cats)

Open Mar-Oct rs Early & late season Last arrival 21.30hrs Last departure noon

This over 18s-only park is set in wooded rural surroundings on the fringe of the Lake District National Park. Touring units are spread out over two sections. The friendly family-run park offers well cared for facilities, and a small indoor swimming pool. A 20 acre site with 73 touring pitches, 30 hardstandings.

Notes ⊛

Sykeside Camping Park *(NY403119)*

▶ ▶ ▶

Brotherswater CA11 0NZ
☎ 017684 82239 ⊫ 017684 82239
e-mail: info@sykeside.co.uk
dir: *Direct access off A592 (Windermere to Ullswater road) at foot of Kirkstone Pass*

PETS: Stables Charges £1.50 per night **Public areas** disp bin **Exercise area** fenced exercise area **Facilities** food food bowl water bowl dog chews leads washing facs walks info vet info **Other** prior notice required disposal bags available

Open all year Last arrival 22.30hrs Last departure 14.00hrs

A camper's delight, this family-run park is sited at the foot of Kirkstone Pass, under the 2000ft Hartsop Dodd in a spectacular area with breathtaking views. The park has mainly grass pitches with a few hardstandings, an area with tipis for hire, and for those campers without a tent there is bunkhouse accommodation. There's a small campers' kitchen and the bar serves breakfast and bar meals. There is abundant wildlife. A 5 acre site with 86 touring pitches, 5 hardstandings.

ENGLAND

George
★★★ 77% HOTEL
Devonshire St CA11 7SU
☎ 01768 862696 📠 01768 868223
e-mail: georgehotel@lakedistricthotels.net
dir: M6 junct 40, 1m to town centre. From A6/A66 to Penrith

PETS: Bedrooms unattended sign **Charges** £10 per night
Public areas except restaurant **Exercise area** 5 min walk
Facilities food bowl water bowl dog walking cage storage
walks info vet info **Other** dogs allowed in standard rooms only

This inviting and popular hotel dates back to a time when
'Bonnie' Prince Charlie made a visit. Extended over the years this
town centre hotel offers well equipped bedrooms. The spacious
public areas retain a timeless charm, and include a choice of
lounge areas that make ideal places for morning coffees and
afternoon teas.

Rooms 35 (4 fmly) **Facilities** Xmas New Year Wi-fi **Parking** 40

Park Foot Caravan & Camping Park
(NY469235)
Howtown Rd CA10 2NA
☎ 017684 86309 📠 017684 86041
e-mail: holidays@parkfootullswater.co.uk
dir: M6 junct 40, A66 towards Keswick, then A592 to Ullswater.
Turn left for Pooley Bridge, right at church, right at x-roads signed
Howtown

PETS: Charges £1 per night **Public areas** except club house
& children's play area **Exercise area** on site **Exercise area**
Lakeland Fells adjacent **Facilities** food food bowl water bowl
scoop/disp bags walks info vet info **Other** prior notice required
Restrictions no dangerous dogs (see page 7)

Open Mar-Oct rs Mar-Apr, mid Sep-Oct clubhouse open wknds
only Last arrival 22.00hrs Last departure noon

A lively park with good outdoor sports facilities, and boat
launching directly onto Lake Ullswater. The attractive mainly
tenting park has many mature trees and lovely views across the
lake. The Country Club bar and restaurant provides good meals,
as well as discos, live music and entertainment in a glorious
location. There are lodges and static caravans for holiday hire. A
18 acre site with 323 touring pitches and 131 statics.

Notes Families & couples only

Waterfoot Caravan Park *(NY462246)*

▶ ▶ ▶

CA11 0JF

☎ 017684 86302   📠 017684 86728

e-mail: enquiries@waterfootpark.co.uk

dir: *M6 junct 40, A66 for 1m, then A592 for 4m, site on right before lake. (NB do not leave A592 until site entrance; Sat Nav not compatible)*

PETS: Public areas except children's area disp bin **Exercise area** allocated dog walking area **Exercise area** adjacent **Facilities** food dog chews scoop/disp bags walks info vet info **Other** prior notice required

Open Mar-14 Nov Last arrival dusk Last departure noon

A quality touring park with neat, hardstanding pitches in a grassy glade within the wooded grounds of an elegant Georgian mansion. Toilets facilities are clean and well maintained, and the lounge bar with a separate family room enjoys lake views, and there is a path to Ullswater. Aira Force waterfall, Dalemain House and garden, and Pooley Bridge are all close by. Please note that there is no access via Dacre. A 22 acre site with 34 touring pitches, 30 hardstandings and 146 statics.

Notes Families only, no tents, no large RVS

The Fat Lamb

★★ 71% HOTEL

Crossbank CA17 4LL

☎ 015396 23242   📠 015396 23285

e-mail: enquiries@fatlamb.co.uk

dir: *On A683, between Kirkby Stephen & Sedbergh*

PETS: Bedrooms (5 GF) **Public areas** except restaurant **Grounds** **Exercise area** 100yds **Facilities** water bowl leads cage storage vet info **On Request** fridge access torch

Solid stone walls and open fires feature at this 17th-century inn, set on its own nature reserve. There is a choice of dining options with an extensive menu available in the traditional bar and a more formal dining experience in the restaurant. Bedrooms are bright and cheerful, and include family rooms and easily accessible rooms for guests with limited mobility.

Rooms 12 (4 fmly) (5 GF) **S** £72-£80; **D** £86-£94 (incl. bkfst)* **Facilities** Private 5-acre nature reserve Xmas Wi-fi **Parking** 60

Royal Oak

★ 75% SMALL HOTEL

CA12 5XB

☎ 017687 77214 & 77695

e-mail: info@royaloakhotel.co.uk

web: www.royaloakhotel.co.uk

dir: *6m S of Keswick on B5289 in town centre*

PETS: Bedrooms (4 GF) unattended **Public areas** except dining room **Grounds Exercise area Facilities** food bowl water bowl leads cage storage walks info vet info **On Request** fridge access torch towels **Resident Pet:** Monty (cat)

Set in a village in one of Lakeland's most picturesque valleys, this family-run hotel offers friendly and obliging service. There is a variety of accommodation styles, with particularly impressive rooms being located in a converted barn across the courtyard and backing onto a stream; family rooms are available. The cosy bar is for residents and diners only, and a set home-cooked dinner is served at 7pm.

Rooms 12 (4 annexe) (5 fmly) (4 GF) **S** £46-£59; **D** £92-£124 (incl. bkfst & dinner)* **Parking** 15 **Notes** LB Closed 4-21 Jan & 5-28 Dec

The Old Post Office Campsite *(NY110016)*

▶ ▶ ▶

CA19 1UY

☎ 01946 726286 & 01785 822866

e-mail: enquiries@theoldpostofficecampsite.co.uk

dir: *A595 to Holmrook and Santon Bridge, 2.5m*

PETS: Charges £1 per night £7 per week **Public areas** disp bin **Exercise area** 100mtrs **Facilities** washing facs walks info vet info

Open Mar-15 Nov Last departure noon

A family-run campsite in a delightful riverside setting next to an attractive stone bridge, with very pretty pitches. Following the devastating floods in November 2009, the enthusiastic owners have taken the opportunity to divide the site into two pitching areas, and upgrading continues in other areas of the site. Permits for salmon, sea and brown trout fishing are available, and there is an adjacent pub serving excellent meals. A 2.2 acre site with 40 touring pitches, 5 hardstandings.

Notes 🐾

ENGLAND

| SILLOTH | Map 11 NY15 |

Golf Hotel

★★ 71% HOTEL

Criffel St CA7 4AB

☎ 016973 31438   ▤ 016973 32582

e-mail: info@golfhotelsilloth.co.uk

PETS: Bedrooms sign Stables nearby Charges £2 per night £14 per week Public areas on leads Exercise area opposite Facilities washing facs cage storage walks info vet info On Request fridge access torch Other charge for damage

A friendly welcome waits at this hotel which occupies a prime position in the centre of the historic market town; it is a popular meeting place for the local community. Bedrooms are mostly well proportioned and are comfortably equipped. The lounge bar is a popular venue for dining, with a wide range of dishes on offer.

Rooms 22 (4 fmly) Facilities FTV Snooker & Games room Notes Closed 25 Dec RS 26 Dec, 1 Jan

Stanwix Park Holiday Centre

(NY108527)

Greenrow CA7 4HH

☎ 016973 32666   ▤ 016973 32555

e-mail: enquiries@stanwix.com

dir: 1m SW on B5300. From A596 (Wigton bypass), follow signs to Silloth on B5302. In Silloth follow signs to site, approx 1m on B5300

PETS: Charges £3 per night £21 per week Public areas except complex, leisure centre, toilets & launderette on leads Exercise area beach 1m Facilities food food bowl water bowl bedding dog chews cat treats scoop/disp bags leads walks info vet info Other prior notice required maximum 2 dogs per pitch Restrictions no dangerous breeds (see page 7)

Open all year rs Nov-Feb (ex New Year) no entertainment/shop closed Last arrival 21.00hrs Last departure 11.00hrs

A large well-run family park within easy reach of the Lake District. Attractively laid out, with lots of amenities to ensure a lively holiday, including a 4-lane automatic, 10-pin bowling alley. Excellent touring areas with hardstandings, one in a peaceful glade well away from the main leisure complex, and there's a campers' kitchen and clean, well maintained toilet facilities. A 4 acre site with 121 touring pitches, 100 hardstandings and 212 statics.

Notes Families only.

Hylton Caravan Park (NY113533)

►►►►

Eden St CA7 4AY

☎ 016973 31707 & 32666   ▤ 016973 32555

e-mail: enquiries@stanwix.com

dir: On entering Silloth on B5302 follow signs Hylton Caravan Park, approx 0.5m on left, (end of Eden St)

PETS: Charges £3 per night £21 per week Public areas except toilets, laundrette & leisure complex on leads disp bin Exercise area beach 1m Facilities walks info Other prior notice required maximum 2 pets per pitch, shop at sister park (Stanwix Park Holiday Centre 1m) Restrictions no dangerous dogs (see page 7)

Open Mar-15 Nov Last arrival 21.00hrs Last departure 11.00hrs

A smart, modern touring park with excellent toilet facilities including several bathrooms. This high quality park is a sister site to Stanwix Park, which is just a mile away and offers all the amenities of a holiday centre. A 18 acre site with 90 touring pitches and 213 statics.

Notes Families only

| TEBAY | Map 7 NY60 |

Westmorland Caravan Park (NY609060)

►►►

Orton CA10 3SB

☎ 01539 711322   ▤ 015396 24944

e-mail: caravans@westmorland.com

dir: Exit M6 at Westmorland Services, 1m from junct 38. Site accessed through service area from either N'bound or S'bound carriageways. Follow park signs

PETS: Stables 3m Public areas disp bin Exercise area walks around woods & grassland Exercise area open countryside (0.5m) Facilities food bowl water bowl washing facs walks info vet info Other disposal bags available

Open Mar-Oct Last arrival anytime Last departure noon

An ideal stopover site adjacent to the Tebay service station on the M6, and handy for touring the Lake District. The park is screened by high grass banks, bushes and trees, and is within walking distance of an excellent farm shop and restaurant. A 4 acre site with 70 touring pitches, 70 hardstandings and 7 statics.

TROUTBECK (NEAR KESWICK)　Map 11 NY32

Troutbeck Camping and Caravanning Club Site *(NY365271)*

▶▶▶▶▶

Hutton Moor End CA11 0SX
☎ 017687 79149
dir: *M6 junct 40, take A66 towards Keswick. After 9.5m take sharp left for Wallthwaite*

PETS: Public areas except in buildings　disp bin　**Exercise area**
walks in adjacent fields　**Facilities** food　food bowl　water
bowl　walks info　vet info　**Other** prior notice required
Resident Pet: Sacha (Shih Tzu)

Open 4 Mar-12 Nov Last arrival 20.00hrs Last departure noon

Beautifully situated between Penrith and Keswick, this quiet, well managed Lakeland park offers two immaculate touring areas, one a sheltered paddock for caravans and motorhomes, with serviced hardstanding pitches, and a newly developed and maturing lower field, which has spacious hardstanding pitches and a superb and very popular small tenting area that enjoys stunning and extensive views of the surrounding fells. The toilet block is appointed to a very high standard and includes two family cubicles, and the log cabin reception/shop stocks local and organic produce. The enthusiastic franchisees offer high levels of customer care and are constantly improving the park, which is well-placed for visited Keswick, Ullswater and the north lakes. A 4.5 acre site with 54 touring pitches, 36 hardstandings and 20 statics.

Notes Site gates closed 23.00hrs-07.00hrs

ULVERSTON　Map 7 SD27

Church Walk House

★★★★ BED AND BREAKFAST
Church Walk LA12 7EW
☎ 01229 582211
e-mail: martinchadd@btinternet.com
dir: *In town centre opposite Stables furniture shop on corner of Fountain St & Church Walk*

PETS: Bedrooms　Stables nearby　**Public areas　Exercise area**
25yds　**Facilities** water bowl　scoop/disp bags　dog walking　cage
storage　walks info　vet info　**On Request** fridge access　torch

This Grade II listed 18th-century residence stands in the heart of the historic market town. Stylishly decorated, the accommodation includes attractive bedrooms with a mix of antiques and contemporary pieces. Service is attentive and there is a small herbal garden and patio.

Rooms 3 rms (2 en suite) (1 pri facs) **S** fr £30; **D** fr £65*
Facilities TVL tea/coffee Cen ht **Notes** LB

WATERMILLOCK　Map 12 NY42

Rampsbeck Country House

★★★ ◎◎◎ HOTEL
CA11 0LP
☎ 017684 86442　📠 017684 86688
e-mail: enquiries@rampsbeck.co.uk
web: www.rampsbeck.co.uk
dir: *M6 junct 40, A592 to Ullswater, at T-junct (with lake in front) turn right, hotel 1.5m*

PETS: Bedrooms (1 GF)　unattended　**Charges** £10 per stay
Public areas hall only　on leads　**Grounds** disp bin　**Exercise area**
meadow adjacent　**Facilities** walks info　vet info　**On Request**
fridge access　torch　towels　**Other** dogs allowed in 3 bedrooms
only

This fine country house lies in 18 acres of parkland on the shores of Lake Ullswater, and is furnished with many period and antique pieces. There are three delightful lounges, an elegant restaurant and a traditional bar. Bedrooms come in three grades; the most spacious rooms are spectacular and overlook the lake. Service is attentive and the award-winning cuisine a real highlight.

Rooms 19 (1 fmly) (1 GF) **S** £95-£170; **D** £140-£290 (incl. bkfst)* **Facilities** STV FTV Putt green 🛶 Private boat trips on Lake Ullswater Xmas New Year Wi-fi **Parking** 25 **Notes** LB Closed 4-27 Jan

Brackenrigg

★★★ INN
CA11 0LP
☎ 017684 86206　📠 017684 86945
e-mail: enquiries@brackenrigginn.co.uk
web: www.brackenrigginn.co.uk
dir: *M6 junct 40, A66 towards Keswick. In 0.5m take A592 after Rheged Services rdbt towards Ullswater. In 5m right at T-junct at lake. 1m to Watermillock sign. Inn 300yds on right. (NB car park entrance before inn)*

PETS: Bedrooms　Charges £10 per stay　**Public areas** except
restaurant　on leads　**Grounds** on leads　**Exercise area**
surrounding area　**Facilities** cage storage　walks info　vet info
On Request fridge access　torch　**Other** charge for damage

An 18th-century coaching inn with superb views of Ullswater and the surrounding countryside. Freshly prepared dishes and daily specials are served by friendly staff in the traditional bar and restaurant. The bedrooms include six attractive rooms in the stable cottages.

Rooms 11 en suite 6 annexe en suite (8 fmly) (3 GF) **S** £30-£55; **D** £60-£130 **Facilities** tea/coffee Dinner available Cen ht Wi-fi **Parking** 40 **Notes** LB

WATERMILLOCK *continued*

The Quiet Site *(NY431236)*

▶ ▶ ▶ ▶

Ullswater CA11 0LS
☎ 07768 727016
e-mail: info@thequietsite.co.uk
dir: *M6 junct 40, A592 towards Ullswater. Right at lake junct, then right at Brackenrigg Hotel. Site 1.5m on right*

PETS: Stables 5m **Charges** £1-£2 per night **Public areas** touring pitch area only disp bin **Exercise area** dog field **Facilities** food food bowl water bowl bedding dog chews scoop/disp bags washing facs walks info vet info **Other** prior notice required maximum 2 dogs per pitch **Resident Pets:** Puzzle (Jack Russell), Arthur (Labrador), Lucky (cat)

Open all year rs Low season park open wknds only Last arrival 22.00hrs Last departure noon

A well-maintained site in a lovely, peaceful location, with good terraced pitches offering great fell views, very good facilities including family bathrooms, and a charming olde-worlde bar. The are four camping pods and a self-catering stone cottage. A 10 acre site with 100 touring pitches, 60 hardstandings and 23 statics.

Notes Quiet from 22.00hrs onwards

Cove Caravan & Camping Park *(NY431236)*

▶ ▶ ▶

Ullswater CA11 0LS
☎ 017684 86549 📠 017684 86549
e-mail: info@cove-park.co.uk
dir: *M6 junct 40 take A592 for Ullswater. Right at lake junct, then right at Brackenrigg Hotel. Site 1.5m on left*

PETS: Charges £1 per dog per night **Public areas** on leads disp bin **Exercise area** 2 dog walks **Facilities** washing facs walks info vet info **Restrictions** well behaved dogs only **Resident Pet:** Molly (Springer Spaniel)

Open Mar-Oct Last arrival 21.00hrs Last departure noon

A peaceful family site in an attractive and elevated position with extensive fell views and glimpses of Ullswater Lake. The ground is gently sloping grass, but there are also hardstandings for motorhomes and caravans, and simple toilet facilities are fresh, clean and well maintained by enthusiastic and welcoming wardens. A 3 acre site with 50 touring pitches, 17 hardstandings and 39 statics.

Notes No open fires 🐾

Holbeck Ghyll Country House Hotel

★★★★ ◉◉◉ COUNTRY HOUSE HOTEL

Holbeck Ln LA23 1LU
☎ 015394 32375 📠 015394 34743
e-mail: stay@holbeckghyll.com
dir: *3m N of Windermere on A591, right into Holbeck Lane (signed Troutbeck), hotel 0.5m on left*

PETS: Bedrooms (11 GF) unattended **Stables** 1.5m **Charges** £8 per night **Public areas** front hall only **Grounds** disp bin **Exercise area** adjacent **Facilities** food (pre-bookable) food bowl water bowl bedding dog chews feeding mat scoop/disp bags leads pet sitting dog walking washing facs cage storage walks info vet info **On Request** fridge access torch towels **Other** charge for damage dog grooming available nearby

Sitting high overlooking the majestic Lake Windermere in well maintained grounds, this is a delightful place where the service is professional and attentive. Beautifully designed, spacious bedrooms are situated in the main house and also in lodges in the grounds; each has amazing lake views and some have patios. The lodge suites are ideal for families. Each room has Egyptian linens, fresh flowers, LCD satellite TV, bathrobes and a decanter of sherry. The restaurant continues to impress with its award-winning cuisine. The hotel also has a health spa, a gym and a boutique store.

Rooms 26 (12 annexe) (5 fmly) (11 GF) **S** £179-£490; **D** £270-£560 (incl. bkfst)* **Facilities** Spa STV 🏌 Putt green 🏌 Gym Sauna Steam room Treatment rooms Beauty massage Xmas New Year Wi-fi **Parking** 34 **Notes** LB

Storrs Hall

★★★★ 78% ◉◉ HOTEL

Storrs Park LA23 3LG
☎ 015394 47111 📠 015394 47555
e-mail: storrshall@elhmail.co.uk
web: www.elh.co.uk/hotels/storrshall
dir: *On A592, 2m S of Bowness, on Newby Bridge road*

PETS: Bedrooms Charges £25 per stay (for up to 2 dogs) **Public areas** except food service areas on leads **Grounds** disp bin **Exercise area** adjacent **Facilities** water bowl cage storage walks info vet info **On Request** torch **Other** charge for damage dogs by prior arrangement only

Set in 17 acres of landscaped grounds by the lakeside, this imposing Georgian mansion is delightful. There are numerous lounges to relax in, furnished with fine art and antiques. Individually styled bedrooms are generally spacious and boast impressive bathrooms. Imaginative cuisine is served in the elegant restaurant, which offers fine views across the lawn to the lake and fells beyond.

Rooms 30 **S** £126-£200; **D** £192-£364 (incl. bkfst) **Facilities** FTV Fishing 🏌 Use of nearby sports/beauty facilities Xmas New Year Wi-fi **Parking** 50 **Notes** LB No children 12yrs

Low Wood

★★★★ 76% HOTEL

LA23 1LP

☎ 015394 33338 & 0845 850 3502   📄 015394 34275

e-mail: lowwood@elhmail.co.uk

dir: *M6 junct 36, A590, A591 to Windermere, then 3m towards Ambleside, hotel on right*

PETS: Bedrooms (21 GF) **Charges** £25 per stay (2 dogs)
Grounds on leads disp bin **Exercise area** woods **Facilities** bedding dog chews cat treats pet sitting dog walking washing facs cage storage walks info vet info **On Request** fridge access torch towels

Benefiting from a lakeside location, this hotel offers an excellent range of leisure and conference facilities. Bedrooms, many with panoramic lake views, are attractively furnished, and include a number of larger executive rooms and suites. There is a choice of bars, a spacious restaurant and the more informal Café del Lago. The poolside bar offers internet and e-mail access.

Rooms 111 (13 fmly) (21 GF) **S** £79-£162; **D** £98-£304 (incl. bkfst)* **Facilities** Spa 🏊 supervised Fishing Gym Squash Water skiing Canoeing Beauty salon Marina Xmas New Year Wi-fi **Services** Lift **Parking** 204 **Notes** LB

Linthwaite House Hotel & Restaurant

★★★ 🏅🏅 COUNTRY HOUSE HOTEL

Crook Rd LA23 3JA

☎ 015394 88600   📄 015394 88601

e-mail: stay@linthwaite.com

web: www.linthwaite.com

dir: *A591 towards The Lakes for 8m to large rdbt, take 1st exit (B5284), 6m, hotel on left. 1m past Windermere golf club*

PETS: Bedrooms (8 GF) **Sep accom** outdoor kennel & caged run
Charges £9 per night **Grounds** **Facilities** water bowl walks info
Other charge for damage prior notice required dogs allowed in 2 bedrooms only; owners to bring dog's own bedding **Restrictions** no breed as large as, or larger, than a Great Dane

Linthwaite House is set in 14 acres of hilltop grounds and enjoys stunning views over Lake Windermere. Inviting public rooms include an attractive conservatory and adjoining lounge and an elegant restaurant. Bedrooms, which are individually decorated, combine contemporary furnishings with classical styles; all are thoughtfully equipped and include CD players. Service and hospitality are attentive and friendly.

Rooms 30 (1 fmly) (8 GF) **S** £160-£190; **D** £238-£576 (incl. bkfst & dinner)* **Facilities** STV FTV Putt green Fishing 🌿 Beauty treatments Massage Access to nearby spa with pool & gym Xmas New Year Wi-fi **Parking** 40 **Notes** LB

Miller Howe Hotel

★★★ 86% 🏅🏅 COUNTRY HOUSE HOTEL

Rayrigg Rd LA23 1EY

☎ 015394 42536   📄 015394 45664

e-mail: info@millerhowe.com

dir: *M6 junct 36 , A591 past Windermere, left at rdbt towards Bowness*

PETS: Bedrooms (1 GF) unattended **Charges** £5 per night
Public areas only at management's discretion on leads **Grounds**
Exercise area 100yds **Facilities** food bowl water bowl cage storage walks info vet info **On Request** fridge access torch towels **Resident Pets:** Betty & Doris (Cocker Spaniels)

This long established hotel of much character enjoys a lakeside setting amidst delightful landscaped gardens. The bright and welcoming day rooms include sumptuous lounges, a conservatory and an opulently decorated restaurant. Imaginative dinners make use of fresh, local produce where possible and there is an extensive, well-balanced wine list. Stylish bedrooms, many with fabulous lake views, include well-equipped cottage rooms and a number with whirlpool baths.

Rooms 15 (3 annexe) (1 GF) **Facilities** Xmas New Year Wi-fi **Parking** 35

ENGLAND

Cedar Manor Hotel & Restaurant

★★ 84% HOTEL

Ambleside Rd LA23 1AX
☎ 015394 43192 & 45970 📠 015394 45970
e-mail: info@cedarmanor.co.uk
dir: *From A591 follow signs to Windermere. Hotel on left just beyond St Mary's Church at bottom of hill*

PETS: Bedrooms (3 GF) unattended sign **Stables** 3m **Charges** £10 per night £30 per week **Public areas Grounds** disp bin **Exercise area** 0.25m **Facilities** washing facs cage storage walks info vet info **On Request** fridge access torch **Other** charge for damage **Restrictions** small to medium size dogs only

Built in 1854 as a country retreat this lovely old house enjoys a peaceful location that is within easy walking distance of the town centre. Bedrooms, some on the ground floor, are attractive and well equipped, with two bedrooms in the adjacent coach house. There is a comfortable lounge bar where guests can relax before enjoying dinner in the well-appointed dining room.

Rooms 11 (2 annexe) (2 fmly) (3 GF) **S** £68-£80; **D** £90-£180 (incl. bkfst)* **Facilities** FTV New Year Wi-fi **Parking** 11 **Notes** LB Closed 3-21 Jan

Wild Boar

★★★★ INN

Crook LA23 3NF
☎ 015394 45225
e-mail: wildboar@elhmail.co.uk
dir: *2.5m S of Windermere on B5284. From Crook 3.5m, on right*

PETS: Bedrooms sign **Charges** £25 for 4 nights **Public areas** except grill room **Grounds Exercise area Facilities** cage storage walks info vet info **On Request** fridge access torch towels **Other** charge for damage

This historic former coaching inn enjoys a peaceful rural location close to Windermere. Public areas include a welcoming lounge, a cosy bar where an extensive choice of wines are served by the glass, and a character restaurant serving wholesome food. Bedrooms, some with four-poster beds, vary in style and size.

Rooms 33 en suite (2 fmly) (9 GF) **S** £69-£108; **D** £78-£156* **Facilities** FTV tea/coffee Direct Dial **Parking** 60

Hill of Oaks & Blakeholme *(SD386899)*

▶ ▶ ▶ ▶

LA12 8NR
☎ 015395 31578 📠 015395 30431
e-mail: enquiries@hillofoaks.co.uk
dir: *M6 junct 36 onto A590 towards Barrow. At rdbt signed Bowness turn right onto A592. Site approx 3m on left*

PETS: Public areas except children's play area **Exercise area** on site **Exercise area** nearby **Facilities** food dog chews scoop/ disp bags walks info vet info

Open Mar-14 Nov Last departure noon

A secluded, heavily wooded park on the shores of Lake Windermere. Pretty lakeside picnic areas, woodland walks and a play area make this a delightful park for families, with excellent serviced pitches, a licensed shop and a heated toilet block. Watersports include sailing and canoeing, with private jetties for boat launching. A 31 acre site with 43 touring pitches and 215 statics.

DERBYSHIRE

ASHBOURNE
Map 7 SK14

von Essen hotels
A PRIVATE COLLECTION
www.vonessenhotels.com

Callow Hall

★★★ 82% HOTEL

Mappleton Rd DE6 2AA
☎ 01335 300900 📠 01335 300512
e-mail: info@callowhall.co.uk
dir: *A515 through Ashbourne towards Buxton, left at Bowling Green pub, then 1st right*

PETS: Bedrooms (2 GF) **Charges** £25 per stay **Public areas** except restaurants **Grounds** on leads disp bin **Exercise area Facilities** walks info vet info **On Request** fridge access **Other** charge for damage **Restrictions** small dogs only

This delightful, creeper-clad, early Victorian house, set on a 44-acre estate, enjoys views over Bentley Brook and the Dove Valley. The atmosphere is relaxed and welcoming, and some of the spacious bedrooms in the main house have comfortable sitting areas. Public rooms feature high ceilings, ornate plasterwork and antique furniture. There is a good range of dishes offered on both the carte and the fixed-price, daily-changing menus.

Rooms 16 (2 fmly) (2 GF) **S** £105-£165; **D** £150-£220 (incl. bkfst)* **Facilities** STV Cycle hire nearby (Tissington Trail) Riding nearby Golf course within 2m Xmas New Year Wi-fi **Parking** 21 **Notes** LB

Mercaston Hall *(SK279419)*

★★★★ FARMHOUSE

Mercaston DE6 3BL

☎ 01335 360263 & 07836 648102 Mr & Mrs A Haddon

e-mail: mercastonhall@btinternet.com

dir: *Off A52 in Brailsford onto Luke Ln, 1m turn right at 1st x-rds, house 1m on right*

PETS: Bedrooms Stables **Charges** £2 per night **Public areas** except dining room **Grounds** disp bin **Exercise area** adjacent fields **Facilities** food bowl water bowl leads washing facs cage storage walks info vet info **On Request** fridge access torch towels **Other** charge for damage

Located in a pretty hamlet, this medieval building retains many original features. Bedrooms are homely, and additional facilities include an all-weather tennis court and a livery service. This is a good base for visiting local stately homes, the Derwent Valley mills and Dovedale.

Rooms 3 en suite **S** fr £45; **D** fr £66* **Facilities** FTV tea/coffee Cen ht Wi-fi ⌨ **Parking Notes** No Children 8yrs Closed Xmas ⌨ 60 acres mixed

Carsington Fields Caravan Park *(SK251493)*

►►

Millfields Ln, Nr Carsington Water DE6 3JS

☎ 01335 372872

dir: *From Belper towards Ashbourne on A517, turn right approx 0.25m past Hulland Ward into Dog Ln. 0.75m right at x-roads signed Carsington. Site on right approx 0.75m*

PETS: Public areas except near toilets disp bin **Exercise area** grass dog run **Facilities** vet info **Other** prior notice required

Open Etr-end Sep Last arrival 21.00hrs Last departure 18.00hrs

A very well presented and spacious park with a good toilet block, open views and a large fenced pond that attracts plenty of wildlife. The popular tourist attraction of Carsington Water is a short stroll away, with its variety of leisure facilities including fishing, sailing, windsurfing and children's play area. The park is also a good base for walkers. A 6 acre site with 10 touring pitches, 10 hardstandings.

Notes No large groups or group bookings

Rutland Arms

★★★ 70% ⚜ HOTEL

The Square DE45 1BT

☎ 01629 812812 📠 01629 812309

e-mail: enquiries@rutlandbakewell.co.uk

dir: *M1 junct 28 to Matlock, A6 to Bakewell. Hotel in town centre*

PETS: Bedrooms (7 GF) unattended **Charges** £10 per night **Public areas** at certain times only on leads **Exercise area** 100yds **Facilities** vet info **Other** charge for damage dogs allowed in courtyard rooms only; may only be left unattended in bedrooms for short periods **Restrictions** small, well behaved dogs only

This 19th-century hotel lies at the very centre of Bakewell and offers comfortable accommodation. The Square restaurant serves an interesting fine dining menu in elegant surroundings. The staff are friendly and welcoming.

Rooms 35 (17 annexe) (2 fmly) (7 GF) **Facilities** New Year Wi-fi **Parking** 25

Monsal Head Hotel

★★ 82% ⚜ HOTEL

Monsal Head DE45 1NL

☎ 01629 640250 📠 01629 640815

e-mail: enquiries@monsalhead.com

web: www.monsalhead.com

dir: *A6 from Bakewell to Buxton. In 2m turn into Ashford-in-the-Water, take B6465 for 1m. Hotel on left through public car park entrance*

PETS: Bedrooms Charges £10 per night £50 per week **Public areas** except restaurant on leads **Grounds** on leads disp bin **Exercise area** 50yds **Facilities** dog grooming cage storage walks info vet info **On Request** fridge access torch **Other** charge for damage please phone for further details of pet facilities **Restrictions** small, well behaved dogs only

Situated three miles from Bakewell and overlooking the picturesque Monsal Dale in the Peak District National Park, this hotel is full of charm and character. The bedrooms have beautiful views, and public areas include the Ashford Room, a quiet residents' lounge, and Longstone Restaurant. The converted stables bar adjacent to the hotel has an excellent choice of cask ales and lagers.

Rooms 7 (1 fmly) **S** £60-£85; **D** £90-£150 (incl. bkfst & dinner)* **Facilities** Xmas New Year **Parking** 20 **Notes** LB RS 25 Dec

BAKEWELL *continued*

Croft Cottages
★★★★ GUEST ACCOMMODATION
Coombs Rd DE45 1AQ
☎ 01629 814101
e-mail: croftco@btinternet.com
dir: *A619 E from town centre over bridge, right onto Station Rd & Coombs Rd*

PETS: Bedrooms unattended **Grounds** on leads **Exercise area** 100yds **Facilities** walks info vet info **On Request** fridge access towels **Restrictions** no breed larger than a Labrador/Retriever **Resident Pet:** Steffi (Belgian Shepherd)

A warm welcome is assured at this Grade II listed stone building close to the River Wye and town centre. Thoughtfully equipped bedrooms are available in the main house or in an adjoining converted barn suite. Breakfast is served in a spacious lounge dining room.

Rooms 3 rms (2 en suite) (1 pri facs) 1 annexe en suite (1 fmly) **S** £40-£50; **D** £60-£80 **Facilities** tea/coffee Cen ht **Parking** 2 **Notes** 🚭

BELPER	Map 8 SK34

Makeney Hall Hotel
★★★★ 73% HOTEL
Makeney, Milford DE56 0RS
☎ 0845 609 9966 📠 01332 842777
e-mail: reservations@akkeron-hotels.com
web: www.akkeron-hotels.com
dir: *Off A6 at Milford, signed Makeney. Hotel 0.25m on left*

PETS: Bedrooms Charges £5 per night **Grounds** on leads **Exercise area** fields adjacent **Facilities** walks info vet info **Other** dogs allowed in courtyard bedrooms only **Restrictions** no dangerous breeds (see page 7)

This restored Victorian mansion stands in six acres of landscaped gardens and grounds above the River Derwent. Bedrooms vary in style and are generally very spacious. They are divided between the main house and the ground floor courtyard. Comfortable public rooms include a lounge, bar and spacious restaurant with views of the gardens.

Rooms 46 (18 annexe) (3 fmly) **Facilities** STV Xmas New Year Wi-fi **Services** Lift **Parking** 150

BUXTON	Map 7 SK07

Barceló Buxton Palace Hotel
★★★★ 72% HOTEL
Palace Rd SK17 6AG
☎ 01298 22001 📠 01298 72131
e-mail: palace@barcelo-hotels.co.uk
web: www.barcelo-hotels.co.uk
dir: *M6 junct 20, follow M56/M60 signs to Stockport then A6 to Buxton, hotel adjacent to railway station*

PETS: Bedrooms unattended sign **Charges** £15 per stay **Public areas** except bar & restaurant on leads **Grounds** on leads **Exercise area** park 600mtrs **Facilities** cage storage walks info vet info **On Request** fridge access **Other** charge for damage dogs allowed in 3rd floor bedrooms only

This impressive Victorian hotel is located on the hill overlooking the town. Public areas are traditional and elegant in style, and include chandeliers and decorative ceilings. The bedrooms are spacious and equipped with modern facilities, and The Dovedale Restaurant provides modern British cuisine. Good leisure facilities are available.

Rooms 122 (18 fmly) **Facilities** Spa 🏊 supervised Gym Beauty facilities Xmas New Year Wi-fi **Services** Lift **Parking** 180

Lime Tree Park *(SK070725)*
▶ ▶ ▶ ▶
Dukes Dr SK17 9RP
☎ 01298 22988 📠 01298 22988
e-mail: info@limetreeparkbuxton.co.uk
dir: *1m S of Buxton, between A515 & A6*

PETS: Charges touring pitches £2 per night **Public areas** on leads disp bin **Exercise area** field available **Facilities** food food bowl water bowl dog chews cat treats leads walks info vet info **Other** prior notice required disposal bags available

Open Mar-Oct Last arrival 21.00hrs Last departure noon

A most attractive and well-designed site, set on the side of a narrow valley in an elevated location. Its backdrop of magnificent old railway viaduct and views over Buxton and the surrounding hills make this a sought-after destination. A 10.5 acre site with 106 touring pitches, 22 hardstandings and 43 statics.

Beech Croft Farm *(SK122720)*

▶▶

Beech Croft, Blackwell in the Peak SK17 9TQ
☎ 01298 85330
e-mail: mail@beechcroftfarm.net
dir: *Off A6 midway between Buxton & Bakewell. Site signed*

PETS: Public areas except toilets & showers **Exercise area** bridlepath 100yds **Facilities** water bowl walks info vet info

Open mid Mar-Nov rs Mar hook up & water tap only, Elsan disposal Last arrival 21.30hrs

A small terraced site in an attractive farm setting with lovely views. Hardstandings are provided for caravans, and there is a separate field for tents. An ideal site for those touring or walking in the Peak District. A 3 acre site with 30 touring pitches, 25 hardstandings.

Thornheyes Farm Campsite *(SK084761)*

▶▶

Thornheyes Farm, Longridge Ln, Peak Dale SK17 8AD
☎ 01298 26421
dir: *1.5m from Buxton on A6 turn E for Peak Dale. After 0.5m S at x-rds to site on right*

PETS: Public areas on leads disp bin **Exercise area** adjacent **Facilities** vet info **Other** prior notice required dogs must be on leads at all times & exercised off site **Resident Pets:** Bart (Alsatian), 4 cats, 1 horse, 2 ponies

Open Etr-Oct Last arrival 21.30hrs Last departure noon

A pleasant mainly-sloping farm site run by a friendly family team in the central Peak District. Toilet and other facilities are very simple but extremely clean. A 2 acre site with 10 touring pitches.

Notes No ball games 🐾

CALVER   Map 8 SK27

Valley View
★★★★ GUEST HOUSE
Smithy Knoll Rd S32 3XW
☎ 01433 631407
e-mail: sue@a-place-2-stay.co.uk
web: www.a-place-2-stay.co.uk
dir: *A623 from Baslow into Calver, 3rd left onto Donkey Ln*

PETS: Bedrooms Exercise area by open fields, dogs can run off lead **Facilities** food (pre-bookable) food bowl water bowl leads washing facs walks info vet info **On Request** fridge access torch towels **Restrictions** no large dogs (ie German Shepherds, Rottweilers) **Resident Pets:** Bailey (Springer Spaniel), Wackey (Border Collie)

This detached stone house is in the heart of the village. It is very well-furnished throughout and delightfully friendly service is provided. A hearty breakfast is served in the cosy dining room, which is well stocked with local guide books.

Rooms 3 en suite 1 annexe en suite (1 GF); **D** £60-£85 **Facilities** tea/coffee Cen ht Wi-fi **Parking** 6 **Notes** LB No Children 5yrs

---

CHESTERFIELD   Map 8 SK37

Ibis Chesterfield
BUDGET HOTEL
Lordsmill St S41 7RW
☎ 01246 221333   🖨 01246 221444
e-mail: h3160@accor.com
web: www.ibishotel.com
dir: *M1 junct 29/A617 to Chesterfield. 2nd exit at 1st rdbt. Hotel on right at 2nd rdbt*

PETS: Bedrooms (8 GF) **Charges** £6 per night **Public areas** except restaurant on leads disp bin **Facilities** walks info vet info **Other** charge for damage

Modern, budget hotel offering comfortable accommodation in bright and practical bedrooms. Breakfast is self-service and dinner is available in the restaurant.

Rooms 86 (21 fmly) (8 GF) **S** £50-£57; **D** £50-£57*

CROMFORD — Map 8 SK25

Alison House

★★★★ GUEST ACCOMMODATION

Intake Ln DE4 3RH

☎ 01629 822211 📠 01629 822316

e-mail: info@alison-house-hotel.co.uk

PETS: Bedrooms unattended Stables 2m Public areas except restaurant on leads Grounds disp bin Exercise area 100yds Facilities scoop/disp bags washing facs walks info vet info On Request fridge access torch towels Other charge for damage

This very well furnished and spacious 18th-century house stands in seven acres of grounds just a short walk from the village. Public rooms are comfortable and bedrooms are mostly very spacious.

Rooms 16 en suite (1 fmly) (4 GF) Facilities tea/coffee Dinner available Direct Dial Cen ht Licensed Wi-fi 🏊 Parking 30

DERBY — Map 8 SK33

Menzies Mickleover Court

★★★★ 73% HOTEL

Etwall Rd, Mickleover DE3 0XX

☎ 01332 521234 📠 01332 521238

e-mail: mickleovercourt@menzieshotels.co.uk

web: www.menzieshotels.co.uk

dir: A50 towards Derby, exit at junct 5. A516 towards Derby, take exit signed Mickleover

PETS: Bedrooms Grounds on leads Facilities walks info vet info Other charge for damage Restrictions small dogs only

Located close to Derby, this modern hotel is well suited to both the conference and leisure markets. Bedrooms are spacious, air conditioned, well equipped and include some smart executive rooms and suites. The smartly presented leisure facilities are amongst the best in the region.

Rooms 99 (20 fmly) (5 smoking) S £50-£165; D £50-£165* Facilities STV 🏊 Gym Beauty salon Steam room Xmas New Year Wi-fi Services Lift Air con Parking 270

Littleover Lodge

★★★ 69% HOTEL

222 Rykneld Rd, Littleover DE23 4AN

☎ 01332 510161 📠 01332 514010

e-mail: enquiries@littleoverlodge.co.uk

web: www.littleoverlodge.co.uk

dir: A38 towards Derby approx 1m on left slip lane signed Littleover/Mickleover/Findon, take 2nd exit off island marked Littleover 0.25m on right

PETS: Bedrooms (6 GF) unattended Grounds disp bin Exercise area Facilities walks info vet info Other charge for damage Restrictions no breed larger than a Labrador

Situated in a rural location this friendly hotel offers modern bedrooms with direct access from the car park. Two styles of dining are available - an informal carvery operation which is very popular locally, and a more formal restaurant which is open for lunch and dinner each day. Service is excellent with the long serving staff being particularly friendly.

Rooms 16 (3 fmly) (6 GF) S £49.50-£80; D £65-£90 (incl. bkfst)* Facilities STV ♫ Xmas New Year Wi-fi Parking 75 Notes LB

DERBY SERVICE AREA (A50) — Map 8 SK42

Days Inn Donington

BUDGET HOTEL

Welcome Break Services, A50 Westbound DE72 2WA

☎ 01332 799666 📠 01332 794166

e-mail: derby.hotel@welcomebreak.co.uk

web: www.welcomebreak.co.uk

dir: M1 junct 24/24a, onto A50 towards Stoke/Derby. Hotel between juncts 1 & 2

PETS: Bedrooms (17 GF) Public areas Grounds on leads Other pets must either be on leads or in carriers

This modern building offers accommodation in smart, spacious and well-equipped bedrooms, suitable for families and business travellers, and all with en suite bathrooms. Continental breakfast is available and other refreshments may be taken at the nearby family restaurant.

Rooms 47 (39 fmly) (17 GF) (8 smoking) S £29-£59; D £39-£69*

Coopers Camp & Caravan Park *(SK121859)*

▶▶

Newfold Farm, Edale Village S33 7ZD
☎ 01433 670372
dir: *From A6187 at Hope take minor road for 4m to Edale. Right onto unclass road, site on left in 800yds opposite school*

PETS: Public areas on leads **Facilities** food leads vet info

Open all year Last arrival 23.30hrs Last departure 15.00hrs

Rising grassland behind a working farm, divided by a wall into two fields, culminating in the 2062ft Edale Moor. Facilities have been converted from original farm buildings, and include a café for backpackers, and a well-stocked shop. A 6 acre site with 135 touring pitches and 11 statics.

Notes

Bentley Brook Inn

★ ★ ★ INN
DE6 1LF
☎ 01335 350278   📠 01335 350422
e-mail: all@bentleybrookinn.co.uk
dir: *2m N of Ashbourne at junct of A515 & B5056*

PETS: Bedrooms unattended sign **Charges** £10 per night
Public areas except restaurant & breakfast room on leads
Grounds on leads **Exercise area** surrounded by fields **Facilities** feeding mat scoop/disp bags cage storage walks info vet info **On Request** fridge access torch towels **Other** charge for damage

This popular inn is located in the Peak District National Park, just north of Ashbourne. It is a charming building with an attractive terrace, sweeping lawns, and nursery gardens. A well-appointed family restaurant dominates the ground floor, where a wide range of dishes is available all day. The character bar serves beer from its own micro-brewery. Bedrooms are well appointed and thoughtfully equipped.

Rooms 11 en suite (1 fmly) (2 GF) **Facilities** TVL tea/coffee Dinner available Direct Dial Cen ht Wi-fi **Parking** 100

The Bulls Head Inn

★ ★ ★ ★ INN
S32 5QR
☎ 01433 630873   📠 01433 631738
e-mail: wilbnd@aol.com
dir: *Off A623 into Foolow*

PETS: Bedrooms Charges £5 per night **Public areas** except restaurant **Exercise area Facilities** food bowl walks info vet info **Other** charge for damage **Resident Pets:** Jack & Holly (West Highland Terriers)

Located in the village centre, this popular inn retains many original features and offers comfortable, well-equipped bedrooms. Extensive and imaginative bar meals are served in the traditionally furnished dining room or in the cosy bar areas. The inn welcomes well-behaved dogs in the bar (and even muddy boots on the flagstone areas).

Rooms 3 en suite (1 fmly); **D** £80-£90 **Facilities** tea/coffee Dinner available Cen ht Golf 18 **Parking** 20

Maynard

★ ★ ★ 79% ◉◉ HOTEL
Main Rd S32 2HE
☎ 01433 630321   📠 01433 630445
e-mail: info@themaynard.co.uk
dir: *From Sheffield take A625 to Castleton. Left into Grindleford on B6521. On left after Fox House Hotel*

PETS: Bedrooms sign **Charges** £20 per night **Public areas** except restaurant on leads **Grounds** disp bin **Exercise area** 250mtrs **Facilities** food (pre-bookable) food bowl water bowl bedding dog chews cat treats feeding mat scoop/disp bags leads washing facs cage storage walks info vet info **On Request** fridge access torch towels **Other** charge for damage prior notice required **Resident Pets:** 2 cats

This building, dating back over 100 years, is situated in a beautiful and tranquil location yet is within easy reach of Sheffield and the M1. The bedrooms are contemporary in style and offer a wealth of accessories. The Peak District views from the restaurant and garden are stunning.

Rooms 10 (1 fmly) **S** £60-£110; **D** £80-£175* **Facilities** STV Wi-fi **Parking** 70 **Notes** LB

ENGLAND

HOPE   Map 7 SK18

Stoney Ridge
★★★★ ≜ GUEST ACCOMMODATION
Granby Rd, Bradwell S33 9HU
☎ 01433 620538
e-mail: toneyridge@aol.com
web: www.stoneyridge.org.uk
dir: *From N end of Bradwell, Gore Ln uphill past Bowling Green Inn, turn left onto Granby Rd*

PETS: **Bedrooms** unattended **Public areas** except dining room on leads **Grounds** on leads disp bin **Exercise area** 100mtrs **Facilities** pet sitting dog walking washing facs cage storage walks info vet info **On Request** fridge access torch towels Resident Pets: Paddy (cockatiel), Bertie & Boris (cockerels), 18 hens

This large, split-level bungalow stands in attractive mature gardens at the highest part of the village and has extensive views. Hens roam freely in the landscaped garden, and their fresh eggs add to the hearty breakfasts. Bedrooms are attractively furnished and thoughtfully equipped, and there is a spacious comfortable lounge and a superb indoor swimming pool.

Rooms 4 rms (3 en suite) (1 pri facs) **S** £48-£58; **D** £60-£74 **Facilities** STV FTV TVL tea/coffee Cen ht Wi-fi **Parking** 3 **Notes** LB No Children 10yrs RS Winter - pool may be closed for maintenance

Round Meadow Barn
★ ★ ★ BED AND BREAKFAST
Parsons Ln S33 6RB
☎ 01433 621347 & 07836 689422 📠 01433 621347
e-mail: rmbarn@bigfoot.com
dir: *Off A625 (Hope Rd) N onto Parsons Ln, over rail bridge, in 200yds right into hay barnyard, through gates, across 3 fields, house on left*

PETS: **Bedrooms Stables Charges** dogs £3, horses £10 per night **Public areas** except at breakfast on leads **Grounds** disp bin **Exercise area Facilities** water bowl feeding mat washing facs vet info **On Request** towels **Restrictions** no Staffordshire Bull Terriers Resident Pets: Puzzle (Jack Russell), Kayti & Jasmin (Welsh ponies), Floss (horse), Lucy (cat)

This converted barn, with original stone walls and exposed timbers, stands in open fields in the picturesque Hope Valley. The bedrooms are large enough for families and there are two modern bathrooms. Breakfast is served at one large table adjoining the family kitchen.

Rooms 3 rms (1 en suite) (2 pri facs) (1 fmly) **S** £35-£40; **D** £60-£70* **Facilities** tea/coffee Cen ht Golf 18 **Parking** 8 **Notes** LB 🐾

MATLOCK   Map 8 SK36

Hodgkinsons Hotel & Restaurant
★★ **69%** HOTEL
150 South Pde, Matlock Bath DE4 3NR
☎ 01629 582170 📠 01629 584891
e-mail: enquiries@hodgkinsons-hotel.co.uk
dir: *On A6 in village centre. On corner of Waterloo Rd & South Parade*

PETS: **Bedrooms** unattended **Charges** £10 per stay **Public areas** except restaurant/bar area **Grounds Exercise area** 200 yds **Facilities** food bowl water bowl bedding dog chews cat treats feeding mat washing facs cage storage walks info vet info **On Request** fridge access torch towels **Other** charge for damage only 1 dog per room

This fine Georgian building was renovated in the Victorian era and has many interesting and unusual features. Bedrooms are equipped with fine antique furniture and a wealth of thoughtful extras. The elegant dining room is the setting for imaginative dinners and a comfortable lounge is also available.

Rooms 8 (1 fmly) **S** £75-£95; **D** £90-£140 (incl. bkfst)* **Facilities** Wi-fi **Parking** 5 **Notes** LB Closed 24-26 Dec

Farley *(SK294622)*
★★★ FARMHOUSE
Farley DE4 5LR
☎ 01629 582533 & 07801 756409 📠 01629 584856
Mrs Brailsford
e-mail: eric.brailsford@btconnect.com
dir: *1m N of Matlock. From A6 rdbt towards Bakewell, 1st right, right at top of hill, left up Farley Hill, 2nd farm on left*

PETS: **Bedrooms Stables Charges** pony £15, horse £20 inc feed/ bedding per night **Public areas** except dining room **Grounds Exercise area** fields surrounding farm **Facilities** food (pre-bookable) food bowl water bowl bedding leads pet sitting dog walking washing facs dog grooming cage storage vet info **On Request** fridge access torch towels Resident Pets: 5 Border Terriers, 1 Labrador, 1 Boxer, 4 horses

Guests can expect a warm welcome at this traditional stone farmhouse. In addition to farming, the proprietors also breed dogs and horses. The bedrooms are pleasantly decorated and equipped with many useful extras. A hearty farm house breakfast offers a good start to any day.

Rooms 2 en suite (3 fmly) **S** £35-£40; **D** £56-£60 **Facilities** TVL tea/coffee Dinner available Cen ht Riding **Parking** 8 **Notes** LB 🐾 165 acres arable/beef/dairy

ENGLAND

Lickpenny Caravan Site *(SK339597)*

▶▶▶▶

Lickpenny Ln, Tansley DE4 5GF
☎ 01629 583040　🖶 01629 583040
e-mail: lickpenny@btinternet.com
dir: *From Matlock take A615 towards Alfreton for 3m. Site signed to left, into Lickpenny Ln, right into site near end of road*

PETS: Public areas disp bin **Exercise area** woodland area **Facilities** food food bowl water bowl dog chews walks info vet info **Other** disposal bags available

Open all year Last arrival 20.00hrs Last departure noon

A picturesque site in the grounds of an old plant nursery with areas broken up and screened by a variety of shrubs, and spectacular views. Pitches, several fully serviced, are spacious and well marked, and facilities are to a very good standard. A bistro/coffee shop is popular with visitors. A 16 acre site with 80 touring pitches, 80 hardstandings.

NEWHAVEN　　　　　　　Map 7 SK16

Newhaven Caravan & Camping Park
(SK167602)

▶▶▶

SK17 0DT
☎ 01298 84300　🖶 01332 726027
e-mail: newhavencaravanpark@btconnect.com
dir: *Between Ashbourne & Buxton at A515 & A5012 junct*

PETS: Public areas except shop disp bin **Exercise area** woodland walks **Facilities** food food bowl water bowl dog chews cat treats scoop/disp bags walks info **Resident Pets:** Basil (Border Collie), Ned (Golden Retriever)

Open Mar-Oct Last arrival 21.00hrs

Pleasantly situated within the Peak District National Park, with mature trees screening the three touring areas. Very good toilet facilities cater for touring vans and a large tent field, and there's a restaurant adjacent to the site. A 30 acre site with 125 touring pitches, 18 hardstandings and 73 statics.

RIPLEY　　　　　　　Map 8 SK35

Golden Valley Caravan & Camping Park
(SK408513)

▶▶▶▶

Coach Rd DE55 4ES
☎ 01773 513881　& 746786　🖶 01773 746786
e-mail: enquiries@goldenvalleycaravanpark.co.uk
dir: *M1 junct 26, A610 to Codnor. Right at lights, then right onto Alfreton Rd. In 1m left onto Coach Rd, park on left. (NB it is advised that Sat Nav is ignored for last few miles & guide directions are followed)*

PETS: Sep accom Stables Charges £2 per night £14 per week **Public areas Exercise area** Topwood Area or field at rear **Exercise area** footpaths adjacent to park **Facilities** dog chews cat treats washing facs walks info vet info **Other** prior notice required disposal bags available **Resident Pets:** Roxy (Labrador), Toby (goat), Gavin (peacock), Brian (goose), rabbits, ducks, chickens

Open all year rs Wknds only in low season Bar/café open Last arrival 21.00hrs Last departure noon

This park is set within 30 acres of woodland in the Amber Valley. The fully-serviced pitches are set out in informal groups in clearings amongst the trees. The park has a cosy bar and bistro with outside patio, a fully stocked fishing lake, an on-site jacuzzi and fully equipped fitness suite. There is also a wildlife pond. A 30 acre site with 45 touring pitches, 45 hardstandings and 1 static.

Notes No open fires or disposable BBQs, no noise after 22.30hrs, no vehicles on grass

ROSLISTON　　　　　　　Map 8 SK21

Beehive Woodland Lakes *(SK249161)*

▶▶

DE12 8HZ
☎ 01283 763981　🖶 01283 763981
e-mail: info@beehivefarm-woodlandlakes.co.uk
dir: *Turn S off A444 at Castle Gresley onto Mount Pleasant Rd, follow Rosliston signs for 3.5m through Linton to T-junct. Turn left signed Beehive Farms*

PETS: Charges dogs £2 per night **Public areas** except farm & lake banks on leads disp bin **Exercise area Facilities** food food bowl water bowl dog chews scoop/disp bags leads washing facs dog grooming walks info vet info **Other** prior notice required **Restrictions** no dangerous breeds (see page 7)

Open Mar-Nov Last arrival 20.00hrs Last departure 10.30hrs

A small, informal caravan area secluded from an extensive woodland park in the heart of The National Forest. Young children will enjoy the on-site animal farm and playground, whilst anglers will appreciate fishing the three lakes within the park. The Honey Pot tearoom provides snacks and is open most days. A 2.5 acre site with 25 touring pitches, 12 hardstandings.

ROWSLEY Map 8 SK26

The Peacock at Rowsley

★★★ ◉◉ HOTEL

Bakewell Rd DE4 2EB

☎ 01629 733518 📄 01629 732671

e-mail: reception@thepeacockatrowsley.com

web: www.thepeacockatrowsley.com

dir: A6, 3m before Bakewell, 6m from Matlock towards Bakewell

PETS: **Bedrooms** unattended **Charges** dog £10 per night
Grounds Exercise area 0.25m **Facilities** food (pre-bookable)
water bowl walks info vet info **On Request** torch towels **Other**
charge for damage

Owned by Lord Manners of Haddon Hall, this hotel combines
stylish contemporary design by India Mahdavi with original
period and antique features. Bedrooms are individually designed
and boast DVD players, complimentary Wi-fi and smart marble
bathrooms. Two rooms are particularly special - one with a
four-poster and one with an antique bed originating from Belvoir
Castle in Leicestershire. Imaginative cuisine, using local,
seasonal produce, is a highlight. Guests are warmly welcomed
and service is attentive. Fly fishing is popular in this area and the
hotel has its own fishing rights on seven miles of the Rivers Wye
and Derwent.

Rooms 16 (5 fmly) **Facilities** Fishing ⛳ Free use of Woodlands
Fitness Centre Free membership to Bakewell Golf Club ♪ New
Year Wi-fi **Parking** 25 **Notes** No children 10yrs

SANDIACRE Map 8 SK43

Holiday Inn Derby/Nottingham

★★★ 73% HOTEL

Holiday Inn

Bostocks Ln NG10 5NJ

☎ 0871 942 9062 📄 0115 949 0469

e-mail: reservations-derby-nottingham@ihg.com

web: www.holidayinn.co.uk

dir: M1 junct 25 follow Sandiacre signs, hotel on right

PETS: **Bedrooms** (53 GF) unattended **Charges** £10 per night
£70 per week **Grounds** on leads disp bin **Facilities** vet info
On Request fridge access torch towels **Other** charge for
damage

This hotel is conveniently located by the M1, ideal for exploring
Derby and Nottingham. The bedrooms are modern and smart. The
restaurant offers a wide range of dishes for breakfast, lunch and
dinner. The lounge/bar area is a popular meeting place, with food
served all day.

Rooms 92 (31 fmly) (53 GF) (2 smoking) **S** £32-£129;
D £42-£139* **Facilities** STV Xmas New Year Wi-fi **Services** Air con
Parking 200 **Notes** LB

THORPE (DOVEDALE) Map 7 SK15

Izaak Walton

★★★ 79% ◉ HOTEL

Dovedale DE6 2AY

☎ 01335 350555 📄 01335 350539

e-mail: reception@izaakwaltonhotel.com

web: www.izaakwaltonhotel.com

dir: A515 onto B5054, to Thorpe, straight over cattle grid & 2
small bridges, 1st right & sharp left

PETS: **Bedrooms** (8 GF) unattended **Charges** £10 per night
Public areas except main restaurant & 1st floor **Grounds** disp
bin **Exercise area** adjacent **Facilities** water bowl washing
facs walks info vet info **On Request** fridge access torch **Other**
charge for damage

This hotel is peacefully situated, with magnificent views over the
valley of Dovedale to Thorpe Cloud. Many of the bedrooms have
lovely views, and the executive rooms are particularly spacious.
Meals are served in the bar area, with more formal dining in the
Haddon Restaurant. Staff are friendly and efficient. Fishing on
the River Dove can be arranged.

Rooms 35 (6 fmly) (8 GF) **D** £70-£200 (incl. bkfst) **Facilities** FTV
Fishing ⛳ Xmas New Year Wi-fi **Parking** 80 **Notes** LB

TIDESWELL — Map 7 SK17

Poppies
★★★ GUEST ACCOMMODATION
Bank Square SK17 8LA
☎ 01298 871083
e-mail: poptidza@dialstart.net
dir: On B6049 in village centre opp NatWest bank

PETS: Bedrooms Charges Public areas on leads Exercise area 200yds Facilities walks info vet info On Request fridge access torch Other charge for damage

A friendly welcome is assured at this non-smoking house, located in the heart of a former lead-mining and textile community, a short walk from the 14th-century parish church. Bedrooms are homely and practical.

Rooms 3 rms (1 en suite) (1 fmly) S £24-£28; D £48-£56 Facilities tea/coffee Cen ht Notes ⊠

DEVON

ASHBURTON — Map 3 SX77

The Rising Sun
★★★★ ⇒ INN
Woodland TQ13 7JT
☎ 01364 652544
e-mail: admin@therisingsunwoodland.co.uk
dir: A38, exit signed Woodland/Denbury, continue straight on for 1.5m Rising Sun on left

PETS: Bedrooms unattended Public areas on leads Grounds disp bin Exercise area 50yds Facilities cage storage walks info vet info Resident Pet: Ruby (rabbit)

Peacefully situated in scenic south Devon countryside, this inn is just a short drive from the A38. A friendly welcome is extended to all guests; business, leisure and families alike. Bedrooms are comfortable and well equipped. Dinner and breakfast feature much local and organic produce. A good selection of homemade puddings, West Country cheeses, local wines and quality real ales are available.

Rooms 5 en suite (2 fmly) (2 GF) S £40-£45; D £50-£65* Facilities FTV tea/coffee Dinner available Cen ht Parking 30 Notes Closed 25 Dec No coaches

River Dart Country Park (SX734700)
►►►►
Holne Park TQ13 7NP
☎ 01364 652511 ◳ 01364 652020
e-mail: info@riverdart.co.uk
dir: M5 junct 31, A38 towards Plymouth. At Ashburton at Peartree junct follow brown site signs. Site 1m on left. (NB Peartree junct is 2nd exit at Ashburton - do not exit at Linhay junct as narrow roads are unsuitable for caravans)

PETS: Charges £3 per night Public areas on leads disp bin Exercise area woodland area on site Facilities vet info Other prior notice required toys & disposal bags available

Open Apr-Sep rs Low season cafe bar restricted opening hours Last arrival 21.00hrs Last departure 11.00hrs

Set in 90 acres of magnificent parkland that was once part of a Victorian estate, with many specimen and exotic trees, and in spring a blaze of colour from the many azaleas and rhododendrons. There are numerous outdoor activities for all ages including abseiling, caving and canoeing, plus high quality, well-maintained facilities. The open moorland of Dartmoor is only a few minutes away. A 90 acre site with 170 touring pitches, 23 hardstandings.

ASHWATER — Map 2 SX39

Blagdon Manor
★★★★★ ⊛⊛ ☲ RESTAURANT WITH ROOMS
EX21 5DF
☎ 01409 211224 ◳ 01409 211634
e-mail: stay@blagdon.com
web: www.blagdon.com
dir: A388 towards Launceston/Holsworthy. Approx 2m N of Chapman's Well take 2nd right for Ashwater. Next right beside Blagdon Lodge, 0.25m

PETS: Bedrooms Stables 5m Charges £8 per night Public areas except restaurant & conservatory on leads Grounds disp bin Exercise area surrounding area Facilities food bowl water bowl bedding dog chews feeding mat scoop/disp bags washing facs cage storage walks info vet info On Request fridge access torch towels Other charge for damage Resident Pets: Nutmeg, Cassia & Meg (Chocolate Labradors)

Located on the borders of Devon and Cornwall within easy reach of the coast, and set in its own beautifully kept yet natural gardens, this small and friendly restaurant with rooms offers a charming home-from-home atmosphere. The tranquillity of the secluded setting, the character and charm of the house and its unhurried pace ensure calm and relaxation. High levels of service, personal touches and thoughtful extras are all part of a stay here. Steve Morey cooks with passion and his commitment to using only the finest local ingredients speaks volumes.

Rooms 7 en suite S £85; D £135-£195* Facilities FTV tea/coffee Dinner available Direct Dial Cen ht Wi-fi ⛷ Parking 13 Notes No Children 12yrs Closed Jan RS Mon & Tue closed No coaches

AXMINSTER
Map 3 SY29

Fairwater Head Hotel
★★★ 75% ◉ HOTEL
Hawkchurch EX13 5TX
☎ 01297 678349 📠 01297 678459
e-mail: stay@fairwaterheadhotel.co.uk
web: www.fairwaterheadhotel.co.uk
dir: *Off B3165 (Crewkerne to Lyme Regis road). Hotel signed to Hawkchurch*

PETS: Bedrooms (8 GF) unattended Sep accom outside pen area Public areas except dining room on leads Grounds on leads disp bin Exercise area surrounding countryside Facilities food (pre-bookable) food bowl water bowl dog chews scoop/disp bags leads pet sitting washing facs cage storage walks info vet info On Request fridge access torch towels Other charge for damage Resident Pets: Mocca (Springer/Cocker Spaniel), Lollipop (Black Labrador)

This elegant Edwardian country house provides a perfect location for anyone looking for a peaceful break. Surrounded by extensive gardens and rolling countryside, the setting guarantees relaxation. Bedrooms are located both within the main house and the garden wing; all provide good levels of comfort. Public areas have much appeal and include lounge areas, a bar and an elegant restaurant. Food is a highlight with excellent local produce prepared with care and skill.

Rooms 16 (4 annexe) (8 GF) S £77.50-£180; D £97.50-£195 (incl. bkfst)* Facilities FTV Library Xmas New Year Wi-fi Parking 30 Notes LB Closed 1-30 Jan

Andrewshayes Caravan Park *(ST248088)*
►►►►
Dalwood EX13 7DY
☎ 01404 831225 📠 01404 831893
e-mail: info@andrewshayes.co.uk
dir: *On A35, 3m from Axminster. Turn N at Taunton Cross signed Stockland/Dalwood. Site 150mtrs on right*

PETS: Charges seasonal £1.50-£2.50 per night Public areas except bar & shop on leads disp bin Exercise area 2 dog walking fields Facilities scoop/disp bags walks info vet info Other prior notice required

Open Mar-Nov rs Sep-Nov shop, bar hrs ltd, pool shut Sep-mid May Last arrival 22.00hrs Last departure 11.00hrs

An attractive family park within easy reach of Lyme Regis, Seaton, Branscombe and Sidmouth in an ideal touring location. This popular park offers modern toilet facilities, an outdoor swimming pool and quiet, cosy bar with a widescreen-TV room. A 12 acre site with 150 touring pitches, 105 hardstandings and 80 statics.

BAMPTON
Map 3 SS92

The Bark House
★★★★ ⬭ GUEST ACCOMMODATION
Oakfordbridge EX16 9HZ
☎ 01398 351236
dir: *A361 to rdbt at Tiverton onto A396 for Dulverton, then onto Oakfordbridge. House on right*

PETS: Bedrooms Charges Public areas if other guests do not object Grounds disp bin Exercise area 10mtrs Facilities feeding mat walks info vet info On Request towels Other charge for damage Resident Pets: Jack & Ellie (dogs)

Located in the stunning Exe Valley and surrounded by wonderful unspoilt countryside, this is a perfect place to relax and unwind. Hospitality is the hallmark here and a cup of tea by the fireside is always on offer. Both breakfast and dinner make use of the excellent local produce, and are served in the attractive dining room, overlooking fields and the river. Bedrooms have a homely, cottage-style feel with comfy beds to ensure a peaceful night's sleep.

Rooms 6 rms (5 en suite) (1 pri facs) (1 fmly) S £50-£60; D £80-£110* Facilities tea/coffee Dinner available Cen ht Licensed Parking 6 Notes LB

BICKINGTON (NEAR ASHBURTON)　　Map 3 SX87

Lemonford Caravan Park *(SX793723)*

►►►►

TQ12 6JR

☎ 01626 821242

e-mail: info@lemonford.co.uk

dir: *From Exeter on A38 take A382, then 3rd exit at rdbt, follow Bickington signs*

PETS: Charges dog £1.50 per night **Public areas** on leads disp bin **Exercise area** 10yds **Facilities** walks info vet info **Other** prior notice required **Restrictions** dog breeds must be approved by owner prior to arrival Resident Pets: 3 cats

Open all year Last arrival 22.00hrs Last departure 11.00hrs

Small, secluded and well-maintained park with a good mixture of attractively laid out pitches. The friendly owners pay a great deal of attention to detail, and the toilets in particular are kept spotlessly clean. This good touring base is only one mile from Dartmoor and ten miles from the seaside at Torbay. A 7 acre site with 82 touring pitches, 55 hardstandings and 44 statics.

BIDEFORD　　Map 2 SS42

Yeoldon Country House

★★★ 81% ◉ SMALL HOTEL

Durrant Ln, Northam EX39 2RL

☎ 01237 474400   📠 01237 476618

e-mail: yeoldonhouse@aol.com

web: www.yeoldonhousehotel.co.uk

dir: *A39 from Barnstaple over River Torridge Bridge. At rdbt right onto A386 towards Northam, 3rd right into Durrant Lane*

PETS: Bedrooms Charges £5 per night **Public areas** lounge only (under strict control) on leads **Grounds** disp bin **Exercise area** North Devon coastal path adjacent **Facilities** washing facs cage storage walks info vet info **On Request** fridge access torch towels **Other** charge for damage Resident Pet: Shaz (Collie cross)

In a tranquil location with superb views over attractive grounds and the River Torridge, this is a charming Victorian house. The well-equipped bedrooms are individually decorated and some have balconies with breathtaking views. The public rooms are full of character with many interesting features and artefacts. The daily-changing dinner menu offers imaginative dishes.

Rooms 10 **S** £75-£85; **D** £115-£135 (incl. bkfst) **Facilities** FTV Wi-fi **Parking** 20 **Notes** LB Closed 24-27 Dec

Royal

★★★ 74% HOTEL

Barnstaple St EX39 4AE

☎ 01237 472005   📠 01237 478957

e-mail: reservations@royalbideford.co.uk

web: www.royalbideford.co.uk

dir: *At eastern end of Bideford Bridge*

PETS: Bedrooms (2 GF) **Stables** 3-5m **Charges** £5 per night **Public areas** reception only **Facilities** cage storage vet info **Other** charge for damage dogs allowed in standard bedrooms only

A quiet and relaxing hotel, the Royal is set near the river within a five-minute walk of the busy town centre and the quay. The bright, well maintained public areas retain much of the charm and style of its 16th-century origins, particularly in the wood-panelled Kingsley Suite. Bedrooms are well equipped and comfortable. The meals at dinner and the lounge snacks are appetising.

Rooms 32 (2 fmly) (2 GF) **S** £59-£80; **D** £65-£100* **Facilities** FTV Xmas New Year Wi-fi **Services** Lift **Parking** 70 **Notes** LB

Pines at Eastleigh

★★★★ 🏠 GUEST ACCOMMODATION

The Pines, Eastleigh EX39 4PA

☎ 01271 860561   📠 01271 861689

e-mail: pirrie@thepinesateastleigh.co.uk

dir: *A39 onto A386 signed East-the-Water. 1st left signed Eastleigh, 500yds next left, 1.5m to village, house on right*

PETS: Bedrooms Stables 2m **Charges** £5 per night **Public areas** except breakfast room, garden room & bar on leads **Grounds** on leads disp bin **Exercise area** nearby **Facilities** food bowl water bowl leads pet sitting dog walking washing facs cage storage walks info vet info **On Request** fridge access torch towels **Other** charge for damage

Friendly hospitality is assured at this Georgian house, set in seven acres of hilltop grounds. Two of the comfortable bedrooms are located in the main house, the remainder in converted barns around a charming courtyard that has a pretty pond and well. A delicious breakfast, featuring local and home-made produce, is served in the dining room, and a lounge and honesty bar are also available.

Rooms 6 en suite (1 fmly) (4 GF) **S** £40-£49; **D** £70-£89 **Facilities** FTV tea/coffee Direct Dial Cen ht Licensed Wi-fi 🍴 **Parking** 20 **Notes** LB No Children 9yrs

BISHOPSTEIGNTON — Map 3 SX97

THE INDEPENDENTS
HOTEL ASSOCIATION

Cockhaven Manor Hotel

★★ 71% HOTEL

Cockhaven Rd TQ14 9RF
☎ 01626 775252 📠 01626 775572
e-mail: cockhaven@btconnect.com
web: www.cockhavenmanor.com
dir: M5/A380 towards Torquay, then A381 towards Teignmouth. Left at Metro Motors. Hotel 500yds on left

PETS: Bedrooms unattended sign **Public areas** except eating areas **Grounds** disp bin **Exercise area** garden & river walks 0.25m **Facilities** food (pre-bookable) food bowl water bowl bedding dog chews cat treats feeding mat scoop/disp bags leads pet sitting dog walking washing facs walks info vet info **On Request** fridge access torch towels **Other** charge for damage **Resident Pet:** Bitsi (dog)

A friendly, family-run inn that dates back to the 16th century. Bedrooms are well equipped and many enjoy views across the beautiful Teign estuary. A choice of dining options is offered, and traditional and interesting dishes, along with locally caught fish, prove popular.

Rooms 12 (2 fmly) **S** £49-£56; **D** £70-£84 (incl. bkfst)*
Facilities FTV Petanque Wi-fi **Parking** 50 **Notes** LB Closed 25-26 Dec RS 25 Dec lunch

BOVEY TRACEY — Map 3 SX87

The Cromwell Arms

★★★★ INN

Fore St TQ13 9AE
☎ 01626 833473 📠 01626 836873
e-mail: info@thecromwellarms.co.uk
dir: From A38 from Exeter towards Plymouth take A382 at Drumbridges rdbt & follow Bovey Tracey signs. At mini rdbt take 2nd exit, follow town centre signs. At next rdbt take 3rd exit into Station Rd (B3344) & up hill

PETS: Bedrooms Charges dog £5 per night **Public areas** except restaurant & lounge on leads **Grounds** on leads disp bin **Exercise area** 2 mins walk **Facilities** feeding mat scoop/ disp bags leads washing facs cage storage walks info vet info **On Request** fridge access torch towels **Other** pets allowed in 2 bedrooms only & may be left unattended for short periods **Resident Pets:** Jasper, Benji & Poppy (Lhasa Apsos)

A traditional country inn situated in the heart of Bovey Tracey, on the southern edge of Dartmoor and approximately three miles from Newton Abbot. The Cromwell dates back from the 1600s, is full of original charm and has been enhanced with 21st-century facilities. This is an atmospheric, friendly pub with lots of character, which is suitable for all ages and is open all day every day.

Rooms 12 en suite (2 fmly) **S** fr £35; **D** fr £70* **Facilities** FTV tea/ coffee Dinner available Direct Dial Cen ht Wi-fi **Parking** 25

BRANSCOMBE — Map 3 SY18

The Masons Arms

[U]

EX12 3DJ
☎ 01297 680300 📠 01297 680500
e-mail: reception@masonsarms.co.uk
dir: Off A3052 towards Branscombe, hotel at hill bottom

PETS: Bedrooms Charges £5 per night **Public areas** except restaurant on leads **Grounds** on leads disp bin **Exercise area** 300yds **Facilities** water bowl washing facs walks info vet info **On Request** fridge access towels **Other** charge for damage **Resident Pet:** Maisy (Parson Russell Terrier)

Currently the rating for this establishment is not confirmed. This may be due to a change of ownership or because it has only recently joined the AA rating scheme. For further details please see the AA website: theAA.com

Rooms 21 (14 annexe) (1 fmly) **S** £80-£175; **D** £80-£175 (incl. bkfst)* **Facilities** Xmas New Year Wi-fi **Parking** 43 **Notes** LB

BRAUNTON — Map 2 SS43

Hidden Valley Park (SS499408)

►►►►

EX34 8NU

☎ 01271 813837

e-mail: relax@hiddenvalleypark.com

dir: *Direct access off A361, 8m from Barnstaple & 2m from Mullacott Cross*

PETS: Charges max £2 per night Public areas except shop & coffee shop disp bin Exercise area exercise field & woods Facilities washing facs walks info vet info Resident Pet: Oscar (Golden Retriever)

Open all year rs 15 Nov-15 Mar all weather pitches only Last arrival 21.00hrs Last departure 10.00hrs

A delightful, well-appointed family site set in a wooded valley, with superb facilities and a café. The park is set in a very rural, natural position not far from the beautiful coastline around Ilfracombe. A 25 acre site with 115 touring pitches, 65 hardstandings.

Lobb Fields Caravan & Camping Park

(SS475378)

►►►

Saunton Rd EX33 1HG

☎ 01271 812090 🖷 01271 812090

e-mail: info@lobbfields.com

dir: *At x-rds in Braunton take B3231 to Croyde. Site signed on right leaving Braunton*

PETS: Charges £2 per night Public areas except shower & toilets disp bin Exercise area dog walk with disposal bin Facilities washing facs walks info vet info Other prior notice required

Open Mar-Oct Last arrival 22.00hrs Last departure 10.30hrs

A bright, tree-lined park with the gently-sloping grass pitches divided into two open areas and a camping field in August. Braunton is an easy walk away, and the golden beaches of Saunton Sands and Croyde are within easy reach. A 14 acre site with 180 touring pitches, 6 hardstandings.

Notes No under 18s unless accompanied by an adult

BRIDGERULE — Map 2 SS20

Highfield House Camping & Caravanning

(SS279035)

►►

Holsworthy EX22 7EE

☎ 01288 381480

e-mail: nikki@highfieldholidays.freeserve.co.uk

dir: *Exit A3072 at Red Post x-rds onto B3254 towards Launceston. Direct access just over Devon border on right*

PETS: Public areas on leads disp bin Exercise area Facilities washing facs walks info vet info Restrictions no Staffordshire Bull Terriers, German Shepherds or Rottweilers Resident Pets: Tilly (West Highland White Terrier), Lucky (Westie/Cairn Terrier), Sparky (Cairn Terrier), Nevja (English Mastiff), goats, chickens, ducks, geese

Open all year

Set in a quiet and peaceful rural location, this park has extensive views over the valley to the sea at Bude, five miles away. The friendly young owners, with small children of their own, offer a relaxing holiday for families, with the simple facilities carefully looked after. A 4 acre site with 20 touring pitches and 4 statics.

Notes 😊

BRIXHAM — Map 3 SX95

Quayside

★★★ 75% ⊛ HOTEL

41-49 King St TQ5 9TJ

☎ 01803 855751 🖷 01803 882733

e-mail: reservations@quaysidehotel.co.uk

web: www.quaysidehotel.co.uk

dir: *A380, at 2nd rdbt at Kinkerswell towards Brixham on A3022*

PETS: Bedrooms Charges £12.50 per night Public areas except restaurant, lounge & Main Mast bar on leads Facilities walks info vet info On Request fridge access Other charge for damage prior notice required Restrictions small dogs only

With views over the harbour and bay, this hotel was formerly six cottages, and the public rooms retain a certain cosiness and intimacy, and include the lounge, residents' bar and Ernie Lister's public bar. Freshly landed fish features on the menus, alongside a number of creative and skilfully prepared dishes, served in the well-appointed restaurant. Good food is also available in the public bar. The owners and their team of local staff provide friendly and attentive service.

Rooms 29 (2 fmly) Facilities FTV ♫ Xmas New Year Wi-fi Parking 30

BRIXHAM *continued*

THE INDEPENDENTS
HOTEL ASSOCIATION

Berry Head Hotel
★★★ 72% HOTEL
Berry Head Rd TQ5 9AJ
☎ 01803 853225 📠 01803 882084
e-mail: stay@berryheadhotel.com
dir: *From marina, 1m, hotel on left*

PETS: Bedrooms Charges £10 per night **Public areas** lounge only at certain times **Grounds Exercise area** 20yds **Other** prior notice required **Restrictions** small dogs only **Resident Pet:** Alfie (Labrador/Poodle cross)

From its stunning cliff-top location, this imposing property that dates back to 1809, has spectacular views across Torbay. Public areas include two comfortable lounges, an outdoor terrace, a swimming pool, together with a bar serving a range of popular dishes. Many of the bedrooms have the benefit of the splendid sea views.

Rooms 32 (7 fmly) **S** £48-£68; **D** £84-£110 (incl. bkfst)*
Facilities FTV 🕑 🏊 Petanque Sailing Deep sea fishing Yacht charter 🎵 Xmas New Year Wi-fi **Services** Lift **Parking** 200 **Notes** LB

BROADWOODWIDGER   Map 2 SX48

Roadford Lake *(SX421900)*
►►
Lower Goodacre PL16 0JL
☎ 01409 211507 📠 01566 778503
e-mail: info@swlakestrust.org.uk
dir: *Exit A30 between Okehampton & Launceston at Roadford Lake signs, across dam wall, watersports centre 0.25m on right*

PETS: Public areas on leads disp bin **Exercise area** lake walks **Facilities** washing facs walks info

Open Apr-Oct

Located right at the edge of Devon's largest inland water, this popular rural park is well screened by mature trees and shrubs. It boasts an excellent watersports school (sailing, windsurfing, rowing and kayaking) with hire and day launch facilities, and is an ideal location for fly fishing for brown trout. A 1.5 acre site with 30 touring pitches, 4 hardstandings.

BUDLEIGH SALTERTON   Map 3 SY08

Hansard House
★★★★ GUEST ACCOMMODATION
3 Northview Rd EX9 6BY
☎ 01395 442773 📠 01395 442475
e-mail: enquiries@hansardhotel.co.uk
web: www.hansardhousehotel.co.uk
dir: *500yds W of town centre*

PETS: Bedrooms unattended sign **Charges** £7.50 per night £45 per week **Grounds** disp bin **Exercise area Facilities** food bowl water bowl bedding feeding mat pet sitting dog walking washing facs cage storage walks info vet info **On Request** fridge access torch towels **Other** charge for damage

Hansard House is quietly situated a short walk from the town centre. Many of the well-presented bedrooms have commanding views across the town to the countryside and estuary beyond. Several are located on the ground floor and have easier access. Guests enjoy a varied selection at breakfast including a range of healthy options. The dining room and lounge are both comfortably furnished, and dinners are sometimes available with prior notification.

Rooms 12 en suite (1 fmly) (3 GF) **S** £46-£57; **D** £84-£99
Facilities STV TVL tea/coffee Direct Dial Cen ht Lift Licensed Wi-fi **Parking** 11 **Notes** LB

Pooh Cottage Holiday Park *(SY053831)*
►►
Bear Ln EX9 7AQ
☎ 01395 442354
e-mail: info@poohcottage.co.uk
dir: *M5 junct 30 onto A376 towards Exmouth. Left onto B3179 towards Woodbury & Budleigh Salterton. Left into Knowle on B3178. Through village, at brow of hill take sharp left into Bear Lane (very narrow). Site 200yds*

PETS: Stables 1m **Public areas** except woodland walkway **Exercise area** common land (150yds), river & coastal paths **Facilities** walks info vet info **Other** prior notice required **Restrictions** no dangerous breeds (see page 7)

Open Apr-Oct Last arrival 20.00hrs Last departure 11.00hrs

A rural park with widespread views of the sea and surrounding peaceful countryside. Expect a friendly welcome to this attractive site, with its lovely play area, and easy access to plenty of walks, as well as the Buzzard Cycle Way. An 8 acre site with 52 touring pitches, 5 hardstandings and 2 statics.

BURRINGTON (NEAR PORTSMOUTH ARMS STATION) Map 3 SS61

Northcote Manor

★★★ ⓜⓜ COUNTRY HOUSE HOTEL

EX37 9LZ

☎ 01769 560501   📠 01769 560770

e-mail: rest@northcotemanor.co.uk

web: www.northcotemanor.co.uk

dir: *Off A377 opposite Portsmouth Arms, into hotel drive.*
NB. Do not enter Burrington village

PETS: Bedrooms Stables 5m **Charges** £5 per night
Public areas except restaurant, top lounge & conservatory
Grounds Exercise area beach (12m) **Facilities** food (pre-bookable) food bowl water bowl dog chews washing facs cage
storage walks info vet info **On Request** fridge access torch
towels

A warm and friendly welcome is assured at this beautiful
country-house hotel. Built in 1716, the house sits in 20 acres of
grounds and woodlands. Guests can enjoy wonderful views over
the Taw River Valley whilst relaxing in the delightful environment
created by the attentive staff. The elegant restaurant is the
highlight of any stay with the finest of local produce used in
well-prepared dishes. Bedrooms, including some suites, are
individually styled, spacious and well appointed.

Rooms 11 **S** £110-£170; **D** £160-£260 (incl. bkfst)*
Facilities FTV Japanese style water garden Xmas New Year
Wi-fi **Parking** 30 **Notes** LB

CHAGFORD Map 3 SX78

Mill End

★★ ⓜⓜ HOTEL

Dartmoor National Park TQ13 8JN

☎ 01647 432282   📠 01647 433106

e-mail: info@millendhotel.com

web: www.millendhotel.com

dir: *From A30 at Whiddon Down follow A382 to*
Moretonhampstead. After 3.5m hump back bridge at Sandy Park,
hotel on right by river

PETS: Bedrooms (3 GF) **Charges** £10 per night **Public areas**
except restaurant **Grounds** disp bin **Exercise area** 500yds
Facilities water bowl leads washing facs cage storage walks
info vet info **On Request** fridge access torch towels **Other**
charge for damage **Resident Pets:** Harry & Orvis (Labradors),
Poppy (cat)

In an attractive location, Mill End, an 18th-century working
water mill, sits by the River Teign that offers six miles of
angling. The atmosphere is akin to a family home where guests
are encouraged to relax and enjoy the peace and informality.
Bedrooms are available in a range of sizes and all are stylishly
decorated and thoughtfully equipped. Dining is certainly a
highlight of a stay here; the menus offer exciting dishes featuring
local produce.

Rooms 14 (3 GF) **S** £100-£170; **D** £100-£230 (incl. bkfst)*
Facilities FTV Fishing Xmas New Year Wi-fi **Parking** 25
Notes LB

Easton Court

★★★★ GUEST ACCOMMODATION

Easton Cross TQ13 8JL

☎ 01647 433469

e-mail: stay@easton.co.uk

web: www.easton.co.uk

dir: *1m E of Chagford at junct A382 & B3206*

PETS: Bedrooms Charges £2.50 per night **Grounds** on leads
Exercise area 0.5m **Facilities** feeding mat washing facs
walks info vet info **On Request** fridge access torch towels
Other charge for damage dogs allowed in 1 bedroom only
Resident Pet: Cassie (German Shepherd)

Set in Dartmoor National Park, the age of this picturesque house
is evident in the oak beams and thick granite walls. Guests can
come and go via a separate entrance. Relaxation is obligatory,
either in the lovely garden or in the snug surroundings of the
lounge. The delightful bedrooms all have country views.

Rooms 5 en suite (2 GF) **S** £45-£65; **D** £60-£80* **Facilities** STV
FTV tea/coffee Cen ht Wi-fi Golf 18 **Parking** 5 **Notes** No Children
10yrs

COMBE MARTIN Map 2 SS54

Newberry Valley Park *(SS576473)*

►►►

Woodlands EX34 0AT

☎ 01271 882334

e-mail: relax@newberryvalleypark.co.uk

dir: *M5 junct 27, A361 to North Aller rdbt. Right onto A399,*
through Combe Martin to sea. Left into site

PETS: Charges peak season £1-£2 per night **Public areas** disp
bin **Exercise area** exercise field (on lead only) **Facilities** walks
info vet info **Other** prior notice required disposal bags available
Resident Pets: Diesel (British Wolfdog), Amber (German
Shepherd), Teyha (Utonagan/Wolfdog cross)

Open Mar-Sep Last arrival 20.45hrs Last departure 10.00hrs

A family owned and run touring park on the edge of Combe
Martin, with all its amenities just five minutes walk away. The
park is set in a wooded valley with its own coarse fishing lake.
The safe beaches of Newberry and Combe Martin are reached by a
short footpath opposite the park entrance, where the South West
coast path is located. A 20 acre site with 120 touring pitches.

Notes No camp fires

ENGLAND

DARTMEET　Map 3 SX67

Hunter's Lodge B & B
★★★★ ⌂ GUEST ACCOMMODATION
PL20 6SG
☎ 01364 631173 & 07840 905624
e-mail: huntlodge@pobox.com
dir: *A38 at Ashburton onto B3357 to Dartmeet, Hunter's Lodge 1st right after 3rd bridge over Dart River*

PETS: Public areas Grounds Exercise area 2min walk **Facilities** washing facs walks info vet info **On Request** fridge access torch **Other** charge for damage dogs accepted in cottage accommodation only **Restrictions** no dangerous dogs (see page 7)

Situated between the East and West Dart rivers, Hunter's Lodge is at the very heart of Dartmoor. The house offers splendid views, and the bedrooms are attractively and comfortably presented. Breakfast features a wide range of fresh foods and local farm produce. German, French and Spanish are spoken here.

Rooms 3 rms (2 en suite) 1 annexe en suite (1 fmly) **S** £35-£45; **D** £50-£80* **Facilities** FTV tea/coffee Dinner available Cen ht Fishing Riding **Parking** 6 **Notes** LB Closed 24-26 Dec RS Mon & Tue closed in low season

Brimpts Farm
★★★ GUEST ACCOMMODATION
PL20 6SG
☎ 01364 631450 ▤ 01364 631179
e-mail: info@brimptsfarm.co.uk
web: www.brimptsfarm.co.uk
dir: *Dartmeet at E end of B3357, establishment signed on right at top of hill*

PETS: Bedrooms Stables Public areas Grounds Exercise area adjacent **Facilities** water bowl washing facs walks info vet info **On Request** fridge access torch towels **Resident Pets:** Kipper (Jack Russell), Fern & Bramble (cats)

A popular venue for walkers and lovers of the great outdoors, Brimpts is peacefully situated in the heart of Dartmoor and has been a Duchy of Cornwall farm since 1307. Bedrooms are simply furnished and many have wonderful views across Dartmoor. Dinner is served by arrangement. Additional facilities include a children's play area and sauna and spa. Brimpts is also home to the Dartmoor Pony Heritage Trust.

Rooms 10 en suite (2 fmly) (7 GF) **S** £32.50; **D** £55* **Facilities** TVL tea/coffee Dinner available Cen ht Licensed Wi-fi Sauna Pool Table **Parking** 50 **Notes** LB

DARTMOUTH　Map 3 SX85

The Dart Marina
★★★★ 80% ◉◉ HOTEL
Sandquay Rd TQ6 9PH
☎ 01803 832580 & 837120 ▤ 01803 835040
e-mail: reservations@dartmarina.com
web: www.dartmarina.com
dir: *A3122 from Totnes to Dartmouth. Follow road which becomes College Way, before Higher Ferry. Hotel sharp left in Sandquay Rd*

PETS: Bedrooms (4 GF) unattended **Charges** £10 per night **Public areas** except restaurants on leads disp bin **Exercise area** 30yds **Facilities** walks info vet info

Boasting a stunning riverside location with its own marina, this is a truly special place to stay. Bedrooms vary in style but all have wonderful views, and some have private balconies to sit and soak up the atmosphere. Stylish public areas take full advantage of the waterside setting with opportunities to dine alfresco. In addition to the Wildfire Bar & Bistro, the River Restaurant is the venue for accomplished cooking.

Rooms 49 (4 annexe) (4 fmly) (4 GF) **Facilities** Spa ⃝ Gym Canoeing Sailing Xmas New Year Wi-fi **Services** Lift **Parking** 50

Royal Castle
★★★ 80% HOTEL
11 The Quay TQ6 9PS
☎ 01803 833033 ▤ 01803 835445
e-mail: enquiry@royalcastle.co.uk
web: www.royalcastle.co.uk
dir: *In centre of town, overlooking Inner Harbour*

PETS: Bedrooms unattended **Charges** £20 per stay **Public areas** except restaurant **Exercise area** 800mtrs **Facilities** bedding dog chews pet sitting walks info vet info **On Request** access torch towels **Other** charge for damage well behaved dogs only **Resident Pet:** Stella (Springer Spaniel)

At the edge of the harbour, this imposing 17th-century former coaching inn is filled with charm and character. Bedrooms are well equipped and comfortable; many have harbour views. A choice of quiet seating areas is offered in addition to both the traditional and contemporary bars. A variety of eating options is available, including the main restaurant which has lovely views.

Rooms 25 (3 fmly) **S** £95-£105; **D** £140-£199 (incl. bkfst)* **Facilities** FTV ♫ Xmas New Year Wi-fi **Parking** 20 **Notes** LB

Stoke Lodge

★★★ 73% HOTEL

Stoke Fleming TQ6 0RA

☎ 01803 770523 📄 01803 770851

e-mail: mail@stokelodge.co.uk

web: www.stokelodge.co.uk

dir: *2m S A379*

PETS: Bedrooms (7 GF) unattended **Grounds** on leads
Exercise area 20yds **Facilities** walks info **On Request** fridge
access torch towels

This family-run hotel continues to attract returning guests and
is set in three acres of gardens and grounds with lovely views
across to the sea. A range of leisure facilities is offered including
both indoor and outdoor pools, along with a choice of comfortable
lounges. Bedrooms are pleasantly appointed. The restaurant
offers a choice of menus and an impressive wine list.

Rooms 25 (5 fmly) (7 GF) **S** £67.50-£73.50; **D** £95-£125 (incl.
bkfst)* **Facilities** FTV 🏊 ⚲ 🏓 Putt green Table tennis Pool &
snooker tables Sauna Xmas New Year Wi-fi **Parking** 50 **Notes** LB

DAWLISH　　　　　　　　　　　　　　　**Map 3 SX97**

Langstone Cliff

★★★ 78% HOTEL

Dawlish Warren EX7 0NA

☎ 01626 868000 📄 01626 868006

e-mail: reception@langstone-hotel.co.uk

web: www.langstone-hotel.co.uk

dir: *1.5m NE off A379 (Exeter road) to Dawlish Warren*

PETS: Bedrooms (10 GF) unattended **Public areas** except
restaurant & pool area **Grounds Exercise area** woods **Facilities**
walks info vet info **Resident Pets:** Buster & Sally (dogs)

A family owned and run hotel, the Langstone Cliff offers a range
of leisure, conference and function facilities. Bedrooms, many
with sea views and balconies, are spacious, comfortable and
well equipped. There are a number of attractive lounges and a
well-stocked bar. Dinner is served, often carvery style, in the
restaurant.

Rooms 66 (4 annexe) (52 fmly) (10 GF) **S** £78-£92; **D** £122-£166
(incl. bkfst)* **Facilities** STV FTV 🏊 ⚲ 🏊 Gym Table tennis Golf
practice area Hair & beauty salon Therapy room Ballroom ♫
Xmas New Year Wi-fi Child facilities **Services** Lift **Parking** 200
Notes LB

Golden Sands Holiday Park *(SX968784)*

Week Ln EX7 0LZ

☎ 01626 863099 📄 01626 867149

dir: *M5 junct 30 onto A379 signed Dawlish. After 6m pass small
harbour at Cockwood, signed on left in 2m*

PETS: Charges £2-£4 per night **Public areas** dogs must be kept
on leads **Facilities** food dog chews walks info vet info **Other**
please phone for further details of pet facilities **Restrictions** no
Rottweilers or dangerous breeds (see page 7)

Open 21 Mar-Oct Last arrival noon Last departure 10.00hrs

A holiday centre for all the family, offering a wide range of
entertainment. The small touring area is surrounded by mature
trees and hedges in a pleasant area, and visitors enjoy free use
of the licensed club, and heated swimming pools. Organised
children's activities are a popular feature, and the facilities of
neighbouring Peppermint Park are open to all visitors. A 12 acre
site with 28 touring pitches.

Lady's Mile Holiday Park *(SX968784)*

EX7 0LX

☎ 0845 0267252 📄 01626 888689

e-mail: info@ladysmile.co.uk

dir: *1m N of Dawlish on A379*

PETS: Charges £1.50-£3.50 per night **Public areas** disp bin
Exercise area fenced area **Facilities** food walks info vet info

Open 17 Mar-27 Oct Last arrival 20.00hrs Last departure
11.00hrs

A holiday site with all grass touring pitches, and plenty of
activities for everyone. Two swimming pools with waterslides, a
large adventure playground, 9-hole golf course, and a bar with
entertainment in high season all add to the enjoyment of a stay
here. Facilities are kept clean, and the surrounding beaches
are easily accessed. A 16 acre site with 243 touring pitches, 30
hardstandings and 43 statics.

ENGLAND

DAWLISH *continued*

Peppermint Park *(SX978788)*

Warren Rd EX7 0PQ
☎ 01626 863436 🖶 01626 866482
e-mail: peppermint@parkholidaysuk.com
dir: *From A379 at Dawlish follow signs for Dawlish Warren. Site 1m on left at bottom of hill*

PETS: Stables 2m **Charges** £2 per night **Public areas** except play area, swimming pool & club house disp bin **Exercise area** 750yds **Facilities** walks info vet info **Other** please phone for further details of pet facilities dog food available

Open Etr-end Oct Last arrival 18.00hrs Last departure 10.00hrs

Well managed, attractive park close to the coast, with excellent facilities including club and bar which are well away from pitches. Nestling close to sandy beaches, the park offers individually marked pitches on level terraces in pleasant, sheltered grassland. The many amenities include a heated swimming pool and water chute, coarse fishing and launderette. A 26 acre site with 180 touring pitches, 15 hardstandings and 82 statics.

Notes Families & couples only

Cofton Country Holidays *(SX967801)*

▶ ▶ ▶ ▶

Starcross EX6 8RP
☎ 01626 890111 & 0800 085 8649 🖶 01626 890160
e-mail: info@coftonholidays.co.uk
dir: *On A379 (Exeter/Dawlish road) 3m from Dawlish*

PETS: Charges £2.50-£4.75 per night **Public areas** except bar, shop & pool area **Exercise area** field for dog walking **Exercise area** woodland walk (0.25m) **Facilities** food food bowl water bowl walks info vet info **Other** prior notice required disposal bags available

Open all year rs Spring BH-mid Sep; Etr-end Oct Pool open; Bar & shop open Last arrival 20.00hrs Last departure 11.00hrs

Set in a rural location surrounded by spacious open grassland, with plenty of well-kept flower beds throughout the park. Most pitches overlook either the swimming pool complex or the fishing lakes and woodlands. An on-site pub serves drinks, meals and snacks for all the family, and a mini-market caters for most shopping needs. A 45 acre site with 450 touring pitches, 30 hardstandings and 76 statics.

Mounts Farm Touring Park *(SX757488)*

▶ ▶ ▶

The Mounts TQ9 7QJ
☎ 01548 521591
e mail: mounts.farm@lineone.net
dir: *A381 from Totnes towards Kingsbridge (NB ignore signs for East Allington). At 'Mounts', site 0.5m on left*

PETS: Public areas except play area disp bin **Exercise area** public footpaths adjacent **Facilities** food bowl water bowl dog chews cat treats scoop/disp bags washing facs walks info vet info **Resident Pets:** Smokie & Dot (cats)

Open 15 Mar-Oct Last arrival anytime Last departure anytime

A neat grassy park divided into four paddocks by mature natural hedges. Three of the paddocks house the tourers and campers, and the fourth is the children's play area. The laundry and well-stocked little shop are in converted farm buildings. A 7 acre site with 50 touring pitches.

Zeacombe House Caravan Park *(SS860240)*

▶ ▶ ▶ ▶

Blackerton Cross EX16 9JU
☎ 01398 341279
e-mail: enquiries@zeacombeadultretreat.co.uk
dir: *M5 junct 27, A361 signed Barnstaple, right at next rdbt onto A396 signed Dulverton & Minehead. In 5m at Exeter Inn left, 1.5m, at Black Cat junct left onto B3227 towards South Molton, site 7m on left*

PETS: Public areas except toilet block & shop on leads disp bin **Exercise area Facilities** washing facs walks info vet info **Other** prior notice required disposal bags availalble **Restrictions** no Pit Bull Terriers

Open 7 Mar-Oct Last arrival 21.00hrs Last departure noon

Set on the southern fringes of Exmoor National Park, this 'garden' park is nicely landscaped in a tranquil location, and enjoys panoramic views towards Exmoor. This adult-only park offers a choice of grass or hardstanding pitches, and a unique restaurant-style delivery service allows you to eat an evening meal in the comfort of your own unit. A 5 acre site with 50 touring pitches, 12 hardstandings.

EGGESFORD — Map 3 SS61

Fox & Hounds Country Hotel

★★★ 72% ⊛ HOTEL

EX18 7JZ

☎ 01769 580345   📠 01271 410200

e-mail: relax@foxandhoundshotel.co.uk

dir: *M5 junct 27, A361 towards Tiverton. Take B3137 signed Witheridge. After Nomans Land follow signs for Eggesford Station. Hotel 50mtrs up hill from station*

PETS: Bedrooms (1 GF) unattended **Stables** 2m **Charges** £10 per night £20 per week **Public areas** except restaurant **Grounds** disp bin **Exercise area** 50mtrs **Facilities** food (pre-bookable) food bowl water bowl bedding dog chews feeding mat scoop/disp bags leads pet sitting dog walking washing facs cage storage walks info vet info **On Request** fridge access torch towels **Resident Pet:** Charlie (Hungarian Viszla)

Situated midway between Exeter and Barnstaple, in the beautiful Taw Valley, this extensively developed hotel was originally a coaching inn dating back to the 1800s. Many of the comfortable, elegant bedrooms have lovely countryside views. Good cooking utilises excellent local produce and can be enjoyed in either restaurant or the convivial bar. For fishing enthusiasts, the hotel has direct access to the River Taw, and equipment and tuition can be provided if required.

Rooms 15 (4 fmly) (1 GF) **S** £60-£75; **D** £120-£180 (incl. bkfst)* **Facilities** FTV Fishing Health & beauty suite Xmas New Year Wi-fi Child facilities **Parking** 100 **Notes** LB

See advert on this page

EXETER — Map 3 SX99

Best Western Lord Haldon Country Hotel

★★★ 73% HOTEL

Dunchideock EX6 7YF

☎ 01392 832483   📠 01392 833765

e-mail: enquiries@lordhaldonhotel.co.uk

web: www.lordhaldonhotel.co.uk

dir: *M5 junct 31, 1st exit off A30, follow signs through Ide to Dunchideock*

PETS: Bedrooms Stables Charges £5 per night **Public areas** except restaurant & lounge **Grounds** disp bin **Exercise area Facilities** cage storage walks info vet info **On Request** fridge access torch towels **Other** charge for damage

Set amidst rural tranquillity, this attractive country house offers well-equipped, comfortable bedrooms; many have stunning views. The daily-changing menu features enjoyable dishes that use mostly locally sourced produce. Guests are assured of a warm welcome from the professional team of staff.

Rooms 23 (3 fmly) **Facilities** FTV Xmas New Year Wi-fi **Parking** 120

EXETER *continued*

Barton Cross Hotel & Restaurant

★★★ 71% ⚜ HOTEL

Huxham, Stoke Canon EX5 4EJ

☎ 01392 841245 📠 01392 841942

e-mail: bartonxhuxham@aol.com

dir: *0.5m off A396 at Stoke Canon, 3m N of Exeter*

PETS: Bedrooms (2 GF) unattended sign **Stables** 1m **Charges Grounds** on leads disp bin **Exercise area Facilities** walks info vet info **On Request** fridge access torch towels **Other** charge for damage **Resident Pets:** Alfie (German Shepherd), Purdy (Greyhound)

17th-century charm combined with 21st-century luxury perfectly sums up the appeal of this lovely country hotel. The bedrooms are spacious, tastefully decorated and well maintained. Public areas include the cosy first-floor lounge and the lounge/bar with its warming log fire. The restaurant offers a seasonally changing menu of consistently enjoyable cuisine.

Rooms 9 (2 fmly) (2 GF) (2 smoking) **Facilities** STV FTV Xmas New Year Wi-fi **Parking** 35 **Notes** LB

Rydon Farm *(SX999871)*

★★★★ FARMHOUSE

Woodbury EX5 1LB

☎ 01395 232341 📠 01395 232341 Mrs S Glanvill

e-mail: sallyglanvill@aol.com

dir: *A376 & B3179 from Exeter into Woodbury, right before 30mph sign*

PETS: Bedrooms Public areas except dining room **Grounds** disp bin **Exercise area** 20mtrs **Facilities** cage storage walks info vet info **On Request** fridge access torch towels

Dating from the 16th century, this Devon longhouse has been run by the same family for eight generations. A stay here is an opportunity to experience a farming lifestyle complete with patient cows steadfastly waiting to be milked. The spacious bedrooms are equipped with many useful extra facilities and one has a four-poster bed. There is a TV lounge and a delightful garden in which to relax. Breakfast is a treat, served in front of an inglenook fireplace.

Rooms 3 en suite (1 fmly) **S** £45-£55; **D** £74-£80* **Facilities** FTV TVL tea/coffee Cen ht **Parking** 3 **Notes** LB 450-acres dairy farm

Horn of Plenty

Ⓤ

PL19 8JD

☎ 01822 832528 📠 01822 834390

e-mail: enquiries@thehornofplenty.co.uk

web: www.thehornofplenty.co.uk

dir: *From Tavistock take A390 W for 3m. Right at Gulworthy Cross. In 400yds turn left, hotel in 400yds on right*

PETS: Bedrooms (4 GF) unattended **Charges** £10 per night **Grounds** disp bin **Facilities** walks info vet info **On Request** torch towels **Other** charge for damage

Currently the rating for this establishment is not confirmed. This may be due to a change of ownership or because it has only recently joined the AA rating scheme For further details please see the AA website: theAA.com

Rooms 10 (6 annexe) (3 fmly) (4 GF) **Parking** 25

Rock Inn

★★ 79% ⚜ HOTEL

TQ13 9XP

☎ 01364 661305 & 661465 📠 01364 661242

e-mail: inn@rock-inn.co.uk

web: www.rock-inn.co.uk

dir: *A38 onto A382 to Bovey Tracey, in 0.5m left onto B3387 to Haytor*

PETS: Bedrooms unattended **Charges** £5.50 per night **Exercise area** woods adjacent **Facilities** walks info vet info **Other** dogs allowed in 3 bedrooms only; not allowed in public rooms

Dating back to the 1750s, this former coaching inn is in a pretty hamlet on the edge of Dartmoor. Each named after a Grand National winner, the individually decorated bedrooms have some nice extra touches. Bars are full of character, with flagstone floors and old beams and offer a wide range of dishes, cooked with imagination.

Rooms 9 (2 fmly) **Facilities** FTV New Year **Parking** 20 **Notes** Closed 25-26 Dec

HOLSWORTHY Map 2 SS30

Headon Farm Caravan Site (SS367023)

► ► ►

Headon Farm, Hollacombe EX22 6NN
☎ 01409 254477 📠 0870 705 9052
e-mail: reader@headonfarm.co.uk
dir: Left off A388, in 0.75m into Staddon Rd, in 1m right into road signed Ashwater. In 0.75m left into road signed Hollacombe. Site on left in 50yds

PETS: Sep accom please phone for details **Stables** 2m **Public areas** on leads disp bin **Exercise area** adjacent fields (on or off lead); forest 3m **Facilities** washing facs dog grooming walks info vet info **Other** prior notice required kennels available locally; campsite on working farm with cattle so please seek guidance concerning exercising dogs etc **Resident Pets:** Joey (Border Collie), Treasure (Dartmoor pony)

Open all year Last arrival 19.00hrs Last departure noon

Set on a working farm in a quiet rural location. All pitches have extensive views of the Devon countryside, yet the park is only two and a half miles from the market town of Holsworthy, and within easy reach of roads to the coast and beaches of North Cornwall. A 2 acre site with 19 touring pitches, 5 hardstandings.

Notes Breathable groundsheets only 📵

Tamarstone Farm (SS286056)

► ►

Bude Rd, Pancrasweek EX22 7JT
☎ 01288 381734
e-mail: camping@tamarstone.co.uk
dir: A30 to Launceston, then B3254 towards Bude, approx 14m. Right onto A3072 towards Holsworthy, approx 1.5m, site on left

PETS: Charges £1 per night £6 per week **Public areas** except wildlife area & woods on leads **Exercise area** small field wth 'dog loo' **Facilities** washing facs vet info **Other** prior notice required **Resident Pets:** Candy & Toffee (cats), chickens

Open Etr-end Oct Last arrival 22.00hrs Last departure noon

Four acres of river-bordered meadow and woodland providing a wildlife haven for those who enjoy peace and seclusion. The wide, sandy beaches of Bude are just five miles away, and coarse fishing is provided free on site for visitors. A 1 acre site with 16 touring pitches and 1 static.

Notes 📵

Noteworthy Caravan and Campsite (SS303052)

►

Noteworthy, Bude Rd EX22 7JB
☎ 01409 253731
e-mail: enquiries@noteworthy-devon.co.uk
dir: On A3072 between Holsworthy & Bude. 3m from Holsworthy on right

PETS: Stables Charges 50p per night **Public areas** except children's play area disp bin **Exercise area** dog walk around field **Facilities** food bowl water bowl washing facs dog grooming walks info vet info **Other** prior notice required **Resident Pets:** cats, horses

Open all year

This campsite is owned by a friendly young couple with their own small children. There are good views from the quiet rural location, and simple toilet facilities. A 5 acre site with 5 touring pitches and 1 static.

Notes No open fires 📵

HONITON — Map 3 ST10

Combe House - Devon
★★★ ◎◎ COUNTRY HOUSE HOTEL

Gittisham EX14 3AD
☎ 01404 540400 🖹 01404 46004
e-mail: stay@combehousedevon.com
web: www.combehousedevon.com
dir: Off A30 1m S of Honiton, follow Gittisham Heathpark signs. From M5 exit 29 for Honiton. Exit Pattasons Cross

PETS: Bedrooms unattended sign **Stables Charges** £9 per night **Public areas** except restaurants **Grounds** on leads disp bin **Exercise area** 1m **Facilities** food bowl water bowl bedding dog chews cat treats feeding mat scoop/disp bags leads washing facs dog grooming cage storage walks info vet info **On Request** fridge access torch towels **Other** charge for damage cottage with dog room & walled garden dog welcome letter & gift, dog map, dog survival box **Resident Pet:** Maverick (cat)

Standing proudly in an elevated position, this Elizabethan mansion enjoys uninterrupted views over acres of its own woodland, meadow and pasture. Bedrooms are a blend of comfort and quality with relaxation being the ultimate objective; the Linen Room suite combines many original features with contemporary style. A range of atmospheric public rooms retain all the charm and history of the old house. Dining is equally impressive - a skilled kitchen brigade maximises the best of local and home-grown produce, augmented by excellent wines.

Rooms 16 (1 annexe) (1 fmly) **S** £159-£379; **D** £179-£399 (incl. bkfst)* **Facilities** Fishing ⤵ Xmas New Year Wi-fi Child facilities **Parking** 39 **Notes** LB Closed 3-18 Jan

Ridgeway Farm
★★★★ GUEST ACCOMMODATION

Awliscombe EX14 3PY
☎ 01404 841331 🖹 01404 841119
e-mail: jessica@ridgewayfarm.co.uk
dir: 3m NW of Honiton. A30 onto A373, through Awliscombe to near end of 40mph area, right opp Godford Farm, farm 500mtrs up narrow lane, sign on entrance

PETS: Bedrooms Stables Charges charge for horses (on request) **Public areas Grounds** disp bin **Exercise area** surrounding fields **Facilities** washing facs cage storage walks info vet info **On Request** fridge access torch **Other** charge for damage **Restrictions** no large dogs (eg Great Danes etc) **Resident Pets:** Chaos (Labrador), Lettuce (Border Terrier), 4 horses

This 18th-century farmhouse has a peaceful location on the slopes of Hembury Hill, and is a good base for exploring nearby Honiton and the east Devon coast. Renovations have brought the cosy accommodation to a high standard and the atmosphere is relaxed and homely. The proprietors and their family pets assure a warm welcome.

Rooms 2 en suite **S** £38-£42; **D** £60-£68 **Facilities** FTV TVL tea/coffee Dinner available Cen ht **Parking** 4 **Notes** LB ⊚

ILFRACOMBE — Map 2 SS54

Darnley
★★ 71% HOTEL

3 Belmont Rd EX34 8DR
☎ 01271 863955
e-mail: darnleyhotel@yahoo.co.uk
web: www.darnleyhotel.co.uk
dir: A361 to Barnstaple & Ilfracombe. Left at Church Hill, 1st left into Belmont Rd. 3rd entrance on left under walled arch

PETS: Bedrooms (2 GF) unattended **Public areas** except restaurant on leads **Grounds** on leads disp bin **Exercise area** 400yds **Facilities** dog chews feeding mat cage storage walks info vet info **On Request** fridge access torch towels **Resident Pet:** Pepsi (cat)

Standing in award-winning, mature gardens, with a wooded path to the High Street and the beach (about a five minute stroll

away), this former Victorian gentleman's residence offers friendly, informal service. The individually furnished and decorated bedrooms vary in size. Dinners feature honest home-cooking, with 'old fashioned puddings' always proving popular.

Rooms 10 (2 fmly) (2 GF) **S** £40; **D** £59-£78 (incl. bkfst)* **Facilities** FTV Xmas New Year Wi-fi **Parking** 10 **Notes** No children 3yrs

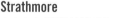

Strathmore

★ ★ ★ ★ GUEST ACCOMMODATION

57 St Brannock's Rd EX34 8EQ
☎ 01271 862248 🖹 01271 862248
e-mail: info@the-strathmore.co.uk
web: www.the-strathmore.co.uk
dir: A361 from Barnstaple to Ilfracombe, Strathmore 1.5m from Mullacot Cross entering Ilfracombe

PETS: **Bedrooms Stables** 1m **Charges** £6.50 (breakfast included) per night **Public areas** in bar & lounge only on leads **Grounds Exercise area** 0.25m **Facilities** water bowl dog chews scoop/disp bags leads washing facs cage storage walks info vet info **On Request** fridge access torch towels **Other** charge for damage **Restrictions** no Bullmastiffs, Staffordshire Bull Terriers, German Shepherds or Rottweilers **Resident Pet:** Holly (Sheltie)

Situated within walking distance of the town centre and beach, this charming Victorian property offers a very warm welcome. The attractive bedrooms are comfortably furnished, while public areas include a well-stocked bar, an attractive terraced garden, and an elegant breakfast room.

Rooms 8 en suite (3 fmly) **S** £35-£40; **D** £65-£80* **Facilities** FTV tea/coffee Cen ht Licensed Wi-fi **Parking** 7 **Notes** LB

Hele Valley Holiday Park *(SS533472)*

▶ ▶ ▶ ▶

Hele Bay EX34 9RD
☎ 01271 862460 🖹 01271 867926
e-mail: holidays@helevalley.co.uk
dir: M5 junct 27 onto A361. Through Barnstaple & Braunton to Ilfracombe. Then A399 towards Combe Martin. Follow brown Hele Valley signs. 400mtrs sharp right, then to T-junct. Reception on left

PETS: **Charges** £2.85 - £4 per night £20 per week **Public areas** except children's play area disp bin **Exercise area** dog walking area **Exercise area** direct access to walks from site **Facilities** food food bowl water bowl dog chews scoop/disp bags washing facs walks info vet info **Other** prior notice required **Resident Pets:** Anna (Rottweiler), Chalky, Maverick & Cody (cats)

Open Etr-Oct Last arrival 18.00hrs Last departure 11.00hrs

A deceptively spacious park set in a picturesque valley with glorious tree-lined hilly views from most pitches. High quality toilet facilities are provided, and the park is close to a lovely beach, with the harbour and other attractions of Ilfracombe just a mile away. A 17 acre site with 50 touring pitches, 18 hardstandings and 80 statics.

Notes Groups by arrangement only

ILSINGTON	Map 3 SX77

Ilsington Country House

★ ★ ★ 86% ◉◉ COUNTRY HOUSE HOTEL

Ilsington Village TQ13 9RR
☎ 01364 661452 🖹 01364 661307
e-mail: hotel@ilsington.co.uk
web: www.ilsington.co.uk
dir: M5 onto A38 to Plymouth. Exit at Bovey Tracey. 3rd exit from rdbt towards Ilsington, then 1st right. Hotel in 5m by Post Office

PETS: **Bedrooms** (6 GF) unattended sign **Stables Charges** £8 per night **Grounds** on leads disp bin **Exercise area** 5 min walk **Facilities** food (pre-bookable) food bowl water bowl dog chews cat treats scoop/disp bags leads washing facs cage storage walks info vet info **On Request** fridge access torch towels **Other** charge for damage dogs not allowed in Superior Rooms or Suites **Restrictions** well behaved dogs only **Resident Pet:** Bilbo (Springer Spaniel/Collie cross)

This friendly, family owned hotel, offers tranquillity and far-reaching views from its elevated position on the southern slopes of Dartmoor. The stylish suites and bedrooms, some on the ground floor, are individually furnished. The restaurant provides a stunning backdrop for the innovative, daily changing menus which feature local fish, meat and game.

Rooms 25 (4 fmly) (6 GF) **S** £85-£120; **D** £105-£210 (incl. bkfst) **Facilities** FTV 🏊 supervised ⛳ Gym Steam room Sauna Beauty treatments Xmas New Year Wi-fi **Services** Lift **Parking** 100 **Notes** LB

ENGLAND

Kennford International Caravan Park

(SX912857)

▶ ▶ ▶ ▶

EX6 7YN

☎ 01392 833046   📄 01392 833046

e-mail: ian@kennfordinternational.com

dir: *At end of M5, take A38, site signed at Kennford slip road*

PETS: Charges dog £1 per night **Public areas** on leads disp bin **Exercise area** small field provided **Exercise area** nearby **Facilities** walks info vet info **Resident Pets:** Jade (Rottweiler), Alfie (British Bulldog), Tigger (cat), guinea pigs

Open all year rs Winter arrival times change Last arrival 21.00hrs Last departure 11.00hrs

Screened by trees and shrubs from the A38, this park offers many pitches divided by hedging for privacy. A high quality toilet block complements the park's facilities. A good, centrally-located base for touring the coast and countryside of Devon, and Exeter is easily accessible via buses that stop nearby. A 15 acre site with 96 touring pitches and 53 statics.

Forest Glade Holiday Park *(ST101073)*

▶ ▶ ▶ ▶

EX15 2DT

☎ 01404 841381   📄 01404 841593

e-mail: enquiries@forest-glade.co.uk

dir: *Tent traffic: from A373 signed at Keepers Cottage Inn (2.5m E of M5 junct 28). Touring caravans: via Honiton/Dunkeswell road: please phone for access details*

PETS: Charges £2 per night **Public areas** except swimming pool, shop, toilets & play areas disp bin **Exercise area** surrounding woodland **Facilities** food dog chews washing facs walks info vet info **Other** prior notice required **Resident Pet:** Poppy (dog)

Open mid Mar-end Oct rs Low season limited shop hours Last arrival 21.00hrs Last departure noon

A quiet, attractive park in a forest clearing with well-kept gardens and beech hedge screening. One of the main attractions is the immediate proximity of the forest, which offers magnificent hillside walks with surprising views over the valleys. Please telephone for route details. A 15 acre site with 80 touring pitches, 40 hardstandings and 57 statics.

Notes Families and couples only

von Essen hotels
A PRIVATE COLLECTION
www.vonessenhotels.com

Lewtrenchard Manor

★★★ 🏵🏵🏵 HOTEL

EX20 4PN

☎ 01566 783256 & 783222   📄 01566 783332

e-mail: info@lewtrenchard.co.uk

web: www.vonessenhotels.co.uk

dir: *A30 from Exeter to Plymouth/Tavistock road. At T-junct turn right, then left onto old A30 (Lewdown road). Left in 6m signed Lewtrenchard*

PETS: Bedrooms (3 GF) **Charges** £15 per night **Public areas** except restaurant **Grounds** on leads disp bin **Exercise area** adjacent **Facilities** water bowl washing facs cage storage vet info **On Request** fridge access torch towels **Other** charge for damage

This Jacobean mansion was built in the 1600s, with many interesting architectural features, and is surrounded by its own idyllic grounds in a quiet valley close to the northern edge of Dartmoor. Public rooms include a fine gallery, as well as magnificent carvings and oak panelling. Meals can be taken in the dining room where imaginative and carefully prepared dishes are served using the best of Devon produce. Bedrooms are comfortably furnished and spacious.

Rooms 14 (2 fmly) (3 GF) **S** £105-£190; **D** £140-£220 (incl. bkfst)* **Facilities** FTV Fishing 🛶 Clay pigeon shooting Falconry Beauty therapies Xmas New Year Wi-fi **Parking** 50 **Notes** LB

Arundell Arms

★★★ 81% ◎◎ HOTEL

PL16 0AA
☎ 01566 784666   📠 01566 784494
e-mail: reservations@arundellarms.co.uk
dir: *1m off A30, 3m E of Launceston*

PETS: Bedrooms (4 GF) unattended **Stables** 1m **Charges** £5 per night plus food **Public areas** except restaurant **Grounds** disp bin **Exercise area** 0.5m **Facilities** food water bowl walks info vet info **On Request** fridge access torch **Other** dogs not allowed on river bank

This former coaching inn, boasting a long history, sits in the heart of a quiet Devon village. It is internationally famous for its country pursuits such as winter shooting and angling. The bedrooms offer individual style and comfort. Public areas are full of character with a relaxed atmosphere, particularly around the open log fire during colder evenings. Award-winning cuisine is a celebration of local produce.

Rooms 21 (4 GF) **Facilities** STV Fishing Skittle alley Game shooting (in winter) Fly fishing school New Year Wi-fi **Parking** 70 **Notes** LB Closed 3 days Xmas

Tors Hotel

★★★ 71% HOTEL

EX35 6NA
☎ 01598 753236   📠 01598 752544
e-mail: info@torshotellynmouth.co.uk
web: www.torslynmouth.co.uk
dir: *Adjacent to A39 on Countisbury Hill just before entering Lynmouth from Minehead*

PETS: Bedrooms unattended **Charges** £5.50 per night **Public areas** except restaurant, luxury suite & pool area **Grounds** disp bin **Exercise area** surrounding woodland **Facilities** food (pre-bookable) food bowl water bowl walks info vet info **On Request** fridge access torch towels

In an elevated position overlooking Lynmouth Bay, this friendly hotel is set in five acres of woodland. The majority of the bedrooms benefit from the superb views, as do the public areas which are generously proportioned and well presented. A fixed-price menu is offered with local, seasonal produce to the fore.

Rooms 31 (6 fmly) **S** £50-£205; **D** £80-£264 (incl. bkfst)*
Facilities ⅋ Table tennis Pool table Xmas New Year Wi-fi **Services** Lift **Parking** 40 **Notes** Closed 4-31 Jan RS Oct-Apr

Bath Hotel

★★ 71% HOTEL

Sea Front EX35 6EL
☎ 01598 752238   📠 01598 753894
e-mail: info@bathhotellynmouth.co.uk
dir: *M5 junct 25, follow A39 to Lynmouth*

PETS: Bedrooms unattended **Public areas** except restaurant **Exercise area** 200yds **Facilities** food (pre-bookable) food bowl water bowl bedding walks info vet info **On Request** fridge access torch towels

This well established, friendly hotel, situated near the harbour offers lovely views from the attractive, sea-facing bedrooms and is an excellent starting point for scenic walks. There are two lounges and a sun lounge. The restaurant menu is extensive and features daily-changing specials that make good use of fresh produce and local fish.

Rooms 22 (9 fmly) **S** £40-£50; **D** £75-£105 (incl. bkfst)*
Parking 12 **Notes** Closed Dec & Jan

ENGLAND

River Lyn View

★ ★ ★ GUEST ACCOMMODATION
26 Watersmeet Rd EX35 6EP
☎ 01598 753501
e-mail: riverlynview@aol.com
dir: *On A39, 200yds past St John's church on right*

PETS: Bedrooms unattended **Public areas Facilities** water bowl cage storage walks info vet info **On Request** fridge access torch towels

A warm welcome awaits at River Lyn View, just a stroll from the picturesque harbour at Lynmouth. Exmoor National Park is a short drive away or you can enjoy a walk along the East Lyn River's tranquil tree-lined banks. Much of the accommodation overlooks the river; all bedrooms are comfortable and include a good range of extras. There is a choice of lounges, and a hearty breakfast is served at individual tables in the open-plan dining area.

Rooms 4 en suite (2 fmly) **S** £40-£42; **D** £54-£60 **Facilities** FTV TVL tea/coffee Cen ht **Parking** 2

LYNTON   **Map 3 SS74**

Lynton Cottage

★ ★ ★ 75% ◎◎ HOTEL
Northwalk EX35 6ED
☎ 01598 752342 🖨 01598 754016
e-mail: mail@lyntoncottage.co.uk
dir: *M5 junct 23 to Bridgwater, then A39 to Minehead & follow signs to Lynton. 1st right after church & right again*

PETS: Bedrooms (1 GF) unattended **Public areas** except restaurant on leads **Grounds** on leads disp bin **Exercise area** beach 1.5m **Facilities** water bowl walks info vet info **Other** charge for damage **Resident Pets:** Chloe & Charlie (cats)

Boasting breathtaking views, this wonderfully relaxing and friendly hotel stands some 500 feet above the sea and makes a peaceful hideaway. Bedrooms are individual in style and size, with the added bonus of the wonderful views; public areas have charm and character in equal measure. Accomplished cuisine is on offer with dishes created with care and skill.

Rooms 16 (1 fmly) (1 GF) **Facilities** FTV Wi-fi **Parking** 20
Notes Closed 2 Dec-12 Jan

Channel View Caravan and Camping Park
(SS724482)

▶ ▶ ▶ ▶

Manor Farm EX35 6LD
☎ 01598 753349 🖨 01598 752777
e-mail: relax@channel-view.co.uk
dir: *A39 E for 0.5m on left past Barbrook*

PETS: Charges £15 per night **Public areas Exercise area** exercise field provided **Facilities** food washing facs walks info vet info **Other** prior notice required

Open 15 Mar-15 Nov Last arrival 22.00hrs Last departure noon

On the top of the cliffs overlooking the Bristol Channel, a well-maintained park on the edge of Exmoor, and close to both Lynton and Lynmouth. Pitches can be selected from a hidden hedged area, or with panoramic views over the coast. A 6 acre site with 76 touring pitches, 15 hardstandings and 31 statics.

Notes Groups by prior arrangement only

Sunny Lyn Holiday Park *(SS719486)*

▶ ▶ ▶

Lynbridge EX35 6NS
☎ 01598 753384 🖨 01598 753273
e-mail: info@caravandevon.co.uk
dir: *M5 junct 27, A361 to South Molton. Right onto A399 to Blackmoor Gate, right onto A39, left onto B3234 towards Lynmouth. Site 1m on right*

PETS: Stables approx 2m **Charges** dog £2.50 per night, other animals negotiable **Public areas** disp bin **Exercise area** National Trust woodland adjacent **Facilities** food food bowl water bowl bedding leads walks info vet info **Other** prior notice required disposal bags available

Open Mar-Oct Last arrival 20.00hrs Last departure 11.00hrs

Set in a sheltered riverside location in a wooded combe within a mile of the sea, in Exmoor National Park. This family-run park offers good facilities including an excellent café. A 4.5 acre site with 9 touring pitches, 5 hardstandings and 7 statics.

Notes No wood fires

Cookshayes Country Guest House

★★★ GUEST HOUSE

33 Court St TQ13 8LG

☎ 01647 440374 ≣ 01647 440453

e-mail: cookshayes@aol.com

web: www.cookshayes.co.uk

dir: *A38 onto A382 to Moretonhampstead. Take B3212 towards Princetown. Cookshayes 400yds on left*

PETS: Bedrooms unattended sign **Public areas** except restaurant **Grounds** disp bin **Exercise area Facilities** scoop/disp bags washing facs walks info vet info **On Request** fridge access torch towels **Other** charge for damage **Resident Pet:** Snitchy (Schnauzer cross)

A genuine welcome awaits at this secluded Victorian house, a perfect base for exploring the delights of Dartmoor. Bedrooms are comfortably furnished and well appointed, and one has a four-poster bed. The smart dining room is the venue for scrumptious breakfasts and excellent dinners, where local produce is cooked with skill and enthusiasm. Additional facilities include a cosy lounge, which overlooks the attractive garden.

Rooms 7 rms (5 en suite) (2 pri facs) (1 fmly) (1 GF) **S** £25-£30; **D** £50-£55 **Facilities** TVL tea/coffee Dinner available Cen ht Licensed **Parking** 10 **Notes** LB No Children 5yrs

 Twitchen House Holiday Park
(SS465447)

Station Rd EX34 7ES

☎ 01647 870343 ≣ 01271 870089

e-mail: goodtimes@woolacombe.com

dir: *From Mullacott Cross rdbt take B3343 (Woolacombe road) to Turnpike Cross junct. Take right fork, site 1.5m on left*

PETS: Charges dogs £1.50 per night (short break £20) **Public areas** except main clubhouse & pool areas **Exercise area** on site & path to beach **Facilities** scoop/disp bags **Other** contact site for further details of facilities & charges for pets

Open Mar-Oct rs mid May & mid Sep outdoor pool closed Last arrival mdnt Last departure 10.00hrs

A very attractive park with good leisure facilities. Visitors can use the amenities at all three of Woolacombe Bay holiday parks, and a bus service connects them all with the beach. The touring features pitches offering either sea views or a country and woodland outlook. A 45 acre site with 334 touring pitches, 110 hardstandings and 278 statics.

Warcombe Farm Caravan & Camping Park
(SS478445)

►►►►

Station Rd EX34 7EJ

☎ 01271 870690 & 07774 428770 ≣ 01271 871070

e-mail: info@warcombefarm.co.uk

dir: *On B3343 towards Woolacombe turn right towards Mortehoe. Site less than 2m on right*

PETS: Charges £1.65 per night **Public areas** except play area & toilets disp bin **Exercise area** 14-acre field provided **Facilities** food food bowl water bowl dog chews cat treats scoop/disp bags leads walks info vet info **Other** prior notice required

Open 15 Mar-Oct rs Low season no take away food Last arrival 21.00hrs Last departure 11.00hrs

Extensive views over the Bristol Channel can be enjoyed from the open areas of this attractive park, while other pitches are sheltered in paddocks with maturing trees. The superb sandy beach with Blue Flag award at Woolacombe Bay is only 1.5m away, and there is a fishing lake with direct access from some pitches. A 19 acre site with 250 touring pitches, 10 hardstandings.

Notes No groups unless booked in advance

Easewell Farm Holiday Park & Golf Club
(SS465455)

►►►

EX34 7EH

☎ 01271 870343 ≣ 01271 870089

e-mail: goodtimes@woolacombe.com

dir: *Take B3343 to Mortehoe. Turn right at fork, site 2m on right*

PETS: Charges Public areas except main clubhouse & pool areas disp bin **Exercise area** adjacent to camping & touring pitches **Other** please contact site for further details of facilities & charges for pets **Resident Pet:** Bonny (Golden Retriever)

Open Mar-Oct rs Etr Last arrival 22.00hrs Last departure 10.00hrs

A peaceful clifftop park with full facility pitches for caravans and motorhomes, and superb views. The park offers a range of activities including indoor bowling and a 9-hole golf course, and all the facilities of the three other nearby holiday centres within this group are open to everyone. A 17 acre site with 302 touring pitches, 50 hardstandings and 1 static.

MORTEHOE *continued*

North Morte Farm
Caravan & Camping Park *(SS462455)*

►►►

North Morte Rd EX34 7EG
☎ 01271 870381   📠 01271 870115
e-mail: info@northmortefarm.co.uk
dir: *From B3343 into Mortehoe, right at post office. Site 500yds on left*

PETS: Charges (seasonal) £1.50-£2 per night Public areas on leads disp bin Exercise area dog areas provided Exercise area beach 500yds Facilities food dog chews scoop/disp bags leads walks info vet info

Open Apr-Oct Last arrival 22.30hrs Last departure noon

Set in spectacular coastal countryside close to National Trust land and 500 yards from Rockham Beach. This attractive park is very well run and maintained by friendly family owners, and the quaint village of Mortehoe with its cafés, shops and pubs, is just a 5-minute walk away. A 22 acre site with 180 touring pitches, 18 hardstandings and 73 statics.

Notes No large groups

NEWTON ABBOT	Map 3 SX87

Bulleigh Park *(SX860660)*

★★★★ 🏠 FARMHOUSE

Ipplepen TQ12 5UA
☎ 01803 872254   📠 01803 872254 Mrs A Dallyn
e-mail: bulleigh@lineone.net
dir: *3.5m S of Newton Abbot. Off A381 at Parkhill Cross by petrol station for Compton, continue 1m, signed*

PETS: Bedrooms Charges dog £5 per night £30 per week Public areas except restaurant & lounge Grounds disp bin Exercise area woods 0.5m Facilities food (pre-bookable) food bowl water bowl dog chews scoop/disp bags leads washing facs cage storage walks info vet info On Request fridge access torch towels Other charge for damage dogs allowed in certain bedrooms only Resident Pet: Nippy (Jack Russell cross)

Bulleigh Park is a working farm, producing award-winning Aberdeen Angus beef. The owners have also won an award for green tourism by reducing the impact of the business on the environment. Expect a friendly welcome at this family home set in glorious countryside, where breakfasts are notable for the wealth of fresh, local and home-made produce, and the porridge is cooked using a secret recipe.

Rooms 2 en suite 1 annexe en suite (1 fmly) S £42-£45;
D £72-£80* Facilities FTV TVL tea/coffee Cen ht Wi-fi Parking 6
Notes LB Closed Dec-1 Feb 60 acres beef/sheep/hens

Dornafield *(SX838683)*

►►►►►

Dornafield Farm, Two Mile Oak TQ12 6DD
☎ 01803 812732   📠 01803 812032
e-mail: enquiries@dornafield.com
dir: *Take A381 (Newton Abbot-Totnes) for 2m. At Two Mile Oak Inn turn right, then left at x-roads in 0.5m to site on right*

PETS: Charges dog £1-£2 per night Public areas disp bin Exercise area 2 exercise areas provided Facilities food food bowl water bowl dog chews cat treats washing facs walks info vet info Other prior notice required disposal bags available (free of charge)

Open 17 Mar-4 Jan Last arrival 22.00hrs Last departure 11.00hrs

An immaculately kept park in a tranquil wooded valley between Dartmoor and Torbay, offering either de-luxe or fully-serviced pitches. A lovely 15th-century farmhouse sits at the entrance, and the park is divided into three separate areas, served by two superb, ultra-modern toilet blocks. The friendly family owners are always available. A 30 acre site with 135 touring pitches, 119 hardstandings.

Ross Park *(SX845671)*

►►►►►

Park Hill Farm, Ipplepen TQ12 5TT
☎ 01803 812983   📠 01803 812983
e-mail: enquiries@rossparkcaravanpark.co.uk
dir: *Off A381, 3m from Newton Abbot towards Totnes, signed opposite Texaco garage towards 'Woodland'*

PETS: Public areas except restaurant disp bin Exercise area 3 fields & orchard Facilities food washing facs walks info vet info Other dog shower room Restrictions dog breeds must be approved by manager Resident Pets: Monty & Zinzan (Labradors)

Open Mar-2 Jan rs Nov-Jan & 1st 3 wks of Mar restaurant/bar closed (ex Xmas/New Year) Last arrival 21.00hrs Last departure 10.00hrs

A top-class park in every way, with large secluded pitches, high quality toilet facilities and lovely floral displays throughout. The beautiful tropical conservatory also offers a breathtaking show of colour. This very rural park enjoys superb views of Dartmoor, and good quality meals to suit all tastes and pockets are served in the restaurant. A 32 acre site with 110 touring pitches, 94 hardstandings.

Notes Bikes, skateboards/scooters only allowed on leisure field

OKEHAMPTON — Map 2 SX59

White Hart Hotel
★★ 71% HOTEL
Fore St EX20 1HD
☎ 01837 52730 & 54514 📠 01837 53979
e-mail: enquiry@thewhitehart-hotel.com
dir: *In town centre, adjacent to lights, car park at rear of hotel*

PETS: **Bedrooms** unattended **Stables Charges** £5 per night
Public areas except restaurant on leads disp bin **Exercise area**
200yds **Facilities** cage storage walks info vet info **Other**
charge for damage

Dating back to the 17th century and situated on the edge of the
Dartmoor National Park, the White Hart offers modern facilities.
Bedrooms are well equipped and spacious. Locally sourced,
home-cooked food is on offer in the bars and the Courtney
Restaurant; or guests can choose to eat in Vines Pizzeria. Wi-fi is
available in public areas.

Rooms 19 (2 fmly) **Facilities** FTV Xmas Wi-fi **Parking** 20

OTTERY ST MARY — Map 3 SY19

Fluxton Farm
★★ BED AND BREAKFAST
Fluxton EX11 1RJ
☎ 01404 812818 📠 01404 814843
web: www.fluxtonfarm.co.uk
dir: *2m SW of Ottery St Mary. B3174, W from Ottery over river, left,
next left to Fluxton*

PETS: **Bedrooms Public areas** except dining room & lounge
Grounds on leads **Exercise area** opposite **Facilities** food bowl
water bowl cat treats feeding mat washing facs cage storage
walks info vet info **On Request** fridge access **Other** cat pens
available cat food available on request **Resident Pets:** the farm
is a cat rescue sanctuary; ducks, chickens

A haven for cat lovers, Fluxton Farm offers comfortable
accommodation with a choice of lounges and a large garden,
complete with pond and ducks. Set in peaceful farmland four
miles from the coast, this 16th-century longhouse has a wealth of
beams and open fireplaces.

Rooms 7 en suite **S** £24.50-£30; **D** £56-£60* **Facilities** FTV TVL
tea/coffee Cen ht **Parking** 15 **Notes** LB No Children 8yrs RS Nov-
Apr pre-booked guests only, wknds only 🐾

PAIGNTON — Map 3 SX86

The Commodore
★★★★ GUEST ACCOMMODATION
14 Esplanade Rd TQ4 6EB
☎ 01803 553107 📠 01803 231186
e-mail: info@commodorepaignton.com
web: www.commodorepaignton.com
dir: *A379 to Paignton, A3022 to seafront. Pass multiplex cinema,
property on right*

PETS: **Bedrooms Charges** £5 per night £35 per week
Public areas on leads **Exercise area** 20mtrs **Facilities** food
(pre-bookable) food bowl water bowl bedding leads washing
facs walks info vet info **On Request** torch towels **Other** charge
for damage **Resident Pet:** Robbie (Springer Spaniel)

With an excellent seafront location, all the popular attractions
of the town including shopping, the harbour, cinema and
restaurants, are all just a short stroll from this family-run
accommodation. Bedrooms are generally spacious and well
furnished and some enjoy sea views. Guests are welcome to use
the lounge and a small downstairs bar is also available.

Rooms 11 en suite (2 fmly) (3 GF) **S** £35-£45; **D** £60-£84*
Facilities FTV TVL tea/coffee Cen ht Licensed **Parking** 10
Notes LB

PAIGNTON *continued*

The Park

★★★ GUEST ACCOMMODATION

Esplanade Rd TQ4 6BQ
☎ 01803 557856 🖷 01803 555626
e-mail: stay@parkhotel.me.uk
web: www.theparkhotel.net
dir: *On Paignton seafront, nearly opposite pier*

PETS: Bedrooms Charges £2 per night £10 per week **Grounds**
on leads **Exercise area** seafront 50yds **Facilities** cage storage
walks info **On Request** fridge access **Other** charge for damage

This large establishment has a prominent position on the seafront
with excellent views of Torbay. The pleasant bedrooms are all
spacious and available in a number of options, and several have
sea views. Entertainment is provided on some evenings in the
lounge. Dinner and breakfast are served in the spacious dining
room, which overlooks the attractive front garden.

Rooms 47 en suite (5 fmly) (3 GF) **Facilities** tea/coffee Dinner
available Cen ht Lift Licensed Wi-fi Pool Table **Parking** 38
Notes LB

The Wentworth Guest House

Ⓤ

18 Youngs Park Rd, Goodrington TQ4 6BU
☎ 01803 557843
e-mail: enquiries@wentworthguesthouse.co.uk
dir: *Through Paignton on A378, 1m left at rdbt, sharp right onto
Roundham Rd, right & right again onto Youngs Park Rd*

PETS: Bedrooms unattended **Charges** £4 per night
Exercise area park opposite, beach 250mtrs **Facilities** food
bowl water bowl bedding feeding mat walks info vet info
On Request torch **Other** charge for damage pets allowed in 1
bedroom only **Restrictions** well behaved, small to meduim size
dogs only **Resident Pets:** Blue (Staffordshire Bull Terrier cross),
Bungle (cat)

At the time of going to press the rating for this establishment was
not confirmed. This may be due to a change of ownership or because
it has only recently joined the AA rating scheme. For further details
please see the AA website: theAA.com

Rooms 10 en suite (2 fmly) (1 GF) **S** £26-£39; **D** £50-£68*
Facilities FTV TVL tea/coffee Cen ht Licensed Wi-fi **Parking** 4

Best Western Duke of Cornwall

★★★ 78% ⊛ HOTEL

Millbay Rd PL1 3LG
☎ 01752 275850 & 275855 🖷 01752 275854
e-mail: enquiries@thedukeofcornwall.co.uk
web: www.thedukeofcornwall.co.uk
dir: *Follow city centre, then Plymouth Pavilions Conference &
Leisure Centre signs. Hotel opposite Plymouth Pavilions*

PETS: Bedrooms unattended sign **Charges** disp bin
Exercise area park 50yds **Facilities** food bowl water bowl
bedding walks info vet info **On Request** fridge access torch
towels

A historic landmark, this city centre hotel is conveniently located.
The spacious public areas include a popular bar, comfortable
lounge and multi-functional ballroom. Bedrooms, many with
far reaching views, are individually styled and comfortably
appointed. The range of dining options includes meals in the bar,
or the elegant dining room for a more formal atmosphere.

Rooms 71 (6 fmly) (20 smoking) **Facilities** STV FTV Xmas New
Year Wi-fi **Services** Lift **Parking** 50

Novotel Plymouth

★★★ 67% HOTEL

Marsh Mills PL6 8NH
☎ 01752 221422 🖷 01752 223922
e-mail: h0508@accor.com
web: www.novotel.com
dir: *Exit A38 at Marsh Mills, follow Plympton signs, hotel on left*

PETS: Bedrooms (18 GF) **Charges** £10 per night **Public areas**
except restaurant on leads **Grounds** on leads **Exercise area**
0.25m **Facilities** water bowl cage storage walks info vet info
On Request torch towels **Other** charge for damage

Conveniently located on the outskirts of the city, close to
Marsh Mills roundabout, this modern hotel offers good value
accommodation. All rooms are spacious and designed with
flexibility for family use. Public areas are open-plan with meals
available throughout the day in either the Garden Brasserie, the
bar, or from room service.

Rooms 100 (17 fmly) (18 GF) **S** £49-£70; **D** £49-£75*
Facilities STV FTV ⚲ Xmas New Year **Services** Lift **Parking** 140
Notes LB

The Cranbourne

★★★ GUEST ACCOMMODATION

278-282 Citadel Rd, The Hoe PL1 2PZ

☎ 01752 263858 & 224646 & 661400 📄 01752 263858

e-mail: cran.hotel@virgin.net

web: www.cranbournehotel.co.uk

dir: *Behind the Promenade, Plymouth Hoe*

PETS: Bedrooms Public areas except dining room on leads **Exercise area** 60yds **Facilities** scoop/disp bags leads walks info vet info **On Request** fridge access towels **Other** pets by prior arrangement only

This attractive Georgian terrace house is located just a short walk from The Hoe, The Barbican and the city centre. Bedrooms are practically furnished and well equipped. Hearty breakfasts are served in the elegant dining room and there is also a cosy bar.

Rooms 40 rms (28 en suite) (5 fmly) (2 GF) **S** £27-£40; **D** £48-£65* **Facilities** FTV TVL tea/coffee Cen ht Licensed Wi-fi **Parking** 14

The Firs Guest Accommodation

★★★ GUEST ACCOMMODATION

13 Pier St, West Hoe PL1 3BS

☎ 01752 262870 & 300010

e-mail: thefirsguesthouse@hotmail.co.uk

PETS: Bedrooms Charges Public areas except dining room on leads **Exercise area** 100yds **Facilities** walks info vet info **On Request** fridge access torch **Resident Pets:** Rosie, Jessica, Tabitha & Fluffy (cats)

A well-located and-well established house on the West Hoe with convenient on-street parking. Friendly owners and comfortable rooms make it a popular destination.

Rooms 7 rms (2 en suite) (2 fmly) **Facilities** FTV tea/coffee Dinner available Cen ht

The Lamplighter

★★★ GUEST ACCOMMODATION

103 Citadel Rd, The Hoe PL1 2RN

☎ 01752 663855 & 07793 360815 📄 01752 228139

e-mail: stay@lamplighterplymouth.co.uk

web: www.lamplighterplymouth.co.uk

dir: *Near war memorial*

PETS: Bedrooms Charges £5 minimum per night **Public areas** except dining room on leads **Exercise area** 50mtrs **Facilities** cage storage walks info vet info **Other** charge for damage

With easy access to The Hoe, The Barbican and the city centre, this comfortable house provides a good base for leisure or business. Bedrooms, including family rooms, are light and airy and furnished to a consistent standard. Breakfast is served in the dining room, which has an adjoining lounge area.

Rooms 9 rms (7 en suite) (2 pri facs) (2 fmly) **S** £30-£35; **D** £50-£55 **Facilities** FTV TVL tea/coffee Cen ht Wi-fi **Parking** 4

PRINCETOWN   Map 2 SX57

The Plume of Feathers Inn (SX592734)

►►

PL20 6QQ

☎ 01822 890240

dir: *Site accessed directly from B3212 rdbt (beside Plume of Feathers Inn) in centre of Princetown*

PETS: Public areas except carvery & B&B disp bin **Exercise area** paddock & field **Exercise area** Dartmoor National Park adjacent **Facilities** food food bowl water bowl dog chews walks info vet info **Other** prior notice required pet menu available at the bar **Resident Pets:** Bonnie (West Highland Terrier), Jeannie (Border Terrier), Dribbles (cat)

Open all year Last arrival 23.30hrs Last departure 11.00hrs

Set amidst the rugged beauty of Dartmoor not far from the notorious prison, this campsite boasts good toilet facilities and all the amenities of the inn. The Plume of Feathers is Princetown's oldest building, and serves all day food in an atmospheric setting - try the 'camp and breakfast' deal that's on offer. The campsite is mainly for tents. A 3 acre site with 85 touring pitches.

Notes No caravans

SALCOMBE — Map 3 SX73

Tides Reach

★★★ 82% ⊛ HOTEL

South Sands TQ8 8LJ

☎ 01548 843466   📄 01548 843954

e-mail: enquire@tidesreach.com

web: www.tidesreach.com

dir: *Off A38 at Buckfastleigh to Totnes. Then A381 to Salcombe, follow signs to South Sands*

PETS: Bedrooms unattended **Charges** £8.50 per night **Public areas** except bar, restaurant & 2 lounges on leads **Grounds** on leads disp bin **Exercise area** adjacent **Facilities** food (pre-bookable) bedding cage storage walks info vet info **On Request** torch towels **Other** charge for damage dogs accepted by prior arrangement only; please phone for further details of pet facilities

Superbly situated at the water's edge, this personally run, friendly hotel has splendid views of the estuary and beach. Bedrooms, many with balconies, are spacious and comfortable. In the bar and lounge, attentive service can be enjoyed along with the view, and the Garden Room restaurant serves appetising and accomplished cuisine.

Rooms 32 **S** £82-£156; **D** £70-£162 (incl. bkfst & dinner)*
Facilities Spa STV FTV ⊗ supervised Gym Squash Windsurfing Sailing Kayaking Scuba diving Hair & beauty treatment Wi-fi **Services** Lift **Parking** 100 **Notes** LB No children 8yrs Closed Dec-early Feb

Bolberry House Farm Caravan & Camping Park *(SX687395)*

►►►

Bolberry TQ7 3DY

☎ 01548 561251

dir: *At Malborough on A381 turn right signed Hope Cove/Bolberry. Take left fork after village signed Soar/Bolberry. 0.6m right again. Site signed in 0.5m*

PETS: Charges high season £1 per night **Public areas** except toilet block on leads disp bin **Exercise area** separate dog walk & exercise paddock **Exercise area** National Trust coastal path adjacent **Other** disposal bags available pets must not be left unattended

Open Etr-Oct Last arrival 20.00hrs Last departure 11.30hrs

A very popular park in a peaceful setting on a coastal farm with sea views, fine cliff walks and nearby beaches. Discount in low season for senior citizens. A shop is open in the high season. A 6 acre site with 70 touring pitches and 10 statics.

Notes ⊗

SAMPFORD PEVERELL — Map 3 ST01

Minnows Touring Park *(SS042148)*

►►►►

Holbrook Ln EX16 7EN

☎ 01884 821770   📄 01884 829199

dir: *M5 junct 27 take A361 signed Tiverton & Barnstaple. In 600yds take 1st slip road, then right over bridge, site ahead*

PETS: Charges 2 dogs free, £1 per extra dog per night **Public areas** except in buildings **Exercise area** canal towpath (with disposal bins) adjacent **Facilities** walks info vet info **Other** water at reception, dog ties by buildings

Open 7 Mar-7 Nov Last arrival 20.00hrs Last departure 11.30hrs

A small, well-sheltered park, peacefully located amidst fields and mature trees. The toilet facilities are of a high quality in keeping with the rest of the park, and there is a good laundry. The park has direct gated access to the canal towpath. A 5.5 acre site with 59 touring pitches, 59 hardstandings and 1 static.

Notes No cycling, no groundsheets on grass

Coast View Holiday Park *(SX935716)*

Torquay Rd TQ14 0BG

☎ 01626 872392   🖷 01626 872719

e-mail: info@coastview.co.uk

dir: *M5 junct 31, A38 then A380 towards Torquay. Then A381 towards Teignmouth. Right in 4m at lights, over Shaldon Bridge. 0.75m, up hill, site on right*

PETS: Charges £2.50 per night £30 per week Public areas except swimming pool, shop & restaurant disp bin Exercise area allocated dog walking area Facilities walks info vet info

Open 15 Mar-1 Nov Last arrival 21.00hrs Last departure 10.30hrs

This park has stunning sea views from its spacious pitches. The family-run park has a full entertainment programme every night for all the family, plus outdoor and indoor activities for children, and will appeal to lively families. A 17 acre site with 110 touring pitches, 6 hardstandings and 86 statics.

Royal Glen

★★★ 74% HOTEL

Glen Rd EX10 8RW

☎ 01395 513221 & 513456   🖷 01395 514922

e-mail: info@royalglenhotel.co.uk

dir: *A303 to Honiton, A375 to Sidford, follow seafront signs, right onto esplanade, right at end into Glen Rd*

PETS: Bedrooms (3 GF) unattended Charges Grounds on leads Facilities walks info

This historic 17th-century, Grade I listed hotel has been owned by the same family for several generations. The comfortable bedrooms are furnished in period style. Guests may use the well-maintained gardens and a heated indoor pool, and can enjoy well-prepared food in the elegant dining room.

Rooms 32 (3 fmly) (3 GF) S £47-£68; D £94-£136 (incl. bkfst)* Facilities STV 🏊 Services Lift Parking 22 Notes LB Closed Dec-1 Feb

Kingswood & Devoran Hotel

★★ 80% HOTEL

The Esplanade EX10 8AX

☎ 01395 516367 & 0800 481731   🖷 01395 513185

e-mail: kingswoodanddevoran@hotels-sidmouth.co.uk

web: www.hotels-sidmouth.co.uk

dir: *M5 junct 30, A3052 signed Sidmouth on right, follow Station Rd down to Esplanade*

PETS: Bedrooms (2 GF) unattended Charges £6 per night

This seafront hotel has been given a new look after joining the two separate establishments in to one. The hotel continues to offer friendly hospitality and service. Many bedrooms enjoy the sea views; all are well appointed and have smart bathrooms. Cuisine is pleasant and offers enjoyable dining featuring freshly prepared dishes.

Rooms 50 (8 fmly) (2 GF) S £57-£82; D £114-£164 (incl. bkfst & dinner)* Facilities FTV Xmas Wi-fi Services Lift Parking 23 Notes LB Closed 27 Dec-10 Feb

Royal York & Faulkner

★★ 80% HOTEL

The Esplanade EX10 8AZ

☎ 01395 513043 & 0800 220714   🖷 01395 577472

e-mail: stay@royalyorkhotel.co.uk

web: www.royalyorkhotel.co.uk

dir: *M5 junct 30 take A3052, 10m to Sidmouth, hotel in centre of Esplanade*

PETS: Bedrooms (5 GF) unattended Charges £5 inc food per night Exercise area 250mtrs Facilities food (pre-bookable) food bowl water bowl walks info vet info On Request fridge access torch towels Other charge for damage

This seafront hotel, owned and run by the same family for over 60 years, maintains its Regency charm and grandeur. The attractive bedrooms vary in size, and many have balconies and sea views. Public rooms are spacious and traditional dining is offered, alongside Blinis Café-Bar, which is more contemporary in style and offers coffees, lunch and afternoon teas. The spa facilities include a hydrotherapy pool, steam room, sauna and a variety of treatments.

Rooms 70 (2 annexe) (8 fmly) (5 GF) S £55-£88; D £110-£193 (incl. bkfst & dinner)* Facilities Spa FTV 🏊 Steam cabin Snooker table Sauna ♫ Xmas New Year Wi-fi Services Lift Parking 20 Notes LB Closed Jan

SIDMOUTH *continued*

The Woodlands Hotel

★★ 72% HOTEL

Cotmaton Cross EX10 8HG
☎ 01395 513120 📠 01395 513348
e-mail: info@woodlands-hotel.com
web: www.woodlands-hotel.com
dir: *Follow signs for Sidmouth*

PETS: Bedrooms (8 GF) unattended sign **Exercise area** 200yds
Facilities cage storage walks info vet info **Other** prior notice
required **Restrictions** no breed larger than a Labrador

Located in the heart of the town and ideally situated for exploring
Devon and Dorset, this listed property has numerous character
features. There is a spacious bar and a lounge where guests
may relax. Freshly prepared dinners can be enjoyed in the smart
dining room. Families with children are made very welcome and
may dine early.

Rooms 20 (4 fmly) (8 GF) **Facilities** Wi-fi **Parking** 20
Notes Closed 20 Dec-15 Jan

The Salty Monk

★★★★★ ◉◉ ▦ RESTAURANT WITH ROOMS

Church St, Sidford EX10 9QP
☎ 01395 513174
e-mail: saltymonk@btconnect.com
web: www.saltymonk.co.uk
dir: *On A3052 opposite church*

PETS: Bedrooms Charges £20 per stay **Public areas** on leads
disp bin **Exercise area** 20mtrs **Facilities** food (pre-bookable)
food bowl water bowl bedding dog chews scoop/disp bags
leads cage storage walks info vet info **On Request** fridge
access torch towels **Other** charge for damage **Resident Pets:**
Finn (Irish Water Spaniel), Isca (Italian Spinone)

Set in the village of Sidford, this attractive property dates from
the 16th century. There's oodles of style and appeal here with
each bedroom having a unique identity. Bathrooms are equally
special with multi-jet showers, spa baths and cosseting robes
and towels. The output from the kitchen is impressive with
excellent local produce very much in evidence, served in the
elegant surroundings of the restaurant. A new mini spa facility
is available.

Rooms 5 en suite 1 annexe en suite (3 GF) **S** £70-£150;
D £110-£200* **Facilities** FTV tea/coffee Dinner available Cen ht
Wi-fi Golf 18 Sauna **Parking** 20 **Notes** LB Closed 2wks Nov &
3wks Jan No coaches

Bramley Lodge Guest House

★★★ GUEST HOUSE

Vicarage Rd EX10 8UQ
☎ 01395 515710
e-mail: haslam@bramleylodge.fsnet.co.uk
dir: *0.5m N of seafront on A375*

PETS: Bedrooms Charges £1 per night **Public areas** except
dining room **Grounds** disp bin **Exercise area** Byes Park
(30mtrs), beach Oct-Apr (600mtrs) **Facilities** water bowl walks
info vet info **On Request** fridge access torch towels **Other**
charge for damage prior notice required **Restrictions** small &
medium size dogs only

Guests are assured of a warm and friendly welcome at this
family-run, small guest house, located about a half mile from
the sea. The neatly furnished bedrooms vary in size, and all are
equipped to a good standard. Home-cooked evening meals are
available, by prior arrangement, with special diets catered for
on request.

Rooms 6 rms (5 en suite) (1 fmly) **S** £30-£33; **D** £62-£66*
Facilities FTV TVL tea/coffee Dinner available Cen ht **Parking** 6
Notes Closed Dec-Jan ⊗

Oakdown Holiday Park *(SY167902)*

►►►►►

Gatedown Ln, Weston EX10 0PT
☎ 01297 680387 📠 01297 680541
e-mail: enquiries@oakdown.co.uk
dir: *Off A3052, 2.5m E of junct with A375*

PETS: Charges touring pitches £2.20 per night **Public areas**
except amenities & children's play area on leads disp bin
Exercise area field trails **Exercise area** 25yds **Facilities** walks
info vet info **Other** prior notice to bring pets is essential in high
season disposal bags available

Open Apr-Oct Last arrival 22.00hrs Last departure 10.30hrs

A quality, friendly, well-maintained park with good landscaping
and plenty of maturing trees that makes it well screened from the
A3502. Pitches are grouped in paddocks surrounded by shrubs,
and include a 50-pitch development replete with an upmarket
toilet block. The park's conservation areas with their natural
flora and fauna offer attractive walks, and there is a hide by the
Victorian reed bed for both casual and dedicated bird watchers.
A 16 acre site with 150 touring pitches, 90 hardstandings and
62 statics.

Notes No bikes/skateboards or kite flying

Salcombe Regis Caravan & Camping Park
(SY153892)

▶▶▶

Salcombe Regis EX10 0JH
☎ 01395 514303 📠 01395 514314
e-mail: contact@salcombe-regis.co.uk
dir: *Off A3052 1m E of junct with A375. From opposite direction turn left past Donkey Sanctuary*

PETS: Charges Public areas except shower & toilet block disp bin **Exercise area** dog exercise area (off lead) with clear-up facilities **Facilities** walks info vet info **Other** prior notice required disposal bags available

Open Etr-end Oct Last arrival 20.15hrs Last departure 10.30hrs

Set in quiet countryside with glorious views, this spacious park has well-maintained facilities, and a good mix of grass and hardstanding pitches. There is a self-catering holiday cottage and static caravans for hire. A footpath runs from the park to the coastal path and the beach. A 16 acre site with 100 touring pitches, 40 hardstandings and 10 statics.

Collaven Manor
★★ 79% COUNTRY HOUSE HOTEL
EX20 4HH
☎ 01837 861522 📠 01837 861614
e-mail: collavenmanor@supanet.com
dir: *A30 onto A386 to Tavistock, hotel 2m on right*

PETS: Bedrooms unattended **Stables** 5m **Charges** £5 per night **Public areas** on leads **Grounds** disp bin **Exercise area** accessed directly from grounds **Facilities** food bowl water bowl cat treats washing facs cage storage walks info vet info **On Request** fridge access torch towels **Other** food available by prior arrangement **Restrictions** no Dobermans, Rottweilers or Pit Bulls **Resident Pets:** Willow, Jas & Jack (cats)

This delightful 15th-century manor house is quietly located in five acres of well-tended grounds. The friendly proprietors provide attentive service and ensure a relaxing environment. Charming public rooms have old oak beams and granite fireplaces, and provide a range of comfortable lounges and a well stocked bar. In the restaurant, a daily-changing menu offers interesting dishes.

Rooms 9 (1 fmly) **S** £59-£65; **D** £98-£146 (incl. bkfst)*
Facilities FTV 🎳 Bowls **Parking** 50 **Notes** LB Closed Dec-Jan

Bundu Camping & Caravan Park *(SX546916)*

▶▶▶

EX20 4HT
☎ 01837 861611
e-mail: frances@bundu.plus.com
dir: *W on A30, past Okehampton. Take A386 to Tavistock. Take 1st left & left again*

PETS: Charges Public areas disp bin **Exercise area** adjacent **Facilities** food washing facs walks info vet info **Resident Pet:** Sophie (German Shepherd)

Open all year Last arrival 23.30hrs Last departure 14.00hrs

Welcoming, friendly owners set the tone for this well-maintained site, ideally positioned on the border of the Dartmoor National Park. Along with fine views and level grassy pitches, the Granite Way cycle track from Lydford to Okehampton along the old railway line, part of the Devon Coast to Coast cycle trail, passes the edge of the park. A 4.5 acre site with 38 touring pitches, 11 hardstandings.

Notes 🐾

Glazebrook House Hotel
★★ 78% ⚜ HOTEL
TQ10 9JE
☎ 01364 73322 📠 01364 72350
e-mail: enquiries@glazebrookhouse.com
web: www.glazebrookhouse.com
dir: *Exit A38 at South Brent, follow brown signs to hotel*

PETS: Bedrooms unattended **Stables** 2m **Charges** £5 per night **Public areas** except restaurant **Grounds** disp bin **Exercise area** 0.5m **Facilities** leads dog walking washing facs cage storage walks info vet info **On Request** fridge access torch towels **Other** charge for damage **Restrictions** only well behaved dogs accepted **Resident Pets:** Bobby (Pointer/Collie cross), Sly (cat)

Enjoying a tranquil and convenient location next to the Dartmoor National Park and set within four acres of gardens, this 18th-century former gentleman's residence offers a friendly welcome and comfortable accommodation. Elegant public areas provide ample space to relax and enjoy the atmosphere, whilst bedrooms are well appointed and include a number with four-poster beds. The dishes on the menus are created from interesting combinations of fresh, locally-sourced produce.

Rooms 10 **S** £50-£55; **D** £80-£145 (incl. bkfst)* **Facilities** FTV Reflexology & other holistic therapies Xmas New Year Wi-fi **Parking** 40 **Notes** LB Closed 2-18 Jan RS 1 wk Aug

SOUTH MOLTON · Map 3 SS72

Riverside Caravan & Camping Park
(SS723274)

▶ ▶ ▶ ▶

Marsh Ln, North Molton Rd EX36 3HQ
☎ 01769 579269   📄 01769 574853
e-mail: relax@exmoorriverside.co.uk
dir: *M5 junct 27 onto A361 towards Barnstaple. Site signed 1m before South Molton on right*

PETS: **Stables** 1m **Public areas** assist dogs only on leads disp bin **Exercise area** wooded field **Facilities** food food bowl water bowl dog chews cat treats leads washing facs walks info vet info **Other** prior notice required disposal bags available

Open all year Last arrival 22.00hrs Last departure 11.00hrs

A family-run park, set alongside the River Mole, where supervised children can play, and fishing is available. This is an ideal base for exploring Exmoor, as well as North Devon's golden beaches. A 40 acre site with 42 touring pitches, 42 hardstandings.

STOKE GABRIEL · Map 3 SX85

Broadleigh Farm Park *(SX851587)*

▶ ▶ ▶

Coombe House Ln, Aish TQ9 6PU
☎ 01803 782422
e-mail: enquiries@broadleighfarm.co.uk
dir: *From Exeter on A38 then A380 towards Torbay. Right onto A385 for Totnes. In 0.5m at Parkers Arms left for Stoke Gabriel. Right after Whitehill Country Park to site*

PETS: **Exercise area** field adjacent **Facilities** vet info
Resident Pets: 2 Border Collies (working dogs), 2 cats

Open Mar-Oct Last arrival 21.00hrs Last departure 11.30hrs

Set in a very rural location on a working farm which borders Paignton and Stoke Gabriel. The large sloping field with a timber-clad toilet block in the centre is sheltered and peaceful, surrounded by rolling countryside but handy for the beaches. A 7 acre site with 80 touring pitches.

Notes 🚭

Higher Well Farm Holiday Park *(SX857577)*

▶ ▶ ▶

Waddeton Rd TQ9 6RN
☎ 01803 782289
e-mail: higherwell@talk21.com
dir: *From Exeter A380 to Torbay, turn right onto A385 for Totnes, in 0.5m left for Stoke Gabriel, follow signs*

PETS: **Public areas** disp bin **Exercise area** fenced off area **Facilities** food vet info

Open 8 Apr-30 Oct Last arrival 22.00hrs Last departure 10.00hrs

Set on a quiet farm yet only four miles from Paignton, this rural holiday park is on the outskirts of the picturesque village of Stoke Gabriel. A toilet block with some en suite facilities is a considerable amenity, and tourers are housed in an open field with some very good views. A 10 acre site with 80 touring pitches, 3 hardstandings and 19 statics.

Notes No commercial vehicles

STOWFORD · Map 2 SX48

Townleigh Farm *(SX425876)*

★ ★ ★ ★ FARMHOUSE

EX20 4DE
☎ 01566 783186   Mr Stubbs
e-mail: mail@townleigh.com
dir: *M5 junct 31, take A30 southbound Roadford, turn off left, left again, follow lane for approx 2m*

PETS: **Stables Charges** £10 per stay **Other** charge for damage
Resident Pets: Bucket (Terrier), Sky (Springer Spaniel), Jude (Labrador), Sting (horse)

This 19th-century farmhouse, in 350 acres of picturesque countryside, has just about something to offer everyone. The Victorian architecture, complemented by all the expected modern luxuries, have much understated grandeur. Bedrooms have much charm, comfort and character together with lovely views, and public areas are equally special with a sumptuous drawing room and elegant dining room. The estate also has a number of self-catering cottages, fishing lakes, an equestrian centre and, in season, pheasant shoots.

Rooms 3 rms (2 en suite) (1 pri facs) **S** £60; **D** £80 **Facilities** TVL tea/coffee Dinner available Cen ht Wi-fi ⛵ Fishing **Parking** 8
Notes LB 250 acres Country sports/horses

STRETE | Map 3 SX84

Strete Barton House
★★★★★ GUEST HOUSE

Totnes Rd TQ6 0RU
☎ 01803 770364 📄 01803 771182
e-mail: info@stretebarton.co.uk
web: www.stretebarton.co.uk
dir: Off A379 coastal road into village, just below church

PETS: Charges £5 per night £35 per week **Grounds** disp bin
Exercise area 20mtrs **Facilities** dog chews cage storage walks
info vet info **On Request** fridge access torch towels **Other** pets
allowed in cottage suite only

This delightful 16th-century farmhouse has been appointed
to blend stylish accommodation with its original character.
Bedrooms are very comfortably furnished and well equipped
with useful extras. Breakfast utilises quality local produce and
is served in the spacious dining room. Guests are also welcome
to use the very comfortable lounge complete with a woodburner
for the cooler months. The village lies between Dartmouth and
Kingsbridge and has easy access to the natural beauty of the
South Hams as well as local pubs and restaurants.

Rooms 5 rms (4 en suite) (1 pri facs) 1 annexe en suite
S £80-£130; **D** £90-£140* **Facilities** FTV tea/coffee Cen ht Wi-fi
Parking 4 **Notes** LB No Children 8yrs

TAVISTOCK | Map 2 SX47

Sampford Manor
★★★ BED AND BREAKFAST

Sampford Spiney PL20 6LH
☎ 01822 853442
e-mail: manor@sampford-spiney.fsnet.co.uk
web: www.sampford-spiney.fsnet.co.uk
dir: B3357 towards Princetown, right at 1st x-rds. Next x-rds
Warren Cross left for Sampford Spiney. 2nd right, house below
church

PETS: Bedrooms Sep accom barn **Stables Charges** £3 per
night **Public areas** except dining room on leads **Grounds** disp
bin **Exercise area** 200yds **Facilities** food bowl water bowl
feeding mat leads washing facs cage storage walks info vet
info **On Request** fridge access torch towels **Other** charge for
damage **Resident Pets:** Spin (Springer/Terrier cross), Cleo
(Springer/Collie cross), Monty (cat), 31 alpacas, 2 horses

Once owned by Sir Francis Drake, this manor house is tucked
away in a tranquil corner of Dartmoor National Park. The family
home is full of character, with exposed beams and slate floors,
while outside, a herd of award-winning alpacas graze in the
fields. Genuine hospitality is assured together with scrumptious
breakfasts featuring home-produced eggs. Children, horses
(stabling available) and pets are all equally welcome.

Rooms 3 rms (2 pri facs) (1 fmly) **S** £30-£40; **D** £55-£75*
Facilities tea/coffee Cen ht **Parking** 3 **Notes** Closed Xmas

Woodovis Park *(SX431745)*
▶ ▶ ▶ ▶

Gulworthy PL19 8NY
☎ 01822 832968 📄 01822 832948
e-mail: info@woodovis.com
dir: A390 from Tavistock signed Callington & Gunnislake. At hill
top right at rdbt signed Lamerton & Chipshop. Site 1m on left

PETS: Public areas except buildings & swimming pool on
leads disp bin **Exercise area** dog walks & woods **Facilities**
washing facs walks info vet info **Other** prior notice required
ground skewer for dog lead by tents; disposal bags available
Resident Pets: Maddie & Molly (Springer Spaniels), Chloe
(mongrel), Zimba (cat)

Open 26 Mar-29 Oct Last arrival 20.00hrs Last departure noon

A well-kept park in a remote woodland setting on the edge of
the Tamar Valley. This peacefully-located park is set at the
end of a half-mile private tree-lined road, and has lots of on-
site facilities. The toilets are excellent, and there is an indoor
swimming pool, all in a friendly atmosphere. A 14.5 acre site with
50 touring pitches, 20 hardstandings and 35 statics.

Harford Bridge Holiday Park *(SX504767)*
▶ ▶ ▶

Peter Tavy PL19 9LS
☎ 01822 810349 📄 01822 810028
e-mail: enquiry@harfordbridge.co.uk
dir: 2m N of Tavistock, off A386 Okehampton Rd, take Peter Tavy
turn, entrance 200yds on right

PETS: Charges £1.50 per night £10.50 per week **Public areas**
on leads disp bin **Exercise area** field opposite **Facilities** walks
info vet info **Other** prior notice required **Resident Pets:** rabbits,
chickens, ducks & horses

Open all year rs Nov-Mar Statics & 5 hardstandings only Last
arrival 21.00hrs Last departure noon

This beautiful spacious park is set beside the River Tavy in the
Dartmoor National Park. Pitches are located beside the river
and around the copses, and the park is very well equipped for
the holidaymaker. An adventure playground and games room
entertain children, and there is fly-fishing and a free tennis court.
A 16 acre site with 120 touring pitches, 5 hardstandings and 80
statics.

Notes No large groups

TAVISTOCK *continued*

Langstone Manor Camping & Caravan Park
(SX524738)

▶▶▶▶

Moortown PL19 9JZ
☎ 01822 613371   📠 01822 613371
e-mail: jane@langstone-manor.co.uk
dir: *Take B3357 from Tavistock to Princetown. Approx 1.5m turn right at x-rds, follow signs. Over bridge, cattle grid, up hill, left at sign then left again. Follow lane to park*

PETS: Public areas disp bin Exercise area moor adjacent Facilities leads washing facs walks info vet info Other prior notice required disposal bags available Resident Pets: Cassie (Collie), Murphy (Springer Spaniel), Mercury (Russian Blue cat)

Open 15 Mar-Oct rs Wkdys in low season restricted hours in bar & restaurant Last arrival 22.00hrs Last departure 11.00hrs

A secluded site set in the well-maintained grounds of a manor house in Dartmoor National Park. Many attractive mature trees provide a screen within the park, and there is a popular lounge bar with an excellent menu of reasonably priced evening meals. Plenty of activities and places of interest can be found within the surrounding moorland. A 6.5 acre site with 40 touring pitches, 10 hardstandings and 25 statics.

Notes No skateboards, scooters, cycles, ball games

THURLESTONE   Map 3 SX64

Thurlestone Hotel
★★★★ 82% ◉ HOTEL
TQ7 3NN
☎ 01548 560382   📠 01548 561069
e-mail: enquiries@thurlestone.co.uk
web: www.thurlestone.co.uk
dir: *A38, A384 into Totnes, A381 towards Kingsbridge, A379 towards Churchstow, onto B3197. Into lane signed to Thurlestone*

PETS: Bedrooms unattended sign Stables 5m Charges £6 per night Public areas front foyer only Grounds on leads Exercise area Facilities (pre-bookable) food bowl water bowl pet sitting dog walking washing facs cage storage walks info vet info On Request fridge access torch towels Other charge for damage

This perennially popular hotel has been in the same family-ownership since 1896 and continues to go from strength to

strength. A vast range of facilities is available for all the family including indoor and outdoor pools, a golf course and a beauty salon. Bedrooms are equipped to ensure a comfortable stay with many having wonderful views of the South Devon coast. A range of eating options includes the elegant and stylish restaurant with its stunning views.

Rooms 64 (23 fmly) S £66-£200; D £132-£400 (incl. bkfst)*
Facilities STV ⬡ ⟋ supervised ⬩ 9 ⬩ Putt green ⬩ Gym Squash Badminton courts Games room Toddler room Snooker room 🎵 Xmas New Year Wi-fi Child facilities Services Lift Parking 121 Notes Closed 1-2 wks Jan

TORQUAY   Map 3 SX96

Barceló Torquay Imperial Hotel
★★★★ 77% HOTEL
Park Hill Rd TQ1 2DG
☎ 01803 294301   📠 01803 298293
e-mail: imperialtorquay@barcelo-hotels.co.uk
web: www.barcelo-hotels.co.uk
dir: *A380 towards seafront. Turn left to harbour, at clocktower right. Hotel 300yds on right*

PETS: Bedrooms unattended Charges £15 per night Public areas muzzled and on leads Grounds on leads disp bin Exercise area 100yds Facilities food bowl water bowl dog chews scoop/disp bags cage storage walks info vet info On Request fridge access torch towels Other charge for damage Restrictions small to medium size dogs only

This hotel has an enviable location with extensive views of the coastline. Traditional in style, the public areas are elegant and offer a choice of dining options including the Regatta Restaurant, with its stunning views over the bay. Bedrooms are spacious, most with private balconies, and the hotel has an extensive range of indoor and outdoor leisure facilities.

Rooms 152 (14 fmly) Facilities Spa STV ⬡ ⟋ supervised ⬩ Gym Squash Beauty salon Hairdresser Steam room 🎵 Xmas New Year Wi-fi Services Lift Parking 140

Corbyn Head Hotel & Orchid Restaurant

★★★ 77% ◉◉◉ HOTEL

Torbay Rd, Sea Front TQ2 6RH
☎ 01803 213611 📠 01803 296152
e-mail: info@corbynhead.com
web: www.corbynhead.com
dir: *Follow signs to Torquay seafront, turn right on seafront. Hotel on right with green canopies*

PETS: Bedrooms (9 GF) **Charges** £7 per night £49 per week
Exercise area 400mtrs **Facilities** vet info **Other** charge for damage

This hotel occupies a prime position overlooking Torbay, and offers well-equipped bedrooms, many with sea views and some with balconies. The staff are friendly and attentive, and a well-stocked bar and comfortable lounge are available. Guests can enjoy fine dining in the award-winning Orchid Restaurant or more traditional dishes in the Harbour View Restaurant.

Rooms 45 (4 fmly) (9 GF) **S** £30-£85; **D** £60-£172 (incl. bkfst)*
Facilities FTV ⤴ Gym Squash ♫ Xmas New Year Wi-fi **Parking** 50
Notes LB

Red House Hotel

★★ 71% HOTEL

Rousdown Rd, Chelston TQ2 6PB
☎ 01803 607811 📠 0871 5289455
e-mail: stay@redhouse-hotel.co.uk
web: www.redhouse-hotel.co.uk
dir: *Follow signs for seafront & Chelston, turn into Avenue Rd, right at 1st lights. Pass shops & church, next left. Hotel on right*

PETS: Bedrooms unattended **Charges** £3 per night **Public areas** except restaurant & lounge on leads **Grounds** on leads
Exercise area 300yds **Facilities** vet info **Other** charge for damage **Restrictions** small - medium size dogs only
Resident Pet: Jemima (cat)

Set just a few minutes' drive from Torquay town and the seafront, this hotel is in an ideal location to explore the Torbay area. The hotel offers comfortably appointed bedrooms, and facilities

include indoor and outdoor swimming pools, plus a gym, sauna, steam room and a treatment room.

Red House Hotel

Rooms 9 (3 fmly) **S** £35-£49; **D** £56-£78 (incl. bkfst)*
Facilities ⓢ ⤴ Gym Sun shower Beauty room Sauna Xmas New Year Wi-fi **Parking** 9 **Notes** LB

Shelley Court

★★ 68% HOTEL

29 Croft Rd TQ2 5UD
☎ 01803 295642 📠 01803 215793
e-mail: shelleycourthotel@hotmail.com
dir: *From B3199 up Shedden Hill Rd, 1st left into Croft Rd*

PETS: Bedrooms (6 GF) unattended sign **Charges** £10 per night **Public areas** except dining room **Grounds** disp bin
Exercise area adjacent **Facilities** scoop/disp bags leads washing facs cage storage walks info vet info **On Request** fridge access torch towels **Other** charge for damage
Resident Pets: Jack (Parson Jack Russell), Vera (Jack Russell)

This hotel, popular with groups, is located in a pleasant, quiet area that overlooks the town towards Torbay. With a friendly team of staff, many guests return here time and again. Entertainment is provided most evenings in the season. Bedrooms come in a range of sizes and there is a large and comfortable lounge bar.

Rooms 27 (3 fmly) (6 GF) **S** £35-£48; **D** £70-£96 (incl. bkfst & dinner) **Facilities** FTV ⤴ Pool table Indoor skittle alley ♫ Xmas New Year **Parking** 20 **Notes** LB Closed 4 Jan-10 Feb

TORQUAY *continued*

Bute Court Hotel

★★ 67% HOTEL

Belgrave Rd TQ2 5HQ

☎ 01803 213408 📠 01803 213429

e-mail: stay@butecourt.co.uk

dir: *A3022 into Torquay. Follow signs for seafront*

PETS: **Bedrooms** (13 GF) **Charges** £5 per night **Grounds** on leads **Exercise area** **Facilities** walks info vet info **On Request** fridge access

This popular hotel is only a short, level walk from the seafront and resort attractions. It still retains many Victorian features, and the comfortable bedrooms offer modern facilities and many have far reaching views. Public areas include a bar and lounges, while the attractive dining room looks across secluded gardens to the sea. Entertainment is also offered during busier periods.

Rooms 43 (2 fmly) (13 GF) **Facilities** FTV ⌘ 𝄞 Xmas New Year Wi-fi **Services** Lift **Parking** 25

The Cary Arms

★★★★★ INN

Babbacombe Beach TQ1 3LX

☎ 01803 327110 📠 01803 323221

e-mail: enquiries@caryarms.co.uk

web: www.caryarms.co.uk

dir: *A380 at Ashcombe Cross onto B3192 to Teignmouth. Right at lights to Torquay on A379, left at lights to Babbacombe. Left onto Babbacombe Downs Rd, left onto Beach Rd*

PETS: **Bedrooms** **Charges** £10 per night **Public areas** on leads **Grounds** on leads disp bin **Exercise area** 100mtrs **Facilities** food bowl water bowl bedding dog chews washing facs walks info vet info **On Request** fridge access torch towels

Located on the water's edge at Babbacombe, this seaside retreat is appointed to high standards with quality shown throughout; the bedrooms have sea views and nearly all have outside terraces or balconies. There is a guest lounge and a dedicated team of 'hosts' who will assist in planning your day or simply impart local knowledge. This is also a popular dining venue, either inside or on the numerous terraces that lead down to the water's edge; in summer months there's a BBQ and wood-fired oven.

Rooms 8 en suite (1 fmly) (3 GF) **S** £100-£200; **D** £150-£250* **Facilities** FTV tea/coffee Dinner available Cen ht Wi-fi Golf 18 Pool Table **Parking** 15 **Notes** LB No coaches

The Downs

★★★★ GUEST ACCOMMODATION

41-43 Babbacombe Downs Rd, Babbacombe TQ1 3LN

☎ 01803 328543 📠 01803 317977

e-mail: manager@downshotel.co.uk

PETS: **Bedrooms** unattended **Charges** £5 per night **Public areas** except restaurant on leads **Exercise area** adjacent **Facilities** cage storage walks info vet info **On Request** fridge access torch towels **Other** charge for damage dogs can accompany guests if breakfast/dinner served in bar lounge (prior notice required)

Originally built in the 1850s, this elegant building forms part of a seafront terrace with direct access to the promenade and Babbacombe Downs. The warmth of welcome is matched by attentive service, with every effort made to ensure a rewarding and relaxing stay. Bedrooms offer impressive levels of comfort and most have spectacular views across Lyme Bay with balconies being an added bonus. For guests with limited mobility, assisted access is available to the first floor. Additional facilities include the convivial lounge/bar and spacious restaurant where enjoyable dinners and breakfasts are offered.

Rooms 12 en suite (4 fmly) **S** £46-£54; **D** £62-£78* **Facilities** FTV TVL tea/coffee Dinner available Direct Dial Cen ht Licensed Wi-fi **Parking** 8 **Notes** LB

Kingsholm

★★★★ 🛏 GUEST HOUSE

539 Babbacombe Rd TQ1 1HQ

☎ 01803 297794 📠 0700 603 7426

e-mail: enquiries@kingsholmhotel.co.uk

dir: *A3022 left onto Torquay seafront, left at clock tower rdbt, Kingsholm 400mtrs on left*

PETS: **Bedrooms** **Charges** £10 per stay **Public areas** except dining room on leads **Grounds** on leads **Exercise area** opposite **Facilities** walks info vet info **On Request** fridge access torch

Guests will no doubt enjoy the friendly and welcoming atmosphere created here by the resident proprietors. A range of well furnished and decorated bedrooms and bathrooms provide guests with plenty of comfort and quality. A relaxing guest lounge, small bar area and car park to the rear are all welcome features. Dinner featuring seasonal, home cooking is available by prior arrangement and should not be missed.

Rooms 9 en suite **S** £26-£33; **D** £52-£65 **Facilities** FTV tea/coffee Dinner available Cen ht Licensed Wi-fi **Parking** 4 **Notes** LB No Children 10yrs

Widdicombe Farm Touring Park *(SX876643)*

▶ ▶ ▶ ▶

Marldon TQ3 1ST
☎ 01803 558325 🖹 01803 559526
e-mail: info@widdicombefarm.co.uk
dir: On A380, midway between Torquay & Paignton ring road

PETS: Charges £1.50-£2.50 per night £10.50-£16 per week
Public areas except buildings on leads disp bin **Exercise area**
small field **Facilities** food food bowl water bowl dog chews cat
treats scoop/disp bags walks info vet info **Other** prior notice
required dogs must be on short lead at all times **Restrictions**
no Alsatians, Dobermans, Rottweilers, Bull Terriers or Ridgebacks
Resident Pets: 2 Border Collies, 3 Jack Russells

Open mid Mar-mid Oct Last arrival 20.00hrs Last departure
10.00hrs

A friendly family-run park on a working farm with good quality
facilities and extensive views. The level pitches are terraced to
take advantage of the views towards the coast and Dartmoor.
This is the only touring park within Torquay, and is also handy for
Paignton and Brixham. There is a well-stocked shop, a restaurant
and a lounge bar. An 8 acre site with 180 touring pitches, 180
hardstandings and 3 statics.

Notes No children

TWO BRIDGES   Map 2 SX67

Two Bridges Hotel

★★★ 77% ◉ HOTEL
PL20 6SW
☎ 01822 890581 🖹 01822 892306
e-mail: enquiries@twobridges.co.uk
web: www.twobridges.co.uk
dir: At junct of B3212 & B3357

PETS: Bedrooms (6 GF) unattended **Public areas** except
restaurant on leads **Grounds** on leads disp bin **Exercise area**
Dartmoor **Facilities** water bowl washing facs cage storage
walks info vet info **On Request** fridge access torch towels
Resident Pet: cat

This wonderfully relaxing hotel is set in the heart of the Dartmoor
National Park, in a beautiful riverside location. Three standards
of comfortable rooms provide every modern convenience, and
include four-poster rooms. There is a choice of lounges and fine
dining is available in the restaurant, where menus feature local
game and seasonal produce.

Rooms 33 (2 fmly) (6 GF) **Facilities** STV Fishing Xmas New Year
Child facilities **Parking** 100 **Notes** LB

WESTWARD HO!   Map 2 SS42

Culloden House

★ ★ ★ GUEST HOUSE
Fosketh Hill EX39 1UL
☎ 01237 479421
e-mail: theAA@culloden-house.co.uk
web: www.culloden-house.co.uk
dir: S of town centre. Off B3236 Stanwell Hill onto Fosketh Hill

PETS: Bedrooms unattended **Public areas** except dining room
Grounds disp bin **Exercise area** short walk **Facilities** cage
storage walks info vet info **On Request** fridge access **Other**
charge for damage dogs allowed unattended in bedrooms only by
prior arrangement

A warm welcome is assured in this family-friendly Victorian
property which stands on a wooded hillside with sweeping views
over the beach and coast. Guests can relax in the spacious
lounge with its log-burning fire and enjoy the wonderful sea
views.

Rooms 7 en suite (3 fmly) (1 GF) **Facilities** FTV tea/coffee Cen ht
Parking 4 **Notes** Closed Xmas & New Year RS Nov-Feb

WOOLACOMBE   Map 2 SS44

Woolacombe Bay Holiday Village
(SS465442)

Sandy Ln EX34 7AH
☎ 01271 870343 🖹 01271 870089
e-mail: goodtimes@woolacombe.com
*dir: From Mullacott Cross rdbt take B3343 (Woolacombe road)
to Turnpike Cross junct. Right towards Mortehoe, site approx 1m
on left*

PETS: Charges £1.50 per night £10 per week **Public areas**
except main clubhouse & pool areas disp bin **Exercise area**
0.5m to Tarka Trail, beach & coastal path **Facilities** food food
bowl water bowl bedding dog chews cat treats litter tray
scoop/disp bags leads washing facs dog grooming walks
info vet info **Other** max 3 dogs free pet pack, toys, Woof Guide
available **Restrictions** Resident Pet: Jess (Boxer)

Open Mar-Oct rs Mar-mid May, mid Sep-Oct no touring, camping
only available Last arrival mdnt Last departure 10.00hrs

A well-developed touring section in a holiday complex with a full
entertainment and leisure programme. This park offers excellent
facilities including a steam room and sauna. For a small charge
a bus takes holidaymakers to the other Woolacombe Bay holiday
centres where they can take part in any of the activities offered,
and there is also a bus to the beach. An 8.5 acre site with 180
touring pitches and 237 statics.

WOOLACOMBE *continued*

Woolacombe Sands Holiday Park
(SS471434)

Beach Rd EX34 7AF
☎ 01271 870569 📠 01271 870606
e-mail: lifesabeach@woolacombe-sands.co.uk
dir: *M5 junct 27, A361 to Barnstaple. Follow Ilfracombe signs, until Mullacott Cross. Turn left onto B3343 to Woolacombe. Site on left*

PETS: Charges £5 per night £35 per week **Public areas** except shop & pools **Exercise area** dog trail & dog exercise area **Facilities** food food bowl water bowl dog chews scoop/disp bags leads walks info vet info **Other** prior notice required

Open Apr-Oct Last arrival 22.00hrs Last departure 10.00hrs

Set in rolling countryside with grassy terraced pitches, most with spectacular views overlooking the sea at Woolacombe. The lovely Blue Flag beach can be accessed directly by footpath in 10-15 minutes, and there is a full entertainment programme for all the family in high season. A 20 acre site with 200 touring pitches, 50 hardstandings and 80 statics.

Europa Park *(SS475435)*

▶ ▶ ▶

Beach Rd EX34 7AN
☎ 01271 871425 📠 01271 871425
e-mail: europaparkwoolacombe@yahoo.co.uk
dir: *M5 junct 27, A361 through Barnstaple to Mullacott Cross. Left onto B3343 signed Woolacombe. Site on right at Spa shop/ garage*

PETS: Charges £3 per night **Public areas** **Exercise area** Woolacoombe Beach 1m **Facilities** vet info

Open all year Last arrival 23.00hrs

A very lively family-run site handy for the beach at Woolacombe, and catering well for surfers but maybe not suitable for a quieter type of stay. Set in a stunning location high above the bay, it provides a wide range of accommodation including surf cabins, and generous touring pitches. Visitors can enjoy the indoor pool and sauna, games room, restaurant/café/bar and clubhouse. Please make sure the site is suitable for you before making your booking. A 16 acre site with 200 touring pitches, 20 hardstandings and 22 statics.

Moorland Links
★ ★ ★ 75% HOTEL

PL20 6DA
☎ 01822 852245 📠 01822 855004
e-mail: moorland.links@forestdale.com
web: www.moorlandlinkshotel.co.uk
dir: *A38 from Exeter to Plymouth, then A386 towards Tavistock. 5m onto open moorland, hotel 1m on left*

PETS: Bedrooms (17 GF) unattended sign **Charges** £7.50 per night **Public areas** except restaurant on leads **Grounds** on leads disp bin **Exercise area** open moorland **Facilities** food (pre-bookable) water bowl walks info vet info **On Request** torch towels **Other** charge for damage

Set in nine acres in the Dartmoor National Park, this hotel offers spectacular views from many of the rooms across open moorland and the Tamar Valley. Bedrooms are well equipped and comfortably furnished, and some rooms have open balconies. The stylish restaurant looks out over the oak fringed lawns.

Rooms 44 (4 fmly) (17 GF) **S** £50-£80; **D** £70-£120 (incl. bkfst)*
Facilities FTV Xmas New Year Wi-fi **Parking** 120 **Notes** LB

Hill Cottage Farm Camping and Caravan Park *(SU119133)*

▶ ▶ ▶ ▶

Sandleheath Rd SP6 3EG
☎ 01425 650513 📠 01425 652339
e-mail: hillcottagefarmcaravansite@supanet.com
dir: *Take B3078 W of Fordingbridge. Turn off at Alderholt, site 0.25m on left after railway bridge*

PETS: Stables Charges £1 per night **Public areas** except in farm fields disp bin **Exercise area** dog walks **Facilities** washing facs dog grooming walks info vet info

Open Mar-Nov Last arrival 19.00hrs Last departure 11.00hrs

Set within extensive grounds this rural, beautifully landscaped park offers all fully-serviced pitches set in individual hardstanding bays with mature hedges between giving adequate pitch privacy. A modern toilet block is kept immaculately clean, and there's a good range of leisure facilities. In high season there is an area available for tenting. A 40 acre site with 35 touring pitches, 35 hardstandings.

BridgeHouse

★★★ 80% HOTEL

3 Prout Bridge DT8 3AY

☎ 01308 862200 📄 01308 863700

e-mail: enquiries@bridge-house.co.uk

web: www.bridge-house.co.uk

dir: Off A3066, 100yds from town square

PETS: Bedrooms (4 GF) Charges £15 per stay Public areas
except dining areas, bar, lounge (at service) Grounds
Exercise area 500yds Facilities food bowl water bowl bedding
pet sitting washing facs cage storage walks info On Request
fridge access torch towels Other charge for damage

Dating back to the 13th century, this property offers friendly
and attentive service. The stylish bedrooms feature finest
Italian cotton linens, flat-screen TVs and Wi-fi plus newly fitted
bathrooms. There are five types of room to choose from including
four-poster and coach house rooms. Smartly presented public
areas include the Georgian dining room, cosy bar and adjacent
lounge, and a breakfast room together with the Beaminster
Brasserie with its alfresco eating area under a canopy overlooking
the attractive walled garden.

Rooms 13 (4 annexe) (2 fmly) (4 GF) Facilities Xmas New Year
Wi-fi Child facilities Parking 20 Notes LB

The Anvil Inn

★★★★ INN

Salisbury Rd, Pimperne DT11 8UQ

☎ 01258 453431 📄 01258 480182

e-mail: theanvil.inn@btconnect.com

dir: 2m NE of Blandford on A354 in Pimperne

PETS: Bedrooms Charges £10 per stay Public areas only in bar
on leads Grounds on leads Exercise area Facilities water bowl
dog chews walks info vet info On Request fridge access torch
towels Other charge for damage

Located in a village near Blandford, this 16th-century thatched
inn provides a traditional country welcome. Bedrooms have been
refurbished to high standards. Dinner is a varied selection of
home-made dishes, plus there is a tempting variety of hand-
pulled ales and wines by the glass.

Rooms 12 en suite S £60-£85; D £85-£105* Facilities STV tea/
coffee Dinner available Direct Dial Cen ht Parking 18 Notes LB
No coaches

St Martin's House

★★★★ BED AND BREAKFAST

Whitecliff Mill St DT11 7BP

☎ 01258 451245 & 07748 887719

e-mail: info@stmartinshouse.co.uk

dir: Off Market Pl onto Salisbury St & left onto White Cliff Mill St,
on right before traffic island

PETS: Bedrooms Charges £5 cleaning charge if necessary
Exercise area 0.25m Facilities food bowl water bowl bedding
feeding mat washing facs walks info vet info On Request torch
towels Other charge for damage

Dating from 1866, this restored property was once part of
the chorister's house for a local church. The bedrooms are
comfortable and well equipped. The hosts offer warm hospitality
and attentive service. Breakfast, which features local and home-
made items, is enjoyed around a communal table. Carefully
prepared dinners are available by arrangement.

Rooms 2 rms (2 pri facs) (1 fmly) S £45-£50; D £65-£70*
Facilities tea/coffee Cen ht Wi-fi Parking 3 Notes Closed 22
Dec-6 Jan 🐾

BLANDFORD FORUM *continued*

The Inside Park *(ST869046)*

▶ ▶ ▶ ▶

Down House Estate DT11 9AD
☎ 01258 453719   📠 01258 459921
e-mail: inspark@aol.com
dir: From town, over River Stour, follow Winterborne Stickland signs. Site in 1.5m

PETS: Sep accom day kennels **Charges** 60p-£1 per night
Public areas except dog-free areas disp bin **Exercise area** private woods & farm walks 6m **Facilities** food food bowl water bowl walks info vet info **Other** prior notice required

Open Etr-Oct Last arrival 22.00hrs Last departure noon

An attractive, well-sheltered and quiet park, half a mile off a country lane in a wooded valley. Spacious pitches are divided by mature trees and shrubs, and amenities are housed in an 18th-century coach house and stables. There are some lovely woodland walks within the park. A 12 acre site with 125 touring pitches.

BOURNEMOUTH   **Map 4 SZ09**

Langtry Manor - Lovenest of a King

★★★ 82% ⬡ HOTEL

Derby Rd, East Cliff BH1 3QB
☎ 0844 3725 432   📠 01202 290115
e-mail: lillie@langtrymanor.com
web: www.langtrymanor.co.uk
dir: A31/A338, 1st rdbt by rail station turn left. Over next rdbt, 1st left into Knyveton Rd. Hotel opposite

PETS: Bedrooms (3 GF) **Charges Public areas** except restaurant & main lounge **Grounds** disp bin **Exercise area** beach & gardens 5 mins **Facilities** washing facs dog grooming cage storage walks info vet info **On Request** fridge access torch towels **Other** charge for damage **Resident Pet:** Tyson (Boxer)

Retaining a stately air, this property was originally built in 1877 by Edward VII for his mistress Lillie Langtry. The individually furnished and decorated bedrooms include several with four-poster beds. Enjoyable cuisine is served in the magnificent dining hall, that displays several large Tudor tapestries. There is an Edwardian banquet on Saturday evenings.

Rooms 20 (8 annexe) (2 fmly) (3 GF) **D** £105-£295 (incl. bkfst)*
Facilities FTV Free use of health club (200yds) ♪ Xmas New Year Wi-fi **Parking** 30 **Notes** LB

Cumberland

★★★ 81% HOTEL

East Overcliff Dr BH1 3AF
☎ 01202 290722   📠 01202 311394
e-mail: info@cumberlandbournemouth.co.uk
dir: A35 towards East Cliff & beaches, right onto Holdenhurst Rd, straight over 2 rdbts, left at junct to East Overcliff Drive, hotel on seafront

PETS: Bedrooms Charges £10 per night £70 per week
Exercise area gardens 10 mins walk **Facilities** walks info vet info **Other** charge for damage **Restrictions** small dogs only

A purpose built, art deco hotel where many of the bedrooms are appointed in keeping with the hotel's original character. Front-facing bedrooms have balconies with superb sea views. The comfortable public areas are spacious and striking in their design. The Mirabelle Restaurant and Red Door Brasserie offer cuisine prepared from local produce.

Rooms 102 (20 fmly) **Facilities** ⬡ ⬡ Squash Sauna ♪ Xmas New Year Wi-fi **Services** Lift **Parking** 50

Carrington House

★★★ 77% HOTEL

31 Knyveton Rd BH1 3QQ
☎ 01202 369988   📠 01202 292221
e-mail: carrington.house@forestdale.com
web: www.carringtonhousehotel.co.uk
dir: A338 at St Paul's rdbt, 200mtrs & left into Knyveton Rd. Hotel 400mtrs on right

PETS: Bedrooms (2 GF) unattended **Charges** £7.50 per night
Public areas except restaurant **Facilities** food (pre-bookable)

This hotel occupies a prominent position on a tree-lined avenue and a short walk from the seafront. The bedrooms are comfortable, well equipped and include many purpose-built family rooms. There are two dining options, Mortimers restaurant, and the Kings bar which serves light meals and snacks. Guests can relax in the comfortable lounge areas whilst the leisure complex offers a whole host of activities including a heated swimming pool.

Rooms 145 (42 fmly) (2 GF) **S** £40-£84; **D** £60-£125 (incl. bkfst)*
Facilities FTV ⬡ Children's play area Xmas New Year Wi-fi
Services Lift **Parking** 85 **Notes** LB

The Riviera

★★★ 77% HOTEL

Burnaby Rd, Alum Chine BH4 8JF
☎ 01202 763653 📄 01202 768422
e-mail: info@rivierabournemouth.co.uk
web: www.rivierabournemouth.co.uk
dir: A338, follow signs to Alum Chine

PETS: Bedrooms (11 GF) **Charges** £7.50 per night £52.50 per week **Public areas** except restaurant on leads **Exercise area** 5 mins walk **Facilities** vet info **Other** charge for damage

The Riviera offers a range of comfortable, well-furnished bedrooms and bathrooms. Welcoming staff provide efficient service delivered in a friendly manner. In addition to a spacious lounge with regular entertainment, there is an indoor and an outdoor pool, and all just a short walk from the beach.

Rooms 73 (4 annexe) (25 fmly) (11 GF) **S** £35-£80; **D** £70-£160 (incl. bkfst)* **Facilities** FTV 🕲 ⚡ Games room Sauna Spa bath Treatments available 🎵 Xmas New Year Wi-fi **Services** Lift **Parking** 45 **Notes** LB

Wessex

★★★ 77% HOTEL

West Cliff Rd BH2 5EU
☎ 01202 551911 📄 01202 297354
e-mail: wessex@forestdale.com
web: www.thewessexhotel.co.uk
dir: Follow M27/A35 or A338 from Dorchester & A347 N. Hotel on West Cliff side of town

PETS: Bedrooms (17 GF) unattended **Charges** £7.50 per night **Public areas** except restaurant **Grounds Facilities** food (pre-bookable) feeding mat

Centrally located and handy for the beach, the Wessex is a popular, relaxing hotel. Bedrooms are well equipped and comfortable with a range of modern amenities. The Lulworth restaurant provides a range of appetising dishes. The excellent leisure facilities boast both indoor and outdoor pools, sauna, ample function rooms and an open-plan bar and lounge.

Rooms 109 (32 fmly) (17 GF) **S** £55-£95; **D** £70-£145 (incl. bkfst)* **Facilities** FTV 🕲 ⚡ Gym Table tennis Sauna Steam room Xmas New Year Wi-fi **Services** Lift **Parking** 160 **Notes** LB

Suncliff

★★★ 75% HOTEL

29 East Overcliff Dr BH1 3AG
☎ 01202 291711 📄 01202 293788
e-mail: info@suncliffbournemouth.co.uk
dir: A338/A35 towards East Cliff & beaches, right into Holdenhurst Rd, straight over 2 rdbts, left at junct into East Overcliff Drive, hotel on seafront

PETS: Bedrooms (14 GF) **Charges** £10 per night **Exercise area** 0.5m **Facilities** walks info vet info **On Request** torch towels **Other** charge for damage **Restrictions** small dogs only

Enjoying splendid views from the East Cliff and catering mainly for leisure guests, this friendly hotel offers a range of facilities and services. Bedrooms are well equipped and comfortable, and many have sea views. Public areas include a large conservatory, an attractive bar and pleasant lounges.

Rooms 97 (29 fmly) (14 GF) **Facilities** 🕲 ⚡ Squash 🎵 Xmas New Year Wi-fi **Services** Lift **Parking** 62

Hotel Collingwood

★★★ 70% HOTEL

11 Priory Rd, West Cliff BH2 5DF
☎ 01202 557575 📄 01202 293219
e-mail: info@hotel-collingwood.co.uk
web: www.hotel-collingwood.co.uk
dir: A338 left at West Cliff sign, over 1st rdbt and left at 2nd rdbt. Hotel 500yds on left

PETS: Bedrooms (6 GF) unattended **Charges** £4 per night £28 per week **Exercise area** park & beach 5 mins **Facilities** cage storage walks info vet info **On Request** fridge access towels **Other** charge for damage

This privately owned and managed hotel is situated close to the BIC. Bedrooms are airy, with the emphasis on comfort. An excellent range of leisure facilities is available and the public areas are spacious and welcoming. Pinks Restaurant offers carefully prepared cuisine and a fixed-price, five-course dinner.

Rooms 53 (16 fmly) (6 GF) **S** £48-£72; **D** £96-£144 (incl. bkfst & dinner)* **Facilities** FTV 🕲 Gym Steam room Sauna Games room Snooker room 🎵 Xmas New Year Wi-fi **Services** Lift **Parking** 55 **Notes** LB

BOURNEMOUTH *continued*

Burley Court
★★★ 61% HOTEL
Bath Rd BH1 2NP
☎ 01202 552824 & 556704 📠 01202 298514
e-mail: info@burleycourthotel.co.uk
dir: *Exit A338 at St Paul's rdbt, take 3rd exit at next rdbt into Holdenhurst Rd. 3rd exit at next rdbt into Bath Rd, over crossing, 1st left*

PETS: Bedrooms (4 GF) unattended sign **Charges** £10 per night **Public areas** disp bin **Exercise area** 50mtrs **Facilities** food (pre-bookable) food bowl water bowl washing facs walks info vet info **On Request** fridge access torch towels **Other** charge for damage

Located on Bournemouth's West Cliff, this well-established hotel is easily located and convenient for the town and beaches. Bedrooms are pleasantly furnished and decorated in bright colours. A daily-changing menu is served in the spacious dining room.

Rooms 38 (8 fmly) (4 GF) **Facilities** ⚲ Xmas **Services** Lift **Parking** 35 **Notes** Closed 30 Dec-14 Jan RS 15-31 Jan

The Whitehall
★★ 78% HOTEL
Exeter Park Rd BH2 5AX
☎ 01202 554682 📠 01202 292637
e-mail: reservations@thewhitehallhotel.co.uk
web: www.thewhitehallhotel.co.uk
dir: *Follow BIC signs then turn into Exeter Park Rd off Exeter Rd*

PETS: Bedrooms (3 GF) unattended **Charges** £2 per night **Grounds** on leads **Exercise area** green 50mtrs **Facilities** vet info **Other** charge for damage **Restrictions** small well behaved dogs only

This friendly hotel enjoys an elevated position overlooking the park and is also close to the town centre and seafront. The spacious public areas include a choice of lounges, a cosy bar and a well-presented restaurant. The well-equipped and inviting bedrooms are spread over three floors.

Rooms 46 (5 fmly) (3 GF) **Facilities** ⚲ Xmas **Services** Lift **Parking** 25

Bourne Hall Hotel
★★ 65% HOTEL
14 Priory Rd, West Cliff BH2 5DN
☎ 01202 299715 📠 01202 552669
e-mail: info@bournehall.co.uk
web: www.bournehall.co.uk
dir: *M27/A31 from Ringwood into Bournemouth on A338, Wessex Way. Follow signs to BIC, onto West Cliff. Hotel on right*

PETS: Bedrooms (5 GF) **Charges** £10 per night £50 per week **Public areas** except restaurant muzzled and on leads **Exercise area** 2mins walk **Facilities** food (pre-bookable) pet sitting dog walking cage storage walks info vet info **On Request** fridge access torch towels **Other** charge for damage

This friendly, comfortable hotel is conveniently located close to the Bournemouth International Centre and the seafront. Bedrooms are well equipped, some located on the ground floor and some with sea views. In addition to the spacious lounge, there are two bars and a meeting room. A daily-changing menu is offered in the dining room.

Rooms 48 (9 fmly) (5 GF) **S** £25-£60; **D** £50-£90 (incl. bkfst)* **Facilities** STV Free leisure facilities for guests at Marriott Highcliff Hotel ⚲ Xmas New Year Wi-fi **Services** Lift **Parking** 35 **Notes** LB

Wood Lodge
★★★★ GUEST ACCOMMODATION
10 Manor Rd, East Cliff BH1 3EY
☎ 01202 290891 📠 01202 290892
e-mail: enquiries@woodlodgehotel.co.uk
web: www.woodlodgehotel.co.uk
dir: *A338 to St Pauls rdbt, 1st exit left. Straight over next 2 rdbts, immediate left*

PETS: Bedrooms Charges £5 per night £35 per week **Public areas** only allowed in halls for access to bedrooms on leads **Grounds** on leads disp bin **Exercise area** many walks nearby **Facilities** vet info **On Request** fridge access torch towels **Other** charge for damage **Restrictions** small dogs only **Resident Pet:** Buster (Yorkshire Terrier)

Expect a warm welcome from this family-run guest accommodation. Set in beautiful gardens minutes from the seafront and a 10 minute walk from the town centre. Bedrooms, which vary in size, are well presented. Home-cooked evening meals and hearty breakfasts are served in the smart dining room.

Rooms 15 rms (14 en suite) (1 pri facs) (1 fmly) (4 GF)
S £35-£48; **D** £70-£100 **Facilities** TVL tea/coffee Dinner available
Cen ht Licensed Wi-fi Pool Table **Parking** 12 **Notes** LB

Carlton Lodge

★ ★ ★ GUEST ACCOMMODATION

12 Westby Rd, Boscombe BH5 1HD
☎ 01202 303650 📄 01202 303650
e-mail: enquiries@thecarltonlodge.com
dir: *A338 Wessex Way turn left signed to football ground, right at
rdbt, left onto Ashley Rd/Christchurch Rd. 1st right onto Crabton
Close Rd, 2nd right onto Westby Rd*

PETS: Bedrooms unattended **Charges Facilities** washing facs
walks info vet info **On Request** fridge access torch towels
Other charge for damage please contact hotel for details of
charges for dogs

This relaxing home-from-home, family run guest accommodation
is only a five minute stroll from the beach and shopping centre at
Boscombe. The en suite bedrooms are spacious and individually
decorated. Hearty breakfasts feature homemade preserves and
excellent locally sourced bacon and sausages. Bournemouth is
a short drive away with Poole, Swanage and Christchurch on the
doorstep.

Rooms 5 en suite (2 fmly) (2 GF) **S** £30-£60; **D** £50-£80
Facilities FTV tea/coffee Cen ht **Parking** 6 **Notes** LB

BRIDPORT   **Map 3 SY49**

THE INDEPENDENTS
HOTEL ASSOCIATION

Bridge House

★ ★ 76% HOTEL

115 East St DT6 3LB
☎ 01308 423371 📄 01308 459573
e-mail: info@bridgehousebridport.co.uk
dir: *Follow signs to town centre from A35 rdbt, hotel 200mtrs on
right*

PETS: Bedrooms Public areas except restaurant, must be
well behaved on leads **Grounds** disp bin **Exercise area** park
adjacent **Facilities** walks info vet info **On Request** fridge
access **Other** charge for damage

A short stroll from the town centre, this 18th-century Grade II
listed property offers well-equipped bedrooms that vary in size.
In addition to the main lounge, there is a small bar-lounge and
a separate breakfast room. An interesting range of home-cooked
meals is provided in the wine bar and brasserie.

Rooms 10 (3 fmly) **S** £69; **D** £98-£108 (incl. bkfst)* **Facilities** FTV
Complimentary membership to leisure park New Year Wi-fi
Parking 13 **Notes** LB

The Shave Cross Inn

★ ★ ★ ★ ★ ⊜ INN

Marshwood Vale DT6 6HW
☎ 01308 868358 📄 01308 867064
e-mail: roy.warburton@virgin.net
web: www.theshavecrossinn.co.uk
dir: *From B3165 exit at Birdsmoorgate, follow brown signs*

PETS: Bedrooms unattended **Stables** nearby **Public areas**
except restaurant on leads **Grounds** on leads **Exercise area**
Facilities washing facs cage storage walks info vet info
On Request fridge access torch towels **Other** charge for
damage **Resident Pets:** Lulu, Liddy, Lotty (Great Danes), Libby
(horse)

This historic inn has been providing refreshment for weary
travellers for centuries and continues to offer a warm and
genuine welcome. The snug bar is dominated by a wonderful
fireplace with crackling logs creating just the right atmosphere.
Bedrooms are located in a separate Dorset flint and stone
building. Quality is impressive throughout with wonderful stone
floors and oak beams, combined with feature beds and luxurious
bathrooms. Food has a distinct Caribbean and international slant
with a number of authentic dishes incorporating excellent local
produce.

Rooms 7 en suite (1 fmly) (3 GF) **Facilities** STV FTV tea/coffee
Dinner available Direct Dial Cen ht Wi-fi Pool Table **Parking** 29
Notes No Children RS Mon (ex BH) Closed for lunch & dinner No
coaches

BRIDPORT *continued*

Britmead House

★★★★ GUEST ACCOMMODATION
West Bay Rd DT6 4EG
☎ 01308 422941 & 07973 725243
e-mail: britmead@talk21.com
web: www.britmeadhouse.co.uk
dir: *1m S of town centre, off A35 onto West Bay Rd*

PETS: Bedrooms Charges Public areas except dining room & lounge **Grounds** on leads disp bin **Exercise area** 100mtrs **Facilities** water bowl washing facs walks info vet info **On Request** fridge access torch towels **Other** charge for damage **Restrictions** no Pit Bull Terriers, Rottweilers or Staffordshire Bull Terriers

Britmead House is located south of Bridport, within easy reach of the town centre and West Bay harbour. Family-run, the atmosphere is friendly and the accommodation well-appointed and comfortable. Suitable for business and leisure, many guests return regularly. A choice of breakfast is served in the light and airy dining room.

Rooms 8 en suite (2 fmly) (2 GF) **S** £40-£58; **D** £60-£80* **Facilities** FTV TVL tea/coffee Cen ht Wi-fi **Parking** 12 **Notes** LB Closed 24-27 Dec

Bingham Grange Touring & Camping Park

(SY478963)

▶ ▶ ▶ ▶ ▶

Melplash DT6 3TT
☎ 01308 488234 📠 01308 488426
e-mail: enquiries@binghamsfarm.co.uk
dir: *From A35 at Bridport take A3066 N towards Beaminster. Site on left in 3m*

PETS: Stables nearby **Charges** £2 per night **Public areas** except washrooms, shop/office, bar/restaurant disp bin **Exercise area** very long woodland trail leading to river bank **Exercise area** park & footpaths adjacent **Facilities** food walks info vet info **Other** disposal bags, tennis balls & dog tethers for ground available **Restrictions** no dangerous dogs (see page 7) **Resident Pets:** Acorn, Wesley, Conker & Bracken (Spaniels), Snoopy (Beagle), Bonzo (Smooth Terrier), Oscar (Golden Labrador) chickens, ducks, geese

Open Mar-Oct rs Restaurant & bar seasonal Last departure 11.00hrs

Set in a quiet rural location but only five miles from the Jurassic coast, this adult-only park enjoys views over the West Dorset countryside. The mostly level pitches are attractively set amongst shrub beds and ornamental trees. There is a restaurant with lounge bar and take away, and all facilities are high quality. A 20 acre site with 150 touring pitches, 70 hardstandings.

Notes No under 18s to stay or visit

Lyons Gate Caravan and Camping Park

(ST660062)

▶ ▶ ▶

Lyons Gate DT2 7AZ
☎ 01300 345260
e-mail: info@lyons-gate.co.uk
dir: *Signed with direct access from A352, 3m N of Cerne Abbas*

PETS: Public areas disp bin **Exercise area** bridle path **Facilities** walks info vet info **Other** prior notice required

Open all year Last arrival 20.00hrs Last departure 11.30hrs

A peaceful park with pitches set out around the four attractive coarse fishing lakes. It is surrounded by mature woodland, with many footpaths and bridleways. Other easily accessible attractions include the Cerne Giant carved into the hills, the old market town of Dorchester, and the superb sandy beach at Weymouth. A 10 acre site with 90 touring pitches, 14 hardstandings.

Notes 🐾

Giant's Head Caravan & Camping Park

(ST675029)

▶ ▶

Giants Head Farm, Old Sherborne Rd DT2 7TR
☎ 01300 341242
e-mail: holidays@giantshead.co.uk
dir: *From Dorchester into town avoiding by-pass, at Top O'Town rdbt take A352 (Sherborne road), in 500yds right fork at Esso (Loder's) garage, site signed*

PETS: Charges dogs £2 per night **Public areas** except dog-free areas on leads disp bin **Exercise area** adjacent **Facilities** walks info vet info **Other** prior notice required

Open Etr-Oct rs Etr shop & bar closed Last arrival anytime Last departure 13.00hrs

A pleasant though rather basic park set in Dorset downland near the Cerne Giant (the landmark figure cut into the chalk) with stunning views. A good stopover site, ideal for tenters and backpackers on the Ridgeway route. A 4 acre site with 50 touring pitches.

Notes 🐾

Wood Farm Caravan & Camping Park
(SY356940)

►►►►►

Axminster Rd DT6 6BT
☎ 01297 560697   🖃 01297 561243
e-mail: holidays@woodfarm.co.uk
dir: *Site entered directly off A35 rdbt, on Axminster side of Charmouth*

PETS: Charges dogs £2 per night Public areas except buildings & play area on leads disp bin Exercise area 2-acre area Facilities food food bowl water bowl walks info vet info Other prior notice required cats are not allowed to roam free Resident Pets: dog, cats, sheep, chickens

Open Etr-Oct Last arrival 19.00hrs Last departure noon

A pleasant, well-established and mature park overlooking Charmouth, the sea and the Dorset hills and valleys. It stands on a high spot, and the four camping fields are terraced, each with its own impressive toilet block. Convenient for Lyme Regis, Axminster, and the famous fossil coastline. A 13 acre site with 216 touring pitches, 175 hardstandings and 81 statics.

Notes No skateboards, scooters, roller skates or bicycles

Christchurch Harbour Hotel
★★★★ 82% ⑩⑩ HOTEL
95 Mudeford BH23 3NT
☎ 01202 483434   🖃 01202 479004
e-mail: christchurch@harbourhotels.co.uk
web: www.christchurch-harbour-hotel.co.uk
dir: *On A35 to Christchurch onto A337 to Highcliffe. Right at rdbt, hotel 1.5m on left*

PETS: Bedrooms (14 GF) unattended Stables Charges Public areas except restaurant on leads Grounds disp bin Exercise area beach Facilities washing facs cage storage walks info vet info On Request fridge access torch towels Other charge for damage dogs allowed in certain rooms only

Delightfully situated on the side of Mudeford Quay close to sandy beaches and conveniently located for Bournemouth Airport and the BIC, the hotel boasts an impressive spa and leisure facility. The bedrooms are particularly well appointed and stylishly finished; many have excellent views and some have balconies. Guests can eat in the award-winning Harbour Restaurant, or the waterside Rhodes South.

Rooms 64 (7 fmly) (14 GF) D £135-£235 (incl. bkfst)* Facilities Spa FTV 🏊 Gym Steam room Sauna Exercise classes Hydrotherapy pool 🎵 Xmas New Year Wi-fi Services Lift Parking 55 Notes LB

Captain's Club Hotel and Spa
★★★★ 80% ⑩⑩ HOTEL
Wick Ferry, Wick Ln BH23 1HU
☎ 01202 475111   🖃 01202 490111
e-mail: enquiries@captainsclubhotel.com
web: www.captainsclubhotel.com
dir: *B3073 to Christchurch. On Fountain rdbt take 5th exit (Sopers Ln) 2nd left (St Margarets Ave) 1st right onto Wick Ln*

PETS: Bedrooms unattended sign Stables 5m Charges £20 per night Public areas outside terrace area only on leads Grounds on leads disp bin Exercise area 2 min walk Facilities walks info vet info On Request fridge access torch towels Other charge for damage Restrictions small - medium size dogs only

Situated in the heart of the town on the banks of the River Stour at Christchurch Quay, and only ten minutes from Bournemouth. All bedrooms, including the suites and apartments have views overlooking the river. Guests can relax in the hydrotherapy pool, enjoy a spa treatment or enjoy the cuisine in Tides Restaurant.

Rooms 29 (12 fmly) S £169-£199; D £169-£229 (incl. bkfst)* Facilities Spa STV FTV Hydro-therapy pool Sauna 🎵 Xmas New Year Wi-fi Services Lift Air con Parking 41

Corfe Castle Camping & Caravanning Club Site *(SY953818)*

►►►►

Bucknowle BH20 5PQ
☎ 01929 480280 & 0845 130 7633
dir: *From Wareham A351 towards Swanage. In 4m turn right at foot of Corfe Castle signed Church Knowle. 0.75m right to site*

PETS: Public areas except facility blocks (ex assist dogs) Exercise area surrounding countryside Facilities food Other prior notice required

Open Mar-Oct Last arrival 20.00hrs Last departure noon

This lovely park is set in woodland near to the famous Corfe Castle. It has modern toilet and shower facilities which are spotless. Although the site is sloping, pitches are level and include 33 spacious hardstandings. The site is perfect for visiting the many attractions of the Purbeck area including Swanage and Studland, as well has having the nearby station at Corfe for the Swanage Steam Railway. A 5 acre site with 80 touring pitches.

Notes Site gates closed between 23.00hrs-07.00hrs

ENGLAND

Summer Lodge Country House Hotel, Restaurant & Spa

★★★★ ◉◉◉ COUNTRY HOUSE HOTEL

DT2 0JR

☎ 01935 482000   📄 01935 482040

e-mail: summer@relaischateaux.com

dir: *1m W of A37 halfway between Dorchester & Yeovil*

PETS: Bedrooms (2 GF) unattended sign **Stables** 5m **Charges** £20 per night £140 per week (negotiable) **Public areas** except restaurant & drawing room **Grounds** disp bin **Exercise area** 20yds **Facilities** food (pre-bookable) food bowl water bowl bedding dog chews feeding mat scoop/disp bags leads pet sitting dog walking washing facs dog grooming cage storage walks info vet info **On Request** fridge access torch towels **Other** charge for damage **Resident Pets:** William & Felix (cats)

This picturesque hotel is situated in the heart of Dorset and is the ideal retreat for getting away from it all, and it's worth arriving in time for the excellent afternoon tea. Bedrooms are appointed to a very high standard; each is individually designed with upholstered walls and come with a wealth of luxurious facilities. The delightful public areas include a sumptuous lounge complete with an open fire, and the elegant restaurant where the cuisine continues to be the high point of any stay.

Rooms 24 (14 annexe) (6 fmly) (2 GF) (1 smoking) **S** £175-£525; **D** £200-£550 (incl. bkfst) **Facilities** Spa STV FTV ⊙ ⊴ ⊷ Gym Sauna Xmas New Year Wi-fi **Services** Air con **Parking** 41 **Notes** LB

The Acorn Inn

★★★★ ◉ INN

DT2 0JW

☎ 01935 83228   📄 01935 83707

e-mail: stay@acorn-inn.co.uk

web: www.acorn-inn.co.uk

dir: *0.5m off A37 between Yeovil & Dorchester, signed Evershot & Holywell*

PETS: Bedrooms unattended **Charges** £10 per night **Public areas** except restaurant on leads **Grounds** on leads **Exercise area** 400yds **Facilities** water bowl dog chews walks info vet info **On Request** torch **Other** charge for damage

This delightful 16th-century coaching inn is located at the heart of the village. Several of the bedrooms feature interesting four-poster beds, and all have been individually decorated and furnished. Public rooms retain many original features including oak panelling, open fires and stone-flagged floors. Fresh local produce is included on the varied menu.

Rooms 10 en suite (2 fmly) **S** £65-£130; **D** £95-£130* **Facilities** STV TVL tea/coffee Dinner available Direct Dial Cen ht Wi-fi Pool Table **Parking** 40 **Notes** LB

The Fox Inn

★★★★ INN

DT2 7PN

☎ 01258 880328   📄 01258 881440

e-mail: fox@anstyfoxinn.co.uk

web: www.anstyfoxinn.co.uk

dir: *Off A354 at Millbourne St Andrew, follow brown signs to Ansty*

PETS: Bedrooms unattended **Public areas** bar only **Grounds** on leads disp bin **Exercise area** public footpath 200yds **Facilities** food bowl water bowl cage storage walks info vet info **On Request** fridge access torch towels **Other** charge for damage **Resident Pet:** Reggie (Labrador)

This popular inn has a long and interesting history including strong links to the Hall & Woodhouse Brewery. Surrounded by beautiful Dorset countryside, this is a great base for exploring the area. Bedrooms are smartly appointed and offer high levels of comfort. The interesting menu focuses on excellent local produce, with a choice of dining options including the oak-panelled dining room. An extensive garden and patio area are also available.

Rooms 11 en suite (7 fmly) **S** £50-£100; **D** £60-£105* **Facilities** TVL tea/coffee Dinner available Direct Dial Cen ht Wi-fi ⊷ **Parking** 30 **Notes** LB

The Orchard Country House
★★★★ GUEST HOUSE

Rousdon DT7 3XW
☎ 01297 442972   📠 01297 443670
e-mail: reception@orchardcountryhotel.com
web: www.orchardcountryhotel.com
dir: *Take A3052 from Lyme Regis towards Sidmouth, on right after garage*

PETS: Bedrooms unattended **Grounds** on leads disp bin **Exercise area** walks nearby **Facilities** water bowl walks info vet info **On Request** fridge access torch **Other** charge for damage pets can only be left unattended in rooms whilst owner is in restaurant

Located in the peaceful village of Rousdon and set in attractive orchard gardens, this friendly and comfortable establishment is a good base for exploring the area. The hop-on/hop-off bus stops just outside which provides an easy transport option for access to many of the local attractions. There is a spacious lounge, and breakfast and dinner are served in the pleasant dining room.

Rooms 11 en suite (1 fmly) (1 GF) **S** £63-£65; **D** £96-£110*
Facilities FTV tea/coffee Dinner available Cen ht Licensed
Parking 25

Hook Farm Caravan & Camping Park
(SY323930)

▶ ▶ ▶

Gore Ln, Uplyme DT7 3UU
☎ 01297 442801   📠 01297 442801
e-mail: information@hookfarm-uplyme.co.uk
dir: *From A35, take B3165 towards Lyme Regis & Uplyme at Hunters Lodge pub. 2m turn right into Gore Lane, site 400yds on right*

PETS: Charges £1 per night **Public areas** except shop, reception & washroom facilities disp bin **Exercise area** apple orchard available **Facilities** leads walks info vet info **Other** tether spikes for sale, tether hook at shop, disposal bags available **Restrictions** no Dobermans, Bullmastiffs, Pit Bulls, Rottweilers or Staffordshire Bull Terriers **Resident Pets:** 4 cats

Open 15 Mar-Oct rs Low season shop closed Last arrival 21.00hrs Last departure 11.00hrs

Set in a peaceful and very rural location with views of Lym Valley and just a mile from the seaside at Lyme Regis. There are modern toilet facilities and good on-site amenities. Most pitches are level due to excellent terracing. The site continues to be upgraded. A 5.5 acre site with 100 touring pitches, 4 hardstandings and 17 statics.

Notes No groups of 6 adults or more 🐕

Huntick Farm Caravan Park *(SY955947)*

▶ ▶ ▶

Huntick Rd BH16 6BB
☎ 01202 622222
e-mail: huntickcaravans@btconnect.com
dir: *Site between Lytchett Minster & Lytchett Matravers. From A31 take A350 towards Poole. Follow Lytchett Minster signs, then Lytchett Matravers signs. Huntick Rd by Red Cow pub*

PETS: Charges £1 per night **Public areas** disp bin **Exercise area** **Facilities** vet info

Open Apr-Oct Last arrival 21.00hrs Last departure noon

A really attractive little park nestling in rural surroundings edged by woodland, a mile from the village amenities of Lytchett Matravers. This neat grassy park is divided into three paddocks offering a peaceful location and yet close to the attractions of Poole and Bournemouth. A 4 acre site with 30 touring pitches.

Notes No ball games on site - field provided

South Lytchett Manor Caravan & Camping Park *(SY954926)*

▶ ▶ ▶ ▶ ▶

Dorchester Rd BH16 6JB
☎ 01202 622577
e-mail: info@southlytchettmanor.co.uk
dir: *On B3067, off A35, 1m E of Lytchett Minster, 600yds on right after village*

PETS: Charges £1 per night £7 per week **Public areas** except play area & toilet blocks disp bin **Exercise area** around pond & woods in adjoining fields **Facilities** food food bowl water bowl dog chews cat treats washing facs walks info vet info **Other** prior notice required disposal bags available **Restrictions** no Rottweilers **Resident Pets:** 2 Labradors, 1 Jack Russell, 1 cat, chickens

Open Mar-2 Jan Last arrival 21.00hrs Last departure 11.00hrs

Situated in the grounds of a historic Manor House the park has modern facilities which are spotless and well maintained. A warm and friendly welcome awaits at this lovely park, which is well located for visiting Poole and Bournemouth, and the Jurassic X53 bus route runs from just outside the park and along the coast between Poole and Exeter. A 20 acre site with 150 touring pitches, 60 hardstandings.

Notes No camp fires or Chinese lanterns

ENGLAND

Fishmore Hill Farm *(ST799013)*

★★★ FARMHOUSE

DT11 0DL

☎ 01258 881122 & 07708 003561 📄 01258 881122

Mr & Mrs N Clarke

e-mail: sarah@fishmorehillfarm.com

dir: *Off A354 signed Milton Abbas, 3m left on sharp bend, up steep hill, 1st left*

PETS: **Stables** Sep accom barn **Charges** dogs £5, horses £10 per night **Public areas** **Grounds** disp bin **Exercise area** National Trust/Forestry Commission land 500yds **Facilities** food bowl water bowl cage storage walks info **On Request** fridge access torch **Other** on-site veterinary practice; paddock for horses **Resident Pets:** dogs (Jack Russells), horses & sheep

This working sheep farm and family home is surrounded by beautiful Dorset countryside, is close to historic Milton Abbey and only a short drive from the coast. Bedrooms, which vary in size, are comfortable and finished with considerate extras. The atmosphere is friendly and relaxed. Breakfast is served in the smart dining room around a communal table.

Rooms 3 en suite **S** £35; **D** £70* **Facilities** TVL tea/coffee Cen ht **Parking** 4 **Notes** Closed Xmas & New Year 🐾 50 acres sheep/horses

Hotel du Vin Poole

★★★★ 78% 🏅 HOTEL

Thames St BH15 1JN

☎ 01202 758570 📄 01202 758571

e-mail: info.poole@hotelduvin.com

web: www.hotelduvin.com

dir: *A31 to Poole, follow channel ferry signs. Left at Poole bridge onto Poole Quay, 1st left into Thames St. Hotel opposite St James Church*

PETS: **Bedrooms** (4 GF) unattended **Charges** £10 per night **Public areas** except bistro on leads **Exercise area** 0.25m **Facilities** cage storage walks info vet info **On Request** fridge access torch **Other** charge for damage

Offering a fresh approach to the well established company style, this property boasts some delightful rooms packed with comfort and all the expected Hotel du Vin features. Situated near the harbour the hotel offers nautically-themed bedrooms and suites that have plasma TVs, DVD players and bathrooms with power showers. The public rooms have been transformed into light and open spaces, and as with the other hotels in this group the bar and restaurant form centre stage.

Rooms 38 (4 GF) **Facilities** STV Xmas New Year Wi-fi **Services** Air con **Parking** **Notes** LB

The Burleigh

★★★ GUEST ACCOMMODATION

76 Wimborne Rd BH15 2BZ

☎ 01202 673889 📄 01202 685283

dir: *Off A35 onto A349*

PETS: **Bedrooms** **Public areas** except dining room on leads **Exercise area** fields nearby **Facilities** walks info vet info **Other** charge for damage guests must bring own pet bedding; cats must be caged **Restrictions** contact proprietor to check size of dog accepted **Resident Pets:** Alfie (Tibetan Terrier), Cassie & Jazz (cats), tortoises

Suited to business and leisure, this well-kept guest accommodation is close to the town centre and ferry terminal. The individually furnished and decorated bedrooms are of a good standard. Breakfast is served at separate tables and there is a small, attractive lounge.

Rooms 8 rms (4 en suite) (1 fmly) **Facilities** TVL tea/coffee Cen ht Wi-fi **Parking** 5

Beacon Hill Touring Park *(SY977945)*

▶▶▶

Blandford Road North BH16 6AB

☎ 01202 631631 📄 01202 624388

e-mail: bookings@beaconhilltouringpark.co.uk

dir: *On A350, 0.25m N of junct with A35, 3m NW of Poole*

PETS: **Stables** 2.5m **Charges** £1-£1.50 per night **Public areas** disp bin **Exercise area** **Facilities** walks info vet info **Other** dog balls & toys available

Open Etr-end Oct rs Low & mid season some services closed/restricted opening Last arrival 23.00hrs Last departure 11.00hrs

Set in an attractive, wooded area with conservation very much in mind. Two large ponds for coarse fishing are within the grounds and the terraced pitches, informally sited so that visitors can choose their favourite spot, offer some fine views. The excellent outdoor swimming pool and tennis court are popular during the summer period. A 30 acre site with 170 touring pitches, 10 hardstandings.

Notes Groups of young people not accepted during high season

PUNCKNOWLE
Map 3 SY58

Offley Bed & Breakfast
★★★★ GUEST ACCOMMODATION

Looke Ln DT2 9BD
☎ 01308 897044 & 07792 624977
dir: *Off B3157 into village centre, left after Crown Inn onto Looke Ln, 1st house on right*

PETS: Bedrooms Public areas on leads **Grounds** disp bin
Exercise area woods & fields adjacent **Facilities** food bowl
water bowl feeding mat leads washing facs cage storage
walks info vet info **On Request** fridge access torch towels

With magnificent views over the Bride Valley, this village house
provides comfortable, quality accommodation. Guests are
assured of a warm, friendly welcome; an ideal venue to enjoy the
numerous local attractions. There are several local inns, one in
the village which is just a gentle stroll away.

Rooms 3 rms (2 en suite) (1 pri facs) **S** £45-£60; **D** £70*
Facilities TVL tea/coffee Cen ht **Parking** 3 **Notes** LB 🚭

ST LEONARDS
Map 4 SU10

Shamba Holidays *(SU105029)*
▶▶▶▶▶

230 Ringwood Rd BH24 2SB
☎ 01202 873302 📠 01202 873392
e-mail: enquiries@shambaholidays.co.uk
dir: *Off A31, from Poole turn left into Eastmoors Lane, 100yds
past 2nd rdbt from Texaco garage. Site 0.25m on right (just past
Woodman Inn)*

PETS: Charges £2.50 per night £17.50 per week **Public areas**
except buildings disp bin **Exercise area** 12-acre field
Exercise area woods 0.5m **Facilities** food walks info vet info

Open Mar-Oct rs Low season some facilities only open at wknds
Last arrival 22.00hrs Last departure 11.00hrs

A relaxed touring park in pleasant countryside between the New
Forest and Bournemouth. The park is very well equipped for
holidaymakers with a swimming pool, a good playground, bar,
shop and takeaway. A 7 acre site with 150 touring pitches.

Notes No large groups, no commercial vehicles

Back of Beyond Touring Park *(SU103034)*
▶▶▶▶

234 Ringwood Rd BH24 2SB
☎ 01202 876968 📠 01202 876968
e-mail: melandsuepike@aol.com
dir: *From E: on A31 over Little Chef rdbt, pass St Leonard's Hotel,
at next rdbt U-turn into lane immediately left to site at end of
lane. From W: on A31 pass Texaco garage & Woodsman Inn,
immediately left to site*

PETS: Charges £1 per night **Public areas** disp bin
Exercise area 18-acre wood **Facilities** food food bowl
water bowl walks info vet info **Other** prior notice required
Resident Pets: Holly, Dusty & Gabby (Dalmatians)

Open Mar-Oct Last arrival 19.00hrs Last departure noon

Set well off the beaten track in natural woodland surroundings,
with its own river and lake yet close to many attractions. This
tranquil park is run by keen, friendly owners, and the quality
facilities are for adults only. A 28 acre site with 80 touring
pitches.

Notes No commercial vehicles

Forest Edge Touring Park *(SU104024)*
▶▶▶

229 Ringwood Rd BH24 2SD
☎ 01590 648331 📠 01590 645610
e-mail: holidays@shorefield.co.uk
dir: *From E: on A31 over 1st rdbt (Little Chef), pass St Leonards
Hotel, left at next rdbt into Boundary Ln, site 100yds on left. From
W: on A31 pass Texaco garage & Woodsman Inn, right at rdbt into
Boundary Ln*

PETS: Stables nearby **Charges** £1.50 per night **Public areas**
Exercise area adjacent **Facilities** food water bowl bedding dog
chews cat treats washing facs walks info vet info **Other** 1 dog
only per pitch free disposal bags

Open Feb-9 Jan rs School & summer hols pool open Last arrival
21.00hrs Last departure 10.00hrs

A tree-lined park set in grassland with plenty of excellent
amenities for all the family, including an outdoor heated
swimming pool and toddlers' pool, an adventure playground, and
two launderettes. Visitors are invited to use the superb leisure
club plus all amenities and entertainment at the sister site of
Oakdene Forest Park less than a mile away. Some pitches may
experience traffic noise from the nearby A31. A 9 acre site with 92
touring pitches and 28 statics.

Notes Families & couples only. 1 car per pitch. Rallies welcome

SHAFTESBURY   Map 3 ST82

Best Western Royal Chase
★★★ 72% ◉ HOTEL
Royal Chase Roundabout SP7 8DB
☎ 01747 853355 ▤ 01747 851969
e-mail: royalchasehotel@btinternet.com
web: www.theroyalchasehotel.co.uk
dir: *A303 to A350 signed Blandford Forum. Avoid town centre, follow road to 3rd rdbt*

PETS: Bedrooms (6 GF) unattended **Charges** £6.50 per night **Public areas** except bar & restaurant **Grounds** disp bin **Facilities** cage storage walks info vet info **On Request** fridge access towels

Equally suitable for both leisure and business guests, this well-known local landmark is situated close to the famous Gold Hill. Both Standard and Crown bedrooms offer good levels of comfort and quality. In addition to the fixed-price menu in the Byzant Restaurant, guests have the option of eating more informally in the convivial bar.

Rooms 33 (13 fmly) (6 GF) **Facilities** ⓢ Turkish steam room Wi-fi **Parking** 100 **Notes** LB

Blackmore Vale Caravan & Camping Park
(ST835233)
▶▶

Sherborne Causeway SP7 9PX
☎ 01747 851523 & 852573 ▤ 01747 851671
e-mail: camping@bmvgroup.co.uk
dir: *From Shaftesbury's Ivy Cross rdbt take A30 signed Sherborne. Site 2m on right*

PETS: Charges £1 per night **Public areas** on leads disp bin **Exercise area** large field adjacent **Facilities** walks info vet info **Other** prior notice required **Restrictions** no Rottweilers, Dobermans or Pit Bulls **Resident Pets:** cats & chickens

Open all year Last arrival 21.00hrs

A pleasant touring park with spacious pitches and well-maintained facilities. A fully-equipped gym is the latest addition to this park, and is open to visitors. Blackmore Vale is set behind a caravan sales showroom and dealership, and about two miles from Shaftesbury. A 5 acre site with 26 touring pitches, 6 hardstandings.

SWANAGE   Map 4 SZ07

The Pines
★★★ 77% HOTEL
Burlington Rd BH19 1LT
☎ 01929 425211 ▤ 01929 422075
e-mail: reservations@pineshotel.co.uk
web: www.pineshotel.co.uk
dir: *A351 to seafront, left then 2nd right. Hotel at end of road*

PETS: Bedrooms (6 GF) unattended **Stables** 4m **Grounds** on leads disp bin **Exercise area Facilities** walks info vet info **On Request** torch towels

Enjoying a peaceful location with spectacular views over the cliffs and sea, The Pines is a pleasant place to stay. Many of the comfortable bedrooms have sea views. Guests can take tea in the lounge, enjoy appetising bar snacks in the attractive bar, and interesting cuisine in the restaurant.

Rooms 41 (26 fmly) (6 GF) **S** £64-£75; **D** £128-£172 (incl. bkfst)* **Facilities** FTV ♫ Xmas New Year Wi-fi **Services** Lift **Parking** 60 **Notes** LB

Ulwell Cottage Caravan Park *(SZ019809)*
▶▶▶▶

Ulwell Cottage, Ulwell BH19 3DG
☎ 01929 422823 ▤ 01929 421500
e-mail: enq@ulwellcottagepark.co.uk
dir: *From Swanage N for 2m on unclass road towards Studland*

PETS: Charges Public areas on leads disp bin **Exercise area** 100yds **Facilities** food food bowl water bowl bedding dog chews scoop/disp bags leads walks info vet info

Open Mar-7 Jan rs Mar-Spring BH & mid Sep-early Jan takeaway closed, shop open variable hrs Last arrival 22.00hrs Last departure 11.00hrs

Nestling under the Purbeck Hills surrounded by scenic walks and only two miles from the beach. This family-run park caters well for families and couples, offering high quality facilities including an indoor heated swimming pool and village inn. A 13 acre site with 77 touring pitches, 19 hardstandings and 140 statics.

ENGLAND

Herston Caravan & Camping Park *(SZ018785)*

▶ ▶ ▶

Washpond Ln BH19 3DJ
☎ 01929 422932 📠 01929 423888
e-mail: office@herstonleisure.co.uk
dir: *From Wareham on A351 towards Swanage. Washpond Ln on left just after 'Welcome to Swanage' sign*

PETS: Public areas on leads Exercise area on site
Exercise area adjacent to park Facilities food food bowl water bowl bedding dog chews leads walks info vet info Other prior notice required disposal bags available

Open all year

Set in a rural area with extensive views of the Purbecks, this tree lined park has many full facility pitches and quality toilet facilities. Herston Halt is within walking distance, a stop for the famous Swanage steam railway between the town centre and Corfe Castle. A 10 acre site with 100 touring pitches, 71 hardstandings and 5 statics.

Notes No noise after 23.00hrs.

The Langton Arms

★★★★ INN

DT11 8RX
☎ 01258 830225 📠 01258 830053
e-mail: info@thelangtonarms.co.uk
dir: *Off A354 in Tarrant Hinton to Tarrant Monkton, through ford, Langton Arms opp*

PETS: Bedrooms Stables 1m Charges £10 per night
Public areas except small bar on leads Grounds Exercise area Facilities cage storage walks info vet info On Request fridge access torch towels

Tucked away in this sleepy Dorset village, the Langton Arms offers stylish, light and airy accommodation and is a good base for touring this attractive area. Bedrooms, all on the ground-floor level in the modern annexe, are very well equipped and comfortable. There is a choice of dining options - the relaxed bar-restaurant or the more formal Stables Restaurant, offering innovative and appetising dishes. Breakfast is served in the conservatory dining room just a few steps through the pretty courtyard.

Rooms 6 annexe en suite (6 fmly) (6 GF) S £70; D £90*
Facilities tea/coffee Dinner available Direct Dial Cen ht
Parking 100

Luckford Wood House

★ ★ ★ GUEST ACCOMMODATION

East Stoke BH20 6AW
☎ 01929 463098 & 07888 719002
e-mail: luckfordleisure@hotmail.co.uk
web: www.luckfordleisure.co.uk
dir: *3m W of Wareham. Off A352, take B3070 to Lulworth, turn right onto Holme Ln, signed East Stoke. 1m right onto Church Ln*

PETS: Bedrooms Charges £5 per night £30 per week
Public areas except dining room & lounge on leads
Exercise area lane adjacent Facilities cage storage walks info vet info On Request fridge access torch towels Restrictions Resident Pet: Sammy (cat)

Rurally situated about three miles west of Wareham, this family home offers comfortable accommodation. Situated on the edge of woodland, there is abundant wildlife to see. Guests can be assured of a friendly welcome and an extensive choice at breakfast.

Rooms 6 rms (3 en suite) (1 pri facs) (3 fmly) (1 GF) S £30-£60; D £55-£85* Facilities FTV TVL tea/coffee Cen ht Wi-fi Parking 6 Notes LB

Wareham Forest Tourist Park *(SY894912)*

▶ ▶ ▶ ▶ ▶

North Trigon BH20 7NZ
☎ 01929 551393 📠 01929 558321
e-mail: holiday@warehamforest.co.uk
dir: *Telephone for directions*

PETS: Charges max £1.50 per night Public areas except buildings on leads disp bin Exercise area woodland walks Exercise area adjacent Facilities washing facs walks info vet info Restrictions well behaved dogs only

Open all year rs Off-peak season limited services Last arrival 21.00hrs Last departure 11.00hrs

A woodland park within the tranquil Wareham Forest, with its many walks and proximity to Poole, Dorchester and the Purbeck coast. Two luxury blocks, with combined washbasin/WCs for total privacy, maintain a high standard of cleanliness. A heated outdoor swimming pool, off licence, shop and games room add to the pleasure of a stay here. A 55 acre site with 200 touring pitches, 70 hardstandings.

Notes Couples & families only, no group bookings

WEST LULWORTH — Map 3 SY88

Cromwell House
★★ 75% HOTEL
Lulworth Cove BH20 5RJ
☎ 01929 400253 & 400332 📠 01929 400566
e-mail: catriona@lulworthcove.co.uk
web: www.lulworthcove.co.uk
dir: *200yds beyond end of West Lulworth, left onto high slip road, hotel 100yds on left opposite beach car park*

PETS: Bedrooms (2 GF) unattended sign Charges £4 per night Public areas except dining room on leads Grounds disp bin Exercise area adjacent Facilities water bowl washing facs cage storage walks info vet info On Request fridge access torch towels Resident Pets: Douglas (Bearded Collie cross), Lily (cat)

Built in 1881 by the Mayor of Weymouth, specifically as a guest house, this family-run hotel now provides visitors with an ideal base for touring the area and for exploring the beaches and coast. The house enjoys spectacular views across the sea and countryside. Bedrooms, many with sea views, are comfortable and some have been specifically designed for family use.

Rooms 18 (1 annexe) (3 fmly) (2 GF) S £45-£67; D £90-£114 (incl. bkfst) Facilities ⚲ Access to Dorset coastal footpath & Jurassic Coast Wi-fi Parking 17 Notes LB Closed 22 Dec-3 Jan RS Xmas & New Year

WEYMOUTH — Map 3 SY67

Bagwell Farm Touring Park (SY627816)
▶▶▶▶
Knights in the Bottom, Chickerell DT3 4EA
☎ 01305 782575 📠 01305 780554
e-mail: aa@bagwellfarm.co.uk
dir: *4m W of Weymouth on B3157 (Weymouth-Bridport), past Chickerell, turn left into site 500yds after Victoria Inn*

PETS: Charges Public areas except washrooms & one eating area on leads Exercise area field available (dogs on leads) Facilities food food bowl water bowl dog chews cat treats scoop/disp bags leads walks info vet info Other prior notice required dogs must be kept on short leads (2mtrs max) & not left unattended.

Open all year rs Winter bar closed Last arrival 21.00hrs Last departure 11.00hrs

An idyllically-placed terraced site on a hillside and a valley overlooking Chesil Beach. The park is well equipped with 25 fully-serviced pitches, mini-supermarket, children's play area and pets corner, and a bar and grill serving food in high season. A 14 acre site with 320 touring pitches, 10 hardstandings.

Notes Families only

WIMBORNE MINSTER — Map 3 SZ09

Les Bouviers Restaurant with Rooms
★★★★★ ◉◉ RESTAURANT WITH ROOMS
Arrowsmith Rd, Canford Magna BH21 3BD
☎ 01202 889555 📠 01202 639428
e-mail: info@lesbouviers.co.uk
web: www.lesbouviers.co.uk
dir: *A31 onto A349. In 0.6m turn left. In approx 1m right onto Arrowsmith Rd. Establishment approx 100yds on right*

PETS: Bedrooms sign Charges £25 per night Public areas except restaurant on leads Grounds on leads disp bin Exercise area 2min walk Facilities food (pre-bookable) food bowl water bowl dog chews feeding mat cage storage walks info vet info On Request fridge access torch Other charge for damage Restrictions no dogs of similar size, or larger than, a Great Dane

An excellent restaurant with rooms in a great location, set in six acres of grounds. Food is a highlight of any stay here as is the friendly, attentive service. Bedrooms are extremely well equipped and beds are supremely comfortable.

Rooms 6 en suite (4 fmly) S £110-£185; D £130-£215*
Facilities FTV tea/coffee Dinner available Direct Dial Cen ht Wi-fi Parking 50 Notes LB RS Sun eve restricted opening & restaurant closed

Wilksworth Farm Caravan Park (SU004018)

▶ ▶ ▶ ▶ ▶

Cranborne Rd BH21 4HW
☎ 01202 885467   📄 01202 885467
e-mail: rayandwendy@wilksworthfarmcaravanpark.co.uk
dir: *1m N of Wimborne on B3078*

PETS: Charges £1.50 per night £10.50 per week **Public areas**
except coffee shop, shop, pool & play area on leads disp bin
Exercise area dog exercise paddock & walk **Facilities** walks
info vet info **Other** prior notice required **Restrictions** max 2 pets
per pitch

Open Apr-Oct rs Oct no shop Last arrival 20.00hrs Last departure
11.00hrs

A popular and attractive park set in the grounds of a listed house,
tranquilly placed in the heart of rural Dorset. The spacious site
has much to offer visitors, including a heated swimming pool,
take-away and café, and games room. The ultra-modern toilet
facilities contain en suite rooms. An 11 acre site with 85 touring
pitches, 20 hardstandings and 77 statics.

Charris Camping & Caravan Park (SY992988)

▶ ▶ ▶

Candy's Ln, Corfe Mullen BH21 3EF
☎ 01202 885970
e-mail: bookings@charris.co.uk
dir: *From E, exit Wimborne bypass (A31) W end. 300yds after
Caravan Sales, follow brown sign. From W on A31, over A350 rdbt,
take next turn after B3074, follow brown signs*

PETS: Public areas except toilet & shop disp bin **Exercise area**
0.25m **Facilities** food bowl water bowl washing facs walks
info vet info **Other** prior notice required disposal bags available
Resident Pets: Spike (cat), 12 doves

Open Mar-Jan Last arrival 21.00hrs Last departure 11.00hrs

A sheltered park of grassland lined with trees, on the edge of the
Stour Valley. The owners are friendly and welcoming, and they
maintain the park facilities to a good standard. Barbecues are a
popular occasional event. A 3.5 acre site with 45 touring pitches,
12 hardstandings.

Notes Earliest arrival time 11.00hrs

The Morritt

★★★★ 77% HOTEL

Greta Bridge DL12 9SE
☎ 01833 627232   📄 01833 627392
e-mail: relax@themorritt.co.uk
web: www.themorritt.co.uk
dir: *Exit A1 (A1(M)) at Scotch Corner onto A66 W'bound towards
Penrith. Greta Bridge 9m on left*

PETS: Bedrooms (4 GF) **Stables** 5m **Charges** £10 per night
Public areas except restaurants on leads **Grounds** on leads
disp bin **Exercise area** countryside adjacent **Facilities** washing
facs cage storage walks info vet info **On Request** fridge access
torch towels **Other** charge for damage dogs allowed in Silver
courtyard rooms only; guests are requested to bring dog's own
bed

Set off the main road at Greta Bridge, this 17th-century former
coaching house provides comfortable public rooms full of
character. The bar, with its interesting Dickensian mural, is very
much focused on food, but in addition a fine dining is offered in
the oak-panelled restaurant. Bedrooms come in individual styles
and of varying sizes. The attentive service is noteworthy.

Rooms 27 (6 annexe) (3 fmly) (4 GF) **S** £80-£175; **D** £90-£175
(incl. bkfst)* **Facilities** FTV Xmas New Year Wi-fi **Parking** 40
Notes LB

Best Western Derwent Manor

OXFORD
HOTELS & INNS

★★★ 73% HOTEL

Allensford DH8 9BB
☎ 01207 592000   📄 01207 502472
e-mail: reservations.derwentmanor@ohiml.com
web: www.oxfordhotelsandinns.com
dir: *On A68*

PETS: Bedrooms (26 GF) **Grounds** **Exercise area** surrounding
countryside **Other** dogs are accepted by prior arrangement only

This hotel, built in the style of a manor house, is set in open
grounds overlooking the River Derwent. Spacious bedrooms,
including a number of suites, are comfortably equipped. A
popular wedding venue, there are also extensive conference
facilities and an impressive leisure suite. The Grouse & Claret bar
serves a wide range of drinks and light meals, and Guinevere's
restaurant offers the fine dining option.

Rooms 48 (3 fmly) (26 GF) **S** £55-£150; (incl. bkfst)*
Facilities STV FTV 🏊 supervised Gym Xmas New Year Child
facilities **Services** Lift **Parking** 100 **Notes** LB

ENGLAND

DARLINGTON — Map 8 NZ21

Headlam Hall
★★★★ 75% ◉ HOTEL

Headlam, Gainford DL2 3HA
☎ 01325 730238 📠 01325 730790
e-mail: admin@headlamhall.co.uk
web: www.headlamhall.co.uk
dir: *2m N of A67 between Piercebridge & Gainford*

PETS: Bedrooms (10 GF) unattended **Stables Grounds** on leads disp bin **Exercise area** 50yds **Facilities** water bowl washing facs cage storage walks info vet info **On Request** fridge access torch **Other** charge for damage dogs allowed in certain bedrooms only **Restrictions** small & medium size dogs only; no Rottweilers, Dobermans, Alsatians or similar breeds

This impressive Jacobean hall lies in farmland north-east of Piercebridge and has its own 9-hole golf course. The main house retains many historical features, including flagstone floors and a pillared hall. Bedrooms are well proportioned and traditionally styled; a converted coach house contains the more modern rooms. There are extensive conference facilities, and the hotel is popular as a wedding venue. There is a stunning spa complex with a 14-metre pool, an outdoor hot spa, drench shower, sauna and steam room. There is also a gym with the latest cardio and resistance equipment, and five treatment rooms offering a range of therapies and beauty treatments.

Rooms 40 (22 annexe) (4 fmly) (10 GF) **S** £90-£115; **D** £115-£140 (incl. bkfst)* **Facilities** Spa STV FTV 🔾 ♨ 🏌 Putt green Fishing 🏊 Gym New Year Wi-fi **Services** Lift **Parking** 80 **Notes** LB Closed 24-26 Dec

The Blackwell Grange Hotel
★★★ 79% HOTEL

Blackwell Grange DL3 8QH
☎ 0870 609 6121 & 01325 509955 📠 01325 380899
e-mail: blackwell.grange@forestdale.com
web: www.blackwellgrangehotel.com
dir: *On A167, 1.5m from central ring road*

PETS: Bedrooms (36 GF) **Charges** £7.50 per night **Public areas** except restaurant **Other** please phone for further details of pet facilities

This beautiful 17th-century mansion is peacefully situated in nine acres of its own grounds yet is convenient for the motorway network. The pick of the bedrooms are in a courtyard building or the impressive feature rooms in the original house. The Havelock Restaurant offers a range of traditional and continental menus.

Rooms 108 (11 annexe) (3 fmly) (36 GF) **S** £69-£104; **D** £79-£114 (incl. bkfst)* **Facilities** FTV 🔾 Gym Beauty room Xmas New Year Wi-fi **Services** Lift **Parking** 250 **Notes** LB

DURHAM — Map 12 NZ24

Marriott
HOTELS & RESORTS

Durham Marriott Hotel, Royal County
★★★★ 78% HOTEL

Old Elvet DH1 3JN
☎ 0191 386 6821 📠 0191 386 0704
e-mail: mhrs.xvudm.frontdesk@marriotthotels.com
web: www.durhammarriottroyalcounty.co.uk
dir: *From A1(M) junct 62, then A690 to Durham, over 1st rdbt, left at 2nd rdbt left at lights, hotel on left*

PETS: Bedrooms (15 GF) **Public areas** except restaurant & bar on leads **Exercise area Facilities** vet info **Other** charge for damage **Restrictions** small dogs only

In a wonderful position on the banks of the River Wear, the hotel's central location makes it ideal for visiting the attractions of this historic city. The building was developed from a series of Jacobean town houses. The bedrooms are tastefully styled. Eating options include the County Restaurant, for formal dining, and the Cruz Restaurant. Marriott Hotels - AA Hotel Group of the Year 2010-11.

Rooms 150 (8 annexe) (10 fmly) (15 GF) (8 smoking) **S** £110-£219; **D** £130-£239 (incl. bkfst)* **Facilities** STV FTV 🔾 supervised Gym Turkish steam room Plunge pool Sanarium Tropical fun shower Wi-fi **Services** Lift **Parking** 76

MIDDLETON-IN-TEESDALE — Map 12 NY92

The Teesdale Hotel
★★ 65% HOTEL

Market Place DL12 0QG
☎ 01833 640264 📠 01833 640651
e-mail: enquiries@teesdalehotel.co.uk
web: www.teesdalehotel.co.uk
dir: *From Barnard Castle take B6278, follow signs for Middleton-in-Teesdale & Highforce. Hotel in town centre*

PETS: Bedrooms Charges £5 per night **Public areas** bar only on leads **Exercise area** 50mtrs **Facilities** walks info vet info **Restrictions** small - medium size dogs only

Located in the heart of the popular village, this family-run hotel offers a relaxed and friendly atmosphere. Bedrooms and bathrooms are well equipped and offer a good standard of quality and comfort. Public areas include a residents' lounge on the first floor, a spacious restaurant and a lounge bar which is popular with locals.

Rooms 14 (1 fmly) **S** £35-£45; **D** £70-£80 (incl. bkfst)* **Facilities** Wi-fi **Parking** 20 **Notes** LB

REDWORTH — Map 8 NZ22

Barceló Redworth Hall Hotel

★★★★ 77% COUNTRY HOUSE HOTEL

DL5 6NL

☎ 01388 770600 📠 01388 770654

e-mail: redworthhall@barcelo-hotels.co.uk

web: www.barcelo-hotels.co.uk

dir: From A1(M) junct 58/A68 signed Corbridge. Follow hotel signs

PETS: Bedrooms Charges £15 per stay **Public areas** only to gain access to bedrooms on leads **Grounds** disp bin **Facilities** food (pre-bookable) food bowl water bowl bedding feeding mat dog grooming walks info vet info **On Request** fridge access **Other** charge for damage grooming treatment details (charges on request)

This imposing Georgian building includes a health club with state-of-the-art equipment and impressive conference facilities making this a popular destination for business travellers. There are several spacious lounges to relax in along with the Conservatory Restaurant. Bedrooms are very comfortable and well equipped.

Rooms 143 (12 fmly) **Facilities** STV ⓣ ⓢ ⓨ Gym Bodysense Health & Leisure Club ♫ Xmas New Year Wi-fi **Services** Lift **Parking** 300

ROMALDKIRK — Map 12 NY92

Rose & Crown

★★ ⚜️⚜️ HOTEL

DL12 9EB

☎ 01833 650213 📠 01833 650828

e-mail: hotel@rose-and-crown.co.uk

web: www.rose-and-crown.co.uk

dir: 6m NW from Barnard Castle on B6277

PETS: Bedrooms (5 GF) **Stables** 0.5m **Charges** £5 per night **Public areas** except restaurant/brasserie on leads **Facilities** walks info vet info **On Request** fridge access torch **Other** charge for damage

This charming 18th-century country inn is located in the heart of the village, overlooking fine dale scenery. The area is renowned for its walking opportunities and many lovely routes lead from the hotel; a walking guide will be found in each bedroom. The attractively furnished bedrooms, including suites, are split between the main house and the rear courtyard. Guests might like to have a drink in the cosy bar with its log fire, after returning from a long walk. Good local produce features extensively on the menus that can be enjoyed in the oak-panelled restaurant with its white linen and gleaming silverware, or in the brasserie and bar. Service is both friendly and attentive.

Rooms 12 (5 annexe) (1 fmly) (5 GF) **S** £92-£120; **D** £140-£180 (incl. bkfst)* **Facilities** STV New Year **Parking** 20 **Notes** LB Closed 24-26 Dec

ESSEX

BIRCHANGER GREEN MOTORWAY SERVICE AREA (M11) Map 5 TL52

Days Inn Bishop's Stortford

BUDGET HOTEL

CM23 5QZ

☎ 01279 656477 📠 01279 656590

e-mail: birchanger.hotel@welcomebreak.co.uk

web: www.welcomebreak.co.uk

dir: M11 junct 8

PETS: Bedrooms Charges £10 per stay **Public areas** on leads **Grounds** on leads **Exercise area** grass area **On Request** towels **Other** charge for damage

This modern building offers accommodation in smart, spacious and well-equipped bedrooms, suitable for families and business travellers, and all with en suite bathrooms. Continental breakfast is available and other refreshments may be taken at the nearby family restaurant.

Rooms 60 (57 fmly) (10 smoking) **S** £29-£59; **D** £29-£69

CANEWDON — Map 5 TQ99

Riverside Village Holiday Park (TQ929951)

►►►

Creeksea Ferry Rd, Wallasea Island SS4 2EY

☎ 01702 258297 📠 01702 258555

e-mail: riversidevillage@tiscali.co.uk

dir: M25 junct 29, A127, towards Southend-on-Sea. Take B1013 towards Rochford. Follow signs for Wallsea Island & Baltic Wharf

PETS: Charges £2 per night **Public areas** except children's play area on leads disp bin **Exercise area** long lakeside 'run', designated dog walk **Facilities** food walks info vet info **Other** prior notice required disposal bags available

Open Mar-Oct

Next to a nature reserve beside the River Crouch, this holiday park is surrounded by wetlands but only eight miles from Southend. A modern toilet block with disabled facilities is provided for tourers. Several restaurants and pubs are within a short distance. A 25 acre site with 60 touring pitches and 162 statics.

CLACTON-ON-SEA — Map 5 TM11

The Sandrock

★★★★ GUEST ACCOMMODATION

1 Penfold Rd, Marine Parade West CO15 1JN
☎ 01255 428215
e-mail: thesandrock@btinternet.com
web: www.thesandrock.co.uk
dir: A133 to seafront, turn right, pass lights at pier, then take 2nd right

PETS: Bedrooms Charges £6 per night £42 per week
Public areas disp bin **Exercise area** 50mtrs **Facilities** vet info **Other** charge for damage dogs only to be left unattended in bedroom at breakfast **Restrictions** well behaved, small & medium size dogs only

A warm welcome is offered at this Victorian property, just off the seafront and within easy walking distance of the town centre. The attractive bedrooms vary in size and style, are thoughtfully equipped, and some have sea views. Breakfast is served in the smart bar-restaurant and there is also a cosy lounge.

Rooms 9 en suite (1 fmly) (1 GF) **S** £38-£43; **D** £58-£63*
Facilities TVL tea/coffee Cen ht Wi-fi **Parking** 5 **Notes** LB

GREAT CHESTERFORD — Map 5 TL54

The Crown House

★★★ 74% ® HOTEL

CB10 1NY
☎ 01799 530515 ≣ 01799 530683
e-mail: reservations@crownhousehotel.com
web: www.crownhousehotel.com
dir: From N exit M11 at junct 9, from S junct 10, follow signs for Saffron Walden & then Great Chesterford (B1383)

PETS: Bedrooms (5 GF) unattended **Charges** £5 per night
Public areas lounge only on leads **Grounds** on leads disp bin
Facilities washing facs walks info vet info **On Request** fridge access torch towels **Other** charge for damage

This Georgian coaching inn, situated in a peaceful village close to the M11, has been sympathetically restored and retains much original character. The bedrooms are well equipped and individually decorated; some rooms have delightful four-poster beds. Public rooms include an attractive lounge bar, an elegant oak-panelled restaurant and an airy conservatory.

Rooms 22 (14 annexe) (2 fmly) (5 GF) **S** £79.50-£109.50;
D £99.50-£145.50 (incl. bkfst)* **Facilities** FTV New Year Wi-fi
Parking 30 **Notes** LB Closed 27-30 Dec

MERSEA ISLAND — Map 5 TM01

Waldegraves Holiday Park (TM33133)

CO5 8SE
☎ 01206 382898 ≣ 01206 385359
e-mail: holidays@waldegraves.co.uk
dir: B1025 to Mersea Island across The Strood. Left to East Mersea, 2nd turn on right, follow tourist signs to site

PETS: Charges touring pitches £2 per night **Public areas** except restaurant, shop, clubhouse & pool on leads disp bin
Exercise area field available **Exercise area** 3m **Facilities** food food bowl water bowl dog chews cat treats litter tray walks info vet info **Other** prior notice required disposal bags available

Open Mar-Nov Last arrival 22.00hrs Last departure 15.00hrs

A spacious and pleasant site, located between farmland and its own private beach on the Blackwater Estuary. Facilities include two freshwater fishing lakes, heated swimming pool, club, amusements, café and golf, and there is generally good provision for families. A 25 acre site with 60 touring pitches and 250 statics.

Notes No large groups or groups of under 21s

GLOUCESTERSHIRE

Tally Ho Bed & Breakfast

★★★★ BED AND BREAKFAST

20 Beckford Rd GL20 8NL

☎ 01242 621482 & 07966 593169

e-mail: tallyhobb@aol.com

dir: M5 junct 9, A46 signed Evesham, through Ashchurch. Take B4077 signed Stow-on-the-Wold & Alderton. Left in 1.5m opp garage signed Alderton

PETS: Bedrooms Exercise area 200yds Facilities walks info vet info Other charge for damage Resident Pets: Springer Spaniels, Fox Terriers

Convenient for the M5, this friendly establishment stands in a delightful quiet village. Bedrooms, including two on the ground floor, offer modern comforts and attractive co-ordinated furnishings. Breakfast is served in the stylish dining room, and for dinner, the village pub is just a stroll away.

Rooms 3 en suite (1 fmly) (2 GF) S £45-£50; D £65-£70 Facilities FTV tea/coffee Cen ht Wi-fi Parking 3 Notes LB

Alveston House Hotel

★★★ 80% ⊚ HOTEL

Davids Ln, Alveston BS35 2LA

☎ 01454 415050 ▨ 01454 415425

e-mail: info@alvestonhousehotel.co.uk

web: www.alvestonhousehotel.co.uk

dir: M5 junct 14 from N or junct 16 from S, on A38

PETS: Bedrooms (6 GF) Stables 5m Public areas except restaurant on leads Grounds Exercise area 0.5m Facilities water bowl cage storage walks info vet info On Request fridge access torch towels Other charge for damage

In a quiet area with easy access to the city and a short drive from both the M4 and M5, this smartly presented hotel provides an impressive combination of good service, friendly hospitality and a relaxed atmosphere. The comfortable bedrooms are well equipped for both business and leisure guests. The restaurant offers carefully prepared fresh food, and the pleasant bar and conservatory area is perfect for enjoying a pre-dinner drink.

Rooms 30 (1 fmly) (6 GF) S £75-£100; D £100-£140 (incl. bkfst)* Facilities FTV Xmas New Year Wi-fi Parking 75 Notes LB

Bibury Court

★★★ 83% ⊚⊚ COUNTRY HOUSE HOTEL

GL7 5NT

☎ 01285 740337 & 741171 ▨ 01285 740660

e-mail: info@biburycourt.com

web: www.biburycourt.com

dir: On B4425, 6m N of Cirencester (A4179). 8m S of Burford (A40), entrance by River Coln

PETS: Bedrooms (1 GF) Charges £20 per stay Public areas except dining room, bar & conservatory on leads Grounds disp bin Facilities food (pre-bookable) food bowl water bowl bedding dog chews walks info vet info On Request fridge access torch Other charge for damage

Dating back to Tudor times, this elegant manor is the perfect antidote to the hustle and bustle of the modern world. Public areas have abundant charm and character. Bedrooms are spacious and offer traditional quality with modern comforts. A choice of interesting dishes is available in the conservatory at lunchtime, whereas dinner is served in the more formal restaurant. Staff are friendly and helpful.

Rooms 18 (3 fmly) (1 GF) S £140-£180; D £170-£250 (incl. bkfst)* Facilities FTV Fishing ⛄ Xmas New Year Wi-fi Parking 40 Notes LB

Swan

★★★ 82% ⊚ HOTEL

GL7 5NW

☎ 01285 740695 ▨ 01285 740473

e-mail: info@swanhotel.co.uk

web: www.cotswold-inns-hotels.co.uk/swan

dir: 9m S of Burford A40 onto B4425. 6m N of Cirencester A4179 onto B4425

Cotswold Inns & Hotels

PETS: Bedrooms unattended Charges £15 per night Public areas except eating areas on leads Exercise area surrounding fields & paths Facilities walks info vet info On Request fridge access torch towels Other charge for damage

This hotel, built in the 17th century as a coaching inn, is set in peaceful and picturesque surroundings. It provides well-equipped and smartly presented accommodation, including four luxury cottage suites set just outside the main hotel. The elegant public areas are comfortable and have feature fireplaces. There is a choice of dining options to suit all tastes.

Rooms 22 (4 annexe) (1 fmly) D £155-£195 (incl. bkfst)* Facilities Fishing Xmas New Year Wi-fi Services Lift Parking 22 Notes LB

Chester House
★★ **79**% HOTEL
Victoria St GL54 2BU
☎ 01451 820286 📠 01451 820471
e-mail: info@chesterhousehotel.com
dir: *On A429 between Northleach & Stow-on-the-Wold*

PETS: Bedrooms (8 GF) unattended **Public areas** except dining areas on leads **Grounds** on leads **Exercise area** 300mtrs **Facilities** cage storage walks info vet info **On Request** fridge access **Other** charge for damage **Resident Pet:** Poppy (Patterdale Terrier)

This hotel occupies a secluded but central location in this delightful Cotswold village. Bedrooms, some at ground floor level, are situated in the main house and adjoining coach house. The public areas are stylish, light and airy. Breakfast is taken in the main building whereas dinner is served in the attractive restaurant just a few yards away.

Rooms 22 (10 annexe) (8 fmly) (8 GF) **Facilities** Beauty therapist New Year Wi-fi **Parking** 18 **Notes** Closed 7 Jan-1 Feb

Hotel du Vin & Bistro

Hotel du Vin Cheltenham
★★★★ **80**% 🏅 HOTEL
Parabola Rd GL50 3AQ
☎ 01242 588450 📠 01242 588455
e-mail: info@cheltenham.hotelduvin.com
web: www.hotelduvin.com
dir: *M5 junct 11, follow signs for city centre. At rdbt opposite Morgan Estate Agents take 2nd left, 200mtrs to Parabola Rd*

PETS: Bedrooms (5 GF) unattended **Public areas** except bistro on leads **Exercise area** 10 min walk **Facilities** walks info **Other** bowl & basket available at a charge

This hotel, in the Montpellier area of the town, has spacious public areas that are packed with stylish features. The pewter-topped bar has comfortable seating and the spacious restaurant has the Hotel du Vin trademark design in evidence; alfresco dining is possible on the extensive terrace area. Bedrooms are very comfortable, with Egyptian linen, deep baths and power showers. The spa is the ideal place to relax and unwind. Although parking is limited, it is a definite bonus. Service is friendly and attentive.

Rooms 49 (2 fmly) (5 GF) **S** £145-£350; **D** £145-£350* **Facilities** Spa STV Wi-fi **Services** Lift Air con **Parking** 26

The Greenway
★★★ **86**% 🏅🏅 COUNTRY HOUSE HOTEL
Shurdington GL51 4UG
☎ 01242 862352 📠 01242 862780
e-mail: info@thegreenway.co.uk
web: www.thegreenway.co.uk
dir: *From Cheltenham centre 2.5m S on A46*

PETS: Bedrooms unattended **Charges** £5 per night **Grounds** **Exercise area** adjacent countryside **Facilities** food bowl water bowl washing facs walks info vet info **On Request** fridge access torch towels **Other** charge for damage

This hotel, with a wealth of history, is peacefully located in a delightful setting close within easy reach of the many attractions of the Cotswolds and also the M5. The Greenway certainly offers something different. The Manor House bedrooms are luxuriously appointed - traditional in style yet with plasma TVs and internet access. The tranquil Coach House rooms, in the converted stable block, have direct access to the beautiful grounds. The attractive dining room overlooks the sunken garden and is the venue for excellent food, proudly served by dedicated and attentive staff.

Rooms 17 (6 annexe) (4 fmly) **S** £150-£455; **D** £150-£455 (incl. bkfst)* **Facilities** Spa FTV 🏊 Clay pigeon shooting Horse riding Mountain biking Archery Xmas New Year Wi-fi **Parking** 50 **Notes** LB

Charlton Kings
★★★ **74**% SMALL HOTEL
London Rd, Charlton Kings GL52 6UU
☎ 01242 231061 📠 01242 241900
e-mail: enquiries@charltonkingshotel.co.uk
dir: *From E (London or Oxford) on A40, hotel 1st building on left on entering Cheltenham. From M5 towards town centre follow Oxford/A40 signs. Through town, hotel last building on right on exiting Cheltenham*

PETS: Bedrooms (3 GF) unattended **Public areas** except restaurant **Grounds** disp bin **Exercise area** 100yds **Facilities** walks info vet info **On Request** fridge access **Resident Pet:** Charlie (Collie cross)

Personally run by the resident proprietors, the relatively small size of this hotel enables a good deal of individual guest care and attention. Bedrooms are very well decorated and furnished and include some welcome extras. Breakfast and dinner, served in the comfortable conservatory-style restaurant, offer a good selection of carefully prepared ingredients. There's a pleasant garden and rear car park.

Rooms 13 (3 GF) **Facilities** STV Wi-fi **Parking** 15

Cotswold Grange

★★ 75% HOTEL

Pittville Circus Rd GL52 2QH

☎ 01242 515119   📠 01242 241537

e-mail: info@cotswoldgrange.co.uk

dir: *From town centre, follow Prestbury signs. Right at 1st rdbt, next rdbt straight over, hotel 100yds on left*

PETS: **Bedrooms Charges** £5 per night **Public areas** except restaurant on leads **Grounds Exercise area** park nearby **Facilities** walks info vet info **On Request** fridge access torch **Other** charge for damage **Restrictions** no very large dogs; no dangerous dogs (see page 7)

A delightful building located in a quieter, mainly residential area of Cheltenham, near Pitville Park and just a short walk to the town centre. The owners have made some impressive changes here and offer a relaxed and welcoming atmosphere; there are many useful extras such as Wi-fi in the bedrooms. A range of carefully cooked and presented dishes is served in the comfortable restaurant.

Rooms 24 (2 fmly) **Facilities** Wi-fi **Parking** 20 **Notes** Closed 25 Dec-1 Jan

Hope Orchard

★★★★ GUEST ACCOMMODATION

Gloucester Rd, Staverton GL51 0TF

☎ 01452 855556   📠 01452 530037

e-mail: info@hopeorchard.com

web: www.hopeorchard.com

dir: *A40 onto B4063 at Arlecourt rdbt, Hope Orchard 1.25m on right*

PETS: **Bedrooms** unattended **Public areas** except in breakfast room **Grounds** disp bin **Exercise area Facilities** food bowl water bowl scoop/disp bags washing facs cage storage walks info vet info **On Request** fridge access torch towels **Other** charge for damage local kennel can provide day sitting service **Resident Pets:** Toby (Staffordshire Bull Terrier), Jessie, Jasper & Louis (cats)

Situated midway between Gloucester and Cheltenham, Hope Orchard is a good base for exploring the area. The comfortable bedrooms are next to the main house, and all are on the ground floor and have their own separate entrances. There is a large garden, and ample off-road parking is available.

Rooms 8 en suite (8 GF) **Facilities** FTV tea/coffee Direct Dial Cen ht Wi-fi **Parking** 10

White Lodge

★★★★ GUEST ACCOMMODATION

Hatherley Ln GL51 6SH

☎ 01242 242347   📠 01242 242347

e-mail: pamela@whitelodgebandb.wanadoo.co.uk

dir: *M5 junct 11, A40 to Cheltenham, 1st rdbt 4th exit Hatherley Ln, White Lodge 1st on right*

PETS: **Bedrooms** unattended **Charges** £5 per night **Public areas** except dining room **Grounds** disp bin **Exercise area Facilities** pet sitting washing facs cage storage walks info vet info **On Request** fridge access torch towels

Built around 1900, this well cared for, smart and friendly establishment is very convenient for access to the M5. Bedrooms, of varying sizes, offer quality and many extra facilities, including fridges and Wi-fi. The very comfortable dining room, where breakfast is served around a grand table, looks out across the pleasant and extensive gardens.

Rooms 4 en suite (1 GF) **S** fr £42; **D** fr £60* **Facilities** FTV tea/coffee Cen ht Wi-fi **Parking** 6 **Notes** 🐾

ENGLAND

CHIPPING CAMPDEN — Map 4 SP13

Three Ways House

★★★ 81% HOTEL

Mickleton GL55 6SB
☎ 01386 438429 ▤ 01386 438118
e-mail: reception@puddingclub.com
web: www.puddingclub.com
dir: *In Mickleton centre, on B4632 (Stratford-upon-Avon to Broadway road)*

PETS: Bedrooms (14 GF) unattended Charges £5 per night Public areas except restaurant on leads Grounds on leads disp bin Exercise area 100mtrs Facilities water bowl walks info vet info On Request fridge access Other charge for damage

Built in 1870, this charming hotel has welcomed guests for over 100 years and is home to the world famous Pudding Club, formed in 1985 to promote traditional English puddings. Individuality is a hallmark here, as reflected in a number of the bedrooms that have been styled around to a pudding theme. Public areas are stylish and include the air-conditioned restaurant, lounges and meeting rooms.

Rooms 48 (7 fmly) (14 GF) S £80-£115; D £140-£225 (incl. bkfst)* Facilities ♫ Xmas New Year Wi-fi Services Lift Parking 37 Notes LB

Noel Arms

★★★ 78% HOTEL

High St GL55 6AT
☎ 01386 840317 ▤ 01386 841136
e-mail: reception@noelarmshotel.com
web: www.noelarmshotel.com
dir: *Off A44 onto B4081 to Chipping Campden, 1st right down hill into town. Hotel on right*

CLASSIC BRITISH HOTELS

PETS: Bedrooms (8 GF) unattended Charges £15 per stay Public areas except restaurant on leads Exercise area car park Facilities vet info Restrictions small - medium size dogs preferred

This historic 14th-century hotel has a wealth of character and charm, and retains some of its original features. Bedrooms are very individual in style, but all have high levels of comfort and interesting interior design. Such distinctiveness is also evident throughout the public areas, which include the popular bar, conservatory lounge and attractive restaurant.

Rooms 28 (1 fmly) (8 GF) S £100-£120; D £130-£200 (incl. bkfst) Facilities Use of spa at sister hotel (charged) Xmas New Year Wi-fi Parking 28 Notes LB

Staddlestones

★★★★★ BED AND BREAKFAST

7 Aston Rd GL55 6HR
☎ 01386 849288
e-mail: info@staddle-stones.com
web: www.staddle-stones.com
dir: *From Chipping Campden take B4081 signed Mickleton, 200mtrs. House on right opposite gravel lane*

PETS: Bedrooms Charges £5 per night Public areas except breakfast room & main house Grounds on leads disp bin Exercise area track adjacent Facilities walks info vet info On Request fridge access torch towels Other charge for damage pets allowed in Garden Room only Restrictions no very large dogs Resident Pet: Phoebe (Border Collie)

A warm welcome can be expected from host Pauline Kirton at this delightful property, situated just a short walk from the Cotswold village of Chipping Campden; this makes an ideal base for walking, cycling, golf or just relaxing. There are three bedrooms offering quality and comfort plus some thoughtful extras. A hearty breakfast is served in the dining room around the communal table, and there's a good choice of mostly organic produce sourced from local farms.

Rooms 2 en suite 1 annexe en suite (1 fmly); D £65-£85* Facilities FTV tea/coffee Cen ht Wi-fi Parking 6 Notes No Children 12yrs

Myrtle House

★★★★ BED AND BREAKFAST

High St, Mickleton GL55 6SA
☎ 01386 430032
e-mail: louanne@myrtlehouse.co.uk
dir: *A46 onto B4632 towards Broadway. In Mickleton, on left opp Three Ways House*

PETS: Bedrooms Stables 4m Charges £10 per stay Public areas except dining room on leads Grounds on leads disp bin Exercise area 200mtrs Facilities water bowl washing facs cage storage walks info vet info On Request fridge access torch towels Other charge for damage dog training available nearby Restrictions pets must be well behaved

Myrtle House stands on the high street of this pleasant Cotswold village. Bedrooms are spacious and well equipped with a range of useful extras and information. The ambience created here by the resident proprietors is relaxed and welcoming. Breakfast is a highlight with a selection of carefully prepared local produce, fresh fruits and home-cooked cakes and croissants. In the evening, a good selection of dining options is just a short stroll away.

Rooms 5 en suite (2 fmly) Facilities tea/coffee Dinner available Cen ht Wi-fi Parking 2

Best Western Stratton House

★★★ 77% HOTEL

Gloucester Rd GL7 2LE
☎ 01285 651761 📠 01285 640024
e-mail: stratton.house@forestdale.com
web: www.strattonhousehotel.co.uk
dir: M4 junct 15, A419 to Cirencester. Hotel on left on A417 or M5 junct 11 to Cheltenham onto B4070 to A417. Hotel on right

PETS: Bedrooms (9 GF) unattended Charges £7.50 per night
Public areas except restaurant

This attractive 17th-century manor house is quietly situated about half a mile from the town centre. Bedrooms are well presented, and spacious, stylish premier rooms are available. The comfortable drawing rooms and restaurant have views over well-tended gardens - the perfect place to enjoy pre-dinner drinks on a summer evening.

Rooms 39 (9 GF) S £50-£110; D £75-£135 (incl. bkfst)*
Facilities FTV Xmas New Year Wi-fi Parking 100 Notes LB

The Crown of Crucis

★★★ 73% HOTEL

Ampney Crucis GL7 5RS
☎ 01285 851806 📠 01285 851735
e-mail: reception@thecrownofcrucis.co.uk
web: www.thecrownofcrucis.co.uk
dir: A417 to Fairford, hotel 2.5m on left

PETS: Bedrooms (13 GF) unattended Stables stable in village, please phone for details Charges £6 per night Public areas in bar only Grounds disp bin Exercise area over bridge nearby Facilities walks info vet info On Request fridge access torch Other charge for damage

This delightful hotel consists of two buildings; one a 16th-century coaching inn, which houses the bar and restaurant, and a more modern bedroom block which surrounds a courtyard. Rooms are attractively appointed and offer modern facilities; the restaurant serves a range of imaginative dishes.

Rooms 25 (2 fmly) (13 GF) (4 smoking) S £72.50; D £99 (incl. bkfst)* Facilities FTV Wi-fi Parking 82 Notes RS 25-26 Dec & 1 Jan

Fleece Hotel

★★★ 73% HOTEL

Market Place GL7 2NZ
☎ 01285 658507 📠 01285 651017
e-mail: relax@fleecehotel.co.uk
web: www.fleecehotel.co.uk
dir: A417/A419 Burford road junct, follow signs for town centre. Right at lights into 'The Waterloo', car park 250yds on left

PETS: Bedrooms (4 GF) unattended Stables 1m Charges £8 per night £56 per week Public areas except restaurant Grounds Exercise area 200yds Facilities walks info vet info On Request fridge access Other charge for damage

This town centre coaching inn, which dates back to the Tudor period, retains many original features such as flagstone-floors and oak beams. Well-equipped bedrooms vary in size and shape, but all offer good levels of comfort and have plenty of character. The bar lounge is a popular venue for morning coffee, and the stylish restaurant offers a range of dishes in an informal and convivial atmosphere.

Rooms 28 (3 fmly) (4 GF) Facilities Xmas New Year Wi-fi Parking 10

Wyndham Arms

★★★ 64% HOTEL

GL16 8JT
☎ 01594 833666 📠 01594 836450
e-mail: nigel@thewyndhamhotel.co.uk
dir: Off B4228, in village centre on B4231

PETS: Bedrooms (6 GF) unattended Stables Charges £5 per night Public areas except restaurant on leads Grounds disp bin Exercise area field at top of car park Exercise area 0.25m Facilities washing facs cage storage walks info vet info On Request fridge access torch towels Other charge for damage Resident Pets: Ruby & Poppy (Irish Red Setters)

The history of this charming village inn can be traced back over 600 years. It has exposed stone walls, original beams and an impressive inglenook fireplace in the friendly bar. Most bedrooms are in a modern extension, whilst the other rooms, in the main house, are more traditional in style. A range of dishes is offered in the bar or restaurant.

Rooms 18 (12 annexe) (3 fmly) (6 GF) S £45-£65; D £75-£115 (incl. bkfst) Facilities FTV Xmas Wi-fi Parking 52 Notes LB

COLEFORD | Map 3 SO51

Dryslade Farm *(SO581147)*

★ ★ ★ ★ FARMHOUSE

English Bicknor GL16 7PA

☎ 01594 860259 📠 01594 860259 Mrs D Gwilliam

e-mail: daphne@drysladefarm.co.uk

web: www.drysladefarm.co.uk

dir: *3m N of Coleford. Off A4136 onto B4432, right towards English Bicknor, farm 1m*

PETS: Bedrooms Public areas except conservatory at breakfast **Grounds** disp bin **Exercise area** paddock on premises **Facilities** scoop/disp bags leads washing facs cage storage walks info vet info **On Request** fridge access torch towels **Other** charge for damage **Resident Pets:** Kay & Milly (Cocker Spaniels)

Visitors are warmly welcomed at this 184-acre working farm, which dates from 1780 and has been in the same family for almost 100 years. The en suite bedrooms are attractively furnished in natural pine and are well equipped. The lounge leads onto a conservatory where hearty breakfasts are served.

Rooms 3 en suite (1 GF); **D** £62-£70 **Facilities** FTV TVL tea/coffee Cen ht Wi-fi **Parking** 6 **Notes** LB 🐾 184 acres beef

The Rock B&B

★ ★ ★ ★ GUEST ACCOMMODATION

GL16 7NY

☎ 01594 837893

e-mail: chris@stayattherock.com

dir: *A40 at Monmouth onto A4136, after 5m turn left at Five Acres onto Park Rd. At Christchurch turn right & immediately left towards Symonds Yat Rock, 0.75m S of Symonds Yat Rock*

PETS: Bedrooms sign **Charges** £8 per stay **Grounds** on leads disp bin **Exercise area** Forest of Dean adjacent **Facilities** scoop/disp bags washing facs cage storage walks info vet info **On Request** fridge access torch towels **Other** all bedrooms have direct outside access some pet facilities are only available on request **Restrictions** well behaved & quiet dogs only **Resident Pets:** 2 English Springer Spaniels, 2 ponies, chickens

The Rock offers stylish modern accommodation and is located on the outskirts of Coleford, near the famous Symonds Yat Rock. Bedrooms are attractively presented and very comfortable, with the garden rooms making the most of the spectacular views over the Wye Valley. Very popular with walkers, the Rock also caters well for business guests. Breakfasts are served in the spacious dining room overlooking the garden.

Rooms 4 en suite (2 GF) **S** £35-£45; **D** £52-£64* **Facilities** tea/coffee Lift Wi-fi **Parking** 20 **Notes** LB

Cor Unum

★ ★ ★ BED AND BREAKFAST

Monmouth Rd, Edge-End GL16 7HB

☎ 01594 837960

e-mail: antony@jones3649.freeserve.co.uk

dir: *On A4136 in village of Edge End*

PETS: Bedrooms Public areas Grounds disp bin **Exercise area** 300yds **Facilities** food (pre-bookable) food bowl water bowl bedding dog chews cat treats pet sitting dog walking washing facs cage storage vet info **On Request** fridge access torch towels **Other** charge for damage pet facilities may be pre-arranged when booking **Restrictions** small - medium size dogs only

A genuine welcome is assured at this comfortably-appointed bungalow which is located in the heart of the Forest of Dean. Bedrooms are neatly furnished, and the lounge has wonderful views across the garden to the Welsh mountains. Breakfast, served in the cosy dining room, is a tasty and fulfilling start to the day.

Rooms 2 en suite (2 GF) **S** £30-£40; **D** £50-£70* **Facilities** FTV TVL tea/coffee Cen ht **Parking** 1 **Notes** LB No Children Closed 20-30 Dec 🐾

CORSE LAWN | Map 3 SO83

Corse Lawn House

★ ★ ★ ◉◉ HOTEL

GL19 4LZ

☎ 01452 780771 📠 01452 780840

e-mail: enquiries@corselawn.com

web: www.corselawn.com

dir: *On B4211 5m SW of Tewkesbury*

PETS: Bedrooms (5 GF) unattended sign **Public areas** except restaurant on leads **Grounds** disp bin **Exercise area** 100yds **Facilities** food (pre-bookable) washing facs walks info vet info **On Request** fridge access torch **Resident Pets:** Sugar & Spice (Black Labradors), Donna & Gigi (horses)

This gracious Grade II listed Queen Anne house has been home to the Hine family for 31 years. Aided by an enthusiastic and committed team, the family continues to preside over all aspects of the hotel, creating a wonderfully relaxed environment. Bedrooms offer a reassuring mix of comfort and quality. The impressive cuisine is based on excellent produce, much of it locally sourced.

Rooms 19 (2 fmly) (5 GF) **S** £90; **D** £160 (incl. bkfst)*
Facilities STV ⊗ ⊗ ⊛ Badminton Table tennis New Year Wi-fi
Parking 62 **Notes** LB Closed 24-26 Dec

EWEN   Map 3 SU09

The Wild Duck

★★ 71% HOTEL

Drakes Island GL7 6BY
☎ 01285 770310 📠 01285 770924
e-mail: wduckinn@aol.com
dir: *From Cirencester take A429 towards Malmesbury. At Kemble left to Ewen. Inn in village centre*

PETS: Bedrooms (7 GF) unattended **Stables** 5m **Charges** £10 per stay **Public areas** except restaurant on leads **Grounds** on leads disp bin **Exercise area** country park & lakes 15 mins' walk **Facilities** dog chews walks info vet info **On Request** fridge access **Resident Pets:** Daisy & Bertie (Spaniels), Archie (Scottish Deerhound)

This lovely 16th-century, family run inn sits in a delightful Cotswold location and offers a wealth of character and interest inside. Log fires crackle and there are heaps of nooks and crannies in the bar and restaurant where guests can enjoy the hearty cuisine and an extensive choice of beers and wines. There is a lovely courtyard for alfresco dining in the warmer weather. The individually designed bedrooms have been re-styled in a contemporary fashion and each room has a black lacquered four poster; the Chinese Suite is in the oldest part of the building.

Rooms 12 (7 GF) **S** £70-£95; **D** £110-£165 (incl. bkfst)*
Facilities FTV Wi-fi **Parking** 50

FAIRFORD   Map 4 SP10

Bull Hotel

★★ 68% HOTEL

The Market Place GL7 4AA
☎ 01285 712535 & 712217 📠 01285 713782
e-mail: info@thebullhotelfairford.co.uk
dir: *On A417 in market square adjacent to post office*

PETS: Bedrooms (2 GF) unattended **Charges** £5 per night £20 per week **Public areas** except restaurant on leads **Grounds Exercise area** 100yds **Facilities** food bowl water bowl dog chews washing facs cage storage walks info vet info **On Request** fridge access torch towels **Other** charge for damage **Resident Pet:** Foxy '5' (Pomeranian)

Located in a picturesque Cotswold market town, this family-run inn dates back to the 15th century and still retains much period character and charm. A wide range of meals can be enjoyed in the popular bar or alternatively in the bistro restaurant. Bedrooms are individual in style, and a number overlook the square.

Rooms 26 (4 annexe) (4 fmly) (2 GF) **Facilities** FTV Fishing Cycle hire Horse riding New Year Wi-fi **Parking** 10 **Notes** LB

FOSSEBRIDGE   Map 4 SP01

The Inn at Fossebridge

★★★★ ⊜ INN

GL54 3JS
☎ 01285 720721 📠 01285 720793
e-mail: info@fossebridgeinn.co.uk
dir: *On A429, 3m S of A40 & 6m N of Cirencester*

PETS: Bedrooms Charges £5 per night **Public areas** on leads **Grounds** on leads disp bin **Exercise area Facilities** water bowl dog chews feeding mat walks info vet info **On Request** fridge access towels **Other** charge for damage **Resident Pet:** Harry (West Highland Terrier)

Located not too far from Cheltenham and Cirencester this welcoming former coaching inn is around 300 years old. Today it is a beautiful Cotswold retreat with wonderful accommodation and grounds. Fine food is served in the character bar and dining areas.

Rooms 8 en suite (1 fmly) **S** £110-£135; **D** £120-£160*
Facilities STV TVL tea/coffee Dinner available Cen ht Fishing **Parking** 30 **Notes** LB No coaches

| **GLOUCESTER** | Map 3 SO81 |

Hatherley Manor

★★★ 78% HOTEL

Down Hatherley Ln GL2 9QA
☎ 01452 730217 📠 01452 731032
e-mail: reservations@hatherleymanor.com
web: www.hatherleymanor.com
dir: *Off A38 into Down Hatherley Lane, signed. Hotel 600yds on left*

PETS: **Bedrooms** (18 GF) unattended sign **Charges** £10 per night **Grounds Exercise area Other** charge for damage

Within easy striking distance of the M5, Gloucester, Cheltenham and the Cotswolds, this stylish 17th-century manor, set in attractive grounds, remains popular with both business and leisure guests. Bedrooms are well appointed and offer contemporary comforts. A particularly impressive range of meeting and function rooms is available.

Rooms 50 (5 fmly) (18 GF) **Facilities** FTV Xmas New Year Wi-fi **Parking** 250 **Notes** LB

Hatton Court

★★★ 73% HOTEL

Upton Hill, Upton St Leonards GL4 8DE
☎ 01452 617412 📠 01452 612945
e-mail: res@hatton-court.co.uk
web: www.hatton-court.co.uk
dir: *From Gloucester on B4073 (Painswick road). Hotel at top of hill on right*

PETS: **Bedrooms** on leads **Exercise area** Painswick Beacon 2m **Facilities** walks info vet info **Other** charge for damage

Built in the style of a 17th-century Cotswold manor house, and set in seven acres of well-kept gardens this hotel is popular with both business and leisure guests. It stands at the top of Upton Hill and commands truly spectacular views of the Severn Valley. Bedrooms are comfortable and tastefully furnished with many extra facilities. The elegant Carringtons Restaurant offers a varied choice of menus, and there is also a newly refurbished bar and foyer lounge.

Rooms 45 (28 annexe) **S** £55-£120; **D** £65-£130 (incl. bkfst) **Facilities** 🏊 Gym Xmas New Year Wi-fi **Parking** 80 **Notes** LB

Red Lion Caravan & Camping Park *(SO849258)*

▶▶▶

Wainlode Hill, Norton GL2 9LW
☎ 01452 730251 & 731810 📠 01452 730251
dir: *Exit A38 at Norton, follow road to river*

PETS: **Stables Charges** 1st dog free, 2nd dog £1.50 per night **Public areas** on leads **Exercise area** river bank adjacent **Facilities** food walks info vet info **Other** prior notice required pets must not roam free

Open all year Last arrival 22.00hrs Last departure 11.00hrs

An attractive meadowland park, adjacent to a traditional pub, with the River Severn just across a country lane. This is an ideal touring and fishing base. A 13 acre site with 60 touring pitches, 10 hardstandings and 85 statics.

Notes

| **LOWER SLAUGHTER** | Map 4 SP12 |

Washbourne Court

★★★ 88% ◉◉ COUNTRY HOUSE HOTEL

GL54 2HS
☎ 01451 822143 📠 01451 821045
e-mail: info@washbournecourt.co.uk
web: www.vonessenhotels.co.uk
dir: *Exit A429 at 'The Slaughters' sign, between Stow-on-the-Wold & Bourton-on-the-Water. Hotel in village centre*

PETS: **Bedrooms** (9 GF) unattended **Charges Public areas** except restaurant on leads **Grounds** on leads **Exercise area** 50mtrs **Facilities** food (pre-bookable) food bowl water bowl dog walking dog grooming cage storage walks info vet info **On Request** fridge access torch towels **Other** charge for damage contact hotel for details of charges

Beamed ceilings, log fires and flagstone floors are some of the attractive features of this part 17th-century hotel, set in four acres of immaculate grounds beside the River Eye. The hotel has an elegant, contemporary style and boasts stunning bedrooms with up-to-the-minute technology and marble bathrooms. Dining, whether in the restaurant or bar is memorable and utilises fine local produce.

Rooms 30 (9 GF) **Facilities** FTV Xmas New Year Wi-fi **Parking** 40 **Notes** LB

MARSHFIELD — Map 3 ST77

Lord Nelson Inn
★★★ INN

SN14 8LP
☎ 01225 891820
e-mail: thelordnelsoninn@btinternet.com
web: www.thelordnelsoninn.info
dir: *M4 junct 18 onto A46 towards Bath. Left at Cold Ashton rdbt towards Marshfield*

PETS: Bedrooms Stables Public areas on leads **Grounds** on leads **Exercise area Facilities** food bowl water bowl walks info vet info **Other** charge for damage

Located at one end of the pleasant village of Marshfield, the Lord Nelson is a traditional coaching inn with a pleasant ambience. The spacious bar provides a good opportunity to mix with the locals, while the candlelit restaurant offers a quieter environment in which to enjoy the excellent selection of carefully prepared homemade dishes. Bedrooms and bathrooms are all well decorated and furnished.

Rooms 3 en suite **S** £27.50-£37.50; **D** £55-£67.50* **Facilities** tea/coffee Dinner available Cen ht **Notes** LB

MICHAEL WOOD MOTORWAY SERVICE AREA (M5) Map 3 ST79

Days Inn Michaelwood
BUDGET HOTEL

Michaelwood Service Area, Lower Wick GL11 6DD
☎ 01454 261513   01454 269150
e-mail: michaelwood.hotel@welcomebreak.co.uk
web: www.welcomebreak.co.uk
dir: *M5 N'bound between junct 13 & 14*

PETS: Bedrooms unattended **Charges Public areas Grounds** on leads disp bin **Facilities** walks info vet info **On Request** fridge access torch towels **Other** charge for damage **Restrictions** no dangerous breeds (see page 7)

This modern building offers accommodation in smart, spacious and well-equipped bedrooms, suitable for families and business travellers, and all with en suite bathrooms. Continental breakfast is available and other refreshments may be taken at the nearby family restaurant.

Rooms 38 (34 fmly) (5 smoking) **S** £29-£59; **D** £29-£69

MORETON-IN-MARSH — Map 4 SP23

White Hart Royal Hotel
★★★ 77% HOTEL

High St GL56 0BA
☎ 01608 650731   01608 650880
e-mail: whr@bpcmail.co.uk
web: www.whitehartroyal.co.uk
dir: *On High St at junct with Oxford Rd*

PETS: Bedrooms (9 GF) **Charges** £10 per night **Public areas** except public bar & courtyard on leads **Grounds** on leads disp bin **Exercise area** 1m **Facilities** food bowl water bowl walks info vet info **On Request** fridge access torch towels **Other** charge for damage

This historic hotel has been providing accommodation for hundreds of years and has now completed a major refurbishment programme that has resulted in high standards of quality and comfort. Public areas are full of character, and the bedrooms, in a wide range of shapes and sizes, include several very spacious and luxurious rooms situated adjacent to the main building. A varied range of well prepared dishes is available throughout the day and evening in the main bar and the relaxing restaurant.

Rooms 28 (8 annexe) (2 fmly) (9 GF) **S** £95; **D** £120-£160 (incl. bkfst)* **Facilities** STV FTV Xmas New Year Wi-fi **Parking** 0 **Notes** LB

Red Lion Inn
★★★ ➡ INN

Little Compton GL56 0RT
☎ 01608 674397
e-mail: info@theredlionlittlecompton.co.uk
dir: *On A44 between Chipping Norton & Moreton-in-Marsh*

PETS: Stables 1m **Public areas** except restaurant on leads **Grounds** on leads disp bin **Exercise area** adjacent **Facilities** feeding mat scoop/disp bags leads washing facs cage storage walks info vet info **On Request** torch towels **Other** charge for damage **Restrictions** no very large dogs

Built in 1748 as a coaching inn the Red Lion retains much of the charm and character of a friendly country pub. It has been sympathetically restored and the inglenook fireplaces, stone walls and oak beams remain a real feature. The comfortable bedrooms are stylishly presented and overlook the neat gardens with the beautiful Cotswold countryside beyond. Comprehensive breakfast choices are available, and evening meals should not be missed.

Rooms 2 en suite; **D** £75-£85* **Facilities** FTV tea/coffee Dinner available Cen ht Wi-fi Pool Table **Parking** 15 **Notes** LB

ENGLAND

Pelerine Caravan and Camping *(SO645183)*

►►►

Ford House Rd GL18 1LQ
☎ 01531 822761
e-mail: pelerine@hotmail.com
dir: *1m from Newent*

PETS: Charges £1 per night **Public areas** disp bin
Exercise area adjacent **Facilities** washing facs vet info **Other**
prior notice required **Resident Pets:** Narla & Simba (Spaniels),
Buttons & Tom (cats)

Open Mar-Nov Last arrival 22.00hrs Last departure 16.00hrs

A pleasant site divided into two areas, one of which is for adults
only, with hardstandings and electric hook ups in each area.
Facilities are very good, especially for families. It is close to
several vineyards, and well positioned in the north of the Forest
of Dean with Tewkesbury and Cheltenham within easy reach. A 5
acre site with 35 touring pitches, 2 hardstandings.

Notes 🐾

Rangeworthy Court

★★ 72% HOTEL

Church Ln, Wotton Rd BS37 7ND
☎ 01454 228347 📄 01454 65089
e-mail: reception@rangeworthycourt.com
dir: *Signed from B4058. Hotel at end of Church Lane*

PETS: Bedrooms Charges £3 per night **Public areas** except
restaurant on leads **Grounds** disp bin **Exercise area Facilities**
food bowl water bowl walks info vet info **On Request** torch
towels **Other** charge for damage **Resident Pet:** Bennie (German
Shepherd/Corgi cross)

This welcoming manor house hotel is peacefully located in its
own grounds, and is within easy reach of the motorway network.
The character bedrooms come in a variety of sizes and there is
a choice of comfortable lounges in which to enjoy a drink before
dinner. The relaxing restaurant offers a selection of carefully
prepared, enjoyable dishes.

Rooms 13 (4 fmly) **S** £66.25-£82.25; **D** £66.25-£99.87 (incl.
bkfst)* **Facilities** FTV 🏹 Wi-fi **Parking** 30 **Notes** LB Closed 24-30
Dec

Tudor Caravan & Camping *(SO728040)*

►►►►

Shepherds Patch GL2 7BP
☎ 01453 890483
e-mail: aa@tudorcaravanpark.co.uk
dir: *From M5 junct 13/14 follow signs for WWT Wetlands Wildlife
Centre-Slimbridge. Site at rear of Tudor Arms pub*

PETS: Stables 2m **Charges** £1 per night **Public areas**
except toilet, shower & laundry buildings on leads disp bin
Exercise area rally field available when not in use **Exercise area**
canal towpath adjacent **Facilities** walks info vet info **Other**
prior notice required local pet sitter/walker available (please
contact for details) dog tethers available

Open all year Last arrival 20.00hrs Last departure noon

An orchard-style park sheltered by mature trees and shrubs, set
in an attractive meadow beside the Sharpness to Gloucester
canal. This tidy site offers both level grass and gravel pitches
complete with electric hook-ups, and there is a separate area for
adults only. Slimbridge Wetlands Centre is close by, and there
is much scope locally for birdwatching. An 8 acre site with 75
touring pitches, 48 hardstandings.

Notes 🐾

Old Stocks

★★ 72% SMALL HOTEL

The Square GL54 1AF
☎ 01451 830666 📄 01451 870014
e-mail: aa@oldstockshotel.co.uk
web: www.oldstockshotel.co.uk
dir: *Exit A429 to town centre. Hotel facing village green*

PETS: Bedrooms (4 GF) unattended **Charges** £5 per stay
Public areas except restaurant on leads **Grounds** on leads
Exercise area 500yds **Facilities** walks info vet info **On Request**
torch **Other** charge for damage patio garden bedrooms most
suitable **Restrictions** well behaved dogs only, no dangerous
breeds (see page 7) **Resident Pet:** Alfie (Golden Retriever)

Overlooking the old market square, this Grade II listed, mellow
Cotswold-stone building is a comfortable and friendly base from
which to explore this picturesque area. There's lots of character
throughout, and the bedrooms offer individuality and charm.
Facilities include a guest lounge, restaurant and bar, whilst
outside, the patio is a popular summer venue for refreshing
drinks and good food.

Rooms 18 (3 annexe) (5 fmly) (4 GF) **S** £35-£55; **D** £70-£130
(incl. bkfst) **Facilities** FTV New Year Wi-fi **Parking** 12 **Notes** LB

Limes

★ ★ ★ GUEST ACCOMMODATION

Evesham Rd GL54 1EJ
☎ 01451 830034 📠 01451 830034
e-mail: thelimes@zoom.co.uk
dir: *500yds from village centre on A424*

PETS: Bedrooms Charges £5 per stay **Public areas** except breakfast room on leads **Grounds** on leads disp bin **Exercise area Facilities** water bowl dog chews leads walks info vet info **On Request** fridge access torch towels **Other** charge for damage **Restrictions** max 2 dogs **Resident Pet:** Casey (Doberman)

Just a short walk from the village centre, this Victorian house provides a comfortable base from which to explore this beautiful area. Bedroom styles vary, with four-poster and ground-floor rooms offered. A warm and genuine welcome is extended, and many guests return on a regular basis. A spacious lounge is available and breakfast is served in the light and airy dining room.

Rooms 4 en suite 2 annexe en suite (2 fmly) (2 GF) **S** £30-£56; **D** £55-£76* **Facilities** FTV TVL tea/coffee Cen ht Wi-fi **Parking** 6 **Notes** Closed Xmas 🐾

STROUD Map 3 SO80

The Bear of Rodborough

Cotswold Inns & Hotels

★ ★ ★ 77% HOTEL

Rodborough Common GL5 5DE
☎ 01453 878522 📠 01453 872523
e-mail: info@bearofrodborough.info
web: www.cotswold-inns-hotels.co.uk/bear
dir: *M5 junct 13, A419 to Stroud. Follow signs to Rodborough. Up hill, left at top at T-junct. Hotel on right*

PETS: Bedrooms unattended sign **Charges** £10 per night **Public areas** except restaurant & lounge on leads **Grounds** disp bin **Exercise area** 2 mins **Facilities** water bowl walks info vet info **On Request** torch **Other** charge for damage

This popular 17th-century coaching inn is situated high above Stroud within acres of National Trust parkland. Character abounds in the lounges and cocktail bar, and in the Box Tree Restaurant where the cuisine utilises fresh local produce. Bedrooms offer equal measures of comfort and style with plenty of extra touches. There is also a traditional and well-patronised public bar.

Rooms 46 (2 fmly) **S** £75-£85; **D** £120-£130 (incl. bkfst)* **Facilities** STV Putt green 🏊 Xmas New Year Wi-fi **Parking** 70

Hyde Crest

★ ★ ★ ★ BED AND BREAKFAST

Cirencester Rd GL6 8PE
☎ 01453 731631
e-mail: anthea@hydecrest.demon.co.uk
dir: *Off A419, 5m E of Stroud, signed Minchinhampton & Aston Down, house 3rd right opp Ragged Cot pub*

PETS: Bedrooms unattended **Public areas Grounds** disp bin **Exercise area** 500-acre common (1m) **Facilities** washing facs walks info vet info **On Request** fridge access torch towels **Resident Pet:** Harry (Cocker Spaniel)

Hyde Crest lies on the edge of the picturesque Cotswold village of Minchinhampton. Bedrooms are located at ground floor level, each with a private patio where welcome refreshments are enjoyed upon arrival (weather permitting). Guests are attentively cared for and scrumptious breakfasts are served in the small lounge-dining room around a communal table.

Rooms 3 en suite (3 GF) **S** £45; **D** £70* **Facilities** TVL tea/coffee Cen ht Wi-fi **Parking** 6 **Notes** No Children 10yrs RS Xmas & New Year no meals available 🐾

TETBURY Map 3 ST89

Cotswold Inns & Hotels

Hare & Hounds

★ ★ ★ ★ 78% 🏅🏅 HOTEL

Westonbirt GL8 8QL
☎ 01666 880233 & 881000 📠 01666 880241
e-mail: reception@hareandhoundshotel.com
web: www.cotswold-inns-hotels.co.uk
dir: *2.5m SW of Tetbury on A433*

PETS: Bedrooms (13 GF) unattended **Charges** £5 per night **Public areas** except restaurant on leads **Grounds** disp bin **Exercise area Facilities** water bowl cage storage walks info vet info **On Request** fridge access **Other** charge for damage

This popular hotel, set in extensive grounds, is situated close to Westonbirt Arboretum and has remained under the same ownership for over 50 years. Bedrooms are individual in style; those in the main house are more traditional and the stylish cottage rooms are contemporary in design. Public rooms include the informal bar and light, airy lounges - one with a log fire in colder months. Guests can eat either in the bar or the attractive restaurant.

Rooms 42 (21 annexe) (8 fmly) (13 GF) **S** £90; **D** £135-£170 (incl. bkfst)* **Facilities** FTV 🏊🏊 Xmas New Year Wi-fi **Parking** 85 **Notes** LB

ENGLAND

HARROW WEALD — Map 4 TQ19

Grim's Dyke Hotel
★★★ 78% ◉◉ HOTEL
Old Redding HA3 6SH
☎ 020 8385 3100 📄 020 8954 4560
e-mail: reservations@grimsdyke.com
web: www.grimsdyke.com
dir: A410 onto A409 north towards Bushey, at top of hill at lights turn left into Old Redding

PETS: Bedrooms (17 GF) **Stables** 5m **Charges** £30 per night **Grounds** on leads **Exercise area Facilities** cage storage vet info **Other** charge for damage **Restrictions** small dogs & assist dogs only

Once home to Sir William Gilbert, this Grade II mansion contains many references to well-known Gilbert and Sullivan productions. The house is set in over 40 acres of beautiful parkland and gardens. Rooms in the main house are elegant and traditional, while those in the adjacent lodge are aimed more at the business guest.

Rooms 46 (37 annexe) (4 fmly) (17 GF) **S** £65-£90; **D** £85-£150 **Facilities** STV ⚓ Gilbert & Sullivan opera dinner Murder mystery & Sabrage evenings ♫ Xmas New Year Wi-fi **Parking** 97 **Notes** LB RS 24-27 Dec

KINGSTON UPON THAMES — Map 4 TQ16

Chase Lodge House
★★★ GUEST ACCOMMODATION
10 Park Rd, Hampton Wick KT1 4AS
☎ 020 8943 1862 📄 020 8943 9363
e-mail: info@chaselodgehotel.com
web: www.chaselodgehotel.com
dir: A308 onto A310 signed Twickenham, 1st left onto Park Rd

PETS: Bedrooms sign **Exercise area Facilities** food food bowl water bowl bedding dog chews cat treats feeding mat litter tray scoop/disp bags leads dog walking cage storage walks info vet info **On Request** fridge access torch towels

This independent establishment is set in a quiet residential area, a short walk from Kingston town centre, Bushey Park and the River Thames. The individually decorated rooms vary in size and are all well-appointed and feature a range of useful extras. An attractive lounge-bar-restaurant is provided where breakfast, snacks and dinner by pre-arrangement are served. Children are most welcome, and on-road parking is available.

Rooms 13 en suite **Facilities** FTV Direct Dial Wi-fi **Notes** LB

ALTRINCHAM — Map 7 SJ78

Best Western Cresta Court Hotel
★★★ 74% HOTEL
Church St WA14 4DP
☎ 0161 927 7272 & 927 2601 📄 0161 929 6548
e-mail: rooms@cresta-court.co.uk
web: www.cresta-court.co.uk

PETS: Bedrooms unattended sign **Public areas** except bar & restaurant on leads **Grounds** on leads **Exercise area On Request** towels **Other** charge for damage

This modern hotel enjoys a prime location on the A56, close to the station, town centre shops and other amenities. Bedrooms vary in style from spacious four-posters to smaller, traditionally furnished rooms. Public areas include a choice of bars and extensive function and conference facilities.

Rooms 140 (9 fmly) **S** £59-£89; **D** £59-£89 (incl. bkfst)* **Facilities** STV FTV Wi-fi **Services** Lift **Parking** 200 **Notes** LB

BOLTON — Map 7 SD70

Broomfield House
★★★ GUEST HOUSE
33-35 Wigan Rd, Deane BL3 5PX
☎ 01204 61570 📄 01204 650932
e-mail: chris@broomfield.force9.net
dir: M61 junct 5, A58 to 1st lights, straight onto A676, premises on right

PETS: Bedrooms unattended **Public areas Exercise area** across road **Facilities** cage storage vet info **On Request** fridge access torch towels **Other** charge for damage

A friendly relaxed atmosphere prevails at Broomfield House, close to the motorway and west of the town centre. There is a comfy lounge and separate bar area. Hearty breakfasts are served in the dining room.

Rooms 20 en suite (2 fmly) (2 GF) (8 smoking) **S** £40-£45; **D** £55 **Facilities** FTV TVL tea/coffee Cen ht Licensed Wi-fi **Parking** 12

DELPH   Map 7 SD90

Wellcroft House
★★★★ GUEST ACCOMMODATION
Bleak Hey Nook OL3 5LY
☎ 01457 875017
e-mail: wellcrofthouse@hotmail.co.uk
web: www.wellcrofthouse.co.uk
dir: Off A62 on Standedge Foot Rd near A670 junct

PETS: Bedrooms Charges £5 per stay **Public areas Grounds Exercise area** 100mtr **Facilities** food (pre-bookable) water bowl bedding washing facs vet info **On Request** torch towels **Other** charge for damage

Commanding superb views down the valley below, this former weaver's cottage offers warm traditional hospitality to walkers on the Pennine Way and those simply touring the Pennine towns and villages. Modern comforts in all bedrooms and transport from local railway or walks is routinely provided by the friendly proprietors.

Rooms 3 rms (2 en suite) (1 GF) **S** £35-£45; **D** £55-£65 **Facilities** FTV TVL tea/coffee Dinner available Cen ht Wi-fi Pool Table **Parking** 1 **Notes** LB

MANCHESTER   Map 7 SJ89

Novotel Manchester Centre

NOVOTEL

★★★ 77% HOTEL
21 Dickinson St M1 4LX
☎ 0161 235 2200 ☐ 0161 235 2210
e-mail: H3145@accor.com
web: www.novotel.com
dir: From Oxford Street, into Portland Street, left into Dickinson Street. Hotel on right

PETS: Bedrooms unattended **Charges** £15 per night disp bin **Exercise area** outside front door - courtyard **Facilities** walks info vet info **On Request** fridge access **Other** charge for damage

This smart, modern property enjoys a central location convenient for theatres, shops, China Town and Manchester's business district. Spacious bedrooms are thoughtfully equipped and brightly decorated. Open-plan, contemporary public areas include an all-day restaurant and a stylish bar. Extensive conference and meeting facilities are available.

Rooms 164 (15 fmly) (10 smoking) **S** £68-£169; **D** £68-£169* **Facilities** STV FTV Gym Steam room Sauna Aromatherapy Wi-fi **Services** Lift Air con **Notes** LB

Ibis Hotel Manchester
BUDGET HOTEL
Charles St, Princess St M1 7DL
☎ 0161 272 5000 ☐ 0161 272 5010
e-mail: H3143@accor.com
web: www.ibishotel.com
dir: M62, M602 towards Manchester Centre, follow signs to UMIST(A34)

PETS: Bedrooms Charges £10 per stay **Facilities** vet info **On Request** fridge access towels

Modern, budget hotel offering comfortable accommodation in bright and practical bedrooms. Breakfast is self-service and dinner is available in the restaurant.

Rooms 126

Ibis Manchester City Centre
BUDGET HOTEL
96 Portland St M1 4GY
☎ 0161 234 0600 ☐ 0161 234 0610
e-mail: H3142@accor.com
web: www.ibishotel.com
dir: In city centre, between Princess St & Oxford St. 10min walk from Piccadilly

PETS: Bedrooms unattended **Charges** £10 per stay **Public areas** except restaurant & bars on leads

Rooms 127 (16 fmly) (7 smoking)

WORSLEY   Map 7 SD70

Novotel Manchester West

NOVOTEL

★★★ 72% HOTEL
Worsley Brow M28 2YA
☎ 0161 799 3535 ☐ 0161 703 8207
e-mail: H0907@accor.com
web: www.novotel.com
dir: Adjacent to M60 junct 13

PETS: Bedrooms (41 GF) unattended **Stables** approx 5m **Charges** £10 per night **Grounds** on leads disp bin **Exercise area** 100yds **Facilities** cage storage walks info vet info **On Request** towels **Other** charge for damage

Well placed for access to the Peak District and the Lake District, as well as Manchester, this modern hotel successfully caters for both families and business guests. The spacious bedrooms have sofa beds and a large work area; the hotel has an outdoor swimming pool, children's play area and secure parking.

Rooms 119 (10 fmly) (41 GF) **Facilities** STV Gym Wi-fi **Services** Lift **Parking** 95

HAMPSHIRE

ALTON | Map 4 SU73

Alton Grange Hotel

★★★ 77% HOTEL

London Rd GU34 4EG

☎ 01420 86565 📠 01420 541346

e-mail: info@altongrange.co.uk

web: www.altongrange.co.uk

dir: From A31 right at rdbt signed Alton/Holybourne/Bordon B3004. Hotel 300yds on left

PETS: Bedrooms (7 GF) unattended Stables Charges £5 per night Public areas bar only on leads Grounds on leads Exercise area 100yds Facilities walks info vet info On Request fridge access torch towels Other charge for damage Resident Pets: Caramel, Barley, Smartie, Treacle, Honey, Cracker (cats)

A friendly family owned hotel, conveniently located on the outskirts of this market town and set in two acres of lovingly tended gardens. The individually styled bedrooms, including three suites, are all thoughtfully equipped. Diners can choose between the more formal Truffles Restaurant or relaxed Muffins Brasserie. The attractive public areas include a function suite.

Rooms 30 (4 annexe) (4 fmly) (7 GF) Facilities Hot air ballooning Wi-fi Parking 48 Notes No children 3yrs Closed 24 Dec-4 Jan

ANDOVER | Map 4 SU34

Esseborne Manor

★★★ 80% HOTEL

Hurstbourne Tarrant SP11 0ER

☎ 01264 736444 📠 01264 736725

e-mail: info@esseborne-manor.co.uk

web: www.esseborne-manor.co.uk

dir: Halfway between Andover & Newbury on A343, just 1m N of Hurstbourne Tarrant

PETS: Bedrooms (6 GF) unattended sign Grounds disp bin Exercise area Facilities food bowl water bowl washing facs walks info vet info On Request fridge access torch Other charge for damage

Set in two acres of well-tended gardens, this attractive manor house is surrounded by the open countryside of the North Wessex Downs. Bedrooms are delightfully individual and are split between the main house, an adjoining courtyard and separate garden cottage. There's a wonderfully relaxed atmosphere throughout, and public rooms combine elegance with comfort.

Rooms 19 (8 annexe) (2 fmly) (6 GF) S £110-£130; D £125-£180 (incl. bkfst)* Facilities STV FTV Xmas New Year Wi-fi Parking 50 Notes LB

Quality Hotel Andover

★★★ 62% HOTEL

Micheldever Rd SP11 6LA

☎ 01264 369111 📠 01264 369000

e-mail: andover@quality-hotels.co.uk

dir: Off A303 at A3093. 1st rdbt take 1st exit, 2nd rdbt take 1st exit. Turn left immediately before Total petrol station, then left again

PETS: Bedrooms (13 GF) Grounds on leads disp bin Exercise area 0.25m Facilities walks info vet info On Request fridge access torch towels

Located on the outskirts of the town, this hotel is popular with business guests. Bedrooms provide useful accessories; public areas consist of a cosy lounge, a hotel bar and a traditional style restaurant serving a range of meals. There is also a large conference suite available and a pleasant garden with patio seating.

Rooms 49 (36 annexe) (13 GF) Facilities Wi-fi Parking 100

BASINGSTOKE | Map 4 SU65

The Hampshire Court Hotel

★★★★ 79% HOTEL

Centre Dr, Chineham RG24 8FY

☎ 01256 319700 📠 01256 319730

e-mail: hampshirecourt@qhotels.co.uk

web: www.qhotels.co.uk

dir: Off A33 (Reading road) behind Chineham Shopping Centre via Great Binfields Rd

PETS: Bedrooms sign Charges dog £15 per night Public areas except food service areas on leads Exercise area adjacent Facilities cage storage walks info vet info On Request fridge access torch Other charge for damage

This hotel boasts a range of smart, comfortable and stylish bedrooms, and leisure facilities that are unrivalled locally. Facilities include indoor and outdoor tennis courts, two swimming pools, a gym and a number of treatment rooms.

Rooms 90 (6 fmly) Facilities Spa STV Gym Steam room Beauty salon Sauna Exercise studios Xmas New Year Wi-fi Services Lift Parking 220

Barceló Basingstoke Country Hotel

★★★★ 74% HOTEL

Scures Hill, Nately Scures, Hook RG27 9JS
☎ 01256 764161 📄 01256 768341
e-mail: basingstokecountry.mande@barcelo-hotels.co.uk
web: www.barcelo-hotels.co.uk
dir: M3 junct 5, A287 towards Newnham. Left at lights. Hotel 200mtrs on right

PETS: Bedrooms (26 GF) sign **Stables** 7m **Charges** £15 per night **Grounds** on leads disp bin **Exercise area** 100mtrs **Facilities** cage storage walks info vet info **On Request** fridge access torch **Other** charge for damage

This popular hotel is close to Basingstoke and its country location ensures a peaceful stay. Bedrooms are available in a number of styles - all have air conditioning, Wi-fi, in-room safes and hairdryers. Guests have a choice of dining in the formal restaurant, or for lighter meals and snacks there is a relaxed café and a smart bar. Extensive wedding, conference and leisure facilities complete the picture.

Rooms 100 (26 GF) **Facilities** Spa STV supervised Gym Sauna Solarium Steam room Dance studio Beauty treatments New Year Wi-fi **Services** Lift Air con **Parking** 200 **Notes** RS 24 Dec-2 Jan

BEAULIEU   Map 4 SU30

The Master Builders at Bucklers Hard

★★★ 79% HOTEL

Buckler's Hard SO42 7XB
☎ 01590 616253 📄 01590 616297
e-mail: enquiries@themasterbuilders.co.uk
web: www.themasterbuilders.co.uk
dir: M27 junct 2, follow Beaulieu signs. At T-junct left onto B3056, 1st left to Buckler's Hard. Hotel 2m on left before village

PETS: Bedrooms (8 GF) unattended **Charges** £15 per night £105 per week **Public areas** except restaurant & lounge on leads **Grounds** on leads disp bin **Facilities** food (pre-bookable) food bowl water bowl bedding **On Request** towels **Other** charge for damage

A tranquil historic riverside setting creates the backdrop for this delightful property. The main house bedrooms are full of historical features and of individual design, and in addition there are some bedrooms in the newer wing. Public areas include a popular bar and guest lounge, whilst grounds are an ideal location for alfresco dining in the summer months. Award-winning cuisine is served in the stylish dining room.

Rooms 25 (17 annexe) (4 fmly) (8 GF) **Facilities** FTV Xmas New Year Wi-fi **Parking** 40 **Notes** LB

Beaulieu Hotel

★★★ 76% HOTEL

Beaulieu Rd SO42 7YQ
☎ 023 8029 3344 📄 023 8029 2729
e-mail: beaulieu@newforesthotels.co.uk
web: www.newforesthotels.co.uk
dir: M27 junct 1/A337 towards Lyndhurst. Left at lights, through Lyndhurst, right onto B3056, continue for 3m

PETS: Bedrooms (4 GF) unattended **Charges** £7.50 per night **Public areas** except food areas on leads **Grounds** **Exercise area** adjacent **Facilities** water bowl walks info vet info **On Request** fridge access

Conveniently located in the heart of the New Forest and close to Beaulieu Road railway station, this popular, small hotel provides an ideal base for exploring this lovely area. Facilities include an indoor swimming pool and an adjoining pub.

Rooms 28 (7 annexe) (5 fmly) (4 GF) **S** £65-£78; **D** £130-£156 (incl. bkfst)* **Facilities** FTV Steam room Xmas New Year Wi-fi **Services** Lift **Parking** 60 **Notes** LB

BROCKENHURST   Map 4 SU30

Balmer Lawn

★★★★ 75% HOTEL

Lyndhurst Rd SO42 7ZB
☎ 01590 623116 📄 01590 623864
e-mail: info@balmerlawnhotel.com
dir: Just off A337 from Brockenhurst towards Lymington

PETS: Bedrooms unattended **Stables** 0.5m **Charges** £20 (1st night), £15 (subsequent nights) £80 per week **Public areas** except restaurant **Grounds** disp bin **Exercise area** direct access to New Forest National Park **Facilities** water bowl washing facs cage storage walks info vet info **On Request** fridge access torch towels **Other** charge for damage dog training available

Situated in the heart of the New Forest, this peacefully located hotel provides comfortable public rooms and a wide range of bedrooms. A selection of carefully prepared and enjoyable dishes is offered in the spacious restaurant. The extensive function and leisure facilities make this popular with both families and conference delegates.

Rooms 54 (10 fmly) **Facilities** FTV Gym Squash Indoor leisure suite Treatment room Xmas New Year Wi-fi **Services** Lift **Parking** 100

ENGLAND

Whitley Ridge Hotel

★★★ ◎◎ COUNTRY HOUSE HOTEL

Beaulieu Rd SO42 7QL
☎ 01590 622354 📄 01590 622856
e-mail: info@whitleyridge.co.uk
web: www.whitleyridge.com
dir: *At Brockenhurst onto B3055 Beaulieu Road. 1m on left up private road*

PETS: (1 GF) **Stables** **Charges** £10 per night **Facilities** cage storage walks info vet info **On Request** torch **Other** charge for damage 2 small cottages available for guests with dogs washing facilities & fridge access at larger cottage, otherwise on request **Resident Pets:** hens

This charming hotel enjoys a secluded picturesque setting in the heart of the New Forest. The relaxing public areas, delightful grounds, the smart and comfortable bedrooms and a team of helpful and attentive staff all contribute to a memorable stay. The cuisine of the well-established Simply at Whitley restaurant is a highlight.

Rooms 15 (3 annexe) (1 GF) **D** fr £125 (incl. bkfst)* **Facilities** ♨ Xmas New Year Wi-fi **Parking** 23

New Park Manor

von Essen hotels

★★★ 80% ◎◎ COUNTRY HOUSE HOTEL

Lyndhurst Rd SO42 7QH
☎ 01590 623467 📄 01590 622268
e-mail: info@newparkmanorhotel.co.uk
web: www.newparkmanorhotel.co.uk
dir: *M27 junct 1, A337 to Lyndhurst & Brockenhurst. Hotel 1.5m on right*

PETS: Bedrooms unattended **Stables** 2m **Charges** £15 per night **Grounds** **Exercise area** 100yds **Facilities** water bowl walks info vet info **Other** charge for damage

Once the favoured hunting lodge of King Charles II, this well presented hotel enjoys a peaceful setting in the New Forest and comes complete with an equestrian centre. The bedrooms are divided between the old house and a purpose-built wing. An impressive spa offers a range of treatments.

Rooms 24 (6 fmly) **Facilities** Spa STV FTV ⊛ ⇄ ⇘ Gym Mountain biking Xmas New Year Wi-fi **Parking** 70

Forest Park

★★★ 73% HOTEL

Rhinefield Rd SO42 7ZG
☎ 01590 622844 📄 01590 623948
e-mail: forest.park@forestdale.com
web: www.forestparkhotel.co.uk
dir: *A337 to Brockenhurst into Meerut Rd, through Waters Green. Right at T-junct into Rhinefield Rd*

PETS: Bedrooms (7 GF) unattended sign **Stables** 10m **Charges** £7.50 per night **Public areas** except restaurant on leads **Grounds** disp bin **Exercise area** across road **Facilities** food (pre-bookable) walks info vet info **On Request** fridge access torch towels

Situated in the heart of the New Forest, this former vicarage and war field hospital is now a hotel which offers a warm and friendly welcome to all its guests. The hotel has a heated pool, riding, a log cabin sauna and tennis courts. The bedrooms and public areas are comfortable and stylish.

Rooms 38 (2 fmly) (7 GF) **S** £69-£93; **D** £89-£125 (incl. bkfst)* **Facilities** FTV ♨ Horse riding stables Sauna Xmas New Year Wi-fi **Parking** 80 **Notes** LB

Watersplash

★★ 63% HOTEL

The Rise SO42 7ZP
☎ 01590 622344
e-mail: bookings@watersplash.co.uk
web: www.watersplash.co.uk
dir: *M3 junct 13/M27 junct 1/A337 S through Lyndhurst & Brockenhurst. The Rise on left, hotel on left*

PETS: Bedrooms (3 GF) unattended **Charges** dogs £5 minimum per night **Public areas** except restaurant; not in bar at busy times **Grounds** disp bin **Facilities** walks info vet info **Resident Pet:** Alfie (dog)

This popular, welcoming hotel that dates from Victorian times has been in the same family for over 40 years. Bedrooms have co-ordinated decor and good facilities. The restaurant overlooks the neatly tended garden and there is also a comfortably furnished lounge, separate bar and an outdoor pool.

Rooms 23 (6 fmly) (3 GF) **Facilities** ⇄ Xmas New Year **Parking** 29

BURLEY — Map 4 SU20

Burley Manor
★★★ 75% HOTEL
Ringwood Rd BH24 4BS
☎ 01425 403522 📄 01425 403227
e-mail: burley.manor@forestdale.com
web: www.theburleymanorhotel.co.uk
dir: Exit A31 at Burley sign, hotel 3m on left

PETS: Bedrooms (17 GF) unattended **Stables Charges** £7.50 per night **Public areas** except restaurant

Set in extensive grounds, this 18th-century mansion house enjoys a relaxed ambience and a peaceful setting. Half of the well-equipped, comfortable bedrooms, including several with four-posters, are located in the main house. The remainder, many with balconies, are in the adjacent converted stable block overlooking the outdoor pool. Cosy public rooms benefit from log fires in winter.

Rooms 38 (17 annexe) (2 fmly) (17 GF) **S** £75-£135; **D** £85-£145 (incl. bkfst)* **Facilities** FTV ⇃ Horse riding stables Xmas New Year Wi-fi **Parking** 60 **Notes** LB

Moorhill House
★★★ 72% ◎ COUNTRY HOUSE HOTEL
BH24 4AH
☎ 01425 403285 📄 01425 403715
e-mail: moorhill@newforesthotels.co.uk
web: www.newforesthotels.co.uk
dir: M27, A31, follow signs to Burley, through village, up hill, right opposite school & cricket grounds

PETS: Bedrooms (3 GF) unattended **Stables** 2m **Charges** £7.50 per night **Public areas** except restaurant & bar on leads **Grounds Exercise area** nearby **Facilities** water bowl walks info vet info **On Request** fridge access

Situated deep in the heart of the New Forest and formerly a grand gentleman's residence, this charming hotel offers a relaxed and friendly environment. Bedrooms, of varying sizes, are smartly decorated. A range of facilities is provided and guests can relax by walking around the extensive grounds. Both dinner and breakfast offer a choice of interesting and freshly prepared dishes.

Rooms 31 (13 fmly) (3 GF) **S** £60-£73; **D** £120-£146 (incl. bkfst)* **Facilities** FTV ⓢ Putt green ⚑ Badminton (Apr-Sep) Xmas New Year Wi-fi **Parking** 50 **Notes** LB

CADNAM — Map 4 SU31

Bartley Lodge Hotel
★★★ 80% ◎ HOTEL
Lyndhurst Rd SO40 2NR
☎ 023 8081 2248 📄 023 8081 2075
e-mail: bartley@newforesthotels.co.uk
web: www.newforesthotels.co.uk
dir: M27 junct 1 at 1st rdbt 1st exit, at 2nd rdbt 3rd exit onto A337. Hotel sign on left

PETS: Bedrooms (2 GF) unattended **Stables** 5m **Charges** £7.50 per night £52.50 per week **Public areas** except restaurant & bar on leads **Grounds** on leads **Exercise area** nearby **Facilities** water bowl walks info vet info **On Request** fridge access

This 18th-century former hunting lodge is very quietly situated, yet is just minutes from the M27. Bedrooms vary in size but all are well equipped. There is a selection of small lounge areas, a cosy bar and an indoor pool, together with a small fitness suite. The Crystal dining room offers a tempting choice of well prepared dishes.

Rooms 31 (12 fmly) (2 GF) **S** £60-£73; **D** £120-£146 (incl. bkfst)* **Facilities** FTV ⓢ Gym Xmas New Year Wi-fi **Parking** 60 **Notes** LB

CRAWLEY — Map 4 SU43

Folly Farm Touring Caravan Park (SU415337)
▶ ▶ ▶
Crawley SO21 2PH
☎ 01962 776486 & 07831 475594
dir: Midway between Winchester & Stockbridge on B3049. Site 0.75m past Rack & Manger pub

PETS: Sep accom Stables Public areas dogs must be kept on leads disp bin **Exercise area** woods, footpaths & bridleways **Facilities** food bowl water bowl litter tray scoop/disp bags leads washing facs walks info vet info **Other** prior notice required **Resident Pets:** Bailey (Labrador), Bridie (Patterdale/Jack Russell cross), Apple, Tabitha & Gussy (cats), 2 Welsh ponies, Sandy & Polack (pigs)

Open all year Last arrival 22.00hrs

A small farm site set in rural mid-Hampshire between Stockbridge and Winchester, ideal for visiting the ancient capital of Wessex or the New Forest, and the south coast is only a short drive away. The clean facilities are located in farm outbuildings, and there is a small campers' kitchen. A 2.5 acre site with 30 touring pitches, 3 hardstandings.

Notes No children in farm area. Adults only 1st May BH

DOGMERSFIELD — Map 4 SU75

Four Seasons Hotel Hampshire
★★★★★ ⚜ HOTEL

Dogmersfield Park, Chalky Ln RG27 8TD
☎ 01252 853000 📠 01252 853010
e-mail: reservations.ham@fourseasons.com
dir: *M3 junct 5 onto A287 Farnham. After 1.5m left for Dogmersfield, hotel 0.6m on left*

PETS: Bedrooms (23 GF) **Public areas** except spa & dining areas on leads **Grounds** on leads disp bin **Exercise area** 500-acre grounds **Facilities** food (pre-bookable) food bowl water bowl bedding dog chews feeding mat scoop/disp bags pet sitting dog walking cage storage walks info vet info **On Request** fridge access torch towels **Other** charge for damage **Restrictions** Dogs must be less than 7kg, less than 18cm to shoulder

This Georgian manor house, set in 500 acres of rolling grounds and English Heritage listed gardens, offers the upmost in luxury and relaxation, just an hour from London. The spacious and stylish bedrooms are particularly well appointed and offer up-to-date technology. Fitness and spa facilities include nearly every conceivable indoor and outdoor activity, in addition to luxurious pampering. An elegant restaurant, a healthy eating spa café and a trendy bar are popular venues.

Rooms 133 (23 GF) **S** £195-£3350; **D** £195-£3350* **Facilities** Spa STV ⓒ ⌇ Fishing ⌇ Gym Clay pigeon shooting Bikes Canal boat Falconry Horse riding Jogging trails ♫ Xmas New Year Wi-fi **Services** Lift Air con **Parking** 165

EAST TYTHERLEY — Map 4 SU22

The Star Inn
★★★★ ⚜ INN

SO51 0LW
☎ 01794 340225
e-mail: info@starinn.co.uk
dir: *1m S of East Tytherley*

PETS: Bedrooms unattended **Public areas** except restaurant on leads **Grounds** on leads disp bin **Exercise area** 500mtrs **Facilities** water bowl dog chews leads washing facs cage storage walks info vet info **On Request** fridge access torch towels **Other** charge for damage **Resident Pets:** Jake (Jack Russell), Gray (cat)

This charming coaching inn offers bedrooms in a purpose-built annexe, separate from the main pub. The spacious rooms have high levels of quality and comfort, and an outdoor children's play area is available. The inn has a loyal following of locals and visitors, drawn especially by the excellent food.

Rooms 3 annexe en suite (3 GF) **Facilities** FTV tea/coffee Dinner available Wi-fi **Parking** 50 **Notes** RS Sun eve & Mon

FAREHAM — Map 4 SU50

Travelrest - Solent Gateway
★★★★ GUEST ACCOMMODATION

22 The Avenue PO14 1NS
☎ 01329 232175 📠 01329 232196
e-mail: solentreservations@travelrest.co.uk
web: www.travelrest.co.uk
dir: *0.5m from town centre on A27. 0.25m from railway station*

PETS: Bedrooms unattended **Charges** £5 per night **Public areas** **Grounds** on leads disp bin **Exercise area** 1m **Facilities** vet info **Other** charge for damage pets allowed in 2 bedrooms only

Situated just west of the town centre, this well-presented accommodation is convenient for the ferry terminals and naval heritage sites. The comfortable bedrooms are spacious and well equipped, and one has a four-poster bed. Breakfast is served in the cosy conservatory-dining room and conference rooms are available.

Rooms 21 en suite (3 fmly) (6 GF) **S** £60-£80; **D** £60-£90 (room only) **Facilities** FTV TVL tea/coffee Dinner available Direct Dial Cen ht Licensed Wi-fi **Parking** 27

FARNBOROUGH — Map 4 SU85

Holiday Inn

Holiday Inn Farnborough
★★★ 81% HOTEL

Lynchford Rd GU14 6AZ
☎ 0871 942 9029 & 01252 894300 📠 01252 523166
e-mail: reservations-farnborough@ihg.com
web: www.holidayinn.co.uk
dir: *M3 junct 4, follow A325 through Farnborough towards Aldershot. Hotel on left at The Queen's rdbt*

PETS: Bedrooms (35 GF) sign **Stables** 5km **Charges** **Public areas** **Grounds** on leads disp bin **Exercise area** 500yds **Facilities** cage storage walks info vet info **On Request** fridge access torch **Other** charge for damage

This hotel occupies a perfect location for events in Aldershot and Farnborough with ample parking on site and easy access to the M3. Modern bedrooms provide good comfort levels, and internet access is provided throughout. Leisure facilities comprise a swimming pool, gym and beauty treatment rooms. Smart meeting rooms are also available.

Rooms 142 (31 fmly) (35 GF) (7 smoking) **Facilities** STV ⓒ supervised Gym Sauna Steam room Beauty room ♫ Xmas New Year Wi-fi **Services** Air con **Parking** 170

FLEET MOTORWAY SERVICE AREA (M3)   Map 4 SU75

Days Inn Fleet
BUDGET HOTEL
Fleet Services GU51 1AA
☎ 01252 815587   📠 01252 815587
e-mail: fleet.hotel@welcomebreak.co.uk
web: www.welcomebreak.co.uk
dir: *Between junct 4a & 5 southbound on M3*

PETS: Bedrooms Charges Public areas Grounds on leads
disp bin **Facilities** food bowl water bowl walks info vet info
On Request fridge access **Other** charge for damage cats must
be caged

This modern building offers accommodation in smart, spacious
and well-equipped bedrooms, suitable for families and business
travellers, and all with en suite bathrooms. Continental breakfast
is available and other refreshments may be taken at the nearby
family restaurant.

Rooms 58 (46 fmly) (5 smoking) **S** £29-£59; **D** £29-£59

FORDINGBRIDGE   Map 4 SU11

Sandy Balls Holiday Centre (SU167148)
Sandy Balls Estate Ltd, Godshill SP6 2JZ
☎ 0845 270 2248   📠 01425 653067
e-mail: post@sandy-balls.co.uk
dir: *M27 junct 1 onto B3078/B3079, W 8m to Godshill. Site 0.25m
after cattle grid*

PETS: Charges touring pitches £4 per night **Public areas** disp
bin **Exercise area** dog exercise field, woodland **Facilities** food
food bowl water bowl dog chews litter tray scoop/disp bags
leads washing facs walks info vet info **Other** prior notice
required max 2 dogs per booking

Open all year rs Nov-Feb pitches reduced, no activities Last
arrival 21.00hrs Last departure 11.00hrs

A large, mostly wooded New Forest holiday complex with good
provision of touring facilities on terraced, well laid-out fields.
Pitches are fully serviced with shingle bases, and groups can
be sited beside the river and away from the main site. Excellent
sport, leisure and entertainment facilities for the whole family;
a bistro, information centre, four tipis and eight ready-erected
tents for hire. A 120 acre site with 233 touring pitches, 233
hardstandings and 233 statics.

Notes Groups by arrangement, no gazebos

HARTLEY WINTNEY   Map 4 SU75

The Elvetham Hotel
★★★ 79% HOTEL
RG27 8AR
☎ 01252 844871   📠 01252 844161
e-mail: enq@theelvetham.co.uk
web: www.theelvetham.co.uk
dir: *M3 junct 4A W, junct 5 E (or M4 junct 11, A33, B3011). Hotel
signed from A323 between Hartley Wintney & Fleet*

PETS: Bedrooms (7 GF) unattended **Charges** £15 per night
Public areas Grounds disp bin **Exercise area Facilities** water
bowl feeding mat washing facs cage storage walks info vet
info **On Request** fridge access torch towels **Other** charge
for damage **Resident Pets:** Harvey (Golden Retriever), Chess
(Golden Labrador)

A spectacular 19th-century mansion set in 35 acres of grounds
with an arboretum. All bedrooms are individually styled and
many have views of the manicured gardens. A popular venue for
weddings and conferences, the hotel lends itself to team building
events and outdoor pursuits.

Rooms 72 (29 annexe) (7 GF) **Facilities** STV Putt green
Gym Badminton Boules Volleyball New Year Wi-fi **Parking** 200
Notes Closed 24-27 Dec

ENGLAND

Red Shoot Camping Park *(SU187094)*

► ► ►

BH24 3QT

☎ 01425 473789   📠 01425 471558

e-mail: enquiries@redshoot-campingpark.com

dir: *A31 onto A338 towards Fordingbridge & Salisbury. Right at brown signs for caravan park towards Linwood on unclassified roads, site signed*

PETS: Stables 2m   **Charges** £1 per night   £7 per week **Public areas** except shop & toilets   disp bin   **Exercise area** New Forest adjacent   **Facilities** food scoop/disp bags   leads   walks info   vet info   **Other** prior notice required   dogs must be on leads at all times on site   **Restrictions** no Pit Bull Terriers

Open Mar-Oct Last arrival 20.30hrs Last departure 13.00hrs

Sitting behind the Red Shoot Inn in one of the most attractive parts of the New Forest, this park is in an ideal spot for nature lovers, walkers and tourers. It is personally supervised by friendly owners, and offers many amenities including a children's play area. There are modern and spotless facilities. A 3.5 acre site with 130 touring pitches.

Notes Quiet after 22.30hrs

Stanwell House

★ ★ ★   83%   ⊛   HOTEL

14-15 High St SO41 9AA

☎ 01590 677123   📠 01590 677756

e-mail: enquiries@stanwellhouse.com

dir: *M27 junct 1, follow signs to Lyndhurst into Lymington centre & High Street*

PETS: Bedrooms (5 GF)   unattended   **Charges** £15 per night **Public areas** except restaurant   **Grounds** on leads   disp bin **Exercise area** 2 min walk   **Facilities** water bowl   dog chews scoop/disp bags   pet sitting   dog walking   washing facs walks info   vet info   **On Request** fridge access   torch   towels **Restrictions** small, well behaved dogs only   **Resident Pets:** Louis & Lola (Terriers)

A privately owned Georgian house situated on the wide high street only a few minutes from the marina, and a short drive from the New Forest. Styling itself as a boutique hotel, the bedrooms are individually designed; there are Terrace rooms with garden access, four-poster rooms, and Georgian rooms in the older part of the building. The four suites include two with their own roof terrace. Dining options include the informal bistro and the intimate Seafood Restaurant. Service is friendly and attentive.

Rooms 30 (4 fmly) (5 GF) **S** fr £99; **D** fr £138 (incl. bkfst)* **Facilities** FTV Xmas New Year Wi-fi **Parking** 12 **Notes** LB

Gorse Meadow Guest House

★ ★ ★ ★   GUEST HOUSE

Sway Rd SO41 8LR

☎ 01590 673354   📠 01590 673336

e-mail: gorsemeadow@btconnect.com

web: www.gorsemeadowguesthouse.co.uk

dir: *Off A337 from Brockenhurst, right onto Sway Rd before Toll House pub, Gorse Meadow 1.5m on right*

PETS: Bedrooms   **Charges** £10 per night   **Grounds** on leads **Facilities** cage storage   walks info   vet info   **On Request** fridge access torch towels   **Other** charge for damage   **Resident Pets:** Camilla & Igor (Great Danes)

This imposing Edwardian house is situated in 14 acres of grounds, and most of the bedrooms enjoy views across the gardens and paddocks. Situated just one mile from Lymington, this is an excellent base to enjoy the many leisure pursuits that the New Forest has to offer. Meals are also available here, and Mrs Tee often uses the local wild mushrooms in her dishes.

Rooms 5 en suite (2 fmly) (2 GF) **S** fr £50; **D** £90-£120* **Facilities** tea/coffee Dinner available Cen ht Licensed Wi-fi **Parking** 20

Best Western Forest Lodge

★ ★ ★   81%   ⊛⊛   HOTEL

Pikes Hill, Romsey Rd SO43 7AS

☎ 023 8028 3677   📠 023 8028 2940

e-mail: forest@newforesthotels.co.uk

web: www.newforesthotels.co.uk

dir: *M27 junct 1, A337 towards Lyndhurst. In village, with police station & courts on right, take 1st right into Pikes Hill*

PETS: Bedrooms (10 GF)   unattended   **Charges** £7.50 per night £52.50 per week   **Public areas** except restaurant & bar   on leads **Grounds** on leads   **Exercise area** adjacent   **Facilities** water bowl walks info   vet info   **On Request** fridge access

Situated on the edge of Lyndhurst, this hotel is set well back from the main road. The smart, contemporary bedrooms include four-poster rooms and family rooms; children are very welcome here. The eating options are the Forest Restaurant and the fine-dining Glasshouse Restaurant. There is an indoor swimming pool and Nordic sauna.

Rooms 36 (11 fmly) (10 GF) **S** £60-£73; **D** £120-£146 (incl. bkfst)* **Facilities** FTV ⊕ Xmas New Year Wi-fi **Parking** 50 **Notes** LB

ENGLAND

Best Western Crown

★★★ 75% HOTEL

High St SO43 7NF
☎ 023 8028 2922   📠 023 8028 2751
e-mail: reception@crownhotel-lyndhurst.co.uk
web: www.crownhotel-lyndhurst.co.uk
dir: *In centre of village, opposite church*

PETS: Bedrooms Charges £7 per night **Public areas** lounge only on leads disp bin **Exercise area** New Forest 200mtrs **Facilities** water bowl dog chews washing facs cage storage walks info vet info **On Request** fridge access torch towels

The Crown, with its stone mullioned windows, panelled rooms and elegant period decor evokes the style of an Edwardian country house. Bedrooms are generally a good size and offer a useful range of facilities. Public areas have style and comfort and include a choice of function and meeting rooms. The pleasant garden and terrace are havens of peace and tranquillity.

Rooms 38 (8 fmly) **S** £61-£72.50; **D** £87-£156 (incl. bkfst)
Facilities FTV Xmas New Year Wi-fi **Services** Lift **Parking** 60
Notes LB

Lyndhurst Park

★★★ 73% HOTEL

High St SO43 7NL
☎ 023 8028 3923   📠 023 8028 3019
e-mail: lyndhurst.park@forestdale.com
web: www.lyndhurstparkhotel.co.uk
dir: *M27 junct 1-3 to A35 to Lyndhurst. Hotel at bottom of High St*

PETS: Bedrooms unattended **Charges** £7.50 per night
Public areas except restaurant

Although it is just by the High Street, this hotel is afforded seclusion and tranquillity from the town due to its five acres of mature grounds. The comfortable bedrooms include home-from-home touches. The bar offers a stylish setting for a snack whilst the oak-panelled Tudor restaurant provides a more formal dining venue.

Rooms 59 (3 fmly) **S** £60-£95; **D** £85-£135 (incl. bkfst)*
Facilities FTV 🏊 ♨ Sauna Xmas New Year Wi-fi **Services** Lift
Parking 100 **Notes** LB

Knightwood Lodge

★★ 67% SMALL HOTEL

Southampton Rd SO43 7BU
☎ 023 8028 2502   📠 023 8028 3730
e-mail: jackie4r@aol.com
web: www.knightwoodlodge.co.uk
dir: *M27 junct 1, A337 to Lyndhurst. Left at lights in village onto A35 towards Southampton. Hotel 0.25m on left*

PETS: Bedrooms (3 GF) unattended **Public areas** except restaurant, bar & swimming pool **Exercise area** New Forest adjacent **Facilities** washing facs walks info vet info **On Request** fridge access torch towels **Other** charge for damage pets allowed in certain bedrooms only

This friendly, family-run hotel is situated on the outskirts of Lyndhurst. Comfortable bedrooms are modern in style and well equipped with many useful extras. The hotel offers an excellent range of facilities including a swimming pool, a jacuzzi and a small gym area. Two separate cottages are available for families or larger groups, and dogs are also welcome to accompany their owners in these units.

Rooms 18 (4 annexe) (2 fmly) (3 GF) **S** £45-£55; **D** £75-£110 (incl. bkfst)* **Facilities** FTV 🏊 Gym Steam room Sauna Spa bath **Parking** 15 **Notes** LB

MILFORD ON SEA   Map 4 SZ29

Westover Hall Hotel

★★★ 88% @@ COUNTRY HOUSE HOTEL

Park Ln SO41 0PT
☎ 01590 643044   📠 01590 644490
e-mail: info@westoverhallhotel.com
dir: *M3 & M27 W onto A337 to Lymington, follow signs to Milford-on-Sea onto B3058, hotel outside village centre towards cliff*

PETS: Bedrooms (2 GF) unattended **Charges** £12 per night **Public areas** except restaurants & bar on leads **Grounds** on leads **Exercise area** beach 100mtrs **Facilities** washing facs walks info vet info **On Request** torch towels **Other** charge for damage **Resident Pet:** Lancelot (Manx cat)

Just a few moments' walk from the beach and boasting uninterrupted views across Christchurch Bay to the Isle of Wight in the distance, this late-Victorian mansion offers a relaxed, informal and friendly atmosphere together with efficient standards of hospitality and service. Bedrooms do vary in size and aspect, but all have been decorated with flair and style. Architectural delights include dramatic stained-glass windows, extensive oak panelling and a galleried entrance hall. The cuisine is prepared with much care and attention to detail.

Rooms 15 (3 annexe) (2 fmly) (2 GF) **S** £90-£140; **D** £160-£310 (incl. bkfst & dinner)* **Facilities** Xmas New Year Wi-fi **Parking** 50 **Notes** LB

THE INDEPENDENTS

175

ENGLAND

MILFORD ON SEA *continued*

Lytton Lawn Touring Park *(SZ293937)*

▶▶▶▶

Lymore Ln SO41 0TX
☎ 01590 648331   📠 01590 645610
e-mail: holidays@shorefield.co.uk
dir: *From Lymington A337 to Christchurch for 2.5m to Everton. Left onto B3058 to Milford on Sea. 0.25m, left onto Lymore Lane*

PETS: Charges £1.50-£3 per night £10.50-£21 per week
Public areas except shop, play area, games room & toilet blocks
disp bin **Exercise area** exercise field **Facilities** food walks info
vet info **Other** prior notice required disposal bags available
Restrictions no Rottweilers or Staffordshire Bull Terriers

Open 6 Feb-2 Jan rs Low season shop/reception limited hrs. No grass pitches Last arrival 22.00hrs Last departure 10.00hrs

A pleasant well-run park with good facilities, located near the coast. The park is peaceful and quiet, but the facilities of a sister park 2.5 miles away are available to campers, including swimming pool, tennis courts, bistro and bar/carvery, and large club with family entertainment. Fully-serviced pitches provide good screening, and standard pitches are on gently-sloping grass. An 8 acre site with 136 touring pitches, 53 hardstandings.

Notes Families & couples only. Rallies welcome

See advert on opposite page

Swan

★★ 67% HOTEL

11 West St SO24 9AD
☎ 01962 732302 & 734427   📠 01962 735274
e-mail: swanhotel@btinternet.com
web: www.swanhotelalresford.com
dir: *Off A31 onto B3047*

PETS: Bedrooms (5 GF) **Public areas** except dining room on
leads **Exercise area** approx 450yds **Facilities** cage storage
walks info vet info **On Request** fridge access **Other** charge for
damage dogs allowed in certain bedrooms only **Restrictions** no
Pit Bull Terriers or Staffordshire Bull Terriers

This former coaching inn dates back to the 18th century and remains a busy and popular destination for travellers and locals alike. Bedrooms are situated in both the main building and the more modern wing. The lounge bar and adjacent restaurant are open all day; for more traditional dining there is another restaurant which overlooks the busy village street.

Rooms 23 (12 annexe) (3 fmly) (5 GF) **Facilities** New Year Wi-fi
Parking 25 **Notes** RS 25 Dec

The Woolpack Inn

★★★★ ◉ INN

Totford SO24 9TJ
☎ 01962 734184   📠 0845 293 8055
e-mail: info@thewoolpackinn.co.uk
web: www.thewoolpackinn.co.uk
dir: *M3 junct 6 take A339 towards Alton, right onto A3046. In Totford on left*

PETS: Bedrooms Stables 1m **Public areas** on leads **Grounds** on
leads **Exercise area** 200mtrs **Facilities** food bowl water bowl
bedding washing facs walks info **On Request** fridge access
towels **Other** charge for damage **Resident Pets:** Buster, Stella
& Olive (dogs)

Situated in the small village of Totford, a tranquil and picturesque location that is within easy reach of main transport routes. This traditional establishment has benefited from extensive refurbishment resulting in a fine balance of contemporary styling and traditional features. The bedrooms (named after game birds) and the bathrooms are well appointed with many thoughtful extras making guest comfort a top priority. The award-winning dining room showcases local produce with regularly changing specials enhancing the carte options.

Rooms 7 en suite (1 fmly) (4 GF) **S** £75-£95; **D** £75-£95*
Facilities FTV tea/coffee Dinner available Direct Dial Cen ht Wi-fi
Pool Table **Parking** 20

OWER — Map 3 SU31

Green Pastures Farm *(SU321158)*

▶▶▶

SO51 6AJ

☎ 023 8081 4444

e-mail: enquiries@greenpasturesfarm.com

dir: *M27 junct 2. Follow Salisbury signs for 0.5m. Then follow brown tourist signs for Green Pastures. Also signed from A36 & A3090 at Ower*

PETS: Sep accom day kennels **Public areas Exercise area** track leading to common **Exercise area** nearby **Facilities** walks info vet info **Other** prior notice required **Resident Pets:** Pudsey (Collie), Nipper (Jack Russell), Molly (cat)

Open 15 Mar-Oct Last departure 11.00hrs

A pleasant site on a working farm, with good screening of trees and shrubs around the perimeter. The touring area is divided by a border of shrubs and, at times, colourful foxgloves. This peaceful location is close to the M27 and New Forest. A 5 acre site with 45 touring pitches, 2 hardstandings.

PORTSMOUTH & SOUTHSEA — Map 4 SU60

Best Western Royal Beach

★★★ 75% HOTEL

South Pde, Southsea PO4 0RN

☎ 023 9273 1281 📠 023 9281 7572

e-mail: enquiries@royalbeachhotel.co.uk

web: www.royalbeachhotel.co.uk

dir: *M27 to M275, follow signs to seafront. Hotel on seafront*

PETS: Bedrooms Public areas except restaurant **Exercise area** nearby park & green **Facilities** walks info vet info

This former Victorian seafront hotel is a smart and comfortable venue suitable for leisure and business guests alike. Bedrooms and public areas are well presented and generally spacious, and the smart Coast Bar is an ideal venue for a relaxing drink.

Rooms 124 (18 fmly) (47 smoking) **S** £60-£95; **D** £80-£125 (incl. bkfst) **Facilities** STV Xmas New Year Wi-fi **Services** Lift **Parking** 50 **Notes** LB

PETERSFIELD — Map 4 SU72

Langrish House

★★★ 75% ◉◉ HOTEL

Langrish GU32 1RN

☎ 01730 266941 📠 01730 260543

e-mail: frontdesk@langrishhouse.co.uk

web: www.langrishhouse.co.uk

dir: *A3 onto A272 towards Winchester. Hotel signed, 2.5m on left*

PETS: Bedrooms (3 GF) unattended **Charges** £10 per night **Public areas** except restaurant **Grounds** on leads **Exercise area** surrounding area **Facilities** bedding scoop/disp bags **On Request** towels **Other** pet pack for dogs (welcome letter, blanket, poop scoop, biscuits & towel) **Resident Pets:** Tonga (Black Labrador), Costanza, Redolfo & Aurora (Siamese cats), chickens, ducks, guinea fowl

Langrish House has been in the same family for seven generations. It is located in an extremely peaceful area just a few minutes drive from Petersfield, halfway between Guildford and Portsmouth. Bedrooms are comfortable and well equipped with stunning views across the gardens to the hills. Guests can eat in the intimate Frederick's Restaurant with views over the lawn, or in the Old Vaults which have an interesting history dating back to 1644. The hotel is licensed for civil ceremonies and various themed events take place throughout the year.

Rooms 13 (1 fmly) (3 GF) **Facilities** ↻ Xmas New Year Wi-fi **Parking** 80 **Notes** LB Closed 2 weeks in Jan

RINGWOOD — Map 4 SU10

Little Forest Lodge
★★★★ GUEST HOUSE
Poulner Hill BH24 3HS
☎ 01425 478848 📠 01425 473564
dir: *1.5m E of Ringwood on A31*

PETS: Bedrooms Charges £5 per night **Public areas** except dining room **Grounds** disp bin **Exercise area Facilities** food bowl water bowl dog chews feeding mat washing facs cage storage walks info vet info **On Request** fridge access torch towels **Resident Pets:** Jade (Retriever/Collie cross), Millie (Doberman/Whippet cross), Harry & Spike (cats), ducks, chickens

A warm welcome is given to guests, and their pets, at this charming Edwardian house set in two acres of woodland. Bedrooms are pleasantly decorated and equipped with thoughtful extras. Both the attractive wood-panelled dining room and the delightful lounge, with bar and wood-burning fire, overlook the gardens.

Rooms 6 en suite (3 fmly) (1 GF) **S** £45-£50; **D** £70*
Facilities tea/coffee Cen ht Licensed 🐾 **Parking** 10

ROMSEY — Map 3 SU32

Hill Farm Caravan Park *(SU287238)*
▶▶▶▶▶
Branches Ln, Sherfield English SO51 6FH
☎ 01794 340402 📠 01794 342358
e-mail: gjb@hillfarmpark.com
dir: *Signed from A27 (Salisbury to Romsey road) in Sherfield English, 4m NW of Romsey & M27 junct 2*

PETS: Charges 2 dogs free, £1.50 per night thereafter
Public areas disp bin **Exercise area** dog walks **Exercise area** 8m **Facilities** food washing facs dog grooming walks info vet info **Other** prior notice required disposal bags availalble

Open Mar-Oct Last arrival 20.00hrs Last departure noon

A small, well-sheltered park peacefully located amidst mature trees and meadows. The two toilet blocks offer smart unisex showers as well as a fully en suite family/disabled room and plenty of privacy in the wash rooms. The owners are continuing to develop this attractive park, and with its proximity to Salisbury and the New Forest, it makes an appealing holiday location. A 10.5 acre site with 70 touring pitches, 60 hardstandings and 6 statics.

Notes Minimum noise at all times and no noise after 23.00hrs, one unit per pitch. Unsuitable for teenagers 🐷

SOUTHAMPTON — Map 4 SU41

Legacy Botleigh Grange Hotel
★★★★ 75% 🏵 HOTEL
Hedge End SO30 2GA
☎ 0844 4119050 📠 08444 119051
e-mail: res-botleighgrange@legacy-hotels.co.uk
web: www.legacy-hotels.co.uk
dir: *M27 junct 7, A334 to Botley, hotel 0.5m on left*

PETS: Bedrooms unattended **Charges** £10 per night £70 per week **Grounds** on leads **Exercise area Facilities** (pre-bookable) vet info **Other** charge for damage dogs allowed in east wing ground floor bedrooms only

This impressive mansion, situated close to the M27, displays good quality throughout. The bedrooms are spacious with a good range of facilities. Public areas include a large conference room and a pleasant terrace with views overlooking the gardens and lake. The restaurant offers interesting menus using fresh, local produce.

Rooms 56 (8 fmly) **S** £71-£150; **D** £79-£200 (incl. bkfst)*
Facilities Spa STV 🎱 Putt green Fishing Gym Relaxation room Steam room Sauna Xmas New Year Wi-fi **Services** Lift **Parking** 200 **Notes** LB

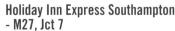

Southampton Park
★★★ 71% HOTEL
Cumberland Place SO15 2WY
☎ 023 8034 3343 ▤ 023 8033 2538
e-mail: southampton.park@forestdale.com
web: www.southamptonparkhotel.com
dir: *At north end of Inner Ring Road, opposite Watts Park & Civic Centre*

PETS: **Bedrooms** unattended sign **Charges** £7.50 per night
Public areas except restaurant **Exercise area Facilities** food
(pre-bookable) food bowl cage storage **On Request** towels
Other charge for damage

This modern hotel, in the heart of the city, provides well-equipped, smartly appointed and comfortable bedrooms. It boasts a well equipped spa with all modern facilities and a beauty salon for those who wish to pamper themselves. The public areas are spacious and include the popular MJ's Brasserie. Parking is available in a multi-storey behind the hotel.

Rooms 72 (10 fmly) **S** £65-£89; **D** £70-£125 (incl. bkfst)*
Facilities Spa FTV ⊗ supervised Gym New Year Wi-fi
Services Lift **Notes** Closed 25 & 26 Dec nights

Elizabeth House
★★ 78% HOTEL
42-44 The Avenue SO17 1XP
☎ 023 8022 4327 ▤ 023 8033 9651
e-mail: mail@elizabethhousehotel.com
web: www.elizabethhousehotel.com
dir: *On A33, hotel on left after Southampton Common, before main lights*

PETS: **Bedrooms** (8 GF) **Grounds** disp bin **Exercise area** 200yds
Facilities cage storage walks info vet info **On Request** fridge
access torch towels **Resident Pet:** Henry (West Highland
Terrier)

This hotel is conveniently situated close to the city centre, so provides an ideal base for both business and leisure guests. The bedrooms are well equipped and are attractively furnished with comfort in mind. There is also a cosy and atmospheric bistro in the cellar where evening meals are served.

Rooms 27 (7 annexe) (9 fmly) (8 GF) **S** £55-£64.50; **D** £65-£77.50
(incl. bkfst)* **Facilities** FTV Wi-fi **Parking** 31

Holiday Inn Express Southampton - M27, Jct 7
BUDGET HOTEL
Botley Rd, West End SO30 3XH
☎ 023 8060 6060 & 8060 6040 ▤ 023 8060 6050
e-mail: reservations@expressbyholidayinn.uk.net
web: www.meridianleisure.com/southampton
dir: *M27 junct 7, follow brown signs to The Rose Bowl. Hotel 1m from junct 7 at entrance to The Rose Bowl*

PETS: **Bedrooms** (38 GF) **Stables** 1.5m **Charges** £10 per night
Grounds on leads **Exercise area Facilities** cage storage walks
info vet info **Other** charge for damage no charge for guide dogs
Restrictions max weight 7kg

This hotel, adjacent to the Rose Bowl, is conveniently located for Southampton Airport and Docks and has ample free parking. There is an air-conditioned restaurant serving conference lunches, evening meals and complimentary hot breakfasts, a fully licensed bar and lounge area with a 42" plasma TV with satellite channels. The hotel offers high speed Wi-fi throughout. Leisure facilities are available at the adjacent Esporta Leisure Centre for a nominal fee.

Rooms 176 (39 fmly) (38 GF) (9 smoking) **S** £49-£109;
D £49-£109 (incl. bkfst) **Parking** 176

SOUTHSEA
See Portsmouth & Southsea

STOCKBRIDGE   Map 4 SU33

York Lodge
★★★★ BED AND BREAKFAST
Five Bells Ln, Nether Wallop SO20 8HE
☎ 01264 781313
e-mail: bradley@york-lodge.co.uk
web: www.york-lodge.co.uk
dir: *Exit A30 or A343 onto B3084, turn into Hosketts Lane, left onto Five Bells Lane, 1st house on right*

PETS: **Bedrooms Public areas Grounds** disp bin **Exercise area**
2 mins' walk **Facilities** washing facs cage storage walks info
vet info **On Request** fridge access torch towels **Resident Pets:**
Ella (Boston Terrier/Pug cross)

Located in the picturesque village famous for Agatha Christie's *Miss Marple* TV series, this charming house has comfortable accommodation in a self-contained wing. Bedrooms are stylishly presented with many thoughtful extra facilities. The dining room overlooks peaceful gardens, and delicious dinners are available by arrangement.

Rooms 2 en suite (2 GF) **S** £35-£55; **D** £70-£75* **Facilities** FTV
tea/coffee Cen ht Wi-fi **Parking** 4 **Notes** No Children 8yrs 🐾

STOCKBRIDGE *continued*

The Three Cups Inn

★ ★ ★ INN

High St SO20 6HB

☎ 01264 810527

e-mail: manager@the3cups.co.uk

PETS: Bedrooms Charges £10 per night **Public areas** bar & lounge only on leads **Grounds Exercise area** adjacent **Facilities** food bowl water bowl cage storage walks info vet info **On Request** fridge access torch **Other** charge for damage

A former coaching inn on the high street in a popular town, with its own parking. Rooms are comfortable and well equipped, and food is available every evening.

Rooms 8 en suite (3 fmly) **S** £72-£79; **D** £79-£89* **Facilities** tea/coffee Dinner available Cen ht Wi-fi Fishing **Parking** 15

The Grosvenor

★ ★ ★ INN

23 High St SO20 6EU

☎ 01264 810606 📠 01264 810747

e-mail: 9180@greeneking.co.uk

PETS: Bedrooms sign **Charges Public areas** on leads **Grounds** on leads disp bin **Exercise area** 150yds **Facilities** washing facs walks info vet info **Other** charge for damage

Located between the historic cathedral cities of Winchester and Salisbury and a stone's throw from the River Test, The Grosvenor, a Georgian building, provides en suite accommodation in a traditional setting. Bedrooms have been designed with guest comfort in mind. The Tom Cannon restaurant is popular with both residents and locals alike, and provides a good range of locally sourced produce including game when in season.

Rooms 14 en suite 12 annexe en suite (6 GF) **Facilities** tea/coffee Dinner available Direct Dial Cen ht Wi-fi Fishing **Parking** 16

SWAY	Map 4 SZ29

Sway Manor Restaurant & Hotel

★ ★ ★ 75% HOTEL

Station Rd SO41 6BA

☎ 01590 682754 📠 01590 682955

e-mail: info@swaymanor.com

web: www.swaymanor.com

dir: *Exit B3055 (Brockenhurst/New Milton road) into village centre*

PETS: Bedrooms unattended **Stables** 2m **Charges** £6 per night **Public areas** except restaurant on leads **Grounds** disp bin **Exercise area** 0.5m **Facilities** walks info vet info **On Request** fridge access **Other** charge for damage **Resident Pets:** Bobby (Chocolate Labrador), Bernard (Golden Labrador)

Built at the turn of the 20th century, this attractive mansion is set in its own grounds, and conveniently located in the village

centre. Bedrooms are well appointed and generously equipped; most have views over the gardens and pool. The bar and conservatory restaurant, both with views over the gardens, are popular with locals.

Rooms 15 (3 fmly) **Facilities** ⊀ 🎵 Xmas New Year Wi-fi **Services** Lift **Parking** 40

The Nurse's Cottage Restaurant with Rooms

★ ★ ★ ★ 🛏 ⌂ GUEST ACCOMMODATION

Station Rd SO41 6BA

☎ 01590 683402

e-mail: stay@nursescottage.co.uk

web: www.nursescottage.co.uk

dir: *Off B3055 in village centre, close to shops*

PETS: Bedrooms unattended sign **Stables** 1m **Exercise area** 200yds **Facilities** food bowl water bowl walks info vet info **On Request** fridge access **Other** charge for damage **Restrictions** accommodation not suitable for large dogs

Enjoying a prominent position in the New Forest village of Sway, the Nurse's Cottage is the recipient of numerous hospitality awards. Quality is paramount in each of the individually styled bedrooms and each room offers a host of thoughtful extras including flat-screen TVs, DVDs, complimentary soft drinks, Wi-fi and delicious handmade chocolates. The conservatory restaurant overlooks the neat garden and the seasonally changing dinner menu features the best in local produce. A wide ranging choice of hot and cold dishes at breakfast guarantees a good start to the day.

Rooms 5 en suite (5 GF) **S** £92.50-£115; **D** £185-£210* (incl. dinner) **Facilities** FTV tea/coffee Dinner available Direct Dial Cen ht Licensed Wi-fi **Parking** 5 **Notes** LB No Children 10yrs Closed Feb-Mar & Nov (3wks)

ENGLAND

Acorn Shetland Pony Stud

★★★★ BED AND BREAKFAST

Meadows Cottage, Arnewood Bridge Rd SO41 6DA
☎ 01590 682000 & 07506 079373
e-mail: meadows.cottage@virgin.net
dir: M27 junct 1, A337 to Brockenhurst, B3055 to Sway, pass
Birchy Hill Nursing Home, over x-rds, 2nd entrance left

PETS: Bedrooms unattended Sep accom barn Stables Charges
dogs £3; other pets by arrangement Public areas possible
restrictions if other guests staying on leads Grounds on leads
disp bin Exercise area Facilities feeding mat leads pet sitting
washing facs cage storage walks info vet info On Request
fridge access torch towels Other charge for damage pets
can be left unattended in bedrooms only by prior arrangement
Resident Pets: Bill & Sir Bobby (cats), 10 Shetland ponies

Located on the outskirts of Sway, this comfortable establishment
is set in over six acres of pony paddocks and a water garden. The
ground-floor bedrooms are well furnished and have direct access
onto patios. The enjoyable, freshly cooked breakfasts use a range
of fine produce including delicious home-made bread.

Rooms 3 en suite (1 fmly) (3 GF) Facilities tea/coffee Cen ht Wi-fi
Parking 30 Notes LB ⊛

WINCHESTER   **Map 4 SU42**

Lainston House

★★★★ ⊛⊛⊛ COUNTRY HOUSE HOTEL

Sparsholt SO21 2LT
☎ 01962 776088   📠 01962 776672
e-mail: enquiries@lainstonhouse.com
web: www.exclusivehotels.co.uk
dir: 2m NW off B3049 towards Stockbridge

PETS: Bedrooms (18 GF) Charges £25 per night Public areas
lounge only on leads Grounds Facilities food (pre-bookable)
water bowl walks info vet info Other charge for damage dog
menu

This graceful example of a William and Mary House enjoys a
countryside location amidst mature grounds and gardens.
Staff provide good levels of courtesy and care with a polished,
professional service. Bedrooms are tastefully appointed and
include some spectacular, spacious rooms with stylish handmade
beds and stunning bathrooms. Public rooms include a cocktail
bar built entirely from a single cedar and stocked with an
impressive range of rare drinks and cigars.

Rooms 50 (6 fmly) (18 GF) Facilities ⌣ Fishing ⌣ Gym Archery
Clay pigeon shooting Cycling Hot air ballooning Walking ♫ Xmas
New Year Wi-fi Parking 200

Mercure Wessex

★★★★ 70% HOTEL

Paternoster Row SO23 9LQ
☎ 01962 861611   📠 01962 841503
e-mail: H6619@accor.com
web: www.mercure.com
dir: M3, follow signs for town centre, at rdbt by King Alfred's
statue past Guildhall, next left, hotel on right

PETS: Bedrooms Charges £10 per night £70 per week
Exercise area park nearby Facilities cage storage walks info
vet info On Request torch Other charge for damage

Occupying an enviable location in the centre of this historic city
and adjacent to the spectacular cathedral, this hotel is quietly
situated on a side street. Inside, the atmosphere is restful and
welcoming, with public areas and some bedrooms enjoying
unrivalled views of the hotel's centuries-old neighbour.

Rooms 94 (6 fmly) S £65-£125; D £65-£135 Facilities STV Gym
Xmas New Year Wi-fi Services Lift Parking 60 Notes LB

The Winchester Royal Hotel

★★★ 77% ⊛ HOTEL

St Peter St SO23 8BS
☎ 01962 840840   📠 01962 841582
e-mail: winchester.royal@forestdale.com
web: www.thewinchesterroyalhotel.co.uk
dir: M3 junct 9 to Winnall Trading Estate. Follow to city centre,
cross river, left, 1st right. Onto one-way system, take 2nd right.
Hotel immediately on right

PETS: Bedrooms (27 GF) Charges £7.50 per night Public areas
except restaurant Other please phone for further details of pet
facilities

Situated in the heart of the former capital of England, a warm
welcome awaits at this friendly hotel, which in parts, dates back
to the 16th century. The bedrooms may vary in style but they are
all comfortable and well equipped; the modern annexe rooms
overlook the attractive well-tended gardens. The conservatory
restaurant makes a very pleasant setting for enjoyable meals.

Rooms 75 (56 annexe) (1 fmly) (27 GF) S £75-£110; D £95-£130
(incl. bkfst)* Facilities FTV Xmas New Year Wi-fi Parking 50
Notes LB

HEREFORDSHIRE

HEREFORD
Map 3 SO54

Three Counties Hotel
★★★ 74% HOTEL

Belmont Rd HR2 7BP
☎ 01432 299955   📠 01432 275114
e-mail: enquiries@threecountieshotel.co.uk
web: www.threecountieshotel.co.uk
dir: On A465 (Abergavenny road)

PETS: Bedrooms (46 GF) Grounds on leads Facilities vet info
Other dogs allowed in certain bedrooms only

Just a mile west of the city centre, this large, privately owned, modern complex has well-equipped, spacious bedrooms; many are located in separate single-storey buildings around the extensive car park. There is a spacious, comfortable lounge, a traditional bar and an attractive restaurant.

Rooms 60 (32 annexe) (4 fmly) (46 GF) S £67-£82; D £77-£102 (incl. bkfst) Facilities STV Wi-fi Parking 250

Sink Green (SO542377)
★★★★ FARMHOUSE

Rotherwas HR2 6LE
☎ 01432 870223   📠 01432 870223 Mr D E Jones
e-mail: enquiries@sinkgreenfarm.co.uk
web: www.sinkgreenfarm.co.uk
dir: 3m SE of city centre. Off A49 onto B4399 for 2m

PETS: Bedrooms Public areas Grounds disp bin Exercise area adjoining fields Facilities water bowl washing facs walks info vet info On Request fridge access torch towels Other charge for damage Resident Pets: Bob & Max (Sheepdogs)

This charming 16th-century farmhouse stands in attractive countryside and has many original features, including flagstone floors, exposed beams and open fireplaces. Bedrooms are traditionally furnished and one has a four-poster bed. The pleasant garden has a summer house, hot tub and barbecue.

Rooms 3 en suite S £33-£40; D £66-£78* Facilities FTV TVL tea/coffee Cen ht Wi-fi Fishing Parking 10 Notes LB 🐾 180 acres beef

LITTLE TARRINGTON
Map 3 SO64

Hereford Camping & Caravanning Club Site
(SO625410)

▶▶▶▶

The Millpond HR1 4JA
☎ 01432 890243 & 0845 130 7633
dir: 300yds off A438 on Ledbury side of Tarrington, entrance on right, 50yds before railway bridge

PETS: Public areas except facility block (ex assist dogs)
Exercise area surrounding countryside Other prior notice required

Open Mar-21 Oct Last arrival 20.00hrs Last departure noon

A much improved grassy park set beside a 3-acre fishing lake

in a peaceful location, and now franchised to the Camping & Caravanning Club. Well-planted trees and shrubs help to divide and screen the park, and the modern toilet block provides very good facilities. Security is excellent. A 4.5 acre site with 55 touring pitches.

Notes Site gates closed between 23.00hrs-07.00hrs

ROSS-ON-WYE
Map 3 SO62

Glewstone Court
★★★ 73% ⚜ COUNTRY HOUSE HOTEL

Glewstone HR9 6AW
☎ 01989 770367   📠 01989 770282
e-mail: glewstone@aol.com
web: www.glewstonecourt.com
dir: From Ross-on-Wye Market Place take A40/A49 Monmouth/Hereford, over Wilton Bridge to rdbt, left onto A40 to Monmouth, in 1m right for Glewstone

PETS: Bedrooms unattended Stables 3m Charges £5 per night Public areas except restaurant Grounds disp bin Exercise area 50mtrs Facilities food (pre-bookable) food bowl water bowl bedding feeding mat litter tray scoop/disp bags leads washing facs cage storage walks info vet info On Request fridge access torch towels Other charge for damage Resident Pets: Buster & Brecon (Golden Retrievers), Barney (Long Haired Miniature Dachshund), Benji (Cocker Spaniel), Toots & Tilly (cats)

This charming hotel enjoys an elevated position with views over Ross-on-Wye, and is set in well-tended gardens. Informal service is delivered with great enthusiasm by Bill Reeve-Tucker, whilst the kitchen is the domain of Christine Reeve-Tucker who offers an extensive menu of well executed dishes. Bedrooms come in a variety of sizes and are tastefully furnished and well equipped.

Rooms 8 (2 fmly) S £80-£99; D £120-£140 (incl. bkfst)*
Facilities ♨ New Year Wi-fi Child facilities Parking 25 Notes LB Closed 25-27 Dec

Pengethley Manor

★★★ **72%** HOTEL

Pengethley Park HR9 6LL

☎ 01989 730211 📄 01989 730238

e-mail: reservations@pengethleymanor.co.uk

web: www.pengethleymanor.co.uk

dir: *4m N on A49 (Hereford road), from Ross-on-Wye*

PETS: Bedrooms (4 GF) unattended **Stables** 5m **Charges** £10 per stay **Public areas** except restaurant & bar on leads **Grounds** on leads disp bin **Exercise area** 100yds **Facilities** washing facs walks info vet info **On Request** fridge access torch towels **Other** charge for damage prior arrangement must be made for pets to ensure correct room is allocated

This fine Georgian mansion is set in extensive grounds with glorious views and two successful vineyards that produce over 1,000 bottles a year. The bedrooms are tastefully appointed and come in a wide variety of styles; all are well equipped. The elegant public rooms are furnished in a style that is in keeping with the house's character. Dinner provides a range of enjoyable options and is served in the spacious restaurant.

Rooms 25 (14 annexe) (3 fmly) (4 GF) **Facilities** ₹ ♿ 9 ♨ Golf improvement course Xmas New Year Wi-fi **Parking** 70

Pencraig Court Country House Hotel

★★★ **70%** COUNTRY HOUSE HOTEL

Pencraig HR9 6HR

☎ 01989 770306 📄 01989 770040

e-mail: info@pencraig-court.co.uk

web: www.pencraig-court.co.uk

dir: *Off A40, into Pencraig 4m S of Ross-on-Wye*

PETS: Bedrooms Charges £5 per night **Public areas** except in restaurant **Grounds** disp bin **Exercise area Facilities** food food bowl water bowl leads washing facs walks info vet info **On Request** fridge access **Other** charge for damage pets only in lounge with other guests' approval **Resident Pets:** Sam (Sussex Spaniel), Ross (cat)

This Georgian mansion commands impressive views of the River Wye to Ross-on-Wye beyond. Guests can be assured of a relaxing stay and the proprietors are on hand to ensure personal attention and service. The bedrooms have a traditional feel and include one room with a four-poster bed. The country-house atmosphere is carried through in the lounges and the elegant restaurant.

Rooms 11 (1 fmly) **Facilities** ♨ Wi-fi **Parking** 20 **Notes** RS 24-27 Dec

King's Head

★★★ **66%** HOTEL

8 High St HR9 5HL

☎ 01989 763174 📄 01989 769578

e-mail: enquiries@kingshead.co.uk

web: www.kingshead.co.uk

dir: *In town centre, past market building on right*

PETS: Bedrooms unattended **Public areas** bar only on leads **Grounds** on leads **Exercise area** 200yds **Facilities** food (pre-bookable) food bowl water bowl cage storage walks info vet info **On Request** torch

This establishment dates back to the 14th century and has a wealth of charm and character. Bedrooms are well equipped and comfortable with thoughtful guest extras provided and include both four-poster and family rooms. The restaurant uses local produce; the menus and specials board reflect a varied selection including fresh fish, free range beef and lamb. There is a well stocked bar serving hand pulled real ales, and like the restaurant, is popular with locals and visitors.

Rooms 15 (1 fmly) **S** £53.50; **D** £90 (incl. bkfst) **Facilities** FTV Wi-fi **Parking** 13 **Notes** LB

Chasedale

★★ **72%** SMALL HOTEL

Walford Rd HR9 5PQ

☎ 01989 562423 & 565801 📄 01989 567900

e-mail: chasedale@supanet.com

web: www.chasedale.co.uk

dir: *From town centre, S on B4234, hotel 0.5m on left*

PETS: Bedrooms (1 GF) unattended **Public areas** except restaurant **Grounds** disp bin **Exercise area** 300mtrs **Facilities** food bowl water bowl cage storage walks info vet info **On Request** fridge access towels **Resident Pets:** Marmite (Chocolate Labrador), Cassis (Black Labrador)

This large, mid-Victorian property is situated on the south-west outskirts of the town. Privately owned and personally run, it provides spacious, well-proportioned public areas and extensive grounds. The accommodation is well equipped and includes ground floor and family rooms, whilst the restaurant offers a wide selection of wholesome food.

Rooms 10 (2 fmly) (1 GF) **S** £42-£45; **D** £84-£90 (incl. bkfst) **Facilities** Xmas Wi-fi **Parking** 14 **Notes** LB

ENGLAND

Orles Barn

★★★★★ ≣ RESTAURANT WITH ROOMS

Wilton HR9 6AE
☎ 01989 562155 📠 01989 768470
e-mail: reservations@orles-barn.co.uk
web: www.orles-barn.co.uk
dir: *A49/A40 rdbt outside Ross-on-Wye, take slip road between petrol station & A40 to Monmouth. 100yds on left*

PETS: Bedrooms sign **Charges** £5 per night **Public areas** except at food service times **Grounds** disp bin **Exercise area** 200mtrs **Facilities** water bowl dog chews feeding mat scoop/disp bags walks info vet info **On Request** towels **Other** charge for damage **Resident Pets:** William (Black Labrador), Twiglet (Jack Russell)

The proprietors of this character property offer a warm welcome to all their guests. Older sections of the property date back to the 14th and 17th centuries when it was a farmhouse with a barn. The property offers comfortable bedrooms, a smart cosy lounge with a bar and a spacious restaurant. Dinner and Sunday lunch are offered from a balanced menu of fresh local and seasonal ingredients. Breakfast utilises quality local produce and makes a good start to the day.

Rooms 5 en suite (1 fmly) (1 GF) **Facilities** FTV tea/coffee Dinner available Cen ht Wi-fi **Parking** 20 **Notes** LB

Wilton Court

★★★★★ ≣ RESTAURANT WITH ROOMS

Wilton Ln HR9 6AQ
☎ 01989 562569 📠 01989 768460
e-mail: info@wiltoncourthotel.com
dir: *M50 junct 4, A40 towards Monmouth at 3rd rdbt left signed Ross-on-Wye, 1st right, hotel on right*

PETS: Bedrooms unattended **Charges** £10 per stay **Public areas** bar only on leads **Grounds** on leads disp bin **Exercise area** **Facilities** food (pre-bookable) washing facs walks info vet info **On Request** fridge access torch **Other** charge for damage **Restrictions** no very large dogs

Dating back to the 16th century, this establishment has great charm and a wealth of character. Standing on the banks of the River Wye and just a short walk from the town centre, there is a genuinely relaxed, friendly and unhurried atmosphere here from hosts Roger and Helen Wynn along with their reliable team. Bedrooms are tastefully furnished and well equipped, while public areas include a comfortable lounge, traditional bar and pleasant restaurant with a conservatory extension overlooking the garden. High standards of food, using fresh, locally sourced ingredients, are offered.

Rooms 10 en suite (1 fmly) **S** £80-£135; **D** £105-£155* **Facilities** FTV TVL tea/coffee Dinner available Direct Dial Cen ht Wi-fi Fishing Pool Table **Parking** 20 **Notes** LB

Lumleys

★★★★ BED AND BREAKFAST

Kern Bridge, Bishopswood HR9 5QT
☎ 01600 890040 📠 0870 706 2378
e-mail: helen@lumleys.force9.co.uk
web: www.thelumleys.co.uk
dir: *Off A40 onto B4229 at Goodrich, over Kern Bridge, right at Inn On The Wye, 400yds opposite picnic ground*

PETS: Bedrooms unattended **Public areas** except dining room **Grounds** disp bin **Exercise area** 20yds **Facilities** water bowl dog chews leads washing facs cage storage walks info vet info **On Request** fridge access torch towels **Resident Pets:** Hector & Barnaby (Cocker Spaniel/Poodle cross)

This pleasant and friendly bed and breakfast overlooks the River Wye, and has been a hostelry since Victorian times. It offers the character of a bygone era combined with modern comforts and facilities. Bedrooms are individually and carefully furnished and one has a four-poster bed and its own patio. Comfortable public areas include a choice of sitting rooms.

Rooms 3 en suite; **D** £65-£75* **Facilities** STV FTV TVL tea/coffee Direct Dial Cen ht Wi-fi **Parking** 15 **Notes**

Lea House

★★★★ ≣ 🛏 GUEST ACCOMMODATION

Lea HR9 7JZ
☎ 01989 750652 📠 01989 750652
e-mail: enquiries@leahouse.co.uk
web: www.leahouse.co.uk
dir: *4m SE of Ross on A40 towards Gloucester*

PETS: Bedrooms Charges £7.50 per stay **Public areas** except dining room during meals on leads disp bin **Exercise area** 30yds **Facilities** washing facs cage storage walks info vet info **On Request** torch towels **Resident Pets:** Piccal & Lilli (cats)

This former coaching inn, near Ross-on-Wye, makes a good base for exploring the Forest of Dean and the Wye Valley, and the atmosphere is relaxed and comfortable. The individually furnished bedrooms are thoughtfully equipped and very homely. Breakfast in the oak-beamed dining room offers home-made breads, freshly squeezed juice, fresh fruit platters, local sausages and a choice of fish. Home-cooked dinners are available by prior arrangement.

Lea House

Rooms 3 rms (2 en suite) (1 pri facs) (1 fmly) **S** £40-£55; **D** £65-£75* **Facilities** TVL tea/coffee Dinner available Cen ht Wi-fi **Parking** 4 **Notes** LB

Thatch Close

★★★★ GUEST ACCOMMODATION

Llangrove HR9 6EL
☎ 01989 770300
e-mail: info@thatchclose.co.uk
web: www.thatchclose.co.uk
dir: *Off A40 at Symonds Yat West/Whitchurch junct to Llangrove, right at x-rds after Post Office & before school. Thatch Close 0.6m on left*

PETS: Bedrooms Charges £2.50 per night £10 per week **Public areas** at discretion of other guests **Grounds** disp bin **Exercise area** adjacent **Facilities** food food bowl water bowl dog chews feeding mat leads washing facs cage storage walks info vet info **On Request** fridge access torch towels **Resident Pets:** Oliver & Tilly (Spaniel/Collie cross), Aku & Zippy (African Grey Parrots)

Standing in 13 acres, this sturdy 18th-century farmhouse is full of character. Expect a wonderfully warm atmosphere with a genuine welcome from your hosts. The homely bedrooms are equipped for comfort with many thoughtful extras. Breakfast and dinner are served in the elegant dining room, and a lounge is available. The extensive patios and gardens are popular in summer, providing plenty of space to find a quiet corner and relax with a good book.

Rooms 3 en suite **S** £40-£50; **D** £60-£70* **Facilities** TVL tea/coffee Dinner available Cen ht Wi-fi **Parking** 8 **Notes** LB

The Whitehouse Guest House

★★★ GUEST HOUSE

Wye St HR9 7BX
☎ 01989 763572
e-mail: whitehouseross@aol.com
dir: *Exit A40 dual-carriageway at Wilton, pass over bridge, take 1st left White House on right*

PETS: Bedrooms sign **Stables** 4.5m **Charges** dog £4 per night **Public areas** except dining room **Exercise area** adjacent **Facilities** food bowl water bowl bedding dog chews feeding mat scoop/disp bags leads walks info vet info **On Request** torch towels **Other** charge for damage **Resident Pet:** Pip (Springer Spaniel)

A warm welcome can be expected at this 18th-century house which is located adjacent to the River Wye and just a short walk to the town centre. The bedrooms are tastefully appointed and provide a thoughtful range of guest extras, including Wi-fi access. There are two four-poster bedrooms plus a double and a single room. A hearty breakfast is provided in the dining room which is set out with separate tables; evening meals are available by prior notice. Parking is on the road to the front.

Rooms 7 en suite (2 fmly) **S** £40-£45; **D** £60-£70* **Facilities** tea/coffee Dinner available Cen ht Licensed Wi-fi **Notes** LB No Children 12yrs Closed 24-25 Dec

SHOBDON	Map 3 SO46

The Bateman Arms

★★★★ INN

HR6 9LX
☎ 01568 708374 📠 08701 236418
e-mail: diana@batemanarms.co.uk
web: www.batemanarms.co.uk
dir: *On B4362 in Shobdon*

PETS: Bedrooms Stables 1.5m **Charges** £5 per stay (donated to charity) **Public areas** except restaurant on leads **Grounds** on leads disp bin **Exercise area** 50mtrs **Facilities** food (pre-bookable) food bowl water bowl scoop/disp bags leads pet sitting dog walking washing facs cage storage walks info vet info **On Request** fridge access torch towels **Other** charge for damage pets allowed in bar only if proprietor's dogs not present **Restrictions** no long haired dogs or dogs likely to moult heavily **Resident Pets:** Bing & Lui (Shih Tzus)

Located in the village, parts of this inn date back over 400 years. The owners offer a warm welcome to all their guests. The accommodation comprises six modern bedrooms located in a separate building, and three bedrooms in the main house; all are comfortable and well appointed. Much character has been retained with plenty of oak beams and a large log fire adding to the warm ambience of the public areas. In addition to the friendly welcome, the food, using carefully prepared local produce, is a key feature.

Rooms 3 en suite 6 annexe en suite (2 fmly) (3 GF) **Facilities** FTV tea/coffee Dinner available Cen ht Wi-fi Pool Table **Parking** 40 **Notes** LB

ENGLAND

STANFORD BISHOP — Map 3 SO65

Boyce Caravan Park (SO692528)

▶▶▶

WR6 5UB

☎ 01886 884248 📄 01886 884187

e-mail: enquiries@boyceholidaypark.co.uk

dir: From A44 take B4220. In Stanford Bishop take 1st left signed Linley Green, then 1st right down private driveway

PETS: Public areas except buildings & play areas disp bin Exercise area dog walking area Facilities walks info vet info Other prior notice required Restrictions no Dobermans, German Shepherds, Bull Terriers, Rottweilers, Japanese Tosa or similar cross breeds

Open Feb-Dec rs Mar-Oct tourers Last arrival 18.00hrs Last departure noon

A friendly and peaceful park with access allowed onto the 100 acres of farmland. Coarse fishing is also available in the grounds, and there are extensive views over the Malvern and Suckley Hills. Many walks available. A 10 acre site with 14 touring pitches, 3 hardstandings and 200 statics.

STAPLOW — Map 3 SO64

The Oak Inn

★★★★ INN

HR8 1NP

☎ 01531 640954

e-mail: oakinn@wyenet.co.uk

dir: 2m N of Ledbury on B4214

PETS: Bedrooms unattended Charges £5 per stay Public areas except restaurant on leads Grounds disp bin Exercise area 50yds Facilities dog chews feeding mat scoop/disp bags leads washing facs cage storage walks info vet info On Request fridge access torch towels Other charge for damage

This delightful country pub, surrounded by a cider apple orchard, is privately owned. Situated north of the market town of Ledbury, yet within easy access of the Malvern Hills, this 17th-century inn has been totally renovated. The bedrooms are modern, spacious and well appointed with under-floor heating and beds with quality pocket-sprung mattresses. The public areas feature log-burning fires, flagstone floors and character wooden beams. Dining is available seven days a week and the open-plan kitchen allows diners to see their meals being prepared. Wi-fi is accessible throughout.

Rooms 4 en suite (1 fmly) S £55-£60; D £80-£90* Facilities FTV tea/coffee Dinner available Cen ht Wi-fi Parking Notes No coaches

SYMONDS YAT (EAST) — Map 3 SO51

The Royal Lodge

★★★★ GUEST ACCOMMODATION

HR9 6JL

☎ 01600 890238 📄 01600 891425

e-mail: info@royalhotel-symondsyat.com

web: www.royallodgesymondsyat.co.uk

dir: Midway between Ross and Monmouth. Exit A40 at signs for Goodrich/B4229 to Symonds Yat East

PETS: Bedrooms unattended Charges £10 per stay Public areas except restaurant on leads Grounds on leads disp bin Exercise area adjacent Facilities cage storage walks info vet info On Request torch Other charge for damage

The Royal Lodge stands at the top end of the village overlooking the River Wye where parking is available. Bedrooms are spacious and comfortable, providing a good range of guest extras including flat-screen TVs; bathrooms offer modern facilities. There is a cosy lounge with an open fireplace and two bars are available. Meals are offered in the welcoming restaurant which provides carefully prepared fresh and local ingredients. The staff are pleasant and friendly.

Rooms 20 en suite (5 fmly) Facilities TVL tea/coffee Dinner available Direct Dial Cen ht Licensed Wi-fi Parking 150

YARKHILL — Map 3 SO64

Garford Farm (SO600435)

★★★★ FARMHOUSE

HR1 3ST

☎ 01432 890226 📄 01432 890707 Mrs H Parker

e-mail: garfordfarm@btconnect.com

dir: Off A417 at Newtown x-rds onto A4103 for Hereford, farm 1.5m on left

PETS: Bedrooms Sep accom Stables Charges dog £4 per night Public areas Grounds disp bin Exercise area 25yds Facilities food bowl water bowl bedding leads washing facs cage storage walks info vet info On Request fridge access torch towels Other charge for damage Resident Pets: Bertie, Sooty & Berry (Black Labradors), Cokie & Soda (cats)

This black and white timber-framed farmhouse, set on a large arable holding, dates from the 17th century. Its character is enhanced by period furnishings, and fires burn in the comfortable lounge during colder weather. The traditionally furnished bedrooms, including a family room, have modern facilities.

Rooms 2 en suite (1 fmly) S fr £35; D fr £60* Facilities tea/coffee Cen ht 🎣 Fishing Parking 6 Notes No Children 2yrs Closed 25-26 Dec 🌐 700 acres arable

HERTFORDSHIRE

BISHOP'S STORTFORD   Map 5 TL42

Down Hall Country House
★★★★ 76% ◉◉ HOTEL

Hatfield Heath CM22 7AS
☎ 01279 731441   📠 01279 730416
e-mail: reservations@downhall.co.uk
web: www.downhall.co.uk
dir: *A1060, at Hatfield Heath keep left. Turn right into lane opposite Hunters Meet restaurant & left at end, follow sign*

PETS: Bedrooms (20 GF) unattended **Charges** £10 per stay **Public areas** only in snooker/games room **Grounds** disp bin **Exercise area Facilities** food bowl water bowl dog chews scoop/disp bags cage storage vet info **On Request** fridge access torch **Other** welcome pack on arrival. Dogs can only be left unattended when owners are on premises

Imposing country-house hotel set amidst 100 acres of mature grounds in a peaceful location just a short drive from Stansted Airport. Bedrooms are generally quite spacious; each one is pleasantly decorated, tastefully furnished and equipped with modern facilities. Public rooms include a choice of restaurants, a cocktail bar, two lounges and leisure facilities.

Rooms 99 (20 GF) **Facilities** FTV ⌨ 🎱 ⛳ Giant chess Whirlpool Sauna Snooker room Gym equipment Xmas New Year Wi-fi **Services** Lift **Parking** 150

See advert on this page

Broadleaf Guest House
★★★ BED AND BREAKFAST

38 Broadleaf Av CM23 4JY
☎ 01279 835467
e-mail: b-pcannon@sky.com
dir: *1m SW of town centre. Off B1383 onto Whittinton Way & Friedburge Ave, Broadleaf Ave 6th left*

PETS: Bedrooms Charges Exercise area surrounding countryside **Facilities** vet info **Other** charge for damage

A delightful detached house situated in a peaceful residential area close to the town centre, and within easy striking distance of the M11 and Stansted Airport. The pleasantly decorated bedrooms are carefully furnished and equipped with many thoughtful touches. Breakfast is served in the smart dining room, which overlooks the pretty garden.

Rooms 2 rms (1 fmly) **S** £35; **D** £50-£65* **Facilities** tea/coffee Cen ht **Parking** 2 **Notes** ⊗

HATFIELD · Map 4 TL20

Hatfield Oak Hotel
★★★ 73% HOTEL
Roehyde Way AL10 9AF
☎ 01707 275701 📠 01707 266033
e-mail: enquiries@hotels-hatfield.com
dir: *M25 junct 23 between juncts 2 & 3 of A1(M). Roehyde Way runs parallel to A1(M)*

PETS: Bedrooms (36 GF) **Public areas** except restaurant on leads **Exercise area** adjacent **Restrictions** small well trained dogs only

The hotel enjoys an enviable location for both leisure and business guests, it is within easy reach of major roads and central London. In addition, the University of Hertfordshire is located nearby. The accommodation has been appointed to a good standard with flat-screen TVs and Wi-fi to name but a few.

Rooms 76 (5 fmly) (36 GF) (6 smoking) **S** £45-£150; **D** £45-£170*
Facilities FTV Wi-fi **Parking** 85 **Notes** LB

ST ALBANS · Map 4 TL10

Avalon House
★★★ GUEST HOUSE
260 London Rd AL1 1TJ
☎ 01727 856757 📠 01727 856750
e-mail: avalon@househotels.co.uk

PETS: Bedrooms Public areas except restaurant on leads **Grounds** disp bin **Exercise area** park (approx 10 mins) **Facilities** pet sitting cage storage walks info vet info **On Request** fridge access torch towels **Other** charge for damage **Resident Pet:** Sasha (King Charles/Jack Russell cross)

A comfortable guest house with en suite accommodation and parking, and in a convenient location for access to the motorway network. The station is only one mile away. There is a residents' lounge with a licensed bar, as well as a dedicated smoking area (although this is a no-smoking establishment).

Rooms 14 en suite (2 fmly) (4 GF) **S** £37.50-£50; **D** £50-£65*
Facilities TVL tea/coffee Cen ht Licensed Wi-fi **Parking** 14 **Notes** No Children 9yrs

SOUTH MIMMS SERVICE AREA (M25) · Map 4 TL20

Days Inn South Mimms
BUDGET HOTEL
Bignells Corner EN6 3QQ
☎ 01707 665440 📠 01707 660189
e-mail: south.mimms@welcomebreak.co.uk
web: www.welcomebreak.co.uk
dir: *M25 junct 23, at rdbt follow signs*

PETS: Bedrooms (18 GF) unattended **Charges Public areas** on leads **Grounds** on leads **Facilities** walks info vet info **Other** charge for damage

This modern building offers accommodation in smart, spacious and well-equipped bedrooms, suitable for families and business travellers, and all with en suite bathrooms. Continental breakfast is available and other refreshments may be taken at the nearby family restaurant.

Rooms 74 (55 fmly) (18 GF) (8 smoking) **S** £29-£69; **D** £29-£79

STEVENAGE · Map 4 TL22

Novotel Stevenage
★★★ 78% HOTEL
Knebworth Park SG1 2AX
☎ 01438 346100 📠 01438 723872
e-mail: H0992@accor.com
web: www.novotel.com
dir: *A1(M) junct 7, at entrance to Knebworth Park*

PETS: Bedrooms (30 GF) **Charges** £6 per night **Public areas** except restaurant on leads **Grounds** disp bin **Exercise area** **Other** charge for damage

Ideally situated just off the A1(M) is this purpose built hotel, which is a popular business and conference venue. Bedrooms are pleasantly decorated and equipped with a good range of useful extras. Public rooms include a large open plan lounge bar serving a range of snacks, and a smartly appointed restaurant.

Rooms 101 (20 fmly) (30 GF) **S** fr £49; **D** fr £49* **Facilities** STV ⚡ Use of local health club New Year Wi-fi **Services** Lift **Parking** 120

WARE — Map 5 TL31

Hanbury Manor, A Marriott Hotel & Country Club

★★★★★ 79% ◎◎ COUNTRY HOUSE HOTEL

SG12 0SD

☎ 01920 487722 & 0870 400 7222 📠 01920 487692

e-mail: mhrs.stngs.guestrelations@marriotthotels.com

web: www.marriotthanburymanor.co.uk

dir: M25 junct 25, take A10 north for 12m, then A1170, right at rdbt, hotel on left

PETS: **Bedrooms Charges** £40 per stay **Grounds** on leads **Exercise area** 100mtrs **Facilities** food bowl water bowl walks info vet info **On Request** torch **Other** charge for damage

Set in 200 acres of landscaped grounds, this impressive Jacobean-style mansion boasts an enviable range of leisure facilities, including an excellent health club and championship golf course. Bedrooms are traditionally and comfortably furnished in the country-house style and have lovely marbled bathrooms. There are a number of food and drink options, including the renowned Zodiac and Oakes restaurants. Marriott Hotels - AA Hotel Group of the Year 2010-11.

Rooms 161 (27 annexe) (60 fmly) **Facilities** Spa STV FTV ⊠ supervised ♨ 18 ⅏ Putt green ⅏ Gym Health & beauty treatments Aerobics Yoga Dance class Xmas New Year Wi-fi **Services** Lift **Parking** 200

Roebuck

★★★ 72% HOTEL

Baldock St SG12 9DR

☎ 01920 409955 📠 01920 468016

e-mail: roebuck@forestdale.com

web: www.theroebuckhotel.co.uk

dir: A10 onto B1001, left at rdbt, 1st left behind fire station

PETS: **Bedrooms** (16 GF) unattended sign **Charges** £7.50 per night £52.50 per week **Public areas** except restaurant on leads **Facilities** food (pre-bookable) food bowl water bowl feeding mat cage storage walks info vet info **On Request** fridge access **Other** charge for damage

The Roebuck is a comfortable and friendly hotel situated close to the old market town of Ware, it is also within easy reach of Stansted Airport, Cambridge and Hertford. The hotel has spacious bedrooms, a comfortable lounge, bar and conservatory restaurant. There is also a range of air-conditioned meeting rooms.

Rooms 47 (1 fmly) (16 GF) **S** £55-£85; **D** £75-£105 (incl. bkfst)* **Facilities** FTV Wi-fi **Services** Lift **Parking** 64 **Notes** LB

ASHFORD — Map 5 TR04

The Croft

★★★ GUEST ACCOMMODATION

Canterbury Rd, Kennington TN25 4DU

☎ 01233 622140 📠 01233 635271

e-mail: info@thecroft.biz

dir: M20 junct 10, 2m on A28 signed Canterbury

PETS: **Bedrooms** unattended **Charges** £7 per night **Grounds** on leads **Exercise area** heath across road **Other** charge for damage cats in cages only, max 2 dogs per room **Resident Pets:** Lina (Dalmatian/Lhasa Apso cross), Alfie (rabbit)

An attractive red-brick house situated in two acres of landscaped grounds just a short drive from Ashford railway station. The generously proportioned bedrooms are in the main house and in pretty cottages; all are pleasantly decorated and thoughtfully equipped. Public rooms include a smart Italian restaurant, a bar, and a cosy lounge.

Rooms 14 en suite (4 GF) **Facilities** tea/coffee Dinner available Direct Dial Cen ht Licensed Wi-fi **Parking** 30

Broadhembury Caravan & Camping Park

(TR009387)

►►►►

Steeds Ln, Kingsnorth TN26 1NQ

☎ 01233 620859 📠 01233 620918

e-mail: holidaypark@broadhembury.co.uk

dir: M20 junct 10, A2070. Left at 2nd rdbt signed Kingsnorth, left at 2nd x-roads in village

PETS: **Public areas** except toilets & play area on leads disp bin **Exercise area** 200yd-walk **Exercise area** public footpaths & woods adjacent **Facilities** water bowl washing facs walks info vet info **Other** prior notice required max 2 dogs per pitch disposal bags available **Resident Pets:** Henry (King Charles Spaniel), Scooby (cross), chickens

Open all year Last arrival 22.00hrs Last departure noon

Well-run and maintained small family park surrounded by open pasture and neatly landscaped, with pitches sheltered by mature hedges. Some super pitches have proved a popular addition, and there is a well-equipped campers' kitchen. A 10 acre site with 60 touring pitches, 24 hardstandings and 25 statics.

ENGLAND

ENGLAND

Heron Cottage

★ ★ ★ ★ GUEST ACCOMMODATION

TN27 8HH
☎ 01580 291358 📠 01580 291358
e-mail: susantwort@hotmail.com
web: www.heroncottage.info
dir: *1m NW of Biddenden. A262 W from Biddenden, 1st right, 0.25m across sharp left bend through stone pillars, left onto unmade road*

PETS: Bedrooms Public areas except dining room **Grounds** disp bin **Facilities** cage storage walks info vet info **On Request** fridge access torch **Restrictions** no dangerous dogs (see page 7)

Expect a warm welcome at this picturesque extended cottage, set in immaculate, mature gardens in peaceful Kent countryside. The bedrooms are thoughtfully equipped and have co-ordinated soft furnishings. Breakfast is served in the smart dining room, and the cosy sitting room has an open fireplace.

Rooms 7 rms (6 en suite) (2 fmly) (1 GF) **S** £45-£60; **D** £55-£70* **Facilities** TVL tea/coffee Dinner available Cen ht Wi-fi 🎣 Fishing **Parking** 8 **Notes** Closed Dec-Feb 🐾

thistle

Thistle Brands Hatch

★ ★ ★ ★ 75% HOTEL

DA3 8PE
☎ 0871 376 9008 📠 0871 376 9108
e-mail: brandshatch@thistle.co.uk
web: www.thistle.com/brandshatch
dir: *Follow Brands Hatch signs, hotel on left of racing circuit entrance*

PETS: Bedrooms (60 GF) **Stables** 2m **Charges** £10 per night **Public areas** except food areas on leads **Grounds** on leads **Exercise area** countryside adjacent **Facilities** washing facs cage storage walks info vet info **On Request** torch towels **Other** charge for damage

Ideally situated overlooking Brands Hatch race track and close to the major road networks (M20/M25). The open-plan public areas include a choice of bars, large lounge and a restaurant. Bedrooms are stylishly appointed and well equipped for both leisure and business guests. Extensive meeting rooms and Otium leisure facilities are also available.

Rooms 121 (5 fmly) (60 GF) (6 smoking) **Facilities** Spa 🏊 Gym New Year Wi-fi **Parking** 200

Best Western

Best Western Abbots Barton Hotel

★ ★ ★ 86% HOTEL

New Dover Rd CT1 3DU
☎ 01227 760341 📠 01227 785442
e-mail: info@abbotsbartonhotel.com
dir: *A2 onto A2050 at bridge, S of Canterbury. Hotel 0.75m past Old Gate Inn on left*

PETS: Bedrooms (6 GF) **Stables** nearby **Charges** £10 per night **Grounds** on leads **Exercise area** 1m **Facilities** food bowl water bowl bedding feeding mat **Other** charge for damage

Delightful property with a country-house hotel feel set amid two acres of pretty landscaped gardens close to the city centre and major road networks. The spacious accommodation includes a range of stylish lounges, a smart bar and the Fountain Restaurant, which serves imaginative food.

Rooms 50 (2 fmly) (6 GF) **S** £65-£125; **D** £80-£140 **Facilities** Xmas New Year Wi-fi **Services** Lift Air con **Parking** 80 **Notes** LB

Yorke Lodge

★ ★ ★ ★ ★ GUEST ACCOMMODATION

50 London Rd CT2 8LF
☎ 01227 451243 📠 01227 462006
e-mail: info@yorkelodge.com
web: www.yorkelodge.com
dir: *From London M2/A2, 1st exit signed Canterbury. At 1st rdbt left onto London Rd*

PETS: Bedrooms unattended **Exercise area** 100yds **Facilities** walks info vet info **On Request** fridge access torch towels **Other** charge for damage **Resident Pets:** Fleur (Dalmatian/Collie cross)

The charming Victorian property stands in a tree-lined road just ten minutes walk from the town centre and railway station. The spacious bedrooms are thoughtfully equipped and carefully decorated; some rooms have four-poster beds. The stylish dining room leads to a conservatory-lounge, which opens onto a superb terrace.

Rooms 8 en suite (1 fmly) **S** £55-£70; **D** £90-£120 **Facilities** FTV tea/coffee Cen ht Wi-fi **Parking** 5 **Notes** LB No Children 5yrs

Bridgewood Manor
★★★★ 72% HOTEL

Bridgewood Roundabout, Walderslade Woods ME5 9AX
☎ 01634 201333 📄 01634 201330
e-mail: bridgewoodmanor@qhotels.co.uk
web: www.qhotels.co.uk
dir: *Adjacent to Bridgewood rdbt on A229. Take 3rd exit signed Walderslade & Lordswood. Hotel 50mtrs on left*

PETS: Bedrooms (26 GF) unattended **Charges** £15 per stay **Public areas** except bar, leisure areas & restaurant on leads **Exercise area** woods adjacent **Other** charge for damage

A modern, purpose-built hotel situated on the outskirts of Rochester. Bedrooms are pleasantly decorated, comfortably furnished and equipped with many thoughtful touches. The hotel has an excellent range of leisure and conference facilities. Guests can dine in the informal Terrace Bistro or experience fine dining in the more formal Squires restaurant, where the service is both attentive and friendly.

Rooms 100 (12 fmly) (26 GF) **S** £50-£85; **D** £65-£125 (incl. bkfst)* **Facilities** Spa STV 🕲 supervised 🏊 Gym Beauty treatments Xmas New Year Wi-fi **Services** Lift **Parking** 170 **Notes** LB

 Campanile

Campanile Dartford
BUDGET HOTEL

1 Clipper Boulevard West, Crossways Business Park DA2 6QN
☎ 01322 278925 📄 01322 278948
e-mail: dartford@campanile.com
dir: *Follow signs for Ferry Terminal from Dartford Bridge*

PETS: Bedrooms Charges £5 per night **Public areas** muzzled and on leads **Grounds** on leads disp bin **Facilities** water bowl vet info **On Request** towels **Other** charge for damage

This modern building offers accommodation in smart, well-equipped bedrooms, all with en suite bathrooms. Refreshments may be taken at the informal bistro.

Rooms 125 (14 fmly) **S** £65; **D** £65*

Sutherland House
★★★★★ GUEST ACCOMMODATION

186 London Rd CT14 9PT
☎ 01304 362853 📄 01304 381146
e-mail: info@sutherlandhouse.fsnet.co.uk
dir: *0.5m W of town centre/seafront on A258*

PETS: Bedrooms unattended sign **Public areas** with consideration for other guests' comfort **Grounds** disp bin **Exercise area Facilities** water bowl washing facs walks info vet info **On Request** fridge access torch towels **Other** charge for damage **Restrictions** small dogs only

This stylish accommodation demonstrates impeccable taste with its charming, well-equipped bedrooms and a comfortable lounge. A fully stocked bar, books, free Wi-fi, Freeview TV and radio are some of the many amenities offered. The elegant dining room is the venue for a hearty breakfast and dinner is available by prior arrangement.

Rooms 4 en suite (1 GF) **S** £60-£70; **D** £70-£80 **Facilities** FTV tea/coffee Dinner available Direct Dial Cen ht Licensed Wi-fi **Parking** 7 **Notes** LB No Children 5yrs

Hubert House Guesthouse & Bistro
★★★★ GUEST HOUSE

9 Castle Hill Rd CT16 1QW
☎ 01304 202253 📄 01304 210142
e-mail: stay@huberthouse.co.uk
web: www.huberthouse.co.uk
dir: *On A258 by Dover Castle*

PETS: Bedrooms Charges £7.50 per night **Exercise area** 300mtrs **Facilities** walks info vet info **On Request** fridge access torch **Other** charge for damage **Resident Pets:** Lillie (Weimaraner), Tullah (Slovakian Pointer)

This charming Georgian house is within walking distance of the ferry port and the town centre. Bedrooms are sumptuously decorated and furnished with an abundance of practical extras. Breakfast, including full English and healthy options, is served in the smart coffee house, which is open all day. Families are especially welcome.

Rooms 6 en suite (4 fmly) **S** £45; **D** £55-£95 **Facilities** FTV tea/coffee Dinner available Cen ht Licensed Wi-fi **Parking** 6 **Notes** LB

FOLKESTONE Map 5 TR23

The Burlington

★★★ 78% HOTEL

Earls Av CT20 2HR

☎ 01303 255301 ▤ 01303 251301

e-mail: info@theburlingtonhotel.com

dir: *M20 junct 13. At rdbt 3rd exit signed A20/Folkestone. At next rdbt 2nd exit into Cherry Garden Lane. To lights, take middle lane into Beachborough Rd, under bridge, left into Shorncliffe Rd. 5th right signed Hythe & Hastings. Hotel at end on right*

PETS: Bedrooms (5 GF) **Charges** £10 per night **Public areas** except restaurant on leads **Grounds** on leads **Facilities** water bowl bedding cage storage walks info vet info **Resident Pets:** Misty & Poppy (cats)

Situated close to the beach in a peaceful side road just a short walk from the town centre. The public rooms include a choice of lounges, the Bay Tree restaurant and a large cocktail bar. Bedrooms are pleasantly decorated and equipped with modern facilities; some rooms have superb sea views.

Rooms 50 (6 fmly) (5 GF) **S** £38–£108; **D** £48–£108* **Facilities** FTV Putt green Xmas New Year Wi-fi **Services** Lift **Parking** 20 **Notes** LB

Langhorne Garden

★★★ GUEST ACCOMMODATION

10-12 Langhorne Gardens CT20 2EA

☎ 01303 257233 ▤ 01303 242760

e-mail: info@langhorne.co.uk

web: www.langhorne.co.uk

dir: *Exit M20 junct 13, follow signs for The Leas, 2m*

PETS: Bedrooms unattended **Public areas** except restaurant on leads **Exercise area** 100yds **Facilities** cage storage walks info vet info **On Request** fridge access torch towels

Once a Victorian villa, Langhorne Garden is close to the seafront, shops and restaurants. Bright spacious bedrooms are traditionally decorated with plenty of original charm. Public rooms include a choice of comfortable lounges and a bar, a spacious dining room and a popular local bar in the basement with billiards, darts and table football.

Rooms 29 en suite (8 fmly) **S** £35–£50; **D** £59–£69* **Facilities** STV FTV tea/coffee Dinner available Direct Dial Cen ht Lift Licensed Wi-fi Pool Table **Notes** LB Closed Xmas RS Jan-Etr no evening meal

Little Satmar Holiday Park *(TR260390)*

▶ ▶ ▶

Winehouse Ln, Capel Le Ferne CT18 7JF

☎ 01303 251188 ▤ 01303 251188

e-mail: info@keatfarm.co.uk

dir: *Signed off B2011*

PETS: Charges £1.50 per night **Public areas** **Exercise area** 100mtrs **Facilities** food dog chews cat treats washing facs walks info vet info **Resident Pets:** 2 Rottweilers, 2 West Highland Terriers, 1 Shih Tzu

Open Mar-Nov Last arrival 23.00hrs Last departure 14.00hrs

A quiet, well-screened site well away from the road and statics, with clean and tidy facilities. A useful base for visiting Dover and Folkestone, and just a short walk from cliff paths with their views of the Channel, and sandy beaches below. A 5 acre site with 47 touring pitches and 75 statics.

Little Switzerland Camping & Caravan Site

(TR248380)

▶ ▶

Wear Bay Rd CT19 6PS

☎ 01303 252168

e-mail: btony328@aol.com

dir: *Signed from A20 E of Folkestone. Approaching from A259 or B2011 on E outskirts of Folkestone follow signs for Wear Bay/ Martello Tower, then tourist sign to site, follow signs to country park*

PETS: Stables 1m **Public areas** disp bin **Exercise area** dog walks, cliff path **Facilities** food bowl water bowl washing facs walks info vet info **Resident Pet:** Fluffy (cat)

Open Mar-Oct Last arrival mdnt Last departure noon

Set on a narrow plateau below the white cliffs, this unusual site has sheltered camping in secluded dells and enjoys fine views across Wear Bay and the Strait of Dover. A licensed café with an alfresco area is popular; the basic toilet facilities are unsuitable for disabled visitors. A 3 acre site with 32 touring pitches and 13 statics.

Notes No open fires 🐾

Mercure Hythe Imperial

★★★★ 74% HOTEL

Princes Pde CT21 6AE

☎ 01303 267441   📠 01303 264610

e-mail: h6862@accor.com

web: www.mercure.com

dir: *M20, junct 11 onto A261. In Hythe follow Folkestone signs. Right into Twiss Rd to hotel*

PETS: Bedrooms (6 GF) unattended sign **Stables** 10m **Charges** £10 per night £60 per week **Public areas** except restaurant, bar & lounge on leads **Grounds** disp bin **Exercise area** 1m **Facilities** water bowl cage storage walks info vet info **On Request** fridge access torch **Other** charge for damage

This imposing seafront hotel is enhanced by impressive grounds including a 13-hole golf course, tennis court and extensive gardens. Bedrooms are varied in style but all offer modern facilities, and many enjoy stunning sea views. The elegant restaurant, bar and lounges are traditional in style and retain many original features. The leisure club includes a gym, a squash court, an indoor pool, and the spa offers a range of luxury treatments.

Rooms 100 (6 fmly) (6 GF) **S** £70-£115; **D** £90-£180*
Facilities Spa STV ③ ♨ 13 ♨ Putt green Gym Squash Snooker & pool table Aerobic studio Table tennis Sauna Steam room Xmas New Year Wi-fi **Services** Lift **Parking** 207 **Notes** LB

The Fayreness

★★★ 79% HOTEL

Marine Dr CT10 3LG

☎ 01843 868641   & 861103   📠 01843 608750

e-mail: info@fayreness.co.uk

web: www.fayreness.co.uk

dir: *A28 onto B2051 which becomes B2052. Pass Holy Trinity Church on right & '19th Hole' public house. Next left, down Kingsgate Ave, hotel at end on left*

PETS: Bedrooms (5 GF) unattended **Stables** 5m **Charges** £5 per night £20 per week **Public areas** except restaurant & conservatory on leads **Grounds** on leads disp bin **Exercise area** clifftop & beach adjacent **Facilities** food bowl water bowl dog chews cage storage walks info vet info **On Request** fridge access torch towels **Other** charge for damage

Situated on the cliff top overlooking the English Channel, just a few steps from a sandy beach and adjacent to the North Foreland Golf Club. The spacious bedrooms are tastefully furnished with many thoughtful touches including free Wi-fi; some rooms have stunning sea views. Public rooms include a large open-plan lounge/bar, a function room, dining room and conservatory restaurant.

Rooms 29 (3 fmly) (5 GF) (4 smoking) **Facilities** STV New Year Wi-fi **Parking** 70

The Black Horse Inn

★★★★ ═ INN

Pilgrims Way, Thurnham ME14 3LD

☎ 01622 737185   & 630830   📠 01622 739170

e-mail: info@wellieboot.net

web: www.wellieboot.net/home_blackhorse.htm

dir: *M20 junct 7, N onto A249. Right into Detling, opposite pub onto Pilgrims Way for 1m*

PETS: Bedrooms unattended sign **Charges** £6 per night **Public areas** in bar area only on leads **Grounds** on leads disp bin **Exercise area** North Downs Way adjacent **Facilities** scoop/disp bags walks info vet info **On Request** fridge access torch towels **Other** charge for damage **Restrictions** no Pit Bull Terriers **Resident Pets:** Sam (Pointer cross), Boston (Staffordshire Terrier), Snowball (cat)

This charming inn dates from the 17th century, and the public areas have a wealth of oak beams, exposed brickwork and open fireplaces. The stylish bedrooms are in a series of cosy cabins behind the premises; each one is attractively furnished and thoughtfully equipped.

Rooms 30 annexe en suite (8 fmly) (30 GF) **S** £60-£75; **D** £80-£95* **Facilities** FTV tea/coffee Dinner available Cen ht Wi-fi **Parking** 40 **Notes** LB No coaches

See advert on page 195

Aylesbury House

★★★★ GUEST ACCOMMODATION

56-58 London Rd ME16 8QL

☎ 01622 762100   📠 01622 664673

e-mail: mail@aylesburyhouse.co.uk

dir: *M20 junct 5, A20 to Maidstone. Aylesbury House on left before town centre*

PETS: Bedrooms unattended **Grounds** on leads **Facilities** walks info vet info **Resident Pet:** Kami (cat)

Located just a short walk from the town centre, this smartly maintained establishment offers a genuine welcome. The carefully decorated bedrooms have co-ordinated soft fabrics and many thoughtful touches. Breakfast is served in the smart dining room overlooking a walled garden.

Rooms 8 en suite **S** £55-£60; **D** £65-£75 **Facilities** FTV tea/coffee Cen ht Wi-fi **Parking** 8

Honeychild Manor Farmhouse *(TR062276)*

★★★★ ≘ FARMHOUSE

St Mary In The Marsh TN29 0DB

☎ 01797 366180 & 07951 237821 🖹 01797 366925

Mrs V Furnival

e-mail: honeychild@farming.co.uk

dir: *2m N of New Romney off A259. S of village centre*

PETS: **Bedrooms Stables Charges** horse £15 per night
Public areas on leads disp bin **Exercise area** approx 100yds
Facilities cage storage walks info vet info **On Request** fridge
access torch towels **Resident Pets:** Georgie (Labrador), Molly
(Collie), Charlie & Eddie (horses)

This imposing Georgian farmhouse is part of a working dairy
farm on Romney Marsh. Walkers and dreamers alike will enjoy
the stunning views and can relax in the beautifully landscaped
gardens or play tennis on the full-sized court. A hearty breakfast
is served in the elegant dining room and features quality local
produce. Bedrooms are pleasantly decorated, well furnished and
thoughtfully equipped.

Rooms 3 rms (1 en suite) (2 pri facs) (1 fmly) **S** £40-£50;
D £70-£85 **Facilities** tea/coffee Dinner available Cen ht Wi-fi 🐾
Parking 10 **Notes** LB 🐾 1500 acres arable/dairy

The Bell

★★★ 80% 🏵 HOTEL

The Quay CT13 9EF

☎ 01304 613388 🖹 01304 615308

e-mail: reservations@bellhotelsandwich.co.uk

web: www.bellhotelsandwich.co.uk

dir: *In town centre*

PETS: **Bedrooms** unattended sign **Stables Charges** £5 per
night **Public areas** except restaurant & bar on leads disp
bin **Exercise area** adjacent **Facilities** food (pre-bookable)
food bowl water bowl bedding dog chews cat treats feeding
mat litter tray scoop/disp bags leads pet sitting dog walking
washing facs cage storage walks info vet info **On Request**
fridge access torch towels **Other** charge for damage

The Bell has been welcoming travellers since the 14th century,
when it looked out over a harbour, now the River Stour; the
existing building dates mainly from the 19th century. The
bedrooms have been refurbished to offer guests much style and
comfort, and some rooms have balconies with river views. The
contemporary Old Dining Room Restaurant offers a seasonally
changing menu that highlights locally caught fish and seafood,
salt marsh lamb and produce from nearby farms. Dating from the
Georgian era, the elegant Regency Room is ideal for conferences,
wedding receptions and parties. Wi-fi is available throughout.

Rooms 37 (4 fmly) **S** £90-£120; **D** £109-£210 (incl. bkfst)*
Facilities FTV Xmas New Year Wi-fi **Parking** 7 **Notes** LB

Hempstead House Country Hotel

★★★ 86% 🏵 HOTEL

London Rd, Bapchild ME9 9PP

☎ 01795 428020 🖹 01795 436362

e-mail: info@hempsteadhouse.co.uk

web: www.hempsteadhouse.co.uk

dir: *1.5m from town centre on A2 towards Canterbury*

PETS: **Bedrooms** (1 GF) unattended **Stables** 1.5m **Public areas**
except restaurant (ex assist dogs) **Grounds** disp bin
Exercise area adjacent **Facilities** food (pre-bookable) food
bowl water bowl scoop/disp bags pet sitting dog walking
washing facs cage storage walks info vet info **On Request**
fridge access torch towels **Resident Pets:** 2 Toy Poodles, 1
Yorkshire Terrier, 1 Labrador

Expect a warm welcome at this charming detached Victorian
property, situated amidst four acres of mature landscaped
gardens. Bedrooms are attractively decorated with lovely
co-ordinated fabrics, tastefully furnished and equipped with
many thoughtful touches. Public rooms feature a choice of
elegant lounges as well as a superb conservatory dining room.
In summer guests can eat on the terraces. There is a spa and
fitness suite.

Rooms 34 (7 fmly) (1 GF) **S** £80-£110; **D** £100-£150 (incl. bkfst)*
Facilities Spa STV FTV 🐾 💪 Gym Fitness studio Steam room
Sauna Hydrotherapy pool Xmas New Year Wi-fi **Services** Lift
Parking 100 **Notes** LB

The Beaumont

★★★★ ≘ GUEST ACCOMMODATION

74 London Rd ME10 1NS

☎ 01795 472536 🖹 01795 425921

e-mail: info@thebeaumont.co.uk

web: www.thebeaumont.co.uk

dir: *From M2 junct 5 or M20 junct 7 take A249 N. Exit at A2, 1m
on left towards Sittingbourne*

PETS: **Bedrooms** unattended **Public areas** on leads **Grounds** on
leads disp bin **Exercise area** 5 mins walk **Facilities** water bowl
scoop/disp bags walks info vet info **On Request** fridge access
torch towels **Restrictions** no large dogs **Resident Pet:** Scooby
(Cocker Spaniel)

This Georgian farmhouse is a charming family-run property that
offers the best hospitality and service. Comfortable bedrooms
and bathrooms are well equipped for business and leisure guests.
Breakfast in the bright, spacious conservatory makes good use
of local produce and homemade preserves. Off-road parking is
available.

Rooms 9 rms (6 en suite) (3 pri facs) (3 GF) **S** £40-£65;
D £65-£75* **Facilities** STV TVL tea/coffee Cen ht Wi-fi **Parking** 9
Notes Closed 24 Dec-1 Jan

Hotel du Vin Tunbridge Wells

★★★★ 71% ⊛ TOWN HOUSE HOTEL

Crescent Rd TN1 2LY

☎ 01892 526455 📠 01892 512044

e-mail: reception.tunbridgewells@hotelduvin.com

web: www.hotelduvin.com

dir: *Follow town centre to main junct of Mount Pleasant Road & Crescent Road/Church Road. Hotel 150yds on right just past Phillips House*

PETS: Bedrooms unattended **Stables** 3m **Public areas** on leads **Grounds** on leads **Exercise area** 200yds **Facilities** (pre-bookable) food bowl water bowl bedding feeding mat cage storage walks info vet info **On Request** fridge access torch towels

This impressive Grade II listed building dates from 1762, and as a princess, Queen Victoria often stayed here. The spacious bedrooms are available in a range of sizes, beautifully and individually appointed, and equipped with a host of thoughtful extras. Public rooms include a bistro-style restaurant, two elegant lounges and a small bar.

Rooms 34 **Facilities** STV Boules court in garden Wi-fi **Services** Lift **Parking** 30 **Notes** LB

Corner Cottage

★ ★ ★ ★ GUEST ACCOMMODATION

Toys Hill TN16 1PY

☎ 01732 750362 📠 01732 750754

e-mail: cornercottagebandb@jshmanco.com

dir: *A25 to Brasted, into Chart Lane signed Fox & Hounds. Right into Puddledock Lane, 1st house on left*

PETS: Bedrooms Public areas Grounds disp bin **Exercise area** adjacent **Facilities** food (pre-bookable) food bowl water bowl pet sitting dog walking washing facs cage storage walks info vet info **On Request** fridge access torch towels **Resident Pet:** Softie (cat)

Set in a charming village this spacious, well-equipped annexe is comfortably furnished and includes many thoughtful touches. In the main cottage a hearty Aga-cooked breakfast is served in the rustic dining room with stunning views of the countryside.

Rooms 1 annexe en suite (1 fmly) **S** £55-£60; **D** £75-£80* **Facilities** tea/coffee Dinner available Cen ht Wi-fi **Parking** 2 **Notes** ⓦ

Seaview Holiday Park *(TR145675)*

► ► ►

St John's Rd CT5 2RY

☎ 01227 792246 📠 01227 792247

e-mail: info@parkholidaysuk.com

dir: *From A299 take A2990 then B2205 to Swalecliffe, site between Herne Bay & Whitstable*

PETS: Stables 5m **Charges** £2-£4 per night **Public areas** except Club House & cafe disp bin **Exercise area Facilities** food dog chews vet info

Open Mar-Oct Last arrival 21.30hrs Last departure noon

A pleasant open site on the edge of Whitstable, set well away from the static area, with a smart, modern toilet block and both super and hardstanding pitches. A 12 acre site with 171 touring pitches, 41 hardstandings and 452 statics.

ENGLAND

BLACKBURN
Map 7 SD62

Foxfields Country Hotel & Suites
★★★ 76% HOTEL

Whalley Rd, Billington BB7 9HY
☎ 01254 822556 ▤ 01254 824613
e-mail: enquiries@hotels-blackburn.com
dir: *Just off A59*

PETS: Bedrooms (13 GF) unattended sign **Charges** £10 per night **Grounds** on leads **Exercise area** 2m **Facilities** food bowl water bowl scoop/disp bags **On Request** torch towels

This modern hotel is easily accessible from major road networks. Bedrooms are comfortable and spacious, and include some suites and others with separate dressing areas. Facilities include a good-sized swimming pool, a small gym and conference suites. The traditional restaurant serves an interesting range of cuisine.

Rooms 44 (16 annexe) (27 fmly) (13 GF) (8 smoking) **S** £50–£110; **D** £60–£120* **Facilities** STV FTV ⊙ Gym Xmas New Year Wi-fi **Parking** 194 **Notes** LB

BLACKPOOL
Map 7 SD33

Barceló Blackpool Imperial Hotel
★★★★ 73% HOTEL

North Promenade FY1 2HB
☎ 01253 623971 ▤ 01253 751784
e-mail: imperialblackpool@barcelo-hotels.co.uk
web: www.barcelo-hotels.co.uk
dir: *M55 junct 2, take A583 North Shore, follow signs to North Promenade. Hotel on seafront, north of tower*

PETS: Bedrooms unattended sign **Charges** £15 per night **Public areas** only in lobby area on leads **Grounds** on leads **Exercise area** beach adjacent **Facilities** vet info **Other** charge for damage dogs allowed in standard bedrooms only

Enjoying a prime seafront location, this grand Victorian hotel offers smartly appointed, well-equipped bedrooms and spacious, elegant public areas. Facilities include a smart leisure club, a comfortable lounge, the No.10 bar and an attractive split-level restaurant that overlooks the seafront.

Rooms 180 (16 fmly) **Facilities** Spa STV ⊙ supervised Gym Xmas New Year Wi-fi **Services** Lift **Parking** 150

Headlands
★★ 68% HOTEL

611-613 South Promenade FY4 1NJ
☎ 01253 341179 ▤ 01253 342657
e-mail: headlandshotel@aol.com
dir: *M55 & filter left, right at rdbt to Promenade, turn right. Hotel 0.5m on right*

PETS: Bedrooms unattended **Charges** £10 per night **Exercise area** 50mtrs **Facilities** water bowl cage storage walks info vet info **On Request** fridge access torch towels **Resident Pets:** Charlie (King Charles Spaniel)

This friendly, family owned hotel stands on the South Promenade, close to the Pleasure Beach and many of the town's major attractions. Bedrooms are traditionally furnished, many enjoying sea views. There is a choice of lounges and live entertainment is provided regularly. Home cooked food is served in the panelled dining room.

Rooms 41 (10 fmly) **S** £30–£49.50; **D** £60–£99 (incl. bkfst)* **Facilities** Darts Games room Pool Snooker ♬ Xmas New Year **Services** Lift **Parking** 46 **Notes** LB Closed 2-15 Jan

BOLTON LE SANDS
Map 7 SD46

Red Bank Farm (SD472681)
▶▶▶

LA5 8JR
☎ 01524 823196 ▤ 01524 824981
e-mail: mark.archer@hotmail.co.uk
dir: *Take A5105 (Morecambe road), after 200mtrs right on Shore Ln. At rail bridge turn right to site*

PETS: Public areas on leads **Exercise area** 50mtrs **Facilities** vet info

Open Mar-Oct

A gently sloping grassy field with mature hedges, close to the sea shore and a RSPB reserve. This farm site has smart toilet facilities, a superb views across Morecambe Bay to the distant Lake District hills, and is popular with tenters. A 3 acre site with 60 touring pitches.

Welcome Lodge Charnock Richard

BUDGET HOTEL

Welcome Break Service Area PR7 5LR
☎ 01257 791746 📄 01257 793596
e-mail: charnockhotel@welcomebreak.co.uk
web: www.welcomebreak.co.uk
dir: *Between junct 27 & 28 of M6 N'bound. 500yds from Camelot Theme Park via Mill Lane*

PETS: Bedrooms (32 GF) **Grounds** disp bin **Exercise area** large field **Exercise area** 20mtrs **Facilities** cage storage vet info

This modern building offers accommodation in smart, spacious and well-equipped bedrooms, suitable for families and business travellers, and all with en suite bathrooms. Continental breakfast is available and other refreshments may be taken at the nearby family restaurant.

Rooms 100 (68 fmly) (32 GF) (20 smoking) **S** £29-£39; **D** £29-£59

Mosswood Caravan Park (SD456497)

▶ ▶ ▶ ▶

Crimbles Ln LA2 0ES
☎ 01524 791041 📄 01524 792444
e-mail: info@mosswood.co.uk
dir: *Approx 4m from A6/M6 junct 33, 1m W of Cockerham on A588*

PETS: Public areas disp bin **Exercise area** 4 acre field (50yds) **Facilities** food food bowl water bowl walks info vet info

Open Mar-Oct Last arrival 20.00hrs Last departure 16.00hrs

A tree-lined grassy park with sheltered, level pitches, located on peaceful Cockerham Moss. The modern toilet block is attractively clad in stained wood, and the facilities include cubicled washing facilities and a launderette. A 25 acre site with 25 touring pitches, 25 hardstandings and 143 statics.

Royal Umpire Caravan Park (SD504190)

▶ ▶ ▶

Southport Rd PR26 9JB
☎ 01772 600257
e-mail: info@royalumpire.co.uk
dir: *From Chorley take A581, 3.5m towards Croston, site on right*

PETS: Public areas disp bin **Exercise area** small fenced grass area **Facilities** washing facs walks info vet info **Other** prior notice required **Restrictions** no Pit Bulls or dangerous dogs (see page 7)

Open all year Last arrival 20.00hrs Last departure 16.00hrs

A pleasant level site set in open countryside, with an attractive sunken garden and seating area. Plenty of leisure opportunities include an interesting children's playground, and a large playing field. The toilets, laundry and dishwashing area are of a very good quality. A restaurant and a pub are within walking distance. A 68 acre site with 200 touring pitches, 190 hardstandings.

Claylands Caravan Park (SD496485)

▶ ▶ ▶ ▶

Cabus PR3 1AJ
☎ 01524 791242 📄 01524 792406
e-mail: alan@claylands.com
dir: *From M6 junct 33 S to Garstang, approx 6m pass Quttros Restaurant, signed off A6 into Weavers Lane, follow lane to end, over cattle grid*

PETS: Stables 5m **Charges** £1 per night £7 per week **Public areas** except bar & restaurant on leads disp bin **Exercise area** walkway near river **Facilities** food scoop/disp bags washing facs walks info vet info

Open Mar-4 Jan Last arrival 23.00hrs Last departure noon

A well-maintained site with lovely river and woodland walks and good views over the River Wyre towards the village of Scorton. This friendly park is set in delightful countryside. Guests can enjoy fishing, and the atmosphere is very relaxed. The quality facilities and amenities are of a high standard, and everything is immaculately maintained. A 14 acre site with 30 touring pitches, 30 hardstandings and 68 statics.

Notes No roller blades or skateboards

GISBURN Map 7 SD84

Stirk House
★★★ 71% HOTEL

BB7 4LJ
☎ 01200 445581 ▤ 01200 445581
e-mail: reservations@stirkhouse.co.uk
dir: W of village, on A59. Hotel 0.5m on left

PETS: Bedrooms (12 GF) unattended Charges Public areas except restaurant Grounds disp bin Exercise area within grounds Facilities food bowl water bowl washing facs walks info vet info On Request fridge access torch towels Other charge for damage

This delightful historic hotel enjoys a peaceful location in its own grounds, amid rolling countryside. Extensive public areas include excellent conference and banqueting facilities, a leisure centre and an elegant restaurant. The stylish bedrooms and suites vary in size and style but all are comfortable and well equipped. Hospitality is warm and friendly, and service attentive.

Rooms 30 (10 annexe) (2 fmly) (12 GF) S £75-£90; D £150-£180 (incl. bkfst) Facilities STV ⊗ supervised ⤫ Gym Aromatherapy Personal training Kick boxing Xmas New Year Wi-fi Parking 400 Notes LB

LANCASTER Map 7 SD46

Lancaster House
★★★★ 76% ◉ HOTEL

CLASSIC
BRITISH HOTELS

Green Ln, Ellel LA1 4GJ
☎ 01524 844822 ▤ 01524 844766
e-mail: lancaster@elhmail.co.uk
web: www.elh.co.uk/hotels/lancaster
dir: M6 junct 33 N towards Lancaster. Through Galgate, into Green Lane. Hotel before university on right

PETS: Bedrooms (44 GF) Charges 1-3 nights £25 Public areas except restaurant & bar on leads Grounds on leads disp bin Exercise area 500mtrs Facilities walks info vet info On Request fridge access torch towels Other charge for damage

This modern hotel enjoys a rural setting south of the city and close to the university. The attractive open-plan reception and lounge boast a roaring log fire in colder months. Bedrooms are spacious, and include 19 rooms that are particularly well equipped for business guests. There are leisure facilities with a hot tub and a function suite.

Rooms 99 (29 fmly) (44 GF) S £79-£156; D £98-£252 (incl. bkfst)* Facilities Spa STV ⊗ supervised Gym Beauty salon Xmas New Year Wi-fi Parking 120 Notes LB

Best Western Royal Kings Arms
★★★ 70% HOTEL

OXFORD
HOTELS & INNS

Market St LA1 1HP
☎ 01524 32451 ▤ 01524 841698
e-mail: reservations.lancaster@ohiml.com
web: www.oxfordhotelsandinns.com
dir: M6 junct 33, A6 to city centre, 1st left, after Market Hotel. Hotel at lights before Lancaster Castle

PETS: Bedrooms unattended Public areas except restaurant on leads disp bin Exercise area 0.5m Facilities walks info vet info On Request fridge access torch Other charge for damage

A distinctive period building located in the town centre, close to the castle. Bedrooms are comfortable and suitable for both business and leisure guests. Public areas include a small lounge on the ground floor and The Castle Bar and Brasserie Restaurant on the first floor. The hotel also has a private car park.

Rooms 55 (14 fmly) Facilities Xmas Services Lift Parking 26

MORECAMBE Map 7 SD46

Clarendon
★★★ 68% HOTEL

76 Marine Road West, West End Promenade LA4 4EP
☎ 01524 410180 ▤ 01524 421616
e-mail: clarendon@mitchellshotels.co.uk
dir: M6 junct 34 follow Morecambe signs. At rdbt (with 'The Shrimp' on corner) 1st exit to Westgate, follow to seafront. Right at lights, hotel 3rd block

PETS: Bedrooms unattended Exercise area 40mtrs Facilities cage storage walks info vet info Other charge for damage Restrictions small to medium size dogs only

This traditional seafront hotel offers views over Morecambe Bay, modern facilities and convenient parking. An extensive fish and grill menu is offered in the contemporary Waterfront Restaurant and guests can relax in the comfortable lounge bar. Davy Jones Locker in the basement has a more traditional pub atmosphere and offers cask ales and regular live entertainment.

Rooms 29 (4 fmly) S £45-£60; D £70-£90 (incl. bkfst)* Facilities Xmas New Year Wi-fi Services Lift Parking 22 Notes LB

The Craigwell

★ ★ ★ GUEST HOUSE

372 Marine Road East LA4 5AH

☎ 01524 410095

e-mail: craigwellhotel@tiscali.co.uk

web: www.craigwellhotel.co.uk

dir: *A589 to seafront, left, Craigwell 400yds*

PETS: Bedrooms Charges £5 per night **Public areas** on leads **Exercise area** 50mtrs **Facilities** walks info vet info **On Request** fridge access towels **Resident Pet:** Kizzy (Lurcher)

This house is part of a Victorian terrace and looks out over Morecambe Bay to the distant Cumbrian hills. There is a stylish lounge with fine views and a spacious breakfast room to the rear. Bedrooms are pleasantly decorated, and have all the expected facilities; six enjoy views of the bay. There is a private car park at the rear.

Rooms 10 en suite (1 fmly) **S** £28-£30; **D** £56-£75* **Facilities** FTV TVL tea/coffee Cen ht Wi-fi **Parking** 4 **Notes** LB

Beach Mount

★ ★ ★ GUEST ACCOMMODATION

395 Marine Road East LA4 5AN

☎ 01524 420753

e-mail: beachmounthotel@aol.com

dir: *M6 junct 34/35, follow signs to Morecambe. Beach Mount 0.5m from town centre on E Promenade*

PETS: Bedrooms unattended **Public areas** except restaurant on leads **Facilities** vet info **On Request** fridge access towels **Resident Pet:** Lola (Labrador/Poodle cross)

This spacious property overlooks the bay and features a range of room styles that includes a family room and a junior suite. Guests have use of a comfortable lounge with fully licensed bar, and breakfasts are served in a pleasant separate dining room.

Rooms 10 en suite (1 GF) (10 smoking) **S** £28.50-£47; **D** £52-£59* **Facilities** FTV tea/coffee Cen ht Licensed **Notes** LB Closed Nov-Mar

Venture Caravan Park *(SD436633)*

▶ ▶ ▶

Langridge Way, Westgate LA4 4TQ

☎ 01524 412986   📠 01524 422029

e-mail: mark@venturecaravanpark.co.uk

dir: *From M6 junct 34 follow Morecambe signs. At rdbt take road towards Westgate & follow site signs. 1st right after fire station*

PETS: Public areas except children's play areas on leads disp bin **Exercise area Facilities** food dog chews cat treats litter tray vet info **Other** prior notice required

Open all year rs winter one toilet block open Last arrival 22.00hrs Last departure noon

A large park with good modern facilities, including a small indoor heated pool, a licensed clubhouse and a family room with children's entertainment. The site has many statics, and is close to the town centre. A 17.5 acre site with 56 touring pitches, 40 hardstandings and 304 statics.

ORMSKIRK   **Map 7 SD40**

Abbey Farm Caravan Park *(SD434098)*

▶ ▶ ▶ ▶

Dark Ln L40 5TX

☎ 01695 572686   📠 01695 572686

e-mail: abbeyfarm@yahoo.com

dir: *M6 junct 27 onto A5209 to Burscough. 4m left onto B5240. Immediate right into Hobcross Ln. Site 1.5m on right*

PETS: Charges £1 per night **Public areas** except recreation field on leads disp bin **Exercise area** field available **Facilities** walks info vet info

Open all year Last arrival 21.00hrs Last departure noon

Delightful hanging baskets and flower beds brighten this garden-like rural park which is sheltered by hedging and mature trees. Modern, very clean facilities include a family bathroom, and there are special pitches for the disabled near the toilets. A superb recreation field caters for children of all ages, and there is an indoor games room, large library, fishing lake and dog walk. Tents have their own area with BBQ and picnic tables. A 6 acre site with 56 touring pitches and 44 statics.

Notes No camp fires

ENGLAND

Ibis Preston North

BUDGET HOTEL

Garstang Rd, Broughton PR3 5JE

☎ 01772 861800   🖷 01772 861900

e-mail: H3162@accor.com

web: www.ibishotel.com

dir: *M6 junct 32, then M55 junct 1. Left lane onto A6. Left at slip road, left again at mini-rdbt. 2nd turn, hotel on right past pub*

PETS: Bedrooms (16 GF) sign **Grounds** on leads **Facilities** walks info vet info **On Request** fridge access torch towels **Other** charge for damage

Modern, budget hotel offering comfortable accommodation in bright and practical bedrooms. Breakfast is self-service, food is available all day and a full dinner menu is available in the restaurant.

Rooms 82 (27 fmly) (16 GF) (12 smoking)

The Inn at Whitewell

★★★★★ ◉ INN

Forest of Bowland, Clitheroe BB7 3AT

☎ 01200 448222   🖷 01200 448298

e-mail: reception@innatwhitewell.com

dir: *M6 junct 31a, B6243 to Longridge. Left at mini-rdbt. After 3 rdbts leave Longridge. Approx 3m, sharp left bend (with white railings), then right. Approx 1m left, right at T-junct. Next left, 3m to Whitewell*

PETS: Bedrooms unattended **Stables** 1m **Public areas** except restaurant **Grounds** disp bin **Exercise area** 50yds **Facilities** water bowl washing facs walks info vet info **On Request** towels

This long-established culinary destination is hidden away in quintessential Lancashire countryside just 20 minutes from the M6. The fine dining restaurant is complemented by two historic and cosy bars with roaring fires, real ales and polished service. Bedrooms are richly furnished with antiques and eye-catching bijouterie, while many of the bathrooms have Victorian brass showers.

Rooms 19 en suite 4 annexe en suite (1 fmly) (2 GF) **S** £83-£150; **D** £113-£191* **Facilities** STV FTV tea/coffee Dinner available Direct Dial Cen ht Wi-fi Fishing **Parking** 60 **Notes** No coaches

The Queen's Head

★★★★ ◉◉ 🍴 RESTAURANT WITH ROOMS

2 Long St LE12 9TP

☎ 01530 222359   🖷 01530 224680

e-mail: enquiries@thequeenshead.org

web: www.thequeenshead.org

dir: *From Loughborough turn left onto B5324, 3m into Belton*

PETS: Bedrooms sign **Charges Public areas Grounds** on leads disp bin **On Request** fridge access torch towels **Other** charge for damage

This well furnished establishment is found in the village centre and has public rooms with a modern feel. The individually designed bedrooms feature crisp white linen, fluffy duvets and pillows, 19-inch LCD TVs with Freeview and DVD players. The restaurant has earned a well deserved reputation for its award-winning cuisine; the menus are based on the freshest, locally sourced produce quality.

Rooms 6 en suite (2 fmly) **Facilities** FTV TVL tea/coffee Dinner available Cen ht Wi-fi **Parking** 20

Ravenstone Guesthouse

★★★★ 🏠 GUEST HOUSE

Ravenstone LE67 2AE

☎ 01530 810536

e-mail: annthorne@ravenstone-guesthouse.co.uk

web: www.ravenstone-guesthouse.co.uk

dir: *1.5m W of Coalville. Off A447 onto Church Ln for Ravenstone, 2nd house on left*

PETS: Bedrooms sign **Sep accom** kennel raised off ground, heated with small run **Public areas** at proprietor's discretion **Grounds** disp bin **Exercise area** 40yds **Facilities** food bowl water bowl bedding feeding mat leads washing facs cage storage walks info vet info **On Request** fridge access torch towels **Other** no charge but contribution to Dogs Trust charity invited **Restrictions** no puppies, Pit Bulls or other fighting dogs **Resident Pet:** Saffron (Yellow Labrador)

Situated in the heart of Ravenstone village, this early 18th-century house is full of character. The bedrooms are individually decorated and feature period furniture, and local produce is used for dinner and in the extensive breakfast menu. The beamed dining room has an honesty bar and there is also a cosy lounge.

Rooms 4 en suite **Facilities** FTV TVL tea/coffee Dinner available Cen ht Licensed Wi-fi **Parking** 6 **Notes** LB Closed 23-30 Dec & 1 Jan RS 31 Dec-1 Jan No breakfast on 1 Jan

EAST MIDLANDS AIRPORT — Map 8 SK42

Donington Manor Hotel
★★★ 78% ⊚ HOTEL
High St DE74 2PP
☎ 01332 810253 📄 01332 850330
e-mail: enquiries@doningtonmanorhotel.co.uk
dir: *1m into village on B5430, left at lights*

PETS: Bedrooms (4 GF) **Charges** £10 per night **Public areas** except restaurant & bar on leads **Grounds** on leads disp bin **Exercise area** 1m **Facilities** cage storage walks info vet info **On Request** fridge access torch towels **Other** charge for damage

Near the village centre, this refined Georgian building offers high standards of hospitality and a professional service. Many of the original architectural features have been preserved; the elegant dining room is particularly appealing. Bedrooms are individually designed, and the newer suites are especially comfortable and well equipped.

Rooms 33 (6 annexe) (8 fmly) (4 GF) **Facilities** STV New Year Wi-fi **Parking** 40 **Notes** RS 24-30 Dec

HINCKLEY — Map 4 SP49

CLASSIC
BRITISH HOTELS

Sketchley Grange
★★★★ 81% ⊚⊚ HOTEL
Sketchley Ln, Burbage LE10 3HU
☎ 01455 251133 📄 01455 631384
e-mail: info@sketchleygrange.co.uk
web: www.sketchleygrange.co.uk
dir: *SE of town, off A5/M69 junct 1, take B4109 to Hinckley. Left at 2nd rdbt. 1st right onto Sketchley Lane*

PETS: Bedrooms (6 GF) unattended **Charges** £10 per night **Public areas** except restaurant & lounge on leads **Grounds** on leads disp bin **Exercise area** **Facilities** walks info vet info **On Request** torch towels **Other** charge for damage **Restrictions** small dogs only

Close to motorway connections, this hotel is peacefully set in its own grounds, and enjoys open country views. Extensive leisure facilities include a stylish health and leisure spa. Modern meeting facilities, a choice of bars, and two dining options, together with comfortable bedrooms furnished with many extras, make this a special hotel.

Rooms 94 (9 fmly) (6 GF) **Facilities** Spa STV ⊛ supervised Gym Steam room Sauna Hairdressing Crèche ♫ Wi-fi Child facilities **Services** Lift **Parking** 270

LEICESTER FOREST MOTORWAY SERVICE AREA (M1) — Map 4 SK50

Welcome Break

Days Inn Leicester Forest East
BUDGET HOTEL
Leicester Forest East, M1 Junction 21 LE3 3GB
☎ 0116 239 0534 📄 0116 239 0546
e-mail: leicester.hotel@welcomebreak.co.uk
web: www.welcomebreak.co.uk
dir: *On M1 northbound between junct 21 & 21A*

PETS: Bedrooms unattended **Public areas** on leads **Grounds** on leads

This modern building offers accommodation in smart, spacious and well-equipped bedrooms, suitable for families and business travellers, and all with en suite bathrooms. Continental breakfast is available, and other refreshments may be taken at the nearby family restaurant.

Rooms 92 (71 fmly) (10 smoking) **S** £29-£59; **D** £29-£69

MARKET HARBOROUGH — Map 4 SP78

Best Western

Best Western Three Swans
★★★ 78% HOTEL
21 High St LE16 7NJ
☎ 01858 466644 📄 01858 433101
e-mail: sales@threeswans.co.uk
web: www.bw-threeswanshotel.co.uk
dir: *M1 junct 20 take A304 to Market Harborough. Through town centre on A6 from Leicester, hotel on right*

PETS: Bedrooms (20 GF) unattended **Stables Charges** £10 per night **Public areas** except restaurant **Grounds** on leads disp bin **Exercise area** 0.75m **Facilities** water bowl dog chews cat treats washing facs cage storage walks info vet info **On Request** fridge access torch towels **Other** charge for damage

Public areas in this former coaching inn include an elegant fine dining restaurant and cocktail bar, a smart foyer lounge and popular public bar areas. Bedroom styles and sizes vary, but are very well appointed and equipped. Those in the wing are particularly impressive, offering high quality and spacious accommodation.

Rooms 61 (48 annexe) (8 fmly) (20 GF) **S** £65-£100; **D** £75-£102 (incl. bkfst) **Facilities** STV Xmas New Year Wi-fi **Services** Lift **Parking** 100 **Notes** LB

ENGLAND

Stapleford Park
★★★★ ◉◉ COUNTRY HOUSE HOTEL
Stapleford LE14 2EF
☎ 01572 787000 🖷 01572 787651
e-mail: reservations@stapleford.co.uk
web: www.staplefordpark.com
dir: 1m SW of B676, 4m E of Melton Mowbray & 9m W of Colsterworth

PETS: Bedrooms Stables 10m Charges £15 per night
Public areas except dining areas & pool area Grounds disp bin
Exercise area Facilities food bowl water bowl bedding dog
chews feeding mat pet sitting walks info vet info On Request
fridge access torch towels Other charge for damage treats for
cats on request; no dogs on golf course

This stunning mansion, dating back to the 14th century, sits in
over 500 acres of beautiful grounds. Spacious, sumptuous public
rooms include a choice of lounges and an elegant restaurant;
an additional brasserie-style restaurant is located in the golf
complex. The hotel also boasts a spa with health and beauty
treatments and gym, plus horse-riding and many other country
pursuits. Bedrooms are individually styled and furnished to a
high standard. Attentive service is delivered with a relaxed yet
professional style. Dinner, in the impressive dining room, is a
highlight of any stay.

Rooms 55 (7 annexe) (10 fmly) Facilities Spa STV FTV ⬡ ᯤ 18 ⬡
Putt green Fishing ᯤ Gym Archery Croquet Falconry Horse riding
Petanque Shooting Billiards Xmas New Year Wi-fi Services Lift
Parking 120

Sysonby Knoll
★★★ 78% HOTEL
Asfordby Rd LE13 0HP
☎ 01664 563563 🖷 01664 410364
e-mail: reception@sysonby.com
web: www.sysonby.com
dir: 0.5m from town centre on A6006

PETS: Bedrooms (7 GF) Charges 1st pet free, additional pet
£5 per stay Public areas except restaurant on leads Grounds
on leads disp bin Exercise area exercise field Exercise area
adjacent Facilities leads washing facs cage storage walks
info vet info On Request fridge access torch towels Other
charge for damage Resident Pets: Stalky & Twiglet (Miniature
Dachshunds)

This well-established hotel is on the edge of town and set in
attractive gardens. A friendly and relaxed atmosphere prevails
and the many returning guests have become friends. Bedrooms,
including superior rooms in the annexe, are generally spacious
and thoughtfully equipped. There is a choice of lounges, a cosy
bar, and a smart restaurant that offers carefully prepared meals.

Rooms 30 (7 annexe) (1 fmly) (7 GF) S £73-£98; D £90-£125
(incl. bkfst)* Facilities FTV Fishing ᯤ Wi-fi Parking 48 Notes LB
Closed 25 Dec-1 Jan

Bryn Barn

★★★★ GUEST ACCOMMODATION

38 High St, Waltham-on-the-Wolds LE14 4AH

☎ 01664 464783 & 07914 222407

e-mail: glenarowlands@onetel.com

web: www.brynbarn.co.uk

dir: *4.5m NE of Melton. Off A607, in Waltham-on-the-Wolds centre*

PETS: Bedrooms Charges £5 per night **Grounds** on leads disp bin **Exercise area** 500mtrs **Facilities** food bowl water bowl feeding mat scoop/disp bags cage storage walks info vet info **On Request** fridge access torch towels **Other** charge for damage ground-floor bedroom with garden access available **Restrictions** no very large dogs; no Alsatians, Pit Bulls, Newfoundlands or Rottweilers

A warm welcome awaits at this attractive, peacefully located cottage within easy reach of Melton Mowbray, Grantham, Rutland Water and Belvoir Castle. Bedrooms are smartly appointed and comfortably furnished, while public rooms include an inviting lounge overlooking a wonderful courtyard garden. Meals are available at one of the nearby village pubs.

Rooms 4 rms (3 en suite) (1 pri facs) (2 fmly) (1 GF) **S** £35-£45; **D** £58-£65* **Facilities** FTV TVL tea/coffee Cen ht Wi-fi **Parking** 4 **Notes** LB Closed 21 Dec-4 Jan

LINCOLNSHIRE

ANCASTER   Map 8 SK94

Woodland Waters *(SK979435)*

▶ ▶ ▶

Willoughby Rd NG32 3RT

☎ 01400 230888 📠 01400 230888

e-mail: info@woodlandwaters.co.uk

dir: *On A153 W of x-roads with B6403*

PETS: Charges £1 per night £7 per week **Public areas** except bar on leads disp bin **Exercise area** lake & park walks **Facilities** walks info vet info **Other** dog bowls at outdoor eating areas on request **Resident Pets:** 2 Black Labradors

Open all year Last arrival 21.00hrs Last departure noon

Peacefully set around five impressive fishing lakes, with a few log cabins in a separate area, this is a pleasant open park. The access road is through mature woodland, and there is an excellent heated toilet block, and a pub/club house with restaurant. A 72 acre site with 62 touring pitches, 2 hardstandings.

BARTON-UPON-HUMBER   Map 8 TA02

Best Western Reeds Country Hotel

★★★ 77% HOTEL

Westfield Lakes, Far Ings Rd DN18 5RG

☎ 01652 632313 📠 01652 636361

e-mail: info@reedshotel.co.uk

dir: *A15 rdbt take 2nd exit (Humber Bridge) & exit at Barton-upon-Humber, left at rdbt. In 200yds right at hotel sign, down hill, hotel at junct*

PETS: Bedrooms unattended sign **Charges** £10 per night **Grounds** on leads **Exercise area** Viking Way adjacent **Facilities** cage storage walks info vet info **Other** charge for damage **Restrictions** smaller bedrooms not suitable for large dogs

This hotel is situated in a quiet wildlife sanctuary just upstream from the Humber Bridge. A very attractive lakeside restaurant commands tranquil views, and there is a health spa offering various alternative therapies. Bedrooms are comfortable and well equipped, and service is both friendly and helpful.

Rooms 26 (5 fmly) **S** £76-£110; **D** £86-£134 (incl. bkfst) **Facilities** Spa STV FTV Xmas New Year Wi-fi **Services** Lift **Parking** 100 **Notes** LB

BOSTON   Map 8 TF34

Orchard Park *(TF274432)*

▶ ▶ ▶ ▶

Frampton Ln, Hubbert's Bridge PE20 3QU

☎ 01205 290328 📠 01205 290247

e-mail: info@orchardpark.co.uk

dir: *On B1192, between A52 (Boston-Grantham) & A1121 (Boston-Sleaford)*

PETS: Stables 1.5m **Public areas** except café & bar on leads disp bin **Exercise area** on site **Exercise area** adjacent **Facilities** food washing facs walks info vet info **Other** disposal bags available

Open all year rs Dec-Feb bar, shop & café closed Last arrival 22.30hrs Last departure 16.00hrs

Ideally located for exploring the unique fenlands, this rapidly-improving park has two lakes - one for fishing and the other set aside for conservation. A very attractive restaurant and bar are popular with visitors. A 51 acre site with 87 touring pitches, 11 hardstandings and 164 statics.

Notes Washing lines not permitted 🐾

Best Western Kings

★★★ 73% HOTEL

North Pde NG31 8AU
☎ 01476 590800 📄 01476 577072
e-mail: kings@bestwestern.co.uk
web: www.bw-kingshotel.co.uk
dir: *S on A1, 1st exit to Grantham. Through Great Gonerby, 2m on left*

PETS: Bedrooms (3 GF) **Public areas** except restaurant on leads **Grounds** on leads disp bin **Exercise area** 200yds **Facilities** cage storage walks info vet info **On Request** fridge access **Other** charge for damage

A friendly atmosphere exists at this extended Georgian house. Modern bedrooms are attractively decorated and furnished, and suitably equipped to meet the needs of corporate and leisure guests. Dining options include the formal Victorian restaurant and the popular Orangery, which also operates as an informal coffee shop and breakfast room; a lounge bar and a comfortable open-plan foyer lounge are also available.

Rooms 21 (3 fmly) (3 GF) **Facilities** STV New Year Wi-fi **Parking** 40 **Notes** Closed 25-26 Dec RS 24 Dec

Beechleigh Guest House

★★★★ GUEST HOUSE

55 North Pde NG31 8AT
☎ 01476 572213 📄 01476 566058
e-mail: info@beechleigh.co.uk
web: www.beechleigh.co.uk
dir: *0.5m N of town centre. A52 onto B1174 by Asda, house 200yds on left*

PETS: Bedrooms Charges £10 per night **Public areas** except dining room disp bin **Exercise area** park, canal & river walks nearby **Facilities** walks info vet info **On Request** fridge access torch **Other** charge for damage **Restrictions** no large breeds; no Pit Bulls, Rottweilers, Dobermans or similar breeds

This Edwardian house sits just a short walk from the town centre on the northern approach. Offering comfortably appointed bedrooms that are equipped with many thoughtful extras including Wi-fi. Freshly cooked breakfasts are taken in the pleasant dining room, and off-road parking is available.

Rooms 3 rms (1 fmly) **Facilities** STV tea/coffee Dinner available Cen ht **Parking** 5 **Notes** No Children 5yrs

Washingborough Hall

★★★ 75% ⊛ HOTEL

Church Hill, Washingborough LN4 1BE
☎ 01522 790340 📄 01522 792936
e-mail: enquiries@washingboroughhall.com
dir: *B1190 into Washingborough. Right at rdbt, hotel 500yds on left*

PETS: Bedrooms Charges £10 per night **Public areas** except restaurants on leads **Grounds** disp bin **Exercise area** 500yds **Facilities** food bowl water bowl leads walks info vet info **On Request** torch **Other** charge for damage **Resident Pets:** Teasel & Higgins (Jack Russells)

This Georgian manor stands on the edge of the quiet village of Washingborough and is set in attractive gardens. Public rooms are pleasantly furnished and comfortable, while the restaurant offers interesting menus. Bedrooms are individually designed and most have views out over the grounds to the countryside beyond.

Rooms 12 (3 fmly) **S** £45-£85; **D** £85-£115 (incl. bkfst)* **Facilities** FTV 🏊 Bicycles for hire New Year Wi-fi **Parking** 40 **Notes** LB

Newport

★★★ GUEST HOUSE

26-28 Newport Rd LN1 3DF
☎ 01522 528590 📄 01522 542868
e-mail: info@newportguesthouse.com
web: www.newportguesthouse.com
dir: *600mtrs N of cathedral*

PETS: Bedrooms Charges Public areas disp bin **Exercise area** 200mtrs **Facilities** walks info vet info **On Request** fridge access **Other** charge for damage

Situated in the quieter upper part of the city and just a few minutes' walk from the cathedral, this double-fronted terrace house offers well-equipped and comfortable bedrooms with broadband access. The pleasing public areas include a very comfortable sitting room and a bright and attractive breakfast room.

Rooms 9 en suite (2 GF) **S** £37-£40; **D** £55-£60* **Facilities** FTV TVL tea/coffee Cen ht Wi-fi **Parking** 4

LOUTH — Map 8 TF38

Best Western Kenwick Park

★★★ 79% HOTEL

Kenwick Park Estate LN11 8NR
☎ 01507 608806 ▤ 01507 608027
e-mail: enquiries@kenwick-park.co.uk
web: www.kenwick-park.co.uk
dir: A16 from Grimsby, then A157 Mablethorpe/Manby Rd. Hotel 400mtrs down hill on right

PETS: Bedrooms unattended **Charges Public areas** on leads **Grounds** on leads disp bin **Exercise area** large grounds **Facilities** water bowl washing facs walks info vet info **On Request** fridge access torch towels **Other** charge for damage please phone for further details of pet facilities

This elegant Georgian house is situated on the 320-acre Kenwick Park estate, overlooking its own golf course. Bedrooms are spacious, comfortable and provide modern facilities. Public areas include a restaurant and a conservatory bar that overlook the grounds. There is also an extensive leisure centre and state-of-the-art conference and banqueting facilities.

Rooms 34 (5 annexe) (10 fmly) **Facilities** Spa ⊗ supervised ↕ 18 ♣ Putt green Gym Squash Health & beauty centre Xmas New Year Wi-fi **Parking** 100

MABLETHORPE — Map 9 TF58

Golden Sands Holiday Park (TF501861)

Quebec Rd LN12 1QJ
☎ 01507 477871 ▤ 01507 472066
e-mail: naomi.mcintosh@bourne-leisure.co.uk
dir: From centre of Mablethorpe turn left on seafront road towards north end. Site on left

PETS: Charges £3 per night **Public areas** except complex area **Exercise area** beach adjacent **Other** prior notice required **Restrictions** maximum 2 dogs per group; certain breeds not accepted

Open mid Mar-Oct Last arrival anytime Last departure 10.00hrs

A large, well-equipped seaside holiday park with separate touring facilities on two sites, including fully modernised toilets. The first floor entertainment rooms are only accessible via stairs (no lifts). A 23 acre site with 214 touring pitches, 20 hardstandings and 1500 statics.

MARTON (VILLAGE) — Map 8 SK88

Black Swan Guest House

★★★★ GUEST ACCOMMODATION

21 High St DN21 5AH
☎ 01427 718878
e-mail: info@blackswanguesthouse.co.uk
web: www.blackswanguesthouse.co.uk
dir: On A156 in village centre at junct A1500

PETS: Bedrooms unattended **Stables** 4m **Public areas** only assist dogs allowed in dining room **Grounds** disp bin **Exercise area** 300yds **Facilities** washing facs cage storage walks info vet info **On Request** fridge access torch **Other** charge for damage **Resident Pets:** Scooby & Patch (cats)

Centrally located in the village, this 18th-century former coaching inn retains many original features, and offers good hospitality and homely bedrooms with modern facilities. Tasty breakfasts are served in the cosy dining room and a comfortable lounge with Wi-fi access is available. Transport to nearby pubs and restaurants can be provided.

Rooms 6 en suite 4 annexe en suite (3 fmly) (4 GF) **S** £45-£55; **D** £68-£75* **Facilities** FTV TVL tea/coffee Cen ht Licensed Wi-fi **Parking** 10 **Notes** LB

ORBY — Map 9 TF46

Heron's Mead Fishing Lake & Touring Park (TF508673)

▶ ▶ ▶ ▶

Marsh Ln PE24 5JA
☎ 01754 811340
e-mail: mail@heronsmeadtouringpark.co.uk
dir: From A158 (Lincoln to Skegness road) turn left at rdbt, through Orby for 0.5m

PETS: Charges £1 per night £5 per week **Public areas** except lakeside disp bin **Exercise area Facilities** walks info vet info

Open Mar-1 Nov Last arrival 21.00hrs Last departure noon

A pleasant fishing and touring park with coarse fishing and an 8-acre woodland walk. The owners have made many improvements to the facilities, which are particularly appealing to quiet couples and elderly visitors. A 16 acre site with 50 touring pitches, 53 hardstandings and 28 statics.

Notes No ball games, no motorbikes.

SCUNTHORPE — Map 8 SE81

Forest Pines Hotel & Golf Resort

★★★★ 79% ⊛ HOTEL

Ermine St, Broughton DN20 0AQ

☎ 01652 650770 📄 01652 650495

e-mail: forestpines@qhotels.co.uk

web: www.qhotels.co.uk

dir: 200yds from M180 junct 4, on Brigg-Scunthorpe rdbt

PETS: Bedrooms (67 GF) unattended **Charges** £15 per stay **Exercise area** 0.5m **Facilities** vet info **Other** charge for damage prior notice required **Restrictions** small, well behaved dogs only

This smart hotel provides a comprehensive range of leisure facilities. Extensive conference rooms, a modern health and beauty spa, and a championship golf course ensure that it is a popular choice with both corporate and leisure guests. The well-equipped bedrooms are modern, spacious, and appointed to a good standard. Extensive public areas include a choice of dining options, with fine dining available in The Eighteen57 fish restaurant, and more informal eating in the Grill Bar.

Rooms 188 (66 fmly) (67 GF) **Facilities** Spa STV FTV 🛞 supervised ⅃ 27 Putt green Gym Mountain bikes Jogging track Xmas New Year Wi-fi **Services** Lift **Parking** 300

Wortley House

★★★ 72% HOTEL

Rowland Rd DN16 1SU

☎ 01724 842223 📄 01724 280646

e-mail: reception@wortleyhousehotel.co.uk

web: www.wortleyhousehotel.co.uk

dir: M180 junct 3 take A18. Follow signs for Grimsby/Humberside airport, 2nd left into Brumby Wood Ln, over rdbt into Rowland Rd. Hotel 200yds on right

PETS: Bedrooms (4 GF) **Stables** 5m **Charges** £10 deposit **Grounds** on leads **Exercise area** 2 mins walk **Facilities** food bowl water bowl cage storage walks info vet info **On Request** torch towels **Other** charge for damage

A friendly hotel with good facilities for conferences, meetings, banquets and other functions. Bedrooms offer modern comfort and good facilities. An extensive range of dishes is available in both the formal restaurant and the more relaxed bar.

Rooms 45 (4 annexe) (5 fmly) (4 GF) **Facilities** FTV Xmas New Year Wi-fi **Parking** 100

SKEGNESS — Map 9 TF56

Best Western Vine

★★★ 70% HOTEL

Vine Rd, Seacroft PE25 3DB

☎ 01754 763018 & 610611 📄 01754 769845

e-mail: info@thevinehotel.com

dir: A52 to Skegness, S towards Gibraltar Point, right into Drummond Rd, 0.5m, right into Vine Rd

PETS: Bedrooms unattended **Charges** £5 per night **Public areas** **Grounds** disp bin **Exercise area** surrounding area **Facilities** cage storage walks info vet info **On Request** fridge access torch towels

Reputedly the second oldest building in Skegness, this traditional style hotel offers two character bars that serve excellent local beers. Freshly prepared dishes are served in both the bar and the restaurant; service is both friendly and helpful. The smartly decorated bedrooms are well equipped and comfortably appointed.

Rooms 25 (3 fmly) **S** £35-£45; **D** £70-£90 (incl. bkfst)* **Facilities** FTV Xmas New Year Wi-fi **Parking** 50

STAMFORD — Map 4 TF00

The George of Stamford

★★★ 86% ⊛ HOTEL

71 St Martins PE9 2LB

☎ 01780 750750 & 750700 (res) 📄 01780 750701

e-mail: reservations@georgehotelofstamford.com

web: www.georgehotelofstamford.com

dir: A1, 15m N of Peterborough onto B1081, hotel 1m on left

PETS: Bedrooms **Public areas** except restaurant (assist dogs only) **Grounds** **Exercise area** meadow 500yds **Facilities** water bowl bedding dog chews feeding mat vet info **On Request** towels **Resident Pets:** Sooty & Sweep (cats)

Steeped in hundreds of years of history, this delightful coaching inn provides spacious public areas that include a choice of dining options, inviting, lounges, a business centre and a range of quality shops. A highlight is afternoon tea, taken in the colourful courtyard when weather permits. Bedrooms are stylishly appointed and range from traditional to contemporary in design.

Rooms 47 (24 fmly) **S** £95-£100; **D** £140-£270 (incl. bkfst)* **Facilities** STV 🏊 Complimentary membership to local gym Xmas New Year Wi-fi **Parking** 110 **Notes** LB

WADDINGHAM　　　　　　　　Map 8 SK99

Brandy Wharf Leisure Park *(TF014968)*

▶ ▶ ▶

Brandy Wharf DN21 4RT

☎ 01673 818010　🖷 01673 818010

e-mail: brandywharflp@freenetname.co.uk

dir: From A15 onto B1205 through Waddingham. Site 3m from Waddingham

PETS: **Stables** 5m **Public areas** disp bin **Exercise area** river bank **Facilities** washing facs walks info vet info **Other** prior notice required **Resident Pets:** Bess, Fizz & Spike (Border Collies), Ruby (Jack Russell), Junior (mongrel), cats, ducks, geese, pigeons

Open all year rs Etr-Oct for tents Last arrival dusk Last departure 17.00hrs

A delightful site in a very rural area on the banks of the River Ancholme, where fishing is available. The toilet block has unisex rooms with combined facilities as well as a more conventional ladies and gents with washhand basins and toilet. All of the grassy pitches have electricity, and there's a playing and picnic area. The site attracts a lively clientele at weekends, and music is allowed until 1am. Advance booking is necessary for weekend pitches. A 5 acre site with 50 touring pitches.

Notes No disposable BBQs on grass, no music after 01.00hrs 🐾

WINTERINGHAM　　　　　　　Map 8 SE92

Winteringham Fields

★ ★ ★ ★ ★ 🏵🏵 ⬛ RESTAURANT WITH ROOMS

DN15 9ND

☎ 01724 733096　🖷 01724 733898

e-mail: wintfields@aol.com

dir: In village centre at x-rds

PETS: **Bedrooms** Sep accom barns **Stables** 200mtrs **Charges** £10 per night **Grounds** disp bin **Exercise area** 20mtrs **Facilities** food (pre-bookable) food bowl water bowl bedding dog chews scoop/disp bags leads walks info vet info **On Request** fridge access torch towels **Other** charge for damage courtyard bedrooms recommended for guests with dogs **Resident Pets:** Juma & Peri (Labradors), Azerah (Great Dane)

This highly regarded restaurant with rooms, located deep in the countryside in Winteringham village, is six miles west of the Humber Bridge. Public rooms and bedrooms, some of which are housed in renovated barns and cottages, are delightfully cosseting. Award-winning food is available in the restaurant.

Rooms 4 en suite 7 annexe en suite (2 fmly) (3 GF) **S** £115-£145; **D** £145-£220 **Facilities** tea/coffee Dinner available Direct Dial Cen ht **Parking** 14 **Notes** LB Closed 25 Dec for 2 wks, last wk Oct, 2 wks Aug No coaches

WOODHALL SPA　　　　　　　Map 8 TF16

Petwood

★ ★ ★　74%　HOTEL

Stixwould Rd LN10 6QG

☎ 01526 352411　🖷 01526 353473

e-mail: reception@petwood.co.uk

web: www.petwood.co.uk

dir: From Sleaford take A153 (signed Skegness). At Tattershall turn left on B1192. Hotel is signed from village

PETS: **Bedrooms** (3 GF) unattended **Charges** £15 per night **Public areas** certain areas only on leads **Exercise area** **Facilities** washing facs walks info vet info **On Request** fridge access torch **Other** charge for damage

This lovely Edwardian house, set in 30 acres of gardens and woodlands, is adjacent to Woodhall Golf Course. Built in 1905, the house was used by 617 Squadron, the famous Dambusters, as an officers' mess during World War II. Bedrooms and public areas are spacious and comfortable, and retain many original features. Weddings and conferences are well catered for in modern facilities.

Rooms 53 (3 GF) **Facilities** Putt green ⚓ 🎵 Xmas New Year Wi-fi **Services** Lift **Parking** 140 **Notes** LB

The Claremont Guest House

★ ★ ★　GUEST HOUSE

9/11 Witham Rd LN10 6RW

☎ 01526 352000

e-mail: claremontgh@live.co.uk

web: www.theclaremontguesthouse.co.uk

dir: In town centre on B1191 near mini-rdbt

PETS: **Bedrooms** unattended sign **Public areas** except restaurant & not before 10am on leads **Grounds** disp bin **Exercise area** 50mtrs **Facilities** water bowl bedding dog chews feeding mat scoop/disp bags leads washing facs cage storage walks info vet info **On Request** fridge access torch towels **Other** charge for damage **Resident Pets:** 2 Miniature Schnauzers

A Victorian townhouse with a lovely dining room, guest lounge and Wi-fi access. Having benefited from a refurbishment by the friendly owners, the bedrooms are well equipped; the rooms vary in size from cosy singles to family rooms. The house has lock up facilities for cyclists and golfers.

Rooms 11 rms (6 en suite) (5 pri facs) (3 fmly) (2 GF) **S** £30-£35; **D** £55-£60 **Facilities** FTV TVL tea/coffee Cen ht Wi-fi **Parking** 4 **Notes** LB

ENGLAND

WOOLSTHORPE · Map 8 SK92

The Chequers Inn
★★★★ ◉ INN
Main St NG32 1LU
☎ 01476 870701 📄 01476 870085
e-mail: justinnabar@yahoo.co.uk
dir: *In village opposite Post Office*

PETS: **Bedrooms** unattended **Stables** next door **Charges**
Public areas except restaurant **Grounds** disp bin **Exercise area**
open countryside adjacent **Facilities** washing facs cage storage
walks info vet info **On Request** fridge access torch towels
Other charge for damage contact inn for details of charges
Restrictions well behaved dogs only

A 17th-century coaching inn set in the lee of Belvoir Castle next
to the village cricket pitch and with its own pétanque pitch.
Exposed beams, open fireplaces and original stone and brickwork,
with 24 wines by the glass, a gastro menu, and real ales.
Comfortable bedrooms are in the former stable block.

Rooms 4 annexe en suite (1 fmly) (3 GF) **S** £50; **D** £70
Facilities FTV TVL tea/coffee Dinner available Cen ht **Parking** 40

LONDON

E14

Four Seasons Hotel Canary Wharf
★★★★★ ◉ HOTEL
Westferry Circus, Canary Wharf E14 8RS
☎ 020 7510 1999 📄 020 7510 1998
e-mail: reservations.caw@fourseasons.com
web: www.fourseasons.com/canarywharf
dir: *From A13 follow Canary Wharf, Isle of Dogs & Westferry
Circus signs. Hotel off 3rd exit of Westferry Circus rdbt*

PETS: **Bedrooms Exercise area** 5 min walk to waterfront
Facilities food (pre-bookable) food bowl water bowl bedding
dog chews litter tray pet sitting dog walking dog grooming
cage storage walks info vet info **On Request** fridge access
torch towels **Other** charge for damage concierge will assist in
arranging kennel space for larger pets **Restrictions** maximum
weight 15lbs

With superb views over the London skyline, this stylish
modern hotel enjoys a delightful riverside location. Spacious
contemporary bedrooms are particularly thoughtfully equipped.
Public areas include the Italian Quadrato Bar and Restaurant,
an impressive business centre and a gym. Guests also have
complimentary use of the impressive Holmes Place health club
and spa. Welcoming staff provide exemplary levels of service and
hospitality.

Rooms 142 (20 smoking) **Facilities** Spa STV FTV ⊕ supervised
⊕ Gym Fitness centre Xmas New Year Wi-fi **Services** Lift Air con
Parking 54

EC1

Malmaison Charterhouse Square
★★★ 88% ◉◉ HOTEL

Malmaison
hotels that dare to be different

18-21 Charterhouse Square, Clerkenwell EC1M 6AH
☎ 020 7012 3700 📄 020 7012 3702
e-mail: london@malmaison.com
web: www.malmaison.com
dir: *Exit Barbican Station turn left, take 1st left. Hotel on far left
corner of Charterhouse Square*

PETS: **Bedrooms** (5 GF) **Charges** £10 per night **Public areas**
except restaurant (assist dogs only) muzzled and on leads
Facilities food bowl water bowl bedding cage storage vet
info **On Request** fridge access torch towels **Other** charge for
damage

Situated in a leafy and peaceful square, Malmaison Charterhouse
maintains the same focus on quality service and food as the
other hotels in the group. The bedrooms, stylishly decorated in
calming tones, have all the expected facilities including power
showers, CD players and free internet access. The brasserie and
bar at the hotel's centre has a buzzing atmosphere and offers
traditional French cuisine.

Rooms 97 (5 GF) **Facilities** STV Gym Wi-fi **Services** Lift Air con
Notes LB

EC3

Novotel London Tower Bridge
★★★★ 71% HOTEL

NOVOTEL

10 Pepys St EC3N 2NR
☎ 020 7265 6000 & 7265 6026 📄 020 7265 6060
e-mail: H3107@accor.com
web: www.novotel.com

PETS: **Bedrooms Charges** £8 per night **Public areas** except
restaurant & bar on leads **Exercise area** park 30mtrs **Facilities**
cage storage walks info vet info **Other** charge for damage

Located near the Tower of London, this smart hotel is convenient
for Docklands, the City, Heathrow and London City airports.
Air-conditioned bedrooms are spacious, modern, and offer a great
range of facilities. There is a smart bar and restaurant, a small
gym, children's play area and extensive meeting and conference
facilities.

Rooms 203 (54 fmly) **Facilities** STV FTV Gym Steam room Sauna
Xmas Wi-fi **Services** Lift Air con

N9

Lee Valley Camping & Caravan Park

(TQ360945)

▶ ▶ ▶

Meridian Way N9 0AR
☎ 020 8803 6900 📄 020 8884 4975
e-mail: leisurecomplex@leevalleypark.org.uk
dir: *M25 junct 25, A10 S, 1st left onto A1055, approx 5m to Leisure Complex. From A406 (North Circular), N on A1010, left after 0.25m, right (Pickets Lock Ln)*

PETS: Charges £1.90 per night £13.30 per week **Public areas** except in toilets, showers, laundry & shop disp bin **Exercise area** adjacent **Facilities** food

Open all year rs Xmas & New Year Last arrival 22.00hrs Last departure noon

A pleasant, open site within easy reach of London yet peacefully located close to two large reservoirs. The very good toilet facilities are beautifully kept by dedicated wardens, and the site has the advantage of being adjacent to a restaurant and bar, and a multi-screen cinema. A 4.5 acre site with 160 touring pitches, 41 hardstandings.

Notes No commercial vehicles

NW1

ibis HOTEL

Ibis London Euston St Pancras

BUDGET HOTEL

3 Cardington St NW1 2LW
☎ 020 7388 7777 📄 020 7388 0001
e-mail: H0921@accor-hotels.com
web: www.ibishotel.com
dir: *From Euston Rd or station, right to Melton St leading to Cardington St*

PETS: Bedrooms unattended **Charges** £5 per night **Public areas** **Exercise area** Regents Park **Facilities** food bowl water bowl **On Request** towels

Modern, budget hotel offering comfortable accommodation in bright and practical bedrooms. Breakfast is self-service and dinner is available in the restaurant.

Rooms 380

SE1

NOVOTEL

Novotel London City South

★★★★ 74% HOTEL

Southwark Bridge Rd SE1 9HH
☎ 020 7089 0400 📄 020 7089 0410
e-mail: H3269@accor.com
web: www.novotel.com
dir: *At junct at Thrale St, off Southwark St*

PETS: Bedrooms Charges £8 per night £56 per week **Public areas** except restaurant & bar; at manager's discretion on leads **Facilities** cage storage walks info vet info **Other** charge for damage

Conveniently located for both business and leisure guests, with The City just across the Thames; other major attractions are also easily accessible. The hotel is contemporary in design with smart, modern bedrooms and spacious public rooms. There is a gym, sauna and steam room on the 6th floor, and limited parking is available at the rear of the hotel.

Rooms 182 (139 fmly) (9 smoking) **Facilities** STV FTV Gym Steam room Sauna Wi-fi **Services** Lift Air con **Parking** 80

SW1

THE RED CARNATION HOTEL COLLECTION

No 41

★★★★★ TOWN HOUSE HOTEL

41 Buckingham Palace Rd SW1W 0PS
☎ 020 7300 0041 📄 020 7300 0141
e-mail: book41@rchmail.com
web: www.41hotel.com
dir: *Opp Buckingham Palace Mews entrance*

PETS: Bedrooms unattended sign **Charges** £500 damage deposit required **Exercise area** St James's Park (5 mins' walk) **Facilities** food (pre-bookable) food bowl water bowl bedding dog chews cat treats feeding mat scoop/disp bags leads pet sitting dog walking dog grooming cage storage walks info vet info **On Request** fridge access torch towels **Other** charge for damage pet menus; dedicated staff member for pets **Restrictions** pets are accepted by prior arrangement only

Small, intimate and very private, this stunning town house is located opposite the Royal Mews. Decorated in stylish black and white, bedrooms successfully combine comfort with state-of-the-art technology. The large lounge is the focal point; food and drinks are available as are magazines and newspapers from around the world plus internet access. Attentive personal service and a host of thoughtful extra touches make No 41 really special.

Rooms 30 (2 fmly) **D** £229-£329* **Facilities** STV Local health club Beauty treatments In-room spa Xmas New Year Wi-fi **Services** Lift Air con

ENGLAND

SW1 *continued*

Sheraton Park Tower
★★★★★ 87% ◉◉◉ HOTEL
101 Knightsbridge SW1X 7RN
☎ 020 7235 8050 📠 020 7235 8231
e-mail: 00412.central.london.reservations@sheraton.com
web: www.luxurycollection.com/parktowerlondon
dir: *Adjacent to Harvey Nichols*

PETS: Bedrooms sign **Charges Public areas** except food areas
& gym on leads **Exercise area** 0.5km **Facilities** food bowl
water bowl bedding dog chews scoop/disp bags walks info vet
info **On Request** towels **Other** charge for damage prior notice
required **Restrictions** maximum weight 40lbs

Superbly located for some of London's most fashionable stores,
the Park Tower offers stunning views over the city. Bedrooms
combine a high degree of comfort with up-to-date decor and a
super range of extras; the suites are particularly impressive. The
hotel offers the intimate Knightsbridge lounge, the more formal
Piano Bar and extensive conference and banqueting facilities.
Restaurant One-O-One is renowned for its seafood.

Rooms 280 (280 fmly) (79 smoking) **Facilities** STV Gym Fitness
room 🎵 Wi-fi **Services** Lift Air con **Parking** 67

The Rubens at the Palace
★★★★ 83% ◉◉ HOTEL
39 Buckingham Palace Rd SW1W 0PS
☎ 020 7834 6600 📠 020 7233 6037
e-mail: bookrb@rchmail.com
web: www.rubenshotel.com
dir: *Opposite Royal Mews, 100mtrs from Buckingham Palace*

RED CARNATION
HOTEL COLLECTION

PETS: Bedrooms sign **Charges** £500 damage deposit required
Public areas disp bin **Exercise area** St James's Park & Green
Park 0.5m **Facilities** food (pre-bookable) food bowl water bowl
bedding dog chews cat treats feeding mat litter tray scoop/
disp bags leads pet sitting dog walking dog grooming cage
storage walks info vet info **On Request** fridge access torch
towels **Other** charge for damage dedicated staff member for
pets **Restrictions** pets accepted by prior arrangement only

This hotel enjoys an enviable location close to Buckingham
Palace. Stylish, air-conditioned bedrooms include the pinstripe-
walled Savile Row rooms, which follow a tailoring theme, and
the opulent Royal rooms, named after different monarchs.
Public rooms include the Library fine dining restaurant and a
comfortable stylish cocktail bar and lounge. The team here pride
themselves on their warmth and friendliness.

Rooms 161 (13 fmly) (14 smoking) **S** £125-£295; **D** £150-£305*
Facilities STV Health club & beauty treatment available nearby 🎵
Xmas New Year Wi-fi **Services** Lift Air con **Notes** LB

Egerton House
★★★★★ 84% TOWN HOUSE HOTEL
17 Egerton Ter, Knightsbridge SW3 2BX
☎ 020 7589 2412 📠 020 7584 6540
e-mail: bookeg@rchmail.com
web: www.egertonhousehotel.com
dir: *Just off Brompton Rd, between Harrods and Victoria & Albert
Museum, opposite Brompton Oratory*

PETS: Bedrooms (2 GF) unattended sign **Public areas** except
restaurant on leads disp bin **Exercise area** Hyde Park (10 mins'
walk) **Facilities** food (pre-bookable) food bowl water bowl
bedding dog chews cat treats litter tray scoop/disp bags leads
pet sitting dog walking dog grooming cage storage walks info
vet info **On Request** fridge access torch towels **Other** charge
for damage 24-hour notice required for all pet provisions

This delightful town house enjoys a prestigious Knightsbridge
location, a short walk from Harrods and close to the Victoria &
Albert Museum. Air-conditioned bedrooms and public rooms are
appointed to the highest standards, with luxurious furnishings
and quality antique pieces; an exceptional range of facilities
include iPods, safes, mini bars and flat-screen TVs. Staff offer
the highest levels of personalised, attentive service.

Rooms 28 (5 fmly) (2 GF) (1 smoking) **D** £276-£581.60*
Facilities STV Xmas New Year Wi-fi **Services** Lift Air con

Baglioni Hotel
★★★★★ ◉ HOTEL
60 Hyde Park Gate, Kensington Rd, Kensington SW7 5BB
☎ 020 7368 5700 📠 020 7368 5701
e-mail: baglioni.london.@baglionihotels.com
dir: *On corner of Hyde Park Gate & De Vere Gardens*

PETS: Bedrooms sign **Public areas** on leads disp bin
Exercise area 20yds **Facilities** cage storage walks info vet info
On Request towels **Other** charge for damage **Restrictions** small
dogs only (max 5kg)

Located in the heart of Kensington and overlooking Hyde Park,
this small hotel buzzes with Italian style and chic. Bedrooms,
predominantly suites, are generously sized, with bold dark colours
and feature espresso machines, interactive plasma-screen TVs
and a host of other excellent touches. Service is both professional
and friendly, with personal butlers for the bedrooms. Public areas
include the main open-plan space with bar, lounge and Brunello
restaurant, all merging together with great elan; there is a small
health club and a fashionable private club bar downstairs.

Rooms 67 (7 fmly) (30 smoking) **S** £235-£970; **D** £235-£970*
Facilities Spa STV FTV Gym Xmas New Year Wi-fi **Services** Lift
Air con **Parking** 2 **Notes** LB

SW10

Wyndham Grand London Chelsea Harbour

★★★★★ 84% ⊛ HOTEL

Chelsea Harbour SW10 0XG

☎ 020 7823 3000 📠 020 7351 6525

e-mail: wyndhamlondon@wyndham.com

web: www.wyndham.com

dir: A4 to Earls Court Rd S towards river. Right into Kings Rd, left down Lots Rd. Chelsea Harbour in front

PETS: Bedrooms Charges Public areas except restaurant on leads **Grounds** on leads disp bin **Exercise area** 5 mins' walk **Facilities** food (pre-bookable) food bowl water bowl bedding dog chews cat treats feeding mat pet sitting dog walking dog grooming cage storage walks info vet info **On Request** fridge access towels **Other** charge for damage please contact hotel for details of charges for pets; maximum of 2 pets per guest room **Restrictions** no heavier than 20lbs

Against the picturesque backdrop of Chelsea Harbour's small marina, this modern hotel offers spacious, comfortable accommodation. All rooms are suites, which are superbly equipped; many enjoy splendid views of the marina. In addition, there are also several luxurious penthouse suites. Public areas include a modern bar and restaurant, excellent leisure facilities and extensive meeting and function rooms.

Rooms 158 (36 fmly) (46 smoking) **S** £181-£1050;
D £181-£1050* **Facilities** Spa STV FTV ⊛ Gym ♫ Xmas New Year Wi-fi **Services** Lift Air con **Parking** 2000 **Notes** LB

SW19

Cannizaro House

★★★★ 80% ⊛⊛ COUNTRY HOUSE HOTEL

West Side, Wimbledon Common SW19 4UE

☎ 020 8879 1464 📠 020 8879 7338

e-mail: info@cannizarohouse.com

dir: From A3 follow A219 signed Wimbledon into Parkside, right onto Cannizaro Rd, sharp right onto Westside Common

PETS: Bedrooms (5 GF) unattended **Stables** 5 mins' walk **Charges Public areas** on leads **Grounds** on leads disp bin **Exercise area** 100yds **Facilities** food bowl water bowl bedding pet sitting dog walking cage storage walks info vet info **On Request** fridge access towels **Other** charge for damage **Restrictions** small to medium size dogs only

This unique, elegant 18th-century house has a long tradition of hosting the rich and famous of London society. A few miles from the city centre, the landscaped grounds provide a peaceful escape and a country-house ambience; fine art, murals and stunning fireplaces feature throughout. Spacious bedrooms are individually furnished and equipped to a high standard. The award-winning restaurant menus proudly herald locally sourced, organic ingredients.

Rooms 46 (10 fmly) (5 GF) **Facilities** STV ⤶ Xmas New Year Wi-fi **Services** Lift **Parking** 95

W1

 RED CARNATION
HOTEL COLLECTION

Chesterfield Mayfair

★★★★ ⊛⊛ HOTEL

35 Charles St, Mayfair W1J 5EB

☎ 020 7491 2622 📠 020 7491 4793

e-mail: bookch@rchmail.com

web: www.chesterfieldmayfair.com

dir: Hyde Park Corner along Piccadilly, left into Half Moon St. At end left & 1st right into Queens St, then right into Charles St

PETS: Bedrooms Charges Public areas on leads **Facilities** food (pre-bookable) food bowl water bowl bedding dog chews cat treats leads pet sitting dog walking cage storage walks info vet info **On Request** fridge access torch towels **Other** charge for damage all pet facilities available on request

Quiet elegance and an atmosphere of exclusivity characterise this stylish Mayfair hotel where attentive, friendly service is paramount. The bedrooms, all with marble-clad bathrooms, have contemporary styles - perhaps with floral fabric walls, an African theme or with Savile Row stripes. In addition to these deluxe bedrooms there are 13 individually designed suites; some with four-poster beds and some with jacuzzis. The Butler's Restaurant is the fine dining option, and The Conservatory, with views over the garden, is just the place for cocktails, light lunches and afternoon teas. The hotel is air conditioned throughout.

Rooms 107 (7 fmly) **S** £158.63-£370.13; **D** £182.13-£393.63* **Facilities** STV ♫ Xmas Wi-fi **Services** Lift Air con

W8

RED CARNATION
HOTEL COLLECTION

Milestone Hotel

★★★★★ ⊛ HOTEL

1 Kensington Court W8 5DL

☎ 020 7917 1000 📠 020 7917 1010

e-mail: bookms@rchmail.com

web: www.milestonehotel.com

dir: From Warwick Rd right into Kensington High St. Hotel 400yds past Kensington underground

PETS: Bedrooms (1 GF) **Charges Public areas** except restaurant disp bin **Exercise area** 30mtrs to Kensington Gardens **Facilities** food (pre-bookable) food bowl water bowl bedding dog chews cat treats feeding mat litter tray scoop/disp bags leads pet sitting dog walking washing facs dog grooming cage storage walks info vet info **On Request** fridge access torch towels **Other** charge for damage **Restrictions** small to medium size dogs only

This delightful town house enjoys a wonderful location opposite Kensington Palace and is near the elegant shops. Individually themed bedrooms include a selection of stunning suites that are equipped with every conceivable extra. Public areas include the luxurious Park Lounge where afternoon tea is served, a delightful panelled bar, a sumptuous restaurant and a small gym and resistance pool.

Rooms 62 (3 fmly) (1 GF) (5 smoking) **S** £235-£280; **D** £265-£330* **Facilities** STV FTV ⊛ Gym Health club ♫ Xmas New Year Wi-fi **Services** Lift Air con **Parking** 1 **Notes** LB

ENGLAND

WC1

The Montague on the Gardens
★★★★ 85% ◎ HOTEL
15 Montague St, Bloomsbury WC1B 5BJ
☎ 020 7637 1001 📄 020 7637 2516
e-mail: bookmt@rchmail.com
web: www.montaguehotel.com
dir: *Just off Russell Square, adjacent to British Museum*

PETS: Bedrooms (19 GF) **Public areas** except food service areas on leads **Exercise area** 100mtrs **Facilities** food bowl water bowl bedding dog chews cat treats pet sitting dog walking cage storage walks info vet info **On Request** fridge access torch towels **Other** charge for damage please phone for further details of pet facilities

This stylish hotel is situated right next to the British Museum. A special feature is the alfresco terrace overlooking a delightful garden. Other public rooms include the Blue Door Bistro and Chef's Table, a bar, a lounge and a conservatory where traditional afternoon teas are served. The bedrooms are beautifully appointed and range from split-level suites to more compact rooms.

Rooms 100 (10 fmly) (19 GF) (5 smoking) **S** £115-£185; **D** £135-£205* **Facilities** STV Gym 🎵 Xmas New Year Wi-fi Child facilities **Services** Lift Air con **Notes** LB

LONDON GATEWAY MOTORWAY SERVICE AREA (M1)   Map 4 TQ29

Days Hotel London North
★★★ 67% HOTEL
Welcome Break Service Area NW7 3HU
☎ 020 8906 7000 📄 020 8906 7011
e-mail: lgw.hotel@welcomebreak.co.uk
web: www.welcomebreak.co.uk
dir: *On M1 between junct 2/4 N'bound & S'bound*

PETS: Bedrooms (80 GF) unattended **Charges Public areas** except restaurant & bar area **Other** charge for damage pets allowed by prior arrangement only - contact hotel at time of booking

This modern building offers accommodation in smart, spacious and well-equipped bedrooms, suitable for families and business travellers, and all with en suite bathrooms. Continental breakfast is available and other refreshments may be taken at the nearby family restaurant.

Rooms 200 (190 fmly) (80 GF) (20 smoking) **S** £29-£59; **D** £29-£89 **Facilities** FTV Wi-fi **Services** Lift Air con **Parking** 160 **Notes** LB

MERSEYSIDE

HAYDOCK   Map 7 SJ59

thistle

Thistle Haydock
★★★★ 76% HOTEL
Penny Ln WA11 9SG
☎ 0871 376 9044 📄 0871 376 9144
e-mail: haydock@thistle.co.uk
web: www.thistle.com/haydock
dir: *M6 junct 23, follow Racecourse signs (A49) towards Ashton-in-Makerfield, 1st left, after bridge 1st turn*

PETS: Bedrooms (65 GF) **Charges** £25 per night (dependent on size of pet) **Public areas** assist dogs only on leads **Grounds** on leads disp bin **Other** charge for damage

A smart, purpose-built hotel which offers an excellent standard of thoughtfully equipped accommodation. It is conveniently situated between Liverpool and Manchester, just off the M6. The wide range of leisure and meeting facilities prove popular with guests.

Rooms 137 (10 fmly) (65 GF) **S** £45-£185; **D** £55-£270* **Facilities** STV FTV supervised Gym Children's play area Sauna Steam room Wi-fi **Parking** 210 **Notes** LB

LIVERPOOL   Map 7 SJ39

Novotel Liverpool Centre
★★★★ 71% HOTEL
40 Hanover St L1 4LY
☎ 0151 702 5100 📄 0151 702 5110
e-mail: h6495@accor.com

PETS: Bedrooms unattended sign **Public areas** except restaurant on leads disp bin **Exercise area** town centre area **Facilities** walks info vet info **On Request** fridge access torch towels **Other** charge for damage

This attractive and stylish city centre hotel is convenient for Liverpool Echo Arena, Liverpool One shopping centre and the Albert Dock; it is adjacent to a town centre car park. The hotel has a range of conference facilities and leisure facilities which include an indoor heated pool and fitness suite. The restaurant offers a contemporary style menu. Bedrooms are comfortable and stylishly designed.

Rooms 209 (127 fmly) **S** £69-£149; **D** £69-£149* **Facilities** STV FTV Gym Steam room Wi-fi **Services** Lift Air con **Notes** LB

Campanile Liverpool

BUDGET HOTEL

Chaloner St, Queens Dock L3 4AJ

☎ 0151 709 8104 📄 0151 709 8725

e-mail: liverpool@campanile.com

dir: *Follow tourist signs marked Albert Dock. Hotel on waterfront*

PETS: Bedrooms (33 GF) **Charges** £5 per night **Public areas** except bar & restaurant **Grounds** on leads disp bin **Other** charge for damage

This modern building offers accommodation in smart, well-equipped bedrooms, all with en suite bathrooms. Refreshments may be taken at the informal bistro.

Rooms 100 (4 fmly) (33 GF) **S** £59-£80; **D** £59-£80*

Campanile

SOUTHPORT
Map 7 SD31

Cambridge House

★★ 81% HOTEL

4 Cambridge Rd PR9 9NG

☎ 01704 538372 📄 01704 547183

e-mail: info@cambridgehouse.co.uk

dir: *A565 N from town centre, over 2 rdbts*

PETS: Bedrooms (2 GF) unattended **Charges** £5 per night **Public areas** except restaurant on leads **Grounds** on leads disp bin **Exercise area** 100yds **Facilities** food water bowl walks info vet info **On Request** fridge access torch towels **Other** charge for damage **Resident Pet:** Samson (Newfoundland cross)

This delightful house is in a peaceful location close to Hesketh Park, a short drive from Lord Street. The spacious, individually styled bedrooms, including a luxurious honeymoon suite, are furnished to a very high standard. Stylish public areas include a lounge, a cosy bar and a dining room. Service is attentive.

Rooms 16 (2 fmly) (2 GF) **S** £60-£85; **D** £70-£94 (incl. bkfst) **Facilities** Wi-fi **Parking** 20 **Notes** LB

Balmoral Lodge Hotel

★★ 74% HOTEL

41 Queens Rd PR9 9EX

☎ 01704 544298 📄 01704 501224

e-mail: balmorallg@aol.com

dir: *On edge of town on A565 (Preston road). E at rdbt at North Lord St, left at lights, hotel 200yds on left*

PETS: Bedrooms (4 GF) sign **Charges** £5 per night £35 per week **Grounds** on leads disp bin **Exercise area** park (5 mins' walk) **Facilities** walks info vet info **Other** charge for damage

Situated in a quiet residential area this popular, friendly hotel is ideally situated just 50 yards from the Lord Street. Bedrooms are comfortably appointed and family rooms are available. In addition to the restaurant which offers freshly prepared dishes, there is a choice of lounges including a comfortable lounge bar.

Rooms 15 (4 annexe) (3 fmly) (4 GF) **S** £30-£40; **D** £40-£90 (incl. bkfst) **Facilities** STV FTV Wi-fi **Parking** 12 **Notes** LB

Bay Tree House B & B

★★★★ ≋ GUEST ACCOMMODATION

No1 Irving St, Marine Gate PR9 0HD

☎ 01704 510555 📄 0870 753 6318

e-mail: baytreehouseuk@aol.com

web: www.baytreehousesouthport.co.uk

dir: *Off Leicester St*

PETS: Bedrooms unattended **Charges** **Public areas** **Exercise area** 100mtrs **Facilities** walks info vet info **On Request** fridge access **Other** charge for damage

A warm welcome is assured at this immaculately maintained house, located a short walk from promenade and central attractions. Bedrooms are equipped with a wealth of thoughtful extras, and delicious imaginative breakfasts are served in an attractive dining room overlooking the pretty front patio garden.

Rooms 6 en suite **S** £45-£69; **D** £68-£110 **Facilities** FTV tea/coffee Dinner available Direct Dial Cen ht Licensed Wi-fi **Parking** 2 **Notes** LB Closed 14 Dec-1 Feb

ENGLAND

SOUTHPORT *continued*

Whitworth Falls

★★★★ GUEST ACCOMMODATION

16 Lathom Rd PR9 0JH

☎ 01704 530074

e-mail: whitworthfalls@rapid.co.uk

dir: *A565 N from town centre, over rdbt, 2nd left onto Alexandra Rd, 4th right*

PETS: Bedrooms Public areas except dining room on leads Exercise area 150yds Facilities walks info vet info Resident Pets: Shelby (King Charles Spaniel), Sherbert (African Grey parrot), Midge, Dexter & Meg (cats), Charlie (rabbit), Caramel (hamster), 4 ducks

Located on a mainly residential avenue within easy walking distance of seafront and Lord Street shops, this Victorian house has been renovated to provide a range of practical but homely bedrooms. Breakfasts and pre-theatre dinners are served in the attractive dining room, and a comfortable sitting room and lounge bar are also available.

Rooms 12 en suite (2 fmly) (1 GF) Facilities TVL tea/coffee Dinner available Direct Dial Cen ht Licensed Parking 8

Willowbank Holiday Home & Touring Park

(SD305110)

►►►

Coastal Rd, Ainsdale PR8 3ST

☎ 01704 571566 📠 01704 571576

e-mail: info@willowbankcp.co.uk

dir: *From A565 between Formby & Ainsdale exit at Woodvale lights onto coast road, site 150mtrs on left. From N: M6 junct 31, A59 towards Preston, A565, through Southport & Ainsdale, right at Woodvale lights*

PETS: Stables approx 5m Charges £1.30 per night Public areas except play area; must be kept on short leads disp bin Exercise area enclosed area (with disposal bins) Exercise area woodland walk 1m Facilities washing facs walks info vet info Other prior notice required Restrictions no Dobermans, Rottweilers, or dangerous dogs (see page 7)

Open Mar-Jan Last arrival 21.00hrs Last departure noon

Set in a wooded clearing on a nature reserve next to the beautiful sand dunes, this attractive park is just off the coastal road to Southport. The immaculate toilet facilities are well equipped. An

8 acre site with 87 touring pitches, 61 hardstandings and 228 statics.

Notes Cannot site continental door entry units. No commercial vehicles

NORFOLK

BELTON   Map 5 TG40

Rose Farm Touring & Camping Park

(TG488033)

►►►►

Stepshort NR31 9JS

☎ 01493 780896 📠 01493 780896

dir: *Follow signs to Belton off A143, right at lane signed Stepshort, site 1st on right*

PETS: Public areas except washing areas, toilet blocks & lounge on leads disp bin Exercise area Facilities walks info vet info Other prior notice required Restrictions no dangerous dogs (see page 7); no dog fouling on site

Open all year

A former railway line is the setting for this very peaceful site which enjoys rural views and is beautifully presented throughout. The ever-improving toilet facilities are spotlessly clean and inviting to use, and the park is brightened with many flower and herb beds. Customer care is truly exceptional. A 10 acre site with 80 touring pitches, 15 hardstandings.

BLAKENEY   Map 9 TG04

Morston Hall

★★★ ◉◉◉ HOTEL

Morston, Holt NR25 7AA

☎ 01263 741041 📠 01263 740419

e-mail: reception@morstonhall.com

web: www.morstonhall.com

dir: *1m W of Blakeney on A149 (King's Lynn to Cromer road)*

PETS: Bedrooms (7 GF) unattended Sep accom 2 kennels with runs (free of charge) Charges £5 per night Grounds Exercise area nearby Facilities bedding feeding mat cage storage walks info vet info On Request fridge access torch towels Other charge for damage

This delightful 17th-century country-house hotel enjoys a tranquil setting amid well-tended gardens. The comfortable public rooms offer a choice of attractive lounges and a sunny conservatory, while the elegant dining room is the perfect setting to enjoy Galton Blackiston's award-winning cuisine. The spacious bedrooms are individually decorated and stylishly furnished with modern opulence.

Rooms 13 (6 annexe) (7 GF) S £120-£190; D £300-£340 (incl. bkfst & dinner)* Facilities STV FTV ⑂ New Year Wi-fi Parking 40 Notes LB Closed Jan-2 Feb & 2 days Xmas

BRANCASTER STAITHE — Map 9 TF74

White Horse

★★★ 79% @@ HOTEL

PE31 8BY
☎ 01485 210262 📠 01485 210930
e-mail: reception@whitehorsebrancaster.co.uk
web: www.whitehorsebrancaster.co.uk
dir: *On A149 (coast road) midway between Hunstanton & Wells-next-the-Sea*

PETS: Bedrooms (8 GF) Charges £10 per night Public areas except restaurant & guest lounge on leads Grounds on leads disp bin Exercise area Norfolk coastal path at end of garden Facilities washing facs walks info vet info On Request fridge access torch towels Other charge for damage dogs allowed in annexe bedrooms only; water bowls outside

A charming hotel situated on the north Norfolk coast with contemporary bedrooms in two wings, some featuring an interesting cobbled fascia. Each room is attractively decorated and thoughtfully equipped. There is a large bar and a lounge area leading through to the conservatory restaurant, with stunning tidal marshland views across to Scolt Head Island.

Rooms 15 (8 annexe) (4 fmly) (8 GF) S £45-£70; D £96-£194 (incl. bkfst)* Facilities Xmas New Year Wi-fi Parking 60 Notes LB

BURNHAM MARKET — Map 9 TF84

Hoste Arms

★★★ 87% @@ HOTEL

The Green PE31 8HD
☎ 01328 738777 📠 01328 730103
e-mail: reception@hostearms.co.uk
web: www.hostearms.co.uk
dir: *Signed on B1155, 5m W of Wells-next-the-Sea*

PETS: Bedrooms (7 GF) unattended sign Charges £10 per stay Public areas bar & lounge only Grounds on leads disp bin Exercise area green opposite Facilities food (pre-bookable) food bowl water bowl bedding walks info vet info On Request torch towels Other charge for damage

A stylish, privately-owned inn situated in the heart of a bustling village close to the north Norfolk coast. The extensive public rooms feature a range of dining areas that include a conservatory with plush furniture, a sunny patio and a traditional pub. The tastefully furnished and thoughtfully equipped bedrooms are generally very spacious and offer a high degree of comfort.

Rooms 35 (7 GF) S £117-£195; D £143-£232 (incl. bkfst)* Facilities STV Xmas New Year Wi-fi Services Air con Parking 45 Notes LB

See advert on this page

CLIPPESBY — Map 9 TG41

Clippesby Hall *(TG423147)*

►►►►►

Hall Ln NR29 3BL
☎ 01493 367800 📠 01493 367809
e-mail: holidays@clippesby.com
dir: *From A47 follow tourist signs for The Broads. At Acle rdbt take A1064, after 2m left onto B1152, 0.5m turn left opposite village sign, site 400yds on right*

PETS: Charges £3.50 per night Public areas except The Pinewoods area on leads disp bin Exercise area dog walk Facilities food food bowl water bowl dog chews cat treats walks info vet info Other prior notice required

Open Etr-end Oct rs Etr-Whit some facilities restricted Last arrival 17.30hrs Last departure 11.00hrs

A lovely country house estate with secluded pitches hidden among the trees or in sheltered sunny glades. The toilet facilities are appointed to a very good standard, providing a wide choice of cubicle. Amenities include a coffee shop with Wi-fi and wired internet access, family bar and restaurant and family golf. There four pine lodges and 13 holiday cottages available for holiday lets. A 30 acre site with 120 touring pitches, 9 hardstandings.

CROMER   Map 9 TG24

The Cliftonville
★★★ 74% HOTEL
NR27 9AS
☎ 01263 512543   🖷 01263 515700
e-mail: reservations@cliftonvillehotel.co.uk
web: www.cliftonvillehotel.co.uk
dir: *From A149 (coast road), 500yds from town centre, N'bound on clifftop by sunken gardens*

PETS: **Bedrooms** unattended **Charges** £5 per night **Public areas** except restaurants on leads **Exercise area** 50mtrs **Facilities** food (pre-bookable) food bowl water bowl bedding cage storage walks info vet info **On Request** fridge access **Other** charge for damage

An imposing Edwardian hotel situated on the main coast road with stunning views of the sea. Public rooms feature a magnificent staircase, minstrels' gallery, coffee shop, lounge bar, a further residents' lounge, Boltons Bistro and an additional restaurant. The pleasantly decorated bedrooms are generally quite spacious and have lovely sea views.

Rooms 30 (5 fmly) **S** £55-£72; **D** £110-£144 (incl. bkfst)* **Facilities** Xmas New Year Wi-fi **Services** Lift **Parking** 21

See advert on opposite page

Glendale
★★★ GUEST HOUSE
33 Macdonald Rd NR27 9AP
☎ 01263 513278
e-mail: glendalecromer@aol.com
dir: *A149 (coast road) from Cromer centre, 4th left*

PETS: **Bedrooms** unattended **Public areas** except breakfast room on leads **Grounds** on leads disp bin **Exercise area** 200mtrs **Facilities** walks info vet info **On Request** fridge access torch towels **Other** pets may only be left unattended at breakfast Resident Pets: Daisy & Megan (Jack Russells), Jess (Collie/Springer Spaniel)

A victorian property situated in a peaceful side road adjacent to the seafront and just a short walk from the town centre. Bedrooms are pleasantly decorated, well maintained and equipped with a good range of useful extras. Breakfast is served at individual tables in the smart dining room.

Rooms 5 rms (1 en suite) **S** £25-£35; **D** £50-£70 **Facilities** tea/coffee **Parking** 2 Notes LB Closed 20 Oct-21 Apr

The Sandcliff
★★★ GUEST HOUSE
Runton Rd NR27 9AS
☎ 01263 512888   🖷 01263 512888
e-mail: bookings@sandcliffcromer.co.uk
dir: *500yds W of town centre on A149*

PETS: **Bedrooms** **Other** please phone for further details of pet facilities

Ideally situated on the seafront overlooking the beach and sea just a short walk from the town centre, many improvements have taken place to this popular establishment in recent years. Public rooms include a large lounge bar with comfortable seating and a spacious dining room where breakfast and dinner are served. The bedrooms are pleasantly decorated, thoughtfully equipped and some have superb sea views.

Rooms 23 rms (17 en suite) (10 fmly) (3 GF) **S** £49.50; **D** £80-£96* **Facilities** TVL tea/coffee Dinner available Licensed Wi-fi Golf 18 **Parking** 10 Notes LB

Manor Farm Caravan & Camping Site
(TG198416)

▶ ▶ ▶ ▶

East Runton NR27 9PR
☎ 01263 512858
e-mail: manor-farm@ukf.net
dir: *1m W of Cromer, exit A148 or A149 at Manor Farm sign*

PETS: Charges £1 per night **Public areas** except dog free areas **Exercise area** farmland & public footpaths adjacent **Facilities** walks info vet info **Other** prior notice required Resident Pets: Mollie (Border Terrier/Lakeland cross),Torro (Lancashire Heeler), Titch & Gerbil (ponies)

Open Etr-Sep rs Oct only one field open (Moll's Meadow) Last arrival 20.30hrs Last departure noon

A well-established family-run site on a working farm enjoying panoramic sea views. There are good modern facilities across the site, which is elevated above Cromer. A 17 acre site with 250 touring pitches.

Notes

DOWNHAM MARKET   Map 5 TF60

Crosskeys Riverside House
★★★ BED AND BREAKFAST
Bridge St, Hilgay PE38 0LD
☎ 01366 387777   📠 01366 387777
e-mail: crosskeyshouse@aol.com
web: www.crosskeys.info
dir: *2m S of Downham Market. Off A10 into Hilgay, Crosskeys on bridge*

PETS: Bedrooms unattended **Stables Charges** £3.50 per stay **Public areas** except dining room **Grounds** disp bin **Exercise area** 500yds **Facilities** leads walks info vet info **On Request** fridge access torch towels Resident Pets: 3 Shih Tzus, 3 horses

Situated in the small village of Hilgay on the banks of the River Wissey, this former coaching inn offers comfortable accommodation that includes a number of four-poster bedrooms; many rooms have river views. Public rooms include a dining room with oak beams and inglenook fireplace, plus a small, rustic residents' bar.

Rooms 4 en suite (1 fmly) (2 GF) **S** £30-£55; **D** £55-£65* **Facilities** FTV tea/coffee Cen ht Fishing **Parking** 10

Lakeside Caravan Park & Fisheries
(TF608013)

▶ ▶ ▶

Sluice Rd, Denver PE38 0DZ
☎ 01366 387074 & 07770 663237   📠 01366 387074
e-mail: richesflorido@aol.com
dir: *Off A10 towards Denver, follow signs to Denver Windmill*

PETS: Stables Charges horse £5 per night **Public areas** except club room, showers & toilets on leads disp bin **Exercise area** large field **Facilities** scoop/disp bags washing facs walks info vet info **Other** quiet lanes & country rides for horses

Open Mar-Oct Last arrival 21.00hrs Last departure noon

A peaceful, rapidly improving park set around four pretty fishing lakes. Several grassy touring areas are sheltered by mature hedging and trees. There is a function room, shop and laundry. A 30 acre site with 100 touring pitches and 1 static.

Map 9 TF92

Abbott Farm (TF975390)

★★★ FARMHOUSE

Walsingham Rd, Binham NR21 0AW

☎ 01328 830519 📠 01328 830519 Mrs E Brown

e-mail: abbot.farm@btinternet.com

web: www.abbottfarm.co.uk

dir: *NE of Fakenham. From Binham SW onto Walsingham Rd, farm 0.6m on left*

PETS: Bedrooms sign Stables 1m Public areas Grounds on leads disp bin Exercise area Facilities food bowl water bowl bedding feeding mat leads washing facs cage storage walks info vet info On Request fridge access torch towels Other charge for damage Resident Pets: Buster (Labrador/Retriever cross), Joss (cat)

A detached red-brick farmhouse set amidst 190 acres of arable farmland and surrounded by open countryside. The spacious bedrooms are pleasantly decorated and thoughtfully equipped; they include a ground-floor room with a large en suite shower. Breakfast is served in the attractive conservatory, which has superb views of the countryside.

Rooms 3 en suite (2 GF) Facilities TVL tea/coffee Cen ht Parking 20 Notes Closed 24-26 Dec 🐾 190 acres arable

Caravan Club M.V.C. Site (TF926288)

►►►

Fakenham Racecourse NR21 7NY

☎ 01328 862388 📠 01328 855908

e-mail: caravan@fakenhamracecourse.co.uk

dir: *From B1146, S of Fakenham follow brown Racecourse signs (with tent & caravan symbols) leads to site entrance*

PETS: Stables Public areas disp bin Exercise area allocated field Facilities food bowl water bowl dog chews washing facs walks info vet info Other disposal bags available

Open all year Last arrival 21.00hrs Last departure noon

A very well laid out site set around the racecourse, with a grandstand offering smart modern toilet facilities. Tourers move to the centre of the course on race days, and enjoy free racing, and there's a wide range of sporting activities in the club house. An 11.4 acre site with 120 touring pitches, 25 hardstandings.

Crossways Caravan & Camping Park
(TF961321)

►►

Crossways, Holt Rd, Little Snoring NR21 0AX

☎ 01328 878335

e-mail: joyholland@live.co.uk

dir: *From Fakenham take A148 towards Cromer. After 3m pass exit for Little Snoring. Site on A148 on left behind Post Office*

PETS: Charges £1 per night Public areas on leads disp bin Exercise area 10mtrs Facilities food dog chews cat treats litter tray scoop/disp bags walks info vet info Other prior notice required

Open all year Last arrival 22.00hrs Last departure noon

Set on the edge of the peaceful hamlet of Little Snoring, this level site enjoys views across the fields towards the North Norfolk coast some seven miles away. Visitors can use the health suite for a small charge, and there is a shop on site, and a good village pub. A 2 acre site with 26 touring pitches, 10 hardstandings and 1 static.

Map 5 TL99

Home Hall B&B

★★★★★ BED AND BREAKFAST

Vicarage Rd IP24 1PE

☎ 01953 498985

e-mail: homehall@btinternet.com

web: www.homehallbedandbreakfast.com

dir: *A11 Thetford left onto A1075 towards Watton. After Wretham turn right into Great Hockham, at village green left then 2nd left onto Vicarage Rd. Home Hall 1st on left*

PETS: Bedrooms unattended Sep accom garage, barn & summer house Stables 200yds Charges £10 per stay Public areas except dining room Grounds disp bin Exercise area 200yds Facilities food (pre-bookable) food bowl water bowl dog chews feeding mat scoop/disp bags leads pet sitting dog walking washing facs cage storage walks info vet info On Request fridge access torch towels Other charge for damage

Enjoy a cream tea on arrival at this delightful detached property, which is set in landscaped gardens. There are three tastefully furnished bedrooms - the Edwardian Suite, the Victorian Suite and the Georgian Suite; each one has beautiful co-ordinated soft fabrics and Freeview TV, DVD, Wi-fi and many thoughtful touches. Organic free-range produce is served at breakfast, with guests seated around a large communal table in the the in the oak-panelled dining room; dinner is also available.

Rooms 3 en suite (2 fmly) S fr £50; D fr £90 Facilities FTV TVL tea/coffee Dinner available Cen ht Wi-fi Parking 3 Notes LB No Children 12yrs

Barnard House

★ ★ ★ ★   BED AND BREAKFAST

2 Barnard Crescent NR30 4DR

☎ 01493 855139

e-mail: enquiries@barnardhouse.com

dir: *0.5m N of town centre. Off A149 onto Barnard Crescent*

PETS: Bedrooms Charges Public areas with other guests' approval **Exercise area Facilities** walks info vet info **On Request** fridge access torch towels **Other** charge for damage **Resident Pets:** Fergus & Flora (Field Spaniels)

A friendly, family-run bed and breakfast, set in mature landscaped gardens in a residential area. The smartly decorated bedrooms are thoughtfully equipped. Breakfast is served in the stylish dining room and there is an elegant lounge with comfy sofas. A warm welcome is assured.

Rooms 3 rms (2 en suite) (1 pri facs) **S** £40-£45; **D** £60-£65 **Facilities** FTV TVL tea/coffee Cen ht Wi-fi **Parking** 3 **Notes** LB Closed Xmas & New Year

Swiss Cottage B&B
Exclusively for Non Smokers

★ ★ ★ ★   GUEST ACCOMMODATION

31 North Dr NR30 4EW

☎ 01493 855742 & 07986 399857   📠 01493 843547

e-mail: info@swiss-cottage.info

dir: *0.5m N of town centre. Off A47 or A12 to to seafront, 750yds N of pier. Turn left at Britannia Pier. Swiss Cottage on left opposite Water Gardens*

PETS: Bedrooms Public areas except breakfast room **Exercise area** 10mtrs **Facilities** walks info vet info **On Request** fridge access **Other** charge for damage dogs must not be left unattended in bedrooms at any time **Restrictions** small to medium size dogs only; no dangerous breeds (see page 7)

A charming detached property situated in the peaceful part of town overlooking the Venetian waterways and the sea beyond. The comfortable bedrooms are pleasantly decorated with co-ordinated fabrics and have many useful extras. Breakfast is served in the smart dining room and guests have use of an open-plan lounge area.

Rooms 8 en suite 1 annexe en suite (2 GF) **S** £31-£40; **D** £52-£67* **Facilities** FTV tea/coffee Cen ht Wi-fi **Parking** 9 **Notes** LB No Children 11yrs Closed Nov-Feb

The Grange Touring Park *(TG510142)*

▶ ▶ ▶ ▶

Yarmouth Rd, Ormesby St Margaret NR29 3QG

☎ 01493 730306   📠 01493 730188

e-mail: info@grangetouring.co.uk

dir: *From A419, 3m N of Great Yarmouth. Site at junct of A419 & B1159. Signed*

PETS: Stables 2m **Charges** 1st dog free, 2nd dog £3.50 per night £24.50 per week **Public areas** except toilets, showers & laundry room disp bin **Exercise area** 100yds **Facilities** walks info vet info **Other** prior notice required information available on dog-friendly beaches & local attractions **Restrictions** no Rottweilers, Pit Bulls or Dobermans

Open Etr-Oct Last arrival 21.00hrs Last departure 11.00hrs

A mature site with plenty of trees, located just one mile from the sea, within easy reach of both coastal attractions and the Norfolk Broads. The level grassy pitches have electric hook-ups, and there are clean, modern toilets. There is Wi-fi access at all pitches. A 3.5 acre site with 70 touring pitches.

Notes No football, no gazebos, no open fires

Caley Hall

★ ★ ★   82%   HOTEL

Old Hunstanton Rd PE36 6HH

☎ 01485 533486   📠 01485 533348

e-mail: mail@caleyhallhotel.co.uk

web: www.caleyhallhotel.co.uk

dir: *1m from Hunstanton, on A149*

PETS: Bedrooms (30 GF) unattended sign **Charges** £5 per night **Public areas** except restaurant & lounge on leads **Grounds** on leads disp bin **Exercise area** 150mtrs **Facilities** food bowl water bowl feeding mat leads washing facs cage storage walks info vet info **On Request** fridge access torch towels **Other** charge for damage **Resident Pet:** Basil (Cocker Spaniel)

Situated within easy walking distance of the seafront. The tastefully decorated bedrooms are in a series of converted outbuildings; each is smartly furnished and thoughtfully equipped. Public rooms feature a large open-plan lounge/bar with plush leather seating, and a restaurant offering an interesting choice of dishes.

Rooms 39 (20 fmly) (30 GF) **S** £59-£109; **D** £80-£200 (incl. bkfst) **Facilities** STV Wi-fi Child facilities **Parking** 50 **Notes** LB Closed 18 Dec-20 Jan

HUNSTANTON *continued*

Claremont

★ ★ ★ ★ GUEST HOUSE

35 Greevegate PE36 6AF

☎ 01485 533171

e-mail: claremontgh@tiscali.co.uk

dir: *Off A149 onto Greevegate, house before St Edmund's Church*

PETS: Bedrooms Public areas except dining room disp bin **Exercise area** adjacent **Facilities** walks info vet info **Other** charge for damage

This Victorian guest house, close to the shops, beach and gardens, has individually decorated bedrooms with a good range of useful extras. There is also a ground-floor room as well as two feature rooms, one with a four-poster, and another with a canopied bed.

Rooms 7 en suite (1 fmly) (1 GF) **S** £26-£30; **D** £52-£60* **Facilities** TVL tea/coffee Cen ht **Parking** 4 **Notes** LB No Children 5yrs Closed 15 Nov-15 Mar 🐾

 Searles Leisure Resort *(TF671400)*

South Beach Rd PE36 5BB

☎ 01485 534211 📠 01485 533815

e-mail: bookings@searles.co.uk

dir: *A149 from King's Lynn to Hunstanton. At rdbt follow signs for South Beach. Straight on at 2nd rdbt. Site on left*

PETS: Stables 5m **Charges** £2.50 per night **Public areas** except buildings **Exercise area** field available for dogs (on leads) **Exercise area** beach 200mtrs **Facilities** food food bowl water bowl washing facs walks info vet info **Other** prior notice required disposal bags available **Restrictions** no Rottweilers, Pit Bulls, Staffordshire Bull Terriers, German Shepherds, Dobermans or similar breeds

Open all year rs 25 Dec & Feb-May limited entertainment & restaurant Last arrival 20.45hrs Last departure 11.00hrs

A large seaside holiday complex with well-managed facilities, adjacent to sea and beach. The tourers have their own areas, including two excellent toilet blocks, and pitches are individually marked by small maturing shrubs for privacy. The bars and entertainment, restaurant, bistro and takeaway, heated indoor and outdoor pools, golf, fishing and bowling green make this park popular throughout the year. A 50 acre site with 332 touring pitches, 100 hardstandings and 460 statics.

Beechwood Hotel

★ ★ ★ ◉ ◉ HOTEL

Cromer Rd NR28 0HD

☎ 01692 403231 📠 01692 407284

e-mail: info@beechwood-hotel.co.uk

web: www.beechwood-hotel.co.uk

dir: *B1150 from Norwich. At North Walsham left at 1st lights, then right at next*

PETS: Bedrooms (4 GF) unattended **Charges** £9 per night **Public areas** except restaurant **Grounds Exercise area** park 400yds **Resident Pets:** Emily & Harry (Airedale Terriers)

Expect a warm welcome at this elegant 18th-century house, situated just a short walk from the town centre. The individually styled bedrooms are tastefully furnished with well-chosen antique pieces, attractive co-ordinated soft fabrics and many thoughtful touches. The spacious public areas include a lounge bar with plush furnishings, a further lounge and a smartly appointed restaurant.

Rooms 17 (4 GF) **S** fr £80; **D** £90-£160 (incl. bkfst) **Facilities** FTV ✈ New Year Wi-fi **Parking** 20 **Notes** LB No children 10yrs

Chimneys

★ ★ ★ ★ ⬛ BED AND BREAKFAST

51 Cromer Rd NR28 0HB

☎ 01692 406172 & 07952 117701

e-mail: jenny.harmer8@virgin.net

dir: *0.5m NW of town centre on A149*

PETS: Bedrooms Public areas on leads **Grounds** on leads disp bin **Exercise area** 1m **Facilities** washing facs cage storage walks info vet info **On Request** fridge access torch towels **Restrictions** no large dogs or long-haired dogs **Resident Pet:** 1 small terrier cross

A delightful Edwardian-style town house set amidst mature secluded grounds close to the town centre. Bedrooms are tastefully furnished and thoughtfully equipped, the superior room has a jacuzzi bath. Breakfast is served in the smart dining room and guests are welcome to sit on the balcony, which overlooks the garden. Dinner is available by prior arrangement.

Rooms 3 en suite (1 fmly) **S** £40-£50; **D** £60-£75 **Facilities** FTV tea/coffee Dinner available Cen ht Wi-fi **Parking** 5 **Notes** 🐾

Two Mills Touring Park *(TG291286)*

▶ ▶ ▶ ▶

Yarmouth Rd NR28 9NA
☎ 01692 405829 📠 01692 405829
e-mail: enquiries@twomills.co.uk
dir: *1m S of North Walsham on Old Yarmouth road past police station & hospital on left*

PETS: Charges 75p per night **Public areas** except in buildings disp bin **Exercise area** dog walks **Facilities** washing facs vet info **Other** max 2 dogs per pitch **Resident Pet:** Pusscat (cat)

Open Mar-3 Jan Last arrival 20.30hrs Last departure noon

Set in superb countryside in a peaceful spot which is also convenient for touring. Some fully-serviced pitches offer panoramic views over the site, and the layout of pitches and facilities is excellent. The very friendly and helpful owners keep the park in immaculate condition. This park does not accept children. A 7 acre site with 81 touring pitches, 81 hardstandings.

| NORWICH | Map 5 TG20 |

Marriott Sprowston Manor Hotel & Country Club

★ ★ ★ ★ 82% 🏵🏵 HOTEL

Sprowston Park, Wroxham Rd, Sprowston NR7 8RP
☎ 01603 410871 📠 01603 423911
e-mail: mhrs.nwigs.frontdesk@marriotthotels.com
web: www.marriottsprowstonmanor.co.uk
dir: *From A11/A47, 2m NE on A115 (Wroxham road). Follow signs to Sprowston Park*

PETS: Bedrooms (5 GF) unattended **Charges** £15 per night **Public areas** except restaurants & bar on leads **Grounds** on leads disp bin **Facilities** food bowl water bowl dog chews cage storage walks info vet info **On Request** fridge access torch

Surrounded by open parkland, this imposing property is set in attractively landscaped grounds and is just a short drive from the city centre. Bedrooms are spacious and feature a variety of decorative styles. The hotel also has extensive conference, banqueting and leisure facilities. Other public rooms include an array of seating areas and the elegant Manor Restaurant. Marriott Hotels - AA Hotel Group of the Year 2010-11.

Rooms 94 (3 fmly) (5 GF) (8 smoking) **S** £104-£128; **D** £138-£150 (incl. bkfst) **Facilities** Spa FTV 🏊 supervised ♨ 18 Putt green Gym Steam room Sauna Xmas New Year Wi-fi **Services** Lift **Parking** 150 **Notes** LB

Stower Grange

★ ★ 85% 🏵 HOTEL

School Rd, Drayton NR8 6EF
☎ 01603 860210 📠 01603 860464
e-mail: enquiries@stowergrange.co.uk
web: www.stowergrange.co.uk
dir: *On Norwich ring road N to Asda supermarket. Take A1067 (Fakenham road) at Drayton, right at lights into School Rd. Hotel 150yds on right*

PETS: Bedrooms unattended **Public areas** except restaurant **Grounds** disp bin **Exercise area** **Facilities** food (pre-bookable) food bowl water bowl dog chews cat treats pet sitting dog walking washing facs cage storage walks info vet info **On Request** torch towels

Expect a warm welcome at this 17th-century, ivy-clad property situated in a peaceful residential area close to the city centre and airport. The individually decorated bedrooms are generally quite spacious; each one is tastefully furnished and equipped with many thoughtful touches. Public rooms include a smart open-plan lounge bar and an elegant restaurant.

Rooms 11 (1 fmly) **S** fr £75; **D** fr £95 (incl. bkfst)* **Facilities** FTV 🏌 New Year Wi-fi **Parking** 40

ENGLAND

NORWICH *continued*

Edmar Lodge

★★★ GUEST ACCOMMODATION

64 Earlham Rd NR2 3DF

☎ 01603 615599 📄 01603 495599

e-mail: mail@edmarlodge.co.uk

web: www.edmarlodge.co.uk

dir: *From A47 S bypass onto B1108 (Earlham Rd), follow university &hospital signs*

PETS: **Bedrooms Grounds** on leads **Exercise area** approx 100yds **Facilities** food bowl water bowl washing facs walks info vet info **On Request** fridge access towels **Other** please phone for further details of pet facilities

Located just a ten-minute walk from the city centre, this friendly family-run guest house offers a convenient location and ample private parking. Individually decorated bedrooms are smartly appointed and well equipped. Freshly prepared breakfasts are served in the cosy dining room; a microwave and a fridge are also available.

Rooms 5 en suite (1 fmly) **S** £38-£45; **D** £45-£50* **Facilities** FTV tea/coffee Cen ht Wi-fi **Parking** 6

Bedingfeld Arms

★★★ INN

PE33 9PS

☎ 01366 328300

e-mail: sam.clark@tiscali.co.uk

web: www.bedingfeldarms.com

PETS: **Bedrooms** unattended **Stables** 5m **Charges Public areas** except restaurants on leads **Grounds** on leads **Exercise area** adjacent **Facilities** water bowl walks info vet info **On Request** fridge access torch towels **Other** charge for damage

This establishment provides five annexe rooms in a refurbished stable block adjacent to the Bedingfeld Arms. The rooms are spacious, smartly presented with en suite facilities. This is a family run, traditional English pub offering friendly hospitality and home-made pub food including a selection of specials plus a range of locally produced ales.

Rooms 5 annexe en suite (1 fmly) (5 GF) **Facilities** TVL tea/coffee Dinner available Cen ht **Parking** 5

OXFORD
HOTELS & INNS

Old Brewery House

★★ 72% HOTEL

Market Place NR10 4JJ

☎ 01603 870881 📄 01603 870969

e-mail: reservations.oldbreweryhouse@ohiml.com

web: www.oxfordhotelsandinns.com

dir: *A1067, right at Bawdeswell onto B1145 into Reepham, hotel on left in Market Place*

PETS: **Bedrooms** (7 GF) unattended sign **Charges Public areas** except bar & restaurant areas on leads **Grounds** on leads **Exercise area** woods 1m **Facilities** water bowl cage storage walks info vet info **On Request** fridge access torch towels **Other** prior notice required

This Grade II listed Georgian building is situated in the heart of this bustling town centre. Public areas include a cosy lounge, a bar, a conservatory and a smart restaurant. Bedrooms come in a variety of styles; each one is pleasantly decorated and equipped with a good range of facilities.

Rooms 23 (2 fmly) (7 GF) **Facilities** Gym Squash Xmas **Parking** 40

RINGSTEAD   Map 9 TF74

The Gin Trap Inn
★★★★ INN

6 High St PE36 5JU
☎ 01485 525264
e-mail: thegintrap@hotmail.co.uk
dir: *A149 from King's Lynn towards Hunstanton. In 15m turn right at Heacham for Ringstead into village centre*

PETS: Bedrooms Public areas except conservatory & dining room **Grounds Exercise area** 500mtrs **Facilities** dog chews walks info vet info **On Request** fridge access torch

This delightful 17th-century inn is in a quiet village just a short drive from the coast. The public rooms include a large open-plan bar and a cosy restaurant. The accommodation is luxurious; each individually appointed bedroom has been carefully decorated and thoughtfully equipped.

Rooms 3 en suite **S** £49-£70; **D** £78-£140* **Facilities** tea/coffee Dinner available Cen ht Wi-fi **Parking** 20 **Notes** No Children No coaches

ST JOHN'S FEN END   Map 9 TF51

Virginia Lake Caravan Park *(TF538113)*
► ► ► ►

Smeeth Rd PE14 8JF
☎ 01945 430585 & 430167
e-mail: louise@virginialake.co.uk
dir: *From A47 E of Wisbech follow tourist signs to Terrington St John. Site on left*

PETS: Public areas except lakeside disp bin **Exercise area** dog walk **Exercise area** 100mtrs **Facilities** food food bowl water bowl litter tray scoop/disp bags leads washing facs walks info vet info **Other** prior notice required **Restrictions** no Pit Bulls, Staffordshire Bull Terriers, Rottweilers or Dobermans **Resident Pets:** 4 Labradors & 2 cats

Open all year Last arrival 21.00hrs Last departure noon

A well-established park beside a 2-acre fishing lake with good facilities for both anglers and tourers. The toilet facilities are very good, and security is carefully observed throughout the park. A clubhouse serves a selection of meals. A 7 acre site with 100 touring pitches, 20 hardstandings.

Notes No camp fires

SCRATBY   Map 9 TG51

Scratby Hall Caravan Park *(TG501155)*
► ► ►

NR29 3SR
☎ 01493 730283
e-mail: scratbyhall@aol.com
dir: *5m N of Great Yarmouth. Exit A149 onto B1159, site signed*

PETS: Stables 0.5m **Public areas** except children's play area & all buildings disp bin **Exercise area** direct access to footpaths & bridleways **Facilities** food food bowl water bowl bedding dog chews leads washing facs walks info vet info **Other** max 2 pets per pitch pet toys available

Open Spring BH-mid Sep Last arrival 22.00hrs Last departure noon

A neatly-maintained site with a popular children's play area, well-equipped shop and outdoor swimming pool with sun terrace. The toilets are kept very clean. The beach and the Norfolk Broads are close by. A 5 acre site with 97 touring pitches.

Notes No commercial vehicles

SWAFFHAM   Map 5 TF80

Breckland Meadows Touring Park *(TF809094)*
► ► ►

Lynn Rd PE37 7PT
☎ 01760 721246
e-mail: info@brecklandmeadows.co.uk
dir: *1m W of Swaffham on old A47*

PETS: Stables 5m **Charges** 50p per night £3.50 per week **Public areas** disp bin **Exercise area Facilities** washing facs walks info vet info

Open all year Last arrival 21.00hrs Last departure 14.00hrs

An immaculate, well-landscaped little park on the edge of Swaffham. The impressive toilet block is well equipped, and there are hardstandings, full electricity and laundry equipment. Plenty of planting is resulting in attractive screening. A 3 acre site with 45 touring pitches, 29 hardstandings.

Notes 🐾

SYDERSTONE   Map 9 TF83

The Garden Caravan Site *(TF812337)*
► ► ►

Barmer Hall Farm PE31 8SR
☎ 01485 578220 & 578178
e-mail: nigel@gardencaravansite.co.uk
dir: *Signed from B1454 at Barmer between A148 & Docking, 1m W of Syderstone*

PETS: Public areas Exercise area 10mtrs **Facilities** walks info vet info **Other** prior notice required max 2 dogs per pitch

Open Mar-Nov Last arrival 21.00hrs Last departure noon

In the tranquil setting of a former walled garden beside a large farmhouse, with mature trees and shrubs, a secluded site surrounded by woodland. The site is run mainly on trust, with a daily notice indicating which pitches are available, and an honesty box for basic foods. An ideal site for the discerning camper, and well placed for touring north Norfolk. A 3.5 acre site with 30 touring pitches.

Notes 🐾

THORNHAM	Map 9 TF74

Lifeboat Inn

★★ 78% ® HOTEL

Ship Ln PE36 6LT

☎ 01485 512236 📄 01485 512323

e-mail: reception@lifeboatinn.co.uk

web: www.lifeboatinn.co.uk

dir: *Follow A149 from Hunstanton for approx 6m. 1st left after Thornham sign*

PETS: Bedrooms (1 GF) unattended **Charges** £8 per stay **Public areas Grounds Exercise area** 0.5m **Other** please phone for further details of pet facilities

This popular 16th-century smugglers' alehouse enjoys superb views across open meadows to Thornham Harbour. The tastefully decorated bedrooms are furnished with pine pieces and have many thoughtful touches. The public rooms have a wealth of character and feature open fireplaces, exposed brickwork and oak beams.

Rooms 13 (3 fmly) (1 GF) **Facilities** FTV Xmas New Year Wi-fi **Parking** 120

THURSFORD	Map 9 TF93

The Old Forge Seafood Restaurant

★★★★ ® RESTAURANT WITH ROOMS

Seafood Restaurant, Fakenham Rd NR21 0BD

☎ 01328 878345

e-mail: sarah.goldspink@btconnect.com

dir: *On A148 (Fakenham to Holt road)*

PETS: Bedrooms Stables Charges horse £10 per night **Grounds** on leads disp bin **Exercise area** adjacent **Facilities** leads pet sitting dog walking cage storage walks info vet info **On Request** fridge access torch towels **Other** charge for damage **Resident Pets:** 3 Labradors, 1 Miniature Schnauzer, 1 mongrel, 4 horses

Expect a warm welcome at this delightful relaxed restaurant with rooms. The open-plan public areas include a lounge bar area with comfy sofas, and an intimate restaurant with pine tables. Bedrooms are pleasantly decorated and equipped with a good range of useful facilities.

Rooms 2 en suite **S** £35-£50; **D** £65 **Facilities** FTV tea/coffee Dinner available Cen ht Wi-fi **Parking** 14 **Notes** No coaches

TITCHWELL	Map 9 TF74

Titchwell Manor

★★★ 86% ®® HOTEL

PE31 8BB

☎ 01485 210221 📄 01485 210104

e-mail: margaret@titchwellmanor.com

web: www.titchwellmanor.com

dir: *On A149 (coast road) between Brancaster & Thornham*

PETS: Bedrooms (16 GF) unattended sign **Sep accom Stables** 2m **Charges** £8 per night **Public areas** except conservatory restaurant on leads **Grounds** on leads disp bin **Exercise area** 1m **Facilities** food bowl water bowl bedding dog chews cat treats feeding mat litter tray scoop/disp bags leads pet sitting washing facs cage storage walks info vet info **On Request** fridge access torch towels **Other** charge for damage

Friendly family-run hotel ideally placed for touring the north Norfolk coastline. The tastefully appointed bedrooms are very comfortable; some in the adjacent annexe offer ground floor access. Smart public rooms include a lounge area, relaxed informal bar and a delightful conservatory restaurant, overlooking the walled garden. Imaginative menus feature quality local produce and fresh fish.

Rooms 26 (18 annexe) (4 fmly) (16 GF) **S** £65-£190; **D** £110-£250 (incl. bkfst)* **Facilities** FTV Xmas New Year Wi-fi **Parking** 50 **Notes** LB

ENGLAND

Broom Hall Country Hotel

★★★ 77% COUNTRY HOUSE HOTEL

Richmond Rd, Saham Toney IP25 7EX

☎ 01953 882125 📠 01953 885325

e-mail: enquiries@broomhallhotel.co.uk

web: www.broomhallhotel.co.uk

dir: *From A11 at Thetford onto A1075 to Watton (12m), B1108 towards Swaffham, in 0.5m at rdbt turn right to Saham Toney, hotel 0.5m on left. From A47 take A1075, left onto B1108*

PETS: Bedrooms (5 GF) unattended **Sep accom** by arrangement **Stables** 6m **Charges** £5 per night (£10 for 2 nights or more) **Public areas** only bar & reception **Grounds** disp bin **Exercise area** 20mtrs **Facilities** bedding leads washing facs walks info vet info **On Request** fridge access torch **Other** charge for damage **Resident Pets:** Megan (Labrador), Maggie & Charlie (Jack Russells)

A delightful Victorian country house situated down a private drive and set in mature landscaped gardens surrounded by parkland. The well-equipped bedrooms are split between the main house and an adjacent building. Public rooms include a relaxing lounge, a brasserie restaurant, a lounge bar, a conservatory and a smart restaurant. There is an indoor swimming pool.

Rooms 15 (5 annexe) (3 fmly) (5 GF) **S** £75-£95; **D** £95-£165 (incl. bkfst) **Facilities** ✿ Massage Reflexology Beauty treatments Wi-fi **Parking** 30 **Notes** LB Closed 24 Dec-4 Jan

The Ollands

★★★★ 🏠 GUEST HOUSE

Swanns Yard NR28 9RP

☎ 01692 535150 📠 01692 535150

e-mail: theollands@btinternet.com

dir: *Off A149 to village x-rds, off Back St*

PETS: Bedrooms Charges £3 per night **Public areas** except dining room **Grounds** disp bin **Exercise area Facilities** walks info vet info **On Request** torch **Other** charge for damage **Restrictions** small to medium size dogs only **Resident Pets:** Candy, Mouse & Abbs (Burmese cats), Storm (cat)

This charming detached property is set in the heart of the picturesque village of Worstead. The well-equipped bedrooms are pleasantly decorated and carefully furnished, and breakfast served in the elegant dining room features local produce.

Rooms 3 en suite (1 GF) **S** £39-£42; **D** £64-£68 **Facilities** TVL tea/coffee Dinner available Cen ht Wi-fi **Parking** 8 **Notes** LB

Broad House Hotel

★★★ 87% 🏵 COUNTRY HOUSE HOTEL

The Avenue NR12 8TS

☎ 01603 783567 📠 01494 400333

e-mail: info@broadhousehotel.co.uk

PETS: Bedrooms unattended **Charges** £11 per night **Grounds** on leads disp bin **Facilities** cage storage vet info **On Request** fridge access torch towels **Other** charge for damage dogs allowed in 2 bedrooms only

A delightful 16th-century Queen Anne residence set amidst 24 acres of secluded parkland in the heart of the Norfolk Broads. The individually styled bedrooms are smartly decorated, and have co-ordinated soft furnishings and have many thoughtful touches. Public rooms include a choice of lounges with plush sofas, the smart Trafford's' restaurant and a function suite.

Rooms 9 (1 fmly) **D** £160-£259 (incl. bkfst)* **Facilities** FTV 🏊 Fishing ⛳ Gym Boat, cycling & canoe hire Xmas New Year Wi-fi **Parking** 60 **Notes** LB

The Falcon

★★★ INN

NN7 1LF

☎ 01604 696200 📠 01604 696673

e-mail: falson.castleashby@oldenglishinns.co.uk

dir: *Off A428*

PETS: Bedrooms sign **Charges** £10 per night **Public areas** except restaurant on leads **Grounds** on leads **Exercise area** 5 mins **Facilities** food bowl water bowl walks info vet info **On Request** torch towels **Other** charge for damage **Restrictions** no Great Danes

Set in the heart of a peaceful village, the inn consists of a main house and a neighbouring cottage. Bedrooms are all individually decorated and provide a wealth of thoughtful extras. Character public rooms, in the main house, include a cellar bar, a choice of lounges and a pretty restaurant serving good quality cuisine.

Rooms 5 en suite 10 annexe en suite (1 fmly) **Facilities** TVL tea/coffee Dinner available Cen ht Wi-fi **Parking** 75 **Notes** LB

CRICK
Map 4 SP57

Holiday Inn Rugby/Northampton

Holiday Inn

★★★ 72% HOTEL

M1 Junction 18 NN6 7XR

☎ 0871 942 9059 & 01788 824800 📠 01788 823 8955

e-mail: rugbyhi@ihg.com

web: www.holidayinn.co.uk

dir: 0.5m from M1 junct 18

PETS: Bedrooms (42 GF) sign **Charges** £10 per night
Public areas except eating areas on leads **Grounds** on leads
Facilities walks info vet info **Other** charge for damage

Situated in pleasant surroundings, located just off the M1, this
modern hotel offers well-equipped and comfortable bedrooms.
Public areas include the popular Traders restaurant and a
comfortable lounge where an all-day menu is available. The Spirit
Health Club provides indoor swimming and a good fitness facility.

Rooms 90 (19 fmly) (42 GF) (12 smoking) **Facilities** STV 🎾 Gym
New Year Wi-fi **Services** Lift Air con **Parking** 250

Ibis Rugby East

BUDGET HOTEL

Parklands NN6 7EX

☎ 01788 824331 📠 01788 824332

e-mail: H3588@accor-hotels.com

web: www.ibishotel.com

dir: M1 junct 18, follow Daventry/Rugby A5 signs. At rdbt 3rd exit
signed DIRFT East. Hotel on right

PETS: Bedrooms (12 GF) **Public areas** except restaurant on
leads **Grounds** on leads **Facilities** vet info

Modern, budget hotel offering comfortable accommodation in
bright and practical bedrooms. Breakfast is self-service and
dinner is available in the café restaurant.

Rooms 111 (47 fmly) (12 GF)

DAVENTRY
Map 4 SP56

 Barceló

Barceló Daventry Hotel

★★★★ 72% HOTEL

Sedgemoor Way NN11 0SG

☎ 01327 307000 📠 01327 706313

e-mail: daventry@barcelo-hotels.co.uk

web: www.barcelo-hotels.co.uk

dir: M1 junct 16/A45 to Daventry, at 1st rdbt turn right to Kilsby/
M1(N). Hotel on right in 1m

PETS: Bedrooms unattended **Charges** £15 per night
Public areas **Grounds** on leads disp bin **Exercise area** parks
nearby **Facilities** washing facs cage storage walks info vet info
On Request fridge access torch **Other** charge for damage

This modern, striking hotel overlooking Drayton Water boasts
spacious public areas that include a good range of banqueting,
meeting and leisure facilities. It is a popular venue for
conferences. Bedrooms are suitable for both business and leisure
guests.

Rooms 155 (17 fmly) **Facilities** STV 🎾 supervised Gym Steam
room Health & beauty salon Xmas New Year Wi-fi **Services** Lift
Parking 350

HELLIDON
Map 4 SP55

 QHOTELS

Hellidon Lakes Golf & Spa Hotel

★★★★ 74% HOTEL

NN11 6GG

☎ 01327 262550 📠 01327 262559

e-mail: hellidonlakes@qhotels.co.uk

web: www.qhotels.co.uk

dir: Off A361 between Daventry & Banbury, signed

PETS: Bedrooms unattended sign **Sep accom** barn by prior
arrangement **Stables** less than 10m **Charges** contact hotel
for details **Public areas** muzzled and on leads **Grounds** on
leads disp bin **Exercise area** **Facilities** food (pre-bookable)
food bowl water bowl bedding dog chews feeding mat scoop/
disp bags leads pet sitting dog walking washing facs dog
grooming cage storage walks info vet info **On Request** fridge
access torch towels **Other** charge for damage

Some 220 acres of beautiful countryside, which include 27
holes of golf and 12 lakes, combine to form a rather spectacular
backdrop to this impressive hotel. Bedroom styles vary, from
ultra smart, modern rooms through to those in the original wing
that offer superb views. There is an extensive range of facilities
available from meeting rooms to a swimming pool, gym and
ten-pin bowling. Golfers of all levels can try some of the world's
most challenging courses on the indoor golf simulator.

Rooms 110 (5 fmly) **Facilities** Spa STV 🎾 ♪ 27 ⛳ Putt green
Fishing 🚣 Gym Beauty therapist Indoor smart golf 10-pin
bowling Steam room Coarse fishing lake Xmas New Year Wi-fi
Services Lift **Parking** 200

ENGLAND

 Campanile

Campanile Northampton

★★★ 67% HOTEL

Cheaney Dr, Grange Park NN4 5FB

☎ 01604 662599   📄 01604 622598

e-mail: northampton@campanile.com

dir: *M1 junct 15, A508 towards Northampton. 2nd exit at 1st rdbt, 2nd exit at 2nd rdbt into Grange Park*

PETS: Bedrooms Charges £5 per night on leads **Exercise area Other** charge for damage

This modern building offers accommodation in smart, well-equipped bedrooms, all with en suite bathrooms. Refreshments may be taken at the informal bistro.

Rooms 87 (18 fmly) **Facilities** STV FTV Xmas New Year Wi-fi **Services** Lift Air con **Parking** 100

Ibis Wellingborough

BUDGET HOTEL

Enstone Court NN8 2DR

☎ 01933 228333   📄 01933 228444

e-mail: H3164@accor-hotels.com

web: www.ibishotel.com

dir: *At junct of A45 & A509 towards Kettering, SW outskirts of Wellingborough*

PETS: Bedrooms (2 GF) **Public areas** except lounge & dining room **Grounds Exercise area** field nearby **Facilities** vet info

Modern, budget hotel offering comfortable accommodation in bright and practical bedrooms. Breakfast is self-service and dinner is available in the restaurant.

Rooms 78 (20 fmly) (2 GF)

Waren House

★★★ 82% 🏵 COUNTRY HOUSE HOTEL

Waren Mill NE70 7EE

☎ 01668 214581   📄 01668 214484

e-mail: enquiries@warenhousehotel.co.uk

web: www.warenhousehotel.co.uk

dir: *2m E of A1 turn onto B1342 to Waren Mill, at T-junct turn right, hotel 100yds on right*

PETS: Bedrooms (3 GF) **Public areas Grounds** on leads disp bin **Exercise area** 20mtrs **Facilities** water bowl cage storage vet info **On Request** fridge access torch towels **Other** charge for damage

This delightful Georgian mansion is set in six acres of woodland and offers a welcoming atmosphere and views of the coast. The individually themed bedrooms and suites include many with large bathrooms. Good, home-cooked food is served in the elegant dining room. A comfortable lounge and library are also available.

Rooms 15 (4 annexe) (3 GF) **S** £125-£155; **D** £140-£190 (incl. bkfst) **Facilities** FTV Xmas New Year Wi-fi **Parking** 20 **Notes** No children 14yrs

ENGLAND

BAMBURGH *continued*

Victoria

★★ 80% HOTEL

Front St NE69 7BP

☎ 01668 214431 📠 01668 214404

e-mail: enquiries@thevictoriahotelbamburgh.co.uk

web: www.thevictoriahotelbamburgh.co.uk

dir: *Off A1, N of Alnwick onto B1342, near Belford & follow signs to Bamburgh. Hotel in town centre*

PETS: Bedrooms (2 GF) unattended sign **Charges** £7.50 per night **Public areas** except restaurant on leads **Facilities** walks info **On Request** fridge access torch **Other** charge for damage

Overlooking the village green, this hotel offers an interesting blend of traditional and modern. Public areas include the Jackie Milburn sports bar with outdoor seating, the traditional lounge bar serving bar snacks, and the brasserie offering a more contemporary dinner menu. Bedrooms come in a variety of styles and sizes; some of the superior rooms have castle views.

Rooms 36 (2 fmly) (2 GF) **S** £40-£70; **D** £70-£200 (incl. bkfst) **Facilities** FTV Xmas New Year Wi-fi **Parking** 18 **Notes** LB Closed 3-8 Jan

Waren Caravan Park *(NU155343)*

▶ ▶ ▶ ▶

Waren Mill NE70 7EE

☎ 01668 214366 📠 01668 214224

e-mail: waren@meadowhead.co.uk

dir: *2m E of town. From A1 onto B1342 signed Bamburgh. Take unclass road past Waren Mill, signed Budle*

PETS: Charges £3 per night **Public areas** except public buildings & play areas disp bin **Exercise area** open field & dog walking areas **Facilities** food food bowl water bowl dog chews feeding mat scoop/disp bags leads washing facs walks info vet info **Other** prior notice required anchor pegs, shampoo & feeding mats available **Restrictions** no Rottweilers, Pit Bulls or Dobermans

Open Apr-Oct Last arrival 20.00hrs Last departure noon

Attractive seaside site with footpath access to the beach, surrounded by a slightly sloping grassy embankment giving shelter to caravans. The park offers excellent facilities including several family bathrooms. There are also wooden wigwams to rent. A 4 acre site with 180 touring pitches, 24 hardstandings and 300 statics.

Glororum Caravan Park *(NU166334)*

▶ ▶ ▶

Glororum Farm NE69 7AW

☎ 01668 214457 📠 01688 214484

dir: *Exit A1 at junct with B1341 (Purdy's Lodge). In 3.5m left onto unclass road. Site 300yds on left*

PETS: Stables 5m **Public areas** except children's play area on leads disp bin **Exercise area** dog walks **Facilities** food food bowl water bowl scoop/disp bags washing facs walks info vet info **Other** prior notice required **Restrictions** well behaved dogs only **Resident Pets:** dogs & cats

Open Mar-end Oct Last arrival 18.00hrs Last departure noon

A pleasantly situated site where tourers have their own well-established facilities. The open countryside setting affords good views of Bamburgh Castle and surrounding farmland. A 6 acre site with 100 touring pitches and 150 statics.

Notes No tents

BELFORD	Map 12 NU13

Purdy Lodge

★★ 76% HOTEL

Adderstone Services NE70 7JU

☎ 01668 213000 📠 01668 213131

e-mail: stay@purdylodge.co.uk

web: www.purdylodge.co.uk

dir: *A1 onto B1341 then immediately left*

PETS: Bedrooms (10 GF) **Public areas** except restaurant & bar on leads **Grounds** on leads **Exercise area** adjacent **Other** charge for damage

Situated off the A1, this family-owned lodge provides modern bedrooms that look out over the fields towards Bamburgh Castle. Food is readily available in the attractive restaurant, Café One, and the lounge bar. This is a great stop-off hotel where a friendly welcome is guaranteed.

Rooms 20 (4 fmly) (10 GF) **S** £54.95-£82.95; **D** £54.95-£82.95* **Facilities** FTV New Year Wi-fi **Parking** 60 **Notes** Closed 25 Dec

BELLINGHAM — Map 12 NY88

Bellingham Camping & Caravanning Club Site (NY835826)

▶ ▶ ▶ ▶

Brown Rigg NE48 2JY
☎ 01434 220175 & 0845 130 7633
dir: *From A69 take A68 N. Then B6318 to Chollerford & B6320 to Bellingham. Pass Forestry Commission land, site 0.5m S of Bellingham*

PETS: Public areas except public buildings disp bin
Exercise area 0.5m **Facilities** leads walks info vet info **Other** free disposal bags

Open 11 Mar-Oct Last arrival 20.00hrs Last departure noon

A beautiful and peaceful site set in the glorious Northumberland National Park. This is a perfect base for exploring this undiscovered part of England, and it is handily placed for visiting the beautiful Northumberland coast. A 5 acre site with 64 touring pitches, 64 hardstandings.

Notes Site gates closed 23.00hrs-07.00hrs

BERWICK-UPON-TWEED — Map 12 NT95

Ord House Country Park (NT982515)

▶ ▶ ▶ ▶ ▶

East Ord TD15 2NS
☎ 01289 305288 ▤ 01289 330832
e-mail: enquiries@ordhouse.co.uk
dir: *On A1, Berwick bypass, turn off at 2nd rdbt at East Ord, follow 'Caravan' signs*

PETS: Charges max £1.50 per night **Public areas** except club house (assist dogs only) **Exercise area** 2km walk **Facilities** food food bowl water bowl bedding dog chews cat treats walks info vet info **Other** prior notice required scoop available; dog tents for sale **Restrictions** max 1 large & 2 small dogs per family; no Rottweilers, Dobermans; no dangerous breeds (see page 7)

Open all year Last arrival 23.00hrs Last departure noon

A very well run park set in the pleasant grounds of an 18th-century country house. Touring pitches are marked and well spaced; some are fully-serviced. The very modern toilet facilities include family bath and shower suites, and first class disabled rooms. There is a six-hole golf course and an outdoor leisure shop with a good range of camping and caravanning spares, as well as clothing and equipment. A 42 acre site with 79 touring pitches, 46 hardstandings and 255 statics.

Old Mill Caravan Site (NU055401)

▶ ▶

West Kyloe Farm, Fenwick TD15 2PG
☎ 01289 381279 & 07971 411625
e-mail: teresamalley@westkyloe.demon.co.uk
dir: *Take B6353 off A1, 9m S of Berwick-upon-Tweed. Road signed to Lowick/Fenwick. Site 1.5m signed on left*

PETS: Public areas on leads disp bin **Exercise area** 600 acres farmland **Exercise area** 20yds **Facilities** walks info vet info **Resident Pets:** Buster (Dachshund), Nipper (Terrier)

Open Etr-Oct Last arrival 19.00hrs Last departure 11.00hrs

Small, secluded site accessed through a farm complex, and overlooking a mill pond complete with resident ducks. Some pitches are in a walled garden, and the amenity block is simple but well kept. Delightful walks can be enjoyed on the 600-acre farm. A 2.5 acre site with 12 touring pitches.

Notes ▣

CORNHILL-ON-TWEED — Map 12 NT83

Tillmouth Park Country House

★ ★ ★ 86% ◉ COUNTRY HOUSE HOTEL

TD12 4UU
☎ 01890 882255 ▤ 01890 882540
e-mail: reception@tillmouthpark.f9.co.uk
web: www.tillmouthpark.co.uk
dir: *Off A1(M) at East Ord rdbt at Berwick-upon-Tweed. Take A698 to Cornhill and Coldstream. Hotel 9m on left*

PETS: Bedrooms unattended **Stables** 4m **Public areas** bar only on leads **Grounds** on leads disp bin **Exercise area** **Facilities** water bowl vet info

An imposing mansion set in landscaped grounds by the River Till. Gracious public rooms include a stunning galleried lounge with a drawing room adjacent. The quiet, elegant dining room overlooks the gardens, whilst lunches and early dinners are available in the bistro. Bedrooms retain much traditional character and include several magnificent master rooms.

Rooms 14 (2 annexe) (4 smoking) **Facilities** FTV ⚓ Game shooting Fishing New Year Wi-fi **Parking** 50 **Notes** Closed 3 Jan-1 Apr

EMBLETON — Map 12 NU22

Dunstanburgh Castle Hotel
★★ 79% HOTEL
NE66 3UN
☎ 01665 576111 📄 0870 706 0394
e-mail: stay@dunstanburghcastlehotel.co.uk
web: www.dunstanburghcastlehotel.co.uk
dir: From A1, take B1340 to Denwick past Rennington & Masons Arms. Take next right signed Embleton

PETS: Bedrooms unattended Grounds disp bin Exercise area 10mtrs Facilities scoop/disp bags walks info vet info On Request fridge access torch towels Resident Pet: Uncle Bob (dog)

The focal point of the village, this friendly, family-run hotel has a dining room and grill room that offer different menus, plus a cosy bar and two lounges. In addition to the main bedrooms, a barn conversion houses three stunning suites, each with a lounge and gallery bedroom above.

Rooms 32 (12 annexe) (6 fmly) S £43.50-£49.50; D £87-£129 (incl. bkfst)* Facilities Wi-fi Parking 16 Notes LB Closed Dec-Jan

FALSTONE — Map 12 NY78

The Blackcock Inn
★★★★ INN
NE48 1AA
☎ 01434 240200
e-mail: thebcinn@yahoo.co.uk
dir: From Hexham take A6079 to Bellingham, then left at church. In village centre, towards Kielder Water

PETS: Bedrooms unattended Stables adjacent Public areas except restaurant Grounds on leads disp bin Exercise area adjacent Facilities food (pre-bookable) food bowl water bowl bedding dog chews cat treats feeding mat litter tray scoop/disp bags leads washing facs cage storage walks info vet info On Request torch Other charge for damage squeaky toys available Resident Pets: Pooch (dog), Eyefull, Banjo & Sno (cats), Rosso (rabbit), Cheese & Onion (fish)

This traditional family-run village inn lies close to Kielder Water. A cosy pub, it has a very homely atmosphere, with welcoming fires in the colder weather. The bedrooms are very comfortable and well equipped, with family rooms available. Evening meals are served here or in the cosy restaurant. The inn is closed during the day on Wednesdays throughout the winter.

Rooms 6 rms (4 en suite) (2 pri facs) (1 fmly) S £45-£60; D £60-£80* Facilities tea/coffee Dinner available Cen ht Wi-fi Fishing Pool Table Parking 15 Notes LB RS Wed Closed during low season

HEXHAM — Map 12 NY96

Hexham Racecourse Caravan Site (NY919623)
▶ ▶ ▶
Hexham Racecourse NE46 2JP
☎ 01434 606847 & 606881 📄 01434 605814
e-mail: hexrace.caravan@uku.co.uk
dir: From Hexham take B6305 signed Allendale/Alston. Left in 3m signed to racecourse. Site 1.5m on right

PETS: Public areas disp bin Exercise area Facilities vet info

Open May-Sep Last arrival 20.00hrs Last departure noon

A part-level and part-sloping grassy site situated on a racecourse overlooking Hexhamshire Moors. The facilities are functional. A 4 acre site with 40 touring pitches.

MATFEN
Map 12 NZ07

Matfen Hall
★★★★ 82% ◉◉ HOTEL

NE20 0RH
☎ 01661 886500 & 855708 🖷 01661 886055
e-mail: info@matfenhall.com
web: www.matfenhall.com
dir: *Off A69 to B6318. Hotel just before village*

PETS: Bedrooms unattended **Charges** £10 per night
Public areas except restaurant on leads **Grounds** on leads
Exercise area Facilities food (pre-bookable)

This fine mansion lies in landscaped parkland overlooking its
own golf course. Bedrooms are a blend of contemporary and
traditional, but all are very comfortable and well equipped.
Impressive public rooms include a splendid drawing room and
the elegant Library and Print Room Restaurant, as well as a
conservatory bar and very stylish spa, leisure and conference
facilities.

Rooms 53 (11 fmly) **Facilities** Spa STV FTV ⌕ supervised ⌕
27 Putt green Gym Sauna Steam room Salt grotto Ice fountain
Aerobics Driving range Golf academy Xmas Wi-fi **Services** Lift
Parking 150

OTTERBURN
Map 12 NY89

The Otterburn Tower Hotel
★★★ 78% ◉◉ HOTEL

NE19 1NS
☎ 01830 520620 🖷 01830 521504
e-mail: info@otterburntower.com
web: www.otterburntower.com
dir: *In village, on A696 (Newcastle to Edinburgh road)*

PETS: Bedrooms (2 GF) sign **Stables** at adjacent stud farm
Charges £10 per night **Public areas** except restaurant on leads
Grounds on leads disp bin **Exercise area Facilities** food (pre-
bookable) food bowl water bowl scoop/disp bags dog walking
washing facs cage storage walks info vet info **On Request**
fridge access torch towels **Other** gun dog training days
Resident Pets: Pete (Jack Russell), Logan (Springer Spaniel)

Built by the cousin of William the Conqueror, this mansion is set
in its own wooded grounds. The property is steeped in history, and
Sir Walter Scott stayed here in 1812. Bedrooms come in a variety
of sizes and some have huge ornamental fireplaces; though
furnished in period style, they are equipped with all modern
amenities. The restaurant features 16th-century oak panelling.

Rooms 18 (2 fmly) (2 GF) **S** £65; **D** £130-£190 (incl. bkfst)
Facilities STV FTV Fishing ⌕ Clay target shooting Xmas New Year
Wi-fi **Parking** 70 **Notes** LB

SEAHOUSES
Map 12 NU23

Bamburgh Castle Inn
★★★ INN

NE68 7SQ
☎ 01665 720283 🖷 01665 720284
e-mail: enquiries@bamburghcastleinn.co.uk
web: www.bamburghcastleinn.co.uk
dir: *A1 onto B1341to Bamburgh, B1340 to Seahouses, follow
signs to harbour*

PETS: Charges £5 per night **Public areas** except bar area on
leads **Grounds** on leads disp bin **Exercise area Facilities**
water bowl cage storage walks info **On Request** fridge access
torch towels

Situated in a prime location on the quayside in the popular
coastal resort of Seahouses, this establishment has arguably
the best viewpoint along the coast. Dating back to the 18th
century, the inn has been transformed in recent years to provide
superb dining and bar areas, with outside seating available in
warmer weather. There are smart, comfortable bedrooms, many
with views of the Farne Islands and the inn's famous namesake,
Bamburgh Castle.

Rooms 27 en suite 2 annexe en suite (6 fmly) (8 GF)
Facilities FTV TVL tea/coffee Dinner available Cen ht Sauna
Solarium Gym **Parking** 35 **Notes** LB

NOTTINGHAMSHIRE

HOLME PIERREPONT
Map 8 SK63

Holme Grange Cottage
★★★ GUEST ACCOMMODATION

Adbolton Ln NG12 2LU
☎ 0115 981 0413
e-mail: jean.colinwightman@talk21.com
dir: *Off A52 SE of Nottingham, opposite National Water Sports
Centre*

PETS: Bedrooms Public areas except dining room on leads
Grounds Exercise area 20yds **Facilities** cage storage vet
info **Restrictions** no Rottweilers, Pit Bulls or Ridgebacks
Resident Pet: Peggy (Cavalier King Charles Spaniel)

A stone's throw from the National Water Sports Centre, this
establishment with its own all-weather tennis court is ideal for
the active guest. Indeed, when not providing warm hospitality
and freshly cooked breakfasts, the proprietor is usually on the
golf course.

Rooms 3 rms (1 en suite) (1 fmly) **S** £30-£34; **D** £50-£54*
Facilities TVL tea/coffee Cen ht Wi-fi ⌕ **Parking** 6 **Notes** LB
Closed Xmas ⌖

Hart's Hotel

★★★★ 82% ◉◉ HOTEL

Standard Hill, Park Row NG1 6GN

☎ 0115 988 1900 📄 0115 947 7600

e-mail: reception@hartshotel.co.uk

web: www.hartsnottingham.co.uk

dir: *At junct of Park Row & Ropewalk, close to city centre*

PETS: Bedrooms (7 GF) Charges £5 per night on leads
Exercise area local walks Facilities walks info vet info
On Request fridge access torch towels Other charge for
damage Restrictions certain breeds may not be accepted, please
phone for details

This outstanding modern building stands on the site of the
ramparts of the medieval castle, overlooking the city. Many of
the bedrooms enjoy splendid views. Rooms are well appointed
and stylish, while the Park Bar is the focal point of the public
areas; service is professional and caring. Fine dining is offered at
nearby Hart's Restaurant. Secure parking and private gardens are
an added bonus.

Rooms 32 (1 fmly) (7 GF) D £120-£260* Facilities STV FTV
Gym Small unsupervised exercise room Xmas New Year Wi-fi
Services Lift Parking 19 Notes LB

Lace Market Hotel

★★★★ 75% ◉◉ TOWN HOUSE HOTEL

29-31 High Pavement NG1 1HE

☎ 0115 852 3232 📄 0115 852 3223

e-mail: stay@lacemarkethotel.co.uk

web: www.lacemarkethotel.co.uk

dir: *Follow tourist signs for Galleries of Justice. Hotel opposite*

PETS: Bedrooms Charges £15 per night Public areas in
gastro-pub only on leads Exercise area 100mtrs Facilities
water bowl cage storage walks info vet info On Request fridge
access torch towels Other charge for damage dogs must not
be left unattended at any time Restrictions small, well behaved
dogs only

This smart town house, a conversion of two Georgian houses,
is located in the trendy Lace Market area of the city. Smart
public areas, including the stylish and very popular Merchants
Restaurant and Saints Bar, are complemented by the 'Cock
and Hoop', a traditional pub offering real ales and fine wines.
Accommodation is stylish and contemporary and includes
spacious superior rooms and split-level suites; are all
thoughtfully equipped with a host of extras including CD players
and mini bars.

Rooms 42 Facilities Complimentary use of nearby health club,
including indoor pool Wi-fi Services Lift

Best Western Bestwood Lodge

★★★ 71% HOTEL

Bestwood Country Park, Arnold NG5 8NE

☎ 0115 920 3011 📄 0115 964 9678

e-mail: bestwoodlodge@btconnect.com

web: www.bw-bestwoodlodge.co.uk

dir: *3m N off A60. Left at lights into Oxclose Ln, right at next
lights into Queens Bower Rd. 1st right. Keep right at fork in road*

PETS: Bedrooms Charges £10 per night Public areas except
restaurant on leads Grounds disp bin Exercise area nearby
country park Facilities walks info vet info On Request fridge
access Other charge for damage Restrictions well behaved
dogs only

Set in 700 acres of parkland this Victorian building, once a
hunting lodge, has stunning architecture that includes Gothic
features and high vaulted ceilings. The bedrooms include modern

comforts suitable for both business and leisure guests, and the popular restaurant serves an extensive menu.

Rooms 39 (5 fmly) **S** £45-£90; **D** £70-£150 (incl. bkfst)
Facilities FTV ⌣ Guided walks Xmas Wi-fi **Parking** 120 **Notes** LB RS 25 Dec & 1 Jan

Nottingham Gateway
★★★ 68% HOTEL
Nuthall Rd, Cinderhill NG8 6AZ
☎ 0115 979 4949 📄 0115 979 4744
e-mail: sales@nottinghamgatewayhotel.co.uk
web: www.nottinghamgatewayhotel.co.uk
dir: M1 junct 26, A610, hotel on 3rd rdbt on left

PETS: Bedrooms unattended **Grounds** on leads disp bin **Exercise area** 0.25m **Facilities** cage storage vet info **On Request** fridge access **Other** charge for damage

Located approximately three miles from the city centre, and with easy access to the M1. This modern hotel provides spacious public areas, with the popular Bows Gallery Restaurant and lounge bar, and the contemporary accommodation is suitably well equipped. Ample parking is a bonus.

Rooms 108 (18 fmly) (10 smoking) **S** £52-£85; **D** £55-£100 (incl. bkfst) **Facilities** STV FTV Xmas New Year Wi-fi **Services** Lift **Parking** 250 **Notes** LB

Rutland Square Hotel
★★★ 68% HOTEL
Saint James St NG1 6FJ
☎ 0115 941 1114 📄 0115 941 0014
e-mail: rutland.square@forestdale.com
web: www.rutlandsquarehotel.co.uk
dir: Follow signs to castle. Hotel on right 50yds beyond castle

PETS: Bedrooms sign **Charges** £7.50 per night **Public areas** except bar & restaurant muzzled and on leads **Facilities** food (pre-bookable) food bowl water bowl vet info **On Request** fridge access towels **Other** charge for damage

The enviable location in the heart of the city adjacent to the castle makes this hotel a popular choice with both leisure and business travellers. The hotel is modern and comfortable with excellent business facilities. Bedrooms offer a host of thoughtful extras to guests and the penthouse has its own jacuzzi. The contemporary Woods Restaurant offers a full range of dining options.

Rooms 87 (3 fmly) **S** £55-£85; **D** £80-£115 (incl. bkfst)*
Facilities FTV Discounted day passes to nearby gym Xmas Wi-fi **Services** Lift **Parking** 30 **Notes** LB

Fairhaven
★★ GUEST ACCOMMODATION
19 Meadow Rd, Beeston NG9 1JP
☎ 0115 922 7509 📄 0870 130 4866
e-mail: info@fairhaven-hotel.com
web: www.fairhavennottingham.com
dir: A52 onto B6005 for Beeston station, 200yds after bridge

PETS: Bedrooms Exercise area 10 mins' walk **Restrictions** no Rottweilers **Resident Pet:** Kevin (dog)

This well-established guest house is in the quiet residential suburb of Beeston on the outskirts of Nottingham. The public rooms offer a stylish reception lounge, and breakfast is served in the cosy dining room. The bedrooms vary in style and size.

Rooms 14 rms (10 en suite) (1 fmly) (1 GF) **S** £27-£35; **D** £52*
Facilities tea/coffee Cen ht Licensed Wi-fi **Parking** 13

RADCLIFFE ON TRENT   **Map 8 SK63**

Thornton's Holt Camping Park (SK638377)
▶ ▶ ▶
Stragglethorpe Rd, Stragglethorpe NG12 2JZ
☎ 0115 933 2125   & 933 4204 📄 0115 933 3318
e-mail: camping@thorntons-holt.co.uk
dir: Take A52, 3m E of Nottingham. Turn S at lights towards Cropwell Bishop. Site 0.5m on left. Or A46 SE of Nottingham. N at lights. Site 2.5m on right

PETS: Public areas except swimming pool area & central toilet block **Exercise area** public footpaths **Exercise area** nearby **Facilities** washing facs walks info vet info **Resident Pets:** Pickle (Border Terrier), Sprocket, Perkins & Scrabble (cats), Eric (horse)

Open Apr-6 Nov Last arrival 20.00hrs Last departure noon

A well-run family site in former meadowland, with pitches located among young trees and bushes for a rural atmosphere and outlook. The toilets are housed in converted farm buildings, and an indoor swimming pool is a popular attraction. A 13 acre site with 155 touring pitches, 35 hardstandings.

Notes Noise curfew at 22.00hrs

ENGLAND

RETFORD (EAST)　　　　　Map 8 SK78

Best Western West Retford

★★★ 77% HOTEL

24 North Rd DN22 7XG

☎ 01777 706333　📠 01777 709951

e-mail: reservations@westretfordhotel.co.uk

web: www.westretfordhotel.co.uk

dir: *From A1 take A620 to Ranby/Retford. Left at rdbt into North Rd (A638). Hotel on right*

PETS: Bedrooms (32 GF) **Stables** 3m **Charges** £20 per night **Public areas Grounds** on leads disp bin **Exercise area** adjacent **Facilities** walks info vet info **Other** charge for damage **Restrictions** dogs accepted only at manager's discretion

Stylishly appointed throughout, and set in very attractive gardens close to the town centre, this 18th-century manor house offers a good range of well-equipped meeting facilities. The spacious, well-laid out bedrooms and suites are located in separate buildings and all offer modern facilities and comforts.

Rooms 63 (15 fmly) (32 GF) **S** £57-£97; **D** £64-£104 (incl. bkfst) **Facilities** FTV Xmas New Year Wi-fi **Parking** 150 **Notes** LB

TEVERSAL　　　　　Map 8 SK46

Teversal Camping & Caravanning Club Site

(SK472615)

▶▶▶▶▶▶

Silverhill Ln NG17 3JJ

☎ 01623 551838

dir: *M1 junct 28 onto A38 towards Mansfield. Left at lights onto B6027. At top of hill straight over at lights & left at Peacock Hotel. Right onto B6014, left at Craven Arms, site on left*

PETS: Public areas except facility block (ex assist dogs) **Exercise area** surrounding countryside **Other** prior notice required

Open all year Last arrival 20.00hrs Last departure noon

A top notch park with excellent purpose-built facilities and innovative, hands-on owners. Each pitch is spacious, the excellent toilet facilities are state-of-the-art, and there are views of and access to the countryside and nearby Silverhill Community Woods. The attention to detail and all-round quality are truly exceptional. A 6 acre site with 126 touring pitches, 92 hardstandings and 1 static.

Notes Site gates closed 23.00hrs-07.00hrs

WORKSOP　　　　　Map 8 SK57

Riverside Caravan Park *(SK582790)*

▶▶▶

Central Av S80 1ER

☎ 01909 474118

dir: *From A57 E of town, take B6040 signed Town Centre at rdbt. Follow international camping sign to site*

PETS: Public areas except toilet block on leads **Exercise area** Clumber Park 4m; Chesterfield canal walk 0.25 **Facilities** washing facs vet info **Resident Pet:** Thomas (cat)

Open all year Last arrival 18.00hrs Last departure noon

A very well maintained park in the attractive market town of Worksop and next door to the cricket/bowls club where Riverside customers are made welcome. This is an ideal park for those wishing to be within walking distance of all amenities and within a 10-minute car journey of the extensive Clumber Park and numerous good garden centres. The towpath of the adjacent Chesterfield Canal provides excellent walking opportunities. A 4 acre site with 60 touring pitches, 59 hardstandings.

Notes No bikes around reception or in toilet block

OXFORDSHIRE

BANBURY　　　　　Map 4 SP44

Fairlawns

★★★ GUEST ACCOMMODATION

60 Oxford Rd OX16 9AN

☎ 01295 262461　& 07831 330220　📠 01295 261296

e-mail: fairlawnsgh@aol.com

dir: *0.5m S of town centre on A4260 near hospital*

PETS: Bedrooms Grounds disp bin **Exercise area** park nearby **Facilities** vet info **On Request** fridge access torch towels **Other** charge for damage **Resident Pets:** Rosie (Boxer), Harley (cat)

This extended Edwardian house retains many original features and has a convenient location. Bedrooms are mixed in size, and all are neatly furnished, some with direct access to the car park. A comprehensive breakfast is served in the traditional dining room and a selection of soft drinks and snacks is also available.

Rooms 11 rms (10 en suite) 6 annexe en suite (5 fmly) (9 GF) **S** £35-£52; **D** £45-£62* **Facilities** tea/coffee Direct Dial Cen ht Wi-fi **Parking** 17

Barnstones Caravan & Camping Site

(SP455454)

▶ ▶ ▶ ▶

Great Bourton OX17 1QU

☎ 01295 750289

dir: *Take A423 from Banbury signed Southam. In 3m turn right signed Gt Bourton/Cropredy, site 100yds on right*

PETS: Public areas disp bin **Exercise area** fenced area (off lead) **Facilities** washing facs dog grooming walks info vet info

Open all year

Popular, neatly laid-out site with plenty of hardstandings, some fully serviced pitches, a smart up-to-date toilet block, and excellent rally facilities. Well run by personable owner. A 3 acre site with 49 touring pitches, 44 hardstandings.

Notes

Bo Peep Farm Caravan Park (SP481348)

▶ ▶ ▶ ▶

Bo Peep Farm, Aynho Rd, Adderbury OX17 3NP

☎ 01295 810605   📠 01295 810605

e-mail: warden@bo-peep.co.uk

dir: *1m E of Adderbury & A4260, on B4100 (Aynho road)*

PETS: Charges dog £1 per stay **Public areas** on leads disp bin **Exercise area** extensive walks **Facilities** food food bowl water bowl dog chews cat treats scoop/disp bags leads washing facs walks info vet info **Resident Pets:** 3 cats

Open Mar-Oct Last arrival 20.00hrs Last departure noon

A delightful park with good views and a spacious feel. Four well laid out camping areas including two with hardstandings and a separate tent field are all planted with maturing shrubs and trees. The two facility blocks are in attractive Cotswold stone. Unusually there is a bay in which you can clean your caravan or motorhome. There are four miles of on-site walks including woods and river bank. A 13 acre site with 104 touring pitches.

BLETCHINGDON   **Map 4 SP51**

The Oxfordshire Inn

★ ★ ★   72% HOTEL

Heathfield Village OX5 3DX

☎ 01869 351444   📠 01869 351555

e-mail: staff@oxfordshireinn.co.uk

web: www.oxfordshireinn.co.uk

dir: *M40 junct 9, A34 towards Oxford, then A4027 towards Bletchingdon. Hotel signed 0.7m on right*

PETS: Bedrooms (15 GF) unattended **Stables** adjacent **Charges** £10 per night **Grounds** on leads disp bin **Exercise area** Large grounds & fields surrounding **Facilities** vet info **Other** charge for damage

A converted farmhouse with additional outbuildings that is located close to major motorway networks. Accommodation is set around an open courtyard, and includes suites that have four-poster beds. There is a spacious bar and restaurant.

Rooms 28 (4 fmly) (15 GF) **S** £59-£94; **D** £69-£101 (incl. bkfst)* **Facilities** Putt green Golf driving range Xmas New Year Wi-fi **Parking** 50 **Notes** LB

Greenhill Leisure Park (SP488178)

▶ ▶ ▶ ▶

Greenhill Farm, Station Rd OX5 3BQ

☎ 01869 351600   📠 01869 350918

e-mail: info@greenhill-leisure-park.co.uk

dir: *M40 junct 9, A34 south for 3m. Take B4027 to Bletchingdon. Site 0.5m after village on left*

PETS: Charges dog £3 per night **Public areas** except play area, shower area & games room disp bin **Exercise area** fenced area of field **Exercise area** 1m **Facilities** food leads walks info vet info **Other** disposal bags available **Restrictions** no pets Oct-Mar

Open all year rs Oct-Mar shop & games room closed Last arrival 21.00hrs Last departure noon

An all-year round park set in open countryside near the village of Bletchingdon. Fishing is available in the nearby river, and the park has its own farm shop. It makes an ideal base for touring the Cotswolds and Oxford. A 7 acre site with 61 touring pitches, 25 hardstandings.

Notes No camp fires, latest arrival time in winter 20.00hrs.

The Lamb Inn

★★★ **83%** SMALL HOTEL

COTSWOLD
INNS & HOTELS

Sheep St OX18 4LR
☎ 01993 823155 📄 01993 822228
e-mail: info@lambinn-burford.co.uk
web: www.cotswold-inns-hotels.co.uk/lamb
dir: A40 into Burford, downhill, 1st left into Sheep St, hotel last on right

PETS: Bedrooms (4 GF) **Public areas** except eating areas **Grounds** on leads **Exercise area** footpaths **Facilities** cage storage walks info vet info **On Request** fridge access torch towels **Other** charge for damage

This enchanting old inn is just a short walk from the centre of this delightful Cotswold village. Inside, an abundance of character and charm is found in the cosy lounge with log fire, and intimate bar with flagged floors. An elegant restaurant offers locally sourced produce in carefully prepared dishes. Bedrooms, some with original features, are comfortable and well appointed.

Rooms 17 (1 fmly) (4 GF) **D** £150-£175 (incl. bkfst)* **Facilities** Xmas New Year Wi-fi

The Bay Tree Hotel

★★★ **81%** HOTEL

COTSWOLD
INNS & HOTELS

Sheep St OX18 4LW
☎ 01993 822791 📄 01993 823008
e-mail: info@baytreehotel.info
web: www.cotswold-inns-hotels.co.uk/bay-tree
dir: A40 or A361 to Burford. From High St turn into Sheep St, next to old market square. Hotel on right

PETS: Bedrooms Charges Public areas except eating areas **Grounds Facilities** cage storage walks info vet info **On Request** torch towels **Other** charge for damage

The modern decorative style combines seamlessly with features from this delightful inn's long history. Bedrooms are tastefully furnished and some have four-poster and half-tester beds. Public areas consist of a character bar, a sophisticated airy restaurant, a selection of meeting rooms and an attractive walled garden.

Rooms 21 (13 annexe) (2 fmly) **D** £165-£175 (incl. bkfst)* **Facilities** ⛲ Xmas New Year Wi-fi **Parking** 50

The Angel at Burford

★★★★ 🍴 RESTAURANT WITH ROOMS

14 Witney St OX18 4SN
☎ 01993 822714 📄 01993 822069
e-mail: paul@theangelatburford.co.uk
web: www.theangelatburford.co.uk
dir: Exit A40 at Burford rdbt, down hill, 1st right into Swan Ln, 1st left to Pytts Ln, left at end into Witney St

PETS: Bedrooms Public areas except restaurant on leads **Grounds** on leads disp bin **Exercise area** 500yds **Facilities** food bowl water bowl dog chews feeding mat scoop/disp bags washing facs walks info vet info **On Request** fridge access torch towels **Restrictions** no Pit Bull Terriers

Once a coaching inn, built in the 16th century, this establishment is situated in the centre of Burford, the 'Gateway to the Cotswolds'. Three attractively decorated en suite bedrooms offer plentiful accessories and share a cosy residents' lounge. The award-winning restaurant is open for lunch and dinner. The peaceful courtyard and walled garden are perfect for relaxing in the summer.

Rooms 3 en suite **Facilities** tea/coffee Dinner available Direct Dial Cen ht Wi-fi **Notes** No Children 9yrs RS Mon & Sun eve No coaches

Tulip Tree House

★★★ BED AND BREAKFAST

Church St OX7 3PP
☎ 01608 810609 📄 01608 810609
dir: A44 onto B4437 into Charlbury, turn onto Church St, behind Bell Hotel

PETS: Bedrooms Public areas Grounds disp bin

Tucked away in the market town of Charlbury, this charming property offers nicely appointed rooms, with good standards of comfort. Breakfast is served in the bright conservatory overlooking the well-tended gardens, which help to create a peaceful and charming atmosphere.

Rooms 3 rms (2 en suite) (1 pri facs) (1 fmly) **S** £58; **D** £75-£85* **Facilities** FTV TVL tea/coffee Cen ht **Parking** 4 **Notes** LB

DORCHESTER (ON THAMES)　　Map 4 SU59

White Hart Hotel

★★★ 77% ◉ HOTEL

High St OX10 7HN

☎ 01865 340074　🖹 01865 341082

e-mail: whitehart@oxfordshire-hotels.co.uk

web: www.oxfordshire-hotels.co.uk

dir: M40 junct 6, B4009 through Watlington & Benson to A4074. Follow Dorchester signs. Hotel on right

PETS: Bedrooms (9 GF) unattended **Charges** £10 per night **Public areas** except bar & restaurant on leads **Grounds** on leads **Exercise area** 200mtrs **Facilities** food bowl water bowl walks info vet info **On Request** fridge access torch towels **Other** charge for damage

Period charm and character are plentiful throughout this 17th-century coaching inn, which is situated in the heart of a picturesque village. The spacious bedrooms are individually decorated and thoughtfully equipped. Public rooms include a cosy bar, a choice of lounges and an atmospheric restaurant, complete with vaulted timber ceiling.

Rooms 26 (4 annexe) (2 fmly) (9 GF) **Facilities** Xmas Wi-fi **Parking** 36

FARINGDON　　Map 4 SU29

Best Western Sudbury House Hotel & Conference Centre

★★★ 74% HOTEL

London St SN7 8AA

☎ 01367 241272　🖹 01367 242346

e-mail: stay@sudburyhouse.co.uk

web: www.sudburyhouse.co.uk

dir: Off A420, signed Folly Hill

PETS: Bedrooms (10 GF) unattended **Charges** £10 per night **Public areas** except restaurant & bar area **Grounds** disp bin **Exercise area Facilities** food bowl water bowl washing facs cage storage walks info vet info **On Request** fridge access torch towels **Other** charge for damage

Situated on the edge of the Cotswolds and set in nine acres of pleasant grounds, this hotel offers spacious and well-equipped bedrooms that are attractively decorated in warm colours. Dining options include the comfortable restaurant for a good selection of carefully presented dishes, and also the bar for lighter options. A comprehensive room service menu is available.

Rooms 49 (2 fmly) (10 GF) (2 smoking) **Facilities** STV 🏊 Gym Boules New Year Wi-fi **Services** Lift **Parking** 100

Chowle Farmhouse Bed & Breakfast (SU272925)

★★★★ FARMHOUSE

SN7 7SR

☎ 01367 241688　Mr & Mrs Muir

e-mail: info@chowlefarmhouse.co.uk

web: www.chowlefarmhouse.co.uk

dir: From Faringdon rdbt on A420, 2m W on right. From Watchfield rdbt 1.5m E on left

PETS: Bedrooms Stables Public areas except dining rooms & upstairs on leads **Grounds** on leads disp bin **Exercise area** fields adjacent **Facilities** feeding mat scoop/disp bags leads washing facs cage storage walks info vet info **On Request** fridge access torch towels **Other** pets allowed in one bedroom only (ground floor) **Resident Pets:** Susie (Yellow Labrador), Winston (Black Labrador), Angus, Lulu, Marvin, Denzel & Lola (cats), Dexter cows, guinea pigs, ferrets, chickens, guinea fowl, quail, tropical fish

Chowle is a delightful modern farmhouse in a quiet setting, just off the A420 and ideally placed for visiting Oxford and Swindon. Bedrooms are very well equipped, and there is a charming and airy downstairs breakfast room. An outdoor pool and jacuzzi are available to guests. Dinner is available, although pre-booking is preferred. There is ample parking space.

Rooms 4 en suite (1 GF) **S** fr £65; **D** fr £85 **Facilities** FTV tea/coffee Dinner available Cen ht Wi-fi ⚡ Golf 9 ⚓ Fishing Riding Sauna Gym **Parking** 10 **Notes** LB 10 acres Pedigree Beef Cattle

GORING　　Map 4 SU68

The Miller of Mansfield

★★★★★ ◉ RESTAURANT WITH ROOMS

High St RG8 9AW

☎ 01491 872829　🖹 01491 873100

e-mail: reservations@millerofmansfield.com

web: www.millerofmansfield.com

dir: M40 junct 7, S on A329 towards Benson, A4074 towards Reading, B4009 towards Goring. Or M4 junct 12, S on A4 towards Newbury. 3rd rdbt onto A340 to Pangbourne. A329 to Streatley, right at rdbt onto B4009 into Goring

PETS: Bedrooms unattended **Charges Public areas** except restaurant **Grounds Exercise area** approx 0.5m **Facilities** water bowl cage storage walks info vet info **On Request** torch towels **Other** charge for damage

The frontage of this former coaching inn hides sumptuous rooms with a distinctive and individual style, an award-winning restaurant that serves appealing dishes using locally sourced ingredients and a comfortable bar, which serves real ales, fine wines, afternoon tea and a bar menu for a quick bite to eat.

Rooms 13 en suite (2 fmly) **Facilities** FTV tea/coffee Dinner available Direct Dial Cen ht Wi-fi **Parking** 2 **Notes** LB

Hotel du Vin Henley-on-Thames
★★★★ 76% ◉◉ TOWN HOUSE HOTEL

New St RG9 2BP
☎ 01491 848400   📠 01491 848401
e-mail: info@henley.hotelduvin.com
web: www.hotelduvin.com
dir: *M4 junct 8/9 signed High Wycombe, 2nd exit onto A404 in 2m. A4130 into Henley, over bridge, through lights, up Hart St, right onto Bell St, right onto New St, hotel on right*

PETS: Bedrooms (4 GF) **Charges** £10 per night £70 per week **Public areas** except restaurant on leads **Grounds** on leads **Exercise area Facilities** food bowl water bowl bedding vet info **On Request** torch

Situated just 50 yards from the water's edge, this hotel retains the character and much of the architecture of the former brewery. Food, and naturally wine, take on a strong focus here and guests will find an interesting mix of dishes to choose from; there are three private dining rooms where the fermentation room and old malt house used to be; alfresco dining is popular when the weather permits. Bedrooms provide comfort, style and a good range of facilities including power showers. Parking is available and there is a drop-off point in the courtyard.

Rooms 43 (4 fmly) (4 GF) **Facilities** STV Use of local spa & gym Xmas New Year Wi-fi **Services** Air con **Parking** 36

The Baskerville
★★★★ INN

Station Rd, Lower Shiplake RG9 3NY
☎ 0118 940 3332
e-mail: enquiries@thebaskerville.com
dir: *2m S of Henley in Lower Shiplake. Off A4155 onto Station Rd, inn signed*

PETS: Bedrooms unattended **Stables** nearby **Charges Public areas** except public bar on leads **Grounds** on leads **Exercise area** village lanes & riverbanks nearby **Facilities** water bowl cage storage vet info **Other** charge for damage

Located close to Shiplake station and just a short drive from Henley, this smart accommodation is perfect for a business or leisure break. It is a good base for exploring the Oxfordshire countryside, and the enjoyable hearty meals served in the cosy restaurant use good local produce.

Rooms 4 en suite (1 fmly) **S** £75; **D** £85* **Facilities** tea/coffee Dinner available Cen ht Wi-fi **Parking** 15 **Notes** RS 23 Dec-2 Jan room only No coaches

Mill House Hotel & Restaurant
★★★ 78% ◉ HOTEL

OX7 6UH
☎ 01608 658188   📠 01608 658492
e-mail: stay@millhousehotel.co.uk
web: www.millhousehotel.co.uk
dir: *Off A44 onto B4450. Hotel signed*

PETS: Bedrooms (7 GF) unattended **Stables** 4m **Charges Grounds** disp bin **Exercise area** 7-acre grounds **Facilities** food (pre-bookable) food bowl water bowl scoop/disp bags cage storage walks info vet info **On Request** fridge access torch towels **Other** charge for damage

This Cotswold-stone, former mill house is a stylish and peaceful hotel, set in well-kept grounds bordered by its own trout stream. The individually designed bedrooms are very comfortable and provide thoughtfully equipped facilities; most rooms have lovely views out over the extensive lawned gardens to the Cotswold Hills beyond. There is a peaceful lounge and bar, plus an atmospheric restaurant. The hotel is a popular venue for weddings.

Rooms 23 (2 annexe) (1 fmly) (7 GF) **S** £65-£85; **D** £80-£100 (incl. bkfst)* **Facilities** STV FTV Fishing ⛳ Xmas New Year Wi-fi Child facilities **Parking** 62 **Notes** LB

Moat End

★ ★ ★ ★ 🏠 BED AND BREAKFAST

The Moat OX7 6XZ

☎ 01608 658090 & 07765 278399

e-mail: moatend@gmail.com

web: www.moatend.co.uk

dir: Off B4450/A436 into village centre

PETS: Bedrooms Stables Charges dog £10 per stay; horse £15 per night (stabling, turn out & hay) **Public areas** on leads **Grounds** on leads disp bin **Facilities** washing facs cage storage walks info vet info **On Request** fridge access torch towels **Resident Pets:** Domino (cat), Heather, Cobweb & Rolo (ponies)

The converted barn lies in a peaceful Cotswold village and has splendid country views. Its well-appointed bedrooms either have a jacuzzi or large shower cubicles (one has hydro-massage jets). The attractive dining room leads to a comfortable beamed sitting room with a stone fireplace. Quality local ingredients are used in the wholesome breakfasts. The owner has won an award for green tourism by reducing the impact of the business on the environment.

Rooms 3 en suite (1 fmly) **S** £50-£65; **D** £68-£75 **Facilities** TVL tea/coffee Cen ht Wi-fi **Parking** 4 **Notes** LB Closed Xmas & New Year 🐾

The Tollgate Inn & Restaurant

★ ★ ★ ★ 🍴 INN

Church St OX7 6YA

☎ 01608 658389

e-mail: info@thetollgate.com

PETS: Bedrooms unattended **Charges** £10 per stay **Public areas** except restaurant & lounge on leads **Grounds Exercise area Facilities** walks info vet info **On Request** fridge access **Other** please phone for further details of pet facilities **Resident Pets:** Guinness (Black Labrador), Tinker (cat)

Situated in the idyllic Cotswold village of Kingham, this Grade II listed Georgian building has been lovingly restored to provide a complete home-from-home among some of the most beautiful countryside in Britain. The Tollgate provides comfortable, well-equipped accommodation in pleasant surroundings. A good choice of menu for lunch and dinner is available with much use made of fresh and local produce. Guests can also be sure of a hearty breakfast provided in the modern, well-equipped dining room.

Rooms 5 en suite 4 annexe en suite (1 fmly) (4 GF) **Facilities** tea/coffee Dinner available Cen ht Wi-fi **Parking** 12

The Oxford Belfry

QHOTELS

★ ★ ★ ★ 76% HOTEL

OX9 2JW

☎ 01844 279381 📠 01844 279624

e-mail: oxfordbelfry@qhotels.co.uk

web: www.qhotels.co.uk

dir: M40 junct 7 onto A329 to Thame. Left onto A40, hotel 300yds on right

PETS: Bedrooms (66 GF) unattended sign **Charges** £15 per night £105 per week **Public areas** except food areas (assist dogs only) on leads **Grounds** on leads **Exercise area** fields adjacent **Facilities** walks info vet info **On Request** torch **Other** charge for damage **Restrictions** max 2 small or 1 large dog per guest

This modern hotel has a relatively rural location and enjoys lovely views of the countryside to the rear. The hotel is built around two very attractive courtyards and has a number of lounges and conference rooms, as well as indoor leisure facilities and outdoor tennis courts. Bedrooms are large and feature a range of extras.

Rooms 154 (20 fmly) (66 GF) **S** £79-£175; **D** £89-£185 (incl. bkfst) **Facilities** Spa STV 🏊 🎾 Gym Steam room Sauna Aerobics studio Xmas New Year Wi-fi **Services** Lift **Parking** 350 **Notes** LB

Barceló Oxford Hotel

Barceló HOTELS & RESORTS

★ ★ ★ ★ 76% HOTEL

Godstow Rd, Wolvercote Roundabout OX2 8AL

☎ 01865 489988 📠 01865 489952

e-mail: oxford@barcelo-hotels.co.uk

web: www.barcelo-hotels.co.uk

dir: Adjacent to A34/A40, 2m from city centre

PETS: Bedrooms (89 GF) sign **Charges** £15 per night **Grounds** on leads **Exercise area** at rear of hotel, canal walk (1m) **Facilities** walks info vet info **Other** charge for damage **Restrictions** small dogs only

Conveniently located on the northern edge of the city centre, this purpose-built hotel offers bedrooms that are bright, modern and well equipped. Guests can eat in the Medio Restaurant or try the Cappuccino Lounge menu. There is the option to eat alfresco on the Patio Terrace when the weather is fine. The hotel offers impressive conference, business and leisure facilities.

Rooms 168 (11 fmly) (89 GF) **Facilities** Spa STV 🏊 supervised Gym Squash Steam room Beauty treatments New Year Wi-fi **Parking** 250

OXFORD *continued*

Old Parsonage

★★★★ 75% TOWN HOUSE HOTEL

1 Banbury Rd OX2 6NN

☎ 01865 310210 📄 01865 311262

e-mail: info@oldparsonage-hotel.co.uk

web: www.oldparsonage-hotel.co.uk

dir: *From Oxford ring road to city centre via Summertown. Hotel last building on right*

PETS: Bedrooms (10 GF) unattended **Charges Public areas** except restaurant on leads **Grounds Exercise area** 2 mins walk **Facilities** food (pre-bookable) food bowl water bowl bedding leads pet sitting dog walking cage storage walks info vet info **On Request** torch towels **Other** charge for damage dog baskets available & special menus on request **Restrictions** well behaved dogs only

Dating back in parts to the 16th century, this stylish hotel offers great character and charm and is conveniently located at the northern edge of the city centre. Bedrooms are attractively styled and particularly well appointed. The focal point of the operation is the busy all-day bar and restaurant; the small garden areas and terraces prove popular in summer months.

Rooms 30 (4 fmly) (10 GF) **D** £135-£214.50* **Facilities** STV FTV Beauty treatments Free use of nearby leisure facilities, punt & house bikes ♫ Xmas New Year Wi-fi **Services** Air con **Parking** 14 **Notes** LB

Westwood Country Hotel

★★★ 78% HOTEL

Hinksey Hill, Boars Hill OX1 5BG

☎ 01865 735408 📄 01865 736536

e-mail: reservations@westwoodhotel.co.uk

web: www.westwoodhotel.co.uk

dir: *Off Oxford ring road at Hinksey Hill junct towards Boars Hill & Wootton. At top of hill road bends to left. Hotel on right*

PETS: Bedrooms (7 GF) **Charges** £100 deposit + £15 per night **Grounds** on leads **Exercise area** 50mtrs **Other** charge for damage **Restrictions** small dogs only

This Edwardian country-house hotel is prominently set in terraced landscaped grounds and is within easy reach of the city centre by car. The hotel is modern in style with very comfortable, well-equipped and tastefully decorated bedrooms. Public areas include a contemporary bar, a cosy lounge and a restaurant overlooking the pretty garden.

Rooms 20 (5 fmly) (7 GF) **S** £70-£110; **D** £95-£135 (incl. bkfst)* **Facilities** FTV Arrangement with local health club, golf club & riding school Xmas New Year Wi-fi **Parking** 50 **Notes** LB

Bath Place Hotel

★★ 58% METRO HOTEL

4-5 Bath Place, Holywell St OX1 3SU

☎ 01865 791812 📄 01865 791834

e-mail: info@bathplace.co.uk

dir: *On S side of Holywell St (parallel to High St)*

PETS: Bedrooms (4 GF) **Charges** £10 per night **Public areas** except dining room on leads **Exercise area** park 500mtrs **Facilities** water bowl walks info vet info **Other** charge for damage **Resident Pet:** Hamish (Border Terrier)

The hotel has been created from a group of 17th-century cottages originally built by Flemish weavers who were permitted to settle outside the city walls. This lovely hotel is very much at the heart of the city today and offers individually designed bedrooms, including some with four-posters.

Rooms 15 (3 fmly) (4 GF) **Facilities** FTV Wi-fi **Parking** 15

OXFORD MOTORWAY SERVICE AREA (M40)   Map 4 SP60

Days Inn Oxford

BUDGET HOTEL

M40 junction 8A, Waterstock OX33 1LJ

☎ 01865 877000 📄 01865 877016

e-mail: oxford.hotel@welcomebreak.co.uk

web: www.welcomebreak.co.uk

dir: *M40 junct 8a, at Welcome Break service area*

PETS: Bedrooms (25 GF) **Public areas** on leads **Grounds** on leads disp bin **Exercise area** adjacent **Facilities** cage storage vet info **On Request** fridge access

This modern building offers accommodation in smart, spacious and well-equipped bedrooms, suitable for families and business travellers, and all with en suite bathrooms. Continental breakfast is available and other refreshments may be taken at the nearby family restaurant.

Rooms 59 (56 fmly) (25 GF) (10 smoking) **S** £29-£79; **D** £29-£79*

STANDLAKE — Map 4 SP30

Lincoln Farm Park Oxfordshire *(SP395028)*

▶ ▶ ▶ ▶ ▶

High St OX29 7RH

☎ 01865 300239 📠 01865 300127

e-mail: info@lincolnfarmpark.co.uk

dir: *In village of Standlake off A415 between Abingdon & Witney, 5m SE of Witney*

PETS: Charges £1.25 per night **Public areas** except children's play area on leads disp bin **Exercise area** 2 small dog runs **Facilities** food food bowl water bowl bedding dog chews cat treats litter tray scoop/disp bags leads walks info vet info **Other** prior notice required **Resident Pets:** Chance (Border Collie), 2 Giant Continental rabbits, 4 rabbits, free range chickens

Open Feb-Nov Last arrival 20.00hrs Last departure noon

An attractively landscaped park in a quiet village setting, with superb facilities and a high standard of maintenance. Family rooms, fully-serviced pitches, two indoor swimming pools and a fully-equipped gym are part of the comprehensive amenities. A 9 acre site with 90 touring pitches, 75 hardstandings.

Notes No gazebos, no noise after 23.00hrs

WALLINGFORD — Map 4 SU68

The Springs Hotel & Golf Club

★ ★ ★ 80% ◉ HOTEL

Wallingford Rd, North Stoke OX10 6BE

☎ 01491 836687 📠 01491 836877

e-mail: info@thespringshotel.com

web: www.thespringshotel.com

dir: *Off A4074 (Oxford-Reading road) onto B4009 (Goring). Hotel approx 1m on right*

PETS: Bedrooms (10 GF) **Charges** £10 per night **Grounds** on leads **Exercise area** **Facilities** vet info **Other** charge for damage dogs allowed in certain bedrooms only

Set on its own 18-hole, par 72 golf course, this Victorian mansion has a timeless and peaceful atmosphere. The generously equipped, individually styled bedrooms vary in size but many are spacious. Some bedrooms overlook the pool and grounds while others have views of the spring-fed lake as does the elegant restaurant. There is also a comfortable lounge, with original features, to relax in.

Rooms 32 (3 fmly) (10 GF) **S** £90-£95; **D** £105-£155 (incl. bkfst)* **Facilities** FTV ⚲ ⚑ 18 Putt green Fishing 🚣 Clay pigeon shooting/horse riding nearby Boat trips from mooring on Thames Xmas New Year Wi-fi **Parking** 150

Shillingford Bridge

★ ★ ★ 74% HOTEL

Shillingford OX10 8LZ

☎ 01865 858567 📠 01865 858636

e-mail: shillingford.bridge@forestdale.com

web: www.shillingfordbridgehotel.com

dir: *M4 junct 12, A4 towards Newbury, A340 to Pangbourne, A329 to Winterbrook rdbt take unclassified road to Wallingford, straight on at lights towards Oxford. Hotel 1.5m. Or M40 junct 6, B4009 through Watlington & Benson, right onto A4074, left at Shillingford rdbt towards Wallingford. Hotel 0.5m*

PETS: Bedrooms (9 GF) unattended sign **Charges** £7.50 per night **Public areas** except restaurant on leads **Grounds** on leads disp bin **Facilities** food (pre-bookable) food bowl water bowl washing facs cage storage walks info vet info **On Request** fridge access torch towels **Other** charge for damage

This hotel enjoys a superb position right on the banks of the River Thames, and benefits from private moorings and has a waterside open-air swimming pool. Public areas are stylish with a contemporary feel and have large picture windows making the best use of the view. Bedrooms are well equipped and furnished with guest comfort in mind.

Rooms 40 (8 annexe) (6 fmly) (9 GF) **S** £60-£100; **D** £80-£140 (incl. bkfst)* **Facilities** FTV ⚲ supervised Fishing Table tennis 🎵 Xmas New Year Wi-fi **Parking** 100 **Notes** LB

WANTAGE — Map 4 SU38

Hill Barn *(SU337852)*

★ ★ ★ FARMHOUSE

Sparholt Firs OX12 9XB

☎ 01235 751236 & 07885 368918 Mrs Joanna Whittington

e-mail: jmw@hillbarn.plus.com

PETS: Bedrooms unattended **Stables Charges** dog £5, horse £10 per night **Public areas Grounds** disp bin **Exercise area** adjacent **Facilities** food (pre-bookable) food bowl water bowl scoop/disp bags leads pet sitting dog walking washing facs cage storage walks info vet info **On Request** fridge access towels **Other** charge for damage

This working farm offers en suite bedrooms with beautiful distant views over the countryside. The atmosphere is friendly, and guests are able to relax either in the sitting room or in the garden. Breakfast is a highlight with home-made jams and produce from the farm when available.

Rooms 2 en suite; **D** £70 **Facilities** TVL tea/coffee Dinner available Cen ht **Parking** 3 **Notes** LB ◉ 100 acres Horses

ENGLAND

The Fleece
★★★ INN

11 Church Green OX28 4AZ
☎ 01993 892270   📠 0871 8130458
e-mail: fleece@peachpubs.com
dir: A40 to Witney town centre, on Church Green

PETS: Bedrooms unattended Charges £10 per night £70 per week Public areas Grounds disp bin Exercise area village green Facilities water bowl washing facs cage storage walks info vet info On Request fridge access towels Other please ask about any specific pet requirements

Set in the centre of Witney overlooking the church green, The Fleece offers ten well equipped en suite modern bedrooms. The popular destination pub offers food all day including breakfast, and a great selection of wines and real ales.

Rooms 7 en suite 3 annexe en suite (1 fmly) (1 GF) Facilities tea/coffee Dinner available Direct Dial Cen ht Wi-fi Parking 12 Notes Closed 25 Dec

The Feathers Hotel
★★★★ 78% ◉◉ HOTEL

Market St OX20 1SX
☎ 01993 812291   📠 01993 813158
e-mail: enquiries@feathers.co.uk
dir: From A44 (Oxford to Woodstock), 1st left after lights. Hotel on left

PETS: Bedrooms (2 GF) unattended Stables 1m Charges £15 per night Public areas except restaurant on leads Grounds on leads disp bin Exercise area 0.5m Facilities food bowl water bowl bedding washing facs cage storage walks info vet info On Request fridge access torch towels Other charge for damage Resident Pet: Johann (African Grey parrot)

This intimate and unique hotel enjoys a town centre location with easy access to nearby Blenheim Palace. Public areas are elegant and full of traditional character from the cosy drawing room to the atmospheric restaurant. Individually styled bedrooms are appointed to a high standard and are furnished with attractive period and reproduction furniture.

Rooms 21 (5 annexe) (4 fmly) (2 GF) D £195-£315 (incl. bkfst)* Facilities FTV Xmas New Year Wi-fi Notes LB

Macdonald Bear
★★★★ 76% ◉◉ HOTEL

Park St OX20 1SZ
☎ 0844 879 9143   📠 01993 813380
e-mail: gm.bear@macdonaldhotels.co.uk
web: www.macdonaldhotels.co.uk
dir: M40 junct 9 follow signs for Oxford & Blenheim Palace. A44 to town centre hotel on left

PETS: Bedrooms (8 GF) unattended sign Charges £10 per night Public areas except restaurant on leads disp bin Exercise area Facilities water bowl bedding cage storage walks info On Request fridge access torch towels Other charge for damage Restrictions small dogs only

With its ivy-clad façade, oak beams and open fireplaces, this 13th-century coaching inn exudes charm and cosiness. The bedrooms are decorated in a modern style that remains in keeping with the historic character of the building. Public rooms include a variety of function rooms, an intimate bar area and an attractive restaurant where attentive service and good food are offered.

Rooms 54 (18 annexe) (1 fmly) (8 GF) Facilities STV Xmas New Year Wi-fi Parking 40

Beech House
★★★★ ◉◉ ⌂ INN

Main St LE15 7SH
☎ 01780 410355   📠 01780 410000
e-mail: rooms@theolivebranchpub.com
dir: From A1 take B668 signed Stretton & Clipsham

PETS: Bedrooms Charges £10 per night Public areas bar only on leads Grounds on leads Exercise area field 200mtrs Facilities water bowl washing facs walks info vet info On Request fridge access towels Other charge for damage dogs allowed in ground-floor bedrooms only

Beech House stands over the road from the Olive Branch restaurant. It offers very well furnished bedrooms which include DVD players. Breakfasts are served in the Olive Branch. Excellent lunches and dinners are also available.

Rooms 5 en suite 1 annexe en suite (2 fmly) (3 GF) S £95-£170; D £110-£190* Facilities tea/coffee Dinner available Direct Dial Cen ht Wi-fi Parking 10 Notes No coaches

EMPINGHAM — Map 4 SK90

The White Horse Inn
★★★ INN

Main St LE15 8PS
☎ 01780 460221 ▤ 01780 460521
e-mail: info@whitehorserutland.co.uk
web: www.whitehorserutland.co.uk
dir: On A606 (Oakham to Stamford road)

PETS: Bedrooms unattended **Charges** £5 per night **Grounds**
Exercise area 10 min walk **Facilities** cage storage walks info
vet info **On Request** fridge access **Resident Pet:** Tia (Chocolate
Labrador)

This attractive stone-built inn, offering bright, comfortable
accommodation, is conveniently located just minutes from the
A1. Bedrooms in the main building are spacious and include a
number of family rooms. Public areas include a well-stocked bar,
a bistro and restaurant where a wide range of meals is served.

Rooms 4 en suite 9 annexe en suite (3 fmly) (5 GF) **S** £53-£63;
D £70-£90* **Facilities** TVL tea/coffee Dinner available Direct Dial
Parking 60 **Notes** Closed 25 Dec

GREETHAM — Map 8 SK91

Rutland Caravan & Camping (SK925148)
▶▶▶▶

Park Ln LE15 7FN
☎ 01572 813520
e-mail: info@rutlandcaravanandcamping.co.uk
dir: From A1 onto B668 towards Greetham. Before Greetham turn
right at x-rds, 2nd left to site

PETS: Charges Public areas except children's play area on
leads disp bin **Exercise area** 2.5-acre area for dog walking
Facilities washing facs walks info vet info **Other** dog wash area
with shower; disposal bags available

Open all year

A pretty caravan park built to a high specification, and
surrounded by well-planted banks which will provide good
screening. The spacious grassy site is close to the Viking Way and
other footpath networks, and well sited for visiting Rutland Water
and the many picturesque villages in the area. A 5 acre site with
130 touring pitches, 65 hardstandings.

LYDDINGTON — Map 4 SP89

The Marquess of Exeter
★★★★ INN

52 Main St LE15 9LT
☎ 01572 822477
e-mail: info@marquessexeter.co.uk
dir: M1 junct 19, A14 to Kettering, then A6003 to Caldecott. Right
onto Lyddington Rd, 2m to village

PETS: Bedrooms Charges £10 per night **Public areas** except
restaurant (accompanied at all times) on leads **Grounds** on
leads disp bin **Exercise area** fields adjacent **Facilities** vet info
On Request fridge access **Resident Pets:** Sammy & Winston
(cats)

Situated in the picturesque Rutland countryside, the inn has
been refurbished with a contemporary touch whilst retaining
many original features such as timber beam ceilings, open log
fires and flagstone floors. The stylish bedrooms, situated across
a courtyard, are individually decorated and comfortable. The food
is imaginative with the chef's 'sharing dishes' being particularly
noteworthy.

Rooms 18 en suite (2 fmly) **S** £65-£65.70; **D** £85-£87.50*
Facilities FTV tea/coffee Dinner available Cen ht Wi-fi **Parking** 60
Notes No coaches

NORMANTON — Map 4 SK90

Best Western Normanton Park
★★★ 70% HOTEL

Oakham LE15 8RP
☎ 01780 720315 ▤ 01780 721086
e-mail: info@normantonpark.co.uk
web: www.normantonpark.com
dir: From A1 follow A606 towards Oakham, 5m. Turn left, 1.5m.
Hotel on right

PETS: Bedrooms (11 GF) sign **Charges** £10 per night £50 per
week **Public areas** except restaurant on leads **Grounds** on
leads disp bin **Exercise area Facilities** food bowl water bowl
bedding dog chews cat treats feeding mat litter tray scoop/
disp bags leads walks info vet info **On Request** fridge access
torch towels **Other** charge for damage **Resident Pet:** Jake (Jack
Russell)

This delightful hotel, on Rutland Water's south shore, is
appointed to a high standard and there are two dining styles
available including an extensive Chinese menu. Bedrooms are
well furnished and there are ample public rooms for guests to
relax in.

Rooms 30 (7 annexe) (6 fmly) (11 GF) **S** £60-£100; **D** £80-£120
(incl. bkfst)* **Facilities** FTV Xmas New Year Wi-fi **Parking** 100
Notes LB

ENGLAND

Hambleton Hall

★★★★ ◎◎◎◎ COUNTRY HOUSE HOTEL

Hambleton LE15 8TH
☎ 01572 756991 ▤ 01572 724721
e-mail: hotel@hambletonhall.com
web: www.hambletonhall.com
dir: 3m E off A606

PETS: Bedrooms Stables 10m **Charges** £10 per night £70 per week **Grounds** on leads **Exercise area** 5 mins **Facilities** vet info **On Request** torch

Established 30 years ago by Tim and Stefa Hart this delightful country house enjoys tranquil and spectacular views over Rutland Water. The beautifully manicured grounds are a delight to walk in. The bedrooms in the main house are stylish, individually decorated and equipped with a range of thoughtful extras. A two-bedroom folly, with its own sitting and breakfast room, is only a short walk away. Day rooms include a cosy bar and a sumptuous drawing room, both featuring open fires. The elegant restaurant serves very accomplished, award-winning cuisine with menus highlighting locally sourced, seasonal produce - some grown in the hotel's own grounds. AA Wine Award Winner for England 2010-11.

Rooms 17 (2 annexe) **S** £175-£205; **D** £205-£375 (incl. bkfst)* **Facilities** STV FTV ↴ ⌣ ↳ Private access to lake Xmas New Year **Services** Lift **Parking** 40 **Notes** LB

Barnsdale Lodge Hotel

★★★ 75% ◎ HOTEL

The Avenue, Rutland Water, North Shore LE15 8AH
☎ 01572 724678 ▤ 01572 724961
e-mail: enquiries@barnsdalelodge.co.uk
web: www.barnsdalelodge.co.uk
dir: Off A1 onto A606. Hotel 5m on right, 2m E of Oakham

PETS: Bedrooms (15 GF) unattended **Charges** £10 per night **Public areas** in bar area only **Grounds** disp bin **Exercise area Facilities** food bowl water bowl walks info vet info **On Request** fridge access torch towels **Resident Pets:** Coco & Maisie (Norfolk Terriers)

A popular and interesting hotel converted from a farmstead overlooking Rutland Water. The public areas are dominated by a very successful food operation with a good range of appealing meals on offer for either formal or informal dining. Bedrooms are comfortably appointed with excellent beds enhanced by contemporary soft furnishings and thoughtful extras.

Rooms 44 (2 fmly) (15 GF) **S** £71.50-£92; **D** £87-£148 (incl. bkfst)* **Facilities** FTV Fishing ↳ Archery Beauty treatments Golf Shooting Xmas New Year **Parking** 200

SHROPSHIRE

Bearwood Lodge Guest House

★★★★ GUEST ACCOMMODATION

10 Kidderminster Rd WV15 6BW
☎ 01746 762159
dir: On A442, 50yds S of Bridgnorth bypass island

PETS: Bedrooms unattended **Public areas** disp bin **Exercise area** 100yds to river walk & park **Facilities** pet sitting washing facs walks info vet info

This friendly guest house is situated on the outskirts of Bridgnorth. It provides soundly maintained modern accommodation, including one bedroom on the ground floor. The bright and pleasant breakfast room has an adjacent conservatory, which opens onto the attractive and colourful garden. There is also a comfortable lounge.

Rooms 5 en suite (1 GF) **S** £45; **D** £65 **Facilities** TVL tea/coffee Cen ht **Parking** 8 **Notes** LB ⊛

The Halfway House Inn
★★★ INN

Cleobury Mortimer Rd WV16 5LS
☎ 01746 762670 📠 01746 768063
e-mail: info@halfwayhouseinn.co.uk
web: www.halfwayhouseinn.co.uk
dir: *1m from town centre on B4363 to Cleobury Mortimer*

PETS: Bedrooms Stables Charges £5 per night £25 per week
Public areas except bar & restaurant on leads **Grounds** on leads
disp bin **Exercise area** 200mtrs **Facilities** leads cage storage
walks info **On Request** fridge access torch **Other** charge for
damage 2 weeks notice required for horses **Restrictions** no
Great Danes, Pit Bull Terriers or Rottweilers

Located in a rural area, this 16th-century inn has been renovated
to provide good standards of comfort, while retaining its original
character. The bedrooms, most of which are in converted stables
and cottages, are especially suitable for families and groups.

Rooms 10 en suite (10 fmly) (6 GF) **S** £50-£75; **D** £60-£95*
Facilities FTV TVL tea/coffee Dinner available Cen ht Wi-fi Golf 18
Fishing Pool Table **Parking** 30 **Notes** LB RS Sun eve (ex BHs)

Stanmore Hall Touring Park *(SO742923)*
►►►►►

Stourbridge Rd WV15 6DT
☎ 01746 761761 📠 01746 768069
e-mail: stanmore@morris-leisure
dir: *2m E of Bridgnorth on A458*

PETS: Charges £1 per night **Public areas** disp bin
Exercise area 2 dog walks **Facilities** food food bowl water bowl
leads **Other** max 2 dogs per pitch disposal bags available

Open all year Last arrival 20.00hrs Last departure noon

An excellent park in peaceful surroundings offering outstanding
facilities. The pitches, many of them fully serviced, are arranged
around the lake in Stanmore Hall, home of the Midland Motor
Museum. Handy for touring Ironbridge and the Severn Valley
Railway, and also Bridgnorth itself which is an attractive old
market town. A 12.5 acre site with 131 touring pitches, 53
hardstandings.

Longmynd Hotel
★★★ 73% HOTEL

Cunnery Rd SY6 6AG
☎ 01694 722244 📠 01694 722718
e-mail: info@longmynd.co.uk
web: www.longmynd.co.uk
dir: *A49 into town centre on Sandford Ave, left at Lloyds TSB, over
mini-rdbt, 1st right into Cunnery Rd, hotel at top of hill on left*

PETS: Bedrooms unattended **Charges** £5 per night **Public areas**
Grounds disp bin **Exercise area Facilities** food (pre-bookable)
scoop/disp bags washing facs cage storage walks info vet
info **On Request** fridge access torch towels **Other** charge for
damage

Built in 1901 as a spa, this family-run hotel overlooks the town,
and the views from many of the rooms and public areas are
breathtaking. The attractive wooded grounds include a unique
wood sculpture trail. Bedrooms, with smart modern bathrooms,
are comfortable and well equipped; suites are available. Facilities
include a choice of relaxing lounges. An ethical approach to
climatic issues is observed, and a warm welcome is assured.

Rooms 50 (3 fmly) **S** £45-£60; **D** £90-£120 (incl. bkfst)*
Facilities ⚒ Putt green Pitch and putt Sauna Xmas New Year
Wi-fi **Services** Lift **Parking** 100 **Notes** LB

Belvedere
★★★★ GUEST HOUSE

Burway Rd SY6 6DP
☎ 01694 722232 📠 01694 722232
e-mail: info@belvedereguesthouse.co.uk
dir: *Off A49 into town centre, over x-rds onto Burway Rd*

PETS: Bedrooms Public areas except restaurant & lounge
Grounds on leads disp bin **Exercise area** 100mtrs **Facilities**
food bowl water bowl washing facs cage storage walks info
vet info **On Request** fridge access torch towels

Popular with walkers and cyclists and located on the lower slopes
of the Long Mynd, this impressive, well-proportioned Edwardian
house has a range of homely bedrooms, equipped with practical
extras and complemented by modern bathrooms. Ground-floor
areas include a cottage-style dining room overlooking the pretty
garden and a choice of lounges.

Rooms 7 rms (6 en suite) (2 fmly) **S** £33-£40; **D** £56-£64*
Facilities TVL tea/coffee Cen ht Wi-fi **Parking** 9 **Notes** LB

CHURCH STRETTON *continued*

North Hill Farm

★★★★ BED AND BREAKFAST

Cardington SY6 7LL

☎ 01694 771532

e-mail: cbrandon@btinternet.com

dir: *From Cardington S onto Church Stretton road, right signed Cardington Moor, farm at top of hill on left*

PETS: **Bedrooms Sep accom** unheated, outdoor kennel with inner bunk; barn **Stables Charges** £2 per night **Public areas** except dining room on leads **Grounds** on leads disp bin **Exercise area** adjacent **Facilities** feeding mat leads washing facs cage storage walks info vet info **On Request** fridge access torch towels **Other** charge for damage giant breeds must stay in kennels **Restrictions** no dangerous dogs (see page 7) **Resident Pets:** Saffron & Kitty (Gordon Setters), Millie & Tilly (Springer Spaniels)

This delightful house has been modernised to provide comfortable accommodation. It is located on a fairly remote 20-acre sheep-rearing holding amid the Shropshire hills. The lounge, with exposed beams, has log fires in colder weather. Guests share one large table in the breakfast room.

Rooms 2 rms (2 pri facs) 2 annexe en suite (2 GF) **S** £35; **D** £55-£64* **Facilities** FTV tea/coffee Cen ht Wi-fi **Parking** 6 **Notes** LB Closed Xmas

Castle View

★★★★ BED AND BREAKFAST

Stokesay SY7 9AL

☎ 01588 673712

e-mail: castleviewb_b@btinternet.com

dir: *On A49 S of Craven Arms opp turning to Stokesay Castle*

PETS: **Bedrooms** unattended **Charges** £5 per stay **Public areas** only assist dogs in dining room **Grounds** disp bin **Exercise area** **Facilities** food (pre-bookable) food bowl water bowl bedding feeding mat leads washing facs cage storage walks info vet info **On Request** fridge access torch towels **Other** charge for damage **Resident Pet:** Cindy (Bearded Collie)

The Victorian cottage, extended about 20 years ago, stands in delightful gardens on the southern outskirts of Craven Arms, close to Stokesay Castle. Bedrooms are thoughtfully furnished, and breakfasts, featuring local produce, are served in the cosy, traditionally-furnished dining room.

Rooms 3 rms (1 en suite) (2 pri facs) **S** £35-£40; **D** £60-£65* **Facilities** tea/coffee Cen ht **Parking** 4 **Notes** LB No Children 3yrs

Woodlands Farm Guest House

★★★★ BED AND BREAKFAST

Beech Rd TF8 7PA

☎ 01952 432741

e-mail: allen.woodlandsfarm@btinternet.com

web: www.woodlandsfarmironbridge.co.uk

dir: *Off B4373 rdbt in Ironbridge onto Church Hill & Beech Rd, house on private lane 0.5m on right*

PETS: **Bedrooms Charges Public areas** except restaurant **Grounds** on leads disp bin **Exercise area** on site **Facilities** vet info **On Request** fridge access torch **Other** charge for damage guests must confirm at time of booking if pet/s will be accepted

Woodlands was originally a brick works and then a working farm before conversion to spacious comfortable en suite bedrooms. Stylish furnishing and comfortable beds feature alongside warm hospitality. Wholesome breakfasts can be enjoyed overlooking the pretty garden.

Rooms 5 en suite (1 fmly) (3 GF) **Facilities** STV FTV tea/coffee Cen ht Wi-fi **Parking** 8 **Notes** No Children 5yrs Closed 24 Dec-2 Jan

Fishmore Hall

★★★ 88% ◉◉ SMALL HOTEL

Fishmore Rd SY8 3DP

☎ 01584 875148   🖷 01584 877907

e-mail: reception@fishmorehall.co.uk

web: www.fishmorehall.co.uk

dir: *A49 onto Henley Rd. 1st right, Weyman Rd, at bottom of hill right onto Fishmore Rd*

PETS: **Bedrooms** (1 GF) unattended **Stables** approx 10m **Charges** £30 per stay **Public areas** except restaurant **Grounds** **Exercise area** adjacent **Facilities** water bowl washing facs cage storage walks info vet info **On Request** fridge access torch towels **Other** charge for damage **Resident Pets:** Fidget & Nismo (cats)

Located in a rural area within easy reach of town centre, this Palladian-style Georgian house has been sympathetically renovated and extended to provide high standards of comfort and facilities. The contemporary interior highlights many period features, and public areas include a comfortable lounge and restaurant, the setting for imaginative cooking.

Rooms 15 (1 GF) **Facilities** FTV ⤳ Beauty treatments Massage Xmas New Year Wi-fi **Services** Lift **Parking** 48 **Notes** LB

Cliffe

★★ 78% SMALL HOTEL

Dinham SY8 2JE

☎ 01584 872063   📄 01584 873991

e-mail: thecliffehotel@hotmail.com

web: www.thecliffehotel.co.uk

dir: *In town centre turn left at castle gates to Dinham, follow over bridge. Take right fork, hotel 200yds on left*

PETS: Bedrooms Charges £5 per night **Public areas** except during food service on leads **Grounds** on leads disp bin **Exercise area** fields surrounding hotel **Restrictions** no Pit Bull Terriers **Resident Pet:** Megan (Black Labrador)

Built in the 19th century and standing in extensive grounds and gardens, this privately owned and personally run hotel is quietly located close to the castle and the river. It provides well-equipped accommodation, and facilities include a lounge bar, a pleasant restaurant and a patio overlooking the garden.

Rooms 9 (2 fmly) **S** £50-£60; **D** £60-£100 (incl. bkfst) **Facilities** Wi-fi **Parking** 22

The Charlton Arms

★★★★ 🍽 INN

Ludford Bridge SY8 1PJ

☎ 01584 872813

dir: *From town centre onto Broad St, over Ludford Bridge, Charlton Arms on right*

PETS: Bedrooms unattended **Charges** £5 per stay **Public areas** except top terrace, restaurant & eating area **Grounds** disp bin **Exercise area** adjacent **Facilities** water bowl cage storage walks info vet info **On Request** fridge access torch towels **Other** charge for damage

This refurbished riverside inn has a restaurant that serves dishes using fresh locally-sourced ingredients and a free house offering a fine selection of local beers. The accommodation reflects the character of this historic building whilst offering all the comforts of modern living. There is one bedroom which has a private terrace and hot tub, and there are decking areas to enjoy drinks or a meal on warmer days.

Rooms 10 en suite (2 fmly) **Facilities** tea/coffee Dinner available Cen ht Wi-fi Fishing **Parking** 25

Church Inn

★★★★ INN

The Buttercross SY8 1AW

☎ 01584 872174   📄 01584 877146

web: www.thechurchinn.com

dir: *In town centre at top of Broad St, behind Buttercross*

PETS: Bedrooms unattended **Charges** £5 per stay **Public areas** except in breakfast area on leads **Facilities** water bowl dog chews **Other** charge for damage prior notice required owners must bring dog's own bedding if required

Set right in the heart of the historic town, this Grade II listed inn has been renovated to provide quality accommodation with smart modern bathrooms, some with spa baths. Other areas include a small lounge, a well-equipped meeting room, and cosy bar areas where imaginative food and real ales are served.

Rooms 8 en suite (3 fmly) **S** £40-£55; **D** £70-£90* **Facilities** TVL tea/coffee Dinner available Direct Dial Cen ht **Notes** No coaches

Moor Hall

★★★★ GUEST HOUSE

Cleedownton SY8 3EG

☎ 01584 823209   📄 01584 824216

e-mail: enquiries@moorhall.co.uk

dir: *A4117 Ludlow to Kidderminster, left to Bridgnorth. B4364, follow for 3.2m, Moor Hall on right*

PETS: Bedrooms unattended **Public areas** except dining room **Grounds** disp bin **Exercise area** fields **Facilities** washing facs cage storage walks info vet info **On Request** fridge access torch towels **Resident Pets:** 2 dogs & 5 cats

This impressive Georgian house, once the home of Lord Boyne, is surrounded by extensive gardens and farmland. Bedrooms are richly decorated, well equipped, and one room has a sitting area. Public areas are spacious and comfortably furnished. There is a choice of sitting rooms and a library bar. Guests eat family-style in an elegant dining room.

Rooms 3 en suite (1 fmly) **S** £40-£45; **D** £60-£70* **Facilities** tea/coffee Dinner available Cen ht Licensed Fishing **Parking** 7 **Notes** LB Closed 25-26 Dec 🏧

ENGLAND

LUDLOW *continued*

Haynall Villa *(SO543674)*

★★★ FARMHOUSE

Little Hereford SY8 4BG

☎ 01584 711589   📠 01584 711589 Mrs R Edwards

e-mail: rachelmedwards@hotmail.com

web: www.haynallvilla.co.uk

dir: *A49 onto A456, at Little Hereford right signed Leysters & Middleton on the Hill. Villa 1m on right*

PETS: Bedrooms Charges £5 per night **Public areas** except dining room **Grounds Exercise area** adjacent **Facilities** leads walks info vet info **On Request** torch **Other** food & water bowl available on request; dogs allowed in lounge only with other guests' approval

Located in immaculate gardens in the pretty hamlet of Little Hereford, this Victorian house retains many original features, which are enhanced by the furnishings and decor. Bedrooms are filled with lots of homely extras and the lounge has an open fire.

Rooms 3 rms (2 en suite) (1 pri facs) (1 fmly); **D** fr £54* **Facilities** FTV TVL tea/coffee Dinner available Cen ht Wi-fi Fishing **Parking** 3 **Notes** LB No Children 6yrs Closed mid Dec-mid Jan 🐾 72 acres arable

LYNEAL (NEAR ELLESMERE)   Map 7 SJ43

Fernwood Caravan Park *(SJ445346)*

▶▶▶▶

SY12 0QF

☎ 01948 710221   📠 01948 710324

e-mail: enquiries@fernwoodpark.co.uk

dir: *From A495 in Welshampton take B5063, over canal bridge, turn right as signed*

PETS: Public areas disp bin **Exercise area** woodland walks **Facilities** food food bowl water bowl washing facs walks info vet info **Other** prior notice required disposal bags available **Resident Pet:** Poppy (Border Collie)

Open Mar-Nov rs Apr-Oct shop open Last arrival 21.00hrs Last departure 17.00hrs

A peaceful park set in wooded countryside, with a screened, tree-lined touring area and coarse fishing lake. The approach is past flower beds, and the static area which is tastefully arranged around an attractive children's playing area. There is a small child-free touring area for those wanting complete relaxation, and the park has 20 acres of woodland walks. A 26 acre site with 60 touring pitches, 8 hardstandings and 165 statics.

MUCH WENLOCK   Map 7 SO69

Yew Tree *(SO543958)*

★★★★ FARMHOUSE

Longville In The Dale TF13 6EB

☎ 01694 771866   Mr & Mrs A Hilbery

e-mail: enquiries@yewtreefarmshropshire.co.uk

dir: *5m SW of Much Wenlock. N off B4371 at Longville, left at pub, right at x-rds, farm 1.2m on right*

PETS: Bedrooms Charges £5 per stay **Public areas** except dining room on leads **Grounds** disp bin **Exercise area** adjacent **Facilities** food bowl water bowl scoop/disp bags leads washing facs cage storage walks info vet info **On Request** fridge access torch towels **Other** charge for damage fields available for horses **Restrictions** giant breeds not accepted **Resident Pets:** Saffy & Tuli (Norfolk Terriers/Jack Russell cross), sheep, chickens, pigs

Peacefully located between Much Wenlock and Church Stretton in ten acres of unspoiled countryside, where pigs, sheep and chickens are reared, and own produce is a feature on the comprehensive breakfast menu. Bedrooms are equipped with thoughtful extras and a warm welcome is assured.

Rooms 2 rms (1 en suite) (1 pri facs) **S** £35-£40; **D** £50-£60* **Facilities** FTV TVL tea/coffee Cen ht **Parking** 4 **Notes** LB Closed 24-30 Dec 🐾 10 acres smallholding/sheep/pigs

OSWESTRY   Map 7 SJ22

Pen-y-Dyffryn Country Hotel

★★★ 83% ◉◉ HOTEL

Rhydycroesau SY10 7JD

☎ 01691 653700   📠 01978 211004

e-mail: stay@peny.co.uk

web: www.peny.co.uk

dir: *A5 into town centre. Follow signs to Llansilin on B4580, hotel 3m W of Oswestry before Rhydycroesau*

PETS: Bedrooms (1 GF) unattended **Stables Public areas** not after 6pm **Grounds** disp bin **Exercise area Facilities** food bowl water bowl scoop/disp bags leads washing facs cage storage walks info vet info **On Request** fridge access torch towels

Peacefully situated in five acres of grounds, this charming old house dates back to around 1840, when it was built as a rectory. The tastefully appointed public rooms have real fires during cold weather, and the accommodation includes several mini-cottages, each with its own patio. This hotel attracts many guests for its food and the attentive, friendly service.

Rooms 12 (4 annexe) (1 fmly) (1 GF) **S** £85-£89; **D** £120-£195 (incl. bkfst)* **Facilities** STV FTV Guided walks Xmas New Year Wi-fi **Parking** 18 **Notes** LB No children 3yrs Closed 18 Dec-19 Jan

The Bradford Arms
★★★★ INN

Llanymynech SY22 6EJ
☎ 01691 830582 📠 01691 839009
e-mail: catelou@tesco.net
dir: 5.5m S of Oswestry on A483 in Llanymynech

PETS: Bedrooms unattended Stables 2m Public areas except restaurant & conservatory on leads Grounds on leads disp bin Exercise area 200yds Facilities water bowl bedding dog chews washing facs cage storage walks info vet info On Request fridge access torch towels Other charge for damage Resident Pet: Charlie (cat)

Once a coaching inn on the Earl of Bradford's estate, the Bradford Arms provides a range of carefully furnished bedrooms with a wealth of thoughtful extras. The elegant ground-floor areas include lounges, bars, and a choice of formal or conservatory restaurants, the settings for imaginative food and fine wines.

Rooms 5 en suite (2 fmly) (2 GF) S £35-£40; D £60-£80* Facilities FTV tea/coffee Dinner available Direct Dial Cen ht Wi-fi Golf 18 Fishing Riding Pool Table Parking 20

Summerfield B&B
★★★★ BED AND BREAKFAST

Sarn Holdings, Sarn Ln, Rhosygadfa SY10 7AU
☎ 01691 661429
web: www.summerfieldbandb.co.uk

PETS: Bedrooms Stables 5 mins' walk Charges from £3.50 per night negotiable per week Public areas Grounds disp bin Exercise area adjacent Facilities food bowl water bowl dog chews cat treats feeding mat litter tray scoop/disp bags leads pet sitting dog walking washing facs cage storage walks info vet info On Request fridge access torch towels Other charge for damage pet food by arrangement Resident Pets: Willow (Collie cross), Thomas & Little Jo (cats)

A warm welcome is assured at this large, rurally located, semi-detached house, standing on pretty gardens close to the village of St Martins. Bedrooms are thoughtfully furnished with a wealth of extras and smart modern en suite showers, or private bathrooms with jacuzzi baths. Comprehensive breakfasts, utilising fresh local produce are served in an attractive dining room, which has a comfortable lounge area.

Rooms 2 rms (1 en suite) (1 pri facs) S £28.50; D £57* Facilities TVL tea/coffee Cen ht Wi-fi Golf 18 Parking 5 Notes LB Closed Xmas & New Year

Park House
★★★★ 76% HOTEL

Park St TF11 9BA
☎ 01952 460128 📠 01952 461658
e-mail: reception@parkhousehotel.net
dir: M54 junct 4, A464 (Wolverhampton road) for approx 2m, under railway bridge, hotel 100yds on left

PETS: Bedrooms (8 GF) unattended Charges £10 per night Grounds Exercise area 500yds Facilities walks info vet info On Request fridge access Restrictions no breeds larger than a Labrador

This hotel was created from what were originally two country houses of very different architectural styles. Located on the edge of the historic market town, it offers guests easy access to motorway networks, a choice of banqueting and meeting rooms, plus leisure facilities. Butlers Bar and Restaurant is the setting for imaginative food. Service is friendly and attentive.

Rooms 54 (16 annexe) (4 fmly) (8 GF) (4 smoking) S £85-£120; D £90-£150 (incl. bkfst)* Facilities STV FTV Gym Steam room Sauna Xmas New Year Wi-fi Services Lift Parking 90 Notes LB

Albright Hussey Manor Hotel & Restaurant
★★★★ 75% HOTEL

Ellesmere Rd SY4 3AF
☎ 01939 290571 & 290523 📠 01939 291143
e-mail: info@albrighthussey.co.uk
web: www.albrighthussey.co.uk
dir: 2.5m N of Shrewsbury on A528, follow signs for Ellesmere

PETS: Bedrooms (8 GF) unattended Charges Public areas disp bin Exercise area Facilities walks info vet info On Request torch Other charge for damage contact hotel for further details

First mentioned in the Domesday Book, this enchanting medieval manor house is complete with a moat. Bedrooms are situated in either the sumptuously appointed main house or in the more modern wing. The intimate restaurant displays an abundance of original features and there is also a comfortable cocktail bar and lounge.

Rooms 26 (4 fmly) (8 GF) Facilities Xmas New Year Wi-fi Parking 100

SHREWSBURY *continued*

Mytton & Mermaid

★★★ 77% ◎◎ HOTEL

Atcham SY5 6QG

☎ 01743 761220 📄 01743 761292

e-mail: reception@myttonandmermaid.co.uk

web: www.myttonandmermaid.co.uk

dir: *From Shrewsbury over old bridge in Atcham. Hotel opposite main entrance to Attingham Park*

PETS: Bedrooms (6 GF) unattended **Charges** £10 per night **Grounds** disp bin **Exercise area Facilities** food bowl water bowl cage storage walks info vet info **On Request** fridge access Resident Pets: dogs

Convenient for Shrewsbury, this ivy-clad former coaching inn enjoys a pleasant location beside the River Severn. Some bedrooms, including family suites, are in a converted stable block adjacent to the hotel. There is a large lounge bar, a comfortable lounge, and a brasserie that has gained a well-deserved local reputation for the quality of its food.

Rooms 18 (7 annexe) (1 fmly) (6 GF) **S** £85-£95; **D** £110-£175 (incl. bkfst)* **Facilities** Fishing ♫ New Year Wi-fi **Parking** 50 **Notes** Closed 25 Dec

Oxon Hall Touring Park (SJ455138)

►►►►►

Welshpool Rd SY3 5FB

☎ 01743 340868 📄 01743 340869

e-mail: oxon@morris-leisure.co.uk

dir: *Exit A5 (ring road) at junct with A458. Site shares entrance with 'Oxon Park & Ride'*

PETS: Charges £1 per night **Public areas Exercise area** 2 dog walks **Facilities** washing facs walks info vet info **Other** prior notice required max 2 dogs per pitch

Open all year Last arrival 21.00hrs

A delightful park with quality facilities, and a choice of grass and fully-serviced pitches. An adults-only section is very popular with those wanting a peaceful holiday, and there is an inviting patio area next to reception and the shop, overlooking a small lake. This site is ideally located for visiting Shrewsbury and the surrounding countryside, and there is always a warm welcome. A 15 acre site with 124 touring pitches, 72 hardstandings and 42 statics.

Telford Hotel & Golf Resort

★★★★ 73% HOTEL

Great Hay Dr, Sutton Heights TF7 4DT

☎ 01952 429977 📄 01952 586602

e-mail: telford@qhotels.co.uk

web: www.qhotels.co.uk

dir: *M54 junct 4, A442. Follow signs for Telford Golf Club*

PETS: Bedrooms (50 GF) sign **Stables** 8m **Charges** £15 per night **Public areas** only for access (except assist dogs) on leads **Grounds** disp bin **Exercise area** public footpath through property **Facilities** walks info vet info **Other** charge for damage maximum of 1 large dog or 2 small dogs per bedroom; dogs are not allowed on golf course **Restrictions** no dogs larger than a Labrador

Set on the edge of Telford with panoramic views of the famous Ironbridge Gorge, this hotel offers excellent standards. Smart bedrooms are complemented by spacious public areas, large conference facilities, a spa with treatment rooms, a golf course and a driving range. Ample parking is available.

Rooms 114 (8 fmly) (50 GF) **Facilities** Spa STV ☜ ♪ 18 Putt green Gym Xmas New Year Wi-fi **Services** Lift **Parking** 200

Church Farm

★★★★ ⊜ GUEST ACCOMMODATION

Wrockwardine Village, Wellington TF6 5DG

☎ 01952 251927 📄 01952 427511

e-mail: info@churchfarm-shropshire.co.uk

dir: *M54 junct 7 towards Wellington, 1st left, 1st right, then right at end of road. 0.5m on left opposite St Peters church*

PETS: Bedrooms Charges £10 per stay **Public areas** except restaurant on leads **Grounds** disp bin **Exercise area** 2m **Facilities** feeding mat leads washing facs cage storage walks info vet info **On Request** fridge access torch towels **Other** charge for damage **Resident Pet:** Basil (Staffordshire Bull Terrier)

Located in the pretty rural village of Wrockwardine, this impressive period former farmhouse provides high standards of comfort and good facilities. Thoughtfully equipped bedrooms, furnished in minimalist style, offer a wealth of thoughtful extras and the spacious day rooms include a comfortable lounge and an elegant dining room, the setting for imaginative cooking.

Rooms 4 rms (3 en suite) (1 pri facs) (1 fmly) **S** £55-£65; **D** £65-£75* **Facilities** FTV tea/coffee Dinner available Cen ht Wi-fi Golf 18 **Parking** 12

Severn Gorge Park *(SJ705051)*

▶ ▶ ▶ ▶

Bridgnorth Rd, Tweedale TF7 4JB
☎ 01952 684789 📠 01952 587299
e-mail: info@severngorgepark.co.uk
dir: *Signed off A442, 1m S of Telford*

PETS: Charges contact for details **Public areas** on leads disp bin **Exercise area** **Facilities** walks info vet info **Other** prior notice required **Restrictions** well behaved dogs only

Open all year Last arrival 22.00hrs Last departure 18.00hrs

A very pleasant wooded site in the heart of Telford, well-screened and maintained. The sanitary facilities are fresh and immaculate, and landscaping of the grounds is carefully managed. This is a really delightful park to stay on, and it is also well positioned for visiting nearby Ironbridge. A 6 acre site with 10 touring pitches, 10 hardstandings and 120 statics.

TELFORD SERVICE AREA (M54)	Map 7 SJ70

Days Inn Telford
BUDGET HOTEL

Telford Services, Priorslee Rd TF11 8TG
☎ 01952 238400 📠 01952 238410
e-mail: telford.hotel@welcomebreak.co.uk
web: www.welcomebreak.co.uk
dir: *At M54 junct 4*

PETS: Bedrooms (21 GF) **Public areas** dogs must be kept on leads **Grounds**

This modern building offers accommodation in smart, spacious and well-equipped bedrooms, suitable for families and business travellers, and all with en suite bathrooms. Continental breakfast is available, and other refreshments may be taken at the nearby family restaurant.

Rooms 48 (45 fmly) (21 GF) (8 smoking) **S** £29-£59; **D** £29-£66

WEM	Map 7 SJ52

Soulton Hall

★ ★ ★ ★ 🍽 GUEST ACCOMMODATION

Soulton SY4 5RS
☎ 01939 232786 📠 01939 234097
e-mail: enquiries@soultonhall.co.uk
web: www.soultonhall.co.uk
dir: *A49 between Shrewsbury & Whitchurch turn onto B5065 towards Wem. Soulton Hall 2m E of Wem on B5065*

PETS: Stables 9m **Charges** **Grounds** on leads **Exercise area** adjacent **Facilities** leads washing facs dog grooming cage storage walks info vet info **On Request** torch towels **Other** charge for damage dogs allowed in Carriage House & Cedar Lodge only (not Sourton Hall)

Located two miles from historic Wem, this 16th-century manor house incorporates part of an even older building. The house stands in 560 acres and provides high levels of comfort. Bedrooms are equipped with homely extras and the ground-floor

areas include a spacious hall sitting room, lounge-bar and an attractive dining room, the setting for imaginative dinners.

Rooms 4 en suite 3 annexe en suite (2 fmly) (3 GF) **Facilities** FTV tea/coffee Dinner available Direct Dial Cen ht Licensed Wi-fi 🍃 Fishing **Parking** 52

Lower Lacon Caravan Park *(SJ534304)*

▶ ▶ ▶

SY4 5RP
☎ 01939 232376 📠 01939 233606
e-mail: info@llcp.co.uk
dir: *Take A49 to B5065. Site 3m on right*

PETS: Public areas except swimming pool area, toilets & licensed premises disp bin **Exercise area** dog walk **Facilities** food dog chews cat treats vet info **Other** prior notice required disposal bags available **Resident Pets:** 1 dog, 4 cats, 1 horse, 11 pigs, 5 alpacas, 5 sheep, chickens, ducks

Open Apr-Oct rs Nov-Mar club wknds only, toilets closed if frosty Last arrival 20.00hrs Last departure 16.00hrs

A large, spacious park with lively club facilities and an entertainments barn, set safely away from the main road. The park is particularly suitable for families, with an outdoor swimming pool and farm animals. A 52 acre site with 270 touring pitches, 30 hardstandings and 50 statics.

Notes No skateboards, no commercial vehicles

WENTNOR	Map 7 SO39

The Green Caravan Park *(SO380932)*

▶ ▶ ▶

SY9 5EF
☎ 01588 650605
e-mail: karen@greencaravanpark.co.uk
dir: *1m NE of Bishop's Castle on A489. Right at brown tourist sign*

PETS: Charges £1 per night **Public areas** on leads disp bin **Exercise area** dog walk & small field for exercising **Facilities** food scoop/disp bags walks info vet info **Other** charge for damage **Resident Pets:** Englebert & Ronnie (Pygmy goats), Sophie, Lily, Tommy & Molly (cats)

Open Etr-Oct Last arrival 21.00hrs Last departure 13.00hrs

A pleasant site in a peaceful setting convenient for visiting Ludlow or Shrewsbury. The grassy pitches are mainly level. A 15 acre site with 140 touring pitches, 5 hardstandings and 20 statics.

SOMERSET

BATH
Map 3 ST76

von Essen hotels
A PRIVATE COLLECTION
www.somersethotels.co.uk

The Royal Crescent
★★★★★ 84% ◉◉ HOTEL
16 Royal Crescent BA1 2LS
☎ 01225 823333 📄 01225 339401
e-mail: info@royalcrescent.co.uk
web: www.vonessenhotels.co.uk
dir: From A4, right at lights. 2nd left onto Bennett St. Continue into The Circus, 2nd exit onto Brock St

PETS: Bedrooms (7 GF) unattended Charges Public areas except restaurant Grounds Exercise area park adjacent Facilities food (pre-bookable) food bowl water bowl bedding pet sitting dog walking cage storage walks info vet info Other charge for damage please contact hotel to confirm which pets are accepted

John Wood's masterpiece of fine Georgian architecture provides the setting for this elegant hotel in the centre of the world famous Royal Crescent. Spacious, air-conditioned bedrooms are individually designed and furnished with antiques. Delightful central grounds lead to a second house, which is home to further rooms, the award-winning Dower House restaurant and the Bath House which offers therapies and treatments.

Rooms 45 (8 fmly) (7 GF) S £195-£900; D £195-£920 (incl. bkfst)* Facilities Spa STV FTV ◎ ⚓ Gym 1920s river launch Xmas New Year Wi-fi Services Lift Air con Parking 27 Notes LB

Best Western The Cliffe
★★★ 83% ◉ HOTEL
Cliffe Dr, Crowe Hill, Limpley Stoke BA2 7FY
☎ 01225 723226 📄 01225 723871
e-mail: cliffe@bestwestern.co.uk
dir: A36 S from Bath onto B3108 at lights left towards Bradford-on-Avon, 0.5m. Right before bridge through village, 2nd hotel on right

Best Western

PETS: Bedrooms (4 GF) Charges £8 per night on leads Grounds on leads disp bin Exercise area Facilities water bowl washing facs walks info vet info On Request fridge access torch towels Other charge for damage

With stunning countryside views, this attractive country house is just a short drive from the City of Bath. Bedrooms vary in size and style but are well equipped; several are particularly spacious and a number of rooms are on the ground floor. The restaurant overlooks the well-tended garden and offers a tempting selection of carefully prepared dishes. Wi-fi is available throughout.

Rooms 11 (3 annexe) (2 fmly) (4 GF) S £111-£150; D £137-£200 (incl. bkfst)* Facilities FTV ⚑ Xmas New Year Wi-fi Parking 20 Notes LB

Pratt's Hotel
★★★ 74% HOTEL
South Pde BA2 4AB
☎ 01225 460441 📄 01225 448807
e-mail: pratts@forestdale.com
web: www.prattshotel.co.uk
dir: A46 into city centre. Left at 1st lights (Curfew Pub), right at next lights. 2nd exit at next rdbt, right at lights, left at next lights, 1st left into South Pde

PETS: Bedrooms unattended sign Charges £7.50 per night Public areas except restaurant on leads Exercise area 2 mins' walk Facilities food food bowl water bowl cage storage walks info vet info

Built in 1743 this popular Georgian hotel still has many original features and is centrally placed for exploring Bath. The bedrooms, each with their own individual character and style, offer great comfort. The lounge has original open fireplaces and offers a relaxing venue for afternoon tea.

Rooms 46 (2 fmly) S £60-£100; D £75-£140 (incl. bkfst)* Facilities FTV Xmas New Year Wi-fi Services Lift Notes LB

Eagle House
★★★★ GUEST ACCOMMODATION
Church St, Bathford BA1 7RS
☎ 01225 859946 📄 01225 859430
e-mail: jonap@eagleho.demon.co.uk
web: www.eaglehouse.co.uk
dir: Off A363 onto Church St

PETS: Bedrooms Stables 2m Charges £5 per night weekly prices on request Public areas except dining room (drawing room on request) Grounds disp bin Exercise area 400yds Facilities water bowl washing facs cage storage walks info vet info On Request fridge access torch towels Resident Pets: Aquilla (Labrador), Inka (cat)

Set in attractive gardens, this delightful Georgian house is pleasantly located on the outskirts of the city. Bedrooms are individually styled, and each has a thoughtful range of extra facilities. The impressive lounge is adorned with attractive pictures, and the dining room has views of the grounds and tennis court.

Rooms 6 en suite 2 annexe en suite (2 fmly) (2 GF) S £48-£88.50; D £62-£112* Facilities tea/coffee Direct Dial Cen ht Wi-fi ◎ ⚓ Parking 10 Notes LB Closed 12 Dec-15 Jan

BREAN Map 3 ST25

Warren Farm Holiday Centre
(ST297564)

Brean Sands TA8 2RP
☎ 01278 751227
e-mail: enquiries@warren-farm.co.uk
dir: *M5 junct 22 , B3140 through Burnham-on-Sea to Berrow & Brean. Site 1.5m past Brean Leisure Park*

PETS: Public areas except buildings, Sunnyside area & field 6 disp bin **Exercise area** farm walk **Facilities** food food bowl water bowl dog chews cat treats litter tray scoop/disp bags walks info vet info **Other** prior notice required

Open Apr-Oct Last arrival 20.00hrs Last departure noon

A large family-run holiday park close to the beach, divided into several fields each with its own designated facilities. Pitches are spacious and level, and enjoy panoramic views of the Mendip Hills and Brean Down. A bar and restaurant are part of the complex, which provide entertainment for all the family, and there is also separate entertainment for children. The park has excellent facilities. A 100 acre site with 575 touring pitches and 800 statics.

Notes No commercial vehicles

Northam Farm Caravan & Touring Park
(ST299556)

TA8 2SE
☎ 01278 751244 📠 01278 751150
e-mail: enquiries@northamfarm.co.uk
dir: *From M5 junct 22 to Burnham-on-Sea. In Brean, park on right 0.5m past Brean Leisure Park*

PETS: Public areas except fields on leads disp bin **Exercise area** dog walks & exercise field **Facilities** food dog chews cat treats scoop/disp bags leads washing facs walks info vet info **Other** prior notice required

Open Mar-Oct rs Mar & Oct shop/café/takeaway open limited hours Last arrival 20.00hrs Last departure 10.30hrs

An attractive site a short walk from the sea and a long sandy beach. This quality park also has lots of children's play areas, and also runs the Seagull Inn about 600 yards away, which includes a restaurant and entertainment. There is a fishing lake on the site which proves very popular. A 30 acre site with 350 touring pitches, 252 hardstandings.

Notes Families & couples only, no motorcycles or commercial vehicles

BRIDGETOWN Map 3 SS93

Exe Valley Caravan Site *(SS923333)*

▶ ▶ ▶ ▶

Mill House TA22 9JR
☎ 01643 851432
e-mail: paul@paulmatt.fsnet.co.uk
dir: *Take A396 (Tiverton to Minehead road). Turn W in centre of Bridgetown, site 40yds on right*

PETS: Charges Public areas on leads disp bin **Exercise area** riverside walks **Facilities** food dog chews scoop/disp bags leads walks info vet info

Open 12 Mar-18 Oct Last arrival 22.00hrs

Set in the Exmoor National Park, this 'adults only' park occupies an enchanting, peaceful spot in a wooded valley alongside the River Exe. There is free fly fishing, and an abundance of wildlife, with excellent walks directly from the park. The inn opposite serves lunchtime and evening meals. A 4 acre site with 50 touring pitches, 10 hardstandings.

Notes

BURTLE Map 3 ST34

Orchard Camping *(ST397434)*

▶

Ye Olde Burtle Inn, Catcott Rd TA7 8NG
☎ 01278 722269 & 722123 📠 01278 722269
e-mail: food@theinn.eu
dir: *M5 junct 23, A39, in approx 4m left onto unclass road to Burtle, site by pub in village centre*

PETS: Stables 0.25m **Public areas Exercise area** surrounding open countryside 0.25m **Facilities** washing facs walks info vet info **Other** prior notice required

Open all year Last arrival anytime

A simple campsite set in an orchard at the rear of a lovely 17th-century family inn in the heart of the Somerset Levels. The restaurant offers a wide range of meals, and breakfast can be pre-ordered by campers. A shower and disabled toilet have been added and these facilities are available to campers outside pub opening hours. Free internet access and Wi-fi available. A 0.75 acre site with 30 touring pitches.

ENGLAND

CHARD
Map 3 ST30

Lordleaze
★★★ 77% HOTEL

Henderson Dr, Forton Rd TA20 2HW
☎ 01460 61066 📠 01460 66468
e-mail: info@lordleazehotel.com
web: www.lordleazehotel.com
dir: A358 from Chard, left at St Mary's Church to Forton & Winsham on B3162. Follow signs to hotel

PETS: Bedrooms (7 GF) unattended Charges £5 per night
Grounds disp bin Exercise area surrounding fields Facilities
vet info On Request fridge access

Conveniently and quietly located, this hotel is close to the Devon, Dorset and Somerset borders, and only minutes from Chard. All bedrooms are well equipped and comfortable. The friendly lounge bar has a wood-burning stove and serves tempting bar meals. The conservatory restaurant offers more formal dining.

Rooms 25 (2 fmly) (7 GF) S £72-£74; D £115-£120 (incl. bkfst)*
Facilities FTV Xmas New Year Wi-fi Parking 55 Notes LB

Watermead
★★★ GUEST HOUSE

83 High St TA20 1QT
☎ 01460 62834 📠 01460 67448
e-mail: trudy@watermeadguesthouse.co.uk
dir: On A30 in town centre

PETS: Bedrooms Charges £5 per night Public areas except
dining room on leads Grounds disp bin Exercise area 100mtrs
Facilities water bowl scoop/disp bags leads washing facs cage
storage walks info vet info On Request torch towels Other
charge for damage Resident Pet: Jasper (Black Labrador)

Guests will feel at home at this family-run house, a smart establishment in a convenient location. Hearty breakfasts are served in the dining room overlooking the garden. Bedrooms are neat, and the spacious, self-contained suite is popular with families. Free Wi-fi access is available.

Rooms 9 rms (6 en suite) 1 annexe en suite (1 fmly) S £35-£49;
D £60-£69* Facilities FTV TVL tea/coffee Cen ht Wi-fi Parking 10
Notes LB

CHEDDAR
Map 3 ST45

Cheddar Bridge Touring Park (ST459529)
▶▶▶▶

Draycott Rd BS27 3RJ
☎ 01934 743048 📠 01934 743048
e-mail: enquiries@cheddarbridge.co.uk
dir: M5 junct 22 (Burnham-on-Sea), A38 towards Cheddar & Bristol, approx 5m. Right onto A371 at Cross, follow Cheddar signs. Through Cheddar village towards Wells, site on right just before Caravan Club site

PETS: Charges £1 (1-2 dogs) per night Public areas dogs must
be kept on leads disp bin Exercise area riverside walk adjacent
Facilities vet info Resident Pets: Belle (dog), Tom & Soxs (cats),
10 ducks

Open Mar-Oct Last arrival 22.00hrs Last departure 11.00hrs

A peaceful adults-only park on the edge of the village of Cheddar, with the River Yeo passing attractively through its grounds. It is handy for exploring the Cheddar Gorge and Wookey Hole, Wells and Bath. The toilet facilities are very good. A 4 acre site with 45 touring pitches, 10 hardstandings and 4 statics.

Notes Quiet 23.00hrs-08.00hrs

CLUTTON
Map 3 ST65

The Hunters Rest
★★★★ INN

King Ln, Clutton Hill BS39 5QL
☎ 01761 452303 📠 01761 453308
e-mail: paul@huntersrest.co.uk
web: www.huntersrest.co.uk
dir: Off A37 onto A368 towards Bath, 100yds right onto lane, left at T-junct, inn 0.25m on left

PETS: Bedrooms unattended Stables 100yds Charges £10 per
stay Public areas on leads Grounds disp bin Exercise area
adjacent Facilities food (pre-bookable) food bowl water
bowl dog chews feeding mat scoop/disp bags leads washing
facs cage storage walks info vet info On Request fridge
access torch Other charge for damage dogs allowed in certain
bedrooms only Resident Pet: Reg (Black Labrador)

This establishment was originally built around 1750 as a hunting lodge for the Earl of Warwick. Set in delightful countryside, it is ideally located for Bath, Bristol and Wells. Bedrooms and bathrooms are furnished and equipped to excellent standards, and the ground floor combines the character of a real country inn with an excellent range of home-cooked meals.

Rooms 5 en suite (1 fmly) S £65-£75; D £90-£125* Facilities FTV
tea/coffee Dinner available Direct Dial Cen ht Wi-fi Parking 90
Notes LB

CREWKERNE   Map 3 ST40

Manor Farm

★ ★ ★ GUEST ACCOMMODATION

Wayford TA18 8QL
☎ 01460 78865 & 0776 7620031 📠 01460 78865
web: www.manorfarm.biz
dir: *B3165 from Crewkerne to Lyme Regis, 3m in Clapton right onto Dunsham Ln, Manor Farm 0.5m up hill on right*

PETS: Sep accom stable block, barns **Stables Public areas**
Grounds disp bin **Exercise area** woods 0.25m **Facilities** food
bowl water bowl bedding leads washing facs cage storage
walks info vet info **On Request** fridge access torch **Other** pet
food on request **Resident Pets:** Charlie & Ginger (cats)

Located off the beaten track, this fine Victorian country house
has extensive views over Clapton towards the Axe Valley. The
comfortably furnished bedrooms are well equipped, and front-
facing rooms enjoy splendid views. Breakfast is served at
separate tables in the dining room, and a spacious lounge is also
provided.

Rooms 4 en suite 1 annexe en suite (2 fmly) **S** £35-£40;
D £70* **Facilities** STV FTV TVL tea/coffee Cen ht Fishing Riding
Parking 14 **Notes** ⊗

DULVERTON   Map 3 SS92

Tarr Farm Inn

★ ★ ★ ★ ★ ⊛ INN

Tarr Steps, Exmoor National Park TA22 9PY
☎ 01643 851507 📠 01643 851111
e-mail: enquiries@tarrfarm.co.uk
web: www.tarrfarm.co.uk
dir: *4m NW of Dulverton. Off B3223 signed Tarr Steps, signs to Tarr Farm Inn*

PETS: Bedrooms Stables 0.5m **Charges** £8 per night £56
per week **Public areas** except restaurant & lounge on leads
Grounds on leads disp bin **Exercise area** 10mtrs **Facilities**
food bowl water bowl bedding dog chews leads cage storage
walks info vet info **On Request** fridge access torch towels
Other charge for damage prior notice required

Tarr Farm, dating from the 16th century, nestles on the lower
slopes of Exmoor overlooking the famous old clapper bridge,
Tarr Steps. The majority of rooms are in the bedroom block that
provides very stylish and comfortable accommodation with an
impressive selection of thoughtful touches. Tarr Farm Inn, with
much character and traditional charm, draws the crowds for
cream teas and delicious dinners which are prepared from good
local produce.

Rooms 9 en suite (4 GF) **Facilities** STV tea/coffee Dinner
available Direct Dial Cen ht Wi-fi Fishing Riding **Parking** 10
Notes No Children 14yrs No coaches

DUNSTER   Map 3 SS94

The Luttrell Arms Hotel

★★★ 73% HOTEL

High St TA24 6SG
☎ 01643 821555 📠 01643 821567
e-mail: info@luttrellarms.fsnet.co.uk
web: www.luttrellarms.co.uk/main.htm
dir: *A39/A396 S towards Tiverton. Hotel on left opposite Yarn Market*

PETS: Bedrooms unattended **Charges** dog £5 per night
Public areas except restaurant on leads **Grounds** on
leads **Exercise area** adjacent **Facilities** walks info vet info
On Request fridge access torch **Resident Pets:** Merlin &
Mordred (cats)

Occupying an enviable position on the high street, this
15th-century hotel looks up towards the town's famous castle.
Beautifully renovated and decorated, high levels of comfort
can be found throughout. Some of the spacious bedrooms have
four-poster beds. The warm and friendly staff provide attentive
service in a relaxed atmosphere.

Rooms 28 (3 fmly) **S** £80-£135; **D** £190-£200 (incl. bkfst &
dinner) **Facilities** FTV Exmoor safaris Historic tours Walking tours
New Year **Notes** LB

ENGLAND

EXFORD — Map 3 SS83

Crown
★★★ 75% ⊛ HOTEL
TA24 7PP
☎ 01643 831554 📄 01643 831665
e-mail: info@crownhotelexmoor.co.uk
web: www.crownhotelexmoor.co.uk
dir: M5 junct 25, follow Taunton signs. Take A358 from Taunton, then B3224 via Wheddon Cross to Exford

PETS: Bedrooms unattended Sep accom stables available as kennels Stables Charges £10 (up to 5 days), £20 (over 5 days) Public areas except restaurant Grounds disp bin Exercise area 25mtrs Facilities water bowl dog chews pet sitting washing facs walks info vet info On Request fridge access torch towels Other charge for damage Resident Pet: Oscar (Patterdale Terrier)

Guest comfort is certainly the hallmark here. Afternoon tea is served in the lounge beside a roaring fire and tempting menus in the bar and restaurant are all part of the charm of this delightful old coaching inn that specialises in breaks for shooting and other country sports. Bedrooms retain a traditional style yet offer a range of modern comforts and facilities, many with views of this pretty moorland village.

Rooms 16 (3 fmly) S £72.50; D £125-£145 (incl. bkfst)*
Facilities Xmas New Year Wi-fi Parking 30 Notes LB

GORDANO SERVICE AREA (M5) — Map 3 ST57

Days Inn Bristol West
BUDGET HOTEL
BS20 7XG
☎ 01275 373709 & 373624 📄 01275 374104
e-mail: gordano.hotel@welcomebreak.co.uk
web: www.welcomebreak.co.uk
dir: M5 junct 19, follow signs for Gordano Services

PETS: Bedrooms (29 GF) Public areas Grounds on leads disp bin Facilities vet info On Request torch towels Other please phone for further details of pet facilities

This modern building offers accommodation in smart, spacious and well-equipped bedrooms, suitable for families and business travellers, and all with en suite bathrooms. Continental breakfast is available and other refreshments may be taken at the nearby family restaurant.

Rooms 60 (52 fmly) (29 GF) (10 smoking) S £29-£59; D £29-£69

HIGHBRIDGE — Map 3 ST34

Sundowner
★★ 68% SMALL HOTEL
74 Main Rd, West Huntspill TA9 3QU
☎ 01278 784766 📄 01278 794133
e-mail: runnalls@msn.com
dir: From M5 junct 23, 3m N on A38

PETS: Bedrooms Public areas except restaurant on leads Grounds on leads Exercise area bridle path adjacent Restrictions small dogs only

Friendly service and an informal atmosphere are just two of the highlights of this small hotel. The open-plan lounge/bar is a comfortable, homely area in which to relax after a busy day exploring the area or working in the locality. An extensive menu, featuring freshly cooked, imaginative dishes, is offered in the popular restaurant.

Rooms 8 (1 fmly) S £50-£55; D £65-£70 (incl. bkfst)*
Facilities FTV Wi-fi Parking 18 Notes Closed 26-31 Dec & 1 Jan RS 25 Dec

The Greenwood

★★★★ GUEST ACCOMMODATION

76 Main Rd, West Huntspill TA9 3QU

☎ 01278 795886 🖨 01278 795886

e-mail: info@the-greenwood.co.uk

web: www.the-greenwood.co.uk

dir: On A38 in West Huntspill, between Orchard Inn & Sundowner Hotel

PETS: Bedrooms unattended **Stables** approx 1m **Public areas** except restaurant on leads **Grounds** on leads disp bin **Exercise area** adjacent **Facilities** water bowl scoop/disp bags washing facs cage storage walks info **On Request** fridge access torch **Other** charge for damage contact for details of stables **Resident Pets:** Paddy (Siberian Husky cross), Guinness (Doberman/Labrador cross)

Set in two acres of land, this 18th-century former farmhouse and family home offers comfortable accommodation in a friendly environment. Breakfast, featuring home-made preserves, is served in the dining room and home-cooked dinners are available by arrangement. There is a lounge for relaxation.

Rooms 7 rms (6 en suite) (1 pri facs) (3 fmly) (1 GF)
S £49.50-£55; **D** £72-£80 **Facilities** FTV TVL tea/coffee Dinner available Cen ht Licensed Wi-fi **Parking** 8 **Notes** LB

von Essen hotels

Homewood Park

★★★ ◎◎◎ HOTEL

BA2 7TB

☎ 01225 723731 🖨 01225 723820

e-mail: info@homewoodpark.co.uk

web: www.homewoodpark.co.uk

dir: 6m SE of Bath on A36, turn left at 2nd sign for Freshford

PETS: Bedrooms (2 GF) **Charges** contact for details **Public areas** except restaurant on leads **Grounds** disp bin **Facilities** food (pre-bookable) food bowl water bowl bedding dog chews feeding mat scoop/disp bags leads pet sitting washing facs cage storage walks info vet info **On Request** fridge access torch towels **Other** charge for damage prior notice required

Homewood Park, an unassuming yet stylish Georgian house set in delightful grounds, offers relaxed surroundings and maintains high standards of quality and comfort throughout. Bedrooms, all individually decorated, include thoughtful extras to ensure a comfortable stay. The hotel has a reputation for excellent cuisine - offering an imaginative interpretation of classical dishes.

Rooms 19 (3 fmly) (2 GF) **Facilities** FTV ⭐ ♨ ♨ Xmas New Year Wi-fi **Parking** 30

Combe House

★★★ 75% ◎ HOTEL

TA5 1RZ

☎ 01278 741382 & 741213 🖨 01278 741322

e-mail: enquiries@combehouse.co.uk

web: www.combehouse.co.uk

dir: From A39 W left in Holford then left at T-junct. Left at fork, 0.25m to Holford Combe

PETS: Bedrooms (2 GF) **Charges** £5 per night **Public areas** in bar & grounds only on leads **Grounds** on leads disp bin **Facilities** food (pre-bookable) food bowl water bowl leads washing facs cage storage walks info vet info **On Request** fridge access torch towels **Other** charge for damage dogs cannot be left unattended in bedrooms unless caged

Located in a peaceful wooded valley with four acres of tranquil gardens to explore, the atmosphere here is relaxed and welcoming. The individually styled bedrooms have lots of comfort - all are designed for a cosseted and pampered stay. Public areas have equal charm with traditional features interwoven with contemporary style. Food comes highly recommended with a dedicated kitchen team producing accomplished, seasonal dishes.

Rooms 18 (1 annexe) (3 fmly) (2 GF) **Facilities** ⊗ ♨ Sauna Small gym Beauty therapy treatments Xmas New Year Wi-fi **Parking** 36 **Notes** LB

von Essen hotels

Hunstrete House

★★★ 82% ◎◎ COUNTRY HOUSE HOTEL

BS39 4NS

☎ 01761 490490 🖨 01761 490732

e-mail: info@hunstretehouse.co.uk

web: www.hunstretehouse.co.uk

dir: From Bath take A4 to Bristol. At Globe Inn rdbt 2nd left onto A368 to Wells. 1m after Marksbury turn right for Hunstrete. Hotel next left

PETS: Bedrooms (8 GF) **Charges** £10 per night **Public areas** except dining areas **Grounds Exercise area** adjacent **Facilities** walks info vet info **Other** charge for damage prior notice required

This delightful Georgian house enjoys a stunning setting in 92 acres of deer park and woodland on the edge of the Mendip Hills. Elegant bedrooms in the main building and coach house are both spacious and comfortable. Public areas feature antiques, paintings and fine china. The restaurant enjoys a well-deserved reputation for its fine cuisine that utilises much home-grown produce.

Rooms 24 (2 fmly) (8 GF) **S** £105; **D** £135-£220 (incl. bkfst)*
Facilities ♨ ♨ Xmas New Year Wi-fi **Parking** 50 **Notes** LB

ENGLAND

Thorney Lakes Caravan Park *(ST430237)*

►►►

Thorney Lakes, Muchelney TA10 0DW
☎ 01458 250811
e-mail: enquiries@thorneylakes.co.uk
dir: *From A303 at Podimore rdbt take A372 to Langport. At Huish Episcopi Church turn left for Muchelney. In 100yds left (signed Muchelney & Crewkerne). Site 300yds after John Leach Pottery*

PETS: Stables Public areas disp bin **Exercise area** 2m walks in fields **Facilities** walks info vet info

Open Etr-Oct

A small, basic but very attractive park set in a cider apple orchard, with coarse fishing in the three well-stocked on-site lakes. The famous John Leach pottery shop is nearby. A 6 acre site with 36 touring pitches.

Notes 🐾

Best Western Northfield

★★★ 74% HOTEL
Northfield Rd TA24 5PU
☎ 01643 705155 & 0845 1302678 📠 01643 707715
e-mail: reservations@northfield-hotel.co.uk
web: www.northfield-hotel.co.uk
dir: *M5 junct 23, follow A38 to Bridgwater then A39 to Minehead*

PETS: Bedrooms (4 GF) unattended **Charges** £8 per night **Public areas** except restaurant, bar & lounge on leads **Grounds** on leads disp bin **Exercise area** 75mtrs **Facilities** vet info **On Request** fridge access torch towels

Located conveniently close to the town centre and the seafront, this hotel is set in delightfully maintained gardens and has a loyal following. A range of comfortable sitting rooms and leisure facilities, including an indoor, heated pool is provided. A fixed-price menu is served every evening in the oak-panelled dining room. The attractively co-ordinated bedrooms vary in size and are equipped to a good standard.

Rooms 30 (7 fmly) (4 GF) (6 smoking) **S** £64-£73; **D** £128-£165 (incl. bkfst & dinner)* **Facilities** STV FTV 🏊 Putt green Gym Steam room Xmas New Year Wi-fi **Services** Lift **Parking** 34 **Notes** LB

Alcombe House Hotel

★★ 85% HOTEL
Bircham Rd, Alcombe TA24 6BG
☎ 01643 705130
e-mail: alcombehouse@talktalkbusiness.net
web: www.alcombehouse.co.uk
dir: *On A39 on outskirts of Minehead opposite West Somerset Community College*

PETS: Bedrooms unattended **Stables** 2m **Grounds** on leads disp bin **Exercise area** 0.25m **Facilities** water bowl cage storage walks info vet info **On Request** fridge access torch towels **Other** prior notice required

Located midway between Minehead and Dunster on the coastal fringe of Exmoor National Park, this Grade II listed, Georgian hotel offers a delightful combination of efficient service and genuine hospitality delivered by the very welcoming resident proprietors. Public areas include a comfortable lounge and a candlelit dining room where a range of carefully prepared dishes is offered from a daily-changing menu.

Rooms 7 **S** £44; **D** £68 (incl. bkfst)* **Facilities** Xmas **Parking** 9 **Notes** LB No children 15yrs Closed 8 Nov-18 Mar

Minehead & Exmoor Caravan & Camping Park *(SS950457)*

►►►

Porlock Rd TA24 8SW
☎ 01643 703074
dir: *1m W of Minehead centre, take A39 towards Porlock. Site on right*

PETS: Public areas except children's play area & toilet block disp bin **Exercise area** 30mtrs **Facilities** walks info vet info **Other** vet available on-site on certain days

Open Mar-Oct rs Nov-Feb Certain wks only (phone to check) Last arrival 22.00hrs Last departure noon

A small terraced park on the edge of Exmoor, spread over five paddocks and screened by the mature trees that surround it. The level pitches provide a comfortable space for each unit on this family-run park. There is a laundrette in nearby Minehead. A 3 acre site with 50 touring pitches, 10 hardstandings.

Notes No open fires 🐾

MUCHELNEY — Map 3 ST42

Muchelney Caravan & Camping Site
(ST429249)

▶▶▶

Abbey Farm TA10 0DQ
☎ 01458 250112 & 07881 524425 ▤ 01458 250112
dir: *From A303 at Podimore rdbt take A372 towards Langport. At church in Huish Episcopi follow Muchelney Abbey sign. In Muchelney left at village cross. Site in 50mtrs*

PETS: Charges dog £1.50 per night £10.50 per week **Public areas** except dog-free area disp bin **Exercise area** grass run with disposal bin **Exercise area** 200mtrs **Facilities** washing facs walks info vet info **Other** prior notice required both dogs & cats must be kept on leads **Restrictions** no Pit Bull Terriers

Open all year Last arrival anytime Last departure flexible

This small developing site is situated opposite Muchelney Abbey, an English Heritage property. This quiet and peaceful site will appeal to all lovers of the countryside, and is well positioned for visiting the Somerset Levels. A 3 acre site with 40 touring pitches, 5 hardstandings.

Notes 🚭

PORLOCK — Map 3 SS84

Porlock Caravan Park *(SS882469)*

▶▶▶▶▶

TA24 8ND
☎ 01643 862269 ▤ 01643 862269
e-mail: info@porlockcaravanpark.co.uk
dir: *Through village fork right signed Porlock Weir, site on right*

PETS: Charges £1 per night £7 per week **Public areas** except toilets, shower, dishwash, laundry & nature garden on leads disp bin **Exercise area** enclosed dog walk **Exercise area** 30yds **Facilities** walks info vet info **Other** prior notice required organised walks with dogs **Resident Pets:** Sid & Alfie (cats)

Open 15 Mar-Oct Last arrival 20.00hrs Last departure 11.00hrs

A sheltered touring park in the centre of lovely countryside on the edge of the village, with Exmoor right on the doorstep. The toilet facilities are superb, and there's a popular kitchen area with microwave and freezer. Holiday statics for hire. A 3 acre site with 40 touring pitches, 14 hardstandings and 55 statics.

Notes No fires

Burrowhayes Farm Caravan & Camping Site *(SS897460)*

▶▶▶▶

West Luccombe TA24 8HT
☎ 01643 862463
e-mail: info@burrowhayes.co.uk
dir: *A39 from Minehead towards Porlock for 5m. Left at Red Post to Horner & West Luccombe, site 0.25m on right, immediately before humpback bridge*

PETS: Stables 2m **Public areas** disp bin **Exercise area** adjacent woods **Facilities** food dog chews cat treats scoop/disp bags leads walks info vet info **Other** ground tethers available

Open 15 Mar-Oct Last arrival 22.00hrs Last departure noon

A delightful site on the edge of Exmoor, sloping gently down to Horner Water. The farm buildings have been converted into riding stables which offers escorted rides on the moors, and the excellent toilet facilities are housed in timber-clad buildings. There are many walks directly into the countryside. An 8 acre site with 120 touring pitches, 10 hardstandings and 20 statics.

PRIDDY — Map 3 ST55

Cheddar Camping & Caravanning Club Site
(ST522519)

▶▶▶▶

Townsend BA5 3BP
☎ 01749 870241 & 0845 130 7633
dir: *From A39 take B3135 to Cheddar. After 4.5m turn left. Site 200yds on right*

PETS: Public areas except facility blocks (ex assist dogs) disp bin **Exercise area** surrounding countryside **Facilities** walks info **Other** prior notice required

Open Mar-15 Nov Last arrival 20.00hrs Last departure noon

A gently sloping site set high on the Mendip Hills and surrounded by trees. This excellent site offers good self-catered facilities especially for families, and fresh bread is baked daily. The site is well positioned for visiting local attractions such as Cheddar, Wookey Hole, Wells and Glastonbury, and is popular with walkers. A 3.5 acre site with 90 touring pitches.

Notes Site gates closed 23.00hrs-07.00hrs

ENGLAND

RUDGE
Map 3 ST85

The Full Moon Inn
★★★ INN
BA11 2QF
☎ 01373 830936
e-mail: info@thefullmoon.co.uk
dir: *From A36 S from Bath, 10m, left at Standerwick by The Bell pub. 4m from Warminster*

PETS: **Bedrooms** unattended **Charges** contact for details per night **Public areas** except restaurant on leads **Grounds** on leads disp bin **Exercise area** local walks **Facilities** vet info **On Request** fridge access **Other** cats must be caged

Peacefully located in the quiet village of Rudge, this traditional inn offers a warm welcome and a proper country pub atmosphere. In the bar area guests can mix with the locals to enjoy a selection of real ales, and a log fire in the colder months. In addition to bar meals, a comfortable restaurant serving excellent home cooked dishes is also available. Bedrooms include some at the main inn and more in an adjacent annexe - all are comfortable and well equipped.

Rooms 5 en suite 12 annexe en suite (2 fmly) (3 GF)
Facilities tea/coffee Dinner available Cen ht ⊗ **Parking** 25

SEDGEMOOR MOTORWAY SERVICE AREA (M5)   Map 3 ST35

Days Inn Sedgemoor
BUDGET HOTEL
Sedgemoor BS24 0JL
☎ 01934 750831   ▤ 01934 750808
e-mail: sedgemoor.hotel@welcomebreak.co.uk
web: www.welcomebreak.co.uk
dir: *M5 northbound junct 21/22*

PETS: **Bedrooms** (19 GF) **Public areas** **Grounds** on leads **Facilities** vet info

This modern building offers accommodation in smart, spacious and well-equipped bedrooms, suitable for families and business travellers, and all with en suite bathrooms. Continental breakfast is available and other refreshments may be taken at the nearby family restaurant.

Rooms 40 (39 fmly) (19 GF) (8 smoking) **S** £29-£69; **D** £29-£69

SPARKFORD
Map 3 ST62

Long Hazel Park *(ST602262)*
▶ ▶ ▶
High St BA22 7JH
☎ 01963 440002   ▤ 01963 440002
e-mail: longhazelpark@hotmail.com
dir: *Exit A303 at Hazlegrove rdbt, follow signs for Sparkford. Site 400yds on left*

PETS: **Stables** 10m **Charges** dogs £1 per night **Public areas** only on pitch occupied by dog owner; dogs must be exercised off site on leads disp bin **Exercise area** 200yds **Facilities** walks info vet info **Other** prior notice required shop 300mtrs; disposal bags available **Restrictions** no Pit Bull Terriers, Rottweilers, Dobermans or dangerous breeds (see page 7) **Resident Pet:** Lola (Jack Russell)

Open all year Last arrival 22.00hrs Last departure 11.00hrs

A very neat, adults-only park next to the village inn in the high street. This attractive park is run by friendly owners to a good standard. There are also luxury lodges on site. A 3.5 acre site with 50 touring pitches, 30 hardstandings and 4 statics.

STANTON DREW
Map 3 ST56

Greenlands *(ST597636)*
★★★★ FARMHOUSE
BS39 4ES
☎ 01275 333487   ▤ 01275 331211   Mrs J Cleverley
dir: *A37 onto B3130, on right before Stanton Drew Garage*

PETS: **Bedrooms** **Public areas** except dining room on leads **Grounds** on leads disp bin **Exercise area** adjacent **Facilities** washing facs cage storage walks info vet info **On Request** fridge access torch **Resident Pet:** Magic (Labrador)

Situated near the ancient village of Stanton Drew in the heart of the Chew Valley, Greenlands is convenient for Bristol Airport and Bath, Bristol and Wells. There are comfortable, well-equipped bedrooms and a downstairs lounge, and breakfast is the highlight of any stay here.

Rooms 4 en suite **Facilities** STV FTV TVL tea/coffee Cen ht **Parking** 8 **Notes** No Children 12yrs ⊛ 3 acres Hobby Farming - Poultry

STON EASTON — Map 3 ST65

Ston Easton Park

★★★★ ⁜⁜ COUNTRY HOUSE HOTEL

von Essen hotels

BA3 4DF

☎ 01761 241631 🖹 01761 241377

e-mail: info@stoneaston.co.uk

web: www.stoneaston.co.uk

dir: On A37

PETS: Bedrooms Stables 0.5m Charges Public areas except restaurant & other areas at manager's discretion Grounds disp bin Exercise area Facilities food (pre-bookable) food bowl water bowl bedding dog chews feeding mat scoop/disp bags leads washing facs dog grooming cage storage walks info vet info On Request fridge access torch towels Other charge for damage

This outstanding Palladian mansion lies in extensive parklands that were landscaped by Humphrey Repton. The architecture and decorative features are stunning and the Saloon is considered to be one of Somerset's finest rooms. The helpful and attentive team provide a very efficient service, and good, award-winning cuisine is on offer. The public areas, bedrooms and bathrooms are all appointed to a very high standard.

Rooms 22 (3 annexe) (2 fmly) S £135-£385; D £175-£495 (incl. bkfst)* Facilities STV ⌇ Fishing 🏹 Archery Clay pigeon shooting Quad bikes Hot air balloon Xmas New Year Wi-fi Parking 120 Notes LB

TAUNTON — Map 3 ST22

The Mount Somerset

★★★ 77% ⁜⁜ HOTEL

von Essen hotels

Lower Henlade TA3 5NB

☎ 01823 442500 🖹 01823 442900

e-mail: info@mountsomersethotel.co.uk

web: www.vonessenhotels.co.uk

dir: M5 junct 25, A358 towards Chard/Ilminster, at Henlade right into Stoke Rd, left at T-junct at end, then right into drive

PETS: Bedrooms unattended Charges Public areas except restaurant & conservatory on leads Grounds Facilities food bowl water bowl bedding feeding mat pet sitting dog walking cage storage walks info On Request fridge access torch towels Other charge for damage

From its elevated and rural position, this impressive Regency house has wonderful views over Taunton Vale. Some of the well-appointed bedrooms have feature bathrooms, and the elegant public rooms are stylish with an intimate atmosphere. In addition to the daily-changing, fixed-price menu, a carefully selected seasonal carte is available in the restaurant.

Rooms 11 (1 fmly) Facilities 🏊 Beauty treatments Xmas New Year Wi-fi Services Lift Parking 100

Farthings Country House Hotel and Restaurant

★★★ 74% ⁜ SMALL HOTEL

Village Rd, Hatch Beauchamp TA3 6SG

☎ 01823 480664 & 0785 668 8128 🖹 01823 481118

e-mail: farthingshotel@yahoo.co.uk

web: www.farthingshotel.co.uk

dir: From A358, between Taunton & Ilminster turn into Hatch Beauchamp for hotel in village centre

PETS: Bedrooms (3 GF) Public areas on leads Grounds on leads disp bin Exercise area adjacent Facilities food (pre-bookable) food bowl water bowl dog chews scoop/disp bags leads washing facs cage storage walks info vet info On Request fridge access torch towels Other please phone for further details of pet facilities; dog grooming locally Resident Pets: Sasha (Cocker Spaniel), Borris, Dorothy & Lucy (pigs) chickens, ducks, geese

This delightful hotel, set in its own extensive gardens in a peaceful village location, offers comfortable accommodation, combined with all the character and charm of a building dating back over 200 years. The calm atmosphere makes this a great place to relax and unwind. Dinner service is attentive, and menus feature best quality local ingredients prepared and presented with care.

Rooms 12 (2 fmly) (3 GF) S £65-£155; D £75-£175 (incl. bkfst)* Facilities FTV 🏊 Xmas New Year Wi-fi Parking 25 Notes LB

Express by Holiday Inn Taunton, M5 Jct 25

BUDGET HOTEL

Blackbrook Business Park, Blackbrook Park Av TA1 2PX

☎ 01823 624000 🖹 01823 624024

e-mail: managertaunton@expressholidayinn.co.uk

web: www.hiexpress.com/taunton

dir: M5 junct 25. Follow signs for Blackbrook Business Park. 100yds on right

PETS: Bedrooms (22 GF) Charges Public areas Grounds on leads disp bin Exercise area On Request torch Other charge for damage well behaved pets only, must be supervised at all times

A modern hotel ideal for families and business travellers. Fresh and uncomplicated, the spacious rooms include Sky TV, power shower and tea and coffee-making facilities. Continental buffet breakfast is included in the room rate; other meals may be taken at the nearby family pub or restaurant.

Rooms 92 (55 fmly) (22 GF) (8 smoking)

TAUNTON *continued*

The Hatch Inn

★★★ INN

Village Rd, Hatch Beauchamp TA3 6SG

☎ 01823 480245

e-mail: jamie@thehatchinn.co.uk

web: www.thehatchinn.co.uk

dir: *M5 junct 25, 3m S off A358*

PETS: **Bedrooms Charges** £5 per night **Public areas** except lounge bar on leads **Exercise area** country walks **Facilities** food bowl water bowl washing facs cage storage walks info vet info **On Request** fridge access torch towels **Other** charge for damage

With easy access to both the A303 and M5, this 18th-century, family-run coaching inn is very much the village local, complete with crackling log fires and a convivial atmosphere. Bedrooms offer good levels of comfort with well appointed bathrooms. Public areas include a choice of bars serving local ales, and the menu features honest, home-cooked cuisine with a focus on local produce.

Rooms 5 en suite (1 fmly) **Facilities** FTV tea/coffee Dinner available Cen ht Wi-fi Pool Table **Parking** 15 **Notes** No coaches

Cornish Farm Touring Park *(ST235217)*

►►►►

Shoreditch TA3 7BS

☎ 01823 327746   ▤ 01823 354946

e-mail: info@cornishfarm.com

dir: *M5 junct 25 towards Taunton. Left at lights. 3rd left into Ilminster Rd (follow Corfe signs). Right at rdbt, left at next. Right at T-junct, left into Killams Dr, 2nd left into Killams Ave. Over motorway bridge. Site on left, take 2nd entrance*

PETS: **Charges** 50p per night £3.50 per week **Public areas** disp bin **Exercise area** public footpath adjacent **Facilities** walks info vet info **Resident Pet:** 1 German Shepherd, cats

Open all year Last arrival anytime Last departure 11.30hrs

This smart park provides really top quality facilities throughout. Although only two miles from Taunton, it is set in open countryside and is a very convenient base for visiting the many attractions of the area such as Clarks Village, Glastonbury and Cheddar Gorge. A 3.5 acre site with 50 touring pitches, 25 hardstandings.

Ashe Farm Camping & Caravan Site

(ST279229)

►►►

Thornfalcon TA3 5NW

☎ 01823 443764

e-mail: info@ashefarm.co.uk

dir: *M5 junct 25, A358 E for 2.5m. Right at Nags Head pub. Site 0.25m on right*

PETS: **Public areas Exercise area** dog walk around fields **Facilities** walks info vet info **Resident Pets:** 3 dogs

Open Apr-Oct Last arrival 22.00hrs Last departure noon

A well-screened site surrounded by mature trees and shrubs, with two large touring fields. A facilities block includes smart toilets and a separate laundry room. Not far from the bustling market town of Taunton, and handy for both coasts. A 7 acre site with 30 touring pitches, 11 hardstandings.

Notes

Holly Bush Park *(ST220162)*

►►►

Culmhead TA3 7EA

☎ 01823 421515

e-mail: info@hollybushpark.com

dir: *M5 junct 25 towards Taunton. At 1st lights left signed Corfe/Taunton Racecourse. 3.5m past Corfe on B3170 right at x-rds at top of hill on unclass road towards Wellington. Right at next junct, site 150yds on left*

PETS: **Charges** contact for details per night **Public areas** except buildings disp bin on leads **Exercise area** field available; Foresty Commission land 50yds **Facilities** food food bowl water bowl dog chews leads washing facs **Other** dogs must be kept on a lead disposal bags available

Open all year Last arrival 21.00hrs Last departure 11.00hrs

An immaculate little park set in an orchard in attractive countryside, with easy access to Wellington and Taunton. The friendly owners are welcoming and keen to help, and keep the facilities in good order. A 2 acre site with 40 touring pitches, 7 hardstandings.

WATCHET Map 3 ST04

Home Farm Holiday Centre *(ST106432)*

▶▶▶

St Audries Bay TA4 4DP
☎ 01984 632487 📄 01984 634687
e-mail: dib@homefarmholidaycentre.co.uk
dir: *Follow A39 towards Minehead, right onto B3191 at West Quantoxhead after St Audries garage, then right in 0.25m*

PETS: Charges £2 per night **Public areas** except bar building, shop & swimming pool disp bin **Exercise area** 2 open grass areas, beach & woodland walk **Facilities** food leads walks info vet info **Other** disposal bags & pet toys available **Resident Pets:** Pickle & Flea (Border Terriers), Oaky & Tarna (Lurchers), Turk (Jack Russell), Tig (Alsatian), Tao & Lace (Huskies), 2 cats

Open all year rs mid Nov-Etr shop & bar closed Last arrival dusk Last departure noon

In a hidden valley beneath the Quantock Hills, this park overlooks its own private beach. The atmosphere is friendly and quiet, and there are lovely sea views from the level pitches. Flower beds, woodland walks, and a koi carp pond all enhance this very attractive site, along with a lovely indoor swimming pool and a beer garden. A 45 acre site with 40 touring pitches, 35 hardstandings and 230 statics.

WELLINGTON Map 3 ST12

The Cleve Spa

★★★★ GUEST ACCOMMODATION

Mantle St TA21 8SN
☎ 01823 662033 📄 01823 660874
e-mail: info@clevehotel.com
web: www.clevehotel.com
dir: *M5 junct 26 follow signs to Wellington town centre. Continue for 600mtrs, entrance on left*

PETS: Bedrooms Charges from £15 per night **Public areas** except restaurant or bar (during service) on leads **Grounds** on leads **Facilities** food bowl water bowl walks info vet info **Other** charge for damage

This elegant Victorian country house is situated in an elevated position with commanding views. Bedrooms provide high levels of comfort and quality with well appointed and stylish bathrooms. Dinner and breakfast are served in the attractive restaurant, after which a stroll around the extensive grounds may be appropriate. An impressive array of leisure facilities is also offered, including indoor pool, spa bath, steam room and fully-equipped fitness studio.

Rooms 20 en suite (5 fmly) (3 GF) **S** £55-£85; **D** £70-£120*
Facilities FTV Dinner available Direct Dial Cen ht Licensed Wi-fi
🕾 Snooker Sauna Solarium Gym **Parking** 100 **Notes** LB

Gamlins Farm Caravan Park *(ST083195)*

▶▶▶

Gamlins Farm House, Greenham TA21 0LZ
☎ 01823 672859 & 07967 683738 📄 01823 673391
e-mail: nataliehowe@hotmail.com
dir: *M5 junct 26, A38 towards Tiverton & Exeter. 5m, right for Greenham, site 1m on right*

PETS: Stables Charges cats & dogs 50p, horses £6-£10 per night **Public areas** except laundry & wash rooms on leads **Exercise area** field available **Facilities** washing facs walks info vet info **Other** prior notice required sand school available (80 x 20mtrs)

Open Mar-Oct

A well-planned site in a secluded position with panoramic views. The friendly owners keep the toilet facilities to a good standard of cleanliness. A 3 acre site with 25 touring pitches, 6 hardstandings and 3 statics.

Notes No loud noise after 22.00hrs 🐾

WELLS Map 3 ST54

Coxley Vineyard

★★ 71% HOTEL

Coxley BA5 1RQ
☎ 01749 670285 📄 01749 679708
e-mail: max@orofino.freeserve.co.uk
dir: *A39 from Wells signed Coxley. Village halfway between Wells & Glastonbury. Hotel off main road at end of village*

PETS: Bedrooms (8 GF) unattended **Stables** 3m **Public areas** except restaurant & lounge bar **Grounds** disp bin **Exercise area** surrounding area **Facilities** water bowl washing facs cage storage walks info vet info **On Request** fridge access towels

This privately owned and personally run hotel was built on the site of an old cider farm. It was later part of a commercial vineyard and some of the vines are still in evidence. It provides well equipped, modern bedrooms; most are situated on the ground floor. There is a comfortable bar and a spacious restaurant with an impressive lantern ceiling. The hotel is a popular venue for conferences and other functions.

Rooms 9 (5 fmly) (8 GF) **S** £55-£72.50; **D** £70-£89.50 (incl. bkfst)* **Facilities** 🕾 Xmas Wi-fi **Parking** 50 **Notes** LB

ENGLAND

The Crown at Wells
★★★★ INN
Market Place BA5 2RP
☎ 01749 673457   📠 01749 679792
e-mail: stay@crownatwells.co.uk
web: www.crownatwells.co.uk
dir: *On entering Wells follow signs for Hotels & Deliveries*

PETS: **Bedrooms** unattended **Charges** £5 per night **Grounds** on leads **Exercise area** **Facilities** food bowl water bowl walks info **On Request** fridge access torch towels **Other** charge for damage

Retaining its original features and period charm, this historic inn is situated in the heart of the city, just a short stroll from the cathedral. The building's frontage has been used in many film productions. Bedrooms, all with modern facilities, vary in size and style. Public areas focus around Anton's, the popular bistro, which offers a light and airy environment and relaxed atmosphere. The Penn Bar offers an alternative eating option and real ales.

Rooms 15 en suite (2 fmly) **S** £60-£90; **D** £90-£110 **Facilities** FTV tea/coffee Dinner available Cen ht Wi-fi Golf 18 **Parking** 10 **Notes** LB

Infield House
★★★★ BED AND BREAKFAST
36 Portway BA5 2BN
☎ 01749 670989   📠 01749 679093
e-mail: infield@talk21.com
web: www.infieldhouse.co.uk
dir: *500yds W of city centre on A371 Portway*

PETS: **Bedrooms** **Public areas** **Grounds** on leads disp bin **Exercise area** 0.5m **Facilities** leads washing facs walks info vet info **On Request** fridge access torch towels **Other** pets are accepted by prior arrangement only **Restrictions** no dogs under 1 year **Resident Pet:** Pepper (Pembroke Corgi)

This charming Victorian house offers comfortable, spacious rooms of elegance and style. The friendly hosts are very welcoming and provide a relaxing home-from-home. Dinners, by arrangement, are served in the pleasant dining room where good home cooking ensures an enjoyable and varied range of options.

Rooms 3 en suite; **D** £66-£68* **Facilities** FTV tea/coffee Dinner available Cen ht Wi-fi **Parking** 3 **Notes** No Children 12yrs

Birdwood House
★★★ GUEST ACCOMMODATION
Birdwood, Bath Rd BA5 3EW
☎ 01749 679250
e-mail: info@birdwood-bandb.co.uk
web: www.birdwood-bandb.co.uk
dir: *1.5m NE of city centre. On B3139 between South & West Horrington*

PETS: **Bedrooms** **Sep accom** large kennel with run **Stables** 4m **Public areas** except dining room on leads **Grounds** on leads disp bin **Exercise area** 100mtrs **Facilities** food (pre-bookable) food bowl water bowl bedding dog chews feeding mat scoop/disp bags leads dog walking washing facs cage storage walks info vet info **On Request** fridge access towels **Restrictions** no Pit Bull Terriers **Resident Pets:** Florrie (Springer Spaniel), Rye & Daisy (cats), cows

Set in extensive grounds and gardens just a short drive from the town centre, this imposing detached house dates from the 1850s. The bedrooms are comfortable and equipped with a number of extra facilities. Breakfast is served around a communal table in the pleasant dining room or conservatory, which is also available for guest use throughout the day.

Rooms 3 rms (2 en suite) (1 pri facs) (1 fmly) **Facilities** TVL tea/coffee Cen ht ⏳ **Parking** 12 **Notes** LB 🐾

Homestead Park *(ST532474)*
▶▶
Wookey Hole BA5 1BW
☎ 01749 673022   📠 01749 673022
e-mail: homesteadpark@onetel.com
dir: *0.5m NW off A371 (Wells to Cheddar road). (NB weight limit on bridge into touring area now 1 tonne)*

PETS: **Charges** 50p per night **Public areas** disp bin **Exercise area** 50mtrs **Facilities** walks info vet info

Open Etr-Sep Last arrival 20.00hrs Last departure noon

This attractive, small site for tents only is by a stream and has mature trees. Set on a wooded hillside and meadowland with access to the river and Wookey Hole. This park is for adults only and the statics are residential caravans. A 2 acre site with 30 touring pitches and 28 statics.

Notes Tents only 🐾

WESTON-SUPER-MARE Map 3 ST36

Camellia Lodge
★★★★ BED AND BREAKFAST
76 Walliscote Rd BS23 1ED
☎ 01934 613534 📠 01934 613534
e-mail: dachefscamellia@aol.com
dir: *200yds from seafront*

PETS: Bedrooms unattended **Exercise area** 400yds beach &
parks **Facilities** walks info vet info **On Request** torch **Other**
charge for damage **Resident Pets:** Jack (dog), Rosie & Riley
(cats)

Guests return regularly for the warm welcome at this immaculate
Victorian family home, which is just off the seafront and within
walking distance of the town centre. Bedrooms have a range
of thoughtful touches, and carefully prepared breakfasts are
served in the relaxing dining room. Home-cooked dinners are also
available by prior arrangement.

Rooms 5 en suite (2 fmly) **S** £30-£35; **D** £60-£70* **Facilities** FTV
tea/coffee Dinner available Cen ht Wi-fi

Country View Holiday Park *(ST335647)*
▶▶▶
Sand Rd, Sand Bay BS22 9UJ
☎ 01934 627595
e-mail: info@cvhp.co.uk
dir: *M5 junct 21, A370 towards Weston-Super-Mare. Immediately
into left lane, follow Kewstoke/Sand Bay signs. Straight over 3
rdbts onto Lower Norton Ln. At Sand Bay right into Sand Rd, site
on right*

PETS: Stables 1m **Charges** £2 per night £14 per week
Public areas except in shop & bar disp bin **Exercise area**
200yds **Facilities** walks info vet info **Other** prior notice required

Open Mar-Jan Last arrival 20.00hrs Last departure noon

A pleasant open site in a rural area a few hundred yards from
Sandy Bay and beach. The park is also well placed for energetic
walks along the coast at either end of the beach. The facilities
are excellent and well maintained. An 8 acre site with 120 touring
pitches, 90 hardstandings and 65 statics.

WHEDDON CROSS Map 3 SS94

North Wheddon Farm *(SS923385)*
★★★★ 🏠 🍽 FARMHOUSE
TA24 7EX
☎ 01643 841791 Mrs R Abraham
e-mail: rachael@go-exmoor.co.uk
dir: *500yds S of village x-rds on A396. Pass Moorland Hall on left,
driveway next right*

PETS: Bedrooms Charges dogs £5 per night **Public areas**
except dining areas at meal times on leads **Grounds** on leads
disp bin **Exercise area** 0.25m **Facilities** washing facs cage
storage walks info vet info **On Request** torch towels **Other**
charge for damage **Resident Pets:** Poppy & Mingming (Border/
Lakeland Terrier cross), sheep, pigs, chickens, ducks, goats,
geese, tortoise

North Wheddon Farm is a delightfully friendly and comfortable
environment with great views, a perfect base for exploring the
delights of Exmoor. The tranquil grounds include a pleasant
garden and guests are welcome to roam the fields and say hello
to the pigs, sheep, goats and any other new arrivals! Memorable
dinners and breakfasts feature excellent produce, much of it
straight from the farm. The bedrooms are thoughtfully equipped
and individual in style with lovely comfy beds.

Rooms 3 rms (2 en suite) (1 pri facs) **S** £38.50; **D** £77*
Facilities FTV tea/coffee Dinner available Cen ht Licensed Wi-fi
Riding **Parking** 5 **Notes** LB 20 acres Mixed

WILLITON Map 4 ST04

The White House
★★★★ GUEST ACCOMMODATION

11 Long St TA4 4QW
☎ 01984 632306
e-mail: whitehouselive@btconnect.com
dir: *A39 Bridgwater to Minehead, in Williton on right prior to Watchet turning*

PETS: Bedrooms unattended Sep accom barn Exercise area 2 mins' walk Facilities washing facs cage storage walks info vet info On Request fridge access torch towels Other charge for damage Resident Pet: 1 Standard Poodle

This Grade II listed Georgian house is in a perfect location for guests wishing to explore this beautiful countryside and the coast. Many original features have been retained which add to the character of this charming establishment. Bedrooms are located both in the main house and an adjacent courtyard; all are impressive and have Egyptian cotton linen and fluffy towels. Breakfast is served in the elegant dining room, and there is a guest lounge for relaxation.

Rooms 8 rms (7 en suite) (1 pri facs) 6 annexe en suite (2 fmly) (6 GF) S £37-£47; D £74-£94* Facilities FTV TVL tea/coffee Cen ht Licensed Wi-fi Parking 12 Notes LB

WINCANTON Map 3 ST72

Holbrook House
★★★ 79% ◉◉ COUNTRY HOUSE HOTEL

Holbrook BA9 8BS
☎ 01963 824466 & 828844 ▤ 01963 32681
e-mail: enquiries@holbrookhouse.co.uk
web: www.holbrookhouse.co.uk
dir: *From A303 at Wincanton left onto A371 towards Castle Cary & Shepton Mallet*

PETS: Bedrooms (5 GF) unattended Charges £10 per night Public areas except restaurant areas on leads Grounds on leads Exercise area 50mtrs Facilities food bowl water bowl leads cage storage walks info vet info On Request fridge access torch towels Other charge for damage

This handsome country house offers a unique blend of quality and comfort combined with a friendly atmosphere. Set in 17 acres of peaceful gardens and wooded grounds, Holbrook House makes a perfect retreat. The restaurant provides a selection of innovative dishes prepared with enthusiasm and served by a team of caring staff.

Rooms 21 (5 annexe) (2 fmly) (5 GF) S £105-£155; D £150-£250 (incl. bkfst)* Facilities Spa FTV ◉ ◉ ◉ Gym Beauty treatment Exercise classes Sauna Steam room Fitness suite ♫ Xmas New Year Wi-fi Parking 100

WITHYPOOL Map 3 SS83

The Royal Oak Inn
★★★★ ⌂ INN

TA24 7QP
☎ 01643 831506 ▤ 01643 831659
e-mail: enquiries@royaloakwithypool.co.uk
dir: *7m N of Dulverton, off B3223*

PETS: Bedrooms Sep accom 1 outdoor kennel Stables 1m Charges £8 per night £56 per week Public areas except restaurant on leads Exercise area 500mtrs Facilities food bowl water bowl bedding dog chews leads walks info vet info On Request torch towels

Set at the heart of Exmoor, this long established and popular inn continues to provide rest and sustenance for weary travellers. The atmosphere is warm and engaging with the bar always frequented by cheery locals. Bedrooms and bathrooms are stylish and very well appointed with added touches of luxury such as Egyptian cotton linen, bath robes and cosseting towels. Menus feature local produce and can be enjoyed either in the bars or in the elegant restaurant.

Rooms 8 rms (7 en suite) (1 pri facs) Facilities tea/coffee Dinner available Direct Dial Cen ht Parking 10 Notes No Children 10yrs No coaches

WIVELISCOMBE Map 3 ST02

Waterrow Touring Park (ST053251)
►►►►►

TA4 2AZ
☎ 01984 623464
e-mail: waterrowpark@yahoo.co.uk
dir: *From M5 junct 25 take A358 (signed Minehead) around Taunton, then B3227 through Wiveliscombe. Site in 3m at Waterrow, 0.25m past Rock Inn*

PETS: Charges £1.50 per night £10.50 per week Public areas except on-site facilities disp bin Exercise area dog exercise field & river walks Facilities walks info vet info Other prior notice required max 2 dogs per unit tick removing tools & disposal bags available Resident Pets: Basil & Smokey (cats)

Open all year Last arrival 19.00hrs Last departure 11.30hrs

This really delightful park for adults only has spotless facilities and plenty of spacious hardstandings. The River Tone runs along a valley beneath the park, accessed by steps to a nature area created by the owners, where fly fishing is permitted. Painting workshops and other activities are available, and the local pub is a short walk away. A 6 acre site with 45 touring pitches, 38 hardstandings and 1 static.

Notes No gazebos

Little Barwick House

★ ★ ★ ★ ★ RESTAURANT WITH ROOMS

Barwick Village BA22 9TD
☎ 01935 423902 📠 01935 420908
e-mail: littlebarwick@hotmail.com
dir: *From Yeovil A37 towards Dorchester, left at 1st rdbt, 1st left, 0.25m on left*

PETS: **Bedrooms** unattended **Charges** £5 per stay **Public areas** except restaurant **Grounds Exercise area** fields & footpaths accessed from house **Facilities** leads pet sitting dog walking washing facs cage storage walks info vet info **On Request** torch towels **Other** charge for damage dogs allowed in lounge if acceptable to other guests **Resident Pets:** Ellie & Archie (Pointers), Rossi & Casey (cats), Pip & Maverick (Hanovarian event horses)

Situated in a quiet hamlet in three and half acres of gardens and grounds, this listed Georgian dower house is an ideal retreat for those seeking peaceful surroundings and good food. Just one of the highlights of a stay here is a meal in the restaurant, where good use is made of local ingredients. Each of the bedrooms has its own character, and a range of thoughtful extras such as fresh flowers, bottled water and magazines is provided.

Rooms 6 en suite **S** £80-£100; **D** £100-£140* **Facilities** FTV tea/coffee Dinner available Direct Dial Cen ht **Parking** 30 **Notes** LB No Children 5yrs RS Sun eve & Mon closed No coaches

The Masons Arms

★ ★ ★ ★ INN

41 Lower Odcombe BA22 8TX
☎ 01935 862591 📠 01935 862591
e-mail: paula@masonsarmsodcombe.co.uk
web: www.masonsarmsodcombe.co.uk
dir: *From A303 take A3088 to Yeovil, follow signs to Montacute after village, 3rd turn on right*

PETS: **Bedrooms** unattended **Stables** 0.5m **Charges** £5 per night **Public areas** on leads **Grounds** disp bin **Exercise area** **Facilities** food (pre-bookable) food bowl water bowl bedding dog chews cat treats feeding mat litter tray scoop/disp bags leads washing facs cage storage walks info vet info **On Request** fridge access torch towels **Other** charge for damage **Resident Pets:** Royce (Springer Spaniel), Ruff (Border Collie), Blake (Jack Russell /Chihuahua cross), Rolo (Jack Russell/Poodle cross), Harley, Duke & Morgan (cats), PJ, Moppet & Fiver (rabbits), chickens

Dating back to the 16th century, this charming inn claims to be the oldest building in this small country village, on the outskirts of Yeovil. The spacious bedrooms are contemporary in style, with clean lines, a high level of comfort and a wide range of considerate extras. The friendly hosts run their own micro-brewery, and their ales are available at the bar along with others.

Public areas include the bar/restaurant, which offers a full menu of freshly prepared dishes, along with a choice of lighter snacks.

The Masons Arms

Rooms 6 en suite (1 fmly) (6 GF) **S** £55-£70; **D** £85*
Facilities FTV tea/coffee Dinner available Direct Dial Cen ht Wi-fi **Parking** 35 **Notes** No coaches

The Helyar Arms

★ ★ ★ ★ INN

Moor Ln, East Coker BA22 9JR
☎ 01935 862332 📠 01935 864129
e-mail: info@helyar-arms.co.uk
dir: *3m S of Yeovil. Off A30 or A37 into East Coker*

PETS: **Bedrooms** unattended **Stables** 1m **Public areas** on leads **Grounds** disp bin **Exercise area** 0.5m **Facilities** walks info vet info **Other** charge for damage

A charming 15th-century inn, serving real food in the heart of a pretty Somerset village. The traditional friendly bar with hand-drawn ales retains many original features while the bedrooms offer well equipped, attractive accommodation and modern facilities.

Rooms 6 en suite (3 fmly) **Facilities** tea/coffee Dinner available Direct Dial Cen ht Wi-fi **Parking** 40 **Notes** LB

The Halfway House Inn Country Lodge

★ ★ ★ INN

Ilchester Rd BA22 8RE
☎ 01935 840350 📠 01935 849006
e-mail: paul@halfwayhouseinn.com
web: www.halfwayhouseinn.com
dir: *A303 onto A37 Yeovil road at Ilchester, inn 2m on left*

PETS: **Bedrooms** sign **Charges** £5 per night **Public areas** except restaurant/main bar (assist dogs only) on leads **Grounds** on leads disp bin **Exercise area** 2m **Facilities** walks info vet info **On Request** fridge access **Other** charge for damage

This roadside inn offers comfortable accommodation, which consists of bedrooms in the main house and other contemporary style rooms, each having its own front door, in the annexe. All rooms are bright and well equipped. Meals are available in the cosy restaurant and bar where friendly staff ensure a warm welcome.

Rooms 11 en suite 9 annexe en suite (7 fmly) (9 GF)
S £49.95-£64.95; **D** £54.95-£135* **Facilities** STV tea/coffee Dinner available Cen ht Wi-fi Fishing Pool table **Parking** 49 **Notes** LB

ENGLAND

Halfway Caravan & Camping Park *(ST530195)*

► ►

Trees Cottage, Halfway, Ilchester Rd BA22 8RE
☎ 01935 840342
e-mail: halfwaycaravanpark@earthlink.net
dir: *On A37 between Ilchester & Yeovil*

PETS: Charges £1 per night £7 per week **Public areas** disp bin **Exercise area** public footpath **Facilities** washing facs walks info vet info **Restrictions** no large dogs; no Rottweilers, Mastiffs, Pit Bulls or Dobermans **Resident Pet:** 1 Belgian Shepherd

Open Mar-Oct Last arrival 19.00hrs Last departure noon

An attractive little park near the Somerset and Dorset border, and next to the Halfway House pub and restaurant, which also has excellent AA-graded accommodation (see previous entry). It overlooks a fishing lake and is surrounded by attractive countryside, with free fishing for people staying at the park. A 2 acre site with 20 touring pitches, 10 hardstandings.

Notes No group parties 🐕

STAFFORDSHIRE

BURTON UPON TRENT   Map 8 SK22

  RAMADA JARVIS

Newton Park

★ ★ ★ ★ 71% COUNTRY HOUSE HOTEL
Newton Solney DE15 0SS
☎ 01283 703568 📠 01283 709235
e-mail: sales.newtonpark@ramadajarvis.co.uk
web: www.ramadajarvis.co.uk
dir: *On B5008 past Repton to Newton Solney. Hotel on left*

PETS: Bedrooms (7 GF) **Charges Grounds** on leads **Facilities** vet info **On Request** torch **Other** charge for damage contact hotel for further details

Set in landscaped grounds, this 18th-century, Grade II listed country-house hotel was once the home of Staffordshire brewer William Worthington. It is now a popular venue for weddings, conferences and meetings. Bedrooms, including executive rooms and suites, are comfortably appointed for both business and leisure guests. Guest can choose to eat in the oak-panelled Folly Restaurant, or in summer relax on the terrace with a drink.

Rooms 50 (5 fmly) (7 GF) (2 smoking) **Facilities** FTV Xmas New Year Wi-fi **Services** Lift **Parking** 120

 Holiday Inn Express

Holiday Inn Express Burton upon Trent

BUDGET HOTEL

2nd Av, Centrum 100 DE14 2WF
☎ 01283 504300 📠 01283 504301
e-mail: info@exhiburton.co.uk
web: www.hiexpress.com/burton-n-trent
dir: *From A38 Branston exit take A5121 signed Town Centre. At McDonalds rdbt, turn left into 2nd Avenue. Hotel on left*

PETS: Bedrooms Stables 0.5m **Charges** £10 per night **Public areas** on leads **Grounds** on leads disp bin **Exercise area Facilities** walks info vet info **On Request** torch towels **Other** charge for damage dogs accepted by prior arrangement only **Restrictions** small dogs only

A modern hotel ideal for families and business travellers. Fresh and uncomplicated, the spacious rooms include Sky TV, power shower and tea and coffee-making facilities. Continental buffet breakfast is included in the room rate; other meals may be taken at the nearby family pub or restaurant.

Rooms 82 (47 fmly)

LONGNOR   Map 7 SK06

Longnor Wood Holiday Park *(SK072640)*

► ► ► ►

SK17 0NG
☎ 01298 83648 📠 01298 83648
e-mail: info@longnorwood.co.uk
dir: *1.25m from Longnor (off Longnor to Leek road), signed from village*

PETS: Public areas except toilet/shower block & on-site shop disp bin **Exercise area** 4-acre field plus woodland walk **Facilities** food bowl water bowl scoop/disp bags leads washing facs walks info vet info

Open Mar-10 Jan Last arrival 21.00hrs Last departure noon

This spacious adult-only park enjoys a secluded setting in the Peak District National Park, an Area of Outstanding Natural Beauty. It is surrounded by beautiful rolling countryside and sheltered by woodland, with wildlife encouraged. The nearby village of Longnor offers pub food, restaurants and shops. A 10.5 acre site with 47 touring pitches, 40 hardstandings and 14 statics.

Hatherton Country House Hotel

★★★ 66% HOTEL

Pinfold Ln ST19 5QP

☎ 01785 712459 📠 01785 715532

e-mail: enquiries@hotels-stafford.com

dir: *A449 to Wolverhampton. In Penkridge turn right after George & Fox pub into Pinfold Ln. Hotel on left in 300yds*

PETS: Bedrooms (18 GF) **Stables** 1.5m **Grounds** on leads disp bin **Exercise area** 0.25m **Facilities** water bowl cage storage vet info **On Request** fridge access towels **Other** charge for damage

The hotel offers comfortable accommodation to both business and leisure guests. The leisure facilities consist of a pool, steam room and jacuzzi with a well-equipped gym and two squash courts. Conference facilities are also available. There is free parking and easy access to the city and countryside.

Rooms 51 (4 fmly) (18 GF) (4 smoking) **S** £49-£110; **D** £49-£110 **Facilities** FTV ⊗ Gym Squash Sauna Xmas New Year Wi-fi **Parking** 200 **Notes** LB

Old School

★★★ BED AND BREAKFAST

Newport Rd, Haughton ST18 9JH

☎ 01785 780358 📠 01785 780358

e-mail: info@theoldsc.co.uk

dir: *A518 W from Stafford, 3m to Haughton, Old School next to church*

PETS: Bedrooms Facilities walks info vet info **On Request** fridge access torch

Located in the heart of Haughton, this Grade II listed former Victorian school has been renovated to provide a range of modern bedrooms equipped with thoughtful extras. The bedrooms comprise a single, a double and a twin; each has a TV. Breakfast is served at a family table in a cosy lounge-dining room.

Rooms 3 rms (3 GF) **S** £25; **D** £50* **Facilities** tea/coffee Cen ht **Parking** 3 **Notes** 🐾

Oak Tree Farm

★★★★★ GUEST ACCOMMODATION

Hints Rd, Hopwas B78 3AA

☎ 01827 56807 📠 01827 67271

e-mail: oaktreefarm1@aol.com

web: www.oaktreefarmhotel.co.uk

dir: *2m NW of Tamworth. Off A51 in Hopwas*

PETS: Bedrooms sign **Charges Grounds Exercise area** woods (5 mins) **Facilities** cage storage walks info vet info **Other** charge for damage

A warm welcome is assured at this sympathetically restored farmhouse, located in peaceful rural surroundings yet only a short drive from the NEC. Spacious bedrooms are filled with homely extras. The elegant dining room, adorned with Oriental artefacts, is the setting for memorable breakfasts. A small conference room is available.

Rooms 2 en suite 5 annexe en suite (2 fmly) (2 GF) **S** £35-£69; **D** £55-£85 **Facilities** FTV TVL tea/coffee Cen ht Wi-fi ⊗ Fishing Sauna **Parking** 20

Brudenell Hotel

★★★★ 85% ⊚⊚ HOTEL

The Parade IP15 5BU

☎ 01728 452071 📠 01728 454082

e-mail: info@brudenellhotel.co.uk

web: www.brudenellhotel.co.uk

dir: *A12/A1094, on reaching town, turn right at junct into High St. Hotel on seafront adjoining Fort Green car park*

PETS: Bedrooms unattended **Charges** £10 per night **Public areas** only on terrace on leads **Exercise area Facilities** food (pre-bookable) food bowl water bowl dog chews vet info **On Request** fridge access torch **Other** charge for damage **Restrictions** well behaved dogs only

Situated at the far end of the town centre just a step away from the beach, this hotel has a contemporary appearance, enhanced by subtle lighting and quality soft furnishings. Many of the bedrooms have superb sea views; they include deluxe rooms with king-sized beds and superior rooms suitable for families. The informal restaurant showcases skilfully prepared dishes that use fresh, seasonal produce especially local fish, seafood and game.

Rooms 44 (15 fmly) **S** £76-£111; **D** £140-£285 (incl. bkfst)* **Facilities** Xmas New Year Wi-fi **Services** Lift **Parking** 16 **Notes** LB

ALDEBURGH *continued*

Wentworth

★★★ 88% ◉◉ HOTEL

Wentworth Rd IP15 5BD

☎ 01728 452312 📄 01728 454343

e-mail: stay@wentworth-aldeburgh.co.uk

web: www.wentworth-aldeburgh.com

dir: *Off A12 onto A1094, 6m to Aldeburgh, with church on left, left at bottom of hill*

PETS: Bedrooms (5 GF) unattended **Charges** £2 per night **Public areas** except restaurant **Grounds** on leads **Exercise area** 300mtrs **Facilities** food bowl water bowl walks info vet info **On Request** fridge access torch **Other** charge for damage **Restrictions** no breed larger than a Labrador

A delightful privately owned hotel overlooking the beach. The attractive, well-maintained public rooms include three stylish lounges as well as a cocktail bar and elegant restaurant. Bedrooms are smartly decorated with co-ordinated fabrics and have many thoughtful touches; some rooms have superb sea views. Several very spacious Mediterranean-style rooms are located across the road.

Rooms 35 (7 annexe) (5 GF) **S** £60.50-£115; **D** £112-£248 (incl. bkfst)* **Facilities** FTV Xmas New Year Wi-fi **Parking** 30 **Notes** LB

Best Western White Lion

★★★ 86% ◉ HOTEL

Market Cross Place IP15 5BJ

☎ 01728 452720 📄 01728 452986

e-mail: info@whitelion.co.uk

web: www.whitelion.co.uk

dir: *A12 onto A1094, follow signs to Aldeburgh at junct on left. Hotel on right*

PETS: Bedrooms unattended **Stables** 2m **Charges** £7.50 per night **Public areas** except restaurant on leads disp bin **Exercise area** beach adjacent (Oct-Apr only) **Facilities** food bowl water bowl washing facs walks info vet info **On Request** fridge access torch **Other** well behaved pets only; pets allowed in certain bedrooms only

A popular 15th-century hotel situated at the quiet end of town overlooking the sea. Bedrooms are pleasantly decorated and thoughtfully equipped, many rooms have lovely sea views. Public areas include two lounges and an elegant restaurant, where locally-caught fish and seafood are served. There is also a modern brasserie.

Rooms 38 (1 fmly) **Facilities** STV Xmas New Year Wi-fi **Parking** 15 **Notes** LB

BILDESTON   Map 5 TL94

Bildeston Crown

★★★ ◉◉◉ HOTEL

104 High St IP7 7EB

☎ 01449 740510 📄 01449 741843

e-mail: hayley@thebildestoncrown.co.uk

web: www.thebildestoncrown.co.uk

dir: *A12 junct 31, turn right onto B1070 & follow signs to Hadleigh. At T-junct turn left onto A1141, then immediately right onto B1115. Hotel 0.5m*

PETS: Bedrooms unattended **Stables** **Charges** £10 per stay **Public areas** except restaurant **Grounds** on leads disp bin **Exercise area** **Facilities** food bowl water bowl **Other** charge for damage

A charming inn situated in a peaceful village close to the historic town of Lavenham. Public areas feature beams, exposed brickwork and oak floors, with contemporary style decor; they include a choice of bars, a lounge and a restaurant. The tastefully decorated bedrooms have lovely co-ordinated fabrics and modern facilities that include a Yamaha music system and LCD TVs. Food here is the real focus and draw; guests can expect fresh, high-quality local produce and accomplished technical skills in both modern and classic dishes.

Rooms 13 **Facilities** STV FTV Xmas New Year Wi-fi **Services** Lift **Parking** 30

BUCKLESHAM   Map 5 TM24

Westwood Caravan Park *(TM253411)*

▶▶▶▶

Old Felixstowe Rd IP10 0BN

☎ 01473 659637 📄 01473 659637

e-mail: info@westwoodcaravanpark.co.uk

dir: *From A14 junct 58 (SE of Ipswich) follow signs for Bucklesham. Site SE of Bucklesham near Kembroke Hall*

PETS: Public areas on leads disp bin **Exercise area** walking area around perimeter of site **Facilities** vet info **Other** prior notice required

Open Mar-15 Jan Last arrival 19.00hrs Last departure 13.00hrs

This site is in the heart of rural Suffolk in an idyllic, peaceful setting. All buildings are of traditional Suffolk style, and the toilet facilities are of outstanding quality. There is also a spacious room for disabled visitors, and plenty of space for children to play. A 5 acre site with 100 touring pitches.

Notes No unruly behaviour

ENGLAND

Angel Hotel

★★★★ 82% @@ TOWN HOUSE HOTEL

Angel Hill IP33 1LT

☎ 01284 714000   🖹 01284 714001

e-mail: staying@theangel.co.uk

web: www.theangel.co.uk

dir: *From A134, left at rdbt into Northgate St. Continue to lights, right into Mustow St, left into Angel Hill. Hotel on right*

PETS: Bedrooms (15 GF) unattended **Charges** £5 per night **Public areas** lounge only on leads **Exercise area** Abbey Gardens, 1 min walk **Facilities** walks info vet info **Other** charge for damage

An impressive building situated just a short walk from the town centre. One of the Angel's more notable guests over the last 400 years was Charles Dickens who is reputed to have written part of the *Pickwick Papers* while in residence. The hotel offers a range of individually designed bedrooms that includes a selection of four-poster rooms and a suite.

Rooms 75 (5 fmly) (15 GF) **S** fr £100; **D** fr £115 (incl. bkfst)* **Facilities** FTV Xmas New Year Wi-fi **Services** Lift **Parking** 20

Ravenwood Hall

★★★ 88% @@ COUNTRY HOUSE HOTEL

Rougham IP30 9JA

☎ 01359 270345   🖹 01359 270788

e-mail: enquiries@ravenwoodhall.co.uk

web: www.ravenwoodhall.co.uk

dir: *3m E off A14, junct 45. Hotel on left*

PETS: Bedrooms (5 GF) unattended **Public areas** except restaurant on leads **Grounds Facilities** walks info vet info **Other** charge for damage please phone for details of pet facilities **Resident Pet:** Minx (Labrador)

A delightful 15th-century property set in seven acres of woodland and landscaped gardens. The building has many original features including carved timbers and inglenook fireplaces. The spacious bedrooms are attractively decorated, tastefully furnished with well-chosen pieces and equipped with many thoughtful touches. Public rooms include an elegant restaurant and a smart lounge bar with an open fire.

Rooms 14 (7 annexe) (5 GF) **Facilities** ⚡ ⛵ Shooting fishing & horse riding can be arranged Xmas New Year Wi-fi **Parking** 150

Best Western Priory

★★★ 83% @@ HOTEL

Mildenhall Rd IP32 6EH

☎ 01284 766181   🖹 01284 767604

e-mail: reservations@prioryhotel.co.uk

web: www.prioryhotel.co.uk

dir: *From A14 take Bury St Edmunds W slip road. Follow signs to Brandon. At mini-rdbt turn right. Hotel 0.5m on left*

PETS: Bedrooms (30 GF) unattended sign **Charges** £10 per pet per night **Public areas Grounds** on leads disp bin **Facilities** washing facs cage storage walks info vet info **On Request** fridge access torch towels **Other** bedding available on request

An 18th-century Grade II listed building set in landscaped grounds on the outskirts of town. The attractively decorated, tastefully furnished and thoughtfully equipped bedrooms are split between the main house and garden wings, which have their own sun terraces. Public rooms feature a smart restaurant, a conservatory dining room and a lounge bar.

Rooms 36 (29 annexe) (1 fmly) (30 GF) **Facilities** FTV Xmas New Year Wi-fi **Parking** 60

Grange

★★★ 74% COUNTRY HOUSE HOTEL

Barton Rd, Thurston IP31 3PQ

☎ 01359 231260   🖹 01359 231387

e-mail: info@grangecountryhousehotel.com

web: www.grangecountryhousehotel.com

dir: *A14 junct 45 towards Gt Barton, right at T-junct. At x-rds left into Barton Rd to Thurston. At rdbt, left after 0.5m, hotel on right*

PETS: Bedrooms (3 GF) **Charges** £15 per night **Exercise area** surrounding countryside **Facilities** walks info vet info **Other** charge for damage **Restrictions** no Rottweilers

A Tudor-style country-house hotel situated on the outskirts of town. The individually decorated bedrooms have co-ordinated fabrics and many thoughtful touches; some rooms have nice views of the gardens. Public areas include a smart lounge bar, two private dining rooms, the Garden Restaurant and banqueting facilities.

Rooms 18 (5 annexe) (1 fmly) (3 GF) **S** £79.50; **D** £100 (incl. bkfst)* **Facilities** FTV Xmas New Year Wi-fi **Parking** 100 **Notes** LB

BURY ST EDMUNDS *continued*

5/6 Orchard Street

★★★ BED AND BREAKFAST

IP33 1EH

☎ 01284 750191 & 07946 590265

e-mail: mariellascarlett@the.com

dir: *In town centre near St John's Church on one-way system; Northgate St turn right onto Looms Ln, 2nd right onto Well St, straight on onto Orchard St*

PETS: Bedrooms Exercise area park 10 mins' walk **Facilities** water bowl walks info vet info **On Request** torch towels **Other** dogs accepted by prior arrangement only **Restrictions** small to medium size dogs only

Expect a warm welcome from the caring hosts at this terrace property situated just a short walk from the town centre. The pleasant bedrooms are comfortably appointed and have a good range of useful extras. Breakfast is served at a large communal table in the cosy dining room.

Rooms 3 rms **S** £25-£28; **D** £40* **Facilities** tea/coffee Cen ht
Notes No Children 6yrs

DUNWICH	Map 5 TM47

The Ship Inn

★★ **80%** SMALL HOTEL

Saint James St IP17 3DT

☎ 01728 648219

e-mail: graeme@agellushotels.co.uk

dir: *From N: A12, exit at Blythburgh onto B1125, then left to village. Inn at end of road. From S: A12, turn right to Westleton. Follow signs for Dunwich*

PETS: Bedrooms unattended **Charges** £5 per night **Public areas** **Grounds** disp bin **Exercise area** adjacent **Facilities** food bowl water bowl dog chews walks info vet info **On Request** fridge access torch

A delightful inn situated in the heart of this quiet village, surrounded by nature reserves and heathland just a short walk from the beach. Public rooms feature a smart lounge bar with an open fire and real ales on tap. The comfortable bedrooms are traditionally furnished; some rooms have lovely views across the sea or marshes.

Rooms 20 **Parking** 0

Haw Wood Farm Caravan Park *(TM421717)*

►►

Hinton IP17 3QT

☎ 01986 784248

dir: *Exit A12, 1.5m N of Darsham level crossing at Little Chef. Site 0.5m on right*

PETS: Public areas on leads disp bin **Exercise area** large field **Facilities** food food bowl water bowl dog chews scoop/disp bags leads washing facs walks info vet info **Resident Pets:** Dyson (Yellow Labrador), cat

Open Mar-14 Jan Last arrival 21.00hrs Last departure noon

An unpretentious family-orientated park set in two large fields surrounded by low hedges. The toilets are clean and functional, and there is plenty of space for children to play. An 8 acre site with 65 touring pitches and 25 statics.

Notes

ELMSWELL	Map 5 TL96

Kiln Farm Guest House

★★★★ GUEST HOUSE

Kiln Ln IP30 9QR

☎ 01359 240442

e-mail: davejankilnfarm@btinternet.com

dir: *Exit A14 junct 47 for A1088. Entrance to Kiln Ln off eastbound slip road*

PETS: Bedrooms Public areas Grounds disp bin **Exercise area** 10mtrs **Facilities** feeding mat cage storage vet info **On Request** fridge access torch towels **Other** charge for damage **Resident Pets:** Barney & Milo (cats)

A delightful Victorian farmhouse situated in a peaceful rural location amid three acres of landscaped grounds. The bedrooms are housed in converted farm buildings; each one is smartly decorated and furnished in country style. Breakfast is served in the smart conservatory and there is also a cosy lounge and bar area.

Rooms 2 en suite 6 annexe en suite (2 fmly) (6 GF); **D** £70-£90*
Facilities TVL tea/coffee Dinner available Cen ht Licensed Wi-fi
Parking 20

FELIXSTOWE — Map 5 TM33

Peewit Caravan Park (TM290338)

► ► ►

Walton Av IP11 2HB
☎ 01394 284511
dir: *Signed from A14 in Felixstowe, 100mtrs past Dock Gate 1, 1st on left*

PETS: Public areas except in shower/toilet block disp bin
Exercise area grass walkway **Facilities** walks info vet info
Restrictions well behaved dogs only

Open Apr or Etr-Oct Last arrival 21.00hrs Last departure 11.00hrs

A grass touring area fringed by trees, with well-maintained grounds and a colourful floral display. This handy urban site is not overlooked by houses, and the toilet facilities are clean and well cared for. A function room contains a TV and library. The beach is a few minutes away by car. A 13 acre site with 45 touring pitches, 4 hardstandings and 200 statics.

Notes Only foam footballs are permitted 🐾

FRAMLINGHAM — Map 5 TM26

Church Farm (TM605267)

★ ★ ★ ★ FARMHOUSE
Church Rd, Kettleburgh IP13 7LF
☎ 01728 723532   Mrs A Bater
e-mail: jbater@suffolkonline.net
dir: *Off A12 to Wickham Market, signs to Easton Farm Park & Kettleburgh 1.25m, house behind church*

PETS: Bedrooms Charges £1 per night **Public areas** if other guests approve on leads **Grounds** on leads **Exercise area**
Facilities leads cage storage walks info vet info **On Request** fridge access torch towels **Resident Pets:** Minnie (Jack Russell), Jessie (Labrador)

A charming 300-year-old farmhouse situated close to the village church amid superb grounds with a duck pond, mature shrubs and sweeping lawns. The converted property retains exposed beams and open fireplaces. Bedrooms are pleasantly decorated and equipped with useful extras, and a ground-floor bedroom is available.

Rooms 2 rms (1 en suite) (1 pri facs) 2 annexe rms 1 annexe en suite (1 pri facs) (3 GF) **S** £30-£35; **D** £60-£70 **Facilities** TVL tea/coffee Dinner available Cen ht Fishing **Parking** 10 **Notes** 🐾 70 acres mixed

HINTLESHAM — Map 5 TM04

Hintlesham Hall Hotel

★ ★ ★ ★ ◉◉ HOTEL
George St IP8 3NS
☎ 01473 652334   📠 01473 652463
e-mail: reservations@hintleshamhall.com
web: www.hintleshamhall.com
dir: *4m W of Ipswich on A1071 to Hadleigh & Sudbury*

PETS: Bedrooms (10 GF) **Public areas** on leads **Grounds** disp bin **Exercise area Facilities** water bowl feeding mat scoop/disp bags pet sitting dog walking cage storage walks info vet info **On Request** torch towels **Other** charge for damage dogs to be muzzled at owner's discretion

Hospitality and service are key features at this imposing Grade I listed country-house hotel, situated in 175 acres of grounds and landscaped gardens. Individually decorated bedrooms offer a high degree of comfort; each one is tastefully furnished and equipped with many thoughtful touches. The spacious public rooms include a series of comfortable lounges and an elegant restaurant, which serves fine classical cuisine. Wi-fi is available throughout.

Rooms 33 (10 GF) **S** £99-£120; **D** £120-£160 (incl. bkfst)*
Facilities FTV ↘ ⌕ 18 ⛳ Putt green ♨ Gym Health & Beauty services Clay pigeon shooting ♫ Xmas New Year Wi-fi **Parking** 60
Notes LB RS Sat

HOLLESLEY — Map 5 TM34

Run Cottage Touring Park (TM350440)

► ► ►

Alderton Rd IP12 3RQ
☎ 01394 411309
e-mail: info@run-cottage.co.uk
dir: *From A12 (Ipswich-Saxmundham) onto A1152 at Melton. 1.5m, right at rdbt onto B1083. 0.75m, left to Hollesley. In Hollesley right into The Street, through village, down hill, over bridge, site 100yds on left*

PETS: Public areas on leads disp bin **Exercise area Facilities** washing facs walks info vet info **Restrictions** max 2 large dogs or 3 small dogs **Resident Pets:** Harvey (Sussex Spaniel), Dudley (Clumber Spaniel)

Open all year Last arrival 20.00hrs Last departure 11.00hrs

Located in the peaceful village of Hollesley on the Suffolk coast, this landscaped park is set behind the owners' house. The generously-sized pitches are serviced by a well-appointed and immaculately maintained toilet block. Handy for Sutton Hoo and the bird reserves at Dunwich and Minsmere. A 2.5 acre site with 20 touring pitches, 6 hardstandings.

Notes No groundsheets, ball games or cycles

ENGLAND

ENGLAND

The Ickworth Hotel & Apartments

★★★★ 73% ◉◉ COUNTRY HOUSE HOTEL

von Essen hotels
A PRIVATE COLLECTION

IP29 5QE

☎ 01284 735350   🖷 01284 736300

e-mail: info@ickworthhotel.co.uk

web: www.ickworthhotel.co.uk

dir: A14 exit for Bury St Edmunds, follow brown signs for Ickworth House, 4th exit at rdbt, cross staggered x-rds. Then onto T-junct, right into village, almost immediately right into Ickworth Estate

PETS: Bedrooms (4 GF) unattended **Public areas** except restaurant & food areas on leads **Grounds Facilities** walks info vet info **Other** prior notice required please contact hotel to confirm which dog breeds are accepted

Gifted to the National Trust in 1956 this stunning property is in part a luxurious hotel that combines the glorious design and atmosphere of the past with a reputation for making children very welcome. The staff are friendly and easy going, there is a children's play area, crèche, horses and bikes to ride, and wonderful 'Capability' Brown gardens to roam in. Plus tennis, swimming, beauty treatments and an impressive dining room.

Rooms 39 (12 annexe) (35 fmly) (4 GF) **Facilities** Spa STV FTV 🕲 ⚒ 🛥 Children's crèche Massage Manicures Adventure playground Vineyard Xmas New Year Wi-fi **Services** Lift **Parking** 40

Novotel Ipswich Centre

★★★ 82% HOTEL

NOVOTEL

Greyfriars Rd IP1 1UP

☎ 01473 232400   🖷 01473 232414

e-mail: h0995@accor.com

web: www.novotel.com

dir: From A14 towards Felixstowe. Left onto A137, follow for 2m into town centre. Hotel on double rdbt by Stoke Bridge

PETS: Bedrooms unattended sign **Charges** £6 per night **Public areas** except restaurant on leads **Grounds** on leads **Exercise area** marina & parks nearby **Facilities** cage storage walks info vet info **Other** charge for damage

A modern, red brick hotel perfectly situated in the centre of town close to shops, bars and restaurants. The open-plan public areas include a Mediterranean-style restaurant and a bar with a small games area. The bedrooms are smartly appointed and have many thoughtful touches; three rooms are suitable for less mobile guests.

Rooms 101 (8 fmly) **Facilities** FTV Gym Sauna Xmas New Year Wi-fi **Services** Lift Air con **Parking** 53

Low House Touring Caravan Centre

(TM227425)

▶ ▶ ▶

Bucklesham Rd, Foxhall IP10 0AU

☎ 01473 659437   & 07710 378029   🖷 01473 659880

e-mail: low.house@btinternet.com

dir: From A14 (south ring road) take slip road to A1156 signed East Ipswich. Right in 1m, right again in 0.5m. Site on left

PETS: Public areas on leads **Exercise area** opposite **Facilities** walks info vet info **Other** max 2 dogs per pitch

Open all year Last arrival anytime Last departure 14.00hrs

A secluded site surrounded by hundreds of mature trees. Buildings have been hand-crafted by the owner in stained timber, and there is a children's play area, and a collection of caged rabbits, bantams and guinea fowl. Tents accepted only if space available. A 3.5 acre site with 30 touring pitches.

Notes ⊛

The Swan

★★★★ 83% ◉◉ HOTEL

High St CO10 9QA

☎ 01787 247477   🖷 01787 248286

e-mail: info@theswanatlavenham.co.uk

web: www.theswanatlavenham.co.uk

dir: From Bury St Edmunds take A134 (S), then A1141 to Lavenham

PETS: Bedrooms (13 GF) unattended **Charges** £10 per night **Public areas** except food service areas on leads **Grounds** on leads **Exercise area** 400yds **Facilities** water bowl walks info vet info **On Request** fridge access torch towels **Other** charge for damage well behaved dogs only

A delightful collection of listed buildings dating back to the 14th century, lovingly restored to retain their original charm. Public rooms include comfortable lounge areas, a charming rustic bar, an informal brasserie and a fine-dining restaurant. Bedrooms are tastefully furnished and equipped with many thoughtful touches. The friendly staff are helpful, attentive and offer professional service.

Rooms 45 (11 fmly) (13 GF) **S** £95-£145; **D** £170-£290 (incl. bkfst)* **Facilities** STV FTV Xmas New Year Wi-fi **Parking** 62 **Notes** LB

Cakes & Ale *(TM432637)*

▶▶▶

Abbey Ln, Theberton IP16 4TE
☎ 01728 831655
e-mail: cakesandalepark@gmail.com
dir: *From Saxmundham E on B1119. 3m follow minor road over level crossing, turn right, in 0.5m straight on at x-rds, entrance 0.5m on left*

PETS: Charges £2 per night **Public areas** disp bin
Exercise area 5 acre field & small copse **Facilities** food washing facs walks info vet info **Other** charge for damage prior notice required **Resident Pet:** Jasper (Blue Merle Border Collie)

Open Apr-Oct rs Low season club, shop & reception limited hours
Last arrival 20.00hrs Last departure 13.00hrs

A large, well spread out site with many trees and bushes on a former Second World War airfield. The spacious touring area includes plenty of hardstandings and super pitches, and there is a good bar and a well-maintained toilet block. Wi-fi access is available on site. A 45 acre site with 50 touring pitches, 50 hardstandings and 200 statics.

Notes No group bookings, no noise between 21.00hrs-08.00hrs

The Black Lion

★★★ 79% HOTEL
Church Walk, The Green CO10 9DN
☎ 01787 312356 📠 01787 374557
e-mail: enquiries@blacklionhotel.net
web: www.blacklionhotel.net
dir: *At junct of A134 & A1092*

PETS: Bedrooms unattended **Charges** **Public areas** except restaurant on leads **Grounds** **Exercise area** opposite **Facilities** water bowl walks info vet info **Other** charge for damage **Resident Pet:** Melford (Labrador/Poodle cross)

This charming 15th-century hotel is situated on the edge of this bustling town overlooking the green. Bedrooms are generally spacious and each is attractively decorated, tastefully furnished and equipped with useful extras. An interesting range of dishes is served in the lounge bar or guests may choose to dine from the same innovative menu in the more formal restaurant.

Rooms 10 (1 fmly) **Facilities** Xmas New Year Wi-fi **Parking** 10

Ivy House Country Hotel

★★★ 83% ◉◉ HOTEL
Ivy Ln, Beccles Rd, Oulton Broad NR33 8HY
☎ 01502 501353 & 588144 📠 01502 501539
e-mail: aa@ivyhousecountryhotel.co.uk
web: www.ivyhousecountryhotel.co.uk
dir: *On A146 SW of Oulton Broad turn into Ivy Ln beside Esso petrol station. Over railway bridge, follow private drive*

PETS: Bedrooms (17 GF) sign **Charges** £15 per stay
Public areas except restaurant on leads **Grounds** on leads disp bin **Exercise area** hotel's fields **Facilities** food bowl bedding dog chews scoop/disp bags washing facs walks info vet info
On Request fridge access torch towels

Peacefully located, family-run hotel set in three acres of mature landscaped grounds just a short walk from Oulton Broad. Public rooms include an 18th-century thatched barn restaurant where an interesting choice of dishes is served. The attractively decorated bedrooms are housed in garden wings, and many have lovely views of the grounds to the countryside beyond.

Rooms 20 (20 annexe) (1 fmly) (17 GF) **S** £99-£115; **D** £135-£170 (incl. bkfst)* **Facilities** FTV Wi-fi **Parking** 50 **Notes** LB Closed 23 Dec-6 Jan

Katherine Guest House

★★★★ ⬚ GUEST ACCOMMODATION
49 Kirkley Cliff Rd NR33 0DF
☎ 01502 567858 📠 01502 581341
e-mail: beauthaicuisine@aol.com
web: www.beauthaikatherine.co.uk
dir: *On A12 seafront road next to Kensington Garden*

PETS: Bedrooms Stables 1m **Charges** by arrangement
Public areas disp bin **Exercise area** adjacent **Other** charge for damage prior notice required **Restrictions** small dogs only (max 10kg)

This large Victorian property lies opposite the beach in the quiet part of town. The spacious public rooms include a smart lounge bar with plush leather sofas and an intimate restaurant serving authentic Thai cuisine. The pleasant bedrooms have co-ordinated fabrics and many thoughtful touches.

Rooms 10 en suite (5 fmly) **S** £35-£39; **D** £65-£69*
Facilities tea/coffee Dinner available Direct Dial Cen ht Licensed Wi-fi **Parking** 4 **Notes** LB

ENGLAND

Somerton House

★ ★ ★ ★ GUEST ACCOMMODATION

7 Kirkley Cliff NR33 0BY

☎ 01502 565665 📄 01502 501176

e-mail: pippin.somerton@btinternet.com

dir: *On old A12, 100yds from Claremont Pier*

PETS: Bedrooms Stables 2m **Charges** £5 per stay **Public areas** except dining room disp bin **Exercise area** 50yds to beach (available for dog walking only out of season) **Facilities** cage storage walks info vet info **On Request** torch **Other** charge for damage

Somerton House is a Grade II Victorian terrace situated in a peaceful area of town overlooking the sea. Bedrooms are smartly furnished in a period style and have many thoughtful touches; some rooms have four poster or half-tester beds. Breakfast is served in the smart dining room and guests have the use of a cosy lounge.

Rooms 7 rms (4 en suite) (2 pri facs) (1 fmly) (1 GF) **S** £36-£46; **D** £57-£62* **Facilities** FTV TVL tea/coffee Cen ht Licensed Wi-fi **Notes** LB Closed 25-26 Dec

Fairways

★ ★ ★ GUEST HOUSE

398 London Road South NR33 0BQ

☎ 01502 572659

e-mail: argi@talktalk.net

dir: *S of town centre on A12, 1m from rail & bus station*

PETS: Bedrooms Public areas except kitchen & restaurant on leads **Exercise area** across road & 5 mins' walk to seafront **Facilities** scoop/disp bags walks info vet info **On Request** fridge access torch towels **Restrictions** small to medium size dogs only **Resident Pet:** Toby (West Highland Terrier)

A friendly, family-run guest house located at the southern end of the town. Bedrooms come in a variety of sizes and styles; each room is pleasantly decorated and thoughtfully equipped. Breakfast is served in the smart dining room and there is also a cosy lounge.

Rooms 7 rms (4 en suite) (2 fmly) **S** fr £22; **D** fr £48* **Facilities** TVL tea/coffee Cen ht

Best Western Heath Court

★ ★ ★ 78% HOTEL

Moulton Rd CB8 8DY

☎ 01638 667171 📄 01638 666533

e-mail: quality@heathcourthotel.com

dir: *Exit A14 for Newmarket & Ely onto A142. Follow town centre signs over mini rdbt. At clocktower left into Moulton Rd*

PETS: Bedrooms unattended sign **Stables** 5m **Grounds** on leads disp bin **Exercise area** 200yds **Facilities** food (pre-bookable) food bowl water bowl bedding feeding mat pet sitting dog walking washing facs dog grooming cage storage walks info vet info **On Request** fridge access torch towels **Other** charge for damage

Modern red-brick hotel situated close to Newmarket Heath and perfectly placed for the town centre. Public rooms include a choice of dining options - informal meals can be taken in the lounge bar or a modern carte menu is offered in the restaurant. The smartly presented bedrooms are mostly spacious and some have air conditioning.

Rooms 41 (2 fmly) **S** £40-£115; **D** £50-£203 (incl. bkfst)* **Facilities** STV New Year Wi-fi **Services** Lift **Parking** 70 **Notes** LB

The Garden Lodge

★ ★ ★ ★ BED AND BREAKFAST

11 Vicarage Ln, Woodditton CB8 9SG

☎ 01638 731116

e-mail: swedishgardenlodge@hotmail.com

web: www.gardenlodge.net

dir: *3m S of Newmarket in Woodditton*

PETS: Bedrooms unattended **Public areas Grounds** disp bin **Facilities** food bowl water bowl vet info **On Request** torch towels **Restrictions** no Bull Terriers

A warm welcome is assured in this home-from-home, not far from the famous racecourse. The accommodation, in quality chalets, is very well equipped and features a wealth of thoughtful extras. Freshly prepared home-cooked breakfasts are served in an elegant dining room in the main house.

Rooms 3 en suite (3 GF) **S** £35-£40; **D** £60-£70* **Facilities** tea/coffee Dinner available Cen ht **Parking** 6 **Notes** 🚭

ORFORD Map 5 TM45

The Crown & Castle
★★★ 86% @@ HOTEL
IP12 2LJ
☎ 01394 450205
e-mail: info@crownandcastle.co.uk
web: www.crownandcastle.co.uk
dir: Turn right from B1084 on entering village, towards castle

PETS: Bedrooms (11 GF) unattended Charges £5 per night
Public areas Grounds on leads disp bin Exercise area
Facilities bedding dog chews scoop/disp bags leads washing
facs walks info vet info On Request fridge access torch towels
Other 1 dog friendly table in restaurant Resident Pets: Teddy &
Anle (Wire-Haired Fox Terriers)

A delightful inn situated adjacent to the Norman castle keep.
Contemporary style bedrooms are spilt between the main house
and the garden wing; the latter are more spacious and have
patios with access to the garden. The restaurant has an informal
atmosphere with polished tables and local artwork; the menu
features quality, locally sourced produce.

Rooms 19 (12 annexe) (1 fmly) (11 GF) Facilities Xmas New Year
Wi-fi Parking 20 Notes No children 4yrs Closed 4-7 Jan

SAXMUNDHAM Map 5 TM36

Sandpit Farm
★★★★ BED AND BREAKFAST
Bruisyard IP17 2EB
☎ 01728 663445
e-mail: smarshall@aldevalleybreaks.co.uk
web: www.aldevalleybreaks.co.uk
dir: 4m W of Saxmundham. A1120 onto B1120, 1st left for
Bruisyard, house 1.5m on left

PETS: Bedrooms sign Sep accom barns & stables Stables
Charges £5 per night £35 per week Public areas except dining
room on leads Grounds on leads disp bin Exercise area
Facilities cage storage walks info vet info On Request fridge
access Other charge for damage pets allowed in one bedroom
only Resident Pets: Twiggy & Inca (Black Labradors), chickens,
guinea fowl

Sandpit Farm is a delightful Grade II listed farmhouse set in
20 acres of grounds. Bedrooms have many thoughtful touches
and lovely country views, and there are two cosy lounges to
enjoy. Breakfast features quality local produce and freshly laid
free-range eggs.

Rooms 2 en suite S £40-£60; D £65-£80 Facilities TVL tea/coffee
Cen ht Wi-fi 🍴 Parking 4 Notes LB Closed 24-26 Dec 📧

Whitearch Touring Caravan Park (TM379610)
►►►
Main Rd, Benhall IP17 1NA
☎ 01728 604646 & 603773
dir: At junct of A12 & B1121

PETS: Public areas Exercise area Facilities walks info vet info

Open Apr-Oct Last arrival 20.00hrs

A small, maturing park set around an attractive coarse-fishing
lake, with good quality toilet facilities and secluded pitches
tucked away among trees and shrubs. The park is popular with
anglers; there is some traffic noise from the adjacent A12. A 14.5
acre site with 50 touring pitches, 50 hardstandings.

Notes No bicycles 📧

SOUTHWOLD Map 5 TM57

Swan Hotel
★★★★ 78% @@ HOTEL
Market Place IP18 6EG
☎ 01502 722186   📠 01502 724800
e-mail: swan.hotel@adnams.co.uk
dir: A1095 to Southwold. Hotel in town centre. Parking via
archway to left of building

PETS: Bedrooms (17 GF) Charges £10 per night Grounds
disp bin Facilities food bowl water bowl bedding dog chews
feeding mat scoop/disp bags washing facs cage storage
walks info vet info On Request fridge access Other charge for
damage dogs allowed in Lighthouse bedrooms only

A charming 17th-century coaching inn situated in the heart of
this bustling town centre overlooking the market place. Public
rooms feature an elegant restaurant, a comfortable drawing
room, a cosy bar and a lounge where guests can enjoy afternoon
tea. The spacious bedrooms are attractively decorated, tastefully
furnished and thoughtfully equipped.

Rooms 42 (17 annexe) (17 GF) Facilities STV FTV Treatment room
Xmas New Year Services Lift Parking 35

The Blyth Hotel
★★ 85% @ SMALL HOTEL
Station Rd IP18 6AY
☎ 01502 722632 & 0845 348 6867
e-mail: reception@blythhotel.com

PETS: Bedrooms unattended Charges £5 per night Public areas
except restaurant & lounge on leads Grounds on leads disp
bin Exercise area 5 mins Facilities food bowl water bowl dog
chews vet info Other charge for damage

Expect a warm welcome at this delightful family run hotel which
is situated just a short walk from the town centre. The spacious
public rooms include a smart residents' lounge, an open-plan bar
and a large restaurant. Bedrooms are tastefully appointed with
co-ordinated fabrics and have many thoughtful touches.

Rooms 13 S £60-£75; D £100-£145 (incl. bkfst)* Facilities FTV
Xmas New Year Wi-fi Parking 8 Notes LB

277

WESTLETON Map 5 TM46

Westleton Crown
★★★ 79% ◉◉ HOTEL

The Street IP17 3AD
☎ 01728 648777 📠 01728 648239
e-mail: reception@westletoncrown.co.uk
web: www.westletoncrown.co.uk
dir: *A12 N, turn right for Westleton just after Yoxford. Hotel opposite on entering Westleton*

PETS: **Bedrooms** (8 GF) unattended **Charges** £7.50 per night **Public areas** except main dining room **Grounds** **Exercise area** outside hotel **Facilities** food bowl water bowl dog chews walks info vet info **On Request** fridge access torch

A charming coaching inn situated in a peaceful village location just a few minutes from the A12. Public rooms include a smart, award-winning restaurant, comfortable lounge, and busy bar with exposed beams and open fireplaces. The stylish bedrooms are tastefully decorated and equipped with many little extras.

Rooms 25 (3 annexe) (3 fmly) (8 GF) **Facilities** Xmas New Year Wi-fi **Parking** 45 **Notes** Closed 25 Dec

WOODBRIDGE Map 5 TM24

Best Western Ufford Park Hotel Golf & Spa
★★★ 82% HOTEL

Yarmouth Rd, Ufford IP12 1QW
☎ 01394 383555 📠 0844 4773727
e-mail: mail@uffordpark.co.uk
web: www.uffordpark.co.uk
dir: *A12 N to A1152, in Melton left at lights, follow B1438, hotel 1m on right*

PETS: **Bedrooms** (32 GF) unattended **Charges** from £5 per night **Public areas** except restaurant on leads **Grounds** on leads **Exercise area** 0.5m **Facilities** food bowl water bowl washing facs cage storage walks info vet info **On Request** fridge access torch towels **Other** charge for damage

A modern hotel set in open countryside boasting superb leisure facilities including a challenging golf course. The spacious public rooms provide a wide choice of areas in which to relax and include a busy lounge bar, a carvery restaurant and the Vista Restaurant. Bedrooms are smartly appointed and pleasantly

decorated, each thoughtfully equipped; many rooms overlook the golf course.

Rooms 87 (20 fmly) (32 GF) **S** £73-£113; **D** £99-£169 (incl. bkfst)* **Facilities** Spa FTV ◎ supervised ♨ 18 Putt green Fishing ⤵ Gym Golf Academy with PGA tuition 2 storey floodlit driving range Dance Studio Xmas New Year Wi-fi **Services** Lift **Parking** 250 **Notes** LB

Moon & Sixpence *(TM263454)*
►►►►►

Newbourn Rd, Waldringfield IP12 4PP
☎ 01473 736650 📠 01473 736270
e-mail: info@moonandsixpence.eu
dir: *Follow caravan & Moon & Sixpence signs from A12 Ipswich (east bypass). 1.5m, left at x-roads*

PETS: **Charges** £1 per night £7 per week **Public areas** except bar & restaurant disp bin **Exercise area** trail around perimeter **Facilities** walks info vet info **Other** prior notice required pet centre & store at nearby retail park **Resident Pet:** 1 Collie

Open Apr-Oct rs Low season club, shop, reception open limited hours Last arrival 20.00hrs Last departure noon

A well-planned site, with tourers occupying a sheltered valley position around an attractive boating lake with a sandy beach. Toilet facilities are housed in a smart Norwegian cabin, and there is a laundry and dishwashing area. Leisure facilities include two tennis courts, a bowling green, fishing, boating and a games room. There is an adult-only area, and a strict no groups and no noise after 9pm policy. A 5 acre site with 65 touring pitches and 225 statics.

Notes No group bookings or commercial vehicles, quiet 21.00hrs-08.00hrs

YOXFORD Map 5 TM36

Satis House
★★★ 88% ◉◉ COUNTRY HOUSE HOTEL

IP17 3EX
☎ 01728 668418 📠 01728 668640
e-mail: enquiries@satishouse.co.uk
web: www.satishouse.co.uk
dir: *Off A12 between Ipswich & Lowestoft. 9m E Aldeburgh*

PETS: **Bedrooms** (2 GF) **Charges** £5 per night £20 per week **Public areas** except restaurant & lounge on leads **Grounds** on leads **Exercise area** walled garden adjacent **Facilities** food (pre-bookable) food bowl water bowl cage storage walks info vet info **On Request** fridge access torch towels **Other** charge for damage prior notice required **Restrictions** small & medium size dogs only

Expect a warm welcome from the caring hosts at this delightful 18th-century, Grade II listed property set in three acres of parkland. The stylish public areas have a really relaxed atmosphere; they include a choice of dining rooms, a smart bar and a cosy lounge. The individually decorated bedrooms are tastefully appointed and thoughtfully equipped.

Rooms 9 (2 annexe) (1 fmly) (2 GF) **Facilities** STV FTV Xmas New Year Wi-fi **Parking** 30

Best Western

SURREY

BAGSHOT — Map 4 SU96

Pennyhill Park Hotel & The Spa

★★★★★ ◉◉◉◉ COUNTRY HOUSE HOTEL

London Rd GU19 5EU

☎ 01276 471774 📄 01276 473217

e-mail: enquiries@pennyhillpark.co.uk

web: www.exclusivehotels.co.uk

dir: M3 junct 3, follow signs to Camberley. On A30 between Bagshot & Camberley

PETS: Bedrooms (26 GF) unattended Stables 5m Charges £50 per stay Public areas except restaurant, bar & spa on leads Grounds Exercise area 2m Facilities food (pre-bookable) food bowl water bowl bedding dog chews cat treats feeding mat leads pet sitting dog walking washing facs cage storage walks info vet info On Request fridge access torch towels Other charge for damage

This delightful country-house hotel set in 120-acre grounds provides every modern comfort. The stylish bedrooms are individually designed and have impressive bathrooms. Leisure facilities include a jogging trail, a golf course and a state-of-the-art spa with a thermal sequencing experience, ozone treated swimming and hydrotherapy pools along with a comprehensive range of therapies and treatments. The Latymer restaurant, overseen by chef Michael Wignall, has become a true dining destination in its own right. The cooking is outstanding and great care is made to source first-rate ingredients, much from local suppliers. There is an eight-seater chef's table. In addition there are other eating options, and lounges and bars to relax in.

Rooms 123 (97 annexe) (6 fmly) (26 GF) Facilities Spa STV ☺ ☃ ♨ 9 ♨ Fishing ♨ Gym Archery Clay shooting Plunge pool Turkish steam room Rugby/football pitch 🎵 Xmas New Year Wi-fi Services Lift Parking 500

CAMBERLEY — Map 4 SU86

Burwood House

★★★★ GUEST ACCOMMODATION

15 London Rd GU15 3UQ

☎ 01276 685686 📄 01276 62220

e-mail: enquiries@burwoodhouse.co.uk

dir: On A30 between Camberley and Bagshot

PETS: Bedrooms Charges £15 per night disp bin Exercise area woods (50mtrs) Facilities food (pre-bookable) cage storage walks info vet info On Request fridge access torch towels Other charge for damage Resident Pets: Luna (Pyrenean Mountain Dog), Caramel (cat)

Burwood House is a very stylish establishment with individually designed bedrooms that offer all modern conveniences including Wi-fi. Every Monday to Thursday evening the kitchen offers a varied menu full of traditional favourites, as well as seasonal house specialties. Breakfast can be taken either buffet-style or as a fresh-cooked meal prepared upon request. Public areas include a lounge, bar and garden.

Rooms 22 en suite (3 fmly) (7 GF) S £75-£115; D £82-£125 Facilities tea/coffee Dinner available Direct Dial Cen ht Licensed Wi-fi ☃ Golf 18 Parking 22 Notes Closed 22 Dec-4 Jan

CHOBHAM — Map 4 SU96

Pembroke House

★★★★ GUEST ACCOMMODATION

Valley End Rd GU24 8TB

☎ 01276 857654 📄 01276 858445

e-mail: pembroke_house@btinternet.com

dir: A30 onto B383 signed Chobham, 3m right onto Valley End Rd, 1m on left

PETS: Bedrooms Public areas except dining room & kitchen Grounds disp bin Exercise area adjacent Facilities food bowl water bowl bedding leads pet sitting washing facs cage storage walks info vet info On Request fridge access torch towels Resident Pets: Puzzle, Carrie, Pandora (Jack Russells)

Proprietor Julia Holland takes obvious pleasure in welcoming guests to her beautifully appointed and spacious home. The elegantly proportioned public areas include an imposing entrance hall and dining room with views over the surrounding countryside. Bedrooms are restful and filled with thoughtful extras.

Rooms 4 rms (2 en suite) (2 pri facs) (1 fmly) S £40-£70; D £90-£150* Facilities STV tea/coffee Cen ht Wi-fi ♨ Parking 10 Notes 🚭

ENGLAND

Mercure White Horse

★★★ 66% HOTEL

High St RH4 1BE
☎ 01306 881138   📠 01306 887241
e-mail: h6637@accor.com
web: www.mercure.com
dir: *M25 junct 9, A24 S towards Dorking. Hotel in town centre*

PETS: Bedrooms (5 GF) unattended sign **Charges** £10 per week **Public areas Grounds** on leads disp bin **Exercise area** 100yds **Facilities** walks info vet info **On Request** fridge access torch towels

The hotel was first established as an inn in 1750, although parts of the building date back as far as the 15th century. Its town centre location and Dickensian charm have long made this a popular destination for travellers. There's beamed ceilings, open fires and four-poster beds; more contemporary rooms can be found in the garden wing.

Rooms 78 (41 annexe) (2 fmly) (5 GF) **S** £85-£125; **D** £95-£145*
Facilities Xmas **Parking** 73 **Notes** LB

Lythe Hill Hotel and Spa

★★★★ 74% 🏵 HOTEL

Petworth Rd GU27 3BQ
☎ 01428 651251   📠 01428 644131
e-mail: lythe@lythehill.co.uk
web: www.lythehill.co.uk
dir: *From High St onto B2131. Hotel 1.25m on right*

PETS: Bedrooms (18 GF) **Stables** 10 mins **Charges** **Public areas Grounds** on leads disp bin **Facilities** food (pre-bookable) food bowl water bowl bedding dog chews dog grooming cage storage walks info vet info **On Request** fridge access torch towels **Other** charge for damage contact hotel for details of charges

This privately owned hotel sits in 30 acres of attractive parkland with lakes, complete with roaming geese. The hotel has been described as a hamlet of character buildings, each furnished in a style that complements the age of the property; the oldest one dating back to 1475. Cuisine in the adjacent 'Auberge de France' offers interesting, quality dishes, whilst breakfast is served in the hotel dining room. The bedrooms are split between a number of 15th-century buildings and vary in size. The stylish spa includes a 16-metre swimming pool.

Rooms 41 (8 fmly) (18 GF) **Facilities** Spa FTV 🏊 Fishing 🎣 Gym Boules Giant chess ♫ Xmas New Year Wi-fi **Parking** 200

The Talbot Inn

★★★★ 🏵 INN

High St GU23 6BB
☎ 01483 225188   📠 01483 211332
e-mail: info@thetalbotinn.com
web: www.thetalbotinn.com
dir: *Exit A3 signed Ripley, on left on High St*

PETS: Bedrooms Charges £10 per night £70 per week **Public areas** bar only on leads **Grounds** on leads **Exercise area** 2mins walk **Facilities** food (pre-bookable) food bowl water bowl dog chews cat treats washing facs cage storage walks info vet info **On Request** fridge access torch towels **Other** charge for damage pet food must be pre-booked

The Talbot Inn simply oozes charm and character and has retained many of its historical features even having undergone a major transformation. Public areas are very comfortable, with real ales and delicious home-cooked food on offer. Alfresco dining is available in summer months. Traditional bedrooms are in the main house and more contemporary-styled rooms are featured in the 'stable block'.

Rooms 9 en suite 30 annexe en suite (17 GF) **S** £45-£70; **D** £80-£110* **Facilities** STV FTV tea/coffee Dinner available Cen ht Wi-fi **Parking** 60

STAINES — Map 4 TQ07

Mercure Thames Lodge
★★★ 73% HOTEL

Thames St TW18 4SJ
☎ 01784 464433 📠 01784 454858
e-mail: h6620-re@accor.com
web: www.mercure.com
dir: M25 junct 13. Follow A30/town centre signs (bus station on right). Hotel straight ahead

PETS: Bedrooms (23 GF) **Stables** 5m **Charges** **Public areas** **Grounds** on leads disp bin **Facilities** food food bowl water bowl litter tray scoop/disp bags cage storage **On Request** fridge access torch towels **Other** charge for damage

Located on the banks of the River Thames in a bustling town, this hotel is well positioned for both business and leisure travellers. Meals are served in the Riverside Restaurant, and snacks are available in the spacious lounge/bar; weather permitting the terrace provides a good place for a drink on a summer evening. Onsite parking is an additional bonus.

Rooms 79 (17 fmly) (23 GF) **Facilities** STV Riverside restaurant & tea gardens with river moorings New Year Wi-fi **Parking** 40

SUSSEX, EAST

ALFRISTON — Map 5 TQ50

Deans Place
★★★ 82% ◉ HOTEL

Seaford Rd BN26 5TW
☎ 01323 870248 📠 01323 870918
e-mail: mail@deansplacehotel.co.uk
web: www.deansplacehotel.co.uk
dir: Off A27 between Eastbourne & Brighton, signed Alfriston & Drusillas Zoo Park. Continue south through village towards Seaford

PETS: Bedrooms (8 GF) unattended **Charges** £5 per night **Public areas** except restaurant & function rooms on leads **Grounds** **Facilities** water bowl washing facs cage storage walks info vet info **On Request** fridge access torch towels

Situated on the southern fringe of the village, this friendly hotel is set in attractive gardens. Bedrooms vary in size and are well appointed with good facilities. A wide range of food is offered including an extensive bar menu and a fine dining option in Harcourt's Restaurant.

Rooms 36 (4 fmly) (8 GF) **S** £78-£90; **D** £115-£170 (incl. bkfst)* **Facilities** STV FTV 🎣 Putt green 🛶 Boules Xmas New Year Wi-fi **Parking** 100 **Notes** LB

The Star Alfriston
★★★ 73% HOTEL

BN26 5TA
☎ 01323 870495 📠 01323 870922
e-mail: bookings@thestaralfriston.co.uk
dir: 2m off A27, at Drusillas rdbt follow Alfriston signs. Hotel on right in centre of High St

PETS: Bedrooms (11 GF) unattended sign **Charges** £5 per night **Public areas** except restaurant on leads **Exercise area** 0.2m **Facilities** water bowl bedding dog chews cage storage vet info **On Request** fridge access torch towels **Other** charge for damage

Built in the 13th century and reputedly one of the country's oldest inns, this charming establishment is ideally situated for walking the South Downs or exploring the Sussex coast. Bedrooms, including two feature rooms and mini suite, are traditionally decorated but with comfortable, modern facilities. Public areas include cosy lounges with open log fires, a bar and a popular restaurant serving a wide choice of dishes using mainly local produce. Guests can also enjoy luxury spa treatments by appointment.

Rooms 37 (1 fmly) (11 GF) **S** £75-£100; **D** £115-£135 (incl. bkfst)* **Facilities** Xmas New Year Wi-fi **Parking** 35 **Notes** LB Closed 3-31 Jan

BATTLE — Map 5 TQ71

Powder Mills
★★★ 80% ◉ HOTEL

Powdermill Ln TN33 0SP
☎ 01424 775511 📠 01424 774540
e-mail: powdc@aol.com
web: www.powdermillshotel.com
dir: M25 junct 5, A21 towards Hastings. At St Johns Cross take A2100 to Battle. Pass Abbey on right, 1st right into Powdermills Ln. 1m, hotel on right

PETS: Bedrooms (5 GF) unattended sign **Stables** **Charges** £10 per night **Public areas** except restaurant **Grounds** disp bin **Exercise area** 150 acres of grounds **Exercise area** **Facilities** leads washing facs cage storage walks info vet info **On Request** fridge access towels **Other** charge for damage **Resident Pets:** Holly & Gemma (English Springer Spaniels)

A delightful 18th-century country-house hotel set amidst 150 acres of landscaped grounds with lakes and woodland. The individually decorated bedrooms are tastefully furnished and thoughtfully equipped; some rooms have sun terraces with lovely views over the lake. Public rooms include a cosy lounge bar, music room, drawing room, library, restaurant and conservatory.

Rooms 40 (10 annexe) (5 GF) **S** £100-£115; **D** £140-£350 (incl. bkfst)* **Facilities** STV FTV 🎣 Fishing Jogging trails Woodland walks Clay pigeon shooting Xmas New Year Wi-fi **Parking** 101 **Notes** LB

ENGLAND

BATTLE *continued*

Brakes Coppice Park *(TQ765134)*

▶ ▶ ▶

Forewood Ln TN33 9AB
☎ 01424 830322
e-mail: brakesco@btinternet.com
dir: *From Battle on A2100 towards Hastings. After 2m turn right for Crowhurst. Site 1m on left*

PETS: Stables 3m **Charges** 25p per night **Public areas** on leads disp bin **Exercise area** woodland walk **Facilities** walks info vet info **Other** prior notice required **Resident Pet:** Marlie (Doberman)

Open Mar-Oct Last arrival 21.00hrs Last departure noon

Secluded farm site in a sunny meadow surrounded by woodland with a small stream and a coarse fishing lake. The basic toilet block is being revamped and modernised, and hardstanding pitches are neatly laid out on a terrace, and tents are pitched on grass edged by woodland. A peaceful base for exploring Battle and the south coast. A 3 acre site with 30 touring pitches, 10 hardstandings.

Notes No fires, footballs or kite flying

BEXHILL   **Map 5 TQ70**

Cooden Beach Hotel

★★★ 80% HOTEL

Cooden Beach TN39 4TT
☎ 01424 842281 📠 01424 846142
e-mail: rooms@thecoodenbeachhotel.co.uk
web: www.thecoodenbeachhotel.co.uk
dir: *A259 towards Cooden. Signed at rdbt in Little Common Village. Hotel at end of road*

PETS: Bedrooms (4 GF) unattended **Public areas** except restaurant (tavern/bar only) **Grounds Exercise area** beach adjacent **Facilities** water bowl walks info vet info **On Request** fridge access **Other** dogs only to be left unattended for short periods **Restrictions** well behaved dogs only

This privately owned hotel is situated in private gardens which have direct access to the beach. With a train station within walking distance the location is perfectly suited for both business and leisure guests. Bedrooms are comfortably appointed, and

public areas include a spacious restaurant, lounge, bar and leisure centre with swimming pool.

Rooms 41 (8 annexe) (10 fmly) (4 GF) **S** £60; **D** £120 (incl. bkfst) **Facilities** FTV ③ Gym Sauna Steam room ♫ Xmas New Year Wi-fi **Parking** 60

BRIGHTON & HOVE   **Map 4 TQ30**

Best Western Princes Marine

★★★ 75% HOTEL

153 Kingsway BN3 4GR
☎ 01273 207660 📠 01273 325913
e-mail: princesmarine@bestwestern.co.uk
dir: *Right at Brighton Pier, follow seafront for 2m. Hotel 200yds from King Alfred leisure centre*

PETS: Bedrooms Stables 4m **Public areas** except restaurant on leads **Grounds** on leads disp bin **Exercise area Facilities** food (pre-bookable) water bowl feeding mat washing facs walks info vet info **On Request** fridge access torch towels

This friendly hotel enjoys a seafront location and offers spacious, comfortable bedrooms equipped with a good range of facilities including free Wi-fi. There is a stylish restaurant, modern bar and selection of roof-top meeting rooms with sea views. Limited parking is available at the rear.

Rooms 48 (4 fmly) **Facilities** Xmas **Services** Lift **Parking** 30

Brighton Pavilions

★ ★ ★ ★ GUEST ACCOMMODATION

7 Charlotte St BN2 1AG
☎ 01273 621750 📠 01273 622477
e-mail: sanchez-crespo@lineone.net
web: www.brightonpavilions.com
dir: *A23 to Brighton Pier, left onto A259 Marine Parade, Charlotte St 15th left*

PETS: Bedrooms unattended **Charges** £10 per night **Public areas** except dining room on leads **Exercise area** 200mtrs **Facilities** walks info vet info **On Request** fridge access **Other** charge for damage **Restrictions** no large breeds **Resident Pet:** Fluffy (budgie)

This well-run operation is in one of Brighton's Regency streets, a short walk from the seafront and town centre. Bedrooms have themes such as Mikado or Pompeii, and are very smartly presented with many thoughtful extras including room service breakfast in superior rooms and free Wi-fi. The bright breakfast room is styled after a Titanic garden restaurant.

Rooms 10 rms (7 en suite) (1 fmly) (1 GF) **S** £45-£47; **D** £85-£152* **Facilities** FTV tea/coffee Direct Dial Cen ht Wi-fi **Notes** LB

ENGLAND

New Steine

★ ★ ★ ★ 🛏 ☕ GUEST ACCOMMODATION

10-11 New Steine BN2 1PB

☎ 01273 695415 & 681546 📠 01273 622663

e-mail: reservation@newsteinehotel.com

dir: *A23 to Brighton Pier, left onto Marine Parade, New Steine on left after Wentworth St*

PETS: Bedrooms Charges £5 per night £35 per week disp bin **Exercise area** 5 mins' walk **Facilities** walks info vet info **On Request** fridge access towels **Other** charge for damage pets allowed in certain bedrooms only **Restrictions** small to medium size dogs only

Close to the seafront off the Esplanade, the New Steine provides spacious bedrooms. There is a cosy lounge, where a wide choice of English, vegetarian, vegan or continental breakfasts is served. There is street parking in front of the property.

Rooms 20 rms (16 en suite) (4 fmly) **S** £24.50-£59; **D** £49.50-£135 **Facilities** FTV tea/coffee Dinner available Direct Dial Cen ht Licensed Wi-fi **Notes** LB No Children 4yrs

Ambassador Brighton

★ ★ ★ ★ GUEST ACCOMMODATION

22-23 New Steine, Marine Pde BN2 1PD

☎ 01273 676869 📠 01273 689988

e-mail: info@ambassadorbrighton.co.uk

web: www.ambassadorbrighton.co.uk

dir: *A23 to Brighton Pier, left onto A259, 9th left, onto Garden Sq, 1st left*

PETS: Bedrooms Public areas except restaurant **Grounds** disp bin **Exercise area** beach nearby **Facilities** dog walking cage storage walks info vet info **On Request** fridge access torch towels **Other** charge for damage

At the heart of bustling Kemp Town, overlooking the attractive garden square next to the seaside, this well-established property has a friendly and relaxing atmosphere. Bedrooms are well equipped and vary in size, with the largest having the best views. A small lounge with a separate bar is available.

Rooms 24 en suite (9 fmly) (3 GF) (8 smoking) **S** £39-£75; **D** £71-£125* **Facilities** tea/coffee Direct Dial Cen ht Licensed **Notes** LB

The Oriental

★ ★ ★ ★ GUEST ACCOMMODATION

9 Oriental Place BN1 2LJ

☎ 01273 205050 📠 01273 205050

e-mail: info@orientalbrighton.co.uk

dir: *A23 right onto A259 at seafront, right into Oriental Place, on right*

PETS: Bedrooms unattended **Public areas** disp bin **Exercise area** 50mtrs **Facilities** food bowl water bowl walks info vet info **On Request** torch towels **Restrictions** well behaved dogs only

The Oriental is situated close to the seafront and enjoys easy access to all areas. The accommodation is comfortable and modern, and there is a licensed bar. A tasty Sussex breakfast using locally sourced produce is offered in a friendly, relaxed atmosphere.

Rooms 9 en suite (4 fmly) (1 GF) **S** £50-£75; **D** £80-£210* **Facilities** FTV tea/coffee Cen ht Licensed Wi-fi

Avalon

★ ★ ★ GUEST ACCOMMODATION

7 Upper Rock Gardens BN2 1QE

☎ 01273 692344 📠 01273 692344

e-mail: info@avalonbrighton.co.uk

dir: *A23 to Brighton Pier, left onto Marine Parade, 300yds at lights left onto Lower Rock Gdns, over lights Avalon on left*

PETS: Bedrooms unattended **Public areas Exercise area** parks & beach nearby **Facilities** food bowl water bowl feeding mat walks info vet info **Other** charge for damage maps & list of dog friendly restaurants & bars available

A warm welcome is assured at this property just a short walk from the seafront and The Lanes. The en suite bedrooms vary in size and style but all are attractively presented with plenty of useful accessories including free Wi-fi. Parking vouchers are available for purchase from the proprietor.

Rooms 7 en suite (3 fmly) (1 GF) **Facilities** FTV tea/coffee Cen ht Wi-fi

ENGLAND

The Grand Hotel
★★★★★ 84% ◎◎ HOTEL

King Edward's Pde BN21 4EQ
☎ 01323 412345 📄 01323 412233
e-mail: reservations@grandeastbourne.com
web: www.grandeastbourne.com
dir: *On seafront W of Eastbourne, 1m from railway station*

PETS: Bedrooms (4 GF) **Charges** £7 per night **Exercise area** park / beach adjacent **Facilities** food (pre-bookable) food bowl water bowl bedding dog chews dog walking dog grooming **On Request** fridge access **Other** football & toys available

This famous Victorian hotel offers high standards of service and hospitality, and is in close proximity to both the beach and the South Downs National Park. The extensive public rooms feature a magnificent Great Hall, with marble columns and high ceilings, where guests can relax and enjoy afternoon tea. The spacious bedrooms provide high levels of comfort; many with stunning sea views and a number with private balconies. Guests can choose to eat in the fine dining The Mirabelle or the Garden Restaurant and there are bars as well as superb spa and leisure facilities.

Rooms 152 (20 fmly) (4 GF) **S** £165-£510; **D** £195-£540 (incl. bkfst)* **Facilities** Spa STV ⊙ supervised ⌐ Putt green Gym Hairdressing Beauty therapy ♫ Xmas New Year Child facilities **Services** Lift **Parking** 80 **Notes** LB

Courtlands
★★★ 70% HOTEL

3-5 Wilmington Gardens BN21 4JN
☎ 01323 723737 📄 01323 732902
e-mail: bookings@courtlandseastbourne.com
dir: *Exit Grand Parade at Carlisle Rd*

PETS: Bedrooms (3 GF) sign **Charges** £7 per night **Public areas** except restaurants on leads **Grounds** on leads disp bin **Exercise area** adjacent park **Facilities** pet sitting dog walking dog grooming walks info vet info **On Request** fridge access **Other** charge for damage

Situated opposite the Congress Theatre, this hotel is just a short walk from both the seafront and Devonshire Park. Bedrooms are comfortably furnished and pleasantly decorated. Public areas are smartly appointed and include a cosy bar, a separate lounge and an attractive dining room.

Rooms 46 (4 fmly) (3 GF) **Facilities** STV FTV ☙ ♫ Xmas New Year **Services** Lift **Parking** 36 **Notes** LB

Congress
★★ 71% HOTEL

31-41 Carlisle Rd BN21 4JS
☎ 01323 732118 📄 01323 720016
e-mail: reservations@congresshotel.co.uk
web: www.congresshotel.co.uk
dir: *From Eastbourne seafront W towards Beachy Head. Right at Wishtower into Wilmington Sq, cross Compton St, hotel on left*

PETS: Bedrooms (8 GF) unattended sign **Grounds** **Exercise area** 200yds **Facilities** walks info vet info **On Request** fridge access

An attractive Victorian property ideally located close to the seafront, Wish Tower and Congress Theatre. The bedrooms are bright and spacious. Family rooms are available plus facilities for less able guests. Entertainment is provided in a large dining room that has a dance floor and bar.

Rooms 62 (6 fmly) (8 GF) **S** £33-£47; **D** £66-£94 (incl. bkfst) **Facilities** FTV Games room ♫ Xmas New Year Wi-fi **Services** Lift **Parking** 12 **Notes** LB RS Jan-Feb

The Berkeley
★★★★★ GUEST ACCOMMODATION

3 Lascelles Ter BN21 4BJ
☎ 01323 645055 📄 01323 400128
e-mail: info@theberkeley.net
dir: *Follow seafront from pier, take 7th turn on right*

PETS: Bedrooms **Public areas** lounge only muzzled and on leads disp bin **Exercise area** beach & grass area 50mtrs **Facilities** walks info vet info

The Berkeley's central location is convenient for the seafront, theatre and town centre. Spacious bedrooms are smartly furnished, and a stylish lounge is provided for guests to relax in; breakfast is served in the attractive dining room.

Rooms 13 en suite (4 fmly) (1 GF) **S** £39-£45; **D** £59-£84 **Facilities** STV tea/coffee Cen ht Wi-fi

Arden House
★★★★ GUEST ACCOMMODATION

17 Burlington Place BN21 4AR
☎ 01323 639639 📄 01323 417840
e-mail: info@theardenhotel.co.uk
dir: *On seafront, towards W, 5th turn after pier*

PETS: Bedrooms **Charges** **Exercise area** 100mtrs **Facilities** food bowl water bowl scoop/disp bags leads walks info vet info **On Request** torch towels

This attractive Regency property sits just minutes away from the seafront and town centre. Bedrooms are comfortable and bright, many with new en suite bathrooms. Guests can enjoy a hearty breakfast at the beginning of the day then relax in the cosy lounge in the evening.

Rooms 11 rms (10 en suite) (1 pri facs) (1 fmly) **S** £35-£42; **D** £58-£68* **Facilities** TVL tea/coffee Cen ht Wi-fi **Parking** 3 **Notes** LB

The Mowbray
★★★★ GUEST ACCOMMODATION
2 Lascelles Ter BN21 4BJ
☎ 01323 720012 📠 01323 733579
e-mail: info@themowbray.com
dir: *Opp Devonshire Park Theatre*

PETS: Bedrooms unattended **Charges Exercise area Facilities**
walks info vet info **On Request** torch **Other** charge for damage
Restrictions small dogs only

This elegant townhouse is located opposite The Devonshire
Theatre and a few minutes' walk from the seafront. Bedrooms,
that are accessible by a lift to all floors, vary in size, but all
are attractively furnished and comfortable. There is a spacious
well presented lounge, small modern bar and a stylish dining
room. Breakfast is home-cooked, as are evening meals that are
available by prior arrangement

Rooms 13 en suite (3 fmly) (1 GF) **S** £35-£46; **D** £74-£100*
Facilities FTV TVL tea/coffee Dinner available Cen ht Lift Licensed
Wi-fi **Notes** LB

The Royal
★★★★ GUEST ACCOMMODATION
8-9 Marine Pde BN21 3DX
☎ 01323 649222 📠 0560 1500 065
e-mail: info@royaleastbourne.org.uk
web: www.royaleastbourne.org.uk
dir: *On seafront 100mtrs E of pier*

PETS: Bedrooms unattended sign **Public areas** except
breakfast room on leads disp bin **Exercise area** beach (20mtrs)
Facilities food (pre-bookable) food bowl water bowl bedding
feeding mat scoop/disp bags leads pet sitting dog walking
cage storage walks info vet info **On Request** fridge access
towels **Other** charge for damage

This property enjoys a central seafront location close to the pier
and within easy walking distance of the town centre. Spectacular
uninterrupted sea views are guaranteed. Now fully renovated
and eco-friendly, the comfortable bedrooms are modern with
flat-screen TVs and free Wi-fi. One of the ten rooms has private
facilities, while the others are fully en suite. A substantial
continental breakfast is served.

Rooms 10 rms (9 en suite) (1 pri facs) (1 fmly) **S** £39-£55;
D £70-£90* **Facilities** STV FTV tea/coffee Cen ht Wi-fi **Notes** LB
No Children 12yrs

Heaven Farm *(TQ403264)*
▶ ▶
TN22 3RG
☎ 01825 790226 📠 01825 790881
e-mail: heavenfarmleisure@btinternet.com
dir: *On A275 between Lewes & East Grinstead, 1m N of Sheffield
Park Gardens*

PETS: Public areas on leads **Exercise area Facilities** walks info
vet info **Other** prior notice required dogs must not worry resident
poultry & ducks **Resident Pets:** 3 cats

Open Apr-Oct Last arrival 21.00hrs Last departure noon

Delightful small rural site on a popular farm complex
incorporating a farm museum, craft shop, organic farm
shop, tea room and nature trail. Good clean facilities in well-
converted outbuildings. A 1.5 acre site with 25 touring pitches, 2
hardstandings.

Notes Prefer no children between 6-18yrs 🐾

The Olde Forge Hotel & Restaurant
★★ 76% HOTEL
Magham Down BN27 1PN
☎ 01323 842893 📠 01323 842893
e-mail: theoldeforgehotel@tesco.net
web: www.theoldeforgehotel.co.uk
dir: *Off Boship rdbt on A271 to Bexhill & Herstmonceux. Hotel
3m on left*

PETS: Bedrooms sign **Charges** £5 per night **Public areas**
except restaurant & guest lounge **Grounds** on leads disp
bin **Exercise area** immediately opposite **Facilities** food (pre-
bookable) food bowl water bowl bedding dog chews feeding
mat scoop/disp bags leads washing facs cage storage walks
info vet info **On Request** fridge access torch towels **Other**
charge for damage please phone for further details of pet
facilities **Resident Pet:** Diesel (Boxer)

In the heart of the countryside, this family-run hotel offers a
friendly welcome and an informal atmosphere. The bedrooms are
attractively decorated with thoughtful extras. The restaurant,
with its timbered beams and log fires, was a forge in the 16th
century; today it has a good local reputation for both its cuisine
and service.

Rooms 7 **S** £48-£58; **D** £85-£95 (incl. bkfst)* **Facilities** Wi-fi
Parking 11 **Notes** LB

ENGLAND

HEATHFIELD   Map 5 TQ52

Holly Grove

★ ★ ★ ★   BED AND BREAKFAST

Little London TN21 0NU

☎ 01435 863375   & 07811 963193

e-mail: joedance@btconnect.com

dir: A267 to Horam, turn right at Little London garage, proceed to bottom of lane

PETS: Bedrooms Stables Charges horses charged (livery) **Public areas** except restaurant **Grounds** disp bin **Exercise area** adjacent **Facilities** food (pre-bookable) food bowl water bowl bedding dog chews cat treats feeding mat litter tray leads pet sitting dog walking washing facs cage storage walks info vet info **On Request** fridge access torch towels **Other** charge for damage **Resident Pets:** Annie, Oscar & Golly (Spaniels), Plessi, Chopin & Sophie (cats), Apache & Josh (horses)

Holly Grove is set in a quiet rural location with heated outdoor swimming pool, satellite TV, Wi-fi and parking facilities. Bedrooms are appointed to a very high standard. There is a separate lounge available for guests, and breakfast is served in the dining room or on the terrace, weather permitting.

Rooms 3 rms (2 en suite) (1 pri facs) (1 fmly) (2 GF) **S** £45–£70; **D** £60–£85* **Facilities** STV TVL tea/coffee Dinner available Cen ht Wi-fi ⚲ Pool Table **Parking** 7

HERSTMONCEUX   Map 5 TQ61

Cleavers Lyng Country House

★ ★ ★ ★   GUEST ACCOMMODATION

Church Rd BN27 1QJ

☎ 01323 833644

e-mail: cleaverslyng@aol.com

web: www.cleaverslyng.co.uk

dir: Exit A271at Herstmonceux into Chapel Row, leads into Church Rd, 1.5m on right

PETS: Bedrooms Stables 1m **Public areas** on leads **Grounds** disp bin **Exercise area** adjacent **Facilities** food (pre-bookable) food bowl water bowl bedding dog chews feeding mat leads washing facs cage storage walks info vet info **On Request** fridge access torch towels **Other** charge for damage

Expect a warm welcome at this Grade II listed country house, parts of which date back to 1577. A spacious downstairs lounge and breakfast room offers the perfect place to relax with its log burning fire. Alternatively guests can enjoy the peaceful, landscaped gardens with fantastic views of beautiful Sussex countryside. Bedrooms are well appointed and offer guests comfortable accommodation; all have LCD TVs, free Wi-fi and many enjoy those amazing views.

Rooms 4 en suite (1 fmly) **S** £50–£90; **D** £75–£110* **Facilities** tea/coffee Cen ht Wi-fi **Parking** 10

HOVE

See Brighton & Hove

NEWICK   Map 5 TQ42

Newick Park Hotel & Country Estate

★ ★ ★   ◉◉   HOTEL

BN8 4SB

☎ 01825 723633   📠 01825 723969

e-mail: bookings@newickpark.co.uk

web: www.newickpark.co.uk

dir: Exit A272 at Newick Green, 1m, pass church & pub. Turn left, hotel 0.25m on right

PETS: Bedrooms (1 GF) unattended sign **Charges** £5 per night **Grounds Facilities** food (pre-bookable) food bowl water bowl washing facs walks info vet info **On Request** fridge access torch towels **Other** dogs allowed in ground-floor bedroom only **Resident Pets:** Maddy (Black Labrador), Tibby (Cocker Spaniel)

Delightful Grade II listed Georgian country house set amid 250 acres of Sussex parkland and landscaped gardens. The spacious, individually decorated bedrooms are tastefully furnished, thoughtfully equipped and have superb views of the grounds; many rooms have huge American king-size beds. The comfortable public rooms include a study, a sitting room, lounge bar and an elegant restaurant.

Rooms 16 (3 annexe) (5 fmly) (1 GF) **S** £125–£245; **D** £165–£285 (incl. bkfst)* **Facilities** FTV ⚲ ⚲ Fishing ⚲ Badminton Clay pigeon shooting Helicopter rides Quad biking Tank driving Xmas Wi-fi **Parking** 52 **Notes** LB

RYE   Map 5 TQ92

Jeake's House

★ ★ ★ ★ ★   🛏 GUEST ACCOMMODATION

Mermaid St TN31 7ET

☎ 01797 222828

e-mail: stay@jeakeshouse.com

web: www.jeakeshouse.com

dir: Approach from High St or The Strand

PETS: Bedrooms Charges £5 per night **Public areas** except dining room (welcome in bar) **Exercise area** 5-10 mins' walk **Facilities** walks info vet info **On Request** fridge access torch towels **Resident Pets:** Princess Yum Yum & Monte (Tonkinese cats)

Previously a 17th-century wool store and then a 19th-century Baptist school, this delightful house stands on a cobbled street in one of the most beautiful parts of this small, bustling town. The individually decorated bedrooms combine elegance and comfort with modern facilities. Breakfast is served at separate tables in the galleried dining room, and there is an oak-beamed lounge as well as a stylish book-lined bar with old pews.

Rooms 11 rms (10 en suite) (1 pri facs) (2 fmly) **S** £70-£79; **D** £90-£130 **Facilities** FTV tea/coffee Direct Dial Cen ht Licensed Wi-fi **Parking** 20 **Notes** No Children 5yrs

Little Saltcote
★ ★ ★ ★ GUEST ACCOMMODATION

22 Military Rd TN31 7NY
☎ 01797 223210 📠 01797 224474
e-mail: info@littlesaltcote.co.uk
web: www.littlesaltcote.co.uk
dir: 0.5m N of town centre. Off A268 onto Military Rd signed Appledore, house 300yds on left

PETS: Bedrooms Charges £5 per night **Public areas** on leads disp bin **Exercise area** 0.5m **Facilities** food bowl water bowl cage storage walks info vet info **On Request** fridge access torch towels **Other** charge for damage **Restrictions** no breed larger than a Labrador **Resident Pets:** Bracken (Labrador/Poodle cross)

This delightful family-run guest accommodation stands in quiet surroundings within walking distance of Rye town centre. The bright and airy en suite bedrooms are equipped with modern facilities including Wi-fi, and you can enjoy afternoon tea in the garden conservatory. A hearty breakfast is served at individual tables in the dining room.

Rooms 4 en suite (2 fmly) (1 GF) **S** £40-£75; **D** £65-£83 **Facilities** tea/coffee Cen ht Wi-fi **Parking** 5 **Notes** LB

Cliff Farm (TQ933237)
★ ★ ★ FARMHOUSE

Military Rd, Iden Lock TN31 7QD
☎ 01797 280331 📠 01797 280331 Mrs P Sullivin
e-mail: info@cliff-farm.com
dir: 2m along Military Rd to Appledore, turn left at hanging milk churn

PETS: Bedrooms Public areas except breakfast room **Grounds Exercise area** surrounding farmland

Beautiful views and wonderful hospitality are what you'll find at this farmhouse situated in a peaceful rural location just a short drive from Rye and Hastings. Bedrooms are pleasantly decorated and comfortably furnished. Breakfast is served at individual tables in the dining room, and there is also a cosy sitting room with a wood-burning stove and TV.

Rooms 3 rms (1 fmly) **Facilities** TVL tea/coffee Cen ht **Parking** 6 **Notes** LB Closed Nov-Feb 🐾 6 acres smallholding

WADHURST	Map 5 TQ63

Little Tidebrook Farm (TQ621304)
★ ★ ★ ★ FARMHOUSE

Riseden TN5 6NY
☎ 01892 782688 & 07970 159988 Mrs Sally Marley-Ward
e-mail: info@littletidebrook.co.uk
web: www.littletidebrook.co.uk
dir: A267 from Tunbridge Wells to Mark Cross, left onto B2100, 2m turn right at Best Beech Inn, left after 1m onto Riseden Rd, farm on left

PETS: Sep accom indoor, heated, (safe & secure) **Stables Charges** £5 per night **Public areas** except at meal times on leads **Grounds** on leads disp bin **Exercise area** farm **Facilities** water bowl scoop/disp bags leads washing facs cage storage walks info vet info **On Request** fridge access torch towels **Resident Pets:** 2 Labradors, 1 Jack Russell, 2 cats, 17 horses

This traditional farmhouse has cosy log fires in winter and wonderful garden dining in warm months. The imaginative decor combines with modern amenities such as Wi-fi to provide leisure and business travellers with the ideal setting. Close to Bewl Water and Royal Tunbridge Wells.

Rooms 3 rms (2 en suite) (1 pri facs) **S** £45-£80; **D** £50-£85* **Facilities** TVL tea/coffee Cen ht Wi-fi **Parking** 8 **Notes** No Children 12yrs 🐾 50 acres horses

ENGLAND

ARUNDEL · Map 4 TQ00

Norfolk Arms
★★★ 74% HOTEL

High St BN18 9AB
☎ 01903 882101 📠 01903 884275
e-mail: norfolk.arms@forestdale.com
web: www.norfolkarmshotel.com
dir: On High St in city centre

PETS: Bedrooms (8 GF) unattended **Charges** £7.50 per night
Public areas except restaurant

Built by the 10th Duke of Norfolk, this Georgian coaching inn
enjoys a superb setting beneath the battlements of Arundel
Castle. Bedrooms vary in sizes and character - all are comfortable
and well equipped. Public areas include two bars serving real
ales, comfortable lounges with roaring log fires, a traditional
restaurant and a range of meeting and function rooms.

Rooms 33 (13 annexe) (4 fmly) (8 GF) **S** £70-£89; **D** £90-£130
(incl. bkfst)* **Facilities** FTV Xmas New Year Wi-fi **Parking** 34
Notes LB

Comfort Inn
★★ 65% HOTEL

Crossbush BN17 7QQ
☎ 01903 840840 📠 01903 849849
e-mail: reservations@comfortinnarundel.co.uk
dir: A27/A284, 1st right into services

PETS: Bedrooms (25 GF) **Charges** £5 per night £35 per
week **Public areas** except restaurant & bar on leads disp bin
Facilities vet info

This modern, purpose-built hotel provides a good base for
exploring the nearby historic town. Good access to local road
networks and a range of meeting rooms, all air-conditioned, also
make this an ideal venue for business guests. Bedrooms are
spacious, smartly decorated and well equipped.

Rooms 53 (4 fmly) (25 GF) (12 smoking) **Facilities** STV FTV Xmas
New Year Wi-fi **Parking** 53

Brooklands Country Guest House
★★★★★ GUEST ACCOMMODATION

Brooklands Barn, Priory Ln BN18 0BG
☎ 01903 889515
e-mail: mail@brooklandsbarn.co.uk
dir: A27/A284 Arundel rdbt, take Ford road, Priory Ln next right
after Maxwell Rd.

PETS: Bedrooms Stables Charges dog £10, horse £25 per
night **Public areas** except main bar & dining area **Grounds**
Exercise area public footpath adjacent **Facilities** vet info
On Request fridge access torch towels **Other** charge for
damage

Brooklands is a stunning barn conversion situated in the
picturesque Arun Valley, just a short distance from the historic
town of Arundel. Stylish bedrooms offer an array of extras such
as Wi-fi. The dining room overlooks the fabulous gardens, and is
ideal for breakfast. There is also an indoor pool.

Rooms 4 en suite (1 fmly) (2 GF) **Facilities** FTV tea/coffee Cen ht
Wi-fi 🐎 Riding **Parking** 13

Ship & Anchor Marina (TQ002040)
▶▶

Station Rd, Ford BN18 0BJ
☎ 01243 551262 📠 01243 555256
e-mail: enquiries@shipandanchormarina.co.uk
dir: From A27 at Arundel take road S signed Ford. Site 2m on left
after level crossing

PETS: Public areas disp bin **Exercise area** riverside walks
Facilities food dog chews cat treats walks info vet info
Resident Pets: 1 dog, 4 cats

Open Mar-Oct Last arrival 21.00hrs Last departure noon

A neat and tidy site with dated but spotlessly clean toilet
facilities enjoying a pleasant position beside the Ship & Anchor
pub and the tidal River Arun. There are good walks from the site
both to Arundel and to the coast. A 12 acre site with 120 touring
pitches, 11 hardstandings.

Notes No music audible to others 🚭

BARNS GREEN — Map 4 TQ12

Sumners Ponds Fishery & Campsite
(TQ125268)

►►►

Chapel Rd RH13 0PR
☎ 01403 732539
e-mail: sumnersponds@dsl.co.uk
dir: *From A272 at Coolham x-rds, N towards Barns Green. In 1.5m take 1st left at small x-rds. 1m, over level crossing. Site on left just after right bend*

PETS: **Stables** 2m **Public areas** disp bin **Exercise area**
Facilities food bowl water bowl walks info vet info **Other**
disposal bags available **Resident Pet:** Skippy (Jack Russell)

Open all year Last arrival 20.00hrs Last departure noon

A touring area on a working farm on the edge of the quiet village of Barns Green, with purpose built facilities of a high standard. There are three well-stocked fishing lakes set in attractive surroundings, and a woodland walk with direct access to miles of footpaths. Horsham and Brighton are within easy reach. A 40 acre site with 61 touring pitches, 31 hardstandings.

Notes Only one car per pitch

BILLINGSHURST — Map 4 TQ02

Limeburners Arms Camp Site *(TQ072255)*

►►

Lordings Rd, Newbridge RH14 9JA
☎ 01403 782311
e-mail: chippy.sawyer@virgin.net
dir: *From A29 take A272 towards Petworth for 1m, left onto B2133. Site 300yds on left*

PETS: **Public areas** **Exercise area** adjacent walks **Facilities**
vet info

Open Apr-Oct Last arrival 22.00hrs Last departure 14.00hrs

A secluded site in rural West Sussex, at the rear of the Limeburners Arms public house, and surrounded by fields. It makes a pleasant base for touring the South Downs and the Arun Valley. The toilets are basic but very clean. A 2.75 acre site with 40 touring pitches.

BIRDHAM — Map 4 SU80

See also Chichester

Tawny Touring Park *(SZ818991)*

►

Tawny Nurseries, Bell Ln PO20 7HY
☎ 01243 512168
e-mail: tawny@pobox.co.uk
dir: *From A27 at Stockbridge rdbt take A286 towards The Witterings. 5m to mini rdbt in Birdham. 1st exit onto B2198. Site 300mtrs on left*

PETS: **Public areas** on leads disp bin **Exercise area** fenced area
Facilities washing facs walks info vet info **Other** prior notice
required **Resident Pet:** 1 Labrador

Open all year Last arrival 21.00hrs Last departure 19.00hrs

A small site for the self-contained tourer only, on a landscaped field adjacent to the owners' nurseries. There six hardstanding pitches for American RVs but no toilet facilities. The beach is one mile away. A 4.5 acre site with 30 touring pitches, 7 hardstandings.

CHICHESTER — Map 4 SU80

Crouchers Country Hotel & Restaurant
★★★ 81%  HOTEL

Birdham Rd PO20 7EH
☎ 01243 784995 📠 01243 539797
e-mail: crouchers@btconnect.com
dir: *From A27 Chichester bypass onto A286 towards West Wittering, 2m, hotel on left between Chichester Marina & Dell Quay*

PETS: **Bedrooms** (15 GF) **Charges** £10 per night £70 per week
Public areas except restaurant & lounge on leads **Grounds**
on leads disp bin **Exercise area** **Facilities** walks info vet
info **On Request** fridge access torch towels **Other** charge for
damage

This friendly, family-run hotel, situated in open countryside, is just a short drive from the harbour. The stylish and well-equipped bedrooms are situated in a separate barn, coach house and stable block, and include four-poster rooms and rooms with patios that overlook the fields. The modern oak-beamed restaurant, with country views, serves award-winning cuisine.

Rooms 26 (23 annexe) (2 fmly) (15 GF) **Facilities** STV FTV Xmas
New Year Wi-fi **Parking** 80

CHICHESTER *continued*

Old Chapel Forge

★ ★ ★ ★ 🛏 BED AND BREAKFAST

Lower Bognor Rd, Lagness PO20 1LR
☎ 01243 264380
e-mail: info@oldchapelforge.co.uk
dir: *4m SE of Chichester. Off A27 Chichester bypass at Bognor rdbt signed Pagham/Runcton, onto B2166 Pagham Rd & Lower Bognor Rd, Old Chapel Forge on right*

PETS: Bedrooms Stables 0.25m **Charges** donation to nature reserve (min £10 per stay) **Public areas** except breakfast area on leads **Grounds** on leads disp bin **Exercise area** 80 acres adjacent & beach 1m **Facilities** walks info vet info **On Request** fridge access torch towels **Other** charge for damage pets accepted by prior arrangement only **Restrictions** no dogs under 1 year; dogs must be house-trained **Resident Pets:** Jade (Labrador), Alphie (Bengal cat), Eddie & Ellie (geese), 4 donkeys

Great local produce features in the hearty breakfasts at this comfortable, eco-friendly property, an idyllic 17th-century house and chapel set in mature gardens with panoramic views of the South Downs. Old Chapel Forge is a short drive from Chichester, Goodwood, Pagham Harbour Nature Reserve and the beach. Bedrooms, including suites in the chapel, are luxurious, and all have internet access.

Rooms 4 annexe en suite (2 fmly) (4 GF) **S** £45-£75; **D** £50-£110*
Facilities tea/coffee Dinner available Cen ht Wi-fi Golf 18
Parking 6 **Notes** LB

Ellscott Park *(SU829995)*

▶ ▶ ▶

Sidlesham Ln, Birdham PO20 7QL
☎ 01243 512003 📠 01243 512003
e-mail: camping@ellscottpark.co.uk
dir: *Take A286 (Chichester/Wittering road) for approx 4m, left at Butterfly Farm sign, site 500yds right*

PETS: Stables 1m **Public areas** on leads disp bin **Exercise area** 3-acre field **Facilities** washing facs walks info vet info **Other** prior notice required **Restrictions** no German Shepherds or dangerous breeds (see page 7) **Resident Pet:** Luckie (Springer Spaniel)

Open Apr-3rd wk in Oct Last arrival daylight Last departure variable

A well-kept park set in meadowland behind the owners' nursery and van storage area. The park attracts a peace-loving clientele, and is handy for the beach and other local attractions. Home-grown produce and eggs are for sale. A 2.5 acre site with 50 touring pitches.

Notes

The Fish House

★ ★ ★ ★ ★ 🏅🏅 RESTAURANT WITH ROOMS

PO18 9HX
☎ 01243 519444 📠 01243 519499
e-mail: info@fishhouse.co.uk
dir: *From Chichester take A286 N, turn left onto B2141 to village*

PETS: Bedrooms Charges Public areas except restaurant on leads **Grounds** on leads **Exercise area** 30yds **Facilities** water bowl washing facs cage storage vet info **On Request** fridge access torch towels **Other** charge for damage **Resident Pets:** Barney & Betty (Bulldogs)

Luxury abounds in the strikingly designed bedrooms, with furniture made from reclaimed Asian teak and bathrooms with stunning marble fixtures. Hot tubs are located in the gardens from where guests can enjoy stunning views of the Sussex Downs. Dining options include the sophisticated restaurant where there is the option to choose the 8-course menu, or the less formal Fish Bar with an array of delicious seafood on offer. In summer an antique Citroën H van, serving seafood and puddings, can be found in the gardens.

Rooms 15 en suite (11 GF) **S** £80-£110; **D** £120-£160*
Facilities STV FTV tea/coffee Dinner available Direct Dial Cen ht Wi-fi Sauna **Parking** 50 **Notes** LB No coaches

CLIMPING — Map 4 SU90

Bailiffscourt Hotel & Spa

★★★ ◉◉ HOTEL

Climping St BN17 5RW

☎ 01903 723511 📄 01903 723107

e-mail: bailiffscourt@hshotels.co.uk

web: www.hshotels.co.uk

dir: *A259, follow Climping Beach signs. Hotel 0.5m on right*

PETS: Bedrooms (16 GF) unattended **Charges** £12 per night **Public areas** except restaurant **Grounds** disp bin **Exercise area** 30-acre grounds, beach 200mtrs **Facilities** food (pre-bookable) food bowl water bowl dog chews feeding mat scoop/disp bags washing facs cage storage walks info vet info **On Request** fridge access torch towels **Other** charge for damage room service menu for dogs

This delightful moated 'medieval manor' dating back only to the 1920s has the appearance of having been in existence for centuries. It was built for Lord Moyne, a member of the Guinness family, who wanted to create an ancient manor house. It became a hotel just over 60 years ago and sits in 30 acres of delightful parkland that leads to the beach. Bedrooms vary from atmospheric feature rooms with log fires, oak beams and four-poster beds to spacious, stylish and contemporary rooms located in the grounds. The Tapestry Restaurant serves award-winning classic European cuisine, and in summer the Courtyard is the place for informal light lunches and afternoon tea. Superb facilities are to be found in the health spa.

Rooms 39 (30 annexe) (25 fmly) (16 GF) **S** £205-£500; **D** £225-£655 (incl. bkfst)* **Facilities** Spa STV FTV ⬚ 🏌 🐾 🏊 Gym Sauna Steam room Dance/fitness studio Yoga/Pilates/gym inductions Xmas New Year Wi-fi Child facilities **Parking** 100 **Notes** LB

CUCKFIELD — Map 4 TQ32

Ockenden Manor

★★★ ◉◉◉ HOTEL

Ockenden Ln RH17 5LD

☎ 01444 416111 📄 01444 415549

e-mail: reservations@ockenden-manor.com

web: www.hshotels.co.uk

dir: *A23 towards Brighton. 4.5m left onto B2115 towards Haywards Heath. Cuckfield 3m. Ockenden Lane off High St. Hotel at end*

PETS: Bedrooms (4 GF) unattended **Charges** £10 per night **Grounds Exercise area** countryside walks **Facilities** walks info vet info **On Request** fridge access torch towels **Other** charge for damage

This charming 16th-century property enjoys fine views of the South Downs. The individually designed bedrooms and suites offer high standards of accommodation, some with unique historic features. Public rooms, retaining much original character, include an elegant sitting room with all the elements for a relaxing afternoon in front of the fire. Imaginative, noteworthy cuisine is the highlight to any stay. The beautiful

rooms and lovely garden make Ockenden a popular wedding venue. A spa is planned for 2011.

Rooms 22 (4 fmly) (4 GF) **S** £110-£205; **D** £187-£485 (incl. bkfst)* **Facilities** STV FTV 🏊 Xmas New Year Wi-fi **Parking** 43 **Notes** LB

DIAL POST — Map 4 TQ11

Honeybridge Park *(TQ152183)*

► ► ► ►

Honeybridge Ln RH13 8NX

☎ 01403 710923 📄 01403 710923

e-mail: enquiries@honeybridgepark.co.uk

dir: *10m S of Horsham, just off A24 at Dial Post. Behind Old Barn Nursery*

PETS: Charges dogs £1.30 per night **Public areas** on leads disp bin **Exercise area** adjacent **Facilities** food walks info vet info

Open all year Last arrival 19.00hrs Last departure noon

An attractive and very popular park on gently-sloping ground surrounded by hedgerows and mature trees. A comprehensive amenities building houses upmarket toilet facilities including luxury family and disabled rooms, as well as a laundry, shop and off-licence. There are plenty of hardstandings and electric hook-ups, and an excellent children's play area. A 15 acre site with 130 touring pitches, 70 hardstandings and 20 statics.

Notes No open fires

GATWICK AIRPORT (LONDON) — Map 4 TQ24

The Lawn Guest House

★★★★ GUEST HOUSE

30 Massetts Rd RH6 7DF

☎ 01293 775751 📄 01293 821803

e-mail: info@lawnguesthouse.co.uk

web: www.lawnguesthouse.com

dir: *M25 junct 7, M23 S towards Brighton/Gatwick Airport. Exit at junct 9. At either South or North Terminal rdbts A23 towards Redhill. At 3rd rdbt (Esso garage on left) take 3rd exit. (Texaco garage on right). In 200yds right at lights into Massetts Rd. Guest house 400yds on left*

PETS: Bedrooms Charges Public areas muzzled **Grounds** on leads **Facilities** walks info **On Request** fridge access towels **Other** charge for damage dogs are required to be muzzled **Restrictions** quiet dogs only; no dangerous breeds (see page 7)

Once a Victorian school, this friendly guest house is well-positioned on a quiet leafy street close to Gatwick. Bedrooms are spacious with thoughtful amenities such as free Wi-fi, and fans for use in warm weather. Airport parking is available.

Rooms 12 en suite (4 fmly) **S** £40-£50; **D** £50-£65* **Facilities** STV tea/coffee Direct Dial Cen ht Wi-fi **Parking** 4

MIDHURST Map 4 SU82

Spread Eagle Hotel and Spa

★★★ 80% ◎◎ HOTEL

South St GU29 9NH
☎ 01730 816911 📠 01730 815668
e-mail: spreadeagle@hshotels.co.uk
web: www.hshotels.co.uk/spread/spreadeagle-main.htm
dir: *M25 junct 10, A3 to Milford, take A286 to Midhurst. Hotel adjacent to market square*

PETS: Bedrooms (8 GF) unattended **Stables** 3m **Charges** £15 per night **Public areas** except restaurant **Grounds Exercise area Facilities** food (pre-bookable) food bowl water bowl bedding walks info vet info **On Request** fridge access torch **Other** charge for damage pets not allowed on beds **Restrictions** very large breeds not allowed **Resident Pet:** Poppy (Boxer)

Offering accommodation since 1430, this historic property is full of character, evident in its sloping floors and inglenook fireplaces. Individually styled bedrooms provide modern comforts; those in the main house have oak panelling and include some spacious feature rooms. The hotel also boasts a well-equipped spa and offers noteworthy food in the oak beamed restaurant.

Rooms 38 (4 annexe) (8 GF) **S** £80-£380; **D** £90-£380 (incl. bkfst)* **Facilities** Spa STV FTV 🏊 Gym Health & beauty treatment rooms Steam room Spa bath Sauna Fitness trainer Xmas New Year Wi-fi **Parking** 75 **Notes** LB

TILLINGTON Map 4 SU92

The Horse Guards Inn

★★★★ ◎ INN

GU28 9AF
☎ 01798 342332 📠 01798 345126
e-mail: info@thehorseguardsinn.co.uk
dir: *Off A272 to Tillington, up hill opposite All Hallows church*

PETS: Bedrooms Stables 0.5km **Charges** £10 per night **Public areas Grounds** on leads **Exercise area** 200yds **Facilities** food bowl water bowl bedding dog chews feeding mat washing facs walks info vet info **On Request** fridge access torch towels **Other** charge for damage **Resident Pets:** Sasha (Siamese cat), Marvin (Russian Blue cat)

The Horse Guards Inn is conveniently located close to Petworth and Midhurst in a quiet village setting opposite the quaint church, and is perfect for exploring the beautiful surrounding countryside. The comfortable bedrooms are simply decorated, and delicious breakfasts are prepared to order using the finest local ingredients. The same principles apply to the substantial and flavoursome meals served in the cosy restaurant/bar dining areas.

Rooms 2 en suite 1 annexe en suite (1 fmly) **S** £75-£120; **D** £75-£120 **Facilities** FTV tea/coffee Dinner available Cen ht Wi-fi

WEST MARDEN Map 4 SU71

Grandwood House

★★★★ GUEST ACCOMMODATION

Watergate PO18 9EG
☎ 07971 845153 & 023 9263 1436 📠 023 9263 1436
e-mail: info@grandwoodhouse.co.uk
web: www.grandwoodhouse.co.uk

PETS: Bedrooms unattended **Stables** 1m **Public areas Grounds** on leads disp bin **Exercise area** adjacent **Facilities** scoop/disp bags washing facs cage storage walks info vet info **On Request** fridge access torch towels **Other** charge for damage proprietor must be informed of size of dog in advance **Resident Pet:** Prince (German Shepherd)

Set in the South Downs and built in 1907, Grandwood House was originally a lodge belonging to Watergate House, which was accidentally burnt down by troops during WWII. Only a short walk away is the local pub in nearby Walderton which serves lunches and evening meals. All rooms are en suite and enjoy views of the garden, open farmland or both. Large security gates leading onto the driveway ensure secure parking at all times.

Rooms 4 annexe en suite (4 GF) **S** £40-£60; **D** £50-£90 **Facilities** FTV tea/coffee Cen ht Wi-fi **Parking** 8 **Notes** LB

WORTHING Map 4 TQ10

THE INDEPENDENTS
HOTEL ASSOCIATION

Cavendish Hotel

[U]

115 Marine Pde BN11 3QG
☎ 01903 236767 📠 01903 823840
e-mail: reservations@cavendishworthing.co.uk
web: www.cavendishworthing.co.uk
dir: *On seafront, 600yds W of pier*

PETS: Bedrooms (1 GF) unattended **Public areas** except restaurant on leads **Exercise area** countryside walks & beach opposite **Facilities** walks info vet info

Currently the rating for this establishment is not confirmed. This may be due to a change of ownership or because it has only recently joined the AA rating scheme. For further details please see the AA website: theAA.com

Rooms 17 (4 fmly) (1 GF) (6 smoking) **Facilities** STV Wi-fi **Services** Air con **Parking** 5

TYNE & WEAR

NEWCASTLE UPON TYNE — Map 12 NZ26

HOTELS & RESORTS

Newcastle Marriott Hotel Gosforth Park
★★★★ 78% HOTEL

High Gosforth Park, Gosforth NE3 5HN
☎ 0191 236 4111 📠 0191 236 8192
web: www.newcastlemarriottgosforthpark.co.uk
dir: Onto A1056 to Killingworth & Wideopen. 3rd exit to Gosforth Park, hotel ahead

PETS: Bedrooms Grounds on leads disp bin Exercise area Facilities walks info vet info Other pets are only accepted by agreement with General Manager at time of booking

Set within its own grounds, this modern hotel offers extensive conference and banqueting facilities, along with indoor and outdoor leisure. There is a choice of dining in the more formal Plate Restaurant or the relaxed Chat's lounge bar. Many of the air-conditioned bedrooms have views over the park. The hotel is conveniently located for the bypass, airport and racecourse. Marriott Hotels - AA Hotel Group of the Year 2010-11.

Rooms 178 (17 smoking) Facilities Spa STV 🕭 supervised 🏊 Gym Squash Jogging trail ♫ New Year Wi-fi Services Lift Air con Parking 340

Kenilworth Hotel
★★ 72% SMALL HOTEL

44 Osborne Rd, Jesmond NE2 2AL
☎ 0191 281 8111 & 281 9111 📠 0191 281 9476
e-mail: info@thekenilworthhotel.co.uk
web: www.thekenilworthhotel.co.uk
dir: A1058 signed Tynemouth for 1m. Left at lights onto Osborne Rd, hotel 0.5m on right

PETS: Bedrooms sign Charges Exercise area 0.5m Facilities food bowl water bowl cage storage walks info vet info On Request torch Other charge for damage

This family-run hotel in the Jesmond area of the city features wooden floors and leather furniture. The smart bedrooms have satellite TVs, DVD players, beverage trays and hairdryers. The main attraction is El Castano, the Spanish tapas restaurant, where the extensive menu features carefully prepared dishes using produce that is sourced both locally and directly from Spain.

Rooms 11 (5 fmly) S £40-£60; D £65-£90 (incl. bkfst)*
Facilities FTV Access to leisure centre 1.5km away Xmas New Year Wi-fi Parking 11 Notes LB

WHICKHAM — Map 12 NZ26

Gibside
★★★ 74% HOTEL

Front St NE16 4JG
☎ 0191 488 9292 📠 0191 488 8000
e-mail: reception@gibside-hotel.co.uk
web: www.gibside-hotel.co.uk
dir: Off A1(M) towards Whickham on B6317, onto Front St, 2m on right

PETS: Bedrooms (13 GF) unattended Exercise area paved area Facilities walks info vet info On Request fridge access

Conveniently located in the village centre, this hotel is close to the Newcastle by-pass and its elevated position affords views over the Tyne Valley. Bedrooms come in two styles, classical and contemporary. Public rooms include the Egyptian-themed Sphinx bar and a more formal restaurant. Secure garage parking is available.

Rooms 44 (2 fmly) (13 GF) S £67.50-£105; D £77.50-£115*
Facilities FTV Golf Academy at The Beamish Park ♫ New Year Wi-fi Services Lift Parking 28

WARWICKSHIRE

ALCESTER — Map 4 SP05

Kings Court
★★★ 73% HOTEL

Kings Coughton B49 5QQ
☎ 01789 763111 📠 01789 400242
e-mail: info@kingscourthotel.co.uk
web: www.kingscourthotel.co.uk
dir: 1m N on A435

PETS: Bedrooms (32 GF) sign Charges Public areas on leads Grounds on leads disp bin Exercise area Facilities food bowl water bowl walks info vet info On Request fridge access torch towels Other charge for damage

This privately owned hotel dates back to Tudor times and the bedrooms in the original house have oak beams. Most guests are accommodated in the well-appointed modern wings. The bar and restaurant offer very good cooking on interesting menus. The hotel is licensed to hold civil ceremonies and the pretty garden is ideal for summer weddings.

Rooms 60 (56 annexe) (3 fmly) (32 GF) S £68; D £90 (incl. bkfst)*
Facilities STV Mini gym Wi-fi Parking 200 Notes LB Closed 24-30 Dec

ENGLAND

BAGINTON   Map 4 SP37

The Oak
★★★ INN
Coventry Rd CV8 3AU
☎ 024 7651 8855 📠 024 7651 8866
e-mail: thebagintonoak@aol.com
web: http://theoak.greatpubs.net

PETS: Bedrooms unattended Stables 0.5m Charges £5 per
night £35 per week Public areas on leads Grounds disp
bin Exercise area adjacent Facilities water bowl dog chews
dog walking washing facs cage storage walks info vet info
On Request fridge access torch towels Other charge for
damage pet washing facilities on request Resident Pets: Beau
& Jasper (Border Collies)

Located close to major road links and Coventry Airport, this
popular inn provides a wide range of food throughout the themed,
open-plan public areas. Families are especially welcome.
Modern, well-equipped bedrooms are situated in a separate
accommodation building.

Rooms 13 annexe en suite (1 fmly) (6 GF) S £40-£65; D £40-£65*
Facilities FTV tea/coffee Dinner available Cen ht Wi-fi
Parking 110

COLESHILL   Map 4 SP28

Grimstock Country House
★★★ 71% COUNTRY HOUSE HOTEL
Gilson Rd, Gilson B46 1LJ
☎ 01675 462121 & 462161 📠 01675 467646
e-mail: enquiries@grimstockhotel.co.uk
web: www.grimstockhotel.co.uk
dir: Off A446 at rdbt onto B4117 to Gilson, hotel 100yds on right

PETS: Bedrooms (13 GF) unattended sign Charges £10 per
stay Public areas except bar and restaurant on leads Grounds
on leads disp bin Exercise area adjacent field Facilities
walks info vet info On Request fridge access Other charge for
damage

This privately owned hotel is convenient for Birmingham
International Airport and the NEC, and benefits from a peaceful
rural setting. Bedrooms are spacious and comfortable.
Public rooms include two restaurants, a wood-panelled bar,
good conference facilities and a gym featuring the latest
cardiovascular equipment.

Rooms 44 (1 fmly) (13 GF) S £60-£95; D £75-£125 (incl. bkfst)*
Facilities STV Gym Xmas New Year Wi-fi Parking 100 Notes LB

CORLEY MOTORWAY SERVICE AREA (M6)   Map 4 SP38

Days Inn Corley - NEC
BUDGET HOTEL
Junction 3-4, M6 North, Corley CV7 8NR
☎ 01676 543800 & 540111 📠 01676 540128
e-mail: corley.hotel@welcomebreak.co.uk
dir: On M6 between juncts 3 & 4 N'bound

PETS: Bedrooms (24 GF) unattended Charges Public areas
except main service area on leads Grounds on leads disp bin
Exercise area Facilities water bowl feeding mat washing facs
cage storage walks info vet info On Request fridge access
torch towels Other charge for damage

This modern building offers accommodation in smart, spacious
and well-equipped bedrooms, suitable for families and business
travellers, and all with en suite bathrooms. Continental breakfast
is available and other refreshments may be taken at the nearby
family restaurant.

Rooms 50 (13 fmly) (24 GF) (8 smoking) S £29-£59; D £29-£69

Harbury Fields *(SP352604)*

▶ ▶ ▶ ▶

Harbury Fields Farm CV33 9JN
☎ 01926 612457
e-mail: rdavis@harburyfields.co.uk
dir: *M40 junct 12 onto B4451 (signed Kenton/Gaydon). 0.75m, right signed Lightborne. 4m, right at rdbt onto B4455 (signed Harbury). 3rd right by petrol station, site in 700yds (by two cottages)*

PETS: Public areas except washrooms **Exercise area** farm walk **Facilities** walks info vet info **Other** prior notice required

Open 2 Jan-19 Dec Last arrival 21.30hrs Last departure noon

This developing park is in a peaceful farm setting with lovely countryside views. All pitches have hardstandings with electric and the facilities are spotless. It is well positioned for visiting Warwick and Leamington Spa as well as the exhibition centres at NEC Birmingham, NAC Stoneleigh Park or Warwick. A 3 acre site with 32 touring pitches, 31 hardstandings.

Notes 🐕

🐾

ⓆHOTELS

Chesford Grange

★★★★ 79% HOTEL
Chesford Bridge CV8 2LD
☎ 01926 859331 📠 01926 859272
e-mail: chesfordgrangereservations@qhotels.co.uk
web: www.qhotels.co.uk
dir: *0.5m SE of junct A46/A452. At rdbt turn right signed Leamington Spa, follow signs to hotel*

PETS: Bedrooms (43 GF) unattended **Charges** £15 per night **Grounds** on leads **Exercise area** acres of grounds **Other** prior notice required well behaved dogs only

This much-extended hotel set in 17 acres of private grounds is well situated for Birmingham International Airport, the NEC and major routes. Bedrooms range from traditional style to contemporary rooms featuring state-of-the-art technology. Public areas include a leisure club and extensive conference and banqueting facilities.

Rooms 205 (20 fmly) (43 GF) **Facilities** Spa STV 🏊 supervised Gym Steam room Solarium Xmas New Year Wi-fi **Services** Lift **Parking** 650

Best
Western

Best Western Falstaff

★★★ 73% HOTEL
16-20 Warwick New Rd CV32 5JQ
☎ 01926 312044 📠 01926 450574
e-mail: sales@falstaffhotel.com
web: www.falstaffhotel.com
dir: *M40 junct 13 or 14, follow Leamington Spa signs. Over 4 rdbts, under bridge. Left into Princes Dr, right at mini-rdbt*

PETS: Bedrooms (16 GF) unattended **Charges** £10 per night **Grounds** on leads **Exercise area** parks nearby **Facilities** vet info **On Request** fridge access towels

Bedrooms at this hotel come in a variety of sizes and styles and are well equipped, with many thoughtful extras. Snacks can be taken in the relaxing lounge bar, and an interesting selection of English and continental dishes is offered in the restaurant; 24-hour room service is also available. Conference and banqueting facilities are extensive.

Rooms 63 (2 fmly) (16 GF) **Facilities** FTV Arrangement with local health club Xmas New Year Wi-fi **Parking** 50

The Red Lion

★★★★ ◉ INN
Main St CV36 5JJ
☎ 01608 684221 📠 01608 684968
e-mail: info@redlion-longcompton.co.uk
dir: *5m S of Shipston on Stour on A3400*

PETS: Bedrooms sign **Stables** nearby **Public areas** except restaurant on leads **Grounds** on leads disp bin **Exercise area** 5 mins' walk **Facilities** water bowl walks info vet info **On Request** torch **Other** charge for damage **Resident Pet:** Cocoa (Chocolate Labrador)

Located in the pretty rural village of Long Compton, this mid 18th-century posting house retains many original features which are complemented by rustic furniture in the public areas. A good range of ales is offered, and interesting menus make good use of quality local produce. Newly refurbished bedrooms are well appointed, and furnished with a good range of facilities.

Rooms 5 en suite (1 fmly) **S** £55; **D** £80-£99* **Facilities** tea/coffee Dinner available Cen ht Wi-fi **Parking** 60 **Notes** No coaches

Best Western Weston Hall

★★★ 68% HOTEL

Weston Ln, Bulkington CV12 9RU
☎ 024 7631 2989   📠 024 7664 0846
e-mail: info@westonhallhotel.co.uk
dir: M6 junct 2, B4065 through Ansty. Left in Shilton, from Bulkington follow Nuneaton signs, into Weston Ln at 30mph sign

PETS: Bedrooms (14 GF) Charges £10 per night Public areas only front bar on leads Grounds Exercise area Facilities (pre-bookable) food bowl water bowl bedding washing facs cage storage walks info vet info On Request torch towels Other charge for damage food by prior arrangement

This Grade II listed hotel, whose origins date back to the reign of Elizabeth I, sits within seven acres of peaceful grounds. The original three-gabled building retains many original features, such as the carved wooden fireplace in the library. Friendly service is provided; and the bedrooms, that vary in size, are thoughtfully equipped.

Rooms 40 (1 fmly) (14 GF) Facilities FTV 🏊 New Year Wi-fi Parking 300 Notes LB

Days Inn Nuneaton

BUDGET HOTEL

St David's Way, Bermuda Park CV10 7SD
☎ 024 7635 7370 & 0870 428 0928   📠 0870 428 0929
e-mail: reservations@daysinnnuneaton.co.uk
web: www.daysinn.com
dir: M6 junct 3 onto A444 Nuneaton. 1m, left onto Bermuda Park. At rdbt right onto St David's Way, hotel on right

PETS: Bedrooms (10 GF) Stables nearby Charges £10 per stay Public areas except lounge 7-9am weekdays, 7-10am weekends on leads Grounds on leads disp bin Exercise area lake 10-min walk Facilities walks info vet info Other charge for damage dogs not allowed on furniture

This modern building offers accommodation in smart, spacious and well-equipped bedrooms, suitable for families and business travellers, and all with en suite bathrooms. Continental breakfast is available and other refreshments may be taken at the nearby family restaurant.

Rooms 101 (4 fmly) (10 GF) (10 smoking) S £50-£67; D £50-£70 (incl. bkfst)*

Lodge Farm Campsite (SP476748)

►►

Bilton Ln, Long Lawford CV23 9DU
☎ 01788 560193
e-mail: adrian@lodgefarm.com
dir: From Rugby take A428 (Lawford road), towards Coventry, 1.5m. At Sheaf & Sickle pub left into Bilton Ln, site 500yds

PETS: Stables 3m Public areas dogs must be on leads & under control at all times disp bin Exercise area 200yds Facilities washing facs walks info vet info Other dogs must be exercised off site Resident Pets: 1 Collie, 1 Jack Russell, 1 German Shorthaired Pointer, 3 cats, chickens

Open Etr-Nov Last arrival 22.00hrs

A small, simple farm site set behind the friendly owner's home and self-catering cottages, with converted stables housing the toilet facilities. Rugby is only a short drive away, and the site is tucked well away from the main road. A 2.5 acre site with 35 touring pitches, 3 hardstandings and 10 statics.

Barceló Billesley Manor Hotel

★★★★ 77% ◉◉ HOTEL

Billesley, Alcester B49 6NF
☎ 01789 279955   📠 01789 764145
e-mail: billesleymanor@barcelo-hotels.co.uk
web: www.barcelo-hotels.co.uk
dir: A46 towards Evesham. Over 3 rdbts, right for Billesley after 2m

PETS: Bedrooms (5 GF) unattended sign Charges £15 per night Grounds on leads disp bin Exercise area 100yds Facilities cage storage walks info vet info On Request fridge access torch towels Other charge for damage

This 16th-century manor is set in peaceful grounds and parkland with a delightful yew topiary garden and fountain. The spacious bedrooms and suites, most in traditional country-house style, are thoughtfully designed and well equipped. Conference facilities and some of the bedrooms are found in the cedar barns. Public areas retain many original features, such as oak panelling, fireplaces and exposed stone.

Rooms 72 (29 annexe) (5 GF) Facilities Spa ⊗ supervised 🏋️🏊 Gym Steam room Beauty treatments Yoga studio Xmas New Year Parking 100

Mercure Shakespeare

★★★★ 71% ⊛ HOTEL

Chapel St CV37 6ER

☎ 01789 294997 📠 01789 415411

e-mail: h6630@accor.com

web: www.mercure.com

dir: M40 junct 15. Follow signs for Stratford town centre on A439. Follow one-way system onto Bridge St. Left at rdbt, hotel 200yds on left opposite HSBC bank

PETS: Bedrooms (3 GF) unattended **Charges** £10 per night **Public areas** disp bin **Exercise area** park 300yds **Other** charge for damage

Dating back to the early 17th century, The Shakespeare is one of the oldest hotels in this historic town. The hotel name represents one of the earliest exploitations of Stratford as the birthplace of one of the world's leading playwrights. With exposed beams and open fires, the public rooms retain an ambience reminiscent of this era. Bedrooms are appointed to a good standard and remain in keeping with the style of the property.

Rooms 74 (11 annexe) (3 GF) **S** £70-£140; **D** £80-£160 (incl. bkfst) **Facilities** Xmas New Year Wi-fi **Services** Lift **Parking** 34 **Notes** LB

Charlecote Pheasant Hotel

★★★ 78% HOTEL

Charlecote CV35 9EW

☎ 0844 855 9126 📠 01789 470222

e-mail: charlecote@foliohotels.com

web: www.foliohotels.com/charlecotepheasant

dir: M40 junct 15, A429 towards Cirencester through Barford. In 2m right into Charlecote, hotel opposite Charlecote Park

PETS: Bedrooms unattended **Charges** £10 per night **Grounds** on leads **Exercise area Facilities** vet info

Located just outside Stratford, this hotel is set in extensive grounds and is a popular conference venue. Various bedroom styles are available within the annexe wings, ranging from standard rooms to executive suites. The main building houses the restaurant and a lounge bar area.

Rooms 70 (39 fmly) **Facilities** FTV 🎣 Children's play area Xmas New Year Wi-fi **Parking** 100

Croft

★★★★ GUEST HOUSE

Haseley Knob CV35 7NL

☎ 01926 484447 📠 01926 484447

e-mail: david@croftguesthouse.co.uk

web: www.croftguesthouse.co.uk

dir: 4.5m NW of Warwick. Off A4177 into Haseley Knob, follow signs

PETS: Bedrooms Charges £3 per night **Public areas Grounds** on leads disp bin **Exercise area** 200mtrs **Facilities** washing facs cage storage walks info vet info **On Request** fridge access **Other** charge for damage

Friendly proprietors provide homely accommodation at this modern detached house, set in peaceful countryside and convenient for Warwick and the NEC, Birmingham. The conservatory dining room overlooks large well-kept gardens. Fresh eggs from home-reared chickens are used for memorable English breakfasts.

Rooms 7 rms (5 en suite) (2 pri facs) 2 annexe rms 1 annexe en suite (1 pri facs) (2 fmly) (4 GF) **Facilities** TVL tea/coffee Cen ht Wi-fi **Parking** 9 **Notes** Closed Xmas wk

Days Inn Warwick North

BUDGET HOTEL

Warwick Services, M40 Northbound Junction 12-13, Banbury Rd CV35 0AA

☎ 01926 651681 📠 01926 651634

e-mail: warwick.north.hotel@welcomebreak.co.uk

web: www.welcomebreak.co.uk

dir: M40 northbound between junct 12 & 13

PETS: Bedrooms Public areas on leads **Grounds** on leads disp bin **Exercise area** large grassed area **Other** prior notice required **Restrictions** small to medium size dogs only

This modern building offers accommodation in smart, spacious and well-equipped bedrooms, suitable for families and business travellers, and all with en suite bathrooms. Continental breakfast is available and other refreshments may be taken at the nearby family restaurant.

Rooms 54 (45 fmly) (8 smoking)

ENGLAND

WARWICK MOTORWAY SERVICE AREA (M40) *continued*

Days Inn Warwick South

BUDGET HOTEL

Warwick Services, M40 Southbound, Banbury Rd CV35 0AA
☎ 01926 650168   📄 01926 651601
e-mail: warwick.south.hotel@welcomebreak.co.uk
web: www.welcomebreak.co.uk
dir: *M40 southbound between junct 14 & 12*

PETS: Bedrooms sign **Charges Public areas** on leads **Grounds** on leads disp bin **Exercise area** adjacent **Facilities** vet info **On Request** fridge access **Other** charge for damage

This modern building offers accommodation in smart, spacious and well-equipped bedrooms, suitable for families and business travellers, and all with en suite bathrooms. Continental breakfast is available and other refreshments may be taken at the nearby family restaurant.

Rooms 40 (38 fmly) (5 smoking) **S** £29-£49; **D** £29-£69*

WOLVEY   Map 4 SP48

Wolvey Villa Farm Caravan & Camping Site

(SP428869)

►►►

LE10 3HF
☎ 01455 220493 & 220630
dir: *M6 junct 2, B4065 follow Wolvey signs. Or M69 junct 1 & follow Wolvey signs*

PETS: Stables Charges dog £1 per night **Public areas** except shop **Exercise area** field **Facilities** food vet info

Open all year Last arrival 22.00hrs Last departure noon

A level grass site surrounded by trees and shrubs, on the borders of Warwickshire and Leicestershire. This quiet country site has its own popular fishing lake, and is convenient for visiting the major cities of Coventry and Leicester. A 7 acre site with 110 touring pitches, 24 hardstandings.

Notes No twin axles

WEST MIDLANDS

BALSALL COMMON   Map 4 SP27

Haigs Hotel

★★★ 72% HOTEL

Kenilworth Rd CV7 7EL
☎ 01676 533004   📄 01676 535132
e-mail: info@haigshotel.co.uk
dir: *A45 towards Coventry, at Stonebridge Island turn right, 4m S of M42 junct 6*

PETS: Bedrooms (5 GF) unattended **Stables** 1m **Charges** £5 per night **Public areas** except restaurant **Grounds** disp bin **Exercise area** 500yds **Facilities** water bowl walks info vet info **On Request** torch **Other** charge for damage

Conveniently located just five miles from Birmingham Airport and twelve miles from Stratford-upon-Avon. This small family-run hotel offers its guests a comfortable stay. Enjoyable meals on a monthly changing menu can be taken in McKee's Restaurant.

Rooms 23 (2 fmly) (5 GF) **S** £50-£80; **D** £60-£90 (incl. bkfst)*
Facilities Xmas New Year Wi-fi **Parking** 23

BIRMINGHAM   Map 7 SP08

Hotel du Vin Birmingham

★★★★ 78% ◎ TOWN HOUSE HOTEL

25 Church St B3 2NR
☎ 0121 200 0600   📄 0121 236 0889
e-mail: info@birmingham.hotelduvin.com
web: www.hotelduvin.com
dir: *M6 junct 6/A38(M) to city centre, over flyover. Keep left & exit at St Chads Circus signed Jewellery Quarter. At lights & rdbt take 1st exit, follow signs for Colmore Row, opposite cathedral. Right into Church St, across Barwick St. Hotel on right*

PETS: Bedrooms unattended **Sep accom Charges** £10 per night **Public areas** except bar & bistro on leads **Facilities** food bowl water bowl bedding cage storage walks info vet info **Other** charge for damage dog bed, blanket & bowls available

The former Birmingham Eye Hospital has become a chic and sophisticated hotel. The stylish, high-ceilinged rooms, all with a wine theme, are luxuriously appointed and feature stunning bathrooms, sumptuous duvets and Egyptian cotton sheets. The Bistro offers relaxed dining and a top-notch wine list, while other attractions include a champagne bar, a wine boutique and a health club.

Rooms 66 **Facilities** Spa STV Gym Treatment rooms Steam room Sauna Xmas New Year Wi-fi **Services** Lift Air con **Parking Notes** LB

Novotel Birmingham Centre

★★★★ 71% HOTEL

70 Broad St B1 2HT

☎ 0121 643 2000 📠 0121 643 9786

e-mail: h1077@accor.com

web: www.novotel.com

dir: A38/A456, hotel on right beyond International Convention Centre

PETS: Bedrooms Charges £5 per night **Public areas** only assist dogs in restaurant & bar on leads disp bin **Facilities** walks info vet info **On Request** torch towels **Other** charge for damage **Restrictions** small dogs only

This large, modern, purpose-built hotel benefits from an excellent city centre location, with the bonus of secure parking. Bedrooms are spacious, modern and well equipped especially for business users; four rooms have facilities for less able guests. Public areas include the Garden Brasserie, function rooms and a fitness room.

Rooms 148 (148 fmly) (11 smoking) **S** £80-£210; **D** £80-£210*
Facilities Gym Fitness room Cardio-vascular equipment Sauna Steam room Wi-fi **Services** Lift Air con **Parking** 53 **Notes** LB

Holiday Inn Birmingham M6 Jct 7

★★★ 72% HOTEL

Chapel Ln, Great Barr B43 7BG

☎ 0870 400 9009 & 0121 357 7303 📠 0121 357 7503

web: www.holidayinn.co.uk

dir: M6 junct 7, A34 signed Walsall. Hotel 200yds on right across carriageway in Chapel Lane

PETS: Bedrooms (67 GF) **Stables** 2m **Charges** £25 per night weekly price on application **Public areas** except restaurant on leads **Grounds** on leads **Facilities** cage storage walks info vet info **On Request** fridge access towels **Other** charge for damage other pets accepted by prior arrangement only

Situated in pleasant surroundings, this modern hotel offers well-equipped and comfortable bedrooms. Public areas include the popular Traders restaurant and a comfortable lounge where a menu is available to guests all day. There is also 24-hour room service; a courtyard patio and a garden.

Rooms 190 (45 fmly) (67 GF) (12 smoking) **Facilities** STV supervised Gym Xmas New Year Wi-fi **Services** Air con **Parking** 250

Campanile Birmingham

Campanile

BUDGET HOTEL

Chester St, Aston B6 4BE

☎ 0121 359 3330 📠 0121 359 1223

e-mail: birmingham@campanile.com

dir: Next to rdbt at junct of A4540/A38

PETS: Bedrooms Charges £5 per night **Grounds** on leads disp bin **Exercise area** 5 mins' walk **Facilities** water bowl walks info vet info **On Request** fridge access torch **Other** charge for damage dogs are required to be muzzled

This modern building offers accommodation in smart, well-equipped bedrooms, all with en suite bathrooms. Refreshments may be taken at the informal bistro.

Rooms 110 (5 fmly)

Ibis Birmingham Bordesley Circus

BUDGET HOTEL

1 Bordesley Park Rd, Bordesley B10 0PD

☎ 0121 506 2600 📠 0121 506 2610

e-mail: H2178@accor.com

web: www.ibishotel.com

PETS: Bedrooms (16 GF) unattended sign **Charges Grounds** on leads **Facilities** food bowl water bowl **Other** charge for damage

Modern, budget hotel offering comfortable accommodation in bright and practical bedrooms. Breakfast is self-service and dinner is available in the restaurant.

Rooms 87 (16 GF)

Ibis Birmingham City Centre

BUDGET HOTEL

Arcadian Centre, Ladywell Walk B5 4ST

☎ 0121 622 6010 📠 0121 622 6020

e-mail: h1459@accor-hotels.com

web: www.ibishotel.com

dir: From motorways follow city centre signs. Then follow Bullring or Indoor Market signs. Hotel adjacent to market

PETS: Bedrooms unattended sign **Charges Public areas** disp bin **Facilities** walks info vet info **Other** charge for damage **Restrictions** small dogs only

Rooms 159 (5 fmly)

Ibis Birmingham Holloway Circus

BUDGET HOTEL

55 Irving St B1 1DH

☎ 0121 622 4925 📠 0121 622 4195

e-mail: H2092@accor.com

web: www.ibishotel.com

dir: From M6 take A38/City Centre, left after 2nd tunnel. Right at rdbt, 4th left (Sutton St) into Irving St. Hotel on left

PETS: Bedrooms Charges £5 per night **Grounds** on leads

Rooms 51 (2 fmly) (26 GF) **S** £51-£155; **D** £51-£155*

BIRMINGHAM *continued*

Rollason Wood

★★ GUEST ACCOMMODATION

130 Wood End Rd, Erdington B24 8BJ
☎ 0121 373 1230 ▤ 0121 382 2578
e-mail: rollwood@globalnet.co.uk
dir: *M6 junct 6, A5127 to Erdington, right onto A4040, establishment 0.25m on left*

PETS: **Bedrooms** sign **Exercise area** 200yds **Facilities** cage storage walks info vet info

Well situated for many road networks and the city centre, this owner-managed establishment is popular with contractors. The choice of three different bedroom styles suits most budgets, and rates include full English breakfasts. Ground-floor areas include a popular bar, cosy TV lounge and a dining room.

Rooms 35 rms (11 en suite) (5 fmly) (9 smoking)
S £21.50-£39.95; **D** £38-£49.50* **Facilities** TVL tea/coffee Dinner available Cen ht Licensed Wi-fi Pool Table **Parking** 35

Novotel Birmingham Airport

★★★ 79% HOTEL

B26 3QL
☎ 0121 782 7000 & 782 4111 ▤ 0121 782 0445
e-mail: H1158@accor.com
web: www.novotel.com
dir: *M42 junct 6/A45 to Birmingham, signed to airport. Hotel opposite main terminal*

PETS: **Bedrooms** **Charges** £20 per night **Other** charge for damage dogs are required to be muzzled

This large, purpose-built hotel is located opposite the main passenger terminal. Bedrooms are spacious, modern in style and well equipped, including Playstations to keep the children busy. Several rooms have facilities for less able guests. The Garden Brasserie is open from noon until midnight; the bar is open 24 hours and a full room service is available.

Rooms 195 (24 fmly) **Facilities** STV Gym Fitness room Wi-fi **Services** Lift Air con

Arden Hotel & Leisure Club

★★★ 71% HOTEL

Coventry Rd, Bickenhill B92 0EH
☎ 01675 443221 ▤ 01675 445604
e-mail: enquiries@ardenhotel.co.uk
dir: *M42 junct 6/A45 towards Birmingham. Hotel 0.25m on right, just off Birmingham International railway island*

PETS: **Bedrooms** (6 GF) **Charges** £10 per night **Grounds** on leads disp bin **Exercise area** **Facilities** vet info **On Request** fridge access **Other** charge for damage

This smart hotel neighbouring the NEC offers modern rooms and well-equipped leisure facilities. After dinner in the formal restaurant, the place to relax is the spacious lounge area. A buffet breakfast is served in the bright and airy Meeting Place.

Rooms 216 (6 fmly) (6 GF) (12 smoking) **S** £55-£135; **D** £65-£160 **Facilities** Spa STV ✪ supervised Gym Sports therapy Beautician ♫ Xmas New Year Wi-fi **Services** Lift **Parking** 300 **Notes** LB Closed 25-28 Dec

Ibis Coventry Centre

BUDGET HOTEL

Mile Ln, St John's Ringway CV1 2LN
☎ 024 7625 0500 ▤ 024 7655 3548
e-mail: H2793@accor.com
web: www.ibishotel.com
dir: *A45 to Coventry, then A4114 signed Jaguar Assembly Plant. At inner ring road towards ring road S. Off exit 5 for Mile Lane*

PETS: **Bedrooms** (25 GF) **Charges** **Public areas** on leads disp bin **Exercise area** 0.5m **Other** charge for damage **Restrictions** small to medium size dogs only

Modern, budget hotel offering comfortable accommodation in bright and practical bedrooms. Breakfast is self-service and dinner is available in the restaurant.

Rooms 89 (25 fmly) (25 GF)

Ibis Coventry South Whitley

BUDGET HOTEL

Abbey Rd, Whitley CV3 4BJ
☎ 024 7663 9922 ▤ 024 7630 6898
e-mail: H2094@accor.com
web: www.ibishotel.com
dir: *Signed from A46/A423 rdbt. Take A423 towards A45. Follow signs for Racquets Health Club & Jaguar Engineering Plant. 1st exit from Jaguar rdbt, hotel at end of lane by The Racquets*

PETS: **Bedrooms** (25 GF) unattended **Charges** £5 per night **Public areas** except restaurant on leads **Grounds** disp bin **Exercise area** 0.1m **Facilities** walks info vet info **On Request** fridge access towels **Other** charge for damage

Rooms 51 (51 annexe) (25 GF) **S** £43-£63; **D** £43-£63*

Manor Hotel
★★★★ 82% ⊚ HOTEL
Main Rd CV7 7NH
☎ 01676 522735   01676 522186
e-mail: reservations@manorhotelmeriden.co.uk
web: www.manorhotelmeriden.co.uk
dir: *M42 junct 6, A45 towards Coventry then A452 signed Leamington. At rdbt take B4102 signed Meriden, hotel on left*

PETS: Bedrooms (20 GF) unattended Stables 3m Public areas assist dogs only on leads Grounds on leads disp bin Exercise area Facilities vet info On Request fridge access Other charge for damage

A sympathetically extended Georgian manor in the heart of a sleepy village is just a few minutes away from the M6, M42 and National Exhibition Centre. The Regency Restaurant offers modern dishes, while Houston's serves lighter meals and snacks. The bedrooms are smart and well equipped.

Rooms 110 (20 GF) S £60-£140; D £70-£180 (incl. bkfst)*
Facilities FTV Wi-fi Services Lift Parking 200 Notes LB RS 24 Dec-2 Jan

Somers Wood Caravan Park *(SP225824)*
► ► ► ►
Somers Rd CV7 7PL
☎ 01676 522978   01676 522978
e-mail: enquiries@somerswood.co.uk
dir: *M42 junct 6, A45 signed Coventry. Keep left (do not take flyover). Then right onto A452 signed Meriden/Leamington. At next rdbt left onto B4102, Hampton Lane. Site in 0.5m on left*

PETS: Charges 2 pets free; £1 per additional pet per night Public areas Exercise area adjacent Facilities washing facs walks info vet info Other prior notice required Resident Pets: Jodie (dog), Tiddles (cat)

Open all year Last arrival variable Last departure variable

A peaceful adults-only park set in the heart of England with spotless facilities. The park is well positioned for visiting the National Exhibition Centre (NEC) or the NEC Arena and National Indoor Arena (NIA), and Birmingham is only 12 miles away. The park also makes an ideal touring base for Warwick, Coventry and Stratford-upon-Avon just 22 miles away. A 4 acre site with 48 touring pitches, 48 hardstandings.

Notes No tents

Novotel Wolverhampton
★★★ 75% HOTEL
Union St WV1 3JN
☎ 01902 871100   01902 870054
e-mail: H1188@accor.com
web: www.novotel.com
dir: *6m from M6 junct 10. A454 to Wolverhampton. Hotel on main ring road*

PETS: Bedrooms unattended Stables 2m Charges £5 per night Public areas on leads Grounds on leads disp bin Exercise area 1m Facilities water bowl cage storage walks info vet info On Request fridge access Other charge for damage

This large, modern, purpose-built hotel stands close to the town centre. It provides spacious, smartly presented and well-equipped bedrooms, all of which contain convertible bed settees for family occupancy. In addition to the open-plan lounge and bar area, there is an attractive brasserie-style restaurant, which overlooks an attractive patio garden.

Rooms 132 (9 fmly) (6 smoking) S £49-£139; D £49-£139*
Facilities STV Wi-fi Services Lift Parking 120 Notes LB RS 23 Dec-4 Jan

Goldthorn Hotel & Leisure Club
★★★ 68% HOTEL
126 Penn Rd WV3 0ER
☎ 01902 429216   01902 710419
e-mail: enquiries@hotels-wolverhampton.com
dir: *A454 then A449 signed Kidderminster. Hotel 1m on right*

PETS: Bedrooms (4 GF) Grounds on leads disp bin Facilities vet info On Request towels Other charge for damage

This hotel is situated just on the outskirts of the old town and offers easy access to major motorway networks. Bedrooms are comfortable and well equipped, with free Wi-fi available throughout. Leisure facilities include a swimming pool, steam and sauna. There is also free on-site parking.

Rooms 74 (16 annexe) (12 fmly) (4 GF) S £40-£110; D £50-£120*
Facilities FTV Gym Sauna Steam room Xmas New Year Wi-fi Parking 100 Notes LB

ENGLAND

WIGHT, ISLE OF

ARRETON
Map 4 SZ58

Blandings
★★★★ BED AND BREAKFAST
Horringford PO30 3AP
☎ 01983 865720 & 865331 📠 01983 862099
e-mail: robin.oulton@horringford.com
web: www.horringford.com/bedandbreakfast.htm
dir: S through Arreton (B3056), pass Stickworth Hall on right,
300yds on left farm entrance signed Horringford Gdns. U-turn to
left, at end of poplar trees turn right. Blandings on left

PETS: Bedrooms Stables nearby Charges £10 per stay
Public areas Grounds on leads disp bin Exercise area
Facilities washing facs cage storage walks info vet info Other
charge for damage dogs to be kept off furniture

This detached home stands in the grounds of Horringford
Gardens. The bedroom has private access and a decking area for
warm summer evenings. Breakfast is a highlight with local island
produce gracing the table.

Rooms 2 en suite (1 GF) S £60-£74* Facilities FTV tea/coffee
Cen ht Parking 3 Notes LB 🐾

BONCHURCH
Map 4 SZ57

The Lake
★★★★ GUEST ACCOMMODATION
Shore Rd PO38 1RF
☎ 01983 852613
e-mail: enquiries@lakehotel.co.uk
dir: 0.5m E of Ventnor. Off A3055 to Bonchurch, opposite village
pond

PETS: Bedrooms Charges £5 per night Public areas one sun
lounge only on leads Grounds on leads disp bin Exercise area
beach 400yds Facilities cage storage vet info On Request
fridge access torch towels Other pet food on request

A warm welcome is assured at this friendly, family-run property
set in two acres of well-tended gardens close to the sea.
Bedrooms are equipped with modern facilities and the elegant

public rooms offer a high standard of comfort. A choice of menus
is offered at dinner and breakfast.

Rooms 11 en suite 9 annexe en suite (7 fmly) (4 GF) S £36-£45;
D £72-£92* Facilities TVL tea/coffee Dinner available Cen ht
Licensed Wi-fi Parking 20 Notes LB No Children 3yrs Closed 20
Dec-2 Jan

COWES
Map 4 SZ49

Best
Western

Best Western New Holmwood
★★★ 70% HOTEL
Queens Rd, Egypt Point PO31 8BW
☎ 01983 292508 📠 01983 295020
e-mail: reception@newholmwoodhotel.co.uk
dir: From A3020 at Northwood Garage lights, left & follow to rdbt.
1st left then sharp right into Baring Rd, 4th left into Egypt Hill. At
bottom turn right, hotel on right

PETS: Bedrooms (9 GF) unattended Charges Public areas
except restaurant on leads Exercise area 2 mins' walk to beach
Facilities water bowl Other charge for damage please contact
hotel for details of charges for dogs

Just by the Esplanade, this hotel has an enviable outlook.
Bedrooms are comfortable and very well equipped, and the light
and airy, glass-fronted restaurant looks out to sea and serves a
range of interesting meals. The sun terrace is delightful in the
summer and there is a small pool area.

Rooms 26 (1 fmly) (9 GF) Facilities STV ♒ Xmas New Year Wi-fi
Parking 20

Duke of York
★★★ INN
Mill Hill Rd PO31 7BT
☎ 01983 295171 📠 01983 295047
e-mail: dukeofyorkcowes@btconnect.com

PETS: Bedrooms Stables 2m Public areas on leads
Exercise area Facilities bedding walks info vet info
On Request fridge access torch towels

This family-run inn is situated very close to the town centre.
Comfortable bedrooms are divided between the main building
and a separate property only seconds away. The menu offers
home-cooked fish and seafood dishes, served every evening in the
redecorated bar and dining area; outdoor, covered dining is also
an option. Parking is a bonus at this location.

Rooms 8 en suite 5 annexe en suite (1 fmly) Facilities FTV tea/
coffee Dinner available Wi-fi Parking 10

ENGLAND

Heathfield Farm Camping *(SZ335879)*

▶ ▶ ▶ ▶

Heathfield Rd PO40 9SH
☎ 01983 407822
e-mail: web@heathfieldcamping.co.uk
dir: *2m W from Yarmouth ferry port on A3054, left to Heathfield Rd, entrance 200yds on right*

PETS: Stables 600mtrs **Charges** £1.75 per night **Public areas** disp bin **Exercise area** adjacent meadow **Facilities** water bowl vet info **Other** prior notice required designated pitches for guests with dogs

Open May-Sep Last arrival 20.00hrs Last departure 11.00hrs

A very good quality park with friendly owners and lovely views across the Solent to Hurst Castle. The toilet facilities, amenities and grounds are very well maintained, and this park is now among the best on the island. A 10 acre site with 60 touring pitches.

Notes Family camping only

Orchards Holiday Caravan Park *(SZ411881)*

▶ ▶ ▶ ▶ ▶

Main Rd PO41 0TS
☎ 01983 531331 & 531350 📄 01983 531666
e-mail: info@orchards-holiday-park.co.uk
dir: *4m E of Yarmouth; 6m W of Newport on B3401. Take A3054 from Yarmouth, after 3m turn right at Horse & Groom Inn. Follow signs to Newbridge. Entrance opposite Post Office*

PETS: Charges £1.50-£2.50 per night **Public areas** disp bin **Exercise area** fenced field **Facilities** food dog chews scoop/disp bags washing facs walks info vet info **Other** prior notice required

Open 11 Feb-2 Jan rs Mar-Oct takeaway, shop, outdoor pool open Last arrival 23.00hrs Last departure 11.00hrs

A really excellent, well-managed park set in a peaceful village location amid downs and meadowland, with glorious downland views. Pitches are terraced, and offer a good provision of hardstandings, including water serviced pitches. A high spec facilities centre was built in 2009. The park has indoor and outdoor swimming pools, a shop, takeaway and licensed coffee shop. There is disabled access to all facilities on site, plus disabled toilets. A 15 acre site with 171 touring pitches, 74 hardstandings and 65 statics.

Notes no cycling, no large single sex groups

Yelf's Hotel

★ ★ ★ 74% HOTEL

Union St PO33 2LG
☎ 01983 564062 📄 01983 563937
e-mail: manager@yelfshotel.com
web: www.yelfshotel.com
dir: *From Esplanade into Union St. Hotel on right*

PETS: Bedrooms (3 GF) **Charges** £10 per night **Public areas Grounds** on leads disp bin **Exercise area** beach (0.5m) **Facilities** water bowl cage storage walks info vet info **On Request** fridge access torch towels

This former coaching inn has smart public areas including a busy bar, a separate lounge and an attractive dining room. Bedrooms are comfortably furnished and well equipped; some are located in an adjoining wing and some in an annexe. A conservatory lounge bar and stylish terrace are ideal for relaxing.

Rooms 40 (9 annexe) (5 fmly) (3 GF) (6 smoking) **Facilities** STV Spa & treatments available at nearby sister hotel Wi-fi **Services** Lift **Parking** 23 **Notes** LB

Whitefield Forest Touring Park *(SZ604893)*

▶ ▶ ▶ ▶ ▶

Brading Rd PO33 1QL
☎ 01983 617069
e-mail: pat&louise@whitefieldforest.co.uk
dir: *From Ryde follow A3055 towards Brading, after Tesco rdbt site 0.5m on left*

PETS: Charges £1-£1.50 per night **Public areas** except toilets disp bin **Exercise area Facilities** walks info vet info **Other** prior notice required **Resident Pets:** Izzy (West Highland White Terrier), Scooby (Black Labrador)

Open Etr-Oct Last arrival 21.00hrs Last departure 11.00hrs

This park is beautifully laid out in Whitefield Forest, and offers a wide variety of pitches, all of which have electricity. It offers excellent modern facilities which are spotlessly clean. The park takes great care in retaining the natural beauty of the forest, and is a haven for wildlife, including the red squirrel, which may be seen on the park's nature walk. A 23 acre site with 80 touring pitches, 20 hardstandings.

ENGLAND

SANDOWN
Map 4 SZ58

The Wight Montrene
★★ 72% HOTEL
11 Avenue Rd PO36 8BN
☎ 01983 403722 📠 01983 405553
e-mail: enquiries@wighthotel.co.uk
web: www.wighthotel.co.uk
dir: *100yds after mini-rdbt between High St & Avenue Rd*

PETS: **Bedrooms** (21 GF) unattended sign **Stables** 8m **Grounds** on leads **Exercise area** 300yds **Facilities** cage storage walks info vet info **Other** charge for damage dogs must be exercised off site **Resident Pets:** Magnum (Great Pyrenean Mountain Dog), Diva & Gizmo (cats)

A family hotel, set in secluded grounds, that is only a short walk from Sandown's beach and high street shops. Bedrooms provide comfort and are either on the ground or first floor. Guests can relax in the heated swimming pool and enjoy the spa facility; there's also evening entertainment in the bar. The dinner menu changes nightly, and a plentiful breakfast is served in the colourful dining room.

Rooms 41 (18 fmly) (21 GF) **Facilities** Spa ✪ Gym Spa, Steam room, Sauna, Solarium, Table tennis, Full size snooker table ♫ Xmas New Year Wi-fi **Parking** 40

Old Barn Touring Park *(SZ573833)*
▶ ▶ ▶ ▶

Cheverton Farm, Newport Rd, Apse Heath PO36 9PJ
☎ 01983 866414 📠 01983 865988
e-mail: oldbarn@weltinet.com
dir: *On A3056 from Newport, site on left after Apse Heath rdbt*

PETS: **Charges** 1st dog free, £1.50 per extra dog per night **Public areas** **Exercise area** adjacent **Facilities** walks info vet info **Other** prior notice required **Resident Pets:** 13 geese, 2 ferrets, chickens, cows

Open May-Sep Last arrival 21.00hrs Last departure noon

A terraced site with good quality facilities, bordering on open farmland. The spacious pitches are secluded and fully serviced, and there is a decent modern toilet block. A 5 acre site with 60 touring pitches, 9 hardstandings.

SHANKLIN
Map 4 SZ58

Hayes Barton
★★★★ 🛏 GUEST ACCOMMODATION
7 Highfield Rd PO37 6PP
☎ 01983 867747
e-mail: williams.2000@virgin.net
web: www.hayesbarton.co.uk
dir: *A3055 onto A3020 Victoria Av, 3rd left*

PETS: **Bedrooms** unattended **Charges** £3.50 per night £22 per week **Public areas** except dining room **Grounds** disp bin **Exercise area** 200yds **Facilities** feeding mat scoop/disp bags pet sitting washing facs cage storage walks info vet info **On Request** fridge access torch towels **Other** charge for damage **Resident Pet:** Katy (Labrador cross)

Hayes Barton has the relaxed atmosphere of a family home and provides well-equipped bedrooms and a range of comfortable public areas. Dinner is available from a short selection of home-cooked dishes, and there is a cosy bar lounge. The old village, beach and promenade are all within walking distance.

Rooms 9 en suite (4 fmly) (2 GF) **S** £34-£42; **D** £68-£84* **Facilities** TVL tea/coffee Dinner available Cen ht Licensed Wi-fi **Parking** 9 **Notes** LB Closed Nov-Mar

Rowborough
★★★★ GUEST ACCOMMODATION
32 Arthurs Hill PO37 6EX
☎ 01983 866072 & 863070 📠 01983 867703
e-mail: susanpatricia@btconnect.com
web: www.rowboroughhotel.com
dir: *Between Sandown & Shanklin*

PETS: **Bedrooms** **Charges** £10 per stay **Public areas** except restaurant at meal times on leads **Grounds** disp bin **Exercise area** 300yds **Facilities** walks info vet info **On Request** fridge access torch towels **Other** charge for damage **Resident Pet:** Penny (Lhasa Apso)

Located on the main road into town, this charming, family-run establishment provides comfortable bedrooms with many extra facilities. The conservatory overlooks the garden, along with a lounge and a bar. Dinner is available by arrangement.

Rooms 9 en suite (5 fmly) (1 GF) **S** £30-£34* **Facilities** TVL tea/coffee Dinner available Cen ht Licensed Wi-fi **Parking** 5 **Notes** LB

TOTLAND BAY — Map 4 SZ38

The Hermitage
★★★ GUEST ACCOMMODATION
Cliff Rd PO39 0EW
☎ 01983 752518
e-mail: blake_david@btconnect.com
web: www.thehermitagebnb.co.uk
dir: Church Hill B3322, right onto Eden Rd, left onto Cliff Rd, 0.5m on right

PETS: Bedrooms unattended Public areas except dining area Grounds Exercise area 5 mins' walk Facilities water bowl washing facs cage storage walks info vet info On Request fridge access torch towels Other charge for damage Resident Pets: 1 German Shepherd, 3 cats, 2 lovebirds

The Hermitage is an extremely pet and people friendly establishment which occupies a stunning and unspoilt location near to the cliff top in Totland Bay. Extensive gardens are well maintained and off-road parking is a bonus. Accommodation is comfortable and you are assured of a genuinely warm welcome and friendly service at this traditionally styled establishment. A range of delicious items at breakfast provide a substantial start to the day.

Rooms 6 rms (5 en suite) (1 pri facs) (1 fmly) Facilities TVL tea/coffee Dinner available Parking 6 Notes LB

VENTNOR — Map 4 SZ57

Eversley
★★★ 71% HOTEL
Park Av PO38 1LB
☎ 01983 852244 & 852462 📠 01983 856534
e-mail: eversleyhotel@yahoo.co.uk
web: www.eversleyhotel.com
dir: On A3055 W of Ventnor, next to Ventnor Park

PETS: Bedrooms (2 GF) Charges £10 per stay Public areas except restaurant on leads Grounds on leads Exercise area private access to Ventnor Park & coastal walks Facilities water bowl Other charge for damage

Located west of Ventnor, this hotel enjoys a quiet location and has some rooms with garden and pool views. The spacious restaurant is sometimes used for local functions, and there is a bar, TV room, lounge area, a card room as well as a jacuzzi and gym. Bedrooms are generally a good size.

Rooms 30 (8 fmly) (2 GF) Facilities ⚡ Gym Pool table Xmas Parking 23 Notes Closed 30 Nov-22 Dec & 2 Jan-8 Feb

See advert on this page

WHITECLIFF BAY — Map 4 SZ68

Whitecliff Bay Holiday Park (SZ637862)
Hillway Rd, Bembridge PO35 5PL
☎ 01983 872671 📠 01983 872941
e-mail: holiday@whitecliff-bay.com
dir: 1m S of Bembridge, signed off B3395 in village

PETS: Charges £1 per night £7 per week Public areas on leads disp bin Exercise area dog field & walkway through park Facilities dog chews cat treats scoop/disp bags vet info Other prior notice required Restrictions no dangerous dogs (see page 7)

Open Mar-Oct Last arrival 21.00hrs Last departure 10.30hrs

A large seaside complex on two sites, with camping on one and self-catering chalets and statics on the other. There is an indoor pool with flume and spa pool, and an outdoor pool with a kiddies' pool, a family entertainment club, and plenty of traditional on-site activities including crazy golf, a soft play area and table tennis plus a restaurant and a choice of bars. There is easy access to a lovely sandy beach. A 49 acre site with 400 touring pitches, 50 hardstandings and 227 statics.

Notes Adults & families only

ENGLAND

WOOTTON BRIDGE — Map 4 SZ59

Kite Hill Farm Caravan & Camping Park
(SZ549906)

►►►

Firestone Copse Rd PO33 4LE
☎ 01983 882543 & 883261 📠 01983 883883
e-mail: welcome@kitehillfarm.co.uk
dir: *Signed off A3054 at Wootton Bridge, between Ryde & Newport*

PETS: **Public areas** on leads disp bin **Exercise area** 2 acres of
uncut meadow, with mown path **Facilities** walks info vet info
Other owners must clean up after pets

Open all year Last arrival anytime Last departure anytime

The park, on a gently sloping field, is tucked away behind the
owners' farm, just a short walk from the village and attractive
river estuary. Facilities are well maintained and the atmosphere
pleasantly relaxing. A 12.5 acre site with 50 touring pitches, 10
hardstandings.

Notes 🐾

WILTSHIRE

ALDBOURNE — Map 4 SU27

The Crown Inn
★★★★ INN
2 The Square SN8 2DU
☎ 01672 540214
e-mail: gant12@hotmail.co.uk
web: www.crownataldbourne.co.uk
dir: *M4 junct 15, N on A419, signed to Aldbourne*

PETS: **Bedrooms** unattended sign **Public areas** except
restaurant on leads **Grounds** on leads **Exercise area** 100yds
Facilities food bowl water bowl leads pet sitting dog walking
cage storage vet info **On Request** fridge access torch towels
Resident Pet: Border Terrier

With a traditional village inn atmosphere, The Crown offers a
relaxed ambience and genuine welcome. The comfortable bar and
dining room provide a very good selection of home-cooked dishes,
with good quality produce used at both dinner and breakfast.
Bedrooms and bathrooms come in a range of shapes and sizes
but are all well decorated and nicely furnished.

Rooms 4 en suite (1 fmly) **S** £49.95; **D** £69.95* **Facilities** FTV TVL
tea/coffee Dinner available Cen ht Wi-fi **Parking** 9 **Notes** LB

AMESBURY — Map 4 SU14

Park House Motel
★★★★ GUEST ACCOMMODATION
SP4 0EG
☎ 01980 629256 📠 01980 629256
e-mail: inof@parkhousemotel.com
dir: *5m E of Amesbury. Junct A303 & A338*

PETS: **Bedrooms** sign **Charges Public areas Grounds** on
leads disp bin **Exercise area Facilities** walks info vet info
On Request fridge access torch towels **Other** charge for
damage **Restrictions** small dogs only **Resident Pets:** Bernard &
Max (Lhasa Apso), Arnie (Yorkshire Terrier)

This family-run establishment offers a warm welcome and is
extremely convenient for the A303. Bedrooms are practically
equipped with modern facilities and come in a variety of sizes.
There is a large dining room where dinner is served during the
week, and a cosy bar in which to relax.

Rooms 30 rms (27 en suite) (1 pri facs) (9 fmly) (25 GF)
S £56-£62; **D** £72* **Facilities** STV FTV TVL tea/coffee Dinner
available Cen ht Licensed Wi-fi **Parking** 40

BRADFORD-ON-AVON — Map 3 ST86

von Essen hotels
A PRIVATE COLLECTION
www.vonessenhotels.com

Woolley Grange
★★★ 82% ◉◉ HOTEL
Woolley Green BA15 1TX
☎ 01225 864705 📠 01225 864059
e-mail: info@woolleygrangehotel.co.uk
web: www.woolleygrangehotel.co.uk
dir: *A4 onto B3109. Bradford Leigh, left at x-roads, hotel 0.5m on
right at Woolley Green*

PETS: **Bedrooms** (3 GF) unattended **Charges** £7-£25 per
stay **Public areas** except dining areas **Grounds** disp bin
Exercise area 14-acre grounds **Exercise area** canal walk (2m)
Facilities food bowl water bowl bedding dog chews scoop/disp
bags leads walks info vet info **On Request** fridge access torch
towels **Other** charge for damage dog owners are advised to keep
dogs on leads due to children staying at hotel **Resident Pet:**
Peanut (Cocker Spaniel)

This splendid Cotswold manor house is set in beautiful
countryside. Children are made especially welcome; there is a
trained nanny on duty in the nursery. Bedrooms and public areas
are charmingly furnished and decorated in true country-house
style, with many thoughtful touches and luxurious extras. The
hotel offers a varied and well-balanced menu selection, including
ingredients from the hotel's own garden.

Rooms 26 (14 annexe) (20 fmly) (3 GF) **S** £90-£185; **D** £90-£210
(incl. bkfst)* **Facilities** Spa FTV 🏊 ⚓ 🏌 Beauty treatments
Football Table tennis Trampoline Boules Cricket Xmas New Year
Wi-fi Child facilities **Parking** 40 **Notes** LB

CALNE
Map 3 ST97

Blackland Lakes Holiday & Leisure Centre
(ST973687)

►►►

Stockley Ln SN11 0NQ
☎ 01249 810943 📠 01249 811346
e-mail: blacklandlakes.bookings@btconnect.com
dir: *From Calne take A4 E for 1.5m, right at camp sign. Site 1m on left*

PETS: Stables Charges £1.50 per night £10.50 per week
Public areas disp bin **Exercise area** dog walk (approx 1m around perimeter) **Facilities** food scoop/disp bags washing facs vet info **Other** prior notice required

Open all year rs 30 Oct-1 Mar pre-paid bookings only Last arrival 22.00hrs Last departure noon

A rural site surrounded by the North and West Downs. The park is divided into several paddocks separated by hedges, trees and fences, and there are two well-stocked carp fisheries for the angling enthusiast. Some excellent walks close by, and the interesting market town of Devizes is a few miles away. A 15 acre site with 180 touring pitches, 25 hardstandings.

CASTLE COMBE
Map 3 ST87

Manor House Hotel and Golf Club
★★★★ ◎◎◎ COUNTRY HOUSE HOTEL
SN14 7HR
☎ 01249 782206 📠 01249 782159
e-mail: enquiries@manorhouse.co.uk
web: www.exclusivehotels.co.uk
dir: *M4 junct 17 follow Chippenham signs onto A420 Bristol, then right onto B4039. Through village, right after bridge*

PETS: Bedrooms (12 GF) unattended **Charges** £50 per stay
Public areas except food service areas on leads **Grounds** on leads **Exercise area** on site **Facilities** food (pre-bookable) food bowl water bowl bedding dog chews cat treats cage storage walks info vet info **On Request** fridge access towels **Other** dogs allowed in cottage bedrooms only Resident Pets: 1 cat, 6 pigs, 6 chickens

This delightful hotel is situated in a secluded valley adjacent to a picturesque village, where there have been no new buildings for 300 years. There are 365 acres of grounds to enjoy, complete with an Italian garden and an 18-hole golf course. Bedrooms, some in the main house and some in a row of stone cottages, have been superbly furnished, and public rooms include a number of cosy lounges with roaring fires. Service is a pleasing blend of professionalism and friendliness. The award-winning food utilises top quality local produce.

Rooms 48 (26 annexe) (8 fmly) (12 GF) **S** £180-£1000;
D £180-£1000 (incl. bkfst)* **Facilities** STV ⚓ 18 ⛳ Putt green Fishing 🚣 Jogging track Hot air ballooning Xmas New Year Wi-fi **Parking** 100 **Notes** LB

LACOCK
Map 3 ST96

At the Sign of the Angel
★★★★ 🏠 🍽 GUEST ACCOMMODATION
6 Church St SN15 2LB
☎ 01249 730230 📠 01249 730527
e-mail: angel@lacock.co.uk
dir: *Off A350 into Lacock, follow 'Local Traffic' sign*

PETS: Bedrooms unattended sign **Public areas** except restaurant **Grounds** on leads **Exercise area** walks in surrounding area **Facilities** water bowl walks info vet info **On Request** fridge access **Other** charge for damage

Visitors will be impressed by the character of this 15th-century former wool merchant's house, set in the National Trust village of Lacock. Bedrooms come in a range of sizes and styles including the atmospheric rooms in the main house and others in an adjacent building. Excellent dinners and breakfasts are served in the beamed dining rooms, and there is also a first-floor lounge and a pleasant rear garden.

Rooms 6 en suite 5 annexe en suite (4 GF) **S** £82; **D** £120-£145*
Facilities FTV tea/coffee Dinner available Direct Dial Cen ht Licensed Wi-fi **Parking** 6 **Notes** Closed 23-27 Dec RS Mon (ex BHs) closed for lunch

LOWER CHICKSGROVE
Map 3 ST92

Compasses Inn
★★★★ ◎ INN
SP3 6NB
☎ 01722 714318 📠 01722 714318
e-mail: thecompasses@aol.com
web: www.thecompassesinn.com
dir: *Off A30 signed Lower Chicksgrove, 1st left onto Lagpond Lane, single-track lane to village*

PETS: Bedrooms unattended **Public areas** **Grounds** disp bin **Exercise area** adjacent **Facilities** food bowl water bowl cage storage walks info vet info **On Request** fridge access torch towels

This charming 17th-century inn, within easy reach of Bath, Salisbury, Glastonbury and the Dorset coast, offers comfortable accommodation in a peaceful setting. Carefully prepared dinners are enjoyed in the warm atmosphere of the bar-restaurant, while breakfast is served in a separate dining room.

Rooms 5 en suite (1 fmly) **S** £50-£85; **D** £70-£130* **Facilities** FTV tea/coffee Dinner available Cen ht Wi-fi **Parking** 40 **Notes** LB Closed 25-26 Dec

ENGLAND

Whatley Manor

★★★★★ ◉◉◉◉ HOTEL

Easton Grey SN16 0RB
☎ 01666 822888 🖨 01666 826120
e-mail: reservations@whatleymanor.com
web: www.whatleymanor.com
dir: *M4 junct 17, follow signs to Malmesbury, continue over 2 rdbts. Follow B4040 & signs for Sherston, hotel 2m on left*

PETS: Bedrooms (4 GF) unattended **Charges** £25 per night **Public areas** except restaurants on leads **Grounds** on leads disp bin **Exercise area Facilities** food (pre-bookable) food bowl water bowl bedding dog chews scoop/disp bags leads pet sitting washing facs walks info **On Request** fridge access torch towels **Other** charge for damage welcome letter, guidelines, luxury dog basket, treats, walk routes & maps

Sitting in 12 acres of beautiful countryside, this impressive country house provides the most luxurious surroundings. Spacious bedrooms, most with views over the attractive gardens, are individually decorated with splendid features. Several eating options are available: Le Mazot, a Swiss-style brasserie, The Dining Room that serves classical French cuisine with a contemporary twist, plus the Kitchen Garden Terrace for alfresco breakfasts, lunches and dinners. The old Loggia Barn is ideal for wedding ceremonies, and the Aquarius Spa is magnificent.

Rooms 23 (4 GF) **S** £295-£855; **D** £295-£855 (incl. bkfst) **Facilities** Spa STV Fishing Gym Cinema Hydro pool - indoor/outdoor Xmas New Year Wi-fi **Services** Lift **Parking** 100 **Notes** LB No children 12yrs

Old Bell

★★★ 80% ◉◉ HOTEL

Abbey Row SN16 0BW
☎ 01666 822344 🖨 01666 825145
e-mail: info@oldbellhotel.com
web: www.oldbellhotel.com
dir: *M4 junct 17, follow A429 north. Left at 1st rdbt. Left at T-junct. Hotel adjacent to abbey*

PETS: Bedrooms (7 GF) unattended sign **Charges** £10 per night **Public areas** except restaurants on leads **Grounds Exercise area** 250mtrs **Facilities** water bowl bedding pet sitting cage storage walks info vet info **Other** charge for damage **Restrictions** no large dogs (eg Newfoundland, Great Dane, Irish Wolfhound)

Dating back to 1220, the wisteria-clad Old Bell is reputed to be the oldest purpose-built hotel in England. Bedrooms vary in size and style; those in the main house tend to be more spacious and are traditionally furnished with antiques, while the newer bedrooms of the coach house have a contemporary feel. Guests have a choice of comfortable sitting areas and dining options, including the main restaurant where the award-winning cuisine is based on high quality ingredients.

Rooms 33 (15 annexe) (7 GF) **S** £87.55; **D** £110-£250 (incl. bkfst)* **Facilities** FTV Xmas New Year Wi-fi **Parking** 33 **Notes** LB

Best Western Mayfield House

Best Western

★★★ 72% ◉ HOTEL

Crudwell SN16 9EW
☎ 01666 577409 🖨 01666 577977
e-mail: reception@mayfieldhousehotel.co.uk
web: www.mayfieldhousehotel.co.uk
dir: *M4 junct 17, A429 to Cirencester. 2m N of Malmesbury on left in Crudwell*

PETS: Bedrooms (8 GF) unattended **Stables** 0.25m **Charges** £15 per stay **Public areas** except restaurant & lounge on leads disp bin **Exercise area** water meadow opposite hotel **Facilities** washing facs cage storage walks info vet info **On Request** torch towels **Other** charge for damage **Restrictions** no dangerous dogs (see page 7)

This popular hotel is in an ideal location for exploring many of the nearby attractions of Wiltshire and The Cotswolds. Bedrooms come in a range of shapes and sizes, and include some on the ground-floor level in a cottage adjacent to the main hotel. In addition to outdoor seating, guests can relax with a drink in the comfortable lounge area where orders are taken for the carefully prepared dinner to follow.

Rooms 28 (8 annexe) (4 fmly) (8 GF) **S** £50-£80; **D** £60-£129 (incl. bkfst)* **Facilities** FTV Xmas New Year Wi-fi **Parking** 50 **Notes** LB

MARLBOROUGH   Map 4 SU16

The Lamb Inn
★★★ ➾ INN

The Parade SN8 1NE
☎ 01672 512668 & 07885 275568 📠 01672 512668
e-mail: thelambinnmarlboro@fsmail.net
dir: From High St, right onto Parade, 50yds on left

PETS: Bedrooms unattended **Public areas Grounds** disp bin **Exercise area** 0.25m **Facilities** food bowl water bowl washing facs walks info vet info **On Request** fridge access towels

Located in a quieter area of Marlborough, yet just a couple of minutes from the bustle of the main street, this traditional inn provides a friendly welcome and relaxed ambience. Bedrooms vary in size and are located above the main inn and in modernised stables adjacent to the pleasant rear garden. Dinner here is a highlight with a good selection of very well cooked and presented dishes using fresh ingredients.

Rooms 6 en suite (1 fmly) **S** £50-£55; **D** £75-£85* **Facilities** tea/coffee Dinner available Cen ht Wi-fi Golf 18 **Notes** No coaches

MELKSHAM   Map 3 ST96

Beechfield House Hotel
★★★ 79% ⊚ COUNTRY HOUSE HOTEL

Beanacre SN12 7PU
☎ 01225 703700 📠 01225 790118
e-mail: reception@beechfieldhouse.co.uk
web: www.beechfieldhouse.co.uk
dir: M4 junct 17, A350 S, bypass Chippenham, towards Melksham. Hotel on left after Beanacre

PETS: Bedrooms (4 GF) unattended **Charges** £15 per night **Grounds** disp bin **Exercise area** fields accessed from grounds **Facilities** cage storage walks info vet info **Other** charge for damage **Restrictions** no large dogs **Resident Pets:** Misty (Black Labrador), Lola & Daisy (cats)

This is a charming, privately owned hotel set within eight acres of beautiful grounds that has its own arboretum. Bedrooms are individual styled and include four-poster rooms, and ground-floor rooms in the coach house. Relaxing public areas are comfortably furnished and there is a beauty salon with a range of pampering treatments available. At dinner there is a very good selection of carefully prepared dishes with an emphasis on seasonal and local produce.

Rooms 24 (6 fmly) (4 GF) **S** £85-£135; **D** £115-£175 (incl. bkfst)* **Facilities** FTV ⭤ 🏊 Table tennis Beauty treatment room Xmas New Year Wi-fi **Parking** 70 **Notes** LB

Shaw Country
★★ 76% SMALL HOTEL

Bath Rd, Shaw SN12 8EF
☎ 01225 702836 & 790321 📠 01225 790275
e-mail: info@shawcountryhotel.com
web: www.shawcountryhotel.com
dir: 1m from Melksham, 9m from Bath on A365

PETS: Bedrooms Grounds on leads **Exercise area** 500yds **Facilities** walks info vet info **On Request** fridge access torch **Other** charge for damage **Resident Pets:** 2 cats

Located within easy reach of both Bath and the M4, this relaxed and friendly hotel sits in its own gardens and includes a patio area ideal for enjoying a drink during the summer months. The house boasts some very well-appointed bedrooms, a comfortable lounge and bar, and the Mulberry Restaurant, where a wide selection of innovative dishes make up both carte and set menus.

Rooms 13 (2 fmly) **S** £61-£66; **D** £85-£105 (incl. bkfst) **Facilities** FTV Wi-fi **Parking** 30 **Notes** RS 26-27 Dec & 1 Jan

ORCHESTON   Map 4 SU04

Stonehenge Touring Park (SU061456)
►►►

SP3 4SH
☎ 01980 620304
e-mail: stay@stonehengetouringpark.com
dir: From A360 towards Devizes turn right, follow lane, site at bottom of village on right

PETS: Public areas except facility block & shop **Exercise area** 50mtrs **Facilities** walks info vet info **Other** prior notice required **Resident Pet:** 1 dog

Open all year Last arrival 21.00hrs Last departure 11.00hrs

A quiet site adjacent to the small village of Orcheston near the centre of Salisbury Plain and four miles from Stonehenge. A 2 acre site with 30 touring pitches, 12 hardstandings.

ENGLAND

PURTON Map 4 SU08

The Pear Tree at Purton
★★★ 81% ◉◉ HOTEL
Church End SN5 4ED
☎ 01793 772100 📠 01793 772369
e-mail: stay@peartreepurton.co.uk
dir: M4 junct 16 follow signs to Purton, At Spar shop turn right.
Hotel 0.25m on left

PETS: Bedrooms (6 GF) Public areas except restaurant Grounds
disp bin Exercise area adjacent Facilities food bowl water
bowl dog chews cat treats scoop/disp bags leads washing
facs walks info vet info On Request fridge access torch towels
Resident Pets: Smudge (dog), Poppy & Buzz (cats)

A charming 15th-century, former vicarage set amidst extensive
landscaped gardens in a peaceful location in the Vale of the
White Horse and near the Saxon village of Purton. The resident
proprietors and staff provide efficient, dedicated service and
friendly hospitality. The spacious bedrooms are individually
decorated and have a good range of thoughtful extras such as
fresh fruit, sherry and shortbread. Fresh ingredients feature on
the award-winning menus.

Rooms 17 (2 fmly) (6 GF) S £115-£145; D £115-£200 (incl. bkfst)
Facilities STV 🏊 Outdoor giant chess Vineyard Wi-fi Parking 60
Notes LB Closed 26-30 Dec

SALISBURY Map 4 SU12

Grasmere House Hotel
★★★ 67% HOTEL
Harnham Rd SP2 8JN
☎ 01722 338388 📠 01722 333710
e-mail: info@grasmerehotel.com
web: www.grasmerehotel.com
dir: On A3094 on S side of Salisbury adjacent to Harnham church

PETS: Bedrooms (9 GF) Charges £10 per night Public areas
except restaurant & bar muzzled and on leads Grounds on leads
Exercise area adjacent to park Facilities walks info vet info
Other charge for damage Restrictions no dangerous dogs (see
page 7) Resident Pet: Sasha (Bulldog)

This popular hotel, dating from 1896, has gardens that overlook
the water meadows and the cathedral. The attractive bedrooms
vary in size, some offer excellent quality and comfort, and some
rooms are specially equipped for less mobile guests. In summer
there is the option of dining on the pleasant outdoor terrace.

Rooms 38 (31 annexe) (16 fmly) (9 GF) Facilities STV FTV Fishing
🏊 Xmas New Year Wi-fi Parking 64 Notes LB

Coombe Touring Park (SU099282)
▶ ▶ ▶ ▶
Race Plain, Netherhampton SP2 8PN
☎ 01722 328451 📠 01722 328451
e-mail: enquiries@coombecaravanpark.co.uk
dir: Exit A36 onto A3094, 2m SW, site adjacent to Salisbury
racecourse

PETS: Charges 20p per night Public areas except toilet,
shower, laundry blocks & shop disp bin Exercise area adjacent
Facilities washing facs walks info vet info Resident Pets: Alfie
(Labrador/Collie cross), Charlie (cat)

Open 3 Jan-20 Dec rs Oct-May shop closed Last arrival 21.00hrs
Last departure noon

A very neat and attractive site adjacent to the racecourse with
views over the downs. The park is well landscaped with shrubs
and maturing trees, and the very colourful beds are stocked from
the owner's greenhouse. A comfortable park with a superb luxury
toilet block, and four static holiday homes for hire. A 3 acre site
with 50 touring pitches and 4 statics.

Notes No disposable BBQs or fires, no mini motorbikes 🐾

Landmark Hotel

★★★ 68% HOTEL

Station Rd, Chiseldon SN4 0PW

☎ 01793 740149   🖹 01793 741326

e-mail: reservations@landmarkhotel.com

dir: M4 junct 15, A346. Right just before Esso garage at Chiseldon. 2nd right into Station Rd. Hotel at bottom of lane on left

PETS: Bedrooms (8 GF) Public areas except restaurant on leads Grounds on leads Exercise area 30mtrs Facilities washing facs walks info vet info On Request fridge access Other charge for damage Resident Pet: Benson (Rough Collie)

Conveniently located just a mile from for the M4, this small hotel is in a quiet, residential setting. Bedrooms and bathrooms provide plenty of quality and comfort with some useful extras including free Wi-fi. A varied selection of food is available in either the main restaurant, conservatory bar or from the extensive room service option.

Rooms 16 (2 fmly) (8 GF) Facilities STV Wi-fi Services Lift Parking 11

Campanile

Campanile Swindon

BUDGET HOTEL

Delta Business Park, Great Western Way SN5 7XG

☎ 01793 514777   🖹 01793 514570

e-mail: swindon@campanile.com

web: www.campanile-swindon.co.uk

dir: M4 junction 16, A3102 towards Swindon. After 2nd rdbt, 2nd exit onto Welton Rd (Delta Business Park), 1st left

PETS: Bedrooms (22 GF) unattended Charges £5 per night Public areas except restaurant & bar on leads Grounds on leads disp bin Exercise area Facilities cage storage walks info vet info Other charge for damage pets may be left unattended in bedrooms for short periods only Restrictions no large dogs

This modern building offers accommodation in smart, well-equipped bedrooms, all with en suite bathrooms. Refreshments may be taken at the informal bistro.

Rooms 120 (6 fmly) (22 GF) S £46.95-£62.95; D £46.95-£62.95

Portquin Guest House

★★★★ GUEST ACCOMMODATION

Broadbush, Broad Blunsdon SN26 7DH

☎ 01793 721261

e-mail: portquin@msn.com

dir: A419 onto B4019 at Blunsdon signed Highworth, continue 0.5m

PETS: Bedrooms Public areas except dining room & upstairs Grounds disp bin Exercise area adjacent Facilities washing facs cage storage walks info vet info On Request fridge access torch towels Restrictions no dogs of similar size or larger than a Great Dane

This friendly guest accommodation, situated not far from Swindon, offers a warm welcome and views of the Lambourn Downs. The rooms vary in shape and size, with six in the main house and three in an adjacent annexe. Full English breakfasts are served at two large tables in the kitchen-dining area.

Rooms 6 en suite 3 annexe en suite (2 fmly) (4 GF) S £45-£50; D £55-£70* Facilities FTV tea/coffee Cen ht Wi-fi Parking 12

Fir Tree Lodge

★★★ GUEST ACCOMMODATION

17 Highworth Rd, Stratton St Margaret SN3 4QL

☎ 01793 822372   🖹 01793 822372

e-mail: info@firtreelodge.com

dir: 1.5m NE of town centre. A419 onto B4006 signed Stratton/Town Centre, premises 200yds opposite Rat Trap pub

PETS: Bedrooms Charges £5 per night £15 per week Grounds Exercise area 50mtrs Facilities walks info vet info On Request torch towels Other charge for damage

Fir Tree Lodge is a modern building offering a range of comfortable bedrooms including rooms on the ground floor. The resident proprietors provide a relaxed and friendly welcome. The guest accommodation benefits from a large secure car park.

Rooms 12 en suite 2 annexe rms (2 pri facs) (1 fmly) (5 GF) S £35-£40; D £55-£60* Facilities FTV tea/coffee Cen ht Wi-fi Parking 13

TROWBRIDGE Map 3 ST85

Fieldways Hotel & Health Club

★★ 68% SMALL HOTEL

Hilperton Rd BA14 7JP
☎ 01225 768336 📄 01225 753649
e-mail: fieldwayshotel@yahoo.co.uk
dir: *A361 from Trowbridge towards Melksham, Chippenham, Devizes. Hotel last property on left*

PETS: Bedrooms (2 GF) **Stables** 3m **Charges** £5 per night **Grounds Exercise area** 50mtrs **Facilities** walks info vet info **On Request** fridge access **Other** charge for damage

Originally part of a Victorian mansion this hotel is quietly set in well-kept grounds and provides a pleasant combination of spacious, comfortably furnished bedrooms. There are two splendid wood-panelled dining rooms, one of which is impressively finished in oak, pine, rosewood and mahogany. The indoor leisure facilities include a gym, a pool and treatment rooms; 'Top to Toe' days are especially popular.

Rooms 13 (5 annexe) (2 fmly) (2 GF) **S** fr £60; **D** £80-£90 (incl. bkfst)* **Facilities** Spa 🏊 Gym Range of beauty treatments/ massage Specialists in pampering days Wi-fi **Parking** 70 **Notes** LB

WARMINSTER Map 3 ST84

Bishopstrow House Hotel

★★★★ 78% ◉◉ HOTEL

BA12 9HH
☎ 01985 212312 📄 01985 216769
e-mail: info@bishopstrow.co.uk
web: www.vonessenhotels.co.uk
dir: *A303, A36, B3414, hotel 2m on right*

PETS: Bedrooms (7 GF) unattended **Charges** dog £10 per night **Public areas** except restaurant, conservatory, pool area **Other** please contact hotel to confirm which pets are accepted **Restrictions** well behaved pets only

This is a fine example of a Georgian country home, situated in 27 acres of grounds. Public areas are traditional in style and feature antiques and some open fires. Most bedrooms offer DVD players. A spa, a tennis court and several country walks ensure there is something for all guests. The restaurant serves top quality, contemporary cuisine.

Rooms 32 (2 annexe) (2 fmly) (7 GF) **Facilities** Spa 🎾 🐾 🏊 Fishing 🛥 Gym Clay pigeon shooting Archery Cycling Xmas New Year Wi-fi **Parking** 100

WESTBURY Map 3 ST85

The Cedar

Ⓤ

Warminster Rd BA13 3PR
☎ 01373 822753 📄 01373 858423
e-mail: info@cedarhotel-wiltshire.co.uk
dir: *On A350, 0.5m S of town towards Warminster*

PETS: Bedrooms (10 GF) **Stables** 2m **Charges** £10 per night £70 per week **Exercise area** 500yds **Facilities** water bowl cage storage walks info vet info **On Request** torch towels **Other** charge for damage

Currently the rating for this establishment is not confirmed. This may be due to a change of ownership or because it has only recently joined the AA rating scheme For further details please see the AA website: theAA.com

Rooms 20 (12 annexe) (4 fmly) (10 GF) **Facilities** FTV Xmas New Year Wi-fi **Parking** 30 **Notes** LB

Brokerswood Country Park *(ST836523)*

▶▶▶▶

Brokerswood BA13 4EH
☎ 01373 822238 📄 01373 858474
e-mail: info@brokerswood.co.uk
dir: *M4 junct 17, S on A350. Right at Yarnbrook to Rising Sun pub at North Bradley, left at rdbt. Left on bend approaching Southwick, 2.5m, site on right*

PETS: Charges dog £1 per night **Public areas** except children's adventure play area disp bin **Exercise area** 80-acre country park **Facilities** food bowl water bowl dog chews scoop/disp bags leads walks info vet info **Other** prior notice required dog/ cat balls, toys & dog pegs available **Restrictions** no Pit Bull Terriers, Japanese Tosas, Fila Braziliero & Dogo Argentino (see also page 7)

Open all year Last arrival 21.30hrs Last departure 11.00hrs

A popular park on the edge of an 80-acre woodland park with nature trails and fishing lakes. An adventure playground offers plenty of fun for all ages, and there is a miniature railway, an indoor play centre, and a café. There are high quality toilet facilities and fully-equipped, ready-erected tents are now available for hire. A 5 acre site with 69 touring pitches, 21 hardstandings.

Notes Families only

WORCESTERSHIRE

ABBERLEY
Map 7 SO76

von Essen hotels
A PRIVATE COLLECTION
www.vonessenhotels.com

The Elms Hotel
★★★ 88% ◉◉ HOTEL
Stockton Rd WR6 6AT
☎ 01299 896666 📠 01299 896804
e-mail: info@theelmshotel.co.uk
web: www.theelmshotel.co.uk
dir: On A443, 2m beyond Great Witley

PETS: Bedrooms (3 GF) unattended Charges £7 per night
Public areas except restaurants on leads Grounds on leads
Facilities cage storage walks info vet info On Request fridge
access torch towels Other charge for damage Resident Pets:
Tickle (Chocolate Labrador), George (cat)

This imposing Queen Anne mansion set in delightful grounds
dates back to 1710 and offers a sophisticated yet relaxed
atmosphere throughout. The spacious public rooms and
generously proportioned bedrooms offer elegance and charm. The
hotel is particularly well geared for families, with a host of child
friendly facilities and features including a crèche, a play area
and wonderful high teas. Imaginative cooking is served in the
elegant restaurant.

Rooms 23 (6 annexe) (1 fmly) (3 GF) Facilities Spa FTV 🕮 🏊 ⛵
Gym Xmas New Year Wi-fi Parking 100

BEWDLEY
Map 7 SO77

Royal Forester Country Inn
★★★★ ◉ INN
Callow Hill DY14 9XW
☎ 01299 266286
e-mail: contact@royalforesterinn.co.uk

PETS: Bedrooms unattended sign Stables Charges dog £10,
horse £30 per night Public areas except bar on leads Grounds
on leads disp bin Exercise area Facilities food (pre-bookable)
food bowl water bowl bedding dog chews cat treats feeding
mat litter tray scoop/disp bags dog walking washing facs dog
grooming cage storage walks info vet info On Request fridge
access torch towels Other charge for damage

Located opposite The Wyre Forest on the town's outskirts, this
inn dates back to 1411 and has been sympathetically restored
to provide high standards of comfort. Stylish modern bedrooms
are complemented by smart bathrooms, and equipped with
many thoughtful extras. Decor styles throughout the public areas
highlight the many retained period features, and the restaurant
serves imaginative food featuring locally sourced produce.

Rooms 7 en suite (2 fmly) S £55; D £79* Facilities STV FTV tea/
coffee Dinner available Cen ht Wi-fi Parking 40 Notes LB No
coaches

Woodcolliers Arms
★★★ INN
76 Welch Gate DY12 2AU
☎ 01299 400589
e-mail: roger@woodcolliers.co.uk
web: www.woodcolliers.co.uk
dir: Exit A456, follow road behind church, left into Welch Gate
(B4190)

PETS: Bedrooms Charges £5 per night £15 per week
Public areas except restaurant on leads disp bin Exercise area
Facilities water bowl walks info vet info On Request fridge
access Other charge for damage Restrictions small to medium
size dogs only Resident Pet: Oliver (Jack Russell)

Dating from before 1780, the Woodcolliers is a family-run
establishment located in the renowned Georgian town of
Bewdley. A traditional inn offering an interesting menu with
both traditional British pub food and a speciality Russian menu.
Accommodation is comfortable and rooms are well equipped.

Rooms 5 rms (4 en suite) (1 pri facs) S £20-£40; D £40-£70
(room only)* Facilities tea/coffee Dinner available Cen ht
Parking 2 Notes LB

BROADWAY
Map 4 SP03

Cotswold
Inns & Hotels

Broadway
★★★ 78% HOTEL
The Green, High St WR12 7AA
☎ 01386 852401 📠 01386 853879
e-mail: info@broadwayhotel.info
web: www.cotswold-inns-hotels.co.uk/broadway
dir: Follow signs to Evesham, then Broadway

PETS: Bedrooms (3 GF) unattended Charges Public areas
except eating areas Grounds Facilities water bowl cage storage
walks info vet info On Request fridge access torch towels
Other charge for damage

A half-timbered Cotswold stone property, built in the 15th century
as a retreat for the Abbots of Pershore. The hotel combines
modern, attractive decor with original charm and character.
Bedrooms are tastefully furnished and well equipped while
public rooms include a relaxing lounge, cosy bar and charming
restaurant; alfresco all-day dining in summer months proves
popular.

Rooms 19 (1 fmly) (3 GF) D £150-£170 (incl. bkfst)* Facilities
Xmas New Year Wi-fi Parking 20 Notes LB

ENGLAND

BROADWAY *continued*

Cowley House
★ ★ ★ ★ GUEST ACCOMMODATION

Church St WR12 7AE
☎ 01386 858148
e-mail: cowleyhouse.broadway@tiscali.co.uk
dir: *Follow signs for Broadway. Church St adjacent to village green, 3rd on left*

PETS: **Bedrooms Charges** £5 per night **Public areas Grounds** disp bin **Exercise area** approx 100yds **Facilities** dog chews feeding mat scoop/disp bags leads washing facs walks info vet info **On Request** fridge access torch towels **Other** charge for damage **Restrictions** small, well behaved dogs only Resident Pets: Holly & Purdey (West Highland Terriers)

A warm welcome is assured at this 18th-century Cotswold-stone house, just a stroll from the village green. Fine period furniture enhances the interiors, and the elegant hall has a polished flagstone floor. Tastefully equipped bedrooms include thoughtful extras and smart modern shower rooms. Comprehensive breakfasts feature local produce.

Rooms 7 rms (6 en suite) (1 pri facs) (1 fmly) (2 GF)
Facilities FTV tea/coffee Cen ht Wi-fi **Parking** 7 **Notes** LB

Horse & Hound
[U]

54 High St WR12 7DT
☎ 01386 852287   ▤ 01386 853784
e-mail: k2mtk@aol.com
dir: *Off A46 to Evesham*

PETS: **Bedrooms** unattended **Charges** £10 per night **Public areas** except restaurant on leads **Exercise area** 100yds **Facilities** dog chews walks info vet info **Other** charge for damage **Restrictions** small dogs only **Resident Pets:** Stella & Gracie (Black Labradors)

Currently the rating for this establishment is not confirmed. This may be due to a change of ownership or because it has only recently joined the AA rating scheme. For further details please see the AA website: theAA.com

Rooms 5 en suite (1 fmly) **Facilities** tea/coffee Dinner available Cen ht Licensed **Parking** 15 **Notes** RS Winter Closed 3pm-6pm

The Evesham
★ ★ ★   77%   HOTEL

Coopers Ln, Off Waterside WR11 1DA
☎ 01386 765566   & 0800 716969 (Res)   ▤ 01386 765443
e-mail: reception@eveshamhotel.com
web: www.eveshamhotel.com
dir: *M5 junct 9, A46 to Evesham. At rdbt on entering Evesham, take B4184 towards town, right at new bridge lights, 800yds, right into Coopers Lane*

PETS: **Bedrooms** (11 GF) unattended **Grounds Exercise area** 400yds **Facilities** vet info **Other** please phone for details of pet facilities

Dating from 1540 and set in extensive grounds, this delightful hotel has well-equipped accommodation that includes a selection of quirkily themed rooms - Alice in Wonderland, Egyptian, and Aquarium (which has a tropical fish tank in the bathroom). A reputation for food is well deserved, with a particularly strong choice for vegetarians. Children are welcome and toys are always available.

Rooms 40 (1 annexe) (3 fmly) (11 GF) **S** £75-£87; **D** £120-£123 (incl. bkfst) **Facilities** FTV ☜ Putt green ⚒ New Year Wi-fi Child facilities **Parking** 50 **Notes** LB Closed 25-26 Dec

The Swan Inn
★ ★ ★ ★   INN

Worcester Rd WR8 0EA
☎ 01684 311870
e-mail: info@theswanhanleyswan.co.uk
web: www.theswanhanleyswan.co.uk
dir: *M5 junct 7, follow signs for Three Counties Showground, 1m before*

PETS: **Bedrooms Sep accom** 1 kennel available on request (quiet dog only) **Public areas** except restaurant on leads **Grounds** on leads disp bin **Exercise area Facilities** cage storage walks info vet info **On Request** fridge access **Other** charge for damage **Resident Pet:** Klaus (German Shepherd)

This 17th-century property, often described as a quintessential country inn, is located right on the village green, and has a warm, cosy, home-from-home atmosphere. Ideally situated at the foot of the beautiful Malvern Hills, it has five en suite bedrooms that are pleasantly furnished, modern and comfortable. Dining, particularly on warmer days in the garden and the patio, is a delight. There is ample parking to the rear of the property.

Rooms 5 en suite (2 fmly) **S** £62.50; **D** £80* **Facilities** tea/coffee Dinner available Cen ht Wi-fi **Parking** 30

Walter de Cantelupe Inn
★★★ INN

Main Road (A38) WR5 3NA
☎ 01905 820572
e-mail: walter.depub@fsbdial.co.uk
web: www.walterdecantelupeinn.com
dir: On A38 in village centre

PETS: Bedrooms sign **Stables** 1.5m **Charges Public areas**
bar only on leads **Grounds** on leads **Exercise area** 0.5m
Facilities water bowl washing facs cage storage walks info vet
info **On Request** fridge access torch towels **Other** charge for
damage dog grooming available nearby

This inn provides cosy bedrooms with smart bathrooms, and
is convenient for the M5 and Worcester. The intimate, open-
plan public areas are the setting for a range of real ales, and
imaginative food featuring local produce and a fine selection of
British cheeses.

Rooms 3 rms (2 en suite) (1 pri facs) **Facilities** tea/coffee Dinner
available Cen ht Wi-fi **Parking** 24 **Notes** No coaches

The Cottage in the Wood Hotel
★★★ 85% ◉◉ HOTEL

Holywell Rd, Malvern Wells WR14 4LG
☎ 01684 588860   01684 560662
e-mail: reception@cottageinthewood.co.uk
web: www.cottageinthewood.co.uk
dir: 3m S of Great Malvern off A449, 500yds N of B4209, on
opposite side of road

PETS: Bedrooms (9 GF) unattended **Stables** 1.5m **Charges**
£7.50 per night **Grounds** disp bin **Exercise area** adjacent
Facilities food bowl water bowl bedding dog chews cage
storage walks info vet info **On Request** fridge access torch
Other charge for damage

Sitting high up on a wooded hillside, this delightful, family-run
hotel boasts lovely views over the Severn Valley. The bedrooms
are divided between the main house, Beech Cottage and the
Pinnacles. The public areas are very stylishly decorated, and

imaginative food is served in an elegant dining room, overlooking
the immaculate grounds.

The Cottage in the Wood Hotel

Rooms 30 (23 annexe) (9 GF) **S** £79-£119; **D** £99-£195 (incl.
bkfst)* **Facilities** Direct access to Malvern Hills Xmas New Year
Wi-fi **Parking** 40

Holdfast Cottage
★★ 82% ◉ HOTEL

Marlbank Rd, Welland WR13 6NA
☎ 01684 310288   01684 311117
e-mail: enquiries@holdfast-cottage.co.uk
web: www.holdfast-cottage.co.uk
dir: M50 junct 1, follow Upton Three Counties/A38 signs, onto
A4104 to Welland

PETS: Bedrooms Stables Charges £5 per night **Public areas**
except lounge & restaurant on leads **Grounds** on leads disp bin
Exercise area 200yds **Facilities** vet info **On Request** torch

At the base of the Malvern Hills this delightful wisteria-covered
hotel sits in attractive manicured grounds. Charming public
areas include an intimate bar, a log fire enhanced lounge
and an elegant dining room. Bedrooms vary in size but all are
comfortable and well appointed. Fresh local and seasonal
produce are the basis for award-winning cuisine.

Rooms 8 (1 fmly) **S** £49-£55; **D** £75-£98 (incl. bkfst)*
Facilities FTV ⚓ Xmas New Year Wi-fi **Parking** 15 **Notes** LB

MALVERN *continued*

The Great Malvern Hotel

★★ 71% HOTEL

Graham Rd WR14 2HN

☎ 01684 563411 🖹 01684 560514

e-mail: sutton@great-malvern-hotel.co.uk

dir: *from Worcester on A449, left beyond fire station into Graham Road. Hotel at end on right*

PETS: **Bedrooms Public areas** except during food service in bar & restaurant on leads disp bin **Exercise area** 0.5m **Facilities** feeding mat pet sitting dog walking washing facs cage storage walks info vet info **On Request** fridge access torch towels **Other** charge for damage **Restrictions** no large dogs (i.e. Dobermans, German Shepherds, Rottweilers)

Close to the town centre this privately owned and managed hotel is ideally situated for many of Malvern's attractions. Accommodation is spacious and well equipped. Public areas include a cosy bar area, popular with locals, and a quiet lounge area.

Rooms 13 (1 fmly) **S** £50-£88; **D** £88 (incl. bkfst) **Facilities** STV FTV ♫ Wi-fi **Services** Lift **Parking** 9 **Notes** LB

Portocks End House

★★★ BED AND BREAKFAST

Little Clevelode WR13 6PE

☎ 01684 310276

e-mail: email@portocksendbandb.co.uk

dir: *On B4424, 4m N of Upton upon Severn, opposite Riverside Caravan Park*

PETS: **Bedrooms Public areas** except dining room **Grounds** disp bin **Facilities** food bowl water bowl scoop/disp bags leads washing facs cage storage walks info vet info **On Request** fridge access torch towels **Resident Pet:** Benji (English Springer Spaniel)

Peacefully located but convenient for the showground and major road links, this period house retains many original features; the traditional furnishings and decor highlight its intrinsic charm. Bedrooms are equipped with lots of thoughtful extras, and breakfasts are taken in a cosy dining room overlooking the pretty garden.

Rooms 2 rms (1 en suite) (1 pri facs) (1 fmly) **S** £28-£30; **D** £50* **Facilities** tea/coffee **Parking** 4 **Notes** Closed Dec-Feb 🐾

Sidney House

★★★ GUEST ACCOMMODATION

40 Worcester Rd WR14 4AA

☎ 01684 574994 🖹 01684 574994

e-mail: info@sidneyhouse.co.uk

web: www.sidneyhouse.co.uk

dir: *On A449, 200yds N from town centre*

PETS: **Bedrooms Public areas** except dining room on leads **Grounds** disp bin **Exercise area** 50yds **Facilities** walks info vet info **On Request** fridge access torch towels

This impressive Grade II listed Georgian house is close to the central attractions and has stunning views. Bedrooms are filled with thoughtful extras, and some have small, en suite shower rooms. The spacious dining room overlooks the Cotswold escarpment and a comfortable lounge is also available.

Rooms 8 rms (6 en suite) (2 pri facs) (1 fmly) **Facilities** FTV TVL tea/coffee Cen ht Licensed Wi-fi **Parking** 9 **Notes** Closed 24 Dec-3 Jan

Four Hedges

★★ GUEST ACCOMMODATION

The Rhydd, Hanley Castle WR8 0AD

☎ 01684 310405

e-mail: fredgies@aol.com

dir: *4m E of Malvern at junct of B4211 & B4424*

PETS: **Bedrooms** unattended **Public areas Grounds** disp bin **Exercise area** adjoining **Facilities** food bowl water bowl leads pet sitting washing facs cage storage walks info vet info **On Request** fridge access torch towels **Other** charge for damage **Resident Pets:** Max (Golden Retriever), Machu & Pichu (cats)

Situated in a rural location, this detached house stands in mature grounds with wild birds in abundance. The bedrooms are equipped with thoughtful extras. Tasty English breakfasts, using free-range eggs, are served in a cosy dining room at a table made from a 300-year-old elm tree.

Rooms 4 rms (2 en suite) **S** fr £25; **D** fr £50* **Facilities** TVL tea/coffee Cen ht 🎣 Fishing **Parking** 5 **Notes** No Children 1yr Closed Xmas 🐾

Express by Holiday Inn Redditch

BUDGET HOTEL

2 Hewell Rd, Enfield B97 6AE

☎ 01527 584658 📄 01527 597905

e-mail: reservations@express.gb.com

web: www.meridianleisure.com/redditch

dir: *M42 junct 2/A441 follow signs to rail station. Before station turn right into Hewell Rd, 1st left into Gloucester Close*

PETS: Bedrooms (10 GF) **Charges** £10 per night **Exercise area** 1m **Facilities** walks info vet info **Other** charge for damage **Restrictions** max weight 7.5kg

A modern hotel ideal for families and business travellers. Fresh and uncomplicated, the spacious rooms include Satellite channels, power shower and tea and coffee-making facilities. Complimentary hot breakfast is included in the room rate; with freshly prepared meals served in the GR Restaurant daily from 18:00 - 22:00.

Rooms 100 (75 fmly) (10 GF) (14 smoking)

MenziesHotels

Menzies Stourport Manor
★★★★ 77% HOTEL

35 Hartlebury Rd DY13 9JA

☎ 01299 289955 📄 01299 878520

e-mail: stourport@menzieshotels.co.uk

web: www.menzieshotels.co.uk

dir: *M5 junct 6, A449 towards Kidderminster, B4193 towards Stourport. Hotel on right*

PETS: Bedrooms (31 GF) **Stables** 0.5m **Charges** £5 per night **Public areas Grounds** on leads disp bin **Exercise area** 500yds **Facilities** washing facs vet info **On Request** torch towels **Other** charge for damage

Once the home of Prime Minister Sir Stanley Baldwin, this much extended country house is set in attractive grounds. A number of bedrooms and suites are located in the original building, although the majority are in a more modern, purpose-built section. Spacious public areas include a range of lounges, a popular restaurant, a leisure club and conference facilities.

Rooms 68 (17 fmly) (31 GF) (10 smoking) **S** £59-£130; **D** £59-£130* **Facilities** STV 🕃 🏊 Putt green Gym Squash Xmas New Year Wi-fi **Parking** 300

White Lion Hotel
★★★ 71% ◉ HOTEL

21 High St WR8 0HJ

☎ 01684 592551 📄 01684 593333

e-mail: reservations@whitelionhotel.biz

dir: *A422, A38 towards Tewkesbury. In 8m take B4104, after 1m cross bridge, turn left to hotel, past bend on left*

PETS: Bedrooms (2 GF) unattended **Charges** £5 per night **Exercise area** car park **Other** please phone for further details of pet facilities **Resident Pets:** Oscar (Giant Schnauzer), 2 cats

Famed for being the inn depicted in Henry Fielding's novel *Tom Jones*, this 16th-century hotel is a reminder of 'Old England' with features such as exposed beams and wall timbers still remaining. The quality furnishing and the decor throughout enhance its character; the bedrooms are smart and include one four-poster room.

Rooms 13 (2 annexe) (2 fmly) (2 GF) **Facilities** FTV Wi-fi **Parking** 14 **Notes** LB Closed 1 Jan RS 25 Dec

The Dewdrop Inn
★★★★ INN

Bell Ln, Lower Broadheath WR2 6RR

☎ 01905 640012 📄 01905 640265

e-mail: enquiries@thedewdrop-inn.co.uk

dir: *From A44 follow signs for Elgar Birthplace Museum, 0.5m past museum turn right at x-rds. 800yds on left*

PETS: Bedrooms Stables nearby **Charges** dog £5 per night **Public areas** except restaurant & bar area on leads **Grounds** on leads disp bin **Exercise area** 800yds **Facilities** walks info vet info **On Request** torch **Other** charge for damage **Resident Pet:** 1 Toy Poodle

This country pub with rooms is set in the pretty village of Lower Broadheath on the outskirts of Worcester. The accommodation offers seven comfortable, en suite bedrooms that are well equipped with thoughtful extras. Dining on the open plan contemporary bar and restaurant is popular for its weekend carvery offering; however a full menu of enticing options is available at other times. Alfresco dining is available in the summer months.

Rooms 7 en suite (7 GF) **S** £48-£55; **D** £60-£72* **Facilities** FTV tea/coffee Dinner available Direct Dial Cen ht Wi-fi **Parking** 40 **Notes** LB

WORCESTER *continued*

Oaklands B&B

★★★★ GUEST ACCOMMODATION

Claines WR3 7RS
☎ 01905 458871   📠 01905 759362
e-mail: barbara.gadd@zoom.co.uk
dir: *M5 junct 6 onto A449. At rdbt take 1st exit signed Claines.
1st left onto School Bank. Oaklands 1st house on right*

PETS: **Bedrooms Stables Charges Public areas Grounds**
disp bin **Exercise area** paddock **Exercise area** approx
200yds **Facilities** washing facs cage storage walks info vet
info **On Request** fridge access torch towels **Other** charge
for damage **Restrictions** no dangerous dogs (see page 7)
Resident Pet: Chloë (Labrador)

A warm welcome is guaranteed at this converted stable, which
is well located in a peaceful setting just a short drive from major
routes. The property stands in abundant mature gardens, and
the well-appointed bedrooms are mostly spacious. There is also a
snooker room and parking is available.

Rooms 4 en suite (2 fmly) **S** £35-£40; **D** £65-£70* **Facilities** tea/
coffee Cen ht Wi-fi Snooker **Parking** 7 **Notes** LB Closed Xmas &
New Year

YORKSHIRE, EAST RIDING OF

BRIDLINGTON   Map 8 TA16

Marton Grange

★★★★★ GUEST ACCOMMODATION

Flamborough Rd, Marton cum Sewerby YO15 1DU
☎ 01262 602034 & 07891 682687   📠 01262 602034
e-mail: info@marton-grange.co.uk
web: www.marton-grange.co.uk
dir: *2m NE of Bridlington. On B1255, 600yds W of Links golf club*

PETS: **Bedrooms Charges** £5 per night **Public areas**
conservatory only on leads **Grounds** on leads disp bin
Exercise area own paddock **Facilities** cage storage walks
info vet info **On Request** fridge access torch **Other** charge
for damage no more than 2 small dogs or 1 medium sized dog
Restrictions no large dogs Resident Pets: cat, chickens

This Grade II listed former farmhouse is set in well maintained
gardens offering high levels of comfort, service and hospitality.
Bedrooms are well appointed with quality fixtures and fittings.
Public areas offer wonderful views of the gardens. Thoughtful
extras are provided as standard and make for a delightful guest
experience.

Rooms 11 en suite (3 GF) **Facilities** FTV tea/coffee Cen ht Lift
Licensed Wi-fi **Parking** 11 **Notes** LB Closed 19-23 Dec & 28
Dec-Jan

The Tennyson

★★★ GUEST ACCOMMODATION

19 Tennyson Av YO15 2EU
☎ 01262 604382 & 07729 149729
e-mail: dianew2@live.co.uk
web: www.thetennyson-brid.co.uk
dir: *500yds NE of town centre. B1254 Promenade from town
centre towards Flamborough, Tennyson Ave on left*

PETS: **Bedrooms Charges** £5 per stay **Public areas** except
dining room on leads disp bin **Exercise area** 300yds **Facilities**
food bowl water bowl bedding feeding mat scoop/disp bags
leads walks info vet info **On Request** fridge access towels
Resident Pets: Shandy & Jerry (dogs)

Situated in a quiet side road close to the town centre and its
attractions, this friendly guest accommodation offers attentive
service, comfortable bedrooms and a cosy bar. Dinner is also
available by prior arrangement.

Rooms 8 rms (7 en suite) (1 pri facs) (2 fmly) (1 GF)
S £27.50-£30; **D** £55-£70* **Facilities** tea/coffee Dinner available
Cen ht Licensed **Notes** LB

KINGSTON UPON HULL   Map 8 TA02

Portland

★★★★ 73% HOTEL

Paragon St HU1 3JP
☎ 01482 326462   📠 01482 213460
e-mail: info@portland-hotel.co.uk
web: www.portland-hull.com
dir: *M62 junct 38 onto A63, to 1st main rdbt. Left at 2nd lights,
over x-rds. Right at next junct onto Carr Lane, follow one-way
system*

PETS: **Bedrooms Exercise area** 5 mins **Facilities** cage storage
vet info **On Request** fridge access torch towels **Restrictions**
small dogs only

A modern hotel situated next to the City Hall providing a good
range of accommodation. Most of the public rooms are on the first
floor and Wi-fi is available. The Bay Tree Café, at street level, is
open during the day and evening. Staff are friendly and helpful
and take care of car parking for hotel guests.

Rooms 126 (4 fmly) **S** £85-£115; **D** £95-£125* **Facilities** STV FTV
Complimentary use of nearby health & fitness centre Xmas New
Year Wi-fi **Services** Lift **Notes** LB

MARKET WEIGHTON — Map 8 SE84

Robeanne House

★ ★ ★ GUEST ACCOMMODATION

Driffield Ln, Shiptonthorpe YO43 3PW

☎ 01430 873312 & 07720 468811   📄 01430 879142

e-mail: enquiries@robeannehouse.co.uk

web: www.robeannehouse.co.uk

dir: *1.5m NW on A614*

PETS: Bedrooms Sep accom kennel in stable **Stables Charges** £5 (dogs), £15 (horses) per night **Public areas Grounds** on leads disp bin **Exercise area Facilities** food (pre-bookable) food bowl water bowl bedding dog chews cat treats feeding mat litter tray scoop/disp bags leads pet sitting dog walking washing facs cage storage walks info vet info **On Request** fridge access torch towels **Other** charge for damage **Resident Pets:** Max (Labrador), Beatty, Josie & Nina (horses), Megan & Dylan (ponies), (Jack, Guinness & Poppy - visiting dogs)

Set back off the A614 in a quiet location, this delightful modern family home was built as a farmhouse. York, the coast, and the Yorkshire Moors and Dales are within easy driving distance. All bedrooms have country views and include a large family room. A charming wooden chalet is available in the garden.

Rooms 2 en suite 6 annexe en suite (2 fmly) (3 GF) **S** £35-£45; **D** £60-£75* **Facilities** FTV TVL tea/coffee Dinner available Cen ht Wi-fi **Parking** 10 **Notes** LB

RUDSTON — Map 8 TA06

Thorpe Hall Caravan & Camping Site

(TA108677)

▶ ▶ ▶

Thorpe Hall YO25 4JE

☎ 01262 420393 & 420574   📄 01262 420588

e-mail: caravansite@thorpehall.co.uk

dir: *5m from Bridlington on B1253*

PETS: Public areas except games room & toilets disp bin **Exercise area** dog walk **Facilities** food food bowl water bowl walks info **Other** disposal bags available **Restrictions** well behaved dogs only

Open Mar-Oct rs limited opening hours reception & shop Last arrival 22.00hrs Last departure noon

A delightful, peaceful small park within the walled gardens of Thorpe Hall yet within a few miles of the bustling seaside resort of Bridlington. The site offers a games field, its own coarse fishery, pitch and putt, and a games and TV lounge, and there are numerous walks locally. There is a refurbished amenity block. A 4.5 acre site with 90 touring pitches.

Notes No ball games (field provided)

ALDBROUGH ST JOHN — Map 8 NZ21

Lucy Cross Farm

★ ★ ★ GUEST ACCOMMODATION

DL11 7AD

☎ 01325 374319 & 07931 545985

e-mail: sally@lucycross.co.uk

web: www.lucycross.co.uk

dir: *A1 junct 56 onto B6275 at Barton, white house 3m from Barton rdbt on left towards Piercebridge*

PETS: Bedrooms unattended **Sep accom** outside kennel & stable available **Stables Charges** dog & cat £6, horse £25 per night £30 per week **Public areas** on leads **Grounds** disp bin **Exercise area Facilities** food (pre-bookable) food bowl water bowl bedding dog chews cat treats feeding mat litter tray scoop/disp bags leads pet sitting dog walking washing facs cage storage walks info vet info **On Request** fridge access torch towels **Other** charge for damage dogs must sleep in own basket; pets allowed in ground-floor bedroom only **Resident Pet:** Spud (Jack Russell)

Located close to major road links, a relaxed atmosphere and friendly welcome is assured. Traditionally furnished bedrooms are very comfortably equipped; one is on the ground floor. A lounge is available and hearty breakfasts are served in the pleasant dining room.

Rooms 5 rms (3 en suite) (2 pri facs) (1 fmly) (1 GF) **S** £35-£45; **D** £65-£75* **Facilities** FTV TVL tea/coffee Dinner available Cen ht Wi-fi Fishing Riding **Parking** 10 **Notes** LB

ALLERSTON — Map 8 SE88

Vale of Pickering Caravan Park *(SE879808)*

▶ ▶ ▶ ▶ ▶

Carr House Farm YO18 7PQ

☎ 01723 859280   📄 01723 850060

e-mail: tony@valeofpickering.co.uk

dir: *On B1415, 1.75m off A170 (Pickering-Scarborough road)*

PETS: Charges dog 50p per night **Public areas** on leads disp bin **Exercise area** large dog walk **Facilities** food leads walks info vet info **Other** prior notice required disposal bags available

Open 5 Mar-3 Jan rs Mar Last arrival 21.00hrs Last departure 11.30hrs

A well-maintained, spacious family park with excellent facilities including a well-stocked shop. Younger children will enjoy the attractive play area, while the large ball sports area will attract older ones. The park is set in open countryside bounded by hedges, and is handy for the North Yorkshire Moors and the attractions of Scarborough. A 13 acre site with 120 touring pitches, 80 hardstandings.

ENGLAND

Alders Caravan Park *(SE497654)*

► ► ► ►

Home Farm YO61 1RY
☎ 01347 838722 📠 01347 838722
e-mail: enquiries@homefarmalne.co.uk
dir: *From A19 exit at Alne sign, in 1.5m turn left at T-junct, 0.5m site on left in village centre*

PETS: **Sep accom** 2 kennels **Stables** 0.5m **Public areas Exercise area Facilities** walks info vet info **Other** max 2 dogs per pitch **Resident Pets:** Digby (Labrador), Spot & Jess (Collies), Molly & Kelly (horses)

Open Mar-Oct Last arrival 21.00hrs Last departure 14.00hrs

A tastefully developed park on a working farm with screened pitches laid out in horseshoe-shaped areas. This well designed park offers excellent toilet facilities including a bathroom and fully-serviced washing and toilet cubicles. A woodland area and a water meadow are pleasant places to walk. A 12 acre site with 87 touring pitches, 6 hardstandings.

Knowles Lodge

★ ★ ★ ★ ★ BED AND BREAKFAST

BD23 6DQ
☎ 01756 720228 📠 01756 720381
e-mail: pam@knowleslodge.com
web: www.knowleslodge.com
dir: *From Bolton Abbey B6160 3.5m, turn right after Barden Tower 1.5m, entrance on left*

PETS: **Bedrooms Charges** £5 per night £30 per week **Public areas** except dining room **Grounds** disp bin **Exercise area** adjacent **Facilities** water bowl bedding washing facs walks info vet info **On Request** fridge access torch towels

Located in the heart of Wharfedale and surrounded by 17 acres of meadow and woodland, this delightful Canadian-style ranch has been lovingly restored. The house is attractively furnished, with well appointed bedrooms, and whether guests are there to walk, cycle, fish, or simply relax and enjoy the scenery, they are sure to be given a warm welcome. Delicious breakfasts featuring home-made dishes are served around a large table.

Rooms 3 en suite (1 fmly) (2 GF) **S** £60-£65; **D** £100
Facilities TVL tea/coffee Cen ht Wi-fi Fishing **Parking** 6
Notes No Children 8yrs

White Rose

★ ★ 72% SMALL HOTEL

Main St DL8 3HG
☎ 01969 650515 📠 01969 650176
e-mail: stay@thewhiterosehotelaskrigg.co.uk
dir: *M6 or A1 onto A684. Follow signs to Askrigg, hotel in village centre*

PETS: **Bedrooms Charges** £5 per night **Public areas** except restaurant (& bar at food service) on leads **Grounds** on leads **Exercise area** field 100yds **Facilities** vet info **Other** charge for damage prior notice required **Restrictions** no breed larger than a Labrador **Resident Pet:** Meg (Black Labrador)

This family-run hotel dates from the 19th century, and is situated in the heart of Askrigg which was the fictional town of Darrowby in the BBC's *All Creatures Great and Small* series. The friendliness of the staff is noteworthy. The accommodation is tastefully decorated and comfortably furnished, and home cooked food is served in the conservatory overlooking the beer garden.

Rooms 12 **S** £45; **D** £70-£80 (incl. bkfst)* **Facilities** New Year **Parking** 20 **Notes** LB Closed 24-25 Dec

The Traddock

★ ★ ★ ★ RESTAURANT WITH ROOMS

LA2 8BY
☎ 015242 51224 📠 015242 51796
e-mail: info@austwicktraddock.co.uk
dir: *From Skipton take A65 towards Kendal, 3m after Settle turn right signed Austwick, cross hump back bridge, 100yds on left*

PETS: **Bedrooms** unattended **Public areas** except restaurant on leads **Grounds** on leads **Exercise area** Yorkshire Dales National Park **Facilities** water bowl scoop/disp bags washing facs walks info vet info **On Request** fridge access torch towels

Situated within the Yorkshire Dales National Park and a peaceful village environment, this fine Georgian country house with well-tended gardens offers a haven of calm and good hospitality. There are two comfortable lounges with real fires and fine furnishings, as well as a cosy bar and an elegant dining room serving fine dinners. Bedrooms are individually styled with many homely touches.

Rooms 12 en suite (2 fmly) (1 GF) **S** £80-£95; **D** £90-£180*
Facilities FTV tea/coffee Dinner available Direct Dial Cen ht Wi-fi Golf 18 **Parking** 20 **Notes** LB No coaches

ENGLAND

BEDALE
Map 8 SE28

Castle Arms
★★★★ ≈ INN
Snape DL8 2TB
☎ 01677 470270 📄 01677 470837
e-mail: castlearms@aol.com
dir: *2m S of Bedale. Off B6268 into Snape*

PETS: Bedrooms Charges £5 per stay **Public areas** except restaurant on leads **Grounds** on leads disp bin **Exercise area** 100mtrs **Facilities** walks info vet info **Other** charge for damage

Nestled in the quiet village of Snape, this former coaching inn is full of character. Bedrooms are in a converted barn, and each room is very comfortable and carefully furnished. The restaurant and public bar offer a good selection of fine ales, along with an interesting selection of freshly-prepared dishes.

Rooms 9 annexe en suite (8 GF) **S** £55-£65; **D** £75-£90*
Facilities tea/coffee Dinner available Cen ht Wi-fi **Parking** 15
Notes LB No coaches

BISHOP MONKTON
Map 8 SE36

Church Farm Caravan Park *(SE328660)*
▶▶▶

Knaresborough Rd HG3 3QQ
☎ 01765 677668 & 07932 158924 📄 01765 677668
e-mail: churchfarmcaravans@uwclub.net
dir: *Turn E off A61. At x-rds turn right. Site approx 500mtrs on right*

PETS: Stables 1m **Public areas** on leads **Exercise area** adjacent **Facilities** washing facs walks info vet info **Other** prior notice required **Resident Pets:** 1 dog (Cocker Spaniel), 1 cat, 3 horses

Open Mar-Oct Last arrival 22.30hrs Last departure 15.30hrs

A very pleasant rural site on a working farm, on the edge of the attractive village of Bishop Monkton with its well-stocked shop and pubs. Whilst very much a place to relax, there are many attractions close by including Fountains Abbey, Newby Hall, Ripon and Harrogate. A 4 acre site with 45 touring pitches, 3 hardstandings and 3 statics.

Notes No ball games 🎦

BOLTON ABBEY
Map 7 SE05

The Devonshire Arms Country House Hotel & Spa
★★★★ ◉◉◉◉ HOTEL
BD23 6AJ
☎ 01756 710441 & 718111 📄 01756 710564
e-mail: res@thedevonshirehotels.co.uk
web: www.devonshirehotels.co.uk
dir: *On B6160, 250yds N of junct with A59*

PETS: Bedrooms (17 GF) unattended sign **Charges** £5 per night **Public areas** except dining rooms **Grounds** on leads disp bin **Exercise area Facilities** food (pre-bookable) food bowl water bowl bedding dog chews scoop/disp bags leads pet sitting dog walking washing facs cage storage walks info vet info **On Request** fridge access torch towels **Resident Pets:** Dexter & Lila (Cocker Spaniels)

With stunning views of the Wharfedale countryside this beautiful hotel, owned by the Duke and Duchess of Devonshire, dates back to the 17th century. Bedrooms are elegantly furnished; those in the old part of the house are particularly spacious and have four-posters and fine antiques. The sitting rooms are delightfully cosy with log fires, and the dedicated staff deliver service with a blend of friendliness and professionalism. The Burlington Restaurant offers award-winning, highly accomplished cuisine together with an impressive wine list, while the Brasserie provides a lighter alternative.

Rooms 40 (1 fmly) (17 GF) **Facilities** Spa STV ® supervised ♨ Fishing 🚣 Gym Classic cars Falconry Laser pigeon shooting Fly fishing Cricket Xmas New Year Wi-fi **Parking** 150

ENGLAND

BURNSALL — Map 7 SE06

Devonshire Fell

★★★★ RESTAURANT WITH ROOMS

BD23 6BT
☎ 01756 729000 📠 01756 729009
e-mail: manager@devonshirefell.co.uk
web: www.devonshirefell.co.uk
dir: On B6160, 6m from Bolton Abbey rdbt A59 junct

PETS: Bedrooms Charges £5 per night **Grounds** on leads **Facilities** food food bowl water bowl bedding dog chews scoop/disp bags cage storage walks info **On Request** fridge access torch towels **Other** charge for damage dogs allowed in certain bedrooms only; goody bag available

Located on the edge of the attractive village of Burnsall, this establishment offers comfortable, well-equipped accommodation in a relaxing atmosphere. There is an extensive menu featuring local produce, and meals can be taken either in the bar area or the more formal restaurant. A function room with views over the valley is also available.

Rooms 12 en suite (2 fmly) **Facilities** STV FTV tea/coffee Dinner available Direct Dial Cen ht Wi-fi Fishing **Parking** 30 **Notes** LB

CATTERICK — Map 8 SE29

Rose Cottage

★★★ GUEST ACCOMMODATION

26 High St DL10 7LJ
☎ 01748 811164
dir: Off A1 in village centre, opposite village pharmacy

PETS: Bedrooms unattended **Exercise area** 5 mins' walk to river, 10 mins' walk to racecourse **Facilities** food bowl water bowl walks info vet info **On Request** torch

Convenient for exploring the Dales and Moors, this well-maintained guest accommodation lies in the middle of Catterick. Bedrooms are nicely presented and comfortable. The cosy public rooms include a cottage-style dining room adorned with Mrs Archer's paintings, and a lounge. Dinner is available by arrangement during the summer.

Rooms 3 rms (2 en suite) (1 fmly) (3 smoking) **S** £30-£36; **D** £48-£54 **Facilities** tea/coffee Dinner available Cen ht **Parking** 3 **Notes** Closed 24-26 Dec

FILEY — Map 8 TA18

Centenary Way Camping & Caravan Park
(TA115798)

▶▶▶

Muston Grange YO14 0HU
☎ 01723 516415 & 512313
dir: Just off A1039 near A165 junct towards Bridlington

PETS: Public areas except toilet block disp bin **Exercise area Facilities** vet info **Other** pet shop in town **Resident Pets:** Fudge (Staffordshire Terrier cross), Clarisa, Jessica & Jethro (cats)

Open Mar-Oct Last arrival 21.00hrs Last departure noon

A well set-out family-owned park, with footpath access to nearby beach. Close to the seaside resort of Filey, and caravan pitches enjoy views over open countryside. A 3 acre site with 75 touring pitches, 25 hardstandings.

Notes No group bookings in peak period, no 9-12 berth tents, no gazebos

Filey Brigg Touring Caravan & Country Park *(TA115812)*

▶▶▶

North Cliff YO14 9ET
☎ 01723 513852
e-mail: fileybrigg@scarborough.gov.uk
dir: 0.5m from Filey town centre on coast road from Scarborough, A165

PETS: Public areas disp bin **Exercise area Other** dogs accepted by prior arrangement only

Open Etr-2 Jan Last arrival 18.00hrs Last departure noon

A municipal park overlooking Filey Brigg with splendid views along the coast, and set in a country park. The beach is just a short walk away, as is the resort of Filey. There is a new, good quality amenity block, and 50 all-weather pitches are available. A 9 acre site with 158 touring pitches, 82 hardstandings.

GREAT AYTON   Map 8 NZ51

Royal Oak
★★★ INN
123 High St TS9 6BW
☎ 01642 722361 & 723270   📠 01642 724047
e-mail: info@royaloak-hotel.co.uk
dir: Off the A173, on High Street

PETS: Bedrooms unattended **Public areas** assist dogs only on leads **Grounds** on leads **Exercise area** local walks **Facilities** water bowl washing facs cage storage walks info vet info **On Request** fridge access torch towels **Other** pet food on request

This 18th-century former coaching inn is very popular with locals and visitors to the village. Bedrooms are all comfortably equipped. The restaurant and public bar retain many original features and offer a good selection of fine ales; an extensive range of food is available all day and is served in the bar or the dining room.

Rooms 5 rms (4 en suite) **Facilities** tea/coffee Dinner available Direct Dial Cen ht Snooker

HARROGATE   Map 8 SE35

Barceló Harrogate Majestic Hotel
★★★★ 75% HOTEL
Ripon Rd HG1 2HU
☎ 01423 700300   📠 01423 502283
e-mail: majestic@barcelo-hotels.co.uk
web: www.barcelo-hotels.co.uk
dir: From M1 onto A1(M) at Wetherby. Take A661 to Harrogate. Hotel in town centre adjacent to Royal Hall

PETS: Bedrooms Charges £15 per stay **Grounds** on leads **Facilities** vet info **Other** charge for damage some bedrooms may not be suitable for larger breeds (please check when booking) **Restrictions** no Rottweilers, Dobermans or Pit Bull Terriers

Popular for conferences and functions, this grand Victorian hotel is set in 12 acres of landscaped grounds that is within walking distance of the town centre. It benefits from spacious public areas, and the comfortable bedrooms, including some spacious suites, come in a variety of sizes.

Rooms 174 (8 fmly) **Facilities** Spa STV 🔍 supervised 🏊 Gym Golf practice net Xmas New Year Wi-fi **Services** Lift **Parking** 250

The Boar's Head Hotel
★★★ 83% ◉◉ HOTEL
Ripley Castle Estate HG3 3AY
☎ 01423 771888   📠 01423 771509
e-mail: reservations@boarsheadripley.co.uk
dir: On A61 (Harrogate to Ripon road). Hotel in town centre

PETS: Bedrooms unattended **Stables Charges** £10 per night **Public areas** except restaurant disp bin **Exercise area** adjacent **Facilities** food bowl water bowl bedding dog chews washing facs walks info vet info **On Request** fridge access torch

Part of the Ripley Castle estate, this delightful and popular hotel is renowned for its warm hospitality and as a dining destination. Bedrooms offer many comforts, and the luxurious day rooms feature works of art from the nearby castle. The banqueting suites in the castle are very impressive.

Rooms 25 (6 annexe) (2 fmly) **Facilities** 🏊 Fishing Clay pigeon shooting Tennis Fishing 🎵 Xmas New Year Wi-fi **Parking** 50

Alexa House
★★★★ GUEST HOUSE
26 Ripon Rd HG1 2JJ
☎ 01423 501988
e-mail: enquiries@alexa-house.co.uk
web: www.alexa-house.co.uk
dir: On A61, 0.25m from junct A59

PETS: Bedrooms sign **Stables** 10m **Public areas** except main building **Grounds** disp bin **Exercise area** 200yds **Facilities** food bowl water bowl feeding mat scoop/disp bags leads washing facs cage storage walks info vet info **On Request** fridge access torch **Other** charge for damage

This popular establishment has stylish, well-equipped bedrooms split between the main house and cottage rooms. All rooms come with homely extras. The opulent day rooms include an elegant lounge with honesty bar, and a bright dining room. The hands-on proprietors ensure high levels of customer care.

Rooms 9 en suite 4 annexe en suite (2 fmly) (4 GF) **S** £45-£60; **D** £75-£90* **Facilities** tea/coffee Cen ht Licensed Wi-fi **Parking** 10 **Notes** Closed 23-26 Dec

HARROGATE *continued*

Rudding Holiday Park *(SE333531)*

►►►►►

Follifoot HG3 1JH
☎ 01423 870439 ░ 01423 870859
e-mail: holiday-park@ruddingpark.com
dir: *From A1 take A59 to A658 signed Bradford. 4.5m then right, follow signs*

PETS: Stables 1m **Public areas** except pub disp bin
Exercise area Facilities food food bowl water bowl dog chews
scoop/disp bags vet info

Open Mar-Jan rs Nov-Jan shop & Deer House pub - limited
opening Last arrival 22.30hrs Last departure 14.00hrs

A spacious park set in the stunning 200 acres of mature
parkland and walled gardens of Rudding Park. The setting has
been tastefully enhanced with terraced pitches and dry-stone
walls. A separate area houses super pitches where all services
are supplied including a picnic table and TV connection, and
there are excellent toilets. An 18-hole golf course, a 6-hole short
course, heated outdoor swimming pool, the Deer House Pub, and
a children's play area complete the amenities. A 55 acre site with
109 touring pitches, 20 hardstandings and 57 statics.

Notes Under 18s must be accompanied by an adult, outside
swimming pool open in summer only

Bilton Park *(SE317577)*

►►►

Village Farm, Bilton Ln HG1 4DH
☎ 01423 863121
e-mail: welcome@biltonpark.co.uk
dir: *Turn E off A59 at Skipton Inn into Bilton Lane. Site approx 1m*

PETS: Public areas Exercise area 8 acres of fields & walks
Facilities food food bowl water bowl walks info vet info **Other**
kennels within 100yds

Open Apr-Oct

An established family-owned park in open countryside yet
only two miles from the shops and tearooms of Harrogate. The
spacious grass pitches are complemented by a well appointed
toilet block with private facilities. The Nidd Gorge is right on the
doorstep. A 4 acre site with 50 touring pitches.

Notes 🐾

Bainbridge Ings Caravan & Camping Site
(SD879895)

►►

DL8 3NU
☎ 01969 667354
e-mail: janet@bainbridge-ings.co.uk
dir: *Approaching Hawes from Bainbridge on A684, left at Gayle
sign, site 300yds on left*

PETS: Public areas disp bin **Exercise area** public footpath
accessed from site **Facilities** walks info vet info

Open Apr-Oct Last arrival 22.00hrs Last departure noon

A quiet, well-organised site in open countryside close to Hawes in
the heart of Upper Wensleydale, popular with ramblers. Pitches
are sited around the perimeter of several fields, each bounded by
traditional stone walls. A 5 acre site with 70 touring pitches, 8
hardstandings and 15 statics.

Notes No noise after 23.00hrs 🐾

Laskill Grange

★★★★ GUEST ACCOMMODATION

YO62 5NB
☎ 01439 798268
e-mail: laskillgrange@tiscali.co.uk
web: www.laskillgrange.co.uk
dir: *From York A19 to Thirsk, A170 to Helmsley then B1257 N,
after 6m sign on left to Laskill Grange*

PETS: Bedrooms sign **Stables Public areas** except dining room
& lounge **Grounds** on leads disp bin **Exercise area** adjacent
Facilities food bowl water bowl feeding mat washing facs cage
storage walks info vet info **On Request** fridge access torch
towels **Other** charge for damage paddock available for horses
Resident Pets: Tosh (dog), swans, ducks, peacock, chickens,
horses

Lovers of the countryside will enjoy this charming 19th-century
farmhouse. Guests can take a walk in the surrounding area of the
property, fish the River Seph, which runs through the grounds,
or visit nearby Rievaulx Abbey. The comfortable, well furnished

bedrooms are in the main house and are supplied with many thoughtful extras.

Rooms 3 rms (2 en suite) (1 pri facs) (3 GF) **Facilities** FTV TVL tea/coffee Dinner available Cen ht Licensed Fishing Riding **Parking** 20 **Notes** LB

Feversham Arms Hotel & Verbena Spa

★★★★ 81% ◉◉ HOTEL

1 High St YO62 5AG

☎ 01439 770766   📠 01439 770346

e-mail: info@fevershamarmshotel.com

web: www.fevershamarmshotel.com

dir: A168 (signed Thirsk) from A1 then A170 or A64 (signed York) from A1 to York North, then B1363 to Helmsley. Hotel 125mtrs from Market Place

PETS: Bedrooms (8 GF) unattended sign **Stables** 2m **Grounds** on leads **Exercise area** 100yds **Facilities** food bowl water bowl washing facs walks info vet info **On Request** fridge access torch towels **Other** charge for damage

This long established hotel lies just round the corner from the main square, and under its caring ownership proves to be a refined operation, yet without airs and graces. There are several lounge areas and a high-ceilinged conservatory restaurant where good local ingredients are prepared with skill and minimal fuss. The bedrooms, including four poolside suites, have their own individual character and decor.

Rooms 33 (9 fmly) (8 GF) **S** £175-£445; **D** £225-£495 (incl. bkfst & dinner) **Facilities** Spa STV FTV ✧ Sauna Saunarium Spa Xmas New Year Wi-fi **Services** Lift **Parking** 50 **Notes** LB

Black Swan Hotel

★★★ 81% ◉◉ HOTEL

Market Place YO62 5BJ

☎ 01439 770466   📠 01439 770174

e-mail: enquiries@blackswan-helmsley.co.uk

web: www.blackswan-helmsley.co.uk

dir: A1 junct 49, A168, A170 east, hotel 14m from Thirsk

PETS: Bedrooms unattended sign **Charges** £10 per night **Public areas** **Grounds** **Exercise area** 0.5m **Facilities** food bowl water bowl bedding dog chews cat treats feeding mat washing facs dog grooming cage storage walks info vet info **On Request** fridge access torch towels **Other** charge for damage **Resident Pet:** Lilly (Old English Sheepdog)

People have been visiting this establishment for over 200 years and it has become a landmark that dominates the market square. The hotel is renowned for its hospitality and friendliness; many of the staff are long-serving and dedicated. The bedrooms are stylish and include a junior suite and feature rooms. Dinner in the award-winning restaurant is the highlight of any stay. The hotel has a Tearoom and Patisserie that is open daily.

Rooms 45 (4 fmly) **Facilities** STV Xmas New Year Wi-fi **Parking** 50

Golden Square Touring Caravan Park

(SE604797)

▶▶▶▶▶

Oswaldkirk YO62 5YQ

☎ 01439 788269   📠 01439 788236

e-mail: reception@goldensquarecaravanpark.com

dir: From Thirsk A19 towards York turn left onto Caravan Route to Helmsley (1m out of Ampleforth village). From York B1363, turn off B1257 to Ampleforth, 0.5m on right

PETS: Stables 3m **Charges** £1.50 per night **Public areas** except playground, shop & toilets; dogs must be kept on leads disp bin **Exercise area** field & wood **Facilities** walks info vet info **Other** prior notice required maximum 2 dogs per pitch **Restrictions** no dangerous breeds (see page 7)

Open Mar-Oct Last arrival 21.00hrs Last departure noon

An excellent, popular and spacious site with very good facilities. This friendly park is set in a quiet rural situation with lovely views over the North Yorks Moors. Terraced on three levels and surrounded by trees, it caters particularly for families. Country walks and mountain bike trails start here; an attractive holiday home development is now completed. Please note that caravans are prohibited from the A170 at Sutton Bank between Thirsk and Helmsley. A 12 acre site with 129 touring pitches, 10 hardstandings and 10 statics.

Notes No skateboards or fires ◉

Foxholme Caravan Park *(SE658828)*

▶▶▶

Harome YO62 5JG

☎ 01439 771904

dir: A170 from Helmsley towards Scarborough, right signed Harome, left at church, through village, follow signs

PETS: Public areas on leads disp bin **Exercise area** dog walking area (off lead) **Facilities** washing facs walks info vet info **Other** prior notice required

Open Etr-Oct Last arrival 23.00hrs Last departure noon

A quiet park set in secluded wooded countryside, with well-shaded pitches in individual clearings divided by mature trees. The facilities are well maintained, and the site is ideal as a touring base or a place to relax. Please note that caravans are prohibited on the A170 at Sutton Bank between Thirsk and Helmsley. A 6 acre site with 60 touring pitches.

Notes ◉

HIGH BENTHAM — Map 7 SD66

Lowther Hill Caravan Park *(SD696695)*

▶

LA2 7AN
☎ 015242 61657
dir: *A65 at Clapham onto B6480 signed Bentham. 3m to site*

PETS: Public areas on leads disp bin **Facilities** vet info
Resident Pet: Lady Di (Maine Coon cat)

Open Mar-Nov Last arrival 21.00hrs Last departure 14.00hrs

A simple site with stunning panoramic views from every pitch. Peace reigns on this little park, though the tourist villages of Ingleton, Clapham and Settle are not far away. All pitches have electricity, and there is a heated toilet/washroom. A 1 acre site with 9 touring pitches, 4 hardstandings.

Notes Payment on arrival 🐾

HINDERWELL — Map 8 NZ71

Serenity Touring and Camping Park
(NZ792167)

▶ ▶ ▶

26A High St TS13 5JH
☎ 01947 841122
e-mail: patandni@aol.com
dir: *Off A174 in Hinderwell*

PETS: Charges 50p per night **Public areas** except laundry, washrooms & toilet areas on leads disp bin **Exercise area** cliff walks 0.5m **Facilities** walks info vet info **Other** prior notice required Resident Pet: D.J. (Black Labrador)

Open Mar-Oct Last arrival 21.00hrs Last departure noon

A charming park mainly for adults, being developed by enthusiastic owners. It lies behind the village of Hinderwell with its two pubs and store, and is handy for backpackers on the Cleveland Way. The sandy Runswick Bay and old fishing port of Staithes are close by, whilst Whitby is a short drive away. A 5.5 acre site with 20 touring pitches, 3 hardstandings.

Notes Mainly adult site, no ball games, kites or frisbees 🐾

HOVINGHAM — Map 8 SE67

Worsley Arms
★★★ 73% HOTEL
High St YO62 4LA
☎ 01653 628234 📠 01653 628130
e-mail: worsleyarms@aol.co.uk
dir: *A64, signed York, towards Malton. At dual carriageway left to Hovingham. At Slingsby left, then 2m*

PETS: Bedrooms (4 GF) unattended **Stables** 5m **Charges** £5 per night **Public areas** lounge only **Grounds** disp bin **Exercise area** **Facilities** dog chews walks info vet info **On Request** fridge access torch towels **Other** welcome dog biscuit on arrival Resident Pet: Badger (Black Labrador)

Overlooking the village green, this hotel has relaxing and attractive lounges with welcoming open fires. Bedrooms are also comfortable and several are contained in cottages across the green. The restaurant provides interesting quality cooking, with less formal dining in the Cricketers' Bar and Bistro to the rear.

Rooms 20 (8 annexe) (2 fmly) (4 GF) **Facilities** FTV 🏊 Shooting Xmas New Year **Parking** 25

HUBY — Map 8 SE56

The New Inn Motel
★★★ GUEST ACCOMMODATION
Main St YO61 1HQ
☎ 01347 810219 📠 01347 810219
e-mail: enquiries@newinnmotel.freeserve.co.uk
web: www.newinnmotel.co.uk
dir: *Off A19 E into village centre, motel on left*

PETS: Bedrooms sign **Charges** £5 per night (reduced rate for multiple nights stay) **Public areas** except dining room on leads **Grounds** on leads **Exercise area** 150mtrs **Facilities** leads washing facs cage storage walks info vet info **On Request** fridge access torch towels **Other** charge for damage pets accepted by prior arrangement only **Restrictions** well behaved dogs only

Located behind the New Inn, this modern motel-style accommodation has a quiet location in the village of Huby, nine miles north of York. Comfortable bedrooms are spacious and neatly furnished, and breakfast is served in the cosy dining room. The reception area hosts an array of tourist information and the resident owners provide a friendly and helpful service.

Rooms 8 en suite (3 fmly) (8 GF) **S** £40-£55; **D** £70-£80* **Facilities** tea/coffee Cen ht **Parking** 8 **Notes** LB Closed mid Nov-mid Dec & part Feb

INGLETON — Map 7 SD67

Gale Green Cottage
★★★★ BED AND BREAKFAST
Westhouse LA6 3NJ
☎ 015242 41245 & 07867 82088
e-mail: jill@galegreen.com
dir: *2m NW of Ingleton. S of A65 at Masongill x-rds*

PETS: Bedrooms Charges Public areas except dining room on leads **Grounds** disp bin **Exercise area** adjacent **Facilities** food bowl water bowl bedding feeding mat scoop/disp bags leads washing facs cage storage walks info vet info **On Request** fridge access torch towels **Other** charge for damage agility equipment under supervision Resident Pets: Jaffa (Red Border Collie), Beau (Golden Retriever), Soxs (cat), ducks, hens

Peacefully located in a rural hamlet, this 300-year-old house has been lovingly renovated to provide modern facilities without compromising original charm and character. Thoughtfully furnished bedrooms feature smart modern en suite shower rooms, and a guest lounge is also available.

Rooms 3 en suite (1 fmly) **S** £30-£35; **D** £58-£64* **Facilities** FTV TVL tea/coffee Cen ht **Parking** 6 **Notes** Closed Xmas & New Year 🐾

ENGLAND

Newton House

★ ★ ★ ★ ⬚ GUEST ACCOMMODATION
5-7 York Place HG5 0AD
☎ 01423 863539 📄 01423 869748
e-mail: newtonhouse@btinternet.com
web: www.newtonhouseyorkshire.com
dir: On A59 in Knaresborough, 200yds from town centre

PETS: Bedrooms Public areas except breakfast room
Exercise area 100mtrs **Facilities** food bowl water bowl bedding
dog chews feeding mat washing facs cage storage walks
info vet info **On Request** fridge access torch towels **Other**
pets allowed in designated bedrooms only (maximum 2 dogs)
Resident Pet: Keema (dog)

The delightful 18th-century former coaching inn is only a short
walk from the river, castle and market square. The property is
entered by an archway into a courtyard. The attractive, very well-
equipped bedrooms include some four-posters and also king-size
doubles. There is a charming lounge, and memorable breakfasts
feature local and home-made produce.

Rooms 9 rms (8 en suite) (1 pri facs) 2 annexe en suite (3 fmly)
(3 GF) **Facilities** FTV TVL tea/coffee Direct Dial Cen ht Licensed
Wi-fi **Parking** 10 **Notes** Closed 1wk Xmas

River House

★ ★ ★ ★ ⬚ ☕ GUEST HOUSE
BD23 4DA
☎ 01729 830315
e-mail: info@riverhousehotel.co.uk
web: www.riverhousehotel.co.uk
dir: Off A65, N to Malham

PETS: Bedrooms Charges £5 per stay **Public areas** except
lounge bar & restaurant (snug only) disp bin **Exercise area**
50yds **Facilities** water bowl leads washing facs cage storage
walks info vet info **On Request** fridge access torch towels
Other charge for damage dogs accepted by prior arrangement
only; dogs must not be left unattended if owners leave the house
Resident Pets: Poppy (Weimaraner), Archie (Jack Russell), Heidi
(English Shorthair cat)

A warm welcome awaits guests at this attractive house, which
dates from 1664. The bedrooms are bright and comfortable, with
one on the ground floor. Public areas include a cosy lounge and a
large, well-appointed dining room. Breakfasts and evening meals
offer choice and quality above expectation.

Rooms 8 en suite (1 GF) **S** £45-£65; **D** £60-£75 **Facilities** tea/
coffee Dinner available Cen ht Licensed Wi-fi Fishing **Parking** 5
Notes LB No Children 9yrs

Beck Hall

★ ★ ★ GUEST HOUSE
Cove Rd BD23 4DJ
☎ 01729 830332
e-mail: alice@beckhallmalham.com
web: www.beckhallmalham.com
dir: A65 to Gargrave, turn right to Malham. Beck Hall 100yds on
right after mini rdbt

PETS: Bedrooms unattended sign **Public areas** with other
guests' permission **Grounds** disp bin **Exercise area** adjacent
Facilities food bowl water bowl pet sitting dog walking
washing facs cage storage walks info vet info **On Request**
fridge access torch towels **Resident Pet:** Harvey (cat)

A small stone bridge over Malham Beck leads to this delightful
property. Dating from 1710, the house has true character, with
bedrooms carefully furnished with four-poster beds. Delicious
afternoon teas are available in the colourful garden in warmer
months, while roaring log fires are very welcoming in winter.

Rooms 11 en suite 7 annexe en suite (4 fmly) (4 GF) **S** £25-£60;
D £48-£80 **Facilities** STV tea/coffee Dinner available Cen ht
Licensed Wi-fi Fishing **Parking** 40 **Notes** LB

MALHAM *continued*

MARKINGTON | Map 8 SE26

Hob Green Hotel
★★★ 82% COUNTRY HOUSE HOTEL

HG3 3PJ

☎ 01423 770031 📠 01423 771589

e-mail: info@hobgreen.com

web: www.hobgreen.com

dir: *From A61, 4m N of Harrogate, left at Wormald Green, follow hotel signs*

PETS: Bedrooms unattended **Charges** on leads **Exercise area** 800 acres of woodland **Facilities** food bowl water bowl walks info vet info **Other** charge for damage pets may only be left in rooms when guests are dining

This hospitable country house is set in delightful gardens amidst rolling countryside midway between Harrogate and Ripon. The inviting lounges boast open fires in season and there is an elegant restaurant with a small private dining room. The individually designed bedrooms are very comfortable and come with a host of thoughtful extras.

Rooms 12 (1 fmly) **S** £95-£105; **D** £120-£140 (incl. bkfst)
Facilities ⬥ Xmas New Year Wi-fi **Parking** 40 **Notes** LB

MASHAM | Map 8 SE28

Swinton Park
★★★★ ⊕⊕⊕ HOTEL

HG4 4JH

☎ 01765 680900 📠 01765 680901

e-mail: enquiries@swintonpark.com

web: www.swintonpark.com

dir: *A1 onto B6267/8 to Masham. Follow signs through town centre & turn right into Swinton Terrace. 1m past golf course, over bridge, up hill. Hotel on right*

PETS: Bedrooms Stables 1.5m (phone for details) **Charges** £25 per night **Grounds** disp bin **Exercise area Facilities** food (pre-bookable) food bowl water bowl bedding dog chews feeding mat leads pet sitting dog walking washing facs cage storage walks info vet info **On Request** fridge access torch towels **Other** please phone for further details of pet facilities
Resident Pet: Myrtle (Golden Labrador)

Although extended during the Victorian and Edwardian eras, the original part of this welcoming castle dates from the 17th century. Bedrooms are luxuriously furnished and come with a host of thoughtful extras. Samuel's restaurant (built by the current owner's great-great-great grandfather) is very elegant and serves imaginative dishes using local produce. The majority of the food is sourced from the 20,000-acre Swinton Estate, as the hotel, winner of several green awards, is committed to keeping the 'food miles' to a minimum. The gardens, including a four-acre walled garden, have been gradually restored over recent years. The Deerhouse is the venue for the hotel's alfresco food festivals.

Rooms 30 (5 fmly) **S** £245-£440; **D** £245-£440 (incl. bkfst & dinner)* **Facilities** Spa FTV ⬥ 9 Putt green Fishing ⬥ Gym Shooting Falconry Pony trekking Cookery school Off-road driving Spa Xmas New Year Wi-fi Child facilities **Services** Lift **Parking** 50 **Notes** LB

MIDDLESBROUGH | Map 8 NZ41

The Grey House
★★★★ GUEST ACCOMMODATION

79 Cambridge Rd, Linthorpe TS5 5NL

☎ 01642 817485 📠 01642 817485

e-mail: denistaylor-100@btinternet.com

web: www.greyhousehotel.co.uk

dir: *A19 N onto A1130 & A1032 Acklam Rd, right at lights*

PETS: Bedrooms Charges £5 per night £35 per week
Public areas except breakfast room muzzled and on leads
Grounds on leads **Facilities** cage storage vet info **On Request** fridge access towels **Other** charge for damage

This Edwardian mansion stands in mature gardens in a quiet residential area, and is lovingly maintained to provide a relaxing retreat. The master bedrooms are well sized, and the upper rooms, though smaller, also offer good comfort. Downstairs there is an attractive lounge and the breakfast room.

Rooms 9 en suite (1 fmly) **Facilities** FTV TVL tea/coffee Direct Dial Cen ht Wi-fi **Parking** 10

MONK FRYSTON   Map 8 SE52

Monk Fryston Hall
★ ★ ★   81%   COUNTRY HOUSE HOTEL
LS25 5DU
☎ 01977 682369   📠 01977 683544
e-mail: reception@monkfrystonhallhotel.co.uk
web: www.monkfrystonhallhotel.co.uk
dir: *A1(M) junct 42/A63 towards Selby. Monk Fryston 2m, hotel on left*

PETS: Bedrooms (5 GF) unattended **Charges** £5 per night
Public areas except restaurant **Grounds Exercise area**
Facilities cage storage vet info **On Request** fridge access torch towels

This delightful 16th-century mansion house enjoys a peaceful location in 30 acres of grounds, yet is only minutes' drive from the A1. Many original features have been retained and the public rooms are furnished with antique and period pieces. Bedrooms are individually styled and thoughtfully equipped for both business and leisure guests.

Rooms 29 (2 fmly) (5 GF) **S** £75-£85; **D** £115-£175 (incl. bkfst)
Facilities STV ♨ Xmas New Year Wi-fi **Parking** 80 **Notes** LB

NORTHALLERTON   Map 8 SE39

Solberge Hall
★ ★ ★   68%   HOTEL
Newby Wiske DL7 9ER
☎ 01609 779191   📠 01609 780472
e-mail: reservations@solbergehall.co.uk
web: www.solbergehall.co.uk
dir: *Exit A1 at Leeming Bar, follow A684, turn right at x-rds, hotel in 2m on right*

PETS: Bedrooms (5 GF) **Charges** £10 per stay **Public areas**
Grounds on leads disp bin **Exercise area Facilities** food bowl water bowl washing facs cage storage walks info vet info **On Request** fridge access torch towels **Other** charge for damage

This Grade II listed Georgian country house is set in parkland and award-winning gardens, and commands panoramic views over open countryside. Bedrooms are comfortable and vary in style, some with four-poster beds. Public areas are split between the main house and the courtyard where Silks Brasserie, the stylish courtyard brasserie is located.

Rooms 24 (7 fmly) (5 GF) **S** £60-£80; **D** £100-£130 (incl. bkfst)*
Facilities STV Clay Pigeon Shooting (charges apply) Walks Xmas Wi-fi **Parking** 100 **Notes** LB

NORTH STANLEY   Map 8 SE27

Sleningford Watermill Caravan Camping Park *(SE280783)*
► ► ►
HG4 3HQ
☎ 01765 635201
dir: *Adjacent to A6108. 5m N of Ripon & 1m N of North Stanley*

PETS: Charges £1.50 per night **Public areas** on leads disp bin
Exercise area Facilities food food bowl water bowl scoop/disp bags walks info vet info **Other** prior notice required only 2 dogs per pitch **Resident Pets:** Loki (Cavalier King Charles Spaniel), Basti & Boots (cats)

Open Etr & Apr-Oct Last arrival 21.00hrs Last departure 12.30hrs

The old watermill and the River Ure make an attractive setting for this touring park which is laid out in two areas. Pitches are placed in meadowland and close to mature woodland, and the park has two enthusiastic managers. A popular place with canoeists. A 14 acre site with 40 touring pitches, 9 hardstandings.

Notes Youth groups by prior arrangement only booked through organisations or associations

---

OSMOTHERLEY   Map 8 SE49

Cote Ghyll Caravan & Camping Park
(SE459979)
► ► ► ► ►
DL6 3AH
☎ 01609 883425
e-mail: hills@coteghyll.com
dir: *Exit A19 dual carriageway at A684 (Northallerton junct). Follow signs to Osmotherley. Left in village centre. Site entrance 0.5m on right*

PETS: Public areas on leads disp bin **Exercise area** dog walk
Exercise area adjacent **Facilities** food food bowl water bowl walks info vet info **Other** disposal bags available

Open Mar-Oct Last arrival 22.00hrs Last departure noon

A quiet, peaceful site in a pleasant valley on the edge of moors, close to the village. The park is divided into terraces bordered by woodland, and the extra well-appointed amenity block is a welcome addition to this attractive park. There are pubs and shops nearby and holiday statics for hire. A 7 acre site with 77 touring pitches, 22 hardstandings and 18 statics.

Notes Family park

PICKERING — Map 8 SE78

The White Swan Inn
★★★ 80% ⊛ HOTEL

Market Place YO18 7AA
☎ 01751 472288   📄 01751 475554
e-mail: welcome@white-swan.co.uk
web: www.white-swan.co.uk
dir: *In town, between church & steam railway station*

PETS: **Bedrooms** (8 GF) unattended **Stables Charges** £12.50 per stay **Public areas Grounds** disp bin **Exercise area** 200mtrs **Facilities** food (pre-bookable) food bowl water bowl pet sitting dog walking washing facs cage storage walks info vet info **On Request** fridge access torch towels

This 16th-century coaching inn offers well-equipped, comfortable bedrooms, including suites, either of a more traditional style in the main building or modern rooms in the annexe. Service is friendly and attentive. Good food is served in the attractive restaurant, in the cosy bar and the lounge, where a log fire burns in cooler months. A comprehensive wine list focuses on many fine vintages. A private dining room is also available.

Rooms 21 (9 annexe) (3 fmly) (8 GF) **S** £115-£135; **D** £150-£260 (incl. bkfst)* **Facilities** FTV Xmas New Year Wi-fi **Parking** 45 **Notes** LB

Fox & Hounds Country Inn
★★ 82% ⊛ HOTEL

Main St, Sinnington YO62 6SQ
☎ 01751 431577   📄 01751 432791
e-mail: foxhoundsinn@easynet.co.uk
web: www.thefoxandhoundsinn.co.uk
dir: *3m W of Pickering, off A170, between Pickering & Helmsley*

PETS: **Bedrooms** (4 GF) **Stables Charges** £5 per night **Public areas** except restaurant & lounge bar **Grounds Exercise area Facilities** washing facs walks info vet info **On Request** fridge access **Resident Pets:** Bracken (Hungarian Vizsla), Flax (Labrador)

This attractive inn lies in the quiet village of Sinnington just off the main road. The smartly maintained, yet traditional public areas are cosy and inviting. The menu offers a good selection of freshly cooked, modern British dishes and is available in the restaurant or informally in the bar. Bedrooms and bathrooms are well equipped and offer a good standard of quality and comfort. Service throughout is friendly and attentive.

Rooms 10 (4 GF) **S** £69-£89; **D** £90-£140 (incl. bkfst)* **Facilities** New Year Wi-fi **Parking** 40 **Notes** Closed 25-26 Dec

RAVENSCAR — Map 8 NZ90

Raven Hall Country House
★★★ 75% HOTEL

YO13 0ET
☎ 01723 870353   📄 01723 870072
e-mail: enquiries@ravenhall.co.uk
web: www.ravenhall.co.uk
dir: *A171 towards Whitby. At Cloughton turn right onto unclassified road to Ravenscar*

PETS: **Bedrooms** (5 GF) **Stables** 3m **Charges** £5 per night £30 per week **Public areas** except lounge, bar & restaurant on leads **Grounds** on leads disp bin **Exercise area** 50yds **Facilities** food (pre-bookable) food bowl water bowl bedding dog chews feeding mat scoop/disp bags leads washing facs cage storage walks info vet info **On Request** fridge access torch towels **Other** charge for damage

This impressive cliff top mansion enjoys breathtaking views over Robin Hood's Bay. Extensive well-kept grounds include tennis courts, putting green, swimming pools and historic battlements. The bedrooms vary in size but all are comfortably equipped, many offer panoramic views. There are also eight environmentally-friendly Finnish lodges that have been furnished to a high standard.

Rooms 52 (20 fmly) (5 GF) **S** £45-£81; **D** £90-£162 (incl. bkfst)* **Facilities** ⊠ ♨ 9 ⌣ Putt green ➟ Gym Bowls Table tennis Xmas New Year **Services** Lift **Parking** 200 **Notes** LB

RICCALL — Map 8 SE63

The Park View
★★★★ GUEST ACCOMMODATION

20 Main St YO19 6PX
☎ 01757 248458   📄 01757 249211
e-mail: mail@parkviewriccall.co.uk
web: www.parkviewriccall.co.uk
dir: *A19 from Selby, left for Riccall by water tower, 100yds on right*

PETS: **Bedrooms Charges** £5 per night **Public areas** except dining room & bar **Grounds** disp bin **Exercise area** 150yds **Facilities** leads walks info vet info **On Request** fridge access torch **Other** charge for damage **Resident Pets:** Merty & Elki (Mini Schnauzers), Dougie (Lhasa Apso)

The well-furnished and comfortable Park View stands in grounds and offers well-equipped bedrooms. There is a cosy lounge plus a small bar, while breakfasts are served in the dining room. Dinner is available midweek.

Rooms 7 en suite (1 fmly) **S** £49-£52; **D** £71-£74* **Facilities** TVL tea/coffee Dinner available Cen ht Licensed Wi-fi **Parking** 10

RICHMOND   **Map 7 NZ10**

Brompton Caravan Park (NZ199002)

▶▶▶▶

Brompton-on-Swale DL10 7EZ
☎ 01748 824629 📠 01748 826383
e-mail: brompton.caravanpark@btinternet.com
dir: Exit A1 signed Catterick, continue on B6271 to Brompton-on-Swale, site 1m on left

PETS: Stables 100mtrs **Charges** £1 per night **Public areas** on leads disp bin **Exercise area** field **Facilities** food scoop/disp bags walks info vet info **Other** prior notice required pet shop adjacent **Resident Pets:** Deefur & Barkley (Bassett Hounds), Marley (Staffordshire Terrier), Cleo (Greyhound), Marmie (cat)

Open mid Mar-Oct Last arrival 21.00hrs Last departure noon

An attractive and well-managed family park where pitches have an open outlook across the River Swale. There is a good children's playground, an excellent family recreation room, a take-away food service, and fishing is available on the river. Holiday apartments are also available. A 14 acre site with 177 touring pitches, 2 hardstandings and 22 statics.

Notes No gazebos, no motor or electric cars or scooters, quiet at midnight

RIPON   **Map 8 SE37**

Best Western Ripon Spa

★★★ 79% HOTEL
Park St HG4 2BU
☎ 01765 602172 📠 01765 690770
e-mail: sales@spahotelripon.co.uk
web: www.riponspa.com
dir: From A61 to Ripon, follow Fountains Abbey signs. Hotel on left after hospital. Or from A1(M) junct 48, B6265 to Ripon, straight on at 2 rdbts. Right at lights towards city centre. Left at hill top. Left at Give Way sign. Hotel on left

PETS: Bedrooms (4 GF) unattended **Public areas** except food areas on leads **Grounds** on leads disp bin **Exercise area** 25yds **Facilities** feeding mat litter tray scoop/disp bags leads washing facs cage storage walks info vet info **On Request** fridge access torch towels **Resident Pets:** Labrador

This privately owned hotel is set in extensive and attractive gardens just a short walk from the city centre. The bedrooms are well equipped to meet the needs of leisure and business

travellers alike, while the comfortable lounges are complemented by the convivial atmosphere of the Turf Bar.

Rooms 40 (5 fmly) (4 GF) **S** £66-£126; **D** £82-£140 (incl. bkfst)*
Facilities FTV ♨ Xmas New Year Wi-fi **Services** Lift **Parking** 60
Notes LB

SCARBOROUGH   **Map 8 TA08**

Best Western Ox Pasture Hall Country Hotel

★★★ 81% ⊚ COUNTRY HOUSE HOTEL
Lady Edith's Dr, Raincliffe Woods YO12 5TD
☎ 01723 365295 📠 01723 355156
e-mail: oxpasture.hall@btconnect.com
web: www.oxpasturehall.com
dir: A171, left onto Lady Edith's Drive, 1.5m, hotel on right

PETS: Bedrooms (14 GF) **Charges** £10 per night **Public areas** except restaurant; allowed in brasserie area **Grounds** disp bin **Exercise area** **Facilities** vet info **Other** charge for damage

This charming country hotel is set in the North Riding Forest Park and has a very friendly atmosphere. Bedrooms (split between the main house, townhouse and the delightful courtyard) are stylish, comfortable and well equipped. Public areas include a split-level bar, quiet lounge and an attractive restaurant. There is also an extensive banqueting area licensed for civil weddings.

Rooms 22 (1 fmly) (14 GF) **Facilities** Xmas New Year Wi-fi **Parking** 100

Delmont

★★ 65% HOTEL
18/19 Blenheim Ter YO12 7HE
☎ 01723 364500 📠 01723 363554
e-mail: enquiries@delmonthotel.co.uk
dir: Follow signs to North Bay. At seafront to top of cliff. Hotel near castle

PETS: Bedrooms (5 GF) unattended **Charges** **Public areas** except restaurant on leads **Grounds** on leads disp bin **Exercise area** adjacent **Facilities** vet info **On Request** fridge access **Other** charge for damage

Popular with groups, a friendly welcome is found at this hotel on the North Bay. Bedrooms are comfortable, and many have sea views. There are two lounges, a bar and a spacious dining room in which good-value, traditional food is served along with entertainment on most evenings.

Rooms 51 (18 fmly) (5 GF) **Facilities** Games Room Pool table ♫ Xmas New Year **Services** Lift **Parking** 2

SCARBOROUGH *continued*

Warwick House
★★ GUEST ACCOMMODATION
70 Westborough YO11 1TS
☎ 01723 374343 🖨 01723 374343
e-mail: warwick-house@talktalk.net
dir: *On outskirts of town centre, just before railway station on left*

PETS: Bedrooms Charges £4 per night disp bin Facilities vet
info Restrictions small dogs only Resident Pets: Sassie & Holly
(cats)

Close to the Stephen Joseph Theatre, station and shops, this
friendly guest accommodation has some en suite and some
shared facility rooms. Hearty breakfasts are served in the
pleasant basement dining room. Private parking is available.

Rooms 6 rms (2 en suite) (4 fmly) Facilities tea/coffee Cen ht
Wi-fi Parking 5 Notes 😵

Jacobs Mount Caravan Park *(TA021868)*
►►►►►
Jacobs Mount, Stepney Rd YO12 5NL
☎ 01723 361178 🖨 01723 361178
e-mail: jacobsmount@yahoo.co.uk
dir: *Direct access from A170*

PETS: Stables 1.5m Charges £2.50 per night £17.50 per week
Public areas except toilet block & public house on leads disp
bin Exercise area woods & field walks Facilities food food bowl
water bowl dog chews cat treats scoop/disp bags washing facs
walks info vet info Resident Pets: 2 Dobermans (working dogs)

Open Mar-Nov rs Mar-May & Oct limited hours at shop/bar Last
arrival 22.00hrs Last departure noon

An elevated family-run park surrounded by woodland and open
countryside, yet only two miles from the beach. Touring pitches
are terraced gravel stands with individual services. A licensed
bar and family room provide meals and snacks, and there is a
separate well-equipped games room for teenagers. An 18 acre
site with 156 touring pitches, 131 hardstandings and 60 statics.

Killerby Old Hall *(TA063829)*
►►►
Killerby YO11 3TW
☎ 01723 583799 🖨 01723 581608
e-mail: killerbyhall@btconnect.com
dir: *Direct access via B1261 at Killerby, near Cayton*

PETS: Charges £1 per night Public areas on leads disp bin
Exercise area adjacent field Facilities walks info vet info Other
pets allowed on caravan site area only

Open 14 Feb-4 Jan Last arrival 20.00hrs Last departure noon

A small secluded park, well sheltered by mature trees and
shrubs, located at the rear of the old hall. Use of the small
indoor swimming pool is shared by visitors to the hall's holiday
accommodation. There is a children's play area. A 2 acre site with
20 touring pitches, 20 hardstandings.

Scotch Corner Caravan Park *(NZ210054)*
►►►
DL10 6NS
☎ 01748 822530 🖨 01748 822530
e-mail: marshallleisure@aol.com
dir: *From Scotch Corner junct of A1 & A66 take A6108 towards
Richmond. 250mtrs then cross central reservation, return
200mtrs to site entrance*

PETS: Charges £2 per night Public areas disp bin
Exercise area 3-acre dog walk Facilities vet info Other prior
notice required Resident Pets: Labrador

Open Etr-Oct Last arrival 22.30hrs Last departure noon

A well-maintained site with good facilities, ideally situated as a
stopover, and an equally good location for touring. The Vintage
Hotel which serves food can be accessed from the rear of the site.
A 7 acre site with 96 touring pitches, 4 hardstandings.

Notes 😵

The Ranch Caravan Park *(SE664337)*
►►►
Cliffe Common YO8 6EF
☎ 01757 638984 🖨 01757 630089
e-mail: contact@theranchcaravanpark.co.uk
dir: *Exit A63 at Cliffe signed Skipwith. Site 1m N on left*

PETS: Public areas except toilet block & bar disp bin
Exercise area surrounding countryside, public footpaths
Facilities walks info vet info Other disposal bags available
Resident Pets: Molly, Frieda & Lottie (Scottish Terriers)

Open 5 Feb-5 Jan Last arrival 20.00hrs Last departure noon

A compact, sheltered park in open countryside offering excellent
amenities. The enthusiastic and welcoming family owners
have created a country club feel, with a tasteful bar serving
food at weekends. A 7 acre site with 50 touring pitches, 50
hardstandings.

SKIPTON — Map 7 SD95

The Coniston

★★★ 81% HOTEL

Coniston Cold BD23 4EA

☎ 01756 748080 📄 01756 749487

e-mail: info@theconistonhotel.com

dir: *On A65, 6m NW of Skipton*

PETS: Bedrooms (25 GF) **Stables** 2m **Charges Public areas** except restaurant areas on leads **Grounds** on leads disp bin **Exercise area Facilities** food (pre-bookable) food bowl water bowl pet sitting cage storage walks info vet info **On Request** fridge access torch towels **Other** charge for damage; paddock available

Privately owned and situated on a 1,400 acre estate centred around a beautiful 24-acre lake, this hotel offers guests many exciting outdoor activities. The modern bedrooms are comfortable and most have king-size beds. Macleod's Bar and the main restaurant serve all-day meals, and fine dining is available in the evening from both carte and fixed-price menus. Staff are very friendly and nothing is too much trouble.

Rooms 50 (13 fmly) (25 GF) **S** £99-£159; **D** £165-£225 (incl. bkfst)* **Facilities** STV Fishing Clay pigeon shooting Falconry Off-road Land Rover driving Archery Target golf Xmas New Year Wi-fi **Parking** 120 **Notes** LB

SLINGSBY — Map 8 SE67

Robin Hood Caravan & Camping Park

(SE701748)

▶ ▶ ▶ ▶

Green Dyke Ln YO62 4AP

☎ 01653 628391 📄 01653 628392

e-mail: info@robinhoodcaravanpark.co.uk

dir: *On edge of Slingsby. Access off B1257 (Malton-Helmsley road)*

PETS: Public areas disp bin **Exercise area Facilities** food leads walks info vet info **Other** prior notice required disposal bags available **Resident Pets:** Violet (guinea pig), Milly, Molly & Mandy (chickens), Rocky (tortoise)

Open Mar-Oct Last arrival 18.00hrs Last departure noon

A pleasant, well-maintained grassy park, in a good position for touring North Yorkshire. Situated on the edge of the village of Slingsby, the park has hardstandings and electricity for every pitch. A 2 acre site with 32 touring pitches, 22 hardstandings and 35 statics.

STILLINGFLEET — Map 8 SE54

Home Farm Caravan & Camping *(SE595427)*

▶ ▶ ▶

Moreby YO19 6HN

☎ 01904 728263 📄 01904 720059

e-mail: home_farm@hotmail.co.uk

dir: *6m from York on B1222, 1.5m N of Stillingfleet*

PETS: Public areas on leads disp bin **Exercise area** fields & woodland **Facilities** washing facs walks info vet info **Other** prior notice required **Resident Pets:** cats

Open Feb-Dec Last arrival 22.00hrs

A traditional meadowland site on a working farm bordered by parkland on one side and the River Ouse on another. Facilities are in converted farm buildings, and the family owners extend a friendly welcome to tourers. An excellent site for relaxing and unwinding in, yet only a short distance from the attractions of York. There are four log cabins for holiday hire. A 5 acre site with 25 touring pitches and 2 statics.

Notes 📵

THIRSK Map 8 SE48

Sowerby Caravan Park *(SE437801)*

▶▶▶

Sowerby YO7 3AG
☎ 01845 522753 📠 01845 574520
e-mail: sowerbycaravans@btconnect.com
dir: *From A19 approx 3m S of Thirsk, turn W for Sowerby. Turn right at junct. Site 1m on left*

PETS: Public areas except children's play area **Exercise area** field adjacent **Facilities** food

Open Mar-Oct Last arrival 22.00hrs

A grassy site beside a tree-lined river bank, with basic but functional toilet facilities. Tourers enjoy a separate grassed area with an open outlook, away from the statics. A 1 acre site with 25 touring pitches, 5 hardstandings and 85 statics.

Notes 🐾

Thirkleby Hall Caravan Park *(SE472794)*

▶▶▶

Thirkleby YO7 3AR
☎ 01845 501360 & 07799 641815
e-mail: greenwood.parks@virgin.net
dir: *3m S of Thirsk on A19. Turn E through arched gatehouse into site*

PETS: Public areas on leads **Exercise area** adjacent wood & field **Other** dogs must be under strict control at all times

Open Mar-Oct Last arrival 20.00hrs Last departure 14.30hrs

A long-established site in the grounds of the old hall, with statics in wooded areas around a fishing lake and tourers based on slightly sloping grassy pitches. Toilet facilities are basic but clean and functional, and this well-screened park has superb views of the Hambledon Hills. A 53 acre site with 50 touring pitches, 3 hardstandings and 185 statics.

Notes 🐾

THORNTON WATLASS Map 8 SE28

Buck Inn

★★★ INN

HG4 4AH
☎ 01677 422461 📠 01677 422447
e-mail: innwatlass1@btconnect.com
web: www.thebuckinn.net
dir: *From A1 at Leeming Bar take A684 towards Bedale, B6268 towards Masham 2m, turn right at x-rds to Thornton Watlass*

PETS: Bedrooms unattended **Charges** £5 per night **Public areas** in residents' lounge only **Grounds** disp bin **Exercise area** 300yds **Facilities** water bowl cage storage walks info vet info **On Request** fridge access torch towels

This traditional country inn is situated on the edge of the village green overlooking the cricket pitch. Cricket prints and old photographs are found throughout and an open fire in the bar adds to the warm and intimate atmosphere. Wholesome lunches and dinners, from an extensive menu, are served in the bar or dining room. Bedrooms are brightly decorated and well equipped.

Rooms 7 rms (5 en suite) (1 fmly) (1 GF) **Facilities** TVL tea/coffee Dinner available Cen ht Wi-fi Fishing Pool Table **Parking** 10 **Notes** RS 24-25 Dec No accommodation, no food 25 Dec

TOWTHORPE Map 8 SE65

York Touring Caravan Site *(SE648584)*

▶▶▶▶

Greystones Farm, Towthorpe Moor Ln YO32 9ST
☎ 01904 499275 📠 01904 499271
e-mail: info@yorkcaravansite.co.uk
dir: *Exit A64 at turn for Strensall/Haxby, site 1.5m on left*

PETS: Public areas except shower/ toilet block disp bin **Exercise area** separate dog walking area on adjoining site **Facilities** walks info vet info

Open all year Last arrival 21.00hrs Last departure noon

This purpose built golf complex and caravan park is situated just over five miles from York. There is a 9-hole golf course, driving range and golf shop with a coffee bar/café. The generous sized, level pitches are set within well-manicured grassland with a backdrop of trees and shrubs. A 6 acre site with 44 touring pitches, 12 hardstandings.

ENGLAND

Wolds Way Caravan and Camping *(SE896743)*

▶ ▶ ▶ ▶

West Farm YO17 8JE

☎ 01944 728463 & 728180

e-mail: knapton.wold.farms@farming.co.uk

dir: *Signed between Rillington & West Heslerton on A64 (Malton to Scarborough road). Site 1.5m*

PETS: Sep accom kennel & run **Stables Public areas** disp bin **Exercise area** walks on 200-acre farm **Facilities** food food bowl water bowl dog chews cat treats scoop/disp bags leads washing facs walks info vet info **Restrictions** no Rottweilers **Resident Pets:** 1 terrier, 2 cats & 4 horses

Open Mar-Oct Last arrival 22.30hrs Last departure 19.00hrs

A park on a working farm in a peaceful, high position on the Yorkshire Wolds, with magnificent views over the Vale of Pickering. This is an excellent walking area, with the Wolds Way passing the entrance to the park. A pleasant 1.5 mile path leads to a lavender farm, with its first-class coffee shop. A 7.5 acre site with 70 touring pitches, 5 hardstandings.

The Wensleydale Heifer

★★★★ ◉◉ RESTAURANT WITH ROOMS

Main St DL8 4LS

☎ 01969 622322 & 622725   📠 01969 624183

web: www.wensleydaleheifer.co.uk

dir: *A1 to Leeming Bar junct, A684 towards Bedale for approx 10m to Leyburn, then towards Hawes 3.5m to West Witton*

PETS: Bedrooms unattended **Charges** £10 per night **Public areas** except bar & lounge on leads **Grounds** disp bin **Exercise area** adjacent **Facilities** food bowl water bowl bedding dog chews walks info **On Request** fridge access towels

Describing itself as boutique style, this 17th-century coaching inn has been transformed in recent years. The bedrooms (a four-poster room and junior suite included) are each designed with a unique and interesting theme - for example, Black Sheep, James Herriott, Malt Whisky, Heifer and Shooter, and for chocolate lovers there's an obvious choice of a room where guests can eat as much chocolate as they like! Food is very much the focus here - the informal fish bar and the contemporary style restaurant. The kitchen prides itself on sourcing the freshest fish and locally reared meats.

Rooms 13 en suite (3 fmly) **Facilities** Direct Dial

Cliffemount

★★★ **80%** ◉◉ SMALL HOTEL

Bank Top Ln, Runswick Bay TS13 5HU

☎ 01947 840103   📠 01947 841025

e-mail: info@cliffemounthotel.co.uk

dir: *Exit A174, 8m N of Whitby, 1m to end*

PETS: Bedrooms (5 GF) **Charges** £7.50 per night **Public areas** bar only & not during food service on leads **Grounds** on leads disp bin **Exercise area** adjacent **Facilities** walks info vet info **On Request** towels **Other** charge for damage **Restrictions** no breed larger than a Spaniel **Resident Pet:** Rosie (Bedlington Terrier)

Overlooking Runswick Bay this property offers a relaxed and romantic atmosphere with open fires and individual, carefully designed bedrooms; some have a private balcony overlooking the bay. Dining is recommended; the food is modern British in style and uses locally sourced fresh seafood and game from nearby estates.

Rooms 20 (4 fmly) (5 GF) **Facilities** FTV Xmas New Year Wi-fi **Parking** 25 **Notes** LB

Chiltern Guest House

★★★★ GUEST HOUSE

13 Normanby Ter, West Cliff YO21 3ES

☎ 01947 604981

e-mail: Jjchiltern@aol.com

dir: *Whalebones next to Harbour, sea on right. Royal Hotel on left, 200yds. Royal Gardens turn left, 2nd road on left, 6th house on right*

PETS: Bedrooms sign **Charges Public areas Grounds** on leads disp bin **Exercise area** 300mtrs **Facilities** leads walks info vet info **On Request** torch **Other** charge for damage **Restrictions** no very large dogs

The Victorian terrace house offers a warm welcome and comfortable accommodation within walking distance of the town centre and seafront. Public areas include a smartly decorated lounge and a bright, attractive dining room. Bedrooms are thoughtfully equipped and many have modern en suites.

Rooms 9 en suite (2 fmly) **S** fr £30; **D** £60-£70* **Facilities** TVL tea/coffee Cen ht Wi-fi Golf 18 **Notes** LB

WHITBY *continued*

Arundel House

★★★ GUEST ACCOMMODATION

Bagdale YO21 1QJ

☎ 01947 603645 📠 08703 121974

e-mail: arundel_house@hotmail.com

dir: *A171 town centre, onto Arundel Place at bottom of hill*

PETS: Bedrooms Charges £5 per night £35 per week
Exercise area 500mtrs Facilities cage storage walks info vet info

In a prime location within walking distance of all the attractions, Arundel House's bedrooms are simply furnished and offer good value for money. Expect a helping of true Yorkshire hospitality, and look out for the unique collection of walking canes on show in the house.

Rooms 12 en suite (2 fmly) (2 GF) S £40-£45; D £70-£90*
Facilities tea/coffee Cen ht Wi-fi Parking 6 Notes LB

Ladycross Plantation Caravan Park

(NZ821080)

Egton YO21 1UA

☎ 01947 895502

e-mail: enquiries@ladycrossplantation.co.uk

dir: *On unclassified road (signed) off A171 (Whitby-Teesside road)*

PETS: Charges 1st dog free, additional dogs £1 per night
Public areas except in reception & shop (ex assist dogs) disp bin
Exercise area heath & woodland Facilities walks info vet info
Other prior notice required

Open end Mar-Oct Last arrival 20.30hrs Last departure noon

A delightful woodland setting with pitches sited in small groups in clearings around an amenities block. An additional toilet block offers excellent facilities. The site is well placed for Whitby and the Moors. Children will enjoy exploring the woodland around the site. A 12 acre site with 130 touring pitches, 18 hardstandings.

YORK Map 8 SE65

The Grange

★★★★ 77% ◉◉ HOTEL

1 Clifton YO30 6AA

☎ 01904 644744 📠 01904 612453

e-mail: info@grangehotel.co.uk

web: www.grangehotel.co.uk

dir: *On A19 York/Thirsk road, approx 500yds from city centre*

PETS: Bedrooms (6 GF) unattended Charges £10 per night
disp bin Exercise area 5 mins' walk Facilities walks info vet info On Request fridge access torch towels Other charge for damage Restrictions small to medium size dogs only

This bustling Regency town house is just a few minutes' walk from the centre of York. A professional service is efficiently

delivered by caring staff in a very friendly and helpful manner. Public rooms are comfortable and have been stylishly furnished; these include two dining options, the popular and informal Cellar Bar, and main hotel restaurant The Ivy Brasserie, which offers fine dining in a lavishly decorated environment. The individually designed bedrooms are comfortably appointed and have been thoughtfully equipped.

Rooms 36 (6 GF) S £120-£278; D £134-£278 (incl. bkfst)*
Facilities STV FTV Use of nearby health club Xmas New Year Wi-fi
Parking 26 Notes LB

Best Western Monkbar

★★★ 80% HOTEL

Monkbar YO31 7JA

☎ 01904 638086 📠 01904 629195

e-mail: sales@monkbarhotel.co.uk

dir: *A64 onto A1079 to city, turn right at city walls, take middle lane at lights. Hotel on right*

PETS: Bedrooms (2 GF) unattended sign Charges £7.50 per night Public areas except bar/restaurant on leads Grounds on leads disp bin Exercise area 100yds Facilities food food bowl water bowl bedding dog chews cat treats scoop/disp bags leads pet sitting dog walking cage storage walks info vet info On Request fridge access torch towels Other charge for damage Resident Pet: Misty Monkbar (Golden Labrador)

This smart hotel enjoys a prominent position adjacent to the city walls, and just a few minutes' walk from the cathedral. Individually styled bedrooms are well equipped for both business and leisure guests. Spacious public areas include comfortable lounges, an American-style bar, an airy restaurant and impressive meeting and training facilities.

Rooms 99 (8 fmly) (2 GF) S £95-£120; D £110-£150 (incl. bkfst)
Facilities STV FTV Xmas New Year Wi-fi Services Lift Parking 66
Notes LB

Holiday Inn York

Holiday Inn

★★★ 79% HOTEL

Tadcaster Rd YO24 1QF
☎ 0871 942 9085 📠 01904 702804
e-mail: reservations-york@ihg.com
web: www.holidayinn.co.uk
dir: *From A1(M) take A64 towards York. In 7m take A1036 to York. Straight over at rdbt to city centre. Hotel 0.5m on right*

PETS: Bedrooms (12 GF) **Stables** adjacent **Exercise area** York racecourse adjacent **On Request** fridge access

Located in a suburban area close to the city centre and overlooking York racecourse, this modern hotel caters equally well for business and leisure guests. Public areas include the spacious family friendly Junction Restaurant, lounge bar and the Cedar Tree Terrace. Seven function rooms are also available for meetings and social events.

Rooms 142 (50 fmly) (12 GF) (7 smoking) **Facilities** STV Xmas New Year Wi-fi **Services** Lift Air con **Parking** 200

Ascot House

★★★★ GUEST ACCOMMODATION

80 East Pde YO31 7YH
☎ 01904 426826 📠 01904 431077
e-mail: admin@ascothouseyork.com
web: www.ascothouseyork.com
dir: *0.5m NE of city centre. Off A1036 Heworth Green onto Mill Ln, 2nd left*

PETS: Bedrooms unattended **Public areas** except dining room **Grounds** disp bin **Exercise area** 300yds **Facilities** dog chews feeding mat leads pet sitting washing facs cage storage walks info vet info **On Request** fridge access torch towels **Other** charge for damage **Resident Pets:** Gemma & Millie (Black Labradors)

June and Keith Wood provide friendly service at the 1869 Ascot House, a 15-minute walk from the town centre. Bedrooms are thoughtfully equipped, many with four-poster or canopy beds and

other period furniture. Reception rooms include a cosy lounge that also retains its original features.

Ascot House

Rooms 13 rms (12 en suite) (1 pri facs) (3 fmly) (2 GF) **S** £55-£80; **D** £70-£80 **Facilities** FTV TVL tea/coffee Cen ht Licensed Wi-fi **Parking** 13 **Notes** LB Closed 21-28 Dec

Greenside

★★★ GUEST HOUSE

124 Clifton YO30 6BQ
☎ 01904 623631 📠 01904 623631
e-mail: greenside@onebillnet.co.uk
web: www.greensideguesthouse.co.uk
dir: *A19 N towards city centre, over lights for Greenside, on left opp Clifton Green*

PETS: Bedrooms unattended **Public areas** disp bin **Exercise area** 50yds **Facilities** food bowl water bowl bedding leads walks info vet info **On Request** towels **Resident Pet:** Jessie (Labrador)

Overlooking Clifton Green, this detached house is just within walking distance of the city centre. Accommodation consists of simply furnished bedrooms and there is a cosy lounge and a dining room, where dinners by arrangement and traditional breakfasts are served. It is a family home, and other families are welcome.

Rooms 6 rms (3 en suite) (2 fmly) (3 GF) **S** fr £30; **D** fr £56* **Facilities** TVL tea/coffee Cen ht Wi-fi **Parking** 6 **Notes** LB Closed Xmas & New Year 🐾

YORKSHIRE, SOUTH

ENGLAND

BARNSLEY Map 8 SE30

Best Western Ardsley House Hotel
★★★ 79% HOTEL

Doncaster Rd, Ardsley S71 5EH
☎ 01226 309955 📠 01226 205374
e-mail: ardsley.house@forestdale.com
web: www.ardsleyhousehotel.co.uk
dir: *On A635, 0.75m from Stairfoot rdbt*

PETS: Bedrooms (14 GF) unattended **Charges** £7.50 per night **Public areas** except restaurant

This late 18th-century building has retained many of its original Georgian features. Bedrooms are both comfortable and well equipped. The excellent leisure facilities including a gym, pool and beauty salon. The Allendale Restaurant, with views of the nearby woodlands, offers an extensive menu.

Rooms 75 (12 fmly) (14 GF) **Facilities** Spa ⊗ supervised Gym Beauty spa 3 treatment rooms ♫ Xmas New Year Wi-fi **Parking** 200

DONCASTER Map 8 SE50

Regent
★★★ 77% HOTEL

Regent Square DN1 2DS
☎ 01302 364180 & 381960 📠 01302 322331
e-mail: reservations@theregenthotel.co.uk
web: www.theregenthotel.co.uk
dir: *On corner of A630 & A638, 1m from racecourse*

PETS: Bedrooms (8 GF) unattended **Charges** £5 per stay **Exercise area** opposite **Facilities** vet info **On Request** towels **Other** charge for damage **Restrictions** small dogs only

This town centre hotel overlooks an attractive small square. There is a choice of bars, including the Beatles themed 'Abbey Road' bar in the basement. A wide range of hearty meals are served throughout. The light, airy restaurant provides a more formal option. Service is friendly and attentive. Bedrooms have been furnished in a contemporary style and are very comfortable.

Rooms 53 (6 fmly) (8 GF) **S** £60-£65; **D** £70-£80 (incl. bkfst)* **Facilities** FTV ♫ Wi-fi **Services** Lift **Parking** 20 **Notes** Closed 25 Dec & 1 Jan RS BH

Danum
★★★ 68% HOTEL

High St DN1 1DN
☎ 01302 342261 📠 01302 329034
e-mail: info@danumhotel.com
dir: *M18 junct 3, A6182 to Doncaster. Over rdbt, right at next. Right at 'give way' sign, left at mini rdbt, hotel ahead*

PETS: Bedrooms unattended **Charges Facilities** vet info **Other** charge for damage

Situated in the centre of the town, this Edwardian hotel offers well equipped conference rooms together with comfortable bedrooms. A contemporary lounge area provides modern dining and especially negotiated rates at a local leisure centre are offered.

Rooms 64 (5 fmly) **S** £45-£80; **D** £50-£95 (incl. bkfst) **Facilities** STV FTV Special rates at Cannons Health Club ♫ Xmas New Year Wi-fi **Services** Lift **Parking** 36 **Notes** RS 26-30 Dec

                          Campanile

Campanile Doncaster
BUDGET HOTEL

Doncaster Leisure Park, Bawtry Rd DN4 7PD
☎ 01302 370770 📠 01302 370813
e-mail: doncaster@campanile.com
dir: *Follow signs to Doncaster Leisure Centre, left at rdbt before Dome complex*

PETS: Bedrooms (25 GF) unattended sign **Stables** 1m **Charges** £5 per night **Public areas** except restaurant (assist dogs only) on leads **Grounds** disp bin **Exercise area** surrounding area **Facilities** walks info vet info **On Request** fridge access **Other** charge for damage

This modern building offers accommodation in smart, well-equipped bedrooms, all with en suite bathrooms. Refreshments may be taken at the informal bistro.

Rooms 50 (25 GF)

Hellaby Hall

★★★★ 71% HOTEL

Old Hellaby Ln, Hellaby S66 8SN

☎ 01709 702701 📠 01709 700979

e-mail: reservations@hellabyhallhotel.co.uk

web: www.hellabyhallhotel.co.uk

dir: *0.5m off M18 junct 1, onto A631 towards Maltby. Hotel in Hellaby. (NB do not use postcode for Sat Nav)*

PETS: Bedrooms (17 GF) unattended **Charges Public areas** except restaurant & bar **Grounds** on leads **Exercise area Facilities** food (pre-bookable) food bowl water bowl bedding feeding mat cage storage walks info vet info **On Request** fridge access towels **Other** charge for damage **Resident Pet:** Savah (cat)

This 17th-century house was built to a Flemish design with high, beamed ceilings, staircases which lead off to private meeting rooms and a series of oak-panelled lounges. Bedrooms are elegant and well equipped, and guests can dine in the formal Attic Restaurant. There are extensive leisure facilities and conference areas, and the hotel holds a licence for civil weddings.

Rooms 90 (2 fmly) (17 GF) **S** £49-£200; **D** £49-£250*

Facilities Spa STV FTV ☉ Gym Beauty room Exercise studio Xmas New Year Wi-fi **Services** Lift **Parking** 250 **Notes** LB

Best Western Elton

★★★ 78% HOTEL

Main St, Bramley S66 2SF

☎ 01709 545681 📠 01709 549100

e-mail: bestwestern.eltonhotel@btinternet.com

web: www.bw-eltonhotel.co.uk

dir: *M18 junct 1 follow A631 Rotherham signs, turn right to Ravenfield, hotel at end of Bramley, follow brown signs*

PETS: Bedrooms (11 GF) unattended **Grounds** on leads **Facilities** walks info vet info **On Request** torch

Within easy reach of the M18, this welcoming, stone-built hotel is set in well-tended gardens. The Elton offers good, modern accommodation, with larger rooms in the extension that are particularly comfortable and well equipped. A civil licence is held for wedding ceremonies, and conference rooms are available.

Rooms 29 (16 annexe) (4 fmly) (11 GF) **S** £33.30-£65.50; **D** £42.30-£98* **Facilities** FTV Wi-fi **Parking** 48 **Notes** LB

Novotel Sheffield

★★★★ 70% HOTEL

50 Arundel Gate S1 2PR

☎ 0114 278 1781 📠 0114 278 7744

e-mail: h1348-re@accor.com

web: www.novotel.com

dir: *Between Registry Office & Crucible/Lyceum Theatres, follow signs to Town Hall/Theatres & Hallam University*

PETS: Bedrooms sign **Charges** £10 per night **Public areas** except restaurant on leads disp bin **Facilities** feeding mat walks info vet info **On Request** torch towels **Other** charge for damage **Restrictions** no fighting dogs (see page 7)

In the heart of the city centre, this new generation Novotel has stylish public areas including a very modern restaurant, indoor swimming pool and a range of meeting rooms. Spacious bedrooms are suitable for family occupation, and the Novation rooms are ideal for business users.

Rooms 144 (136 fmly) **S** £69-£179; **D** £69-£199 (incl. bkfst)

Facilities STV FTV ☉ Local gym facilities free for residents use Xmas New Year Wi-fi **Services** Lift Air con **Parking** 60 **Notes** LB

Ibis Sheffield

BUDGET HOTEL

Shude Hill S1 2AR

☎ 0114 241 9600 📠 0114 241 9610

e-mail: H2891@accor.com

web: www.ibishotel.com

dir: *M1 junct 33, follow signs to Sheffield City Centre (A630/A57), at rdbt take 5th exit, signed Ponds Forge, for hotel*

PETS: Bedrooms (3 GF) **Charges Public areas** on leads **Facilities** water bowl **On Request** towels **Other** charge for damage **Restrictions** well behaved dogs only

Modern, budget hotel offering comfortable accommodation in bright and practical bedrooms. Breakfast is self-service and dinner is available in the restaurant.

Rooms 95 (15 fmly) (3 GF) (8 smoking) **S** £35-£89; **D** £35-£89*

ENGLAND

WOODALL MOTORWAY SERVICE AREA (M1)   Map 8 SK48

Days Inn Sheffield
BUDGET HOTEL
Woodall Service Area S26 7XR
☎ 0114 248 7992 📄 0114 248 5634
e-mail: woodall.hotel@welcomebreak.co.uk
web: www.welcomebreak.co.uk
dir: *M1 southbound, at Woodall Services, between juncts 30 & 31*

PETS: Bedrooms (16 GF) unattended **Public areas** on leads
Grounds Exercise area Facilities food bowl water bowl walks
info vet info **On Request** fridge access torch towels **Other**
charge for damage

This modern building offers accommodation in smart, spacious
and well-equipped bedrooms, suitable for families and business
travellers, and all with en suite bathrooms. Continental breakfast
is available and other refreshments may be taken at the nearby
family restaurant.

Rooms 38 (32 fmly) (16 GF) (6 smoking) **S** £29-£59; **D** £29-£59

WORSBROUGH   Map 8 SE30

Greensprings Touring Park *(SE330020)*
►►
Rockley Abbey Farm, Rockley Ln S75 3DS
☎ 01226 288298 📄 01226 288298
dir: *M1 junct 36, A61 to Barnsley. Left after 0.25m signed Pilley.
Site 1m at bottom of hill*

PETS: Stables Public areas except toilets disp bin
Exercise area dog walking area **Facilities** walks info vet info
Other prior notice required max 2 dogs per caravan

Open Apr-Oct Last arrival 21.00hrs Last departure noon

A secluded and attractive farm site set amidst woods and
farmland, with access to the river and several good local walks.
There are two touring areas, one gently sloping. Although not
far from the M1, there is almost no traffic noise, and this site is
convenient for exploring the area's industrial heritage, as well
as the Peak District. A 4 acre site with 65 touring pitches, 5
hardstandings.

Notes 😊

YORKSHIRE, WEST

BINGLEY   Map 7 SE13

Five Rise Locks Hotel & Restaurant
★★ 74% SMALL HOTEL
Beck Ln BD16 4DD
☎ 01274 565296 📄 01274 568828
e-mail: info@five-rise-locks.co.uk
dir: *Off Main St onto Park Rd, 0.5m left onto Beck Ln*

PETS: Bedrooms (2 GF) unattended **Stables** 3m **Charges** £5
per night **Grounds** disp bin **Exercise area** 300yds **Facilities**
scoop/disp bags washing facs cage storage walks info vet
info **On Request** fridge access torch towels **Other** charge for
damage **Resident Pets:** Ruby & Tilly (Bassett Hounds)

A warm welcome and comfortable accommodation await you at
this impressive Victorian building. Bedrooms are of a good size
and feature homely extras. The restaurant offers imaginative
dishes and the bright breakfast room overlooks open countryside.

Rooms 9 (2 GF) **Facilities** FTV Wi-fi **Parking** 20

BRADFORD   Map 7 SE13

Best Western Guide Post Hotel
★★★ 75% HOTEL
Common Rd, Low Moor BD12 0ST
☎ 0845 409 1362 & 01274 607866 📄 01274 671085
e-mail: sue.barnes@guideposthotel.net
web: www.guideposthotel.net
dir: *From M606 rdbt take 2nd exit. At next rdbt take 1st exit
(Cleckheaton Rd). 0.5m, turn right at bollard into Common Rd*

PETS: Bedrooms (13 GF) unattended **Public areas** except
restaurant & bar on leads **Exercise area** 2 mins **Facilities**
washing facs cage storage vet info **On Request** fridge access
torch towels **Other** charge for damage

Situated south of the city, this hotel offers attractively styled,
modern, comfortable bedrooms. The restaurant offers an
extensive range of food using fresh, local produce; lighter snack
meals are served in the bar. There is also a choice of well-
equipped meeting and function rooms. There is disabled access
to the hotel, restaurant and one function room.

Rooms 42 (10 fmly) (13 GF) (8 smoking) **S** £48.50-£68.50;
D £56-£76 (incl. bkfst) **Facilities** STV FTV Complimentary use of
nearby swimming & gym facilities Wi-fi **Parking** 100

DEWSBURY **Map 8 SE22**

Heath Cottage Hotel & Restaurant

★★★ 72% HOTEL

Wakefield Rd WF12 8ET

☎ 01924 465399 🖩 01924 459405

e-mail: info@heathcottage.co.uk

dir: *M1 junct 40/A638 for 2.5m towards Dewsbury. Hotel before lights, opposite Earlsheaton Cemetery*

PETS: Bedrooms (3 GF) unattended **Charges** £7.50 per night **Public areas** except restaurant & bar on leads **Grounds** on leads disp bin **Exercise area** 150mtrs **Facilities** food (pre-bookable) **Other** charge for damage

Standing in an acre of grounds, Heath Cottage is just two and a half miles from the M1. The service is friendly and professional. All the bedrooms are modern and well appointed, and some are in a converted stable building. The lounge bar and restaurant are air conditioned. Extensive parking is available.

Rooms 28 (6 annexe) (3 fmly) (3 GF) **S** £40-£89; **D** £55-£99 (incl. bkfst)* **Facilities** Wi-fi **Parking** 60 **Notes** LB RS 23-27 Dec

GARFORTH **Map 8 SE43**

Holiday Inn Leeds Garforth

★★★ 83% HOTEL

Wakefield Rd LS25 1LH

☎ 0113 286 6556 🖩 0113 286 8326

e-mail: reservations@hileedsgarforth.com

web: www.holidayinn.co.uk

dir: *At junct of A63/A642. Hotel opposite rdbt*

PETS: Bedrooms (35 GF) unattended **Charges** £10 per night **Public areas Grounds** on leads disp bin **Exercise area** 200yds **Facilities** walks info vet info **Other** charge for damage

Located just outside Leeds, this hotel has excellent access to the M1 and M62 making it an ideal base for exploring the area. Well-equipped accommodation includes executive bedrooms. Public areas are attractively designed and include meeting rooms and leisure club. Aioli's Restaurant serves contemporary cuisine.

Rooms 144 (30 fmly) (35 GF) (15 smoking) **Facilities** FTV 🖭 supervised Gym New Year Wi-fi **Services** Air con **Parking** 250

Best Western Milford Hotel

★★★ 81% HOTEL

A1 Great North Rd, Peckfield LS25 5LQ

☎ 01977 681800 🖩 01977 681245

e-mail: enquiries@mlh.co.uk

web: www.mlh.co.uk

dir: *On A63, 1.5m W of A1(M) junct 42 & 4.5m E of M1 junct 46*

PETS: Bedrooms (13 GF) unattended **Stables** 3m **Charges** £7.50 per night disp bin **Exercise area** 200yds **Facilities** food (pre-bookable) food bowl water bowl walks info vet info **On Request** torch **Other** charge for damage pets allowed in standard bedrooms only

This friendly, family owned and run hotel is conveniently situated, and provides very comfortable, modern accommodation. The air-conditioned bedrooms are particularly spacious and well equipped, and ten boutique-style superior rooms are available. Public areas include a relaxing lounge area, the contemporary Watermill Restaurant and lounge bar which has a working waterwheel.

Rooms 46 (13 GF) (6 smoking) **S** £53.10-£79; **D** £60.30-£87* **Facilities** FTV Xmas New Year Wi-fi **Services** Air con **Parking** 80 **Notes** LB

GOMERSAL **Map 8 SE22**

Gomersal Park

★★★ 79% HOTEL

Moor Ln BD19 4LJ

☎ 01274 869386 🖩 01274 861042

e-mail: enquiries@gomersalparkhotel.com

web: www.gomersalparkhotel.com

dir: *A62 to Huddersfield. At junct with A65, by Greyhound Pub right, after 1m take 1st right after Oakwell Hall*

PETS: Bedrooms (32 GF) unattended **Charges Public areas** except restaurant & bar on leads **Grounds** disp bin **Exercise area** 100yds **Facilities** food bowl water bowl washing facs cage storage walks info vet info **On Request** fridge access torch towels **Other** charge for damage **Resident Pet:** Teal (English Pointer)

Constructed around a 19th-century house, this stylish, modern hotel enjoys a peaceful location and pleasant grounds. Deep sofas ensure comfort in the open-plan lounge and imaginative meals are served in the popular Brasserie 101. The well-equipped bedrooms provide high quality and comfort. Extensive public areas include a well-equipped leisure complex and pool, and a wide variety of air-conditioned conference rooms.

Rooms 100 (3 fmly) (32 GF) **S** £50-£120; **D** £50-£120 **Facilities** FTV 🖭 supervised Gym Wi-fi **Services** Lift **Parking** 150 **Notes** LB

HALIFAX Map 7 SE02

Holdsworth House
★★★ 85% ◉◉ HOTEL

Holdsworth HX2 9TG
☎ 01422 240024 📄 01422 245174
e-mail: info@holdsworthhouse.co.uk
web: www.holdsworthhouse.co.uk
dir: *From town centre take A629 (Keighley road). Right at garage up Shay Ln after 1.5m. Hotel on right after 1m*

PETS: Bedrooms (15 GF) **Charges** £10 per night **Public areas** except restaurant area on leads **Grounds** on leads
Exercise area 500yds **Facilities** walks info vet info **On Request** fridge access **Other** charge for damage **Restrictions** small to medium sized dogs only

This delightful 17th-century Jacobean manor house, set in well tended gardens, offers individually decorated, thoughtfully equipped bedrooms. Public rooms, adorned with beautiful paintings and antique pieces, include a choice of inviting lounges and superb conference and function facilities. Dinner provides the highlight of any stay and is served in the elegant restaurant by friendly, attentive staff.

Rooms 40 (2 fmly) (15 GF) **Facilities** FTV New Year Wi-fi **Parking** 60 **Notes** LB

HARTSHEAD MOOR MOTORWAY SERVICE AREA (M62) Map 8 SE12

Days Inn Bradford
BUDGET HOTEL

Hartshead Moor Service Area, Clifton HD6 4JX
☎ 01274 851706 📄 01274 855169
e-mail: hartshead.hotel@welcomebreak.co.uk
web: www.welcomebreak.co.uk
dir: *M62 between junct 25 and 26*

PETS: Bedrooms (16 GF) unattended **Public areas** **Grounds** on leads disp bin **Exercise area** surrounding fields **Facilities** vet info **On Request** fridge access **Other** charge for damage

This modern building offers accommodation in smart, spacious and well-equipped bedrooms, suitable for families and business travellers, and all with en suite bathrooms. Continental breakfast is available and other refreshments may be taken at the nearby family restaurant.

Rooms 38 (33 fmly) (16 GF) **S** £29-£49; **D** £29-£49

HUDDERSFIELD Map 7 SE11

The Huddersfield Central Lodge
★★★★ GUEST ACCOMMODATION

11/15 Beast Market HD1 1QF
☎ 01484 515551 📄 01484 432349
e-mail: enquiries@centrallodge.com
web: www.centrallodge.com
dir: *In town centre off Lord St, signs for Beast Market from ring road*

PETS: Bedrooms unattended **Charges** **Public areas** except breakfast room at meals time **Grounds** on leads disp bin
Exercise area 500mtrs **Facilities** washing facs cage storage walks info vet info **On Request** fridge access torch towels
Other charge for damage

This friendly, family-run operation offers smart spacious bedrooms with modern en suites. Some rooms are in the main building, while new rooms, many with kitchenettes, are situated across a courtyard. Public rooms include a bar and a conservatory, and there are arrangements for local restaurants to charge meals to guests' accounts. Secure complimentary parking.

Rooms 9 en suite 13 annexe en suite (2 fmly) (6 smoking)
S £52-£58; **D** £68* **Facilities** FTV TVL tea/coffee Direct Dial Cen ht Licensed Wi-fi **Parking** 50

Griffin Lodge Guest House

★★★ GUEST HOUSE

273 Manchester Rd HD4 5AG

☎ 01484 431042 📠 01484 431043

e-mail: info@griffinlodge.co.uk

web: www.griffinlodge.co.uk

PETS: **Bedrooms Public areas Grounds** on leads disp bin **Facilities** walks info vet info **Resident Pets:** Ben (German Shepherd cross) & Polly (mongrel)

Located on the outskirts of Huddersfield and close to the villages of Holmfirth and Marsden, Griffin Lodge is family run and offers comfortable well appointed accommodation. Either continental or a full hearty cooked breakfast is served in the small dining room and there is parking to the rear.

Rooms 6 en suite (4 fmly) (6 GF) **S** £35-£45; **D** fr £45*

Facilities FTV tea/coffee Cen ht Wi-fi **Parking** 10

ILKLEY   Map 7 SE14

Best Western Rombalds Hotel & Restaurant

★★★ 83% ◉ HOTEL

11 West View, Wells Rd LS29 9JG

☎ 01943 603201 📠 01943 816586

e-mail: reception@rombalds.demon.co.uk

web: www.rombalds.co.uk

dir: A65 from Leeds. Left at 3rd main lights, follow Ilkley Moor signs. Right at HSBC Bank onto Wells Rd. Hotel 600yds on left

PETS: **Bedrooms** sign **Stables** 6m **Charges** £10 per night £50 per week **Grounds** on leads disp bin **Exercise area** adjacent **Facilities** water bowl walks info vet info **On Request** fridge access torch

This elegantly furnished Georgian townhouse is located in a peaceful terrace between the town and the moors. Delightful day rooms include a choice of comfortable lounges and an attractive restaurant that provides a relaxed venue in which to sample the skilfully prepared, imaginative meals. The bedrooms are tastefully furnished, well equipped and include several spacious suites.

Rooms 15 (2 fmly) **Facilities** STV Xmas Wi-fi **Parking** 28 **Notes** Closed 28 Dec-2 Jan

KEIGHLEY   Map 7 SE04

Dalesgate

★★ 70% HOTEL

406 Skipton Rd, Utley BD20 6HP

☎ 01535 664930 📠 01535 611253

e-mail: stephen.e.atha@btinternet.com

dir: In town centre follow A629 over rdbt onto B6265. Right after 0.75m into St. John's Rd. 1st right into hotel car park

PETS: **Bedrooms** (3 GF) unattended **Charges Public areas** except bar & restaurant **Exercise area** 300yds **Facilities** food bowl water bowl leads washing facs cage storage walks info vet info **On Request** fridge access torch towels **Other** charge for damage **Resident Pets:** Dan & Silk (German Shepherds)

Originally the residence of a local chapel minister, this modern, well-established hotel provides well-equipped, comfortable bedrooms. It also boasts a cosy bar and pleasant restaurant, serving an imaginative range of dishes. A large car park is provided to the rear.

Rooms 20 (2 fmly) (3 GF) **Parking** 25 **Notes** RS 22 Dec-4 Jan

LEEDS   Map 8 SE33

Malmaison Leeds

★★★ 83% ◉ HOTEL

1 Swinegate LS1 4AG

☎ 0113 398 1000 📠 0113 398 1002

e-mail: leeds@malmaison.com

web: www.malmaison.com

dir: M621/M1 junct 3, follow city centre signs. At KPMG building, right into Sovereign Street. Hotel at end on right

PETS: **Bedrooms** unattended **Charges** £10 per stay **Public areas** except bar & restaurant on leads **Facilities** food (pre-bookable) food bowl water bowl bedding dog chews cat treats feeding mat vet info **On Request** fridge access torch towels **Other** charge for damage

Close to the waterfront, this stylish property offers striking bedrooms with CD players and air conditioning. The popular bar and brasserie feature vaulted ceilings, intimate lighting and offer a choice of a full three-course meal or a substantial snack. Service is both willing and friendly. A small fitness centre and impressive meeting rooms complete the package.

Rooms 100 (4 fmly) **S** £75-£140; **D** £75-£375* **Facilities** STV Gym Xmas New Year Wi-fi **Services** Lift Air con **Notes** LB

ENGLAND

OSSETT   Map 8 SE22

Heath House
★ ★ ★ ★ GUEST ACCOMMODATION
Chancery Rd WF5 9RZ
☎ 01924 260654 & 07890 385622   📠 01924 263131
e-mail: bookings@heath-house.co.uk
web: www.heath-house.co.uk
dir: M1 junct 40, A638 towards Dewsbury, at end dual
carriageway exit rdbt 2nd left, house 20yds on right

PETS: Bedrooms sign **Sep accom** room specifically for dogs
Public areas Grounds disp bin **Exercise area** 600yds **Facilities**
food (pre-bookable) food bowl water bowl bedding leads pet
sitting dog walking washing facs cage storage walks info vet
info **On Request** fridge access torch towels **Other** charge for
damage **Resident Pets:** Sally (Greyhound), Diesel (Japanese
Akita)

The spacious Victorian family home stands in four acres of
tranquil gardens a short distance from the M1. It has elegant en
suite bedrooms, and the courteous and friendly owners provide
healthy, freshly-cooked breakfasts.

Rooms 2 en suite 2 annexe en suite (1 fmly) (2 GF) **S** £35-£40;
D £50-£55* **Facilities** tea/coffee Cen ht Fishing **Parking** 16

OTLEY   Map 7 SE24

Chevin Country Park Hotel & Spa
★ ★ ★ 74% HOTEL
Yorkgate LS21 3NU
☎ 01943 467818   📠 01943 850335
e-mail: chevin@crerarhotels.com
dir: From Leeds/Bradford Airport rdbt take A658 N, towards
Harrogate, for 0.75m to 1st lights. Turn left, then 2nd left onto
'Yorkgate'. Hotel 0.5m on left

PETS: Bedrooms (45 GF) unattended **Charges** £10 per night
Grounds on leads **Facilities** walks info vet info **On Request**
torch towels **Other** pet allowed in lodge rooms only; 44 acres of
woodland available

Peacefully located in its own woodland yet convenient for major
road links and the airport. Bedrooms are split between the
original main log building and chalet-style accommodation in
the extensive grounds. Public areas include a bar and several
lounges. The Lakeside Restaurant provides views over the small
lake and good leisure facilities are available.

Rooms 49 (30 annexe) (7 fmly) (45 GF) **Facilities** FTV 🎾 🛁
Fishing Gym Xmas New Year Wi-fi **Parking** 100 **Notes** LB

WAKEFIELD   Map 8 SE32

Holiday Inn Leeds - Wakefield
★ ★ ★ 75% HOTEL
Queen's Dr, Ossett WF5 9BE
☎ 0870 400 9082   📠 01924 230684
e-mail: wakefield@ichotelsgroup.com
web: www.holidayinn.co.uk
dir: M1 junct 40 follow signs for Wakefield. Hotel on right in
200yds

PETS: Bedrooms (35 GF) sign **Charges Grounds** on leads
Exercise area field adjacent **Other** charge for damage dogs are
required to be muzzled & on leads

Situated close to major motorway networks, this modern hotel
offers well-equipped and comfortable bedrooms. Public areas
include the popular Traders restaurant and a comfortable lounge
where a menu is available throughout the day. Conference
facilities are also available.

Rooms 104 (32 fmly) (35 GF) (9 smoking) **Facilities** STV Xmas
New Year Wi-fi **Services** Lift Air con **Parking** 105

Stanley View Guest House
★ ★ ★ GUEST HOUSE
226-230 Stanley Rd WF1 4AE
☎ 01924 376803   📠 01924 369123
e-mail: enquiries@stanleyviewguesthouse.co.uk
dir: M62 junct 30, follow Aberford Rd 3m. Signed on left

PETS: Bedrooms Public areas except dining area on leads
Exercise area Facilities vet info **Other** charge for damage dogs
in ground floor bedrooms only

Part of an attractive terrace, this well established guest house
is just half a mile from the city centre and has private parking
at the rear. The well equipped bedrooms are brightly decorated,
and there is a licensed bar and comfortable lounge. Hearty home-
cooked meals are served in the attractive dining room.

Rooms 17 rms (13 en suite) (6 fmly) (7 GF) **S** £30-£37; **D** £50*
Facilities STV TVL tea/coffee Dinner available Direct Dial Cen ht
Licensed **Parking** 10

WETHERBY Map 8 SE44

Days Inn Wetherby

BUDGET HOTEL

Junction 46 A1(M), Kirk Deighton LS22 5GT
☎ 01937 547557 📄 01937 547559
e-mail: reservations@daysinnwetherby.co.uk
dir: *A1(M) junct 46 at Moto Service Area*

PETS: Bedrooms (35 GF) unattended **Charges** £10 per room
per night **Public areas** on leads **Grounds** on leads disp bin
Facilities vet info **Other** charge for damage **Restrictions** small
dogs only

This modern building offers accommodation in smart, spacious
and well-equipped bedrooms, suitable for families and business
travellers, and all with en suite bathrooms. Continental breakfast
is available and other refreshments may be taken at the nearby
family restaurant.

Rooms 129 (33 fmly) (35 GF)

CHANNEL ISLANDS
GUERNSEY

CASTEL Map 16

Fauxquets Valley Campsite

▶ ▶ ▶ ▶

GY5 7QL
☎ 01481 236951 & 07781 413333
e-mail: info@fauxquets.co.uk
dir: *Off pier. 2nd exit off rdbt. Top of hill left onto Queens Rd.
Continue for 2m. Turn right onto Candie Rd. Opposite sign for
German Occupation Museum*

PETS: Public areas on leads disp bin **Exercise area** field
Facilities washing facs walks info vet info **Other** prior notice
required **Resident Pets:** Bracken (Jack Russell), Morley
(Chocolate Labrador), Blackie (Black Labrador)

Open mid Jun-Aug

A beautiful, quiet farm site in a hidden valley close to the sea.
Friendly helpful owners, who understand campers' needs, offer
good quality facilities and amenities, including upgraded toilets,
an outdoor swimming pool, bar/restaurant, nature trail and
sports areas. A 3 acre site with 120 touring pitches.

VALE Map 16

La Bailloterie Camping & Leisure

▶ ▶ ▶

Bailloterie Ln GY3 5HA
☎ 01481 243636 & 07781 103420 📄 01481 243225
e-mail: info@campinginguernsey.com
dir: *3m N of St Peter Port, take Vale road to Crossways, turn right
into Rue du Braye. Site 1st left at sign*

PETS: Public areas except building & outdoor eating areas
Exercise area suitable areas nearby **Facilities** washing facs
vet info **Other** prior notice required disposal bags available
Restrictions no dangerous dogs (see page 7)

Open 15 May-15 Sep Last arrival 23.00hrs

A pretty rural site with one large touring field and a few small,
well-screened paddocks. This delightful site has been in the
same family ownership for over 30 years, and offers super
facilities in converted outbuildings. A 12 acre site with 100
touring pitches.

JERSEY

GOREY Map 16

Old Court House

★ ★ ★ 71% HOTEL

JE3 9FS
☎ 01534 854444 📄 01534 853587
e-mail: ochhotel@itl.net
web: www.ochhoteljersey.com

PETS: Bedrooms (9 GF) **Charges** £6 per night **Exercise area**
50yds **Facilities** bedding pet sitting washing facs cage storage
walks info vet info **On Request** fridge access torch towels
Other charge for damage

Situated on the east of the island, a short walk from the beach,
this long established hotel continues to have a loyal following for
its relaxed atmosphere and friendly staff. Bedrooms are of similar
standard throughout and some have balconies overlooking the
gardens. Spacious public areas include a comfortable, quiet
lounge, a restaurant, and a large bar with a dance floor.

Rooms 58 (4 fmly) (9 GF) **S** £50-£69; **D** £100-£151 (incl. bkfst)*
Facilities STV ⚲ ♫ Wi-fi **Services** Lift **Parking** 40 **Notes** LB
Closed Nov-Mar

ENGLAND

ENGLAND

ROZEL — Map 16

Château la Chaire

★★★ ◎◎ HOTEL

Rozel Bay JE3 6AJ

☎ 01534 863354 📄 01534 865137

e-mail: res@chateau-la-chaire.co.uk

web: www.chateau-la-chaire.co.uk

dir: *From St Helier on B38 turn left in village by Rozel Bay Inn, hotel 100yds on right*

PETS: Bedrooms (1 GF) **Charges** £10 per night **Grounds Exercise area** 50yds **Facilities** food bowl water bowl walks info vet info **On Request** fridge access torch towels **Other** charge for damage dogs allowed in suite only **Resident Pet:** Jasmine (Labrador)

Built as a gentleman's residence in 1843, Château la Chaire is a haven of peace and tranquillity, set within a secluded wooded valley. Picturesque Rozel Harbour is within easy walking distance and the house is surrounded by terraced gardens. There is a wonderful atmosphere here and the helpful staff deliver high standards of guest care. Imaginative menus, making the best use of local produce, are served in the oak-panelled dining room. Bedrooms styles and sizes are varied - all are beautifully appointed and include many nice touches such as flowers and mineral water.

Rooms 14 (2 fmly) (1 GF) **D** £95-£295 (incl. bkfst)* **Facilities** STV Xmas New Year Wi-fi **Parking** 30 **Notes** LB No children 7yrs

ST BRELADE — Map 16

Hotel Miramar

★★ 72% HOTEL

Mont Gras d'Eau JE3 8ED

☎ 01534 743831 📄 01534 745009

e-mail: miramarjsy@localdial.com

dir: *From airport take B36 at lights, turn left onto A13, 1st right into Mont Gras d'Eau*

PETS: Bedrooms (12 GF) unattended **Public areas** on leads disp bin **Exercise area** 100yds **Facilities** cage storage walks info vet info

A friendly welcome awaits at this family-run hotel set in delightful sheltered gardens, overlooking the beautiful bay. Accommodation is comfortable with well-appointed bedrooms; some are on the ground floor, and there are two on the lower ground with their own terrace overlooking the outdoor heated pool. The restaurant offers a varied set menu.

Rooms 38 (2 fmly) (12 GF) (4 smoking) **S** £33-£50.90; **D** £66-£101.80 (incl. bkfst)* **Facilities** 🏊 Wi-fi **Parking** 30 **Notes** LB Closed Oct-mid Apr

ST MARTIN — Map 16

Beuvelande Camp Site

►►►►►

Beuvelande JE3 6EZ

☎ 01534 853575 📄 01534 857788

e-mail: info@campingjersey.com

dir: *Take A6 from St Helier to St Martin & follow signs to site before St Martins Church*

PETS: Charges dog £2 per night **Public areas** on leads disp bin **Exercise area Facilities** walks info **Other** prior notice required **Restrictions** no Staffordshire Bull Terriers or Rottweilers

Open Apr-Sep rs Apr-May & Sep pool & restaurant closed, shop hours limited

A well-established site with excellent toilet facilities, accessed via narrow lanes in peaceful countryside close to St Martin. An attractive bar/restaurant is the focal point of the park, especially in the evenings, and there is a small swimming pool and playground. Motorhomes and towed caravans will be met at the ferry and escorted to the site if requested when booking. A 6 acre site with 150 touring pitches and 75 statics.

ST OUEN — Map 16

Bleu Soleil Campsite

►►►►

La Route de Vinchelez, Leoville JE3 2DB

☎ 01534 481007 📄 01534 481525

e-mail: info@bleusoleilcamping.com

dir: *From St Helier ferry port take A2 towards St Aubin then turn right onto A12 passing airport to Leoville. Site on right of La Route de Vinchelez*

PETS: Stables 1m **Public areas** except café, shop, TV lounge & swimming pool area disp bin **Exercise area** beach nearby **Facilities** food bowl water bowl washing facs walks info vet info **Other** prior notice required owners must clean up after their pets **Resident Pets:** 1 dog, cats

Open all year Last arrival 23.00hrs Last departure 10.00hrs

A compact tent park set in the NW corner of the island and surrounded by beautiful countryside. Greve-de-Lacq beach is close by, and the golden beaches at St Ouen's Bay and St Brelade's Bay are only a short drive away. There are 45 ready-erected tents and 6 family tipis for hire. A 1.5 acre site with 55 touring pitches, 8 hardstandings and 45 statics.

Notes No noise after 22.00hrs

ST SAVIOUR — Map 16

Longueville Manor
★★★★★ @@@ HOTEL
JE2 7WF
☎ 01534 725501 📄 01534 731613
e-mail: info@longuevillemanor.com
web: www.longuevillemanor.com
dir: A3 E from St Helier towards Gorey. Hotel 1m on left

PETS: Bedrooms (7 GF) unattended **Grounds** disp bin
Exercise area beach 0.5m **Facilities** feeding mat cage storage
walks info vet info **On Request** fridge access torch towels

Dating back to the 13th century, there is something very special
about Longueville Manor, which is why so many guests return
time and again. It is set in 17 acres of grounds including
woodland walks, a spectacular rose garden and a lake. Bedrooms
have great style and individuality boasting fresh flowers, fine
embroidered bed linen and a host of extras. The committed team
of staff create a welcoming atmosphere and every effort is made
to ensure a memorable stay. The very accomplished cuisine is
also a highlight of any stay.

Rooms 30 (1 annexe) (7 GF) (6 smoking) **S** £195-£370;
D £220-£630 (incl. bkfst)* **Facilities** STV 🎾 ☺️🏊 Xmas New
Year Wi-fi **Services** Lift **Parking** 40 **Notes** LB

ISLE OF MAN

PORT ERIN — Map 6 SC16

Falcon's Nest
★★ 71% HOTEL
The Promenade IM9 6AF
☎ 01624 834077 📄 01624 835370
e-mail: falconsnest@enterprise.net
web: www.falconsnesthotel.co.uk
dir: Follow coast road S from airport or ferry. Hotel on seafront,
immediately after steam railway station

PETS: Bedrooms unattended sign **Public areas** except food
areas, bars & restaurant on leads **Grounds** on leads disp bin
Exercise area 50mtrs to beach/park **Facilities** walks info vet
info **On Request** fridge access towels

Situated overlooking the bay and harbour, this Victorian hotel
offers generally spacious bedrooms. There is a choice of bars,
one of which attracts many locals. Meals can be taken in the
lounge bar, the conservatory or in the attractively decorated main
restaurant.

Rooms 39 (9 fmly) (15 smoking) **S** £35-£42.50; **D** £70-£100 (incl.
bkfst)* **Facilities** FTV Xmas New Year Wi-fi **Parking** 20

Scotland

CITY OF ABERDEEN

ABERDEEN　　　　　　　　　　Map 15 NJ90

Doubletree by Hilton Aberdeen

★★★★　78%　HOTEL

Beach Boulevard AB24 5EF
☎ 01224 633339 & 380000　🖷 01224 638833
e-mail: sales.doubletreeaberdeen@hilton.com
web: www.hilton.co.uk/aberdeencity
dir: *From A90 follow signs for city centre, then for beach. On Beach Blvd, left at lights, hotel on right*

PETS: **Bedrooms** (22 GF) **Charges** £10 per night **Public areas** on leads **Grounds** on leads disp bin **Exercise area** 100yds **Other** charge for damage **Restrictions** small dogs only

This modern, purpose-built hotel lies close to the seafront. Bedrooms come in two different styles - the retro-style Classics and spacious Premiers. In addition the Platinum Club offers a unique experience of 44 superb high-spec bedrooms that have their own reception bar, lounge and dinner and breakfast room. The restaurant and striking Atrium bar are housed in the main building.

Rooms 168 (44 annexe) (8 fmly) (22 GF) **S** £65-£165; **D** £65-£165 **Facilities** Spa STV ☜ Gym Steam room Treatment rooms Nail bar Sauna Solarium Fitness Studio New Year Wi-fi **Services** Lift **Parking** 172 **Notes** LB

Malmaison Aberdeen

Malmaison
hotels that dare to be different

★★★　86%　◉◉　HOTEL

49-53 Queens Rd AB15 4YP
☎ 01224 327370　🖷 01224 327371
e-mail: info.aberdeen@malmaison.com
dir: *A90, 3rd exit onto Queens Rd at 3rd rdbt, hotel on right*

PETS: **Bedrooms** (10 GF) unattended **Stables** 2m **Charges** £10 for dog bowl and bed **Public areas** except restaurant on leads **Exercise area** 2m **Facilities** food bowl water bowl bedding cage storage walks info vet info **On Request** fridge access torch towels

Popular with business travellers and as a function venue, this well-established hotel lies east of the city centre. Public areas include a reception lounge and an intimate restaurant; however the extensive bar menu remains a preferred choice for many regulars. There are two styles of accommodation, with the superior rooms being particularly comfortable and well equipped.

Rooms 79 (8 fmly) (10 GF) **D** £95-£395* **Facilities** Spa STV FTV Gym Steam room Xmas New Year Wi-fi **Services** Lift **Parking** 50 **Notes** LB

ABERDEENSHIRE

ABOYNE　　　　　　　　　　Map 15 NO59

Aboyne Loch Caravan Park *(NO538998)*

►►►

AB34 5BR
☎ 013398 86244 & 013398 82589　🖷 013398 82589
dir: *On A93, 1m E of Aboyne*

PETS: **Public areas** disp bin **Exercise area** dog walks **Facilities** walks info vet info

Open 31 Mar-Oct Last arrival 20.00hrs Last departure 11.00hrs

Attractively sited caravan park set amidst woodland on the shores of the lovely Aboyne Loch in scenic Deeside. The facilities are modern and immaculately maintained, and amenities include boat-launching, boating and fishing. An ideally situated park for touring Royal Deeside and the Aberdeenshire uplands. A 6 acre site with 20 touring pitches, 25 hardstandings and 120 statics.

Notes ⊗

BALLATER　　　　　　　　　　Map 15 NO39

Darroch Learg

★★★　◉◉◉　SMALL HOTEL

Braemar Rd AB35 5UX
☎ 013397 55443　🖷 013397 55252
e-mail: enquiries@darrochlearg.co.uk
web: www.darrochlearg.co.uk
dir: *On A93, W of Ballater*

PETS: **Bedrooms** (1 GF) **Stables** 1m **Public areas** except restaurant & drawing room **Grounds** disp bin **Exercise area** adjacent **Facilities** food bowl water bowl bedding walks info vet info **On Request** fridge access torch towels **Resident Pet:** Isla (Black Labrador)

Set high above the road in extensive wooded grounds, this long-established hotel offers superb views over the hills and countryside of Royal Deeside. Nigel and Fiona Franks are caring and attentive hosts who improve their hotel every year. Bedrooms, some with four-poster beds, are individually styled, bright and spacious. Food is a highlight of any visit, whether it is a freshly prepared breakfast or the fine cuisine served in the delightful conservatory restaurant.

Rooms 17 (5 annexe) (1 GF) **S** £130-£190; **D** £210-£320 (incl. bkfst & dinner)* **Facilities** New Year **Parking** 25 **Notes** LB Closed Xmas & Jan (ex New Year)

Banchory Lodge Hotel
★★★ 81% ⊛ COUNTRY HOUSE HOTEL

AB31 5HS

☎ 01330 822625 & 822681   🖷 01330 825019

e-mail: enquiries@banchorylodge.co.uk

web: www.banchorylodge.co.uk

dir: *Off A93, 13m W of Aberdeen, hotel off Dee St*

PETS: Bedrooms Stables 5m **Charges** £10 per night £60 per week **Public areas Grounds** on leads disp bin **Facilities** food food bowl water bowl bedding walks info vet info **On Request** fridge access torch towels **Other** charge for damage **Restrictions** no Rottweilers

This hotel enjoys a scenic setting in grounds by the River Dee. Inviting public areas include a choice of lounges, a cosy bar and a restaurant with views of the river. Bedrooms come in two distinct styles; those in the original part of the house contrasting with the newer wing rooms which are particularly spacious.

Rooms 22 (10 fmly) (3 smoking) **S** £90-£120; **D** £130-£150 (incl. bkfst) **Facilities** Fishing Children's play area Xmas New Year Child facilities **Parking** 50 **Notes** LB

Brownmuir Caravan Park *(NO740772)*
▶ ▶ ▶

AB30 1SJ

☎ 01561 320786   🖷 01561 320786

e-mail: brownmuircaravanpark@talk21.com

dir: *From N: A90 take B966 signed Fettercairn, site 1.5m on left. From S: A90, exit 4m N of Laurencekirk signed Fordoun, site 1m on right*

PETS: Public areas except children's play area disp bin **Exercise area Facilities** walks info vet info

Open Apr-Oct Last arrival 23.00hrs Last departure noon

A mainly static site set in a rural location with level pitches and good touring facilities. The area is ideal for cyclists, walkers and golfers, as well as those wanting to visit Aberdeen, Banchory, Ballater, Balmoral, Glamis and Dundee. A 7 acre site with 11 touring pitches, 7 hardstandings and 49 statics.

Notes 🐾

Gordon Arms Hotel
★★ 64% SMALL HOTEL

The Square AB54 8AF

☎ 01466 792288   🖷 01466 794556

e-mail: reception@gordonarms.demon.co.uk

dir: *Off A96 (Aberdeen to Inverness road) at Huntly. Hotel immediately on left after entering town square*

PETS: Bedrooms Stables 2m **Charges** £5 per night **Facilities** cage storage walks info vet info **On Request** fridge access torch towels **Other** charge for damage

This friendly, family-run hotel is located in the town square and offers a good selection of tasty, well-portioned dishes served in the bar, and also in the restaurant at weekends or midweek by appointment. Bedrooms come in a variety of sizes, but all have a good range of accessories.

Rooms 13 (3 fmly) **Facilities** FTV ♫ Wi-fi

Kildrummy Castle Hotel
★★★★ 75% COUNTRY HOUSE HOTEL

AB33 8RA

☎ 019755 71288   🖷 019755 71345

e-mail: kildrummy@btconnect.com

web: www.kildrummycastlehotel.co.uk

dir: *Off A97 (Huntly to Ballater road)*

PETS: Bedrooms sign **Grounds** on leads disp bin **Exercise area Facilities** cage storage walks info vet info **On Request** fridge access torch towels **Other** charge for damage

Set in landscaped gardens and accessed via a tree lined drive, Kildrummy Castle enjoys a peaceful rural location in the heart of the beautiful Grampian Highlands. The comfortable bedrooms have fabulous views, often with the ruin of the original castle as a backdrop. The current owners have sympathetically restored much of the original features, and the cosy lounges provide a perfect setting for afternoon tea or that post dinner drink. A relaxed atmosphere supported by friendly service is another obvious attraction here. Dinner features the best in local produce, along with an extensive wine list. The hotel is just a 35-minute drive from Aberdeen.

Rooms 16 (2 fmly) **S** fr £95; **D** £169-£213 (incl. bkfst)* **Facilities** FTV Fishing Xmas New Year Wi-fi **Parking** 25 **Notes** Closed 3-24 Jan RS 5-15 Nov

NORTH WATER BRIDGE   Map 15 NO66

Dovecot Caravan Park *(NO648663)*

►►►

AB30 1QL

☎ 01674 840630 📱 01674 840630

e-mail: adele@dovecotcaravanpark.co.uk

dir: *Take A90, 5m S of Laurencekirk. At Edzell Woods sign turn left. Site 500yds on left*

PETS: Public areas disp bin **Exercise area** riverside dog walk **Facilities** walks info vet info

Open Apr-Oct Last arrival 20.00hrs Last departure noon

A level grassy site in a country area close to the A90, with mature trees screening one side and the River North Esk on the other. The immaculate toilet facilities make this a handy overnight stop in a good touring area. A 6 acre site with 25 touring pitches, 8 hardstandings and 44 statics.

PETERHEAD   Map 15 NK14

Palace

★★★ 80% HOTEL

Prince St AB42 1PL

☎ 01779 474821 📱 01779 476119

e-mail: info@palacehotel.co.uk

web: www.palacehotel.co.uk

dir: *A90 from Aberdeen, follow signs to Peterhead, on entering town turn into Prince St, then right into main car park*

PETS: Bedrooms (14 GF) **Public areas** except restaurant & bars on leads **Grounds Restrictions** small to medium size dogs only **Resident Pet:** Morgan (Boxer)

This town centre hotel is popular with business travellers and for social events. Bedrooms come in two styles, with the executive rooms being particularly smart and spacious. Public areas include a themed bar, an informal diner reached via a spiral staircase, and a brasserie restaurant and cocktail bar.

Rooms 64 (2 fmly) (14 GF) **Facilities** Pool table Snooker room ♫ Xmas New Year Wi-fi **Services** Lift **Parking** 50

ANGUS

MONIFIETH   Map 11 NO43

Riverview Caravan Park *(NO502322)*

►►►►

Marine Dr DD5 4NN

☎ 01382 535471 📱 01382 811525

e-mail: info@riverview.co.uk

dir: *From Dundee on A930 follow signs to Monifieth, past supermarket, right signed golf course, right under rail bridge. Site signed on left*

PETS: Public areas except toilets & showers disp bin **Exercise area** park & field adjacent **Facilities** food bowl water bowl leads **Other** dog grooming nearby disposal bags available

Open Apr-Oct Last arrival 22.00hrs Last departure 12.30hrs

A well-landscaped seaside site with individual hedged pitches, and direct access to the beach. The modernised toilet block has excellent facilities which are immaculately maintained. Amenities include a multi-gym, sauna and steam rooms. A 5.5 acre site with 40 touring pitches, 40 hardstandings and 46 statics.

ARGYLL & BUTE

ARDUAINE   Map 10 NM71

Loch Melfort

★★★ 81% @@ HOTEL

PA34 4XG

☎ 01852 200233 📱 01852 200214

e-mail: reception@lochmelfort.co.uk

web: www.lochmelfort.co.uk

dir: *On A816, midway between Oban & Lochgilphead*

PETS: Bedrooms (10 GF) unattended **Charges** £8 per night **Grounds** disp bin **Exercise area** large field **Exercise area Facilities** washing facs cage storage walks info vet info **On Request** fridge access torch towels **Other** charge for damage **Resident Pets:** Rosie (Beagle), Evie & Bethan (horses)

Enjoying one of the finest locations on the West Coast, this popular, family-run hotel has outstanding views across Asknish Bay towards the Islands of Jura, Scarba and Shuna. Accommodation is provided in either the balconied rooms of the Cedar wing or the more traditional rooms in the main hotel. Dining options include the main restaurant offering stunning views or the more informal bistro.

Rooms 25 (20 annexe) (2 fmly) (10 GF) **S** £174; **D** £298 (incl. bkfst & dinner)* **Facilities** 4 moorings Beauty treatments ♫ Xmas New Year Wi-fi Child facilities **Parking** 50 **Notes** LB Closed 4-20 Jan

SCOTLAND

BARCALDINE — Map 10 NM94

Barcaldine House

★ ★ ★ ★ ★ ◉◉ GUEST ACCOMMODATION

PA37 1SG
☎ 01631 720219
e-mail: enquiries@barcaldinehouse.co.uk
web: www.barcaldinehouse.co.uk

PETS: Bedrooms unattended **Stables** 5m **Charges Public areas Grounds** disp bin **Exercise area** 50yds **Facilities** food (pre-bookable) food bowl water bowl bedding dog chews scoop/disp bags leads pet sitting dog walking washing facs cage storage walks info vet info **On Request** fridge access torch towels **Other** charge for damage **Restrictions** well behaved dogs only **Resident Pet:** Stan (Cocker Spaniel)

Originally built in 1709 by Patrick Campbell IV of Barcaldine, this fine country house enjoys a peaceful location on lands that were once part of the extensive estates of the Campbells of Breadalbane. The house has been sympathetically restored, and the attractive bedrooms are spacious and very well equipped. The award-winning restaurant serves the best in local produce and has a well deserved reputation. Guests have a choice of comfortable lounges with real fires and the billiard room is a popular feature. The house is an ideal base when exploring Argyll & Bute, the Highlands and the islands of Scotland.

Rooms 8 en suite (1 fmly) **S** £100-£140; **D** £120-£190*
Facilities STV FTV tea/coffee Dinner available Direct Dial Cen ht Licensed Snooker **Parking** 16 **Notes** LB

CARRADALE — Map 10 NR83

Carradale Bay Caravan Park (NR815385)

▶ ▶ ▶

PA28 6QG
☎ 01583 431665
e-mail: info@carradalebay.com
dir: A83 from Tarbert towards Campbeltown, left onto B842 (Carradale road), right onto B879. Site 0.5m

PETS: Charges 1st pet free, 2nd pet £1 per night **Public areas** except shower block disp bin **Exercise area** walks & beach **Facilities** walks info vet info

Open Apr-Sep Last arrival 22.00hrs Last departure noon

A beautiful, natural site on the sea's edge with superb views over Kilbrannan Sound to the Isle of Arran. Pitches are landscaped into small bays broken up by shrubs and bushes, and backed by dunes close to the long sandy beach. Lodges and static caravans for holiday hire. An 8 acre site with 75 touring pitches and 12 statics.

CONNEL — Map 10 NM93

Falls of Lora Hotel

★ ★ ★ 77% HOTEL

PA37 1PB
☎ 01631 710483 ▤ 01631 710694
e-mail: enquiries@fallsoflora.com
web: www.fallsoflora.com
dir: From Glasgow take A82, A85. Hotel 0.5m past Connel sign. (5m before Oban)

PETS: Bedrooms (4 GF) **Public areas** except dining areas & lounge on leads **Grounds** disp bin **Exercise area** 100mtrs **Facilities** washing facs cage storage **On Request** fridge access torch towels **Other** charge for damage

Personally run and welcoming, this long-established and thriving holiday hotel enjoys inspiring views over Loch Etive. The spacious ground floor takes in a comfortable, traditional lounge and a cocktail bar with over a hundred whiskies and an open log fire. Guests can eat in the popular, informal bistro, which is open all day. Bedrooms come in a variety of styles, ranging from the cosy standard rooms to high quality luxury rooms.

Rooms 30 (4 fmly) (4 GF) (30 smoking) **S** £49.50-£59.50; **D** £59-£147 (incl. bkfst)* **Facilities** Wi-fi Child facilities **Parking** 40 **Notes** LB Closed mid Dec & Jan

ERISKA — Map 10 NM94

Isle of Eriska

★ ★ ★ ★ ★ ◉◉◉ COUNTRY HOUSE HOTEL

PA37 1SD
☎ 01631 720371 ▤ 01631 720531
e-mail: office@eriska-hotel.co.uk
dir: Exit A85 at Connel, onto A828, follow for 4m, then follow hotel signs from N of Benderloch

PETS: Bedrooms (2 GF) **Sep accom** dog run; barn **Charges Grounds** disp bin **Exercise area Facilities** food (pre-bookable) food bowl water bowl dog chews leads washing facs walks info vet info **On Request** fridge access torch towels **Other** charge for damage **Resident Pets:** Marti, Dibley & Sula (Labradors)

Situated on its own private island with delightful beaches and walking trails, this hotel is in a tranquil setting, perfect for total relaxation. The spacious bedrooms are very comfortable and boast some fine antique pieces. Local seafood, meats and game feature prominently on the award-winning menu, as do vegetables and herbs grown in the hotel's kitchen garden. Leisure facilities include an indoor swimming pool, gym, spa treatment rooms and a small golf course.

Rooms 23 (2 GF) **S** £245-£325; **D** £325-£450 (incl. bkfst)* **Facilities** Spa FTV ❄ supervised ♨ 9 ⛳ Putt green Fishing 🎣 Gym Sauna Steam room Skeet shooting Nature trails Xmas New Year Wi-fi **Parking** 40 **Notes** Closed Jan

SCOTLAND

Glendaruel Caravan Park *(NR005865)*

▶ ▶ ▶

PA22 3AB

☎ 01369 820267   📄 01369 820367

e-mail: mail@glendaruelcaravanpark.com

dir: *A83 onto A815 to Strachur, 13m to site on A886. By ferry from Gourock to Dunoon then B836, then A886 for approx 4m N. (NB this route not recommended for towing vehicles - 1:5 uphill gradient on B836)*

PETS: Public areas reception, shop, toilets & children's play area on leads disp bin **Exercise area** woodland walk **Facilities** food food bowl water bowl washing facs vet info **Other** prior notice required **Resident Pet:** Black Labrador

Open Apr-Oct Last arrival 22.00hrs Last departure noon

A very pleasant, well-established site in the beautiful Victorian gardens of Glendaruel House. The level grass and hardstanding pitches are set in 23 acres of wooded parkland in a valley surrounded by mountains, with many rare specimen trees. The owners are hospitable and friendly. Static caravans are available for hire. A 3 acre site with 25 touring pitches, 15 hardstandings and 33 statics.

The Ardanaiseig

★★★ ◉◉◉ COUNTRY HOUSE HOTEL

by Loch Awe PA35 1HE

☎ 01866 833333   📄 01866 833222

e-mail: ardanaiseig@clara.net

dir: *A85 at Taynuilt onto B845 to Kilchrenan. Left in front of pub (road very narrow) signed 'Ardanaiseig Hotel' & 'No Through Road'. Continue for 3m*

PETS: Bedrooms (5 GF) unattended **Charges** £10 per stay **Public areas** Grounds disp bin **Facilities** pet sitting washing facs walks info vet info **On Request** fridge access torch towels **Resident Pet:** Patch (Jack Russell)

Set amid lovely gardens and breathtaking scenery beside the shore of Loch Awe, this peaceful country-house hotel was built in a Scottish baronial style in 1834. Many fine pieces of furniture are evident in the bedrooms and charming day rooms, which include a drawing room, a library bar and an elegant dining room. Dinner provides the highlight of any visit with skilfully cooked dishes making excellent use of local, seasonal produce.

Rooms 18 (4 fmly) (5 GF) **S** £94-£242; **D** £128-£424 (incl. bkfst)* **Facilities** FTV Fishing 🎣 Boating Clay pigeon shooting Bikes for hire Xmas New Year Wi-fi Child facilities **Parking** 20 **Notes** Closed 2 Jan-1 Feb

Taychreggan

★★★ 86% ◉◉ COUNTRY HOUSE HOTEL

PA35 1HQ

☎ 01866 833211 & 833366   📄 01866 833244

e-mail: info@taychregganhotel.co.uk

dir: *W from Crianlarich on A85 to Taynuilt, S for 7m on B845 (single track) to Kilchrenan*

PETS: Bedrooms Charges £10 per night **Public areas** except restaurant **Grounds** on leads disp bin **Facilities** walks info vet info **On Request** torch towels **Other** charge for damage

Surrounded by stunning Highland scenery this stylish and superbly presented, family-friendly hotel, once a drover's cottage, enjoys an idyllic setting in 40 acres of wooded grounds on the shores of Loch Awe. The hotel has a smart bar with adjacent courtyard Orangerie and a choice of quiet lounges with deep, luxurious sofas. A well earned reputation has been achieved by the kitchen for the skilfully prepared dinners that showcase the local and seasonal Scottish larder.

Rooms 18 **S** £87.50-£168.50; **D** £115-£277 (incl. bkfst) **Facilities** FTV Fishing 🎣 Air rifle range Archery Clay pigeon shooting Falconry Mock deer stalk New Year Wi-fi **Parking** 40 **Notes** Closed 24-26 Dec & 3 Jan-10 Feb

The Columba Hotel

★★★ 72% HOTEL

The Esplanade PA34 5QD

☎ 01631 562183   📄 01631 564683

e-mail: columba@mckeverhotels.co.uk

dir: *A85 to Oban, at 1st lights in town turn right*

PETS: Bedrooms Stables 5m **Charges** £10 (cleaning charge) **Public areas** except restaurant & café lounge on leads **Exercise area** 30mtrs **Facilities** cage storage walks info vet info **On Request** fridge access torch **Other** charge for damage please ask about any specific pet requirements

One of Oban's landmarks this Victorian hotel is located on the seafront with stunning views out over the Firth of Lorne to the Isle of Mull. The well-appointed, contemporary bedrooms offer guests comfortable accommodation. Alba Restaurant provides a menu of modern Scottish dishes.

Rooms 49 (5 fmly) **Facilities** FTV 🎵 Xmas New Year Wi-fi **Services** Lift **Parking** 6 **Notes** LB

Lancaster

★★ GUEST ACCOMMODATION

Corran Esplanade PA34 5AD

☎ 01631 562587 📠 01631 562587

e-mail: lancasteroban@btconnect.com

dir: *On seafront next to Columba's Cathedral*

PETS: Bedrooms unattended **Public areas** except dining room on leads **Exercise area** beach & woods adjacent **Facilities** leads cage storage walks info vet info **On Request** fridge access torch towels

A family-run establishment on the esplanade that offers budget accommodation; many bedrooms boast lovely views out over the bay towards the Isle of Mull. Public areas include a choice of lounges and bars that also benefit from the panoramic views. A swimming pool, sauna and jacuzzi are added benefits.

Rooms 27 rms (24 en suite) (3 fmly) (10 smoking) **S** £35-£40; **D** £74-£82* **Facilities** TVL tea/coffee Cen ht Licensed ☜ Sauna Pool Table **Parking** 20 **Notes** LB

PORT APPIN   Map 14 NM94

Airds Hotel

★★★★ ◉◉◉ SMALL HOTEL

PA38 4DF

☎ 01631 730236 📠 01631 730535

e-mail: airds@airds-hotel.com

web: www.airds-hotel.com

dir: *From A828 (Oban to Fort William road), turn at Appin signed Port Appin. Hotel 2.5m on left*

PETS: Bedrooms (2 GF) **Charges** £10 per night **Grounds** **Exercise area** surrounding area **Facilities** bedding walks info vet info **On Request** fridge access torch towels **Other** charge for damage

The views are stunning from this small, luxury hotel on the shores of Loch Linnhe and where the staff are delightful and nothing is too much trouble. The well-equipped bedrooms provide style and luxury whilst many bathrooms are furnished in marble and have power showers. Expertly prepared dishes, utilising the finest of ingredients, are served in the elegant dining room. Comfortable lounges with deep sofas and roaring fires provide the ideal retreat for relaxation. A real get-away-from-it-all experience.

Rooms 11 (3 fmly) (2 GF) **S** £181-£351; **D** £245-£415 (incl. bkfst & dinner)* **Facilities** FTV Putt green 🏌 Xmas New Year Wi-fi **Parking** 20 **Notes** LB RS Nov-Jan

TARBERT LOCH FYNE   Map 10 NR86

OXFORD
HOTELS & INNS

Stonefield Castle

★★★★ 73% ◉ HOTEL

PA29 6YJ

☎ 01880 820836 📠 01880 820929

e-mail: reservations.stonefieldcastle@ohiml.com

web: www.oxfordhotelsandinns.com

dir: *From Glasgow take M8 towards Erskine Bridge, follow signs for Loch Lomond on A82. From Arrochar follow signs for A83 through Inveraray & Lochgilphead, hotel on left 2m before Tarbert*

PETS: Bedrooms (10 GF) unattended **Charges** £10 per night **Public areas** except restaurant & bar on leads **Grounds** on leads disp bin **Facilities** food bowl water bowl walks info vet info **On Request** fridge access torch towels **Other** charge for damage

This fine baronial castle commands a superb lochside setting amidst beautiful woodland gardens renowned for their rhododendrons - visit in late spring to see them at their best. Elegant public rooms are a feature, and the picture-window restaurant offers unrivalled views across Loch Fyne. Bedrooms are split between the main house and a purpose-built wing.

Rooms 32 (2 fmly) (10 GF) **Facilities** Xmas New Year Wi-fi **Services** Lift **Parking** 50 **Notes** LB

CLACKMANNANSHIRE

DOLLAR   Map 11 NS99

Castle Campbell Hotel

★★★ 77% SMALL HOTEL

11 Bridge St FK14 7DE

☎ 01259 742519 📠 01259 743742

e-mail: bookings@castle-campbell.co.uk

web: www.castle-campbell.co.uk

dir: *On A91 (Stirling to St Andrews road), in centre of Dollar, by bridge overlooking Dollar Burn & Clock Tower*

PETS: Bedrooms Charges £10 per night **Public areas** except restaurant on leads **Exercise area** 100yds **Facilities** walks info vet info **Other** charge for damage

Built in 1821 as a coaching inn, this small hotel has a warm and inviting interior, and guests can choose to eat in either the stylish restaurant or the relaxing bar. Bedrooms are comfortable with many thoughtful extras provided as standard. It is within easy striking distance for Edinburgh, Glasgow and Perth, and Gleneagles is just a few miles away.

Rooms 9 (1 fmly) **S** £46-£69; **D** £65-£108 (incl. bkfst)* **Facilities** Wi-fi **Parking** 8 **Notes** LB

SCOTLAND

DUMFRIES & GALLOWAY

AUCHENCAIRN
Map 11 NX75

Balcary Bay Hotel

★★★ 86% ◉◉ HOTEL

DG7 1QZ

☎ 01556 640217 & 640311 📠 01556 640272

e-mail: reservations@balcary-bay-hotel.co.uk

web: www.balcary-bay-hotel.co.uk

dir: *On A711 between Dalbeattie & Kirkcudbright, hotel 2m from village*

PETS: Bedrooms (3 GF) unattended **Charges Public areas Grounds** disp bin **Exercise area** beach adjacent **Facilities** food bowl water bowl scoop/disp bags leads washing facs cage storage walks info vet info **On Request** fridge access torch towels **Other** charge for damage **Resident Pets:** Rusty & Barney (Irish Red Setters)

Taking its name from the bay on which it lies, this hotel has lawns running down to the shore. The larger bedrooms enjoy stunning views over the bay, whilst others overlook the gardens. Comfortable public areas invite relaxation. Imaginative dishes feature at dinner, accompanied by a good wine list.

Rooms 20 (1 fmly) (3 GF) **S** £72; **D** £130-£160 (incl. bkfst)* **Facilities** FTV **Parking** 50 **Notes** LB Closed 1st Sun Dec-1st Fri Feb

ECCLEFECHAN
Map 11 NY17

Hoddom Castle Caravan Park *(NY154729)*

▶▶▶▶▶

Hoddom DG11 1AS

☎ 01576 300251 📠 01576 300757

e-mail: hoddomcastle@aol.com

dir: *M74 junct 19, follow signs to site. From A75 W of Annan take B723 for 5m, follow signs to site*

PETS: Charges £1.50 per night **Public areas** except bar & restaurant on leads disp bin **Exercise area** woodland walk **Exercise area** adjacent **Facilities** food food bowl water bowl walks info vet info **Other** prior notice required **Resident Pet:** Oscar (Jack Russell)

Open Etr or Apr-Oct rs Early season cafeteria closed Last arrival 21.00hrs Last departure 14.00hrs

The peaceful, well-equipped park can be found on the banks of the River Annan, and offers a good mix of grassy and hard pitches, beautifully landscaped and blending into the surroundings. There are signed nature trails, maintained by the park's countryside ranger, a 9-hole golf course, trout and salmon fishing, and plenty of activity ideas for children. A 28 acre site with 200 touring pitches, 150 hardstandings and 54 statics.

Notes No electric scooters, no gazebos, no fires

GATEHOUSE OF FLEET
Map 11 NX55

Anwoth Caravan Site *(NX595563)*

▶▶▶▶

DG7 2JU

☎ 01557 814333 & 840251 📠 01557 814333

e-mail: enquiries@auchenlarie.co.uk

dir: *From A75 into Gatehouse of Fleet, site on right towards Stranraer. Signed from town centre*

PETS: Stables 10m **Public areas** disp bin **Exercise area** 300yds **Facilities** washing facs walks info vet info **Other** charge for damage prior notice required

Open Mar-Oct Last arrival 20.00hrs Last departure noon

A very high quality park in a peaceful sheltered setting within easy walking distance of the village, ideally placed for exploring the scenic hills, valleys and coastline. Grass, hardstanding and fully serviced pitches are available and guests may use the leisure facilities at the sister site, Auchenlarie Holiday Park. A 2 acre site with 28 touring pitches, 13 hardstandings and 44 statics.

GRETNA Map 11 NY36

Braids Caravan Park *(NY313674)*

▶▶▶▶

Annan Rd DG16 5DQ
☎ 01461 337409
e-mail: enquiries@thebraidscaravanpark.co.uk
dir: *On B721, 0.5m from village on right, towards Annan*

PETS: Public areas on leads disp bin **Exercise area** 0.5m
Facilities walks info vet info **Other** dogs must be exercised off site

Open all year Last arrival 21.00hrs Last departure noon

A well-maintained grassy site in the centre of the village just inside the Scottish border. A good toilet block provides a high standard of facilities, and several hard pitches further enhance this busy and popular park. A 6 acre site with 93 touring pitches, 29 hardstandings.

Notes No skateboards, last arrival time 20.00hrs in winter

King Robert the Bruce's Cave Caravan & Camping Park *(NY266705)*

▶▶▶▶

Cove Estate, Kirkpatrick Fleming DG11 3AT
☎ 01461 800285 & 07779 138694 📠 01461 800269
e-mail: enquiries@brucescave.co.uk
dir: *Exit A74(M) junct 21 for Kirkpatrick Fleming, follow N through village, pass Station Inn, left at Bruce's Court. Over rail crossing to site*

PETS: Public areas except toilet block, shop & children's play area on leads disp bin **Exercise area** river walk **Facilities** food scoop/disp bags washing facs walks info vet info **Resident Pets:** Scamp, Cally, Bruce & Bruno (dogs), Silver & Buttercup (cats), Daisy (Shetland pony), Silver & Prince (horses), ducks

Open Apr-Nov rs Nov-Mar shop closed, water restriction Last arrival 22.00hrs Last departure 16.00hrs

The lovely wooded grounds of an old castle and mansion are the setting for this pleasant park. The mature woodland is a haven for wildlife, and there is a riverside walk to Robert the Bruce's Cave. A toilet block with en suite facilities is of special appeal to families. A 80 acre site with 75 touring pitches, 60 hardstandings and 35 statics.

GRETNA SERVICE AREA (A74(M)) Map 11 NY36

Days Inn Gretna Green

BUDGET HOTEL

Welcome Break Service Area DG16 5HQ
☎ 01461 337566 📠 01461 337823
e-mail: gretna.hotel@welcomebreak.co.uk
web: www.welcomebreak.co.uk
dir: *Between junct 21/22 on M74 - accessible from both N'bound & S'bound carriageway*

PETS: Bedrooms (64 GF) **Public areas** **Grounds** on leads disp bin **Exercise area** 20yds **Facilities** walks info vet info **On Request** torch

This modern building offers accommodation in smart, spacious and well-equipped bedrooms suitable for families and business travellers, and all with en suite bathrooms. Continental breakfast is available and other refreshments may be taken at the nearby family restaurant.

Rooms 64 (54 fmly) (64 GF) **S** £29-£59; **D** £29-£59

KIRKBEAN Map 11 NX95

Cavens

★★★ ⊛ COUNTRY HOUSE HOTEL

DG2 8AA
☎ 01387 880234 📠 01387 880467
e-mail: enquiries@cavens.com
web: www.cavens.com
dir: *On entering Kirkbean on A710, hotel signed*

PETS: Bedrooms (1 GF) **Sep accom** please enquire when booking **Stables** 1m **Charges** £10 per stay **Public areas** **Grounds** disp bin **Exercise area** adjacent **Facilities** walks info vet info **Other** charge for damage **Resident Pet:** Hamish (Labrador)

Set in six acres of parkland gardens, Cavens encapsulates all the virtues of an intimate country-house hotel. Quality is the keynote, and the proprietors spared no effort in the fine renovation of the house. Bedrooms are delightfully individual and very comfortably equipped; choose between the Country rooms or the more spacious Estate rooms. A choice of charming lounges invites peaceful relaxation. The dinner menu offers the best of local and home-made produce.

Rooms 5 (1 GF) **Facilities** ⅃ Shooting Fishing Horse riding New Year **Parking** 12 **Notes** LB Closed Jan

SCOTLAND

SCOTLAND

Best Western Selkirk Arms

★★★ 77% HOTEL

Old High St DG6 4JG
☎ 01557 330402 📄 01557 331639
e-mail: reception@selkirkarmshotel.co.uk
web: www.selkirkarmshotel.co.uk
dir: On A71, 5m S of A75

PETS: Bedrooms (1 GF) **Charges** £5 per night **Public areas** bar only on leads **Grounds** on leads disp bin **Exercise area** 2 mins' walk **Facilities** water bowl dog chews cage storage walks info vet info **On Request** fridge access torch **Other** charge for damage

The Selkirk Arms is aptly named, as it was originally the hostelry where Robert Burns wrote the *Selkirk Grace*. It is now a smart and stylish hotel set in secluded gardens just off the town centre. Inviting public areas include the attractive Artistas restaurant, bistro, air-conditioned lounge bar and the Burns Lounge.

Rooms 17 (3 annexe) (2 fmly) (1 GF) **Facilities** STV FTV New Year Wi-fi **Parking** 10 **Notes** Closed 24-26 Dec

Arden House Hotel

★★ 72% HOTEL

Tongland Rd DG6 4UU
☎ 01557 330544 📄 01557 330742
dir: Exit A57, 4m W of Castle Douglas onto A711. Follow Kirkcudbright signs, over Telford Bridge. Hotel 400mtrs on left

PETS: Bedrooms unattended sign **Public areas Grounds** disp bin **Exercise area Facilities** vet info

Set well back from the main road in extensive grounds on the northeast side of town, this spotlessly maintained hotel offers attractive bedrooms, a lounge bar and adjoining conservatory serving a range of popular dishes, which are also available in the dining room. It boasts an impressive function suite in its grounds.

Rooms 9 (7 fmly) (5 smoking) **S** £55-£60; **D** £75-£80 (incl. bkfst)* **Parking** 70

Dryfesdale Country House

★★★★ 71% HOTEL

Dryfebridge DG11 2SF
☎ 01576 202427 📄 01576 204187
e-mail: reception@dryfesdalehotel.co.uk
web: www.dryfesdalehotel.co.uk
dir: From M74 junct 17 follow Lockerbie North signs, 3rd left at 1st rdbt, 1st exit left at 2nd rdbt, hotel 200yds on left

PETS: Bedrooms (19 GF) unattended sign **Stables** 100yds **Charges** £5 per night £15 per week **Public areas Grounds** disp bin **Facilities** food (pre-bookable) food bowl water bowl bedding dog chews feeding mat scoop/disp bags washing facs cage storage walks info vet info **On Request** fridge access torch towels **Other** charge for damage **Resident Pet:** Buddy (Long Haired German Shepherd)

Conveniently situated for the M74, yet discreetly screened from it, this friendly hotel provides attentive service. Bedrooms, some with access to patio areas, vary in size and style; all offer good levels of comfort and are well equipped. Creative, good value dinners make use of local produce and are served in the airy restaurant that overlooks the manicured gardens and rolling countryside.

Rooms 28 (5 fmly) (19 GF) **Facilities** STV FTV Putt green 🏌 Clay pigeon shooting Fishing 🎵 Xmas New Year Wi-fi **Parking** 60

Kings Arms Hotel

★★ 78% HOTEL

High St DG11 2JL
☎ 01576 202410 📄 01576 202410
e-mail: reception@kingsarmshotel.co.uk
web: www.kingsarmshotel.co.uk
dir: A74(M), 0.5m into town centre, hotel opposite town hall

PETS: Bedrooms unattended **Public areas** except restaurant & 1 bar on leads disp bin **Exercise area** 1 min walk **Facilities** food bowl water bowl washing facs cage storage walks info vet info **On Request** fridge access torch towels **Resident Pet:** Bailey (Yellow Labrador)

Dating from the 17th century this former inn lies in the town centre. Now a family-run hotel, it provides attractive well-equipped bedrooms with Wi-fi access. At lunch a menu ranging from snacks to full meals is served in both the two cosy bars and the restaurant at dinner.

Rooms 13 (2 fmly) **S** £50; **D** £83 (incl. bkfst) **Facilities** FTV Xmas New Year Wi-fi **Parking** 8

Ravenshill House

★★ 74% HOTEL

12 Dumfries Rd DG11 2EF

☎ 01576 202882

e-mail: aaenquiries@ravenshillhotellockerbie.co.uk

web: www.ravenshillhotellockerbie.co.uk

dir: *From A74(M) Lockerbie junct onto A709. Hotel 0.5m on right*

PETS: Bedrooms Grounds disp bin **Exercise area** 400yds **Facilities** walks info vet info **On Request** fridge access **Other** dogs must be supervised at all times

Set in spacious gardens on the fringe of the town, this friendly, family-run hotel offers cheerful service and good value, home-cooked meals. Bedrooms are generally spacious and comfortably equipped, including a two-room unit ideal for families.

Rooms 8 (2 fmly) **S** £50-£65; **D** £78-£85 (incl. bkfst)* **Facilities** FTV Wi-fi **Parking** 35 **Notes** LB Closed 1-3 Jan

---

MOFFAT **Map 11 NT00**

Annandale Arms Hotel

★★★ 77% ◉ HOTEL

High St DG10 9HF

☎ 01683 220013   📠 01683 221395

e-mail: reception@annandalearmshotel.co.uk

web: www.annandalearmshotel.co.uk

dir: *M74 junct 15/A701. Hotel on west side of central square that forms High St*

PETS: Bedrooms (5 GF) unattended **Public areas** except restaurant on leads **Grounds** disp bin **Exercise area** 0.5m Resident Pets: Jago (Labrador), Zach (Cocker Spaniel)

With a history dating back 250 years old, this family run hotel in the heart of Moffat has undergone a refurbishment to provide well-appointed, modern bedrooms and bathrooms. There is a welcoming bar and restaurant serving real ales and quality food. Wi-fi and off-road parking are added benefits.

Rooms 16 (2 fmly) (5 GF) (5 smoking) **S** £60-£75; **D** £98 (incl. bkfst)* **Facilities** FTV New Year Wi-fi **Parking** 20 **Notes** LB Closed 25-26 Dec

Best Western Moffat House

★★★ 77% HOTEL

High St DG10 9HL

☎ 01683 220039   📠 01683 221288

e-mail: reception@moffathouse.co.uk

dir: *M74 junct 15 into town centre*

PETS: Bedrooms (4 GF) unattended **Stables Charges** £5 per night **Grounds** on leads **Exercise area Facilities** food bowl water bowl cage storage walks info vet info **On Request** fridge access torch towels **Other** charge for damage

This fine Adam mansion, in its own neatly tended gardens, is set back from the main road in the centre of this popular country town. Inviting public areas include a quiet sun lounge to the rear, a comfortable lounge bar serving tasty meals and an attractive restaurant for the more formal occasion. Bedrooms present a mix of classical and modern styles.

Rooms 21 (4 fmly) (4 GF) **S** £49-£69; **D** £79-£99 (incl. bkfst)* **Facilities** STV Xmas New Year Wi-fi **Parking** 30 **Notes** LB

Limetree House

★★★★ GUEST ACCOMMODATION

Eastgate DG10 9AE

☎ 01683 220001

e-mail: info@limetreehouse.co.uk

web: www.limetreehouse.co.uk

dir: *Off High St onto Well St, left onto Eastgate, house 100yds on left*

PETS: Bedrooms Public areas except dining room on leads **Exercise area** 0.25m **Facilities** cage storage walks info vet info **On Request** fridge access torch **Other** charge for damage 1 dog per guest, max 2 dogs in house **Restrictions** no large breeds Resident Pets: Sully, Mike & Beattie (cats)

A warm welcome is assured at this well-maintained guest accommodation, quietly situated behind the main high street. Recognisable by its colourful flower baskets in season, it provides an inviting lounge and bright cheerful breakfast room. Bedrooms are smartly furnished and include a large family room.

Rooms 6 en suite (1 fmly) (1 GF) **S** £42.50-£45; **D** £65-£80* **Facilities** FTV TVL tea/coffee Cen ht Wi-fi Golf 18 **Parking** 3 **Notes** LB No Children 5yrs RS Xmas & New Year

MOFFAT *continued*

Barnhill Springs Country Guest House

★★ GUEST ACCOMMODATION

DG10 9QS

☎ 01683 220580

e-mail: barnhillsprings@yahoo.co.uk

dir: *A74(M) junct 15, A701 towards Moffat, Barnhill Rd 50yds on right*

PETS: **Bedrooms** unattended **Public areas** except dining room **Grounds** disp bin **Exercise area** 2 acres of wooded grounds for dogs to exercise **Facilities** food bowl water bowl dog chews scoop/disp bags leads washing facs cage storage walks info vet info **On Request** fridge access torch towels **Resident Pet:** Kim (Collie cross)

This former farmhouse has a quiet, rural location south of the town and within easy reach of the M74. Bedrooms are well proportioned; and have private bathrooms. There is a comfortable lounge and separate dining room. Barnhill Spring continues to welcome pets.

Rooms 5 rms (5 pri facs) (1 fmly) (1 GF) **S** £33-£35; **D** £66-£70 **Facilities** TVL tea/coffee Dinner available Cen ht **Parking** 10 **Notes** LB

The Bruce Hotel

★★★ 73% HOTEL

88 Queen St DG8 6JL

☎ 01671 402294   📠 01671 402294

e-mail: mail@the-bruce-hotel.com

web: www.the-bruce-hotel.com

dir: *Off A75 Newton Stewart rdbt towards town. Hotel 800mtrs on right*

PETS: **Bedrooms** unattended **Public areas** except restaurant on leads **Grounds** on leads **Exercise area Facilities** walks info **Other** charge for damage **Restrictions** please phone for advice on which breeds are accepted

Named after the Scottish patriot Robert the Bruce, this welcoming hotel is just a short distance from the A75. One of the well-appointed bedrooms features a four-poster bed, and popular family suites contain separate bedrooms for children. Public areas include a traditional lounge, a formal restaurant and a lounge bar, both offering a good choice of dishes.

Rooms 20 (3 fmly) **S** £50-£70; **D** £60-£90 (incl. bkfst) **Facilities** FTV New Year Wi-fi **Parking** 14 **Notes** LB

Creebridge Caravan Park *(NX415656)*

►►►

Minnigaff DG8 6AJ

☎ 01671 402324 & 402432   📠 01671 402324

e-mail: john_sharples@btconnect.com

dir: *0.25m E of Newton Stewart at Minnigaff on bypass, signed off A75*

PETS: **Stables** 0.5m **Charges** £5 per night £30 per week **Public areas** disp bin **Exercise area** 500mtrs **Facilities** food bowl water bowl washing facs cage storage walks info vet info **Other** charge for damage

Open all year rs Mar only one toilet block open Last arrival 20.00hrs Last departure 10.00hrs

A small family-owned site a short walk from the town's amenities. The site is surrounded by mature trees, and the toilet facilities are clean and functional. A 5.5 acre site with 36 touring pitches, 12 hardstandings and 50 statics.

Notes 🐾

Loch Ken Holiday Park *(NX687702)*

►►►

DG7 3NE

☎ 01644 470282

e-mail: penny@lochkenholidaypark.co.uk

dir: *On A713, N of Parton*

PETS: **Charges** £2 per night **Public areas** except shop on leads disp bin **Exercise area** field provided **Exercise area** 50mtrs **Facilities** food leads walks info vet info **Other** prior notice required **Resident Pets:** 12 ducks

Open Mar-mid Nov rs Mar/Apr (ex Etr) & late Sep-Nov restricted shop hours Last departure noon

A busy and popular park with a natural emphasis on water activities, set on the eastern shores of Loch Ken, with superb views. Family owned and run, it is in a peaceful and beautiful spot opposite the RSPB reserve, with direct access to the loch for fishing and boat launching. The park offers a variety of water sports, as well as farm visits and nature trails. Static caravans for hire. A 7 acre site with 52 touring pitches, 4 hardstandings and 35 statics.

Knockinaam Lodge

★★★ ◎◎◎ HOTEL

DG9 9AD

☎ 01776 810471   📠 01776 810435

e-mail: reservations@knockinaamlodge.com

web: www.knockinaamlodge.com

dir: *From A77 or A75 follow signs to Portpatrick. Through Lochans. After 2m left at signs for hotel*

PETS: Bedrooms unattended **Charges** £20 per stay
Grounds Exercise area beach 20mtrs **Other** dogs allowed
in certain bedrooms only; owners to bring dog's own bedding
Resident Pets: Jack, Jerry & Lucy (Black Labradors)

Any tour of Dumfries & Galloway would not be complete without
a night or two at this haven of tranquillity and relaxation.
Knockinaam Lodge is an extended Victorian house, set in an
idyllic cove with its own pebble beach and sheltered by majestic
cliffs and woodlands. A warm welcome is assured from the
proprietors and their committed team, and much emphasis is
placed on providing a sophisticated but intimate home-from-
home experience. The cooking is a real treat and showcases
superb local produce. Dinner is a set meal, but choices can be
discussed in advance.

Rooms 10 (1 fmly) **S** £155-£300; **D** £260-£420 (incl. bkfst &
dinner)* **Facilities** FTV Fishing ⛳ Shooting Walking Sea fishing
Clay pigeon shooting Xmas New Year Wi-fi **Parking** 20

Fernhill

★★★ 79% HOTEL

Heugh Rd DG9 8TD

☎ 01776 810220   📠 01776 810596

e-mail: info@fernhillhotel.co.uk

web: www.fernhillhotel.co.uk

dir: *From Stranraer A77 to Portpatrick, 100yds past Portpatrick
village sign, turn right before war memorial. Hotel 1st on left*

PETS: Bedrooms (8 GF) **Public areas** except restaurant & bar on
leads disp bin **Exercise area** wooded area 0.5m **Facilities** cage
storage walks info vet info **On Request** torch towels

Set high above the village, this hotel looks out over the harbour
and Irish Sea; many of the bedrooms take advantage of the views.
A modern wing offers particularly spacious and well-appointed
rooms; some have balconies. The smart conservatory restaurant
offers interesting, freshly prepared dishes.

Rooms 36 (9 annexe) (3 fmly) (8 GF) **Facilities** Leisure facilities
available at sister hotel in Stranraer Xmas New Year Wi-fi
Parking 45 **Notes** LB Closed mid Jan-mid Feb

Kings Green Caravan Site *(NX340430)*

►►►

South St DG8 9SG

☎ 01988 700489

dir: *Direct access from A747 at junct with B7085, towards
Whithorn*

PETS: Public areas except toilet, shower & laundry blocks
Exercise area beach **Facilities** walks info vet info **Other** pet
supplies available at shop (500yds), dog grooming service (2m)

Open Etr, May & Jul-Aug Last arrival 20.00hrs Last departure
noon

Set beside the unspoilt village with all its amenities and the
attractive harbour, this level grassy park is community owned
and run. Approached via the coast road, the park has views
reaching as far as the Isle of Man. A 3 acre site with 30 touring
pitches.

Notes No golf or fireworks on site 😊

Sands of Luce Holiday Park *(NX103510)*

►►►►

Sands of Luce DG9 9JN

☎ 01776 830456   📠 01776 830477

e-mail: info@sandsofluceholidaypark.co.uk

dir: *From S & E: left from A75 onto B7084 signed Drummore.
Site signed at junct with A716. From N: A77 through Stranraer
towards Portpatrick, 2m, follow A716 signed Drummore, site
signed in 5m*

PETS: Stables 5m **Public areas** on leads disp bin **Exercise area**
Facilities washing facs walks info vet info **Other** prior notice
required owners must clear up after their pets Resident Pets:
Penny (Springer Spaniel), Skye (Labrador), Noosa & Whinn (cats)

Open Mar-Jan Last arrival 20.00hrs Last departure noon

This is a large park with a balance of static and touring caravans
and enjoys a stunning position with direct access to a sandy
beach and with views across Luce Bay. It has its own boat
storage area and boasts an excellent static hire fleet and a
tastefully decorated well-managed club. A 30 acre site with 100
touring pitches and 190 statics.

Notes No quad bikes

SCOTLAND

SCOTLAND

Blackaddie House Hotel

★★★ 78% ◉◉ COUNTRY HOUSE HOTEL

Blackaddie Rd DG4 6JJ

☎ 01659 50270

e-mail: ian@blackaddiehotel.co.uk

dir: *Off A76 just N of Sanquhar at Burnside Service Station. Private road to hotel 300mtrs on right*

PETS: Bedrooms (3 GF) **Charges** £5 per night £25 per week **Public areas** except restaurant on leads **Grounds** disp bin **Exercise area** adjacent **Facilities** food (pre-bookable) food bowl water bowl dog chews leads cage storage walks info vet info **On Request** fridge access torch towels **Other** charge for damage **Resident Pets:** 2 Cocker Spaniels, 1 cat

Overlooking the River Nith, this family run country house hotel offers hands on service, friendly and attentive. Accommodation is well presented and comfortable with many useful extras provided as standard. Award-winning food features highly here, and the restaurant has views of the gardens.

Rooms 9 (3 annexe) (2 fmly) (3 GF) **S** £80-£150; **D** £100-£200 (incl. bkfst)* **Facilities** Xmas New Year Wi-fi **Parking** 20 **Notes** LB

Corsewall Lighthouse Hotel

★★★ 78% HOTEL

Corsewall Point, Kirkcolm DG9 0QG

☎ 01776 853220 🖨 01776 854231

e-mail: lighthousehotel@btinternet.com

web: www.lighthousehotel.co.uk

dir: *A718 from Stranraer to Kirkcolm (approx 8m). Follow hotel signs for 4m*

PETS: Bedrooms (2 GF) sign **Charges** £10 per night **Public areas** except restaurant **Grounds** disp bin **Exercise area** 20-acre grounds **Exercise area Facilities** washing facs walks info vet info **On Request** torch towels **Other** charge for damage dogs allowed in Loch Ryan, Lighthouse & North Channel suites only **Restrictions** no breed larger than a Labrador

Looking for something completely different? A unique hotel converted from buildings that adjoin a listed 19th-century lighthouse set on a rocky coastline. Bedrooms come in a variety of sizes, some reached by a spiral staircase, and like the public areas, are cosy and atmospheric. Cottage suites in the grounds offer greater space.

Rooms 10 (4 annexe) (4 fmly) (2 GF) (2 smoking) **S** £130-£150; **D** £150-£230 (incl. bkfst & dinner)* **Facilities** FTV Xmas New Year **Parking** 20

Aird Donald Caravan Park *(NX075605)*

▶ ▶ ▶ ▶

London Rd DG9 8RN

☎ 01776 702025

e-mail: enquiries@aird-donald.co.uk

dir: *From A75 left on entering Stranraer (signed). Opposite school, site 300yds*

PETS: Public areas disp bin **Exercise area** wooded area **Exercise area** 0.25m **Facilities** walks info vet info

Open all year Last departure 16.00hrs

A spacious touring site, mainly grass but with tarmac hardstanding area, with pitches large enough to accommodate a car and caravan overnight without unhitching. On the fringe of town screened by mature shrubs and trees. Ideal stopover en route to Northern Irish ferry ports. A 12 acre site with 100 touring pitches, 30 hardstandings.

Notes Tents Apr-Sep only 🚐

Drumroamin Farm Camping & Touring Site *(NX444512)*

▶ ▶ ▶

1 South Balfern DG8 9DB

☎ 01988 840613 & 07752 471456

e-mail: enquiry@drumroamin.co.uk

dir: *A75 towards Newton Stewart, onto A714 for Wigtown. Left on B7005 through Bladnock, A746 through Kirkinner. Take B7004 signed Garlieston, 2nd left opposite Kilsture Forest, site 0.75m at end of lane*

PETS: Public areas except shower block disp bin **Exercise area** woodland walk **Facilities** washing facs walks info vet info **Resident Pet:** Maggie (Chocolate Labrador)

Open all year Last arrival 21.00hrs Last departure noon

An open, spacious park in a quiet spot a mile from the main road, and close to Wigtown Bay. A superb toilet block offers spacious showers, and there's a lounge/games room and plenty of room for children to play. A 5 acre site with 48 touring pitches and 3 statics.

Notes No fires

EAST AYRSHIRE

KILMARNOCK — Map 10 NS43

The Fenwick Hotel

★★★ 78% HOTEL

Fenwick KA3 6AU

☎ 01560 600478 📠 01560 600334

e-mail: info@thefenwickhotel.co.uk

web: www.thefenwickhotel.co.uk

dir: M77 junct 8, hotel between motorway & B7061

PETS: Bedrooms (9 GF) **Charges** £10 per night £70 per week **Grounds** disp bin **Exercise area Facilities** walks info vet info **On Request** fridge access towels **Other** charge for damage

Benefiting from a great location alongside the M77 and offering easy links to Ayr, Kilmarnock and Glasgow. The spacious bedrooms are thoughtfully equipped; complimentary Wi-fi is available throughout the hotel. The bright restaurant offers both formal and informal dining and there are two bars to choose from.

Rooms 30 (1 fmly) (9 GF) **S** £50-£75; **D** £55-£85 (incl. bkfst)* **Facilities** STV Xmas New Year Wi-fi **Parking** 64

EAST LOTHIAN

DUNBAR — Map 12 NT67

Thurston Manor Holiday Home Park

(NT712745)

▶ ▶ ▶ ▶ ▶

Innerwick EH42 1SA

☎ 01368 840643 📠 01368 840261

e-mail: mail@thurstonmanor.co.uk

dir: 4m S of Dunbar, signed off A1

PETS: Charges Public areas except buildings & children's play area disp bin **Facilities** food food bowl water bowl dog chews leads vet info **Other** prior notice required max 2 dogs per unit; contact site for details of charges disposal bags available

Open Mar-8 Jan rs 1-22 Dec site open wknds only Last arrival 23.00hrs Last departure noon

A pleasant park set in 250 acres of unspoilt countryside. The touring and static areas of this large park are in separate areas. The main touring area occupies an open, level position, and the toilet facilities are modern and exceptionally well maintained. The park boasts a well-stocked fishing loch, a heated indoor swimming pool, steam room, sauna, jacuzzi, mini-gym and fitness room and seasonal entertainment. A 250 acre site with 100 touring pitches, 45 hardstandings and 500 statics.

Belhaven Bay Caravan & Camping Park

(NT661781)

▶ ▶ ▶

Belhaven Bay EH42 1TS

☎ 01368 865956 📠 01368 865022

e-mail: belhaven@meadowhead.co.uk

dir: From A1 onto A1087 towards Dunbar. Site (1m) in John Muir Park

PETS: Charges £3 per night **Public areas** except play area on leads disp bin **Exercise area** lakeside grass area **Exercise area** adjacent **Facilities** food bowl water bowl washing facs walks info vet info **Other** prior notice required disposal bags available **Restrictions** no dangerous breeds (see page 7)

Open Mar-13 Oct Last arrival 20.00hrs Last departure noon

Small, well-maintained park in a sheltered location and within walking distance of the beach. This is an excellent spot for seabird watching, and there is a good rail connection with Edinburgh from Dunbar. A 40 acre site with 52 touring pitches, 11 hardstandings and 64 statics.

MUSSELBURGH — Map 11 NT37

Drum Mohr Caravan Park (NT373734)

▶ ▶ ▶ ▶

Levenhall EH21 8JS

☎ 0131 665 6867 📠 0131 653 6859

e-mail: admin@drummohr.org

dir: Exit A1 at A199 junct through Wallyford, at rdbt onto B1361 signed Prestonpans. 1st left, site 400yds

PETS: Stables 1km **Charges** £1.50 per night **Public areas** except children's play area on leads disp bin **Exercise area** perimeter walk **Facilities** food vet info **Other** maximum of 2 dogs per pitch

Open all year rs Winter arrivals by arrangement Last arrival 17.00hrs Last departure noon

This attractive park is sheltered by mature trees on all sides, and carefully landscaped within. The park is divided into separate areas by mature hedging and planting of trees and ornamental shrubs. Pitches are generous in size, and there are a number of fully serviced pitches plus first-class amenities. A 9 acre site with 120 touring pitches, 50 hardstandings and 12 statics.

SCOTLAND

CITY OF EDINBURGH

EDINBURGH — Map 11 NT27

Prestonfield

★★★★★ ⊛⊛ TOWN HOUSE HOTEL

Priestfield Rd EH16 5UT

☎ 0131 225 7800 📄 0131 220 4392

e-mail: reservations@prestonfield.com

web: www.prestonfield.com

dir: A7 towards Cameron Toll. 200mtrs beyond Royal
Commonwealth Pool, into Priestfield Rd

PETS: Bedrooms (6 GF) unattended Charges Public areas on
leads Grounds disp bin Facilities food (pre-bookable) food
bowl water bowl dog chews dog walking cage storage walks
info vet info On Request torch towels Other charge for damage
Resident Pets: Archie & Brodie (Jack Russells), Highland cattle,
peacocks

This centuries-old landmark has been lovingly restored and
enhanced to provide deeply comfortable and dramatically
furnished bedrooms. The building demands to be explored: from
the tapestry lounge and the whisky room to the restaurant, where
the walls are adorned with pictures of former owners. Facilities
and services are up-to-the-minute, and carefully prepared meals
are served in the award-winning Rhubarb restaurant.

Rooms 23 (6 GF) S £285; D £285 (incl. bkfst) Facilities STV FTV ↨
18 Putt green ⛳ Free bike hire Xmas New Year Wi-fi Services Lift
Parking 250 Notes LB

Novotel Edinburgh Park

★★★★ 78% HOTEL

15 Lochside Av EH12 9DJ

☎ 0131 446 5600 📄 0131 446 5610

e-mail: h6515@accor.com

dir: Near Hermiston Gate shopping area

PETS: Bedrooms unattended Stables 3m Charges £10 per night
Grounds on leads Other charge for damage Restrictions no Pit
Bull Terriers

Located just off the city by-pass and within minutes of the
airport, this modern hotel offers bedrooms that are spacious and
comfortable. The public areas include the open-plan lobby, bar
and a restaurant where some tables have their own TVs.

Rooms 170 (130 fmly) Facilities ⊛ Gym Wi-fi Services Lift
Parking 96

Novotel Edinburgh Centre

★★★★ 73% HOTEL

Lauriston Place, Lady Lawson St EH3 9DE

☎ 0131 656 3500 📄 0131 656 3510

e-mail: H3271@accor.com

web: www.novotel.com

dir: From Edinburgh Castle right onto George IV Bridge from
Royal Mile. Follow to junct, then right onto Lauriston Place. Hotel
700mtrs on right

PETS: Bedrooms unattended Charges £10 per night
Public areas except restaurant on leads Exercise area park 5
mins' walk Facilities walks info Other charge for damage

One of the new generations of Novotels, this modern hotel is
located in the centre of the city, close to Edinburgh Castle. Smart
and stylish public areas include a cosmopolitan bar, brasserie-
style restaurant and indoor leisure facilities. The air-conditioned
bedrooms feature a comprehensive range of extras and
bathrooms with baths and separate shower cabinets.

Rooms 180 (146 fmly) Facilities STV ⊛ Gym Sauna Steam room
Xmas Wi-fi Services Lift Air con Parking 15

Dalhousie Castle and Aqueous Spa

★★★ 82% ⊛⊛ HOTEL

Bonnyrigg EH19 3JB

☎ 01875 820153 📄 01875 821936

e-mail: info@dalhousiecastle.co.uk

web: www.dalhousiecastle.co.uk

dir: A7 S from Edinburgh through Lasswade/Newtongrange, right
at Shell Garage (B704), hotel 0.5m from junct

PETS: Bedrooms Stables 5m Charges £20 per stay (refundable
deposit) Public areas except library & food/beverage areas
on leads Grounds on leads disp bin Exercise area 500yds
Facilities vet info On Request fridge access Other charge for
damage dogs allowed in standard bedrooms only Restrictions
well behaved dogs only

A popular wedding venue, this imposing medieval castle sits
amid lawns and parkland and even has a falconry. Bedrooms
offer a mix of styles and sizes, including richly decorated themed
rooms named after various historical figures. The Dungeon
restaurant provides an atmospheric setting for dinner, and the
less formal Orangery serves food all day. The spa offers many
relaxing and therapeutic treatments and hydro facilities.

Rooms 36 (7 annexe) (3 fmly) Facilities Spa FTV Fishing Falconry
Clay pigeon shooting Archery Laserday Xmas New Year Wi-fi
Parking 110 Notes LB

Best Western Kings Manor

★★★ 78% HOTEL

100 Milton Road East EH15 2NP

☎ 0131 669 0444 & 468 8003 📠 0131 669 6650

e-mail: reservations@kingsmanor.com

web: www.kingsmanor.com

dir: *A720 E to Old Craighall junct, left into city, right at A1/A199 junct, hotel 400mtrs on right*

PETS: Bedrooms (13 GF) **Charges** £5 per night **Public areas** except dining areas on leads **Grounds** disp bin **Exercise area** 600yds **Facilities** washing facs vet info **On Request** fridge access torch towels **Other** charge for damage

Lying on the eastern side of the city and convenient for the by-pass, this hotel is popular with business guests, tour groups and for conferences. It boasts a fine leisure complex and a bright modern bistro, which complements the quality, creative cooking in the main restaurant.

Rooms 95 (8 fmly) (13 GF) **S** £50-£90; **D** £60-£165*
Facilities Spa STV FTV 🐾 🏊 Gym Health & beauty salon Steam room Sauna Xmas New Year Wi-fi **Services** Lift **Parking** 130 **Notes** LB

Arden Guest House

★★★ GUEST HOUSE

126 Old Dalkeith Rd EH16 4SD

☎ 0131 664 3985 📠 0131 621 0866

e-mail: ardenguesthouse@btinternet.com

dir: *2m SE of city centre nr Craigmillar Castle. On A7 200yds W of hospital*

PETS: Bedrooms unattended **Public areas** **Grounds** disp bin **Exercise area** 0.25m **Facilities** food (pre-bookable) food bowl water bowl bedding dog chews scoop/disp bags leads pet sitting dog walking washing facs cage storage walks info vet info **On Request** fridge access torch towels

Well situated on the south side of the city, close to the hospital. Benefiting from off-road parking and refurbishment in a number of areas. Many thoughtful extras are provided as standard, including Wi-fi. Attentive and friendly service enhances the guest experience.

Rooms 8 en suite (2 fmly) (3 GF) **Facilities** STV tea/coffee Cen ht Wi-fi **Parking** 8 **Notes** Closed 22-27 Dec

Pitbauchlie House

★★★ 77% HOTEL

Aberdour Rd KY11 4PB

☎ 01383 722282 📠 01383 620738

e-mail: info@pitbauchlie.com

web: www.pitbauchlie.com

dir: *M90 junct 2, A823, then B916. Hotel 0.5m on right*

PETS: Bedrooms (19 GF) unattended sign on leads **Grounds** **Exercise area** 3-acre wooded grounds **Facilities** walks info vet info **On Request** fridge access torch towels

Situated in three acres of wooded grounds this hotel is just a mile south of the town and has a striking modern interior. The bedrooms are well equipped, and the deluxe rooms have 32-inch LCD satellite TVs and CD micro systems; there is one bedroom designed for less able guests. The eating options include Harvey's Conservatory bistro and Restaurant 47 where Scottish and French influenced cuisine is offered.

Rooms 50 (3 fmly) (19 GF) **Facilities** STV FTV Gym Wi-fi **Parking** 80

Woodland Gardens Caravan & Camping Site *(NO418031)*

►►►

Blindwell Rd KY8 5QG

☎ 01333 360319

e-mail: enquiries@woodland-gardens.co.uk

dir: *Off A915 (coast road) at Largo at E end of Lundin Links, turn N off A915, 0.5m signed*

PETS: Charges £5 per stay **Public areas** except public wash facilities, dogs may not roam free (tether on site) on leads disp bin **Exercise area** 100yds **Facilities** walks info vet info **Other** prior notice required 1 dog per unit disposal bags available; **Restrictions** no dangerous breeds (see page 7) Resident Pet: Bramble (Golden Retriever)

Open Apr-Oct Last arrival 21.00hrs Last departure noon

A secluded and sheltered 'little jewel' of a site in a small orchard under the hill called Largo Law. This very attractive site is family owned and run to an immaculate standard, and pitches are grouped in twos and threes by low hedging and gorse. A 1 acre site with 20 touring pitches, 6 hardstandings and 5 statics.

Notes 🐾

SCOTLAND

ST ANDREWS   Map 12 NO51

The Inn at Lathones
★★★★ @@ INN

Largoward KY9 1JE
☎ 01334 840494   📄 01334 840694
e-mail: lathones@theinn.co.uk
web: www.theinn.co.uk
dir: *5m S of St Andrews on A915, 0.5m before village of Largoward on left just after hidden dip*

PETS: **Bedrooms** unattended **Charges** £10 per stay **Grounds** **Exercise area** **Facilities** vet info **On Request** fridge access torch **Other** charge for damage

This lovely country inn, parts of which are 400 years old, is full of character and individuality. The friendly staff help to create a relaxed atmosphere. Smart contemporary bedrooms are in two separate wings. The colourful, cosy restaurant is the main focus, where the menu offers modern interpretations of Scottish and European dishes.

Rooms 21 annexe en suite (1 fmly) (18 GF) **S** £99-£129; **D** £120-£180* **Facilities** STV TVL tea/coffee Dinner available Direct Dial Cen ht Wi-fi **Parking** 35 **Notes** LB Closed 26 Dec & 3-16 Jan RS 24 Dec

CITY OF GLASGOW

GLASGOW   Map 11 NS56

Malmaison Glasgow

★★★ 83% @ HOTEL

278 West George St G2 4LL
☎ 0141 572 1000   📄 0141 572 1002
e-mail: glasgow@malmaison.com
web: www.malmaison.com
dir: *From S & E: M8 junct 18 (Charing Cross). From W & N: M8 city centre*

PETS: **Bedrooms** (19 GF) unattended **Charges** £10 per night **Public areas** except restaurant on leads **Exercise area** 50yds **Facilities** (pre-bookable) food bowl water bowl **On Request** fridge access towels **Other** charge for damage

Built around a former church in the historic Charing Cross area, this hotel is a smart, contemporary establishment offering impressive levels of service and hospitality. Bedrooms are spacious and feature a host of modern facilities, such as CD players and mini bars. Dining is a treat here, with French brasserie-style cuisine, backed up by an excellent wine list, served in the original crypt.

Rooms 72 (4 fmly) (19 GF) **D** £125-£355* **Facilities** STV Gym Cardiovascular equipment New Year Wi-fi **Services** Lift **Notes** LB

Georgian House
★★★ GUEST HOUSE

29 Buckingham Ter, Great Western Rd, Kelvinside G12 8ED
☎ 0141 339 0008 & 07973 971563
e-mail: thegeorgianhouse@yahoo.com
web: www.thegeorgianhousehotel.com
dir: *M8 junct 17 towards Dumbarton, through 4 sets of lights & right onto Queen Margaret Dr, then right onto Buckingham Ter*

PETS: **Bedrooms** sign **Stables** 7m **Charges** **Public areas** **Grounds** on leads disp bin **Exercise area** across road **Facilities** food bowl water bowl feeding mat dog walking washing facs walks info vet info **On Request** fridge access torch towels **Other** charge for damage

Georgian House offers good value accommodation at the west end of the city in a peaceful tree-lined Victorian terrace near the Botanic Gardens. Bedrooms vary in size and are furnished in modern style. Only a continental style breakfast is served which is in the first-floor lounge-dining room.

Rooms 11 rms (10 en suite) (1 pri facs) (4 fmly) (3 GF) **S** £35-£55; **D** £50-£80* **Facilities** FTV TVL tea/coffee Cen ht Wi-fi **Parking** 7 **Notes** LB

The Kelvin
★★★ GUEST HOUSE

15 Buckingham Ter, Great Western Rd, Hillhead G12 8EB
☎ 0141 339 7143   📄 0141 339 5215
e-mail: enquiries@kelvinhotel.com
web: www.kelvinhotel.com
dir: *M8 junct 17, A82 Kelvinside/Dumbarton, 1m on right before Botanic Gardens*

PETS: **Bedrooms** **Charges** **Public areas** except dining room & lounge on leads **Grounds** disp bin **Exercise area** **Facilities** food bowl water bowl walks info vet info **On Request** fridge access torch towels **Other** charge for damage

Two substantial Victorian terrace houses on the west side of the city have been combined to create this friendly establishment close to the Botanical Gardens. The attractive bedrooms are comfortably proportioned and well equipped with flat-screen TVs offering an array of channels; Wi-fi is also available. The dining room on the first floor is the setting for breakfasts served at individual tables.

Rooms 21 rms (9 en suite) (4 fmly) (2 GF) (14 smoking) **S** £30-£48; **D** £56-£68 **Facilities** FTV tea/coffee Cen ht Wi-fi **Parking** 5

ARISAIG Map 13 NM68

Cnoc-na-Faire

★ ★ ★ ★ ⚙ 🍴 INN

Back of Keppoch PH39 4NS

☎ 01687 450249   📄 01687 450249

e-mail: cnocnafaire@googlemail.com

dir: On A830, 1m past Arisaig, left onto B0080. 0.5m on left into drive

PETS: **Bedrooms** unattended **Stables** 1m **Charges** **Public areas** except restaurant on leads **Grounds** disp bin **Exercise area** 500yds **Facilities** food bowl water bowl dog chews feeding mat scoop/disp bags leads washing facs cage storage walks info vet info **On Request** fridge access torch towels **Restrictions** no dangerous breeds (see page 7) **Resident Pets:** Harris & Lewis (Cocker Spaniels)

Gaelic for 'Hill of Vigil' the property boasts picture-postcard views down to the white sandy beach and beyond to the Inner Hebridean isles. The modern bedrooms and bathrooms cater well for guests' needs. Award-winning food is served in the cosy bar and restaurant. Warm and genuine service and hospitality complete a wonderful guest experience.

Rooms 6 en suite **S** £85-£95; **D** £90-£125* **Facilities** STV tea/coffee Dinner available Cen ht Wi-fi Golf 9 **Parking** 15 **Notes** Closed 23-27 Dec No coaches

BALLACHULISH Map 14 NN55

The Isles of Glencoe Hotel & Leisure Centre

★ ★ ★ 71% HOTEL

PH49 4HL

☎ 0845 906 9966   📄 01855 811770

e-mail: reservations@akkeron-hotels.com

web: www.akkeron-hotels.com

dir: A82 N, slip road on left into village, 1st right, hotel in 600yds

PETS: **Bedrooms** (21 GF) unattended sign **Charges** £10 per night **Public areas** except restaurant on leads **Grounds** on leads disp bin **Exercise area** **Facilities** food bowl water bowl bedding dog chews cat treats scoop/disp bags washing facs cage storage walks info vet info **On Request** fridge access torch towels **Other** charge for damage

Enjoying a spectacular setting beside Loch Leven, this friendly modern establishment has spacious bedrooms, and guests have a choice of Loch or Mountain View rooms. Public areas include a popular restaurant and a family friendly leisure centre.

Rooms 59 (21 fmly) (21 GF) **S** £69-£135; **D** £69-£145 (incl. bkfst)* **Facilities** STV ⊗ Gym Hydroseat Bio-sauna 🎵 Xmas New Year Wi-fi **Parking** 100

Lyn-Leven

★ ★ ★ ★ GUEST HOUSE

West Laroch PH49 4JP

☎ 01855 811392   📄 01855 811600

e-mail: macleodcilla@aol.com

web: www.lynleven.co.uk

dir: Off A82 signed on left West Laroch

PETS: **Bedrooms** **Charges** £5 per night **Public areas** disp bin **Exercise area**

Genuine Highland hospitality and high standards are part of the appeal of this comfortable guest house. The attractive bedrooms vary in size, are well equipped, and offer many thoughtful extra touches. There is a spacious lounge, and a smart dining room where delicious home-cooked evening meals and breakfasts are served at individual tables.

Rooms 8 en suite 4 annexe en suite (3 fmly) (12 GF); **D** £50-£66* **Facilities** TVL tea/coffee Dinner available Cen ht Licensed **Parking** 12 **Notes** LB Closed Xmas

BOAT OF GARTEN Map 14 NH91

Boat Hotel

★ ★ ★ 82% ⚙⚙ HOTEL

PH24 3BH

☎ 01479 831258   & 831696   📄 01479 831414

e-mail: info@boathotel.co.uk

dir: Off A9 N of Aviemore onto A95, follow signs to Boat of Garten

PETS: **Bedrooms** unattended **Charges** £10 per night **Public areas** except restaurant on leads **Grounds** **Facilities** walks info vet info **Other** charge for damage dogs allowed in certain bedrooms only

This well established hotel is situated in the heart of the pretty village of Boat of Garten. The public areas include a choice of comfortable lounges and the restaurant has a well deserved reputation for fine dining; in addition the bistro serves meals until late. Individually styled bedrooms reflect the unique character of the hotel; all are comfortable, well equipped and have a host of thoughtful extras.

Rooms 34 (2 fmly) **S** £39-£69; **D** £69-£159 (incl. bkfst)* **Facilities** FTV Xmas New Year Wi-fi **Parking** 36

SCOTLAND

BRORA
Map 14 NC90

CLASSIC BRITISH HOTELS

Royal Marine Hotel, Restaurant & Spa
★★★★ 75% ⊛ HOTEL

Golf Rd KW9 6QS
☎ 01408 621252 🖷 01408 621181
e-mail: info@royalmarinebrora.com
web: www.royalmarinebrora.com
dir: Off A9 in village towards beach & golf course

PETS: Bedrooms (2 GF) unattended Charges £10 per stay
Exercise area beach (300mtrs) Facilities washing facs cage
storage walks info vet info On Request fridge access towels
Other charge for damage disposal bags available

A distinctive Edwardian residence sympathetically extended,
the Royal Marine attracts a mixed market. Its leisure centre
is popular, and the restaurant, Hunters Lounge and café bar
offer three contrasting eating options. A modern bedroom wing
complements the original bedrooms, which retain period style.
There are also luxury apartments just a short walk away.

Rooms 21 (1 fmly) (2 GF) Facilities FTV 🕙 🏊 Putt green Fishing
🏊 Gym Steam room Sauna Xmas New Year Wi-fi Parking 40
Notes LB

CARRBRIDGE
Map 14 NH92

Dalrachney Lodge
★★★ 75% SMALL HOTEL

PH23 3AT
☎ 01479 841252 🖷 01479 841383
e-mail: dalrachney@aol.com
web: www.dalrachney.co.uk
dir: Follow Carrbridge signs off A9. In village on A938

PETS: Charges £5 per night Public areas Grounds on leads
disp bin Exercise area Facilities cage storage walks info
vet info Other charge for damage Restrictions no Pit Bulls or
dangerous breeds (see page 7) Resident Pets: 2 cats

A traditional Highland lodge, Dalrachney lies in grounds by the
River Dulnain on the edge of the village. Spotlessly maintained
public areas include a comfortable and relaxing sitting room and
a cosy well-stocked bar, which has a popular menu providing an
alternative to the dining room. Bedrooms are generally spacious
and furnished in period style.

Rooms 11 (3 fmly) S £83-£90; D £83-£95 (incl. bkfst)
Facilities Fishing Xmas New Year Wi-fi Parking 10 Notes LB

CONTIN
Map 14 NH45

Coul House
★★★ 79% ⊛ COUNTRY HOUSE HOTEL

IV14 9ES
☎ 01997 421487 🖷 01997 421945
e-mail: stay@coulhousehotel.com
dir: Exit A9 north onto A835. Hotel on right

PETS: Bedrooms (4 GF) unattended Charges £5 per
night Public areas except dining areas Grounds disp bin
Exercise area adjacent Facilities cage storage walks info vet
info On Request fridge access torch

This imposing mansion house is set back from the road in
extensive grounds. A number of the generally spacious bedrooms
have superb views of the distant mountains and all are
thoughtfully equipped. The Octagonal Restaurant offers guests
the chance to enjoy contemporary Scottish cuisine.

Rooms 20 (3 fmly) (4 GF) Facilities 9 hole pitch & putt New Year
Wi-fi Child facilities Parking 60 Notes LB Closed 24-26 Dec

CORPACH
Map 14 NN07

Linnhe Lochside Holidays (NN074771)
►►►►►

PH33 7NL
☎ 01397 772376 🖷 01397 772007
e-mail: relax@linnhe-lochside-holidays.co.uk
dir: On A830, 1m W of Corpach, 5m from Fort William

PETS: Charges £5 per night £35 per week Public areas except
pet-free areas disp bin Exercise area dog walk area & long
beach Facilities washing facs walks info vet info Other prior
notice required Resident Pets: dogs, cats, ferrets, ducks,
chickens

Open Etr-Oct Last arrival 21.00hrs Last departure 11.00hrs

An excellently maintained site in a beautiful setting on the shores
of Loch Eil, with Ben Nevis to the east and the mountains and
Sunart to the west. The owners have worked in harmony with
nature to produce an idyllic environment, where they offer the
highest standards of design and maintenance. A 5.5 acre site
with 85 touring pitches, 63 hardstandings and 20 statics.

FORT AUGUSTUS — Map 14 NH30

The Lovat, Loch Ness
★★★ 87% ◎◎ HOTEL

Loch Ness Side PH32 4DU
☎ 0845 450 1100 & 01456 459250 ▤ 01320 366677
e-mail: info@thelovat.com
web: www.thelovat.com
dir: In town centre on A82

PETS: Bedrooms (7 GF) Stables 30m Charges £6.50 per night
Public areas only in bar area outside dining hours on leads
Grounds on leads disp bin Exercise area 15-20 mins Facilities
food (pre-bookable) food bowl water bowl dog chews cat treats
feeding mat scoop/disp bags leads cage storage walks info
vet info On Request fridge access torch towels Other charge
for damage pets accommodated in 1 bedroom only Restrictions
2 small dogs or 1 large dog only

This charming country-house hotel enjoys an elevated position
in the pretty town of Fort Augustus. It has impressively styled
bedrooms with a host of thoughtful extras. Inviting public areas
include a comfortable lounge with a log fire, a stylish bar, and
contemporary restaurant were food is cooked with skill and care.
The hospitality and commitment to guest care will leave a lasting
impression.

Rooms 28 (6 annexe) (3 fmly) (7 GF) S £60-£135; D £80-£260
(incl. bkfst)* Facilities FTV Xmas New Year Wi-fi Services Lift
Parking 30 Notes LB

FORT WILLIAM — Map 14 NN17

Moorings
★★★ 82% ◎ HOTEL

Banavie PH33 7LY
☎ 01397 772797 ▤ 01397 772441
e-mail: reservations@moorings-fortwilliam.co.uk
web: www.moorings-fortwilliam.co.uk
dir: Take A830 (N from Fort William), cross Caledonian Canal,
1st right

PETS: Bedrooms (1 GF) Charges £5 per stay Public areas
except restaurant during food service on leads Grounds on leads
disp bin Exercise area canal bank walk adjacent Facilities
bedding washing facs cage storage walks info On Request
torch towels Other charge for damage pet blanket provided;
dogs accepted by prior arrangement only & allowed in standard
ground-floor bedroom only

Located on the Caledonian Canal next to a series of locks
known as Neptune's Staircase and close to Thomas Telford's
house, this hotel with its dedicated team offers friendly service.
Accommodation comes in two distinct styles and the newer rooms
are particularly appealing. Meals can be taken in the bars or the
spacious dining room.

Rooms 27 (1 fmly) (1 GF) S £50-£135; D £95-£145 (incl. bkfst)*
Facilities STV New Year Wi-fi Parking 60 Notes LB RS 24-27 Dec

Lime Tree Hotel & Restaurant
★★★ 78% ◎ SMALL HOTEL

Lime Tree Studio, Achintore Rd PH33 6RQ
☎ 01397 701806 ▤ 01397 701806
e-mail: info@limetreefortwilliam.co.uk
dir: On A82 at entrance to Fort William

PETS: Bedrooms (4 GF) Charges £5 per night Public areas
except restaurant on leads Grounds disp bin Exercise area
100mtrs Other charge for damage Restrictions small to
medium sized dogs only; no puppies Resident Pet: Maggie (dog)

A charming small hotel with an inspirational art gallery on the
ground floor, with lots of original artwork displayed throughout.
Evening meals can be enjoyed in the restaurant which has a loyal
following. The hotel's comfortable lounges with their real fires
are ideal for pre or post dinner drinks or maybe just to relax in.
Individually designed bedrooms are spacious with some nice little
personal touches courtesy of the artist owner.

Rooms 9 (4 fmly) (4 GF) Facilities New Year Wi-fi Parking 9
Notes Closed Nov

Glen Nevis Caravan & Camping Park
(NN124722)

▶▶▶▶

Glen Nevis PH33 6SX
☎ 01397 702191 ▤ 01397 703904
e-mail: holidays@glen-nevis.co.uk
dir: In northern outskirts of Fort William follow A82 to mini-rdbt.
Exit for Glen Nevis. Site 2.5m on right

PETS: Public areas on leads disp bin Exercise area Facilities
walks info vet info

Open 13 Mar-9 Nov rs Mar & mid-Oct-Nov limited shop &
restaurant facilities Last arrival 22.00hrs Last departure noon

A tasteful site with well-screened enclosures, at the foot of Ben
Nevis in the midst of some of the Highlands' most spectacular
scenery; an ideal area for walking and touring. The park boasts a
restaurant which offers a high standard of cooking and provides
good value for money. A 30 acre site with 380 touring pitches,
150 hardstandings and 30 statics.

Notes Quiet 23.00hrs-08.00hrs

SCOTLAND

FOYERS · Map 14 NH42

Craigdarroch House

★★★★ 🍴 RESTAURANT WITH ROOMS

IV2 6XU

☎ 01456 486400   📠 01456 486444

e-mail: info@hotel-loch-ness.co.uk

dir: *Take B862 from either end of loch, then B852 signed Foyers*

PETS: Bedrooms Charges £10 per week **Public areas** except restaurant on leads **Grounds** on leads disp bin **Exercise area** adjacent **Facilities** walks info vet info **On Request** towels **Other** charge for damage **Resident Pets:** 2 dogs, Harris Hawk

Craigdarroch is located in an elevated position high above Loch Ness on the south side. Bedrooms vary in style and size but all are comfortable and well equipped; those that are front-facing have wonderful views. Dinner is well worth staying in for, and breakfast is also memorable.

Rooms 10 en suite (1 fmly) **S** £40-£80; **D** £60-£160*
Facilities FTV TVL tea/coffee Dinner available Direct Dial Cen ht Wi-fi **Parking** 24 **Notes** No coaches

GLENCOE · Map 14 NN15

Invercoe Caravan & Camping Park

(NN098594)

▶ ▶ ▶ ▶

PH49 4HP

☎ 01855 811210   📠 01855 811210

e-mail: holidays@invercoe.co.uk

dir: *Exit A82 at Glencoe Hotel onto B863 for 0.25m*

PETS: Public areas Exercise area 100yds **Facilities** food food bowl water bowl walks info vet info

Open all year Last departure noon

Level grass site set on the shore of Loch Leven, with excellent mountain views. The area is ideal for both walking and climbing, and also offers a choice of several freshwater and saltwater lochs. Convenient for the good shopping at Fort William. A 5 acre site with 60 touring pitches and 4 statics.

Notes No large group bookings

GLENFINNAN · Map 14 NM98

The Prince's House

★★★ 78% ◉◉ SMALL HOTEL

PH37 4LT

☎ 01397 722246   📠 01397 722323

e-mail: princeshouse@glenfinnan.co.uk

web: www.glenfinnan.co.uk

dir: *On A830, 0.5m on right past Glenfinnan Monument. 200mtrs from railway station*

PETS: Bedrooms unattended **Charges** £5 per stay **Public areas** except restaurant **Grounds** disp bin **Exercise area** 250mtrs **Facilities** walks info vet info **On Request** torch **Other** charge for damage **Resident Pet:** Floren (cat)

This delightful hotel enjoys a well deserved reputation for fine food and excellent hospitality. The hotel has inspiring views and sits close to where 'Bonnie' Prince Charlie raised the Jacobite standard. Comfortably appointed bedrooms offer pleasing decor. Excellent local game and seafood can be enjoyed in the restaurant and the bar.

Rooms 9 **S** £65-£75; **D** £100-£150 (incl. bkfst) **Facilities** STV FTV Fishing New Year **Parking** 18 **Notes** LB Closed Xmas & Jan-Feb (ex New Year) RS Nov-Dec & Mar

GOLSPIE · Map 14 NC80

Granite Villa Guest House

★★★★ GUEST ACCOMMODATION

Fountain Rd KW10 6TH

☎ 01408 633146

e-mail: info@granite-villa.co.uk

dir: *Left from A9 (N'bound) onto Fountain Rd, immediately before pedestrian crossing lights*

PETS: Bedrooms Charges £5 per stay **Public areas** except dining room on leads **Grounds** on leads disp bin **Exercise area** 500yds **Facilities** washing facs walks info vet info **On Request** towels **Other** charge for damage **Resident Pets:** Indi & Keera (Labradors)

Originally built in 1892 for a wealthy local merchant, this traditional Victorian house has been sympathetically restored in recent years. Bedrooms are comfortable and all come with a range of thoughtful extras. Guests can relax in the large lounge, with its views over the landscaped garden; complimentary tea and coffee are often served here. A warm welcome is assured in this charming period house.

Rooms 5 en suite (1 fmly) (1 GF) (2 smoking) **S** £45-£70; **D** £70-£80* **Facilities** FTV tea/coffee Cen ht Wi-fi Golf **Parking** 6 **Notes** ☺

Culloden House

★★★★ 80% ◉◉ HOTEL

Culloden IV2 7BZ

☎ 01463 790461   📠 01463 792181

e-mail: info@cullodenhouse.co.uk

web: www.cullodenhouse.co.uk

dir: *A96 from Inverness, right for Culloden. 1m after 2nd lights, left at church*

PETS: Bedrooms (3 GF) sign **Stables** 6m **Public areas** except restaurant & bar on leads **Grounds** disp bin **Exercise area** 500mtrs **Facilities** food food bowl water bowl bedding feeding mat washing facs cage storage walks info vet info **On Request** fridge access torch towels **Other** charge for damage

Dating from the late 1700s this impressive mansion is set in extensive grounds close to the famous Culloden Battlefield. High ceilings and intricate cornices are particular features of the public rooms, including the elegant Adam dining room. Bedrooms come in a range of sizes and styles, with a number situated in a separate house.

Rooms 28 (5 annexe) (1 fmly) (3 GF) **S** £100-£175; **D** £125-£250 (incl. bkfst) **Facilities** FTV ◗ Putt green ⚑ Boules Badminton Golf driving net Putting green New Year Wi-fi **Parking** 50 **Notes** No children 10yrs Closed 24-28 Dec

Loch Ness Country House Hotel

★★★★ 79% ◉ SMALL HOTEL

Loch Ness Rd IV3 8JN

☎ 01463 230512   📠 01463 224532

e-mail: info@dunainparkhotel.co.uk

web: www.dunainparkhotel.co.uk

dir: *On A82, 1m from Inverness town boundary*

PETS: (3 GF) **Charges** £10 per night £70 per week **Grounds** on leads **Exercise area Facilities** food bowl water bowl bedding cage storage walks info vet info **On Request** fridge access torch towels **Other** charge for damage pets allowed in garden cottages only

Built in the Georgian era, this fine house is perfectly situated in its own six acre private Highland estate. The hotel has luxurious bedrooms; some are garden cottage suites. The stylish restaurant serves the best of local produce and guests have a choice of cosy well-appointed lounges for after dinner drinks. The garden terrace is ideal for relaxing and has splendid views over the landscaped gardens towards Inverness.

Rooms 13 (2 annexe) (8 fmly) (3 GF) **S** £75-£135; **D** £159-£195 (incl. bkfst)* **Facilities** FTV Xmas New Year Wi-fi Child facilities **Parking** 50 **Notes** LB

Kingsmills

★★★★ 74% HOTEL

Culcabock Rd IV2 3LP

☎ 01463 237166 & 257100   📠 01463 225208

e-mail: reservations@kingsmillshotel.com

web: www.kingsmillshotel.com

dir: *From A9 S, exit Culduthel/Kingsmills 5th exit at rdbt, 0.5m, over mini-rdbt past golf club. Hotel on left after lights*

PETS: Bedrooms (34 GF) **Grounds** on leads **Exercise area Facilities** walks info vet info **Other** please advise hotel of any dogs at time of booking

This manor house hotel is located just a short drive from the city, and is set in four acres of landscaped grounds. There is a range of spacious, well-equipped modern bedrooms; the rooms in the newer wing are especially impressive. There is a choice of restaurants, a comfortable lounge, a leisure club and conference facilities.

Rooms 114 (5 fmly) (34 GF) (6 smoking) **Facilities** Spa STV ⊠ supervised Putt green Gym Hairdresser Sauna Steam room Pitch & putt ♫ Xmas New Year Wi-fi **Services** Lift **Parking** 140

Royal Highland

★★★ 77% HOTEL

Station Square, Academy St IV1 1LG

☎ 01463 231926 & 251451   📠 01463 710705

e-mail: info@royalhighlandhotel.co.uk

web: www.royalhighlandhotel.co.uk

dir: *From A9 into town centre. Hotel next to rail station & Eastgate Retail Centre*

PETS: Bedrooms (2 GF) **Charges Facilities** vet info **Other** charge for damage cats accepted in carriers only **Restrictions** small to medium size, well behaved, non threatening dogs only

Built in 1858 adjacent to the railway station, this hotel has the typically grand foyer of the Victorian era with comfortable seating. The contemporary ASH Brasserie and bar offers a refreshing style for both eating and drinking throughout the day. The generally spacious bedrooms are comfortably equipped especially for the business traveller.

Rooms 85 (12 fmly) (2 GF) (25 smoking) **S** £45-£109; **D** £59-£179 (incl. bkfst)* **Facilities** FTV Gym Xmas New Year Wi-fi **Services** Lift **Parking** 8

SCOTLAND

Express by Holiday Inn Inverness

BUDGET HOTEL

Stoneyfield IV2 7PA

☎ 01463 732700 🖨 01463 732732

e-mail: inverness@expressholidayinn.co.uk

web: www.hiexpress.com/inverness

dir: *From A9 follow A96 & Inverness Airport signs, hotel on right*

PETS: Bedrooms (24 GF) **Charges** £10 per stay ß **Public areas** except lounge on leads disp bin **Facilities** walks info vet info **Other** charge for damage pets allowed in certain bedrooms only **Restrictions** small to medium size dogs only

A modern hotel ideal for families and business travellers. Fresh and uncomplicated, the spacious rooms include Sky TV, power shower and tea and coffee-making facilities. Continental buffet breakfast is included in the room rate; other meals may be taken at the nearby family pub or restaurant.

Rooms 94 (43 fmly) (24 GF) (10 smoking)

JOHN O'GROATS   Map 15 ND37

John O'Groats Caravan Site *(ND382733)*

▶ ▶ ▶

KW1 4YR

☎ 01955 611329 & 07762 336359

e-mail: info@johnogroatscampsite.co.uk

dir: *At end of A99*

PETS: Public areas dogs must be kept on leads **Exercise area** adjacent **Facilities** washing facs walks info vet info **Other** local shop 0.25m

Open Apr-Sep Last arrival 22.00hrs Last departure 11.00hrs

An attractive site in an open position above the seashore and looking out towards the Orkney Islands. Nearby is the passenger ferry that makes day trips to the Orkneys, and there are grey seals to watch, and sea angling can be organised by the site owners. A 4 acre site with 90 touring pitches, 30 hardstandings.

Notes 🐾

LOCHINVER   Map 14 NC02

Inver Lodge

★★★★ ◎◎ HOTEL

IV27 4LU

☎ 01571 844496 🖨 01571 844395

e-mail: stay@inverlodge.com

web: www.inverlodge.com

dir: *A835 to Lochinver, through village, left after village hall, follow private road for 0.5m*

PETS: Bedrooms (11 GF) unattended **Charges Public areas** front foyer lounge only **Grounds Exercise area** nearby **Facilities** washing facs cage storage walks info vet info **On Request** fridge access torch towels **Other** charge for damage **Resident Pet:** Sam (Cairn Terrier)

Genuine hospitality is a real feature at this delightful, purpose-built hotel. Set high on the hillside above the village all bedrooms and public rooms enjoy stunning views. There is a choice of lounges and a restaurant where chefs make use of the abundant local produce. Bedrooms are spacious, stylish and come with an impressive range of accessories. There is no night service between 11pm and 7am.

Rooms 21 (11 GF) **S** £110-£140; **D** £200-£450 (incl. bkfst)* **Facilities** FTV Sauna Wi-fi **Parking** 30 **Notes** LB Closed Nov-Mar

---

MUIR OF ORD   Map 14 NH55

THE CIRCLE

Ord House

★★ 72% ◎ SMALL HOTEL

IV6 7UH

☎ 01463 870492 🖨 01463 870297

e-mail: admin@ord-house.co.uk

dir: *Exit A9 at Tore rdbt onto A832. 5m, through Muir of Ord. Left towards Ullapool (A832). Hotel 0.5m on left*

PETS: Bedrooms (3 GF) unattended **Stables** 1m **Charges Public areas** except restaurant **Grounds** disp bin **Exercise area** adjacent **Facilities** food (pre-bookable) food bowl water bowl bedding scoop/disp bags leads pet sitting washing facs cage storage walks info vet info **On Request** fridge access torch towels **Other** charge for damage **Resident Pet:** Poppy (Black Labrador)

Dating back to 1637, this country-house hotel is situated peacefully in wooded grounds and offers brightly furnished and well-proportioned accommodation. Comfortable day rooms reflect the character and charm of the house, with inviting lounges, a cosy snug bar and an elegant dining room where wide-ranging, creative menus are offered.

Rooms 12 (3 GF) **S** £60-£75; **D** £110-£140 (incl. bkfst)* **Facilities** Putt green 🎯 Clay pigeon shooting Wi-fi **Parking** 30 **Notes** LB Closed Nov-Apr

Boath House

★★★ ◉◉◉◉ HOTEL

Auldearn IV12 5TE
☎ 01667 454896 📠 01667 455469
e-mail: info@boath-house.com
web: www.boath-house.com
dir: *2m past Nairn on A96, E towards Forres, signed on main road*

PETS: Bedrooms (1 GF) **Stables** 1m **Grounds** disp bin
Exercise area 1m **Facilities** water bowl dog chews scoop/
disp bags washing facs cage storage walks info vet info
On Request fridge access torch **Other** charge for damage pet
policy which owners are required to sign **Resident Pet:** Pippin
(Jack Russell)

Standing in its own grounds, this splendid Georgian mansion has
been lovingly restored. Hospitality is first class. The owners are
passionate about what they do, and have an ability to establish
a special relationship with their guests that will be particularly
remembered. The food is also memorable here - the five-course
dinners are a culinary adventure, matched only by the excellence
of breakfasts. The house itself is delightful, with inviting
lounges and a dining room overlooking a trout loch. Bedrooms
are striking, comfortable, and include many fine antique pieces.
AA Hotel of the Year for Scotland 2010-11.

Rooms 8 (1 fmly) (1 GF) **S** £180-£250; **D** £220-£320 (incl. bkfst)
Facilities FTV Fishing ⤵ Beauty salon Xmas New Year Wi-fi
Parking 20 **Notes** LB

Crubenbeg House

★★★★ GUEST HOUSE

Falls of Truim PH20 1BE
☎ 01540 673300
e-mail: enquiries@crubenbeghouse.com
web: www.crubenbeghouse.com
dir: *4m S of Newtonmore. Off A9 for Crubenmore, over railway
bridge & right, signed*

PETS: Bedrooms Public areas except kitchen & dining room
Grounds disp bin **Exercise area** adjacent **Facilities** food (pre-
bookable) food bowl water bowl dog chews feeding mat scoop/
disp bags leads pet sitting dog walking washing facs cage
storage walks info vet info **On Request** fridge access torch
towels **Resident Pet:** Rajah (Saluki/Alsatian cross)

Set in a peaceful rural location, Crubenbeg House has stunning
country views and is well located for touring the Highlands. The
attractive bedrooms are individually styled and well equipped,
while the ground-floor bedroom provides easier access. Guests
can enjoy a dram in front of the fire in the inviting lounge, while
breakfast features the best of local produce in the adjacent
dining room.

Rooms 4 rms (3 en suite) (1 pri facs) (1 GF) **Facilities** STV
tea/coffee Dinner available Cen ht Licensed Wi-fi **Parking** 10
Notes LB No Children

Scourie

★★★ 73% SMALL HOTEL

IV27 4SX
☎ 01971 502396 📠 01971 502423
e-mail: patrick@scourie-hotel.co.uk
dir: *N'bound on A894. Hotel in village on left*

PETS: Bedrooms (5 GF) unattended **Public areas** except dining
areas **Grounds** disp bin **Exercise area** 200yds **Facilities** cage
storage walks info vet info **On Request** fridge access **Other**
charge for damage **Resident Pets:** Tilly (Springer Spaniel),
Jessie & Clemmie (cats)

This well-established hotel is an angler's paradise with extensive
fishing rights available on a 25,000-acre estate. Public areas
include a choice of comfortable lounges, a cosy bar and a
smart dining room offering wholesome fare. The bedrooms are
comfortable and generally spacious. The resident proprietors and
their staff create a relaxed and friendly atmosphere.

Rooms 20 (2 annexe) (2 fmly) (5 GF) **S** £40-£51; **D** £59-£69 (incl.
bkfst)* **Facilities** Fishing Wi-fi **Parking** 30 **Notes** LB Closed mid
Oct-end Mar RS winter evenings

Grants at Craigellachie

★★★★ ◉ RESTAURANT WITH ROOMS

Craigellachie, Ratagan IV40 8HP
☎ 01599 511331
e-mail: info@housebytheloch.co.uk
dir: *From A87 exit for Glenelg, 1st right to Ratagan, opposite
Youth Hostel sign*

PETS: Bedrooms Charges £5 per night £35 per week **Grounds**
on leads disp bin **Exercise area** 200mtrs **Facilities** leads
walks info vet info **On Request** torch **Resident Pets:** Morgan &
Magda (Boxers)

Sitting on the tranquil shores of Loch Duin and overlooked by
the Five Sisters Mountains, Grants really does have a stunning
location. The restaurant has a well deserved reputation for
its fine cuisine, and the bedrooms are stylish and have all the
creature comforts. Guests are guaranteed a warm welcome at
this charming house.

Rooms 2 en suite 2 annexe en suite (3 GF); **D** £155-£220* (incl.
dinner) **Facilities** STV tea/coffee Dinner available Cen ht Wi-fi
Riding **Parking** 8 **Notes** LB No Children 12yrs Closed Dec-mid Feb
RS Oct-Apr reservation only No coaches

SCOTLAND

SHIELDAIG — Map 14 NG85

Tigh an Eilean
★ ◎◎ SMALL HOTEL
IV54 8XN
☎ 01520 755251 📠 01520 755321
e-mail: tighaneilean@keme.co.uk
dir: Off A896 onto village road signed Shieldaig, hotel in centre

PETS: Bedrooms unattended sign Stables 400yds Grounds disp bin Exercise area 400mtrs Facilities food (pre-bookable) food bowl water bowl bedding dog chews cat treats feeding mat scoop/disp bags leads washing facs cage storage walks info vet info On Request fridge access torch towels Resident Pets: Ella & Katy (Black Labradors), Woody (cat)

A splendid location by the sea, with views over the bay, is the icing on the cake for this delightful small hotel. It can be a long drive to reach Sheildaig but guests remark that the journey is more than worth the effort. The brightly decorated bedrooms are comfortable though don't expect television, except in one of the lounges. For many, it's the food that attracts, with fish and seafood featuring strongly.

Rooms 11 (1 fmly) Facilities Birdwatching Kayaks Wi-fi Parking 15 Notes Closed late Oct-mid Mar

SPEAN BRIDGE — Map 14 NN28

The Smiddy House
★★★★ ◎◎ 🍴RESTAURANT WITH ROOMS
Roy Bridge Rd PH34 4EU
☎ 01397 712335 📠 01397 712043
e-mail: enquiry@smiddyhouse.co.uk
web: www.smiddyhouse.co.uk
dir: In village centre, A82 onto A86

PETS: Bedrooms Charges £5 per night Exercise area 200yds Facilities food food bowl water bowl walks info vet info Other charge for damage Restrictions small dogs only Resident Pets: Cara (Cavalier King Charles Spaniel)

Set in the Great Glen which stretches from Fort William to Inverness, this was once the village smithy, and is now a friendly establishment. The attractive bedrooms, named after places in Scotland, are comfortably furnished and well equipped. A relaxing garden room is available for guest use. Delicious evening meals are served in Russell's restaurant.

Rooms 4 en suite (1 fmly) S £55-£80; D £60-£85* Facilities tea/coffee Dinner available Wi-fi Parking 15 Notes No coaches

Achnabobane (NN195811)
★★★ FARMHOUSE
PH34 4EX
☎ 01397 712919 Mr and Mrs N Ockenden
e-mail: enquiries@achnabobane.co.uk
web: www.achnabobane.co.uk
dir: 2m S of Spean Bridge on A82

PETS: Bedrooms Charges £5 per stay Public areas except lounge & restaurant on leads Grounds on leads disp bin Facilities scoop/disp bags cage storage walks info vet info On Request fridge access torch towels Other charge for damage Resident Pets: Morse (Cavalier King Charles Spaniel), Bea, Korky & Dyllon (cats), chickens, 1 cockerel

With breathtaking views of Ben Nevis, Aonach Mhor and the Grey Corries, the farmhouse offers comfortable, good-value accommodation in a friendly family environment. Bedrooms are traditional in style and well equipped. Breakfast and evening meals are served in the conservatory-dining room.

Rooms 4 rms (1 en suite) (1 fmly) (1 GF) S £29; D £58-£72* Facilities TVL tea/coffee Dinner available Cen ht Wi-fi Parking 5 Notes Closed Xmas Red Deer/Woodland

STRONTIAN — Map 14 NM86

Kilcamb Lodge
★★★ ◎◎ COUNTRY HOUSE HOTEL
PH36 4HY
☎ 01967 402257 📠 01967 402041
e-mail: enquiries@kilcamblodge.co.uk
web: www.kilcamblodge.co.uk
dir: Off A861, via Corran Ferry

PETS: Bedrooms sign Charges dog £5 per night £30 per week Public areas Grounds disp bin Exercise area 22 acres of grounds & lochside Facilities food (pre-bookable) dog chews scoop/disp bags washing facs cage storage walks info vet info On Request fridge access torch towels Other charge for damage

This historic house on the shores of Loch Sunart was one of the first stone buildings in the area, and was used as military barracks around the time of the Jacobite uprising. It is situated on the beautiful and peaceful Ardamurchan Peninsula where otters, red squirrels and eagles can be spotted. The suites and bedrooms, with either loch or garden views, are stylishly decorated using designer fabrics and have flat-screen TVs,

DVD/CD players, plus bath robes, iced water and even guest umbrellas. Accomplished cooking, utilising much local produce, can be enjoyed in the stylish dining room. Warm hospitality is assured.

Rooms 10 (2 fmly) **S** £151-£198; **D** £239-£359 (incl. bkfst & dinner)* **Facilities** FTV Fishing Boating Hiking Bird/whale/otter watching Stalking Clay pigeon shooting Xmas New Year Wi-fi **Parking** 20 **Notes** LB No children 10yrs Closed 2 Jan-1 Feb

TONGUE · Map 14 NC55

Ben Loyal Hotel

★★★ 70% ◉ SMALL HOTEL

Main St IV27 4XE

☎ 01847 611216 🖹 01847 611212

e-mail: benloyalhotel@btinternet.com

web: www.benloyal.co.uk

dir: At junct of A838/A836. Hotel by Royal Bank of Scotland

PETS: Bedrooms Stables 10m **Public areas** except bar & restaurant during food service **Grounds** disp bin **Exercise area** adjacent **Facilities** walks info vet info **On Request** fridge access

Enjoying a super location close to Ben Loyal and with views of the Kyle of Tongue, this hotel, more often that not, marks the completion of a stunning highland and coastal drive. Bedrooms are thoughtfully equipped and brightly decorated whilst day rooms extend to a traditionally styled dining room and a cosy bar. Extensive menus ensure there's something for everyone. Staff are especially friendly and provide useful local information.

Rooms 11 (1 fmly) **S** £40; **D** £90 (incl. bkfst)* **Facilities** FTV Fishing Fly fishing tuition and equipment New Year Wi-fi **Parking** 20 **Notes** LB Closed 30 Nov-1 Mar

TORRIDON · Map 14 NG95

The Torridon

★★★★ ◉◉ COUNTRY HOUSE HOTEL

By Achnasheen, Wester Ross IV22 2EY

☎ 01445 791242 🖹 01445 712253

e-mail: info@thetorridon.com

web: www.thetorridon.com

dir: From A832 at Kinlochewe, take A896 towards Torridon. (Do not turn into village) continue 1m, hotel on right

PETS: (2 GF) **Charges** £5 per night **Public areas** only bar area **Grounds** on leads disp bin **Other** charge for damage pets allowed in cottage suite only; dogs allowed off lead in certain areas of grounds only

Delightfully set amidst inspiring loch and mountain scenery, this elegant Victorian shooting lodge has been beautifully restored to make the most of its many original features. The attractive bedrooms are all individually furnished and most enjoy stunning Highland views. Comfortable day rooms feature fine wood panelling and roaring fires in cooler months. The whisky bar

is aptly named, boasting over 300 malts and in-depth tasting notes. Outdoor activities include shooting, cycling and walking.

Rooms 19 (2 GF) **S** £180-£460; **D** £295-£505 (incl. bkfst & dinner)* **Facilities** STV Fishing ⚓ Abseiling Archery Climbing Falconry Kayaking Mountain biking Xmas New Year Wi-fi **Services** Lift **Parking** 20 **Notes** LB Closed 2 Jan-9 Feb RS Nov-14 Mar

ULLAPOOL · Map 14 NH19

Broomfield Holiday Park *(NH123939)*

►►►

West Shore St IV26 2UT

☎ 01854 612020 & 612664 🖹 01854 613151

e-mail: sross@broomfieldhp.com

dir: Take 2nd right past harbour

PETS: Public areas except toilet facilities & children's play area on leads disp bin **Exercise area** beach **Facilities** washing facs walks info vet info

Open Etr/Apr-Sep Last departure noon

Set right on the water's edge of Loch Broom and the open sea, with lovely views of the Summer Isles. The park is close to the harbour and town centre with their restaurants, bars and shops. A 12 acre site with 140 touring pitches.

Notes No noise at night

WHITEBRIDGE · Map 14 NH41

Whitebridge Hotel

★★ 69% HOTEL

IV2 6UN

☎ 01456 486226 🖹 01456 486413

e-mail: info@whitebridgehotel.co.uk

dir: A9 onto B851, follow signs to Fort Augustus. Or A82 onto B862 at Fort Augustus

PETS: Bedrooms Public areas except restaurant on leads **Grounds Exercise area** nearby **Facilities** water bowl walks info vet info

Close to Loch Ness and set amid rugged mountain and moorland scenery, this hotel is popular with tourists, fishermen and deerstalkers. Guests have a choice of more formal dining in the restaurant or lighter meals in the popular cosy bar. Bedrooms are thoughtfully equipped and brightly furnished.

Rooms 12 (3 fmly) **S** £42-£48; **D** £65-£75 (incl. bkfst)* **Facilities** Fishing Wi-fi **Parking** 32 **Notes** Closed 11 Dec-9 Jan

SCOTLAND

MIDLOTHIAN

ROSLIN
Map 11 NT26

The Original Rosslyn Inn
★★★★ INN

4 Main St EH25 9LE
☎ 0131 440 2384 📄 0131 440 2514
e-mail: enquiries@theoriginalhotel.co.uk
dir: Off city bypass at Straiton for A703 (inn near Rosslyn Chapel)

PETS: Bedrooms Charges Public areas bar only Grounds
Exercise area 10yds Facilities food bowl water bowl cage
storage walks info vet info On Request towels Other charge
for damage

Whether you find yourself on the Da Vinci Code trail or in the area
on business, this property a very short walk from the famous
Rosslyn Chapel which is well worth a visit. A delightful village
inn offers well-equipped bedrooms with upgraded en suites.
Four of the rooms have four-poster beds. The Grail Restaurant,
the lounge and conservatory offer a comprehensive selection of
dining options.

Rooms 6 en suite (2 fmly) (1 smoking) Facilities STV tea/coffee
Dinner available Cen ht Wi-fi Parking 8 Notes LB

MORAY

ABERLOUR
Map 15 NJ24

Aberlour Gardens Caravan Park (NJ282434)
▶▶▶

AB38 9LD
☎ 01340 871586 📄 01340 871586
e mail: info@aberlourgardens.co.uk
dir: Midway between Aberlour & Craigellachie on A95 turn onto
unclass road. Site signed. (NB vehicles over 10' 6" use A941 to
Dufftown)

PETS: Public areas on leads disp bin Exercise area numerous
walks accessed from park Facilities food bowl water bowl
washing facs walks info vet info Other pets must be either on
leads or in cages as appropriate

Open Mar-27 Dec Last arrival 19.00hrs Last departure noon

This attractive parkland site is set in the five-acre walled garden
of the Victorian Aberlour House, surrounded by the full range of
spectacular scenery from the Cairngorm National Park, through
pine clad glens, to the famous Moray coastline; the park is
also well placed for the world renowned Speyside Malt Whiskey
Trail. It offers a small, well-appointed toilet block, laundry and
small licensed shop. A 5 acre site with 34 touring pitches, 16
hardstandings and 32 statics.

Notes No ball games, max 5mph speed limit, no noise after
23.00hrs

NORTH LANARKSHIRE

CUMBERNAULD
Map 11 NS77

The Westerwood Hotel & Golf Resort
★★★★ 80% HOTEL

1 St Andrews Dr, Westerwood G68 0EW
☎ 01236 457171 📄 01236 738478
e-mail: westerwood@qhotels.co.uk
web: www.qhotels.co.uk

PETS: Bedrooms (49 GF) unattended Charges Public areas
except leisure club & restaurant Grounds on leads disp bin
Exercise area Facilities walks info Other charge for damage
pet food on request Restrictions small dogs only

This stylish, contemporary hotel enjoys an elevated position
within 400 acres at the foot of the Campsie Hills. Accommodation
is provided in spacious, bright bedrooms, many with super
bathrooms, and day rooms include sumptuous lounges and an
airy restaurant; extensive golf, fitness and conference facilities
are available.

Rooms 148 (15 fmly) (49 GF) Facilities Spa 🔄 ⅃ 18 ⛳ Putt green
Gym Beauty salon Relaxation room Sauna Steam room Xmas New
Year Wi-fi Services Lift Parking 250

PERTH & KINROSS

ALYTH
Map 15 NO24

Tigh Na Leigh Guesthouse
★★★★★ 🏠 ☕ GUEST ACCOMMODATION

22-24 Airlie St PH11 8AJ
☎ 01828 632372 📄 01828 632279
e-mail: bandcblack@yahoo.co.uk
web: www.tighnaleigh.co.uk
dir: In town centre on B952

PETS: Bedrooms unattended Charges £7.50 per night
Public areas except dining room Grounds on leads
Exercise area 200yds Facilities food bowl water bowl dog
chews scoop/disp bags washing facs cage storage walks info
vet info On Request fridge access torch towels Resident Pets:
Tom & Bunny (cats)

Situated in the heart of this country town, Tigh Na Leigh is Gaelic
for 'The House of the Doctor'. Its location and somewhat sombre
façade are in stunning contrast to what lies inside. The house
has been completely restored to blend its Victorian architecture
with contemporary interior design. Bedrooms, including a
superb suite, have state-of-the-art bathrooms. There are three
entirely different lounges, while delicious meals are served in the
conservatory/dining room overlooking a spectacular landscaped
garden. The owners were finalists in the AA Friendliest Landlady
of the Year award 2010-11.

Rooms 5 en suite (1 GF) S £39-£47; D £80-£120* Facilities FTV
TVL tea/coffee Dinner available Cen ht Licensed Wi-fi Golf 18
Parking 5 Notes No Children 12yrs Closed Dec-Feb

SCOTLAND

Atholl Arms Hotel
★★★ 72% HOTEL
Old North Rd PH18 5SG
☎ 01796 481205   📠 01796 481550
e-mail: hotel@athollarms.co.uk
web: www.athollarmshotel.co.uk
dir: *Off A9 to B8079, 1m into Blair Atholl, hotel near entrance to Blair Castle*

PETS: Bedrooms Stables 1m **Charges** £5 per night £35 per week **Public areas** except restaurant on leads **Grounds** on leads disp bin **Exercise area** village green adjacent **Facilities** cage storage walks info vet info **Other** charge for damage

Situated close to Blair Castle and conveniently adjacent to the railway station, this stylish hotel has historically appointed public rooms that include a choice of bars, and a splendid baronial-style dining room. Bedrooms vary in size and style. Staff throughout are friendly and very caring.

Rooms 30 (3 fmly) **Facilities** Fishing Rough shooting 🎵 New Year Wi-fi **Parking** 103

Blair Castle Caravan Park *(NN874656)*
▶ ▶ ▶ ▶ ▶
PH18 5SR
☎ 01796 481263   📠 01796 481587
e-mail: mail@blaircastlecaravanpark.co.uk
dir: *From A9 junct with B8079 at Aldclune, then NE to Blair Atholl. Site on right after crossing bridge in village*

PETS: Charges £1 per night **Public areas** except reception, toilet blocks & children's play area disp bin **Exercise area** dog walk adjacent **Facilities** food food bowl water bowl walks info vet info **Other** prior notice required disposal bags available **Restrictions** no dangerous breeds (see page 7)

Open Mar-Nov Last arrival 21.30hrs Last departure noon

Attractive site set in impressive seclusion within the Atholl Estate, surrounded by mature woodland and the River Tilt. Although a large park, the various groups of pitches are located throughout the extensive parkland, and each has its own sanitary block with all-cubicled facilities of a very high standard. There is a choice of grass pitches, hardstandings, or fully-serviced pitches. This park is particularly suitable for the larger type of motorhome. A 32 acre site with 248 touring pitches and 109 statics.

Notes Family park, no noise after 23.00hrs

Royal
★★★ 83% HOTEL
Melville Square PH6 2DN
☎ 01764 679200   📠 01764 679219
e-mail: reception@royalhotel.co.uk
web: www.royalhotel.co.uk
dir: *Off A9 on A822 to Crieff, then B827 to Comrie. Hotel in main square on A85*

PETS: Bedrooms unattended **Stables** 3m **Public areas Grounds** disp bin **Exercise area** 500yds **Facilities** food bowl water bowl scoop/disp bags leads washing facs walks info vet info **On Request** fridge access torch towels **Other** charge for damage **Resident Pet:** Ella (Labrador)

A traditional façade gives little indication of the style and elegance inside this long-established hotel located in the village centre. Public areas include a bar and library, a bright modern restaurant and a conservatory-style brasserie. Bedrooms are tastefully appointed and furnished with smart reproduction antiques.

Rooms 13 (2 annexe) **S** £85-£105; **D** £140-£180 (incl. bkfst) **Facilities** STV Fishing Shooting arranged New Year Wi-fi **Parking** 22 **Notes** LB Closed 25-26 Dec

Kenmore Hotel
★★★ 78% HOTEL
The Square PH15 2NU
☎ 01887 830205   📠 01887 830262
e-mail: reception@kenmorehotel.co.uk
web: www.kenmorehotel.com
dir: *Off A9 at Ballinluig onto A827, through Aberfeldy to Kenmore, hotel in village centre*

PETS: Bedrooms (7 GF) **Stables** 1m **Charges** £7.50 per night £52.50 per week **Public areas** except restaurant on leads **Grounds** on leads disp bin **Exercise area** 0.5m **Facilities** food (pre-bookable) food bowl water bowl dog chews cat treats scoop/disp bags washing facs cage storage walks info vet info **On Request** fridge access torch towels **Other** charge for damage **Restrictions** no dangerous dogs (see page 7)

Dating back to 1572, this riverside hotel is Scotland's oldest inn and has a rich and interesting history. Bedrooms have tasteful decor, and meals can be enjoyed in the restaurant which has panoramic views of the River Tay. The choice of bars includes one with real fires.

Rooms 40 (13 annexe) (4 fmly) (7 GF) (4 smoking) **Facilities** STV Fishing Salmon fishing on River Tay Xmas New Year Wi-fi **Services** Lift **Parking** 40

Ballathie House Hotel

★★★★ 78% ⊛⊛ COUNTRY HOUSE HOTEL

PH1 4QN

☎ 01250 883268   📄 01250 883396

e-mail: email@ballathiehousehotel.com

web: www.ballathiehousehotel.com

dir: *From A9, 2m N of Perth, B9099 through Stanley & signed, or from A93 at Beech Hedge follow signs for hotel, 2.5m*

PETS: Bedrooms (10 GF) **Charges** £10 per stay **Public areas Grounds** disp bin **Exercise area Facilities** food bowl water bowl dog chews vet info **On Request** fridge access towels **Other** charge for damage

Set in delightful grounds, this splendid Scottish mansion house combines classical grandeur with modern comfort. Bedrooms range from well-proportioned master rooms to modern standard rooms, and many boast antique furniture and art deco bathrooms. There are also Riverside Rooms, a purpose-built development right on the banks of the river, complete with balconies and terraces. The elegant restaurant has views over the River Tay.

Rooms 41 (16 annexe) (2 fmly) (10 GF) **S** £95-£130; **D** £190-£260 (incl. bkfst)* **Facilities** FTV Putt green Fishing ⛴ Xmas New Year Wi-fi **Services** Lift **Parking** 50 **Notes** LB

 MACDONALD HOTELS & RESORTS

Macdonald Loch Rannoch Hotel

★★★ 73% HOTEL

PH16 5PS

☎ 0844 879 9059 & 01882 632201   📄 01882 632203

e-mail: loch_rannoch@macdonald-hotels.co.uk

web: www.macdonald-hotels.co.uk

dir: *Off A9 onto B847 Calvine. Follow signs to Kinloch Rannoch, hotel 1m from village*

PETS: Bedrooms Charges £10 per stay **Public areas** except lounge, bar & restaurant on leads **Grounds** on leads disp bin **Exercise area** 100yds **Facilities** walks info vet info **On Request** fridge access torch towels **Other** charge for damage

Set deep in the countryside with elevated views across Loch Rannoch, this hotel is built around a 19th-century hunting lodge and provides a great base for exploring this beautiful area. The

superior bedrooms have views over the loch. There is a choice of eating options - The Ptarmigan Restaurant and the Schiehallan Bar for informal eating. The hotel provides both indoor and outdoor activities.

Rooms 44 (25 fmly) **Facilities** 🎣 Fishing Gym Xmas New Year Wi-fi **Services** Lift **Parking** 52

Dunalastair Hotel

🆄

PH16 5PW

☎ 01882 632323 & 632218   📄 01882 632371

e-mail: info@dunalastair.co.uk

dir: *A9 to Pitlochry, on N side take B8019 to Tummel Bridge then A846 to Kinloch Rannoch*

PETS: Bedrooms (9 GF) unattended sign **Charges** £5 per night **Public areas** except restaurant on leads **Grounds** disp bin **Exercise area Facilities** food (pre-bookable) food bowl water bowl dog chews feeding mat scoop/disp bags walks info vet info **Other** charge for damage **Resident Pet:** Kiita (Blue Merle Border Collie)

Currently the rating for this establishment is not confirmed. This may be due to a change of ownership or because it has only recently joined the AA rating scheme. For further details please see the AA website: theAA.com

Rooms 28 (4 fmly) (9 GF) **Facilities** Fishing 4x4 safaris Rafting Clay pigeon shooting Bike hire Archery Xmas New Year Child facilities **Parking** 33 **Notes** LB

The Green Hotel

★★★★ 73% ⊛ HOTEL

2 The Muirs KY13 8AS

☎ 01577 863467   📄 01577 863180

e-mail: reservations@green-hotel.com

web: www.green-hotel.com

dir: *M90 junct 6 follow Kinross signs, onto A922 for hotel*

PETS: Bedrooms (14 GF) **Stables** 4m **Public areas** except restaurant, lounge & bar on leads **Grounds** on leads **Exercise area** across rd **Facilities** cage storage walks info vet info **On Request** fridge access towels

A long-established hotel offering a wide range of indoor and outdoor activities. Public areas include a classical restaurant, a choice of bars and a well-stocked gift shop. The comfortable, well-equipped bedrooms, most of which are generously proportioned, boast attractive colour schemes and smart modern furnishings.

Rooms 46 (3 fmly) (14 GF) **S** £70-£110; **D** £95-£175 (incl. bkfst)* **Facilities** STV 🎣 supervised ♨ 36 ⛳ Putt green Fishing ⛴ Gym Petanque Curling (Sep-Apr) New Year Wi-fi **Parking** 60 **Notes** LB Closed 23-24 & 26-28 Dec RS 25 Dec

The Anglers Inn

★ ★ ★ INN

Main Rd, Guildtown PH2 6BS

☎ 01821 640329

e-mail: info@theanglersinn.co.uk

web: www.theanglersinn.co.uk

dir: *6m N of Perth on A93*

PETS: Bedrooms unattended **Public areas** in bar only on leads **Grounds** on leads disp bin **Exercise area** 10mtrs **Facilities** water bowl dog chews scoop/disp bags washing facs cage storage walks info vet info **On Request** fridge access torch towels **Other** charge for damage disposal bags available

This charming country inn enjoys a peaceful rural setting and yet is only a short drive from Perth city centre and is a favourite with race-goers. The inn has been totally refurbished and the accommodation consists of tastefully styled en suite bedrooms, each equipped with a flat-screen TV and complimentary Wi-fi. The restaurant has a loyal following, and the dinner menu is supplemented by nightly-changing blackboard specials.

Rooms 5 en suite (1 fmly) **Facilities** FTV TVL tea/coffee Dinner available Cen ht Wi-fi 🏊 Pool Table **Parking** 40 **Notes** LB No Children

Green Park

★ ★ ★ 87% ◉ COUNTRY HOUSE HOTEL

Clunie Bridge Rd PH16 5JY

☎ 01796 473248　📄 01796 473520

e-mail: bookings@thegreenpark.co.uk

web: www.thegreenpark.co.uk

dir: *Exit A9 at Pitlochry, follow signs 0.25m through town*

PETS: Bedrooms (16 GF) unattended **Public areas Grounds** disp bin **Exercise area** 20yds **Facilities** food bowl water bowl bedding scoop/disp bags leads washing facs cage storage walks info vet info **On Request** fridge access torch towels **Resident Pets:** Dan (Golden Retriever), Squeaky & Speedy (guinea pigs)

Guests return year after year to this lovely hotel that is situated in a stunning setting on the shores of Loch Faskally. Most of the thoughtfully designed bedrooms, including a splendid wing, the restaurant and the comfortable lounges enjoy these views. Dinner utilises fresh produce, much of it grown in the kitchen garden.

Rooms 51 (3 fmly) (16 GF) **S** £70-£100; **D** £140-£200 (incl. bkfst & dinner) **Facilities** FTV Putt green New Year Wi-fi **Services** Lift **Parking** 51 **Notes** LB

Milton of Fonab Caravan Site *(NN945573)*

▶ ▶ ▶ ▶

Bridge Rd PH16 5NA

☎ 01796 472882　📄 01796 474363

e-mail: info@fonab.co.uk

dir: *0.5m S of town off A924*

PETS: Public areas disp bin **Exercise area Facilities** food scoop/disp bags walks info vet info

Open Apr-Oct Last arrival 21.00hrs Last departure 13.00hrs

Set on the banks of the River Tummel, with extensive views down the river valley to the mountains, this park is close to the centre of Pitlochry, adjacent to the Pitlochry Festival Theatre. The sanitary facilities are exceptionally good, with most contained in combined shower/wash basin and toilet cubicles. A 15 acre site with 154 touring pitches and 36 statics.

Notes Couples & families only, no motor cycles ♿

SCOTLAND

ST FILLANS Map 11 NN62

The Four Seasons Hotel

★★★ 83% ◉◉ HOTEL

Loch Earn PH6 2NF
☎ 01764 685333 📄 01764 685444
e-mail: info@thefourseasonshotel.co.uk
web: www.thefourseasonshotel.co.uk
dir: On A85, towards W of village

PETS: Bedrooms unattended Public areas except restaurants
Grounds on leads disp bin Exercise area behind hotel
Facilities food (pre-bookable) food bowl water bowl bedding
dog chews scoop/disp bags leads pet sitting dog walking
washing facs dog grooming cage storage walks info vet
info On Request fridge access torch towels Other charge for
damage pet concierge service Resident Pets: Sham & Pagne
(Münsterlanders)

Set on the edge of Loch Earn, this welcoming hotel and many
of its bedrooms benefit from fine views. There is a choice of
lounges, including a library, warmed by log fires during winter.
Local produce is used to good effect in both the Meall Reamhar
restaurant and the more informal Tarken Room.

Rooms 18 (6 annexe) (7 fmly) S £55-£90; D £110-£150 (incl.
bkfst) Facilities FTV Xmas New Year Wi-fi Parking 40 Notes LB
Closed 2 Jan-Feb RS Nov, Dec, Mar

TUMMEL BRIDGE Map 14 NN75

Tummel Valley Holiday Park (NN764592)

PH16 5SA
☎ 0844 335 3756 📄 01882 634302
e-mail: touringandcamping@parkdeanholidays.com
dir: From Perth take A9 N to bypass Pitlochry. 3m after Pitlochry
take B8019 signed Tummel Bridge. Site 11m on left

PETS: Charges vary (please phone) on leads disp bin
Exercise area 200yds Facilities food litter tray walks info
vet info Other prior notice required disposal bags available
Restrictions no American Pit Bull Terriers, Japanese Tosas, Dogo
Argentinos, Fila Brasilieros (see also page 7)

Open Mar-Oct Last arrival 21.00hrs Last departure 10.00hrs

A well-developed site amongst mature forest in an attractive
valley, beside the famous bridge on the banks of the River
Tummel. Play areas and the bar are sited alongside the river,
and there is an indoor pool, children's clubs and live family
entertainment. This is an ideal base in which to relax. A 55 acre
site with 34 touring pitches, 34 hardstandings and 159 statics.

Notes No tents or trailer tents

SCOTTISH BORDERS

BROUGHTON Map 11 NT13

The Glenholm Centre

★★★ 🏠 GUEST ACCOMMODATION

ML12 6JF
☎ 01899 830408
e-mail: info@glenholm.co.uk
dir: 1m S of Broughton. Off A701 to Glenholm

PETS: Bedrooms unattended Public areas Grounds disp bin
Exercise area adjacent Facilities leads cage storage walks
info vet info On Request fridge access torch Resident Pets:
Minty & Sage (Bearded Collies)

Surrounded by peaceful farmland, this former schoolhouse has a
distinct African theme. The home-cooked meals and baking have
received much praise and are served in the spacious lounge-
dining room. The bright airy bedrooms are thoughtfully equipped,
and the service is friendly and attentive. Computer courses are
available.

Rooms 3 en suite 1 annexe en suite (1 fmly) (2 GF) Facilities TVL
tea/coffee Dinner available Cen ht Licensed Wi-fi ♿ Parking 14
Notes Closed 20 Dec-1 Feb

SCOTLAND

Crailing Old School

★★★★  GUEST HOUSE

TD8 6TL
☎ 01835 850382
e-mail: jean.player@virgin.net
web: www.crailingoldschool.co.uk
dir: *A698 onto B6400 signed Nisbet, Crailing Old School also signed*

PETS: Bedrooms Sep accom large kennel with run/raised bed **Stables** 0.5m **Charges** £2 per night £14 per week **Public areas** except main house **Grounds** disp bin **Exercise area** 0.2m **Facilities** food (pre-bookable) food bowl water bowl bedding dog chews scoop/disp bags leads dog walking washing facs cage storage walks info vet info **On Request** fridge access torch towels **Other** charge for damage dogs allowed in ground floor annexe bedrooms only **Resident Pet:** Reiver (Lurcher/ Scottish Deerhound cross)

This delightful rural retreat, built in 1887 as the village school, has been imaginatively renovated to combine Victorian features with modern comforts. The spacious bedrooms are beautifully maintained and decorated, and filled with homely extras. The lodge annexe suite located 10 yards from the house offers easier ground-floor access. The best of local produce produces tasty breakfasts, served in the stylish lounge-dining room (evening meals by arrangement).

Rooms 3 rms (1 en suite) (1 pri facs) 1 annexe en suite (1 GF) **S** £38.50-£45; **D** £60-£80* **Facilities** FTV TVL tea/coffee Dinner available Cen ht Wi-fi **Parking** 7 **Notes** No Children 9yrs Closed 24 Dec-2 Jan, 1wk Feb & 2wks Autumn

Kingsknowes

★★★ 75% HOTEL

Selkirk Rd TD1 3HY
☎ 01896 758375 📠 01896 750377
e-mail: enq@kingsknowes.co.uk
web: www.kingsknowes.co.uk
dir: *Off A7 at Galashiels/Selkirk rdbt*

PETS: Bedrooms Public areas except meal times **Grounds Exercise area Resident Pets:** Isla & Hector (Labradors)

An imposing turreted mansion, this hotel lies in attractive gardens on the outskirts of town close to the River Tweed. It boasts elegant public areas and many spacious bedrooms, some with excellent views. There is a choice of bars, one with a popular menu to supplement the restaurant.

Rooms 12 (2 fmly) **Facilities** Wi-fi **Parking** 65 **Notes** LB

Ferniehirst Mill Lodge

★★ GUEST HOUSE

TD8 6PQ
☎ 01835 863279
e-mail: ferniehirstmill@aol.com
web: www.ferniehirstmill.co.uk
dir: *2.5m S of Jedburgh on A68, onto private track to end*

PETS: Bedrooms unattended **Stables Charges** horses £6-£12 per night **Grounds** disp bin **Exercise area** 30mtrs **Facilities** washing facs cage storage walks info vet info **On Request** fridge access torch towels **Resident Pets:** Arctic-maremma (Sheepdog), Flight & Mac (Whippets), 11 horses

Reached by a narrow farm track and a rustic wooden bridge, this chalet-style house has a secluded setting by the River Jed. Bedrooms are small and functional but there is a comfortable lounge in which to relax. Home-cooked dinners are available by arrangement, and hearty breakfasts are served in the cosy dining room.

Rooms 7 en suite (1 GF) **S** £28; **D** £56* **Facilities** TVL tea/coffee Dinner available Direct Dial Cen ht Fishing Riding **Parking** 10

SCOTLAND

KELSO · Map 12 NT73

The Roxburghe Hotel & Golf Course
★★★ 85% COUNTRY HOUSE HOTEL

Heiton TD5 8JZ
☎ 01573 450331 📄 01573 450611
e-mail: hotel@roxburghe.net
web: www.roxburghe.net
dir: *From A68 Jedburgh take A698 to Heiton, 3m SW of Kelso*

PETS: Bedrooms (3 GF) unattended **Sep accom** 2 outdoor kennels **Stables** 10.2m **Charges** £10 per night **Grounds Exercise area Facilities** food bowl water bowl washing facs cage storage walks info vet info **On Request** torch towels **Other** charge for damage dogs allowed in Courtyard rooms only; cats must be caged

Outdoor sporting pursuits are popular at this impressive Jacobean mansion owned by the Duke of Roxburghe, and set in 500 acres of woods and parkland bordering the River Teviot. Gracious public areas are the perfect settings for afternoon teas and carefully prepared meals. The elegant bedrooms are individually designed, some by the Duchess herself, and include superior rooms, some with four posters and log fires.

Rooms 22 (6 annexe) (3 fmly) (3 GF) **Facilities** Spa STV ⚓ 18 Putt green Fishing ⚓ Clay shooting Health & beauty salon Mountain bike hire Falconry Archery Xmas New Year **Parking** 150

Ednam House
★★★ 77% HOTEL

Bridge St TD5 7HT
☎ 01573 224168 📄 01573 226319
e-mail: contact@ednamhouse.com
web: www.ednamhouse.com
dir: *50mtrs from town square*

PETS: Bedrooms (3 GF) **Public areas** except restaurant & function room **Grounds** disp bin **Exercise area Facilities** food bowl water bowl walks info vet info **On Request** fridge access torch **Restrictions** no Bernese Mountain Dogs or similar sized breeds

Overlooking a wide expanse of the River Tweed, this fine Georgian mansion has been under the Brooks family ownership for over 75 years. Accommodation styles range from standard to grand, plus The Orangerie, situated in the grounds, that has been converted into a gracious two-bedroom apartment. Public areas include a choice of lounges and an elegant dining room that has views over the gardens.

Rooms 32 (2 annexe) (4 fmly) (3 GF) **S** £78-£88; **D** £115-£161 (incl. bkfst)* **Facilities** FTV ⚓ Free access to Abbey Fitness Centre Wi-fi **Parking** 60 **Notes** Closed 22 Dec-6 Jan

LAUDER · Map 12 NT54

The Black Bull
★★★★ INN

Market Place TD2 6SR
☎ 01578 722208 📄 01578 722419
e-mail: enquiries@blackbull-lauder.com
dir: *On A68 in village centre*

PETS: Bedrooms Stables 0.5m **Charges** £5 per stay **Public areas** bar only on leads **Grounds Exercise area** nearby **Facilities** food bowl water bowl walks info vet info **On Request** fridge access **Other** charge for damage **Restrictions** very large dogs are not accepted; no Rottweilers

This 18th-century coaching inn has been completely transformed. The lovely bedrooms are furnished in the period character and thoughtfully equipped with modern amenities. The wooden floored cosy bar and four dining areas are charming, the main dining room being a former chapel. A very good range of food makes this a popular gastro-pub.

Rooms 8 en suite (2 fmly) **S** £60-£70; **D** £85-£95 **Facilities** FTV tea/coffee Dinner available Direct Dial Cen ht Wi-fi **Parking** 8 **Notes** LB

Thirlestane Castle Caravan & Camping Site
(NT536473)

▶ ▶ ▶

Thirlestane Castle TD2 6RU
☎ 01578 718884 & 07976 231032
e-mail: thirlestanepark@btconnect.com
dir: *Signed off A68 & A697, just S of Lauder*

PETS: Public areas on leads disp bin **Exercise area** 1 min **Facilities** walks info vet info **Restrictions** no dangerous breeds (see page 7) **Other** maximum 2 dogs per guest; dogs must not be left unattended at any time; dog fouling is the responsibility of owner

Open Apr-1 Oct Last arrival 20.30hrs Last departure noon

Set in the grounds of the impressive Thirlestane Castle, with mainly level grassy pitches. The park and facilities are kept in sparkling condition. A 5 acre site with 60 touring pitches, 17 hardstandings and 24 statics.

Notes 🐾

Cringletie House

★★★★ ◎◎ COUNTRY HOUSE HOTEL

Edinburgh Rd EH45 8PL
☎ 01721 725750 📠 01721 725751
e-mail: enquiries@cringletie.com
web: www.cringletie.com
dir: *2m N on A703*

PETS: Bedrooms (2 GF) unattended **Charges** £10 per stay
Grounds Exercise area nearby **Facilities** food bowl water
bowl dog chews cage storage walks info vet info **On Request**
fridge access torch **Other** all dogs welcomed with a dog biscuit
Resident Pet: Daisy (cat)

This romantic baronial mansion, built in 1861, is set in 28
acres of beautiful gardens and woodland; there is a walled
garden with a 400-year-old yew hedge (perhaps the oldest in
Scotland), a waterfall, sculptures and croquet lawn. In 1971
Scottish Heritage granted the property a Grade B listing, and in
the same year the house became a hotel. The delightful public
rooms, with welcoming fires, include a cocktail lounge with
adjoining conservatory, and there are service bells in each room
which still work. The award-winning, first-floor restaurant has a
a magnificent hand-painted ceiling. The individually designed
bedrooms have grace and charm, and for the ultimate luxury
there's the Selkirk Suite.

Rooms 13 (2 GF) **S** £170-£295; **D** £210-£335 (incl. bkfst)*
Facilities STV Putt green ⛳ Petanque Giant chess & draughts In-
room spa Xmas New Year Wi-fi **Services** Lift **Parking** 30 **Notes** LB

Macdonald Cardrona Hotel & Golf Course

★★★★ 76% ◎ HOTEL

Cardrona Mains EH45 8NE
☎ 01896 833600 📠 01896 831166
e-mail: general.cardrona@macdonald-hotels.co.uk
web: www.macdonald-hotels.co.uk/cardrona
dir: *On A72 between Peebles & Innerleithen, 3m S of Peebles*

PETS: Bedrooms (16 GF) unattended **Stables** 2m **Charges**
£10 per stay **Public areas** except lounge & restaurant on leads
Grounds on leads disp bin **Exercise area** 1m **Facilities** food
bowl water bowl dog chews washing facs cage storage walks
info vet info **On Request** fridge access torch towels **Other**
charge for damage

The rolling hills of the Scottish Borders are a stunning backdrop
for this modern, purpose-built hotel. Spacious bedrooms are
traditional in style, equipped with a range of extras, and most
enjoy fantastic countryside. The hotel features some impressive
leisure facilities, including an 18-hole golf course, 18-metre
indoor pool and state-of-the-art gym.

Rooms 99 (24 fmly) (16 GF) **S** £85-£179; **D** £94-£189 (incl.
bkfst)* **Facilities** Spa STV 🎱 ♨ 18 Putt green Gym Sauna Steam
room Xmas New Year Wi-fi **Services** Lift **Parking** 200 **Notes** LB

Tontine

★★★ 81% HOTEL

High St EH45 8AJ
☎ 01721 720892 📠 01721 729732
e-mail: info@tontinehotel.com
web: www.tontinehotel.com
dir: *In town centre*

PETS: Bedrooms unattended **Stables** 2m **Public areas** assist
dogs only disp bin **Exercise area** Tweed Green behind hotel
Facilities walks info vet info **On Request** fridge access torch
towels **Other** charge for damage dogs allowed in certain
bedrooms only **Restrictions** well behaved dogs only

Conveniently situated in the main street, this long-established
hotel offers comfortable public rooms including the elegant Adam
Restaurant and an inviting lounge and 'clubby' bar. Bedrooms,
contained in the original house and the river-facing wing, offer a
smart, classical style of accommodation. The lasting impression
is of the excellent level of hospitality and guest care.

Rooms 36 (3 fmly) **S** £45-£55; **D** £75-£95* **Facilities** STV FTV
Xmas New Year Wi-fi Child facilities **Parking** 24 **Notes** LB

Crossburn Caravan Park *(NT248417)*

▶ ▶ ▶ ▶

Edinburgh Rd EH45 8ED
☎ 01721 720501 📠 01721 720501
e-mail: enquiries@crossburncaravans.co.uk
dir: *0.5m N of Peebles on A703*

PETS: Public areas except shop on leads disp bin
Exercise area dog walk **Facilities** walks info vet info **Other** max
2 dogs per pitch **Resident Pets:** Zara (Rhodesian Ridgeback),
Ginty (Jack Russell)

Open Apr-Oct Last arrival 21.00hrs Last departure 14.00hrs

A peaceful site in a relatively quiet location, despite the proximity
of the main road which partly borders the site, as does the
Eddleston Water. There are lovely views, and the park is well
stocked with trees, flowers and shrubs. Facilities are maintained
to a high standard, and fully-serviced pitches are available. A
large caravan dealership is on the same site. A 6 acre site with
45 touring pitches, 15 hardstandings and 85 statics.

SCOTLAND

ST BOSWELLS — Map 12 NT53

Dryburgh Abbey Hotel
★★★★ 74% ◉◉ COUNTRY HOUSE HOTEL
TD6 0RQ
☎ 01835 822261 📠 01835 823945
e-mail: enquiries@dryburgh.co.uk
web: www.dryburgh.co.uk
dir: B6356 signed Scott's View & Earlston. Through Clintmains, 1.8m to hotel

PETS: Bedrooms (8 GF) unattended **Sep accom** paddock available for horses **Stables** 0.5m **Charges** £7 per night **Public areas** except restaurant **Grounds** disp bin **Exercise area** surrounding countryside **Facilities** food bowl water bowl washing facs cage storage walks info vet info **On Request** fridge access torch towels **Other** charge for damage **Resident Pets:** Bracken & Harry (Cocker Spaniels)

Found in the heart of the Scottish Borders, and sitting beside to the ancient ruins of Dryburgh Abbey and the majestic River Tweed. This country house hotel, dating from the mid 19th century, offers comfortable public areas and an array of bedrooms and suites, each still displaying original features. The award-winning Tweed Restaurant, overlooking the river, has now been refurbished, and offers an 8-course dinner menu showcasing the chef's dedication to producing modern Scottish cuisine. The Abbey Bar offers food throughout the day.

Rooms 38 (31 fmly) (8 GF) **S** £65-£231; **D** £130-£362 (incl. bkfst & dinner)* **Facilities** FTV ⊗ Putt green Fishing 🛁 Sauna Xmas New Year Wi-fi **Services** Lift **Parking** 70 **Notes** LB

SOUTH AYRSHIRE

BALLANTRAE — Map 10 NX08

Glenapp Castle
★★★★★ ◉◉◉ HOTEL
KA26 0NZ
☎ 01465 831212 📠 01465 831000
e-mail: enquiries@glenappcastle.com
web: www.glenappcastle.com
dir: S through Ballantrae, cross bridge over River Stinchar, 1st right, hotel in 1m

PETS: Bedrooms (7 GF) **Grounds Exercise area** adjacent **Facilities** food bowl water bowl feeding mat scoop/disp bags leads pet sitting dog walking washing facs cage storage walks info vet info **On Request** fridge access torch towels **Other** charge for damage **Resident Pets:** Midge & Mozzy (Springer Spaniels)

Friendly hospitality and attentive service prevail at this stunning Victorian castle, set in extensive private grounds to the south of the village. Impeccably furnished bedrooms are graced with antiques and period pieces. Breathtaking views of Arran and Ailsa Craig can be enjoyed from the delightful, sumptuous day rooms and from many of the bedrooms. Accomplished cooking, using quality local ingredients is a feature of all meals; dinner is offered on a well crafted and imaginative, no-choice, five-course menu. Guests should make a point of walking round the wonderful grounds, to include the azalea lake and walled vegetable gardens with their fine restored greenhouses.

Rooms 17 (2 fmly) (7 GF) **S** £260-£445; **D** £405-£610 (incl. bkfst & dinner)* **Facilities** STV FTV 🛁 🛁 New Year Wi-fi **Services** Lift **Parking** 20 **Notes** LB Closed Jan-mid Mar & Xmas wk

BARRHILL — Map 10 NX28

Barrhill Holiday Park (NX216835)
►►►►
KA26 0PZ
☎ 01465 821355 📠 01465 821355
e-mail: barrhill@surfree.co.uk
dir: On A714 (Newton Stewart to Girvan road). 1m N of Barrhill

PETS: Public areas on leads **Exercise area** adjacent to park **Facilities** scoop/disp bags washing facs walks info vet info

Open Mar-Jan

A small, friendly park in a tranquil rural location, screened from the A714 by trees. The park is terraced and well landscaped, and a high quality amenity block includes disabled facilities. A 6 acre site with 30 touring pitches, 30 hardstandings and 39 statics.

Notes ⊕

SOUTH LANARKSHIRE

ABINGTON   Map 11 NS92

Mount View Caravan Park *(NS935235)*

▶ ▶ ▶

ML12 6RW
☎ 01864 502808
e-mail: info@mountviewcaravanpark.co.uk
dir: *M74 junct 13, A702 S into Abington. Left into Station Rd, over river & railway. Site on right*

PETS: **Public areas** pets to be kept on own pitch & exercised off site on leads **Exercise area** adjacent **Facilities** walks info vet info **Other** prior notice required **Restrictions** no Pit Bull Terriers **Resident Pet:** Hollie (Retriever)

Open Mar-Oct

A delightfully maturing family park, surrounded by the Southern Uplands and handily located between Carlisle and Glasgow. It is an excellent stopover site for those travelling between Scotland and the South. The West Coast railway passes beside the park. A 5.5 acre site with 51 touring pitches, 51 hardstandings and 20 statics.

Notes 5mph speed limit

ABINGTON MOTORWAY SERVICE AREA (M74)   Map 11 NS92

Days Inn Abington

BUDGET HOTEL
ML12 6RG
☎ 01864 502782   ⌕ 01864 502759
e-mail: abington.hotel@welcomebreak.co.uk
web: www.welcomebreak.co.uk
dir: *M74 junct 13, accessible from N'bound and S'bound carriageways*

PETS: **Bedrooms** unattended **Public areas** dogs must be kept on leads **Grounds**

This modern building offers accommodation in smart, spacious and well-equipped bedrooms, suitable for families and business travellers, and all with en suite bathrooms. Continental breakfast is available and other refreshments may be taken at the nearby family restaurant.

Rooms 52 (50 fmly) (8 smoking) **S** £29-£49; **D** £29-£59

NEW LANARK   Map 11 NS84

New Lanark Mill Hotel

★ ★ ★ 83% HOTEL
Mill One, New Lanark Mills ML11 9DB
☎ 01555 667200   ⌕ 01555 667222
e-mail: hotel@newlanark.org
web: www.newlanark.org
dir: *Signed from all major roads, M74 junct 7 & M8*

PETS: **Bedrooms** unattended **Charges** £5 per night **Grounds** **Exercise area** adjacent **Facilities** cage storage vet info **Other** charge for damage

Originally built as a cotton mill in the 18th century, this hotel forms part of a fully restored village, now a UNESCO World Heritage Site. There's a bright modern style throughout which contrasts nicely with features from the original mill. There is a comfortable foyer-lounge with a galleried restaurant above. The hotel enjoys stunning views over the River Clyde.

Rooms 38 (5 fmly) (6 smoking) **S** £69-£109; **D** £79-£119 (incl. bkfst) **Facilities** STV ⊗ Gym Beauty room Steam room Sauna Aerobics studios Xmas New Year Wi-fi **Services** Lift **Parking** 75 **Notes** LB

STIRLING

BLAIRLOGIE   Map 11 NS89

Witches Craig Caravan & Camping Park *(NS821968)*

▶ ▶ ▶ ▶

FK9 5PX
☎ 01786 474947
e-mail: info@witchescraig.co.uk
dir: *3m NE of Stirling on A91 (Hillfoots-St Andrews road)*

PETS: **Public areas** except amenity block & children's play area disp bin **Exercise area** woods **Facilities** vet info

Open Apr-Oct Last arrival 20.00hrs Last departure noon

In an attractive setting with direct access to the lower slopes of the dramatic Ochil Hills, this is a well-maintained family-run park. It is in the centre of 'Braveheart' country, with easy access to historical sites and many popular attractions. A 5 acre site with 60 touring pitches, 26 hardstandings.

CALLANDER — Map 11 NN60

Roman Camp Country House

★★★ 87% ◉◉◉ COUNTRY HOUSE HOTEL

FK17 8BG

☎ 01877 330003 📠 01877 331533

e-mail: mail@romancamphotel.co.uk

web: www.romancamphotel.co.uk

dir: *N on A84, left at east end of High Street. 300yds to hotel*

PETS: Bedrooms (7 GF) **Grounds** disp bin **Exercise area** woods 10 mins' walk **Facilities** cage storage walks info vet info **On Request** fridge access torch towels **Other** charge for damage well behaved dogs only; paddock for horses

Originally a shooting lodge, this charming country house has a rich history. Twenty acres of gardens and grounds lead down to the River Teith, and the town centre and its attractions are only a short walk away. Food is a highlight of any stay and menus are dominated by high-quality Scottish produce that is sensitively treated by the talented kitchen team. Real fires warm the atmospheric public areas and service is friendly yet professional.

Rooms 15 (4 fmly) (7 GF) **S** £95-£145; **D** £145-£195 (incl. bkfst) **Facilities** STV FTV Fishing Xmas New Year Wi-fi **Parking** 80 **Notes** LB

CRIANLARICH — Map 10 NN32

The Crianlarich Hotel

★★★ 75% ◉ HOTEL

FK20 8RW

☎ 01838 300272 📠 01838 300329

e-mail: info@crianlarich-hotel.co.uk

web: www.crianlarich-hotel.co.uk

dir: *At junct of A85 & A82*

PETS: Bedrooms Public areas except restaurant & public bar on leads **Exercise area** 2 mins **Facilities** water bowl cage storage walks info vet info **On Request** fridge access torch towels

Standing at what has been an important transport junction for many years, this hotel continues to cater to travellers' needs. The impressive ground-floor areas have benefited from investment, and the pleasant bedrooms are smartly appointed and offer all the usual amenities. Friendly relaxed service and high quality food makes this an enjoyable place to stay especially as it is close to Loch Lomond and the Trossachs National Park.

Rooms 36 (1 fmly) **S** £50-£75; **D** £60-£135 (incl. bkfst)* **Facilities** FTV ♫ Xmas New Year Wi-fi **Services** Lift **Parking** 30 **Notes** LB

LOCHEARNHEAD — Map 11 NN52

Mansewood Country House

★★★★ GUEST HOUSE

FK19 8NS

☎ 01567 830213

e-mail: stay@mansewoodcountryhouse.co.uk

dir: *A84 N to Lochearnhead, 1st building on left; A84 S to Lochearnhead*

PETS: Bedrooms Charges Public areas Grounds on leads disp bin **Exercise area Facilities** food bowl water bowl walks info vet info **On Request** fridge access **Other** charge for damage dogs accepted in log cabin only

Mansewood Country House is a spacious former manse that dates back to the 18th century and lies in a well-tended garden to the south of the village. Bedrooms are well appointed and equipped and offer high standards of comfort. Refreshments can be enjoyed in the cosy bar or the elegant lounge, and meals prepared with flair are served in the attractive restaurant.

Rooms 6 en suite (1 GF) **S** £45-£65; **D** £60-£65* **Facilities** TVL tea/coffee Dinner available Cen ht Licensed Wi-fi **Parking** 6 **Notes** LB RS Nov-Mar Phone for advance bookings

STIRLING — Map 11 NS79

Barceló
HOTELS & RESORTS

Barceló Stirling Highland Hotel

★★★★ 75% HOTEL

Spittal St FK8 1DU

☎ 01786 272727 📠 01786 272829

e-mail: stirling@barcelo-hotels.co.uk

web: www.barcelo-hotels.co.uk

dir: *A84 into Stirling. Follow Stirling Castle signs as far as Albert Hall. Left, left again, follow Castle signs*

PETS: Bedrooms unattended **Charges** £15 per stay **Public areas** assist dogs only on leads **Exercise area** 5 mins' walk **Facilities** walks info vet info **Other** charge for damage prior notice required

Enjoying a location close to the castle and historic town, this atmospheric hotel was previously a high school. Public rooms have been converted from the original classrooms and retain many interesting features. Bedrooms are more modern in style and comfortably equipped. Scholars Restaurant serves traditional and international dishes, and the Headmaster's Study is the ideal venue for enjoying a drink.

Rooms 96 (4 fmly) **Facilities** Spa STV ☜ supervised Gym Squash Steam room Dance studio Beauty therapist Xmas New Year Wi-fi **Services** Lift **Parking** 96

Linden Guest House

★★★★ GUEST HOUSE

22 Linden Av FK7 7PQ

☎ 01786 448850 & 07974 116573 📠 01786 448850

e-mail: fay@lindenguesthouse.co.uk

web: www.lindenguesthouse.co.uk

dir: *0.5m SE of city centre off A9*

PETS: Bedrooms Grounds disp bin **Exercise area** 50mtrs **Facilities** (pre-bookable) food bowl water bowl feeding mat scoop/disp bags leads washing facs cage storage walks info vet info **On Request** fridge access torch towels **Other** charge for damage dog grooming available locally **Resident Pet:** Finn (Red Setter)

Situated within walking distance of the town centre, this friendly guest house offers attractive and very well-equipped bedrooms, including a large family room that sleeps five comfortably. There is a bright dining room where delicious breakfasts are served at individual tables with quality Wedgwood crockery.

Rooms 4 en suite (2 fmly) (1 GF); **D** £60-£70* **Facilities** STV tea/coffee Cen ht Wi-fi **Parking** 2 **Notes** LB

STRATHYRE   Map 11 NN51

Creagan House

★ ★ ★ ★ ★ 🍴🍴 RESTAURANT WITH ROOMS

FK18 8ND

☎ 01877 384638 📠 01877 384319

e-mail: eatandstay@creaganhouse.co.uk

web: www.creaganhouse.co.uk

dir: *0.25m N of Strathyre on A84*

PETS: Bedrooms unattended **Public areas** except restaurant & lounge **Grounds** disp bin **Exercise area** National Park accessible from car park **Facilities** food bowl water bowl leads washing facs cage storage walks info vet info **On Request** fridge access torch towels

Originally a farmhouse dating from the 17th century, Creagan House has operated as a restaurant with rooms for many years. The baronial-style dining room provides a wonderful setting for sympathetic cooking. Warm hospitality and attentive service are the highlights of any stay.

Rooms 5 en suite (1 fmly) (1 GF) **S** £72.50-£92.50; **D** £125-£145 **Facilities** FTV tea/coffee Dinner available Cen ht Wi-fi **Parking** 26 **Notes** LB Closed 9-24 Nov, Xmas & 19 Jan-10 Mar RS closed Wed & Thu

WEST DUNBARTONSHIRE

BALLOCH   Map 10 NS38

Sunnyside

★★★ BED AND BREAKFAST

35 Main St G83 9JX

☎ 01389 750282 & 07717 397548

e-mail: enquiries@sunnysidebb.co.uk>aa

dir: *From A82 take A811 then A813 for 1m, over mini-rdbt 150mtrs on left*

PETS: Bedrooms unattended **Charges** £5 per week **Public areas** on leads **Grounds** disp bin **Exercise area** surrounding countryside **Facilities** food (pre-bookable) food bowl water bowl bedding dog chews scoop/disp bags leads washing facs cage storage walks info vet info **On Request** torch towels **Other** charge for damage

Set in its own grounds well back from the road by Loch Lomond, Sunnyside is an attractive, traditional detached house, parts of which date back to the 1830s. Bedrooms are attractively decorated and provide comfortable modern accommodation. Free Wi-fi is also available. The dining room is located on the ground floor, and is an appropriate setting for hearty Scottish breakfasts.

Rooms 6 en suite (2 fmly) (1 GF) **S** £28-£40; **D** £46-£60* **Facilities** tea/coffee Dinner available Cen ht Wi-fi **Parking** 8

Lomond Woods Holiday Park *(NS383816)*

▶ ▶ ▶ ▶

Old Luss Rd G83 8QP

☎ 01389 755000 📠 01389 755563

e-mail: lomondwoods@holiday-parks.co.uk

dir: *From A82, 17m N of Glasgow, take A811(Stirling to Balloch road). Left at 1st rdbt, follow holiday park signs, 150yds on left*

PETS: Charges £25 per week **Public areas** except children's play area on leads **Exercise area** perimeter walk **Facilities** walks info vet info **Other** prior notice required **Restrictions** no dangerous breeds (see page 7)

Open all year Last arrival 20.00hrs **Last departure** noon

A mature park with well-laid out pitches and self-catering lodges screened by trees and shrubs, surrounded by woodland and hills. The park is within walking distance of 'Loch Lomond Shores', a leisure and retail complex which is the main gateway to Scotland's first National Park. Amenities include the Loch Lomond Aquarium, an Interactive Exhibition, and loch cruises. A 13 acre site with 110 touring pitches, 110 hardstandings and 35 statics.

Notes No tents, no jet skis

SCOTLAND

WEST LOTHIAN

SCOTLAND

BATHGATE
Map 11 NS96

The Cairn Hotel
★★★ 73% HOTEL
Blackburn Rd EH48 2EL
☎ 01506 633366 📠 01506 633444
e-mail: cairn@mckeverhotels.co.uk
dir: M8 junct 3A (E'bound), at rdbt 1st left, next rdbt 2nd left, at mini rdbt straight on, tkae 1st slip road signed Blackburn, right at T-junct turn, hotel next right

PETS: Bedrooms (12 GF) sign **Stables** 2m **Facilities** washing facs **On Request** fridge access torch towels **Other** charge for damage

Ideally located for both Edinburgh and Glasgow, being just minutes from the M8, this property has well appointed bedrooms and spacious public areas; Wi-fi is an added benefit. The service in the informal bar and restaurant is relaxed and friendly. Ample parking is available.

Rooms 61 (2 fmly) (12 GF) **S** £29-£59; **D** £39-£99 (incl. bkfst) **Facilities** STV FTV Xmas New Year Wi-fi **Services** Lift **Parking** 80 **Notes** LB

EAST CALDER
Map 11 NT06

Linwater Caravan Park *(NT104696)*
▶ ▶ ▶
West Clifton EH53 0HT
☎ 0131 333 3326 📠 0131 333 1952
e-mail: linwater@supanet.com
dir: M9 junct 1, signed from B7030 or from Wilkieston on A71

PETS: Public areas except toilet block disp bin **Exercise area** walks to parks & canal **Facilities** walks info vet info **Other** prior notice required **Resident Pets:** Mimi (Black Labrador), Minnow (Cocker Spaniel), Beth (Golden Retriever), Cobbles (cat), sheep, pigs, ducks, hens

Open late Mar-late Oct Last arrival 21.00hrs Last departure noon

A farmland park in a peaceful rural area within easy reach of Edinburgh. The very good facilities are housed in a Scandinavian-style building, and are well maintained by resident owners. There are three 'timber tents' for hire and nearby are plenty of pleasant woodland walks. A 5 acre site with 60 touring pitches, 18 hardstandings.

LINLITHGOW
Map 11 NS97

Bomains Farm
★★★★ GUEST HOUSE
Bo'Ness EH49 7RQ
☎ 01506 822188 & 822861 📠 01506 824433
e-mail: bunty.kirk@onetel.net
web: www.bomains.co.uk
dir: A706, 1.5m N towards Bo Ness, left at golf course x-rds, 1st farm on right

PETS: Bedrooms unattended **Stables Charges** £5 per night **Grounds Exercise area** adjacent **Facilities** walks info vet info **Other** pets may be left unattended by arrangement only **Resident Pets:** Minnie (Bichon Frise), Penny (Mini Schnauzer)

From its elevated location this friendly farmhouse has stunning views of the Firth of Forth. The bedrooms which vary in size are beautifully decorated, well equipped and enhanced by quality fabrics, with many thoughtful extra touches. Delicious home-cooked fare featuring the best of local produce is served in a stylish lounge-dining room.

Rooms 6 rms (4 en suite) (1 pri facs) (1 fmly) **S** fr £35; **D** £60-£90* **Facilities** STV FTV TVL tea/coffee Cen ht Wi-fi Golf 18 Fishing **Parking** 12

Beecraigs Caravan & Camping Site
(NT006746)
▶ ▶ ▶ ▶
Beecraigs Country Park, The Park Centre EH49 6PL
☎ 01506 844516 📠 01506 846256
e-mail: mail@beecraigs.com
dir: From Linlithgow on A803 or from Bathgate on B792, follow signs to country park. Reception either at restaurant or park centre

PETS: Public areas except buildings, dogs must be kept on leads on site disp bin **Exercise area** main country park area **Exercise area** field & woodland adjacent **Facilities** walks info vet info **Other** disposal bags available at visitor centre

Open all year rs 25-26 Dec, 1-2 Jan no new arrivals Last arrival 21.00hrs Last departure noon

A wildlife enthusiast's paradise where even the timber facility buildings are in keeping with the environment. Beecraigs is situated peacefully in the open countryside of the Bathgate Hills. Small bays with natural shading offer intimate pitches, and there's a restaurant serving lunch and evening meals. The smart toilet block includes en suite facilities. A 6 acre site with 36 touring pitches, 36 hardstandings.

Notes No ball games near caravans, no noise after 22.00hrs

SCOTTISH ISLANDS

ISLE OF ARRAN

BRODICK — Map 10 NS03

Kilmichael Country House

★★★ ◉◉ COUNTRY HOUSE HOTEL

Glen Cloy KA27 8BY
☎ 01770 302219 📠 01770 302068
e-mail: enquiries@kilmichael.com
web: www.kilmichael.com
dir: *From Brodick ferry terminal towards Lochranza for 1m. Left at golf course, inland between sports field & church, follow signs*

PETS: Bedrooms (7 GF) unattended Grounds on leads disp bin Exercise area adjacent Facilities washing facs walks info vet info On Request torch towels Other charge for damage Resident Pets: Guiseppe (Dalmation), chickens, ducks, turkeys, geese & peafowl

Reputed to be the oldest on the island, this lovely house lies in attractive gardens in a quiet glen less than five minutes' drive from the ferry terminal. It has been lovingly restored to create a stylish, elegant country house, adorned with ornaments from around the world. There are two inviting drawing rooms and a bright dining room, serving award-winning contemporary cuisine. The delightful bedrooms are furnished in classical style; some are contained in a pretty courtyard conversion.

Rooms 8 (3 annexe) (7 GF) Facilities Wi-fi Parking 14 Notes LB No children 12yrs Closed Nov-Feb (ex for prior bookings)

ISLE OF HARRIS

SCARISTA — Map 13 NG09

Scarista House

★★★★ ◉◉ RESTAURANT WITH ROOMS

HS3 3HX
☎ 01859 550238 📠 01859 550277
e-mail: timandpatricia@scaristahouse.com
dir: *On A859, 15m S of Tarbert*

PETS: Bedrooms unattended Public areas library only Grounds on leads disp bin Exercise area 200yds Facilities food bowl water bowl pet sitting washing facs cage storage walks info vet info On Request fridge access torch towels Resident Pets: Molly (Cavalier King Charles Spaniel), Misty (cat)

A former manse, Scarista House is a haven for food lovers who seek to explore this magnificent island. It enjoys breathtaking views of the Atlantic and is just a short stroll from miles of golden sandy beaches. The house is run in a relaxed country-house manner by the friendly hosts. Expect wellies in the hall and masses of books and CDs in one of two lounges. Bedrooms are cosy, and delicious set dinners and memorable breakfasts are provided.

Rooms 3 en suite 2 annexe en suite (2 GF) Facilities tea/coffee Dinner available Direct Dial Cen ht Parking 12 Notes Closed Xmas, Jan & Feb No coaches

ISLE OF MULL

CRAIGNURE — Map 10 NM73

Shieling Holidays *(NM724369)*

▶▶▶▶

PA65 6AY
☎ 01680 812496
e-mail: sales@shielingholidays.co.uk
dir: *From ferry left onto A849 to Iona. 400mtrs left at church, follow site signs towards sea*

PETS: Charges £1 per night £7 per week Public areas except public buildings & toilets disp bin Exercise area 2m of coastline Facilities washing facs walks info vet info

Open 12 Mar-1 Nov Last arrival 22.00hrs Last departure noon

A lovely site on the water's edge with spectacular views, and less than one mile from ferry landing. Hardstandings and service points are provided for motorhomes, and there are astro-turf pitches for tents. The park also offers unique, en suite cottage tents for hire and bunkhouse accommodation for families. A 7 acre site with 90 touring pitches, 30 hardstandings and 15 statics.

TOBERMORY — Map 13 NM55

Highland Cottage

★★★ ◉◉ SMALL HOTEL

Breadalbane St PA75 6PD
☎ 01688 302030
e-mail: davidandjo@highlandcottage.co.uk
web: www.highlandcottage.co.uk
dir: *A848 Craignure/Fishnish ferry terminal, pass Tobermory signs, straight on at mini rdbt across narrow bridge, turn right. Hotel on right opposite fire station*

PETS: Bedrooms (1 GF) Charges Public areas Grounds on leads disp bin Exercise area 3 mins walk Facilities washing facs cage storage walks info vet info On Request fridge access torch towels Other charge for damage Restrictions no large, long-haired dogs (ie German Shepherds, St Bernards etc)

Providing the highest level of natural and unassuming hospitality, this delightful little gem lies high above the island's capital. Don't be fooled by its side street location, a stunning view over the bay is just a few metres away. 'A country house hotel in town' it is an Aladdin's Cave of collectables and treasures, as well as masses of books and magazines. There are two inviting lounges, one with an honesty bar. The cosy dining room offers memorable dinners and splendid breakfasts. Bedrooms are individual; some have four-posters and all are comprehensively equipped to include TVs and music centres.

Rooms 6 (1 GF) S £110-£135; D £150-£190 (incl. bkfst)*
Facilities FTV Wi-fi Parking 6 Notes LB No children 10yrs Closed Nov-Mar

SCOTLAND

TOBERMORY *continued*

Tobermory

★★ 76% HOTEL

53 Main St PA75 6NT

☎ 01688 302091 📄 01688 302254

e-mail: tobhotel@tinyworld.co.uk

web: www.thetobermoryhotel.com

dir: On waterfront

PETS: Bedrooms (2 GF) **Public areas** only in reception on leads **Exercise area** 200yds **Facilities** cage storage walks info vet info **Other** charge for damage

This friendly hotel, with its pretty pink frontage, sits on the seafront amid other brightly coloured, picture-postcard buildings. There is a comfortable and relaxing lounge where drinks are served prior to dining in the stylish restaurant (there is no bar). Bedrooms come in a variety of sizes; all are bright and vibrant.

Rooms 16 (2 fmly) (2 GF) **S** £38-£61; **D** £76-£122 (incl. bkfst)* **Facilities** supervised New Year Wi-fi Child facilities **Notes** Closed Xmas

ISLE OF SKYE

EDINBANE
Map 13 NG35

Skye Camping & Caravanning Club Site

(NG343524)

▶ ▶ ▶ ▶

Borve, Arnisort IV51 9PS

☎ 01470 582230 📄 01470 582230

e-mail: skye.site@thefriendlyclub.co.uk

dir: Approx 12m from Portree on A850 (Dunvegan road). Site by loch shore

PETS: Public areas except facility block (ex assist dogs) **Exercise area** surrounding countryside **Other** prior notice required dogs must be under control at all times & exercised off site

Open Apr-Oct Last arrival 22.00hrs Last departure noon

The Club site on Skye stands out for its stunning waterside location and glorious views, the generous pitch density, the overall range of facilities, and the impressive ongoing improvements under enthusiastic franchisee owners. Layout maximises the beauty of the scenery and genuine customer care is very evident with an excellent tourist information room and campers' shelter being just two examples. The new amenities block (opened in 2010) has that definite 'wow' factor with smart modern fittings, including excellent showers and the generously proportioned disabled room and family bathroom. There are several wooden camping pods for hire. A 7 acre site with 105 touring pitches, 36 hardstandings.

ISLEORNSAY
Map 13 NG71

Kinloch Lodge

★★★ COUNTRY HOUSE HOTEL

IV43 8QY

☎ 01471 833214 & 833333 📄 01471 833277

e-mail: reservations@kinloch-lodge.co.uk

web: www.kinloch-lodge.co.uk

dir: 6m S of Broadford on A851, 10m N of Armadale on A851

PETS: Bedrooms (1 GF) **Charges** £15 per night **Grounds** on leads **Exercise area** 500mtrs **Facilities** vet info **Other** charge for damage **Restrictions** no large breeds

Owned and ran in a hands-on fashion by Lord and Lady MacDonald and their family, this hotel enjoys beautiful scenery, being surrounded by hills and a sea loch. Bedrooms and bathrooms are well appointed and comfortable, and public areas boast numerous open fires and relaxing areas to sit. There is a cookery school ran by Claire MacDonald and a shop selling her famous cookery books and produce.

Rooms 15 (8 annexe) (1 GF) **S** £150-£300; **D** £198-£380 (incl. bkfst & dinner) **Facilities** STV FTV Fishing New Year Wi-fi **Parking** 40 **Notes** LB

PORTREE
Map 13 NG44

Bosville Hotel

★★★ 81% HOTEL

Bosville Ter IV51 9DG

☎ 01478 612846 📄 01478 613434

e-mail: bosville@macleodhotels.co.uk

web: www.macleodhotels.com

dir: A87 signed Portree, then A855 into town. After zebra crossing follow road to left

PETS: Bedrooms **Public areas** bar only, not during food service on leads **Grounds** on leads **Exercise area** 200yds **Facilities** water bowl walks info vet info

This stylish, popular hotel enjoys fine views over the harbour. Bedrooms are furnished to a high specification and have a fresh, contemporary feel. Public areas include a smart bar, bistro and the Chandlery restaurant where fantastic local produce is treated with respect and refreshing restraint.

Rooms 19 (2 fmly) **Facilities** STV Use of nearby leisure club (charged) Xmas New Year Wi-fi **Parking** 10

Flodigarry Country House

★★★ 78% ◎ COUNTRY HOUSE HOTEL

IV51 9HZ

☎ 01470 552203   📄 01470 552301

e-mail: info@flodigarry.co.uk

web: www.flodigarry.co.uk

dir: *Take A855 from Portree, through Staffin, N to Flodigarry, signed on right*

PETS: **Bedrooms** unattended **Grounds** disp bin **Facilities** (pre-bookable) leads washing facs walks info vet info **On Request** torch towels **Other** charge for damage dogs allowed in Flora Macdonald cottage only

This hotel is located in woodlands on The Quiraing in north-east Skye overlooking the sea towards the Torridon Mountains. The dramatic scenery is a real inspiration here, and this charming house was once the home of the Scotland's heroine, Flora MacDonald. Guests are assured of real Highland hospitality and there is an easy going atmosphere throughout. A full range of activities is offered, with mountain walks, fishing and boat trips proving to be the most popular.

Rooms 18 (7 annexe) (3 fmly) (4 GF) **S** £80-£130; **D** £100-£200 (incl. bkfst)* **Facilities** FTV Xmas New Year Wi-fi **Parking** 40 **Notes** LB Closed Nov-15 Dec & Jan

The Glenview

★★★ ◎ RESTAURANT WITH ROOMS

Culnacnoc IV51 9JH

☎ 01470 562248

e-mail: enquiries@glenviewskye.co.uk

dir: *12m N of Portree on A855*

PETS: **Bedrooms Charges** £3 per night £21 per week **Grounds** on leads **Facilities** cage storage walks info vet info **On Request** torch **Other** charge for damage

The Glenview is located in one of the most beautiful parts of Skye with stunning seas views; it is close to the famous Old Man of Storr rock outcrop. The individually styled bedrooms are very comfortable and front-facing rooms enjoy the dramatic views. Evening meals should not to be missed as the restaurant has a well deserved reputation for its locally sourced produce.

Rooms 5 en suite (1 GF) **S** £57.50-£67.50; **D** £80-£110* **Facilities** tea/coffee Dinner available Wi-fi **Parking** 12 **Notes** RS Sun & Mon closed

Staffin Camping & Caravanning *(NG492670)*

▶ ▶ ▶

IV51 9JX

☎ 01470 562213   📄 01470 562213

e-mail: staffincampsite@btinternet.com

dir: *On A855, 16m N of Portree. Turn right before 40mph signs*

PETS: **Public areas** except toilet area disp bin **Exercise area** adjacent **Facilities** walks info vet info **Resident Pet:** Henry (Briard)

Open Apr-Oct Last arrival 22.00hrs Last departure 11.00hrs

A large sloping grassy site with level hardstandings for motor homes and caravans, close to the village of Staffin. The toilet block is appointed to a very good standard and the park now has a laundry. A 2.5 acre site with 50 touring pitches, 18 hardstandings.

Notes No music after 22.00hrs 🐾

Wales

WALES (side tab)

BEAUMARIS   Map 6 SH67

Best Western Bulkeley Hotel

★★★ 77% HOTEL

Castle St LL58 8AW

☎ 01248 810415 📠 01248 810146

e-mail: reception@bulkeleyhotel.co.uk

web: www.bulkeleyhotel.co.uk

dir: From A55 junct 8a to Beaumaris. Hotel in town centre

PETS: **Bedrooms** unattended **Charges** £7.50 per night
Public areas lounge & bar only on leads **Grounds** on leads
Exercise area 2 mins' walk **Facilities** food bowl water bowl
walks info vet info **On Request** torch towels **Other** charge for
damage please phone for further details of pet facilities

A Grade I listed hotel built in 1832, the Bulkeley is just 100 yards
from the 13th-century Beaumaris Castle in the centre of town; the
friendly staff create a relaxed atmosphere. Many rooms, including
18 of the bedrooms, have fine panoramic views across the
Menai Straits to the Snowdonian Mountains. The well-equipped
bedrooms and suites, some with four-posters, are generally
spacious, and have pretty furnishings. There is a choice of bars, a
coffee shop, a restaurant and bistro.

Rooms 43 (5 fmly) **S** £47-£75; **D** £75-£115 (incl. bkfst)*
Facilities FTV Xmas New Year Wi-fi **Services** Lift **Parking** 25
Notes LB

Bishopsgate House Hotel

★★ 85% ⊛ SMALL HOTEL

54 Castle St LL58 8BB

☎ 01248 810302 📠 01248 810166

e-mail: hazel@bishopsgatehotel.co.uk

dir: From Menai Bridge onto A545 to Beaumaris. Hotel on left in
main street

PETS: **Bedrooms Charges** £5 per night **Public areas** disp bin
Exercise area opposite beach & green **Facilities** food (pre-
bookable) food bowl water bowl dog chews cat treats scoop/
disp bags leads pet sitting dog walking washing facs cage
storage walks info vet info **On Request** fridge access torch
towels **Other** charge for damage **Resident Pets:** Bonnie (Jack
Russell cross), Polly Anna (cat)

This immaculately maintained, privately owned and personally
run small hotel dates back to 1760. It features fine examples
of wood panelling and a Chinese Chippendale staircase.
Thoughtfully furnished bedrooms are attractively decorated
and two have four-poster beds. Quality cooking is served in the
elegant restaurant and guests have a comfortable lounge and
cosy bar to relax in.

Rooms 9 **Parking** 8 **Notes** LB

DULAS — Map 6 SH48

Tyddyn Isaf Caravan Park *(SH486873)*

►►►►►

Lligwy Bay LL70 9PQ
☎ 01248 410203 & 01248 410667 📠 01248 410667
e-mail: mail@tyddynisaf.co.uk
dir: *Take A5025 through Benllech to Moelfre rdbt, left towards Amlwch to Brynrefail village. Turn right opposite craft shop. Site 0.5m down lane on right*

PETS: Public areas except shop, bar & children's play area on leads disp bin Exercise area surrounding walks Facilities food bowl water bowl scoop/disp bags walks info vet info Other prior notice required Resident Pets: 1 Labrador, cat, sheep, cattle

Open Mar-Oct rs Mar-Jul & Sep-Oct bar & shop opening limited Last arrival 21.30hrs Last departure 11.00hrs

A beautifully situated, very spacious family park on rising ground adjacent to a sandy beach, with magnificent views overlooking Lligwy Bay. A private footpath leads directly to the beach and there is an excellent nature trail around the park. There are very good toilet facilities, including two family rooms, a well-stocked shop, and café/bar serving meals, which are best enjoyed on the terrace. A 16 acre site with 30 touring pitches, 50 hardstandings and 56 statics.

Notes No groups, maximum 3 units together 🐾

PENTRAETH — Map 6 SH57

Rhos Caravan Park *(SH517794)*

►►►

Rhos Farm LL75 8DZ
☎ 01248 450214 📠 01248 450214
e-mail: rhosfarm@googlemail.com
dir: *Site on A5025, 1m N of Pentraeth*

PETS: Charges £1.50 per night Public areas except toilets & children's play area Exercise area 4-acre field Facilities walks info vet info Other prior notice required Resident Pets: Tess (Springer Spaniel), Jack (Chocolate Labrador)

Open Etr-Oct Last arrival 22.00hrs Last departure 16.00hrs

A warm welcome awaits families at this spacious park on level, grassy ground with easy access to the main road to Amlwch. This 200-acre working farm has two play areas and farm animals to keep children amused, with good beaches, pubs, restaurants and shops nearby. The two toilet blocks are kept to a good standard by enthusiastic owners, who are constantly improving the facilities. A 15 acre site with 98 touring pitches and 66 statics.

Notes 🐾

RHOSNEIGR — Map 6 SH37

Ty Hen *(SH327738)*

►►►

Station Rd LL64 5QZ
☎ 01407 810331 📠 01407 810331
e-mail: info@tyhen.com
dir: *From A55 exit 5 follow signs to Rhosneigr, at clock turn right. Entrance 50mtrs before Rhosneigr railway station*

PETS: Public areas except toilet block, swimming pool & children's play area on leads disp bin Exercise area fields Exercise area beach (10 mins) Facilities walks info vet info Resident Pets: Scruff (Longhaired Terrier), Lunar (Black Labrador/Collie cross), Twix, Thomas & Meow (cats), Phebe & Maisey (Shetland ponies), Percy & Petal (donkeys)

Open mid Mar-Oct Last arrival 21.00hrs Last departure noon

Attractive seaside position near a large fishing lake and riding stables, in lovely countryside. A smart toilet block offers a welcome amenity at this popular family park, where friendly owners are always on hand. A 7.5 acre site with 38 touring pitches, 5 hardstandings and 42 statics.

Notes 1 motor vehicle per pitch, children must be in tents/tourers/statics by 22.00hrs

BRIDGEND

BRIDGEND — Map 3 SS97

Best Western Heronston

★★★ 74% HOTEL

Ewenny Rd CF35 5AW
☎ 01656 668811 & 666085 📠 01656 767391
e-mail: reservations@bestwesternheronstonhotel.co.uk
web: www.bw-heronstonhotel.co.uk
dir: *M4 junct 35, follow signs for Porthcawl, at 5th rdbt turn left towards Ogmore-by-Sea (B4265), hotel 200yds on left*

PETS: Bedrooms (37 GF) Charges £10 per night Public areas only for access on leads Grounds on leads Exercise area Facilities walks info vet info Other charge for damage

Situated within easy reach of the town centre and the M4, this large modern hotel offers spacious well-equipped accommodation, including ground floor rooms. Public areas include an open-plan lounge/bar, attractive restaurant and a smart leisure and fitness club. The hotel also has a choice of function/conference rooms, and ample parking is available.

Rooms 75 (4 fmly) (37 GF) (8 smoking) Facilities STV 🐾 Gym Steam room Sauna Xmas New Year Wi-fi Services Lift Parking 160

WALES

SARN PARK MOTORWAY SERVICE AREA (M4) Map 3 SS98

Days Inn Cardiff West

BUDGET HOTEL

Sarn Park Services, M4 Junct 36 CF32 9RW

☎ 01656 659218 📄 01656 768665

e-mail: sarn.hotel@welcomebreak.co.uk

web: www.welcomebreak.co.uk

dir: *M4 junct 36*

PETS: Bedrooms (20 GF) **Public areas Grounds** disp bin
Exercise area country walks nearby **Facilities** vet info

This modern building offers accommodation in smart, spacious and well-equipped bedrooms, suitable for families and business travellers, and all with en suite bathrooms. Continental breakfast is available and other refreshments may be taken at the nearby family restaurant.

Rooms 40 (39 fmly) (20 GF) (5 smoking) **S** £29-£45; **D** £29-£69

CARDIFF

CARDIFF Map 3 ST17

Copthorne Hotel Cardiff-Caerdydd

★★★★ 74% @ HOTEL

Copthorne Way, Culverhouse Cross CF5 6DA

☎ 029 2059 9100 📄 029 2059 9080

e-mail: reservations.cardiff@millenniumhotels.co.uk

web: www.millenniumhotels.co.uk

dir: *M4 junct 33, A4232 for 2.5m towards Cardiff West. Then A48 W to Cowbridge*

PETS: Bedrooms (27 GF) **Public areas** lobby & lounge only on leads **Grounds** on leads **Exercise area** lakeside walk nearby **Facilities** cage storage walks info vet info **On Request** fridge access torch towels **Other** charge for damage

A comfortable, popular and modern hotel, conveniently located for the airport and city. Bedrooms are a good size and some have a private lounge. Public areas are smartly presented and include a gym, pool, meeting rooms and a comfortable restaurant with views of the adjacent lake.

Rooms 135 (7 fmly) (27 GF) **S** £56.40-£200; **D** £56.40-£200*
Facilities STV ⊙ Gym Sauna Steam room 🎵 Xmas New Year Wi-fi
Services Lift **Parking** 225 **Notes** LB

Barceló Cardiff Angel Hotel

★★★★ 70% HOTEL

Castle St CF10 1SZ

☎ 029 2064 9200 📄 029 2039 6212

e-mail: angel@barcelo-hotels-co.uk

web: www.barcelo-hotels.co.uk/hotels/wales/barcelo-cardiff-angel-hotel

dir: *Opposite Cardiff Castle*

PETS: Bedrooms unattended **Charges** £15 per stay **Public areas** except dining room on leads **Facilities** vet info **On Request** fridge access torch **Other** charge for damage

This well-established hotel is in the heart of the city overlooking the famous castle and almost opposite the Millennium Stadium. All bedrooms offer air conditioning and are appointed to a good standard. Public areas include an impressive lobby, a modern restaurant and a selection of conference rooms. There is limited parking at the rear of the hotel.

Rooms 102 (3 fmly) **Facilities** STV Xmas New Year Wi-fi
Services Lift Air con **Parking** 60

Best Western St Mellons Hotel & Country Club

★★★ 70% HOTEL

Castleton CF3 2XR

☎ 01633 680355 📄 01633 680399

e-mail: reservations.stmellons@ohiml.com

web: www.oxfordhotelsandinns.com

dir: *M4 junct 28 follow A48 Castleton/St Mellons. Hotel on left past garage*

PETS: Bedrooms (5 GF) **Charges Public areas** assist dogs only **Grounds** on leads disp bin **Facilities** cage storage walks info vet info **On Request** fridge access torch towels **Other** charge for damage **Restrictions** no large dogs; no Great Danes, Rottweilers or Bull Terriers

This Regency mansion has been tastefully converted into an elegant hotel with an adjoining leisure complex that attracts a strong local following. Bedrooms, some in purpose-built wings, are spacious and smart. The public areas retain pleasing architectural proportions and include relaxing lounges and a restaurant serving a varied choice of carefully prepared, enjoyable dishes.

Rooms 41 (20 annexe) (9 fmly) (5 GF) **S** £55-£190; **D** £60-£200 (incl. bkfst)* **Facilities** Spa ⊙ Gym Squash Beauty salon Xmas Wi-fi **Parking** 100 **Notes** LB

Campanile Cardiff

BUDGET HOTEL

Caxton Place, Pentwyn CF23 8HA

☎ 029 2054 9044 ▤ 029 2054 9900

e-mail: cardiff@campanile.com

dir: *Take Pentwyn exit from A48(M), follow signs for hotel*

PETS: Bedrooms Charges £5 per night **Exercise area** park 5 mins walk **Facilities** water bowl walks info vet info **Other** charge for damage

This modern building offers accommodation in smart, well-equipped bedrooms, all with en suite bathrooms. Refreshments may be taken at the informal bistro.

Rooms 47 (47 annexe)

Ibis Cardiff Gate

BUDGET HOTEL

Malthouse Av, Cardiff Gate Business Park, Pontprennau CF23 8RA

☎ 029 2073 3222 ▤ 029 2073 4222

e-mail: H3159@accor.com

web: www.ibishotel.com

dir: *M4 junct 30, follow Cardiff Service Station signs. Hotel on left*

PETS: Bedrooms (22 GF) unattended sign **Public areas** except restaurant disp bin **Exercise area** 200mtrs **Facilities** cage storage walks info **On Request** fridge access torch towels **Other** charge for damage

Modern, budget hotel offering comfortable accommodation in bright and practical bedrooms. Breakfast is self-service provided in the spacious dining area. Meeting rooms are available for conferences and dinner is available from nearby restaurants.

Rooms 78 (19 fmly) (22 GF) (7 smoking)

CARMARTHENSHIRE

HARFORD
Map 3 SN64

Springwater Lakes *(SN637430)*

►►►

SA19 8DT

☎ 01558 650788

dir: *4m E of Lampeter on A482, entrance well signed on right*

PETS: Charges 1st dog free, £2 per extra dog per night **Public areas** on leads disp bin **Exercise area** 2 dog walks & exercise areas **Facilities** walks info vet info **Other** prior notice required

Open Mar-Oct Last arrival 20.00hrs Last departure 11.00hrs

In a rural setting overlooked by the Cambrian Mountains, this park is adjoined on each side by four spring-fed and well-stocked fishing lakes. All pitches have hardstandings, electricity and TV hook-ups, and there is a small and very clean toilet block and a shop. A 20 acre site with 20 touring pitches, 20 hardstandings.

Notes Children must be supervised around lakes, no cycling on site, no ball games ⊛

LLANDOVERY
Map 3 SN73

Erwlon Caravan & Camping Park *(SN776343)*

►►►►

Brecon Rd SA20 0RD

☎ 01550 721021 & 720332

e-mail: peter@erwlon.co.uk

dir: *0.5m E of Llandovery on A40*

PETS: Stables 1m **Charges** max £1 per night **Public areas** on leads disp bin **Exercise area** fenced area provided **Exercise area** 200mtrs **Facilities** washing facs walks info vet info

Open all year Last arrival anytime Last departure noon

Long-established family-run site set beside a brook in the Brecon Beacons foothills. The town of Llandovery and the hills overlooking the Towy Valley are a short walk away. The superb, Scandinavian-style facilities block has cubicled washrooms, family and disabled rooms and is an impressive feature; ongoing improvements include a campers' kitchen. An 8 acre site with 75 touring pitches, 15 hardstandings.

Notes Quiet after 22.30hrs ⊛

LLANELLI
Map 2 SN50

Best Western Diplomat Hotel

★★★ 78% HOTEL

Felinfoel SA15 3PJ

☎ 01554 756156 ▤ 01554 751649

e-mail: reservations@diplomat-hotel-wales.com

web: www.diplomat-hotel-wales.com

dir: *M4 junct 48, A4138 then B4303, hotel 0.75m on right*

PETS: Bedrooms (4 GF) unattended **Charges** £10 per night **Public areas Grounds** on leads disp bin **Exercise area Facilities** cage storage walks info vet info **On Request** fridge access torch towels **Other** charge for damage **Resident Pets:** Heidi & Duke (Alsatian/Collie cross)

This Victorian mansion, set in mature grounds, has been extended over the years to provide a comfortable and relaxing hotel. The well-appointed bedrooms are located in the main house and there is also a wing of comfortable modern bedrooms. Public areas include Trubshaw's Restaurant, a large function suite and a modern leisure centre.

Rooms 50 (8 annexe) (2 fmly) (4 GF) **S** £70-£80; **D** £80-£95 (incl. bkfst)* **Facilities** FTV ⊗ supervised Gym Sauna Steam room Sun beds Hairdresser ♫ Xmas New Year Wi-fi **Services** Lift **Parking** 250 **Notes** LB

WALES

Afon Teifi Caravan & Camping Park
(SN338405)

▶ ▶ ▶

Pentrecagal SA38 9HT
☎ 01559 370532
e-mail: afonteifi@btinternet.com
dir: *Signed off A484, 2m E of Newcastle Emlyn*

PETS: **Public areas** disp bin **Exercise area** 15 acres **Facilities** washing facs walks info vet info

Open Apr-Oct Last arrival 23.00hrs

Set on the banks of the River Teifi, a famous salmon and sea trout river, this park is secluded with good views. Family owned and run, and only two miles from the market town of Newcastle Emlyn. A 6 acre site with 110 touring pitches, 22 hardstandings and 10 statics.

Notes ✆

Argoed Meadow Caravan and Camping Site
(SN268415)

▶ ▶ ▶

Argoed Farm SA38 9JL
☎ 01239 710690
dir: *From Newcastle Emlyn on A484 towards Cenarth, take B4332. Site 300yds on right*

PETS: **Stables** 2m **Public areas** on leads disp bin **Exercise area** 3-acre field, walk by river **Facilities** washing facs walks info vet info

Open all year Last arrival anytime Last departure noon

Pleasant open meadowland on the banks of the River Teifi, very close to Cenarth Falls gorge. A modern toilet block adds to the general appeal. A 3 acre site with 30 touring pitches, 5 hardstandings.

Notes No bikes or skateboards ✆

Moelfryn Caravan & Camping Park *(SN321370)*

▶ ▶ ▶

Ty-Cefn, Pant-y-Bwlch SA38 9JE
☎ 01559 371231
e-mail: moelfryn@moelfryncaravanpark.co.uk
dir: *A484 from Carmarthen towards Cynwyl Elfed. Pass Blue Bell Inn on right, in 200yds left onto B4333 towards Hermon. In 7m at brown sign on left turn left, site on right*

PETS: **Public areas** except shower block & play area on leads disp bin **Exercise area** dog run **Facilities** vet info **Resident Pets:** Kai (German Shepherd), Ginger, Patch & Kat (cats), Tara & Sultan (horses)

Open Mar-10 Jan Last arrival 22.00hrs Last departure noon

A small, beautifully maintained, family-run park in a glorious elevated location overlooking the valley of the River Teifi. Pitches are level and spacious, and well screened by hedging and mature trees. Facilities are spotlessly clean and tidy, and the playing field is well away from the touring area. Home-cooked meals can be ordered and Sunday breakfast delivered to the tent/caravan door. A 3 acre site with 25 touring pitches, 13 hardstandings.

Notes Games to be played in designated area only

Aromatherapy Reflexology Centre
★ ★ ★ BED AND BREAKFAST

The Barn House, Pennant Rd SY23 5LZ
☎ 01974 202581
e-mail: aromareflex@googlemail.com
web: www.aromatherapy-breaks-wales.co.uk
dir: *S of Aberystwyth to Llanon; exit village turn left at 40mph sign. 2nd left to Barn House*

PETS: **Bedrooms** **Sep accom** 2 large kennels in open shed **Charges** £3.50 per night **Grounds** disp bin **Exercise area** 5 mins **Facilities** food bowl water bowl washing facs cage storage walks info vet info **On Request** fridge access **Resident Pet:** Celt (Welsh Terrier)

Expect a warm welcome from this family run bed and breakfast where Welsh is spoken. The house is set in its own grounds in a tranquil position with lovely views of Cardigan Bay. Bedrooms are comfortable and smartly presented. There is a choice of traditional, vegetarian or vegan breakfasts. As its name implies aromatherapy and reflexology are available at the centre.

Rooms 3 rms (2 en suite) (1 pri facs) **S** £25-£50; **D** £50-£100 **Facilities** FTV tea/coffee **Parking** 7 **Notes** LB ✆

WALES

Llety Ceiro Country House
★★★★ GUEST HOUSE

Peggy Ln, Bow St, Llandre SY24 5AB
☎ 01970 821900 📠 01970 820966
e-mail: marinehotel1@btconnect.com
dir: *4m NE of Aberystwyth. Off A487 onto B4353 for 300yds*

PETS: Bedrooms unattended **Stables Charges** £5 per night £35 per week **Public areas** except restaurant on leads **Grounds** disp bin **Exercise area** 100yds **Facilities** food bowl water bowl cage storage walks info vet info **On Request** fridge access **Other** charge for damage

Located north of Aberystwyth, this house is well maintained throughout. Bedrooms are equipped with a range of thoughtful extras in addition to smart modern bathrooms. Morning coffees, afternoon teas and dinner are available in an attractive dining room, with a conservatory extension, and bicycle hire is also available.

Rooms 11 en suite (2 fmly) (3 GF) (1 smoking) **Facilities** FTV TVL tea/coffee Dinner available Direct Dial Cen ht Licensed Wi-fi **Parking** 21

The Hafod Hotel
★★★ 68% HOTEL

SY23 3JL
☎ 01970 890232 📠 01970 890394
e-mail: hafodhotel@btconnect.com
dir: *Exit A44 in Ponterwyd signed Devil's Bridge/Pontarfynach onto A4120 for 3m, over bridge. Hotel opposite*

PETS: Bedrooms Public areas with consent on leads **Grounds Exercise area** adjacent **Facilities** washing facs walks info vet info **On Request** torch towels **Other** charge for damage prior notice required

This former hunting lodge dates back to the 17th century and is situated in six acres of grounds. Now a family-owned and run hotel, it provides accommodation suitable for both business and leisure guests. Family rooms and a four-poster room are available. In addition to the dining area and lounge, there are tea rooms.

Rooms 17 (2 fmly) **S** £50; **D** £80-£130 (incl. bkfst)* **Facilities** Xmas New Year Wi-fi **Parking** 200

Ynyshir Hall
★★★ ◉◉◉ COUNTRY HOUSE HOTEL

SY20 8TA
☎ 01654 781209 & 781268 📠 01654 781366
e-mail: ynyshir@relaischateaux.com
web: www.ynyshir-hall.co.uk
dir: *Off A487, 5.5m S of Machynlleth, signed from main road*

PETS: Bedrooms unattended sign **Sep accom** outside kennel **Public areas Grounds** disp bin **Exercise area Facilities** food (pre-bookable) food bowl water bowl walks info vet info **On Request** torch towels **Other** charge for damage dogs allowed in ground-floor bedrooms only

Set in beautifully landscaped grounds and surrounded by a RSBP reserve, Ynyshir Hall is a haven of calm. Lavishly styled bedrooms, each individually themed around a great painter, provide high standards of luxury and comfort. The lounge and bar have different moods, and both feature abundant fresh flowers. The dining room offers outstanding cooking using best ingredients with modern flair.

Rooms 9 (2 annexe) **S** £180-£320; **D** £280-£395 (incl. bkfst)* **Facilities** 🍃 Xmas New Year **Parking** 20 **Notes** LB No children 9yrs

The Cliff Hotel
★★★ 77% HOTEL

SA43 1PP
☎ 01239 613241 📠 01239 615391
e-mail: reservations@cliffhotel.com
dir: *Exit A487 into Cardigan, take B4548 towards Gwbert, 2m to hotel*

PETS: Bedrooms (5 GF) unattended **Charges** £5 per night **Public areas** except restaurant & bars on leads **Grounds Exercise area** 20yds **Facilities** cage storage walks info vet info **On Request** fridge access **Other** charge for damage prior notice required

Set in 30 acres of grounds with a 9-hole golf course, this hotel commands superb sea views from its cliff-top location overlooking Cardigan Bay. Bedrooms in the main building offer excellent views and there is also a wing of modern rooms. Public areas are spacious and comprise a choice of bars, lounges and a fine dining restaurant. The spa offers a wide range of up-to-the-minute leisure facilities.

Rooms 70 (6 fmly) (5 GF) **S** £59-£85; **D** £70-£150 (incl. bkfst) **Facilities** Spa STV FTV ⊗ ⅃ 9 Putt green Fishing Gym Xmas New Year **Services** Lift **Parking** 100 **Notes** LB

WALES

LAMPETER — Map 2 SN54

Falcondale Mansion

★★★ 86% ◉◉ COUNTRY HOUSE HOTEL
SA48 7RX
☎ 01570 422910 📠 01570 423559
e-mail: info@falcondalehotel.com
web: www.falcondalehotel.com
dir: 800yds W of High St (A475) or 1.5m NW of Lampeter (A482)

PETS: Bedrooms unattended sign Stables Charges £10 per
night Public areas except restaurants & with other guests'
comfort in mind Grounds disp bin Exercise area hotel grounds
Facilities food (pre-bookable) food bowl water bowl bedding
dog chews feeding mat scoop/disp bags leads washing facs
cage storage walks info vet info On Request fridge access
torch towels Other charge for damage Resident Pets: Pudgeley
& Major (Cocker Spaniels)

Built in the Italianate style, this charming Victorian property is
set in extensive grounds and beautiful parkland. The individually-
styled bedrooms are generally spacious, well equipped and
tastefully decorated. Bars and lounges are similarly well
appointed with additional facilities including a conservatory
and function room. Guests have a choice of either the Valley
Restaurant for fine dining or the less formal Peterwells Brasserie.

Rooms 19 (2 fmly) D £145-£185 (incl. bkfst)* Facilities FTV ⛳
Xmas New Year Wi-fi Services Lift Parking 60

CONWY

BETWS-Y-COED — Map 6 SH75

Craig-y-Dderwen Riverside Hotel

★★★★ 71% ◉ COUNTRY HOUSE HOTEL
LL24 0AS
☎ 01690 710293 📠 01690 710362
e-mail: info@snowdoniahotel.com
web: www.snowdoniahotel.com
dir: A5 to town, cross Waterloo Bridge, take 1st left

PETS: Bedrooms (1 GF) unattended sign Stables 3m Charges
£7.50 per night Public areas except restaurant on leads
Grounds disp bin Exercise area 16 acres of fields Facilities
food (pre-bookable) food bowl water bowl cat treats feeding
mat litter tray scoop/disp bags washing facs cage storage
walks info vet info On Request fridge access torch towels
Other charge for damage

This Victorian country-house hotel is set in well-maintained
grounds alongside the River Conwy, at the end of a tree-lined
drive. Very pleasant views can be enjoyed from many rooms, and
two of the bedrooms have four-poster beds. There are comfortable
lounges and the atmosphere throughout is tranquil and relaxing.

Rooms 18 (2 fmly) (1 GF) (2 smoking) S £95-£105; D £110-£190
(incl. bkfst)* Facilities STV FTV Fishing ⛳ Badminton Volleyball
New Year Wi-fi Parking 50 Notes Closed 23-26 Dec & 2 Jan-1 Feb

Best Western Waterloo

★★★ 78% HOTEL
LL24 0AR
☎ 01690 710411 📠 01690 710986
e-mail: reservations@waterloo-hotel.info
web: www.waterloo-hotel.info
dir: A5, near Waterloo Bridge

PETS: Bedrooms (31 GF) unattended Charges £6.50 per night
Grounds on leads disp bin Exercise area 25mtrs Facilities
cage storage walks info vet info On Request fridge access
towels

This long-established hotel, named after the nearby Waterloo
Bridge, is ideally located for visiting Snowdonia. Stylish
accommodation is split between rooms in the main hotel and
modern, cottage-style rooms located in buildings to the rear.
The attractive Garden Room Restaurant serves traditional Welsh
specialities, and the vibrant Bridge Inn provides a wide range of
food and drink throughout the day and evening.

Rooms 45 (34 annexe) (12 fmly) (31 GF) S £77.75-£90;
D £115.50-£140 (incl. bkfst)* Facilities ⛹ Gym Steam room
Sauna New Year Wi-fi Parking 100 Notes LB Closed 25-26 Dec

Plas Farm Caravan Park *(SH897744)*

▶▶▶▶

LL22 8AU

☎ 01492 680254   & 07831 482176

e-mail: info@plasfarmcaravanpark.co.uk

dir: *A547 Abergele, right Rhyd y Foel Rd, 3m then left signed B5381, 1st farm on right*

PETS: Sep accom large wooden pen **Charges** dog £1 per night £7 per week **Public areas** except children's play area disp bin **Exercise area** field & woodland **Facilities** washing facs walks info vet info **Other** disposal bags available

Open Mar-Oct Last departure 11.00hrs

A small, quiet caravan park on a working farm, surrounded by rolling countryside and farmland. The park is an ideal holiday location for both families and couples, with its modern facilities, fully-serviced pitches, and well-equipped children's play area, as well as spacious fields to roam through. A 10 acre site with 40 touring pitches, 40 hardstandings.

The Northwood

★ ★ ★   GUEST HOUSE

47 Rhos Rd, Rhos-on-Sea LL28 4RS

☎ 01492 549931

e-mail: welcome@thenorthwood.co.uk

web: www.thenorthwood.co.uk

dir: *Exit at A55 junct 22 (Old Colwyn), at T-junct right to next T-junct (facing sea). Left, pass pier, left opposite harbour into Rhos Rd. On left adjacent to church*

PETS: Bedrooms unattended **Public areas** except dining room or lounge on leads **Grounds** disp bin **Exercise area** adjacent **Facilities** food (pre-bookable) food bowl water bowl dog chews cat treats feeding mat litter tray scoop/disp bags leads pet sitting dog walking washing facs cage storage walks info vet info **On Request** fridge access torch towels **Other** charge for damage a sausage for dogs at breakfast! **Resident Pets:** Sam (cat), Sticky & Fluffy (lovebirds)

A short walk from the seafront and shops, this constantly improving guest house has a warm and friendly atmosphere and welcomes back many regular guests. Bedrooms are furnished in modern style, and freshly prepared meals, utilising fresh produce (some home grown), can be enjoyed in the spacious dining room overlooking the pretty patio rear garden.

Rooms 11 rms (10 en suite) (1 pri facs) (3 fmly) (2 GF)

Facilities TVL tea/coffee Dinner available Cen ht Licensed Wi-fi

Parking 12

    WELSH RAREBITS

Castle Hotel Conwy

★ ★ ★ ★   79% ◉◉   TOWN HOUSE HOTEL

High St LL32 8DB

☎ 01492 582800   📠 01492 582300

e-mail: mail@castlewales.co.uk

web: www.castlewales.co.uk

dir: *A55 junct 18, follow town centre signs, cross estuary (castle on left). Right then left at mini-rdbts onto one-way system. Right at Town Wall Gate, right into Berry St then High St*

PETS: Bedrooms Charges small pet £5, large pet £10 per night **Public areas** on leads **Grounds** on leads disp bin **Exercise area** 50mtrs **Facilities** feeding mat leads pet sitting dog grooming cage storage walks info vet info **On Request** fridge access torch towels **Other** charge for damage **Resident Pet:** Tizzy (Cocker Spaniel)

This family-run, 16th-century hotel is one of Conwy's most distinguished buildings and offers a relaxed and friendly atmosphere. Bedrooms are appointed to an impressive standard and include a stunning suite. Public areas include a popular modern bar and the award-winning restaurant.

Rooms 28 (2 fmly) **S** £84-£94; **D** £125-£135 (incl. bkfst)

Facilities New Year Wi-fi **Parking** 34 **Notes** LB

WALES

CONWY *continued*

The Groes Inn

★ ★ ★ ★ ★ ◉ INN

Tyn-y-Groes LL32 8TN
☎ 01492 650545 📄 01492 650855
e-mail: enquiries@thegroes.com
web: www.groesinn.com
dir: *A55, over Old Conwy Bridge, 1st left through Castle Walls on B5106 (Trefriw Road), 2m on right*

PETS: Bedrooms unattended **Stables** stabling can be arranged (0.5m) **Charges** £10 per night **Public areas** in hall area only on leads **Grounds Exercise area** adjacent **Facilities** dog chews feeding mat washing facs cage storage walks info vet info **On Request** torch **Other** charge for damage pets allowed in two bedrooms only **Resident Pets:** Buff (Wire Haired Fox Terrier), Hemi & Mica (Lurchers)

Located in the picturesque Conwy Valley, this historic inn dates from 1573 and was the first licensed house in Wales. The exterior and gardens have an abundance of shrubs and seasonal flowers and create an immediate welcome, which is matched by a friendly and professional staff. Public areas are decorated and furnished with flair to highlight the many period features, and a formal dining room is also available. Spacious bedrooms, in sympathetically renovated former outbuildings are equipped with a wealth of thoughtful extras, and many have balconies overlooking the surrounding countryside.

Rooms 14 en suite (1 fmly) (6 GF) **S** £85-£160; **D** £105-£180* **Facilities** FTV tea/coffee Dinner available Direct Dial Cen ht Wi-fi ⛳ Golf 18 Squash Riding **Parking** 100 **Notes** LB Closed 25 Dec

The Old Rectory Country House

★ ★ ★ ★ ★ 🛏 GUEST ACCOMMODATION

Llanrwst Rd, Llansanffraid Glan Conwy LL28 5LF
☎ 01492 580611
e-mail: info@oldrectorycountryhouse.co.uk
web: www.oldrectorycountryhouse.co.uk
dir: *0.5m S from A470/A55 junct on left, by 30mph sign*

PETS: Bedrooms unattended **Charges** £10 per stay **Public areas** **Grounds** on leads disp bin **Exercise area** adjacent **Facilities** washing facs cage storage walks info vet info **On Request** fridge access torch towels **Other** charge for damage dogs allowed in Coach House only **Restrictions** no breed larger than a Labrador

This very welcoming accommodation has fine views over the Conwy estuary and towards Snowdonia. The elegant day rooms are luxurious and afternoon tea is available in the lounge. Bedrooms share the delightful views and are thoughtfully furnished, while the genuine hospitality creates a real home-from-home.

Rooms 3 en suite 2 annexe en suite (1 fmly) (2 GF) **S** £79-£119; **D** £99-£159* **Facilities** STV FTV tea/coffee Direct Dial Cen ht **Parking** 10 **Notes** LB No Children 5yrs Closed 14 Dec-15 Jan

LLANDDULAS　　　　　　　　　　　　　　**Map 6 SH97**

Bron-Y-Wendon Caravan Park *(SH903785)*

▶ ▶ ▶ ▶ ▶

Wern Rd LL22 8HG
☎ 01492 512903 📄 01492 512903
e-mail: stay@northwales-holidays.co.uk
dir: *Take A55 W. Turn right at sign for Llanddulas A547 junct 23, then sharp right. 200yds, under A55 bridge. Park on left*

PETS: Charges £1 per night / £7 per week **Public areas** except reception, shower block & games room; all pets under strict control disp bin **Exercise area** adjacent **Facilities** walks info vet info

Open all year Last arrival anytime Last departure 11.00hrs

A good quality site with sea views from every pitch, and excellent purpose-built toilet facilities. Staff are helpful and friendly, and everything from landscaping to maintenance has a stamp of excellence. An ideal seaside base for touring Snowdonia, with lots of activities available nearby. An 8 acre site with 130 touring pitches, 85 hardstandings.

WALES

LLANDUDNO **Map 6 SH78**

  WELSH RAREBITS

St Tudno Hotel and Restaurant

★★★ HOTEL

The Promenade LL30 2LP
☎ 01492 874411 📄 01492 860407
e-mail: sttudnohotel@btinternet.com
web: www.st-tudno.co.uk
dir: *On Promenade towards pier, hotel opposite pier entrance*

PETS: **Bedrooms Charges** £10 per night **Public areas** on leads **Exercise area** beach adjacent **Facilities** food bowl water bowl walks info vet info **Other** charge for damage **Restrictions** small to medium dogs preferred; no boisterous or noisy dogs **Resident Pet:** Tarkwell (cat)

A high quality family-owned hotel with friendly, attentive staff, and enjoying fine sea views. The stylish bedrooms are well equipped with mini-bars, robes, satellite TVs and many other thoughtful extras. Public rooms include a lounge, a welcoming bar and a small indoor pool. The Terrace Restaurant, where seasonal and daily-changing menus are offered, has a delightful Mediterranean atmosphere. Afternoon tea is a real highlight.

Rooms 18 (4 fmly) **S** £65-£90; **D** £90-£210 (incl. bkfst)
Facilities FTV 🏊 🎵 Xmas New Year Wi-fi Child facilities
Services Lift **Parking** 12 **Notes** LB

Dunoon

★★★ 81% HOTEL

Gloddaeth St LL30 2DW
☎ 01492 860787 📄 01492 860031
e-mail: reservations@dunoonhotel.co.uk
web: www.dunoonhotel.co.uk
dir: *Exit Promenade at war memorial by pier onto wide avenue. 200yds on right*

PETS: **Bedrooms** unattended sign **Charges** £9 per night £63 per week **Grounds** on leads **Exercise area** beach 500mtrs, park 1m **Facilities** washing facs cage storage walks info vet info **On Request** fridge access torch towels **Other** charge for damage **Restrictions** small dogs only

This impressive privately owned hotel is centrally located and offers a variety of styles and sizes of attractive, well-equipped bedrooms. Elegant public areas include a tastefully appointed restaurant, where competently prepared dishes are served together with a good choice of notable wines that are reasonably priced. The caring and attentive service is noteworthy.

Rooms 49 (7 fmly) **S** £60-£120; **D** £90-£157 (incl. bkfst)*
Facilities FTV Pool table Wi-fi **Services** Lift **Parking** 24 **Notes** LB Closed 22 Dec-early Mar

Can-Y-Bae

★★★★ GUEST ACCOMMODATION

10 Mostyn Crescent, Central Promenade LL30 1AR
☎ 01492 874188 📄 01492 868376
e-mail: canybae@btconnect.com
web: www.can-y-baehotel.com
dir: *A55 junct 10 onto A470, signed Llandudno/Promenade. Can-Y-Bae on seafront promenade between Venue Cymru Theatre & Band Stand*

PETS: **Bedrooms** sign **Charges** 1st night £5, extra nights £3 £23 per week **Public areas** except restaurant (assist dogs only) on leads disp bin **Exercise area** beach 10mtrs (restrictions apply) **Facilities** food bowl water bowl feeding mat dog grooming walks info vet info **Other** charge for damage dog grooming by appointment (charged) **Resident Pet:** Rolo (Airedale Terrier)

A warm welcome is assured at this tastefully renovated house, centrally located on the Promenade. Bedrooms are equipped with both practical and homely extras and upper floors are serviced by a modern lift. Day rooms include a panoramic lounge, cosy bar and attractive basement dining room.

Rooms 16 en suite (1 fmly) (2 GF) **S** £35-£45; **D** £70-£80*
Facilities FTV tea/coffee Dinner available Direct Dial Cen ht Lift Licensed Wi-fi **Notes** LB No Children 12yrs

Epperstone

★★★★ GUEST ACCOMMODATION

15 Abbey Rd LL30 2EE
☎ 01492 878746 📄 01492 871223
e-mail: epperstonehotel@btconnect.com
dir: *A550/A470 to Mostyn St. Left at rdbt, 4th right onto York Rd, Eppestone on junct of York Rd & Abbey Rd*

PETS: **Bedrooms** sign **Stables** 5m **Charges** approx £4 per night **Grounds Exercise area** adjacent & beach (1km) **Facilities** washing facs cage storage vet info **On Request** fridge access torch **Other** charge for damage **Restrictions** small dogs only

Rooms 8 en suite (pri facs) annexe en suite (pri facs) (5 fmly) (GF) (smoking) **S** £30-£35; **D** £60-£70* **Facilities** FTV tea/coffee Direct Dial Wi-fi **Parking** 8 **Notes** No Children

LLANRWST
Map 6 SH86

Maenan Abbey
★★★ 78% HOTEL

Maenan LL26 0UL
☎ 01492 660247 ▤ 01492 660734
e-mail: reservations@manab.co.uk
dir: *3m N on A470*

PETS: **Bedrooms** unattended **Charges** £5 per night **Public areas** except dining area & bar during food service **Grounds** **Exercise area** surrounding area **Facilities** food (pre-bookable) cage storage vet info **On Request** fridge access towels **Other** charge for damage **Resident Pets:** Poppy (Staffordshire cross), Harvey (Spaniel), Olliecat & Kittie (cats)

Set in its own spacious grounds, this privately owned hotel was built as an abbey in 1850 on the site of a 13th-century monastery. It is now a popular venue for weddings as the grounds and magnificent galleried staircase make an ideal setting for photographs. Bedrooms include a large suite and are equipped with modern facilities. Meals are served in the bar and restaurant.

Rooms 14 (3 fmly) (4 smoking) **Facilities** Fishing Guided mountain walks Xmas New Year Wi-fi **Parking** 60

Bodnant Caravan Park *(SH805609)*
▶ ▶ ▶ ▶

Nebo Rd LL26 0SD
☎ 01492 640248
e-mail: ermin@bodnant-caravan-park.co.uk
dir: *S in Llanrwst, exit A470 opposite Birmingham garage onto B5427 signed Nebo. Site 300yds on right, opposite leisure centre*

PETS: **Charges** dog 50p per night **Public areas** except children's play area disp bin **Exercise area** fenced area, short illuminated dog walk **Exercise area** Gwydyr Forest 1m **Facilities** walks info vet info **Other** prior notice required pet store 0.5m, kennels nearby (day boarding) **Resident Pets:** Besi, Bobi & Loli (working dogs), cats, sheep, geese, ducks, guinea fowl

Open Mar-end Oct Last arrival 21.00hrs Last departure 11.00hrs

This well maintained and stunningly attractive park is filled with flower beds, and the landscape includes shrubberies and trees. The statics are unobtrusively sited, and there are 35 fully-serviced pitches and the quality toilet blocks are spotlessly clean. There is a separate playing field and rally field. A 5 acre site with 54 touring pitches, 20 hardstandings and 2 statics.

Notes Main gates locked 23.00hrs-08.00hrs, no noise after 23.00hrs

TAL-Y-BONT (NEAR CONWY)
Map 6 SH76

Tynterfyn Touring Caravan Park *(SH768695)*
▶

LL32 8YX
☎ 01492 660525
dir: *5m S of Conwy on B5106, signed Tal-y-Bont, 1st on left*

PETS: **Charges** £1 per night £7 per week **Public areas** disp bin **Exercise area** large field **Facilities** food bowl water bowl scoop/disp bags walks info vet info **Other** prior notice required **Resident Pets:** Nel & Suzie (Border Collies)

Open Mar-Oct rs 28 days in year tent pitches only Last arrival 22.00hrs Last departure noon

A quiet, secluded little park set in the beautiful Conwy Valley, and run by family owners. The grounds are tended with care, and the older-style toilet facilities sparkle. There is lots of room for children and dogs to run around. A 2 acre site with 15 touring pitches, 4 hardstandings.

Notes ⊘

Hafod Country House

★★★★ GUEST ACCOMMODATION

LL27 0RQ

☎ 01492 640029

e-mail: stay@hafod-house.co.uk

dir: *On B5106 entering Trefriw from S, 2nd house on right*

PETS: Bedrooms unattended **Charges** £5 per night **Public areas**
Grounds disp bin **Exercise area** 100yds **Facilities** food
(pre-bookable) food bowl water bowl dog chews scoop/disp
bags leads washing facs cage storage walks info vet info
On Request fridge access torch towels **Other** all bedrooms have
balcony with steps to garden **Resident Pets:** Isla (Deerhound),
Ricky (Greyhound)

This former farmhouse is personally run with a wealth of charm
and character. The tasteful bedrooms feature period furnishings
and thoughtful extras such as fresh fruit. There is a comfortable
sitting room and a cosy bar. The fixed-price menu is imaginative
and makes good use of fresh, local produce while the breakfast
menu offers a wide choice.

Rooms 6 en suite; **D** £70-£90 **Facilities** FTV tea/coffee Dinner
available Direct Dial Cen ht Licensed **Parking** 14 **Notes** LB No
Children 11yrs RS Jan-mid Feb Mon & Tue no meals for non-
residents

Llawr-Betws Farm Caravan Park *(SJ016424)*

► ►

LL21 0HD

☎ 01490 460224 & 460296

dir: *3m W of Corwen off A494 (Bala road)*

PETS: Public areas Facilities walks info vet info

Open Mar-Oct Last arrival 23.00hrs Last departure noon

A quiet grassy park with mature trees and gently sloping pitches.
The friendly owners keep the facilities in good condition. A 12.5
acre site with 35 touring pitches and 68 statics.

Notes ⊗

Hendwr Country Park *(SJ042386)*

► ► ►

LL21 0SN

☎ 01490 440210

dir: *From Corwen (A5) take B4401 for 4m. Right at Hendwr sign.*
Site 0.5m on right down wooded driveway. Or follow brown signs
from A5 at Corwen

PETS: Stables Charges dogs & cats free; charges for horses
on application **Public areas** except shop & toilets disp bin
Exercise area 6-acre wood adjacent (dogs must be on leads)
Exercise area 1m **Facilities** food walks info vet info **Other**
prior notice required **Restrictions** no dangerous breeds (see page
7) **Resident Pets:** dogs, cats, horses, cattle, sheep

Open Apr-Oct Last arrival 22.00hrs Last departure 16.00hrs

Set in parkland at the end of a tree-lined lane, Hendwr (it means
'old tower') has a stream meandering through its grounds, and
all around is the stunning Snowdonia mountain range. The toilet
facilities are good. Self-catering holiday lodges and 29 seasonal
touring pitches are available. An 11 acre site with 40 touring
pitches, 3 hardstandings and 80 statics.

Notes ⊗

WALES

LLANDYRNOG
Map 6 SJ16

Pentre Mawr Country House

★ ★ ★ ★ ★ 　 GUEST ACCOMMODATION

LL16 4LA
☎ 01824 790732 📄 01824 790441
e-mail: info@pentremawrcountryhouse.co.uk
dir: *From Denbigh follow signs to Bodfari/Llandyrnog. Left at rdbt to Bodfari, after 50yds turn left onto country lane, follow road and Pentre Mawr on left*

PETS: Bedrooms unattended **Stables Charges** horse £25 per night **Public areas** except restaurant & pool areas **Grounds** disp bin **Exercise area Facilities** food (pre-bookable) water bowl bedding dog chews scoop/disp bags leads washing facs walks info vet info **On Request** fridge access torch towels **Other** charge for damage **Resident Pets:** Mollie, Maisie & Millie (Collies), Morris & Oscar (cats), 4 ponies

Expect a warm welcome from Graham and Bre at this superb family country house set in nearly 200 acres of meadows, park and woodland. The property has been in Graham's family for over 400 years. Bedrooms are individually decorated, very spacious and each is thoughtfully equipped. Breakfast is served in either the morning room or, on warmer mornings, on the Georgian terrace. Dinner is served in the formal dining room. There is a salt water swimming pool in the walled garden.

Rooms 8 en suite (4 GF) **S** £80-£160; **D** £100-£180*
Facilities tea/coffee Dinner available Cen ht Licensed Wi-fi 🕏 🌳
🎣 Fishing **Parking** 8 **Notes** LB No Children 13yrs 🐾

LLANGOLLEN
Map 7 SJ24

Bryn Meirion B&B

★ ★ ★ ★ 　 GUEST ACCOMMODATION

Abbey Rd LL20 8EF
☎ 01978 861911
e-mail: j.hurle@globalnet.co.uk
web: www.users.globalnet.co.uk/~jhurle/

PETS: Bedrooms Public areas except dining room **Grounds** disp bin **Exercise area** 50yds **Facilities** food bowl water bowl washing facs cage storage walks info vet info **On Request** fridge access torch towels **Other** charge for damage **Resident Pet:** Charlie (cat)

This spacious Edwardian house is set in large gardens, just on the outskirts of the town of Llangollen. The attractive bedrooms are well equipped and a comfortable beamed lounge is available. Breakfast and dinners by prior arrangement are served in the conservatory style dining room, with views over the River Dee and the steam railway.

Rooms 3 rms (2 en suite) (1 pri facs) (1 fmly) **S** £25-£35; **D** £50-£60* **Facilities** FTV TVL tea/coffee Dinner available Cen ht **Parking** 3 **Notes** 🐾

RHUALLT
Map 6 SJ07

Penisar Mynydd Caravan Park *(SJ093770)*

▶ ▶ ▶ ▶

Caerwys Rd LL17 0TY
☎ 01745 582227 📄 01745 582227
e-mail: contact@penisarmynydd.co.uk
dir: *From Llandudno 1st left at top of Rhuallt Hill (junct 29). From Chester take junct 29, follow Dyserth signs, site 500yds on right*

PETS: Charges dog £1 per night **Public areas** on leads disp bin **Exercise area** dog walking area **Facilities** washing facs walks info vet info **Resident Pets:** Meg (Jack Russell), George (Border Terrier)

Open Mar-15 Jan Last arrival 21.00hrs Last departure 21.00hrs

A very tranquil, attractively laid-out park set in three grassy paddocks with superb facilities block including a disabled room and dishwashing area. The majority of pitches are super pitches. Everything is immaculately maintained, and the amenities of the seaside resort of Rhyll are close by. A 6.6 acre site with 75 touring pitches, 75 hardstandings.

Notes No cycling 🐾

WALES

RUABON   Map 7 SJ34

James' Caravan Park *(SJ300434)*

▶ ▶ ▶

LL14 6DW
☎ 01978 820148   📠 01978 820148
e-mail: ray@carastay.demon.co.uk
dir: *Approach on A483 South, at rdbt with A539, turn right (signed Llangollen) over dual carriageway bridge, site 500yds on left*

PETS: Charges £2 per night **Public areas** on leads disp bin
Exercise area large field **Facilities** walks info vet info

Open all year Last arrival 21.00hrs Last departure 11.00hrs

A well-landscaped park on a former farm, with modern heated toilet facilities. Old farm buildings house a collection of restored original farm machinery, and the village shop, four pubs, take away and launderette are a 10-minute walk away. A 6 acre site with 40 touring pitches, 4 hardstandings.

Notes

RUTHIN   Map 6 SJ15

Eyarth Station

★ ★ ★ ★ GUEST ACCOMMODATION
Llanfair Dyffryn Clwyd LL15 2EE
☎ 01824 703643   📠 08717 146743
e-mail: stay@eyarthstation.com
dir: *1m S of Ruthin. Off A525 turn right onto lane, 600yds to Eyarth Station*

PETS: Bedrooms Charges £8 per night **Public areas** except dining room & lounge on leads **Grounds** on leads disp bin
Exercise area adjacent **Facilities** food bowl water bowl feeding mat scoop/disp bags leads washing facs cage storage walks info vet info **On Request** fridge access torch towels **Other** charge for damage pets accepted by prior arrangement only **Restrictions** no Rottweilers or Pit Bull Terriers **Resident Pet:** cat

Until 1964 and the Beeching cuts, this was a sleepy country station. A comfortable lounge and outdoor swimming pool occupy the space once taken up by the railway and platforms. Bedrooms are carefully decorated and full of thoughtful extras. Family rooms are available, and two rooms are in the former stationmaster's house adjoining the main building.

Rooms 4 en suite 2 annexe en suite (2 fmly) (4 GF) (1 smoking)
S £50-£70; **D** £75* **Facilities** TVL tea/coffee Dinner available Cen ht Licensed Wi-fi ⚡ Golf 9 **Parking** 6 **Notes** LB

The Wynnstay Arms

★ ★ ★ ★ INN
Well St LL15 1AN
☎ 01824 703147   📠 01824 705428
e-mail: resevations@wynnstayarms.com
web: www.wynnstayarms.com
dir: *In town centre*

PETS: Bedrooms Charges £5 per night **Public areas** except restaurant on leads disp bin **Exercise area** park nearby
Facilities washing facs cage storage walks info vet info
On Request fridge access torch **Other** charge for damage
Restrictions small dogs only

Established in 1549 this former coaching inn in the town centre has been sympathetically renovated to provide good quality accommodation and a smart café-bar. Imaginative food is served in Fusions Brasserie, where the contemporary decor highlights the many retained period features.

Rooms 7 en suite (1 fmly) **S** £45-£60; **D** £65-£105* **Facilities** FTV tea/coffee Dinner available Cen ht Wi-fi **Parking** 14 **Notes** LB

FLINTSHIRE

MOLD   Map 7 SJ26

Beaufort Park Hotel

★ ★ ★ 74% HOTEL
Alltami Rd, New Brighton CH7 6RQ
☎ 01352 758646   📠 01352 757132
e-mail: info@beaufortparkhotel.co.uk
web: www.beaufortparkhotel.co.uk
dir: *A55/A494. Through Alltami lights, over mini rdbt by petrol station towards Mold, A5119. Hotel 100yds on right*

PETS: Bedrooms (32 GF) unattended **Charges** £10 per night
Public areas except restaurant on leads **Grounds** on leads disp bin **Facilities** walks info vet info **On Request** towels **Other** charge for damage **Restrictions** small, well behaved dogs only

This large, modern hotel is conveniently located a short drive from the North Wales Expressway and offers various styles of spacious accommodation. There are extensive public areas, and several meeting and function rooms are available. There is a wide choice of meals in the formal restaurant and in the popular Arches bar.

Rooms 106 (8 fmly) (32 GF) **S** £50-£95; **D** £60-£110 (incl. bkfst)
Facilities FTV Squash 🎵 Xmas New Year Wi-fi **Parking** 200
Notes LB

WALES

GWYNEDD

Porth Tocyn

★★★ 80% ◉◉ COUNTRY HOUSE HOTEL
Bwlch Tocyn LL53 7BU
☎ 01758 713303 & 07789 994942 📠 01758 713538
e-mail: bookings@porthtocyn.fsnet.co.uk
web: www.porth-tocyn-hotel.co.uk
dir: 2.5m S follow Porth Tocyn signs after Sarnbach

PETS: Bedrooms (3 GF) unattended **Exercise area** adjacent
Other charge for damage **Restrictions** certain breeds not
accepted, please phone to check

Located above Cardigan Bay with fine views over the area, Porth
Tocyn is set in attractive gardens. Several elegantly furnished
sitting rooms are provided and bedrooms are comfortably
furnished. Children are especially welcome and a playroom is
provided. Award-winning food is served in the restaurant.

Rooms 17 (1 fmly) (3 GF) **S** £70-£85; **D** £95-£170 (incl. bkfst)*
Facilities FTV ⚹ 🏊 Table tennis Wi-fi **Parking** 50 **Notes** LB
Closed mid Nov-wk before Etr RS some off season nights

Deucoch Touring & Camping Park (SH301269)

▶ ▶ ▶ ▶

Sarn Bach LL53 7LD
☎ 01758 713293 & 07740 281770 📠 01758 713293
e-mail: info@deucoch.com
dir: From Abersoch take Sarn Bach road, at x-rds turn right, site
on right in 800yds

PETS: Stables nearby **Public areas** except shower block on leads
disp bin **Exercise area** 1m **Facilities** walks info vet info **Other**
prior notice required **Restrictions** authorisation from site owners
required for large dogs & for more than 1 dog **Resident Pets:**
Chara (Samoyed), Cassie (Staffie cross)

Open Mar-Oct Last arrival 22.00hrs Last departure 11.00hrs

A sheltered site with sweeping views of Cardigan Bay and
the mountains, just a mile from Abersoch and a long sandy
beach. The facilities block is well maintained, and this site is
of special interest to watersports enthusiasts and those touring
the Llyn Peninsula. A 5 acre site with 70 touring pitches, 10
hardstandings.

Notes Families only 🐾

Rhydolion (SH283276)

▶ ▶ ▶

Rhydolion, Llangian LL53 7LR
☎ 01758 712342
e-mail: enquiries@rhydolion.co.uk
dir: From A499 take unclassified road to Llangian for 1m, turn
left, through Llangian. Site 1.5m after road fork towards Hell's
Mouth/Porth Neigwl

PETS: Charges horse £20 per week **Public areas** on leads disp
bin **Exercise area** lane adjacent **Facilities** vet info **Other** prior
notice required field available for horses

Open Mar-Oct Last arrival 22.00hrs Last departure noon

A peaceful small site with good views, on a working farm close
to the long sandy surfers beach at Hell's Mouth. The simple toilet
facilities are kept to a high standard by the friendly owners, and
nearby Abersoch is a mecca for boat owners and water sports
enthusiasts. A 1.5 acre site with 28 touring pitches.

Notes Families and couples only 🐾

Pen-y-Bont Touring Park (SH932350)

▶ ▶ ▶ ▶

Llangynog Rd LL23 7PH
☎ 01678 520549 📠 01678 520006
e-mail: penybont-bala@btconnect.com
dir: From A494 take B4391. Site 0.75m on right

PETS: Charges £1 per night **Public areas** disp bin
Exercise area wood & footpath **Facilities** food food bowl water
bowl dog chews scoop/disp bags leads washing facs walks
info vet info **Other** prior notice required dogs accepted only at
manager's discretion

Open Mar-Oct Last arrival 21.00hrs Last departure noon

A family run attractively landscaped park in a woodland country
setting. Set close to Bala Lake and the River Dee, with plenty of
opportunities for water sports including kayaking and white water
rafting. The park offers good facilities including Wi-fi, and many
pitches have water and electricity. A 7 acre site with 95 touring
pitches, 59 hardstandings.

Notes No camp fires, BBQ's must be kept off ground, quiet after
22.30hrs

WALES

Tyn Cornel Camping & Caravan Park

(SH895400)

▶ ▶ ▶ ▶

Frongoch LL23 7NU
☎ 01678 520759 ▤ 01678 520759
e-mail: tyncornel@mail.com
dir: *From Bala take A4212 (Porthmadog road) for 4m. Site on left before National Whitewater Centre*

PETS: Stables 4m **Charges** £2 per night **Public areas** except shop & near toilet block disp bin **Exercise area** 4-acre field **Exercise area** adjacent **Facilities** walks info vet info **Other** prior notice required **Resident Pets:** China (Labrador), Mrs Cat (cat)

Open Etr-Oct Last arrival 20.00hrs Last departure noon

A delightful riverside park with mountain views, popular with those seeking a base for river kayaks and canoes, with access to the nearby White Water Centre and riverside walk with tearoom. The helpful, resident owners keep the modern facilities, including a laundry and dishwashing room, very clean. A 10 acre site with 67 touring pitches, 10 hardstandings.

Notes Quiet after 23.00hrs, no cycling, latest arrival time 22.00hrs on Fri, no campfires or woodburning

Treborth Hall Farm Caravan Park *(SH554707)*

▶ ▶

The Old Barn, Treborth Hall Farm LL57 2RX
☎ 01248 364399 ▤ 01248 364333
e-mail: enquiries@treborthleisure.co.uk
dir: *A55 junct 9, 1st left at rdbt, straight over 2nd rdbt, site approx 800yds on left*

PETS: Public areas dogs must be on leads **Exercise area** numerous walks adjacent **Facilities** vet info **Other** prior notice required **Restrictions** no Bull Terriers, Rottweilers, Dobermans or Alsatians

Open Etr-end Oct Last arrival 22.30hrs Last departure 10.30hrs

Set in eight acres of beautiful parkland with its own trout fishing lake and golf course, this well-run park offers serviced pitches in a sheltered, walled orchard. Tents have a separate grass area, and there is a good clean toilet block. An excellent base for families with easy access for the Menai Straits, Anglesey beaches, Snowdon and the Lleyn peninsula. An 8 acre site with 34 touring pitches, 34 hardstandings and 4 statics.

Llwyndu Farmhouse

★★★★ ⬤ GUEST ACCOMMODATION
Llanaber LL42 1RR
☎ 01341 280144
e-mail: intouch@llwyndu-farmhouse.co.uk
web: www.llwyndu-farmhouse.co.uk
dir: *A496 towards Harlech where street lights end, on outskirts of Barmouth, take next right*

PETS: Bedrooms Public areas except dining room **Grounds** on leads disp bin **Exercise area** 0.25m **Facilities** washing facs cage storage walks info vet info **On Request** fridge access torch towels **Resident Pets:** Juke (Jack Russell), Holly, Khalilah & J.P.(horses)

This converted 16th-century farmhouse retains many original features including inglenook fireplaces, exposed beams and timbers. There is a cosy lounge and meals can be enjoyed in the licensed restaurant; two and three course dinners are offered. Bedrooms are modern and well equipped, and some have four-poster beds. Four rooms are in nearby buildings.

Rooms 3 en suite 4 annexe en suite (2 fmly); **D** £96-£120* **Facilities** FTV TVL tea/coffee Dinner available Cen ht Licensed Wi-fi **Parking** 10 **Notes** LB Closed 25-26 Dec RS Sun no dinner

WALES

BARMOUTH *continued*

Hendre Mynach Touring Caravan & Camping Park *(SH605170)*

▶▶▶▶▶

Llanaber Rd LL42 1YR
☎ 01341 280262 📄 01341 280586
e-mail: mynach@lineone.net
dir: *0.75m N of Barmouth on A496*

PETS: Charges 1st dog free, £1 per extra dog per night
Public areas disp bin **Exercise area** 50yds **Facilities** food food bowl water bowl dog chews leads walks info vet info **Other** toys, disposal bags available

Open Mar-9 Jan rs Nov-Jan shop closed Last arrival 22.00hrs Last departure noon

A lovely site with immaculate facilities, just off the A496 and near to the railway, with almost direct access to promenade and beach. Caravanners should not be put off by the steep descent, as park staff are always on hand if needed. Pitches have TV and satellite hook-up as well as water and electricity. A small café serves light meals and takeaways. A 10 acre site with 240 touring pitches, 75 hardstandings and 1 static.

Trawsdir Touring Caravans & Camping Park *(SH596198)*

▶▶▶▶▶

Llanaber LL42 1RR
☎ 01341 280611 & 280999 📄 01341 280740
e-mail: enquiries@barmouthholidays.co.uk
dir: *3m N of Barmouth on A496, just past Wayside pub on right*

PETS: Public areas disp bin **Exercise area** dog field provided **Facilities** food food bowl water bowl leads washing facs vet info **Other** disposal bags available

Open Mar-Jan Last arrival 20.00hrs Last departure noon

A quality park with spectacular views to the sea and hills, and very accessible to motor traffic. The facilities are appointed to a very high standard, and include spacious cubicles containing showers and washbasins, individual showers, smart toilets with sensor operated flush, and under-floor heating. Tents and caravans have their own designated areas divided by dry-stone walls, and the site is very convenient for large recreational vehicles. Luxury holiday lodges for hire. A 15 acre site with 70 touring pitches, 70 hardstandings.

Notes Families & couples only

BEDDGELERT Map 6 SH54

THE CIRCLE

The Royal Goat

★★★ 77% HOTEL

LL55 4YE
☎ 01766 890224 📄 01766 890422
e-mail: info@royalgoathotel.co.uk
web: www.royalgoathotel.co.uk
dir: *On A498 at Beddgelert*

PETS: Bedrooms Charges £10 per night **Exercise area** 100yds **Facilities** walks info vet info **Other** charge for damage **Restrictions** small dogs only

An impressive building steeped in history, the Royal Goat provides well-equipped accommodation, and carries out an annual programme of refurbishment that has included the smart, modern bathrooms. Attractively appointed, comfortable public areas include a choice of bars and restaurants, a residents' lounge and function rooms.

Rooms 32 (4 fmly) **Facilities** FTV Fishing Xmas New Year **Services** Lift **Parking** 100 **Notes** LB Closed Jan-1 Mar RS Nov-1 Jan

---

CAERNARFON Map 6 SH46

Plas Dinas Country House

★★★★ ⬤ GUEST ACCOMMODATION

Bontnewydd LL54 7YF
☎ 01286 830214
e-mail: info@plasdinas.co.uk
web: www.plasdinas.co.uk
dir: *3m S, off A487, 0.5m down private drive*

PETS: Bedrooms unattended **Charges** £10 per night **Public areas** except restaurant **Grounds** disp bin **Exercise area** **Facilities** food food bowl water bowl dog chews scoop/disp bags cage storage walks info vet info **On Request** fridge access torch towels **Other** charge for damage **Restrictions** no dogs larger than a Labrador **Resident Pet:** Patsy (Miniature Schnauzer)

Situated in 15 acres of beautiful grounds in Snowdonia, this delightful Grade II listed building dates back to the mid-17th century, but with many Victorian additions. Once the home of the Armstrong-Jones family; there are many family portraits, memorabilia and original pieces of furniture for guests to view. The bedrooms, including four-poster rooms, are individually decorated and have modern facilities. There is a stylish drawing room where a fire burns in the winter. Fresh local produce features on the dinner menu.

Rooms 10 en suite (1 GF) **S** £89-£169; **D** £99-£179*
Facilities FTV tea/coffee Dinner available Direct Dial Cen ht Licensed Wi-fi **Parking** 10 **Notes** LB No Children 13yrs Closed Xmas & New Year

Plas Gwyn Caravan & Camping Park

(SH520633)

► ► ►

Llanrug LL55 2AQ

☎ 01286 672619

e-mail: info@plasgwyn.co.uk

dir: *A4086, 3m E of Caernarfon, site on right. Between River Seiont & Llanryg village*

PETS: Charges 50p per night **Public areas** disp bin **Exercise area** field adjacent **Facilities** dog chews washing facs walks info vet info **Other** prior notice required dog scoop available **Resident Pets:** Kiri (Bichon Frisé), Millie (Springer Spaniel), Beth & Abbie (Cocker Spaniels)

Open Mar-Oct Last arrival 22.00hrs Last departure 11.30hrs

A secluded park handy for the beaches, historic Caernarfon, and for walking. The site is set within the grounds of Plas Gwyn House, a Georgian property with colonial additions, and the friendly owners are gradually upgrading the park. There is a wooden camping pod and five static caravans for hire. A 3 acre site with 30 touring pitches, 8 hardstandings and 18 statics.

Riverside Camping *(SH505630)*

► ► ►

Seiont Nurseries, Pont Rug LL55 2BB

☎ 01286 678781   📠 01286 677223

e-mail: brenda@riversidecamping.co.uk

dir: *2m from Caernarfon on right of A4086 towards Llanberis, also signed Seiont Nurseries*

PETS: Charges £2 per night £14 per week **Public areas** except restaurant, garden centre & shower blocks on leads disp bin **Exercise area** walk by disused railway **Facilities** vet info **Other** prior notice required

Open Etr-end Oct Last arrival anytime Last departure noon

Set in the grounds of a large garden centre beside the small River Seiont, this park is approached by an impressive tree-lined drive. Immaculately maintained by the owners, there are good grassy riverside tent pitches, clean and tidy toilet facilities and an excellent café/restaurant. A haven of peace close to Caernarfon. A 4.5 acre site with 60 touring pitches, 8 hardstandings.

Notes No fires, no loud music 🐾

Min y Gaer

★ ★ ★ ★ GUEST HOUSE

Porthmadog Rd LL52 0HP

☎ 01766 522151   📠 01766 523540

e-mail: info@minygaer.co.uk

dir: *On A497 200yds E of junct with B4411*

PETS: Bedrooms Charges £2.50 per night **Public areas** except dining room on leads **Grounds** on leads disp bin **Exercise area** 200mtrs **Facilities** feeding mat scoop/disp bags leads cage storage vet info **On Request** fridge access torch towels **Other** charge for damage **Restrictions** no breed larger than a Labrador **Resident Pet:** Daisy (Cocker Spaniel)

The friendly, family-run Min y Gaer has superb views from many of the rooms. The smart, modern bedrooms are furnished in pine, and the welcoming proprietors also provide a bar and a traditionally furnished lounge.

Rooms 10 en suite (2 fmly) **S** £35; **D** £64-£70* **Facilities** FTV TVL tea/coffee Cen ht Licensed Wi-fi **Parking** 12 **Notes** Closed Nov-14 Mar

Eisteddfa *(SH518394)*

► ► ► ►

Eisteddfa Lodge, Pentrefelin LL52 0PT

☎ 01766 522696

e-mail: eisteddfa@criccieth.co.uk

dir: *From Porthmadog take A497 towards Criccieth. After approx 3.5m, through Pentrefelin, site signed 1st right after Plas Gwyn Nursing Home*

PETS: Charges 50p per night **Public areas** on leads disp bin **Exercise area** on site **Exercise area** 3m **Facilities** walks info vet info **Other** prior notice required **Resident Pet:** Max (Chocolate Labrador)

Open Mar-Oct Last arrival 22.30hrs Last departure 11.00hrs

A quiet, secluded park on elevated ground, sheltered by the Snowdonia Mountains and with lovely views of Cardigan Bay; Criccieth is nearby. The owners are carefully improving the park whilst preserving its unspoilt beauty, and are keen to welcome families, who will appreciate the cubicled facilities. There's a field and play area, woodland walks, a tipi and three static holiday caravans for hire. An 11 acre site with 100 touring pitches, 17 hardstandings.

WALES

DOLGELLAU
Map 6 SH71

WELSH RAREBITS

Penmaenuchaf Hall
★★★ ◉ COUNTRY HOUSE HOTEL
Penmaenpool LL40 1YB
☎ 01341 422129   📠 01341 422787
e-mail: relax@penhall.co.uk
web: www.penhall.co.uk
dir: *Off A470 onto A493 to Tywyn. Hotel approx 1m on left*

PETS: Bedrooms Charges £10 per night **Public areas** in hall lounge only **Grounds** on leads disp bin **Exercise area** 50yds **Facilities** food (pre-bookable) food bowl water bowl dog chews cat treats washing facs cage storage walks info vet info **On Request** fridge access torch towels **Other** charge for damage pets allowed in certain bedrooms only

Built in 1860, this impressive hall stands in 20 acres of formal gardens, grounds and woodland, and enjoys magnificent views across the River Mawddach. Sympathetic restoration has created a comfortable and welcoming hotel with spacious day rooms and thoughtfully furnished bedrooms, some with private balconies. Fresh produce cooked in modern British style is served in an elegant conservatory restaurant, overlooking the countryside.

Rooms 14 (2 fmly) **S** £95-£145; **D** £150-£240 (incl. bkfst) **Facilities** STV FTV Fishing 🎣 Complimentary salmon & trout fishing Xmas New Year **Parking** 30 **Notes** LB No children 6yrs

Dolserau Hall
★★★ 81% ◉ HOTEL
LL40 2AG
☎ 01341 422522   📠 01341 422400
e-mail: welcome@dolserau.co.uk
web: www.dolserau.co.uk
dir: *1.5m outside Dolgellau between A494 to Bala & A470 to Dinas Mawddy*

PETS: Bedrooms (3 GF) unattended **Grounds** disp bin **Exercise area** adjacent **Facilities** walks info vet info **On Request** fridge access torch **Other** charge for damage pets allowed in Coach house rooms only **Restrictions** small dogs preferred **Resident Pet:** Charlie (Golden Retriever)

This privately owned, friendly hotel lies in attractive grounds that extend to the river and are surrounded by green fields. Several comfortable lounges are provided and welcoming log fires are lit during cold weather. The smart bedrooms are spacious, well equipped and comfortable. A varied menu offers very competently prepared dishes.

Rooms 20 (5 annexe) (1 fmly) (3 GF) **Facilities** Fishing Xmas New Year **Services** Lift **Parking** 40 **Notes** No children 10yrs Closed Dec-Jan (ex Xmas & New Year)

FFESTINIOG
Map 6 SH74

Ty Clwb
★★★★ BED AND BREAKFAST
The Square LL41 4LS
☎ 01766 762658   📠 01766 762658
e-mail: tyclwb@talk21.com
web: www.tyclwb.co.uk
dir: *On B4391 in Ffestiniog, opp church*

PETS: Bedrooms unattended **Public areas** except dining room disp bin **Exercise area** 100yds **Facilities** scoop/disp bags washing facs cage storage walks info vet info **On Request** fridge access torch towels **Resident Pets:** Ben (Lurcher/Old English Sheepdog cross), Casper (Border Collie)

Located opposite the historic church, this elegant house has been carefully modernised and is immaculately maintained throughout. Bedrooms are thoughtfully furnished and in addition to an attractive dining room, a spacious lounge with sun patio provides stunning views of the surrounding mountain range.

Rooms 3 en suite; **D** £54-£70 **Facilities** TVL tea/coffee Cen ht

LLANBEDR
Map 6 SH52

Ty Mawr
★★ 72% SMALL HOTEL
LL45 2NH
☎ 01341 241440   📠 01341 241440
e-mail: tymawrhotel@onetel.com
web: www.tymawrhotel.org.uk
dir: *From Barmouth A496 (Harlech road). In Llanbedr turn right after bridge, hotel 50yds on left, brown tourist signs on junct*

PETS: Bedrooms unattended **Stables** 0.5m **Public areas** except restaurant **Grounds** disp bin **Exercise area** approx 200yds **Facilities** water bowl cage storage walks info vet info **On Request** fridge access **Resident Pets:** Carlo (Welsh Sheepdog), Chelly (Border Collie), Tara (Sheepdog)

Located in a picturesque village, this family-run hotel has a relaxed, friendly atmosphere. The attractive grounds opposite the River Artro provide a popular beer garden during fine weather. The attractive, rustically furnished bar offers a blackboard selection of food and a good choice of real ales. A more formal menu is available in the restaurant. Bedrooms are smart and brightly decorated.

Rooms 10 (2 fmly) **S** £45-£50; **D** £70-£80 (incl. bkfst)* **Facilities** STV **Parking** 30 **Notes** LB Closed 24-26 Dec

WALES

LLANDWROG
Map 6 SH45

White Tower Caravan Park *(SH453582)*

▶▶▶▶

LL54 5UH

☎ 01286 830649 & 07802 562785 ▤ 01286 830649

e-mail: whitetower@supanet.com

dir: *1.5m from village on Tai'r Eglwys road. From Caernarfon take A487 (Porthmadog road). Cross rdbt, 1st right. Site 3m on right*

PETS: Stables 1.5m Public areas except club house & swimming pool disp bin Exercise area 100mtrs Facilities walks info vet info

Open Mar-10 Jan rs Mar-mid May & Sep-Oct bar open wknds only Last arrival 23.00hrs Last departure noon

There are lovely views of Snowdonia from this park located just two miles from the nearest beach at Dinas Dinlle. A well-maintained toilet block has key access, and the hard pitches have water and electricity. Popular amenities include an outdoor heated swimming pool, a lounge bar with family room, and a games and TV room. A 6 acre site with 104 touring pitches, 80 hardstandings and 54 statics.

LLANRUG
Map 6 SH56

Llys Derwen Caravan & Camping Site
(SH539629)

▶▶▶▶

Ffordd Bryngwyn LL55 4RD

☎ 01286 673322

e-mail: llysderwen@aol.com

dir: *From A55 junct 13 (Caernarfon) take A4086 to Llanberis, through Llanrug, turn right at pub, site 60yds on right*

PETS: Public areas caravan fields only on leads disp bin Exercise area separate field from caravans & tents Facilities walks info vet info Resident Pets: Lacey, Buffy, Brenna, Ria & Odin (Bernese Mountain Dogs)

Open Mar-Oct Last departure noon

A pleasant, beautifully maintained small site set in woodland within easy reach of Caernarfon, Snowdon, Anglesey and the Lleyn Peninsula. Visitors can expect a warm welcome from enthusiastic, hands-on owners, who keep the toilet facilities spotlessly clean. A 5 acre site with 20 touring pitches and 2 statics.

Notes No open fires 😊

PORTHMADOG
Map 6 SH53

Royal Sportsman

★★★ 77% ⊛ HOTEL

131 High St LL49 9HB

☎ 01766 512015 ▤ 01766 512490

e-mail: enquiries@royalsportsman.co.uk

dir: *By rdbt, at A497 & A487 junct*

PETS: Bedrooms (9 GF) unattended Stables Charges £5 per night Public areas except dining room Grounds disp bin Exercise area countryside Facilities food (pre-bookable) food bowl water bowl pet sitting dog walking washing facs dog grooming cage storage walks info vet info On Request fridge access torch towels Other charge for damage Resident Pet: Gelert (Sheepdog)

Ideally located in the centre of Porthmadog, this former coaching inn dates from the Victorian era and has been restored into a friendly, privately owned and personally run hotel. Rooms are tastefully decorated and well equipped, and some are in an annexe close to the hotel. There is a large comfortable lounge and a wide range of meals is served in the bar or restaurant.

Rooms 28 (9 annexe) (7 fmly) (9 GF) S £56-£80; D £84-£96 (incl. bkfst)* Facilities STV FTV Xmas New Year Wi-fi Parking 17 Notes LB

PWLLHELI
Map 6 SH33

Hafan Y Mor Holiday Park *(SH431368)*

LL53 6HJ

☎ 0871 231 0887 ▤ 01766 810379

dir: *From Caernarfon A499 to Pwllheli. A497 to Porthmadog. Park on right, approx 3m from Pwllheli. Or from Telford, A5, A494 to Bala. Right for Porthmadog. Left at rdbt in Porthmadog signed Criccieth & Pwllheli. Park on left 3m from Criccieth*

PETS: Charges depending on length of stay £20-£40 Public areas except restaurants, food servery & swimming pool area disp bin Exercise area grassed areas & beaches Facilities food food bowl water bowl walks info vet info Other prior notice required disposal bags available Restrictions no fighting or dangerous breeds (see page 7)

Open 20 Mar-2 Nov rs Mar-May & Sep-Oct reduced facilities Last arrival 21.00hrs Last departure 10.00hrs

Set between the seaside towns of Pwllheli and Criccieth on the sheltered Llyn Peninsula, this is an all-action caravan park with direct beach access. Facilities include an indoor splash pool with flumes and bubble pools, wave rider, aqua jet racer, and boating lake. A 500 acre site with 73 touring pitches and 800 statics.

WALES

TYWYN Map 6 SH50

Eisteddfa *(SH651055)*
★★★★ FARMHOUSE
Eisteddfa, Abergynolwyn LL36 9UP
☎ 01654 782385   📄 01654 782385 Mrs G Pugh
e-mail: hugh.pugh01@btinternet.com
dir: *5m NE of Tywyn on B4405 nr Dolgoch Falls*

PETS: **Bedrooms Charges** £10 per stay **Public areas Grounds**
disp bin **Exercise area Facilities** cage storage walks info
On Request torch

Eisteddfa is a modern stone bungalow situated less than a mile
from Abergynolwyn, in a spot ideal for walking or for visiting the
local historic railway. Rooms are well equipped and stunning
views are a feature from the attractive dining room.

Rooms 3 rms (2 en suite) (3 GF) **S** £30-£35; **D** £55-£60*
Facilities STV FTV TVL tea/coffee Cen ht **Parking** 6 **Notes** LB
Closed Dec-Feb 🐾 1200 acres mixed

MONMOUTHSHIRE

ABERGAVENNY Map 3 SO21

   WELSH RAREBITS

Llansantffraed Court
★★★★ 77% ◉◉ COUNTRY HOUSE HOTEL
Llanvihangel Gobion, Clytha NP7 9BA
☎ 01873 840678   📄 01873 840674
e-mail: reception@llch.co.uk
web: www.llch.co.uk
dir: *At A465/A40 Abergavenny junct take B4598 signed Usk (do
not join A40). Continue towards Raglan, hotel on left in 4.5m*

PETS: **Bedrooms** unattended **Charges** dogs £10 per night,
charges for cats - please enquire disp bin **Exercise area** 20
acres of grounds **Facilities** food bowl water bowl bedding dog
walking walks info vet info **Other** prior notice required

In a commanding position and in its own extensive grounds, this
very impressive property, a privately owned country-house hotel,
has enviable views of the Brecon Beacons. Extensive public areas
include a relaxing lounge and a spacious restaurant offering
imaginative and enjoyable award-winning dishes. Bedrooms
vary in size and reflect the individuality of the building; all are
comfortably furnished and provide some thoughtful extras.
Extensive parking is available.

Rooms 21 (1 fmly) **S** £90-£110; **D** £125-£175 (incl. bkfst)*
Facilities STV FTV ⛳ Putt green Fishing 🎣 Clay pigeon shooting
school Wi-fi Child facilities **Services** Lift **Parking** 250 **Notes** LB

Angel Hotel
★★★ 78% ◉ HOTEL
15 Cross St NP7 5EN
☎ 01873 857121   📄 01873 858059
e-mail: mail@angelhotelabergavenny.com
web: www.angelhotelabergavenny.com
dir: *Follow town centre signs from rdbt, S of Abergavenny, past
rail & bus stations. Turn left along side of hotel*

PETS: **Bedrooms** unattended **Charges** £10 per night
Public areas except restaurant on leads **Grounds** on leads
Exercise area 50mtrs **Facilities** water bowl bedding pet sitting
dog walking cage storage walks info vet info **On Request**
towels

Once a coaching inn this has long been a popular venue for both
local people and visitors; the two traditional function rooms and
a ballroom are in regular use. In addition there is a comfortable
lounge, a relaxed bar and a smart restaurant. In warmer weather
there is a central courtyard that is ideal for alfresco eating. The
bedrooms include a four-poster room and some that are suitable
for families.

Rooms 32 (2 fmly) **S** £69-£120; **D** £89-£150 (incl. bkfst)*
Facilities FTV ♫ Xmas New Year Wi-fi **Services** Lift **Parking** 30
Notes LB Closed 25 Dec RS 24 & 26-30 Dec

Pyscodlyn Farm Caravan & Camping Site
(SO266155)
▶ ▶ ▶
Llanwenarth Citra NP7 7ER
☎ 01873 853271 & 07816 447942
e-mail: pyscodlyn.farm@virgin.net
dir: *From Abergavenny take A40 (Brecon road), site 1.5m from
entrance of Nevill Hall Hospital, on left 50yds past phone box*

PETS: **Sep accom Stables Public areas** disp bin **Exercise area**
adjacent field **Facilities** washing facs walks info **Other** prior
notice required **Resident Pets:** 2 dogs, 2 cats, 2 horses

Open Apr-Oct

With its outstanding views of the mountains, this quiet park in
the Brecon Beacons National Park makes a pleasant venue for
country lovers. The Sugarloaf Mountain and the River Usk are
within easy walking distance, and despite being a working farm,
dogs are welcome. A 4.5 acre site with 60 touring pitches and 6
statics.

Notes 🐾

CHEPSTOW — Map 3 ST59

Castle View
★★★ 64% HOTEL

16 Bridge St NP16 5EZ
☎ 01291 620349 📄 01291 627397
e-mail: castleviewhotel@btconnect.com
dir: *M48 junct 2, A466 for Wye Valley, at 1st rdbt right onto A48 towards Gloucester. Follow 2nd sign to town centre, then to Chepstow Castle, hotel directly opposite*

PETS: Bedrooms unattended sign Stables 1m Charges £8 per night Public areas except restaurant on leads Grounds on leads disp bin Exercise area castle green, park green & riverside 100mtrs Facilities washing facs cage storage walks info vet info On Request fridge access torch towels Other charge for damage Resident Pets: Lillie (Jack Russell)

This hotel was built around 300 years ago and offers unrivalled views of Chepstow Castle. Accommodation is comfortable - there are family rooms, double-bedded rooms, and some bedrooms that are situated in a separate building; a good range of extras for guest comfort are provided. There is a cosy bar area and a small restaurant where home-cooked food using fresh, local ingredients is offered.

Rooms 13 (4 annexe) (7 fmly) Facilities Xmas New Year Wi-fi Parking Notes LB

MONMOUTH — Map 3 SO51

Church Farm
★★★ GUEST HOUSE

Mitchel Troy NP25 4HZ
☎ 01600 712176
e-mail: info@churchfarmguesthouse.eclipse.co.uk
dir: *From A40 S, left onto B4293 for Trelleck before tunnel, left in 150yds, follow signs to Mitchel Troy. Guest house on main road, on left 200yds beyond campsite*

PETS: Bedrooms Public areas except dining room Grounds disp bin Exercise area Facilities cage storage walks info vet info On Request fridge access Resident Pet: Ollie (Labrador)

Located in the village of Mitchel Troy, this 16th-century former farmhouse retains many original features including exposed beams and open fireplaces. There is a range of bedrooms and a spacious lounge, and breakfast is served in the traditionally furnished dining room. Dinner is available by prior arrangement.

Rooms 9 rms (7 en suite) (2 pri facs) (3 fmly) S £32-£34; D £64-£68 Facilities TVL tea/coffee Dinner available Cen ht Parking 12 Notes LB Closed Xmas 🌐

SKENFRITH — Map 3 SO42

The Bell at Skenfrith
★★★★★ ◉◉ 🍴RESTAURANT WITH ROOMS

NP7 8UH
☎ 01600 750235 📄 01600 750525
e-mail: enquiries@skenfrith.co.uk
web: www.skenfrith.co.uk
dir: *On B4521 in Skenfrith, opposite castle*

PETS: Bedrooms Charges £5 per night Public areas except restaurant Grounds Exercise area surrounding countryside Facilities water bowl walks info vet info On Request torch

The Bell is a beautifully restored, 17th-century former coaching inn which still retains much of its original charm and character. It is peacefully situated on the banks of the Monnow, a tributary of the River Wye, and is ideally placed for exploring the numerous delights of the area. Natural materials have been used to create a relaxing atmosphere, while the bedrooms, which include full suites and rooms with four-poster beds, are stylish, luxurious and equipped with DVD players.

Rooms 11 en suite (2 fmly) S £75-£120; D £110-£220* Facilities tea/coffee Dinner available Direct Dial Cen ht Wi-fi Parking 36 Notes No Children 8yrs Closed last wk Jan-1st wk Feb RS Nov-Mar Closed Tue No coaches

TINTERN PARVA — Map 3 SO50

Best Western Royal George
★★★ 75% HOTEL

Wye Valley Rd NP16 6SF
☎ 01291 689205 📄 01291 689448
e-mail: royalgeorgetintern@hotmail.com
web: www.bw-royalgeorgehotel.co.uk
dir: *Off M48/A466, 4m to Tintern, 2nd on left*

PETS: Bedrooms (10 GF) Charges £10 per night Public areas except restaurant & lounge at food service Grounds on leads disp bin Exercise area 50yds Facilities water bowl cage storage walks info vet info On Request fridge access torch Other charge for damage

This privately owned and personally run hotel provides comfortable, spacious accommodation, including bedrooms with balconies overlooking the well-tended garden; there are a number of ground-floor bedrooms. The public areas include a lounge bar and a large function room, and a varied and popular menu is available in either the bar or restaurant. This hotel is an ideal base for exploring the counties of Monmouthshire and Herefordshire.

Rooms 15 (14 annexe) (6 fmly) (10 GF) S £65-£110; D £75-£120 (incl. bkfst)* Facilities STV Xmas New Year Wi-fi Parking 50 Notes LB

WALES

The Abbey Hotel
★★★ 64% HOTEL

NP6 6SF
☎ 01291 680020
e-mail: abbeyhotel@live.com

PETS: **Bedrooms** unattended sign **Public areas** except restaurant on leads **Grounds** on leads disp bin **Exercise area** 0.2m **Facilities** bedding dog chews scoop/disp bags pet sitting washing facs cage storage walks info vet info **On Request** fridge access torch towels **Other** charge for damage

Situated in the heart of the Wye Valley, this hotel offers many bedrooms that have views of Tintern Abbey. In addition to the main restaurant, a comfortable bar area is available for lighter dining options. Two function rooms are available and the hotel is a popular venue for weddings.

Rooms 22 (2 fmly) **S** £45-£65; **D** £75-£120 (incl. bkfst)
Facilities FTV Xmas New Year Wi-fi **Parking** 60 **Notes** LB

Parva Farmhouse Riverside Guest House
★★★★ 🍴 GUEST HOUSE

Monmouth Rd NP16 6SQ
☎ 01291 689411 📠 01291 689941
e-mail: parvahoteltintern@fsmail.net
dir: *On A466 at N edge of Tintern. Next to St Michael's Church on the riverside*

PETS: **Bedrooms Charges** £3 per night **Public areas** except restaurant **Grounds** disp bin **Exercise area** countryside adjacent **Facilities** water bowl vet info **On Request** fridge access torch **Restrictions** small to medium size dogs only **Resident Pet:** Frodo (Border Terrier cross)

This relaxed and friendly, family-run guest house is situated on a sweep of the River Wye with far-reaching views of the valley. Originally a farmhouse dating from the 17th century, many features have been retained, providing character and comfort in an informal atmosphere. The cosy Inglenook Restaurant is the place where quality ingredients are offered at breakfast and dinner. The individually designed bedrooms are tastefully decorated and enjoy pleasant views; one has a four-poster.

Rooms 8 en suite (2 fmly) **S** £47-£65; **D** £62-£95* **Facilities** tea/coffee Dinner available Cen ht Licensed **Parking** 8 **Notes** No Children 12yrs

Glen-yr-Afon House
★★★ 79% HOTEL

Pontypool Rd NP15 1SY
☎ 01291 672302 & 673202 📠 01291 672597
e-mail: enquiries@glen-yr-afon.co.uk
web: www.glen-yr-afon.co.uk
dir: *A472 through High St, over river bridge, follow to right. Hotel 200yds on left*

PETS: **Bedrooms Charges** £10 per night **Grounds** on leads **Facilities** walks info vet info **Other** charge for damage

On the edge of this delightful old market town, Glen-yr-Afon, a unique Victorian villa, offers all the facilities expected of a modern hotel combined with the warm atmosphere of a family home. Bedrooms are furnished to a high standard and several overlook the well-tended gardens. There is a choice of comfortable sitting areas and a stylish and spacious banqueting suite.

Rooms 28 (1 annexe) (2 fmly) **S** £94-£118; **D** £136-£159 (incl. bkfst)* **Facilities** STV FTV ♨ Complimentary access to Usk Tennis Club New Year Wi-fi **Services** Lift **Parking** 101 **Notes** LB

The Three Salmons Hotel
★★★ 77% ◉ HOTEL

Bridge St NP15 1RY
☎ 01291 672133 📠 01291 673979
e-mail: general@threesalmons.co.uk
dir: *M4 junct 24/A449, 1st exit signed Usk. On entering town hotel on main road*

PETS: **Bedrooms** (4 GF) unattended **Stables** 2m **Charges** £5 per night **Grounds** on leads disp bin **Exercise area** 500mtrs **Facilities** water bowl cage storage walks info vet info **On Request** fridge access torch towels

A 17th-century coaching inn located in the centre of a small market town with friendly, efficient staff who help create a welcoming atmosphere. Following a change of ownership many improvements are now taking place. The food is one of the main attractions and the contemporary restaurant proves popular. Bedrooms are comfortable and a good range of extras are provided. There is a large function suite ideal for weddings and parties, and parking is secure.

Rooms 24 (14 annexe) (3 fmly) (4 GF) **S** £75-£95; **D** £85-£105 (incl. bkfst)* **Facilities** FTV Wi-fi **Parking** 25

WALES

NEATH PORT TALBOT

PORT TALBOT   Map 3 SS79

Best Western Aberavon Beach Hotel

★★★ 78% HOTEL

Neath SA12 6QP
☎ 01639 884949 📠 01639 897885
e-mail: sales@aberavonbeach.com
web: www.aberavonbeachhotel.com
dir: *M4 junct 41/A48 & follow signs for Aberavon Beach & Hollywood Park*

PETS: Bedrooms unattended **Public areas** except restaurant on leads **Grounds** on leads **Exercise area** beach 100yds (restricted access May-Sep) **Facilities** water bowl walks info vet info **On Request** fridge access **Other** charge for damage pets allowed unattended in bedrooms only if owners are on premises **Restrictions** no dangerous dogs (see page 7)

This friendly, purpose-built hotel enjoys a prominent position on the seafront overlooking Swansea Bay. Bedrooms, many with sea views, are comfortably appointed and thoughtfully equipped. Public areas include a leisure suite with swimming pool, open-plan bar and restaurant plus a choice of function rooms.

Rooms 52 (6 fmly) **S** £56-£80; **D** £66-£130 (incl. bkfst)*
Facilities FTV 🏊 All weather leisure centre Sauna 🎵 Xmas New Year Wi-fi **Services** Lift **Parking** 150 **Notes** LB

PEMBROKESHIRE

BROAD HAVEN   Map 2 SM81

Creampots Touring Caravan & Camping Park *(SM882131)*

▶ ▶ ▶

Broadway SA62 3TU
☎ 01437 781776
dir: *From Haverfordwest take B4341 to Broadway. Turn left, follow brown tourist signs to site*

PETS: Public areas except children's play area disp bin **Exercise area** beach 1.5m **Facilities** walks info vet info **Other** prior notice required **Restrictions** no Bull Terriers

Open Mar-Jan Last arrival 21.00hrs Last departure noon

Set just outside the Pembrokeshire National Park, this quiet site is just one and a half miles from a safe sandy beach at Broad Haven, and the coastal footpath. The park is well laid out and carefully maintained, and the toilet block offers a good standard of facilities. The owners welcome families. An 8 acre site with 71 touring pitches, 12 hardstandings and 1 static.

FISHGUARD   Map 2 SM93

The Cartref Hotel
★★ 65% HOTEL

15-19 High St SA65 9AW
☎ 01348 872430 & 0781 330 5235 📠 01348 873664
e-mail: cartrefhotel@btconnect.com
web: www.cartrefhotel.co.uk
dir: *On A40 in town centre*

PETS: Bedrooms unattended **Stables** 4m **Charges** £5 per night £20 per week **Public areas** on leads **Exercise area** 100mtrs **Facilities** food bowl water bowl cage storage walks info vet info **On Request** fridge access torch towels **Resident Pets:** Tofie (Terrier), Toby (Jack Russell)

Personally run by the proprietor, this friendly hotel offers convenient access to the town centre and ferry terminal. Bedrooms are well maintained and include some family rooms. There is also a cosy lounge bar and a welcoming restaurant that looks out onto the high street.

Rooms 10 (2 fmly) **S** £35-£41; **D** £62-£68 (incl. bkfst)*
Facilities FTV **Parking** 4 **Notes** LB

WALES

Gwaun Vale Touring Park *(SM977356)*

▶ ▶ ▶

Llanychaer SA65 9TA
☎ 01348 874698
e-mail: margaret.harries@talk21.com
dir: *From Fishguard take B4313. Site 1.5m on right*

PETS: **Public areas** except toilet block, laundry area, children's play area & other pitches disp bin **Exercise area** fenced area provided **Facilities** walks info vet info

Open Apr-Oct Last arrival anytime Last departure 11.00hrs

Located at the opening of the beautiful Gwaun Valley, this well-kept park is set on the hillside with pitches tiered on two levels. There are lovely views of the surrounding countryside, and good facilities. A 1.6 acre site with 29 touring pitches, 5 hardstandings and 1 static.

Notes No skateboards 🐾

HASGUARD CROSS	Map 2 SM80

Hasguard Cross Caravan Park *(SM850108)*

▶ ▶ ▶

SA62 3SL
☎ 01437 781443 📠 01437 781443
e-mail: hasguard@aol.com
dir: *From Haverfordwest take B4327 towards Dale. In 7m right at x-rds. Site 1st right*

PETS: **Public areas** disp bin **Exercise area** dog walk on site **Facilities** washing facs walks info vet info **Other** prior notice required

Open all year rs Aug tent field for 28 days Last arrival 21.00hrs Last departure 10.00hrs

A very clean, efficient and well-run site in Pembrokeshire National Park just one and a half miles from the sea and beach at Little Haven, and with views of the surrounding hills. The toilet and shower facilities are immaculately clean, and there is a licensed bar (evenings only) serving a good choice of food. A 4.5 acre site with 12 touring pitches and 42 statics.

Redlands Touring Caravan & Camping Park *(SM853109)*

▶ ▶ ▶

SA62 3SJ
☎ 01437 781300
e-mail: info@redlandscamping.co.uk
dir: *From Haverfordwest take B4327 towards Dale. Site 7m on right*

PETS: **Charges** 1st dog free, 2nd dog £1 per night **Public areas** dogs must not roam free on leads disp bin **Exercise area** small fenced dog walk area **Facilities** food walks info vet info **Other** prior notice required no more than 2 dogs per pitch in high season **Restrictions** no Rottweilers or dangerous breeds (see page 7)

Open Mar-Dec Last arrival 21.00hrs Last departure 11.30hrs

A family owned and run park set in five acres of level grassland with tree-lined borders, close to many sandy beaches and the famous coastal footpath. Ideal for exploring the Pembrokeshire National Park. A 6 acre site with 60 touring pitches, 32 hardstandings.

Notes No commercial vans or mini buses 🐾

HAVERFORDWEST	Map 2 SM91

Hotel Mariners

★★ 71% HOTEL

Mariners Square SA61 2DU
☎ 01437 763353 📠 01437 764258
e-mail: hotelmariners@aol.com
dir: *Follow town centre signs, over bridge, up High St, 1st right down Dark St, hotel at end in Mariners Square*

PETS: **Bedrooms** **Public areas** assist dogs only **Grounds** on leads disp bin **Exercise area** 1m **Facilities** walks info vet info **On Request** fridge access torch towels **Other** cats must be caged

Located a few minutes' walk from the town centre, this privately owned and friendly hotel is said to date back to 1625. The bedrooms are equipped with modern facilities and are soundly maintained. A good range of food is offered in the popular bar, which is a focus for the local community. Facilities include a choice of meeting rooms.

Rooms 28 (5 fmly) **Facilities** STV Wi-fi **Parking** 50 **Notes** LB Closed 25 Dec-2 Jan

WALES

College Guest House
★★★★ GUEST HOUSE
93 Hill St, St Thomas Green SA61 1QL
☎ 01437 763710 📠 01437 763710
e-mail: colinlarby@aol.com
dir: *In town centre, along High St, pass church, keep in left lane. 1st exit by Stonemason Arms pub, follow signs for St Thomas Green. 300mtrs on left by No Entry sign*

PETS: Bedrooms Charges Public areas except restaurant **Grounds** disp bin **Exercise area** 90mtrs **Facilities** food bowl water bowl feeding mat scoop/disp bags leads pet sitting washing facs cage storage walks info vet info **On Request** fridge access torch towels **Other** charge for damage **Resident Pets:** Bartie (Jack Russell/Collie cross), Alfie (Yorkshire Terrier), Zag (cat)

Located in a mainly residential area within easy walking distance of the attractions, this impressive Georgian house has been upgraded to offer good levels of comfort and facilities. There is range of practically equipped bedrooms, along with public areas that include a spacious lounge (with internet access) and an attractive pine-furnished dining room, the setting for comprehensive breakfasts.

Rooms 8 en suite (4 fmly) **Facilities** FTV TVL tea/coffee Cen ht Wi-fi

Nolton Cross Caravan Park *(SM879177)*
▶▶
Nolton SA62 3NP
☎ 01437 710701 📠 01437 710329
e-mail: info@noltoncross-holidays.co.uk
dir: *1m off A487 (Haverfordwest to St David's road) at Simpson Cross, towards Nolton & Broadhaven*

PETS: Stables nearby **Public areas** disp bin **Exercise area** 200mtrs **Facilities** walks info vet info **Other** prior notice required

Open Mar-Dec Last arrival 22.00hrs Last departure noon

High grassy banks surround the touring area of this park next to the owners' working farm. It is located on open ground above the sea and St Bride's Bay (within 1.5 miles), and there is a coarse fishing lake close by - equipment for hire and reduced permit rates for campers are available. A 4 acre site with 15 touring pitches and 30 statics.

Notes No youth groups

THE CIRCLE

Castlemead
★★ 72% HOTEL
SA70 7TA
☎ 01834 871358 📠 01834 871358
e-mail: castlemeadhotel@aol.com
web: www.castlemeadhotel.com
dir: *A4139 towards Pembroke, B4585 into village, follow signs to beach & castle. Hotel on left*

PETS: Bedrooms (3 GF) unattended **Public areas Grounds** disp bin **Exercise area** beach 500yds **Facilities** washing facs cage storage walks info vet info **On Request** fridge access torch towels **Resident Pets:** Rosie (Border Collie), Max & Polly (cats)

Benefiting from a superb location with spectacular views of the bay, the Norman church and Manorbier Castle, this family-run hotel is friendly and welcoming. Bedrooms which include some in a converted former coach house, are generally quite spacious and have modern facilities. Public areas include a sea-view restaurant, bar and residents' lounge, as well as an extensive garden.

Rooms 8 (3 annexe) (2 fmly) (3 GF) **Facilities** FTV Wi-fi **Parking** 20 **Notes** LB Closed Dec-Feb RS Nov

WALES

NEWPORT
Map 2 SN03

Llysmeddyg
★★★★ 🏵️🏵️ RESTAURANT WITH ROOMS

East St SA42 0SY
☎ 01239 820008
e-mail: contact@llysmeddyg.com
dir: *On A487 in centre of town on Main St*

PETS: Bedrooms unattended **Stables** 5m **Public areas**
except restaurant on leads **Grounds** on leads **Exercise area**
estuary walk (2mins) **Facilities** pet sitting walks info vet info
On Request fridge access torch **Other** charge for damage

Llysmeddyg is a Georgian townhouse offering a blend of old and
new, with elegant furnishings, deep sofas and a welcoming fire.
The owners of this property have used local craftsmen to create a
lovely interior that creates an eclectic style throughout. The focus
of the restaurant menu is on quality food through use of fresh,
seasonal ingredients sourced locally. The spacious bedrooms are
comfortable and contemporary in design; bathrooms vary in style.

Rooms 5 en suite 3 annexe en suite (3 fmly) (1 GF) **Facilities** tea/
coffee Dinner available Cen ht Wi-fi **Parking** 8 **Notes** LB No
coaches

ROSEBUSH
Map 2 SN02

Rosebush Caravan Park *(SN073293)*
▶ ▶

Rhoslwyn SA66 7QT
☎ 01437 532206 & 07831 223166 📠 01437 532206
dir: *From A40, near Narberth, take B4313, between Haverfordwest*
& Cardigan B4329, site 1m

PETS: Public areas disp bin **Exercise area Facilities** food
walks info vet info **Other** prior notice required **Resident Pet:**
Cindy (Labrador)

Open 14 Mar-Oct Last arrival 23.00hrs Last departure noon

A most attractive park with a large ornamental lake at its centre
and good landscaping. Set off the main tourist track, it offers
lovely views of the Presely Hills which can be reached by a scenic
walk. Rosebush is a quiet village with a handy pub, and the park
owner also runs the village shop. Due to the deep lake on site,
children are not accepted. A 12 acre site with 65 touring pitches
and 15 statics.

Notes

ST DAVID'S
Map 2 SM72

Warpool Court
★★★ 81% 🏵️🏵️ COUNTRY HOUSE HOTEL

SA62 6BN
☎ 01437 720300 📠 01437 720676
e-mail: info@warpoolcourthotel.com
web: www.warpoolcourthotel.com
dir: *At Cross Square left by The Bishops Restaurant (Goat St).*
Pass Farmers Arms pub, after 400mtrs left, follow hotel signs,
entrance on right

PETS: Bedrooms unattended **Charges** £10 per night **Grounds**
disp bin **Exercise area Facilities** water bowl washing facs
cage storage walks info vet info **On Request** fridge access
torch towels

Originally the cathedral choir school, this hotel is set in
landscaped gardens looking out to sea and is within easy walking
distance of the Pembrokeshire Coastal Path. The lounges are
spacious and comfortable, and the bedrooms are well furnished
and equipped with modern facilities. The restaurant offers
delightful cuisine.

Rooms 22 (3 fmly) **S** £110-£195; **D** £130-£360 (incl. bkfst)*
Facilities 🎾 🏊 🚣 Table tennis Pool table Xmas New Year Wi-fi
Parking 100 **Notes** Closed Nov & 1st half Dec

SAUNDERSFOOT · Map 2 SN10

St Brides Spa Hotel

St Brides Hill SA69 9NH
☎ 01834 812304   ▤ 01834 811766
e-mail: reservations@stbridesspahotel.com
web: www.stbridesspahotel.com
dir: A478 onto B4310 to Saundersfoot. Hotel above harbour

PETS: (9 GF) Charges £15 per night Public areas except bar, restaurant & spa on leads Exercise area beach & woods 5 mins Facilities food bowl water bowl bedding walks info vet info On Request fridge access Other charge for damage pets allowed in apartments only (lounge area)

Currently the rating for this establishment is not confirmed. This may be due to a change of ownership or because it has only recently joined the AA rating scheme. For further details please see the AA website: theAA.com

Rooms 46 (12 annexe) (6 fmly) (9 GF) S £125-£190; D £150-£280 (incl. bkfst)* Facilities Spa FTV Gym Sauna Steam room Xmas New Year Wi-fi Services Lift Parking 65 Notes LB

Vine Cottage

★★★★ GUEST HOUSE
The Ridgeway SA69 9LA
☎ 01834 814422
e-mail: enquiries@vinecottageguesthouse.co.uk
web: www.vinecottageguesthouse.co.uk
dir: A477 S onto A478, left onto B4316, after railway bridge right signed Saundersfoot, cottage 100yds beyond 30mph sign

PETS: Bedrooms Charges £5 per stay Public areas except dining room Grounds disp bin Exercise area beach 0.5m Facilities dog chews feeding mat scoop/disp bags leads washing facs walks info vet info On Request fridge access torch towels Other charge for damage Resident Pets: Ruby & Megan (English Springer Spaniels)

A warm welcome awaits guests at this pleasant former farmhouse located on the outskirts of Saundersfoot, yet within easy walking distance of this delightful village. Set in extensive, mature gardens which include some rare and exotic plants. Vine Cottage also has a summer house where guests can sit and relax on warmer evenings. Bedrooms, including a ground-floor room, are modern and well equipped, and some are suitable for families. There is a comfortable, airy lounge. Breakfast is served in the cosy dining room.

Rooms 5 en suite (2 fmly) (1 GF) S £40-£50; D £70-£80* Facilities FTV tea/coffee Dinner available Cen ht Parking 10 Notes LB No Children 6yrs 🐾

SOLVA · Map 2 SM82

Lochmeyler Farm Guest House (SM855275)

★★★★★ 🏠 FARMHOUSE
Llandeloy, Pen-y-Cwm SA62 6LL
☎ 01348 837724   ▤ 01348 837622 Mrs M Jones
e-mail: stay@lochmeyler.co.uk
web: www.lochmeyler.co.uk
dir: From Haverfordwest A487 (St David's road) to Pen-y-Cwm, right to Llandeloy

PETS: Bedrooms Sep accom outside kennel with secure run Stables 4m Grounds disp bin Exercise area adjacent Facilities washing facs cage storage vet info On Request fridge access towels Other charge for damage Resident Pets: George (Labrador), Patch (Collie), Sooty (Cocker Spaniel)

Located on a 220-acre dairy farm in an outstandingly beautiful area, Lochmeyler provides high levels of comfort and excellent facilities. The spacious bedrooms, some in converted outbuildings, are equipped with a wealth of thoughtful extras and four have private sitting rooms. Comprehensive breakfasts are served in the dining room as well as dinner on request; a sumptuous lounge is also available.

Rooms 12 en suite (6 GF) S £40-£50; D £70-£80* Facilities FTV tea/coffee Dinner available Direct Dial Cen ht Licensed Wi-fi Parking 12 Notes LB No Children 10yrs 220 acres dairy

Clarence House

★★ 63% HOTEL

Esplanade SA70 7DU
☎ 01834 844371 📄 01834 844372
e-mail: clarencehotel@freeuk.com
dir: *Off South Parade by town walls onto St Florence Parade & Esplanade*

PETS: Bedrooms unattended **Charges** £3 per night **Public areas** except restaurant on leads **Grounds** disp bin **Exercise area** beach 5 mins' walk **Facilities** walks info vet info **On Request** fridge access torch towels

Owned by the same family for over 50 years, this hotel has superb views from its elevated position. Many of the bedrooms have sea views and all are comfortably furnished. The bar leads to a sheltered rose garden or a number of lounges. Entertainment is provided in high season, and this establishment is particularly popular with coach tour parties.

Rooms 76 (6 fmly) **S** £32-£53; **D** £64-£106 (incl. bkfst)*
Facilities ♫ **Services** Lift **Notes** LB Closed 18-28 Dec

Rosendale Guesthouse

★★★★ GUEST HOUSE

Lydstep SA70 7SQ
☎ 01834 870040
e-mail: rosendalewales@yahoo.com
web: www.rosendalepembrokeshire.co.uk
dir: *3m SW of Tenby. A4139 W towards Pembroke. Rosendale on right after Lydstep*

PETS: Bedrooms Charges £2 per night **Grounds** on leads disp bin **Exercise area** Lydstep Headland 0.5m **Facilities** food bowl water bowl feeding mat cage storage walks info vet info **On Request** fridge access torch **Other** charge for damage **Restrictions** no large dogs (eg Great Danes, St Bernards etc)

A warm welcome awaits all guests at this family-run establishment that is ideally located on the outskirts of the pretty village of Lydstep, not far from the seaside town of Tenby. Rosendale provides modern, well-equipped bedrooms; some with coast or country views, and three rooms that are on the ground floor of a separate building to the rear of the main house. The attractive dining room is the setting for breakfast served at separate tables.

Rooms 6 en suite (3 GF) **Facilities** FTV tea/coffee Cen ht Wi-fi **Parking** 6 **Notes** No Children 16yrs

Esplanade

★★★★ GUEST ACCOMMODATION

The Esplanade SA70 7DU
☎ 01834 842760 & 843333 📄 01834 845633
e-mail: esplanadetenby@googlemail.com
web: www.esplanadetenby.co.uk
dir: *Follow signs to South Beach, premises on seafront next to town walls*

PETS: Bedrooms Public areas except restaurant at meal times on leads **Exercise area** beach 20mtrs **Facilities** washing facs walks info vet info **On Request** fridge access torch towels **Other** charge for damage

Located beside the historic town walls of Tenby and with stunning views over the sea to Caldey Island, the Esplanade provides a range of standard and luxury bedrooms, some ideal for families. Breakfast is offered in the elegant front-facing dining room, which contains a comfortable lounge-bar area.

Rooms 14 en suite (4 fmly) (1 GF) **S** £50-£100; **D** £70-£130 **Facilities** tea/coffee Direct Dial Cen ht Licensed Wi-fi **Notes** LB Closed 15-27 Dec

Trefalun Park *(SN093027)*

▶▶▶▶

Devonshire Dr, St Florence SA70 8RD
☎ 01646 651514 📄 01646 651746
e-mail: trefalun@aol.com
dir: *1.5m NW of St Florence & 0.5m N of B4318*

PETS: Charges £1 per night (touring pitches) **Public areas** disp bin **Exercise area** field available **Facilities** walks info vet info **Other** prior notice required **Resident Pets:** Rio (Great Dane), Buzz (Miniature Schnauzer), Ellar (German Shepherd), Lizzie (donkey)

Open Etr-Oct Last arrival 19.00hrs Last departure noon

Set within 12 acres of sheltered, well-kept grounds, this quiet country park offers well-maintained level grass pitches separated by bushes and trees, with plenty of space to relax in. Children can feed the park's friendly pets. Plenty of activities are available at the nearby Heatherton Country Sports Park, including go-karting, indoor bowls, golf and bumper boating. A 12 acre site with 90 touring pitches, 54 hardstandings and 10 statics.

Notes No motorised scooters

WALES

WOLF'S CASTLE   Map 2 SM92

 WELSH RAREBITS

Wolfscastle Country Hotel
★★★ 78% COUNTRY HOUSE HOTEL
SA62 5LZ
☎ 01437 741688 & 741225 📄 01437 741383
e-mail: enquiries@wolfscastle.com
web: www.wolfscastle.com
dir: On A40 in village at top of hill. 6m N of Haverfordwest

PETS: Bedrooms unattended Charges £5 per night Public areas except restaurant & bar Grounds on leads disp bin Exercise area 200mtrs Facilities food bowl water bowl dog chews feeding mat washing facs cage storage walks info vet info On Request fridge access torch towels Other dogs not allowed in executive bedrooms

This large stone house, a former vicarage, dates back to the mid-19th century and is now a friendly, privately owned and personally run hotel. It provides stylish, modern, well-maintained and well-equipped bedrooms. There is a pleasant bar and an attractive restaurant, which has a well deserved reputation for its food.

Rooms 20 (2 fmly) S £75-£95; D £105-£135 (incl. bkfst)*
Facilities FTV New Year Wi-fi Parking 60 Notes LB Closed 24-26 Dec

POWYS

BRECON   Map 3 SO02

The Felin Fach Griffin
★★★★ INN
Felin Fach LD3 0UB
☎ 01874 620111
e-mail: enquiries@eatdrinksleep.ltd.uk
dir: 4m NE of Brecon on A470

PETS: Bedrooms unattended Public areas except dining room Grounds Exercise area Facilities food bowl water bowl dog chews scoop/disp bags walks info vet info On Request fridge access torch towels Resident Pets: Max (Kelpie Collie), Gizmo (Chihuahua)

This delightful inn stands in an extensive garden at the northern end of the village of Felin Fach. The public areas have a wealth of rustic charm and provide the setting for the excellent food that is served. The bedrooms are carefully appointed and have modern equipment and facilities. The service and hospitality are commendable here.

Rooms 7 en suite (1 fmly) S £85-£100; D £110-£155*
Facilities tea/coffee Dinner available Direct Dial Cen ht 🦤
Parking 61 Notes LB Closed 24-25 Dec No coaches

Borderers
★★★ GUEST ACCOMMODATION
47 The Watton LD3 7EG
☎ 01874 623559
e-mail: info@borderers.com
web: www.borderers.com
dir: 200yds SE of town centre on B4601, opp church

PETS: Bedrooms unattended Grounds disp bin Exercise area 100mtrs Facilities food bowl water bowl bedding washing facs walks info vet info On Request fridge access torch towels Resident Pets: Ella (Black Labrador), Breagh (Chocolate Labrador)

This house was originally a 17th-century drovers' inn. The courtyard, now a car park, is surrounded by many of the bedrooms, and pretty hanging baskets are seen everywhere. The bedrooms are attractively decorated with rich floral fabrics. A room with easier access is available.

Rooms 4 rms (3 en suite) (1 pri facs) 5 annexe en suite (2 fmly) (4 GF) S £40-£50; D £56-£60* Facilities FTV tea/coffee Cen ht Wi-fi Parking 6

The Lansdowne
★★★ GUEST ACCOMMODATION
The Watton LD3 7EG
☎ 01874 623321 📄 01874 610438
e-mail: reception@lansdownehotel.co.uk
dir: A40/A470 onto B4601

PETS: Bedrooms Public areas except restaurant on leads Exercise area 2 min walk Facilities washing facs walks info vet info On Request torch towels

Privately-owned and personally-run, this Georgian house is conveniently located close to the town centre. The accommodation is well equipped and includes family rooms and a bedroom on ground-floor level. There is a comfortable lounge, a small bar and an attractive split-level dining room where dinner is available to residents.

Rooms 9 en suite (2 fmly) (1 GF) S £40-£45; D £60-£65
Facilities FTV tea/coffee Dinner available Direct Dial Cen ht Licensed Notes LB No Children 5yrs

WALES

BUILTH WELLS
Map 3 SO05

THE INDEPENDENTS
HOTEL ASSOCIATION

Caer Beris Manor
★★★ 77% COUNTRY HOUSE HOTEL
LD2 3NP
☎ 01982 552601 📄 01982 552586
e-mail: caerberis@btconnect.com
web: www.caerberis.com
dir: From town centre follow A483/Llandovery signs. Hotel on left

PETS: Bedrooms (3 GF) unattended Stables Charges £5 per night Public areas except main restaurant & conservatory Grounds disp bin Exercise area Facilities washing facs cage storage walks info vet info On Request torch towels Other charge for damage

Guests can expect a relaxing stay at this friendly and privately owned hotel that has extensive landscaped grounds. Bedrooms are individually decorated and furnished to retain an atmosphere of a bygone era. The spacious and comfortable lounge and a lounge bar continue this theme, and there's an elegant restaurant, complete with 16th-century panelling.

Rooms 23 (2 fmly) (3 GF) Facilities FTV Fishing ⛵ Clay pigeon shooting Bird watching Xmas New Year Wi-fi Parking 100

Fforest Fields Caravan & Camping Park
(SO100535)

▶▶▶

Hundred House LD1 5RT
☎ 01982 570406
e-mail: office@fforestfields.co.uk
dir: From town follow New Radnor signs on A481. 4m to signed entrance on right, 0.5m before Hundred House village

PETS: Public areas except toilets disp bin Exercise area extensive woodland trails; fenced 'toilet' areas Facilities washing facs walks info vet info Other prior notice required Restrictions no noisy, aggressive or badly behaved dogs

Open Etr & Apr-Oct Last arrival 21.00hrs Last departure 18.00hrs

A sheltered park in a hidden valley with wonderful views and plenty of wildlife. Set in unspoilt countryside, this is a peaceful park with delightful hill walks beginning on site. The historic town of Builth Wells and the Royal Welsh Showground are only four miles away, and there are plenty of outdoor activities in the vicinity. A 12 acre site with 60 touring pitches, 17 hardstandings.

Notes No loud music or revelry 🐾

CRICKHOWELL
Map 3 SO21

WELSH RAREBITS

Bear Hotel
★★★ 75% ◉ HOTEL
NP8 1BW
☎ 01873 810408 📄 01873 811696
e-mail: bearhotel@aol.com
dir: On A40 between Abergavenny & Brecon

PETS: Bedrooms (6 GF) unattended Public areas except restaurant on leads Grounds disp bin Exercise area 350yds Facilities food bowl water bowl dog chews scoop/disp bags washing facs walks info vet info On Request fridge access torch towels Other freshly cooked chicken offered to all visiting dogs

A favourite with locals as well as visitors, the character and friendliness of this 15th-century coaching inn are renowned. The bedrooms come in a variety of sizes and standards including some with four-posters. The bar and restaurant are furnished in keeping with the style of the building and provide comfortable areas in which to enjoy some of the very popular dishes that use the finest locally-sourced ingredients.

Rooms 34 (13 annexe) (6 fmly) (6 GF) S £73-£123; D £90-£159 (incl. bkfst)* Facilities STV FTV Wi-fi Parking 45 Notes LB RS 25 Dec

Manor
★★★ 75% ◉ HOTEL
Brecon Rd NP8 1SE
☎ 01873 810212 📄 01873 811938
e-mail: info@manorhotel.co.uk
web: www.manorhotel.co.uk
dir: On A40, Crickhowell/Brecon, 0.5m from Crickhowell

PETS: Bedrooms unattended Stables 7m to establishment's own farm Charges £5 per night Public areas except restaurant Grounds Exercise area adjoining footpaths Facilities walks info vet info Other charge for damage pets allowed in certain bedrooms only Resident Pets: Honey & Henry (Golden Retrievers), Cerys (Welsh Cob)

This impressive manor house, set in a stunning location, was the birthplace of Sir George Everest. The bedrooms and public areas are elegant, and there are extensive leisure facilities. The restaurant, with panoramic views, is the setting for excellent modern cooking.

Rooms 22 (1 fmly) **S** £55-£80; **D** £75-£140 (incl. bkfst)* **Facilities** STV FTV 🏊 Gym Fitness assessment Sunbed Xmas New Year Wi-fi **Parking** 200

CRIGGION · Map 7 SJ21

Brimford House (SJ310150)

★ ★ ★ ★ FARMHOUSE

SY5 9AU

☎ 01938 570235   Mrs Dawson

e-mail: info@brimford.co.uk

dir: Off B4393 after Crew Green turn left for Criggion, Brimford 1st on left after pub

PETS: Bedrooms Grounds Exercise area Facilities washing facs cage storage walks info vet info **On Request** fridge access torch towels **Resident Pets:** Emma (Black Labrador), 3 cats

This elegant Georgian house stands in lovely open countryside and is a good base for touring central Wales and the Marches. Bedrooms are spacious, and thoughtful extras enhance guest comfort. A cheery log fire burns in the lounge during colder weather and the hospitality is equally warm, providing a relaxing atmosphere throughout.

Rooms 3 en suite **S** £45-£60; **D** £65-£75 **Facilities** FTV TVL tea/coffee Cen ht Fishing **Parking** 4 **Notes** LB 🐾 250 acres arable/beef/sheep

ERWOOD · Map 3 SO04

Hafod-y-Garreg

★ ★ ★ ★ BED AND BREAKFAST

LD2 3TQ

☎ 01982 560400

e-mail: john-annie@hafod-y.wanadoo.co.uk

web: www.hafodygarreg.co.uk

dir: 1m S of Erwood. Off A470 at Trericket Mill, sharp right, up track past cream farmhouse towards pine forest, through gate

PETS: Bedrooms Charges £5 per night **Public areas** except at dinner **Grounds** on leads **Exercise area** adjacent **Facilities** washing facs cage storage walks info vet info **On Request** fridge access torch **Other** charge for damage **Restrictions** no puppies **Resident Pets:** Ginger & Puss (cats), Rosie (goat), chickens

This remote Grade II listed farmhouse dates in part from 1401 and has been confirmed, by dendrochronology, as the 'oldest dwelling in Wales'. As you would expect the house has tremendous character, and is decorated and furnished to befit its age although the bedrooms have all the modern facilities. There is an impressive dining room and a lounge with an open fireplace. Warm hospitality from John and Annie McKay is a major strength here.

Rooms 2 en suite; **D** £72* **Facilities** STV tea/coffee Dinner available Cen ht Wi-fi **Parking** 6 **Notes** No Children Closed Xmas 🐾

LLANDRINDOD WELLS · Map 3 SO06

   CLASSIC BRITISH HOTELS

The Metropole

★ ★ ★ ★ 75% ◉ HOTEL

Temple St LD1 5DY

☎ 01597 823700 📠 01597 824828

e-mail: info@metropole.co.uk

web: www.metropole.co.uk

dir: On A483 in town centre

PETS: Bedrooms unattended **Charges** £10 per night £70 per week **Public areas** except restaurants & food outlets on leads **Grounds** on leads disp bin **Exercise area** park adjacent to hotel **Facilities** walks info **On Request** fridge access

The centre of this famous spa town is dominated by this large Victorian hotel, which has been personally run by the same family for well over 100 years. The lobby leads to Spencers Bar and Brasserie and to the comfortable and elegantly styled lounge. Bedrooms vary in style, but all are spacious and well equipped. Facilities include an extensive range of modern conference and function rooms, as well as the impressive leisure centre. Extensive parking is provided to the rear of the hotel.

Rooms 120 (11 fmly) **S** £87-£120; **D** £87-£150 (incl. bkfst) **Facilities** Spa FTV 🏊 Gym Beauty & holistic treatments Sauna Steam room Xmas New Year Wi-fi Child facilities **Services** Lift **Parking** 150 **Notes** LB

Disserth Caravan & Camping Park (SO035583)

▶ ▶ ▶

Disserth, Howey LD1 6NL

☎ 01597 860277

e-mail: disserthcaravan@btconnect.com

dir: 1m off A483, between Howey & Newbridge-on-Wye, by church. Follow brown signs from A483 or A470

PETS: Stables 4m **Public areas** except reception & bar on leads disp bin **Exercise area** adjacent fields with footpaths **Facilities** food food bowl water bowl walks info vet info **Other** prior notice required dogs must be kept on short leads & must not be left unattended for lengthy periods on own pitch

Open Mar-Oct Last arrival 22.00hrs Last departure noon

A delightfully secluded and predominantly adult park nestling in a beautiful valley on the banks of the River Ithon, a tributary of the River Wye. This little park is next to a 13th-century church, and has a small bar open at weekends and busy periods. The chalet toilet block offers spacious combined cubicles. A 4 acre site with 30 touring pitches, 6 hardstandings and 25 statics.

Notes 🐾

Cain Valley

★★ 78% HOTEL

High St SY22 5AQ
☎ 01691 648366 📠 01691 648307
e-mail: info@cainvalleyhotel.co.uk
dir: At end of A490. Hotel in town centre, car park at rear

PETS: Bedrooms Charges £5 per night **Facilities** vet info
On Request torch

This Grade II listed coaching inn has a lot of charm and character including features such as exposed beams and a Jacobean staircase. The comfortable accommodation includes family rooms and a wide range of food is available in a choice of bars, or in the restaurant, which has a well-deserved reputation for its locally sourced steaks.

Rooms 13 (2 fmly) (13 smoking) **Parking** 10

The Lake Country House & Spa

★★★ ◉◉ COUNTRY HOUSE HOTEL

LD4 4BS
☎ 01591 620202 & 620474 📠 01591 620457
e-mail: info@lakecountryhouse.co.uk
web: www.lakecountryhouse.co.uk
dir: W from Builth Wells on A483 to Garth (approx 6m). Left for Llangammarch Wells, follow hotel signs

PETS: Bedrooms (7 GF) **Charges** £8 per night **Public areas**
Grounds disp bin **Exercise area Facilities** water bowl scoop/
disp bags leads pet sitting dog walking walks info vet
info **On Request** fridge access torch **Other** charge for
damage owners to bring own dogs bedding & feeding bowls
Resident Pets: Belle (Labrador), Cassie (Collie/Labrador)

Expect good old-fashioned values and hospitality at this Victorian country house hotel. In fact, the service is so traditionally English, guests may believe they have a butler! The establishment offers a 9-hole, par 3 golf course, 50 acres of wooded grounds and a spa where the hot tub overlooks the lake. Bedrooms, some located in an annexe, and some at ground-floor level, are individually styled and have many extra comforts. Traditional afternoon teas are served in the lounge and award-winning cuisine is provided in the spacious and elegant restaurant.

Rooms 30 (7 GF) **S** £225; **D** £305 (incl. bkfst & dinner)*
Facilities Spa FTV ⊙ ⅃ 9 ⌢ Putt green Fishing ⅊ Gym Archery
Horse riding Mountain biking Quad biking Xmas New Year Wi-fi
Parking 72 **Notes** LB

The Old Vicarage

★★★★ GUEST HOUSE

SY18 6RN
☎ 01686 440280 📠 01686 440280
e-mail: info@theoldvicaragellangurig.co.uk
dir: A470 onto A44, signed

PETS: Bedrooms Charges £2 per night **Public areas** except
dining areas on leads **Grounds** on leads disp bin **Exercise area**
100yds **Facilities** water bowl feeding mat washing facs
cage storage walks info vet info **On Request** torch towels
Resident Pet: Madge (Jack Russell)

Located on pretty mature grounds, which feature a magnificent holly tree, this elegant Victorian house provides a range of thoughtfully furnished bedrooms, some with fine period items. Breakfast is served in a spacious dining room and a comfortable guest lounge is also available. Afternoon teas are served in the garden during the warmer months.

Rooms 4 en suite (1 fmly) **S** £34-£40; **D** £56-£68* **Facilities** TVL
tea/coffee Dinner available Cen ht Licensed Wi-fi **Parking** 6
Notes LB 🐾

Carlton Riverside

★★★★ ◉◉◉ RESTAURANT WITH ROOMS

Irfon Crescent LD5 4SP
☎ 01591 610248
e-mail: info@carltonriverside.com
dir: In town centre beside bridge

PETS: Bedrooms unattended **Stables** 0.25m **Exercise area**
0.25m **Facilities** walks info vet info **On Request** towels

Guests become part of the family at this character property, set beside the river in Wales's smallest town. Carlton Riverside offers award-winning cuisine for which Mary Ann Gilchrist relies on the very best of local ingredients. The set menu is complemented by a well-chosen wine list and dinner is served in the delightfully stylish restaurant which offers a memorable blend of traditional comfort, modern design and river views. Four comfortable bedrooms have tasteful combinations of antique and contemporary furniture, along with welcome personal touches.

Rooms 4 en suite **S** £50; **D** £75-£100 **Facilities** tea/coffee Dinner
available Cen ht Wi-fi **Notes** LB Closed 20-30 Dec No coaches

Lasswade Country House

★★★★ ◎◎ RESTAURANT WITH ROOMS

Station Rd LD5 4RW

☎ 01591 610515 ▤ 01591 610611

e-mail: info@lasswadehotel.co.uk

dir: *Off A483 into Irfon Terrace, right onto Station Rd, 350yds on right*

PETS: Sep accom indoor kennels (no charge) grazing for horses **Stables** 400yds **Charges** charge for horses only **Grounds** on leads disp bin **Exercise area** walks & forest nearby **Facilities** walks info vet info **Other** charge for damage **Resident Pets:** Chaff (Border Collie), Steel (horse)

This friendly establishment on the edge of the town has impressive views over the countryside. Bedrooms are comfortably furnished and well equipped, while the public areas consist of a tastefully decorated lounge, an elegant restaurant with a bar, and an airy conservatory which looks out on to the neighbouring hills. The kitchen utilises fresh, local produce to provide an enjoyable dining experience.

Rooms 8 en suite **S** £55-£70; **D** £75-£100* **Facilities** TVL Dinner available Cen ht **Parking** 6 **Notes** LB No coaches

Bank Farm Caravan Park *(SJ293123)*

▶▶▶

SY21 8EJ

☎ 01938 570526

e-mail: bankfarmcaravans@yahoo.co.uk

dir: *13m W of Shrewsbury, 5m E of Welshpool on A458*

PETS: Public areas dogs must be on leads **Exercise area** fields & woodland outside public area **Facilities** walks info vet info

Open Mar-Oct Last arrival 20.00hrs

An attractive park on a small farm, maintained to a high standard. There are two touring areas, one on either side of the A458, and each with its own amenity block, and immediate access to hills, mountains and woodland. A pub serving good food, and a large play area are nearby. A 2 acre site with 40 touring pitches and 33 statics.

Notes ⊜

Dragon Hotel

★★ 79% ◎ HOTEL

SY15 6PA

☎ 01686 668359 ▤ 0870 011 8227

e-mail: reception@dragonhotel.com

web: www.dragonhotel.com

dir: *Behind town hall*

PETS: Bedrooms unattended **Stables** 0.5m **Public areas** except dining areas on leads **Grounds** on leads **Exercise area** countryside nearby **Facilities** pet sitting dog walking vet info **On Request** torch towels **Other** charge for damage

This fine 17th-century coaching inn stands in the centre of Montgomery. Beams and timbers from the nearby castle, which was destroyed by Cromwell, are visible in the lounge and bar. A wide choice of soundly prepared, wholesome food is available in both the restaurant and bar. Bedrooms are well equipped and family rooms are available.

Rooms 20 (6 fmly) (2 smoking) **S** fr £56; **D** fr £94.50 (incl. bkfst)* **Facilities** FTV ⊗ Sauna ♫ Xmas New Year Wi-fi **Parking** 21 **Notes** LB

Miskin Manor Country Hotel

★★★★ 75% ◎◎ COUNTRY HOUSE HOTEL

Pendoylan Rd CF72 8ND

☎ 01443 224204 ▤ 01443 237606

e-mail: reservations@miskin-manor.co.uk

web: www.miskin-manor.co.uk

dir: *M4 junct 34, A4119, signed Llantrisant, hotel 300yds on left*

PETS: Bedrooms (7 GF) **Charges** £50 per stay **Public areas** except restaurant & dining areas on leads **Grounds** on leads disp bin **Facilities** water bowl washing facs dog grooming walks info vet info **On Request** fridge access torch towels **Other** charge for damage **Resident Pets:** 2 cats

This historic manor house is peacefully located in 22 acres of grounds yet only minutes away from the M4. Bedrooms are furnished to a high standard and include some located in converted stables and cottages. Public areas are spacious and comfortable and include a variety of function rooms. The relaxed atmosphere and the surroundings ensure this hotel remains popular for wedding functions. There is a separate modern health and fitness centre which includes a gym, sauna, steam room and swimming pool.

Rooms 43 (9 annexe) (2 fmly) (7 GF) **Facilities** ⊗ supervised ⚑ Gym Wi-fi **Parking** 200

WALES

PONTYPRIDD — Map 3 ST08

Llechwen Hall
★★★ 73% COUNTRY HOUSE HOTEL
Llanfabon CF37 4HP
☎ 01443 742050 & 743020 🖹 01443 742189
e-mail: steph@llechwen.co.uk
dir: *A470 N towards Merthyr Tydfil. At large rdbt take 3rd exit. At mini rdbt take 3rd exit, hotel signed 0.5m on left*

PETS: Bedrooms (4 GF) unattended **Stables** 2m **Public areas Grounds** on leads disp bin **Exercise area** 300mtrs **Facilities** cage storage walks info vet info **On Request** fridge access torch towels

Set on top of a hill with a stunning approach, this country house hotel has served many purposes in its 200-year-old history including a private school and a magistrates' court. The spacious, individually decorated bedrooms are well equipped; some are situated in the separate coach house nearby. There are ground-floor, twin, double and family bedrooms on offer. The Victorian-style public areas are attractively appointed and the hotel is a popular venue for weddings.

Rooms 20 (8 annexe) (6 fmly) (4 GF) **S** £45-£75; **D** £55-£85 (incl. bkfst)* **Facilities** FTV Xmas New Year Wi-fi **Parking** 150

SWANSEA

LLANGENNITH — Map 2 SS49

Kings Head
★★★★ INN
Town House SA3 1HX
☎ 01792 386212 🖹 01792 386477
e-mail: info@kingsheadgower.co.uk

PETS: Bedrooms sign **Stables** 150yds **Charges** £5 per dog, £15 per horse per night **Public areas** on leads **Grounds** on leads disp bin **Exercise area** beach 1m (access all year) **Facilities** water bowl walks info vet info **Other** charge for damage **Resident Pets:** Skinny (Greyhound), Frank (Connemara pony)

This establishment is made up from three 17th-century buildings set behind a splendid rough stone wall; it stands opposite the church in this coastal village. In two separate buildings the comfortable, well-equipped bedrooms, including some on the ground floor, can be found. This is an ideal base for exploring the Gower Peninsula, whether for walking, cycling or surfing. Evening meals and breakfasts can be taken in the inn.

Rooms 27 en suite (3 fmly) (14 GF) **S** £75-£110; **D** £75-£130* **Facilities** FTV tea/coffee Dinner available Direct Dial Cen ht Wi-fi Pool Table **Parking** 35 **Notes** LB

PORT EINON — Map 2 SS48

Carreglwyd Camping & Caravan Park
(SS465863)

►►►
SA3 1NL
☎ 01792 390795 🖹 01792 390796
dir: *A4118 to Port Einon, site adjacent to beach*

PETS: Public areas on leads **Exercise area** on site **Exercise area** walks accessible from site **Facilities** food vet info **Other** disposal bags available **Resident Pets:** Bruno (Black Labrador), Dare (German Shepherd), Emma (cat)

Open Mar-Dec Last arrival 18.00hrs Last departure 15.00hrs

Set in an unrivalled location alongside the safe sandy beach of Port Einon on the Gower Peninsula, this popular park is an ideal family holiday spot. Close to an attractive village with pubs and shops, most pitches offer sea views. The sloping ground has been partly terraced, and facilities are excellent. A 12 acre site with 150 touring pitches.

RHOSSILI — Map 2 SS48

Pitton Cross Caravan & Camping Park
(SS434877)

►►►
SA3 1PH
☎ 01792 390593 🖹 01792 391010
e-mail: admin@pittoncross.co.uk
dir: *2m W of Scurlage on B4247*

PETS: Stables 3m **Charges** dog £1 per night £7 per week **Public areas** except dog free area on leads disp bin **Exercise area** connecting field **Facilities** food food bowl water bowl leads washing facs walks info vet info **Other** prior notice required disposal bags available **Resident Pets:** Buster & Dave (dogs), Tipsy, Minnie & Amy (cats)

Open all year rs Nov-Apr no bread, milk or papers Last arrival 20.00hrs Last departure 11.00hrs

Surrounded by farmland close to sandy Menslade Bay, which is within walking distance across the fields. This grassy park is divided by hedging into paddocks. Nearby Rhossili Beach is popular with surfers. Performance kites are sold, and instruction in flying is given. A 6 acre site with 100 touring pitches, 21 hardstandings.

Notes Quiet at all times, charcoal BBQ's off ground

WALES

WALES

SWANSEA — Map 3 SS69

The White House

★★★★ GUEST ACCOMMODATION

4 Nyanza Ter SA1 4QQ
☎ 01792 473856 📠 01792 455300
e-mail: reception@thewhitehousehotel.co.uk
dir: *On A4118, 1m W of city centre at junct with Eaton Crescent*

PETS: Bedrooms Stables 5m **Grounds** on leads **Exercise area** 200yds **Facilities** food bowl water bowl washing facs cage storage walks info vet info **On Request** fridge access torch towels

Part of a short early-Victorian terrace in fashionable Uplands, this house retains many original features. It has been restored to provide thoughtfully furnished and equipped quality accommodation. Bedrooms are filled with many extras, and the memorable Welsh breakfasts include cockles and laverbread.

Rooms 9 en suite (4 fmly) **S** £54-£66; **D** £84* **Facilities** FTV TVL tea/coffee Dinner available Direct Dial Cen ht Licensed Wi-fi **Parking** 8 **Notes** LB

VALE OF GLAMORGAN

LLANTWIT MAJOR — Map 3 SS96

Acorn Camping & Caravan Site *(SS973678)*

►►►

Ham Lane South CF61 1RP
☎ 01446 794024
e-mail: info@acorncamping.co.uk
dir: *B4265 to Llantwit Major, follow camping signs. Approach site through Ham Manor residential park*

PETS: Charges 70p per night **Public areas** except shop, games room & shower block disp bin **Exercise area** adjacent **Facilities** food food bowl water bowl dog chews cat treats washing facs walks info vet info **Other** prior notice required disposal bags available

Open Feb-8 Dec Last arrival 21.00hrs Last departure 11.00hrs

A peaceful country site in level meadowland, with some individual pitches divided by hedges and shrubs. About one mile from the beach, which can be approached by a clifftop walk, and the same distance from the historic town of Llantwit Major. An internet station and a full size snooker table are useful amenities. A 5.5 acre site with 90 touring pitches, 10 hardstandings and 15 statics.

Notes No noise 23.00hrs-07.00hrs

WREXHAM

EYTON — Map 7 SJ34

The Plassey Leisure Park *(SJ353452)*

►►►►►

The Plassey LL13 0SP
☎ 01978 780277 📠 01978 780019
e-mail: enquiries@plassey.com
dir: *From A483 at Bangor-on-Dee exit onto B5426 for 2.5m. Site entrance signed on left*

PETS: Charges £2 per night £14 per week **Public areas** except bars, restaurants & shops on leads disp bin **Exercise area** 1-acre grounds, 2m of walks **Facilities** food dog chews cat treats litter tray scoop/disp bags vet info **Other** prior notice required **Restrictions** no dangerous breeds (see page 7)

Open Feb-Nov Last arrival 20.30hrs Last departure noon

A lovely park set in several hundred acres of quiet farm and meadowland in the Dee Valley. The superb toilet facilities include individual cubicles for total privacy and security, while the Edwardian farm buildings have been converted into a restaurant, coffee shop, beauty studio, and various craft outlets. There is plenty here to entertain the whole family, from scenic walks and swimming pool to free fishing, and use of the 9-hole golf course. A 10 acre site with 90 touring pitches, 45 hardstandings and 15 statics.

Notes No footballs, bikes or skateboards

WALES

The Hanmer Arms

★★★★ INN

SY13 3DE
☎ 01948 830532   📠 01948 830740
e-mail: info@hanmerarms.co.uk
web: www.hanmerarms.co.uk
dir: On A539, just off A525 Whitchurch/Wrexham road

PETS: Bedrooms Stables 2m Charges £6 per night Public areas
in bar only on leads Grounds Exercise area surrounding
countryside Facilities water bowl vet info On Request fridge
access torch towels Other charge for damage

Located in the centre of the village and also home to the
local crown-green bowling club, this former farm has been
sympathetically renovated to provide a good range of facilities.
Well-equipped bedrooms are situated in the former stables or
barns, and rustic furniture styles highlight the many period
features in the public areas, which also feature an attractive
first-floor function room.

Rooms 12 annexe en suite (2 fmly) (8 GF) S fr £55; D fr £76*
Facilities FTV tea/coffee Dinner available Cen ht Wi-fi Parking 50
Notes LB

The Hand at Llanarmon

★★★★ ⊚ INN

LL20 7LD
☎ 01691 600666   📠 01691 600262
e-mail: reception@thehandhotel.co.uk
dir: Exit A5 at Chirk onto B4500 signed Ceiriog Valley, continue
for 11m

PETS: Bedrooms Stables 2m Charges contact for details
Public areas except restaurant on leads on leads disp bin
Exercise area adjacent, country lane Facilities water bowl
walks info vet info Other prior notice required; dogs allowed in
certain bedrooms only

Refurbished to a high standard, this owner managed inn provides
a range of thoughtfully furnished bedrooms, with smart modern
bathrooms. Public areas retain many original features including
exposed beams and open fires. Imaginative food utilises the

finest of local produce. A warm welcome and attentive service
ensure a memorable guest experience.

Rooms 13 en suite (4 GF) Facilities tea/coffee Dinner available
Direct Dial Cen ht Wi-fi Pool Table Parking 19 Notes RS 24-26
Dec

West Arms

★★★★ ⊚⊚ INN

LL20 7LD
☎ 01691 600665 & 600612   📠 01691 600622
e-mail: gowestarms@aol.com
dir: Off A483/A5 at Chirk, take B4500 to Ceiriog Valley

PETS: Bedrooms Sep accom kennels with hay Stables 4m
Charges £6 per night Public areas except restaurant on leads
Grounds disp bin Exercise area 300yds Facilities water bowl
bedding litter tray scoop/disp bags leads washing facs cage
storage walks info vet info On Request fridge access torch
towels Other charge for damage Resident Pet: Gem (Sheepdog/
Border Collie cross)

Set in the beautiful Ceiriog Valley, this delightful 17th-century
inn has a wealth of charm and character. There is a comfortable
lounge, a room for private dining and two bars, as well as an
elegant, award-winning restaurant offering a set-price menu of
imaginative dishes, utilising quality local produce. The attractive
bedrooms have a mixture of modern and period furnishings.

Rooms 15 en suite (2 fmly) (3 GF) S £53-£125; D £87-£225*
Facilities FTV tea/coffee Dinner available Direct Dial Cen ht Wi-fi
Fishing Parking 22 Notes LB

Ireland

NORTHERN IRELAND

CO ANTRIM

ANTRIM — Map 1 D5

Six Mile Water Caravan Park *(J137870)*

▶ ▶ ▶

Lough Rd BT41 4DG
☎ 028 9446 4963 & 9446 3113
e-mail: sixmilewater@antrim.gov.uk
dir: *1m from town centre, follow Antrim Forum/Loughshore Park signs. On Dublin road take Lough road (pass Antrim Forum on right). Site at end of road on right*

PETS: **Public areas** except toilets, showers, TV room & games room on leads disp bin **Facilities** walks info vet info **Other** prior notice required dogs must be under control & on leads at all times

Open Mar-Oct rs Feb-Nov Weekends only Last arrival 21.45hrs Last departure noon

A pretty tree-lined site in a large municipal park, within walking distance of Antrim and the Antrim Forum leisure complex yet very much in the countryside. The modern toilet block is well equipped, and other facilities include a laundry and electric hook-ups. A 9.61 acre site with 67 touring pitches, 37 hardstandings.

Notes Max stay 14 nights, no noise between 22.00hrs-08.00hrs

BALLYMONEY — Map 1 C6

Drumaheglis Marina & Caravan Park

(C901254)

▶ ▶ ▶ ▶

36 Glenstall Rd BT53 7QN
☎ 028 2766 0280 & 2766 0227 📠 028 2766 0222
e-mail: drumaheglis@ballymoney.gov.uk
dir: *Signed off A26, approx 1.5m outside Ballymoney towards Coleraine, & also off B66 S of Ballymoney*

PETS: **Public areas** except play area on leads **Facilities** vet info

Open 17 Mar-Oct Last arrival 20.00hrs Last departure 13.00hrs

Exceptionally well-designed and laid out park beside the Lower Bann River, with very spacious pitches and two quality toilet blocks. Ideal base for touring Antrim or for watersports enthusiasts. A 16 acre site with 55 touring pitches, 55 hardstandings.

BUSHMILLS — Map 1 C6

Ballyness Caravan Park *(C944393)*

▶ ▶ ▶ ▶ ▶

40 Castlecatt Rd BT57 8TN
☎ 028 2073 2393 📠 028 2073 2713
e-mail: info@ballynesscaravanpark.com
dir: *0.5m S of Bushmills on B66, follow signs*

PETS: **Public areas** except amenity building disp bin **Exercise area** on site **Exercise area** 1m **Facilities** dog chews cat treats washing facs walks info vet info **Other** disposal bags & pet toys available **Resident Pet:** Gyp (German Shepherd)

Open 17 Mar-Oct Last arrival 21.00hrs Last departure noon

A quality park with superb toilet and other facilities, on farmland beside St Columb's Rill, the stream that supplies the famous nearby Bushmills distillery. The friendly owners built this park with the discerning camper in mind, and they continue to improve it to ever higher standards. There is a pleasant walk around several ponds, and the park is peacefully located close to the beautiful north Antrim coast. A 16 acre site with 48 touring pitches, 48 hardstandings and 65 statics.

Notes No skateboards or roller blades

LARNE — Map 1 D5

Derrin House

★ ★ ★ ★ GUEST ACCOMMODATION

2 Princes Gardens BT40 1RQ
☎ 028 2827 3269 📠 028 2827 3269
e-mail: info@derrinhouse.co.uk
dir: *Off A8 Harbour Highway onto A2 (coast route), 1st left after lights at Main St*

PETS: **Bedrooms Exercise area** 5 mins' walk **Facilities** cage storage walks info

Just a short walk from the town centre, and a short drive from the harbour, this comfortable Victorian house offers a very friendly welcome. The bedrooms are gradually being refurbished to offer smartly presented modern facilities. Public areas are light and inviting, hearty breakfasts are offered in the stylish dining room.

Rooms 7 rms (6 en suite) (1 pri facs) (2 fmly) (2 GF) **S** £35-£40; **D** £55-£60* **Facilities** TVL tea/coffee Cen ht Wi-fi **Parking** 3 **Notes** LB

BELFAST

BELFAST
Map 1 D5

Malmaison Belfast
★★★ 83% ◉ HOTEL
34 - 38 Victoria St BT1 3GH
☎ 028 9022 0200   📠 028 9022 0220
e-mail: hcaters@malmaison.com
web: www.malmaison.com
dir: *M1 along Westlink to Grosvenor Rd. Follow city centre signs. Pass City Hall on right, turn left onto Victoria St. Hotel on right*

PETS: **Bedrooms** **Charges** **Public areas** except bar or brasserie on leads **Facilities** food bowl water bowl bedding vet info **Other** please contact hotel for details of charges for dogs charge for dog basket & bowl

Situated in a former seed warehouse, this luxurious, contemporary hotel is ideally located for the city centre. Comfortable bedrooms, boast a host of modern facilities, whilst the deeply comfortable, stylish public areas include a popular bar lounge. The 'Home Grown and Local' menu in the brasserie showcases local seasonal ingredients. The warm hospitality is notable.

Rooms 64 **Facilities** STV Gym Wi-fi **Services** Lift

DUNDONALD
Map 1 D5

Dundonald Touring Caravan Park *(J410731)*
▶ ▶ ▶
111 Old Dundonald Rd BT16 1XT
☎ 028 9080 9123 & 9080 9129   📠 028 9048 9604
e-mail: sales@castlereagh.gov.uk
dir: *From Belfast city centre follow M3 & A20 to City Airport. Then A20 to Newtownards & follow signs to Dundonald & Ulster Hospital. At hospital right at sign for Dundonald Ice Bowl. Follow to end, turn right. (Ice Bowl on left)*

PETS: **Public areas** dogs must be kept on leads & under control at all times disp bin **Exercise area** park (5 mins' walk) **Facilities** walks info vet info

Open 17 Mar-Oct rs Nov-Mar Aire de Service restricted to motorhomes Last arrival 23.00hrs Last departure noon

A purpose-built park in a quiet corner of Dundonald Leisure Park on the outskirts of Belfast. This peaceful park is ideally located for touring County Down and exploring the capital. In the winter it offers an 'Aire de Service' for motorhomes. A 1.5 acre site with 22 touring pitches, 22 hardstandings.

Notes No commercial vehicles

CO LONDONDERRY

AGHADOWEY
Map 1 C6

Brown Trout Golf & Country Inn
★★★ 71% HOTEL
209 Agivey Rd BT51 4AD
☎ 028 7086 8209   📠 028 7086 8878
e-mail: jane@browntroutinn.com
dir: *At junct of A54 & B66 junct on road to Coleraine*

PETS: **Bedrooms** unattended **Public areas** except upstairs restaurant on leads **Grounds** disp bin **Exercise area** 60 acres of woodland **Facilities** scoop/disp bags leads walks info vet info **On Request** fridge access torch towels **Other** charge for damage **Resident Pets:** Muffin & Lucy (Chocolate Labradors)

Set alongside the Agivey River and featuring its own 9-hole golf course, this welcoming inn offers a choice of spacious accommodation. Comfortably furnished bedrooms are situated around a courtyard area whilst the cottage suites also have lounge areas. Home-cooked meals are served in the restaurant and lighter fare is available in the charming lounge bar which has entertainment at weekends.

Rooms 15 (11 fmly) **S** £60-£70; **D** £80-£110 (incl. bkfst) **Facilities** STV FTV ♨ 9 Putt green Fishing Gym Game fishing ♫ Xmas New Year Wi-fi **Parking** 80 **Notes** LB

CO TYRONE

DUNGANNON
Map 1 C5

Cohannon Inn & Auto Lodge
★★ 72% HOTEL
212 Ballynakilly Rd BT71 6HJ
☎ 028 8772 4488   📠 028 8775 2217
e-mail: info@cohannon.com
dir: *400yds from M1 junct 14*

PETS: **Bedrooms** (21 GF) **Charges** disp bin **Exercise area** 50mtrs **Facilities** walks info vet info **Other** charge for damage

Handy for the M1 and the nearby towns of Dungannon and Portadown, this hotel offers well-maintained bedrooms, located behind the inn complex in a smart purpose-built wing. Public areas are smartly furnished and wide-ranging menus are served throughout the day.

Rooms 42 (20 fmly) (21 GF) (5 smoking) **S** fr £44.95; **D** fr £49.95* **Facilities** New Year **Parking** 160 **Notes** RS 25 Dec

IRELAND

DUNGANNON *continued*

Dungannon Park *(H805612)*

▶ ▶ ▶

Moy Rd BT71 6DY
☎ 028 8772 8690 ▤ 028 8772 9169
e-mail: dpreception@dungannon.gov.uk
dir: *M1 junct 15, A29, left at 2nd lights*

PETS: Public areas except play area & amenity buildings on leads disp bin **Exercise area Facilities** walks info vet info
Other prior notice required no fouling on site

Open Mar-Oct Last arrival 20.30hrs Last departure 14.00hrs

Modern caravan park in a quiet area of a public park with fishing lake and excellent facilities, especially for disabled. A 2 acre site with 20 touring pitches, 12 hardstandings.

REPUBLIC OF IRELAND

CO CORK

BALLYLICKEY	Map 1 B2

Sea View House Hotel

★★★ ◉◉ HOTEL

☎ 027 50073 & 50462 ▤ 027 51555
e-mail: info@seaviewhousehotel.com
web: www.seaviewhousehotel.com
dir: *5km from Bantry, 11km from Glengarriff on N71*

PETS: Bedrooms (5 GF) **Charges Public areas** on leads
Grounds on leads disp bin **Exercise area** walks nearby
Facilities cage storage walks info vet info **Other** charge for damage **Restrictions** small dogs only

Colourful gardens and glimpses of Bantry Bay through the mature trees frame this delightful country house. Owner Kathleen O'Sullivan's team of staff are exceptionally pleasant and there is a relaxed atmosphere in the cosy lounges. Guest comfort and good cuisine are the top priorities. Bedrooms are spacious and individually styled; some on the ground floor are appointed to suit less able guests.

Rooms 25 (3 fmly) (5 GF) **Parking** 32 **Notes** Closed mid Nov-mid Mar

BANDON	Map 1 B2

Glebe Country House

★★★★ BED AND BREAKFAST

Ballinadee
☎ 021 4778294 ▤ 021 4778456
e-mail: glebehse@indigo.ie
dir: *Off N71 at Innishannon Bridge signed Ballinadee, 8km along river bank, left after village sign*

PETS: Bedrooms Stables nearby **Public areas Grounds** disp bin
Facilities food (pre-bookable) food bowl water bowl bedding dog chews cat treats feeding mat leads washing facs cage storage walks info vet info **On Request** fridge access torch towels **Resident Pets:** Tarka (Dalmatian), Mini (Miniature Schnauzer), Fluffy & Ginger (cat)

This lovely bed and breakfast stands in well-kept gardens, and is run with great attention to detail. Antique furnishings predominate throughout this comfortable house, which has a lounge and an elegant dining room. An interesting breakfast menu offers unusual options, and a country-house style dinner is available by arrangement.

Rooms 4 en suite (2 fmly) **S** €50-€60; **D** €90-€100*
Facilities TVL tea/coffee Dinner available Direct Dial Cen ht Wi-fi
Parking 10 **Notes** LB Closed 21 Dec-3 Jan

IRELAND

Blarney Golf Resort

★★★★ 76% HOTEL

Tower

☎ 021 4384477 ☐ 021 4516453

e-mail: reservations@blarneygolfresort.com

dir: *Exit N20 for Blarney, 4km to Tower, right onto Old Kerry Rd. Hotel 2km on right*

PETS: Bedrooms (30 GF) unattended **Charges** €12 per night **Grounds** on leads disp bin **Exercise area Facilities** walks info vet info **On Request** towels **Other** pets allowed in lodges only; dogs are required to be muzzled bowls & bedding available by prior arrangement

Set on a John Daly designed golf course on the outskirts of the village of Tower, this hotel offers a range of well-equipped comfortable bedrooms. Excellent standards of cuisine are on offer in the Inniscarra Restaurant, with more casual eating available throughout the afternoon in Cormac's bar. The hotel also features a Sentosa Spa.

Rooms 117 (56 annexe) (56 fmly) (30 GF) **S** €65; **D** €85 (incl. bkfst)* **Facilities** Spa FTV supervised ♨ 18 Putt green Gym Steam room Sauna ♫ Xmas New Year Wi-fi **Services** Lift Air con **Parking** 250 **Notes** LB

Ashlee Lodge

★★★★★ GUEST HOUSE

Tower

☎ 021 4385346 ☐ 021 4385726

e-mail: info@ashleelodge.com

dir: *4km from Blarney on R617*

PETS: Bedrooms Public areas Grounds on leads disp bin **Exercise area Facilities** walks info vet info **On Request** towels **Other** pets allowed in 1 bedroom only **Resident Pet:** Tammy (cat)

Ashlee Lodge is a purpose-built guest house, situated in the village of Tower, close to Blarney and local pubs and restaurants. Bedrooms are decorated with comfort and elegance in mind, some with whirlpool baths, and one room has easier access. The extensive breakfast menu is memorable for Ann's home baking. Guest can unwind in the sauna or the outdoor hot tub. Transfers to the nearest airport and railway station can be arranged, and tee times can be booked at many of the nearby golf courses.

Rooms 10 en suite (2 fmly) (6 GF) **S** €65-€95; **D** €80-€140* **Facilities** STV FTV TVL tea/coffee Dinner available Direct Dial Cen ht Licensed Wi-fi Sauna **Parking** 12 **Notes** LB

Castlemartyr Resort

[U]

☎ 021 4219000 ☐ 021 4623359

e-mail: reception@castlemartyrresort.ie

dir: *N25, 3rd exit signed Rosslare. Continue past Carrigtwohill & Midleton exits. Right at lights in village*

PETS: Bedrooms (30 GF) unattended **Grounds** on leads **Exercise area** 250mtrs **Facilities** food (pre-bookable) food bowl water bowl bedding washing facs walks info vet info **Restrictions** max weight 70lb **Resident Pets:** Earl & Countess (Irish Setters)

Currently the rating for this establishment is not confirmed. This may be due to a change of ownership or because it has only recently joined the AA rating scheme. For further details please see the AA website: theAA.com

Rooms 109 (98 annexe) (6 fmly) (30 GF) **Facilities** Spa STV FTV supervised ♨ 18 ⛳ Gym Leisure facility Bicycles Horse & carriage rides Target archery ♫ New Year Wi-fi **Services** Lift Air con **Parking**

Friar's Lodge

★★★★★ GUEST HOUSE

5 Friars St

☎ 086 289 5075 & 021 4777384 ☐ 021 4774363

e-mail: mtierney@indigo.ie

dir: *In town centre next to parish church*

PETS: Bedrooms unattended **Stables Exercise area Facilities** walks info vet info **On Request** fridge access towels **Other** charge for damage

This new, purpose-built property near the Friary, has been developed with every comfort in mind. Bedrooms are particularly spacious. Located on a quiet street just a short walk from the town centre, with secure parking to the rear. A very good choice is offered from the breakfast menu.

Rooms 18 en suite (2 fmly) (4 GF) (2 smoking) **S** €50-€80; **D** €80-€120* **Facilities** STV tea/coffee Direct Dial Cen ht Lift Wi-fi **Parking** 20 **Notes** Closed Xmas

SHANAGARRY — Map 1 C2

Ballymaloe House

★ ★ ★ ★ ★ ◎◎ GUEST HOUSE

☎ 021 4652531 📄 021 4652021
e-mail: res@ballymaloe.ie
dir: From R630 at Whitegate rdbt, left onto R631, left onto Cloyne. Located on Ballycotton Rd

PETS: Bedrooms Stables 1m Grounds disp bin Exercise area on grounds Facilities food bowl water bowl bedding dog walking cage storage walks info vet info On Request fridge access torch towels Other charge for damage dogs permitted in bedrooms with porches only Restrictions no dangerous dogs (see page 7) Resident Pets: Tommy & Flicker (dogs)

This charming country house is on a 400-acre farm, part of the Geraldine Estate in East Cork. Bedrooms upstairs in the main house retain many original features. The ground-floor and courtyard rooms feature garden patios. The relaxing drawing room and dining rooms have enchanting old-world charm. Ballymaloe is renowned for excellent meals, many of which are created using ingredients produced on the farm. There is a craft shop, café, tennis and small golf course on the estate.

Rooms 21 en suite 9 annexe en suite (2 fmly) (3 GF) Facilities TVL Dinner available Direct Dial Cen ht Licensed Wi-fi ⚘ ♨⚓ Golf 9 ⚓ Fishing Parking 50 Notes LB Closed 23-26 Dec RS Jan

YOUGHAL — Map 1 C2

Ahernes

★ ★ ★ ★ ★ ◎ GUEST HOUSE

163 North Main St
☎ 024 92424 📄 024 93633
e-mail: ahernes@eircom.net

PETS: Bedrooms Public areas assist dogs only on leads Exercise area many walks adjacent Facilities walks info vet info On Request fridge access Other charge for damage Restrictions small dogs & assist dogs only

In the same family since 1923, Ahernes offers a warm welcome, with turf fires and a traditional atmosphere. Spacious bedrooms are furnished to the highest standard and include antiques and modern facilities. There is a restaurant, well known for its daily-changing menu of the freshest seafood specialities, in addition to a cosy drawing room.

Rooms 12 en suite (2 fmly) (3 GF) S €110-€120; D €130-€150* Facilities FTV tea/coffee Dinner available Direct Dial Cen ht Licensed Wi-fi Parking 20 Notes LB Closed 23-26 Dec

CO DONEGAL

DONEGAL — Map 1 B5

Harvey's Point Country Hotel

★ ★ ★ ★ 87% ◎◎ HOTEL

Lough Eske
☎ 074 9722208 📄 074 9722352
e-mail: sales@harveyspoint.com
web: www.harveyspoint.com
dir: N56 from Donegal, then 1st right (Loch Eske/Harvey's Point)

PETS: Bedrooms (34 GF) unattended Stables Grounds disp bin Exercise area Facilities food bowl water bowl pet sitting cage storage walks info vet info On Request fridge access torch Other pets allowed in courtyard bedrooms only Resident Pets: Paddy (Labrador), geese, swans

Situated by the lake shore, this hotel is an oasis of relaxation; comfort and attentive guest care are the norm here. A range of particularly spacious suites and bedrooms is available, together with smaller rooms in the courtyard annexe. The kitchen brigade maintains consistently high standards in The Restaurant, with less formal dining in The Steakhouse at peak periods. A very popular Sunday buffet lunch is served weekly, with dinner entertainment on selected dates.

Rooms 70 (34 GF) S €99-€195; D €158-€580 (incl. bkfst) Facilities Treatment rooms Pitch 'n' putt Bicycle hire Walking tours ♫ Xmas New Year Wi-fi Services Lift Parking 300 Notes LB Closed Mon & Tue Nov-Mar

Ard Na Breatha

★ ★ ★ ★ 📄 GUEST HOUSE

Drumrooske Middle
☎ 074 972 2288 & 086 842 1330 📄 074 974 0720
e-mail: info@ardnabreatha.com
web: www.ardnabreatha.com
dir: From town centre onto Killybegs road, 2nd right, sharp right at Vivo shop

PETS: Bedrooms Grounds on leads disp bin Exercise area country road from house to forest Facilities walks info vet info On Request towels Resident Pets: Labrador, horse

This family-run guest house is just a short drive from the town centre. Bedrooms are all well-appointed and very comfortable, with a relaxing lounge for residents. Evening meals are served in the popular restaurant at weekends and during high season, but can be arranged for residents at other times. The menu features much of the produce of the family farm which surrounds the house.

Rooms 6 en suite (1 fmly) (3 GF) Facilities TVL tea/coffee Dinner available Direct Dial Cen ht Licensed Parking 16 Notes Closed Dec-Jan RS wknds Restaurant only open with prior reservation

DUNKINEELY — Map 1 B5

Castle Murray House and Restaurant

★★★★ RESTAURANT WITH ROOMS

St Johns Point
☎ 074 9737022   📠 074 9737330
e-mail: info@castlemurray.com
dir: *From Donegal take N56 towards Killybegs. Left to Dunkineely*

PETS: **Bedrooms Public areas** lounge area until 6pm on leads **Grounds Exercise area** small beach (1 min), large beach (6km) **Facilities** cage storage walks info vet info **On Request** fridge access torch **Other** charge for damage **Restrictions** small dogs only

Situated on the coast road of St Johns Point, this charming family-run house and restaurant overlooks McSwynes Bay and the castle. The bedrooms are individually decorated with guest comfort very much in mind, as is the cosy bar and sun lounge. There is a strong French influence in the cooking; locally landed fish, and prime lamb and beef are featured on the menus.

Rooms 10 en suite (2 fmly) **Facilities** FTV tea/coffee Dinner available Direct Dial Cen ht Wi-fi **Parking** 40 **Notes** LB Closed mid Jan-mid Feb No coaches

PORTNOO — Map 1 B5

Boyle's Caravan Park *(G702990)*

▶▶

☎ 074 9545131 & 086 8523131   📠 074 9545130
e-mail: pboylecaravans@gmail.com
dir: *Exit N56 at Ardra onto R261 for 6m. Follow signs for Santa Anna Drive*

PETS: **Public areas** dogs must on leads at all times; owners must clear up after their pets disp bin **Exercise area Facilities** washing facs walks info vet info **Restrictions** no Dobermans, Alsatians, Bull Terriers or similar breeds

Open 18 Mar-Oct Last arrival 23.00hrs Last departure 11.00hrs

Set at Narin Beach and close to a huge selection of water activities on a magnificent stretch of the Atlantic. This open park nestles among the sand dunes, and offers well-maintained facilities. A 1.5 acre site with 20 touring pitches and 80 statics.

Notes No skateboards

RATHMULLAN — Map 1 C6

Rathmullan House

★★★★ 79% ◉◉ COUNTRY HOUSE HOTEL

☎ 074 9158188   📠 074 9158200
e-mail: info@rathmullanhouse.com
dir: *From Letterkenny, then Ramelton then Rathmullan R243. Left at Mace shop, through village, hotel gates on right*

PETS: **Bedrooms** (9 GF) unattended **Stables** 500yds **Charges** €10 per dog per night **Grounds** on leads disp bin **Exercise area** 500yds **Facilities** food (pre-bookable) food bowl water bowl bedding dog chews scoop/disp bags cage storage walks info vet info **On Request** fridge access torch towels **Restrictions** max height 80cm no Pit Bull Terriers **Resident Pets:** Suzy (Labrador), Brush & Odie (Jack Russells)

Dating from the 18th century, this fine property has been operating as a country-house hotel for the last 40 years or so under the stewardship of the Wheeler family. Guests are welcome to wander around the well-planted grounds and the walled garden, from where much of the ingredients for the Weeping Elm Restaurant are grown. The many lounges are relaxing and comfortable, while many of the bedrooms benefit from balconies and patio areas.

Rooms 34 (4 fmly) (9 GF) **Facilities** Spa New Year Wi-fi **Parking** 80 **Notes** LB Closed 11 Jan-5 Feb RS 15 Nov-12 Mar

DUBLIN

DUBLIN — Map 1 D4

Glenshandan Lodge

★★★★ GUEST ACCOMMODATION

Dublin Rd, Swords
☎ 01 8408838   📠 01 8408838
e-mail: glenshandan@eircom.net
dir: *Beside Statoil on airport side of Swords Main St*

PETS: **Bedrooms** sign **Stables** 0.5m **Public areas Grounds** disp bin **Exercise area** 200mtrs **Facilities** food (pre-bookable) food bowl water bowl bedding scoop/disp bags leads pet sitting dog walking washing facs cage storage walks info vet info **On Request** fridge access torch towels

Glenshandan Lodge is a family and pet-friendly house with hospitable owners and good facilities including e-mail access. Bedrooms are comfortable and one room has easier access. Secure parking available. Close to pubs, restaurants, golf courses and the airport.

Rooms 9 en suite (5 fmly) (5 GF) **Facilities** TVL tea/coffee Cen ht Wi-fi **Parking** 10 **Notes** Closed Xmas/New Year

IRELAND

CO GALWAY

CASHEL | Map 1 A4

Cashel House

★★★ ◎◎ COUNTRY HOUSE HOTEL
☎ 095 31001 📄 095 31077
e-mail: res@cashel-house-hotel.com
web: www.cashel-house-hotel.com
dir: S off N59, 1.5km W of Recess, well signed

PETS: Bedrooms (6 GF) unattended **Sep accom** 2 stables
suitable for bigger dogs & gun dogs **Stables Charges** horse
€20 per night **Grounds** disp bin **Exercise area Facilities**
food (pre-bookable) washing facs cage storage walks info vet
info **On Request** fridge access torch towels **Other** charge for
damage **Resident Pets:** cats, horses

Cashel House is a mid-19th century property, standing at
the head of Cashel Bay, in the heart of Connemara. Quietly
secluded in award-winning gardens with woodland walks.
Attentive service comes with the perfect balance of friendliness
and professionalism from McEvilly family and their staff. The
comfortable lounges have turf fires and antique furnishings. The
restaurant offers local produce such as the famous Connemara
lamb, and fish from the nearby coast.

Rooms 29 (4 fmly) (6 GF) (4 smoking) **Facilities** STV FTV 🌊
Garden school Xmas New Year Wi-fi **Parking** 40 **Notes** LB

Zetland Country House

★★★ 78% HOTEL
Cashel Bay
☎ 095 31111 📄 095 31117
e-mail: info@zetland.com
dir: N59 from Galway towards Clifden, right after Recess onto
R340, left after 4m (R341), hotel 1m on right

PETS: Bedrooms (3 GF) sign **Stables Charges** negotiable
Public areas bar only **Grounds** on leads disp bin **Exercise area**
Facilities food (pre-bookable) food bowl water bowl bedding
feeding mat scoop/disp bags leads pet sitting dog walking
washing facs dog grooming cage storage walks info vet info
On Request torch towels **Other** charge for damage

Standing on the edge of Cashel Bay, this former sporting lodge
dating from the early 1800s is a cosy and relaxing hotel that
exudes charm. Many of the comfortable rooms have sea views,
as has the restaurant where seafood is a particular feature. The
atmospheric bar makes a popular meeting place for locals.

Rooms 19 (10 fmly) (3 GF) **Facilities** STV FTV 🌊 Fishing 🎿
Shooting Cycling Xmas New Year Wi-fi **Parking** 32 **Notes** LB

GALWAY | Map 1 B3

Ardilaun Hotel & Leisure Club

★★★★ 81% ◎ HOTEL
Taylor's Hill
☎ 091 521433 📄 091 521546
e-mail: info@theardilaunhotel.ie
web: www.theardilaunhotel.ie
dir: M6 to Galway City West, then follow signs for N59 Clifden,
then N6 towards Salthill

PETS: Bedrooms (8 GF) **Charges** €10 per night **Public areas**
lobby only on leads **Grounds** on leads disp bin **Exercise area**
Facilities food bowl water bowl bedding dog chews walks info
vet info **On Request** fridge access towels

This very smart country house style hotel is located on the
outskirts of the city and has lovely landscaped gardens.
Bedrooms have been thoughtfully equipped and furnished, and
the deluxe rooms and suites are particularly spacious. Public
areas include a selection of comfortable lounges, the Camilaun
Restaurant overlooking the garden, Blazers bistro and bar plus
extensive banqueting and leisure facilities.

Rooms 125 (17 fmly) (8 GF) (16 smoking) **S** €79-€150;
D €99-€290 (incl. bkfst)* **Facilities** Spa STV 🕏 supervised Gym
Treatment & analysis rooms Beauty salon Spinning room 🎵 New
Year Wi-fi **Services** Lift **Parking** 380 **Notes** LB Closed pm 23,
24-26 Dec

RECESS | Map 1 A4

Lough Inagh Lodge

★★★ ◎ COUNTRY HOUSE HOTEL
Inagh Valley
☎ 095 34706 & 34694 📄 095 34708
e-mail: inagh@iol.ie
dir: From Recess take R344 towards Kylemore

PETS: Bedrooms (4 GF) unattended **Public areas** except at
food service **Grounds** on leads **Exercise area** countryside
walks nearby **Facilities** food bowl water bowl bedding dog
chews walks info vet info **On Request** fridge access torch
towels **Other** please phone for further details of pet facilities
Resident Pets: Sophie (Mixed Terrier), Sasha (cat)

Dating from 1880, this former fishing lodge is akin to a family
home, where guests are encouraged to relax and enjoy the peace.
Overlooking Lough Inagh, and nestled among the mountains of

Connemara, it is in an ideal location for those who enjoy walking and fishing. Bedrooms are individually decorated, some with spacious seating areas, and each is dedicated to an Irish literary figure. A choice of two cosy lounges is offered, often featuring a welcoming turf fire. Informal dining from a bar menu is available during the day. Dinner is a highlight of a visit to the Lodge, featuring locally sourced produce cooked with care, with seafood a speciality.

Rooms 13 (1 fmly) (4 GF) **Facilities** Fishing Hill walking Fly fishing Cycling **Services** Air con **Parking** 16 **Notes** Closed mid Dec-mid Mar

CO KERRY

CASTLEGREGORY   Map 1 A2

Griffin's Palm Beach Country House *(Q525085)*
★★★ FARMHOUSE
Goulane, Conor Pass Rd
☎ 066 7139147   📠 066 7139073 Mrs Catherine Griffin
e-mail: griffinspalmbeach@eircom.net
dir: *1.5km from Stradbally*

PETS: Bedrooms unattended sign **Sep accom** barn **Charges** €5 per night €35 per week **Public areas Grounds** on leads disp bin **Exercise area** beach 0.5m **Facilities** water bowl scoop/disp bags washing facs cage storage walks info **On Request** fridge access torch towels **Other** charge for damage **Resident Pets:** Daisy (Jack Russell), Scott (Sheepdog)

This farmhouse is a good base for exploring the Dingle Peninsula and unspoiled beaches. The comfortable bedrooms have fine views over Brandon Bay, and the delightful garden can be enjoyed from the dining room and sitting room. Mrs Griffin offers a warm welcome and her home baking is a feature on the breakfast menu.

Rooms 8 rms (6 en suite) (2 pri facs) (3 fmly) (1 GF) **S** €48-€50; **D** €70-€80* **Facilities** TVL tea/coffee Cen ht 🏌 Golf 9 **Parking** 10 **Notes** LB Closed Nov-Feb 150 acres mixed

---

KENMARE   Map 1 B2

Sheen Falls Lodge
★★★★★ ◉◉ COUNTRY HOUSE HOTEL
☎ 064 6641600   📠 064 6641386
e-mail: info@sheenfallslodge.ie
dir: *From Kenmare take N71 to Glengarriff over suspension bridge, take 1st left*

PETS: Sep accom kennels **Stables Public areas** disp bin **Exercise area Facilities** food bowl water bowl bedding walks info vet info **On Request** fridge access torch towels

This former fishing lodge has been developed into a beautiful hotel with a friendly team of professional staff. The cascading Sheen Falls are floodlit at night, forming a romantic backdrop to the enjoyment of award-winning cuisine in La Cascade restaurant. Less formal dining is available in Oscar's Restaurant. Bedrooms are very comfortably appointed; many of the suites are particularly spacious. The leisure centre and beauty therapy facilities offer a number of exclusive treatments.

Rooms 66 (14 fmly) (14 GF) **S** €150-€220; **D** €210-€420 (incl. bkfst)* **Facilities** Spa STV 🕹 supervised 🎣 Fishing 💪 Gym Table tennis Steam room Clay pigeon shooting Cycling Vintage car rides Library 🎵 Xmas New Year Wi-fi **Services** Lift **Parking** 76 **Notes** Closed 2 Jan-1 Feb

---

KILLARNEY   Map 1 B2

Randles Court
★★★★ 81% HOTEL
Muckross Rd
☎ 064 6635333   📠 064 6639301
e-mail: info@randlescourt.com
dir: *N22 towards Muckross, right at T-junct. From N72 3rd exit on 1st rdbt into town, follow signs for Muckross, hotel on left*

PETS: Bedrooms unattended **Public areas** on leads **Grounds** on leads **Exercise area Facilities** pet sitting dog walking dog grooming cage storage walks info vet info **On Request** fridge access **Other** charge for damage **Resident Pet:** Ruby (Bichon Frise)

Close to all the town's attractions, this is a friendly family-run hotel with an emphasis on customer care. Bedrooms are particularly comfortable. Guests can enjoy a relaxing drink in the cosy bar then dine in the chic Checkers bistro where good food is served in the evenings. A swimming pool and other leisure facilities are available.

Rooms 78 (4 fmly) **Facilities** STV 🕹 supervised Sauna Steam room Hydrotherapy suite New Year Wi-fi **Services** Lift **Parking** 110 **Notes** LB Closed 22-27 Dec

IRELAND

KILLARNEY *continued*

Fairview

★★★★★ 🏠 GUEST HOUSE

College St
☎ 064 6634164   📠 064 6671777
e-mail: info@fairviewkillarney.com
dir: *In town centre off College St*

PETS: **Bedrooms Stables** 3km **Charges Public areas** disp bin **Exercise area** 1km **Facilities** bedding cage storage walks info vet info **On Request** fridge access towels **Other** charge for damage dogs are required to be muzzled

This guest house is situated in the town centre and close to the railway station. Great attention to detail has been taken in the furnishing and design to ensure guest comfort in bedrooms. There is a lift to all floors and a penthouse suite enjoys views to the mountains. Dinner is served nightly in the Fifth Season Restaurant.

Rooms 29 en suite (1 GF) (2 smoking) **Facilities** STV TVL tea/coffee Dinner available Direct Dial Cen ht Lift Licensed Wi-fi **Parking** 11

Kingfisher Lodge

★★★★ GUEST HOUSE

Lewis Rd
☎ 064 6637131   📠 064 6639871
e-mail: info@kingfisherlodgekillarney.com
dir: *Dublin link straight through 1st rdbt. Right at next rdbt towards town centre, Lodge on left*

PETS: **Sep accom** shed with dog area provided **Grounds** disp bin **Exercise area** National Park 0.5m **Facilities** pet sitting walks info vet info **On Request** fridge access torch Resident Pets: Bronasha (Sussex Spaniel), Jazz (Labrador)

This welcoming, family-run modern guest house, situated within walking distance of the town centre, has comfortable well-appointed bedrooms. A delicious breakfast is served in the attractively decorated dining room and there is also a relaxing lounge. A drying room is available for fishing and wet gear. Golf, walking and fishing trips can be arranged.

Rooms 10 en suite (1 fmly) (2 GF) **S** €40-€65; **D** €60-€100 **Facilities** STV FTV TVL tea/coffee Direct Dial Cen ht Wi-fi Golf 18 **Parking** 11 **Notes** LB Closed 15 Dec-13 Feb

---

Coursetown Country House

★★★★★ BED AND BREAKFAST

Stradbally Rd
☎ 059 8631101   📠 059 8632740
e-mail: coursetown@hotmail.com
dir: *3km from Athy. N78 at Athy onto R428*

PETS: **Sep accom Stables** 6m **Public areas** on leads **Grounds** on leads **Exercise area Facilities** food bowl water bowl washing facs cage storage vet info **On Request** fridge access towels **Other** charge for damage Resident Pet: Leopold & Ophilia (cats)

This charming Victorian country house stands on a 100-hectare tillage farm and bird sanctuary. It has been extensively refurbished, and all bedrooms are furnished to the highest standards. Convalescent or disabled guests are especially welcome, and Iris and Jim Fox are happy to share their knowledge of the Irish countryside and its wildlife.

Rooms 5 en suite (1 GF) **Facilities** TVL tea/coffee Direct Dial Cen ht **Parking** 22 **Notes** No Children 12yrs Closed 15 Nov-15 Mar

---

The Ice House

★★★★ 77% ◉◉ HOTEL

The Quay
☎ 096 23500   📠 096 23598
e-mail: chill@theicehouse.ie
dir: *On Sligo road turn right at Judge's Garage into Riverside Estate. Right at T junct onto Quay Rd. Hotel on left*

PETS: **Bedrooms** (10 GF) unattended sign **Public areas** except restaurant & lounge on leads **Exercise area** riverside walk **Facilities** food food bowl water bowl bedding dog chews feeding mat scoop/disp bags leads pet sitting dog walking washing facs dog grooming cage storage walks info vet info **On Request** fridge access torch towels **Other** charge for damage **Restrictions** small to medium size dogs only

With a fascinating history, this property, a mile or so from the town centre, is a stunning mix of old and new. The contemporary decor features lots of wood, steel and glass creating a very light and airy interior, contrasted with Victorian features and furnishings in the original house. The stylish bedrooms include suites that have river views from their balconies. An interesting menu is offered at dinner in the vaulted Pier Restaurant, once the ice store for the Moy fishery, with lighter fare offered during the day in the bright riverside bar.

Rooms 32 (7 fmly) (10 GF) **Facilities** Spa STV Laconium Steam room New Year Wi-fi **Services** Lift **Parking** 32 **Notes** Closed 25-26 Dec

KNOCK — Map 1 B4

Knock Caravan and Camping Park (M408828)

▶ ▶ ▶

Claremorris Rd

☎ 094 9388100 ▤ 094 9388295

e-mail: caravanpark@knock-shrine.ie

dir: From rdbt in Knock, through town. Site entrance on left 1km, opp petrol station

PETS: Public areas on leads Exercise area 200mtrs Facilities walks info vet info Other prior notice required Restrictions no type of Bull Terrier; no Bull Mastiffs, Dobermans, Alsatians, Rottweilers, Rhodesian Ridgebacks or any breed listed under Dangerous Dogs Act (see page 7)

Open Mar-Nov Last arrival 22.00hrs Last departure noon

A pleasant, very well maintained caravan park within the grounds of Knock Shrine, offering spacious terraced pitches and excellent facilities. A 10 acre site with 88 touring pitches, 88 hardstandings and 12 statics.

CO SLIGO

CASTLEBALDWIN — Map 1 B4

Cromleach Lodge Country House Hotel

★ ★ ★ ★ 79% ◉ HOTEL

Lough Arrow

☎ 071 9165155 ▤ 071 9165455

e-mail: info@cromleach.com

dir: 6km from N4 (Dublin-Sligo road)

PETS: Bedrooms (9 GF) Charges Public areas Grounds on leads disp bin Exercise area 100mtrs Facilities pet sitting dog walking washing facs dog grooming walks info vet info On Request fridge access torch towels Other charge for damage

A feeling of welcome and homeliness fills this hotel, set in the hills overlooking Lough Arrow. Luxuriously furnished and a haven of peace it is justly renowned for its fine cuisine. Additional contemporary bedrooms have been added, many of which have great views. The whole team here will ensure a memorable stay.

Rooms 57 (9 fmly) (9 GF) S €105-€160; D €150-€260 (incl. bkfst)* Facilities Spa Steam room Sauna New Year Wi-fi Services Lift Parking 50 Notes LB Closed Mon, Tue, Nov & 21-27 Dec

CO TIPPERARY

NENAGH — Map 1 B3

Ashley Park House

★ ★ ★ ★ BED AND BREAKFAST

☎ 067 38223 & 38013 ▤ 067 38013

e-mail: margaret@ashleypark.com

web: www.ashleypark.com

dir: 6.5km N of Nenagh. Off N52 across lake, signed on left & left under arch

PETS: Bedrooms unattended Sep accom Stables Charges horses €20 per night horses €110 per week Public areas Grounds disp bin Exercise area 20yds Facilities food bowl water bowl pet sitting dog walking washing facs cage storage walks info vet info On Request fridge access torch towels Resident Pets: horses, ducks, peacocks, hens, lambs in spring

The attractive, colonial style farmhouse was built in 1770. Set in gardens that run down to Lake Ourna, it has spacious bedrooms with quality antique furnishings. Breakfast is served in the dining room overlooking the lake, and dinner is available by arrangement. There is a delightful walled garden, and a boat for fishing on the lake is available.

Rooms 5 en suite (3 fmly) S €45-€70; D €90-€120* Facilities TVL tea/coffee Dinner available Cen ht Licensed Wi-fi Golf 18 Fishing Parking 30 Notes LB 🌫

IRELAND

CO WATERFORD

ARDMORE · Map 1 C2

Cliff House

★★★★ 82% ◉◉ HOTEL

☎ 024 87800 & 87801 ▤ 024 87820

e-mail: info@thecliffhousehotel.com

dir: *From Dungarvan: N25, signed Cork. Left onto R673. From Youghal: N25 signed Waterford. Right onto R673 signed Ardmore. In Ardmore take Middle Rd to hotel*

PETS: Sep accom kennel & dog run **Stables** 5km **Public areas** only on outdoor terrace on leads **Grounds** on leads disp bin **Exercise area** 100mtrs **Facilities** water bowl cage storage walks info vet info **On Request** fridge access torch towels

This is a unique property that is virtually sculpted into the cliff face overlooking Ardmore Bay, just a few minutes' walk from the village. Most of the individually designed bedroom suites and the public rooms enjoy the same great views, as do the relaxing leisure and spa facilities. Dinner in the award-winning House Restaurant is a particular highlight of any visit here; the menu features seasonal and local produce cooked with flair.

Rooms 39 (8 fmly) (7 GF) **S** €180-€200; **D** €200-€450 (incl. bkfst)* **Facilities** Spa STV FTV ⊗ Fishing Gym Sauna Steam room Relaxation room Outdoor pursuits New Year Wi-fi Child facilities **Services** Lift Air con **Parking** 52 **Notes** LB Closed 2 wks in Jan

CO WEXFORD

CAMPILE · Map 1 C2

Kilmokea Country Manor & Gardens

★★★★★ GUEST ACCOMMODATION

Great Island

☎ 051 388109 ▤ 051 388776

e-mail: stay@kilmokea.com

dir: *R733 from New Ross to Campile, right before village for Great Island & Kilmokea Gardens*

PETS: Bedrooms unattended sign **Sep accom** kennels in courtyard barns & stables **Stables Charges Public areas** except restaurant, lounge & conservatory on leads **Grounds** on leads disp bin **Exercise area** orchard & fields **Facilities** food (pre-bookable) food bowl water bowl bedding dog chews cat treats feeding mat litter tray scoop/disp bags leads pet sitting dog walking washing facs cage storage walks info vet info **On Request** fridge access torch towels **Other** charge for damage **Resident Pets:** Jasmine (Labrador), Rosa (Springer Spaniel), Jackie (horse), chickens, peacocks, ducks

An 18th-century stone rectory now restored and located in wooded gardens (open to the public) where peacocks wander and trout fishing is available on the lake. Comfortable bedrooms and public rooms are richly furnished, and a country-house style

dinner is served nightly (booking essential). Take breakfast in the conservatory and tea overlooking the beautiful gardens.

Rooms 4 en suite 2 annexe en suite (1 fmly) (2 GF) **S** €75-€120; **D** €180-€300 **Facilities** STV TVL tea/coffee Dinner available Direct Dial Cen ht Licensed Wi-fi ⊗ ⊰ ⊰ Fishing Riding Sauna Gymnasium **Parking** 23 **Notes** LB RS Nov-end Jan

CO WICKLOW

DUNLAVIN · Map 1 C3

Rathsallagh House

★★★★★ ◉ ▤ GUEST HOUSE

☎ 045 403112 ▤ 045 403343

e-mail: info@rathsallagh.com

dir: *M9 S exit junct 3 onto R747, left signed Baltinglass. At junct with R448 left for Crookstown, 1st right to Dunlavin*

PETS: Sep accom 2 heated indoor pens with heat lamps (various sizes) **Stables** 10km **Grounds Exercise area Facilities** scoop/ disp bags leads washing facs cage storage walks info vet info **On Request** fridge access torch towels **Other** over 500 acres of grounds available to walk in **Restrictions** no Rottweilers or Bull Terriers **Resident Pets:** Becket (Golden Retriever), Tilly (Labrador), Truffle, Tigger & Treacle (Terriers)

Surrounded by its own 18-hole championship golf course this delightful house was converted from Queen Ann stables in 1798 and has the addition of spacious and luxurious bedrooms with conference and leisure facilities. Food is country-house cooking at its best, and there is a cosy bar and comfortable drawing room to relax in. Close to Curragh and Punchestown racecourses.

Rooms 29 en suite (11 GF) **Facilities** FTV TVL tea/coffee Dinner available Direct Dial Cen ht Licensed Wi-fi ⊰ ⊰ Golf 18 ⚑ Snooker Sauna **Parking** 150 **Notes** LB No Children 6yrs

IRELAND

Tynte House *(N870015)*

★★★★ FARMHOUSE

☎ 045 401561 📄 045 401586 Mr & Mrs J Lawler

e-mail: info@tyntehouse.com

web: www.tyntehouse.com

dir: *N81 at Hollywood Cross, right at Dunlavin, follow finger signs for Tynte House, past market house in town centre*

PETS: Bedrooms Public areas Grounds on leads disp bin **Exercise area Facilities** cage storage walks info vet info **On Request** fridge access torch towels **Resident Pet:** Sasha (West Yorkshire Terrier)

The 19th-century farmhouse stands in the square of this quiet country village. The friendly hosts have carried out a lot of restoration resulting in comfortable bedrooms and a relaxing guest sitting room. Breakfast, featuring Caroline's home baking, is a highlight of a visit to this house.

Rooms 7 en suite (2 fmly) **Facilities** TVL tea/coffee Direct Dial Cen ht Wi-fi 🏊 Golf 18 Pool Table **Parking** 16 **Notes** Closed 16 Dec-9 Jan 200 acres beef/tillage

---

The Ritz Carlton Powerscourt

[U]

Powerscourt Estate

☎ 01 2748888 📄 01 2749999

e-mail: powerscourtreservations@ritzcarlton.com

dir: *From Dublin take M50, M11, then N11, follow Enniskerry signs. In Enniskerry left up hill, hotel on right*

PETS: Bedrooms (39 GF) unattended sign **Charges** €50 per night **Grounds** on leads disp bin **Exercise area Facilities** food (pre-bookable) food bowl water bowl bedding dog chews cat treats litter tray cage storage walks info vet info **On Request** torch towels **Restrictions** dogs must be 10kg or under

This very stylish hotel, built in the Palladian style, has a tranquil setting with stunning views over the gardens and woodlands to the Sugar Loaf. The bedrooms and suites are particularly spacious and well appointed with very impressive bathrooms that have TVs, deep tubs and walk-in showers. The luxuriously appointed public areas are airy and spacious with a variety of food options that includes the Gordon Ramsay at Powerscourt restaurant. The hotel also has a stunning spa, two golf courses, and includes fly fishing and equestrian pursuits among its many leisure facilities.

Rooms 200 (39 GF) **D** €215-€385 (incl. bkfst)* **Facilities** Spa STV 🐾 🏋 36 Putt green Fishing 🎣 Gym Cycling Mega chess Xmas New Year Wi-fi Child facilities **Services** Lift Air con **Parking** 384 **Notes** LB

BrookLodge Hotel & Wells Spa

★★★★ 86% 🌟🌟 HOTEL

☎ 0402 36444 📄 0402 36580

e-mail: info@brooklodge.com

web: www.brooklodge.com

dir: *N11 to Rathnew, R752 to Rathdrum, R753 to Aughrim follow signs to Macreddin Village*

PETS: Bedrooms (4 GF) sign **Sep accom** dogs can sleep in stables if available **Stables** on leads **Grounds** disp bin **Exercise area On Request** towels **Other** charge for damage

A luxury country-house hotel in a village style setting, which includes horse riding, an 18-hole golf course, a pub, café and food shop. There is a choice of dining options, the award-winning Strawberry Tree Restaurant specialising in organic and wild foods and a more casual Italian restaurant. Bedrooms and lounges in the original house are very comfortable; there are bedrooms also in Brookhall for guests attending weddings and conferences. The Wells Spa offers extensive treatments and leisure facilities.

Rooms 90 (32 annexe) (27 fmly) (4 GF) **Facilities** Spa STV FTV 🐾 🏹 🏋 18 Putt green Gym Archery Clay pigeon shooting Falconry Off road driving Xmas New Year Wi-fi **Services** Lift **Parking** 200

IRELAND

Maps

County Maps

The county map shown here will help you identify the counties within each country. You can look up each county in the guide using the county names at the top of each page. To find towns featured in the guide use the atlas and the index.

England

1 Bedfordshire
2 Berkshire
3 Bristol
4 Buckinghamshire
5 Cambridgeshire
6 Greater Manchester
7 Herefordshire
8 Hertfordshire
9 Leicestershire
10 Northamptonshire
11 Nottinghamshire
12 Rutland
13 Staffordshire
14 Warwickshire
15 West Midlands
16 Worcestershire

Scotland

17 City of Glasgow
18 Clackmannanshire
19 East Ayrshire
20 East Dunbartonshire
21 East Renfrewshire
22 Perth & Kinross
23 Renfrewshire
24 South Lanarkshire
25 West Dunbartonshire

Wales

26 Blaenau Gwent
27 Bridgend
28 Caerphilly
29 Denbighshire
30 Flintshire
31 Merthyr Tydfil
32 Monmouthshire
33 Neath Port Talbot
34 Newport
35 Rhondda Cynon Taff
36 Torfaen
37 Vale of Glamorgan
38 Wrexham

KEY TO ATLAS

Shetland Islands

16

Orkney Islands

- ● Establishment location
- ○ Town name
- Ⓜ Motorway junction
- ㉚ Restricted motorway junction

13 **14** **15**

Inverness

Aberdeen

Fort William

Perth

Glasgow Edinburgh

10 **11** **12**

Stranraer

Carlisle

Newcastle upon Tyne

Londonderry Larne

Belfast

Middlesbrough

Kendal

York

Leeds Kingston upon Hull

1

Liverpool Manchester **8** **9**

Galway

Dublin

Sheffield

Holyhead **6** **7**

Lincoln

Limerick

Nottingham

Rosslare

Aberystwyth

Norwich

Cork

Birmingham

Cambridge

Carmarthen

Gloucester

Colchester

Cardiff

Oxford

4 LONDON **5**

Bristol

Guildford

2 **3** Taunton

Southampton Maidstone

Dover

Barnstaple

Dorchester

Brighton

Exeter

Plymouth

Penzance

Isles of Scilly

Channel Islands **16**

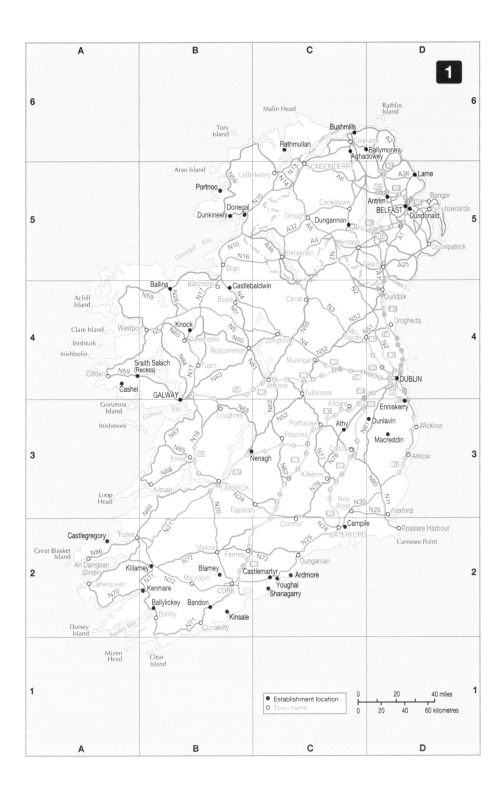

A   B   C   D

6

Malin Head

Rathlin Island

Bushmills

Tory Island

Rathmullan

Coleraine
Ballymoney
Aghadowey

Aran Island

Letterkenny

LONDONDERRY

A2

Larne

A36

Portnoo

N56

N13

N14

A6

M2

Antrim
BELFAST
Dundonald

Bangor
Newtownards

Donegal

N15

Cookstown

M2

Dunkineely

Omagh

Dungannon

Downpatrick

Donegal Bay

A32

A5

Enniskillen

A4

Armagh

N2

Newry

A25

Sligo

N15

N16

Dundalk

M1

Achill Island

Ballina

Ballymote

Castlebaldwin

Cavan

N52

Drogheda

N59

N26

N17

Boyle

N4

N3

N51

Clare Island

Westport

N5

Knock

N60

Claremorris

N5

N60

Roscommon

Longford

N4

N52

Navan

N2

M1

Tal

Inishturk
Inishbofin

Sraith Salach (Recess)

N84

N17

Tuam

N61

Mullingar

M4

Tal

DUBLIN

Clifden

N59

Cashel

GALWAY

N63

Athlone

M6

M4

M7

Tullamore

M50

Gorumna Island

Galway Bay

N65

Loughrea

N62

Kildare

Enniskerry

Inishmore

N67

N18

N52

Portlaoise

M7

N81

Dunlavin

Wicklow

N85

Ennis

M18

Nenagh

Roscrea

Athy

Macreddin

N68

N62

N77

N78

Arklow

Loop Head

Kilrush

M7

N24

LIMERICK

Kilkenny

Carlow

M9

M11

N80

N69

N20

Tipperary

N76

New Ross

N30

N11

Wexford

Castlegregory

Tralee

N21

Clonmel

N24

N25

Rosslare Harbour

Great Blasket Island

N86

Mallow

Fermoy

N72

Dungarvan

Campile

WATERFORD

Carnsore Point

An Daingean (Dingle)

Killarney

N72

Blarney

Castlemartyr

Ardmore

Cahersiveen

N71

N22

Macroom

Youghal

N70

Kenmare

CORK

Shanagarry

Ballylickey

Bandon

Kinsale

Dursey Island

Bantry

N71

Clonakilty

Bantry Bay

Mizen Head

Clear Island

● Establishment location
○ Town name

0   20   40 miles

0   20   40   60 kilometres

A   B   C   D

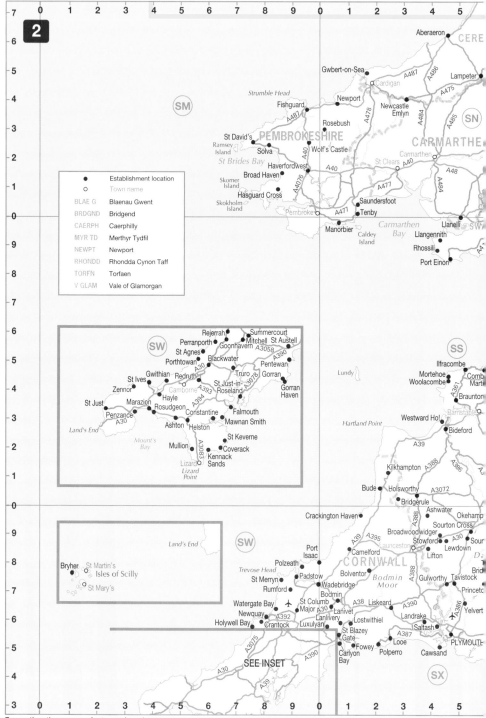

2

| | 0 | 1 | 2 | 3 | 4 | 5 | 6 | 7 | 8 | 9 | 0 | 1 | 2 | 3 | 4 | 5 |

Establishment location
○ Town name

BLAE G	Blaenau Gwent
BRDGND	Bridgend
CAERPH	Caerphilly
MYR TD	Merthyr Tydfil
NEWPT	Newport
RHONDD	Rhondda Cynon Taff
TORFN	Torfaen
V GLAM	Vale of Glamorgan

SM

Strumble Head
Fishguard
St David's
Ramsey Island
Solva
St Brides Bay
Skomer Island
Broad Haven
Skokholm Island
Hasguard Cross
PEMBROKESHIRE
Rosebush
Wolf's Castle
Haverfordwest
Saundersfoot
Pembroke
Tenby
Manorbier
Caldey Island

Gwbert-on-Sea
Cardigan
Newport
Newcastle Emlyn
CARMARTHE
Carmarthen
St Clears

Aberaeron
CERE
Lampeter

SN

Carmarthen Bay
Llanelli
Llangennith
Rhossili
Port Einon

SW

Rejerrah
Perranporth
St Agnes
Porthtowan
Gwithian
St Ives
Zennor
St Just
Marazion
Penzance
Land's End
Mount's Bay
Summercourt
Mitchell
St Austell
Goonhaven
Blackwater
Redruth
Camborne
Hayle
Rosudgeon
Ashton
Mullion
Lizard
Lizard Point
Truro
Pentewan
Gorran
Gorran Haven
St Just-in-Roseland
Constantine
Helston
Mawnan Smith
St Keverne
Coverack
Kennack Sands
Falmouth

SS
Lundy
Ilfracombe
Mortehoe
Woolacombe
Comb
Marti
Braunton
Barnstaple
Westward Ho!
Bideford
Hartland Point

SW
Land's End
Bryher
St Martin's
Isles of Scilly
St Mary's

Kilkhampton
Bude
Holsworthy
Bridgerule
A3072
Crackington Haven
Ashwater
Okeham
Broadwoodwidger
Sourton Cross
Launceston
Stowford
Lewdown
Sour
Camelford
Lifton
Polzeath
Port Isaac
Padstow
Bolventor
Bodmin Moor
Gulworthy
Tavistock
Brid
St Merryn
Wadebridge
Bodmin
Princeto
Rumford
Watergate Bay
St Columb Major
Lanivet
Liskeard
Yelvert
Newquay
Holywell Bay
Crantock
Lanlivery
Lostwithiel
Landrake
Saltash
PLYMOUTH
Luxulyan
St Blazey Gate
Fowey
Looe
Carlyon Bay
Polperro
Cawsand
CORNWALL
SEE INSET

SX

| | 0 | 1 | 2 | 3 | 4 | 5 | 6 | 7 | 8 | 9 | 0 | 1 | 2 | 3 | 4 | 5 |

For continuation pages refer to numbered arrows

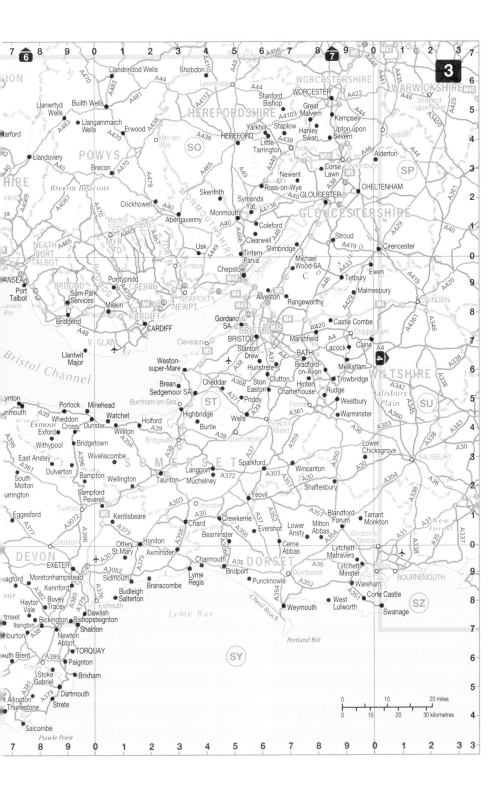

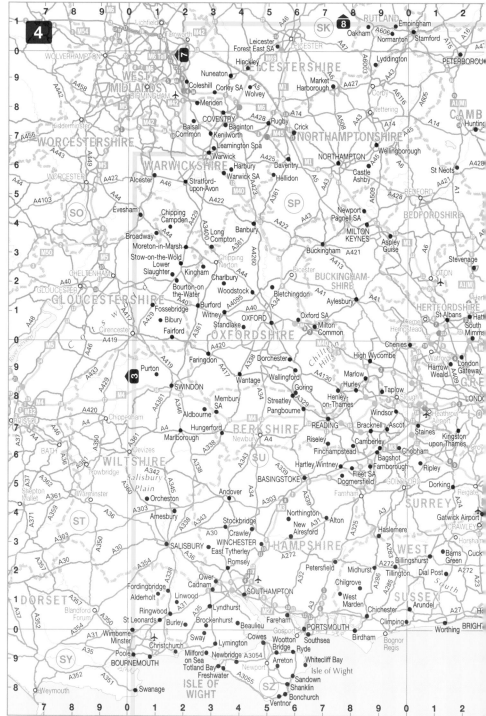

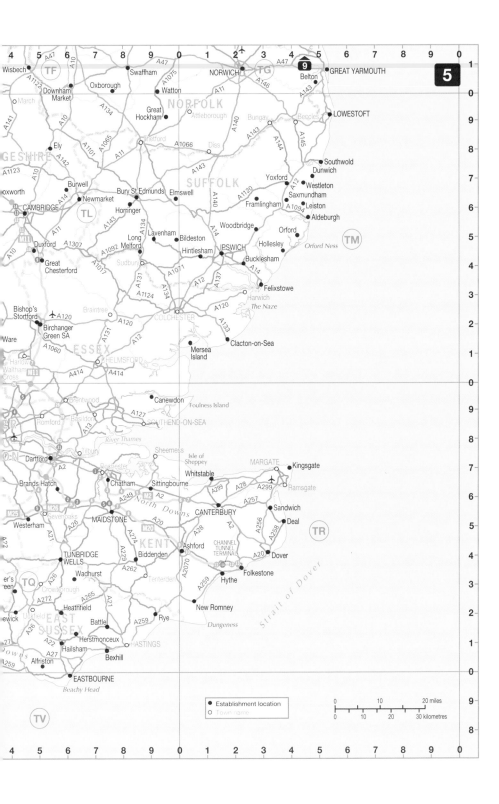

A10   Point of Ayre
Isle of Man
Ramsey
A3
Maughold Head
ISLE
OF
A4
MAN
Peel
A1
A2
DOUGLAS
A3
A5
Port Erin   Castletown
Dreswick Point

Santon Bridg
Ravenglass

(SC)

*Irish
Sea*

MI

Carmel Head
Dulas
Great
Ormes
Head
Holyhead   Pentraeth   Llandudno   Colwyn   Rhyl
A5025   Beaumaris   Bay   Llanddulas
Holy Island   Conwy   Betws-yn-Rhos   A55   A55   Rhuallt
Rhosneigr   A55   Bangor   Tal-y-Bont   A470   Llandyrno
ISLE OF   A4080   Llanrug   A5   Trefriw   Llanrwst   A525
ANGLESEY   Caernarfon   A4086   Betws-y-Coed   A543   Ruthi
Llandwrog   A4085   DENBIG
Caernarfon   (SH)   A498   A470   A5   A4
Bay   A499   Beddgelert   Cor
A487   Ffestiniog
A497   Porthmadog   A4212   Bala   Llandr
Lleyn Peninsula   Criccieth   A470   A494
Pwllheli   GWYNEDD   Llanfy
Abersoch   Llanbedr
Bardsey   A496
Island   Barmouth   Dolgellau   A470   A458
A470   POWYS
Tywyn   A493   Machynlleth   A470   Newto

Cardigan Bay   Eglwysfach   A470   A483

(SN)   A487   A44   Devil's   Llangurig
Aberystwyth   Bridge   A470
CEREDIGION   Rhayader
A485

● Establishment location
○ Town name
FLINTS Flintshire

0   10   20 miles
0   10   20   30 kilometres

For continuation pages refer to numbered arrows

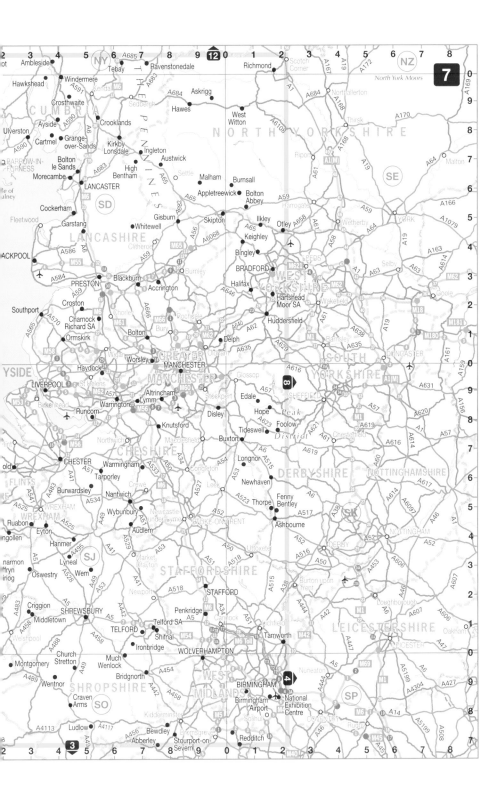

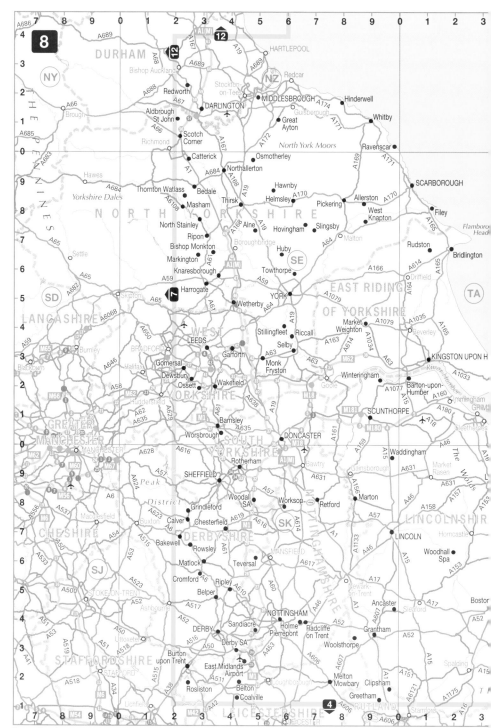

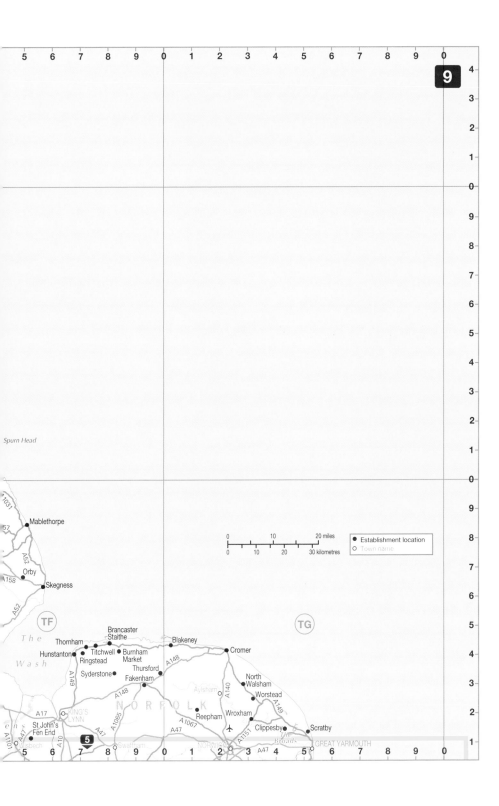

9

Spurn Head

Mablethorpe

Orby

Skegness

TF

TG

The
Wash

Thornham
Brancaster
Staithe
Blakeney
Cromer
Hunstanton
Titchwell
Burnham
Ringstead
Market
Syderstone
Thursford
North
Walsham
Fakenham
Worstead
Aylsham
NORFOLK
A140
KING'S
LYNN
Reepham
Wroxham
St John's
Fen End
A1067
Clippesby
Scratby
The
Broads
GREAT YARMOUTH

0   10   20 miles
0   10   20   30 kilometres

● Establishment location
○ Town name

5

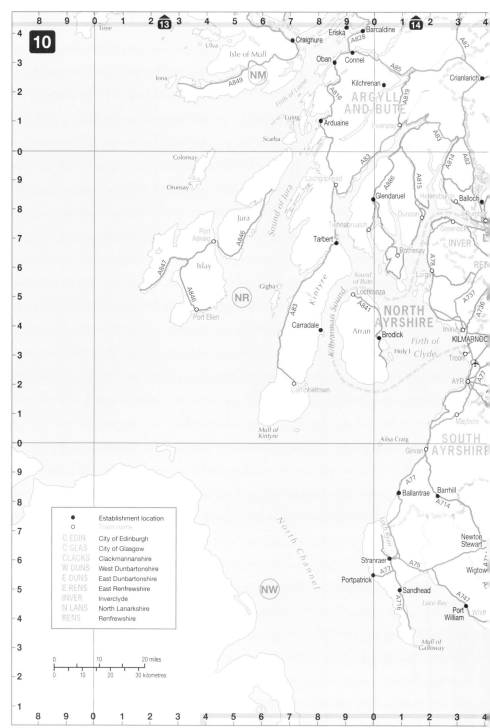

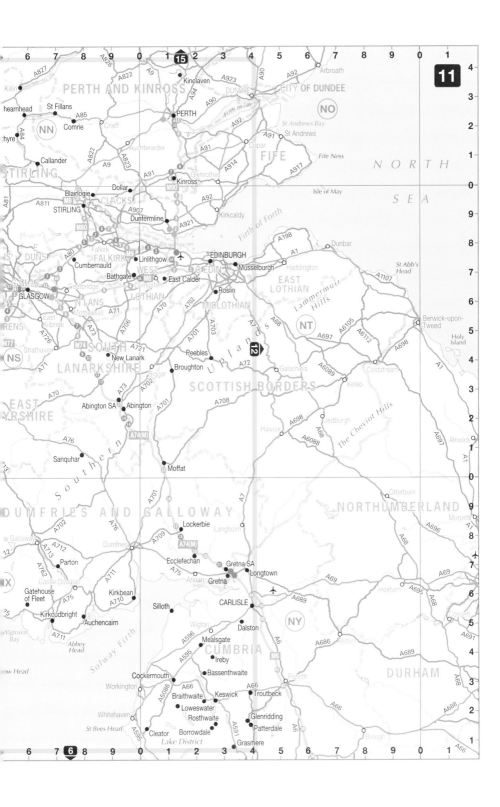

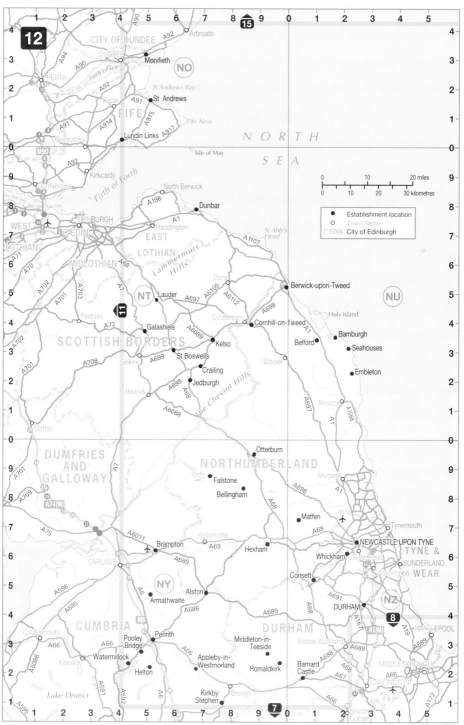

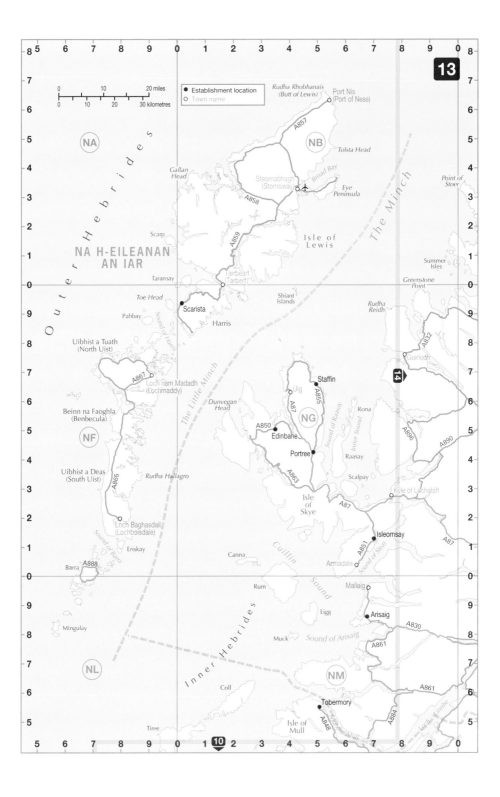

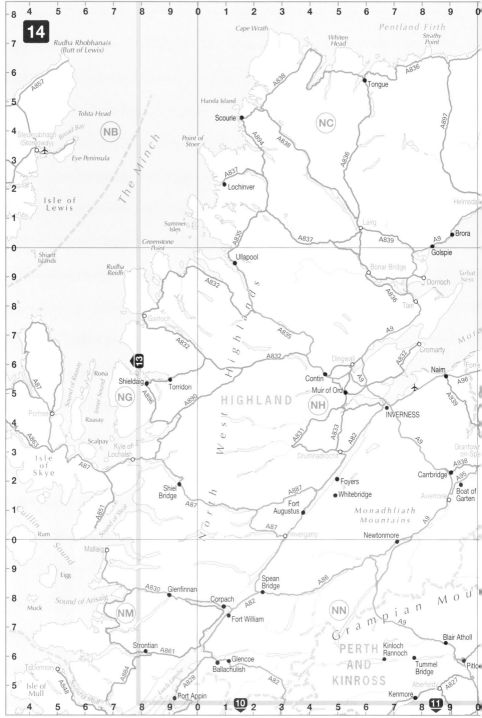

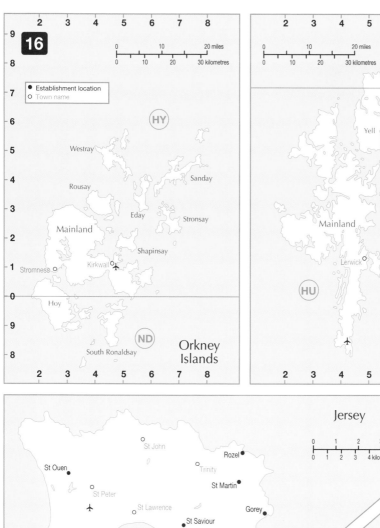

Establishment location
Town name

Orkney Islands

HY

ND

Westray

Rousay

Sanday

Eday

Stronsay

Mainland

Shapinsay

Stromness

Kirkwall

Hoy

South Ronaldsay

Shetland Islands

HP

HU

Unst

Yell

Fetlar

Whalsay

Mainland

Lerwick

Bressay

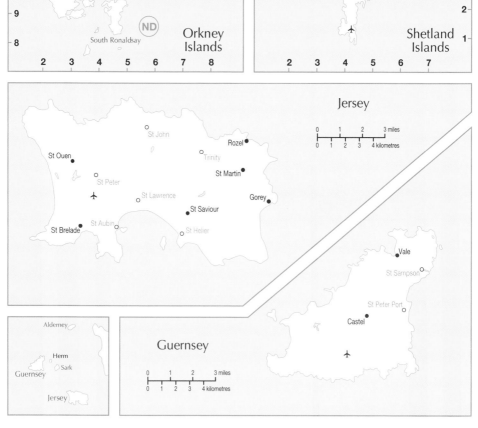

Jersey

St John

Rozel

St Ouen

Trinity

St Peter

St Martin

St Lawrence

St Saviour

Gorey

St Aubin

St Helier

St Brelade

Vale

St Sampson

St Peter Port

Castel

Alderney

Herm

Sark

Guernsey

Jersey

Guernsey

Index

Index

C

E

INDEX

M

AA Media Limited would like to thank the following photographers, companies and picture libraries for their assistance in the preparation of this book.

Abbreviations for the picture credits are as follows: (t) top; (b) bottom; (l) left; (r) right; (c) centre; (AA) AA World Travel Library

1 Keith Blair; 2t Samantha Warner; 2c Keith Blair; 2b Paul Collett; 3t Kerina Turner; 3bl Jean Parry; 3br Helen Woodvine; 5t Kerina Turner; 5b C E Brew; 6t Jean Parry; 7t Kerina Turner; 8t Jean Parry; 8bl Samantha Warner; 8br Karen Smith; 9t Kerina Turner; 9bl ActiveShot; 9br Jean Parry; 10t Jean Parry; 11t Kerina Turner; 11bl David Earl; 11br Neil Matthews; 12t Jean Parry; 12r Lisa Knight; 13t Kerina Turner; 13br Chris Cawston; 14t Jean Parry; 14cl Sarah Montgomery; 14cr Stuart Callister; 15t Kerina Turner; 15c Jean Parry; 17t Kerina Turner; 17c RSPCA; 18b Sarah Montgomery; 19t Kerina Turner; 19c Jane Croft; 20 AA/J Miller; 24 AA/J A Tims; 347 AA; 348 AA/S Day; 381 AA/K Blackwell; 384 AA/S Anderson; 391 AA/S Whitehorn; 392 AA/C Jones; 394 AA/G Matthews; 401 AA/M Bauer; 429 Rachel Marsh; 431 AA/C Warren; 434 AA/I Dawson; 446 AA/T Mackie; 467 AA/J Wood; 492 AA/M Short

Every effort has been made to trace the copyright holders, and we apologise in advance for any accidental errors. We would be happy to apply any corrections in the following edition of this publication.

Please send this form to:
Editor, AA Pet Friendly Places to Stay,
Lifestyle Guides,
The Automobile Association,
13th Floor, Fanum House,
Basingstoke RG21 4EA

Readers' Report Form

or e-mail: lifestyleguides@theAA.com

Please use this form to tell us about any establishment you have visited, whether it is in the guide or not currently listed. Feedback from readers helps us to keep our guide accurate and up to date. However, if you have a complaint to make during a visit, we do recommend that you discuss the matter with the management there and then, so that they have a chance to put things right before your visit is spoilt.

Please note that the AA does not undertake to arbitrate between you and the establishment's management, or to obtain compensation or engage in protracted correspondence.

Date:

Your name (block capitals)

Your address (block capitals)

....

....

....

....

....

e-mail address:

Comments (Please include the name & address of the establishment) ....

....

....

....

....

....

....

....

(please attach a separate sheet if necessary)

Please tick here if you DO NOT wish to receive details of AA offers or products ☐

PTO

AA Pet Friendly Places to Stay 2011

Have you bought this guide before?   Yes   No

Do you regularly use any other accommodation, restaurant, pub or food guides?
If yes, which ones?

....

....

Why did you buy this guide? (circle all that apply)

holiday   short break   attending a show (eg Crufts)

other ....

How often do you stay in a Hotel, B&B or at a Campsite with your pets?
(circle one choice)

more than once a month   once a month   once in 2-3 months

once in six months   once a year   less than once a year

Please answer these questions to help us make improvements to the guide:

Which of these factors are most important when choosing pet-friendly
accommodation?

price   location   awards/rating   service

decor/surroundings   previous experience   recommendation   proximity to exercise area

facilities for pets   extent of freedom for pets

other (please state) ....

Do you use the location atlas?   Yes   No

What elements of the guide do you find the most useful when choosing an
establishment?

description   photo   advertisement   star/pennant rating

information on pet facilities

What do you like best about the guide?

....

....

....

Can you suggest any improvements to the guide?

....

....

....

Thank you for returning this form

Please send this form to:
Editor, AA Pet Friendly Places to Stay,
Lifestyle Guides,
The Automobile Association,
13th Floor, Fanum House,
Basingstoke RG21 4EA

Readers' Report Form

or e-mail: lifestyleguides@theAA.com

Please use this form to tell us about any establishment you have visited, whether it is in the guide or not currently listed. Feedback from readers helps us to keep our guide accurate and up to date. However, if you have a complaint to make during a visit, we do recommend that you discuss the matter with the management there and then, so that they have a chance to put things right before your visit is spoilt.

Please note that the AA does not undertake to arbitrate between you and the establishment's management, or to obtain compensation or engage in protracted correspondence.

Date:

Your name (block capitals)

Your address (block capitals)

....

....

....

....

....

e-mail address:

Comments (Please include the name & address of the establishment) ....

....

....

....

....

....

....

....

(please attach a separate sheet if necessary)

Please tick here if you DO NOT wish to receive details of AA offers or products ☐

PTO

AA Pet Friendly Places to Stay 2011

Have you bought this guide before?　　　　Yes　　　　No

Do you regularly use any other accommodation, restaurant, pub or food guides?
If yes, which ones?

....

....

Why did you buy this guide? (circle all that apply)

holiday　　　　　　short break　　　　　attending a show (eg Crufts)

other ....

How often do you stay in a Hotel, B&B or at a Campsite with your pets?
(circle one choice)

more than once a month　　　　　once a month　　　　　once in 2-3 months

once in six months　　　　　　　once a year　　　　　　less than once a year

Please answer these questions to help us make improvements to the guide:

Which of these factors are most important when choosing pet-friendly
accommodation?

price　　　　　　　location　　　　　　awards/rating　　　　service

decor/surroundings　previous experience　recommendation　　proximity to exercise area

facilities for pets　　extent of freedom for pets

other (please state) ....

Do you use the location atlas?　　　　　Yes　　　　No

What elements of the guide do you find the most useful when choosing an
establishment?

description　　　　photo　　　　　　advertisement　　　　star/pennant rating

information on pet facilities

What do you like best about the guide?

....

....

....

Can you suggest any improvements to the guide?

....

....

....

Thank you for returning this form